Stamp Duty Land Tax

Third Edition

R. S. Nock
Barrister

JORDANS

Stamp Duty Land Tax

Third Edition

Published by
Jordan Publishing Limited
21 St Thomas Street
Bristol BS1 6JS

Whilst the publishers and the author have taken every care in preparing the material included in this work, any statements made as to the legal or other implications of particular transactions are made in good faith purely for general guidance and cannot be regarded as a substitute for professional advice. Consequently, no liability can be accepted for loss or expense incurred as a result of relying in particular circumstances on statements made in this work.

© Jordan Publishing Limited, 2010

Crown Copyright material is reproduced with kind permission of the Controller of Her Majesty's Stationery Office.

British Library Cataloguing-in-Publication Data

A catalogue record for this book is available from the British Library.

ISBN 978 1 84661 183 4

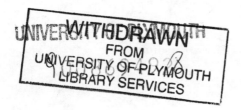

Typeset by Letterpart Ltd, Reigate, Surrey

Printed in Great Britain by Antony Rowe Limited

PREFACE

The Finance Act 2003 made the most fundamental revision of stamp duties since their initial introduction in 1694, although its structure and drafting do bear the signs of hurried preparation. Interestingly about two-thirds of the Act is concerned with the compliance regime, which applies to all transactions and so represents a disproportionate cost for small routine transactions such as house purchases. It was soon recognised that the charging provisions were not adequate and fundamental changes were made in November 2003. The initial regulations also had to be withdrawn and replaced late in the day. This process of continual fundamental change continues with currently the sixth set of provisions for leases, third set of changed provisions for partnerships and numerous detailed amendments including a general anti-avoidance provision. Significant changes have continued without proper consideration of the necessary consequential changes and consistency. It is not surprising that even after six years years of tinkering the legislation which does not fit comfortably with land law and conveyancing because of the absence of property lawyers on the official team, is an increasing mess with internal inconsistencies increasing. Opportunities to clarify the legislation are not taken up.

A special mention of thanks is again due to Lynn Gower for coping with rushed typewriting and messy semi-legible drafts and coping with a broken 'typing foot' and a new grandchild at 'rush hour'. Much is due to her patience and skill with the word processor and the fax. Appreciation is also required for the help and co-operation from Tony Hawitt at Jordans and Tracy Robinson.

R. S. Nock
December 2009

CONTENTS

TABLE OF CASES

References are to paragraph numbers.

Stamp Duty Land Tax

TABLE OF STATUTES

References are to paragraph numbers.

t

TABLE OF STATUTORY INSTRUMENTS

References are to paragraph numbers.

Chapter 1

STAMP TAXES – THE GENERAL STRUCTURE

BACKGROUND

1.1   The Finance Act (FA) 2003 made substantial changes in relation to the structure of stamp taxes[1] with effect from 1 December 2003 ('the implementation date'),[2] namely that stamp duties have been removed from all property other than shares and marketable securities[3] and a limited range of dealings in partnership interests,[4] which include stock and marketable securities in their assets and until FA 2008 limited certain fixed duties survived for share and land transactions.[5] These were essentially the fixed duties other than those imposed by FA 1999, Sch 13 as applied to shares and other property.[6] A landlord's counterpart of the lease is no longer subject to the fixed duty as a 'duplicate or counterpart'.[7] However, for those few items of property still subject to stamp duty the full range of *ad valorem* duties remains in full effect.[8] Dealings in land are subject to stamp duty land tax and certain fixed duties.[9]

Transition

1.2   In general the changes apply to transactions that take effect on or after 1 December 2003; but:

- completion of certain land transactions after 1 December 2003 remain subject to stamp duty; although it must also be noted that there is significant retrospective operation of the new stamp duty land tax to 11 July 2003 for land transactions entered into or varied in certain ways on or after that date but completed after the implementation of stamp duty land tax;[10] The provisions of FA 2003, Sch 19 are complex but are of considerable practical importance. Notwithstanding that many years have elapsed since the introduction of stamp duty land tax there will remain uncompleted contracts entered into before 1 December 2003. Careful use of the transitional provisions can save taxpayers a significant amount of tax, particularly in relation to leases where the stamp duty land tax charge is frequently significantly higher, in some cases up to 20 times higher, than the equivalent stamp

---

[1]   Ie stamp duty, stamp duty reserve tax and stamp duty land tax.
[2]   FA 2003, Sch 19, para 2(2); Stamp Duty Land Tax (Appointment of the Implementation Date) Order 2003, SI 2003/2899.
[3]   Companies Act 2006, s 555 no longer imposes stamp duty upon a return of allotments.
[4]   FA 2003, Sch 15, paras 31–33.
[5]   FA 2008, Sch 32, para 18.
[6]   FA 2008 made further reductions.
[7]   FA 2003, s 125(5)(a) (as amended).
[8]   Ibid, s 125(5); Sch 15, paras 9–14 (as amended).
[9]   FA 2008, Sch 32, para 22.
[10]   FA 2003, Sch 19 (as amended).

duty charge, if still applicable. In addition reliefs may be available that are not currently available from stamp duty land tax. For example, completion of agreements for sale or lease or rent reviews in transactions entered into before the removal of disadvantaged land relief[11] may still be eligible for that relief. The taxpayer will also be relieved from the cumbersome and expensive compliance provisions which arise because of the lack of finality in relation to many forms of stamp duty land tax and the fact that many transactions have to be reported and retrospectively adjusted having been dealt with on a provisional basis. This does mean that dealing with a transaction that has not been completed requires careful planning. For example, where the parties are considering varying an agreement for lease or a lease that was granted subject to stamp duty they should avoid structuring the transaction in such a way that either an express or implied surrender and regrant operates.[12] Such a transaction would create a new stamp duty land tax lease losing the benefits attaching to a stamp duty lease such as the fact that HMRC Stamp Taxes do not apply the new legislation where there is a holding over of a stamp duty lease pursuant to the Landlord and Tenant Act 1954 (as amended). Moreover, although there are certain exclusions from the land exchange rules there is no credit in respect of the stamp duty paid upon the rent against the stamp duty land tax arising.[13] It will need to be investigated whether it is possible to vary the lease in some way or change the relationship of the parties without generating a surrender and regrant. However, it is fundamental to the continuation of the beneficial stamp duty regime for agreements for lease that the contract is not altered or varied. The transitional provisions apply to benefit conditional agreements[14] so that these remain within the stamp duty regime notwithstanding that they were unconditional on 1 December 2003. A variation of a contract can, therefore, cause a loss of the beneficial treatment by moving into stamp duty land tax. In many situations taxpayers have found it beneficial to complete the transaction and pay the appropriate generally lower stamp duty and then enter into some variation of the arrangement that attracts little or no stamp duty land tax. In such situations it may be possible to produce an aggregate charge to stamp duty and stamp duty land tax that is significantly lower than the stamp duty land tax that would arise by a simple variation of the agreement.

- completions of pre-1 December 2003 contracts for property other than land or shares and marketable securities are free of *ad valorem* stamp duty and since FA 2008[15] free of all remaining fixed duties.[16] The removal applies to instruments executed on or after implementation date, notwithstanding that the instrument is executed pursuant to a contract entered into prior to that date. Generally there is an exemption for 'conveyances' executed after that date, but this is of little benefit since most of the items of property affected by the change are subject to stamp duty at the contract stage[17] pursuant to FA 1999, Sch 13, para 7 for which there is no retrospective relief in general. However, where parties have for some time been resting upon such an arrangement such as an offer letter orally accepted to

---

[11]   Ibid, Sch 6.
[12]   See further **7.1** and **7.83**.
[13]   FA 2003, Sch 17A, paras 9 and 16.
[14]   Although options are subject to a special regime restricting the benefit of the transactional reliefs; FA 2003, Sch 19, para 9.
[15]   Schedule 32.
[16]   FA 2003, Sch 20.
[17]   Which includes conditional contracts; also see Stamp Duty and Stamp Duty Land Tax (Consequential Amendment of Enactments) Regulations 2003, SI 2003/2868, reg 2.

constitute a binding contract,[18] the new regime offers them the opportunity of tidying up the transaction free of stamp duty, by executing any assignments after the implementation date;[19]

- considerable areas of difficulty exist in determining whether the particular charging provisions of stamp duty land tax apply to transactions involving leases which were granted subject to stamp duty. This is separate from the problem outlined above concerning whether a transaction entered into prior to the implementation of stamp duty land tax is subject to that tax. This discussion relates to situations where a transaction has been entered into subject to stamp duty and completed before 1 December 2003 or even if completed after that date was subject to stamp duty. The question is whether the variation of that arrangement is itself a chargeable transaction. Where the arrangement is simply a contract the variation may affect the transitional provisions but there is also the question as to whether the transaction itself is subject to charge. There is no general statutory principle dealing with these situations and it is necessary to consider the particular detailed legislation. The question is whether the transaction is viewed as a standalone transaction taxable in its own right or whether it applies to operate on a retrospective basis which raises difficulties for the purposes of transactions that are subject to stamp duty. For example, the question is how are the stamp duty land tax provisions to apply in a context where the basic transaction was subject to stamp duty, particularly where there may be 'tax credits' available. Moreover, much of stamp duty land tax is provisional and retrospectively adjusted. Where there are retrospective adjustments that apply to transactions entered into before 1 December 2003 there is a fundamental question as to how this retrospection is to operate. In some cases such as abnormal increases in rent there are specific provisions.[20] In other cases the transitional effect is implicit because there is a reference to the effective date[21] or reference to rent previously subject to stamp duty land tax[22] or where the lease was eligible for a stamp duty land tax relief[23] which must exclude stamp duty leases. In other cases such as variations or surrenders of leases the position is open on the legislation so that the transaction is *prima facie* taxable. There is also the question of the practice of HMRC Stamp Taxes such as currently regarding the holding over of stamp duty leases as not being within the stamp duty land tax regime.[24] Unfortunately each case depends upon its own particular circumstances because of the absence of clear transitional rules;

- reliefs from stamp duty may be available such as disadvantaged land which are not available for a stamp duty land tax transaction.

---

[18]   *Carlill v Carbolic Smokeball Co* [1892] 2 QB 484.
[19]   FA 2003, s 125.
[20]   Ibid, Sch 17A, para 14(7).
[21]   Such as linked successive leases; FA 2003, Sch 17A, para 6.
[22]   See, for example, FA 2003, Sch 17A, para 4(3)(c) and 3(3)(c).
[23]   FA 2003, Sch 17A, para 11.
[24]   See **7.163**.

REMOVAL OF STAMP DUTY UPON 'OTHER PROPERTY'

1.3   The position after FA 2003 and 2008 now is as follows:

- stamp duty upon shares and marketable securities, including bearer instruments and dealings in partnership interests;

- stamp duty reserve tax in relation to shares and marketable securities;

- stamp duty land tax upon land transactions and certain dealings in partnership interests.

Potential problem areas

1.4   Notwithstanding the removal of stamp duty from all 'other property' there are certain items of property that are not obviously land or shares or marketable securities but which remain within the charge to stamp taxes. However, the existence of 'other property' in the transaction does not mean that it will necessarily be free of stamp taxes. Whilst a transfer of shares or marketable securities for a consideration other than shares[25] is not a sale since other forms of consideration are not chargeable consideration and there is no longer a problem in relation to fixed duties for transfers not on sale.[26] However, the charges to stamp duty reserve tax apply to consideration in kind.[27] This will leave problems of valuation;[28] however, production of an appropriately 'stamped' transfer which includes an instrument that is not liable to stamp duty because it is not a transfer on sale will cancel the liability to stamp duty reserve tax[29] but this may be increasingly difficult because of computerised share trading although transactions within CREST will usually be for a cash consideration and therefore sales. The main importance of this arrangement is for off-market transactions such as dealings in shares in private or unlisted companies.

Goodwill

1.5   Although stamp duty upon goodwill was *prima facie* abolished by the FA 2002,[30] there is the problem of embedded goodwill.[31] Various cases[32] suggest that certain types of goodwill may in reality be related to the premises concerned and form part of the land value, and so be subject to stamp duty land tax as part of the consideration to be allocated to the land.[33] Failure to take this into account and allocate an appropriate part of the consideration to the land value may expose the parties to penalties for negligence or fraud. HMRC Stamp Taxes are taking a strict approach to this issue and in practice

---

[25]   Which are equated with 'cash' for stamp duty purposes; see *J&P Coats Ltd v IRC* [1897] 2 QB 427.

[26]   FA 2003, s 125; FA 2008, Sch 32, para 22.

[27]   FA 1986, s 87(1) referring to consideration in 'money's worth' (see *Secretan v Hart* 45 TC 701).

[28]   See **Chapter 27**.

[29]   FA 1986, s 92.

[30]   Section 116.

[31]   See the treatment of embedded goodwill in intellectual property in *Stamp Taxes Bulletin* Issue 1, August 2001. This allowed the exemption of embedded goodwill. The same line of reasoning would make goodwill embedded in land taxable.

[32]   See, eg, *Mullins v Wessex Motors* [1947] 2 All ER 727; *Whiteman Smith Motor Co Ltd v Chaplin* [1934] 2 KB 35.

[33]   Compare the treatment of embedded goodwill in intellectual property in *Stamp Taxes Bulletin* Issue 1, August 2001. This allowed the exemption of embedded goodwill. The same line of reasoning would make goodwill embedded in land taxable.

previously contended that where there is the sale of a business including land the entirety of consideration allocated by the parties to goodwill is really part of the value of the land from which the business is conducted. This was based upon the analysis in the Capital Gains Tax Manual which has recently been criticised and rejected by the Special Commissioners as incorrect,[34] and certain of these comments in the Manual have been modified by the capital gains tax section of HMRC. It is considered that this view, that all goodwill is embedded, is incorrect and overlooks the fact that goodwill is transferable apart from land involved in the business although it may not be capable of sale apart from a business. 'Goodwill' comprises many elements such as the absence of competition, lists of customers, the reputation of the persons carrying on the business for quality service and products. This can be seen in covenants that such persons will not carry on a competing business.[35] There are long-term contracts and brand names such as the name of the business and the right to utilise it. There is also a form of goodwill attached to the site which makes it convenient for customers. Not all of these will be land value, since it will be possible to sell the business separate from the land and pass the goodwill to the purchaser by means of a non-competition clause and assigning the right to make use of the business name. It seems unlikely that such a transaction would constitute the acquisition of a chargeable interest in the land from which the business was previously carried on.[36] The problem with HMRC Stamp Taxes is likely to arise where the land is sold together with the business as a going concern; but even here there is no established principle that all of that item described as goodwill is part of the land price even where the land is a major part of the business structure such as hotels, betting shops, nursing homes and retail shops and where some form of licence is required to carry on the business on the premises. It will be necessary to identify the aspects of goodwill involved and to isolate these in the valuation process.

1.6　　HMRC, in general, have issued a long statement concerning their views on embedded and free goodwill.[37] This statement suffers from the usual defect of many HMRC publications in that it deals with consequences such as the machinery for allocating consideration where there is embedded goodwill and free goodwill but very little upon the principles to be applied by HMRC in determining whether the goodwill referred to in the agreement is 'embedded'. It seems that HMRC intend to apply this backwards namely to assume that there is embedded goodwill and seek to apportion the consideration attributed to 'goodwill' on the various bases set out in the statement. However, there will be many issues as to whether the goodwill is 'embedded' even in the extended sense in which HMRC intend to apply this statement. The context of the agreement and its drafting will, therefore, remain a key issue for many years to come until these issues are litigated and adequately resolved. This can involve the preparation and clearly instructions to business valuers and similar advisers will be important including, in particular, the instructions as to how to value the land[38] in order to deal with the issues of apportionment of the consideration later. For example, if there is an instruction to the valuers to prepare the valuation of the property on the basis it is included in the business on a going concern basis in accordance with the various possibilities in the Valuation Manual for surveyors this will, in a sense, pre-empt many of the arguments as to whether the goodwill is part of the land value. The land will have

---

34　*Balloon Promotions Ltd v Wilson* [2006] STC SpC 167.
35　*Eastern National Omnibus Co Ltd v IRC* [1939] 1 KB 161; *Kirby v Thorn-EMI* [1987] STC 621; *Kent Food v HMRC* [2007] STC SpCD 47.
36　Even where the seller grants a lease of the premises to the purchaser of the business at a full rent HMRC Stamp Taxes may allege that the payment for the goodwill is in whole or in part a hidden premium for the lease.
37　HMRC Guidance Note 30 January 2009; STI 2009, p 460.
38　Or other assets for other tax purposes.

been valued taking into account the business relationship.[39] There will also be important issues as to what is included in the contract such as the right to the name, list of customers, and, where relevant, such as in relation to nursing homes, whether the medical and nursing staff continue in employment. Possibly more important would be the conduct of the purchaser. For example, on the purchase of a restaurant a change from Italian to Indian cuisine might indicate that the goodwill which may be related to the type of food and the chef was not a key factor in the transaction and that the price was being paid predominantly for the land and its location. Other issues might arise where the purchaser changes the name and, for example, in relation to a supermarket or convenience store changes the style of the premises, staff uniforms, reorganises the shelving and has different 'own brands'. Obviously, if there is a major discontinuity between the business being sold and the business being carried on and, in particular, certain types of reorganisation and rationalisation of the business by the purchaser this may indicate that there is no 'free goodwill' involved. To some extent the issue may depend upon whether there is some form of restriction upon the vendors carrying on business. It is not unusual to find some provision to the effect that the vendors of a business will not carry on competing business within a specified radius. This might indicate that the goodwill was related to the location because of the territorial restriction but it may also be a factor in indicating that the goodwill was 'personal' to the vendors and therefore a form of 'free' goodwill.[40] As regards restrictions upon the vendor it is well established that, as a matter of general law, a restrictive covenant against competition namely the basic protection that a purchaser requires in order to prevent the vendor from opening up a competing business for which the purchaser has paid is a form of 'goodwill'.[41] A restrictive covenant is, therefore, a species of property. HMRC Stamp Taxes have not considered this principle for which they contended in relation to stamp duty for many generations in the context of the definition of chargeable interest for stamp duty land tax.[42] This includes the benefit of an obligation, restriction or condition affecting the value of any estate, interest, right or power in or over land in the United Kingdom. This is a wide-ranging provision since it has been necessary to deal with certain standard covenants in leases. However, there is a specific exclusion from the relieving provisions in relation to arrangements that affect the rent that a tenant might pay in the open market.[43] A restrictive covenant against competition or a covenant in a lease restricting user which might be regarded as a form of 'goodwill' by preventing the person from carrying on a competing business could, on a general interpretation of this legislation, constitute a chargeable interest especially where the 'goodwill' might be embedded. In consequence, a restrictive covenant against competition, if valid, could be an obligation affecting the value of land and, therefore, a chargeable interest in its own right. Restrictive covenants against competition have been treated as a form of

---

[39]   To attach such an arrangement on the basis that it was not 'just and reasonable' might be close to HMRC having to allege that the parties were operating fraudulently and on a criminal basis pursuant to *Re Wragge* [1897] 1 Ch 796.

[40]   Issues may arise where there is not a transfer of the existing land interest but some form of lease or sublease being granted by the vendors of the business. In this situation there would be a question as to whether the payment describes 'goodwill' was some form of 'premium' for the grant of the lease and subject to stamp duty land tax accordingly.

[41]   *Eastern National Omnibus Co Ltd v IRC* [1939] 1 KB 161; *Kirby v Thorn-EMI* [1987] STC 621; and this can apply even as between a seller and purchaser of shares in a company as in *Connors v Connors Brothers* [1940] 4 All ER 179.

[42]   FA 2003, s 48(1)(b); see **2.11**.

[43]   Ibid, Sch 17A, para 10. This has raised fundamental questions as to whether every lease is potentially a land exchange because covenants in leases are recognised by the draftsman of the legislation as being covenants or obligations that could affect the value of land for the purposes of FA 2003, s 48(1)(b).

goodwill,[44] and where these relate to carrying on business within a geographical area relating to the premises being sold, the appropriate part of the consideration for the covenant may be part of the land value. However, these are unlikely to constitute restrictive covenants over land as a chargeable interest because there may not be any dominant land to be benefited, but they may nevertheless be chargeable interests as 'restrictions' affecting the value of an estate and interest in land.[45] In this situation, the vendor by asking for this covenant may be entering into a land exchange[46] because he is receiving the benefit of an obligation that restricts the value of land within FA 2003, s 48(1)(b). This could mean that goodwill that is not embedded but is effective to affect the value of land is a chargeable interest in its own right with appropriate taxation consequences such as a potential charge where the right is created[47] or is released for a payment. A release of a chargeable interest which may occur with a release of a user covenant in a lease is a chargeable transaction.[48]

1.7   Since 'goodwill' is frequently a balancing item between the fair value of the assets and the total price paid for the business HMRC Stamp Taxes are faced with certain important contrary arguments of fundamental principle and the extent of their powers, including the power to reallocate the consideration[49] differently from the amounts allocated by the parties. It may be difficult for them to suggest that the allocation was made negligently and not in good faith where independent advice has been received. These suggestions by HMRC Stamp Taxes have been treated by the courts over a long period as allegations involving fraud and the criminal law burden of proof will be applied.[50] It will be important that the parties obtain independent advice and that this is prepared upon the basis of the land as part of the business. Useful evidence will be independent advice as to the value of the land if sold separately from the business. A higher consideration allocated to the land above its stand-alone value in the contract will indicate that the valuers took into account the value of the land to the business.

Debt

1.8   Most forms of indebtedness,[51] including mortgages, are exempt from stamp duty,[52] but indebtedness that constitutes a 'marketable security'[53] remains subject to stamp duty at 0.5 per cent unless it constitutes exempt loan capital[54] or is an alternative finance instrument[55] This charge to stamp duty is underpinned by the liability to the principal charge to stamp duty reserve tax which is self-assessed, notifiable within a limited time and directly enforceable.[56] However, simply because debt is not itself a chargeable interest it may give rise to a liability to stamp taxes. For example, a transfer of shares or land in satisfaction of a debt is a chargeable transaction.[57]

---

[44]   *Connors v Connors Brothers* [1940] 4 All ER 179; *Eastern National Omnibus Co Ltd v IRC* [1939] 1 KB 161; *Kirby v Thorn-EMI* [1987] 2 All ER 947.

[45]   FA 2003, s 48(1)(b).

[46]   Ibid, s 47.

[47]   Ibid, Sch 4, para 5.

[48]   Ibid, s 43(3)(b).

[49]   Ibid, Sch 4, para 4.

[50]   See, for example, *Re Wragge* [1897] 1 Ch 796.

[51]   Certain types of fundraising within the alternative finance regime designed to evade the ethical restrictions upon usury create problems but limited relief has been made available; FA 2009, Sch 61; FA 2003, s 75C.

[52]   And stamp duty land tax: FA 2003, s 48(2)(a).

[53]   Stamp Act 1891, s 122.

[54]   Pursuant to FA 1986, s 79.

[55]   FA 2009, Sch 61; see **10.60**.

[56]   FA 1986, s 86; see **1.22**.

[57]   Stamp Act 1891, s 57; FA 2003, Sch 4, paras 8 and 8A.

Leasing contracts

1.9 Contracts for the hire or lease of goods or for their hire purchase or lease purchase are exempt from stamp duty. However, where the equipment that is the subject-matter of the contract has become attached to the land, particularly where it has become a fixture, there will be issues as to whether the benefit of that contract is some form of chargeable interest in land for the purposes of stamp duty land tax.[58] In some situations there may be a lease of equipment which is *prima facie* a lease of chattels but the lessee may attach the equipment to the land and may incorporate it into the land or building in circumstances where it might be regarded as a fixture for certain purposes.[59] The question is whether in relation to future disposals of the land (ie the lease) is the disposal of a chargeable interest or a chattel ie the consideration for the equipment has to be treated as part of the price for the lease, and whether the disposal of the interest of the lessor of the equipment is a disposal of a chattel or some form of interest in land. In the latter case there is a *prima facie* chargeable transaction as the acquisition of a chargeable interest for the purposes of stamp duty land tax.

Partnership interests

1.10 Although shares or interests in partnerships are not, in general,[60] chargeable interests in land,[61] notwithstanding the look-through provisions in FA 2003, Sch 15, Part 1,[62] the transfer (as defined)[63] of an interest in a partnership (not defined but different from a 'share' which is defined)[64] is subject to stamp duty land tax where the partnership is a 'property investment partnership' and there is consideration for the transfer or it is to a relevant company.[65] The charge is not on the actual consideration but a proportion of the market value of any relevant land held by the partnership.[66] There are also charges to stamp duty (but not the principal charge to stamp duty reserve tax[67]) where the assets of the partnership include shares and marketable securities.[68] There are three issues:

- essentially a transfer of an interest in a partnership is no longer subject to *ad valorem* stamp duty;

- where the assets of the property investment partnership[69] include shares or marketable securities there is a charge to stamp duty upon a relevant part of the consideration;[70] and

---

[58]   See **4.39**.
[59]   See, for example, *Stokes v Costain Property Investments Ltd* [1984] STC 204 and *Barclays Mercantile and Business Finance v Mawson* (2005) STC 1; *Drages v IRC* 46 TC 389.
[60]   They are treated as chargeable interests for certain purposes; see **13.18**.
[61]   See **Chapter 13**.
[62]   See **Chapter 13**.
[63]   FA 2003, Sch 15, paras 31 and 32; s 125 and Sch 19.
[64]   See **13.19**.
[65]   FA 2003, Sch 15, para 14 (as amended) and Stamp Duty Land Tax (Variation of Finance Act 2003) Regulations 2006, SI 2006/3237. See **Chapter 13**.
[66]   FA 2003, Sch 15, paras 14 and 12A.
[67]   FA 1986, s 87.
[68]   FA 2003, Sch 15, paras 31–33.
[69]   But note the effect of anti-avoidance provisions for other partnerships pursuant to FA 2003, Sch 15, paras 17 and 17A.
[70]   FA 2003, Sch 15, para 14.

- where the partnership is a property investment partnership there is a charge to stamp duty land tax upon a proportion of the market value.[71]

In addition to these basic charges there are situations where a transfer of an interest in a partnership may have stamp tax implications:

- in some situations the retirement or dealings in a partnership interest may operate to trigger anti-avoidance provisions for stamp duty land tax such as FA 2003, Sch 15, paras 17 and 17A; and

- a dealing in a partnership interest may operate as a scheme transaction which has to be taken into account when calculating the charge pursuant to the general anti-avoidance provisions for stamp duty land tax.[72]

THE CHARGE TO STAMP DUTY

1.11 Stamp duty remains in effect:

- for the completion of certain land contracts entered into before 1 December 2003.[73] This may have other advantages in that reliefs that were available for stamp duty may be available for transactions that might otherwise fall into charge pursuant to stamp duty land tax. However, this relief is dependent upon the relevant contract not having been altered since the introduction of stamp duty land tax.[74] In this situation the parties may find it more tax efficient to mitigate the overall liability by completing the transaction and attracting stamp duty upon the basis of the original contract and subsequently varying the completion arrangements which may attract little or no stamp duty land tax notwithstanding that the variation of a chargeable interest is a potentially chargeable transaction.[75] Completions of contracts involving 'all other property' on or after that date are not subject to stamp duty whether or not the contract was stampable;

- for the completion of transactions relating to shares and marketable securities; contracts for the sale of stock and marketable securities are not subject to stamp duty[76] unless, perhaps, this is a contract simply for the sale of an equitable interest in shares.[77] However, an uncompleted contract for the sale of shares where stamp duty has not been paid or the instrument has not qualified for some form of exemption remains liable to the principal charge to stamp duty reserve tax;[78]

- for transfers of shares in partnerships which include shares and marketable securities in their assets;[79] and

---

Ibid, Sch 15, para 14 (as amended).
[72] Ibid, ss 75A–75C.
[73] Ibid, Sch 19 (as amended).
[74] Ibid, Sch 19, paras 3–4B.
[75] Ibid, s 43.
[76] FA 1999, Sch 13, para 7.
[77] See, for example, *Peter Bone v IRC* [1995] STC 921; *Oughtred v IRC* [1960] AC 206 but note the effective reversal of this decision by the Court of Appeal in *Neville v Wilson* [1997] Ch 144.
[78] FA 1986, s 87.
[79] FA 2003, Sch 15, paras 31–33.

- as regards certain fixed duties for transfers of land subject to certification pursuant to the Stamp Duty (Exempt Instrument) Regulations 1987.[80]

The full traditional stamp duty continues to apply[81] so that, for example, the computational principles including the contingency principle will apply such as where there is a sale of shares on an earnout basis.[82]

Transitional benefits

1.12   The stamp duty regime is, in general, considerably more favourable for leases than stamp duty land tax such as the lower charge upon most rents and it is important to present the protection for stamp duty arrangements wherever possible.

This is especially important in relation to the treatment of stamp duty leases in the new regime ie transactions entered into in relation to leases granted before 1 December 2003, and in some cases after that date where the grant was subject to stamp duty.[83] Certain transactions are not subject to stamp duty land tax and are free of stamp duty. For example, in practice HMRC Stamp Taxes accept that the charges relating to the holding over of expired leases[84] do not apply where the old lease was subject to stamp duty and the rules relating to abnormal increases of rent after the fifth year of the term do not apply.[85] The legislation is not always clear on these points such as renewals of stamp duty leases and the linked transaction rules[86] so that each charge has to be looked at in the context of its particular wording. For example, where the charge refers to an earlier effective date it cannot apply to stamp duty leases which cannot have an effective date. These benefits will be lost if the parties effect a surrender and regrant or other arrangement replacing the stamp duty lease with a new stamp duty land tax lease. Negotiations should keep this point in mind. There may be other methods of dealing with the situation. For example, rather than extending the term of a lease that is within the stamp duty regime there may be benefits in inserting an option to renew the lease or the parties enter into an agreement for a reversionary lease.[87] No charge to stamp duty land tax would arise unless and until the option to renew is exercised and the new agreement for lease comes into effect and such agreement for lease is either completed or substantially performed. Whilst there are technical difficulties in relation to the grant of a reversionary lease which HMRC Stamp Taxes regard as being immediately taxable in respect of the rent which will arise only when the lease takes effective possession so that estimates may be required, there is no chargeable event in relation to an agreement for reversionary lease since the tenant is in occupation under the existing lease and this is not substantial performance of the agreement for lease.

---

[80]   SI 1987/516; FA 2003, Sch 32, para 22.

[81]   It seems that foreign shares and marketable securities remain subject to stamp duty where there is something done or to be done in the UK; Stamp Act 1891, s 14; *Maples (Paris) Ltd v IRC* [1908] AC 22.

[82]   And the traditional principle of stamp duty in relation to chargeable consideration and the computation thereof, including the contingency principle, continues to apply in full.

[83]   FA 2003, Sch 19, para 8; note also the possible credit for stamp duty upon the agreement for lease against the stamp duty land tax pursuant to paras 7 and 7A and the special favourable penalty regime continues to apply (FA 1994, s 111; FA 1994, ss 240 and 240A; FA 2003, Sch 19, para 8(2)); see **1.16**.

[84]   FA 2003, Sch 17A, paras 3 and 4.

[85]   On stamp duty leases granted after 1 December 2003 see FA 2003, Sch 17A, para 14(7) (as amended).

[86]   FA 2003, Sch 19, para 7.

[87]   But note the restrictions imposed by the Law of Property Act 1925, s 149.

Land

1.13 Although stamp duty land tax has become the primary tax in relation to land transactions, stamp duty at rates of up to 4 per cent where the consideration exceeds £500,000 continues to be charged[88] upon land transactions in relation to instruments executed on or after the implementation date in the following cases.

Completion of pre-11 July 2003 contracts[89]

1.14 Stamp duty applies where there is a completion in the form of a conveyance[90] or lease pursuant to an agreement for sale or lease entered into on or before Royal Assent.[91] This is dependent upon the agreement not having been altered. Where this applies it may be more stamp tax efficient to complete the stamp duty transaction attracting the lower charge to tax and varying the arrangements after completion which may attract little or no stamp duty land tax. The aggregate of the stamp duty and the stamp duty land tax will frequently be significantly lower than a full stamp duty land tax charge upon the varied agreement. This continuation of the stamp duty charge is beneficial in three situations:

(1) it enables the parties, by deferring the execution of the formal instrument of conveyance or lease to postpone the payment of the tax without interest or penalty;

(2) it may enable the parties to claim that a lower charge to stamp duty applies such as in the case of a lease at a rent where the stamp duty charge will almost always be a small fraction of the equivalent stamp duty land tax liability; and

(3) the taxpayer is not subject to the onerous and expensive stamp duty land tax compliance regime.[92]

These situations are particularly important in relation to the following agreements:

Conditional agreements

1.15 Although there are special provisions bringing transactions arising pursuant to the exercise of options or pre-emptive rights granted on or after 17 April 2003 into the charge to stamp duty land tax,[93] this does not apply to conditional agreements. In consequence, where these were entered into prior to 11 July 2003 the fact that they may not have become unconditional until after that date or even after the implementation of stamp duty land tax does not affect the position that the completion of such contracts remains subject to stamp duty.

---

[88] But subject to whatever exemptions might be available.

[89] Contracts entered into on or after that date and completed after 1 December 2003 are within the new tax.

[90] 'Conveyance' is widely defined by Stamp Act 1891, FA 1999, Sch 13, para 1 and case law has extended these definitions to items such as powers of attorney (*Diplock v Hammond* (1854) 5 De GM & G 320) and written memoranda (*Horsfall v Hey* (1848) 2 Ex 778). It remains an open question in practice whether these principles will be carried forward by HMRC Stamp Taxes in practice into stamp duty land tax.

[91] FA 2003, s 125(5); Sch 19, paras 3 and 4.

[92] FA 2003, Sch 10; see **Chapters 15–20** below.

[93] Ibid, Sch 19, para 9.

Agreements for lease

1.16   In general, the stamp duty upon rents reserved by leases of land in the United Kingdom is significantly lower than the stamp duty land tax charged upon such rent.[94] It is, therefore, important that nothing is done to jeopardise this special position (such as the transaction set out below). Moreover, the stamp duty penalty and late payment interest regime continues to apply so that, no matter how long the actual grant of the lease is deferred, provided that it and the agreement for lease are presented together for stamping,[95] although the agreement for lease is subject to duty the interest and penalties do not begin to run until 30 days after the execution of the lease.[96] In consequence, there are cash flow benefits in remaining within the stamp duty regime.

Restrictions upon transitional stamp duty regime for land

Variations of contracts

1.17   This favourable stamp duty regime does not apply and the transaction falls into the more onerous stamp duty land tax regime (including the compliance requirements) where, notwithstanding that the contract, whether or not conditional, was entered into prior to 11 July 2003,[97] either:

- there is a variation of the contract on or after that date. There is, significantly, no qualification or explanation of which types of variation cancel the preservation of the stamp duty regime for such contracts. In consequence, it seems that any amendment of the contract, no matter how trivial, will bring the transaction into charge to stamp duty land tax. Clearly, changes to the completion date[98] or payment schedule or building specifications will jeopardise the benefit of the continued application of the stamp duty regime. HMRC Stamp Taxes has merely indicated that this provision will not apply to totally trivial changes such as a different colour scheme; or

- there is an assignment of the rights under the contract on or after that date. The transaction is taken into stamp duty land tax, notwithstanding that any arrangements relating to the assignment of the contract prior to implementation date will be subject to stamp duty.[99] There is a potential double charge to tax in these situations which should be investigated; or

- the contract arises pursuant to the exercise of an option, right of pre-emption or similar right on or after that date regardless of the date when the option or right was granted;[100] or

---

[94]   Ibid, Sch 5; see **7.98** below.

[95]   For the procedure see FA 2003, Sch 19, para 8; FA 1994, ss 240 and 240A.

[96]   FA 1994, ss 240 and 240A.

[97]   For the credit arrangements where the agreement for lease is subject to stamp duty but the lease is subject to stamp duty land tax see FA 2003, Sch 19, para 8.

[98]   There may also be an issue where the completion date is extended informally such as where the purchaser defaults temporarily, particular if the vendor concurs in the delay.

[99]   FA 1999, Sch 13, para 7; *Western Abyssinian Mining Syndicate Ltd v IRC* (1935) 46 TC 407.

[100] See also the special rules for options and similar rights entered into on or after 17 April 2003 in FA 2003, Sch 19, para 9.

- the 'purchaser', which would appear to include a lessee or other taxpayer, is a person other than the original party to the contract because of a further contract made on or after that date,[101] such as where a subsale agreement has been entered into;[102] or

- the stamp duty transaction may be 'linked' with a stamp duty land tax transaction and so increase the charge to stamp duty land tax. Such prior stamp duty transactions cannot be 'linked transactions' for the purposes of either stamp duty or stamp duty land tax but it is provided that in relation to a transaction that is not a stamp duty land tax transaction but is linked to it in the sense of forming part of an overall arrangement or scheme it will be recognised for the purpose of stamp duty land tax and when determining the rate of stamp duty land tax for the stamp duty land tax transaction the chargeable consideration in respect of the stamp duty land tax transaction to be aggregated with the later 'linked' stamp duty land tax transaction is the consideration in respect of which the *ad valorem* stamp duty was calculated.[103]

Any such contract, if completed after the implementation of stamp duty land tax, is subject to the tax, notwithstanding that it was entered into prior to 11 July 2003 and would not have been subject to stamp duty.

Subsale and pre-11 July 2003 contracts

1.18 The terms of FA 2003, Sch 19, para 3(3)(c), would suggest that where a pre-11 July 2003 contract which is the subject-matter of a subsale agreement entered into on or after that date is completed after the implementation of stamp duty land tax,[104] it ceases to be exempt from stamp duty and became subject to stamp duty land tax. However, this is not an accurate picture:

- where the contract has been substantially performed[105] prior to 11 July 2003 it is specifically provided that the completion after the implementation of stamp duty land tax of any contract that is varied, assigned or subsold on or after 11 July 2003 does not bring the original contract into charge to stamp duty land tax.[106] However, the substantial performance or completion of the subsale contract will be subject to stamp duty land tax upon the assignee;[107]

---

[101] FA 2003, Sch 19, para 3(3).
[102] The same point would arise where there has been an assignment, but, as this is specifically dealt with, there appears to be a duplication in the legislation.
[103] FA 2003, Sch 19, para 7(1).
[104] If completed prior to such implementation of stamp duty land tax, the subsale relief of Stamp Act 1891, s 58(4) and (5) continues to apply. It is worthwhile considering where part only of the land has been subsold and the contracts completed by transfers or leases whether to take a transfer of the balance of the land to the original purchaser and pay stamp duty only upon the reduced amount (*Maples v IRC* [1914] 3 KB 303) rather than resting upon the contract and completing that outstanding subsale of part, since these would bring the full charge to stamp duty land tax into operation so that the full original purchase price and not merely the balance became retrospectively taxable. The subsale provisions in FA 2003, s 45 indicate that the full charge to stamp duty land tax would apply since the effective date is deferred from substantial performance to 'completion', i e any transfer by way of subsale (FA 2003, Sch 19, para 4). In consequence it seems probable that not taking a transfer of the legal title to the balance of the land is unnecessary and a more expensive charge to stamp duty land tax will be incurred.
[105] FA 2003, s 44; see **Chapters 10** and **13** below.
[106] Ibid, Sch 19, para 4(3).
[107] Pursuant to ibid, s 45; see **6.28**.

- where the original contract was not substantially performed before 11 July 2003, then:

- if it is not substantially performed and subsold until after the implementation of stamp duty land tax, it will be within the charge to that tax but would appear to qualify for the limited relief contained in FA 2003, s 45 which provides for a form of subsale relief where the original agreement to acquire the property has not been substantially performed;[108]

- if the original contract is substantially performed between 11 July 2003 and the implementation date for stamp duty land tax, completion after that latter date by way of subsale means that the original contract will be subject to stamp duty land tax.[109] For these purposes it does not matter that the substantial performance took place before the implementation of stamp duty land tax since it is provided that the effective date for the purposes of that tax is the date of completion.[110]

These points can be of considerable importance in practice since the stamp duty land tax legislation is designed to prevent parties from resting upon contract. However, parties may be resting upon uncompleted contracts entered into within the stamp duty regime for many years or awaiting the outcome of planning applications. It is not unusual for parties to enter into contracts but to leave the completion paperwork open, possibly even intending to subsell. Such transactions where these remain outstanding in the stamp duty land tax regime will, therefore, need to be considered in the context of the above provisions which can move the original transaction from stamp duty into stamp duty land tax.

1.19 Finance Act 2003, Sch 19, para 3(3)(c) is modified to bring into charge retrospectively contracts for the acquisition of land entered into prior to 10 July 2003 where there is a subsequent subsale. Paragraph 3(3)(c) is amended so that as regards pre-10 July 2003 agreements not completed before 17 March 2004, the transaction is subject to stamp duty land tax if on or after the latter date there is an assignment, subsale or other transaction (relating to the whole or part of the subject-matter of the contract) as a result of which a person other than the purchaser under the contract becomes entitled to call for a conveyance. The charge does not apply if the contract was substantially performed before 17 March 2004.[111] However, this may not have significant practical impact if the original contract is not substantially performed and the subsale meets the conditions of Finance Act 2003, s 45. It, nevertheless, remains a risk for persons who entered into conditional arrangements some years ago where planning permission has not yet been obtained.

Completion of contracts entered into between 11 July and 30 November 2003

1.20 Where a contract was entered into prior to 1 December 2003 but was not substantially performed before 11 July 2003 the effective date is the date of 'completion' ie it becomes a stamp duty land tax transaction.[112]

---

108   See **6.36**.
109   FA 2003, Sch 19, para 4.
110   Ibid, Sch 19, para 4(3).
111   Ibid, Sch 39, paras 12 and 13(4).
112   Ibid, Sch 19, para 4.

1.21 However, in these situations the parties may escape a charge to stamp duty or stamp duty land tax should the transaction qualify for subsale relief pursuant to FA 2003, s 45 (as amended).[113]

Shares and marketable securities

1.22 These are subject to numerous possible regimes of stamp taxes including:

- transfers of shares and marketable securities are subject to stamp duty. The rules as to computation, timing of instruments, reliefs and exemptions[114] continue to apply to transfers on sale or the fixed duties in respect of transfers of shares or marketable securities were removed by FA 2008[115] and there is now a nil rate for transactions involving shares where the consideration does not exceed £1000 provided that the stock transfer form contains a certificate to the effect that it does not form part of a series or a larger transaction where the consideration exceeds the £1000 limit. The standard form of certificate has been incorporated into the back of stock transfer forms which no longer contain the long list of certificates required for the exemption from the £5 fixed duty.[116]

- there is, in general, no stamp duty upon a contract for the sale of a legal interest in stock and marketable securities,[117] although there is a charge upon contracts for the sale of equitable interests in such securities;[118] but

- contracts for the sale of shares, are subject to the principal charge to stamp duty reserve tax[119] unless there has been a duly stamped transfer.[120] The interaction of stamp duty reserve tax and stamp duty is important. For example, it is important to understand the rules concerning stamp duty upon share transactions since there are few exemptions from stamp duty reserve tax; such relief as is available generally depends upon obtaining an exemption from stamp duty for the share transfer.[121] However, the payment of the correct amount of stamp duty will cancel the principal charge to stamp duty reserve tax. The latter is the principal charge following the FA 1996 and this is cancelled by the production of appropriate instruments of transfer within the stamp duty regime.[122] It is, however, necessary to produce the 'duly stamped' instrument. It is not sufficient to contend that had there been a stamp duty instrument the amount would have been nil or negligible. This does not cancel the charge; there must be the production of the appropriate instrument. This includes instruments that are exempt from stamp duty although where such exemption depends adjudication it is necessary to go through the appropriate procedure. There are, however, certain transaction indicators within CREST which may enable transactions on the Stock Exchange to avoid the need

---

[113] This is, however, complicated by retrospective 'clarifications' of the law relating to subsales and assignments; FA 2003, Sch 19, paras 4A and 4B.

[114] The obtaining of these reliefs will also be important in certain cases in order to prevent the clawback of any exemptions from stamp duty land tax pursuant to FA 2003, Sch 7; see **Chapter 12**.

[115] Schedule 32.

[116] Stamp Duty (Exempt Instrument) Regulations 1987, SI 1987/516.

[117] FA 1999, Sch 13, para 7.

[118] Note the drafting issues in cases such as *Peter Bone v IRC* [1995] STC 921.

[119] FA 1986, s 87; payment of stamp duty upon a transfer within a six-year period cancels the charge: see s 92 thereof.

[120] FA 1986, s 91.

[121] Ibid, s 91 which cancels the charge to stamp duty reserve tax where there is a 'duly stamped' transfer.

[122] FA 1986, s 92.

to make an immediate payment of stamp duty reserve tax where certain exemptions from stamp duty may be available.

- the issue of bearer instruments by UK companies remains subject to stamp duty.[123] Certain bearer documents issued before 1 October 1999 remain subject to stamp duty pursuant to the provisions of FA 1963, ss 59 et seq; instruments executed on or after that date are subject to stamp duty pursuant to the provisions of Finance Act 1999, Sch 15;

- the transfer of bearer instruments issued by non-UK companies are subject to stamp duty upon first transfer on sale in this country;[124]

- in certain cases, dealings in bearer instruments issued by UK companies may be subject to the principal charge to stamp duty reserve tax;[125]

- although there is no stamp duty upon the issue of shares in general, the issue of chargeable securities[126] into depository and clearance schemes are subject to a special charge to stamp duty reserve tax of 1.5 per cent;[127]

- transfers of shares in UK companies into depository and clearance schemes will be subject to stamp duty or stamp duty reserve tax at the rate of 1.5 per cent;[128]

- a special regime for stamp duty reserve tax applies to dealings in units and shares in unit trusts and open-ended investment companies.[129]

Shares, land or assets

1.23   The threatened charge to stamp duty land tax upon shares in land rich companies has not been introduced which makes transfers of shares considerably more stamp tax efficient than acquisitions of land, especially where the company is incorporated outside the United Kingdom so that its shares can be transferred free of stamp duty[130] and stamp duty reserve tax.[131] There are, however, numerous anti-avoidance provisions designed to prevent parties 'converting' land into shares.[132]

1.24   The converse of the situation of there being no provisions for land rich companies is that there is no relief for the transfer of shares in respect of assets of the company that are not taxable so that the purchase of the undertaking may be more cost effective. For example, the company may have debtors and creditors, intellectual property, goodwill as well as chattels, trading stock and the benefit of long-term contracts. There may be issues as to whether there is some form of embedded goodwill in the land but subject to that all of the assets in the company other than shares in

---

[123]   This charge may be unlawful pursuant to the capital duty directive (EC Directive 69/335 (as amended)); see *Kingdom of Belgium v European Commission* [2004] ECJ.

[124]   FA 1999, Sch 15, para 2.

[125]   FA 1986, s 90 (as amended).

[126]   Ibid, s 99 (as amended).

[127]   Ibid, ss 93 et seq. This charge may be unlawful pursuant to the capital duty directive (EC Directive 69/335 (as amended)); see *Kingdom of Belgium v European Commission* [2004] ECJ.

[128]   Ibid, ss 67 et seq, certain aspects of which are unlawful *HSBC Holdings v HMRC* [2009] ECJ.

[129]   FA 1999, Sch 19 and the various statutory instruments issued pursuant thereto.

[130]   Stamp Act 1891, s 14(4).

[131]   FA 1986, s 99(4) (as amended).

[132]   Such as the connected company charge; FA 2003, ss 53 and 54.

subsidiaries can be transferred free of stamp duty. This, of course, raises an acute issue of whether a purchaser should acquire assets or shares. Obviously, where the company is 'land rich' there are benefits in acquiring the shares, particularly if the relevant parties have, with foresight, established a company outside the United Kingdom where there will be no charge to stamp duty or stamp duty reserve tax if the transaction is carefully planned. This will pass the value of the land without stamp duty. On the other hand, where the company has no land in the United Kingdom but has considerable debtors, goodwill and similar property the transfer of the shares effectively imposes an indirect charge to stamp duty of 0.5 per cent upon the transfer of those assets. In this situation the purchaser, subject to other taxes, may find it more efficient to acquire the assets rather than the shares.

'Stocks' and 'marketable securities' defined

1.25 The current charges to stamp duty are limited to 'stock or marketable securities' with an exclusion for alternative finance instruments.[133] These are words that have acquired a special meaning in stamp duty which has to be borne in mind. 'Stock' is defined[134] as including 'any share in any stocks or funds transferable at the Bank of England or at the Bank of Ireland and India promissory notes and any share in the stocks or funds of any foreign or colonial state or government, or in the capital stock or funded debt[135] of any county council, corporation, company or society in the United Kingdom or of any foreign or colonial corporation, company or society'. It would, therefore, appear to include shares and many forms of debt instrument of companies. A limited liability partnership incorporated pursuant to the Limited Partnership Act 2000 is a body corporate[136] and is governed by the provisions of the companies legislation with modifications as set out in regulations.[137] In consequence, the interests of partners may well be 'stock'.[138] The attitude of HMRC Stamp Taxes is not clear on this point. It appears to regard such interests as 'transparent'[139] and not as 'shares' but this is not supported by the legislation.[140] The area is important in relation to the charges to stamp duty reserve tax since this applies to 'chargeable securities'[141] and the definition specifically excludes instruments relating to property that are exempt from stamp duty.[142] In consequence, although certain aspects of the definition for stamp duty reserve tax refer to rights to be allotted shares and options to acquire securities this aspect of the definition has become redundant and overtaken by events after 1986. Such arrangements are no longer subject to stamp duty and, in consequence, are no longer chargeable securities. There are differences in the drafting of the two sets of provisions but the practical effect is considered to be that where the security in question is not subject to stamp duty it is also no longer a chargeable security for the purposes of stamp duty reserve tax.

1.26 'Stock' does not include 'interests in stock' for stamp duty so that options relating to stock and marketable securities are not 'stock' and, in consequence, the grant

---

[133] FA 2009, Sch 61; see **10.60**.

[134] Stamp Act 1891, s 122(1).

[135] *Reed International v IRC* [1975] STC 427.

[136] Limited Liability Partnership Act 2000, s 1(2).

[137] Limited Liability Partnership Regulations 2001, SI 2001/1090.

[138] This also raises questions as to whether they are bodies corporate for the purposes of the reliefs from stamp duty.

[139] Inland Revenue Tax Bulletin, Issue 50.

[140] Specific provisions provide for transparency in relation to stamp duty land tax: FA 2003, Sch 15, para 2.

[141] Defined in FA, 1986, s 99 (as much amended).

[142] FA 1986, s 99(5) (as amended).

and assignment of options relating to property other than land[143] are free of stamp duty on or after implementation date. However, dealings in options, as opposed to their issue, are subject to stamp duty reserve tax.[144]

1.27 This area is important in relation to the issue of new shares which is significant not only in relation to the charge to stamp duty and stamp duty reserve tax, but also can affect the availability of relief.[145] For the purposes of stamp duty, there are various stages in the creation of new shares:

- the right to be allotted shares. This is the stage where a person has entered into a contract to subscribe or to transfer property to the company in consideration of shares, but the board of directors has not yet resolved to allot the shares.[146] In this case, HMRC Stamp Taxes has consistently for decades maintained that the contractual right is not 'stock'[147] and has claimed the full 4 per cent rate of stamp duty. Such rights will now be exempt from stamp duty upon transfer. Moreover, the transfer of such rights would not appear to fall into charge for the purposes of stamp duty reserve tax;[148] as they are now exempt from all stamp duties, they would not be chargeable securities[149] notwithstanding the reference to rights to be allotted shares etc in the definition;[150]

- the right to an allotment of shares. This is the stage where the board of directors has resolved to allot the shares. As this point, the shares come into existence[151] and dealings are subject to stamp duty or stamp duty reserve tax; and

- the shares are entered in the register, ie are 'issued'.[152]

These various stages are important not merely in deciding whether there is a charge to tax but also whether the conditions for exemption from stamp duty, stamp duty reserve tax[153] or stamp duty land tax upon corporate takeovers and reconstructions have been satisfied.[154] They may also be important in deciding whether the contract has been substantially performed because the consideration has been provided.[155]

1.28 'Marketable security' is defined[156] as being a security of such a description as to be capable of being sold in any stock market in the United Kingdom. This definition has two limbs, namely:

---

[143] Options (and pre-emption rights) relating to land are chargeable interests within the charge to stamp duty land tax; see FA 2003, s 46.

[144] FA 1986, s 99 (as amended) defining 'chargeable securities'.

[145] See, for example, *Oswald Tillotson v IRC* [1933] 1 KB 134.

[146] See, eg, *Letts v IRC* [1957] 1 WLR 201.

[147] See Press Releases, 27 June 1985 and August 1985.

[148] FA 1986, s 99 (as amended).

[149] Ibid, s 99(5)(a).

[150] Ibid, s 99(3)(c) (as amended).

[151] *Pye-Smith v IRC* [1958] 1 WLR 905; *Re Simo Securities* [1971] 3 All ER 999; *Re Pool Shipping* [1920] 1 Ch 251; *Letts v IRC* [1957] 1 WLR 201. These cases may have relevance in determining the effective date for acquisitions by companies in consideration of shares such as incorporations and reorganisations.

[152] *National Westminster Bank v IRC* [1995] 1 AC 119.

[153] There is a rare direct exemption from stamp duty reserve tax in relation to the issue of securities with a depository or clearance scheme in connection with certain takeovers; FA 1986, ss 95 and 97.

[154] *Oswald Tillotson Ltd v IRC* [1933] 1 KB 134; *Brotex Cellulose Fibres Ltd v IRC* [1933] 1 KB 158; *Murex v IRC* [1933] 1 KB 173; *National Westminster Bank v IRC* [1994] STC 580.

[155] FA 2003, s 44; see **14.10**.

[156] Stamp Act 1891, s 122.

(i)   *Security*: A security for stamp duty purposes is a debt instrument such as a debenture. Notwithstanding popular usage of 'security' as including a wide range of investments such as equities and preference shares, this does not apply for stamp duty. It is necessary to note that the words 'security' is used in different sense in relation to stamp duty and stamp duty reserve tax. In the latter case it bears its wider meaning of some form of interest in shares including not merely the shares themselves but rights to dividends and other derivative arrangements. This gives rise to apparent inconsistencies in the legislation but most of these problems are resolved by the fact that there is an exclusion from the definition of chargeable 'securities' for the purposes of stamp duty reserve tax for those 'securities' that are exempt from stamp duties. However, since 'security' for the purposes of stamp duty reserve tax is wider than the definition of 'security' for the purposes of stamp duty there may be 'securities' that remain subject to the former charge. However, since such arrangements are not usually 'marketable securities' and are, in consequence, not 'stock' they will be instruments exempt from stamp duty and therefore specifically excluded from the definition of 'chargeable securities' for the purposes of stamp duty reserve tax;[157]

(ii) *Marketable*: This is a special definition because of the limited concept of 'marketability'. An actual listing on the Stock Exchange in the United Kingdom is not necessary[158] and a listing on an overseas Stock Exchange is not, of itself, sufficient to create a marketable security. The test is whether the instrument is of such a character that it could qualify for a listing in the United Kingdom. The longstanding practice is that, since private companies cannot as a matter of law list their securities, these are not marketable securities. Similarly, certain types of debt instrument issued by companies whose ordinary securities are listed may not themselves qualify for listing because, for example, the amounts in which they are transferable are inconveniently large or may be only partly paid or of a revolving nature. These will not be 'marketable securities'. Dealings in such instruments continue to be free of stamp duty and stamp duty reserve tax, as the FA 1986 provides that that tax does not apply to securities which are exempt from all stamp duty.[159]

Foreign securities

1.29   Securities issued by foreign companies remain within the charge to various stamp taxes.

- Stamp Act 1891, s 14(4) is not repealed or amended so that a transfer of stock or marketable securities of a company incorporated outside the United Kingdom will be subject to stamp duty if:
  - the transfer or contract for the sale of the equitable interest[160] is executed in the United Kingdom; or

---

[157] FA 2003, s 99(5) (as amended).
[158] *Texas Land and Cattle Co v IRC* (1888) 16 R 69, 26 SLR 49.
[159] FA 1986, s 99(5) (as amended).
[160] On the problems of determining equitable interests in foreign property for these purposes, see *Farmer & Co v IRC* [1898] 2 QB 141; but to the extent that these may depend upon the availability of equitable relief; see, for example, the power of the English courts in relation to foreign property as in *Penn v Baltimore* (1750) 1 Ves Sen 444.

–   if the transfer relates to something done or to be done in the United
      Kingdom, such as the provision of the consideration in this country.[161]

•   The principal charge to stamp duty reserve tax applies to unstamped
      arrangements for the transfer of chargeable securities of companies incorporated
      outside the United Kingdom where the securities are entered in a register[162]
      maintained in the United Kingdom by or on behalf of the company.[163]

•   The first transfer on sale in the United Kingdom of bearer securities issued
      outside the United Kingdom by a non-UK company is subject to bearer
      instrument duty.[164]

---

[161]   *Maples & Co (Paris) Ltd v IRC* [1908] AC 22.
[162]   On what is a 'register', especially in the context of branch or duplicate registers, see *Standard Chartered Bank
        v IRC* [1978] 3 All ER 644. It is important to note the requirement that the register or recording of the
        movements in title of the shares is maintained by or on behalf of the company. Frequently, companies may
        employ outside parties to maintain their share register. It is obviously important that such parties are located
        and operating and can maintain their main records outside the UK. Unfortunately, HMRC Stamp Taxes
        have, from time to time, taken the point that such offshore registrars may maintain some form of presence in
        the UK where they are to be notified of any dealings in relation to the shares in the company in question.
        This will require the keeping of records. HMRC Stamp Taxes have taken 2 points. The first of these is that
        such records are a 'share register' in their own right. This is manifestly incorrect because such records are
        simply the basis upon which the persons within the UK assess what needs to be forwarded to the offshore
        registrars who maintain the overseas or branch register. Their records are not in any way inclusive or
        indicative of the current title to the shares. They are simply indications of the current state of the
        information relating to dealings in the shares. To supplement this bad point, HMRC Stamp Taxes also take
        the second point that this is a share register of a company. Apart from the fact that it is not a share register
        it is a record that is maintained by or on behalf of the UK representatives of the offshore registrar for their
        own purposes. Provided that it can be shown that the registrars have no power or authority to maintain a
        share register and are specifically prohibited from doing so by the terms of their contract with the company
        then it is difficult for HMRC Stamp Taxes to maintain that any records in the UK of share movements that
        may need to collated and forwarded to the offshore registrars before appropriate changes can be made in the
        company's register are not a register maintained by or on behalf of the company in the UK.
[163]   FA 1986, s 99(4).
[164]   FA 1999, s 125(7); Sch 15, para 11.

Chapter 2

STAMP DUTY LAND TAX – GENERAL PRINCIPLES AND BASIC ISSUES

INTERPRETATION OF THE LEGISLATION

2.1 This chapter deals with the basic structure of the tax in order to provide a framework for understanding the legislation. The topics covered are dealt with in detail in subsequent chapters. The interpretation principles to be applied to stamp duty land tax legislation and regulations are extremely obscure. The drafting was apparently based upon 'plain English' concepts,[1] but it is clear that the legislation cannot work in anything approaching a reasonable fashion on this basis because taking the words at face value of their plain English or dictionary meaning produces utterly nonsensical results and represents a danger for professional advisers acting on this basis. It is also important to bear in mind that, although the legislation is closely based upon the model of the conveyance on sale in terms of both structure and terminology, the words utilised in the legislation have to bear special definitions if the legislation is to make sense and these definitions have to be much distorted from their ordinary 'plain English' and even their normal legal meanings. Failure to appreciate the non-plain English drafting and attaching too much significance to the ordinary usage of words either as plain English or as traditional conveyancing terms is dangerously misleading. There are fundamental issues of principle which those responsible for drafting and structuring the legislation have not addressed such as:

- where the words have a longstanding technical meaning as a matter of general law whether this is the meaning to be applied or whether there is some special 'plain English' meaning to be adopted. There is also a question of whether words which have over three centuries acquired a particular meaning in relation to stamp duty are intended to bear the same meaning in stamp duty land tax. Although there is a certain amount of evidence in practice that suggests that HMRC Stamp Taxes are applying a similar meaning there is no general principle to this effect, particularly since there are many cases where a word well-known in stamp duty has to bear a novel meaning for stamp duty land tax. This raises issues of whether there is an overlap in the meaning of such terms. Words bearing widespread or routine conveyancing meanings tend, in practice, to bear a special meaning and this introduces an additional problem of construction, namely whether words in regular use in conveyancing bear their popular non-specialist or dictionary meaning or their general technical meaning or a special meaning derived from the peculiar context of the stamp duty land tax legislation;

---

[1]   But this is a problem for the draftsman such as the reference to 'this Schedule' in FA 2003, s 52(3). Even the word 'above' seems to be a challenge; see FA 1986, s 88(1B)(iia).

- there is also the question as to whether the draftsman's concept of 'plain English' coincides with that of practitioners and taxpayers and whether dictionary definitions, and if so which dictionary, are appropriate;

- the extent to which words that have a long stamp tax history and have acquired a specific meaning widely known amongst practitioners are to bear the same meaning in stamp duty land tax. There is a fundamental question, not merely as a matter of construction but as a matter of the general application of the tax, as to how far the 'baggage' of 300 years of stamp duty is to be carried across into the construction and administration of stamp duty land tax. There is considerable evidence in practice that certain members of former Stamp Office have retained their employment in relation to stamp duty land tax and are bringing with them the views and practices to which they have become accustomed in stamp duty. These constructions and practices are not necessarily consistent with a 'plain English' construction of the legislation; and

- there is also the bizarre drafting of the legislation upon the basis of a theory that 'one-size-fits-all'. The basic model of the legislation is that of a transfer of a freehold interest for a consideration upon sale. However, the tax base in terms of the types of transaction that are involved and the types of consideration that are made chargeable defers fundamentally from the basic stamp duty model of the conveyance or transfer on sale. The so-called 'plain English' legislation must, therefore, be twisted and distorted in order to make it applicable to transactions that are not conveyances on sale. For example, the taxpayer is described as a purchaser although he need not be a purchaser because there is no consideration[2] or he is a person becoming entitled to pre-emptive rights or even a person who was not a party to the original transaction. In addition, 'conveyance' has to include 'lease' for the purposes of stamp duty land tax, but this leaves open the question of whether it continues to bear the wide stamp duty meaning such that a power of attorney given to a purchaser continues to be a 'conveyance'[3] which may affect questions of whether the contract has been completed by conveyance between the same parties for the purposes of notification and payment of additional tax pursuant to FA 2003, s 44(8). It will be some considerable time before these many fundamental issues of construction are satisfactorily resolved. For example, there are questions as to what is a 'conveyance' which is fundamental, as indicated above, to certain aspects of the doctrine of substantial performance;[4]

- the legislation refers to the 'purchaser' rather than the 'taxpayer'. This must mean that 'purchaser' includes lessee and grantee of rights such as the persons to whom an option is granted and persons who become entitled to rights of way or rights to light or restrictive covenants;

- the plain English style or drafting means that there is a lack of precision and consistency in the legislation because the English of the draftsman reflects its flexibility as a spoken rather than a written language. For example, it is significant where the word 'consideration' is utilised whether it is intended to be 'chargeable consideration' or is 'consideration' in general which may or may not be chargeable. Similarly, there are issues around words of general usage such as 'conveyance'. For

---

2   FA 2003, s 43(4).
3   *Diplock v Hammond* (1854) 5 De GM & G 320.
4   FA 2003, s 44(1) and (10)(b).

some purposes this is defined as any written instrument.[5] In addition to the problem of what is a 'conveyance'[6] the legislation from time to time uses the words 'transfer'[7] and 'transfer' is sometimes used as a substitute word for 'acquisition'.[8] It is provided that 'company' includes 'bodies corporate' but there is no explanation as to whether there is intended to be any difference in usage where the words 'company' is used rather than 'body corporate';

• the plain English as applied to 'acquisition' involves property passing and besting but the related explanation is rather obscurely defined in such a way that it includes 'release or surrender'. It is therefore possible to 'acquire' an interest that disappears so that nothing vests in the 'acquirer'. In addition, because of the rules of substantial performance a charge to tax can arise notwithstanding that the purchaser has not been vested with any interest in the property at the particular time;

• this problem is increased because there are few general definitions.[9] Although there are certain definitions these apply only for limited purposes being expressed to apply only for certain parts of the stamp duty land tax legislation.

In consequence, it is clear that there is no simple approach to the legislation, particularly as it is frequently amended without adequate thought being given to the consequential changes that need to be made in order for the changes to apply consistently and without anomalies throughout the tax. There is, therefore, no simple or single basis for approaching the legislation as a matter of construction and it is necessary to be aware of the policy and purposes of the legislation in order to be able to understand how the 'plain English' legislation has to be distorted in order to fit in with conveyancing terminology and practices and former stamp duty practices or to overcome the 'one-size-fits-all' approach to the structuring of the legislation.

2.2 Given the drafting and structural deficiencies in the legislation it is helpful to be aware of the policy and intentions when seeking to interpret the provisions. Stamp duty land tax is essentially a package of anti-avoidance measures hurriedly put together in order to attack certain basic techniques utilised for the mitigation of stamp duty such as avoiding documentation. It is provided that stamp duty land tax applies notwithstanding there is no documentation.[10] Delay in the execution of an instrument subject to stamp duty such as delaying completion.[11] This arrangement is achieved by linking the tax charge to substantial performance rather than completion was tax efficient. Notwithstanding the terminology of FA 2003, s 108 referring to 'completion' as the effective date the numerous special rules will be applied to produce a tax charge between contract and completion.[12] It is also intended to avoid value shifting without a written instrument. For this purpose the definition of 'chargeable interest' is widely

---

5   See, for example, FA 2003, s 44(10)(b). However, an 'agreement' that is not a contract it is not supported by consideration is potentially an exempt transaction pursuant to FA 2003, Sch 3, para 1. It is, therefore, a matter for debate as to how far non-consensual 'agreements' that are unsupported by consideration and fall short of a contract can have any effect.

6   See further **1.14** and **3.32**.

7   See, for example, FA 2003, Sch 15.

8   Compare FA 2003, Sch 15, paras 9(2) and 35 and s 44 thereof.

9   FA 2003, s 122 with other definitions of a general nature in ss 116–119 and 121.

10 Ibid, s 42(2)(a).

11 The contract is not a conveyance and not, in principle, subject to stamp duty in the absence of specific charging provisions; see, for example, *Angus v IRC* (1889) 23 QBD 579.

12 See, for example, FA 2003, s 44(4).

defined as including many forms of contract affecting the value of land;[13] and the definition of 'acquisition'[14] applies to transactions that are not conveyances or completions in the traditional sense but include the actions of the parties and other transactions which may move value from one party to another. An awareness of the former planning techniques being attacked may provide some assistance in the search for the meaning of the current legislation. It also means that such techniques are no longer effective for reducing the stamp duty land tax cost.[15]

2.3   Unfortunately, there are particular problems in relation to the structuring of the legislation. There is much apparent self-serving drafting and structuring by HMRC Stamp Taxes. There are provisions that, upon any reasonable view of the legislation or the general law, are unnecessary. For example, it would seem to be a general principle that where a person acquires property and has an inherent liability imposed upon him, such as the obligation of the assignee of the lease to pay rent, this is not chargeable consideration.[16] Similarly, it is a general principle that consideration must move in the opposite direction from the property. In consequence, an inducement or reverse premium payable by a landlord to a tenant to accept the lease or by an assignor to a tenant of an onerous lease to accept the assignment of the lease or by a tenant as an inducement to a landlord to accept early termination of the lease these would not be consideration because the land and the payment are moving in the same direction. However, there is legislation specifically dealing with these situations. For example, it is provided that covenants given by an assignee of a lease in relation to the future rent are, in general, not taxable[17] and there are specific exemptions for reverse payments.[18] Clearly those responsible for the legislation have some bizarre theories as to inherent liabilities and reverse consideration. The legislation must, therefore, be approached on the basis that non-orthodox principles apply to stamp duty land tax and the normal rules of contract and land law may not be appropriate. To apply decisions such as *Swayne v IRC*[19] would mean that the provisions dealing with such covenants would be redundant and it would be impossible to persuade HMRC Stamp Taxes and their supporting judiciary that the legislation is redundant. In consequence, there is much self-serving legislation of this nature ie designed to provide support for bizarre theories of general law. There is much legislation enacted on the basis of certain assumptions that are very dubious but because the legislation making the amendment is in place then the bad assumption of HMRC Stamp Taxes becomes a good principle. The implications of such legislation is wide-ranging and any amendment or exception will need to be carefully considered because it may validate a dubious argument of HMRC Stamp Taxes in a wider context.

---

[13]   FA 2003, s 48(1)(b); see also Sch 17A, para 10(c).

[14]   Ibid, s 43(3) (as amended).

[15]   These techniques have very limited relevant to the surviving stamp duties following the restriction of stamp duty by FA 2003, s 125 to shares and marketable securities and the removal of most fixed duties by FA 2003, Sch 32. There may be certain advantages in relation to dealings in partnership interests where there is a charge to stamp duty on transfers of interests in partnerships where the partnership includes amongst its assets shares and marketable securities (FA 2003, Sch 15, para 31). There is no specific provision extending this charge to be within stamp duty reserve tax. In consequence, transactions where there is no written contract or instrument that can operate as a 'transfer or conveyance' there can be no charge to stamp duty. The techniques may, therefore, be useful in a limited range of circumstances. Many of these techniques such as the absence of documentation and resting on contract are irrelevant in relation to shares and marketable securities because of the application of stamp duty reserve tax which is a transaction based tax (FA 1986, s 86 and following).

[16]   See, for example, *Swayne v IRC* [1900] 1 QB 172.

[17]   FA 2003, Sch 17A, para 17.

[18]   Ibid, Sch 17A, para 18.

[19]   [1900] 1 QB 172.

STAMP DUTY MITIGATION

2.4 In order to have a basis for understanding the approach to the legislation it is necessary to understand the policy. The following techniques are attacked:

Avoiding documentation – transaction tax

2.5 The charge to stamp duty land tax applies whether or not there is a document.[20] The opportunity at present for unwritten land transactions is restricted by the general legislation relating to land and conveyancing which frequently requires deeds[21] or writing[22] or written memoranda[23] for the transaction to be valid or effective to pass title;[24] but, many transactions can be entered into without writing, such as leases for less than 3 years,[25] holding over, surrenders of leases by operation of law, and constructive trusts.[26]

---

[20] FA 2003, s 43(2)(a); compare the stamp duty cases of *IRC v G Angus & Co* (1889) 23 QBD 579 and *Carlill v Carbolic Smokeball Co* [1892] 2 QB 484; see **2.5**. There can be a tax charge notwithstanding that the contract is conditional so that, for example, where there is an agreement to assign a lease that is subject to the consent of the landlord the entry of the assignee into possession in order to fit out the premises or to make modifications could constitute taking possession and substantial performance giving rise to a charge to tax even before the contract becomes unconditional let alone being 'completed' by the formal assignment of the right. In some situations the actions of the parties between contract and completion may mean that there is a charge to tax because there is an event that constitutes substantial performance of the agreement. This may affect the amount of the tax such as where building works or fitting out are involved and the parties take steps that do not constitute 'substantial performance' in which case the exemption for building works upon the land to be acquired will not be available (FA 2003, Sch 4, para 10). Since solicitors will frequently be required to sign the declaration (SDLT 1) as to the effective date of the transaction it is important that they are aware of the activities of the parties between contract and completion and whether these constitute substantial performance in order to avoid suggestions that they are involved in the preparation of a form which they 'know' to be incorrect which would expose them to a penalty of £3000 (FA 2003, s 96).

[21] Law of Property Act 1925, s 52.

[22] Ibid, s 53(1)(c); Law of Property (Miscellaneous Provisions) Act 1989, s 2.

[23] Law of Property Act 1925, s 53(2).

[24] For what is required in order to satisfy these provisions in general see, for example, *First Post Homes v Johnson* [1995] 4 All ER 355; but note *Spiro v Glencrown Properties* Ltd [1991] 1 All ER 600 in relation to the exercise of options.

[25] Law of Property Act 1925, s 52.

[26] Ibid, s 53(2); *Yaxley v Gotts* [1999] 2 WLR 1217; *Carlill v Carbolic Smokeball Co* [1892] 2 QB 484; *IRC v G Angus & Co* (1889) 23 QBD 579; *Neville v Wilson* [1997] Ch 144 but note the limitations on these principles as implicit in *Yeoman Row Management v Crabbe* [2008] 4 All ER 713. This decision with its criticism of *Oughtred v IRC* [1960] AC 206 indicates a level of judicial lack of integrity where taxation issues are involved. The decision in *Oughtred v IRC* indicated that s 53(1)(c) of the Law of Property Act 1925 prevailed over s 53(2) thereof. However, in *Neville v Wilson* [1997] Ch 144 the Court of Appeal recognised that this produced preposterous conveyancing consequences and effectively re-wrote the ratio decidendi and recast the majority in *Oughtred v IRC supra* in order to produce the appropriate result. The decisions are manifestly inconsistent but show that judges are reluctant to go and follow taxpayers into areas where they are beyond their competence but are not deterred from re-tracing their steps when it is convenient to do so (see also Lord Hoffmann in *Commissioner of Inland Revenue v Mitsubishi Motors New Zealand* [1995] STC 989). In order to prevent parties avoiding the charge to tax by means of subsale arrangements the relief is restricted and is potentially vulnerable to the general anti-avoidance provisions. In other cases, to prevent parties postponing the duty by 'resting upon contract' it is provided that the charge arises by reference to 'substantial performance' which can precede completion. In consequence, it is not possible to escape the charge to tax by resting simply upon the contract and not completing since 'substantial performance' can trigger the tax charge ahead of completion. This can arise even where it is not necessary to refer the matter to the Land Registry. For example, land may be held by a nominee as bare trustee for several beneficial owners. In this situation the relevant parties are the beneficial owners not the nominee. Dealings between the nominees will, therefore, be dealings in chargeable interests, notwithstanding no entry is to be made at the Land Registry. In this situation it will be easy to produce a tax charge since this can arise where a relevant beneficial owner becomes entitled to possession which includes the right to receive the rents in respect of any leases that have been granted by the nominee on behalf of the beneficial owner. It must, however, be noted

2.6   This change from a documentary to a transaction tax has many consequences. For example, although in the majority of routine cases the execution and delivery of the documentation will coincide with the effective date for the tax, this is not necessarily the case. The coincidence of completion and the tax charge[27] is not a universal or necessary principle but is expressly made subject to numerous 'special provisions'.[28] It is the action of the parties not paperwork that trigger the tax; the charge can arise even without documentation such as entry into possession ahead of completion.[29] The actions of the parties between contract and completion need to be carefully monitored. Moreover, by removing the need for documentation those responsible for the tax have provided a trap for the unwary layman. Parties may enter into arrangements and not consult appropriate professional advisers because they do not need documentation. For example, where a tenant commences holding over pursuant to the Landlord and Tenant Act 1954 he may consult a surveyor for advice as to the rent negotiations but may not consult a solicitor until such time as the parties have agreed a new lease. Similarly, where there is a rent review the parties may consult estate agents or valuers in the rent negotiations but will not necessarily consult solicitors unless they decide to have a memorandum endorsed upon the lease. These are situations where the layman is unlikely to be aware that there is a complex tax issue which may have retrospective effects and could impose problems for his title upon future sales and incur substantial penalties. Similarly, many domestic arrangements are informal such as where parents and child enter into some form of arrangement for the purchase of a house when they may use a solicitor for the conveyancing but they may not disclose that there is some domestic arrangement whereby if the child pays off the mortgage the house will be passed to the child.[30] If, as seems likely, such an arrangement is intended to have legal consequences notwithstanding its domestic nature[31] the parties have embarked upon a chargeable transaction unaware of the risks and issues involved.

E-conveyancing

2.7   One of the policies underlying the legislation is to provide for e-conveyancing which may be document free[32] so that no stamp duty would be payable. The transaction basis of the stamp duty land tax means that it can be adapted to e-conveyancing.

---

that in the context of equitable principles such as proprietary estoppel or constructive trusts Walker LJ stated in *Yaxley v Gotts* [1999] 2 WLR 1217 that the equitable principles applied to create a contract which overrode the need for writing imposed by Law of Property (Miscellaneous Provisions) Act 1989, s 2.

[27]   FA 2003, s 119.

[28]   In fact there are so many 'special provisions' providing for events other than 'completion' in the traditional sense being the effective date that it will only be, in a sense, accidental that the completion is the time at which the tax charge arises and the primary or initial obligation to report occurs. In practice there will be a high correlation between those acts that constitute substantial performance such as payment of 90 per cent or more of the purchase price or taking possession of the property and the completion of the transaction in the form of the delivery of the appropriate conveyance, transfer, lease or deed.

[29]   See **Chapter 14**.

[30]   *Errington v Errington & Woods* [1952] 1 KB 290.

[31]   See, for example, *Parker v Clark* [1961] All ER 93.

[32]   There is also power for the notification period to be reduced from the current 30 days to instant notification at the effective date but detailed rules and mechanics will be needed to enable payment to move from, for example, the client's account to the account of HMRC Stamp Taxes. This is still under discussion between HMRC Stamp Taxes and mortgagees and lenders so that payment will need HMRC Stamp Taxes at the moment that the taxpayer implements the computer systems to transfer title into his name or the name of his nominee.

2.8   Various provisions have been made to deal with the transition to e-conveyancing.[33] This includes the power to reduce the time for filing and payment of tax from 30 days to nil requiring instant settlement of the tax; presumably intended to require payment simultaneously with entering the Land Registry computer. Complex banking arrangements may be required. There are also powers to make the information in land transaction returns widely available,[34] and powers to extend the information required in such returns and to enlarge the power of the various Land Registries in enforcing the tax.[35]

Resting on contract and subsales

2.9   Since stamp duty is a tax on instruments the actions of the parties had no tax consequences. It was possible to postpone and possibly avoid tax by exchanging contracts and then acting upon the contract such as by entering upon the land since there was no conveyance. The deferral could become avoidance where the parties subsold themselves out of the property.[36] This has been attacked. Although, except in the case of options and pre-emption rights,[37] entering into a contract or an agreement for lease or a contract to assign the benefit of a land contract is not a chargeable transaction,[38] and this now applies to entering into agreements for lease which do not as such attract a tax charge, simply relying upon the contract and not taking a conveyance or grant of a lease is attacked in numerous ways; namely:

- the charge to stamp duty land tax will usually arise upon 'substantial performance' of the contract even where this is not accompanied by completion;[39]

- subsale relief is severely restricted and remodelled[40] with special rules where an agreement for lease is completed by a grant to a third party.[41] The intention of the legislation is that a taxpayer cannot escape or postpone the tax charge by resting upon the contract and avoiding a transfer or a lease. The charge arises if the parties perform the contract without executing documents. There is, however, a limited general relief and several focused specific reliefs.[42] Where there is a subsale or assignment or novation or other arrangement and the first or assigned contract has not been substantially performed there will be no charge to stamp duty land tax in respect of this contract upon the original party when the conveyance to the third party is executed notwithstanding that this is completion[43] or substantial performance of the original contract. It seems that the transfer by way of subsale or to the assignee is not to be regarded as substantial performance or completion

---

[33]   Apart from the charge arising without a document see also F(No 2)A 2005, s 47 and FA 2003, s 78A; for electronic communications see Stamp Duty Land Tax (Electronic Communications) Regulations 2005, SI 2005/844.

[34]   FA 2003, s 78A.

[35]   F(No 2)A 2005, s 47.

[36]   Similar structures applied to agreements for lease and taking advantage of the special penalty regime (FA 1984, s 111; FA 2003, Sch 19, para 8).

[37]   FA 2003, s 46(3).

[38]   Ibid, ss 44(2), 45 and Sch 17A, para 12B; on subsale relief see **Chapter 6**; on directing the grant of lease to third parties see **6.57**.

[39]   See ibid, s 44(3); see **14.12**.

[40]   Ibid, s 45; and significantly amended by Stamp Duty Land Tax (Variation of Finance Act 2003) Regulations 2006, SI 2006/3237 now FA 2003, ss 75A–75C; see **Chapter 6**.

[41]   FA 2003, Sch 17A, para 12A; see **Chapter 7**.

[42]   See **Chapter 11**.

[43]   FA 2003, s 44(10)(a) does not apply in this case because that is limited to completion between the same parties.

of the original contract.[44] The effect of the provision is that, provided the original contract has not been substantially performed:

–   the purchaser or lessee or grantee or release under the first contract is not liable to stamp duty land tax in respect of that contract;

–   the assignee, or subpurchaser or other third party is not subject to stamp duty land tax in relation to the contract whereby he becomes entitled to 'acquire' the chargeable interest;

–   where there is substantial performance or completion with the assignee or subpurchaser, this will trigger a charge to stamp duty land tax upon that party; but

–   the performance of that contract is not to be regarded as substantial performance of the original contract pursuant to s 45(3).

2.10   In consequence:

•   the person making the acquisition pursuant to the original contract, not having previously substantially performed, is not liable to stamp duty land tax; and

•   the assignee, subpurchaser or other third party is liable to stamp duty land tax upon the balance of the consideration outstanding under the original contract.[45]

However, where the subsale is caught by the general anti-avoidance provisions there is a special charge upon the third party when the identity of the person described as 'P' has been ascertained.[46]

Moving value without transferring property

2.11   Since stamp duty depends upon the transfer or vesting of property by means of a written instrument, the mere movement of value between different items of property, such as by shifting value between shares in a company by means of a resolution varying the rights attached to the shares, is not subject to duty.[47] This could be achieved by creating or reserving rights in or over land which were not subject to stamp duty either upon their creation or their variation or their release or surrender. This value shifting is attacked in a variety of ways such as:

•   including within the basic charge transactions that do not involve the transfer of property such as releases or variations but not, it seems, disclaimers or exceptions and reservations;[48] but which are chargeable interests for the purposes of stamp duty land tax;[49]

---

[44]   FA 2003, s 45(3).
[45]   Which will usually be the price less any deposit paid by the first purchaser which is provided by the third party or a person connected with him (FA 2003, s 45(3)(b)(i)) and the consideration paid by the third party to the first purchaser as consideration for the assignment or subsale or other transfer of rights (FA 2003, s 45(3)(b)(ii)).
[46]   FA 2003, ss 75A–75C; see **2.19**.
[47]   This is not an agreement to 'transfer' chargeable securities for the purposes of Stamp Duty Reserve Tax.
[48]   *Re Paradise Motors Ltd* [1968] 1 WLR 1125. Although there are problems with HMRC Stamp Taxes as to what may be excepted and reserved and what has to take the form of a transfer and regrant. See **5.154**.
[49]   Special reliefs are introduced for alternative finance investment land which are technically chargeable interests; see FA 2009, Sch 61.

- bringing into charge interests in property that were not subject to stamp duty[50] including the benefit of an obligation, restriction or condition affecting the value of any estate, interest, right or power in or over land. This would include contracts or covenants.[51] Although entering into a contract is not of itself a chargeable contract dealings in the rights arising may be dealings in chargeable interests.

- the introduction of the general anti-avoidance provisions.[52] These apply where there are a number of 'scheme transactions' whereby a person acquires a chargeable interest in circumstances where there have been intervening steps so that the person acquiring the chargeable interest pays less than if he had entered into a direct acquisition from the relevant vendor of the property.[53] These provisions include transactions that are not 'chargeable transactions' or indeed, are transactions that would not be described as 'transactions' on any normal meaning of the term. It will, therefore, attempt to catch not merely subsale arrangements which are identified as primary targets of the legislation[54] these can include value shifting where there is no dealing in any chargeable interest such as, for example, where A proposing to sell the land to B grants a licence to C who may be connected with A or may be connected with B for a lump sum that takes the value out of the land owned by A but which does not give rise to a charge to tax because C is not acquiring a chargeable interest.[55] A transfers the land for its much reduced value to B who removes the encumbrance of C's licence by making a payment to C without attracting a charge to stamp duty land tax because B is not acquiring a chargeable interest from C. In this situation C may be vulnerable to an attack by HMRC Stamp Taxes on the basis of a notional acquisition from A for the consideration paid for the licence.[56]

2.12   Particular illustrations of the attack on value shifting include the following:

- variations of leases, such as payments to commute rent;[57]

- the grant, release or modification of restrictive covenants, options and similar arrangements;[58]

- the inclusion within chargeable consideration of obligations undertaken by a tenant such as affect the rent that a tenant will be prepared to pay in the open market[59] and any payment pursuant to such an obligation;[60]

---

[50]   See **4.39**.
[51]   FA 2003, s 48(1)(b).
[52]   Ibid, ss 75A–75C; see **2.19**.
[53]   There are considerable difficulties owing to the rather poor quality of the drafting of this legislation in identifying the original party described as 'V' and the ultimate acquirer of the property described as 'P'. These issues and some of the many other problems related to this abysmal legislation are considered at **2.19**.
[54]   See the illustrative list of transactions that 'may' be caught by these provisions set out FA 2003, s 75A(3); see also 'may' in s 46(1).
[55]   FA 2003, s 48(2); but note the special treatment for alternative finance FA 2003, ss 73(b), 75A(7)(a) and 45(3).
[56]   FA 2003, s 75A(5).
[57]   Ibid, Sch 17A, para 15A(1).
[58]   Ibid, s 44(3).
[59]   FA 2003, Sch 17A, para 10(1)(c); but without any provisions dealing with the computation of the chargeable amount.
[60]   Ibid, Sch 17A, para 11(2).

- the benefit of obligations or restrictions affecting the value of an interest in land being included as chargeable interests[61] so that payment to vary these will be chargeable transactions.

This list of illustrations has been much enlarged by the introduction of the general anti-avoidance provisions which is designed to attack, *inter alia*, value shifting.[62] There is a list of 'illustrative transactions' to which these provisions 'may' apply such as leases where break clauses are involved and value moves by reason of the existence, creation or cancellation or release of a break clause. Dealings in break clauses are, *prima facie*, not chargeable interests because they are not rights in or over land and may not be obligations affecting the value of land since they are powers rather than duties or restrictions.[63] The creation and removal or other dealing in relation to a break clause can, therefore, pass value without dealing in a chargeable interest. It is, therefore, potentially within the general anti-avoidance provisions.

Drafting[64]

2.13   It was frequently possible to mitigate the charge to stamp duty by suitable drafting. For example, the drafting of variable consideration provisions could reduce the stamp duty charge by avoiding a *prima facie* sum.[65] When producing a transaction tax HMRC Stamp Taxes boasted that drafting would be irrelevant for the purposes of stamp duty land tax; but this has proved to be a major error on their part. There are issues relating to variable consideration;[66] but the drafting of documents can have a significant impact upon the ultimate liability to stamp duty land tax. It may affect what is consideration for the transaction[67] and the question of lease or licence depends upon a detailed investigation of the terms of the agreement between the parties.[68] There may be questions as to whether the provisions are a condition or consideration that is potentially chargeable.[69] The drafting may affect whether there is a chargeable interest or obligation affecting the value of land.[70] Where parties are seeking to enlarge a lease by extending the term there may be a difference between a deed of variation that operates as a surrender and regrant, albeit with credits but of a limited nature where rent is concerned unless the original lease was itself subject to stamp duty land tax;[71] and a grant of a reversionary lease[72] which HMRC Stamp Taxes regard as immediately taxable bringing in the tax upon the rent payable for the first years of the lease

---

61   Ibid, s 48(1)(b).
62   Ibid, ss 75A–75C; **see 2.19**.
63   Ibid, s 48(1)(b).
64   See **Chapter 26**.
65   *Independent Television Authority v IRC* [1961] AC 427; *L M Tenancies v IRC* [1996] STC 880 on appeal [1998] STC 326.
66   FA 2003, s 51; see **5.187**.
67   *Crane Fruehauf v IRC* [1975] STC 51; *Shop and Stores Developments v IRC* [1967] 1 All ER 42; *Central and District Properties v IRC* [1966] 2 All ER 433; *Snell v HMRC* [2006] STC (SCD) 295.
68   *Addiscombe Garden Estates Ltd v Crabbe* [1957] 3 All ER 563 and note especially *Ogwr v Dykes* [1989] 2 All ER 880 to the effect that a statement that the parties do not intend to create a lease may tip the balance in favour of a licence at least outside protected residential properties; for similar consequences in other areas see, for example, *Massey v Crown Life* [1978] 2 All ER 576; *Ready Mixed Concrete (South East) Limited v Minister of Pensions* [1968] 1 All ER 433.
69   See, for example, *Eastham v Leigh, London and Provincial Properties Limited* [1971] 2 All ER 887; FA 2003, Sch 4, para 10; *Errington v Errington & Woods* [1952] 1 KB 290; *GUS Merchandise v Customs and Excise* [1981] 1 WLR 1309.
70   FA 2003, s 48(1)(b) particularly in the context of whether it is possible to 'except and reserve' interests or whether transactions have to take the form of a surrender and regrant.
71   FA 2003, Sch 17A, paras 9 and 16.
72   Assuming that this is permissible pursuant to Law of Property Act 1925.

notwithstanding the lease does not take effect for some time and an agreement for a reversionary lease which is, *prima facie*, not taxable because the prospective tenant is already in occupation under an existing lease he will not be taking possession under the agreement for reversionary lease thereby avoiding any substantial performance or tax charge in respect of that agreement. Similarly, where it is proposed to enlarge the lease by including additional premises there may be important differences between a deed of variation that operates as a surrender and regrant with potential tax charges but with the benefit of possible credits at least where the original lease was a stamp duty land tax lease[73] or the grant of a parallel lease upon the same terms and conditions which is a separate lease or is a partial surrender which does not involve a surrender and regrant imposing a potential charge upon a deemed new lease. It may also affect whether the consideration has been paid in cash or otherwise provided or is left outstanding as unpaid purchase price[74] such as in relation to company reorganisations which require the payment of cash which may affect whether substantial performance has occurred or subsale relief is available.

No finality and retrospection

2.14   Stamp duty land tax is somewhat unique in that it lacks a definite date when a taxpayer can be reasonably confident that his tax position is settled. The tax was intended to facilitate electronic conveyancing and to remove some of the difficulties concerned with registration of title by removing the need for definitive stamping before registration and producing a situation where any disputes as to tax are behind the registration and do not impede title, security and subsequent dealings.[75] In consequence, the filing of the initial return on a self-assessment basis is subject only to minimal scrutiny by HMRC Stamp Taxes who have very limited power to intervene at this stage.[76] In consequence, the acceptance of a land transaction return (SDLT 1) by HMRC Stamp Taxes is no indication whatsoever that the return is correct although any challenges to the return will take place behind the registered title and cannot affect title once registered. Moreover, many of the filings are on a provisional basis to be adjusted subsequently on a retrospective basis. In consequence, a taxpayer who has filed a return, paid the tax and received an SDLT 5 cannot regard his position as finally settled in two major respects:

- it may take many years for the tax liability to be finally settled. This is a particular problem for variable consideration such as rent review, overage and clawback arrangements where the tax remains open and any tax paid provisional until the consideration or rent is finally agreed when the position is retrospectively adjusted; Given the modern regrettable practice[77] of 80 year periods for overage and clawback arrangements it is easy to see that a taxpayer's position can remain open for about a century. Similarly the rent charging provisions apply throughout the

---

[73]   FA 2003, Sch 17A, paras 9 and 16.

[74]   *Coren v Keighley* 48 TC 370; FA 2003, Sch 7, Part 2. There may be key issues in many stamp duty land tax contexts as to whether there is a debt or lease.

[75]   Unfortunately this has proved an optimistic approach by the draftsman particularly since self-certificates (SDLT 60) have been abolished and the Land Registry, under the disguise of local discretion, have claimed even greater powers than those available to HMRC Stamp Taxes to challenge the stamp duty land tax position. There also appears to be a tendency for the Land Registry to refer transactions to HMRC Stamp Taxes for 'guidance' and to pass on information where the Land Registry believe there may have been an element of tax mitigation or tax efficiency.

[76]   FA 2003, Sch 10, para 7.

[77]   But, *prima facie*, obligatory; see *Akazuc Enterprises v Farmar* [2003] PL SCS 127.

term of the lease and beyond if the lease is held over or renewed as a successive linked lease;[78] where there may be a protracted Enquiry by HMRC Stamp Taxes;[79] and

- the compliance regime is somewhat open-ended. Although the basic period for HMRC Stamp Taxes to challenge the return is 9 months by means of an Enquiry they may issue a discovery assessment during the next 6 years or 21 years if there is evidence of negligence or fraud.[80] Moreover a new Enquiry or discovery period may open as each stage of the transaction is reported and, in particular, if HMRC wants to enquire into certain land transaction returns this entitles them to launch an Enquiry into earlier land transaction returns in respect of the same land transaction.[81] There are obligations to file further returns such as where variable consideration becomes ascertained[82] where there is a clawback of reliefs[83] or where there is a subsequent linked transaction[84] which may include a lease renewal.[85] This power to launch an Enquiry into a previous phase of the transaction applies notwithstanding that the 9 month Enquiry period has elapsed in relation to that phase.[86] Even the conclusion of an Enquiry does not necessarily prevent HMRC Stamp Taxes from issuing a discovery assessment because of the statutory limitations upon what they are regarded as 'knowing' at the termination of an Enquiry.[87]

New title problems

2.15 This provisional and retrospective nature of much of the tax has given rise to problems for title, requisitions and due diligence so that there are now documents and information that form a key part of the title. These open tax positions and risks are by statute passed to third parties in many cases, particularly where leases are involved.[88] Moreover, although third parties may not take over the tax position of the original taxpayer but his tax position and information used in the form may form the basis of his assessments and contain key information that he may need. For example, an assignee of a lease who holds over will retrospectively be treated as being a person to whom an extended lease was granted;[89] similarly, where there is a successive linked lease this relates back to the original tax calculation which is adjusted on the basis of the aggregate term.[90] Where the abnormal rent increase regime[91] applies the current tenant, who may be an assignee of the lease, will require detailed information from the original taxpayer's own calculations in order to determine, for example, what is the base rent to be taken into account. In a reasonable number of situations it may be sufficient to produce a copy of the land transaction return (SDLT 1 to SDLT 4) and a copy of the

---

78 FA 2003, Sch 17A, para 5.
79 Ibid, Sch 10, para 24 on power to close an Enquiry.
80 Taxpayers are themselves liable to penalty if they do not correct returns (FA 2003, Sch 10, para 8) and there is no time limit expressed to apply in their favour; see *Slattery v Moore Stephens* [2003] STC 1379 on failure to ask the right questions as negligence.
81 FA 2003, Sch 10, para 12(2A).
82 Ibid, s 80.
83 Ibid, s 81.
84 Ibid, s 81A.
85 Ibid, Sch 17A, para 5.
86 Ibid, Sch 10, para 12(2A).
87 Ibid, Sch 10, para 30(4).
88 See, for example, FA 2003, s 81A; Sch 17A, para 12.
89 FA 2003, Sch 17A, paras 3 and 4.
90 Ibid, Sch 17A, para 5.
91 Ibid, Sch 17A, paras 13, 14 and 15.

Revenue certificate (SDLT 5). Unfortunately, in many cases this will not be sufficient. The land transaction return and the Revenue certificate simply deal in global figures. For example, these merely state the relevant net present value of the rent. However, where a tenant believes that his review may have produced an abnormal increase in the rent the global net present value of the rent will be of no benefit. He will require a detailed breakdown as to how that net present value was arrived at ie he will require details of the actual figures inserted in the calculation for each of the years and, in particular, the assumed rent taken into account for all years after the expiration of the fifth year of the term.[92] Similarly, where a tenant holds over an assigned lease pursuant to the Landlord and Tenant Act 1954 his holding over involves a retrospective re-calculation of the initial self-assessment and any subsequent returns such as on the first rent review or the expiration of the fifth year of the term. This will, again, require a detailed breakdown for each year's rent and, in particular, the assumed rent for all years after the expiration of the fifth year of the term. These problems of calculation have become more of a long-term issue now that HMRC Stamp Taxes have indicated that they regard rents which include Value Added Tax as being variable rents within the normal regime requiring adjustments to be made and re-calculations submitted whenever there is a change in the rate of Value Added Tax.[93] Assignees may, therefore, require details of the rate of Value Added Tax taken into account in respect of the rent for any relevant years and this will continue into the need for information for subsequent potential abnormal rent increases.

2.16 In relation to overage and clawback payments[94] the lack of finality related to the open-ended nature of the contract means that 'exit strategies' are required when entering into these arrangements particularly where lease premiums are involved.[95] However, whilst these exit strategies can deal with situations where there is the sale of a freehold interest or the assignment of an existing lease, there are additional complications and title issues in relation to the grant of new leases where there is some form of variable premium. It is provided that the assignee of the lease takes over the open tax position of the original tenant including the liability to make returns as and when variable premium payments become ascertained in whole or in part and to pay any tax in relation thereto.[96] A key part of the original tenant's title will, therefore, be details of the clawback premium arrangements and a detailed breakdown of the calculation made in the initial, provisional, land transaction return[97] together with details of any arrangements whereby the tax was postponed in respect of the overage or clawback payment. Without this information an assignee of the lease cannot deal with the outstanding tax position that is forced upon him by statute.

2.17 Other title issues arise in relation to the assignment of leases that were exempt when granted. In relation to leases granted to charities,[98] or leases granted as part of a sale and leaseback or lease and underlease back transactions[99] or leases granted on an intra-group basis[100] or in connection with a reorganisation or reconstruction,[101] the first taxable assignment of the lease is taxed as if it were the grant of a new lease. The term

---

[92]   Ibid, Sch 17A, paras 7 and 8, 14 and 15.
[93]   Ibid, Sch 17A, para 12(1)(a); see **15.39**.
[94]   Ibid, ss 51 and 80.
[95]   See **5.206**.
[96]   FA 2003, Sch 17A, para 12.
[97]   Ibid, s 51.
[98]   Ibid, Sch 8.
[99]   Ibid, s 57A.
[100] Ibid, Sch 7, Part 1.
[101] Ibid, Sch 7, Part 2.

of the new lease is the unexpired term of the original lease. The stampable consideration will include any lump sum being paid by the assignee for the acquisition of the lease and the assignee will be liable for tax upon the future rents.[102] This will be calculated by reference to the passing rent at the time of the assignment and the normal rules for variable rents will apply since these will almost inevitably be appropriate.[103] In this situation, which applies without time limit from the original grant, the assignee of the lease may feel that it is appropriate that he receives some form of reverse payment or inducement[104] because of the additional liability that he is incurring. It will also mean additional enquiries into the title of the assigning tenant in order to determine whether the lease fall to those or any other exemptions which may be added by the Treasury from time to time.[105] This liability in respect of the future rent may surprise assignees since it is specifically provided that upon the assignment of a lease the usual covenant to pay the future rent is not part of the taxable consideration;[106] but this exemption is overridden by the specific charging provisions.[107] In addition to the need for relevant stamp duty land tax information to be maintained and preserved effectively as a document of title potentially extends for a longer period than that applying for the preservation of stamp duty land tax records.[108] This information will need to be held throughout the life of the lease, for example, since it will be relevant when a holding over begins[109] or the lease is renewed in certain circumstances.[110] The documentation will, therefore, have a life longer than the normal keeping of tax records.[111] In addition, an assignee who is unable to obtain the requisite information in acceptable form or in a form that will be acceptable by HMRC Stamp Taxes should any Enquiry or challenge be made, may find it prudent to refuse to proceed with the transaction since he will be exposed to potential unquantifiable tax liabilities. Alternatively, he may require some form of reduction in the price. In theory, an indemnity against difficulties would appear to be acceptable; however, the problem will be enforcing the indemnity many years down the line when the original parties may have disappeared or become untraceable in other ways or have died.

Completion documentation

2.18   This question of documents of title including stamp duty land tax records means that it is necessary to reconsider what documentation is required at completion. As a minimum the purchaser or tenant will require all such documentation as will enable him to deal not only with HMRC Stamp Taxes in the form of the land transaction return[112] but also with the Land Registry, particularly in those circumstances where the revenue certificate (SDLT 5) is not available because the transaction is not notifiable or there are differences between the Land Registry documentation and the stamp duty land tax documentation. These issues are considered in more detail later[113] but it is necessary to understand how these principles work in the context of the general policy of the legislation. There are many situations arising in practice where the person on the Land

---

102   Compare FA 2003, Sch 17A, para 17.
103   FA 2003, Sch 17A, para 7.
104   Not taxable; FA 2003, Sch 17A, para 17; Sch 4, para 16.
105   FA 2003, Sch 17A, para 11.
106   Ibid, Sch 17A, para 17.
107   Ibid, Sch 17A, para 11; see **5.40**.
108   Ibid, Sch 10, para 9.
109   Ibid, Sch 17A, para 3.
110   Ibid, Sch 17A, para 5.
111   Ibid, Sch 10, para 9(2).
112   Ibid, Sch 10, para 9.
113   See **Chapter 22**.

Register is not the same as the person involved in the transaction. For example, there may be a subsale where the intermediate purchaser is not subject to tax.[114] In this situation there may be a single transfer directly from the original seller to the third party or two transfers where there are restrictions upon subsales in the contract so that there is a transfer from the original seller to the first purchaser which will be unsupported by a revenue certificate and a transfer from the first purchaser to the second purchaser. In this situation the revenue certificate will refer to the first purchaser and the second purchaser but the Land Registry transfer will be from the original seller. Alternatively, the land may be held by nominees and land transaction returns have to be filed and signed by the beneficial owners.[115] The Land Registry frequently requires some explanation as to the discrepancies between the two sets of documents. This may require certain information from third parties such as the first purchaser indicating that he is not expecting to produce a return because his transaction is not taxable. It would seem prudent to stipulate in the contract that such documentation will be delivered. Ideally this should be at completion because it may not be easy to pursue the other parties after completion and when difficulties arise with the Land Registry or HMRC Stamp Taxes. Express provision will make the position clear rather than parties seeking to rely upon the usual arrangements concerning 'further assurances' or the obligations of persons who contract with full title guarantee. If the taxpayer cannot produce the relevant information for the purpose of the Land Registry then his title may be blocked or frozen for some time, to the irritation of his mortgagee, notwithstanding that he has a valid and effective revenue certificate (SDLT 5).

Planning and anti-avoidance

2.19   FA 2003, ss 75A–75C[116] introduces with effect from 4 December 2006 general anti-avoidance provisions for the purposes of stamp duty land tax. HMRC Stamp Taxes can recast a number of transactions (known as 'scheme transactions'[117] which have to be involved with each other) into a notional transaction for a deemed consideration. It applies where a person eventually to be identified as V disposes of a chargeable interest and at some stage[118] a person who is eventually identified as P acquires all or part of

---

[114]   FA 2003, s 45; see **Chapter 6**.

[115]   Ibid, Sch 16, para 3; although, in practice, HMRC Stamp Taxes have accepted land transaction returns signed by the nominee upon the basis that the actions of the nominee are deemed to be the actions of the beneficial owner.

[116]   Stamp Duty Land Tax (Variation of Finance Act 2003) Regulations 2006, SI 2006/3237.

[117]   FA 2003, s 75A(1)(b); but although they are described as 'scheme transactions' this is misleading in two respects. There is not, as such, a requirement that there is a 'scheme'; it seems that the provisions are intended to operate largely upon an objective basis regardless of the intention of the parties. Clearly this is because the resources available to HMRC Stamp Taxes and their experience mean it would be difficult for them to raise the appropriate questions in an Enquiry and would require much time and resource. The merest suggestion that there has to be some form of 'scheme' is that the transactions have to be 'involved in connection with each other' which is likely to prove a key condition and which will raise many questions of fact and evidence. Also this is misleading because the definition of 'transaction' is not limited to a chargeable transaction but includes other matters including 'transactions' that would not normally be regarded as 'transactions'. This definition suggests that there may be 'transactions' that are not 'schemes' and therefore would not be within the normal meanings of 'arrangement'.

[118]   This requires more than one step; it is, however, uncertain whether HMRC Stamp Taxes intend to make any point concerning the traditional distinction between contract and completion namely two steps in a single transaction. This position becomes even more of a problem where, for the purposes of stamp duty land tax, there are at least three steps namely contract, substantial performance and completion. Unless HMRC Stamp Taxes are prepared to regard these as being incidental transactions or part of a 'process' for transferring the property between the parties (see FA 2003, s 75B) there will be very few arrangements which have only a single step. Options will clearly be vulnerable since there will be the steps relating to the grant of the option and the subsequent steps relating to the exercise of the option and the completion of the contract arising.

that chargeable interest[119] and the aggregate stamp duty land tax on the various transactions is less than the stamp duty land tax that would have been payable on a direct acquisition from V by P (known as 'the lower tax condition'. Consideration given for certain relieved transactions is ignored when computing the consideration in respect of the notional transaction[120] and transactions within Sch 6A ie the reliefs for residential property or Sch 8 (the reliefs for charities); however, the market value charge pursuant to the connected company rules applies for the purposes of computing the charge[121] as does the market value charge upon the value of the interest received for the purposes of land exchanges.[122] When the many conditions are satisfied there is a notional transaction between V and P for the highest consideration provided or received by any one person including third parties other than V and P. The notional transaction is entitled to any relief which it would attract if it were an actual transaction.[123] Unfortunately, the structure of the notional transaction means that most of the reliefs that would be available such as company reorganisations cannot be satisfied because the parties to the notional transaction will not be the same as the party to the actual transaction.[124]

2.20 The provision is bizarrely structured. Not only are its terms of reference obscure but the legislation contains an illustrative list of transactions to which it 'may' apply including popular arrangements such as:

- subsales of residential property for less than market value:

- sales of reversions subject to leases with break clauses;

- termination or variation of break clauses in leases.

There is no indication in the legislation as to when the legislation is intended to apply to the transactions within the illustrative list and when not. No doubt every transaction within that illustrative list is vulnerable and will have to be scrutinised in order to see whether the 'lower tax condition' has been satisfied. Certain transactions are excluded from the concept of 'scheme transactions' because they are regarded as 'incidental'.[125] These are expressed as potentially including construction of a building on the chargeable interest in question or relates to the supply of property other than land such as chattels, or relates to loans and the funding of the transaction.[126] However, a transaction is not incidental where it forms part of a process or series of transactions by which the transfer is effected or the transfer is conditional on the completion of the transaction or it is a subsale or other arrangement within the illustrative list.[127] Unfortunately, no explanation is given of what is a 'process' or series of transactions to effect the transfer. There is a suspicion that HMRC Stamp Taxes may seek to rely upon

---

119   For these purposes an interest in a property investment partnership is a chargeable interest to the extent that it relates to land owned by the partnership and where either V or P is a partnership the market value charge applies but it seems that there may be a reduction in the market value charge for the sum of the lower proportions provided that the parties involved in the notional transaction and the actual transaction can meet the criteria for the application of the market value charge.

120   These are FA 2003, ss 60, 61, 63, 64, 65, 66, 67, 69, 71, 74 and 75.

121   Ibid, ss 53 and 75C(6).

122   Ibid, s 75C(7) and Sch 4, para 5.

123   Ibid, Sch 5; s 75C(2) and (3).

124   Ibid, s 75C(2).

125   Ibid, s 75B.

126   Ibid, s 75B(3).

127   Ibid, s 75B(2).

the traditional distinction between contract and completion to claim that there are two steps in every transaction which may rise to three where there is substantial performance between contract and completion. Transactions within the alternative finance relief are also excluded[128] as are transactions within the shared ownership relief.[129]

2.21 HMRC Stamp Taxes have issued a Technical Bulletin setting out their views on certain aspects of this legislation. Unfortunately, the document is utterly useless in practice. It contains two lists one of which illustrates the consequences of the legislation applying; the other dealing with the situation where the legislation does not apply. Since these two lists contain essentially the same fact situations in each of the illustrations it is difficult to see what are the criteria being adopted by HMRC Stamp Taxes for singling out transactions as falling within the first of the lists, namely those that are attacked by the legislation.

2.22 However, the provision is much wider in terms than the illustrative list and the Technical Bulletin would suggest and may affect routine commercial transactions such as structuring the acquisition of reversionary interests in blocks of flats where the tenants seek to avoid the double charge to tax when they take new leases or extend their existing leases. Seeking to take the benefit of the relief for leases granted to third parties[130] as part of a developer's financing agreement or establishing a new management company as part of an enfranchising exercise is clearly vulnerable to attack by HMRC Stamp Taxes because the parties may adopt a circuitous route for commercial reasons which also has a degree of stamp duty land tax efficiency.[131] For example, the parties may form a management company to acquire the interest from the landlord. This will attract stamp duty land tax in the normal way. However, alternative routes might involve the tenants acquiring the interest from the landlord and subselling this with the benefit of relief.[132] They may then enter into some form of deed of variation bringing their leases into line with their new involvement with the property and changing management arrangements etc; this may qualify for reliefs.[133] Alternatively, the parties might enter into an arrangement with the landlord for modernising their leases for an additional payment which would probably not attract stamp duty land tax because it would be below the nil rate threshold for taxable premiums with the benefit of the reliefs. Having stripped the value out of the freehold interest this can be bought by the management company for a token sum attracting little or not stamp duty land tax.[134] In this way the aggregate tax paid upon the transactions being negligible would be less than would have been paid on the first illustration of a direct acquisition by the management company by the landlord. It is, therefore, potentially subject to stamp duty land tax general anti-avoidance provisions in respect of the other variations. The lower tax condition would have been satisfied. This particular route by producing a lower tax charge than other routes would appear to fail the lower tax condition ie the total tax paid on all the scheme transactions is less than the tax that would have been paid on the notional transaction. It is important to note that when determining the chargeable consideration for the notional transaction ie the highest amount paid in respect of any scheme transaction the scheme transactions are

---

[128] Ibid, s 75A(7)(a).
[129] Ibid, Sch 9; s 75A(7)(a).
[130] Ibid, Sch 17A, para 12B.
[131] Note also the extended special rate treatment for collective enfranchisement arrangements; FA 2003, s 74 (as amended).
[132] FA 2003, s 45; see **Chapter 6**.
[133] Ibid, Sch 17A, paras 9 and 16.
[134] And avoiding funding problems that might involve loans that could constitute taxable premiums for the grant of their modernised leases on the deed of variation pursuant to FA 2003, Sch 17A, para 18A.

not limited to chargeable transactions and may relate to other forms of property and the consideration need not be within the definition of 'chargeable consideration' for the purposes of stamp duty land tax. For example, a sale of shares in a company has no stamp duty land tax implications whatsoever but such a sale of the shares is potentially a scheme transaction[135] and the consideration for the share transaction can be taken into account in respect of determining the chargeable consideration for the notional transaction.[136] Moreover, although the share transaction may have paid stamp duty or stamp duty reserve tax this tax is not available as a credit to reduce the full charge to stamp duty land tax.

2.23 These provisions appear to operate on an objective basis in that a tax avoidance motive is not required; but the legislation cannot operate on a sensible basis without a degree of subjectivity, intention or purpose. A 'number' of transactions are required. It is assumed that a 'number' involves more than one but 'transaction' is defined as not being limited to chargeable transactions but to any form of event including events that would not normally be described as 'transactions'.[137] The use of the word 'number' is important since it carries a different connotation from a 'series' or a 'scheme'. Series and scheme require some form of linkage or overall plan or purpose. A 'number' seems to refer simply to a chronological basis for the tax namely one event follows another. Moreover, the number can be determined in a sense retrospectively because scheme transactions can include those that precede the disposal by V[138] notwithstanding that is ultimately identified as being the initial disposal of the chargeable interest by the person identified as V for the purpose of the notional transaction and can include events after what is determined to be the acquisition of the chargeable interest by the person eventually identified as P.[139] Indeed, it may only be subsequently a run of events over which P may not be involved that he becomes a party to a notional transaction within the general anti-avoidance rules. His actual acquisition may not have been obviously tainted.

2.24 The main safeguard for the taxpayer will be the question of the lower tax condition ie the aggregate stamp duty land tax[140] paid upon the scheme transactions is lower than the tax that would have been paid on the notional transaction. However, it is possible for transactions to have a substantial consideration without attracting stamp duty land tax and many gifts or transfers for no chargeable consideration will not attract stamp duty land tax. The main alternative defence will be that the disposal by V and the acquisition by P are not involved in connection with each other.

2.25 It is provided that the scheme transactions are to be 'disregarded' although the meaning of this is completely unclear. It seems that the scheme transactions do actually take place and have effect in stamp tax. Therefore, a share transaction which is ultimately found to be a 'scheme transaction' remains subject to stamp duty and

---

[135] Unless the transfer of the shares is the first step; FA 2003, s 75C(1). This refers to 'transfer' and presumably means a transfer of shares and will not include a subscription for shares or the allotment of new shares or any other arrangement to create or issue securities.

[136] FA 2003, s 75A(5)(a).

[137] Ibid, s 75A(2)(c).

[138] This emerges because the chargeable consideration for the notional transaction ignores any consideration paid for a transfer of shares provided that this is the first step ie precedes the disposal by V; FA 2003, s 75C(1).

[139] FA 2003, s 75A(2)(d).

[140] But not other taxes such as stamp duty or stamp duty reserve tax upon share transactions that are scheme transactions notwithstanding that the consideration paid for the shares can be taken into account when calculating the special charge.

although disregarded the charge is not cancelled and the tax is not, apparently, to be repaid. Similarly parties to 'disregarded' chargeable transactions remain chargeable and have to notify. The fact that their transaction is disregarded does not appear to mean that they are entitled to a refund of any stamp duty land tax paid in respect of that disregarded chargeable transaction. Indeed, the tax paid on the scheme transactions is dealt with in a very unusual manner. It seems that the tax is not refundable but is available as a credit for the person ultimately identified as P in order to enable him to reduce the amount of tax payable in respect of the notional transaction.[141] Unfortunately, this credit is available only in respect of stamp duty land tax payable; there is no credit available in respect of stamp duty or stamp duty reserve tax in respect of share transactions notwithstanding that these have borne a full charge to stamp duty. The chargeable consideration for the notional transaction can, therefore, produce a liability to 4.5 per cent stamp taxes overall, because the same consideration[142] is taxed twice.

2.26 Since it is fundamental to the charge that P acquires an interest in land he will have an obligation to report his actual acquisition.[143] However, this is not his only notification obligation because he is also required to notify the notional transaction.[144] For these purposes and for payment the effective date of the notional transaction is the last date of completion for the scheme transactions or, if earlier, the last date on which a contract in respect of the scheme transactions is substantially performed. This can be an event after P's actual acquisition.[145]

Other anti-avoidance provisions

2.27 Certain reliefs incorporate a qualifying condition to the effect that the transaction does not form part of some tax avoidance scheme or is part of a *bona fide* commercial arrangement.[146] There is no advance clearance procedure although, in general, HMRC Stamp Taxes will be prepared to accept a clearance obtained in respect of capital gains tax in relation to company reorganisations.[147]

Notification of schemes

2.28 Stamp duty land tax, along with other taxes, now require various scheme to be disclosed in advance to HMRC who, by being advised early, can bring in rapid anti-avoidance or amending legislation to deal with the situation.[148] Nevertheless it

---

[141] FA 2003, s 75C(10).
[142] But not the same transaction FA 2003, Sch 10, para 33.
[143] FA 2003, s 77.
[144] Ibid, s 77(1)(d).
[145] Ibid, s 75B(6).
[146] See, for example, FA 2003, Sch 7 relating to intra-group and company reorganisations; Sch 8 relating to relief for charities.
[147] But note the use to which such a clearance was put by HMRC Stamp Taxes as a means of attacking the relief that the taxpayer was seeking in *Swithland Investments v IRC* [1990] STC 448. Also note the comments of the judge to the effect that the setting out of a series of steps in a clearance application could have the effect of a contract between the shareholders and may affect the scope of what is the scheme of reconstruction and may also cause the company to lose the beneficial ownership of its assets insofar as these are affected by the scheme.
[148] FA 2004, Part 7, ss 306 and following.

seems that all parties have to be involved in the original planning of the scheme. There may be advantages where a seller or landlord refuses to co-operate in the purchaser's tax planning.[149]

Disclosure of stamp duty land tax savings schemes[150]

2.29 Legislation[151] and regulations[152] require disclosure of certain arrangements designed or intended to reduce the charge to stamp duty land tax. Forms have also been issued.

2.30 Disclosure is required where the main benefit of the arrangement is a stamp duty land tax advantage. A stamp duty land tax 'advantage' is:

- relief or increased relief from or repayment or increased repayment of stamp duty land tax; or
- the avoidance or reduction of a charge to stamp duty land tax; or
- the deferral of any payment of tax; or
- the accelerated repayment of tax; or
- the avoidance of any obligation to deduct or account for tax,

unless the arrangement falls within the list of exclusions from disclosure namely:

- the arrangement relates solely to residential property;
- the market value of the land does not exceed £5,000,000. There is considerable explanation of this requirement. If the value of the property is not known it is assumed to be more than £5,000,000. Where the scheme is intended to be utilised generally the market value is assumed to be in excess of £5,000,000.

Excluded steps

2.31 Arrangements are excluded from disclosure if they comprise the steps set out below, or certain combinations of the steps.

A acquisitions of chargeable interests by a special purpose vehicle.

B claims to reliefs.

C sale of shares in a special purpose vehicle.

D not exercising the option to tax for VAT.

---

149 Note the availability of the various forms of subsale and similar reliefs where the seller does not co-operate.
150 There is power to apply these arrangements to stamp duty reserve tax.
151 FA 2004, s 306.
152 Stamp Duty Land Tax Avoidance (Prescribed Descriptions of Arrangements) Regulations 2005, SI 2005/1868); Tax Avoidance Schemes (Information) (Amendment) Regulations 2005, SI 2005/1869; Tax Avoidance Schemes (Information) Regulations 2004, SI 2004/1864.

E   transfer of a business as a going concern for the purposes of VAT.

F   entering into a joint venture by means of a partnership.

Where there is a combination of the above steps disclosure is not required except where:

- there is a combination of all or any of steps A, C and D; or

- step A, C or D is involved on two or more occasions.

Person to disclose

2.32   The basic duty to disclose falls upon the 'promoter', unless he is covered by legal professional privilege. A promoter is a person who is to any extent responsible for the design arrangements or he makes the arrangements available for implementation or the organisation or management of such arrangements in the case of a business which involves the provision of services relating to taxation or the business is carried on by a bank or securities house.[153] Where there is no promoter or legal professional privilege applies the taxpayer is required to disclose. Certain persons are not treated as promoters:

- tax advisers who are instructed to advise only on the technical details of the scheme but who are not the persons involved in the design of the arrangements;

- conveyancers who occasionally provide tax advice notwithstanding that they provide advice as to the non-tax issues such as property law;

- tax advisers who may have designed part of the scheme but do not know the details of the overall scheme and are not in a position to know whether the overall arrangement is one requiring disclosure.

A promoter[154] has to notify[155] where there is a notifiable arrangement or a notifiable proposal.[156] Certain UK persons inside the United Kingdom may have to make a notification where the promoter is outside the United Kingdom and there is no other promoter in the United Kingdom.[157] Where there is no promoter then any person entering into a notifiable arrangement will have to notify the scheme.[158] The scheme will be issued with a number which has to be given to the client.[159]

Information required

2.33   Detailed information is required but forms are to be made available to ease this process. These include details of the promoter and of the steps including information explaining each element in the arrangement; information explaining the proposals and

---

[153]   Income and Corporation Taxes Act 1988, ss 209A(4) and 840A.
[154]   FA 2004, s 307.
[155]   Ibid, s 308.
[156]   Ibid, s 306.
[157]   Ibid, s 309.
[158]   Ibid, s 310.
[159]   Ibid, ss 311 and 312.

the statutory provisions upon which is based in such detail that HMRC will comprehend the manner in which the operations will be implemented.

2.34   Sometimes the notification has to be delivered to HMRC before the expiration of 5 days.

The arrangements that have to be notified are prescribed in regulations.[160] The arrangements[161] are those whose subject-matter does not consist wholly of residential property in respect of which the applicable value is at least £5,000,000.[162] However, numerous arrangements involving non-residential property are excluded by the schedule to the Regulations. The excluded arrangements are:

Arrangements are excluded from being prescribed arrangements for the purposes of these Regulations if they:

(a)   comprise one or more of steps A to F listed below (subject to Rules 1 and 2 which specify arrangements involving combinations of those steps which are not excluded arrangements); but

(b)   do not include any step, which is necessary for the purpose of securing a tax advantage, other than one listed below.

Rule 1

Arrangements involving Steps B, D, E and F are excluded arrangements unless rule 2 applies.

Rule 2

Arrangements are not excluded arrangements if they:

(a)   include all, or at least two of, steps A, C and D; or

(b)   involve more than one instance of step A, C or D.

The steps are as follows.

Step A: Acquisition of a chargeable interest by special purpose vehicle

The acquisition of a chargeable interest in land by a company created for that purpose ('a special purpose vehicle').

Step B: Claims to relief

Making:

---

[160]   Stamp Duty Land Tax Avoidance Schemes (Prescribed Descriptions of Arrangements) Regulations 2005, SI 2005/1868.

[161]   Ibid, reg 2(3).

[162]   See the assumption where there is a proposal to make the scheme available generally pursuant Stamp Duty Land Tax Avoidance Schemes (Prescribed Descriptions of Arrangements) Regulations 2005, SI 2005/1868, reg 2(5).

(a)   a single claim to relief under any of the following provisions of the Finance
       Act 2003—
       (i)   section 57A (sale and leaseback arrangements);
       (ii)   section 60 (compulsory purchase facilitating development);
       (iii) section 61 (compliance with planning obligation);
       (iv)   section 64 (demutualisation of building society);
       (v)   section 64A (initial transfer of assets to trustees of unit trust scheme);
       (vi)   section 65 (incorporation of limited liability partnership);
       (vii) section 66 (transfers involving public bodies);
       (viii) section 67 (transfer in consequence of reorganisation of parliamentary
              constituencies);
       (ix)   section 69 (acquisition by bodies established for national purposes);
       (x)   section 71 (certain acquisitions by registered social landlords);
       (xi)   section 74 (collective enfranchisement by leaseholders);
       (xii) section 75 (crofting community right to buy);
       (xiii) Schedule 6 (disadvantaged areas relief);
       (xiv) Schedule 6A (relief for certain acquisitions of residential property);
       (xv)   Schedule 7 (group relief and reconstruction acquisition reliefs);
       (xvi) Schedule 8 (charities relief); or
       (xvii) Schedule 9 (right to buy, shared ownership leases etc.);

(b)   one or more claims to relief under any one of the following provisions of the
       Finance Act 2003:
       (i)   section 71A (alternative property finance: land sold to financial institution
              and leased to individual);
       (ii)   section 72 (alternative property finance in Scotland: land sold to financial
              institution and leased to individual);
       (iii) section 72A (alternative property finance in Scotland: land sold to financial
              institution and individual in common); or
       (iv)   section 73 (alternative property finance: land sold to financial institution
              and resold to individual).

Step C: Sale of shares in special purpose vehicle

The sale of shares in a special purpose vehicle, which holds a chargeable interest in land,
to a person with whom neither the special purpose vehicle, nor the vendor, is connected.

Step D: Not exercising election to waive exemption from VAT

No election is made to waive exemption from value added tax contained in para 2 of
Sch 10 to the Value Added Tax Act 1994 (treatment of buildings and land for value
added tax purposes).

Step E: Transfer of a business as a going concern

Arranging the transfer of a business, connected with the land which is the subject of the arrangements, in such a way that it is treated for the purposes of value added tax as the transfer of a going concern.

Step F: Undertaking a joint venture

The creation of a partnership (within the meaning of para 1 of Sch 15 to the Finance Act 2003) to which the property which subject to a land transaction is to be transferred.

Judicial intervention

2.35 There is a judge-made anti-avoidance regime.[163] This 'principle' is of an extremely fluctuating and uncertain scope and there must be debate whether it can co-exist with general or specific anti-avoidance legislation. There have been decisions that it can apply to stamp taxes[164] although there is also judicial recognition that stamp taxes are unique as an irrecoverable cost of purchase and not a tax on sales and gains and not within the principle.[165] Notwithstanding judicial encouragement, HMRC Stamp Taxes did not seek to apply the 'principle' because they were not equipped to investigate the evidence fundamental to the findings of facts that needed to be established. There was one ill-considered attempt to apply the 'principle' to stamp duty reserve tax which was quickly abandoned for the same reason. It was thought that as stamp duty land tax was a transaction tax it, like stamp duty reserve tax, was vulnerable to the 'approach' but the operational difficulties of being unable to develop the issues in the absence of evidence has meant that a recent attempt to apply the 'principle' to stamp duty land tax has been abandoned.

---

[163]   *Ramsay v IRC* [1981] STC 174; *Furniss v Dawson* [1984] STC 153.
[164]   *Ingram v IRC* [1981] STC 835; *Collector of Stamp v Arrowtown Hong Hong*, Dec 2003; *Stamp Commissioners v Carreras* [2004] UKPC 16.
[165]   *McNiven v Westmoreland* [2003] 1 AC 311.

Chapter 3

THE CHARGE TO STAMP DUTY LAND TAX

3.1 Stamp duty land tax is imposed upon a land transaction[1] which involves:[2]

- an acquisition;

- of a chargeable interest;[3]

- in land;[4]

- in the United Kingdom;

- which interest in land is not exempt[5] from the charge to stamp duty land tax. It is important to note that this excludes dealings in the specified interests from the charge to stamp duty land tax altogether;[6] and

- the transaction is not 'exempt'.[7] There are provisions 'exempting' certain land transactions[8] and there are other provisions relieving an otherwise chargeable transaction from liability to stamp duty land tax.[9] Although the drafting regrettably uses the word 'exempt' in both contexts, there are important differences between them. A transaction involving an 'exempt interest' and a transaction that is 'exempt' because it is listed in FA 2003, Sch 3, is altogether outside the scope of stamp duty land tax – in general it need not be notified[10] and is ignored in relation to linked transactions. This is a wide exclusion from the tax since many forms of 'relief' from the tax take the form of ignoring the actual consideration and deeming the consideration for most of the tax to be 'nil' or 'exempt' or otherwise to be ignored.[11] In such cases because there is no chargeable consideration the transaction falls within FA 2003, Sch 3, para 1 and is *prima facie* not notifiable.[12]

---

[1]   FA 2003, s 43(1).
[2]   Ibid, s 49(1).
[3]   See **Chapter 4**.
[4]   See **4.7**.
[5]   See **Chapter 4**.
[6]   See **Chapter 16**.
[7]   On the problems of the meaning of the word 'exempt' see **11.18**. The full list and details of exempt transactions are considered below but for present purposes it is important to note that a transaction is also exempt if there is no 'chargeable consideration' for the transaction: see FA 2003, Sch 3, para 1; see **11.13**; but different compliance rules may apply.
[8]   FA 2003, Sch 3.
[9]   Note the bizarre drafting dealing with 'exemption' in FA 2003, s 49(2).
[10]   FA 2003, s 77A; see **18.2**.
[11]   See further **Chapter 11**.
[12]   However, certain types of transaction were made notifiable notwithstanding the 'nil consideration' the situation such as dealings with connected companies, partnerships and certain PFI projects. However,

On the other hand, a transaction involving a chargeable interest which is 'exempt' or relieved may not produce a charge to tax but may require the production of a land transaction return. In these cases the effect is that the amount of the chargeable consideration remains unaltered, it is the rate of tax which is reduced.

Since documentation and registration of title issues are no longer core issues for the tax or compliance regimes, notwithstanding the need to have made some attempt to address the tax issues involved so that an appropriate certificate (SDLT 5) can be produced to the Land Registry,[13] there are cases when notification and/or payment is required even though there is no change in the title position requiring registration.

CHARGEABLE CONSIDERATION

3.2   Although not specifically mentioned in the charging provisions there must be chargeable consideration[14] before a charge arises because there is a general exemption for transactions where there is no chargeable consideration.[15]

'Consideration'

3.3   There must be consideration provided by the purchaser or a person connected with him.[16] However this presupposes some concept of 'consideration' as there is no general specific provision. This will raise questions as to whether the arrangement is some form of promise for a consideration or a conditional gift[17] and what appears to be a condition may be consideration.[18] There may also be questions as to whether inducements provided by third parties are part of the consideration.[19] These are key issues since without some form of 'consideration' it may affect whether there is a transaction and it will, *prima facie*, form the basis for calculating the charge to tax.[20]

Need for consideration

3.4   It must, however, not be overlooked that an 'acquisition' of a chargeable interest by itself is not sufficient – it must be an acquisition where there is a chargeable consideration. There is a general provision which exempts transactions for no chargeable consideration.[21] This may be a key issue in relation to certain arrangements where there

---

although these restrictions upon FA 2003, Sch 3, para 1 were not dealt with in the consequential legislation it seems that such transactions are not notifiable because there being no chargeable consideration the transaction will be covered by the exclusion for transactions where the chargeable consideration does not exceed the £40,000 threshold pursuant to FA 2003, s 77A; see **18.2**.

13   Unless the transaction is non-taxable or non-notifiable when a covering letter may be sufficient; see **Chapter 6**.
14   See **3.5** and **Chapter 5**.
15   FA 2003, Sch 3, para 1.
16   Ibid, Sch 4, para 1; note also the definition of 'purchaser' FA 2003, s 43(5); see **15.6**.
17   See, for example, *GUS Merchandise v Customs and Excise* [1981] 1 WLR 1309.
18   See, for example, *Eastham v Leigh, London and Provincial Properties Limited* [1971] 2 All ER 887.
19   See, for example, *Crane Fruehauf v IRC* [1975] STC 51; *Central and District Properties v IRC* [1966] 2 All ER 433.
20   See **3.6**.
21   Ibid, Sch 3, para 1.

may not be a formal enforceable contract[22] or situations where there is no such contract but equity may intervene[23] to create some form of proprietary interest pursuant to a constructive trust.[24]

However, this is counterbalanced by certain anti-avoidance rules such as those where connected companies or partnerships are involved where there is deemed to be a chargeable consideration related to market value.[25] This requirement may restrict the charge since, for example, there may be a point that, in relation to certain acquisitions by operation of law, these are not consensual and 'consideration' in the broad sense is related to the agreement by the promisee to provide the benefit requested by the promisor. Situations where the obligation is 'imposed' upon the 'acquirer' may, therefore, mean that the obligation is not consideration. An illustration of this would be the assumption by an assignee of a lease of the obligation to pay future rent. As he cannot accept the benefit of the lease without assuming the inherent liability it will not be chargeable consideration,[26] and this particular point has been accepted by HMRC Stamp Taxes notwithstanding FA 2003, Sch 4, para 8.[27] This issue of the extent to which consideration needs to be by agreement is likely to give rise to significant debate with HMRC Stamp Taxes.[28]

Chargeable consideration and actual consideration

3.5   There is an important distinction between chargeable consideration and actual consideration. In general, stamp duty land tax works upon the basis of the actual consideration.[29] There is, for example, no basic rule treating all transactions as taking place at not less than market value. Therefore, gifts such as distributions in specie and advancements by trustees are treated as being for no chargeable consideration if there is no actual consideration. Nevertheless, there are various rules affecting the situation. For example, there are situations deeming consideration to exist such as dealings with connected companies[30] and there are situations where the actual consideration is to be ignored or treated as nil.[31]

Quantifying the consideration

3.6   Since stamp duty land tax is wider than cash transactions there have to be detailed rules for identifying and quantifying certain types of consideration. For example, since much of the consideration that is chargeable is consideration in kind there are rules for dealing with the computation of the amount[32] and there are special

---

[22]   See, for example, Law of Property (Miscellaneous Provisions) Act 1989, s 2; *First Post Homes v Johnson* [1995] 4 All ER 355; *Spiro v Glencrown Properties Ltd* [1991] 1 All ER 600 but note *Tootal Clothing v Guinea Properties Management* (1992) 64 P&CR 452.

[23]   See, for example, *Yaxley v Gotts* [1999] 2 WLR 1217.

[24]   However, in what may be a key comment, Walker LJ in *Yaxley v Gotts* [1999] 2 WLR 1217 stated that equitable principles overrode the need for writing imposed by Law of Property (Miscellaneous Provisions) Act 1989, s 2, so that notwithstanding the absence of writing there was a valid and enforceable contract. Note the limitations on this suggested by *Yeoman Row Management v Crabbe* [2008] 4 All ER 713.

[25]   FA 2003, ss 53 and 54; Sch 15, Part 3 (as amended). This is not the same as there being actual consideration where the legislation deems the consideration to be a different amount.

[26]   See *Swayne v IRC* [1900] 1 QB 172; FA 2003, Sch 17A, para 16; but see para 11 thereof; see **7.238**.

[27]   FA 2003, Sch 17A, para 17.

[28]   See **3.50** and **5.98**.

[29]   FA 2003, Sch 4, para 1.

[30]   Ibid, ss 53 and 54; see **5.208**.

[31]   See, for example, FA 2003, Sch 4, para 17 and FA 2003, Sch 17A, para 16.

[32]   See, for example, FA 2003, Sch 4.

rules for attributing a value to certain types of the consideration such as variable payments where there are clawback arrangements or there is a variable rent.[33] In other situations the legislation may identify a particular type of consideration or deemed consideration. For example, in relation to land exchanges where major interests ie freeholds and leaseholds are involved, the chargeable amount is the value of what is received rather than the value of the consideration provided.[34] Apart from the questions of determining the market value of the actual or deemed consideration there are few situations where market value of an interest is itself made the consideration. The main situations are dealings with connected companies where the consideration is deemed to be not less than the market value of the property concerned;[35] dealings between partners and partnerships and connected parties.[36]

Other situations have special rules. Since building works and services may have no open market value special rules are applied and the tax is calculated by reference to the open market cost[37] of the works or fitting out.[38]

TRANSACTION TAX

3.7   Stamp duty land tax is payable whether or not there is an instrument effecting the transaction.[39] Paperwork may be important and may operate to trigger an event with tax or compliance consequences but other non-documentary events also produce a tax charge. There are frequent illustrations of the principle that although entering into or exchanging contracts is not, as such, a taxable event, the actions of the parties after entering into the contract may have taxation consequences notwithstanding that the contract is conditional.[40] This requires professional advisers to have an awareness of what is to happen between contract and completion even where the contract is conditional.[41] If there is an instrument, the tax charge applies:

–   whether or not it is executed in the United Kingdom;[42] or

–   whether or not any party to the transaction is present or resident in the United Kingdom.[43]

Certain provisions deal with the enforcement of tax where non-resident 'purchasers' are involved.[44] Regulations may be issued for the recovery of tax from non-residents.[45]

---

[33]   FA 2003, s 51 and Sch 17A, paras 7, 8, 13, 14 and 15.
[34]   Ibid, Sch 4, para 5.
[35]   Ibid, ss 53 and 54.
[36]   Ibid, Sch 15.
[37]   Ibid, Sch 4, para 11(1).
[38]   Ibid, Sch 4, paras 10 and 11; see also s 80 and Stamp Duty Land Tax (Administration) Regulations 2003, SI 2003/2835, Part 4.
[39]   FA 2003, s 42(2)(a).
[40]   See **Chapter 14**.
[41]   See **26.4**.
[42]   FA 2003, s 42(2)(b).
[43]   Ibid, s 42(2)(c).
[44]   See FA 2003, s 100(4)(b) which deals with the situation of non-residents is that stamp duty land tax due from a company incorporated outside the United Kingdom may be recovered from, *inter alia*, the proper officer of the company.
[45]   Ibid, s 100(4).

This charge can arise even where it is not necessary to refer the matter to the Land Registry. For example, land may be held by a nominee or bare trustee for several beneficial owners. In this situation the relevant parties are the beneficial owners not the nominee. Dealings between the nominees will, therefore, be dealings in chargeable interests, notwithstanding no entry is to be made at the Land Registry. In this situation it will be easy to produce a tax charge since this can arise where a relevant beneficial owner becomes entitled to possession which includes the right to receive the rents in respect of any leases that have been granted by the nominee on behalf of the beneficial owner.

3.8   The tax is intended to be equally applicable when present conveyancing is replaced by electronic transfers of land[46] and applies whether or not there is a document[47] and to transactions taking effect by operation of law.[48] In consequence it is linked to transactions rather than documentation although the execution of documentation may have an effect on the timing of the tax charge and/or notification obligations. Given basic land law and conveyancing legislation requiring the execution of documentation, most land transactions will be 'completed' in writing which may operate to trigger a charge to the tax;[49] but this is not necessarily the true position. Although the legislation[50] defines the effective date, ie the tax date, by reference to the date of completion this is expressly made subject to special rules of which there are many.[51] This superficial link between written 'completion' and the charge to stamp duty land tax is, however, not necessarily always the case. In consequence, the tax may arise notwithstanding the parties have not 'completed' in the traditional sense. Similarly, the fact that there is a written instrument does not mean there will be a tax charge. For example, in order to prevent parties avoiding the charge to tax by means of subsale arrangements the relief is restricted and is potentially vulnerable to the general anti-avoidance provisions. In other cases, to prevent parties postponing the duty by 'resting upon contract'[52] it is provided that the charge arises by reference to 'substantial performance' which can precede completion. In consequence, it is not possible to escape the charge to tax by resting simply upon the contract and not completing since 'substantial performance' can trigger the tax charge ahead of completion. Certain arrangements concerned with subsales of property are not subject to tax notwithstanding that the parties have completed their transaction.[53]

3.9   This means that it is important for professional advisers to monitor arrangements between the parties to a transaction between contract and completion. Moreover, since the tax can arise even where the contract is conditional it may be necessary to be aware of the actions of the parties or potential parties during

---

[46]   Indeed, it appears to be a key part of the introduction of electronic conveyancing that the stamp duty land tax will be payable instantly. HMRC Stamp Taxes are given power to reduce the 30 day period to instant settlement ie payment must be made before the transaction can be presented to the Land Registry by the FA 2003, s 76(2). This is obviously likely to give rise to considerable problems in relation to banking and payment arrangements and may require greater flexibility as to drawdown of mortgage funds. However, there are many practical difficulties in this area, not least being a suggestion by HMRC Stamp Taxes that they have absolute power to veto or control the person eligible to utilise the Land Registry computerised system; for example, to have firms whose clients have a poor record in relation to stamp duty land tax.

[47]   FA 2003, s 42(2)(c).

[48]   Ibid, s 43(2); see **3.50**.

[49]   Ibid, ss 44(3) and 119; see **Chapter 13**.

[50]   Ibid, s 119.

[51]   Ibid, s 119(2) referring to ss 44(4), 44A(3), 45A(8), 46(3), Sch 17A, paras 12A(2), 12B(3) and 19(3); see **Chapter 14**.

[52]   See **2.9** and **Chapter 14**.

[53]   FA 2003, s 45(3).

negotiations or whilst the conditions are being satisfied.[54] Moreover, there may be situations where the actions of the parties before completion have beneficial effects such as the exemption for building works and fitting out to be carried out on the land to be acquired.[55]

3.10 The tax applies to transactions taking effect by operation of law[56] or to transactions where there is no documentation (although these will be rare for the time being because so many land transactions require written instruments of some description due to the requirements of the various Law of Property Acts). The creation or passing of interests by reason of constructive trusts which do not require writing[57] may be chargeable transactions.[58] However, the rules for substantial performance and for constructive trusts are not identical and there will, in practice, be many problems in determining at what point in the transaction the effective date for notification and payment occurs or is deemed to occur.[59]

THE CHARGEABLE TRANSACTION

3.11 As indicated elsewhere[60] the chargeable transaction is the acquisition of a chargeable interest for a consideration. By referring to the 'acquisition' which is itself defined in relation to creations and surrenders and other actions it implies that, in accordance with the basic definition of the 'effective date'[61] the chargeable transaction arises only when the transaction is perfected and the interest is 'acquired' or 'released' or the actual variation actually takes effect. However, this is a misleading set of legislative provisions and the chargeable transaction is somewhat different since there are many 'special provisions' which indicate that in effectively every transaction the chargeable event will be the actions of the parties prior to completion.

---

54 Different rules apply to options FA 2003, s 46 notwithstanding that in some respects options and conditional contracts may be regarded as very similar; see, for example, *Spiro v Glencrown Properties Ltd* [1991] 1 All ER 600.

55 FA 2003, Sch 4, para 10.

56 See **3.50**.

57 Law of Property Act 1925, s 53(2); *Neville v Wilson* [1997] Ch 144; *Yaxley v Gotts* [1999] 2 WLR 1217. This decision with its criticism of *Oughtred v IRC* [1960] AC 206 indicates a level of judicial lack of integrity where taxation issues are involved. The decision in *Oughtred v IRC supra* indicated that s 53(1)(c) of the Law of Property Act 1925 prevailed over s 53(2) thereof. However, in *Neville v Wilson* [1997] Ch 144 the Court of Appeal recognised that this produced preposterous conveyancing consequences and effectively re-wrote the ratio decidendi and recast the majority in *Oughtred v IRC* in order to produce the appropriate result. The decisions are manifestly inconsistent but show that judges are reluctant to go and follow taxpayers into areas where they are beyond their competence but are not deterred from re-tracing their steps when it is convenient to do so (see also Lord Hoffmann in *Commissioner of Inland Revenue v Mitsubishi Motors New Zealand* [1995] STC 989).

58 There is a basic technical issue as to whether transactions taking effect by operation of law are capable of having consideration which requires a consensual if not a contractual basis. This issue goes to the root of the extent of the charge since transactions, even where there is a consideration in the technical sense, are not subject to the tax if there is no 'chargeable consideration'. See **3.50** and **5.98**.

59 Note especially the deemed effective date for the notional transaction for the general anti-avoidance provisions (FA 2003, s 75A(6)) which is likely to be different from the effective date for the actual acquisition by the person eventually identified as 'P' which has to be separately notified notwithstanding that it forms the basis of the charge for the general anti-avoidance provisions.

60 See **3.1**.

61 FA 2003, s 119.

Contract as chargeable event

3.12   The tax is based upon chargeable transactions. In consequence it is not the contract as such which triggers the liability to report and pay the stamp duty land tax.[62] This would cause the tax charge to arise too early. The trigger for most transactions is the earlier of 'completion' in the traditional sense or 'substantial performance' of the contract.[63] Substantial performance is *prima facie* unrelated either to the date of the contract or to the date at which the equitable interest passes pursuant to any constructive trust arising.[64] Both substantial performance and completion require notification ie direct reporting and possible payment of tax,[65] and the possibility of a tax charge arising between contract and completion may mean that professional advisers may be subject to a professional duty of care to monitor the actions of their client during this period. Special rules apply in relation to options and rights of pre-emption[66] where the tax trigger is the grant[67] of the option or rights, not the date when they became exercisable.

Contracts as chargeable interests

3.13   Contracts relating to land may themselves be chargeable interests. The legislation focuses upon dealings in 'chargeable interests' and there is no specific provision stating that contracts to acquire land are not 'chargeable interests'. There are various provisions indicating that merely entering into the contract or the agreement for lease is not, of itself, a chargeable event[68] but this does not mean that a contract to acquire an interest in land or an agreement for lease is not itself a chargeable interest. Indeed, it would seem to be contrary to the policy of the legislation for a contract to acquire an interest in land not to be a chargeable interest since this would offer opportunities of value shifting and other arrangements.[69] Indeed, it is specifically provided that an obligation affecting the value of a chargeable interest or an estate or interest in land is itself a chargeable interest.[70] In consequence, a contract for the sale of the benefit of a contract would be a contract for the sale of a chargeable interest and it has proved necessary to provide that entering into a contract to assign the benefit of a contract is not a chargeable transaction as such.[71] In consequence, dealings in relation to or variations of a contract relating to land may involve some form of dealing with a chargeable interest giving rise to a chargeable transaction although the time of the actual charge will not necessarily be the making of the contract to sell the benefit of the contract.

---

[62]   Ibid, s 44(2).
[63]   See **Chapter 14**.
[64]   *Michaels v Harley House (Marylebone) Ltd* [1999] 3 WLR 229.
[65]   FA 2003, s 44(8).
[66]   Ibid, s 46(3).
[67]   It would seem that the grant of a conditional option is taxable with no refund if the condition is satisfied, whereas a conditional grant of an option is not taxable until the condition is satisfied. There may, in consequence, be important drafting differences between an option that may be exercised if a certain event occurs and an agreement to grant an option if an event happens. This means that there is a need to determine when an option is 'granted' as there is a difference between the grant of an option and an agreement to grant which was significant for stamp duty purposes as discussed in *George Wimpey Ltd v IRC* [1975] 2 All ER 45 which also illustrates the need for careful drafting in order to avoid a double charge upon the option premium which may not be cancelled by the provisions against double taxation of the same transaction; FA 2003, Sch 10, para 33.
[68]   See, for example, FA 2003, ss 44(2) and 45(2).
[69]   Subject, of course, to the application of the general anti-avoidance provisions of FA 2003, ss 75A–75C.
[70]   FA 2003, s 48(1)(b); see **4.39**.
[71]   See, for example, FA 2003, ss 45, 45A and Sch 17, para 12B.

'ACQUISITION'

3.14   'Acquisition' is widely extended largely by implication and applies to, *inter alia*:[72]

- the creation of a chargeable interest;

- the surrender of a chargeable interest;

- the release of a chargeable interest;[73] and

- the variation of a chargeable interest; but with special rules for the variation of leases whether relating to the rent[74] or other terms and covenants.[75]

There are many questions as to the meaning of these subsidiary applications of the word 'acquisition' and the probable answers to it are not always plain English but are special meanings necessary to make the tax work on a reasonable basis.

3.15   Although the structure of the legislation and the terminology is based upon the model of the conveyance on sale it is clear from the extended definition of 'acquisition' that the terminology and structure has to be stretched to fit a whole range of transactions. This approach to distorting the terminology (which terminology has a long history in traditional stamp duty as well as routine conveyancing) to fit is increased by the types of transaction to which the tax is intended to apply. Although the conveyance on sale is essentially a consensual arrangement it is clear that this simple contract for sale model is not intended to be quite so obvious in relation to stamp duty land tax.

3.16   The tax, in consequence, extends beyond transfers and assignments of freeholds and leaseholds where property passes between or vests in another party which is the normal meaning of 'acquisition' to cover a whole range of other transactions where nothing is acquired by the taxpayer. In consequence, references to 'conveyance' and 'completion' will include leases, deeds and delivery of other documents. Unfortunately, none of these extensions are themselves defined or explained and in consequence give rise to a large set of sub-problems of interpretation.

3.17   The mechanics of 'the acquisition' are also widely defined in that it applies to an 'acquisition' whether effected:

- by act of the parties;

- by order of the court or other authority; or

- by or under any statutory provision; or

- by operation of law.[76]

---

[72]   Ibid, s 43(3).
[73]   See *Belch v IRC* (1877) 4R (Ct of Sess) 592 (release of a rent charge), but for a release pursuant to the terms of instrument creating right, see *Gibb v IRC* (1880) 8R (Ct of Ses) 120; *Cormack's Trustees v IRC* [1924] SC 819; *Great Northern Railway v IRC* [1899] 2 QB 652; appd [1901] KB 416.
[74]   FA 2003, Sch 17A, paras 7, 8, 13–15A.
[75]   Ibid, s 43(3)(d) and Sch 17A, para 15A (as amended).
[76]   See **3.50**.

This is an extremely ambiguous set of drafting. Apart from any explicit guidance on the particular extensions of the plain English meaning of 'acquisition' which is not defined but has to be used in a very specific sense since the tax charge arises where nothing is 'acquired'. The term 'operation of law' is used indiscriminately and without consistency throughout the legislation and seems to have different meanings in each separate context. In relation to 'acquisition' it is ambiguous because it is not made clear whether it refers to rights arising by operation of law such as constructive trusts[77] or constructive arrangements being completed by law rather than act of the parties or pursuant to statute. Obviously the context of 'acquisition' refines these problems but does not totally resolve them.[78]

3.18 Each of the elements in the definition of a chargeable transaction requires detailed explanation.

'Creation'

3.19 There is no definition of 'creation'. Obviously, entering into the grant of a new lease will involve the creation of a new interest in land similarly the grant of an option or pre-emption right or the grant of a right of way will involve the creation of a new right.

There is a fundamental issue in relation to what is involved in 'creation'. A person may dispose of only part of his interest in the land such as a freeholder agreeing to grant a lease or a tenant agreeing to grant a sublease. In this situation it is clear that there is only a part disposal and the creation of one interest.[79] However, other situations are not so clear and, as with other taxes, there is a detailed question as to the nature of the subject-matter of the transaction and whether there is only a part-disposal or a total disposal with a regrant of rights out of the interest transferred such as in the case of a sale and leaseback.[80] There is the question whether the purported 'exclusion' of certain interests or rights from the transaction means that there is a part-disposal or whether there is the 'creation' back in favour of the original disposer of new rights.[81] For example, where A transfers land to B and excepts and reserves certain rights in relation to the land transferred it is considered that these rights have not necessarily been 'created'; there is no movement of interest from B to A, simply a restriction or limitation upon the interest passing from A to B.[82] It is considered that this does not involve a chargeable transaction and the appropriate entries can be made on the land register without the production of a certificate.[83] However, if the land is conveyed to B without restriction and B 'regrants' the right to A, this regrant will be the creation of new chargeable interests which may form part of the chargeable consideration.[84] Obviously once the rights are separated they are likely to be 'chargeable interests' in their own right so that subsequent dealings for a consideration may be separate chargeable transactions.

---

[77] See *Yaxley v Gotts* [1999] 2 WLR 1217.

[78] See **3.19** and following.

[79] *Lady Ingram v IRC* [1999] STC 37.

[80] For which special rules apply see, for example, FA 2003, s 57A.

[81] Should there be the creation of new rights there is likely to be a land exchange with multiple charges to tax; FA 2003, s 47, Sch 4, para 5; see **5.150**.

[82] This is a different issue from that of whether the market value of the interest being acquired is to be determined on the basis that the interest is subject to the rights 'excepted or reserved' or to be regranted.

[83] FA 2003, s 79, which applies only to 'land transactions'.

[84] *Prima facie* the transaction will fall into the land exchange rules and the extent of the charge to stamp duty land tax will depend upon whether the transaction involves exchanges of major interests or only non-major interest: see FA 2003, s 47 and Sch 4, para 5.

3.20 Unfortunately, HMRC Stamp Taxes are currently taking an aggressive approach in this area contending that all excepting and reserving is a regrant unless either the rights are separately in existence prior to the transaction or they are specific rights which appear to be limited to mineral rights.[85] This has far reaching consequences since it has the effect of converting many routine transactions into land exchanges pursuant to FA 2003, s 47.[86] It might be thought that this is not a significant issue in practice but problems do lurk in the background should there be an Enquiry. The charge upon exchanges is based upon the market value of the chargeable interest received. For the types of interest, normally excepted and reserved, usually minor interests, these will have a negligible market value because they cannot be sold in the 'open market'.[87] No doubt the rights may have a 'value' if only because of the nuisance for the holder of the rights who can demand some form of compensation from the landowner as a means of cancelling his rights[88] but it is doubtful whether this arrangement of only one possible potential 'purchaser' constitutes a 'market' and whether, in the circumstances of one limited and very special purchaser, such a market is 'open'. Moreover, since the rights will be interests in the dominant land they will not be capable of separate sale and can only exist as part of the dominant land therefore, there is no market for the rights as such[89] and fall within the nil rate band so that there is no reporting obligation.[90] Also for the major interest conveyed subject to the exceptions and reservation the actual consideration is likely to be the market value; but this is not necessarily the case. For example, a developer may be offering a discount for a bulk sale or purchase from plan. HMRC Stamp Taxes take the view that arm's length negotiations are not conclusive of market value such as where the seller is anxious to obtain a quick sale or as a receiver or personal representative is 'anxious' rather than 'willing' to sell.[91] Should HMRC Stamp Taxes persist in this approach there are potential traps for many purchasers, vendors and lessors in what appear to be routine transactions.

Disclaimer, renunciation and waiver[92]

3.21 There may also be issues as to whether interests have been 'created' or there is merely a recognition of an existing situation which has been dormant or irrelevant. It is considered that a disclaimer does not involve a surrender or release even if for a consideration,[93] even though the effect of the disclaimer is that the property or interest effectively passes to another person. This is not the termination of an interest – it is an action which prevents an interest from arising. It seems that renunciation[94] is not

---

85 For example, in their view latent rights which take effect pursuant to Law of Property Act 1925, s 62 are 'regrants'. Difficulties have arisen in practice in relation to delayed completions ie situations where the property has been sold in the sense that the consideration money has been paid but the seller has been allowed to remain in occupation on a temporary basis. HMRC Stamp Taxes appear to have been advised that this is not simply a delayed completion but is a transfer or acquisition of the land and the grant of some interest back. The question is the nature of the interest 'retained' or 'regranted' by or to the seller and whether this is some form of chargeable interest having a value that can attract a charge to tax.
86 See **5.153**.
87 See **Chapter 27**.
88 See, for example, *Alexander v IRC* [1991] STC 112.
89 However, where attempts are made to 'reserve' or 'except' such interests and there is no dominant land to be benefitted the right will have a separate existence and may well be a chargeable interest pursuant to FA 2003, s 48(1)(b); see **4.39**.
90 FA 2003, s 77(4).
91 See, for example, *Lap Shun Textiles Industrial Co v Collector of Stamp Revenue* [1976] AC 530; *Cowan de Groot Properties Ltd v Eagle Trust plc* [1991] BCLC 1045.
92 Note also the exemption for variations of estates which may also apply to such transactions (FA 2003, Sch 3, paras 3A and 4).
93 *Re Paradise Motors Ltd* [1968] 1 WLR 1125.
94 'Renunciation' has a special meaning in Scotland which is different from its meaning in England. This adds

chargeable notwithstanding that it operates to pass property. It is not included in the list of events constituting 'acquisitions' but it does appear in the definition of 'transfer' for certain partnership purposes[95] so that its absence indicates that such transactions are not chargeable.

3.22 However, there may be issues about releases, waivers and payments of compensation.[96] Each case will require careful consideration and suitably prudent drafting because of the effect of the arrangement may be something more than a mere payment of compensation and may involve some modification in the rights for the future. This is a particular problem in relation to leases since only certain 'variations' of leases are taxable[97] ie whether a variation that is not taxable is subject to tax as a release of a covenant in the lease. This arises because what may appear to be a potentially taxable variation of a covenant in a lease because the tenant is paying for it[98] is taxable but another variation of a similar nature where the landlord is paying the tenant for the variation and so may not be taxable, there is also an event which is a 'release' or 'waiver' of all or part of the covenant in the lease. The question is whether the provisions relating to the 'waiver' or 'release' of part of the covenant apply notwithstanding the implication that this type of 'variation' is not intended to be taxable. It is thought that because of the structure of the legislation the 'waiver' or 'partial release' of covenants in a lease are not intended to be taxable. However, HMRC Stamp Taxes have not made their views known on this point. Although, for example, covenants in leases relating to repairs and any sums of money paid by the tenant as damages for breach of covenant are not subject to stamp duty land tax,[99] there is the issue of whether, where the covenant has been broken and a sum is paid as compensation for dilapidations, this involves some form of variation of the covenant,[100] which is taxable.[101] To the extent that the underlying covenant is modified there would appear to be a risk of liability to stamp duty land tax.[102] It is considered that the settlement of litigation is not a dealing in land, although it terminates a right, nor is a lock-out agreement.[103] However, it remains to be discovered in practice how far HMRC Stamp Taxes intend to impose charges upon the termination of litigation or potential litigation between the parties, particularly where the litigation relates to the compromise of a dispute based upon a breach of covenant in a lease.[104]

---

to the confusion in the drafting because it is unclear whether the word is intended to bear its general (ie English) meaning or is limited to its special Scottish meaning. As the tradition of drafting tax legislation is to utilise English terms and leave Scottish lawyers to make sense of this alien terminology it is considered that 'renunciation' bears its English, not its Scottish meaning. On the concept of 'renunciation' in English law it is clear that a 'renunciation' is not a 'transfer', which may be a key issue in relation to the exclusion of initial share transfers from the general anti-avoidance provisions (FA 2003, s 75C(1)) but as being some other form of transaction; see, for example, *Re Pool Shipping* [1920] 1 Ch 251; *Re Simo Securities Trusts Ltd* [1971] 3 All ER 999.

[95]   FA 2003, Sch 15, paras 9(2) and 35; but it is questionable whether this is an attempt by the draftsman to deal with the specific Scottish terminology or is just an oversight when copying in other similar legislation.

[96]   See, for example, FA 2003, 43(3).

[97]   FA 2003, s 43(3)(d), Sch 17A, para 15A; see **7.218**.

[98]   Ibid, Sch 17A, para 15A(1A).

[99]   Ibid, Sch 4, para 13.

[100] See, eg, *Banning v Wright* 48 TC 421.

[101] FA 2003, Sch 17A, para 15A (as amended).

[102] See, eg, *Banning v Wright* 48 TC 421.

[103] See, eg, *Pitt v PHH Asset Management* [1993] 4 All ER 961.

[104] Note, however, that many types of covenant in leases are excluded from the charge to tax as is any payment made in respect of the covenant which presumably includes payments of compensation by reference to the breach of covenant; FA, 2003, Sch 17A, para 10(1) and (2).

Statutory extensions – deemed acquisitions[105]

3.23   Notwithstanding the width of the basic definition of 'acquisitions'[106] there have
been extensions of the charge to transactions where land is not acquired in an attempt
to forestall attempts to mitigate the charge to tax by utilising land 'derivatives' for value
shifting.[107] This anti-avoidance legislation has been enacted after the main legislation
and appears to be hurriedly drafted and does not always fit comfortably with the
original legislation or apply to the types of arrangement intended to be attacked. It can,
in consequence, provide a trap for the unwary.

3.24   FA 2003, s 44A[108] provides that where a person acquires a right to direct a
conveyance a chargeable transaction arises where that contract is substantially
performed. It is difficult to reconcile these provisions with the subsale and similar
arrangements legislation[109] where the contract for sale or lease may entitle the purchaser
to direct that the transfer or lease be made to a third party, but it is intended to charge
arrangements such as those where a developer rather than agreeing to purchase the land
agrees with the landowner to construct buildings on the land for a consideration to be
calculated by reference to the realisation proceeds of the sale or leasing of the
development in due course.[110]

3.25   This provision is potentially extremely wide-ranging. It does not define the
circumstances under which the power to direct the conveyance arises. It can arise to
genuine commercial situations and certain powers of attorney are situations where the
attorney or agent is potentially subjected to stamp duty land tax. For example, A may
have significant assets, including land, and is proposing to take a long vacation or be
working abroad for many years. In consequence, he may appoint some person in the UK
to manage his assets and give them powers to purchase and to sell. This may be
embodied in some form of power of attorney in order to enable the person to execute
conveyances. In this situation the attorney has power to enter into contracts and to
execute and direct conveyances. Technically such a person will be liable to stamp duty
land tax upon any sale that he effects. It might be thought that this is a somewhat limited
situation but there seems to be no reason, in principle, why the type of protected power
of attorney that is given to persons to manage the estates of people subject to disability
or to members of the family where a person is suffering from dementia are not caught.
The legislation can clearly apply to these situations because the person has power to
direct a conveyance ie to make a contract in the name of the donor of the power and to
execute the conveyance. It is assumed that HMRC Stamp Taxes would not wish to
pursue such parties for stamp duty land tax particularly where the purchaser of the
property has paid tax in respect of the same transaction. However, should they do so,
this would be regarded as an unfair dispensation of the law operating without statutory
authority disadvantageously to other persons.

---

[105]   There are two situations potentially applicable; namely: (i) situations where no charge would otherwise arise;
and (ii) situations where there is a basic chargeable transaction but which is to be taxed upon a basis
different from its primary characterisation such as abnormal increases in rent (FA 2003, Sch 17A, paras 14
and 15) or certain variations of leases taxed as acquisitions of chargeable interest Sch 17A, para 15A.

[106]   FA 2003, s 43(3).

[107]   This is in addition to other hidden anti-avoidance provisions such as the extended definition of 'chargeable
interest' such as FA 2003, s 48(1)(b).

[108]   See also FA 2003, s 45A; now also vulnerable to s 75A.

[109]   FA 2003, s 45 (as amended); Sch 17A, para 12B; see **Chapter 6**.

[110]   See further **Chapter 8**.

3.26 The chargeable transaction arises where a chargeable interest is to be 'conveyed' by the one party to the contract (usually the landowner) at the direction of the other party to the contract to a third person who is not a party to the contract or to such a third person or the party with the power to direct the 'conveyance'. The legislation has many problems.[111] It utilises the word 'conveyed' which is defined and only for limited purposes solely by reference to instruments. However, it seems likely that it will be applied to the power to direct the grant of leases.[112]

3.27 The entering into the building or similar contract is not a chargeable transaction but if the contract is substantially performed, the party with the power to direct the conveyance is deemed to acquire a chargeable interest, the nature of which is unexplained, and is taxable.[113] 'Substantial performance' bears its normal meaning; but this is not particularly relevant to contracts where there is no land interest being acquired. The rules as to substantial payment will not apply because the chargeable consideration would normally be moving from the developer to the landowner, whereas in this case the consideration for the building works is moving from the vendor, the landowner to the developer and has not been provided by the 'other party' to the contract. It is, therefore, difficult to find a chargeable consideration because payments will be moving in the opposite direction from the land obligations.[114] The payment for the building works cannot be chargeable consideration for the deemed land acquisition by the 'other party'.[115] The charge cannot, therefore, arise where the builder merely has power to 'recommend' purchasers or tenants which the landowner can accept or reject. There are no connected party provisions so that a selling agency granted to an associate of the developer (ie the other party) does not bring these provisions into operation.

CHARGEABLE INTEREST WHICH IS NOT EXEMPT[116]

3.28 A chargeable interest means:[117]

- an estate, interest, right or power in or over land in the United Kingdom, or

- the benefit of an obligation, restriction or condition affecting the value of any such estate, interest, right or power,

- other than an exempt interest.

3.29 In general the terms utilised are relatively clear. Estates and interests are well known as are rights in or over land such as easements and rights to light. Powers over land would include trustees' powers of appointment as well as other powers of

---

[111] It is a classic illustration of professional advisers acting in what may be a breach of duty to clients passing on planning ideas contained in counsel's advice which is in breach of the rules of client confidentiality which the advisers do not fully understand to HMRC Stamp Taxes who themselves do not fully understand the issues involved when preparing what they regard as anti-avoidance legislation. It suffers from serious defects because of the poor quality of those 'consulting' with HMRC Stamp Taxes in various groups and associations.

[112] Where leases are not intended to be involved, the draftsman tends to utilise the word 'transfer'; but this, unhelpfully, does not appear to be a consistently adopted policy; but see FA 2003, Sch 17A, para 12B.

[113] Such arrangements produce a notifiable transaction FA 2003, s 77(1)(c).

[114] But see **2.3** on the possible HMRC Stamp Taxes theory of 'reverse consideration'.

[115] But see **2.3** on the draftsman's bizarre theory of reverse consideration.

[116] See further **Chapter 4**.

[117] FA 2003, s 48.

appointment such as testamentary powers. The key area will be the meaning of obligation and restrictions affecting the value of land. There may be a contractual arrangement restricting the development of land thereby affecting its value.[118] Whilst entering into such a contract would not be a chargeable transaction any subsequent dealings in relation to such an arrangement could involve 'acquisitions' such as variations or releases. In consequence all contracts relating to land are likely to be chargeable interests, not merely options or pre-emptive rights. Merely entering into a contracts to sell the benefit of contracts relating to land are not as such immediately taxable,[119] but all other arrangements in relation to such a contract, such as a formal assignment for payment, appear to be vulnerable to tax on completion or substantial performance of a contract to acquire a chargeable interest.

Exempt interests

3.30   The 'acquisition' or deemed acquisition must relate to a chargeable interest other than certain interests in or over land which are 'exempt' ie they are not chargeable interests. This dealing in an interest which is exempt ie not a chargeable interest, is not the same as a transaction being 'exempt'.

Exempt interests include:

*   *any security interest*: this is defined as being any interest or right, other than a rent charge,[120] held for the purpose of securing the payment of money or performance of any other obligation.[121] In Scotland the reference to 'rent charge' is a reference to a feu duty or a payment mentioned in s 56(1) of the Abolition of Feudal Tenure etc (Scotland) Act 2000 (ASP 5) s 56(1). The definition appears to be wide enough to exclude security interests such as the liens of an unpaid vendor for the purchase price;[122]

*   *a licence to use or occupy land*: this will give rise to difficult technical issues when deciding whether there is a notifiable transaction or if the transaction is to be self-certified or not returned as non-notifiable transactions ie a non-taxable transaction because it is considered to be a licence – if this decision ultimately proves after an Enquiry[123] to be incorrect, interest and penalties will arise.[124] It must, however, be noted that, although licenses either as regards grant or dealing are not chargeable interests, entry into possession of land as a licensee may operate as 'substantial performance' of a contract and so give rise to a charge to tax;[125]

---

[118]   This may be a key issue where there is an attempt to create a restrictive covenant which is ineffective because there is no dominant land to be benefited. This could apply, for example, where vendors seek to create protection or security for the payment of overage or clawback consideration.

[119]   FA 2003, s 45, Sch 17A, para 12B.

[120]   Three problems exist in relation to rent charges; namely whether: since rent charges are chargeable interests a transfer subject to the grant of a rent charge is to be treated as an exchange; the creation of the rent charge involves chargeable consideration of a periodical nature; where the property is conveyed subject to a pre-existing rent charge whether this is to be treated as the assumption of a liability within FA 2003, Sch 4, para 8. It remains to be seen whether HMRC Stamp Taxes continue their previous stamp duty practice of, effectively, treating estate rent charges as a form of security for payment of service and similar charges.

[121]   FA 2003, s 48(3); query if this applies to a restrictive covenant to secure overage payments.

[122]   Note the effect of such liens upon the beneficial ownership in the property as in *Musselwhite v Musselwhite* [1962] 1 Ch 210.

[123]   Pursuant to FA 2003, Sch 10; see **Chapter 9**.

[124]   On lease or licence, see **Chapter 7**.

[125]   FA 2003, s 44(5)(b).

- in England and Wales or Northern Ireland:
  - *a tenancy at will*;
  - *an advowson*;
  - *a franchise* (this is defined as a grant from the Crown such as the right to hold a market or fair or the right to take tolls); or
  - *a manor*.[126]

- *interest held as part of alternative finance arrangements*.[127] An interest held by the financial institution as part of an alternative finance transaction is an exempt interest. In addition, the concept of 'exempt interests' has been extended by legislation in order to cope with the need for alternative finance to assist people who are prohibited from straightforward lending and mortgage arrangements by reason of the rules of usury relating to their particular beliefs. These reliefs are, however, not limited to members of any particular community and are available to all persons who may find that the alternative finance regime[128] are more efficient than the general reliefs. Two areas relating to the alternative finance regime have been introduced:
  - since it is not possible to enter into a straightforward loan arrangement and the 'lender' or provider of funds has to acquire some interest in the land which generates an income that is really interest, the transactions tend to take the form of a sale and saleback or a sale and leaseback. Exemptions are available for such transactions although there are restrictions upon the relief particularly in relation to subsales;[129]
  - persons who provide funds in this situation may themselves also be restricted in relation to the raising of money by way of loan and the payment of interest. It may be necessary for them to provide an interest in land or shares generating income so that the loan is in fact some form of sale of an interest in the property with possibly some form of right of reacquisition. It is provided that where the provider of funds in relation to some form of sale and saleback or sale and leaseback in respect of the acquisition of the property is a qualifying company such as a bank subsidiary or a company holding a consumer credit licence the interest held by that company for the time being as the provider of funds is an exempt interest.[130] It is also provided[131] that where there is a raising of funds by means of an alternative finance investment bond which represents an interest in the assets whether land or shares there is an exemption from stamp duty land tax and stamp duty in respect of dealings in the bond.

HMRC Stamp Taxes is given power to extend the list of exempt interests by regulation,[132] but this power has not hitherto been exercised.

---

126 Ibid, s 48(2)–(4).
127 Ibid, s 73B.
128 Ibid, ss 71A–73B. These may be more beneficial than the basic leaseback relief pursuant to FA 2003, s 57A.
129 Ibid, s 45(3) (as amended).
130 Ibid, s 73AB.
131 FA 2009, Sch 61.
132 FA 2003, s 48(5).

WHETHER OR NOT THERE IS AN INSTRUMENT

Transactions not documents

3.31   Although writing is required for most land transactions to be effective in law,[133] all arrangements that may give rise to a constructive trust upon equitable principles may be effective contracts notwithstanding the absence of writing.[134] Nevertheless, the existence of writing is not a condition of liability to stamp duty land tax but the production of a 'conveyance' or any written instrument itself may constitute 'completion' which may be the effective date for the transaction and so produce a taxable or notifiable event.[135] It must, however, be noted that the absence of sufficient writing[136] or writing in the proper form (such as where deeds are required) may mean that as a matter of general law[137] there is no transaction or no passing of title unless the conduct of the parties is such that an interest passes by reason of some form of constructive trust[138] not requiring writing.[139] This issue of documentation is, therefore, important in determining:

- whether there is a transaction;

- when that transaction becomes effective;

- whether there is a tax charge; and

- the effect upon the tax by reason of the drafting and/or structuring of the documents.[140]

3.32   The transactional nature of the tax means that it can apply however the interest is 'acquired', at least if it falls within the list in the legislation.[141] It is not necessary for there to be a document and title can pass by other means such as because it 'completes' the transaction or constitutes substantial performance such as a direction in writing to a tenant to pay the rent to a third party.[142] This is a different question from the issue of whether such documentation as may be created is a 'conveyance' which triggers a tax

---

[133]   Such as Law of Property Act 1925, ss 52 and 53(1); but note s 53(2); *Neville v Wilson* [1997] Ch 144; Law of Property (Miscellaneous Provisions) Act 1989; on the type of contract required see *First Post Homes v Johnson* [1995] 4 All ER 355 but note *Spiro v Glencrown Properties Ltd* [1991] 1 All ER 600.

[134]   Note the comments of Walker LJ in *Yaxley v Gotts* [1999] 2 WLR 1217; but note the limits on the scope of these arrangements indicated by *Yeoman Row Management v Crabbe* [2008] 4 All ER 713.

[135]   FA 2003, s 44(8), (10)(b).

[136]   *First Post Homes v Johnson* [1995] 4 All ER 355.

[137]   But note that it is possible to proceed from ineffective oral arrangements to a valid completion in writing: *Tootal Clothing v Guinea Properties Management* (1992) 64 P & CR 452; it may also be possible to exercise an option over land orally since, according to *Spiro v Glencrown Properties Ltd* [1991] 2 WLR 931, the only contract required to be in writing pursuant to Law of Property (Miscellaneous Provisions) Act 1989, s 2 is the option itself, treating it as a conditional agreement to sell rather than an irrevocable offer – a point upon which there is great divergence in the cases depending upon how the particular judge viewed the policy of the legislation. Note also the comments in *Yaxley v Gotts* [1999] 2 WLR 1217 that equitable notions may override the statutory requirements for writing and create not merely a constructive trust but a valid and binding oral contract.

[138]   *Yaxley v Gotts* [1999] 2 WLR 1217; *Binions v Evans* [1972] Ch 359; *Inwards v Baker* [1965] 2 QB 29; *ER Ives (Investments) v High* [1967] 2 QB 379; on the extent to which such transactions may not be taxable, see **5.98**.

[139]   Law of Property Act 1925, s 53(2); Law of Property (Miscellaneous Provisions) Act 1989, s 2(6); but since such arrangements are not obviously contractual there may not be a chargeable consideration and so not a chargeable transaction (FA 2003, Sch 3, para 1).

[140]   See **Chapter 26**.

[141]   FA 2003, 43(3).

[142]   *Re Whiting* (1879) 10 Ch D 615; FA 2003, s 44(4) and (10)(b).

charge.[143] This is not generally defined although it is defined for the purposes of FA 2003, s 44, as being 'any instrument';[144] this must be between the same parties.[145] Clearly the word 'conveyance' must include leases and declarations of trust.[146] It remains to be seen whether there will be an attempt by HMRC Stamp Taxes to bring over the wide stamp duty meaning of the term notwithstanding that this was based on a statutory provision.[147] It means that, for the time being, parties run the risk of inadvertently triggering a tax charge by producing receipts[148] or powers of attorney enabling a purchaser to complete the transaction by executing a transfer in the name of the seller in favour of a third party.[149]

TRANSACTIONS HOWEVER EFFECTED

3.33   There is an ambiguity in this legislation in referring to the transaction being 'effected'. This usually suggests a transaction being completed such as by act of the parties executing a lease or by a Court order vesting the property. The word 'effected' does not usually refer to the entry into the contract, but it is difficult to apply this in the context of substantial performance which must be an act of the parties. It is considered that this refers to the completion or vesting of title not the contract.

The tax applies to chargeable transactions however effected.[150]

Act of the parties

3.34   The tax applies where the acquisition is by act of the parties ie the title passes as a result of something done by the parties such as the execution of a conveyance or lease. Unfortunately, it is unclear how far the 'act of the parties' is intended to stretch. The utilisation of the plural 'parties' suggests that there needs to be a bilateral transaction – a unilateral transaction would it seems, in the absence of specific charging provisions, not be a chargeable transaction such as a declaration of trust by the owner of property in favour of other persons. In principle, such a transaction is likely to be exempt because it will be for no chargeable consideration[151] but there may be a completion of a contract for sale by means of a declaration of trust such as where property is held by the vendor as a nominee and it is provided that as at completion of the contract the nominee will execute an appropriate declaration of trust including the purchaser amongst the list of beneficiaries. In such a situation it would seem that notwithstanding the use of the plural 'parties' this would be a sufficient 'act of the parties' because of the agreement

143   FA 2003, s 44(8) which means that subsales or the grant of leases to third parties may not be completion for these purposes (FA 2003, s 45; Sch 17A, para 12B).
144   Ibid, s 44(10)(b).
145   Ibid, s 44(10)(a).
146   See, for example, *Peter Bone v IRC* [1995] STC 921; *West London Syndicate Ltd v IRC* [1898] 2 QB 507; *Angus v IRC* (1889) 23 QBD 579; *City and Permanent Building Society v Miller* [1952] Ch 840.
147   FA 1999, Sch 13, para 1 which re-enacted provisions with a long history; see Stamp Act 1891, ss 54 and 61.
148   As in *Garnett v IRC* (1899) 81 LT 633.
149   *Diplock v Hammond* (1854) 5 De GM & G 320; but this may turn upon the nature of the authority of the purchaser. Frequently, contracts for sale provide that if the vendor or landlord should default in his obligation to produce a transfer or the grant of a lease the purchaser or tenant may complete the transaction executing documents in the name of the registered owner. This would not be a 'conveyance' because it is not immediately effective but is a power which arises only in the event of the default of the seller or landlord. Compare also *Roddick v Gandell* (1852) 1 De G M & G 763 concerning powers of attorney given to third parties and not to the purchaser.
150   FA 2003, s 42(2).
151   Ibid, Sch 3, para 1.

that this is the way in which the transaction is to proceed, and it is far from clear how far
unilateral acts can constitute chargeable transactions given the need for 'chargeable
consideration'.[152] For example, a transfer of land out of a settlement pursuant to the
exercise of a power of advancement exercisable without consent would not, in the
absence of a charge upon the land,[153] be a chargeable transaction because it arises as the
act of only one of the parties (ie the trustees) to the transaction.[154] Given the fact that
there is a general exemption for transactions where there is no chargeable
consideration[155] it would seem that there may need to be a consensual element.[156]

3.35   For example, there may be a problem of whether unilateral actions are
chargeable transactions for persons administering the estate of deceased persons
although there have been several statutory interventions in this area alleviating many of
the difficulties.[157] The parties may agree that the executors can appropriate a chargeable
interest in land in full or part satisfaction of the interest of a pecuniary legatee and such
a transaction being in satisfaction of indebtedness[158] would be an acquisition by way of
chargeable consideration and consensual.[159] However, there is a power to appropriate
property in satisfaction of a legacy or devise without consent.[160] Such an arrangement
was not regarded as a conveyance on sale because there was no consent to the
arrangement or even a deemed consent.[161] However, this transaction would now appear
to be, *prima facie*, subject to stamp duty land tax[162] since even if it does not take effect
by act of the parties it is 'by or under any statutory provision' – but this depends upon
the question of whether a transfer in satisfaction of a debt such as a pecuniary legacy
without the consent of the creditors/legatee is a transfer for a chargeable consideration.
It is arguable that 'consideration' requires a contract or agreement and that something
done without consent being non-contractual does not involve chargeable consideration[163] and so is exempt,[164] and not notifiable.[165]

3.36   Reliefs have been introduced[166] for many variations of estates involving the
appropriation of property in or towards a beneficiary's entitlement in the estate of a
deceased, whether testate or intestate,[167] and allocations of trust assets by trustees with

---

[152]   See **Chapter 5**.

[153]   FA 2003, Sch 4, para 8 (as amended) but if done without consent of the beneficiary there would not be an
assumption of liability and so it would fall outside para 4; see **5.134**.

[154]   It remains to be seen in practice whether in any Enquiry into such transactions HMRC Stamp Taxes intend
to investigate any preliminary discussions between the trustees and beneficiaries as a possible springboard
for the argument that there is a bilateral agreement between the parties; but see the possible reliefs such as
that for the reallocation of assets with consent pursuant to FA 2003, Sch 16, para 8; see **Chapter 9**.

[155]   FA 2003, Sch 3, para 1; see **11.8** and **11.19**.

[156]   HMRC Stamp Taxes cannot exploit the inclusion of FA 2003, Sch 3, para 1 since this refers to chargeable
not actual consideration. Unilateral transactions may, therefore, not be chargeable transactions on general
principles.

[157]   See FA 2003, Sch 3, paras 3 and 3A; Sch 4, paras 8 and 8A.

[158]   FA 2003, Sch 4, para 8.

[159]   Cf *Jopling v IRC* [1940] 2 KB 282.

[160]   Administration of Estates Act 1925, s 41.

[161]   Note the possible implications of consent by beneficiaries because of the introduction of relief for the
reallocation of assets with consent; FA 2003, Sch 16, para 8.

[162]   Subject to the possibility of exemption pursuant to FA 2003, Sch 3, para 4; see also Sch 16, para 8.

[163]   Note the relevance of consent for the charge on the reallocation of assets in relation to FA 2003, Sch 16,
para 8.

[164]   Pursuant to FA 2003, Sch 3, para 1; see further **11.18**.

[165]   FA 2003, s 77A.

[166]   Ibid, Sch 3, para 3A; see **9.36**.

[167]   Ibid, Sch 3, para 3A. The relief for variations of estates within 2 years after the death is enlarged. Where the
consideration for the acquisition of the chargeable interest includes consideration that is not other property
within the estate the charge to stamp duty land tax is limited to that consideration. For example, if a

the agreement of the beneficiary.[168] The fact that it was thought necessary to introduce reliefs indicates that the official view is that the exercise of a power without consent is a chargeable transaction, and the satisfaction of an entitlement or obligation without consent is chargeable consideration. The basic issues of principle in other cases are, therefore, unaffected by these limited exemptions. This relief is restricted if the legatee or devisee gives consideration other than the assumption of liability in respect of a charge upon the property to secure a sum of money payable whether certainly or contingently,[169] and the relief is available where the acceptance of the property is in satisfaction of, for example, a pecuniary legacy. This appears to exempt appropriations by a widow of the matrimonial home in or towards the satisfaction of her statutory legacy. Any other interpretation would deprive the exemption of virtually any worthwhile application. As the relief is included in FA 2003, Sch 3, it is not a notifiable transaction.[170]

By order of the court or other authority[171]

3.37 Court orders can take a variety of forms. They may vest property[172] or they may declare the rights of the parties or they may sanction an arrangement such as in relation to the reconstruction of companies[173] or supply consent on behalf of persons who are unable to consent. In these latter situations further action by the parties may be necessary.[174] Clearly, where the court order vests property or the court supplies consent on behalf of those persons so that there can be an effective transfer (ie some form of contract) who are unable to consent there will either be a transfer or some form of agreement to transfer or acquire property of a consensual nature within the charge should there be consideration.

3.38 It was well settled law that for the purposes of stamp duty that Court orders could be conveyances on sale and accordingly were stampable and undertakings were required from the parties to stamp the documentation.[175] Such orders are now clearly within the charge to stamp duty land tax. Much may turn upon the nature of the order which will depend upon the initial drafting of the claim for relief or defence in the litigation. It seems probable that HMRC Stamp Taxes will seek to impose a charge if the order is for the vesting of property, although there will be considerable debate with them if the order sought is merely a declaration of rights so drafted that there may not be chargeable consideration.

---

daughter agrees to take the house in consideration of the son receiving shares out of the estate and cash provided by the daughter from her own assets only the cash is taxable. It seems that the rate of tax is related to the cash and not the total value of the consideration, so that the lower rates of tax are available; see also Sch 4, paras 8(1A) and 8A.

[168] FA 2003, Sch 16, para 8 (as amended).
[169] Ibid, Sch 3, para 4(2) and (2A); Sch 4, paras 8 and 8A; see **Chapter 9**.
[170] Ibid, s 77A.
[171] Note that the relief for transactions entered into in connection with the breakdown of matrimonial relations or civil partnerships require Court orders; FA 2003, Sch 3, paras 3 and 3A (but note the existence of 2 paras 3A).
[172] See, for example, *Sun Alliance v IRC* [1971] 1 All ER 135; the Court order operating as the equivalent of a stock transfer form.
[173] Such as reconstructions Insolvency Act 1980, s 110 and Companies Act 2006, s 899; see also returns of capital Companies Act 2006, s 645; other reconstructions may require other sanctions such as insurance companies.
[174] Variation of Trusts Act 1958; *Re Holt* [1969] 1 Ch 100; *Re Ball* [1968] 1 WLR 899.
[175] *Sun Alliance Insurance Ltd v IRC* [1971] 1 All ER 135; *Terrapin v IRC* [1967] 1 WLR 665.

3.39   The declaration of rights of parties raises more difficult issues. This may simply be an order that the interests of the parties have not been changed by the events in dispute, in which case there would seem to be no acquisition or disposal of any property. On the other hand, the order may recognise that there have been changes of title to property.[176] The type of case which may now give rise to problems, subject to the difficult question of 'chargeable consideration', in equitable arrangements such as constructive trusts and similar concepts,[177] would be illustrated by cases such as *Ives v High*[178] and *Binions v Evans*.[179] These are cases where parties, in reliance upon statements made by or the inactivity of other parties, have incurred expenditure or altered their position and so become entitled to some form of interest in the property[180] and there is some indication[181] that in such circumstances equitable principles may intervene so that there is a valid contract notwithstanding the absence of writing as required by Law of Property (Miscellaneous Provisions) Act 1989, s 2.[182] The Court may, therefore, find some form of enforceable obligation to transfer an interest in property whether by means of an 'equitable oral but binding contract' or some form of constructive trust and given that there is now a very fine but vital line between what is a condition and what is consideration[183] the recognition by the court of some form of interest passing by reason of the events including the party acting upon the promise as a 'request'[184] could be the trigger for the liability to tax.

3.40   Whether there is such an effective oral passing of title is possibly dependent upon the exercise of judicial discretion since equitable reliefs may be a matter of discretion and the circumstances. The Court may decide that a cash payment possibly secured by a charge upon the land may be a more appropriate remedy than the vesting of some interest in the land or compromise of litigation. There is, obviously, a question as to when the 'effective date' of such transactions occurs. The cases suggest that there may be two stages in the transaction which will be of crucial significance. There is the initial commencement of activity which may be sufficient to preclude the landowner from withdrawing or revoking his 'promise' but is insufficient to satisfy the terms of the promise and there is completion in the sense of the full performance of the conditions when the 'promisee' becomes entitled in equity to call for the transfer of the relevant interest. For example, in *Yaxley v Gotts*[185] the plaintiff embarked upon certain building operations in reliance upon an oral and therefore ineffective promise by the landowner to give him an interest in the land when the work was completed.[186] Clearly it would be possible to allege that the landowner could not withdraw from his offer or promise once

---

[176]   The discretionary nature of equitable relief and the possibility of relief in quasi-contract by way of *quantum meruit* and *quantum valebant* will leave open doubts as to whether there is a constructive trust passing property and quasi-contract which does not until the final decision of the Courts. This uncertainty of the rights of the parties raises questions of whether settlements of disputes involve the acquisition of rights; but agreeing to compromise litigation may be consideration but may not necessarily be money or money's worth.

[177]   See **3.4**.

[178]   [1967] 2 QB 379.

[179]   [1972] Ch 359.

[180]   There is, of course, the question of whether the mere payment of money which can easily be refunded is a sufficient alteration of position by the person to his detriment to justify the application of the principles of equitable estoppel.

[181]   See the comments of Walker LJ in *Yaxley v Gotts* [1999] 2 WLR 1217.

[182]   But note the limitations on this approach in *Yeoman Row Management v Crabbe* [2008] 4 All ER 713.

[183]   *Eastham v Leigh, London and Provincial Properties Limited* [1971] 2 All ER 887; *Yaxley v Gotts* [1999] 2 WLR 1217.

[184]   Note the judicial reluctance to treat such arrangements as unenforceable promises of a gift as in *GUS Merchandise v Customs and Excise* [1981] 1 WLR 1309.

[185]   [1999] 2 WLR 1217.

[186]   Such building works would now be chargeable consideration: see FA 2003, Sch 4, para 10; **Chapter 8**.

the works had started[187] but at that point no interest would have accrued to or vested in the plaintiff who has not 'earned' the property by fulfilling the promise. The problem is whether the interest passes once the building works are complete or when the court relying upon equitable principles states the nature of that interest. Alternative remedies might have been available such as some form of equitable charge on the land or a claim in quasi-contract for reasonable remuneration for services rendered[188] but in that case the Court indicated that in this type of situation the equitable notions intervene to create a valid oral contract binding upon the parties and override the statutory requirements of Law of Property (Miscellaneous Provisions) Act 1989, s 2. If this is a general principle[189] then many constructive trusts arrangements will be essentially contract arrangements for a consideration. It is a difficult decision as to whether the effective date of that transaction would be the completion of the works or only when the nature of the interest that had passed by reason of the constructive trust was declared by the court.[190]

3.41 Difficulties are likely to arise frequently in practice in situations such as that illustrated by *Errington v Errington and Woods*.[191] For example, when A purchases land utilising a mortgage and allows B to occupy the land upon the basis that B may be entitled to the land or an interest therein as and when the mortgage is fully repaid by B. Such transactions will frequently be oral and so technically may not constitute binding contracts to sell the land.[192] If in writing there will be a contract for sale which is substantially performed when B enters onto the land albeit as a licensee.[193] Where there is no contract in writing B may be dependent upon equitable relief, which may take a variety of forms, assuming that he can produce satisfactory evidence of the oral arrangement. *Prima facie* he will have no right to the land or any interest therein until the court so orders. There will undoubtedly have been a chargeable transaction – the problem is when it has occurred.

Pre-contract activities

3.42 A particular area of difficulty is where the parties may be negotiating in good faith and in relying upon the good faith of the other party to a contract and embark upon activities that are consistent only with the contract coming into existence. Alternatively, the parties may be closely connected such as the family who are shareholders in a family company and even without embarking upon formal negotiations or instructing lawyers to formalise the situation, may undertake activities in relation to land. For example, a family carrying on a farming business in relation to a partnership may have not formalised the ownership of the land on which the partnership carries on business so that the partnership may have some form of tenancy or may have a licence but notwithstanding the lack of definition in the rights[194] the partnership may construct new farm buildings. There are difficulties in implying any

---

[187] See, eg, *Errington v Errington and Woods* [1952] 1 KB 290.

[188] See, for example, *Brewer Street Investments Limited v Barclays Woollens* [1953] 2 All ER 1330.

[189] But note that it may be restricted to cases where there is a promise to perform a particular act rather than a promise to enter into a contract as in *Yeoman Row Management v Crabbe* [2008] 4 All ER 713 since it is very difficult to have a contract to enter into a contract where there are no obligatory standard forms; see, for example, *Scammell v Ouston* [1941] AC 251; *Sweet & Maxwell v Universal News Services* [1964] 3 All ER 30.

[190] There is also the question of whether, as there was not a valid contract because of the lack of writing, the acting upon the statement could be regarded as 'consideration'; see **3.50** and **5.98**.

[191] [1952] 1 KB 290.

[192] Law of Property (Miscellaneous Provisions) Act 1989, s 2; but note *Yaxley v Gotts* [1999] 2 WLR 1217.

[193] FA 2003, s 44(5)(a) and (6)(b).

[194] Which will probably not be referred to in the accounts of the partnership.

form of constructive trust or equitable interests that could constitute an oral but effective contract notwithstanding Law of Property (Miscellaneous Provisions) Act 1989, s 2,[195] but there may be questions as to whether the entry upon the land and the carrying out of works or other activities create some form of equitable principle whereby 'in consideration of the works' there is to be the acquisition of some form of interest in the land. The parties may have entered into some arrangement, possibly on advice, which could be 'subject to contract' in which case there will be no obligations and no consideration or there may be some informal arrangement that binds the parties whilst the lawyers prepare the paperwork.[196] In the circumstances it would seem that if the parties proceed to a formal contract or the grant of a lease the works will not, *prima facie*, be chargeable consideration since past consideration is no consideration.[197] This could be important since it would mean that the works would not be subject to the charge to stamp duty land tax since they would not be chargeable consideration. However, should the parties by their drafting, refer to the transaction taking place such as the lease being granted in consideration of the works having been carried out and HMRC Stamp Taxes seek to treat this as being chargeable consideration there would be difficulties in establishing that the works were excluded from the charge because they were carried out after the effective date.[198] There may have to be a complicated and expensive analysis of the situation in order to determine what, if any, rights are created and whether there is consideration in the form of the works or services being supplied or carried out.

Domestic Arrangements

3.43 Frequently arrangements within a family will be of an informal nature. This may include situations such as that referred to above in relation to *Errington v Errington & Woods*.[199] These arrangements may include the promise that should X move in and care for Y, the property of Y will pass to X upon death. This may constitute a contract to transfer the property on death in consideration of the services. Although services are not money's worth[200] they are now chargeable by reference to the open market cost.[201] There will be an initial difficulty in establishing the precise terms of the arrangement because they will be informal and no doubt disputes between the parties as to whether the property forms part of the estate or is subject to a contract outside the estate of the deceased individual. There may also be difficulties where parents and a child combine to acquire a property with the benefit of a mortgage and the whole or the bulk of the deposit being provided by the parents but upon the basis that the child will discharge the mortgage and will become the owner of the property. There will obviously be difficulties in regard to the lack of formality in recording the arrangement by the parties which may not have been made known to their advisers when acquiring the property so there will be issues as to whether the parents actually purchased an interest in the property or made a gift of the cash or entered into some form of loan arrangement[202] with the child. This could mean that there is a chargeable transaction by reference to the passing of an interest to the child when the property is acquired or when the child becomes entitled to the property when the mortgage is discharged or the property is sold in due course.

195   See, for example, *Yeoman Row Management v Crabbe* [2008] 4 All ER 713.
196   Compare *Winn v Bull* (1877) 7 Ch D 29; *Branca v Cobarro* [1947] 2 All ER 101; see also *Brewer Street Investments Limited v Barclays Woollens* [1953] 2 All ER 1330.
197   See, for example, *Eastwood v Kenyon* (1840) 11 A&E 438; *Re McArdle* [1951] 1 All ER 905.
198   FA 2003, Sch 4, para 10.
199   [1952] 1 KB 290.
200   *Secretan v Hart* 45 TC 701.
201   FA 2003, Sch 4, para 11.
202   On loans and deposits note FA 2003, Sch 17A, para 18A.

3.44 Even if the terms of the arrangement can be clarified to the satisfaction of HMRC Stamp Taxes there is the question as to whether there is a chargeable transaction since frequently the Courts may decide that because the arrangement is of a domestic nature the parties do not intend to enter into legal relations. They may be more willing to find some form of gift than some form of contract. This is a matter of inference and presumption. Obviously, where there are significant items of property and money involved or something approaching a commercial venture then the Court may be more willing to impute some intention to enter into legal relations which may, when coupled with other equitable principles, be sufficient to create a valid oral contract notwithstanding Law of Property (Miscellaneous Provisions) Act 1989, s 2.[203] In other situations there is a reluctance to hold domestic or family arrangements to be binding.[204]

Practical issues

3.45 There are obviously numerous difficulties in this area as to whether the Court will find some form of contract that is capable of forming the basis for a chargeable transaction or whether there will simply be some other form of equitable relief such as a cash payment possibly secured by a charge on the property until the property is sold. Should the situation be a contract as found by the Court or as agreed by the parties, this would 'confirm' the existence of a chargeable transaction.[205] Comprises of litigation are usually contractual[206] the question will be whether the agreement to transfer the property is for a chargeable consideration since foregoing the right to litigate is not necessarily money's worth[207] and there may be no action based upon a pre-existing contract which could supply consideration for the original transaction that was being performed by the compromise.

3.46 Should the circumstances be established and there is a chargeable transaction there will be the key question as to when the tax charge arises. In this type of case the interpretation of the general definition of the effective date[208] as the date of 'completion' will be crucial since it seems that the transaction will not be covered by any of the special rules because there is not a 'contract' contemplating completion by 'conveyance' unless HMRC Stamp Taxes successfully persuade the current judiciary to follow the suggestion of Walker LJ in *Yaxley v Gotts*[209] that equitable principles can override the need for writing pursuant to Law of Property (Miscellaneous Provisions) Act 1989, s 2 so that such arrangements, although oral, are valid and binding contracts.[210] The practical problem is that in many cases the issues will not be addressed until some time after the event which may entitle the person to the property has

---

[203] *Yaxley v Gotts* [1999] 2 WLR 1217 indicating that the equitable principles could override s 2 of the Act.

[204] See, for example, *Parker v Clark* [1961] All ER 93; *Beesley v Hallwood Estates* [1960] 2 All ER 314; on appeal [1961] 1 All ER 90; *Simpkins v Pays* [1955] 3 All ER 10; *Davis v Sweet* [1962] 2 QB 300; *Powell v Braun* [1954] 1 All ER 484.

[205] There may obviously be questions as to whether any compromise between the parties to resolve the uncertainties is itself some form of contract for the acquisition of a chargeable interest.

[206] *Fisher v Apollinaris* (1875) 10 Ch App 297; *Miles v New Zealand Alford Estate* (1886) 32 ChD 266; *Horton v Horton* [1961] 1 QB 215.

[207] FA 2003, Sch 4, paras 1 and 7.

[208] Ibid, s 119.

[209] [1999] 2 WLR 1217.

[210] The current judiciary may in consequence be forced to address the as yet unresolved highly technical and fundamental argument as to whether such equitable relief, arising from reliance upon the good faith of the 'promisor', is a right or a remedy, particularly where the relief is discretionary and whether there can be a valid oral contract rather than some potentially discretionary equitable remedy where the terms are less than certain as to the property interest in question; see, for example, *Yeoman Row Management v Crabbe* [2008] 4 All ER 713.

occurred and conveyances are required or there is litigation as to the rights of the various parties which will involve the Court having to decide between the conflicting testimony of the various parties and in the absence of a key witness such as the deceased individual who promised the transfer of the house. Where there is writing there is the question of whether this is a non-testamentary contract[211] to make a will in a particular form or whether it is a contract outside the will to leave the house in consideration of the performance of 'services' which are now a taxable consideration.[212] Where there is no writing there are issues as to whether the arrangement is rendered void pursuant to Law of Property (Miscellaneous Provisions) Act 1989, s 2 and the parties have to rely upon a constructive trust. If the will is made and the property devised as promised or if the promisor dies intestate but a constructive trust arises there would appear to be a charge to stamp duty land tax upon the carer who inherits outside the will, but possibly no charge to stamp duty land tax arises upon a straightforward devise.[213] By the time that the matter is resolved by the Court or compromised by the parties there may have been considerable delay and problems where the 'effective date' took place sometime earlier which might occur where, for example, a person goes into a house or a flat to act as a carer for the current owner and HMRC Stamp Taxes establish that this constitutes some form of 'joint possession' sufficient to constitute substantial performance of the informal contract between the parties. Substantial penalties and interest charges may have arisen because HMRC Stamp Taxes' view of the effective date was some time prior to the formal transfer of the property ie 'completion'.[214] This would apply should there be a contract since it will be the clear understanding ie a term of the arrangement that the property is to be conveyed into the name of the carer.

3.47 Similar issues arise where the court sanctions an arrangement such as a merger of insurance companies ie those situations where there is essentially an agreement between the parties and the Court supplies the consent of certain parties who, for example, may not be able to consent,[215] or whose consent is necessary to override or protect the interests of minorities or the public where there may be dissenters to the arrangement.[216] Here the statutory mechanism is designed to produce something that can operate as a contract or even a conveyance.[217] For many years for the purposes of stamp duty it was accepted that there was no 'sale' in these situations, since the transaction took effect by order of the court or by operation of law, which operation as specified in the statute was triggered by the sanction of the court. It would seem to be the intention of the legislation that such sanctioning exercises by the court are to be equated with the consensual order, ie giving approval on behalf of persons who are unable to consent, and so to be within the charge to stamp duty land tax. The court is in effect merely implementing an agreement between appropriate parties so that there may be sufficient consensual element for there to be consideration.

---

[211] Which, like undertakings relating to mutual wills, may create trust relationships.

[212] FA 2003, Sch 4, para 11.

[213] Attempts to treat this as a disposition within the estate of the deceased promisor and so not subject to tax are likely to be regarded by HMRC Stamp Taxes as 'fraud' ie presenting the transaction on a totally false basis of being a testamentary tax-free transaction rather than a taxable *inter vivos* agreement to the Land Registry.

[214] FA 2003, s 44.

[215] Such as Variation of Trusts Act 1958.

[216] Such as Companies Act 2006, s 895.

[217] Such as *Sun Alliance Insurance Ltd v IRC* [1971] 1 ALL ER 135; see also *Terrapin International v IRC* [1967] 2 All ER 461, 1 WLR 665.

By or under any statutory provision

3.48 This is clearly meant to bring in transactions where a private Act of Parliament is used to convey or vest property.[218] It would also seem to apply where transactions are carried out under statutory authority, although there are certain exemptions for land transactions entered into in connection with compulsory purchase of property.[219] Matters done under statutory authority would appear to apply to right to buy and similar transactions[220] and collective enfranchisement and other arrangements by leaseholders.[221] The fact that there are specific provisions dealing with the computation and relief of such transactions indicates that they are *prima facie* within the charge.

3.49 Other areas where persons are exercising statutory powers would include appropriations by personal representatives in or towards the satisfaction of legacies and devises[222] and statutory powers of advancement for trustees.[223] Again, statutory provisions dealing with such arrangements indicate clearly that they are potentially chargeable.

By operation of law

3.50 This is clearly meant to catch the transactions that take effect regardless of how the parties view the situation such as a deed of variation of a lease operating as a surrender and regrant by operation of law,[224] or a lease terminating by operation of law ie by the actions of the parties and without writing but it raises questions as to whether it is intended to apply to transactions that arise by reason of the operation of statutory provisions such as the protection of tenants holding over pursuant to the Landlord and Tenant Act 1954. In the first situation the property is actually transferred by the legislation and does not require any further act by the parties other than, perhaps, tidying up at the Land Registry. In other cases the exercise of a statutory power may enable the party to carry out the transaction but it does not actually execute the transfer of the title such as compulsory acquisitions by local authorities where the title passes pursuant to statutory powers but by reference to the general vesting declaration or similar arrangements. There are general issues such as the acquisition of interests by reason of those trusts which arise by operation of law, such as the types of constructive trust considered above.[225] The charge is, potentially, much wider, but unfortunately those devising the tax have failed to address the ambiguities in this concept. It may be either:

- a transaction where the law imposes rights and liabilities upon the parties regardless of their prior arrangements such as certain types of constructive trusts[226] where the property passes possibly contrary to the wishes of one or more of the parties. In many such cases the charge may not arise because there is no

---

[218] *Great Western Railways v IRC* [1894] 1 QB 507; *Ridge Nominees Ltd v IRC* [1962] CH 376.
[219] *IRC v Glasgow and Southwestern Railway* (1887) 12 App Cas 315; *Kirkness v John Hudson Ltd* [1955] AC 696; FA 2003, ss 60 and 61; see **11.31** and **11.34**.
[220] FA 2003, s 70; Sch 9 (as amended).
[221] Ibid, s 74.
[222] See **3.50** and **5.98**.
[223] Trustee Act 1925, s 32; FA 2003, Sch 16, para 7.
[224] *Friends Provident Life Office v British Railways Board* [1996] 1 All ER 336; *Gable Construction v IRC* [1968] 1 WLR 1426.
[225] See **3.4**.
[226] Such as *ER Ives (Investments) v High* [1967] 2 QB 379; *Binions v Evans* [1972] Ch 359.

chargeable consideration, but dealings with family companies and partnerships where deemed consideration arises[227] could be a problem; or

- the law imputes certain consequences to the parties' actions such as the parties entering into a deed of variation of a lease that operates as some form of surrender and regrant by operation of law.[228] It is also intended to deal with situations where a transaction is completed by operation of law without the need for documentation by the parties such as a surrender of a lease by a tenant to the landlord simply by handing over the documents and vacating the premises. This is effective to terminate the lease and writing is not necessary; or

- a transaction where as a precondition there is a contract or binding obligation entered into by the parties but the title passes between the parties without the need for any further action or documentation on their part. Frequently the title passing will be equitable and so action by the parties will be needed to pass the legal title, such as administrative mergers of foreign companies.

3.51 There is, therefore, an inherent ambiguity in the situation in that it is unclear whether this is intended to apply to situations where obligations arise because the law implies them in the circumstances or whether the transaction is 'effected' ie completed by the law without the intervention of the parties other than as a purely formal tidying up exercise. The title will pass without the parties taking any further real or significant action. The issue is one of considerable importance since various provisions in the legislation refer to events 'by operation of law' such as tenants holding over by operation of law.[229] Such holding over may be pursuant to statute such as the Landlord and Tenant Act 1954 or it may be in a situation outside the Landlord and Tenant Act 1954 where the tenant continues in occupation without statutory protection or entitlement but the law may create some new form of tenancy such as a common law tenancy from year to year upon the same terms of the existing lease but modified for a yearly tenancy if that should be the nature of the rental payments.[230]

It is believed that HMRC Stamp Taxes intend to take the widest possible interpretation of this concept so that potential taxpayers under attack may need to investigate other aspects of the charge such as the need for consideration.[231]

3.52 The last of bullet points would seem to be potentially within the charge to stamp duty land tax because there may be 'chargeable consideration'. In the latter cases a charge may not arise because in the absence of a contract there cannot be 'chargeable

---

[227]   FA 2003, ss 53 and 54; Sch 15, Part 3.
[228]   *Gable Construction v IRC* [1968] 1 WLR 1426; *Friends Provident v British Rail* [1996] 1 All ER 336.
[229]   FA 2003, Sch 17, para 3.
[230]   At present it seems that HMRC Stamp Taxes are not seeking to allege that holding over not pursuant to statutory provisions such as the Landlord and Tenant Act 1954 or possibly the agricultural holdings legislation constitutes some form of chargeable transaction for the purposes of stamp duty land tax. They have not sought to enquire into transactions in order to determine whether a yearly tenancy has arisen. This is probably because there is little tax benefit for them at present. Frequently the holding over will be in respect of stamp duty leases and holding over such leases is not within the charge to stamp duty land tax because there is no 'effective date' to which the holding over can relate back as required by FA 2003, Sch 17A, para 3. Moreover, even if HMRC Stamp Taxes could establish that there was some form of common law yearly tenancy the net present value of the rent is likely to be below the £150,000 nil rate slice and therefore would not be taxable and being a lease for less than 7 years would not be notifiable (FA 2003, Sch 17A, paras 3(5) and 4(4A); s 77A).
[231]   See **3.4**.

consideration' pursuant to FA 2003, Sch 3, para 1.[232] It would appear to apply to the implementation of agreements such as mergers of foreign companies and variations of leases. The latter would appear to apply to many cases of constructive trusts where because of the absence of writing there cannot be a binding agreement,[233] as in *Yaxley v Gotts*[234] and *Errington v Errington and Woods*[235] but interests in land pass in reliance upon unenforceable promises. There would seem to be a risk that because there is a promise, albeit oral and not as such enforceable, the recognition and enforcement of such arrangement by constructive trust is sufficiently 'consensual' to convert the actions requested into consideration of a chargeable nature.

3.53 Certain aspects of how the charge is intended to operate are clear. For example, it applies to those variations of leases such as enlarging the term which by law can only take effect as surrenders and regrants.[236] There was for many years in the area of stamp duty an argument that where transactions took effect by operation of law there was either no contract or agreement for lease or any interest moving and thus there was no consideration in the sense required to give rise to a charge. Certain consequences happened as a result of some other event but not a 'sale'. This occurred in relation to the merger of insurance companies which flowed from the court sanctioning or approving the scheme.

3.54 Other situations that are potentially within the area of 'operation of law' would be certain administrative mergers or demergers or *fusions* and *fissions* of companies incorporated abroad. These are situations where the local law of the state of incorporation provides that, subject to various conditions being satisfied upon entry upon the Register or some other administrative act by the local equivalent of the Companies Registry, the entire assets and liabilities of one of the companies would be absorbed into the other company.[237] Beneficial title having passed by operation of the foreign law as a form of universal succession the need for a transfer of the bare legal title in the United Kingdom did not operate to convey anything upon sale. Such transactions may now be taxable.

---

[232] See **3.31**.
[233] Law of Property (Miscellaneous Provisions) Act 1989, s 2.
[234] [1999] 2 WLR 1217.
[235] [1952] 1 KB 290.
[236] See, for example, *Gable Construction v IRC* [1968] 1 WLR 1426; specific charges apply to variations of rent in such circumstances, FA 2003, Sch 17A, para 13; *Friends Provident v British Rail* [1996] 1 All ER 336.
[237] Compare the powers of the Courts in the United Kingdom to vest asset such as Companies Act 2006, ss 895 and following; see also *Sun Alliance Insurance Ltd v IRC* [1971] 1 ALL ER 135.

Chapter 4

CHARGEABLE INTERESTS

BASIC DEFINITION

4.1   The charge[1] requires an 'acquisition'[2] of a 'chargeable interest' which includes other property as part of the subject-matter of the transaction, and which is defined[3] as being either:[4]

- an estate;

- an interest;

- a right;

- a power;

- in or over land;

or

- the benefit of:
  - – an obligation;
  - – a restriction, which may include goodwill;
  - – right; or
  - – power,

which is

- in land;[5] or

- over land;

in the United Kingdom and which is not an exempt interest.[6]

---

[1]   See **Chapter 3**.
[2]   FA 2003, s 43(1).
[3]   Ibid, s 48(1).
[4]   The definition uses the word 'means' which indicates that it is exhaustive.
[5]   See **4.8** on 'land' and, *inter alia*, crops, fixtures and goodwill.
[6]   HMRC Stamp Taxes is given power to extend the list of exempt interests by regulation, FA 2003, s 48(5) but this power has not hitherto been exercised; the extensions for alternative finance have been dealt with by mainstream legislation.

Statutory extensions

4.2   A chargeable interest has been extended so that now, in effect, it includes a power to direct a sale whether or not linked to a licence to enter upon the land.[7] It also includes certain deemed interests, ie situations where a person is deemed to acquire a chargeable interest such as where there are certain variations of a lease.[8]

Exempt interests[9]

4.3   Chargeable interests do not include 'exempt interests',[10] which are:

- any security interest. This is defined as being any interest or right, other than a rent charge,[11] held for the purpose of securing the payment of money or performance of any other obligation[12] such as mortgages.[13] In Scotland the reference to 'rent charge' is a reference to a feu duty or a payment mentioned in Abolition of Feudal Tenure etc (Scotland) Act 2000 (ASP 5), s 56(1);

- a licence to use or occupy land.[14] This will give rise to difficult technical issues when deciding whether there is a notifiable transaction or if the transaction is to be self-certified or not returned as a non-taxable transaction because it is considered to be a licence – if this decision ultimately proves after a challenge by HMRC Stamp Taxes[15] to be incorrect, interest and penalties will arise.[16] There are many problems to be investigated such as:

---

[7]   FA 2003, ss 44A and 45A; see **3.24**.

[8]   Ibid, Sch 17A, paras 15A(1A) and 14(2); see **7.218**.

[9]   Defined FA 2003, s 48(2), see **3.30**.

[10]   In addition to the issue of those interests in or rights over land that are exempt, ie not chargeable interests, it is provided that certain transactions that are 'exempt' or relieved from tax may not be chargeable transactions, but may require notification. There is a key issue in relation to the nature of reliefs from stamp duty land tax. This may provide that the interest in land in question is an exempt interest in which case there will be no chargeable transaction (FA 2003, s 48). The exemption or relief may provide that the actual consideration is to be ignored and the chargeable consideration is to be treated as nil or exempt when there will be a transfer for no chargeable consideration which is exempt from stamp duty land tax pursuant to FA 2003, Sch 3, para 1 so that the transaction is not taxable and not notifiable (FA 2003, s 77A) in situations where the transaction is, in a sense, chargeable, but is 'relieved' in that the tax charge is reduced to nil but there remains chargeable consideration subject to a nil rate of tax. In the last case it is clear that the transaction, although not being for a chargeable consideration, it is chargeable and notifiable notwithstanding it falls into a zero tax liability band. There is a distinction between a dealing in an exempt interest, a dealing in a chargeable interest that is 'exempt' for certain reasons (largely because it falls within FA 2003, Sch 3) and a chargeable transaction that does not attract stamp duty land tax because there is a relieving provision and the notification provisions refer to notifiable transactions that would have attracted tax but for some exemption or relief (FA 2003, s 77A(1)). The restricted nature of this issue must be noted, since not being liable to stamp duty land tax is based upon several different bases not all of which qualify as an 'exemption' within the peculiar terminology of stamp duty land tax. Eg a land transaction remains a chargeable transaction for the purposes of deciding whether it is notifiable within FA 2003, s 77, notwithstanding that some provisions reduce the chargeable consideration to nil; but these are now probably removed indirectly from the obligation to notify because the chargeable consideration being nil brings the transaction below the £40,000 notification threshold; FA 2003, s 77A; but see **Chapter 18**.

[11]   On rent charges see **4.55**.

[12]   FA 2003, s 48.

[13]   Ibid, s 48(3)(a). It is unclear whether substance or form will be applied; such as where a restrictive covenant or similar arrangement is entered into for the sole purpose of securing an overage payment whether it will be treated as a covenant and taxable or as merely a security arrangement.

[14]   Which does not confer an interest in land *Thames Conservators v IRC* (1886) 18 QBD 279.

[15]   It is difficult to predict the nature of the likely challenge. A no return will have been filed an Enquiry is unlikely; the possibility is an assessment or determination issued by HMRC Stamp Taxes pursuant to FA

    −   whether there is a lease or a licence;[17]

    −   whether there is a licence or some other interests such as a *profit a prendre* such as mineral rights;[18] and

    −   what restrictions upon the exemption are implied by the requirement that it must be a licence 'to use or occupy land'.

It must, however, be noted that, although licences to use or occupy are not chargeable interests either as regards grant or dealing, entry into possession of land as a licensee may operate as 'substantial performance' of a contract and so give rise to a charge to tax;[19]

- in England and Wales or Northern Ireland:
  - a tenancy at will;[20]
  - an advowson;
  - a franchise (namely grant from the Crown such as the right to hold a market or fair or the right to take tolls; not a right to carry on business under a licensing arrangement); or
  - a manor.[21]

- an interest held by a financial company in connection with an exempt alternative financing arrangement;[22]

- certain fundraising instruments issued under the alternative finance regime where these are not loans but are interests in the underlying assets that are there to generate the income to service the investment bond.[23]

'SUBJECT-MATTER OF THE TRANSACTION'

4.4   Although the charge is by reference to the acquisition of a chargeable interest the charge is in terms of the 'subject-matter of the transaction' which is referred to on several occasions.[24] This is defined as:[25]

- the chargeable interest acquired[26] together with

- any interest or right which is

2003, Sch 10, paras 25 and 28, is theoretically a possibility but it remains to be seen how HMRC Stamp Taxes, as at present organised, will discover information or become aware of the transaction in order to have the basis for a justifiable claim.

16   On lease or licence, see **Chapter 7**.

17   *Addiscombe Garden Estates Ltd v Crabbe* [1957] 3 All ER 563; the drafting is an issue but note *Ogwr v Dykes* [1989] 2 All ER 880.

18   See, for example, *T&E Homes Limited v Robinson* [1979] STC 4351; *Lowe v JW Ashmore* [1970] 46 TC 597.

19   FA 2003, s 44(5)(b); see **14.16**.

20   But these are treated as a tenancy for a year which grows over time (FA 2003, Sch 17A, paras 3 and 4); but no obvious consequences arise from this treatment at present.

21   FA 2003, s 48(2)–(4).

22   Ibid, s 73C.

23   FA 2009, Sch 61.

24   See, eg, FA 2003, ss 48(5), 55(3)(a) and Sch 4, para 1.

25   Ibid, s 43(6).

26   This is given the label of the 'main subject-matter' of the transaction but no or little use of the term is made subsequently in the legislation.

- appurtenant or pertaining to the chargeable interest acquired

- that is acquired with it.

This is particularly important in relation to determining the rate of stamp duty land tax. The rate is fixed by reference to the nature of the 'relevant land', ie the main subject-matter of the transaction, and not by reference to anything which pertains or is appurtenant thereto.[27]

'Appurtenant'

4.5   This is an old-fashioned conveyancing term used to describe land or rights and profits attached to or arising out of land[28] which is annexed to other land.

Contracts and agreements for lease or acquisition

4.6   Contracts raise two fundamental issues for stamp duty land tax; namely:

- the temporal relationship between entry into the contract and the occurrence of the tax charge; and

- whether a contact relating to land is a chargeable interest in its own right.[29]

Merely entering into a contract to 'acquire' or to lease a chargeable interest is not itself a chargeable transaction,[30] and there are various provisions to the effect that contracts for the assignments of the benefit of contracts are not chargeable transactions.[31] However, it is specifically provided that options and pre-emption rights are chargeable upon 'grant' not exercised[32] but the exercise is a separate land transaction[33] so that the subsequent exercise of the option 'may' be a linked transaction requiring retrospective adjustment of the initial self-assessment.[34] This together with the definition of chargeable interests as including contracts affecting the value of land[35] means that the contracts themselves are chargeable interests.[36] It is clear that the variation of an option such as an extension of the exercise period is a chargeable transaction. It also seems clear that the variation of a contract to purchase or lease land or to move a right of way or alter rights to light is a chargeable transaction.[37] It remains to be seen whether

---

[27]   FA 2003, s 55.
[28]   It has been held to bring in money held in trust to be used to purchase land: *Re Gosselin* [1906] 1 Ch 120.
[29]   See **4.39**.
[30]   FA 2003, s 44(2).
[31]   See, eg, FA 2003, ss 45 (as amended), 45A and Sch 17A, para 12B.
[32]   But note the judicial confusion in *George Wimpey Ltd v IRC* [1975] 2 All ER 45 between contracts to grant and actual grant of options.
[33]   FA 2003, s 46.
[34]   See **5.37**.
[35]   FA 2003, s 48(1)(b) and Sch 17A, para 10(1)(c).
[36]   See **4.39**.
[37]   There is also the important question of whether the variation of a pre-1 December 2003 contract cancels the transitional reliefs in the FA 2003, Sch 19 (as much amended retrospectively). Contracts entered into before July 2003 may remain subject to stamp duty rather than stamp duty land tax at completion after the 1 December 2003. This is dependent upon the contract not having been varied. It may be more efficient to complete the contract and pay the stamp duty and then vary the completion arrangements which may attract little or no liability to stamp duty land tax. This is important since continuing with the stamp duty regime is usually more tax efficient and subject to less onerous compliance and reporting obligations. In addition, certain of the transitional arrangements such as those concerned with the removal or relief for

HMRC Stamp Taxes will pursue this area of liability vigorously in practice. The consequences of such a variation are wide-ranging such as the need to file a return, which depends upon the question of whether a contract to acquire a major interest is itself a major interest.[38]

'LAND'

Definitions

4.7   The fundamental limitation of the stamp duty land tax is that it applies only to chargeable interests in 'land' in the United Kingdom.[39] This is defined by FA 2003, s 121 as including building and structures and land covered by water. This is not a particularly extensive definition and problems have already arisen in relation to goodwill[40] and equipment that has been attached to the land which may have become a fixture and part of the land[41] and certain contractual arrangements.[42]

4.8   This is similar to, but probably supplants, a general definition of 'land' is contained in Interpretation Act 1978, Sch 1, which states that it 'includes' 'buildings and other structures, land covered with water, and any estate, interest, easement, servitude or right in or over land'. This definition and FA 2003, s 121 are not helpful statutory definitions since each of them is itself merely an extension of some other undisclosed general definitions. Where there is an extension to the definition (ie the word is defined as 'including' something which assumes that the basic meaning of the word has been established elsewhere in the legislation), this helps to indicate the basic scope of the word as being its basic general law meaning, which appears to include everything on or under the soil, all buildings erected thereon and mines sunk beneath it.[43] It seems that land does not include annual growing crops.[44] It may include a share in the proceeds of the sale of land.[45] It means that there is some general meaning outside the legislation which is extended by the statutory provision. The Interpretation Act 1978 is not, therefore, exhaustive nor indeed providing the basic guidance since it appears to extend beyond the definition in FA 2003. There is, therefore, a need to look beyond the statutory provision. The issue is, therefore, dealing with basic law in several areas, namely land itself, fixtures, interests in land, rights over land. Two areas are in practice giving rise to difficulties, namely fixtures[46] and goodwill.[47] However, most of the

---

transactions involving disadvantaged land remain available for completions in respect of contracts entered into before March 2005 (FA 2003, s 96) this depends upon the contract not having been varied. In addition, there is a form of transitional relief in that many tax computations such as those concerned with lease rents are of a provisional nature and are retrospectively reviewed in the light of subsequent events. In consequence, where the original lease was eligible for relief such as the grant of a charity or to a partnership where there is a substantial reduction for the sum of the lower proportions or the land in question was disadvantaged land at the time that the lease was granted the relief may continue to be available in respect of the retrospective adjustment in the light of rent reviews etc.

[38]   FA 2003, s 117.

[39]   Ibid, s 48(1)(a); see also Sch 4, para 4(1)(b) and (c) which provide for the apportionment of the consideration between the land transaction and other matters; and it is only the chargeable consideration attributable to the land transaction which is subject to stamp duty land tax.

[40]   See **1.5**.

[41]   See **4.10**.

[42]   FA 2003, s 48(1)(b); Sch 17A, para 10(1).

[43]   *Newcomen v Coulson* (1877) 5 Ch D 133 at 142–143.

[44]   *Evans v Roberts* (1826) 5 B & C 829; *Brantom v Griffits* (1876) 1 CPD 349; for natural crops, see *Carrington v Roots* (1837) 2 M & W 242; *Teal v Auty* (1820) 2 Brod & B 99.

[45]   See, eg, *Re Glassington* [1906] 2 Ch 305; cf *Re Newman* [1930] 2 Ch 409.

[46]   See **4.10**.

legislation relating to stamp duty land tax will not make sense if easements and other interests referred to in the Interpretation Act 1978 are not treated as land or interests in land. The inclusion of these items is vital to the success of HMRC Stamp Taxes' attempt to attack value shifting as was the extension of chargeable interests[48] to include contracts and obligations affecting the value of estates or interests in or rights over land.[49]

4.9   Other statutes contain definitions of 'land',[50] but these apply only for the purposes of those Acts and have at most a limited value in relation to the meaning of 'land' for the purposes of stamp duty land tax. They may provide illustrations in support of an argument but they cannot be conclusive on the issue. The different definitions of land for different purposes[51] does mean that something may be land for conveyancing purposes but not for stamp duty land tax or vice versa. Thus an item may be land for certain purposes but a chattel for other purposes; it is purely a question of what legislation is involved for the purposes of the particular transaction.[52] It may also depend upon the judicial view of the policy of the legislation, as in the case in relation to options over land and the question whether they are some form of contract or merely an irrevocable offer.[53] This can be a significant factor when organising transactions in a manner which is effective to produce a reasonable stamp duty land tax outcome.

Fixtures

General

4.10   Consideration properly allocated to equipment related to the land that is a fixture, ie part of the land, is subject to stamp duty land tax[54] but is not chargeable consideration if the equipment has retained its character as a chattel.[55] The consideration for the transaction has to be apportioned between the land and the chattels on a just and reasonable basis.[56] In addition, although the chattels may be acquired at the same time as the land along with other property, the rate of stamp duty land tax is related only to the land price.[57] The importance of the distinction is:

- those items which have retained their character as chattels and movable property are not subject to stamp duty land tax and that part of the price which is allocated to them on a just and reasonable basis[58] can be ignored for the purposes of

---

[47]   See **1.5** and **4.11**.

[48]   FA 2003, s 48(1)(b).

[49]   In addition, attempts to manipulate the stamp duty land tax charge by means of various transactions involving interests that are not chargeable interests such as granting licences etc. will no doubt be scrutinised by HMRC Stamp Taxes in order to determine whether they form part of the 'scheme transactions' for the purposes of the general anti-avoidance provisions contained in FA 2003, ss 75A–75C (see **2.19**).

[50]   Eg Law of Property Act 1925, s 205(1)(ix), which differs from the definition in Law of Property (Miscellaneous Provisions) Act 1989, s 2(6).

[51]   See the discussion in *Lavery v Pursell* (1889) 39 Ch D 508.

[52]   *Lavery v Pursell* (above).

[53]   See the discussions in *Spiro v Glencrown Properties Ltd* [1991] 2 WLR 931; see **3.26**.

[54]   It may be necessary to file an SDLT 4 where there is the sale of a business.

[55]   FA 2003, Sch 4, para 1 limiting the chargeable consideration to the subject-matter of the transaction (defined in s 43(6)). In consequence, consideration allocated to other items of property cannot be 'chargeable' and is ignored for the purposes of the lower rates of tax; see also the limited exclusion for computing the tax pursuant to the general anti-avoidance provisions (FA 2003, s 75(3)(b)).

[56]   FA 2003, Sch 4, para 4.

[57]   And this consideration for the other property may not be involved in the scheme but may be an incidental transaction for the purposes of the general anti-avoidance charges pursuant to FA 2003, ss 75A–75C.

[58]   FA 2003, Sch 4, para 4; but note *Saunders v Edwards* [1987] 2 All ER 651; *Re Wragge* [1897] 1 Ch 796.

computing the rate and the application of the linked transaction rules.[59] This means that the amount of the consideration allocated to goods but not fixtures can be deducted from the total price when calculating the stamp duty land tax and, in particular, in considering the availability of the lower rates of stamp duty land tax;

- as regards true fixtures, as these are part of the land they pass as part of the land and the consideration attributable to them attracts stamp duty land tax;[60] and

- as regards sales of land whether freehold or leasehold, whether equipment that is attached to the land but is held under a lease or similar arrangement from a third party is in the case of the seller a chargeable interest or an item of property not subject to stamp duty land tax; but there may be a separate issue where the lessor of the equipment sells his interest therein.[61]

This will, in practice, prove a vital issue for persons purchasing newly constructed or refurbished commercial buildings where the equipment is likely to constitute a high proportion of the value of the transaction.[62] The same issues arise for acquisitions of dwellings for a consideration near a rate increase threshold and the purchaser wishes to allocate part of the price to items such as carpets, kitchen units and other fitted furniture.[63] Purchasers should consider whether the potential tax saving is worth the risk of the potential costs and hardship of an Enquiry,[64] since it seems that the sale of land and 'chattels' at around the thresholds for the rate bands were intended to be a high priority area for Enquiries, and allegations of negligent or fraudulent returns[65] may be made where the allocation between land and chattels is not made on what HMRC Stamp Taxes are likely to regard as the proper statutory just and reasonable basis,[66] when not supported by an independent valuation. This will be a particular issue where the price is arbitrarily reduced below the threshold without appropriate advice as to the value of the chattels. Where clients decline to obtain that advice, solicitors may need to consider whether it is prudent for them to continue to act.[67]

Test for 'fixtures'

4.11 There is no specific provision in the stamp duty land tax legislation dealing with 'fixtures' which is, in consequence, an important issue left to the general law both as regards the applicability of the charge and the determination of what is land and what remains a chattel. Fixtures have been described as anything so attached to the land as to

---

59 See **5.37**.
60 Unless sold separately from the land and are to be detached as part of the sale terms.
61 Compare *Drages v IRC* 46 TC 389.
62 There are, however, currently unresolved issues, possibly more of a presentational rather than a substantive nature, where the vendor is retaining the benefit of the capital allowances and the elections or other arrangements are on the basis that the purchaser's expenditure for capital allowance purposes is negligible. It remains to be seen whether HMRC Stamp Taxes will equate such elections with a just and reasonable allocation of the purchase price for stamp duty land tax purposes. This may make the drafting of the contract a delicate issue.
63 *Leigh v Taylor* [1902] AC 157; *D'Elyncourt v Gregory* (1866) LR 3 Eq 382.
64 Vendors and other professionals may also be unwilling to risk exposure to allegations of conspiracy to defraud HMRC by agreeing to such an allocation of the consideration.
65 *Saunders v Edwards* [1987] 2 All ER 651.
66 FA 2003, Sch 4, para 4.
67 Ibid, stating that such activity is professional misconduct and perhaps makes them liable as parties to a conspiracy to defraud HMRC, including the vendor and the vendor's advisers; see also FA 2003, ss 95 and 96.

become legally part of the land[68] and, as shown in *Stokes v Costain Property Investments*,[69] pass with the land or in the case of a lease, subject to issues such as 'tenant's fixtures'[70] belong to the landlord as the person entitled to the freehold reversion. As a matter of general law, the question of fixture or chattel depends upon the application of the two tests namely:

- the purpose of annexation; and

- the degree of annexation.

It seems to be the current position that the purpose of annexation is the primary or initial test.[71] If the purpose of the annexation is simply to enable the chattel to be utilised or enjoyed, such as attaching tapestries to a wall[72] or securing equipment to the land for the purposes of industrial safety,[73] it will, *prima facie*, retain its character as a chattel.[74] It is after the stage where it has been determined that the chattel has been attached to the land for the purpose of enjoying the asset rather than with the intention of making it part of the land that the degree of annexation becomes important. Whilst the equipment may retain its character as a chattel under the purpose of annexation test, it may lose this status if it is so attached to the land that it cannot be removed without substantial damage to the premises.[75] Affixation and the degree of damage to the premises are merely aspects of the tests and an item can retain its character as a chattel notwithstanding affixation.

4.12   *HMRC Stamp Taxes Manual 2000* originally attached great significance to the question of whether the equipment is in a state of severance on the day of the execution of the stampable instrument, which may be equated with the effective date of the transaction for the purposes of stamp duty land tax[76] with the return of allotments, also refers to the question of the state of severance upon the relevant date rather than the strict legal analysis. To a significant extent the position was modified and replaced by the *Stamp Taxes Bulletin*;[77] but it is by no means obvious that even these more reasonable views are consistent with the case law. Fortunately whilst the errors of emphasis are in favour of the equipment being a fixture, the general case law is in favour of the taxpayer.[78] It seems that in relation to stamp duty land tax the same approach is

---

[68]   *Hulme v Brigham* [1943] KB 152; *Reynolds v Ashby & Son* [1904] AC 466.

[69]   [1984] STC 204.

[70]   See **4.16**.

[71]   *Holland v Hodgson* (1872) LR 7 CP 328; *Smith v City Petroleum Co Ltd* [1940] 1 All ER 260; *Lombard and Ulster Banking Ltd v Kennedy* [1974] NI 20; *H E Dibble Ltd v Moore* [1970] 2 QB 181.

[72]   *Leigh v Taylor* [1902] AC 157.

[73]   *Tate & Lyle Food Distribution Ltd v Greater London Council* [1983] 2 AC 509.

[74]   *Chelsea Yacht and Boat Club v Pope* [2001] 2 All ER 409.

[75]   *Lancaster v Eve* (1859) 5 CBNS 717. In these cases the terms of any lease may be important since the tenant may be responsible for the repair and maintenance of the asset and may be required to remove certain equipment from the land at the end of the lease. The fact that the tenant has these obligations is an indication that there is no intention to make it part of the land and the fact that the equipment can be repaired or removed, at least in part, is an indication that there is a substantial chattel element in the arrangement. The issue is, however, not helped by the fact that definitions in relation to land and in relation to sale of goods are not entirely consistent and there are suggestions, such as in *Lavery v Pursell* (1889) 19 CH D 508, to the effect that whether an item is land or goods may depend upon the purpose for which the question is being raised.

[76]   See **Chapter 14**.

[77]   Issue 1, August 1995.

[78]   *HMRC Stamp Taxes Manual 2002* sets out the modified view of what are 'fixtures' reflecting the change in practice in *Stamp Taxes Bulletin* Issue 1, August 2002. It is assumed that in practice a similar stance will be taken by HMRC Stamp Taxes in relation to stamp duty land tax.

being applied in practice and the fact that the equipment is attached to the land is no longer a conclusive factor that it is a fixture; although if the removal of the equipment would involve substantial damage to the premises this will point to its being a fixture.

Purpose of affixation

4.13 This whole area of land law was fundamentally reviewed and more items were made chattels by the Court of Appeal in *TSB v Botham*,[79] with greater emphasis being placed upon the purpose rather than the degree of annexation. In *TSB v Botham*[80] the older cases, where emphasis was placed upon annexation itself rather than the reasons for the annexation, were treated somewhat critically as being concerned primarily with the competing rights of mortgagees and lessors rather than the basic issue of ownership of the equipment, ie issues different from those relevant for the purposes of stamp duty land tax.

4.14 It is also part of the test for the legal nature of the asset that the purpose of affixation has to be investigated. If the asset is attached to the land not with the intention of making it part of the land but for its better utilisation as a chattel, it will retain its character as a chattel, at least if it can be removed without substantial change to the premises. Thus tapestries attached to a wall have been treated as chattels because this was necessary for their use as decorations.[81] Similarly, attaching equipment to the land for reasons of industrial safety, even where this may require significant attachment including bolting and embedding in concrete will not necessarily affect its character as a chattel. However, where the removal of the chattel would cause substantial damage to the land, ie the building to which it is attached, the fact that it is attached to the land simply for its better enjoyment as a chattel will not prevent the chattel from becoming a fixture.[82]

Degree of Affixation

4.15 HMRC Stamp Taxes began with the presumption, irrebuttable as far as their practice was concerned, that if a chattel is attached to land it is a fixture[83] and it appeared to have been of little relevance that the equipment is attached to the land for the purposes of industrial safety or necessity[84] or convenient use or enjoyment of the asset. On this basis a tapestry or painting would be a fixture if attached to a frame that is screwed to the wall, although the cases are quite clear that such an arrangement does not involve the asset in losing its character as a chattel.[85] In general law attachment to the land was not conclusive on the point, as in *Tate & Lyle Food and Distribution Ltd v GLC*,[86] where a jetty built under a licence remained a chattel.[87] A free-standing structure

---

[79]   [1996] ECGS 149.
[80]   Ibid.
[81]   *Leigh v Taylor* [1902] AC 157.
[82]   *Wake v Hall* (1883) 8 App Cas 195.
[83]   See, eg, Stamps Form 22 which requires an actual state of severance at the date of the sale.
[84]   *Holland v Hodgson* (1872) LR 7 CP 328 – spinning loom bolted to the factory floor; *Smith v City Petroleum* [1940] 1 All ER 260 – petrol pumps on forecourt; *Lombard and Ulster Banking Ltd v Kennedy* [1974] NI 20 – automatic car wash equipment bolted to the floor.
[85]   *Hulme v Brigham* (above).
[86]   [1983] 2 AC 509; see also *Thames Conservators v IRC* (1886) 18 QBD 279 – a licence to occupy land does not involve a transfer of property.
[87]   See also *Hulme v Brigham* [1943] KB 152.

is not necessarily a fixture[88] and this may also be the position where the structure is inserted into holes or sockets built into the ground.[89] But where the free-standing chattel is somehow an integral part of the building it may nevertheless become a fixture.[90] Insofar as this treatment suggests that simply because the equipment is attached to the land it is a fixture, it is considered to be wrong in law. It appears that the chattel may not become a fixture if it is capable of being removed without significant damage to the land[91] or where there is an agreement between the landowner and the owner of the chattel that it can be removed.[92] It may be that attachment to the land is necessary so that the chattel can be used because of industrial safety which indicates that it is still a chattel.

Tenant's fixtures[93]

4.16   The question of whether an item is a chattel or a fixture applies to both the sale of freehold land and of leases; but there is a further issue in relation to the sale of leases because of the status of certain tenant's fixtures – ie those items of equipment which are attached to the land but which the tenant is entitled to remove during and at the termination of the tenancy or may by the terms of the lease be required to remove.

4.17   In relation to leases, certain equipment attached to the land by the tenant may become a fixture and belong to the landlord, but the right of the landlord is subject to the right and power of the tenant to detach the equipment at any time and to take it away at the termination of the lease. Indeed, there may be obligations in the lease requiring the tenant to install the equipment or permitting him to do so but requiring him during the term of the lease to keep it in repair and to replace parts as necessary with a clear obligation to remove the equipment at the expiration of the lease. The covenants or obligations are potentially indications that the equipment is not intended to form part of the land and *prima facie* evidence that it has retained it s character as a chattel.[94] Such items are generally described as 'tenant's fixtures'. The rights of the tenant have been described as neither land nor goods but an intangible right to sever the equipment and remove the goods.[95] This raises the question of what is the treatment in practice of arrangements relating to such severable 'tenant's fixtures' under the current regime. There is also a question whether the contract for the sale of equipment attached to the land is a contract for the sale of goods or of an interest in land.[96] This may depend upon whether the equipment is sold together with the land or is sold under a contract pursuant to which it is to be detached from the land and removed by the purchaser who does not acquire any interest in the land.[97]

---

[88]   *HE Dibble Ltd v Moore* [1970] 2 QB 181 – a free-standing greenhouse remained a chattel; see also *Mather v Fraser* (1886) 2 K & J 523; *Webb v Frank Bevis Ltd* [1940] 1 All ER 247.

[89]   *Culling v Tufnol* (1694) Bull NP 34.

[90]   *D'Elyncourt v Gregory* (1866) LR 3 Eq 382.

[91]   *Lancaster v Eve* (1859) 5 CBNS 717 at 726.

[92]   Ibid at 727; *Simmons v Midford* [1969] 2 All ER 1269 at 1271.

[93]   This point does not arise in relation to freehold interests since the owner of that interest is entitled to remove the equipment at any time so that it forms part of the land and there cannot be a 'right to sever' as against a person entitled to a superior interest.

[94]   Further support for the equipment being a chattel would be the issue of rent and whether the benefit of the equipment is part of the rent or is to be excluded from any rent reviews because the equipment was purchased or leased by the tenant at his own expense.

[95]   *Lee v Gaskell* (1876) 1 QBD 700.

[96]   See, for example, Sale of Goods Act 1979, s 61; and see *Lavery v Pursell* (1889) 19 CH D 508.

[97]   See, eg, *Underwood v Burgh Castle Brick and Cement Syndicate* [1922] 1 KB 343.

4.18 Under certain circumstances where the land is leased and equipment has become attached to the land for use in connection with the lease in circumstances where it has ceased to be a chattel, a tenant is entitled, or possibly required by the terms of the lease, to remove the chattels which he or his predecessor as tenant has attached to the land notwithstanding that they have in consequence of the affixation technically become 'fixtures'.[98] The principle is that the chattel would lose its identity as a chattel and vest in the landlord but his title is defeasible in that the tenant is entitled in law to remove the equipment at any time.[99] This is a difficult point for analysis since the tenant may in the course of his carrying on a business on the land attach equipment which over the lifetime of the lease may wear out or be damaged and require replacement from time to time, and it may be an obligation under the terms of the lease that the tenant removes all such equipment and structures at the end of the lease and/or maintains it in reasonable repair, in the meantime replacing worn or damaged parts from time to time as necessary, which is a clear indication that so far as the parties are concerned the title to the equipment is not intended to pass to the landlord. In these circumstances, where the tenant has a right to remove or where the lease itself expressly provides that the tenant will remove all such equipment at the termination of the lease, the degree of annexation and the amount of damage to the premises in removing or replacing the equipment may be less of a factor in determining the status of the equipment on land as chattels. This general power to remove does not apply to all chattels installed by tenants, but only those which can be regarded as trade,[100] ornamental and domestic,[101] and agricultural.[102]

4.19 For many years HMRC Stamp Taxes has sought to impose a charge to stamp duty based upon the analysis contained in several cases[103] on the Statute of Frauds 1640 which held that:

(1)   the item, by reason of affixation of the land becomes a fixture,[104] and part of the land and so loses its character as a chattel;[105]

(2)   whilst attached to the land it is land;[106] but

(3)   it does not become land permanently because the tenant can remove it.[107]

---

[98]   The right may be lost under the terms of the lease: see, eg, *Re British Red Ash Collieries Ltd* [1920] 1 Ch 326.

[99]   *Crossley Bros v Lee* [1908] 1 KB 86.

[100]   See, eg, *Climie v Wood* (1869) LR 4 Exch 328; *New Zealand Government Property Corporation v HM & S Ltd* [1982] QB 1145; *Penton v Robart* (1801) 2 East 88; *Wardell v Usher* (1841) 3 Scott NR 508; *Elliott v Bishop* (1854) 10 Exch 496; *Smith v City Petroleum Co Ltd* [1940] 1 All ER 260.

[101]   *Spyer v Phillipson* [1931] 2 Ch 183.

[102]   Agricultural Holdings Act 1986, s 10; on settlements see, eg, *Lawton v Lawton* (1743) 3 A & K 13; *Re Hulse* [1905] 1 Ch 406; *Registrar of Titles v Spencer* (1909) 9 CLR 641; *Re De Falbe* [1901] 1 Ch 523; *Re Whaley* [1908] 1 Ch 615; *Norton v Dashwood* [1896] 2 Ch 497.

[103]   *Hallen v Runder* (1834) 1 Cr M & R 266; *Lee v Gaskell* (1876) 1 QBD 700.

[104]   Ie it is a pre-condition to this issue arising that the asset has lost its character as a chattel; contrary to the HMRC Stamp Taxes' contention, the point does not arise simply because the equipment is attached to the land on the date upon which the written agreement to sell the leasehold interest is executed or exchanged.

[105]   *Crossley Bros v Lee* [1908] 1 KB 86.

[106]   *Lee v Risdan* (1816) 7 Taunt 188.

[107]   It seems that the right to sever may continue beyond the expiration or termination of the lease where the tenant remains in occupation in the capacity of tenant: *New Zealand Government Property Corporation v HM & S* [1982] 1 All ER 624.

In consequence, when selling the lease together with the equipment a tenant is selling neither land nor goods,[108] but his right to sever and remove, and it seems that this may not be an interest in land[109] although it is a form of 'property'. However, as the asset is apparently not 'land', the consideration attributable to the tenant's fixture may fall outside the charge to stamp duty land tax, but this issue may ultimately turn upon whether the interest of the tenant is a right in or over land or the benefit of a right or power in or over land within the definition of chargeable interests.[110] The point is debatable and would appear to be in favour of the taxpayer since it is a right in relation to the equipment which, although attached to and temporarily forming part of the land, is to be detached and removed, which points to the interest being in the equipment, ie a chattel interest rather than a right in or over land.[111]

Sale of land or goods

4.20 It frequently happens that a person with an estate in land will contract to sell equipment on or attached to the land on terms which require its removal, or severing them.[112] This is not to be within FA 2003, s 75A. This can arise where a landowner arranges for the demolition of a structure and the removal of the materials from the land, or the sale by a farmer of a crop. The point can also arise in relation to the sale of freehold land since not everything attached to the land will be 'land'. The question to be considered in such cases is whether this is a sale of an interest in land or goods. The cases on the point are confusing because both the definition of 'land' in the Law of Property Act 1925[113] and the definition of 'goods' in the Sale of Goods Act 1979[114] overlap, and include certain fixtures which are to be removed under the contract of sale. In consequence, it seems that a contract for the demolition of a building and removal of the materials may be both a sale of land and a sale of goods.[115] These cases are concerned with definitions in particular statutes which do not apply for stamp duty land tax purposes, and it remains to be seen whether HMRC Stamp Taxes will contend that an acquisition involves an interest in land within the charge to stamp duty land tax. This will depend upon how the current pro-Revenue judiciary will view the policy of the legislation. The technical issues are unlikely to carry much weight with the current judiciary, who rely upon HMRC's arguments somewhat uncritically and will treat the matter as a policy of enlarging the tax base. Badly drafted legislation will assist them in finding against taxpayers notwithstanding the technical merit of their position upon general land law. It is probable, therefore, that HMRC Stamp Taxes will seek to include the consideration allocated to such items within the charge to stamp duty land tax. This represents, at present, a difficult decision for parties when completing a land transaction return.

Leased equipment

4.21 Moreover, in practice, many items of equipment that are on or attached to the land may not be owned by him but leased or be held under some lease purchase or

---

[108] This analysis may have implications for the treatment of the landlord's interest in the equipment. Since this is an interest that can be defeated it may not be an interest in land but some other form of property.

[109] *Thomas v Jennings* (1896) 66 LJQB 5.

[110] FA 2003, s 48.

[111] If it were an interest in land the Statute of Frauds 1640 would probably have produced a different result.

[112] See, eg, *Underwood v Burgh Castle Brick and Cement Syndicate* [1922] 1 KB 343.

[113] Section 205(1)(ix).

[114] Section 61.

[115] See, eg, *Lavery v Pursell* (1889) 39 Ch D 508; *Sims v Thomas* (1840) 12 A & E 536; *ex parte Foss* (1858) 2 De G & J 230; *Jarvis v Jarvis* (1893) 63 LJ Ch 10.

hire-purchase arrangement with a third party who, *prima facie*, remains the owner of the goods. Here there is a question of whether such equipment has become a fixture and lost its character as a chattel notwithstanding the ownership of the equipment and there may be a difference between a lease and a lease purchase agreement since in the latter case the lessee of the equipment may become the owner. The older cases concerned with the competing claims of a mortgagee and the owner of leased equipment attached by the hiring tenant to the land indicate that the equipment is capable of becoming a fixture, although it is an open question whether such old cases are inconsistent with the correct application of the modern approach to the correctness of the test of affixation. Moreover, as the equipment is not provided by the landlord, the lease may require the tenant to remove the equipment at the end of the tenancy indicating an absence of intention that the equipment should not become a permanent part of the land although the precise nature of his rights in relation to the goods whilst they are attached to the land has not been examined in detail by recent cases. Two areas of, as yet unresolved problems of stamp duty land tax arise; namely:

- whether the owner or lessor of the equipment has an interest in or over land that is a 'chargeable interest'. It may be that he has some right to enter upon the land in order to inspect and/or remove the goods, which may be a chargeable interest where they are attached to the land;

- whether the lessee of the equipment, who may be a freeholder or a lessee of the land, has attached them to the land so as to make them fixtures or part of the land for the purposes of any sale of his interest in the land whilst they are attached to the land. It may be that the rights of the lessee of the equipment in relation to these goods is neither goods nor land but simply the benefit of the lease or lease purchase agreement,[116] which is not 'land', so that any consideration allocated to the equipment is ignored in computing the stamp duty land tax. Such an arrangement is likely to contain a provision that the tenant will be responsible for the repair and maintenance of the equipment, its replacement as necessary and its removal on the expiration of the lease. This is a powerful indication that the equipment is not a fixture, especially where the tenant is only a hirer of the equipment.

The issue may also arise indirectly: such as where a person carrying on a leasing business has hired equipment to a tenant, who has attached it to the land in such a way that it has become a fixture (albeit possibly severable) and the owner of the equipment sells the benefit of the hiring agreement to another party,[117] it may have retained its character as a chattel or where the lessee of the equipment sells his business as a going concern. In this situation although the point is not immediately obvious there is a question as to whether the interests being sold include some form of chargeable interest which may include an obligation affecting the value of an estate or interest in land.[118]

Two issues arise as follows.

---

[116] Compare the cases on the Statute of Frauds 1640 such as *Lee v Gaskell* (1876) 1 QB 700.

[117] A sale of goods subject to a lease or hiring agreement is a sale of goods, although it is potentially a sale of a contractual right in the case of lease purchase or hire purchase: see *Drages Ltd v IRC Ltd* (1927) 46 TC 389 and **4.24**.

[118] FA 2003, s 48.

Interest of tenant/lessee of equipment

4.22   There is the question of what an assignee from a tenant who is disposing of his interest in the land is purchasing in such a situation, namely whether it is the right to remove the equipment or the benefit of the leasing or hire-purchase agreement or the equipment has become part of the land notwithstanding that it is leased equipment.[119] The latter would seem to be the correct analysis. In addition, the benefit of the agreement will usually be of little value because of the obligation to pay the ongoing rental instalments. In consequence, as this agreement is not an interest in or over land, no charge should arise but should stamp duty land tax apply it would be likely to be small since the consideration may be negligible.

Interest of third party/lessor of equipment

4.23   The position in relation to third party interests is more difficult because the old cases indicate that 'the title to chattels may[120] clearly be lost by being affixed to real property by a person who is not the owner of the chattels'.[121] This can occur even where the equipment is hired and attached to the land.[122] The nature of the equipment lessor's interest is less clear. It may be that where the leased equipment has become a fixture this interest of the lessor is something in the nature of an intangible interest similar to the right of the tenant of the land, so that there is potentially a charge to stamp duty land tax upon the sale by the equipment lessor of the leasing portfolio. The right of the lessor of the equipment to retake possession in the event of breach or default by the lessee appears to create an equitable interest in the land in the form of a right of entry[123] in favour of the lessor of the equipment.

4.24   An owner of goods who leases them to a person who attaches them to the land may find that his right of ownership has been replaced by a right of re-entry and to remove the equipment. Notwithstanding that the effect of the arrangement is to create an equitable interest in the land for certain purposes, it is thought that (as between the parties themselves for stamp duty land tax purposes) there remains a contract for the hire of goods rather than an agreement for lease of an interest in land[124] which does not attract stamp duty land tax.[125] There will be a question as to whether the lessor of the equipment is disposing of a right to chattels notwithstanding their degree of affixation to the land[126] or he is disposing of some interest in or right over land into which his interest in the chattel has, for the time being at least, mutated.

---

[119]   It seems possible that outside the area of taxation the current judiciary would treat the equipment as land and the sale would be at the benefit of the leasing contract (*TSB v Botham* [1996] ECGS 149); but where tax is a stake the position is less optimistic, compare *Oughtred v IRC* [1960] AC 206 and *Neville v Wilson* [1997] Ch 144 where tax because tax was not involved the Court of Appeal applied the correct law effectively overruling the House of Lords in a tax matter.

[120]   'May' is clearly important in that it implies that the property does not automatically become part of the land.

[121]   *Reynolds v Ashby & Son* [1904] AC 466.

[122]   See, eg, *Hobson v Gorringe* [1897] 1 Ch 182; *Reynolds v Ashby & Son* (above), holding that title will pass to a mortgagee of the land.

[123]   *Re Morrison, Jones and Taylor Ltd* [1914] 1 Ch 50; it confers protection against all persons other than persons acquiring legal interest for value without notice: see *Re Samuel Allen & Sons Ltd* [1907] 1 Ch 575; but may not be registerable as a profit in gross: *Poster v Slough Estates Ltd* [1968] 1 WLR 1515; *Shiloh Spinners Ltd v Harding* [1973] AC 691.

[124]   See now *Melluish v BMI* [1995] STC 964 and note the definition of 'lease' in FA 2003, Sch 17A, para 1; but compare 'major interest' in s 117.

[125]   See *Jones v IRC* [1895] 1 QB 484.

[126]   Note the analysis for lease and lease purchase in *Drages v IRC* 46 TC 389.

Estates, interest and other rights

An estate in or over land

4.25 There is no definition of 'estate'. The Law of Property Act 1925, s 1 provides that only certain estates and interests may exist as legal estates and that all other estates and interests take effect as equitable interests.[127] However, these provisions are not definitions of what is an estate or interest and in the context of the definition of major interests in FA 2003, s 117 it is clearly immaterial whether the interest or estate subsists at law or in equity. The word 'estate' is in essence the description of the relationship of a person with, *inter alia*, land. Presumably it was intended to indicate that freeholds and leaseholds are chargeable interests.

Interests in land and rights over land

4.26 The issues here are largely related to the rights of persons who do not have an interest such as freeholder or leaseholder in the land, but have, in effect, rights exercisable over or in relation to the land such as right of way, rights to light, mineral rights. It is a different issue from that considered above as to the nature of the interests, if any, of a third party whose chattels have become attached to the land.

4.27 It would seem that incorporeal hereditaments[128] and easements[129] may not be 'land' in the strict sense but a vein of coal under land[130] and presumably other minerals may be land. However, the issue for stamp duty land tax purposes is whether they are interests in or rights over land or obligations affecting the value of estates and interests in or rights over land.[131]

4.28 The following is a list of cases which have been held not to be sales of goods but possibly sales of land, some of which were applied for the purposes of the Stamp Act 1891 or its predecessors:

- an agreement to quarry stone;[132]

- an agreement to sell freehold fixtures unsevered.[133] However, an agreement whereby the purchaser is to sever equipment attached to the land and to remove it has been treated as a sale of goods for the purposes of the sales of goods legislation.[134]

---

[127] Law of Property Act 1925, s 1(3).
[128] *Re Dawson* 11 TLR 455, but see *Smith D Jerdon v Milward* (1782) 3 Doug KB 70.
[129] *Chelsea Waterworks Co v Bowley* (1851) 17 QB 358; *Metropolitan Railway Co v Fowler* [1893] AC 416; *Heath v Pugh* 7 App Cas 235: a mortgagee's action for foreclosure was an action for the recovery of land; see also *Nevill v IRC* [1924] AC 385; *Marlborough v AG* [1945] Ch 145.
[130] *Wilkinson v Proud* (1843) 11 M & W 33.
[131] FA 2003, s 48(1)(b).
[132] *Hughes v Budd* (1840) 8 Dowl 478.
[133] *Horsfall v Hey* (1848) 17 LJ Ex 266; but note that it appears to have been assumed in *Underwood Ltd v Burgh Castle Brick and Cement Syndicate* [1922] 1 KB 343 that the sale of a piece of equipment cemented into the floor was a sale of goods.
[134] *Underwood v Burgh Castle* [1922] 1 KB 343; but note the possibility that this might also be land depending upon the legislation involved as described in *Lavery v Pursell* (1889) 39 Ch D 569.

4.29   It has been held for various purposes that the following are interests in land:

- easements and profits;[135]

- an interest under a trust for sale of land;[136]

- a lease of land;

- a sale of heaps of cinders and slag which were not in specific or separate mounds;[137]

- sale of future rents,[138] but this may depend upon whether the transaction is drafted as a transfer of the right to receive the rent as such or as the benefit of the personal covenant of the tenant to pay the rent. (This latter course may have difficulties in relation to rents arising pursuant to later leases with different tenants. In this case it may amount to a contract to assign the benefit of the expectation of future property.);

- a share in the proceeds of the sale of land.[139] This may raise a question in relation to attempts to escape from the problems of mortgages as chargeable consideration where there is an attempt to put property into joint names and there is a charge upon the property. Notwithstanding former practices have now been put on a statutory basis[140] and only a proportion of the mortgage is brought into charge to tax there will still be problems where the amount of the mortgage exceeds a particular level so that the proportion of the property takes the transaction above the nil rate band for the time being. It might be thought that a possible method of dealing with the situation is to avoid any dealings in the legal title or the equitable interest and simply to find that the property is to be held upon some form of trust or fiduciary arrangement under which the incoming party is to be entitled to a share in the net proceeds of sale after dealing with the mortgage. This would appear to avoid the question of the mortgage being brought into charge since there is no assumption of the liability in respect of the mortgage.[141] However, it may nevertheless be a chargeable transaction because it is a dealing in a chargeable interest. The main safeguard will be that such arrangements are frequently of a domestic nature and there is no actual consideration being involved the transaction may well be exempt because there is no chargeable consideration[142] and so not notifiable[143] or consideration is below the nil rate threshold being a small proportion of the equity of redemption rather than a deemed participation in the total value of the property.

---

135   *Webber v Lee* (1882) 9 QBD 315; on money held upon trust to purchase land see *Re Gosselin* [1906] 1 Ch 120.
136   This raises interesting questions of analysis where at the time the trust assets include property other than land in the United Kingdom.
137   *Morgan v Russell & Sons* [1909] 1 KB 357.
138   *Ex parte Hall, Re Whiting* (1879) 10 Ch D 615; see also *IRC v John Lewis* [2001] STC 1118. However, during the discussion relating to the introduction of the tax certain statements were made that the tax would not apply to securitisation of land notwithstanding that this involved sales of rent.
139   *Re Glassington* [1906] 2 Ch 305; cf *Re Newman* [1930] 2 Ch 409.
140   FA 2003, Sch 4, para 8.
141   Ibid, Sch 4, paras 8 and 8A; see **5.133**.
142   Ibid, Sch 3, para 1.
143   Ibid, s 77A; Sch 3, para 1.

4.30 The following have been held not to be 'land' or interests in or matters relating to land:

- an agreement compromising litigation relating to land is not itself a contract relating to land within the Law of Property (Miscellaneous Provisions) Act 1989, s 2;

- a lock-out agreement controlling negotiations for the sale of land;[144]

- possibly a partner's share[145] where the partnership assets include land, although this is generally regarded as correct law since a partner's share is a separate asset in its own right and not a bundle of separate rights in the underlying assets of the partnership, at least as a general principle. Transfers of partnership shares remain subject to stamp duty[146] and there are specific provisions dealing with transfers of interests in partnerships for the purposes of stamp duty land tax;[147]

- a mere expectation of inheriting property is not itself property or an interest in property being a mere spes.[148] This also applies to the rights of a person who is the object of a special power of appointment prior to its exercise;[149] but a general power of appointment may be an interest in land;[150]

- proceeds of sale of land held subject to an immediate trust for sale are not 'land' within the Interpretation Act 1978.[151]

Contracts and options

Contracts as chargeable interests

4.31 It is provided that:

- merely entering into a contract is not, of itself, a chargeable transaction;[152] and

- a contract to assign the benefit of a contract or agreement for lease is not a chargeable transaction.[153]

However, this leaves open the question of whether contracts relating to interests in land are themselves chargeable interests so that dealings in contracts not within the above two situations such as variations or releases of contractual rights for a consideration are chargeable transactions. This is a particular issue in relation to arrangements for the assignment of rights arising under a contract such as an assignment of the contract to acquire land or an assignment of the right to call for a lease under an agreement for lease.[154] There is a clear issue since it is specifically provided that entering into a contract

---

[144] *Pitt v PHH Asset Management* [1993] 4 All ER 961.
[145] *IRC v Gray* [1994] STC 360 at 377.
[146] FA 2003, Sch 15.
[147] See **Chapter 13**.
[148] *Allcard v Walker* [1896] 2 Ch 369; *Re Parsons* (1890) 45 Ch D 51.
[149] *Re Brooks' Settlement Trusts* [1939] Ch 993.
[150] *Fleming v Buchanan* (1853) 22 LJ Ch 886.
[151] *Re Sidebottom* [1902] 2 Ch 389.
[152] FA 2003, s 44(2), see **3.23**.
[153] Ibid, ss 45(2) and 45A(2); Sch 17A, para 12B.
[154] See for various possible analyses *Attorney General v Brown* (1849) 3 Exch 662.

to assign a contract is not, of itself, an event giving rise to an immediate charge to tax but this does not state that the arrangement is not itself a potentially chargeable transaction since it could involve the acquisition of a chargeable interest namely the benefit of a contract. Clearly, where the first contract has been performed to some extent or the equitable interest may have passed at a certain stage in the transaction a vendor may become a bare trustee of nominee for the purchaser although this, it would seem, is dependent upon the consideration having been paid or provided in full. An unpaid or partly paid vendor who retains the legal title has some form of lien or interest in the property of a significant nature that prevents the equitable interest vesting fully in the purchaser.[155] It seems clear that, since options and pre-emption rights have special provisions making their grant chargeable, contracts and agreements for lease even where conditional, are chargeable interests so that many dealings in such contracts will be chargeable transactions in their own right. However, this restatement of the general rule that merely entering into a contract is not a chargeable event[156] does not mean that substantial performance or completion of that contract by assignment or other means is not a chargeable event because it is the assignment of a chargeable interest. This emerges rather obliquely from the limited exemption for, *inter alia*, assignments pursuant to FA 2003, s 45.[157] Although the rules regarding the creation of rights will not apply to the contractual rights coming into existence, variation of contractual rights such as the extension of the completion date or variation of the building specifications for a consideration will be chargeable transactions. There will be an important issue of principle where a contract is terminated as to whether this is a rescission with a return of the consideration paid or is a release or surrender for a consideration.[158]

4.32 Where the consideration has been fully provided or the right to specific performance has arisen, the relevant party will have acquired an equitable interest in the land pursuant to the constructive trust that arises by operation of law.[159] In consequence, any dealing in such a contract whether between the original parties or the 'purchaser' under the contract and a third party would, it seems, apart from FA 2003, s 45, which merely states that the entry into the contract is not, as such, a chargeable transaction (ie defers the chargeable or effective date) as far as the subpurchaser or assignee is concerned, involve an immediately chargeable transaction in a chargeable interest being a dealing in a potential equitable interest.[160]

---

[155]   *Re Kidner* [1929] 2 Ch 121; *Musselwhite v Musselwhite* [1962] 1 Ch 210; *Michaels v Harley House (Marylebone) Ltd* [2000] Ch 104; *Warmington v Miller* [1973] 2 All ER 372; *Langen and Wind Ltd v Bell* [1972] Ch 685; it must be noted that these cases may be different from those concerned with whether the vendor has lost the beneficial ownership as opposed to the equitable interest vesting in the purchaser because of the ability on beneficial ownership, at least of shares, to be suspended for the time being as in *Commissioners of Inland Revenue v Livingston* [1965] AC 604; *Ayerst v C & K (Construction) Ltd* [1976] AC 167. However, notwithstanding attempts by the Courts to apply this arrangement in relation to shares and land in a commercial context as opposed to a statutory regime where questions of priorities and abatement may affect the ownership of the assets by decisions such as *Wood Preservation v Prior* [1969] 1 All ER 364 has not been wholly successful and has been criticised and suggested may be wrong in subsequent decisions such as *J Sainsbury v O'Connor* [1991] STC 5156. There is also the question as to whether it is possible to suspend beneficial ownership of land because the right to rent arises and cannot be postponed or deferred such as can easily take place in relation to dividends and shares.

[156]   FA 2003, ss 44(2) and 45(2).

[157]   See **Chapter 6**, and see also FA 2003, s 45A and Sch 17A, para 12B.

[158]   See FA 2003, s 45(8), and **Chapter 6**.

[159]   See, eg, *Neville v Wilson* [1997] Ch 144; *Walsh v Lonsdale* (1882) 21 Ch D 9.

[160]   Note the possible implications of Law of Property Act 1925, s 53(1)(c) as to what may be involved in relation to the former requirements for dealing and completing such a contract and the questions of the impact of s 53(2) thereof as consequences of *Oughtred v IRC* [1960] AC 206; *Neville v Wilson* [1997] Ch 144 and Law of Property (Miscellaneous Provisions) Act 1989, s 2.

4.33 A more difficult question arises where the constructive trust has not arisen because, for example, the vendor has a lien for the unpaid purchase price or the balance[161] which prevents the equitable interest from vesting in the purchaser. Similar problems arise where the contract is conditional upon the happening of some event such as obtaining planning permission, or the co-operation of adjoining landowners in selling their property. *Prima facie*, the contract is a chargeable interest but subsequent assignments thereof are possibly excluded from the charge to stamp duty land tax pursuant to FA 2003, s 45. In other cases, a charge to stamp duty land tax will arise.

4.34 As options are specifically treated as 'chargeable interests',[162] it is inconceivable that HMRC Stamp Taxes cannot have intended that contracts, whether conditional or unconditional, should not be chargeable interests, since, if the contracts are not in themselves chargeable interests, the opportunities for mitigating stamp duty land tax by utilising conditional contracts rather than options[163] are obvious.

Options and pre-emption rights

4.35 The acquisition of an option by the grantor to enter into a land transaction or of a right of pre-emption preventing the grantor from entering into or restricting the right of the grantor to enter into a land transaction[164] is a land transaction distinct from any land transaction resulting from the exercise of the option or the right. In consequence, there will be charges to stamp duty land tax in respect of:

- the grant of an option or pre-emption right;

- the exercise of the option or pre-emption right. Such exercise will produce a contract which may relate to the acquisition of a chargeable interest the subject-matter of the option or pre-emption right and this may be a 'linked transaction' involving the exercise of the option, the grant of the option so that the premium for the grant of the option and the strike price payable upon the exercise thereof will have to be aggregated for determining the amount of stamp duty land tax payable[165] and in order to determine whether the lower rates are available or not. There will also need to be separate reporting and notification of the grant and the exercise of the option;

- the assignment of the option or pre-emption right;

- the variation of the terms of the option or pre-emptive right; and

- the release of the option or pre-emption right.

4.36 Each of these is a separate transaction for the purposes of stamp duty land tax; but there may be a timing issue between:

---

[161] *Michaels v Harley House (Marylebone) Ltd* [1999] 3 WLR 229; *Musselwhite v Musselwhite* [1962] 1 Ch 210; *Langen and Wind Ltd v Bell* [1972] Ch 685; but note the possible implication of drafting and set-off as in *Coren v Keighley* 48 TC 370.
[162] FA 2003, s 46.
[163] On the nature of options or contracts to purchase or irrevocable offers, see *Spiro v Glencrown Properties Ltd* [1991] 2 WLR 931.
[164] On the possible impact of pre-emptive rights on ownership see *Hunter v Hunter* [1936] AC 222; *Hawks v McArthur* [1951] 1 All ER 22; *Tett v Phoenix* (1985) SJ 869.
[165] FA 2003, ss 55(4) and 108.

- a grant of an option which is exercisable if planning permission is obtained – i e an immediate grant of an option exercisable conditionally – which seems to be taxable; and

- an agreement to grant an option if planning permission is obtained – i e there is no grant of an option unless and until the condition is satisfied – which is not taxable until the condition is met.

The difference between conditional grant and conditional exercise may have important consequences for taxpayers if the above analysis is accepted as correct.

A right

4.37   There may be certain rights which are interests in land but this provision is clearly intended to ensure that all rights whether easements, profits à prendre, restrictive covenants or rights to light are within the charge to tax. The question is whether the use of the word 'right' coupled with the use of 'benefit of a contract' affecting land will enlarge the scope of the stamp duty land tax beyond the traditional list. It would seem wide enough to cover contracts to acquire land, options and pre-emption rights.

A power

4.38   This reference to a 'power' in relation to land would seem to have been included to bring into charge interest such as the powers of trustees to appoint or advance land out of settlements. The mortgagee's power of sale is presumably not within this charge because security arrangements are exempt interests,[166] but other forms of power such as powers of attorney held by persons entitled to interests in the land such as purchasers or lessees are likely to be regarded as chargeable interests. General and possibly special powers of appointment would seem to be chargeable interests. In some situations such powers may be exercised without consent so that there may be no chargeable consideration[167] and so no chargeable transaction.[168] In other cases, such as powers of compulsory acquisition of land, may have the statutory effect of producing a contract and so a chargeable transaction.[169]

The benefit of an obligation

4.39   'Chargeable interests' extend beyond traditional estates and interests and include the benefit of an obligation, restriction or condition affecting the value[170] of any estate, interest, right or power in or over land in the United Kingdom.[171] Clearly, this is part of the policy behind stamp duty land tax designed to prevent value shifting by means of arrangements that do not involve chargeable interest. This is presumably intended to include contractual and other arrangements falling short of rights over land but which affect its value. For example, it is thought that a contractual arrangement limiting development of or dealings in land which is not a valid restrictive covenant could fall within this term. This might occur where land is sold with a condition prohibiting

---

[166]   But such rights may constitute 'arrangements' for other anti-avoidance purposes.
[167]   See FA 2003, Sch 16, para 8.
[168]   Ibid, Sch 3, para 1; see **11.19**.
[169]   *IRC v Glasgow and South Western Railway* (1887) 12 App Cas 315.
[170]   It appears to be irrelevant whether the obligation restriction or condition depresses or enhances the value of the land.
[171]   FA 2003, s 48(1)(b); see also on leasehold covenants Sch 17A, para 10(1)(c).

development where the vendor does not retain any neighbouring land that could benefit from the restriction and qualify as the 'dominant' land. Since there is no dominant land[172] the contractual condition cannot qualify as an interest in or over land but since it may affect value it is deemed to be a chargeable interest. The effect is that there will be some form of land exchange which as a double chargeable transaction may create a liability to the tax for the vendor. There will be a transfer of the main chargeable interest requiring the 'purchaser' to enter into another land transaction namely the 'creation' or grant of the obligation affecting the vendor of the main interest.[173] This imposes a charge upon the vendor upon the market value of the contractual restriction.[174] As this is not a traditional interest in land it may be an item of property that can be sold as a separate chose in action in the open market unlike traditional rights and interests in and over land such as a valid restrictive covenant. Since these traditional interests cannot exist in gross they may not, as such, be capable of sale in the open market. They may have o market value although valuable,[175] but a contractual obligation not qualifying as a restrictive covenant is not subject to any such restrictions. The purchaser will also be subject to tax upon the market value of the interest being acquired which will not necessarily be the price being paid even in an arm's length transaction.[176]

In the United Kingdom

4.40 Foreign land is not included, and it seems that for these purposes the United Kingdom ends somewhere near the tide level.

EQUITABLE AND SIMILAR INTERESTS

4.41 Equitable interests in land are within the charge. The draftsman has made this assumption that the interests of beneficiaries in a trust are equitable interests in the underlying investments rather than a separate interest being a bundle of rights rather than a single separate chose in action or other item of property of an equitable nature and prepared legislation that brings other forms of interests in trusts into the charge to tax such as foreign trusts.[177] For example, it is provided that major interests may subsist at law or in equity[178] and, where land is held by a 'nominee',[179] the dealings arc attributed to the beneficial owner.[180] These issues also affect the persons to be identified as vendors or purchasers and required to sign the declaration for compliance purposes.[181]

---

[172] It seems that a ransom strip will not necessarily qualify as the dominant land since it cannot benefit from the restriction because it is too small.

[173] FA 2003, ss 47, 43(3) and 48(1)(b); see **4.39**.

[174] Ibid, Sch 4, para 5; see **5.150** and **4.39**.

[175] For the difference between 'value' and 'market value' see *Stanton v Drayton Commercial Investment Co Ltd* [1982] STC 585; see **Chapter 27**.

[176] *Lap Shun Textiles Industrial Co v Collector of Stamp Revenue* [1976] AC 530.

[177] FA 2003, Sch 16, para 2; see **9.12**.

[178] Ibid, s 117; but in most cases equitable interests will be non-major interests because they are limited interests.

[179] Defined in FA 2003, Sch 16, para 1(3).

[180] Ibid, Sch 16, para 3; see **9.1**.

[181] This has been carried to a somewhat extreme by HMRC Stamp Taxes but which is potentially of assistance to taxpayers and beneficial owners. Since the acts of the nominee are deemed to be the acts of the beneficial owner HMRC Stamp Taxes have indicated that a signature by the nominee who is on the legal title will be regarded for the purposes of the validity of the land transaction return (SDLT 1) as being the signature of the beneficial owner; see **9.8** and **15.26**.

4.42 It must, however, be noted that the provisions which provide a form of fiscal transparency for interests in trusts and deem certain types of trust interest to be interests in land mean that the tax may depend upon the nature of the interest. There are important differences between major interests ie freeholds and leaseholds which include equitable interests in freeholds and leaseholds, and other interests in property.[182] In consequence, interests in a settlement or a testamentary trust would appear to be minor interests because they are limited interests in the underlying trust asset and the fact that the trust asset is, for example, a freehold does not convert the equitable interest into an interest that is a major interest. It is only a limited interest in the freehold and not the freehold itself. This has important implications for dealings in relation to the variation of trusts and estates because exchanges where major interests are involved are dealt with at market value whereas exchanges of minor interests, such as the exchange of a life interest in part of the trust assets for the reversionary interest in other trust assets, will be a dealing in limited interests ie minor interests with tax only upon the equality payment.[183] The fact that the parties may become entitled to a freehold interest or the transfer of the property out of the trust to the relevant beneficiary in order to complete the variation of the equitable interest may produce the transfer of a major interest does not change the nature of the interests that were the subject-matter of the various transactions involved in the restructuring of the trust. The difficulty is where the transaction is not formally completed and there are subsequent arrangements since, at the particular stage, the beneficiary may have become absolutely entitled as against the trustees and therefore entitled to an equitable freehold interest or the benefit of the equitable interest in the entire lease ie will have acquired an equitable interest that is a major interest so that any subsequent dealings will fall into different computational rules because major interests are involved.[184]

Bare trustees, nominees and settlements

4.43 The existence of the nominee or bare trustee is ignored and the beneficial owner is treated as the owner of the interest in the land. The legislation[185] is to the effect that the acts of the nominee are to be treated for tax purposes as being the acts of the beneficial owner.[186] In these situations any return for stamp duty land tax purposes has to include the name of the beneficial owner as seller or purchaser and this should appear on the Revenue certificate (SDLT 5).[187] This means that there will be a discrepancy between the persons involved in a Land Registry documentation such as the nominee as registered owner of the legal title and the persons identified for the purposes of stamp duty land tax. This will require extra work on behalf of those acting for the purchaser in determining what documentation will be required in order to persuade the Land Registry that the stamp duty land tax documentation relates to the same dealings in the property.

---

[182] FA 2003, ss 77A and 117 and Sch 4, para 5.
[183] Ibid, Sch 4, para 5(4).
[184] Ibid, Sch 4, para 5(2).
[185] Ibid, Sch 16, para 3.
[186] Ibid, Sch 16, para 3(1).
[187] Stamp Duty Land Tax (Administration) Regulations 2003, SI 2003/2837, reg 5(3).

Settlements – the basic position

4.44 The charge to stamp duty land tax extends to interests in trusts whether *inter vivos* or testamentary[188] and the estates of deceased persons[189] which can include chargeable interests. Where there is some form of interest in possession trusts such as a life interest or a remainder then the interest of the beneficiary includes an interest in the underlying assets. This is regarded correctly or otherwise by the draftsman as being a separate interest in each individual asset of the trust and so, if the assets or investments held by the trustees include land in the United Kingdom, the interest of the beneficiary will include an equitable interest that is a chargeable interest to some extent.[190] In consequence, variations of trusts involving, *inter alia*, exchanges or releases of interests for consideration will be chargeable transactions where the trust investment includes land.[191] Dealings in such interests will require apportionment of the consideration between that part of the equitable interest that relates to land in the United Kingdom and the other assets. Such apportionment must be made on a just and reasonable basis.[192]

Power of appointment

4.45 A power of appointment is a chargeable interest;[193] but being the object of a power is not a chargeable interest since the object of the power merely has a hope but no immediate interest in the assets. The exercise of a power of appointment will not normally be a chargeable transaction since there will be no chargeable consideration[194] but where there is consideration as the appointee 'purchased' his right to be included in the class of relevant beneficiaries special anti-avoidance provisions may apply.[195]

---

[188] There may be an issue as to whether, and if so when, a beneficiary in the estate of a deceased individual acquires an interest in the assets forming part of the estate; see **4.50**.

[189] If it did not apply, then the limited exemption for variations of such estates in FA 2003, Sch 3, para 4 would be unnecessary; see **9.36**.

[190] However, this approach has not been adopted by HMRC Stamp Taxes in relation to stamp duty or stamp duty reserve tax where shares are involved. The interest of the beneficiary has been regarded as a separate form of interest and is not an interest in shares as such. Nor is it regarded as being a bundle of rights or interests for each of the individual assets or investments of the trust. In consequence, dealings in equitable interests were stampable as dealings in separate assets which are now free of stamp duty and are not stamp duty reserve tax because the limited interest of the beneficiary is not an interest in shares. This clearly indicates a lack of consistency or sophistication in the analysis of the situation but the legislation in relation to stamp duty land tax clearly indicates that it is contemplated that there is to be a charge in respect of part of the equitable interest by the underlying assets include land so that there is a part equitable interest in part of the assets that is a chargeable interest. This analysis also differs from the treatment of dealings in interests in partnerships because these are regarded as separate assets rather than as being a bundle of interest in the underlying partnership assets so that there have to be special rules dealing with dealings in interest in partnerships where the partnership owns shares (FA 2003, s 125 and Sch 15, paras 31–33) or land since a partnership interest is not, as such, a chargeable interest notwithstanding that the partnership includes land and it has been necessary to include various provisions deeming a partnership interest to be a chargeable interest for particular purposes.

[191] But the nature of the interest may be that it is a minor interest because it is a limited equitable interest and it will not be a major interest simply because the underlying trust investment is the freehold interest in land.

[192] Any other basis is likely to be regarded by HMRC Stamp Taxes as fraud: see *Saunders v Edwards* [1987] 2 All ER 651.

[193] FA 2003, s 48(1)(a).

[194] The existence of consideration may mean that the exercise is a fraud on the power.

[195] FA 2003, Sch 16, para 7.

Discretionary trusts

4.46   Certain trusts such as discretionary trusts and certain foreign trusts[196] do not have interests in possession and the interests of the beneficiaries are not interests in the underlying property but merely personal rights exercisable against trustees to compel proper administration of the trusts.[197] Such interests are not chargeable interests because they are located at the residence of the trustee or within the jurisdiction of the legal system pursuant to which the trust was established and confer no tracing or similar rights against the assets. In consequence, they do not relate to land in the United Kingdom.

4.47   However, two issues arise:

*   there is a provision[198] to the effect that had the trust been situate subject to English law the interests of the beneficiary would have been some form of interest in the underlying property an interest '*in rem*' relating to the underlying assets rather than purely '*in personam*' ie a claim or power gainable against the trustees to administer the assets properly, the foreign interest is to be treated on the same basis as English interests notwithstanding that it provides only limited rights and powers to the beneficiary; and

*   in order to prevent parties dealing with the passing of property by holding it within discretionary trusts or foreign trusts which do not involve equitable interests in the underlying property in English law,

it is provided[199] that where a chargeable interest is acquired by virtue of either the exercise of a power of appointment or the exercise of a discretion vested in trustees of a settlement in favour of a person who has provided consideration in order to be included within the class of beneficiaries, it is treated as being an acquisition for any such consideration given by the person in whose favour the appointment was made or the discretion was exercised for becoming an object of the power or discretion.

Foreign trusts

4.48   Foreign law trusts, including the law of Scotland,[200] do not always recognise equitable interests in the sense of this term in English law and the position of the beneficiaries is not a proprietary interest in the underlying investments within the trust fund but only a personal right against the trustees and possibly only a contractual or similar personal right such as a *ius crediti*.[201] It is, however, provided that where there is a trust which, if it were governed by English law, would confer upon the beneficiary a proprietary or equitable interest in the underlying investments held in the trust fund, then the interests of the beneficiaries are to be treated as though they were such equitable interests. Foreign trusts are, therefore, to be treated as though they were governed by English law and the nature of the interests of the beneficiary are to be determined accordingly.

---

[196]   See **4.48** and **9.25**.
[197]   Difficult issues may arise where on the effective date there is only one existing discretionary beneficiary: see *Holmden v IRC* [1968] AC 685.
[198]   FA 2003, Sch 16, para 2.
[199]   Ibid, Sch 16, para 7; see **9.26**.
[200]   See, for example, *Sharp v Woolwich Building Society* [1997] 1 BCLC 603.
[201]   See, for illustrations of this, *Garland v Archer-Shee* (1928) 15 TC 693; *Archer-Shee v Baker* 15 TC 1.

4.49 In consequence, where the trustees own land in the United Kingdom then, notwithstanding any foreign law applicable, the interests of the beneficiaries are chargeable interests in land in the United Kingdom. Clearly there will be interesting questions of whether such trustees have properly performed their duties when they invest directly in land in the United Kingdom rather than indirectly through a company or even as a partner in a partnership because, subject to certain special provisions, an interest in a partnership is not, as such, a chargeable interest notwithstanding that the partnership owns interests in land.[202] In such a situation the trustees, and therefore the beneficiaries, do not have chargeable interest subject to the tax where the interests of the beneficiaries are not affected by the current legislation and, at most, are interests in the shares or partnership interest rather than chargeable interests in the land in the United Kingdom.

Estates of deceased persons

Interests in suspense

4.50 In relation to dispositions arising upon death, whether testamentary or on intestacy, interests of specific devisees of land or chargeable interests situate in the United Kingdom are, *prima facie*, chargeable interests so that disposals of their interests in the estate or variations of the estate, if for consideration, *prima facie*, give rise to liability to stamp duty land tax, although there are exemptions for certain variations of the estates of deceased persons entered into within 2 years after the death.[203] However, this does not appear to be the view of HMRC Stamp Taxes. As regards residuary beneficiaries, these essentially have no interest in the underlying assets held for the time being as part of the residue. There is merely a personal claim against the personal representatives for proper administration of the estate.[204] However, once the administration of the estate is completed and the residuary assets defined, the beneficial ownership will vest in the residuary devisees and they will acquire chargeable interests. HMRC Stamp Taxes appear to take a similar view as regards participation in specific legacies or devises and do not restrict this to the situation of participation in the residuary estate. The residuary estate is subject to a statutory regime which cannot be regarded as passing an interest to the beneficiary because of the rules dealing with the application of the assets in the estate where the estate is insolvent or there are insufficient assets to provide all of the specific legacies or cash payments or liabilities and assets that might form part of the residuary or main estate may have to be sold. In consequence, they appear to take the view that at least until the estate is fully administered and all of the liabilities have been paid for or provided for by the appropriation of particular assets to their discharge, there is no relationship between the legatees or devisees of the particular assets and the assets themselves. On this view where there is a possibility that, for example, the estate may be 'insolvent' in the sense that there may be a need to have recourse to the particular assets for sale in order to generate the cash to pay off liabilities, there cannot be a form of relationship between the specific legatee or devisee and a particular asset since his claim is not absolute but provisional or conditional, the interest is not regarded as vested but defeasible but as not being an interest in the asset at all. The contrary view, that there is an interest in the underlying asset, raises very different consequences from those where the specific devisee or legatee is regarded as having invested the defeasible interest in the underlying property.

---

[202] See **Chapter 13**.
[203] FA 2003, Sch 3, para 4; see **9.36**.
[204] *Commissioner of Stamp Duties (Queensland) v Livingston* [1964] 3 All ER 692 (PC).

Change of status

4.51   It will be a routine event for trustees to become bare trustees or executors to become nominees. This can arise, for example, where a beneficiary becomes absolutely entitled as against the trustees,[205] or they exercise a power of appointment or advancement without transferring the legal title. Executors will, such as upon the execution of an assent or upon completing the administration, become trustees or possibly nominees. Whilst this change of status does not, of itself, normally give rise to a charge to stamp duty land tax, the charge does have implications such as who is the 'purchaser' or vendor in relation to any particular transaction, and, most importantly, in practice who is liable for the tax and who is the person who must sign the declaration at the end of the basic stamp duty land tax return or self-assessment.

Foreign estates of deceased persons

4.52   There are no specific statutory provisions, unlike the case of trusts, dealing with foreign estates holding land in the United Kingdom where the interests of the beneficiaries are not similar to those in England and Wales. However, it is assumed that the normal principles will apply such as *Livingston*[206] so residuary beneficiaries or legatees or devisees in insolvent estates or possible beneficiaries in all estates[207] have no interest in the assets of the estates at least until the administration is completed or the creditors have been provided for. However, there would seem to be no reason why when the interests in the assets being to vest in the beneficiaries during the administration of the estate[208] the specific provisions dealing with foreign trusts and discretionary trusts,[209] which do not appear to be restricted to discretionary trusts and powers of appointment governed by the laws of England and Wales or Northern Ireland, should not apply to settlements arising pursuant to wills or intestacies of persons dying domiciled outside the United Kingdom where the disposition of their estates, whether testate or intestate, is governed by foreign legal systems. There may, therefore, be interesting questions as to whether the administration of the estate, particularly in relation to interests in the equivalent of the residuary estate, which is governed by a law of a jurisdiction outside the United Kingdom, has progressed to such a state that the interests of the specific, general or residuary legatees or devisee have reached a point where the law of England and Wales would regard the relevant persons as having a proprietary interest in the land or chargeable interest in land in the United Kingdom.

Liability of deceased for unpaid tax

4.53   As the law of England and Wales does not recognise, as part of domestic law, the concept of universal succession which exists in many foreign legal systems, successors to, beneficiaries of, or the equivalent of the personal representatives of, deceased individuals who died domiciled outside England and Wales or whose estates are for whatever reason to be administered in accordance with a legal system outside England and Wales, are likely to be faced with difficult questions of whether they are subject to stamp duty land tax either in respect of the liability of the deceased such as where the

---

[205]   Pursuant to rules such as *Saunders v Vautier* (1841) 10 LJ Ch 354; and see FA 2003, Sch 16, paras 1 and 3.

[206]   *Commissioner of Stamps v Livingston* [1964] 3 All ER 692 (PC).

[207]   There may, however, be a need for some form of written assent may be necessary to convert the personal representatives into trustees; see Administration of Estates Act 1925, s 36(4) and (7); *Re King's Will Trust* [1964] Ch 542; *Re Hodge* [1940] Ch 260; but see *Re Ponder* [1921] 2 Ch 59.

[208]   See **9.25**.

[209]   FA 2003, Sch 16, para 2.

deceased acquired the land with a deferred consideration which has been postponed or not disclosed to HMRC Stamp Taxes or whether they are required to notify and pay tax in respect of a transaction relating to the interests of persons in the estate.[210] The obtaining of ancillary probate or administration and the resealing of foreign grants will lead to some difficult issues for such persons as a consequence of ill thought through provisions which were not adequately understood or reviewed by those advising the opposition parties in Standing Committee during the debate.

Partnerships

4.54 Although there are certain 'look-through' provisions for partnerships[211] including those partnerships which have corporate personality such as limited liability partnerships, the interests of partners are, as a basic principle, not chargeable interests. However, special rules apply to bring transfers of interests in property investment partnerships into charge[212] and the general anti-avoidance provisions[213] whereby the interest of a partner is deemed to be a chargeable interest.[214]

Rent charges

4.55 The exclusion of rent charges from excluded interests raises various issues which did not arise in stamp duty because estate rent charges were, in practice, treated as security interests. The issues include:

- where land is conveyed subject to the creation of an estate rent charge, it is unclear whether this will be treated as either:
    - a regrant giving rise to a land exchange with two chargeable transactions[215] taxable upon the market value[216] which can be a problem where the purchaser is paying a discounted price;[217] or
    - a single sale for a purchase price which includes a periodical payment of a variable nature;[218] and

- where land is conveyed subject to an existing rent charge whether this involves the assumption of a liability which is added to the consideration.[219] It is thought that this situation falls within the principle[220] that the assumption of an interest liability or a covenant to make future payments is not consideration. It is uncertain whether this principle has survived into stamp duty land tax because of certain specific provisions dealing with this type of situation[221] but which may not be sufficiently wide to apply to estate rent charges. The attitude of HMRC Stamp

---

[210] Details of the provision for recovery of tax and the imposition of penalties upon non-resident taxpayers remain to be published as regulations or practice statements.

[211] FA 2003, Sch 15, paras 2 and 4.

[212] Ibid, Sch 15, para 14 (as amended).

[213] Ibid, ss 75A–75C.

[214] See **Chapter 13**.

[215] The seller is unlikely to be taxable since the estate rent charge is a minor interest having a value within the nil rate band and so also may not be notifiable; FA 2003, s 77A.

[216] FA 2003, s 47; Sch 4, para 5; see **5.160**.

[217] See **Chapter 27**.

[218] FA 2003, s 52; see **5.121**.

[219] Ibid, Sch 4, para 8.

[220] *Swayne v IRC* [1900] 1 QB 172, 69 LJQB 63.

[221] FA 2003, Sch 14, para 16, Sch 17A, para 17.

Stamp Duty Land Tax

Taxes is not known but there has hitherto been no evidence of any attempt to impose a charge in these circumstances which suggests that the inherent liability principle has been carried forward.

In relation to stamp duty estate rent charges[222] were not charged to tax because they represented a payment for services and were not consideration for the payment for the conveyance of the land; but rent charges were otherwise within the charging provisions of Stamp Act 1981, s 56.[223] No guidance on whether this approach has been provided by HMRC Stamp Taxes in relation to stamp duty land tax.

---

[222] Estate Rent Charges Act 1977.
[223] FA 2003, s 52 is in essentially the same terms.

Chapter 5

COMPUTATION

PART I – RATES

5.1   Stamp duty land tax is charged, initially on a self-assessment basis[1] as a percentage of the chargeable consideration[2] or the net present value of the rent,[3] both of which have to be determined by reference to complex statutory provisions (which is not necessarily the same amount as the actual consideration[4]) whether in the form of lump sums, instalments or rent and similar periodical payments. Unfortunately in many cases the consideration and rent may be variable because of overage or clawback arrangements or the rent is reviewable or subject to VAT when changes in the rate may produce a situation where further tax is payable or a refund becomes available and the possibility of which has to be taken into account when making the initial calculation for any actual or deemed lease such as may arise by reason of particular events. This involves a multi-stage process of the initial return and tax computation being determined on a provisional or estimated basis[5] with obligations to deal with the situation as the variables or uncertainties become settled,[6] which obligations may pass to third parties who have to re-compute the tax liability of the original 'purchaser'.[7] Additionally, the tax rate has to be calculated at the rate applicable to the guestimated figures and not the basic price or rent; notwithstanding that part of the tax may be deferred[8] the rate is on the total guestimate not the initial payment. Repayments may also be necessary where the guestimates are excessive and a lower rate applies by reason of subsequent events.[9] The provisional and retrospective nature of the tax means that even the possibility of linked transactions[10] may be a factor to be taken into account when dealing with the rate of tax, as is the possibility that a landlord may exercise the option to subject the rent to VAT.

---

[1]   There is no automatic review of the complex calculations and valuations involved in the initial or subsequent return; the challenge depends upon the random possibility of HMRC Stamp Taxes initiating an Enquiry pursuant to FA 2003, Sch 10, para 12 or making a 'discovery' etc enabling them to issue an assessment pursuant to FA 2003, Sch 10, para 28.

[2]   FA 2003, s 55(1).

[3]   See **7.108**.

[4]   This basic list of chargeable considerations is contained in FA 2003, Sch 4, although this is supplemented by charging and computational provisions scattered at random throughout the legislation. It must also be noted that the legislation refers to both 'chargeable consideration' and 'consideration' without giving any express indication as to whether on any particular occasion the two bear the same or a different meaning, i e 'consideration' without the word 'chargeable' may mean either 'chargeable consideration' or 'actual consideration which is not chargeable'. Taxpayers and their advisers will have to give detailed attention to the particular context which may require that there is actual 'consideration' but the chargeable amount is totally different (FA 2003, Sch 15, para 14 (as amended)).

[5]   See **7.157**; such guestimated figures are also relevant in determining whether there has been substantial performance; see **Chapter 14**.

[6]   See, for example, FA 2003, s 80, Sch 17A, paras 7 and 8.

[7]   See **2.15**.

[8]   See **16.32**.

[9]   Such as the transaction being accepted by HMRC Customs and Exercise as a transfer of a going concern.

[10]   See **5.113**.

5.2   The rate depends upon:

- the amount of the chargeable consideration whether actual or deemed including any guestimated figures subject to later retrospective adjustment;

- whether the transaction is a linked transaction with other chargeable transactions;[11]

- whether the property is residential or non-residential[12] although as a consequence of the early removal of the reliefs for land in a disadvantaged area this distinction is of only minor significance in practice;[13] and

- whether the consideration consists solely of or includes rent, since in relation to premiums for leases of non-residential premises the level of rent (ie in excess of £1000) may mean that there is no nil rate for the premium,[14] as well as the rules for calculating the amount of 'rent' that is chargeable.

5.3   The legislation provides for a complex rate structure particularly when attempting to deal with nil rate or exempt bands and linked transactions[15] where the consideration includes both rent and other consideration in the case of leases of land, because there is an attempt to avoid the creation of two nil rate bands, ie for both the tax upon premium and rent. Where the consideration consists of both rent and other consideration, the stamp duty land tax appears to be the aggregate of the tax upon the rent plus the tax upon the consideration other than the rent but the computation of the tax upon the premium and upon the rent are governed by different principles and have to be dealt with in different parts of the land transaction return (SDLT 1).[16]

---

[11]   FA 2003, ss 55(4) and 108. See ibid, Sch 19, para 7 for the transitional provisions arising in relation to linking with pre-implementation date transactions.

[12]   HMRC Stamp Taxes did promise that there would be two separate regimes one dealing with a much simplified and less sophisticated chargeable and compliance regime for residential property and another dealing with commercial and complex transactions. Unfortunately, this promise that was made has not been delivered but the basically straightforward residential property transactions are subject to the same regime as large scale commercial transactions with the difficulties of seeking to understand the legislation designed to deal with the latter in relation to the former. There are few situations where special provisions apply to residential transactions such as the restriction upon the nil rate premium where the property relates to non-residential property and the rent exceeds £1000 or there are certain transactions within FA 2003, Sch 6A dealing with part-exchanges etc of residential property. However, subject to these very limited and special exemptions the same regime applies to small residential transactions as applies to very large transactions with complex issues.

[13]   This early removal is a clear indication of a self-inflicted wound occasioned by a taxpayer publicly boasting of the benefits to him of the relief where these benefits were not intended to arise. Taxpayers and their professional advisers should be aware of the need to exercise discretion in these areas especially where they are directors of companies with outside shareholders whose investments are jeopardised by such ill-considered public statements and who may take the view that the directors and their advisers are liable for negligent management of the company's business.

[14]   FA 2003, Sch 5, paras 9 and 9A.

[15]   Ibid, Sch 5, para 2(5) and (6).

[16]   However, owing to the design of the form the tax upon the rent although dealt with in a later part of the form has to be 'carried back' to an earlier part of the form dealing with the tax payable which has to deal with the aggregate figure (less any tax paid previously) notwithstanding that it is contained in the part of the form dealing with sales and not with leases.

TERMINOLOGY

'Residential property'

5.4   The rate structure depends upon whether the relevant land,[17] ie the land or an interest in which the chargeable interest is acquired,[18] is wholly or partly 'residential'.[19] Other situations where residential property is significant include:

- the transitional relief for disadvantaged land;

- the need to file SDLT 4;

- the availability of a nil rate for lease premiums.[20]

'Residential property' is defined[21] as meaning:[22]

- a building that is used or suitable for use as a dwelling;[23]

- a building that is in the process of being constructed or adapted for use as a dwelling;

- land that is or forms part of a garden or grounds of a building that is used or suitable for use or is being constructed or adapted for use as a dwelling; or

- an interest in or right over land that subsists for the benefit of a building or land suitable for use with a dwelling.

5.5   These provisions appear to require at least some completed construction works on the land, and land that is intended for the construction of a dwelling but no works of construction such as foundations have occurred is not residential.[24] This means that there may be a difference between agreeing to buy property that is to be constructed on the land so that there is a single contract for the purchase of the land and the building when constructed[25] and the chargeable consideration being fixed by reference the total of the land and the building prices and which may exceed the nil rate threshold for the time being and the situation where there is a purchase of the land from land with a related building agreement and only the land price may be subject to tax and since there is no building or start of a building upon the land at the relevant time it cannot be the purchase of a dwelling' so the transaction will qualify for the appropriate treatment as non-residential property.[26]

---

17   FA 2003, s 44(3)(a).
18   Ibid, s 44(6).
19   This, of course, provides the basis for significant increases in the rate of tax upon such property; see also **Chapter 10**.
20   FA 2003, Sch 5, paras 9 and 9A.
21   Ibid, s 116.
22   Ie this definition is exhaustive and not merely illustrative.
23   A purchase or lease from plan before work commences appears to be non-residential and the building works may escape tax; *Prudential Assurance Co Ltd v IRC* [1992] STC 863; see **Chapter 8**.
24   Demolition of pre-exiting works may be an intriguing issue.
25   FA 2003, Sch 4, para 10; *Prudential Assurance Co Ltd v IRC* [1992] STC 863; see **Chapter 8**.
26   See, for the question of related land and building works, the old stamp duty decisions such as *Prudential Assurance Co Ltd v IRC* [1992] STC 863 which HMRC Stamp Taxes have accepted as being relevant for the purposes of the charge to stamp duty land tax; see **5.93**.

'Dwelling'

5.6   There is no basic definition of a 'dwelling' but there is some guidance on a limited number of practical issues. It seems that this is likely to be extended by HMRC Stamp Taxes to apply to residential property that is not a totally self-contained unit but which involves shared utilisation of facilities such as kitchens and bathrooms. This basic concept of shared facilities as a dwelling is supported by certain specific statutory provisions.

Use as a dwelling

5.7   A 'dwelling' apparently in addition to its 'plain English' meaning is 'illustratively' extended to include certain situations. It is provided that a building is used as a dwelling when used as:

- residential accommodation for school pupils;

- residential accommodation for students other than accommodation as a hall of residence for students in further or higher education;

- residential accommodation for members of the armed forces;

- an institution that is the sole or main residence of at least 90 per cent of its residents and which is not used as:
  - a home or other institution providing residential accommodation for children;
  - a hall of residence for students in further or higher education;
  - a home or other institution providing residential accommodation with personal care for persons in need of personal care by reason of old age, disablement, past or present dependence on alcohol or drugs or past or present mental disorder. This, it would seem, would not necessarily cover the provision of hostel accommodation for unemployed or other homeless persons;
  - a hospital or hospice. This would seem to be limited to hospices providing accommodation with some form of medical treatment;
  - a prison or similar establishment;
  - a hotel, inn or similar establishment.[27] As hotels and inns are run for providing temporary accommodation on a profit-making basis, it is considered that 'similar establishments' will not extend to hostels and similar accommodation for homeless and other persons.

Where at the effective date the building is actually being used for any of the institutional purposes that are not regarded as the provision of dwellings, it is that actual use that is taken into account and the fact that it is suitable for any other use is to be ignored.

5.8   Where the building[28] is not in use at the relevant date but is suitable for a purpose that is to be treated as use as a dwelling and at least one other purpose that is not to be regarded as use as a dwelling (such as a hall of residence for students in further or higher education) then, if there is one such use for which it is more or most suitable, it is that

---

[27]   FA 2003, s 116(2) and (3); there is power to amend by statutory instrument in s 116(8)(a).
[28]   Again it seems that there must be some building on the land, not a clear site.

use that is the purpose to be taken into account when deciding whether it is a dwelling or not;[29] but otherwise the building is to be treated as suitable for use as a dwelling.[30]

5.9   It would seem that actual use or suitability for use at the time of the transaction governs the status of the property as residential or non-residential. The future use of the property does not appear to be a relevant consideration. This may mean that the timing and structure of transactions could be important. For example, where there is the acquisition of commercial property with a view to redevelopment as residential, such as the conversion of a hotel into flats, then its non-residential status will be the factor governing the liability or level of the nil rate for stamp duty land tax for that transaction; the future intended use will not be appropriate. On the other hand, if the property acquired consists of several dwellings and does not meet the relief for six or more dwellings acquired under a single transaction, the fact that the dwellings are empty and about to be demolished would indicate that the property is to be regarded as residential, and the fact that the existing buildings are to be demolished and converted into non-residential property is irrelevant.

Mixed property

5.10   For these purposes, 'building' includes part of a building[31] so that issues will arise where there is sale of a single structure with mixed use such as a shop with a flat above or a public house with accommodation. There is no specific procedure for dealing with such mixed use structures but it would seem that where there is a single transaction that includes such a structure it will be treated as one that is for 'mixed property', where special tables of rates apply;[32] For 'mixed' property the nil rate band extends to £150,000.[33] However, when determining the availability of the nil rate for small premiums a lease of mixed property is treated as two separate leases provided that any premium and/or rent is apportioned between the residential and the non-residential parts on a just and reasonable basis.[34]

Six or more properties

5.11   It is specifically provided that where there is a single transaction involving the transfer of major interests in or the grant of a lease over six or more separate dwellings those dwellings are treated as not involving residential property,[35] so that there is a slight increase in the nil rate threshold, which means that, in practice, the point is scarcely worth arguing in economic terms. Unfortunately there is no explanation of what is a 'single transaction' for these purposes but it is obviously not the same as a 'linked transaction',[36] since where there are linked transactions these remain 'a number' of separate chargeable transactions and consideration is aggregated for the purpose of the lower rates being the total chargeable consideration for 'all those transactions'. It is likely that, for example, a person proposing to redevelop by acquiring several adjacent properties or flats within a block with a view to demolition and construction of new

---

29   FA 2003, s 116(5)(a).
30   Ibid, s 116(5)(b).
31   Ibid, s 116(6).
32   Ibid, s 55(2), Table B.
33   Ibid, s 55(2), Table B, but note the restriction upon the availability of the nil rate band where the annual rent exceeds £1000 for non-residential property (FA 2003, Sch 5, paras 9(2) and 9A); for shared ownership transactions see FA 2003, Sch 9, para 2(4A).
34   FA 2003, Sch 5, paras 9 and 9A.
35   Ibid, s 116(7).
36   Ibid, s 108; see **5.113**.

premises or the refurbishment of existing premises will be dealing with separate vendors. Technically, this would be several separate transactions and not a single transaction but, *prima facie*, provided that he various vendors are not connected parties these would be unlinked transactions each separately entitled to the appropriate lower rate.[37] This is, however, clearly the type of transaction for which the relief was intended to be made available. The provision can, therefore, only be made to work on a reasonable basis if the words 'a single transaction' are interpreted in a wide sense of a 'single commercial transaction' which comprises several independent legal transactions; but, since as a general principle of construction 'transaction' means a 'chargeable transaction', this approach is technically not open and because the transaction may be unlinked the potential benefit of the lower rates may be lost. Moreover, the phrase 'a single transaction', by using the word 'single', would appear to preclude the application of the principle of statutory construction that the singular includes the plural. The extended definition applies only where there is a single seller. Separate acquisitions from different vendors do not qualify even where completion is linked, or the vendors are connected persons.

5.12   The effect of the legislation would seem to be that the policy is to make as much property residential (ie not exempt) as possible because this, generally, has a lower nil rate threshold compared with non-residential property although the temporary increase to £175,000 gives residential property a slight advantage where the transactions are not linked. There is also a benefit in that the nil rate band for lease premiums is not affected by the level of the rent for residential property,[38] but there is no nil rate for non-residential property where the annual rent exceeds £1000 and it is likely that in any borderline cases HMRC Stamp Taxes will seek to argue that the property is to be regarded as a 'dwelling'. However, where there is a proposed acquisition of several properties that will not or may not qualify for the favourable treatment as non-residential property, it may be appropriate to consider making the contracts entirely independent although the linked transaction principles make this a difficult exercise.[39] This could make the nil rate of stamp duty land tax available for each transaction.

5.13   It is important to note that the linked transaction rules which aggregate separate transactions for the purposes of the nil rate of stamp duty land tax require each of the transactions that are to be linked to be between the same parties or persons, or between persons connected with either of them. In consequence, it would seem that acquisition by a developer from five separate vendors, where the consideration falls into the nil rate band for each transaction, would not involve a 'linked transaction' and would be eligible for the nil rate or lower rate.

TRANSACTIONS INVOLVING WHOLLY RESIDENTIAL PROPERTY[40]

5.14   The basic charging structure is linked to residential property not in a disadvantaged area. There are minor variations in the structure where:

---

37   See **6.53**.
38   FA 2003, Sch 5, paras 9 and 9A.
39   See **5.113**.
40   FA 2003, s 55(2)(a) (as amended by FA 2006, s 162); for shared ownerships arrangements see FA 2003, Sch 9, para 2(4A).

- the ground rent reserved by a lease for non-residential property exceeds £1,000;[41] and

- the property is non-residential.

Consideration not including rent[42]

5.15   Where there is a sale of land or the grant of a lease which does not involve the payment of rent, ie a peppercorn only is payable.[43]

Relevant consideration	Percentage
Not more than £125,000 (temporarily £175,000)	0%
More than £125,000 (temporarily £175,000) but not more than £250,000	1%
More than £250,000 but not more than £500,000	3%
More than £500,000	4%

Consideration consisting solely of rent[44]

5.16   The stamp duty land tax is charged as a percentage of the net present value of the rent payable over the term of the lease.[45]

Relevant consideration, ie relevant rental value	Percentage
Not more than £125,000	0%
More than £125,000	1%

The 1 per cent rate applies only to the excess of the net present value over the nil rate threshold, not to the whole value.[46]

Consideration including premium and rent[47]

5.17   Stamp duty land tax is payable in respect of the rent in addition to the tax chargeable upon any other chargeable consideration[48] such as where the lease is granted for a ground rent but the tenant enters into obligations to carry out works that constitute a taxable premium[49] in accordance with the above tables.[50]

---

[41]   FA 2003, Sch 5, paras 9 and 9A for shared ownership see Sch 9, para 2(4A).
[42]   This Table includes premiums for leases.
[43]   There is a technical distinction between a peppercorn rent (no chargeable consideration) and a rent of £1 if demanded (chargeable consideration).
[44]   For the meaning of rent and the formula for the computation of the relevant rental value, see **7.108**.
[45]   FA 2003, Sch 5, para 2(4)(b).
[46]   Ibid, Sch 5, para 2 (as amended).
[47]   Eg a lease for a premium and a ground rent.
[48]   FA 2003, Sch 5, para 9(4).
[49]   FA 2003, Sch 4, para 10; see **Chapter 8**.

Stamp Duty Land Tax

TRANSACTIONS INVOLVING WHOLLY NON-RESIDENTIAL PROPERTY

5.18 However, the legislation looks towards the transaction taking effect, ie the acquisition arising by reason of statute rather than pursuant to the exercise of the statutory power. The exercise of a statutory power is, essentially, likely to be regarded as some form of contractual or consensual arrangement.

Consideration not including rent

5.19

Relevant consideration	Percentage
Not more than £150,000	0%
More than £150,000 but not more than £250,000	1%
More than £250,000 but not more than £500,000	3%
More than £500,000	4%

Consideration consisting solely of rent – basic charge

5.20

Relevant rental value	Percentage
Not more than £150,000	0%
The excess above £150,000	1%

Consideration including premium and rent

Rent

5.21

Relevant rental value	Percentage
Not more than £150,000	nil/exempt
The excess above £150,000	1%

Plus:

---

[50] The previous restriction of the nil rate for premiums where the average annual rent exceeded £600 has been removed for residential property; FA 2003, Sch 5, paras 9 and 9A.

Premium and annual rent not exceeding £1000 for non-residential premises

5.22

Relevant consideration	Percentage
Not more than £150,000	nil/exempt
More than £150,000 but not more than £250,000	1%
More than £250,000 but not more than £500,000	3%
More than £500,000	4%

Premium with annual rent exceeding £1000

5.23   Where there is a lease of non-residential property and the annual rent exceeds £1000 there is no nil rate for the premium. The average annual rent means the average annual rent over the term of the lease.[51] However, where different amounts of rent are payable for different parts of the term and those amounts (or any of them) are ascertainable at the effective date of the transaction, the average annual rent is the average annual rent over the period for which the highest ascertainable rent is payable. It seems, however, that where there is merely a ground rent which is 'variable' such as rent for a lease of a shop that is to double every 25 years, this is not treated initially as variable because the rent is fixed during the first 5 years of the term and this forms the general basis for taxing the rent. Subsequent increases are ignored unless producing an 'abnormal increase' in the rent and, it seems, do not retrospectively cancel the nil rate for the premium.

5.24   For these purposes the 'annual rent' means the average annual rent over the term of the lease.[52] However, if different amounts of rent are payable for different parts of the term and those amounts, or any of them, are ascertainable at the effective date of the transaction the average annual rent over the period for which the highest ascertainable rent is payable is the 'annual rent'. This can give rise to some difficulties in interpretation. Substituting £1000 for £600 in the following illustrations for what they are worth the views of HMRC Stamp Taxes are as follows:[53]

Lease premium: Relevant Rental Figure (May 2007)

5.25   This page relates only to the calculation of the relevant rental figure for the purposes of calculating stamp duty land tax (SDLT) on premiums, under paras 9(2A) and (3) of Sch 5 Finance Act 2003. Where consideration for a lease is in the form of both premium and rental payments, these are considered together for the purposes of SDLT so that the tax-free threshold is not available twice for the same transaction (*see*

---

[51]   FA 2003, Sch 5, para 9(3).
[52]   Consequential changes have been made in relation to disadvantaged land, the relief for charities where the £600 figures is increased to £1000. Similar adjustments are made in relation to partnerships and for the provisions dealing with loans or deposits in connection with the grant or assignment of a lease that are treated as premiums; FA 2003, Sch 17A, para 18A.
[53]   These refer to £600 but the principles are useful for non-residential property and the £1,000 rent threshold.

SDLTM13010). The rental figures used for determining net present value and for calculating SDLT on the rental element may be different – *see* SDLTM13075.

The relevant rental figure is determined by the rent each year.

If the annual rent is the same for each year of the lease, this is the relevant rental figure.

If the rent is variable, you need to determine what the ascertainable rent is each year. Rent is ascertainable if you know you are going to have to pay at least this amount for the year. The relevant rental figure is then the highest ascertainable annual rent during the term of the lease.

Lease premium: Relevant Rental Figure: Example 1 (May 2007)

5.26 This page relates only to the calculation of the relevant rental figure for the purposes of calculating stamp duty land tax (SDLT) on premiums, under paras 9(2A) and (3) of Sch 5 Finance Act 2003. Where consideration for a lease is in the form of both premium and rental payments, these are considered together for the purposes of SDLT so that the tax-free threshold is not available twice for the same transaction (*see* SDLTM13010). The rental figures used for determining net present value and for calculating SDLT on the rental element may be different – *see* SDLTM13075.

> *Example 1*
>
> A residential lease for 999 years is granted on 1 December 2005 for a premium of £90,000 and a ground rent of £200 per year. The ground rent does not change.
>
> The relevant rental figure is £200 which does not exceed £600 so **does not** cause the residential threshold to be modified for the purposes of calculating tax on the premium.
>
> No SDLT is payable on the premium as it is below the threshold of £120,000 for the 0 per cent rate band for residential property. However, the transaction is notifiable as the lease is for 7 years or more and chargeable consideration has been given (*see* SDLTM12010).

Calculation of stamp duty land tax: Lease premium: Relevant Rental Figure: Example 2 (May 2007)

5.27 This page relates only to the calculation of the relevant rental figure for the purposes of calculating stamp duty land tax (SDLT) on premiums, under paras 9(2A) and (3) of Sch 5 Finance Act 2003. Where consideration for a lease is in the form of both premium and rental payments, these are considered together for the purposes of SDLT so that the tax-free threshold is not available twice for the same transaction (see SDLTM13010). The rental figures used for determining net present value and for calculating SDLT on the rental element may be different – *see* SDLTM13075.

> *Example 2*
>
> A residential lease for 999 years is granted on 1 December 2005 for a premium of £90,000 and a ground rent of £750 per year. The ground rent does not change.

The relevant rental figure is the same as the annual rent in this case, ie £750. As this is more than £600, the 0 per cent threshold is not available for the purposes of calculating tax on the premium. As the premium is below the £250,000 threshold, it is taxable at 1 per cent.

Calculation of stamp duty land tax: Lease premium: Relevant Rental Figure: Example 3 (May 2007)

5.28 This page relates only to the calculation of the relevant rental figure for the purposes of calculating stamp duty land tax (SDLT) on premiums, under paras 9(2A) and (3) of Sch 5 Finance Act 2003. Where consideration for a lease is in the form of both premium and rental payments, these are considered together for the purposes of SDLT so that the tax-free threshold is not available twice for the same transaction (*see* SDLTM13010). The rental figures used for determining net present value and for calculating SDLT on the rental element may be different – *see* SDLTM13075.

Example 3

A residential lease for 999 years is granted on 1 December 2005 for a premium of £275,000 and a ground rent of £250 per year. The ground rent does not change.

The relevant rental figure is the annual rent of £250. As this is below £600, the 0 per cent threshold would be available for the purposes of calculating SDLT on the premium element of the consideration. However the premium exceeds the £250,000 threshold so is taxable at 3 per cent.

Calculation of stamp duty land tax: Lease premium: Relevant Rental Figure: Example 4 (May 2007)

5.29 This page relates only to the calculation of the relevant rental figure for the purposes of calculating stamp duty land tax (SDLT) on premiums, under paras 9(2A) and (3) of Sch 5 Finance Act 2003. Where consideration for a lease is in the form of both premium and rental payments, these are considered together for the purposes of SDLT so that the tax-free threshold is not available twice for the same transaction (*see* SDLTM13010). The rental figures used for determining net present value and for calculating SDLT on the rental element may be different – *see* SDLTM13075.

Example 4

A residential lease for 999 years is granted on 1 December 2005 for a premium of £90,000 and a ground rent of £200 per year. The ground rent doubles every 25 years for the first 100 years.

The rent in this case is variable so, per Paragraph 9(3) Schedule 5 FA 2003, the relevant rental figure is the highest ascertainable annual rent during the term of the lease:

The ground rent payable in years 1 – 25 is £200;

The ground rent payable in years 26 – 50 is £400;

The ground rent payable in years 51 – 75 is £800; and

The ground rent payable in years 76 – 100 is £1,600.

The relevant rental figure is therefore £1,600.

As this is more than £600, the 0 per cent residential threshold is not available for the purposes of calculating tax on the premium. The premium is taxable at 1 per cent as it is below the £250,000 threshold.

5.30   This has been amended by the insertion of a new para 9A where the transaction involves non-residential property. Broadly with effect on and after 12 March 2008 the rental limit is increased to £1000. It is provided that where the relevant land consists entirely of non-residential property the nil rate band does not apply to the premium if the relevant rent is at least £1000. Where the relevant land is partly residential and partly non-residential property the nil rate band does not apply if the rent attributable on a just and reasonable apportionment to the non-residential land is at least £1000. For these purposes where there are residential and non-residential properties involved the transaction is treated as if it were two separate transactions or two sets of linked transactions namely:

• one consisting of all the residential property interests and another consisting of all of the non-residential property. The annual rent has essentially the same definition as that considered above.

5.31

Relevant consideration	Percentage
Not more than £250,000	1%
More than £250,000 but not more than £500,000	3%
More than £500,000	4%

LAND WHICH IS PARTLY RESIDENTIAL AND PARTLY NON-RESIDENTIAL

5.32   A special regime applies to mixed property transactions including leases of property such as a sale of a shop with a flat above it.

Sales of mixed land

5.33   It is treated as non-residential property, ie the nil rate threshold is £150,000.[54]

Leases of mixed property

5.34   The level of the rent no longer affects the nil rate threshold for residential property but rent in excess of £1000 for non-residential property cancels the nil rate for lease premiums.[55] In the case of a lease of mixed property this is treated as two separate leases, one residential and one non-residential taxable accordingly provided that any premium and rent is apportioned on a just and reasonable basis.[56]

---

[54]   FA 2003, s 55(2)(b), Table B.
[55]   Ibid, Sch 5, paras 9 and 9A.
[56]   Ibid, Sch 4, para 4.

SPECIAL RATES

5.35   It should be noted that there are certain special rates,[57] namely:

*   0.5 per cent stamp duty land tax applicable in relation to certain corporate reorganisations contained in para 8 of Sch 7 to the FA 2003;[58]

*   acquisitions by collective enfranchisement by qualifying companies and crofters' right to buy[59] where average rates apply.

In some cases the rate is not adjusted but special rules may apply to determine the amount of the consideration which is chargeable such as by substituting market value[60] or by excluding certain consideration as in partitions of jointly owned land,[61] or exchanges of non-major interests[62] or surrenders and regrants of leases.[63]

Lower rates of stamp duty land tax

5.36   The lower rates of stamp duty land tax are dependent upon the chargeable transaction not being a linked transaction with other chargeable transactions where the aggregate consideration exceeds £500,000 or the aggregate net present value of the rents for the various leases exceeds £125,000 (£175,000 temporarily) or £150,000. It is provided[64] that if the transaction is a linked transaction the relevant consideration for the purchaser of determining the rate of stamp duty land tax is the aggregate of the chargeable consideration for all of the linked transactions.[65] Consideration that is not 'chargeable' because, for example, it relates to chattels is not to be aggregated for these purposes.[66] Obviously, where there are linked transactions and the consideration aggregated over the transactions is below £500,000, then the relevant lower rate will apply.

LINKED TRANSACTIONS

Basic principles[67]

5.37   The chargeable consideration[68] for several different transactions such as transactions involving different contracts to acquire several separate properties may

---

[57]   Exemptions and reliefs are described in more detail in **Chapters 11** and **12**.
[58]   See **12.34**.
[59]   FA 2003, ss 55(5) (as amended), 74 and 75; see **Chapter 11**.
[60]   Ibid, s 53 (connected companies).
[61]   Ibid, Sch 4, para 6; see **5.169**.
[62]   Ibid, Sch 4, para 5(4); see **5.151**.
[63]   Ibid, Sch 17A, para 16.
[64]   FA 2003, s 55(4)(b).
[65]   The linked transaction test also applies in identifying the relevant chargeable interests where consideration has to be aggregated for those purposes: ibid, s 55(4)(a).
[66]   On this important issue of fixtures, see **4.10**.
[67]   There are certain practical benefits in these rules such as the ability to use a single land transaction return for several transactions where these have the same effective date thereby reducing the compliance costs. Unfortunately, in practice HMRC Stamp Taxes have taken the position that if several chargeable transactions have the same effective date they are automatically linked and are likely to launch an Enquiry which will reduce and possibly cancel the cost saving of a single return. The tactics of filing returns have considerable practical consequences for cost saving.
[68]   The linked transaction principles are concerned only with the aggregation of chargeable consideration; but

have to be aggregated where there are linked transactions. In other situations involving leases the renewal of the lease may produce an aggregated term for the two leases requiring a retrospective adjustment which may affect the rates.[69] The purpose of the linked transaction rules is to prevent taxpayers from mitigating the charge to stamp duty land tax by fragmenting their transaction so that the chargeable consideration falls below a tax rate threshold thereby attracting a lower rate of tax. Contrary to popular opinion amongst many practitioners,[70] it is not possible to reduce the tax charge simply by entering into different contracts even where these are entered into on different dates and provide for separate completions on different dates. The definitions and the transaction-based structure of the tax mean that it is the commercial or negotiated basis of the arrangements such as a discount for purchasing several new properties not the legal structure which is important.

5.38   The rules, however, do not empower HMRC Stamp Taxes to change the nature of the transaction and to convert separate contracts for the purchase or lease of land and for building works into a single contract for the sale or lease of a completed building.[71] Since the linked transactions relate only to chargeable consideration, it is important to note that the charging provisions sometimes refer to transactions below a certain level as 'exempt' and sometimes states that a particular area of consideration, whether rent or other consideration, does not constitute chargeable consideration or is to be treated as nil. It seems that the variable use of language is important in the context of linked transactions and notification obligations. In the case of the former, the rate threshold is determined by aggregating the chargeable consideration for all linked transactions.[72] Obviously where the legislative provisions state that the chargeable consideration is deemed to be 'nil' there is nothing to aggregate and other transactions may qualify for a reduced rate. The status of transactions to be treated as 'exempt' is unclear. *Prima facie*, it is open to HMRC Stamp Taxes to take the point that such consideration is chargeable notwithstanding that the particular transaction is itself 'exempt'. However, as the aggregation of such consideration would, to some extent, nullify the benefit of the exemption and because a transaction which is 'exempt' is not meant to be a transaction giving rise to an actual charge to tax,[73] the transaction would appear to escape from the aggregation requirement of linked transactions, because being 'exempt' it does not generate chargeable consideration. It remains to be seen whether, in practice, HMRC Stamp Taxes accept what would seem to be the correct view in practice.

5.39   Unfortunately, the linked transaction rules operate on a retrospective basis. As part of the provisional basis of much of stamp duty land tax,[74] a subsequent linked transaction such as the renewal of a lease[75] will require a recalculation of the tax originally paid when the lease was granted. In some situations these obligations are by statute passed to third parties.[76]

---

where there are linked transaction with the same effective date a single land transaction return for all the transactions may be filed; FA 2003, s 108(2) but this is a problem since multiple Revenue certificates (SDLT 5) may be necessary where the various properties are in different Land Registries since HMRC Stamp Taxes seem to have difficulty in producing multiple certificates.

69   FA 2003, Sch 17A, para 5; see **7.105**.
70   Which exposes them and their clients to risks of significant penalties; see FA 2003, ss 95 and 96.
71   See **Chapter 8**; note the treatment for the general anti-avoidance provisions; FA 2003, s 75B(3)(a).
72   FA 2003, s 55(3)(b).
73   Ibid, s 49(1).
74   See **Chapter 1**.
75   FA 2003, Sch 17A, para 6.
76   Ibid, s 81A; Sch 17A, para 12.

Exchanges and linked transactions

5.40   HMRC Stamp Taxes take the views that linked transactions can move in opposite directions and special rules apply where the parties to the transaction are connected persons. In their view a transfer from A to B is linked with B's provision of the consideration from B to A. This would seem to provide a very different policy from that normally associated with the linked transaction rules namely it is designed to prevent parties from fragmenting movements of separate items[77] of property from A to B not with preventing B from providing consideration in a variety of forms. In consequence, it has been their view that land exchanges are linked transactions. This view was gradually abandoned on the basis that only transactions moving in the same direction could be linked but this was not accepted by HMRC Stamp Taxes in relation to land exchanges between connected parties. Thus where a mother was transferring her house to daughter in exchange for daughter's flat these were linked transactions notwithstanding the movement in opposite directions and the values had to be aggregated in order to determine the rate. This was abandoned only by legislation which is no doubt a deliberate policy by HMRC Stamp Taxes in order to provide themselves with support for the view that movement in opposite directions are linked transactions for other purposes. It remains to be seen in what other context HMRC Stamp Taxes would wish to link and aggregate transactions in opposite directions.

5.41   The problem in relation to exchanges between connected parties was also based upon a further argument which is the reason why there was self-serving legislation to deal with the situation rather than accepting a particular line of principle. This was that transactions were automatically linked if they were between the same parties or persons connected with either of them. Therefore, transactions are, in the view of HMRC Stamp Taxes, automatically linked if A is connected with B such as where there is a renewal of an expired lease by the exercise of an option to review where the landlord and tenant at the time of the exercise of the option are connected regardless of the identity of the parties at the time of the grant of the lease and regardless of and dealings in the lease or the landlord's interest during the term of the lease. This is clearly a totally flawed analysis since the linked transaction rules are intended to deal with situations of connected vendors or landlords or connected purchasers or tenants for the original transaction. The reference is to the parties on one side of the transaction being connected, not to the parties on both sides of the transaction being connected. Nevertheless, it seems that HMRC Stamp Taxes are intending to press this argument that transactions are automatically linked if the parties are connected. The areas where this is apparently giving rise to difficulties in practice from time to time relate to holding over where the tenant holding over pursuant to the Landlord and Tenant Act 1954 is connected with the landlord or where there are negotiations for a new lease or the exercise of an option to renew a lease and the landlord and the tenant are connection. In this case HMRC Stamp Taxes do not require any pre-existing scheme or arrangement; in their view it is sufficient to link the transactions if the parties are connected. This analysis is doubly flawed because it order to be linked transactions there has to be a scheme or arrangement linking the two events and whilst the fact that the parties are connected might provide the basis for some form of assumption or inference that there was the possibility of a scheme or arrangement it does not provide the basis for an argument that the connection of the parties automatically overrides the requirement for a scheme or arrangement such as where A grants a lease to B Ltd which is a subsidiary of C Ltd and at that time is totally unconnected with A. Subsequently A's company,

---

[77]   But the successive linked leases principles relate to transactions affecting the same property; FA 2003, Sch 17A, para 5; see **7.105**.

D Ltd, acquires the undertaking of B Ltd including the lease which it renews. There can be no scheme for the holding over or renewal notwithstanding that the parties are connected. This view of HMRC Stamp Taxes is also manifest nonsense since if land exchanges are not linked simply because the parties are the same, the fact that they are connected is irrelevant. Connected parties only become relevant if there is a commercial linkage of acquisitions moving in the same direction; they cannot of themselves link a transaction where there is no linkage on the facts or in law such as a basic land exchange.

Definition

5.42   FA 2003, s 108, provides that transactions are linked if they form part:

• of a[78] single scheme, arrangement or series of transactions,[79]

• between the same vendor and purchaser or, in either case, persons connected with them.[80]

There are also certain provisions deeming transactions to be linked[81] or unlinked.[82]

Single scheme[83]

5.43   The terminology utilising words such as 'arrangement'[84] raises practical problems. The linked transaction principles are clearly intended to be wider than the certificate of value test, which required some form of contractual linkage so that independent gifts and unlinked contracts were separate transactions. However, the drafting suggests that it is intended to bring within linked transactions those transactions which are merely commercially linked in the sense that, although the contracts are legally independent, one agreement would not have been signed unless the other agreements were also executed at the same time.[85] Linkage would also appear to apply to a series of gifts where these are part of a pre-arranged scheme designed, for example, to reduce the effect of the connected company charges[86] or the effect upon the

---

[78]   The use of 'a' reinforces the need or HMRC Stamp Taxes to prove that there is one scheme and not two. It may be that if there is a change of intention the various steps may, for certain purposes, be connected (*Clarke Chapman John Thompson Ltd v IRC* [1975] STC 567) but it cannot make the various steps 'a' single transaction. HMRC Stamp Taxes have taken the contrary interpretation in relation to 'a' scheme of reconstruction on advice abandoned the argument literally at the doors of the Court of the appeal. In that case the original intention was to acquire both the ordinary shares and the preference shares in the target company. Initially the preference shareholders indicated that they would accept the first proposal. The offer was circulated on the basis of being only for the ordinary shares. Subsequent discussions produced a proposal that was acceptable to the preference shareholder and a formal offer was made that was accepted. The effect of the capitulation by HMRC Stamp Taxes was that because of the original interest the two offers were connected but were two separate schemes.

[79]   Note the possible arguments on these terms from the similar wording for certificates of value for lower rates of stamp duty based upon *A-G v Cohen* [1936] 2 KB 246.

[80]   Income and Corporation Taxes Act 1988, s 839.

[81]   See, for example, FA 2003, Sch 17A, para 14(5)(b).

[82]   FA 2003, Sch 17A, paras 12A(2), 14.

[83]   A series of transactions would require some form of contractual linkage rather than a mere commercial arrangement.

[84]   Not defined for these purposes.

[85]   Cf the approach for stamp duty in *Kimbers & Co v IRC* [1936] 1 KB 132; *Prudential Assurance Co Ltd v IRC* [1992] STC 863 where such commercial interdependence was held to be irrelevant.

[86]   FA 2003, s 53.

market value for the special partnership charges[87] or the charge upon gifts of land subject to a mortgage intended to reduce the amount of the mortgage brought into charge on each occasion. Such transactions are now linked even though they are not contractually interdependent. Attempts to obtain the benefit of the lower rates by having separate contracts[88] separate parties or separate completions will no longer be certain of success depending upon the background negotiations.[89]

5.44 There are, however, wide-ranging issues concerning what, as a matter of fact and/or law, will be regarded as a single arrangement. For example, in order to mitigate the stamp duty land tax upon the rent the parties may agree to grant and take a short lease with an option to renew. Clearly the new lease may[90] be linked with the option; the question is whether the fact that the option to renew is contained within the lease itself means that the new lease is linked with the original lease so that the terms of the two leases have to be aggregated into a retrospective single lease.[91] To some extent this may depend upon the facts of the particular case, i e whether there was a clear understanding between the parties that the option would be exercised so that there is a single arrangement. Notwithstanding that this approach requires a recalculation of the stamp duty land tax upon the original lease,[92] and involves an unacceptable level of retroactive effect,[93] it may mean that any exemption originally available, such as disadvantaged land relief, remains, in effect, available for the new lease because this is an extension of the original lease. HMRC Stamp Taxes should they manage to find evidence upon what they can justifiably challenge the taxpayer's self-assessment return are likely to press this point ingenuously if they believe that there has been a significant change in the pattern of leasing leading to a loss of revenue.

5.45 Problems will arise over whether there is 'a' scheme for the acquisition of several properties or 'several' independent schemes for the acquisition of numerous properties. In the latter case the transaction will not be linked. This raises many difficult questions of evidence and whether the evidence obtained by HMRC Stamp Taxes justifies finding of facts that in law constitute the existence of a 'scheme' etc relating to the negotiations for the purchase or lease of the several properties involved. Broadly, and at some risk to accuracy, the test is likely to be whether the parties would not have entered into the various purchase agreements or the terms such as the price and any discount would have been the same unless all agreements were signed or had entered into an agreement (not necessarily contractual) for one of the properties before discussing the purchase of the second or subsequent properties. The lapse of time between events may also be a significant factor. In the latter case there are several schemes or arrangements and the first or prior agreements were intended to proceed notwithstanding that there might or might not be subsequent sales. Obviously other factors may be relevant such as a discount on the price because several properties are being acquired and the discount would not have been available unless there was a multiple purchase. Establishing the separateness of the different purchases or leases will be difficult. It is, therefore, important that when completing the relevant land transaction return a detailed

---

[87]   Ibid, Sch 15, Part 3 (as amended).

[88]   Note the comments on incorrect use of certificates of value in *Lloyds and Scottish v Prentice* 121 SJ 847 (on appeal *Lloyds and Scottish v Cyril Lord* [1992] BCLC 609).

[89]   Professional advisers dealing with the form may find it prudent to obtain a detailed contemporaneous file note from the taxpayer and hope that the vendor and his advisers will, if questioned during any Enquiry, tell the same version of the events leading to the contract or contracts.

[90]   But not necessarily; and is not linked where the current tenant is an assignee; see **5.52**.

[91]   For the issues where the option has been exercised after the lease has been assigned, see **5.49**.

[92]   FA 2003, Sch 17A, para 5.

[93]   Including the reallocation of the nil rate band to other leases.

contemporaneous file note of the client's view of the facts is prepared. There is, however, the risk that the subsequent recollection of the vendor or its agents as to the nature of the negotiations will not be identical with the statements by the client which will be a problem upon any subsequent Enquiry where HMRC Stamp Taxes utilise their powers to obtain information from third parties.[94]

5.46 Separate acquisitions at an auction would not appear to be linked notwithstanding that they are between the same parties because they are not a single arrangement.[95] In this case each individual property is acquired and the contract made and is not affected by the fact that an attempt by the purchaser to acquire property put up by the same vendor are or are not successful. It is not a case of the first property being acquired only if the second property is acquired or vice versa.

Retrospection

5.47 The transaction-based nature of stamp duty land tax and the statutory references to 'schemes' and 'arrangements' means that the linked transaction principles operate on a retrospective basis ie the original land transaction return (SDLT 1) will have to be adjusted in the light of the subsequent event.[96] Thus the tax upon the grant of an option may have to be retrospectively adjusted when it is exercised and the relevant contract is substantially performed or completed.[97] However, there have to be at least two transactions before there can be anything to link. In consequence, as at its own effective date the first chargeable transaction stands alone and there is no other transaction with which it can be 'linked' at that time, subsequent events may be linked transactions. In general, linked transactions arise only where the parties to the related transaction are the same persons or persons connected with either of them.[98] However, third parties may be affected, particularly assignees of leases.[99] Their transactions may not themselves be linked transactions but they may be affected by linked transactions between the original parties such as retrospective increases in the tax liabilities relating to their chargeable interest for which they are liable.[100] Surprisingly, therefore, subsequent transactions may retrospectively change the provisional nature of the initial land transaction return,[101] even where there are transactions involving other persons and in which the taxpayer is not only not involved but of which he may also be unaware unless he has taken prudent commercial steps in negotiating the contracts and leases. Due diligence by prospective purchasers is essential.

5.48 This retrospection has a wide-ranging application. Subsequent events can increase the tax on the chargeable transaction requiring a totally new land transaction return and the payment of the additional tax.[102] This problem is particularly acute for lease renewals[103] where the successive linked lease will require a retrospective adjustment

---

[94]   See **Chapter 21**.
[95]   *Cohen and Moore v IRC* [1933] 2 KB 126.
[96]   FA 2003, s 81A; see also Sch 17A, para 12.
[97]   Ibid, s 46; see **4.35** and **5.78**.
[98]   Ibid, s 108.
[99]   Ibid, s 81A; Sch 17A, para 12.
[100] Ibid, Sch 17A, para 12; Sch 5, para 2(6); s 81A.
[101] The completion of the land transaction return (SDLT 1) on the basis that the transaction is not linked will be correct at the time but this will become retrospectively incorrect if there are appropriate subsequent transactions.
[102] FA 2003, s 81A.
[103] Ibid, Sch 17A, para 5.

of the tax on both the original lease and any other leases of other property with which it is linked notwithstanding these leases are vested in third parties not involved in the lease renewal itself.[104]

Subsequent problems

5.49   As it is possible for a later lease, including, it seems, the renewal of a lease pursuant to the exercise of an option, to be linked with the initial grant of the lease of those premises, it would appear to be the case that a subsequent lease may be linked with the grant of the original leases of other premises.[105] This will require, *inter alia*, a retrospective re-allocation of the nil rate relief between the leases in the initial tax computation. This will, in consequence, require additional calculations and possibly notifications to be made in respect of each of the leases that were linked upon the initial grant. This will arise every time there is a linked transaction by renewal of any of the leases concerned. An assignee of any of those leases will need to know the amount of nil rate relief that has been allocated to the lease that he is acquiring and of any subsequent adjustment thereof by reasonable later linked transactions to which he is not a party. It is necessary for him to require information of any adjustments made by the assignor or any third assignees of any of the leases as a result of linked transactions, since the obligation to make further returns in respect of land transactions attaches to the lease and passes to the assignee.[106]

5.50   Additionally this general principle of construction is reinforced by specific legislation. It is provided[107] that options 'may be' linked with the subsequent exercise and there are detailed provisions dealing with the renewal of leases.[108]

Subsales and assignments

5.51   Where there is a subsale or a partial assignment of the benefit of an unperformed contract[109] there will be no linkage between the balance of the original contract and the part assigned since these will be treated[110] in many cases as separate contracts between different parties ie the taxable transaction ie the taxable transaction is the secondary contract between the first purchaser and the second purchaser and it will, in consequence, have to be viewed in the context of its own surrounding circumstances such as whether it is part of an arrangement. The fact that the first purchaser is a party to a contract for the acquisition of several properties does not, of itself, taint the subsale or assignment arrangements.

The same parties

5.52   It is important to note that linked transactions apply predominantly only between the same parties, ie the same acquirer and the same disposer. The starting point of HMRC Stamp Taxes is based on this, namely if the parties to the various transactions are the same it is, in their view, automatically linked particularly if the

[104]   Ibid, Sch 17A, para 12.
[105]   Ibid, Sch 17A, para 5.
[106]   Ibid, s 81A.
[107]   Ibid, s 46; see **14.32** and **5.78**.
[108]   Ibid, Sch 17A, para 6; see **7.105**.
[109]   See **Chapter 6**.
[110]   Pursuant to FA 2003, s 45.

parties are connected.[111] However, this is clearly incorrect; notwithstanding their refusal to consider the factual circumstances of each case, these evidentiary issues are important and their rigid approach can be challenged although this will require patience and persistence.

Assignees and other third parties

5.53   It is stated that the linked transaction rules apply only as between the same parties or persons connected with either of them. This raises problems for assignees of property interests in two respects, namely:

- how far assignees are affected by linked transactions between the original party and the assignor. Specific statutory provisions impose surprising obligations upon such arrangements and these are considered elsewhere;[112] and

- how far transactions entered into by an assignee such as the exercise of an option to renew a lease are themselves linked transactions.

There are also unresolved issues as to whether these problems are complicated by the fact that the assignee is a person connected with the assignor, especially where the assignment is unconnected with the original transaction.

5.54   There are two basic issues for the latter situation, namely:

- whether in law the assignee is to be treated as an original party to the transaction because he steps into the shoes of the assignor and becomes a party to the original contract and so in the view of HMRC Stamp Taxes becomes a substitute party to the original 'arrangements' or scheme and, if he is 'the same party';

- whether on the facts the assignment means that there cannot be a single scheme or arrangement notwithstanding the original understandings between the original parties.

Assignee as same person

5.55   As regards the first question, if, for example, A may grant an option to B, who assigns it to C, who exercises the option. In such a case there is a question whether C's contract pursuant to the exercise of the option is to be linked with the premium paid for the grant of the option. For other purposes, HMRC Stamp Taxes have accepted that an assignee may qualify as being the same person as the assignor but this is in a context as to the performance of the original contract ie whether the performance of a contract is between appropriate parties notwithstanding the change of purchaser by reason of the assignment; it is the same contract but a different person entitled to the right. It is considered that for the purposes of stamp duty land tax the assignor and the assignee are not the same person notwithstanding they occupy the same position in relation to the same contract,[113] so that the grant of the option and the substantial performance of

---

[111]   In their incorrect view the connection of the parties is itself sufficient to link transactions; no 'scheme' being required; see **5.41**.

[112]   FA 2003, s 81A; Sch 17A, para 12; see **7.235**.

[113]   See, eg, FA 2003, s 45.

the contract arising pursuant to its exercise by an assignee is not a linked transaction. This will be a significant issue in practice in a few years' time when assignees of leases begin to exercise the options to renew.

5.56 The fact that one of the parties to the transaction is connected to another party to the transaction such as a subsidiary of a purchaser or grantee of an option means that the transaction is between the same parties because the relevant parties are connected persons. Therefore, it will not be easy to fragment transactions by arranging for various interests to be acquired by separate companies within the same group or different members of the family.

Assignee and linked event

5.57 Should the assignee be the same person as the assignor for these purposes, it is an open question whether the assignee of a lease who exercises the option to renew the lease will be tainted by the fact that there was an arrangement between the landlord and the original tenant that the option would be exercised and the consideration provided for the assignment of the lease was influenced by the existence of the option to renew.[114] It is thought that such a situation is not a linked transaction because the decision to exercise the option to renew is *prima facie* made upon independent circumstances relevant to the assignee of the lease or other chargeable interest. This problem is likely to be particularly acute in relation to the assignment of options to purchase land such as part of a corporate reconstruction.

Connected parties

5.58 Unfortunately, the linked transactions legislation is not limited solely to transactions between the same parties; it extends to transactions that are otherwise linked but are between different parties where the parties are connected with either the vendor or the purchaser. For example, where there is an arrangement to sell or lease several properties by the same vendor or to the person who negotiated the arrangement but the intention is to operate the splitting of the agreement into several contracts between members of that person's family or the family company or separate subsidiaries within the same group,[115] this will not 'unlink' the various acquisitions.

5.59 Linked transaction problems arise where there are 'connected vendors'. *Prima facie,* the acquisition of several properties by a purchaser from different vendors will not be linked; but if the various vendors are connected with each other the transactions will be linked if the other conditions for linkage are present. For example, A agrees to acquire the freehold interest from B and the leasehold interest from C Ltd. Notwithstanding that A would not sign or complete either agreement unless both were exchanged the transactions are, *prima facie*, not linked because there are different vendors. However, if B is either solely or together with members of his family, the controller of C Ltd the linkage will be reinstated because the two sellers are connected.

---

[114] It is considered that the assignment and the exercise of the option are not linked transactions because they are between different parties. It is only the original grant and the subsequent exercise that may be linked.

[115] On the definition of 'connected persons' see Income and Corporation Taxes Act 1988, s 839.

Multiple parties

5.60   There are often situations where there are multiple sellers to a single purchaser or multiple purchasers from a single vendor or multiple subpurchasers of parts of the property from a single purchaser and there may be some 'arrangement' involved in the transaction. For example, there may be the situation where someone has organised a property investment syndicate whereby numerous purchasers or tenants are combining to acquire a block of flats from the developer, probably at the stage before the building works commence.[116] In this situation the person organising the syndicate will have, no doubt, negotiated a favourable price because the developer is guaranteed that all of the properties will be sold. Clearly there is a commercial negotiation which provides the necessary 'a single' scheme. However, there will be individual and separate purchasers and tenants for each flat, although some may take several flats. Clearly if a particular tenant is taking several leases then it will be almost inevitable that these leases are linked transactions and he will not be in a position to unlink the transactions by directing the leases be granted to members of his family or to a connected company or to trustees of settlements. However, there may be numerous participants and it is necessary for any person acquiring a property to investigate whether any of the other participants in the arrangements are connected with him. This is a difficult problem for solicitors and licensed conveyancers, since they may be acting for only one purchaser and may not be aware either that there is a single scheme for the acquisition of numerous properties nor will they necessarily be aware, without investigation, of whether any of the other participants are connected with their particular client. Nevertheless, it is necessary to carry out the investigation before advising on whether the transaction is linked. However, the fact that one or more of the parties may be connected with other parties does not necessarily taint the whole arrangement. The connected party principle will link or maintain the linkage only between those contracts to which the connected persons are parties. A genuinely unconnected third party, who is buying one of the properties, will not be linked and will be entitled to whatever lower rate, if any, may be appropriate.

5.61   Similarly a developer may wish to acquire the whole of a block of flats or a terrace of houses. In this situation there will be a negotiation by a single purchaser with numerous sellers. The linkage will become quite strong because the contracts will almost inevitably contain a provision that one contract will not complete unless all of the other related contracts also complete at the same time. However, the contracts will be 'unlinked' where the sellers are not connected persons. In this situation there may, of course, be situations where some or all of the sellers are connected because, being members of the same family, they are living in adjoining properties. This connection between particular vendors will maintain the linkage as regards those contracts but as regards the agreements with unconnected persons the separate identity rules will unlink the transaction giving the purchaser the benefit of whatever lower rates may be appropriate for that individual transaction. The fact that some of the vendors are connected and their transactions are linked does not, automatically, taint all of the contracts in the arrangement as linked transactions for these purposes. This can be a significant practical problem for solicitors acting for the purchaser where the vendors have different surnames; but it is necessary to investigate whether they are connected because the surname may represent changes of name such as on marriage. The issues for investigation by solicitors acting for purchasers will be immediately obvious because they are likely to be acting for the purchaser knowing that there are multiple vendors but

---

[116]   In these circumstances the impact of FA 2003, Sch 17A, para 12B may need to be watched in order to avoid potential downside consequences for the individual tenants.

they need to be spotted at the inception of the transaction so that the costs can be taken into account when quoting to the potential clients.

Notification obligations in relation to simultaneous linked transactions

5.62 Where there are simultaneous linked transactions such as disposals or leases of various properties notification will be required, particularly in the case of leases because of the need to apportion the nil rate slice between the rents for the various leases by reference to their proportion of total net present value.[117]

5.63 HMRC Stamp Taxes offered the facility of simultaneous filing of linked transactions upon the same SDLT 1 in order to reduce the costs of taxpayers. Where there are two or more and including persons connected with the purchaser(s) linked transactions with the same effective date,[118] the purchaser, or all of the purchasers[119] if more than one, may make a single land transaction return as if all of those transactions that are notifiable[120] were a single notifiable transaction.[121] If a single return is made the persons making the return are treated as purchasers acting jointly in relation to a single transaction.[122] This is related to a facility offered by the land transaction return of separate certificates for the various items of property included in the land transaction return. Unfortunately, it seems that in practice HMRC Stamp Taxes and their computer systems have great difficulty in providing the facility of single filing for multiple acquisitions even on the same date and the provision of separate certificates for each title where this is necessary because the properties are dealt with by different Land Registries.

Notification obligations for later linked transactions

5.64 Subsequent transactions may be linked such as linked successive leases[123] or performance or completion of contracts arising pursuant to the exercise of an option which may be linked.[124] Such subsequent transactions may have to be notified,[125] and these obligations pass to assignees of leases and this applies notwithstanding that the lease assigned to them is not directly involved in the linked transaction such as the renewal of another lease to which the assignee is not a party.[126]

5.65 A transaction when entered into may not be notifiable because, for example, the chargeable consideration is below the notification threshold of £40,000 or the nil rate threshold,[127] but as a result of a later chargeable transaction that is linked to it, may become notifiable 'retrospectively'. Similarly, the initial transaction may be taxed at a

---

[117] FA 2003, Sch 5, para 2(5) and (6).
[118] It must be noted that this is not necessarily the same as the contract date or the date of completion by written instrument and/or payment in full (FA 2003, s 44). In consequence, the notification provision may apply to linked contracts entered into on different dates.
[119] Because different purchasers may be linked if they are connected persons.
[120] FA 2003, s 77; see **Chapter 16**.
[121] Ibid, s 108(2).
[122] Ibid, s 108(4); see **Chapter 14**.
[123] Ibid, Sch 17A, para 5.
[124] Ibid, s 46.
[125] Ibid, s 81A.
[126] Ibid, Sch 17A, para 12; see further **7.235**.
[127] Ibid, s 77A.

lower rate for stamp duty land tax, but as a result of a later linked transaction that taxation liability may be increased. Alternatively, the transaction may become notifiable for the first time.

Problems for leases

5.66   Leases may be linked in two distinct ways:

- there may be linked transactions where there are several leases of different properties; and/or

- the renewal of a lease may be linked with the grant of the original lease.[128]

These two principles may be interlinked so that a renewal of a lease may be linked with a prior grant of a lease of other property. In addition, problems may arise for assignees of leases.[129]

Leases – special rules

5.67   If the lease is one of a number of linked transactions the relevant rental value is the aggregate of the net present value of the rent payable over the terms of all of the linked leases.[130]

Premiums and linked transactions

5.68   Where the chargeable consideration consists of or includes rent then, when applying the provisions as to linked transactions, no account is taken of rent in determining the relevant consideration for the determination of the band for the purposes of the tax upon the premiums, if any;[131] but the nil rate band for the premium is not available for non-residential property where the average annual rent exceeds £1000.[132]

Rents and linked transactions

5.69   The slice system for rents means that it is necessary to allocate the appropriate portion of the nil rents slice between leases when granted.[133] This is done by reference to the relative net present value of the rents of the linked leases.

The introduction of a slice system so that the first £125,000 (temporarily £175,000) or £150,000 of rent is also subject to nil rate tax has caused problems in relation to linked transactions. Where there are several leases granted as part of a linked transaction, such as where a landlord grants leases of a chain of shops or several units on an industrial site to a single tenant or a purchaser of the reversionary interest negotiates new leases with the existing tenants in order to harmonise the covenants and simplify management issues, it is necessary to apportion the nil rate band of stamp duty land tax in respect of

---

[128]   Ibid, Sch 17A, para 5.
[129]   Ibid, Sch 17A, para 12(1)(b). See **7.235** and **15.39**.
[130]   Ibid, Sch 5, para 2(4)(b).
[131]   Ibid, Sch 5, para 9(5).
[132]   Ibid, Sch 5, paras 9 and 9A (as amended).
[133]   Ibid, Sch 5, para 2.

the rent reserved by those leases. A not infrequent situation arises from the renegotiation of existing leases. For example, a person may purchase a portfolio of reversions and negotiation with the tenants for variations in the covenants in the leases so as to harmonise the management of the leases. Such variations may be chargeable transactions in their own right and so be linked.[134] On occasion the variations may be sufficiently fundamental to involve a surrender and regrant by operation of law or the parties may decide to tidy up the documentation by re-issuing the leases incorporating the variation. Such new leases, whether actual or deemed, will arise by reason of single commercial negotiation and, in consequence, will be linked not only for the immediate transaction but also all future transactions relating to those leases.[135] This apportionment is done between the leases on the basis of their proportionate net present value of the rent calculated. It would seem that this amount of nil rate band will be carried forward for any future computations of stamp duty land tax upon the lease such as upon any 5-year review.

5.70 However, subsequent leases may be linked as successive leases to the original lease. This will impact upon the initial allocation of the nil rate band by reason of the retrospective recalculation of the stamp duty land tax ie the nil rate allocated to the original lease has to be reduced.[136] This may affect assignee of a leases[137] who may find that, as a result of subsequent linked transactions to which he will not be a party[138] but which he may have to notify,[139] may find that he has an additional tax liability because the retrospective reallocation of the nil rate slice will reduce the amount allocated to his lease thereby increasing the charge. There is nothing in the legislation to indicate that the assignee of the lease as the current tenant, is not liable for any increased tax arising by reason of the reduction of the nil rate slice allocated to his please as a consequence of one or more later linked transactions notwithstanding that he is not a party to them.[140]

5.71 It seems to be the intention that the effect of being linked transactions is not merely to aggregate the chargeable consideration but also to aggregate the terms of successive linked leases.[141] The exercise of an option to renew a 5-year lease may produce not two leases but one retrospective lease for 10 years. This will change the notification requirements for both leases and will retrospectively affect the allocation of the lower rates of stamp duty land tax for any other leases that are linked. The initial allocation of the nil rate band for rents between linked leases will need to be recalculated for all linked leases including those relating to different premises. In such a situation, the 'purchaser'[142] under the initial transaction must deliver a return or further return in respect of that transaction before the end of the period of 30 days after the effective date of the subsequent transaction. This, like all returns, must include a self-assessment of the tax chargeable as a result of the subsequent transaction, but this is to be calculated

---

[134] This may involve a change of rent review dates which of itself raises the fundamental question of whether this is merely a variation of the lease or is an increase or reduction of rent which are all taxed on different bases.

[135] The parties should also consider an incidental but fundamentally important consequence. Such exercises may effectively convert a stamp duty lease into a stamp duty land tax lease with many adverse consequences such as charges associated with holding over or renewal.

[136] Moreover, it seems that this consequence occurs notwithstanding that some of the earlier leases may have terminated ie there appears to be a need to pay additional retrospective tax upon expired leases because their nil rate has been reduced.

[137] FA 2003, s 81A, Sch 17A, para 12.

[138] Linked transactions apply only as between the same parties and connected persons (FA 2003, s 108).

[139] FA 2003, s 81A and Sch 17A, para 12.

[140] Note especially FA 2003, s 81A and Sch 17A, para 12(10(b).

[141] Ibid, Sch 17A, para 5.

[142] Which includes assignees of the lease; ibid, s 81A and Sch 17A, para 12; see **5.73** and **7.235**.

by reference to the rate in force at the effective date of the initial transaction.[143] This return falls fully within the provisions of FA 2003, Sch 10 and the rules for penalties[144] and Enquiries by HMRC Stamp Taxes apply.[145] However, the 30-day period for filing and late payment interest is calculated from the effective date of the subsequent transaction.[146]

Successive leases and lease renewals

5.72 It appears to be the view of the draftsman that the renewal of an expired or existing lease whether by the exercise of an option in an existing lease or otherwise can be a linked transaction.[147] This means that the later lease will be linked with the original lease and, presumably, the tax in respect of the original lease will have to be recalculated upon the basis of the net present value of a single lease for the longer term. It would seem, however, that this only applies where the option is exercised by the original grantee of the lease since, *prima facie*, linked transactions apply only as between the same parties or persons connected with them.[148] This is, of course, aimed at preventing parties from obtaining two or more nil rate reliefs in respect of rents below the net present value of £125,000 (or the temporary £175,000) or £150,000, as appropriate. As the option and its exercise only 'may' be linked,[149] it remains to be seen what form of scheme or arrangement will be regarded by HMRC Stamp Taxes as sufficient to link transactions. The concept of linked successive leases is, however, fundamentally flawed since it operates for the benefit of the taxpayer. For example, a lease for 21 years with a break clause is taxed as a lease for 21 years and there is no adjustment in the tax should the break clause be exercised by either the landlord, the tenant or an assignee of either. However, a lease for 7 years with an option to renew is taxed as a lease for 7 years with a further charge as and when the option to renew is exercised and the agreement arising is substantially performed or the new lease is granted. Should this new lease be treated as a linked transaction the tax will be calculated by reference to a heavily discounted rent which is also the assumed rent for all years after the expiration of the fifth year of the original lease term as extended, ie is likely to be a lower figure than the actual passing rent. This assumed rent as discounted will usually produce a much lower tax charge than a new lease where the net present value of the new rent significantly exceeds £125,000 (or the temporary £175,000) or £150,000. The taxpayer may lose the benefit of a further nil rate slice on the rent but in those cases where the rent is sufficiently large the benefit of a lower tax charge together with the cash flow benefits of deferred payment with interest or penalty can be significant. Taxpayers may, therefore, wish to argue for linked transactions which will create considerable policy questions for HMRC Stamp Taxes.

---

[143] Ibid, s 81A.
[144] It is an open question of whether assignees are by statute also made liable for penalties in respect of the defects in or default relating to the original filing by the assignor where the statutory obligations have to amend the return retrospectively ie the deal with the open tax position of the original taxpayer/assignor.
[145] It will have been noticed that the power to Enquire into the later returns effectively extends the power of HMRC Stamp Taxes to attack the earlier returns since it provides an opportunity to make a 'discovery' into the earlier return.
[146] FA 2003, s 87(3)(aa).
[147] Ibid, Sch 17A, para 5.
[148] However, other provisions in the legislation such as those dealing with assignees of leases in FA 2003, s 81A seem to envisage that assignees may become involved in linked transactions.
[149] FA 2003, s 46.

Lease renewals and assignees

5.73 Difficult issues arise where a lease containing an option to renew is assigned. FA 2003, s 81A, states that the assignee of a lease is subject to the same obligations including, it seems, both compliance and payment of tax as the assignor if the original taxpayer. This means that the assignee has to report and pay any additional stamp duty land tax imposed upon the original taxpayer notwithstanding that his exercise of the option is not a linked transaction and he is not a party to the later linked transaction that retrospectively affects the chargeable interest.

5.74 It is thought that HMRC Stamp Taxes may seek to argue that the exercise of an option to renew a lease by an assignee is a linked transaction producing a successive linked lease.[150] However, in many cases this will benefit the assignee since the tax upon the rent reserved by the reserved lease will be significantly discounted. There is a problem for HMRC Stamp Taxes in balancing the second nil rate slice for the rent against the discounting in determining the net present value.

5.75 More important in practice will be the legislation which states that the assignee[151] of a lease takes over totally the provisional tax position of the original tenant.[152] For example, the assignee of a lease is responsible for dealing with the rent adjustment taxation during or at the end of the fifth year of the term and for abnormal increases in rent thereafter. Although certain of these transactions may not be linked upon the general principles the anti-avoidance provisions may deem them to be linked so that the fact that the transaction in question is not between the same parties is irrelevant and the transactions are automatically linked.[153] However, the deemed grant of a lease on substantial performance and the subsequent grant are not linked.[154]

5.76 It may seem invidious rather than stealthy that, for example, an assignee of a lease may become responsible for stamp duty land tax obligations initially imposed upon the original tenant who may not be the immediate assignor of the lease but merely one of the several predecessors in title. However, the legislation seems to be quite clear. The assignee of a lease becomes responsible for the compliance and other obligations of the original tenant in relation to the specified events. The separate references to compliance and other obligations make it clear that the latter refers to payment of the tax and not merely record-keeping.[155] There is, therefore, a situation of persons becoming responsible for someone else's tax not simply as a requirement for deducting tax for payments and there is no statutory indemnity. Conversely the assignee may become entitled to refunds but this is extremely unlikely in the context of linked transactions which are intended simply to increase the tax charge.

---

[150] But see **7.105**.

[151] This set of problems is not limited to the first assignee of the lease; the difficulties apply to whoever happens to be the legal tenant at the time any chargeable transaction arises and the chargeable transactions include transactions to which the current tenant is not a direct or indirect party; see **6.61**.

[152] FA 2003, Sch 17A, para 12.

[153] See, eg, ibid, Sch 17A, para 14(5).

[154] Ibid, Sch 17A, para 12A(3).

[155] It seems at least arguable that the record-keeping obligations of the original tenant (see **Chapter 20**) do not pass to the assignees of the lease and their successor; but the contrary point is not unarguable by HMRC Stamp Taxes.

Land only linkage

5.77 HMRC Stamp Taxes sought to apply the linked transaction principles where there are separate contracts for the sale or lease of land and the construction of a building by the seller or lessor at the expense of the purchaser or tenant.[156] A typical problem will be the question of an agreement to sell land or to grant a lease where the parties enter into a more or less simultaneous contract for the seller or landlord to construct a building upon the land. HMRC Stamp Taxes initially contended that the chargeable consideration for the sale or lease include the building contract, since FA 2003, Sch 4, para 10(2)(c) excluded payments made by the purchaser or tenant only if it is not a condition of the arrangement (ie a term of the land contract) that the works are to be carried out by the vendor or lessor or a person connected with him.[157] However, this would not necessarily link the land and the building contracts for the purposes of the lower rates. The fact that the land and the building contracts are commercially related is not effective within the land transaction legislation to create a single contract for the sale or lease of the completed building.[158] It is considered that linking can apply only to land transactions;[159] it does not apply to link land transactions with contracts relating to other matters such as the simultaneous sale of land and chattels.[160] In consequence, if the land transaction and the building contract are not so related that they form a single contract and the building works are an integral part of that contract, they cannot be 'linked' so as to bring the consideration for the building works into charge to stamp duty land tax. Such building works are chargeable, if at all, only where they constitute chargeable consideration the subject-matter of the contract or fall within FA 2003, Sch 4, para 10.[161] HMRC Stamp Taxes have confirmed that they have eventually accepted the advice of leading counsel that their position on building agreements is not sustainable on the current legislation.

Options and pre-emption rights and linked transactions

5.78 It is provided that the grant of an option, although a land transaction in its own right,[162] only 'may' also be linked with the contracts or transaction resulting from the exercise of the option.[163] If linked, although the option may be granted for a premium below the £500,000 threshold and so may initially be taxed at a lower rate of stamp duty land tax, when the option is exercised or the resulting contract is substantially performed or completed so that an effective date for that transaction arises, the consideration for the option and the price payable for the acquisition of the land have to be aggregated and increased stamp duty land tax will be payable in respect of the option premium.[164] Therefore, attempts to obtain the benefit of lower rates by granting numerous options for small consideration between the same grantor and same grantee

---

[156] See **Chapter 8**.

[157] See further **8.8**.

[158] See *Kimbers & Co v IRC* [1936] 1 KB 132; *Prudential Assurance Co Ltd v IRC* [1993] 1 WLR 211.

[159] It is considered that, as a general matter of construction of FA 2003, 'transaction' and 'land transaction' are synonymous and that a reference to a 'transaction' does not apply to commercially related matters.

[160] See **Chapter 8**; on fixtures see **4.10**.

[161] See **8.8**.

[162] FA 2003, s 46(1).

[163] Ibid.

[164] There should not be any interest or penalty arising in such a case since the additional stamp duty land tax becomes notifiable and payable only by reference to the effective date for the substantial performance or completion of the contract arising pursuant to the exercise of the option.

will not be effective, and a full second 'retrospective' return (SDLT 1) is required for the grant of the option in addition to the land transaction return required for the main transaction.[165]

5.79 It would seem, therefore, arguable that since an option and its exercise are not automatically linked there must be something in the nature of a cut and dried plan that the option will be exercised. Clearly, if there are significant possibilities that the option may not be exercised, such as where it is conditional upon obtaining planning permission, or not exercisable for many years in the future, then it may not be linked. On the other hand, cross-options exercised within a short period after grant are likely to be regarded by HMRC Stamp Taxes as *prima facie* part of a series of transactions. This is likely to arise where parties for the purposes of capital gains tax enter into a series of options exercisable in successive tax years. Here it would, *prima facie*, be relatively easy for HMRC Stamp Taxes to establish that there was a pre-arranged timetable under which the options would almost inevitably be exercised. Similarly, an option granted for a very large premium where it would be commercially unrealistic not to exercise the option is also likely to form part of a single arrangement in the view of HMRC Stamp Taxes.

PART II – CHARGEABLE CONSIDERATION

5.80 This part of the Chapter is concerned with the second part of the process for computing stamp duty land tax, ie the nature and the amount of chargeable consideration which determines both the rate and the amount to which that rate is applied. This is complicated because of several factors:

- there are different regimes for rent and other consideration;

- there is a wide range of consideration in kind which has to be valued;[166] and

- much of the tax is initially self-assessed on a provisional and estimated basis to be adjusted in the light of subsequent events.

However, the rules as to what is 'consideration' although based upon contractual principles the application of such rules to the tax are far more complex. In particular, there is a fundamental distinction between actual and chargeable consideration which affects not only whether there is a tax charge and if so the amount of tax payable but also the compliance procedures.

5.81 Unlike stamp duty consideration in kind is now a major area of charge.[167] There is a major area of cost for taxpayers because of the need to self-assess the stamp duty land tax and to determine on the basis of proper professional, and expensive, advice the value of the relevant assets. Failure to take proper advice will almost invariably be regarded by HMRC Stamp Taxes as involving a negligent return and professional advisers will be on risk of penalty as co-operating in the preparation of a land

---

[165] It is not possible to combine these linked transactions on the same return because they do not have the same effective date.

[166] See **Chapter 27**; note the possibility of challenge on valuation methods and principles in *Langham v Veltema* [2004] STC 544.

[167] FA 2003, Sch 4; especially para 1 referring to 'money's worth'.

transaction return knowing it to be incorrect,[168] ie they are aware that the figures
inserted in the land transaction return were not prepared on a proper basis or they did
not ask the necessary questions.[169]

5.82   Also of great practical significance is the treatment of variable consideration. It
is not unusual[170] for contracts or agreements for lease to provide for consideration or
rent that depends upon future events such as overage payments. The principles dealing
with such arrangements introduce a significant lack of finality into the tax.[171] This
retrospective uncertainty is extended to contracts even where the contractual
consideration is certain but there are later linked transactions as described in the
previous part of this chapter which require that previous consideration or the rate to be
adjusted.

DEFINITION

5.83   The chargeable consideration[172] is, except as otherwise provided:[173]

- any consideration[174]

- in money or money's worth[175]

- given or deemed to be given

- for the subject-matter of the transaction[176]

- directly or indirectly[177]

- by either:
    - the purchaser;[178] or
    - by a person connected[179] with him.[180]

Apart from certain routine situations relating to contingent, uncertain or unascertained
consideration,[181] stamp duty land tax, like stamp duty, is *prima facie* a once-and-for-all

---

168 Ibid, ss 95 and 96.
169 *Slattery v Moore Stephens* [2003] STC 1379.
170 It may even be necessary; see *Akazuc Enterprises v Farmar* [2003] PL SCS 127.
171 See **2.14**.
172 FA 2003, Sch 4, para 1(1).
173 Such as the connected company charge upon not less than the market value of the land (FA 2003, ss 53 and
     54) or dealings involving partners and partnerships within the special regime (ibid, Sch 15, Part 3) or the
     land exchange charges (ibid, s 47 and Sch 4, para 5) and related matters such as surrenders and regrants of
     leases. Note the ease with which HMRC Stamp Taxes can make a discovery in self-assessment and
     valuations as in *Langham v Veltema* [2004] STC 544.
174 See **5.90**.
175 See **5.87**.
176 See **4.4**.
177 See **5.103**.
178 See **Chapter 15**.
179 See **15.9**.
180 FA 2003, Sch 4, para 1(2).
181 Ibid, ss 51 and 80.

tax and it is far from clear whether there is a general 'wait-and-see' principle.[182] There are many situations where there is a provisional filing, possibly on an estimated or more accurately 'guestimated'[183] basis, which has to be adjusted in the light of subsequent circumstances such as in relation to variable consideration[184] or variable rents including the impact of VAT changes.[185] Subject to these specific provisions there are situations where, for example, it is a condition for the relief in respect of corporate reorganisations[186] that the consideration shares are 'issued' to the relevant parties. This involves registration in the right names and there is the question as to whether these conditions have to be satisfied as at the effective date. However, such a transaction may have numerous stages particularly in the context of contract, potential substantial performance and completion when the number of documents involved, such as many leases involving landlord's consent, there may be considerable delay in completing the paperwork. There may also be a delay between the directors resolving to allot the consideration shares and these actually being entered upon the register.[187] The question is whether, where the shares are not actually allotted and registered on the effective date, that there is an obligation to do so the mere existence of the obligation is sufficient to satisfy the conditions for relief. It is thought that, technically, the conditions would not have been satisfied simply by reason of the obligation to issue the shares. However, whilst this was a fundamental point in relation to the equivalent reliefs from stamp duty for company reorganisations,[188] the point was never taken by HMRC Stamp Taxes.

5.84 Similar wait-and-see issues arise in relation to potential VAT. For example, there are questions concerning the treatment of the VAT that might arise should a transaction not be accepted as a transfer of a going concern.[189] In such a case there is a form of deferred obligation of a conditional nature upon the purchaser to pay the VAT should the vendor issue an appropriate tax invoice. In relation to a company reconstruction there may be many situations where the question of whether the VAT actually or potentially payable should the transaction not be a transfer of a going concern the acquisition of the undertaking is or is not a payment of cash or other consideration but it is certainly not the issue of shares. It is considered that there is no wait-and-see in this situation in order to determine whether the VAT would be paid in the form of cash. The strict application of the rules relating to variable consideration which will include such provisional VAT[190] means that the potential VAT has to be taken into account in making the initial self-assessment. The provisional consideration will, therefore, include the obligations in relation to VAT and this will, under most circumstances,[191] mean that the conditions for the relief are not satisfied as at the effective date because the final form of the consideration remains uncertain. It is potentially arguable that where the special rules for variable consideration apply, the initial assessment is provisional only, the eligibility for the relief can be reassessed in the light of the subsequent events because this is a retrospective adjustment of the original return by reference to the effective date. In this situation there could be a retrospective qualification for the

---

[182] See **11.9**.
[183] Based upon guess because there are no established rules for predicting future value or rents over an eighty year period.
[184] FA 2003, s 51.
[185] Ibid, Sch 17A, paras 7 and 8.
[186] Ibid, Sch 7, Part 2.
[187] Registration is fundamental to the question of whether the shares have been 'issued'; see *Oswald Tillotson v IRC* [1933] 1 KB 134; *Brotex Cellulose Fibres Ltd v IRC* [1933] 1 KB 158; *Murex v IRC* [1933] 1 KB 173; *National Westminster Bank v IRC* [1995] 1 AC 119.
[188] See, for example, FA 1927, s 55; FA 1986, ss 75–77.
[189] See **5.130**.
[190] FA 2003, s 51.
[191] But see, for possible methods of dealing with the situation in **12.26**.

exemption. However, where there is no such retrospective adjustment of the provisional consideration the relief would not be available because there is no general wait-and-see. There is no suggestion that a potential claim for damages or a claim pursuant to an indemnity or warranty is some form of contingent liability which has to be taken into account in computing the liability.[192]

5.85   Moreover, there does not appear to be any express provision for recovery of overpaid tax because the consideration is effectively reduced by a later successful claim for damages or indemnity for breach of contractual terms or otherwise.[193]

However, as described elsewhere,[194] much of the tax is initially self-assessed on a provisional basis and subsequent events require retrospective adjustments and even where the consideration is certain and not subject to possible variation the retrospective linked transaction rules can change the tax charge. Many of these situations affect the amount of the chargeable consideration.

5.86   Each of the components in the above definition of 'chargeable consideration' requires explanation. For example:

- it is worthy of note that the consideration must be provided by 'the purchaser' as defined by the FA 2003, s 44(4) and (5)[195] or a person connected with him. In consequence, when consideration is provided by a third party who does not 'acquire' a chargeable interest and is not reimbursed in some way by the person benefiting, the consideration may not be 'chargeable consideration';[196]

- it seems that merely because there is consideration for the transaction it will not necessarily be chargeable. For example, in relation to land exchanges where A agrees to transfer land to B who in consideration thereof agrees to transfer or lease land or grant or vary rights to or in favour of C, C is a 'purchaser' because he is a party to the transaction,[197] but the consideration for that transaction is not provided by C but by A, who is not a purchaser because he is not 'acquiring' any interest in land[198] even within the extended definition of that term.[199]

---

[192]   Compare Taxation of Chargeable Gains Act 1992, s 49; *Zim Properties v Proctor* [1985] STC 90 ESC D 53; *Wardhaugh v Penrith Rugby Club* [2002] STC 776.

[193]   In effect, a successful damages claim reduces the costs of the purchaser but there is no clear right to a refund. However, the possibility of such a claim may not be regarded as a circumstance which, of itself, makes the consideration uncertain where there is a fixed price, so that no adjustment can be made. The position may differ where the consideration is variable for other reasons so that the final calculation of the tax has not been made at the time of the damages claim. There may also be issues as to the nature of the claim for damages and whether this does represent a reduction in the price.

[194]   See **2.14**.

[195]   See **Chapter 15**.

[196]   See further **5.99** and **5.103**.

[197]   FA 2003, s 43(5).

[198]   Ibid, s 43(4).

[199]   Ibid, s 43(3).

SOME GENERAL ISSUES

What is money's worth?

Consideration in kind – market value

5.87 As the reference to 'money's worth' indicates the scope of consideration within the charge to stamp duty land tax is considerably wider than that applicable to stamp duty. There is no definition of 'money's worth' but because it refers to the sale proceeds[200] it is clear that this must be something that is capable of both being turned into money and is capable of being sold.[201] This will apply to consideration including shares issued in relation to corporate reorganisations and incorporations.[202] This raises the issue of whether certain types of consideration can have a market value;[203] but there may be no 'market value' for rights and interests 'excepted and reserved' on the transfer which may be the regrant of minor interests which can exist only as part of the dominant land and are not separately saleable.[204] The basic provision is subject to 'contrary express provision' such as other provisions relating to chargeable consideration where this is not related to market value such as services,[205] works,[206] or debts.[207] This means that many forms of consideration or deemed consideration will have to be valued at the cost and at the risk of the taxpayer. Failure to take the appropriate steps to determine the market value is a basis upon which HMRC Stamp Taxes can make a discovery[208] and issue a discovery assessment. The absence of proper steps to determine the market value may also be regarded by HMRC Stamp Taxes as 'negligence' in the preparation of the form enabling them to issue a discovery assessment for up to 21 years after the effective date.[209]

5.88 FA 2003, Sch 4, para 7, provides that 'except as otherwise provided' the value of any chargeable consideration for a land transaction other than cash, whether sterling or other currency,[210] or indebtedness being satisfied or assumed is its market value at the effective date of the transaction. 'Market value' is to be determined[211] in accordance with Taxation of Chargeable Gains Act 1992, ss 272–274. It is, however, a relatively easy matter to state the principles upon which market value is to be determined it is a much

---

[200] FA 2003, Sch 4, para 7.
[201] *Secretan v Hart* 45 TC 701; *Re M C Bacon Ltd* [1990] BCLC 324. There might be questions of money's worth where, although a person cannot sell an asset but can convert it into cash by entering into an arrangement to deal with the asset in a manner that would enable him to reduce the value; but this argument is not open to HMRC Stamp Taxes since the definition of market value refers not to the value or cash to be derived from sale, albeit hypothetical, in the open market.
[202] Note the comments in *Crane Fruehauf v IRC* [1975] STC 51 that the parties must do the best they can when dealing with the value of future shares.
[203] Such as where the consideration consists of the surrender or variation of a chargeable interest which may disappear and so is no longer capable of being sold on the open market, i e the difference between the value of the transaction to the 'purchaser' whose land may be substantially benefited by a major increase in value and the market value of something which cannot be sold separately from land which is not included in the transaction. There is the important distinction between something being 'valuable' and something having a 'market value'. This distinction is crucial to the dealing with minor interests.
[204] See **4.39**.
[205] FA 2003, Sch 4, para 11.
[206] Ibid, Sch 4, para 10; see **Chapter 8**.
[207] Ibid, Sch 4, para 8; see **5.133**.
[208] *Langham v Veltema* [2004] STC 544; FA 2003, Sch 10, paras 25 and 28.
[209] See *Slattery v Moore Stephens* [2003] STC 1379.
[210] On foreign currency see **5.116**.
[211] FA 2003, s 118.

more difficult task on determining what those principles mean and how they apply in any particular case such as the relative waiting to be given to various factors.[212]

5.89   It is, therefore, necessary to go through various stages, namely to determine:

(1)   whether there is consideration;[213] and, if so,

(2)   whether it is chargeable, which involves two issues:
   (a)   whether it is within the list of considerations falling into charge; and, if so,
   (b)   whether it is provided directly or indirectly by the 'purchaser' or a person connected with him;[214] and, if not

(3)   whether there are provisions deeming there to be consideration. Such deeming arrangements can take various forms, namely:
   (a)   deeming there to be chargeable consideration where there is no actual consideration;
   (b)   deeming the chargeable consideration to be something different or of a different amount from the actual consideration; or
   (c)   deeming the actual consideration not to be chargeable consideration which affects the compliance regime because this is not the same as an 'exemption' although in both situations no actual tax is payable.

CONSIDERATION

5.90   The issue of what is 'consideration' appears to rest basically upon normal contractual principles. There are, however, several preliminary issues which need to be considered because there is some confusion in the legislation as to the nature of 'consideration' and this confusion has caused some amazingly nonsensical utterances in the debates in Parliament upon the FA 2003, in particular in relation to building works and some very odd additions to the legislation.

Which direction?

5.91   The traditional concept of 'consideration' is that it moves from the provider or promisor in the opposite or different direction to the property but not necessarily to the promisee. This raises problems for multipartite arrangements given the definition of 'chargeable consideration' being provided by a third party connected with the 'purchaser'. In addition, there can be consideration where the transferee or 'purchaser' makes a payment to a third party. To some extent the arrangement may be a matter of

---

[212]   See **Chapter 27**. When determining the 'market value', FA 2003, s 118 does not apply in relation to certain arrangements relating to shared ownership leases and the statement of the 'market value' of the dwelling contained in the lease: see ibid, Sch 9, para 2(5).

[213]   This will raise the basic analysis of whether there is a condition or it is consideration; see, for example, *Errington v Errington & Woods* [1952] 1 KB 290. More significantly, however, is the question of there being no chargeable transaction where there is no chargeable consideration (FA 2003, Sch 3, para 1) and whether transactions 'by operation of law' are consensual should 'by operation of law' extend beyond statutory completions of the arrangement (see **3.50**) so that constructive trusts and similar arrangements can be regarded as contracts for this purpose. It should, however, be noted that in *Yaxley v Gotts* [1999] 2 WLR 1217 Walker LJ stated that equitable notions of constructive trust or proprietary estoppel could override the provisions requiring writing such as Law of Property (Miscellaneous Provisions) Act 1989, s 2 so that there could be a valid oral contract.

[214]   FA 2003, Sch 4, para 1(1).

drafting since stating that part of the consideration is to be allocated to a third party does not mean that it is not consideration.[215] In a traditional subsale where A agrees to sell to B and B agrees to sell to C it is frequently provided that C will pay part of the consideration due from him to A in discharge of B's liability to A. In this circumstance the payment by C, although made to a third party, will be part of the consideration received by or due to B.[216]

Reverse payments

5.92 Where the property and cash move in the same direction, such as when a tenant pays the landlord to accept the early surrender of a lease, the payment by the tenant is not consideration for the surrender; it is consideration for the landlord agreeing to accept the surrender.[217] Those responsible for the structure of stamp duty land tax have either overlooked this basic principle of the law of contract or have a very obscure charging provision in mind. This problem surfaced from time to time in the HMRC Stamp Taxes' argument that land exchanges are linked transactions notwithstanding that the properties (ie the considerations) are moving in opposite directions. Other illustrations of this confused analysis exist but these have been, unnecessarily, given the benefit of reliefs. For example, a 'reverse premium', ie a sum paid by a landlord to the tenant as an inducement to take the lease,[218] is not, on general principles, consideration, ie a premium for the grant of the lease. However, the draftsman[219] thought it necessary to provide specifically that a 'premium' moving from the landlord to the tenant, ie a cash payment moving in the same direction as the lease, is not to count as chargeable consideration.[220] This exclusion also applies to payments by tenants to the landlord in relation to a surrender and payments by assignors to assignees in relation to an assignment, such as where the outgoing tenant pays the assignee a sum because of dilapidations which will have to be made good by the assignee or because the current rent is in excess of the market rent. However, the basic principle of 'reverse consideration' being chargeable consideration continues to be applied by HMRC Stamp Taxes. Obviously, the scope for such an approach is limited by reason of the specific exemptions for reverse payments.[221] Nevertheless, situations have arisen where a seller or landlord may agree to pay or contribute to the purchaser or lessee's costs whether in the form of stamp duty land tax or simply a contribution towards relocation or damage to the business. HMRC Stamp Taxes have taken the view that such a 'compensation' payment is chargeable consideration or a premium for the grant of the new lease.[222] It is

---

[215] Note *Spectros International plc v Maddern* [1997] STC 114; although Lightman J in that case indicated that had it not been a straightforward statement as to the cash amount of the consideration but simply an obligation upon the purchaser to procure the release or discharge of the indebtedness in question this might have produced a different result.

[216] On such directions to pay third parties as equitable arrangements see, for example, *Diplock v Hammond* (1854) 5 De GM & G 320.

[217] See the analysis in VAT cases such as *Gleneagles Hotel v Customs and Excise* [1988] VATTR 196; *Neville Russell v Customs and Excise* [1987] VATTR 194.

[218] Or possibly a consideration for entering into the agreement for lease.

[219] Who appears not to be alone in this confusion, since the Government was apparently persuaded that it was necessary to amend the original FA 2003 provisions to include payments to assignees. The problem appears to include lack of technical competence of the self-proclaimed 'advisers' to HMRC in matters of tax; a point which in the writer's view is a reason for taxpayers not utilising such advisers since client confidentiality is not always properly safeguarded.

[220] FA 2003, Sch 17A, para 18.

[221] However, HMRC Stamp Taxes may be somewhat nervous about the approach because indemnities by purchasers to vendors might be utilised as a basis for claiming that the chargeable consideration had been reduced by a reverse payment or compensation by way of damages for breach of contract.

[222] There is, from time to time, a dispute with HMRC Stamp Taxes as to where there is a payment of such compensation in connection with the relocation of a business which involves the surrender of a lease of one

also, in the view of HMRC Stamp Taxes, a factor in relation to transactions where the chargeable consideration is market value rather than the actual consideration. It is their view, apparently upon advice, that the undertaking by the seller or landlord to meet these expenses enhances the value of the land and is not an indication of the land being less valuable than the asking price.[223]

5.93 A similar issue arose in the debates in relation to building works where the Government rather bizarrely suggested that the taxing provisions in relation to works[224] had somehow reversed the decision in *Prudential Assurance Co Ltd v IRC*.[225] That was a case where the landlord agreed to grant a lease and to construct a building in consideration of a cash payment by the tenant. The court held that there was a separate building contract and agreement for lease, ie the building costs were not part of the price paid for the land.[226] The debate stated that somehow the building works as opposed to the costs being paid for them constitute the chargeable consideration for the purposes of stamp duty land tax ie the landlord's obligations to construct the building rather than the tenant's obligation to pay for the building was consideration being provided by the tenant (purchaser) for the grant of the lease ie the landlord was providing the consideration for his own disposal.[227] It is, however, difficult to see how this can arise. FA 2003, Sch 4, para 10 refers to the consideration for a land transaction, ie the consideration for the acquisition of a chargeable interest,[228] and this clearly cannot apply where the acquisition of the chargeable interest (eg the lease) and the benefit of the building works are moving in the same direction in return for a cash payment. On this particular issue, HMRC Stamp Taxes have accepted that the basic position as illustrated by *Kimbers & Co v IRC*[229] and *Prudential Assurance Co Ltd v IRC*[230] has not been fundamentally changed. It has been altered only where the consideration for the land contract includes an undertaking by the purchaser or tenant to carry out the building works, which is considered to be an unusual analysis,[231] and it is a term of the land contract that the purchaser or tenant will employ the vendor or landlord or a connected party to carry out those building works. Provided that the undertaking is not consideration or it is not a term of the land contract requiring the employment of the vendor or lessor, and the two contracts are legally independent, the consideration paid for the building works will escape stamp duty land tax[232] and the two contracts cannot be 'linked'[233] to create a single contract for these purposes.[234]

5.94 However, since the draftsman thought it necessary both to include and extend the exemption for certain reverse payments and the Government team accepted the odd

---

set of premises in consideration of the grant of a lease of other premises and the landlord agrees to contribute to the tenant's expenses then notwithstanding the exemption from the land exchange rules (pursuant to FA 2003, Sch 17A, para 16) this payment is some form of consideration for the surrender of the existing lease. Clearly there are major drafting issues involved.

[223] There are also questions as to whether such arrangements are a fraud upon the lender of funds and other persons by misrepresenting the amount or value of the consideration and the worth of the property.

[224] FA 2003, Sch 4, para 10.

[225] [1992] STC 863.

[226] See further **Chapter 8**.

[227] These types of misconceived analysis have been raised by HMRC Stamp Taxes in relation to valuation where the seller or landlord undertakes to contribute to the costs of the purchaser or tenant; note the implications of purchaser's costs and enfranchising pursuant to FA 2003, Sch 4, para 16C.

[228] FA 2003, s 43(1).

[229] [1936] 1 KB 132.

[230] [1992] STC 863.

[231] But see *Eastham v Leigh, London and Provincial Properties Limited* [1971] 2 All ER 887 considered at **5.97**.

[232] See further **8.8**.

[233] Pursuant to FA 2003, s 108.

[234] See **5.37**.

analysis of HMRC Stamp Taxes in the debates, there may be difficulties of analysis where two items are moving in the same direction if HMRC Stamp Taxes believe, as manifestly appears to be the case, in such a situation that one of those items represents consideration for the acquisition of the other, notwithstanding a traditional consideration is being provided by the person acquiring both interests.[235]

5.95   For example, the legislation provides that 'services' are now chargeable consideration[236] and it is arguable, for example, that by accepting the lease the tenant is providing a service, ie agreeing to do something,[237] the market cost of such services being the reverse premium but the 'service' is being provided for the reverse premium; and it is difficult for HMRC Stamp Taxes to argue that the lease is being granted in consideration of a separate service by the tenant accepting the grant of the lease. It remains to be seen what use, if anything, HMRC Stamp Taxes intend to make of this bizarre new concept of 'reverse consideration' outside the area of the specific exemptions, in practice.

Conditions or consideration

5.96   Although there are numerous illustrations of how to compute stamp duty land tax which indirectly indicate what is to be regarded as chargeable consideration,[238] there is no explanation of the general meaning of 'consideration', in consequence of which the general common law approach to what is consideration will be applied.

5.97   It will be a difficult issue of analysis whether any particular part of the arrangement is 'consideration' or is, for example, a conditional arrangement as in *Eastham v Leigh, London and Provincial Properties Ltd*[239] where a provision in an agreement for lease that the grant of the lease was conditional upon the tenant satisfactorily completing the building works was held to be part of the consideration not a true condition precedent.

Non-consensual and non-contractual arrangements

5.98   There is a fundamental question as to transactions pursuant to non-consensual arrangements, such as trustees appointing or advancing property without the need for the consent of all or any of the beneficiaries and, in particular, without the need for the consent of the appointee or of the trustee of the fund into which the property is appointed,[240] appropriations by executors without the devisee's consent,[241] which, because of the absence of consent, was not regarded as a sale for the purposes of stamp duty[242] or more importantly in practice, consensual arrangements falling short of binding contracts for some technical reasons but which are effective to pass some form of chargeable interest in the property such as constructive or similar trusts.[243] The

---

[235]   See further **5.217** and **7.208** (reverse premiums) and **Chapter 8**, **7.70** and **7.213** (works).

[236]   FA 2003, Sch 4, para 11; Stamp Duty Land Tax (Administration) Regulations 2003, SI 2003/2837, Part 4; see **16.32**.

[237]   See, eg, the cases on VAT such as *Neville Russell v Customs and Excise* [1987] VATTR 194.

[238]   If there are provisions for computation the consideration and the transaction must be chargeable; compare *J&P Coats Ltd v IRC* [1897] 2 QB 427.

[239]   [1971] 2 All ER 887; see also *GUS Merchandise v Customs and Excise* [1981] 1 WLR 1309 on the question of conditional gift or consideration: arrangements for donees to bear the inheritance tax may be taxable.

[240]   See, for example, FA 2003, Sch 16, para 8.

[241]   Administration of Estates Act 1925, s 41.

[242]   Compare *Jopling v IRC* [1940] 2 KB 282.

[243]   See **3.50**; although oral arrangements may, by reason of the application of equitable principles may be valid

emphasis in the legislation on 'acquisition', ie the vesting of title in the 'purchaser', implies that non-consensual arrangements may be vulnerable provided that non-consensual arrangements involve 'consideration'.[244] There is no test such as 'sale' in the former stamp duty regime that carries with it the implication of a 'contract' or legislation which effectively deems there to be a contract to sell unless the need for 'chargeable consideration' implies an agreement. Unfortunately the overall drafting is not helpful such as the connected company charge and its reliefs. For example, a dividend *in specie* or a distribution in a winding up need not have the agreement of the members but the passing of any resolution by the members agreeing to this arrangement would *prima facie* make the arrangement one taking effect with consent[245] it was felt necessary to exclude these from the charging provisions. It is considered that the absence of consent means that there is no consideration,[246] but the enactment of numerous provisions including amendments (such as the exemption for the allocation of assets by trustees with the consent of the beneficiary to the termination of his interest in other assets, where the consent of the beneficiary is not chargeable consideration),[247] intended to provide limited areas of relief which specifically apply to situations where there is no consent[248] clearly indicates that HMRC Stamp Taxes intend to develop an argument that 'chargeable consideration' can exist outside the context of non-contractual arrangements. Such reliefs would not be necessary if non-consensual arrangements were not *prima facie* taxable and the mere giving of consent of itself constituted some form of chargeable consideration.[249]

Third party issues

5.99   In connection with who is the provider of 'consideration' to make it 'chargeable' the 'purchaser' is the person acquiring the subject-matter of the transaction[250] provided that he is providing consideration or is a party to the transaction whether or not providing consideration.[251] This suggests technical issues may arise where there are tripartite and similar arrangements. Payments by third parties who, *prima facie*, are not necessarily parties but may, in the view of HMRC Stamp Taxes, be parties to the transaction because they are providing consideration for the transaction as some form of inducement to enter into the contract, although consideration for the transaction, may not be chargeable consideration because they are not provided directly or indirectly by the purchaser, ie the person 'acquiring' the benefit of the transaction. Obviously, there would need to be an investigation as to whether the purchaser was somehow procuring the provision of that consideration by paying such of those fees or agreeing to indemnify the third party who is actually making the payment or providing the consideration.

---

contracts ie equitable notions override the need for writing imposed by Law of Property (Miscellaneous Provisions) Act 1989, s 2; see *Yaxley v Gotts* [1999] 2 WLR 1217.

244   FA 2003, Sch 3, para 1.

245   Note Companies Forms (Tables A to E) 1986, SI 1986/805; see also Companies (Forms) Regulations 1985, SI 1985/854, Article 135 (Table A).

246   In the case of distributions of capital the transfer is in satisfaction of the rights of the members which is a form of consideration but not one that is chargeable.

247   FA 2003, Sch 16, para 8.

248   Ibid, Sch 16, para 8 (as amended).

249   Since HMRC Stamp Taxes have no revealed their fundamental concept of 'consideration' there are, as yet, undisclosed issues as to how 'consent' can be 'money's worth' but changes such as FA 2003, Sch 16, para 8, indicate that 'consent' is sufficient to produce chargeable consideration.

250   FA 2003, s 43(4).

251   Ibid, s 43(5).

5.100 The basic principle would suggest that if the consideration comes from an unconnected person it is not chargeable consideration since he may not be a party to the transaction. Unfortunately this is not as simple an issue as might appear on the surface since third parties may offer some form of 'inducement' for the party to enter into the transaction. These may be illustrated by cases such as *Crane Freuhauf v IRC*[252] and *Central and District Properties v IRC*,[253] as to whether the third party arrangement was somehow being guaranteed or underwritten by the purchaser and therefore somehow formed part of the total package so as to be consideration. However, there will be questions as to whether such guarantees that the consideration will be forthcoming from the third party even though part of the scheme is part of the chargeable consideration.[254] Presumably, in this case, if there is such a warranty or guarantee by the purchaser or taxpayer the consideration may not be the benefit of the warranty or undertaking.[255] It may, ultimately, be the amount of consideration derived from the third party.

5.101 Third parties may become involved in land transactions in two ways. They may either:

• acquire a chargeable interest in the land as part of a subsale or assignment; or

• be providers of consideration, whether or not chargeable[256] by offering some inducement such as the giving of guarantees or other benefits[257] to the owner of the chargeable interest to enter into a contract whereby some other person acquires that interest.[258]

The issue is whether an inducement offered by the third party is part of the chargeable consideration upon which the person acquiring the chargeable interest is required to pay stamp duty land tax;[259] but such arrangements also raise the question of whether, should the inducement being provided by the third party be consideration, it is chargeable consideration, ie whether it is being provided by the 'purchaser' or a person connected with him as required by the FA 2003, Sch 4, para 1. This involves the issue of whether the third party is a purchaser or a party to the transaction. This requires an understanding of who is a 'purchaser' and who is a party to the transaction. There is the obvious point for HMRC Stamp Taxes to take that any person who provides consideration is a party to the transaction. There is, however, the difficulty of trying to explain the legislation upon the basis that it is not intended to apply to a person who is providing an inducement but which is not consideration so that he may not be a party.[260] It would seem that if a third party offers an inducement in the sense of agreeing to

---

[252] [1975] STC 51.

[253] [1966] 1 WLR 1015.

[254] The giving of guarantees will be part of the consideration not as in relation to stamp duty because it might be regarded by HMRC Stamp Taxes as the assumption of a contingent liability but because 'services' are chargeable consideration pursuant to FA 2003, Sch 4, para 11.

[255] This will depend upon how guarantees etc are regarded, whether as services or as contingent or uncertain consideration.

[256] FA 2003, Sch 4, para 1; see **5.83**.

[257] *Curzon Offices Ltd v IRC* [1944] 1 All ER 163; *IRC v Wachtel* [1971] 1 All ER 271; *Crane Fruehauf v IRC* [1975] STC 51; *Central and District Properties v IRC* [1966] 2 All ER 433; assuming that such guarantees are proper exercises of the powers of the boards of directors – see *Rolled Steel Products Ltd v British Steel Corporation* [1984] BCLC 466.

[258] See the illustration of a 'land exchange' in **5.153**.

[259] The other issues of subsale etc are considered in **Chapter 6**.

[260] See, for example, *Crane Fruehauf v IRC* [1975] STC 51; *Central and District Properties v IRC* [1966] 2 All ER 433; *Shop and Stores Developments v IRC* [1967] 1 All ER 42. These are also key issues in whether there is a

purchase part of the property under a separate transaction such as where the purchaser is entering into some form of sale and leaseback arrangement in order to fund the basic acquisition of the land from A agrees to sell part of the land to B who agrees to lease back that land this will not be provision of consideration by B for the main transaction and the third party is unlikely to be a party to the transaction. The mere fact that the person receives cash,[261] however, if the basic acquisition and the onward movement of the property are all included in a single contract there is a danger that the payment may form part of the consideration in some way or make the third party a party to the transaction.[262] There is a definition of 'purchaser'[263] to the effect that the person 'acquiring' the chargeable interest and any interest or right appurtenant or pertaining thereto that is acquired with it.[264] This applies even if there is no consideration given for the transaction;[265] but a person is not treated as a purchaser unless he has given consideration for, or is a party to, the transaction.[266] This would suggest that if the consideration is provided by an unconnected party such as a bank giving a guarantee for overage payments and the person 'acquiring' the interest is 'the purchaser' the consideration in the form of the inducement is not chargeable consideration,[267] although HMRC Stamp Taxes are likely to contend that if the third party is a party to the contract because it signs the contract fiving the guarantee it is a party to the transaction.

5.102 There are many situations where third parties are involved in the transaction: for example, A may be a developer who is acquiring a site and has an arrangement with the local authority whereby, with the help of the local authority's compulsory powers,[268] he will arrange[269] for all the interests in the land to be vested in the local authority, which will grant him a lease of the assembled site in due course subject to whatever arrangements may be appropriate. In that situation, the costs of acquiring the land fall upon the developer.[270] The question of the provision of the chargeable consideration by the purchaser is important bearing in mind that the definition refers to the purchaser as the person acquiring the subject-matter of the transaction.[271] In this situation, X may be a tenant under a lease from Y. A, the developer, pays a sum of money to X and to Y in

---

scheme of reconstruction and whether the other conditions for the various reliefs for corporate restructuring pursuant to FA 2003, Sch 7 are satisfied; see **Chapter 12**.

261   *Shop and Stores Developments v IRC* [1967] 1 All ER 42.
262   See the comments of Scarman LJ in *Crane Fruehauf v IRC* [1975] STC 51.
263   FA 2003, s 43(4).
264   Ibid, s 43(4) and (6).
265   Ibid, s 43(4). The use of the word 'purchaser' is misleading since it should refer to 'taxpayer'. It emerges, albeit indirectly, from the definition of purchaser as 'acquirer' of a chargeable interest that it covers a wide-range of situations. Moreover, the reference to a person being a 'purchaser' without providing consideration is essentially a compliance obligation. Were there is no consideration there may be no chargeable transaction (FA 2003, Sch 3, para 1) but it may be necessary to identify the 'taxpayer' ie the person who may be responsible for filing returns etc. Also it should be noted that there may be no actual consideration but there may be chargeable consideration such as where there is a gift to a connected company. In this situation the person would not be a 'purchaser' in the general sense because he is not 'buying for consideration'. He is, however, a 'deemed purchaser' in the general sense because he is treated as supplying consideration. He is, therefore, the person to be identified as responsible for paying the tax and filing any returns.
266   Ibid, s 43(5).
267   Ibid, Sch 4, para 1; but there are many problems to be resolved and likely to involve expensive litigation such as where the cost of the inducement is ultimately borne by the purchaser whether by way of express contractual indemnity to the third party or an indemnity implied by the general law entitling a party to restitution in equity.
268   FA 2003, s 60.
269   Relying upon the exemption for land acquired pursuant to compulsory powers in FA 2003, s 60.
270   But query whether this is an acquisition by the local authority that is a land exchange; FA 2003, s 47.
271   FA 2003, s 43(4).

consideration of which Y transfers the freehold and X surrenders the lease to the local authority which does not make a payment to the persons transferring or surrendering the property but may be providing consideration to the developer in the form of an undertaking to grant a lease of the site when assembled or the development is completed. The local authority is a party to the transaction ie receives the property and so is a 'purchaser'[272] but it is questionable whether the local authority has provided the consideration.[273] A, the developer, has undoubtedly provided the consideration but he is not the person acquiring the subject-matter of the transaction, ie the freehold or leasehold interest. There is, therefore, a basic question which has to be resolved by HMRC Stamp Taxes as to whether in this situation an inducement provided by a third party which is consideration for some form of bargain is chargeable consideration.[274] The local authority may have agreed to grant a lease to A after A has completed the social housing for the local authority as part of the consideration and the development has been completed satisfactorily. The difference in the consideration provided by A to the local authority from that passing between the local authority and X and Y clearly indicates that A cannot be indirectly providing the consideration passing between the local authority and X and Y. Moreover, the local authority will be entering into a land exchange for a deemed consideration equal to market value,[275] and there are conceptual problems as to whether a third party inducement can be added to the deemed consideration. It is considered that the third party involvement has to be ignored.[276] The attempt to provide anti-avoidance legislation manifestly failed to take into account the structure of the basic charging provisions and appears to have missed the intended mark if the current judiciary apply the legislation in accordance with its express terms.

'Directly or indirectly'

5.103 It is specifically stated that to be 'chargeable' the actual or, presumably, any deemed consideration where appropriate (although deemed consideration is frequently a value rather than an asset) has to be provided[277] 'directly or indirectly' by the 'purchaser' or a person connected with him. These words, although superficially restricting the scope of chargeable consideration, are clearly intended to enlarge the scope of stamp duty land tax significantly. However, although as, a general principle, consideration has to be provided by the promisee it does not have to move to the promisor. The obvious case here is company reconstructions where the existing company agrees to transfer land to the new company in consideration of the latter issuing shares to the existing company's shareholders.[278]

---

[272] Ibid, s 43(5).

[273] This illustration raises the ambiguity referred to above in the words 'provision of the consideration'. The developer may be providing consideration where he is a party to the contract agreeing to make the payment in return for the transfer or surrender to the local authority. On the other hand, the local authority may make a payment without the developer being an executing party to the agreements. However, there may be some form of funding or other arrangement such as the payment of a premium for the lease to be granted by the local authority in due course, which provides the cash required by the local authority in order to discharge the obligations to the persons transferring or surrendering the land to it whether pursuant to contract or pursuant to the threat or exercise of compulsory powers; note the possible relief for the local authority pursuant to FA 2003, s 60.

[274] See also *Central and District Properties v IRC* [1966] 2 All ER 433; *Crane Fruehauf v IRC* [1975] STC 51; *Shop and Stores Developments v IRC* [1967] 1 All ER 42.

[275] FA 2003, s 47.

[276] The developer, C, will not be involved in a land exchange because any consideration that he may provide does not involve entering into another land transaction.

[277] It is difficult to see how 'deemed consideration' can be 'provided' by anyone. This may require treating 'provided' as being 'deemed to be provided' unless the legislation itself expressly provides that the deemed consideration is to be regarded as paid by the 'purchaser'.

[278] There is, however, a theory that in this case the consideration is receivable by the transferor company which

5.104 The 'direct' provision of the consideration is obvious, ie the purchaser or lessee pays the vendor or lessor, which will be the majority of cases in practice. In most cases the taxpayer 'directly' provides the consideration, but given the apparent importance of the consideration deriving from the 'purchaser' or a connected person, the word 'indirectly' is likely to become extremely important in practice. No statutory guidance is provided but it may apply to subsales where the first purchaser directs the subpurchaser to pay the consideration to the original vendor in satisfaction of the first purchaser's liability although such a direction to pay which may be an equitable assignment[279] would seem in 'plain English' to be the direct provision of the consideration. 'Indirect' it seems may refer to persons who agree to bear another's costs. The general case-law may provide some help in dealing with this issue particularly in the context of payments being made or other participation by third parties. There are fundamental and highly technical issues of drafting, structuring and analysis as to whether such third party involvement is consideration for the chargeable transaction[280] or represents a separate transaction and, if the former, whether its provided by the purchaser, as widely defined for these purposes, indirectly such as whether an agreement to indemnify, fund or purchase property from the third party in order to provide or to lend the necessary cash can amount to the 'indirect' provision of the consideration. It will be noted that there is no requirement that there is any form of 'arrangement' for the provision of the consideration. It is probable, therefore, that HMRC Stamp Taxes will seek to investigate cash movements and if, as a matter of fact, the cash moves in the appropriate direction the fact that there is no contractual commitment to that effect will be ignored. For example, if a sublease is granted out of a head lease and the rent is paid into a bank account out of which the rent or instalments of the premium are paid to the landlord, it is probable that HMRC Stamp Taxes will allege in an Enquiry that the subtenant is providing the consideration.[281] Similar contentions were raised from time to time in relation to leases for the purposes of stamp duty. Although, because such points are unconvincing, they were rarely effectively raised in practice, they have never been formally abandoned and given the much enlarged power of HMRC Stamp Taxes to interfere in transactions the potential risk of attack may have become more significant.

5.105 It is clear that the consideration is basically the *quid pro quo* provided under the contract,[282] not what ultimately, pursuant to the overall development of the transaction, is received by the 'vendor'. The fact that there are wider arrangements is irrelevant even where these arrangements relate to consideration provided under the agreement such as the onward sale. Although there is a fine line between consideration that is part of the arrangement and consideration for some larger arrangement of which the contract forms a part.[283]

5.106 Where the consideration or part thereof in the form of an inducement is provided by a third party, this may be 'guaranteed' expressly or impliedly by the 'purchaser'. If it is not so underwritten and is a genuinely independent offer by the third party, it cannot be said to be provided by the purchaser, in particular since it will not be

---

directs the consideration to be registered in the names of its shareholders because this has certain tax benefits. There may, on this theory, be a distribution or dividend by the transferor company.

279   *Diplock v Hammond* (1854) 5 De GM & G 320.
280   See, eg, *Crane Fruehauf v IRC* [1975] STC 51; *Shop and Stores Developments Ltd v IRC* [1967] 1 All ER 42.
281   Note decisions such as *Diplock v Hammond* (1854) 5 De GM & G 320 and *Roddick v Gandell* (1852) 1 De G M & G 763 on whether such arrangements are equitable assignments. This may have stamp duty land tax implications since a right to receive rents would appear to be a chargeable interest (see *Re Whiting* (1879) 10 Ch D 615) and may be chargeable if assigned in satisfaction of a debt (FA 2003, Sch 4, para 8).
282   *Central and District Properties v IRC* [1966] 2 All ER 433.
283   *Crane Fruehauf v IRC* [1975] STC 51.

part of the consideration for the transaction. This would seem to apply notwithstanding that the third party is receiving a 'fee' from the purchaser; but where this 'fee' is an indemnity or similar arrangement to meet the obligations of the third party who is to be fully reimbursed for his expenditure, the 'indirect' point is likely to be decided in favour of HMRC Stamp Taxes. Overall, it seems that such third party transactions are likely to involve close scrutiny upon an Enquiry.

5.107 FA 2003, Sch 4, para 1(1) limits the chargeable consideration to whatever is provided directly or indirectly by the purchaser or person connected with him. Two issues arise in such cases where 'inducements are involved':

- whether the inducement is part of the consideration for the transaction and whether it is offered to the vendor or the purchaser since an inducement to the purchaser to enter into the contract would not appear to be consideration for the 'acquisition' since it is moving in the same direction as the chargeable interest and is a 'reverse payment' but those responsible for the drafting of the legislation have a bizarre theory that such reverse consideration can be chargeable.[284] It does, however, raise real questions as to whether guarantees of unpaid purchase monies are part of the chargeable consideration;[285] and

- the amount or value of such third party inducements to be included as chargeable consideration.[286]

Consideration for the subject-matter of the transaction

5.108 In order to be chargeable the consideration must be given for the subject-matter of the transaction.[287] The subject-matter of a land transaction is defined by FA 2003, s 43(6) as being the chargeable interest acquired (which is also occasionally referred to as the 'main subject matter') together with any interest or right appurtenant or pertaining to the main chargeable interest that is acquired with that main interest.[288] This apparently simple proposition contains many sub-problems where there is a reverse payment which is accompanying the subject-matter of the transaction; it is not given 'for' the chargeable interest but for the service of accepting that interest;[289] but this obvious point appears not to have been understood by those responsible for the legislation. The problem is where A pays money to B to surrender a lease to C,[290] A's payment is not for the subject-matter of the transaction (ie the lease); it is for B's service of surrendering the lease to the freeholder C. There will, therefore, need to be a careful analysis of the transaction and considerable thought given to the drafting in order to avoid the consideration being given 'for' the chargeable interest.

---

[284] Exemptions for certain reverse payments are contained in the legislation. This would not be necessary if those consulting with HMRC Stamp Taxes had not advised on the basis that the law is contrary to longstanding general contractual principles and stamp duty practice and law.
[285] See, eg, *Curzon Offices v IRC* [1944] 1 All ER 163.
[286] See *Fielder v Vedlynn Ltd* [1992] STC 553 for the suggestion that guarantees may not add value to the consideration. In some contexts, however, the legislation may include a guarantee as a contingent liability for the amount of the principal debt outstanding plus interest regardless of the likelihood that payment will ever be made because of the financial stability of the principal debtor; FA 2003, Sch 4, para 8 including 'contingent' debts and liabilities.
[287] FA 2003, Sch 4, para 1.
[288] See **4.4**.
[289] See **5.92**.
[290] Where the consideration provided by A includes land the possible application of the land exchange rules must be considered; see **5.150**.

Global consideration – apportionment – subject-matter of the transaction

5.109 In many cases, the consideration may be 'global' in the sense there is a single consideration for a whole parcel of assets including land and other matters such as chattels but any consideration that is attributable to other matters will not be chargeable consideration for the purposes of stamp duty land tax. Where there is a contract for the acquisition of land including related equipment, and insofar as that equipment is not a fixture but retains its character as a chattel, there will be no charge to stamp duty land tax upon that part of the consideration.[291] The questions will arise in such cases, whether the payments are consideration for the acquisition of the chargeable interest, ie the subject-matter of the transaction or some other asset or service, ie for what is the consideration being provided.

Apportionment – just and reasonable – not market value

5.110 It is provided in FA 2003, Sch 4, para 4(1) that the consideration attributable:

•   to two or more land transactions; or

•   to a transaction that is part land transaction and part other matters; or

•   in part to matters making it a chargeable consideration and in part to other matters where it is not chargeable consideration,

must be apportioned on a just and reasonable basis.[292] If the consideration is not apportioned between the various components or if apportioned by the parties otherwise than on a just and reasonable basis then the stamp duty land tax applies as though it had been so apportioned, ie HMRC Stamp Taxes are given power to challenge the allocation of the consideration made by the parties.[293] The situation likely to arise most frequently in practice will be the entering into two separate agreements whereby A agrees to transfer or lease land to B for a consideration and agrees to construct a building upon that land for a consideration. Provided that, as was the case with stamp duty, there are two separate agreements and not a single agreement for the sale or lease of the land with the building thereon,[294] the consideration under the separate building agreement is for the building services and is not for the acquisition of the subject-matter of the land contract.[295] However, the consideration must be properly allocated between the land and the building works. Similar problems will arise where there is a sale of land as part of a business so that there will be trading stock and other items that are not subject to stamp duty land tax. In this context a key issue is the treatment of 'goodwill'. This may be 'embedded goodwill' ie a special value attributable to the land so that the consideration may be related to an interest in land and there is the question of the

---

[291] See **4.10**; on situations where there is residential and non-residential property some of which is within a disadvantaged area see FA 2003, Sch 6, paras 6(1) and 7(2) or the rent exceeds £1000; Sch 5, paras 9 and 9A.

[292] FA 2003, Sch 4, para 4(1). It is important to note that this is not the same as appointment on a 'market value' basis. This will be significant where there are transactions between connected parties, where the arrangement does not take place at market value pursuant to the connected company charges in ibid, s 53 or where a clawback of relief is obtained pursuant to one of the reliefs contained in ibid, Sch 7, paras 3(2) and 8(2) but the actual consideration is related to cost or book value.

[293] Ibid, Sch 4, para 4(2).

[294] *Paul v IRC* [1936] SC 443; *Kimbers & Co v IRC* [1936] 1 KB 132; *Prudential Assurance Co Ltd v IRC* [1992] STC 863.

[295] See also **8.8** and especially **5.181** on the defects in the drafting of the charging provisions in FA 2003, Sch 4, para 10.

apportionment between embedded goodwill and other items of goodwill.[296] HMRC, including Stamp Taxes, have issued a statement on certain aspects of selling goodwill with a business. Unfortunately, this is of little real benefit because it concentrates predominantly upon the valuation of the goodwill and the apportionment of the consideration to it; it does not deal with the fundamental question of how to identify embedded goodwill and true goodwill.

5.111 It is also provided that where there is consideration given for what is in substance one bargain then this can be attributable to the whole bargain even though separate consideration is, or purports to be, given for different elements of the bargain or, it seems, separate contracts.[297] This would appear to enable HMRC Stamp Taxes to reallocate consideration.[298] The fact that the apportionment has to be just and reasonable, ie is on an objective basis, makes it easier for HMRC Stamp Taxes to attack even arm's length agreements.[299] It must, however, not be overlooked that allocation on a basis solely or mainly with the object of reducing the charge to stamp duty land tax is likely to be treated as fraud.[300] This applies to wrongful allocation of a consideration with a view to obtaining the benefit of the lower rates of stamp duty land tax[301] or reducing the tax by producing an artificially low consideration. In addition to any general criminal sanctions that may be applicable for attempts to defraud HMRC Stamp Taxes or conspiracy to achieve the same,[302] there is a tax-related penalty for any person who fraudulently delivers a land transaction return or fails to make a correction.[303] Further, a person who assists in or induces the preparation or delivery of any information, return or other document that he knows will be or is likely to be used for any purposes of stamp duty land tax and he knows to be incorrect is liable to a penalty not exceeding £3,000.[304] However, more significantly, a person who is knowingly concerned in fraudulent evasion of tax by himself or any other person is guilty of an offence which carries with it:

- on summary conviction, imprisonment for a term not exceeding 6 months or a fine not exceeding the statutory maximum, or both;

- on conviction on indictment, imprisonment for a term not exceeding 7 years or a fine, or both.[305]

Wrongful allocation of the consideration could, however, easily be regarded by HMRC Stamp Taxes as falling within these areas. The allocation may be taken at face value by

---

[296]   See further **1.5**.
[297]   FA 2003, Sch 4, para 4(3).
[298]   If the parties allocate consideration on something other than a just and reasonable basis, they may be committing some form of fraud on HMRC Stamp Taxes: *Saunders v Edwards* [1987] 2 All ER 651; *Re Wragge* [1897] 1 Ch 796.
[299]   Where the test is more subjective in approach such as agreeing the price or value (*Stanton v Drayton Commercial Investment Co Ltd* [1982] STC 585) it is more difficult for HMRC Stamp Taxes to attack the arrangement since this may require allegations of bad faith which impose the criminal law burden of proof (*Re Wragge* [1897] 1 Ch 796).
[300]   *Saunders v Edwards* (above); *Lloyds and Scottish v Prentice* 121 SJ 847 (on appeal as *Lloyds and Scottish v Cyril Lord* [1992] BCLC 609.
[301]   See, eg, *Lloyds and Scottish v Prentice* (above).
[302]   See *Saunders v Edwards* (above).
[303]   FA 2003, Sch 10, para 8.
[304]   Ibid, s 96.
[305]   Ibid, s 95.

other divisions of the Revenue with adverse consequences[306] and possibly may involve company law downsides for transactions at other than market value.[307]

5.112 Where parties are engaged in part-exchange or similar exercises it will be important to ensure that any market values[308] or other figures that are required by the land transaction return are *bona fide* and can be corroborated by contemporaneous written expert evidence.[309]

Linked transactions, allocation and aggregation

5.113 This allocation of the chargeable consideration is important in relation to the lower rates of stamp duty land tax.[310] Although this question of lower rates is affected by the issue of linked transactions,[311] pursuant to the principles relating to linked transactions, the consideration for each of the separate linked transactions has to be aggregated in order to determine the 'relevant consideration' for the purposes of identifying the rates of stamp duty land tax which, since transactions can be linked retrospectively with subsequent transactions requiring recalculation of the tax and a fresh land transaction return. However, this requires aggregation only of the 'chargeable consideration' for the individual linked transaction,[312] ie the chargeable consideration[313] allocated to the chargeable interest and any interest or right appurtenant or pertaining to it that is acquired with it in each of the contracts.[314] The linking does not aggregate all of the actual consideration. This means that consideration properly allocated to property other than the land component or any other 'subject-matter of the transaction' is not chargeable consideration and is therefore ignored in deciding whether the lower rate of stamp duty land tax is applicable. For example, where there is a lease of business premises and an agreement to sell the business being carried on in those premises, although the contracts may be related, the lease will be eligible for the lower rates of stamp duty land tax. Notwithstanding that the aggregate consideration for the lease and the business assets[315] may exceed the threshold, this will not affect the rate and computation of stamp duty land tax.[316]

Provided by the purchaser or connected party

5.114 The consideration is chargeable only if it is 'provided' directly or indirectly by the purchaser or a person connected with him. The concept of the 'provision' of the consideration is essentially ambiguous and has been approached in different ways by

---

[306] *Re Hollebone* [1959] 2 All ER 152. They may not regard themselves as bound by the reallocation of the consideration by HMRC Stamp Taxes.

[307] *Aveling Barford v Perrion Ltd* [1989] BCLC 626; *Barclays Bank plc v British and Commonwealth Holdings plc* [1996] 1 All ER 381; including unlawful financial assistance: *Plaut v Steiner* [1989] BCLC 352; although this has been much reduced by Companies Act 2006.

[308] FA 2003, Sch 4, para 5.

[309] In practice it seems that HMRC Stamp Taxes are not anxious to challenge up-to-date independent professional valuations unless large amounts are involved.

[310] See **5.37**.

[311] FA 2003, s 55(4).

[312] But note the special principles applying to premiums and rent for linked leases; FA 2003, Sch 5, para 2(5) and (6).

[313] Actual consideration is, as such, not necessarily the appropriate amount in the aggregate process.

[314] FA 2003, s 43(6), Sch 4, para 1.

[315] Subject to the question of whether any element of the goodwill is 'embedded' in the land and should form part of the land price.

[316] See **5.38** on linked transactions where the consideration is 'exempt' or the transaction is relieved from liability.

different judges.[317] In a narrow sense a person 'provides' the consideration only if he supplies something to the relevant party under the terms of the contract. The consideration is the quid-pro-quo for the acquisition of the property.[318] On this analysis a person provides the consideration only if he is a party to the contract and his contribution is directly receivable by the vendor as part of the purchase price. Other views include the suggestion that a person 'provides' the consideration if he puts the relevant party in a position to be able to pay the consideration. For example, a bank which lends money to a purchaser provides the cash that enables the transaction to proceed. On this view consideration is providing the resources that enable the consideration to be paid. It can include loans by third parties to the purchaser and it has been suggested that it can include a person totally unconnected and possibly unaware of the transaction who buys assets from the purchaser which provides the purchaser with the cash to complete his transaction with the vendor. These views have been taken in practice from time to time by HMRC Stamp Taxes and although unsuccessful have attracted a certain amount of judicial sympathy. For example, in relation to intra-group transactions HMRC Stamp Taxes have for many decades taken the view that a loan by a third party to the purchaser,[319] if connected with the purchase, such as providing the cash or resources to pay the seller or landlord, is the provision of the consideration. This approach has been limited[320] but the fact that there are situations where the point could be taken indicates that there is a potential policy in HMRC Stamp Taxes to look to this wider view of 'provision of the consideration' ie enabling the purchaser to pay although the provider of the funds is not a purchaser himself or a party to the contract.

CALCULATING THE CONSIDERATION IN PARTICULAR CASES

Money

5.115 In most cases where the consideration is a monetary payment it will be easy to determine the amount chargeable, subject, of course, to the need to apportion the consideration on a just and reasonable basis in any particular case.[321] However, particular provisions need to be noted.

Foreign currency

5.116 Where a transaction is carried out in a currency other than sterling, the chargeable consideration is the sterling equivalent ascertained by reference to the London closing exchange rate effective on the date of the transaction, unless the parties used a different rate for the purposes of the transaction.[322]

---

[317] Note also the comments in *Ensign Tankers (Leasing) Ltd v Stokes* [1992] STC 226 to the effect that the funding arrangement in that case meant that the parties had not 'incurred expenditure'.

[318] *Shop and Stores Developments v IRC* [1967] 1 All ER 42.

[319] HMRC Stamp Taxes have also taken the point that an interest free or low rate loan or an interest free unpaid consideration is not a *bona fide* commercial transaction see **12.88** and **12.101**.

[320] Statement of Practice 3/98; which appears to have been carried over from stamp duty to stamp duty land tax in the relevant Manual.

[321] See **5.109**.

[322] FA 2003, Sch 4, para 9.

Unpaid consideration

5.117 The fact that the consideration is left outstanding as a debt, whether or not bearing interest so that the 'value' of the debt may be below its face value, does not provide a basis for discounting the chargeable amount because of the delayed payment.

Instalments

5.118 Where all or part of the consideration other than rent is payable by instalments which are not, for these purposes, regarded as an annuity[323] or other periodical payment,[324] over a period of time, the amount or value of the chargeable consideration for a transaction is determined without any discount for the postponement of the right to receive it or any part of it.[325]

There will be some interesting technical debates with HMRC Stamp Taxes on the differences between instalments and periodical payments. The point seems likely to turn upon the drafting.[326] If the consideration is expressed as a fixed sum payable by specified amounts, this is likely to be regarded as an arrangement involving instalments, particularly if the amounts of the various payments are not the same but are different only because an interest element is added to the various payments. On the other hand, if there is no fixed sum divided into specified payments but simply a statement that the consideration is a series of payments of substantially the same amount, this will be regarded as an annual or periodical payment.

5.119 There is no power given to the taxpayer to apply to pay the tax by instalments even where the consideration is payable by instalments or periodically, or where part of the consideration treated as an 'annuity' is either 'contingent' or 'uncertain' or 'unascertained'.[327]

Annuities and annual and similar payments other than rent and instalments[328]

Basics

5.120 Where the chargeable consideration for a land transaction consists of or includes an annuity or any consideration, other than rent or instalments, that falls to be paid or provided periodically[329] and the period of the consideration is payable either:

- for life; or

- in perpetuity;[330] or

---

323   Ibid, s 52; see **5.102**.
324   Ibid, s 52(6); see **5.120** and, eg, *Quietlece Ltd v IRC* [1984] STC 95.
325   Ibid, Sch 4, para 3.
326   See **5.123**.
327   FA 2003, s 52(7)(a); see **5.121**.
328   On the question of whether VAT that is reserved separately from the rent is 'rent' or is some form of premium payable periodically as indicated in Statements of Practice SP6/91 and SP11/91 in relation to stamp duty see **7.64**.
329   See *Quietlece Ltd v IRC* [1984] STC 95.
330   Note the issue of irredeemable debentures and long-term debt as an annuity – *Mersey Docks and Harbour Board v IRC* [1897] 1 QB 786.

- for an indefinite term; or

- for a definite term exceeding 12 years,

this chargeable consideration is limited to 12 years of annual payments.[331] Presumably, where the period does not fall within the above list, such as for a definite term not exceeding 12 years, the chargeable consideration for the purposes of stamp duty land tax is treated as consideration payable by instalments upon the aggregate amount[332] or, where 'uncertain', upon the basis of an initial reasonable estimate[333] adjusted for each payment as necessary.[334] Annual payments are payments in respect of each successive period of 12 months beginning with the effective date of the transaction,[335] which may not coincide with the contractual provisions relating to the timing of the payments so that separate calculations may be required for this purpose. The planning of home annuity or reversionary or similar value release schemes is important because this 12-year arbitrary principle of assessing the chargeable consideration may bear no relationship to the actuarial or commercial value of the transaction. In general it may be more stamp duty land tax efficient to dispose of the interest in the land for a fixed sum which is then utilised to provide the premium for the grant of the annuity.[336] A transfer of an interest, if for a fixed sum, is subject to stamp duty land tax upon the actual price; the fact that the consideration is to be applied in the purchase of an annuity is irrelevant.[337] The grant of the annuity is not the consideration for the acquisition of the chargeable interest or subject-matter of the transaction.[338]

Variable annuities

5.121 Where the annual amount varies[339] then the tax has to be paid upon the basis of a reasonable estimate of the amount expected to be paid over the appropriate period;[340] except where the annuity or periodical payment is adjustable in line with the Retail Prices Index is ignored,[341] although linking to any other form of index or a modified Retail Prices Index will bring the uncertain consideration rules into play; but the provisions for subsequent, retrospective adjustment in relation to other forms of variable consideration where these cease to be uncertain or contingent and the application to apply to defer payment do not apply.[342] It would seem, therefore, that where there is a variable annuity the original reasonable estimate stands and no adjustments are required but serious penalties and interest are likely to be imposed if, with the benefit of hindsight, HMRC Stamp Taxes discover that the original estimate was below the actual outcome, especially if the taxpayer cannot produce contemporaneous written advice from independent professional advisers to support the original figures in the land transaction return. There is, however, a particular quirk in

---

[331] FA 2003, s 52(1) and (2). There is no subsequent repayment if the annuity terminates within the 12-year period because, eg, of the death of the annuitant.
[332] Ibid, Sch 4, para 3.
[333] Ibid, s 51(3).
[334] Ibid, s 80.
[335] Ibid, s 52(4).
[336] It may be prudent to have actual cash movements rather than a mere set-off since the latter route may be easier for HMRC Stamp Taxes to attack as a sale for an annuity.
[337] Unless HMRC Stamp Taxes seek to apply the general anti-avoidance provisions aggressively.
[338] FA 2003, Sch 4, para 1.
[339] Presumably taking into account possible variations in the rate of VAT or any other tax should this apply such as an annuity for a net sum after deduction of tax.
[340] FA 2003, s 51.
[341] Ibid, s 52(3).
[342] Ibid, s 52(5) and (7).

that where the amount payable varies or may vary, the 12 years taken into account are the 12 highest annual payments. No guidance is provided as to how to determine the 12 highest payments where consideration is 'uncertain' – presumably the parties have to make their reasonable estimate of the 12 highest amounts expected during the lifetime of the annuity but the term of the annuity may also be uncertain such as an annuity for life.[343] This may mean that in the case of annuities that have a life or deemed life of greater than 12 years will be taxed upon the basis of estimates of annuity payments after the expiration of the first 12 years. This is no doubt designed as some form of anti-avoidance measure designed to prevent parties postponing the benefits in some way. However, there may be questions as to whether any later payments are in fact instalments of the annuity or some other form of payment such as a return of premium[344] or possible compensation on early redemption or other matters.[345]

5.122 The taxpayer is, therefore, upon a significant risk. There is no ability to claim a refund if the original estimate is too high; but there is a risk that if the estimate is too low HMRC Stamp Taxes will almost certainly allege negligence in any Enquiry or use this as a basis for alleging negligence when making a discovery in order to enlarge the period for attack to 21 years.[346] and the possibility of an allegation of fraud cannot be totally ruled out. There is also a difficult technical question as to whether the 'purchaser', ie the party 'acquiring' the chargeable interest and granting the annuity, will be regarded as not being negligent or fraudulent if he completes the land transaction return form upon the basis of the actuarial value of the annuity, rather than making an estimate of the amount that might be payable upon the statutory assumption that the annuitant will survive for the 12-year period regardless of age and health. If the annuity is not variable, the 12-year period will apply automatically, but if the annuity is 'variable' there is an argument that the 12-year period is, in effect, replaced by the reasonable estimate requirement,[347] when the actuarial value may be the relevant, non-reviewable basis. The official attitude is not known.

'Periodical payments' or 'instalments'

5.123 The difference between the computation rules for deferred consideration and periodical payments is clearly important. It would seem that this may be a matter of drafting:

- a consideration of £1,000,000 payable by ten equal instalments of £100,000 would appear to be a deferred consideration;

- a consideration consisting of ten annual payments of £100,000 without any fixed sum being specified would appear to be a periodical payment.

In the above illustration, the charge to stamp duty land tax would be the same, but if the payment period exceeded 12 years then the difference might become important. For example:

---

[343] Ibid, s 52(4).
[344] See *General Accident v IRC* [1904] 2 KB 658.
[345] *Knights Deep v IRC* [1900] 1 QB 217; *Western United Investment Co v IRC* [1958] 1 All ER 257.
[346] On inappropriate valuations or estimates as a basis for making a discovery see *Langham v Veltema* [2004] STC 544; on the extended powers to issue discovery assessments see FA 2003, Sch 10, para 28.
[347] FA 2003, s 51(2).

- a consideration of £20,000,000 payable by 20 annual instalments, if treated as a deferred consideration, would be subject to stamp duty land tax upon £20,000,000; but

- a consideration consisting of £1,000,000 payable annually for 20 years would, it seems, be taxable upon a consideration of 12 years, namely £12,000,000.

5.124 In relation to stamp duty, an arrangement for periodical payments which contained the provision for payment of the balance forthwith upon default in any instalment was held not to affect the position, since the payment of 'compensation' or damages for breach was not an item that could be included in the computation of stamp duty.[348] Similarly, arrangements in a policy for the return of the premium, was not a payment of insurance monies or an annuity instalment.[349] It remains to be seen whether such arrangements would be equally effective to escape the charge for the purposes of stamp duty land tax.

Lease payments[350]

5.125 It would seem that, notwithstanding the exclusion of rents from these provisions, a 'premium' payable by instalments could qualify as a periodical payment within these provisions. This may raise interesting questions of drafting in relation to instalment payments and leases as to whether the payments are premium or rent. In many cases in practice the issue is not important provided that the payment is separately apportioned from the main rent so that it is not taxable as 'rent'[351] since most such payments related to leases are specifically exempt from tax.[352] Unfortunately there is no such exclusion for VAT payable in respect of rent which is, *prima facie*, taxable as a periodical premium. It seems that if the VAT is reserved either as part of the rent[353] it is, in practice, subject to stamp duty land tax as rent;[354] but if it is not reserved as rent it may be a premium payable periodically subject to stamp duty land tax upon the total amount of VAT payable, broadly, over the life of the lease or 12 years, whichever is the shorter.[355]

Value Added Tax[356]

General issues

5.126 Stamp duty land tax is charged upon any VAT actually chargeable in respect of the transaction.[357] The fact that the purchaser or tenant or other person paying the VAT may be able to recover the input tax in whole or in part is not a relevant factor and stamp duty land tax is payable upon the entirety of the VAT.[358] It may not apply to any VAT chargeable by virtue of an exercise of the option to tax pursuant to Value Added

---

[348] *Western United Investment Co v IRC* [1958] Ch 392; see also *Photo Productions Ltd v Securicor Transport Ltd* [1981] 2 WLR 283; especially Lord Diplock.
[349] See *Stevenson Securities v IRC* [1959] SLT 125; *Commercial Union Assurance Co. v IRC* [1938] 2 KB 551; *General Accident Corporation v IRC* (1906) 8 F (Ct of Sess) 477.
[350] See **Chapter 7**.
[351] FA 2003, Sch 17A, para 6.
[352] Ibid, Sch 17A, para 10.
[353] See **7.147** on VAT making rent variable.
[354] FA 2003, Sch 5, para 4(1).
[355] Ibid, s 52.
[356] On VAT and rent see **7.68**.
[357] FA 2003, Sch 4, para 2.
[358] Compare *Glenrothes Development Corporation v IRC* [1994] STC 74.

Tax Act 1994, Sch 10, para 2, made after the effective date of the transaction but this may be a factor in determining whether there has been an abnormal rent increase,[359] or when carrying out the review of at the end of the fifth year. This applies so that:

- if the transaction is exempt as at the effective date, the existence of the as yet unexercised option to tax does not, of itself, make the consideration uncertain within FA 2003; s 51(2);[360] but it seems that the exercise of the option to tax is regarded by HMRC Stamp Taxes as an increase in the rent; and

- the subsequent exercise of the option to tax is an unlikely event except in relation to leases and rents. There appear to be relatively few cases other than leases where there can be an effective exercise of the option to tax. However, there may be an issue where there is a difference between the effective date for stamp duty land tax and the tax point for the purpose of VAT. For example, there may be substantial performance of the agreement before the tax point for the purpose of VAT so that the exercise is too late for the computation of the consideration as at the effective date. However, it is provided that where substantial performance is followed by completion between the same parties a further return is required and additional tax payable.[361] The introduction of the two separate charges in relation to new leases[362] complicates this simple principle. It seems that if the option to tax is exercised after substantial performance of the agreement[363] for lease but before the actual grant the new calculation of the tax upon the rent when the lease is granted (or the new periodical premium) will have to take into account the VAT now payable. The exemption for substantial performance does not carry over to the grant of the lease; and

- it is the view of HMRC Stamp Taxes that where the rate of VAT changes so that, for example, rent increases or reduces this means that the rent is a variable rent governed by the rules applicable thereto.[364] This means, for example, should the rate of VAT change during the first five years of the term there may be a need to file several stamp duty land tax returns depending upon how far the variation in the rate of VAT coincides with the years of the lease for the purposes of computing the rent and possible liability to pay additional tax or claims for refund of VAT because the rate is lower than that included in the original return.[365] It seems that if the rate of VAT takes effect outside the five year period it may be a factor in determining whether there has been an abnormal increase in the rent.

Value Added Tax and Land exchanges

5.127 In some cases an actual charge to VAT may be ignored. In the case of land exchanges involving major interests the charge is upon the market value of the interest

---

[359]   FA 2003, Sch 17A, paras 14 and 15.
[360]   See **7.66**.
[361]   FA 2003, s 44(8).
[362]   Ibid, Sch 17A, para 12A; see **7.25**.
[363]   Different issues arise where the lease is varied by deed to introduce a charge to VAT or power to charge VAT as an increase of 'rent'; see **Chapter 7**.
[364]   FA 2003, Sch 17A, paras 7, 8, 13, 14 and 15.
[365]   The question of the number and timing of returns and payments has been complicated by the reason of HMRC Stamp Taxes to the temporary reduction in the rate of VAT. Since this view is that rent that is subject to VAT is a variable rent which can be affected by a rate change at any time it seems that the rent for the first 5 years of the term does not become 'ascertained' until the expiration of the first 5 years (FA 2003, s 80) so that no return is required, for example, for a rent review during the first 5 years.

being acquired. Cash adjustments between the parties are ignored.[366] This means that if either or both of the land transfers are actually or potentially subject to VAT because they are not transfers of going concerns any cash payments whether made in full or by way of set-off are irrelevant in computing the tax. However, there is the wider question in relation to market value namely whether when determining market value or 'costs'[367] VAT has to be included. There is a question as to whether the fiscal valuation assumptions take account of VAT and, in particular, whether it is to be assumed that the transaction giving rise to the valuation would include VAT or would be exempt or possibly affected by the transfer of the going concern provisions.[368]

Value Added Tax and Market value

5.128 The problem here that is being raised with HMRC Stamp Taxes is whether the 'market value' chargeable consideration, which can arise in contexts other than exchanges such as the connected company charge or dealings between partners and partnerships, includes VAT. The issue is what assumptions in relation to VAT are to be made as regards the hypothetical market sale that is the basis for valuation. This raises the question of the terms of the sale in the open market such as whether the transaction would be subject to VAT and, in particular, where land is involved whether the option to tax would or would not be assumed to be exercised or whether the transaction might, in the hypothetical sale, qualify as a transfer of a going concern. These are, of course, assumptions as to the identity of the vendor in the hypothetical sale although questions as to the identity of the hypothetical purchaser in the open market would be entitled to credit for the input tax. However, since the 'price' includes VAT the fact that the purchaser might be able to recover the VAT would appear to be irrelevant. This is obviously a key issue that will need to be raised at a preliminary stage with HMRC Stamp Taxes where valuation disputes arise as will the question of the identity of the parties to the hypothetical sale although it seems that at present HMRC Stamp Taxes do not require the parties to increase the amount because of VAT.

5.129 'Market value' is defined[369] as being the 'price' which the property would realise on a sale on the open market. 'Price' is regarded as what the other party would pay, rather than what the seller would receive so that, *prima facie*, it could include any VAT that would arise upon the hypothetical transaction.[370] There are, however, complex issues of principle where the chargeable interest in question has not been opted to tax and the transaction would be exempt from VAT or whether it can be assumed that the hypothetical transaction can be notionally structured as a successful transfer of a going concern. It is considered that in these types of situation the market value will ignore VAT since this either cannot or may not arise. For example, where there is a sale from A to B is it to be assumed that the seller in the open market is A selling to someone other than B in order to produce a better price because there may be a special purchaser from A or whether B is the hypothetical seller of the property that he has acquired in the open market.[371] The VAT is ignored as a general matter.

---

[366] FA 2003, Sch 4, para 5.
[367] Ibid, Sch 4, para 11.
[368] See **5.130**.
[369] FA 2003, Sch 4, para 7.
[370] Compare *Glenrothes Development Corporation v IRC* [1994] STC 74.
[371] There are also issues as to the terms of the hypothetical sale in the open market and whether this takes into account the terms of the actual transaction between the parties, should there be one. See **Chapter 27**.

Value Added Tax and Transfer of Going Concern

5.130 Parties frequently enter into a transaction that they believe is excluded from the charge to VAT because it is a transfer of a going concern;[372] but in order to protect the vendor the contract will usually contain a clause to the effect that if the transaction is not a transfer of a going concern the vendor will issue a tax invoice and upon receipt the purchaser will pay the extra amount. It seems to be obvious that such an arrangement forms part of the consideration ie making it variable or adjustable.

5.131 It appears to be the view of HMRC Stamp Taxes that in such circumstance the provisions for payment of the VAT will not be an 'uncertain sum', since all of the circumstances relating to liability to VAT or the availability of the treatment as a transfer of a going concern are *prima facie* known at the effective date (ie it is in their view an 'unascertained sum') which has to be included in the 'estimate' of the chargeable consideration but the taxpayer cannot postpone the payment of stamp duty land tax upon the potential VAT element[373] which may also push the transaction into a higher tax rate. On the surface, the VAT is either payable or not and the stamp duty land tax is applicable accordingly. The fact that HMRC Customs and Excise might disagree with the analysis of the parties is irrelevant since the ultimate outcome depends upon the facts. Taking the view that the transaction is a transfer of a going concern which later proves to be incorrect means that the self-assessment and reporting obligations have not been properly observed. Interest and penalties may be imposed.

5.132 However, in certain circumstances this view may appear to be overly simplistic since it appears to be based on the view that the effective date for stamp duty land tax will always be the same as the tax point for VAT so that there can be no difference in the fact situation for both taxes. A wrong assumption since, in the view of HMRC Stamp Taxes, there can be two effective dates for stamp duty land tax and both of these cannot correspond with the tax point for VAT, and there is no necessity that one of these two effective dates will correspond with the VAT tax point. It also fails to take into account the fact that the availability of the treatment as a transfer of a going concern depends, *inter alia*, upon the transferee (ie the stamp duty land tax 'purchaser') carrying on the same business as the disposer for a certain, unspecified time after the transaction. In consequence, the treatment as a transfer of a going concern depends, in part at least, upon the conduct of the 'purchaser'. This introduces an element of 'uncertainty' into the situation but it seems inconceivable that those responsible for the structuring of stamp duty land tax can have intended the application of the variable consideration rules in FA 2003, s 51(1) and (2), to depend upon whether or not there might at the effective date be a 'retrospective' loss of the treatment by reason of subsequent actions of the purchaser. There is currently a dispute as to how this situation should be reported. It is the view of HMRC Stamp Taxes that this is a case of 'unascertained' consideration and the potential VAT has to be included in the assessment. The full stamp duty land tax is payable since there is no power to defer the payment of tax on 'unascertained consideration' although this is estimated or provisional; the extra tax can be reclaimed when the transaction is officially confirmed as a transfer of a going concern, although it will be difficult to point to such a date in many cases. The contrary, more widely held view is that the VAT is a 'contingent sum', ie it is payable only if demanded by the vendor. In such a case although the potential VAT has to be included in the initial return it is possible to apply to defer the payment of the tax upon the potential VAT. However, notwithstanding the postponement the potential VAT still has

---

[372]   Value Added Tax Act 1994, s 49; Value Added Tax (Special Provisions) Order 1995, SI 1995/1268, reg 5.
[373]   FA 2003, s 90; Stamp Duty Land Tax (Administration) Regulations 2003, SI 2003/2837, Part 4.

to be included in the initial computation of the tax and may increase the rate of stamp duty land tax which has to be applied to the net of VAT price. Should the transaction be confirmed as a transfer of a going concern the deferred tax ceases to be payable, the rate will be reduced and the tax paid in respect of the higher rate can be reclaimed. HMRC Stamp Taxes are resisting such applications. Failure to deal with the land transaction return on either of the above bases referring to the potential VAT could expose the parties to penalties and late payment interest charges particularly if the VAT does become payable.[374]

Debts and liabilities satisfied or assumed

5.133 FA 2003, Sch 4, para 8, provides that, where the chargeable consideration for a land transaction consists in whole or in part of the satisfaction or release of a pre-existing debt due to the purchaser or landlord or a debt owed by the vendor or lessor or grantor or other party benefiting from the transaction or consists of the assumption of an existing debt by the purchaser or tenant or other taxpayer, the amount of the debt satisfied, released or assumed is to be taken as being the whole or part of the chargeable consideration for the transaction.

Assumption or satisfaction of liabilities

5.134 Three areas of potential charge to stamp duty land tax arise in this context:

- transfers of property in satisfaction of a debt (which includes contingent as well as certain, immediate and future debts) such as where a mortgagee forecloses;[375]

- transfer of property where the transferee assumes liabilities of the vendor such as on the purchase of a business; or

- a transfer of property which is subject to a charge.[376]

There are numerous exemptions from these basic charges such as the administration or variation of the estates of deceased individuals.[377]

5.135 The general assumption of liabilities can arise as a potential trap for the unwary where there is a sale of a business as a going concern with the purchaser taking over, *inter alia*, the debtors and creditors of the business. The effect of the

---

[374] Also failure to refer to this possible payment may be indicative that the taxpayer has not been fully advised as to his ongoing liabilities in relation to the tax and may fail to declare the tax should the VAT become payable.

[375] In other situations there is unlikely to be a charge to stamp duty land tax. The transfer by way of foreclosure is a transfer in full or partial satisfaction of the debt clearly within the charging provisions. Other methods of enforcement such as exercising the power of sale or appointing a receiver are not chargeable events because there is no transfer pursuant to the exercise of the relevant power. However, the Revenue Solicitor advised HMRC Stamp Taxes, in a previous recession, that where the mortgagee takes possession of property where there is a negative equity the ownership of the property passes to the mortgagee giving rise to a potential charge to tax. It is considered that this view is totally unsupported by the authorities and correct analysis. See also *English Sewing Cotton Co Ltd v IRC* [1947] 1 All ER 679.

[376] It is unclear whether the former practice relating to gifts of property subject to a mortgage where the donee did not expressly or impliedly assume liability in respect of the mortgage or was to be indemnified by the donor will be carried over into the new regime as being a situation where the liability is not assumed by the transferee. See Statement of Practice SP6/90.

[377] FA 2003, Sch 3, paras 3A and 4; Sch 4, paras 8 and 8A; see **Chapter 9**.

charging/computational provisions is that the actual cash consideration is increased by the amount of the liabilities taken over on a gross basis, ie the total liabilities involved not the net figure after deducting debtors to the business. This then has to be apportioned between the individual assets or groups of assets on a just and reasonable basis.[378] Although the assumption of liabilities does not apply to any VAT arising in respect of the particular transaction, it may include the outstanding VAT or other tax liabilities of the vendor in relation to the business.[379] The liabilities may also include contingent liabilities such as liabilities in respect of guarantees this may give rise to considerable problems where the business is insolvent because the liabilities, including contingent liabilities, exceed the current value of the assets.

Debt

5.136 The chargeable interest may be transferred where a 'debt' is involved in the consideration such as where the transferee accepts the property in full or partial satisfaction of a pre-existing debt. This is taxed upon the relevant amount outstanding including interest as at the effective date[380] or the market value if smaller than the debt.[381] For these purposes 'debt' means an obligation, whether certain or contingent, to pay a sum of money either immediately or in the future;[382] and an existing debt means a debt created or arising before the effective date on or otherwise than in connection with the transaction.[383] These include both the principal and any interest which has accrued due on or before the effective date.[384] This limits the charge to liabilities assumed which existed before the transaction; it does not apply to the question of unpaid consideration for the particular land transaction.[385]

Contingent obligations – guarantees etc

5.137 The definition of 'debt' as including contingent obligations to pay money or future obligations raises many problems. It clearly includes transfers of property subject to a mortgage where the mortgage was given to secure a guarantee or indemnity. This can be a major problem where, for example, there is a transfer of the matrimonial home into joint names[386] which is subject to a charge or guarantee to the bank in respect of a loan to or indebtedness of the family company or business. It is possible that many transfers into joint names do not declare the existence of such guarantees and should the parties be unfortunate enough to be selected for an Enquiry the potential tax and related penalty and interest issues could be significant. In such a case the definition of the amount of the debt as being the principal amount payable together with any interest as accrued on the day on or before the effective date of the transaction means that in such a case the consideration will be the full face value of the guaranteed debt plus any outstanding interest. In this case the restriction of the charge to market value could be important.[387]

---

[378] This is an additional problem to that of whether the payment for 'goodwill' is really a misdescribed payment of a premium price for the land, see **1.5**.

[379] See, for example, *Ponsonby v Customs and Excise* [1988] STC 28.

[380] FA 2003, Sch 4, para 8.

[381] Ibid, Sch 4, para 8(2).

[382] Ibid, Sch 4, para 8(3)(a).

[383] Ibid, Sch 4, para 8(3)(b).

[384] Ibid, Sch 4, para 8(3)(c).

[385] Such unpaid consideration is consideration payable on a deferred or postponed basis within ibid, Sch 4, para 3; see **5.118**.

[386] See for relief FA 2003, Sch 3, para 3; Sch 4, paras 8 and 8A.

[387] Ibid, Sch 4, para 8(2).

Assumption of liabilities – indemnities

5.138 The assumption of liabilities frequently takes the form of an agreement to give an indemnity since it is not possible to assign a liability. This means that, in practice, properly advised vendors will require the purchaser to undertake to pay the liabilities and to indemnify the vendor should he be required to discharge any such outstanding liabilities.[388] Such an indemnity is undoubtedly the assumption of the liability within the computational provisions and so fully chargeable. There may be an issue between agreeing to indemnify a vendor in the event of liability arising to the vendor as a result of some form of breach. Such an indemnity, it is thought, would not form part of the chargeable consideration.[389] In this context it should be noted that it is provided[390] that, where a purchaser agrees to indemnify the vendor in respect of liability to a third party arising from breach of an obligation owed by the vendor in relation to the land that is the subject-matter of the transaction,[391] neither the agreement nor any payment made in pursuance of the indemnity counts as chargeable consideration.[392] Not all breaches will be within its protection because it refers to obligations or covenants affecting the vendor. It is not a contingent liability but a compensation payment arising in certain circumstances.[393] However, not all indemnities will be so limited. It may amount to an undertaking, as mentioned previously, and the drafting may give rise to problems. For example, where a vendor is selling land with the benefit of planning permission he may require some comfort from the purchaser in relation to the performance of the obligations contained in the 'Section 106 Agreement'. Whilst it seems that an indemnity in relation to any liability arising upon the vendor in the event of breach by the purchaser is unlikely to form part of the chargeable consideration, a positive obligation imposed by the vendor upon the purchaser to carry out the terms of the planning arrangements will constitute part of the consideration being supplied by the purchaser. In consequence, the obligations pursuant to the Section 106 Agreement such as to pay cash to the local authority or to carry out works upon land retained by the local authority such as building new schools or social housing would become part of the consideration for the transfer of the land and would appear to be, *prima facie*, taxable consideration by reference to the amount of the cash and the costs of the works not being carried out upon the land to be acquired.[394] This is not a simple indemnity in the event of a breach or default but is a positive obligation. It is, therefore, more likely to be regarded by HMRC Stamp Taxes as chargeable consideration.

Inherent liabilities – future rent etc

5.139 It also appears that the assumption of inherent liabilities is not within these charging provisions, bringing forward the principle of *Swayne v IRC*[395] that such liabilities were not subject to stamp duty. In consequence, an agreement, for example, by an assignee of a lease to indemnify the tenant against future payments of rent will not be included within the chargeable consideration.[396] Unfortunately, this legislation raises

[388] Note the drafting issues such as *Spectros International plc v Maddern* [1997] STC 114.
[389] See FA 2003, Sch 4, para 16.
[390] Ibid, Sch 4, para 16.
[391] Defined in ibid, s 43(6).
[392] Ibid, Sch 4, para 16.
[393] Compare *Western United Investment Co v IRC* [1958] 1 All ER 257.
[394] And so not within the protection for such works pursuant to FA 2003, Sch 4, para 10.
[395] [1900] 1 QB 172.
[396] FA 2003, Sch 17A, para 17 but note that this does not apply to the special charge upon future rents reserved by leases which were exempt when granted – ibid, Sch 17A, para 11.

considerable problems. The decision in *Swayne v IRC*[397] indicated that as a matter of general principle inherent liabilities such as rent and obligations relating to covenants and, possibly, liabilities automatically transferring upon the purchase of land in relation to Section 106 Agreements were not chargeable consideration. The argument is that if the purchaser has no choice but to take the property with the liability then it is not consideration.[398] The liability is imposed upon him rather than voluntarily assumed. Unfortunately, the fact that those responsible for preparing the legislation took the view that it was necessary to exclude inherent liabilities of a particular nature indicates that, in their view, they intend to take the argument that inherent liabilities are chargeable consideration. Obviously, arguments for the general principle will be faced with the argument by HMRC Stamp Taxes that if that general principle were correct, the legislation would be redundant and there could be no such thing as redundant tax legislation.

Transfers subject to a charge

5.140 The transfer of property that is subject to a mortgage is *prima facie* within this charge where the taxpayer assumes liability in respect of the mortgage.[399] If the transferee provides other consideration or merely assumes liability in respect of the mortgage the chargeable consideration will consist of or be increased by the amount of the mortgage together with any unpaid interest outstanding at the effective date.[400] The charge requires the assumption of a liability; the mere fact that the property is transferred subject to a charge no longer automatically increases the chargeable consideration. The stamp duty land tax liability depends upon the undertaking given by the transferee. If the transferee agrees to discharge the debt or to indemnify the transferor the mortgage and accrued, unpaid interest will be taxable as part of the consideration. However, if the transferee merely takes over the property subject to the charge, such as where he acknowledges the existence of the mortgage but on a without recourse basis so that there is no fresh covenant to pay the debt there is no assumption of liability.[401] This is subject to anti-avoidance legislation. Where the property is transferred subject to a charge and the liability is not assumed at the time of the transaction but subsequently the rights or liabilities in relation to the debt charged on the property are changed as a result of or in connection with the transaction there is deemed to be an assumption of that secured debt[402] without the assumption of liability no charge to tax will arise. Unfortunately owing to the desire of certain persons to be cosy with HMRC and who paid little regard to client confidentiality, certain preliminary planning ideas were leaked to HMRC Stamp Taxes who introduced anti-avoidance legislation at a very late stage in that year's Finance Bill. These amendments were prepared in a hurry and were not debated so that there are many issues arising, some of which were the result of the persons leaking the arrangements not being as technically competent as they believed themselves to be.

---

[397] [1900] 1 QB 172.

[398] Note *Halsall v Brizell* [1957] Ch 169; he who takes the benefit must take the burden.

[399] See FA 2003, Sch 4, para 8(1)(b).

[400] Attempts to escape from these problems by not transferring the land but an interest in the proceeds of sale will operate to mean that only a net cash figure is being involved; but it appears that a right to participate in the proceeds of sale may be some form of interest in property and therefore is potentially a chargeable interest for the purposes of stamp duty land tax; see **4.30**.

[401] It was formerly stamp duty practice not to impose the charge where the transferor agreed to indemnify the transferee in respect of the mortgage. It seems that this practice has been carried over into the new regime since there is no assumption of liability if properly drafted.

[402] FA 2003, Sch 4, para 8(1A).

5.141 These provisions[403] are to the effect that if, pursuant to or in connection with[404] a transfer of property subject to a charge where there is no assumption of liability, there is subsequently a change in the mortgage arrangements, the subsequent variation is treated retrospectively as an assumption of the mortgage liability and the original land transaction return has to be replaced by a further form prepared on a retrospective basis.

5.142 There will, in practice, be significant problems as to what are offending arrangements such as whether any subsequent arrangements are variations relating to the mortgage such as voluntary repayment by the purchaser[405] or repayment on a subsequent spontaneous arrangement re-financing arrangement. These would appear to be potentially unconnected with the transfer of the chargeable interest but will be vulnerable to attack by HMRC Stamp Taxes. Notwithstanding that there would be no technical or other merit in such an attack HMRC Stamp Taxes will be tempted and likely not to resist the temptation to apply these provisions on the basis that the costs of an Enquiry or discovery assessment and subsequently litigation will exceed the amount of the stamp duty land tax involved so that the taxpayer will as in many stamp tax situations, in any reasonable commercial assessment of the situation, be economically coerced into capitulating to an unreasonable view of HMRC Stamp Taxes. The fact that the subsequent arrangements were the consequence of subsequent events and not part of the original transaction is most unlikely, in the writer's experience, to be accepted by HMRC Stamp Taxes and it will be an expensive and a probably futile exercise to attempt to prove otherwise before the current judiciary.

Joint names

5.143 Parties, such as spouses, frequently transfer property that is subject to a mortgage from the name of one party into joint names or transfer out of joint names into the name of one of them. The mortgage may constitute chargeable consideration.[406] The previous stamp duty concession[407] for transfers of part interests has been carried forward into the stamp duty land tax legislation.[408] Where the mortgage liability is secured on property and immediately before the transaction there were two or more persons each holding an undivided share of the property or where there are two or more such persons immediately afterwards only part of the mortgage is included in the chargeable consideration. It seems, also, the transaction will apply to cases where one of two joint owners transfers the property into a single name such as the matrimonial home held in joint names or jointly owned property is put into a single name.[409] However, in such a case the transferee may already be jointly and severally liable in respect of the whole of the mortgage. It is, therefore, arguable that in such a case the transferee is not assuming any liability since he was already obliged to the mortgagee. For these purposes, it is provided that the amount of the secured debt assumed is to be determined as if the amount of the debt were the proportion of the corresponding liability by each of the persons. It seems that HMRC Stamp Taxes may take the view that there is a deemed assumption of liability by reason of these provisions.[410] Where a part interest in the

---

[403] Ibid, Sch 4, para 8.

[404] Words of wide meaning intended to catch a wide range of variations of mortgages included in the planning; *Clarke Chapman – John Thompson Ltd v IRC* [1975] STC 567.

[405] Compare *Chandos v IRC* 6 Exch 464; *Mortimore v IRC* 2 H&C 838.

[406] FA 2003, Sch 4, para 8.

[407] SDLT 6, p 27.

[408] FA 2003, Sch 4, para 8(1B).

[409] Such arrangements may alternatively benefit from the exemption for transactions in connection with matrimonial breakdown (FA 2003, Sch 3, para 3).

[410] FA 2003, Sch 4, para 8(1B).

property transferred only an equivalent proportion of the mortgage will be subject to stamp duty land tax.[411] Frequently putting the property into joint names is combined with a refinancing. In practice HMRC Stamp Taxes calculate the tax by reference to the original mortgage being replaced and not the amount of the new mortgage being taken out.

Exclusions

5.144 The charge does not apply where there is an appropriation or assent by a personal representative within the exemption or there is an exempt variation of the estate of a deceased individual pursuant to FA 2003, Sch 3, paras 3 and 38. The chargeable consideration does not include the amount of any secured debt assumed by the legatee.[412]

Limitations on the amount of chargeable consideration

5.145 There is, however, one safeguard in that FA 2003, Sch 4, para 8(2) provides that if the amount of the chargeable consideration exceeds the market value of the chargeable interest being acquired by the transaction, the amount of the chargeable consideration is limited to the market value. This is obviously quite an important restriction in relation to negative equity, contingent consideration[413] and indemnities such as those mentioned above.

Side effects

5.146 The treatment of liabilities has other problems in addition to the difficulties affect upon the amount of chargeable consideration. In particular, there are reliefs and reduced rates in respect of certain company reconstructions and reorganisations.[414] These allow for relief where there is the assumption of liabilities as part of the consideration but, in many situations, not where there is any consideration other than the assumption of liabilities and the issue of shares.[415] There must be no other form of consideration other than, in certain circumstances, a very small amount of cash not exceeding 10 per cent of the nominal value of the consideration shares. The treatment of liabilities, including potential liabilities, is, therefore, important. To the extent that the liabilities may exceed the relevant figure the relief may be lost. This is a potential risk where the parties 'backdate' the effect of the transaction ie treat the transaction as having taken place at some earlier date with, for example, the vendor being deemed to have carried on the business as agent for the purchaser. This is not a valid or effective

---

[411] For these purposes in England, Wales and Northern Ireland a joint tenant of property is treated as holding an equal undivided share of the property; FA 2003, Sch 4, para 8(1C).

[412] FA 2003, Sch 3, para 3A; Sch 4, para 8A(1); see **Chapters 9** and **11**.

[413] Such as guarantees secured on the land by of the benefit of members of the group. The writer has encountered such situations where, eg, a parcel of land valued at £150,000 was subject to contingent liabilities of £300 million.

[414] FA 2003, Sch 7, Part 2; see **Chapter 12**.

[415] Which is itself subject to considerable technical issues such as the proportion of shares to be issued which can affect whether there is a scheme of reconstruction as in *Brooklands Selangor Holdings Ltd v IRC* [1970] 1 WLR 429 or whether the consideration has been 'issued' (ie registered) *Oswald Tillotson v IRC* [1933] 1 KB 134; *Brotex Cellulose Fibres Ltd v IRC* [1933] 1 KB 158; *Murex v IRC* [1933] 1 KB 173; *National Westminster Bank v IRC* [1994] STC 580; *Baytrust Holdings Ltd v IRC* [1971] 1 WLR 1333.

exercise as such; it is simply a mechanism for adjusting the consideration and may produce a situation where the consideration provided at the relevant time falls outside the qualifying conditions.[416]

Employment

5.147 Land transactions entered into by reason of employment, such as rights to occupy residential accommodation, which give rise to benefits in kind for the purposes of income tax are treated as transactions entered into for a chargeable consideration.[417] Where there is a tenancy and not a licence and the terms of the arrangement produce a benefit in kind for income tax purposes taxable upon the employee,[418] the benefit in kind is deemed to be rent or to be additional rent added to any actual rent payable. As the level of the benefit in kind may vary from year to year as the elements in the income tax calculation, this will make the rent 'uncertain' within FA 2003, s 51, so that the initial return will have to be made and tax paid initially upon the basis of a reasonable estimate with a consequent obligation to recalculate and notify at the end of the tenancy or the end of the fifth year.[419]. If there is an actual rent the rent is the cash equivalent for the other tax. If the tenancy is treated as accommodation for the performance of duties the chargeable consideration is the actual consideration if any. There is also a difficult issue of determining the length of the lease for the purposes of applying the formula for calculating the stamp duty land tax upon the rent being for a possibly indeterminate period, the tenancy will *prima facie* be treated initially as a lease for 1 year increasing to a deemed lease for 2, 3 or more years as the employment and the tenancy continue.[420] Fortunately the arrangement is notifiable only if the rent and deemed rent become taxable ie if the employment continues beyond 6 years (ie becomes a deemed 7 year lease) the fact that there is a 7 year lease is not automatically notifiable.[421] However, if tax has been paid previously or becomes payable the notification and payment becomes an annual event.

5.148 The problems for employees are not limited to deemed rents. There is a charge upon the market value of a chargeable interest in land where there is a benefit in kind. In cases not within the above two charging provisions ie broadly cases where accommodation is not involved such as where a chargeable interest is transferred to an employee as a benefit in kind the chargeable consideration is an amount not less than the market value of the subject-matter of the transaction as at the effective date of the transaction.[422] It appears that this charge does not apply to dividends *in specie* since these are not made to the employee as such but as shareholder. However, arrangements wholly intended to mitigate other taxes and National Insurance involving bonus payments etc in land are possibly subject to this charge.[423]

---

[416] See, for example, *Metal Box Plastic Films Limited v IRC* [1969] 1 All ER 1620.
[417] FA 2003, Sch 4, para 12; and Sch 17A, para 17.
[418] Income Tax (Earnings and Pensions) Act 2003, Part 3, Chapter 5, especially ss 105 and 106.
[419] FA 2003, Sch 17A, paras 7 and 8; or each year, para 3.
[420] The application of these principles to tenancies created before 1 December 2003 is confused.
[421] FA 2003, Sch 17A, paras 3(5) and 4(4A).
[422] Ibid, Sch 4, para 12(1)(c).
[423] Ibid, Sch 4, para 12.

Reliefs for employee situations[424]

5.149 There are two limited reliefs in connection with the relocation of employed persons. Employers[425] and relocation[426] companies who acquire the employee's existing house may be exempt from stamp duty land tax, although the employee remains liable in full for the tax on his newly acquired residence but the conditions for and the restrictions upon the relief differ depending upon whether the taxpayer is the employer or a relocation company.

Land exchanges

General principles

5.150 It is crucial to the understanding of the land exchange principles to appreciate the distinction between the highly technical definition of land exchange and the concept of 'transfer' for a consideration in kind (ie something other than cash or debt), particularly since the same transaction may be as regards certain participants a land exchange and for others a transaction for a consideration in kind.[427] This requires a detailed investigation of whether the actual consideration for the transaction is the entry into another land transaction (ie a 'land exchange') or an 'acquisition' of a chargeable interest in land for a consideration that does not consist of or include the entry into another land transaction. Where there is an acquisition of a chargeable interest that is not a land exchange but involves 'barter', ie a consideration in kind, the stamp duty land tax is, in general,[428] computed upon the market value of the consideration provided.[429] Where there is a land exchange very different principles apply.

5.151 The chargeable consideration for stamp duty land tax includes other interests in land.[430] It is, however, specifically provided that where one land transaction is entered into by a purchaser wholly or partly in consideration of another land transaction being entered into by him whereby he is to receive the benefit of other land, then each side of the transaction is to be treated as if it is a separate and distinct chargeable transaction.[431] Thus, in a simple case, where A agrees to exchange land with B there will be two chargeable transactions:

(1)   A will be acquiring B's land in consideration, *inter alia*, of his land; and

(2)   B will be treated as acquiring A's land in consideration, *inter alia*, of his land.

There are, therefore, two sets of chargeable transactions, but the chargeable considerations differ from the actual considerations and any payments of equality money or VAT are ignored in computing the tax.[432]

---

[424]   See **Chapter 11**.
[425]   FA 2003, Sch 6A, para 5.
[426]   Ibid, Sch 6A, para 6.
[427]   Ibid, Sch 4, para 1.
[428]   In some cases, such as works and services, the charge is based upon open market costs; FA 2003, Sch 4, paras 10 and 11.
[429]   Ibid, Sch 4, paras 1 and 4, dealing with consideration in money's worth.
[430]   Ibid, s 47; Sch 4, para 5.
[431]   Ibid, s 47(1) (as amended).
[432]   Ibid, Sch 4, paras 5 and 6.

5.152 It is specifically provided that where one land transaction is entered into by a 'purchaser'[433] wholly or partly in consideration of another land transaction being entered into by him as the 'seller' (which will include entering into the transaction as landlord or tenant or person releasing a right) then each of the land transactions is treated as a separate chargeable transaction attracting its own separate charges to stamp duty land tax.[434] Each party is in consequence taxable. However, it is provided[435] that exchanges are no longer regarded as linked transactions even where they involve connected parties.[436] These rules are intended to apply to not merely exchanges of land such as a freehold for freehold swap and sales of land in consideration of leases back or grants of leases in consideration of the grant of other leases but also surrenders of leases in consideration of leases of other property.

'Exchanges'

5.153 It is, therefore, necessary to determine what is a 'land exchange' for these purposes and whether the particular transaction qualifies for relief since there is, in effect, a double charge upon exchanges.[437] The definition of 'land exchange' is wide and can produce surprising consequences in many routine situations. The definition is that there is a land exchange where A enters into a land transaction with B and the consideration includes B entering into a land transaction. It is not a requirement that B's land transaction is with A; it can be with a third party, C. The charge is, therefore, not limited to simple mutual transfers between A and B. The charge applies to tripartite and similar arrangements such as where A agrees to transfer land to B who agrees to transfer land to C who pays cash to A. B is involved in a land exchange since his consideration to A is entering into the land contract with C.[438] However, C will not necessarily be involved in a land exchange since the consideration that he is providing to B does not involve C entering into a land transaction with anyone. C will, in consequence, be *prima facie*, taxable upon the consideration, if any, that he provides. It is this question of the consideration provided by C that will cause great difficulties in practice. It is provided that actual consideration is 'chargeable consideration' only if it is provided by either the taxpayer or a party to the chargeable transaction or a connected person. There will, therefore, be issues as to whether the transaction between A and B constitutes chargeable consideration for the transaction between B and C[439] and, in particular, whether A is a party to the transaction or is connected with C. The broad effect of the provisions is that B and C are likely to be taxed upon totally different bases:

- B is taxed as a party to a land exchange pursuant to FA 2003, Sch 4, para 5;

- C is taxed upon general principles, namely the amount or value of the chargeable consideration which he or a person connected with him has provided which is a

---

[433] Which includes tenants or grantees of rights, such as sale and leaseback and surrender or regrant.

[434] FA 2003, s 47(1).

[435] Ibid, 47(1) (as amended).

[436] It should, however, be noted that this is another illustration of the self-serving nature of amendments to the legislation (see **2.3**). The amendments take the form of excluding linked transactions as they apply to connected persons. The legislation assumes that where the parties are connected the transactions are automatically linked. By excluding the linked transaction rules for exchanges HMRC Stamp Taxes have created for themselves legislative support for their extremely dubious argument that where the parties are connected they are automatically linked whether or not there was 'a scheme or arrangement'.

[437] FA 2003, Sch 4, para 5.

[438] This, however, raises the issue of whether the consideration for C's transaction is provided by A and whether the legislation can be stretched so that because of A's involvement converts C's arrangement into a land exchange.

[439] On the issue of third party inducements and consideration see **5.99**.

difficult technical issue in its own right and can easily distort the overall tax charge upon the transaction as well as add to the compliance costs and expense of dealing with an Enquiry whilst HMRC Stamp Taxes struggle to understand the basic principles and valuation issues involved.

5.154 The above definition indicates that a land exchange is an extremely wide concept. It applies when chargeable interests whether major interest such as freeholds or leaseholds or minor interests are involved. In consequence, a land exchange within these provisions can arise in circumstances that may take practitioners by surprise. It will apply wherever chargeable interests are moving in opposite directions and may supplant the charging provisions that people may think would otherwise apply. For example, a sale and leaseback is a land exchange.[440] Similarly, a deed of variation entered into by a tenant with a lease of a flat enlarging the term which operates by way of surrender and regrant[441] will be a land exchange.[442] Unfortunately, the definition of chargeable interests means that routine drafting such as 'excepting and reserving' could give rise to potential difficulties. It is essentially the view of HMRC Stamp Taxes that the words 'excepting and reserving' do not restrict the interest that passes to the transferee by keeping out of the transaction the relevant interest. It is the view of HMRC Stamp Taxes that virtually nothing can be kept back and excluded from the transferred interest; such transactions, in their view, take effect as transfers of the entire interest plus the regrant of the interests that the transferor sought to 'except and reserve'. In consequence, there is a transfer of a major interest in consideration of the acquisition ie grant of new interests back to the seller or landlord. In consequence, where a person transfers land to a developer 'excepting and reserving' rights of way over the land transferred or rights to access to the mains drainage and facilities to be installed on the land or imposes restrictions on the development of the land there will be a transfer and a 'regrant' of the rights that the party claims to have 'excepted and reserved'. In consequence, there will be a transfer by way of exchange of the freehold interest to the purchaser. This will take place at market value[443] although, in practice, this is likely to be regarded by HMRC Stamp Taxes as the cash price passing between the parties, at least in those cases where they are not connected persons and are acting at arm's length. This is quite a significant development since originally HMRC Stamp Taxes took the view that the interest being acquired by the purchaser had to be valued ignoring the obligation to grant back the rights to the other party. They now accept that the interest has to be valued subject to these restrictions, which makes it more likely that the purchase price will equate with the open market value of the land subject to the rights. This will be an important issue where there is an overage or clawback arrangement where the tax may be assessed on an artificial figure.[444] It may be possible to argue for a land exchange which could exclude the overage arrangements and to try to persuade HMRC Stamp Taxes that in the circumstances the market value is the basic price since the overage or clawback is unlikely to produce any payment.

5.155 This, however, leaves the vendor with a problem since he will be a party to a land exchange acquiring an interest probably involving a major interest which means that he is subject to tax upon the market value of the interest that is 'regranted' ie acquired by him. In cases where the right regranted is some form of right over land such as a restrictive covenant or easement it may have a value but does not have an open market

---

[440]   But see FA 2003, s 57A (as much amended) for a limited relief.
[441]   See, for example, **5.173**.
[442]   But special reliefs may apply; see, for example, FA 2003, Sch 17A, paras 9 and 16.
[443]   FA 2003, Sch 4, para 5.
[444]   Ibid, s 51; see **5.187**.

value and therefore the acquisition of a minor interest for a consideration of nil or no chargeable consideration.[445] However, rights that are not rights in or over land may be chargeable interests.[446] In consequence, a reservation of a 'benefit' by a seller that is not a properly reserved interest but involves a 'regrant' will involve the acquisition of a chargeable interest in land that may be capable of sale in the open market. The vendor may be subject to tax where the right 'reserved' ie in the view of HMRC Stamp Taxes 'regranted' exceeds the nil rate threshold for the time being.[447]

Computation of 'chargeable consideration' for exchanges

5.156 Special rules apply for computing the charge to stamp duty land tax in relation to such exchanges and these depend upon whether the transaction relates to major or minor interests in land,[448] partitions of interests in land[449] and there is limited relief for surrenders and regrants and certain part-exchanges involving new dwellings which are really modifications of the subsale regime.[450] These reliefs are described below.

Trusts and estates and exchanges[451]

5.157 These problems of exchange or consideration in kind or mixed consideration ie a bundle[452] of equitable interests in the underlying investments which include land and other property such as shares can apply where there are variations of trusts or the estates of deceased persons[453] where the respective interests being 'exchanged' or released and granted are or include equitable interests in land[454] held by the trustees as part of the trust fund. In consequence the stamp duty land tax implications of the variation of an estate or trust[455] will differ significantly depending upon the underlying assets in respect of which the equitable interests subsist. For example, there may be:

---

[445]   Ibid, Sch 5, para 4; s 77A and Sch 3, para 1; see **Chapters 17** and **18**.

[446]   Ibid, s 48(1)(b); see **4.39**.

[447]   Ibid, s 77A.

[448]   Ibid, Sch 4, para 5.

[449]   Ibid, Sch 4, para 6.

[450]   Ibid, s 58; see **Chapter 6**.

[451]   See further **Chapter 9**.

[452]   There is, however, a fundamental issue of principle as to whether, in general law, the equitable interest of a beneficiary in a trust is a single interest in property or chose in action in the entirety of the underlying investments or is a separate equitable interest in each of the underlying assets. The same issue arises in relation to partnerships where, however, HMRC Stamp Taxes have for many decades accepted that the partnership interest is a single interest and a separate interest. In consequence, the nature of the interest in a partnership is not influenced by the nature of the underlying assets. Certain legislation has been required to deal with that particular problem; but it also appears that the draftsman was of the view that the interest of beneficiaries in a trust was a collection of individual equitable interests in each of the separate investments held by the trustees. However, this view has not been applied consistently by HMRC Stamp Taxes in that no claims have been made that dealings in equitable interests in trusts that hold a mixture of assets or consist solely of shares are chargeable interests for the purposes of stamp duty land tax. This issue of partnerships owning shares has been dealt with separately but there has never been any attempt to claim that beneficiaries in trusts owned interests in shares although the taxpayer did not take full advantage of this possible argument in relation to the charge to stamp duty in *Oughtred v IRC* [1960] AC 206. There is, therefore, a lack of consistency in this area.

[453]   But note the exemption for certain variations of the estates of deceased persons in FA 2003, Sch 3, para 4.

[454]   Or deemed equitable interest in the case of foreign trusts: ibid, Sch 16, para 2.

[455]   See **Chapter 9**.

- a variation of trust involving life and reversionary interests in land and no other property which will be treated as a land exchange but consisting of an exchange of minor interests[456] to which special rules apply;[457]

- a variation of a trust involving an interest in land for a consideration relating solely to an equitable interest in personal property which is not a land exchange but a barter transaction for a consideration in kind with only one potential charge to stamp duty land tax;

- a variation of trust involving a release of an equitable interest in a mixture of land and other property for a consideration not involving land which is not a land transaction and so is a barter transaction;

- a variation involving an equitable interest in property not involving land for an equitable interest in land which is a 'barter' transaction not a land exchange; and

- a variation involving the mutual adjustments of equitable interests in a mixture of property including but not comprising solely of interests in land. This will frequently be the situation in practice such as where the life tenant in a mixed fund enters into a partition arrangement with a remainderman in the same mixed fund. There is no direct guidance in the legislation as to how such transactions should be treated in the self-assessment regime. The mixed nature of the consideration on both sides of the transaction raises fundamental issues as to whether a land exchange extends to a situation where the relevant land contract is merely a part of a larger contract not involving only land. To some extent these issues may be simplified should the transaction be treated as a land exchange and thus could be supported by a reasonable construction of the definition of 'land exchange'. Unfortunately, the attitude of HMRC Stamp Taxes has not been published in any binding or helpful format.

Two computational regimes for land exchanges

5.158 The detailed provisions for computing the stamp duty land tax upon each of the separate transactions involved in the exchange ie the acquisition by the transferee and the separate chargeable acquisition by the transferor are contained in FA 2003, Sch 4, para 5. For each transaction, the consideration for the respective acquisition of the chargeable interest rules depend upon whether the subject-matter of the transaction is a major interest in land. This is defined by FA 2003, s 117. The definition depends upon whether the land is in England and Wales, Scotland or Northern Ireland. In England and Wales a major interest is a freehold or a term of years absolute.[458] It will be noted that although the latter part of the definition refers to leases it differs from the definition of 'lease' for the general purposes of stamp duty land tax,[459] and appears to be based upon the definition in the Law of Property Act 1925.[460] There are therefore issues as to whether these differences are simply the product of poor drafting or are intended to have real consequences in the treatment of transactions.[461] It is considered that it is the consequence of poor drafting and technical skill and there is a risk that a 'lease' of a

---

[456] FA 2003, s 117.
[457] Ibid, Sch 4, para 5(4); see **5.161**.
[458] Ibid, s 117.
[459] Ibid, Sch 17, para 1.
[460] Section 205(1)(xxvii).
[461] Such as whether 'leases' can apply to all interests in land having a limited duration.

minor interest such as a right of way solely for the duration of a development will be treated as a major interest by HMRC Stamp Taxes notwithstanding that the overall impression from the legislation that such interests are intended to remain minor interests.[462] In relation to Scotland, a major interest is the interest of an owner of land or the right of a tenant over property subject to a lease. In Northern Ireland, the major interest is a freehold estate or any leasehold estate whether subsisting at law or in equity.

Major interests

5.159 These charging provisions apply[463] where either:

- there is an exchange of major interests, for example, a freehold is swapped for another freehold or a freehold is transferred in consideration of the grant of a leaseback.[464] In such a case each of the parties to the exchange is taxable upon the market value[465] of the property received plus on rent reserved by any leases granted as part of the arrangement.[466] Any cash sum paid as equality is ignored; or

- there is an exchange of a major interest for a non-major interest such as a freehold interest in land or transfer in consideration of the grant or release of a restrictive covenant or a variation of a right of way or rights to light. There is a charge upon the market value of the two interests received[467] but there may be issues as to the market value of:
  - the transferred freehold; and
  - the restrictive covenant being acquired.[468]

5.160 Where the acquisition involves major interests together with any other interests appurtenant or pertaining thereto, ie there is a transfer of a major interest or several major interests or, it seems, a mixture of major and minor interests in 'exchange for'[469] either one or major interests or the acquisition of one or more minor interests or, it seems, a mixture of major and minor interests such as a transfer of a freehold interest for a cash sum and the variation of a restrictive covenant over land held by the transferor of the freehold or for the grant of easements or rights to light in favour of

---

[462] See also **5.161**.

[463] FA 2003, Sch 4, para 5(3)(a)(ii) and (b)(ii).

[464] Taxpayers may find that it is more tax efficient to grant the lease to a nominee prior to the disposal of the freehold interest.

[465] See **27.19** on whether the market value may include VAT.

[466] Special rules apply to land exchanges in PFI projects; FA 2003, Sch 4, paras 5(7) and 17.

[467] In such contexts the grant of the easement or variation of the right to light may be only part of the total package. Eg there may be a purchase of land and a variation of rights by the vendor for a cash sum. Here there is no exchange and the tax is charged upon the cash payment. However, there may be a transfer of land in consideration of a cash payment by the purchaser and the grant by the purchaser of new rights back to the vendor. Here there is an exchange and the tax is upon market value rather than the cash price. In practice where the parties are at arm's length it is probable that, in the absence of special factors, HMRC Stamp Taxes will accept that the agreed cash price is the market value (but note their reliance upon *Lap Shun Textiles Industrial Co v Collector of Stamp Revenue* [1976] AC 530 to the effect that arm's length negotiation is not conclusive of market value; see also *Cowan de Groot Properties Ltd v Eagle Trust plc* [1991] BCLC 1045). This is more likely now that HMRC Stamp Taxes appear to have abandoned their longstanding argument that market value has to be determined ignoring the obligations to grant back the new rights and seem prepared in practice to accept that the interest value can be depressed by the existence of the contractual obligation of the taxpayer to grant the new rights.

[468] See also FA 2003, s 48(1)(b) on contracts as chargeable interests and see **5.155** on valuation.

[469] Where there is not an exchange but a barter transaction the charge is upon the consideration provided with problems for 'mixed transactions' and apportioning the consideration and valuations – see **Chapter 9**.

land retained by the transfer or, as a conveyance of a freehold in consideration of a conditional agreement to grant a lease back and a temporary right of way during the development over the freehold land,[470] then:

- if there is an acquisition of a single interest whether major or not, the chargeable consideration for the acquisition is either:
  - the market value of the interest being acquired;[471] or
  - if the acquisition is the grant or deemed grant[472] of a lease at a rent, that rent,[473] the stamp duty land tax in this case being the aggregate of tax upon the market value, if any, of the lease plus the tax upon the rent;

- if there are several acquisitions of interests, the chargeable consideration for each of those interests is either:
  - the market value of each of the interests being acquired.[474] In addition to the issue of the value of minor interests which can, in law, subsist only as part of the dominant land and do not have independent existence there is the question of whether there is a transfer and regrant of the new right or a 'reservation' of the interest since on the latter case there is no land exchange. However, there is also an issue whether the right 'retained' is a chargeable interest. Although it may not constitute an estate or right in or over land it may be a chargeable interest as a contract affecting the value of land and so a chargeable interest[475] so that subsequent dealings in the right are potentially chargeable transactions. Also, as mentioned above, there may be questions as to how the actual consideration is allocated by the parties and whether this is effective to avoid the double charge or escape from the definition of a 'land exchange';[476] plus
  - if the acquisition of any of those interests is the grant of a lease at a rent, that rent.[477] This charge is in addition to the charge upon the market value, ie where the rent is below the market rent there is a possible charge upon a deemed premium on an amount equal to the amount that a lease on such favourable terms would realise if sold on the open market.

---

[470] There is, of course, the question of whether the temporary right of way is a lease or a term of years absolute and, in consequence, a major interest.

[471] FA 2003, Sch 4, para 5(3)(a)(i).

[472] Problems of interpretation arose because of the special meaning of 'grant' of a lease, which does not include an agreement for lease (see **7.4**) but in such a case substantial performance of an agreement for lease triggers the charge to stamp duty land tax and this is currently taxed as the 'grant' of a lease; FA 2003, Sch 17A, para 12A.

[473] FA 2003, Sch 4, para 5(3)(a)(ii). Presumably this will have to be converted into its net present value in accordance with the provisions of ibid, Sch 5.

[474] FA 2003, Sch 4, para 5.

[475] FA 2003, s 48(1)(b).

[476] There is an interesting exercise in valuation since, where there is the acquisition of a non-major interest, this interest may not have a market value for various reasons, although there may be considerable enhancement of the value of the land of the person 'acquiring'. Eg it may be a restrictive covenant available only for the land retained, rights of light or way existing only for the benefit of the 'dominant land'. These can only be sold as rights attaching to the land and are not capable of separate sale. They can be 'sold' to the owner of the servient land who is the only possible purchaser of the rights as such. It will need to be determined whether a sole rather than special purchaser represents the 'open market' within FA 2003, Sch 4, para 7. Alternatively, the non-major interest may disappear such as upon the release of a restrictive covenant – and it seems difficult to sell something which has 'disappeared' in the open market. It may also be a variation of a minor interest, which for the reasons set out above may not be saleable in the 'open market'.

[477] FA 2003, Sch 4, para 5(3)(b)(i).

This would appear to exclude from the charge to stamp duty land tax any consideration consisting of a chargeable interest so that the charge, *prima facie*, falls only upon any cash paid by way of equality or similar adjustment in land.

Other ('non-major') interests – non-major interest for non-major interest

5.161 Different rules apply where all of the interests in the chargeable transaction are minor interests; broadly there is one charge to tax upon the equality consideration, if any. Where none of the relevant acquisitions involves a major interest in land[478] then:

- where there is only one relevant acquisition of a non-major interest which is made in consideration of one or more disposals by the other party to the transaction,[479] the chargeable consideration for the acquisition is the amount or value of any chargeable consideration other than the disposal or disposals given for the acquisition;[480]

- where there are two or more relevant acquisitions of non-major interests made in consideration of one or more relevant disposals, the chargeable consideration for each relevant acquisition is the appropriate proportion of the amount or value of any chargeable consideration other than the disposal or disposals given for the acquisitions.[481] The appropriate proportion of the chargeable consideration is to be determined in accordance with the fraction:

$$\frac{MV}{TMV}$$

where:

- MV is the market value of the subject-matter for the acquisition for which the chargeable consideration is being determined; and

- TMV is the total market value of the subject-matter of all relevant acquisitions.[482]

If only one of the interests involved is a major interest these rules do not apply which suggests that fragmentation of contracts and transactions may be a strategy worth investigating, since this could produce a different chargeable consideration should this be commercially feasible and effective for other taxes, especially VAT, where the restrictive anti-avoidance principles of the transfer of a going concern and the related long-term problems are unlikely to apply producing cash flow difficulties. Although such fragmented transactions may be 'linked' this merely alters the rate of tax; it does not nullify the strategy.[483] The transactions remain separate transactions for the purposes of analysis and determining the category into which they fall for the purposes

---

[478] There is no express provision dealing with the situation of a mixed acquisition of major and other interests, such as where the subject-matter of the transaction involves the acquisition of freeholds with easements over adjoining land as part of an 'exchange' where the purchaser 'regrants' certain rights to the vendor which will be minor interests.

[479] FA 2003, Sch 4, para 5(2)(b).

[480] Ibid, Sch 4, para 4(a).

[481] Ibid, Sch 4, para 4(b).

[482] Ibid, Sch 4, para 5.

[483] There are questions as to whether HMRC Stamp Taxes might seek to apply the general anti-avoidance provisions pursuant to FA 2003, ss 77A–77C and **2.19**.

of determining the chargeable consideration and the rate. The linked transaction rules cannot amalgamate the different contracts to convert an exchange of minor interests into an overall transaction involving major interests or to package the interests involved in separate contracts or for separately allocated consideration and change the overall basis for computing the stamp duty land tax.

5.162 Non-major interest transactions with the limited charge upon the equality adjustment apply to transactions such as:

- variations of trusts holding land involving the mutual exchange of interests;

- grant of mutual or cross-options;

- variations of estates of deceased persons outside the scope of the variation exemptions;[484]

- mutual adjustments of rights of way.

No guidance is provided in relation to the balancing consideration. Usually this will be a cash payment and if sufficiently small may be eligible for a lower rate of tax notwithstanding the overall value of the transaction. An unresolved problem likely to affect trusts and jointly owned assets is the treatment of mortgages charged upon the property and whether the relevant part of the mortgage is to be treated as the equality payment.[485]

Exchanges – special cases

5.163 This brutal rule of a double charge on certain land exchanges is mitigated in several special cases. To some extent these are a confused mixture of specific variations on subsale relief and special reliefs applicable only to the land exchange regime. Thus a surrender and regrant relief[486] can apply only to the land exchange regime whereas reliefs such as the relocation of employees[487] is predominantly a form of subsale relief. The precise scope of applicable reliefs must, therefore, be closely investigated in each case because there are long-term problems arising from anti-avoidance legislation which depend upon the nature of the exemption applied to the original transaction which can have significant and expensive consequences for third parties who are not properly advised and as a result fail to take the necessary steps for their own protection.[488]

Part-exchanges of new houses

5.164 Two variations on subsale relief are available for residential property for corporate builders of new houses.

---

[484]   FA 2003, Sch 3, para 4.
[485]   FA 2003, Sch 4, para 8; see **5.134**.
[486]   FA 2003, Sch 17A, paras 9 and 16.
[487]   Ibid, Sch 6A, paras 5 and 6.
[488]   See ibid, Sch 7, Part 1 and s 45 (as amended).

Acquisition by builder

5.165 There is a relief for a new housebuilder in a part exchange. The relief is available only to the corporate developer; the individual acquiring the new dwelling remains fully liable on his acquisition, but this is based upon market value not necessarily the price of what the new dwelling was offered in the market.

5.166 Finance Act 2003, Sch 6A, para 1, provides that an acquisition is exempt from stamp duty land tax where:

- there is the acquisition of a new dwelling which can include freeholds and leasehold interests in both houses and flats by an individual[489] (whether alone or with other individuals[490]) from a house building company.[491] A building is a new dwelling if it has been constructed for use as a single dwelling and has not been previously occupied or it has been adapted for use as a single dwelling and has not been occupied since its adaptation.[492] The acquisition of the old dwelling is acquisition by way of transfer of a major interest in the dwelling. The individual must, therefore, transfer the whole of his interest in the existing dwelling to a new dwelling by way of grant or transfer of a major interest in the dwelling;

- the acquisition of the new dwelling is made in consideration[493] of the transfer[494] of an existing dwelling which includes land occupied and enjoyed with the dwelling as its garden or grounds;

- the existing dwelling is acquired by a house building company, which is defined as a company that carries on the business of constructing or adapting buildings or part of buildings for use as dwellings. The relief is, therefore, available only to companies and not to individual builders or partnerships;

---

[489] These situations are likely to arise in connection with matrimonial breakdown where the matrimonial home is changed for one or two smaller dwellings. In these cases the meaning of 'the' individual on the two sides of the transaction will be crucial, especially where the property was in joint names. It seems that where there is a transfer by joint owners the relief is available notwithstanding that the new dwelling is acquired by only one of the parties. Given the rules relating to nominees the legal title will not necessarily be the crucial test in this type of situation. It remains to be seen how far HMRC Stamp Taxes will require the builder company to investigate the title as affected by the stamp duty land tax rules in order to identify the correct 'individual'.

[490] It seems that whilst there must be at least one individual in common the individual's who are acquiring the property need not be totally identical with the individuals who are disposing of the existing property. There is nothing in the legislation to indicate that the reference to 'with other individuals' refers to 'with the same other individuals'.

[491] The relief is not available for non-corporate builders so that many small developers will not be eligible for relief. A builder acquiring an existing plot intending to demolish a house and construct flats or dwellings on the basis that the plot holder will receive a new flat or dwelling may not be eligible for this limited relief. The intentions of HMRC Stamp Taxes as regards partnerships and land syndicates are unclear. It is on the legislation expected that where the partnership consists solely of bodies corporate it will be eligible for the relief because of the look-through provisions in FA 2003, Sch 7, Part 1; but it may be that because of the provision that partnerships continue notwithstanding changes in partners that HMRC Stamp Taxes intend to develop a residual argument that there is a separate quasi-entity where partnerships are involved of a non-corporate nature and so outside the relief.

[492] FA 2003, Sch 6A, para 7(1) and (2).

[493] Although not made clear by the legislation it seems that the relief will be available where there is some form of cash equality in the transaction whether in the form of the individual paying additional consideration for the acquisition of the new dwelling or where the developer pays consideration to the individual because the individual's existing house is more valuable than the property being acquired.

[494] The relief is not available where the individual merely leases his house.

172 *Stamp Duty Land Tax*

- the existing dwelling is acquired from an individual[495] (whether alone or with other individuals) but not from other persons;

- the individual occupied the existing dwelling as his only or main residence at some time in the period of 2 years ending with the date of the acquisition of the existing dwelling by the house building company;

- the individual intends to occupy the new dwelling as his only or main residence. This appears to be a matter of intention and there does not appear to be a clawback of the relief if the individual does not take up residence or leaves shortly after the transaction is completed;

- the area of land acquired, ie the existing dwelling, by the house building company does not exceed the permitted area, which means that the land occupied and enjoyed with the dwelling as its garden or grounds does not exceed an area of 0.5 of a hectare, inclusive of the site of the existing dwelling, or such larger area as is required for the reasonable enjoyment of the existing dwelling as a dwelling having regard to its size and character.[496] For these purposes, the permitted area is taken to consist of that part of the land that would be most suitable for occupation and enjoyment with the dwelling as its garden or grounds if the rest of the land were separately occupied.[497] If the condition as to permitted area is not satisfied the chargeable consideration for the acquisition by the house building company is the amount calculated by deducting the market value of the permitted area from the market value of the old dwelling.[498]

Acquisitions by 'finance company'

5.167 A similar relief is available to companies which assist house builders by operating a form of part-exchange. In this situation there is not a direct exchange since the developer transfers or leases the new dwelling to the relevant individual who transfers his existing dwelling to a company which may or may not be associated with the developer. In such a situation since there are notional cash movements there is no land exchange and the transaction with the financing company is a variation on the subsale relief regime. The relief is available to the financing company; the existing householder remains fully liable on the acquisition of the newly constructed residential premises; but the charge is based upon the market value of the new dwelling which is not necessarily the same as the price at which the new dwelling was offered for sale by the developer. The conditions for the relief are:

- the acquisition of the existing dwelling is by a property trader, ie a company, a limited liability partnership or a partnership whose members are all either companies or limited liability partnerships.[499] It does not apply to individuals, general partnerships, trustees or limited partnerships within the Limited Partnerships Act 1907;

---

[495] See *Jasmine Trustees Ltd v Wells & Hind* [2007] STC 660; see also footnote 489 above.
[496] FA 2003, Sch 6A, para 7(3). This test is similar to that adopted for capital gains tax and the principal private residence; it is probable that the same approach as that adopted in these cases will apply for stamp duty land tax given the manifest heavy reliance upon capital gains tax advice that has seemingly been revealed by HMRC Stamp Taxes notwithstanding the fundamental differences in structure between the two taxes.
[497] Ibid, Sch 6A, para 7(4).
[498] Ibid, Sch 6A, para 1(4).
[499] Ibid, Sch 6A, para 8(1).

- there is the acquisition of a new dwelling by an individual (whether alone or with other individuals)[500] from a house building company.[501] A building is a new dwelling if it has been constructed for use as a single dwelling and has not been previously occupied or it has been adapted for use as a single dwelling and has not been occupied since its adaptation.[502] The acquisition of the old dwelling is acquisition by way of transfer of a major interest in the dwelling. The individual must, therefore, transfer the whole of his interest in the existing dwelling;

- the acquisition is made in consideration[503] of the transfer[504] of an existing dwelling which includes land occupied and enjoyed with the dwelling as its garden or grounds;

- the existing dwelling is acquired by a house building company, which is defined as a company that carries on the business of constructing or adapting buildings or part of buildings for use as dwellings. The relief is available only to companies and not to individual builders or partnerships;

- the existing dwelling is acquired from an individual (whether alone or with other individuals[505]) but not from other persons;[506]

- the individual occupied the old dwelling as his only or main residence at some time in the period of 2 years ending with the date of the acquisition of the existing dwelling by the house building company;

- the property trader does not intend to spend more than the permitted amount on the refurbishment of the old dwelling or to grant a lease or licence of the old dwelling other than a limited licence to the individual for a period of not more than 6 months.[507] The reference to a licence for not more than 6 months is meant to deal with the situation where there is a delayed completion because the new dwelling is not ready at the time that it is proposed to complete the acquisition of the existing dwelling;[508]

---

[500] It seems that as long as there is at least one individual in common with those disposing of the original dwelling and those acquiring the new dwelling there need not be total identity of all of the individuals involved in the joint disposal or acquisition; see also footnote 489 above.

[501] The relief is not available for non-corporate builders so that many small developers will not be eligible for relief. A builder acquiring an existing plot intending to demolish a house and construct flats or dwellings on the basis that the plot holder will receive a new flat or dwelling may not be eligible for this limited relief. The intentions of HMRC Stamp Taxes as regards partnerships and land syndicates are unclear. It is on the legislation expected that where the partnership consists solely of bodies corporate it will be eligible for the relief because of the look-through provisions in FA 2003, Sch 7, Part 1; but it may be that because of the provision that partnerships continue notwithstanding changes in partners that HMRC Stamp Taxes intend to develop a residual argument that there is a separate quasi-entity where partnerships are involved of a non-corporate nature and so outside the relief.

[502] FA 2003, Sch 6A, para 7(1) and (2).

[503] It seems that this does not refer to the sole consideration. It would appear that the relief is available where the transfers involve some form of equality adjustment such as the individual paying because the new premises are more valuable than his existing premises or the developer or other party paying the cash adjustment because the new property is less valuable than the individual's existing dwelling.

[504] The relief is not available where the individual merely leases his house.

[505] See footnote 489 above.

[506] There may be problems where trustees own the existing dwelling; see *Jasmine Trustees Ltd v Wells & Hind* [2007] STC 660.

[507] FA 2003, Sch 6A, para 2(2)(d).

[508] HMRC Stamp Taxes have taken points in relation to delayed completions such as where the seller having delivered title is allowed to remain in occupation pursuant to the terms of the contract upon the basis that

- the property trader must not intend to permit any of its principals are employees or any person connected with any of them to occupy the old dwelling.[509] The permitted amount in relation to the refurbishment of the dwelling is £10,000 or 5 per cent of the consideration for the acquisition of the dwelling whichever is the greater but subject to a maximum of £20,000;[510]

- the individual intends to occupy the new dwelling as his only or main residence. This appears to be a matter of intention and there does not appear to be a clawback of the relief if the individual does not take up residence or leaves shortly after the transaction;

- the area of land acquired by the house building company does not exceed the permitted area, which means that the land occupied and enjoyed with the dwelling as its garden or grounds does not exceed an area of 0.5 of a hectare, inclusive of the site of the dwelling, or such larger area as is required for the reasonable enjoyment of the dwelling as a dwelling having regard to its size and character.[511] For these purposes, the permitted area is taken to consist of that part of the land that would be most suitable for occupation and enjoyment with the dwelling as its garden or grounds if the rest of the land were separately occupied.[512] If the condition as to permitted area is not satisfied the chargeable consideration for the acquisition by the house building company is the amount calculated by deducting the market value of the permitted area from the market value of the old dwelling.[513]

This relief is withdrawn if the property trader either spends more than the permitted amount on refurbishment of the old dwelling or grants a lease or licence of the old dwelling or permits any of its principals or employees or any person connected with any of them to occupy the old dwelling other than the grant of a lease or licence to the individual for a period of not more than 6 months.[514]

PFI projects

5.168 Certain land exchanges involving a sale and leaseback or a lease and underlease back where a relevant public is involved can qualify for exemption pursuant to FA 2033, Sch 4, para 17.[515]

---

this involves the 'regrant' of some interest in the land producing a land exchange. It will be necessary, therefore, for the delayed completion to operate as some form of 'licence' subject to the prescribed time limit.

[509] FA 2003, Sch 6A, para 2(2)(d)(iii).

[510] Ibid, Sch 6A, para 9(2).

[511] Ibid, Sch 6A, para 7(3). This test is similar to that adopted for capital gains tax and the principal private residence; it is probable that the same approach as that adopted in these cases will apply for stamp duty land tax given the manifest heavy reliance upon capital gains tax advice that has seemingly been revealed by HMRC Stamp Taxes notwithstanding the fundamental differences in structure between the two taxes.

[512] Ibid, Sch 6A, para 7(4).

[513] Ibid, Sch 6A, para 1(4).

[514] Ibid, Sch 6A, para 11(2). A principal in relation to a property trader means in the case of a company a director, in the case of a limited liability partnership a member and in the case of any other qualifying partnership a person who is a member or who is a principal of a member in the partnership (FA 2003, Sch 6A, para 8(2)).

[515] See **11.35** and **7.258**.

Partitions

5.169 A partition of a jointly owned chargeable interest involves an element of exchange since each party is giving up his partial or undivided interest in the asset or in a specified part of the asset to the other party or parties jointly interested in return for their giving up in his favour his, her or their partial interests in that asset or other assets.[516] Where land is concerned this would involve an 'exchange'[517] with the transaction *prima facie* being treated as two or more separate 'acquisitions', each of which is chargeable to stamp duty land tax at the appropriate rate. However, a limited relief is available in respect of this exchange of the part or joint or undivided interests in the respective parts. It is specifically provided by FA 2003, Sch 4, para 6, that, in the case of a land transaction giving effect to a partition or division of the chargeable interest to which persons are jointly entitled,[518] the share of the interest held by the person acquiring immediately before the partition or division but passing to the other party does not become a 'chargeable consideration'.

5.170 There are certain conceptual difficulties as to the scope of this relief because of longstanding ambiguities in the practice of HMRC Stamp Taxes in this area. These problems arise because of the failure to define 'partition' which existed even in relation to stamp duty. There are numerous situations which are in plain English described as partitions, for example:

- A and B may be jointly entitled in equity to land held under a single title. A division of the land in such a case is undoubtedly a 'partition';

- A and B may be jointly entitled to land which geographically constitutes a single area but was acquired on separate occasions and is held under separate titles,[519] but the arrangement does not constitute a partnership where special rules apply.[520] There is, therefore, *prima facie*, not a single asset jointly held but a pool of assets. This situation can be muddied even further where, although there is a single geographical unit, there is a mixture of titles such as where certain parcels of the land held jointly are freehold interest and others are held by leases for terms of different duration. This may frequently occur where several property developers agreed to co-operate[521] in the acquisition[522] of a land bank which is to be physically divided between them as and when the planning permission is obtained and the 'section 106 agreement' is signed. The land bank will usually represent the acquisition of numerous interests or estates in land. There may be acquisitions of freehold reversion and various leases and subleases of all or part of one parcel of land and numerous similar acquisitions of different parcels of land. All of this will involve different titles and numbers at the Land Registry. It seems, however, that in practice HMRC Stamp Taxes treat such break-ups of pooled interests in land as a

---

[516] This relief does not apply to the majority of trusts and estates where the interests will be successive rather than concurrent (see **Chapter 9**).
[517] FA 2003, s 47.
[518] Ibid, s 121.
[519] Parties involved in these and similar situations may, justifiably, take the view that their long-term stamp duty land tax requires a consolidation of the various titles at the Land Registry.
[520] FA 2003, Sch 15, para 16; see **Chapter 13**; **13.63**.
[521] It is probably important that such a situation is carefully structured since different rules and significantly more expensive consequences apply to 'partitions' of chargeable interests held by partnerships; FA 2003, Sch 15, para 16.
[522] It should be noted that there may be a land exchange subject to tax where the participants agree to pool or contribute land which they own individually as well as acquire new land on a joint basis.

'partition' for the purposes of these provisions so that the only charge will be upon the person who is providing equality money.

5.171 Notwithstanding the foregoing it is possible that HMRC Stamp Taxes may change their unpublished practice which is not consistently applied and take a more technical approach. In consequence the possible limitations upon this relief[523] need to be noted:

• it is available only where there is a division of a single chargeable interest;

• it does not apply where there is a pool of chargeable interests that are jointly owned where these are divided between the co-owners. This will have important implications for the partition of assets on the dissolution or winding-up of partnerships and similar ventures;

• the parties must be jointly entitled, ie:
    – in England and Wales, the parties are beneficially entitled as joint tenants or tenants in common;
    – in Scotland, the parties are entitled as joint owners or owners in common; and
    – in Northern Ireland, the parties are beneficially entitled as joint tenants, tenants in common or coparceners.

The relief is therefore available only for persons holding the interest concurrently.[524] It does not apply to partition of assets where the interests are held in succession, such as A for life, remainder to B (eg as on a variation of a trust).[525] The charge is intended to apply only to any adjustment between the parties to deal with differences in the value between the parts of the chargeable interest allocated to each participant. This raises two issues which have not been publicly addressed by HMRC Stamp Taxes; namely:

• the effect of the parties making the adjustment by allocating other property such as debts jointly owned to make up the balance; and

• the impact of the computational provisions where the partitioned asset or assets is subject to a charge.[526]

Partnerships

5.172 Special rules apply to partitions involving partnerships. Dealings between partners and partnerships are subject to a special regime.[527] The special regime for partitions does not apply to transactions involving partnerships and partitions.[528] This means that the partitions do not apply to the acquisition of an interest in a partnership in consideration of entering into a land transaction with an existing partner.[529] In such a

---

[523] Where this relief does not apply the parties will need to consider whether the exchange of interests involve major or non-major interests and the special charging provisions apply: FA 2003, Sch 4, para 5 (see **5.150**).
[524] FA 2003, s 121.
[525] See **4.42** and **9.19** on variations of trust.
[526] FA 2003, Sch 4, para 8.
[527] Ibid, Sch 15, Part 3 (as amended); see **Chapter 13**.
[528] Ibid, Sch 15, para 16(3).
[529] Ibid, Sch 15, para 16; but note that in some situations the special rules for transfers to partners may apply; ibid, Sch 15, paras 18 and following; see **13.45**.

case the interest in the partnership is to be treated as a major interest in land for the purposes of the partnership if the relevant partnership property includes a major interest in land.[530] The effect would be that where the relevant exchanges operate the transaction will be taxed at market value upon the interest being acquired.[531]

Surrenders and regrants

5.173 The surrender of an existing lease in consideration of the grant of a new lease, whether of the same or different land, is technically a land exchange. The landlord receiving the surrender is doing so in consideration of the entry into another land transaction namely the grant of the new lease. This will apply where there is the surrender and regrant of a lease of the same premises or the tenant surrenders the lease of an existing premises in consideration of the grant of a lease of new premises such as where the landlord is seeking to persuade the tenant to relocate in order to enable developments or refurbishment programmes to proceed. This would, *prima facie*, involve two charges upon the market value of the various interests involved, namely the existing lease being surrendered and the new lease granted.[532] The provisions apply only to terminations of existing leases whether express or by operation of law and the grant of new leases; they do not apply to transfers of land and leases back or assignments of existing leases and the grant of underleases back. These are land exchanges and are subject to the full charge upon the relevant market values but subject to certain specialist reliefs such as the relief for leases back in sale and leaseback transactions[533] and certain transactions involved in connection with the alternative finance regime.[534]

5.174 The original provisions relating to surrenders and regrants were amended[535] and special rules apply to the chargeable premium and the chargeable rent. The land exchange rules are largely disapplied[536] and there is a limited credit for the tax on the new rent.[537] Essentially, as regards the taxable 'premium' the surrender of a lease and the grant of a new lease is no longer treated as a land exchange. The chargeable consideration for the grant of the new lease excludes the value of the lease surrendered and the new lease is not consideration for the surrender of the existing lease. There is no requirement as regards this relief that the premises involved in the old lease and the new lease are substantially the same. As indicated above, the relief is available in relation to the relocation of tenants. Obviously, any compensation or inducement being paid by the landlord will be carefully scrutinised by HMRC Stamp Taxes in order to discover whether it could represent some form of additional consideration for the surrender

---

[530] Ibid, Sch 15, para 16(1).

[531] It must also be noted that such land exchanges and partitions in relation to a partnership may operate to trigger certain anti-avoidance provisions which apply where there has been a transfer of land from a partner to a connected partnership consisting of individuals and there are changes in the composition of the partnership pursuant to arrangements in place when the transfer was made or where, within three years of the transfer of the land, there is a withdrawal of cash or assets from the partnership (FA 2003, Sch 15, paras 17 and 17A).

[532] These provisions will also apply to deemed surrenders and regrants where the parties entering into a deed of variation such as enlarging the term of an existing lease or changing the demised premises. There is, of course, the question of where there is a land exchange for consideration where the parties enter into a deed of variation that is a surrender and regrant by operation of law which in a sense is a non-consensual arrangement; see **5.98**.

[533] FA 2003, s 57A (as much amended).

[534] Ibid, ss 71A–73BA.

[535] See ibid, Sch 17A, para 16.

[536] Ibid, Sch 17A, para 16; but note the limits where there is a transfer and leaseback see **7.78**.

[537] Ibid, Sch 17A, paras 9 and 9A.

rather than a reverse inducement for the taking of the new lease.[538] There will, therefore, be questions as to payments of costs related to removal, disturbance to business or other factors and whether these are 'consideration' or are attributable to some other aspect of the transaction. The major requirement is that it is between the same parties. There does not appear to be any 'connected person' eligibility so that a change between parent company and subsidiary in respect of the existing lease and the new lease could take the transaction out of the exemption and into a full charge to tax on both sides of the transaction.

Surrender

5.175 This latter provision means that in routine cases involving the enlargement of the terms of leases of residential flats the landlord will not be providing chargeable consideration and any changes in his title at the Land Registry can be dealt with on the basis that there is not a notifiable transaction.

New lease 'premium'

5.176 The taxpayer is chargeable only upon any actual other consideration provided for the variation such as cash paid for the extra term. This relief applies whether or not the new lease relates to the same premises as the surrendered lease. In calculating the rate of tax only the equality or premium payment is usually taken into account other items such as the value of the surrendered lease is ignored.[539]

New rent – credit

5.177 The tenant is also taxable upon the rent reserved by the new lease. Since this cannot involve tax upon rent already taxed there is a reduction in the rent reserved by the new lease equal to rent that would have been 'payable' over the balance of the surrendered term,[540] which is described as the 'overlap period'. However, this reduction is available only where the old and new leases are between the same parties,[541] and the surrendered lease has paid stamp duty land tax,[542] and only where the existing and new leases relate to the same or substantially the same premises. Obviously, it is easy to discover whether the conditions as to the same parties is satisfied and whether the existing lease has paid stamp duty land tax are satisfied but there is a major practical problem in relation to the question as to whether the new lease relates to the same or substantially the same premises. Frequently the surrender and regrant will arise by operation of law where the parties change the demised premises by deed of variation.[543] There will, therefore, be an important practical difference between a partial surrender or a variation of the terms of the lease as regards demised premises. The latter will be a part-surrender not involving the grant of a new lease but will not be a full surrender and regrant whereas the latter will involve a grant of a new stamp duty land tax lease. Where there is an actual or deemed grant of a new lease the question is what will be regarded as

---

538   Ibid, Sch 17A, para 18.
539   There are, however, potential issues for the connected company charge (FA 2003, ss 53 and 62) but it seems that since exemptions apply to the special regime for partnerships (FA 2003, Sch 15, para 25(2)) the charge will be limited and not include the market value.
540   FA 2003, Sch 17A, para 9.
541   Ibid, Sch 17A, para 9(1)(a).
542   Ibid, Sch 17A, para 9(4). Surrenders and regrants of 'stamp duty leases' are fully taxable upon the whole of the new rent but apparently qualify for exclusion from the land exchange charges.
543   Which operates by way of surrender and regrant; see *Friends Provident Life Office v British Railways Board* [1996] 1 All ER 336.

being 'substantially' the same premises.[544] HMRC Stamp Taxes have not really published any safe harbour so that there is a significant risk that the relief will not be available where a significant amount of property is brought into the demised premises or a significant amount is taken out. The relief should be available where there is a minor variation of the terms of the demised premises because of a need to rectify where there has been property included or excluded from the demised premises but it would seem that anything more than 5 per cent of the area of the demised premises would be on risk. Also it is not clear how the difference between the old and the new premises is measured. For example, there may be a 5 storey building where there is an extension on the ground floor. This may represent a very small percentage of the total area of the building in terms of floor space but may represent a 'substantial' increase in the area of land if this is the sole criteria. HMRC Stamp Taxes have not really indicated very clearly whether they intend to look simply at the ground involved or whether the substantial identity depends upon the total square footage of the building.

5.178 The rent credit mechanism is fraught with problems unless HMRC Stamp Taxes adopt a simple route. The problem is the definition of 'rent payable' in respect of the original lease. This is[545] the amount of rent taken into account in calculating the tax on the original lease. This will not be the current passing rent, but a deemed figure. Where the surrender or deemed surrender takes effect during the first 5 years of the term; in subsequent years it will be based upon the assumed rent, ie the highest rent during the first 5 years of the term.[546] This rent will be discounted by reference to the expired length of the lease. However, the rent for the new lease will be commencing its discounting only from the date of the new grant or deemed regrant. In consequence there will be an element of double taxation of the rent even in those cases where there is no actual increase in the current or future passing rent.

5.179 Where the rent for the new lease is variable the normal complexities during the first 5 years will apply but with a reduction by reference to the discounted previously taxed rent, which will have to be taken into account in the initial estimate of the tax and the subsequent adjustment.[547]

The carrying out of 'works'

5.180 There has been a major change in the taxation of contracts for the disposal of land where there are related building or other works and many transactions that were not subject to stamp duty are now fully taxable. This major practice area is considered in detail in Chapter 8.[548]

Services (other than works)

5.181 Although the passage from *Secretan v Hart*[549] defining 'money's worth' refers to 'services', it is generally considered that services are not 'money's worth', since it is not

---

[544] It seems that the new lease need not be for substantially the same term and there are no restrictions upon the length of the new lease.

[545] FA 2003, Sch 17A, para 9(4).

[546] Since abnormal increases are deemed to be new leases it is probable that HMRC Stamp Taxes will not include any such increases in the deductible rent calculation so that there will be a double taxation of the rent.

[547] Where there is a subsequent increase or abnormal increase in the rent, it seems that the effect of this reduction is ignored.

[548] See **Chapter 8**.

[549] 45 TC 701.

usually possible to sell the benefit of service contracts in the open market.[550] It is, therefore, provided[551] that services are chargeable consideration for the purposes of stamp duty land tax and this is done by reference to the price that would have to be paid if acquired in the open market.[552] This will be a problem where the services may not be widely available as in the case referred to above[553] of a person who acts as a carer of an aged parent on the basis of a promise to inherit the house on the death of the parent,[554] especially since there have been no attempts either in the legislation or practice statements to give detailed guidance as to what 'services' are included.[555] The main argument against significant liability is that most such arrangements do not have an open market cost.[556]

5.182 In situations where there are services other than the carrying out of works within FA 2003, Sch 4, para 10, which form the whole or part of the consideration for a land transaction, the services form chargeable consideration. There arises an initial question of what are 'services' for these purposes; in particular whether the giving of guarantees is a service and if so whether the 'service' is provided directly or indirectly by the 'purchaser' as possibly required by FA 2003, Sch 4, para 1.[557] For example, where a parent company guarantees the performance of its obligations by a subsidiary company there is a question of whether the giving of the guarantees is a 'service' and, if so, how is the tax calculated. This should be relatively straightforward since there will be a fee charged by a commercial bank for giving an equivalent guarantee as it is generally assumed that payment made pursuant to a guarantee is not chargeable consideration.

5.183 No doubt an agreement to manage or to act as agent selling property constitutes services.[558] However, there may be difficult issues of whether services are being supplied as consideration for the acquisition of the chargeable interest where the relevant party agrees to 'procure' that some event will happen. Such terminology in the drafting suggests a 'service'.[559]

5.184 There may be a question of whether such services are chargeable consideration where they are to be separately paid for but form part of a development package, such as an agreement whereby, for example, a landowner agrees to dispose of certain land to a developer in consideration of, *inter alia*, the construction of buildings upon other land owned by the landlord for a fee and an arrangement whereby the developer or an associated company will market and manage the property in return for a commission and a fee. The amount of the chargeable consideration is the open market cost of the services, ie the amount that would have to be paid in the open market to obtain those services – an intriguing new basis for calculating tax.[560] It means that taxpayers may not know the final stamp duty land tax cost of their transaction for many years;

---

[550]   See *Noakes v Doncaster Amalgamated Collieries* [1940] 3 All ER 549.

[551]   FA 2003, Sch 4, para 11.

[552]   Ibid, Sch 4, para 11(1).

[553]   See **3.46**.

[554]   Assuming that this is not void for uncertainty and there is the necessary intention to create legal relations; but see *Yaxley v Gotts* [1999] 2 WLR 1217.

[555]   Eg a reverse premium to a tenant can be regarded as a payment for the 'service' of the tenant in accepting the lease; the exemption for such situations indicates that such 'services' would be taxable.

[556]   There may be issues as to the cost for caring for the landowner but this may not be such an issue where the arrangement is to pay off the mortgage; *Errington v Errington & Woods* [1952] 1 KB 290.

[557]   See **5.83**.

[558]   Note the potential trap in FA 2003, ss 44A and 45A.

[559]   See, eg, *Brocklesby v Merricks* (1934) 18 TC 576; *Bradbury v Arnold* (1957) 37 TC 665.

[560]   Little, if any, guidance is obtainable from Stamp Duty Land Tax (Administration) Regulations 2003, SI 2003/2837, Part 4.

nevertheless, they have to submit a figure on the stamp duty land tax return and if, upon Enquiry, HMRC Stamp Taxes takes a different view as to the open market cost of the services, claims for interest for late payment and penalties for incorrect returns[561] can be expected.

Trusts[562]

5.185 Most transactions involving trusts will not attract an actual obligation to pay stamp duty land tax because they will be gifts or other transactions for no chargeable consideration,[563] although where the trustees are bodies corporate the possible application of the charge upon not less than the market value needs to be noted.[564] Corporate trustees can be companies connected with the settlor[565] so that the transaction is *prima facie* within the charge but there are various exclusions where the company is connected with the settlor only by reason of the settlor/trustee relationship so that commercial corporate trustees are not within the charge. It is undesirable to use family companies as trustees. Where there is no chargeable consideration for the transfer into the trust fund the transaction will not be notifiable.[566] This will apply to transfers of chargeable interests into and out of trusts such as contributions to the capital made by the settlor or advances or appointments by the trustees out of the trust fund to beneficiaries in exercise of their powers.[567] as well as appropriations within a single trust between 'subfunds'. This has been extended so that even where the allocation of the property is with the consent of the beneficiaries it is not for a chargeable consideration.[568] Such transactions being for no chargeable consideration will not be notifiable.[569]

Anti-avoidance for trusts

5.186 Needless to say in addition to the general anti-avoidance provisions[570] there are special anti-avoidance provisions producing a chargeable transaction. Where a chargeable interest is acquired by virtue of either:

- the exercise of a power of appointment; or

- the exercise of a discretion vested in trustees of a settlement,

there is *prima facie* no charge to stamp duty land tax[571] in most cases. However, a chargeable transaction arises where the person acquiring the land 'bought' his way into the class of eligible beneficiaries. There is to be treated as consideration for the acquisition of the interest by virtue of the exercise of the power or discretion any consideration given for the person in whose favour the appointment was made or the

---

[561] FA 2003, Sch 10, para 8.
[562] See further **Chapter 9**.
[563] FA 2003, Sch 3, para 1.
[564] Ibid, ss 53 and 54; see **5.208**.
[565] Income and Corporation Taxes Act 1988, s 839.
[566] FA 2003, s 77A; Sch 3, para 1.
[567] But note the anti-avoidance provisions dealing with discretionary trusts and similar arrangements where there is an appointment or an advancement to a beneficiary who has purchased his eligibility pursuant to FA 2003, Sch 16, para 7.
[568] FA 2003, Sch 16, para 8 (as amended).
[569] Ibid, s 77A.
[570] Ibid, ss 75A–75C.
[571] See **Chapter 9**.

discretion was exercised becoming an object of the power or discretion.[572] Therefore, if a person pays a sum of money, whether to the trustees or to the settlor or to any other party, in order to be included within the class of discretionary beneficiaries or appointees, that money will rank as chargeable consideration in respect of any land transferred out of the trust.[573] Additionally the rules relating to the market value charge upon acquisitions by companies connected with the 'vendor' have to be considered.[574] This will apply even where the transaction is an appointment into a subtrust where the trustee is a body corporate unless the exclusions for certain corporate trustees apply.[575]

Variable consideration

5.187 There are many forms of variable consideration in relation to land transactions such as overage payments or 'clawback', sums that are linked to a possible re-sale of lease of the property within a specified time, the ultimate success of the proposed development, or to capture a share of windfall profits if planning consent is obtained,[576] consideration that may vary depending upon the terms of the planning permission, lease rents that may depend upon the final net lettable area of the building or the percentage of the turnover, whether gross or net of certain special expenses derived from sublettings or the price for the purchase of a reversion may depend upon the outcome of a review of the rents. There is also a complex regime dealing with the normal situation of variable rents such as reviews to market rent, turnover rents, shares of rents received from some tenants and the impact of the changes in the rate of VAT upon rents.[577] There are two unbelievably cumbersome – and therefore expensive and burdensome to the taxpayer[578] – sets of legislation relating to rents and to other consideration and the latter has a subset of principles relating to leases with a variable premium.[579] This represents a multi-stage problem of reporting, calculation and payment and dealings with the property; broadly with reference to:

- substantial performance;

- completion, such as delivery of the conveyance or grant of the lease;

- subsequent payments;

---

[572] FA 2003, Sch 16, para 7. There may, however, be some fundamental questions of the law governing the exercise of fiduciary powers as to whether the exercise of the power of appointment or advancement in favour of a 'purchaser' of the interest is open to attack as a fraud upon the power being made to a person not within the persons originally selected as objects of the power by the settlor or person conferring the power.

[573] Assuming that the exercise is not tainted as a fraud on a power or similar breach of trust.

[574] FA 2003, ss 53 and 54; see **5.208**.

[575] Ibid, s 54.

[576] Attempts are made to protect or secure such potential consideration by way of restrictions upon the land. Such arrangements are unlikely to be restrictive covenants because they do not benefit dominant land but they may be chargeable interests in their own right. This may convert the transaction from a sale for a variable consideration into a land exchange changing the computation basis for the vendor (subject to the complex issue of how HMRC Stamp Taxes can treat transactions where there are two or more separately applicable charging provisions). It also exposes the vendor to a potential tax charge since such rights to a deferred consideration can have a substantial market value.

[577] See **7.157**.

[578] And which raise major commercial issues for onward sales and leases of the property as well as potentially inhibiting business reorganisations and dealing with insolvency.

[579] See, for example, FA 2003, s 81A, Sch 17A, para 12.

- subsequent onward sales of the property and the need for an effective 'exit strategy' and dealing with those situations where the legislation passes the liability to third parties who may not unreasonably require indemnities.[580] In some situations the liability for the open tax position passes to the third party;[581] in other situations it remains the liability of the original taxpayer notwithstanding that he has parted with the land and is not necessarily in a position to know that an event which triggers the obligation to pay the additional consideration has occurred especially in those transactions where the fashionable drafting requires the obligation to subsist for a period of 80 years. There are, therefore, difficult technical issues as regards the drafting and structuring of the original agreement and the dealing with the open tax position on a subsequent onward sale, or administering an estate or winding-up of a company as well as the due diligence required to discover the existence and extent of the risks to the purchaser.[582] Indeed, the structuring of the initial transaction can fundamentally affect the subsequent dealings in the property, especially where the original taxpayer has obtained the benefit of postponing the tax upon the variable consideration. These issues are discussed elsewhere.[583] The present section deals with the initial tax computation which produces the open or non-final tax position, although it has to be noted that these principles can also affect a subsequent purchaser of the chargeable interest if the arrangement was not initially set up in the most efficient format;

- in addition to the complications of this regime for computing stamp duty land tax with its provisional basis and subsequent retrospective adjustments there are many implications for title, due diligence and the sort of warranties and indemnities that vendors and purchasers may require. For example, the taxpayer, if an individual, may have an outstanding provisional tax liability and obligation to report against his estate and a company may have similar problems of potential tax so that personal representatives of individuals and liquidators and receivers of companies may be restricted in their ability to wind-up the affairs of the individual or the company;

- assignees of leases are affected in a variety of ways, they may be by statute compelled to deal with variable premiums,[584] they are subject to obligations in relation to rent reviews which deal with the open tax position of the original tenant. To complicate matters even further, assignees of leases are dependent upon obtaining an accurate stamp duty land tax history of the lease since his actions may give rise to liabilities to tax such as whether rent reviews produce an abnormal increase[585] or the turnover has a similar effect or he may hold over the lease within the Landlord and Tenant Act 1954 so that his tax liability relates back to the original grant of the lease.[586] Without a detailed record of the tax positions of the previous tenants he will be unable to comply with his obligations to determine whether there is a liability and, if so, whether tax is payable and the amount of such tax. In effect, HMRC Stamp Taxes have converted stamp duty land tax into an additional and complicated title issue.[587] Without this information prospective

---

[580] See, for example, **7.53**.
[581] On the lack of finality and open tax positions see **2.14**; for assignees of leases see **7.238**.
[582] FA 2003, s 81A; Sch 17A, para 12.
[583] **Chapter 16**; Stamp Duty Land Tax (Administration) Regulations 2003, SI 2003/2837, Part 4.
[584] FA 2003, s 81A and Sch 17A, para 12.
[585] Ibid, Sch 17A, paras 14 and 15.
[586] Ibid, Sch 17A, paras 3, 4, 9 and 9A.
[587] See **2.13**.

purchasers of land or persons proposing to act as executors[588] or liquidators[589] should consider whether it is safe to proceed because they may be entering into situations where there is an unquantifiable liability to tax and HMRC Stamp Taxes have consistently refused to assist in dealing with this situation such as producing detailed records. Moreover, even if HMRC Stamp Taxes were able to produce such records those that they have would be effectively useless. Copies of the original land transaction return are frequently meaningless in this context since they deal in global figures whereas, for example, an assignee of a lease requires a detailed breakdown of the rents for each of the years in question that form the basis for the calculation of the net present value. It is the information that was used to calculate the figures inserted on the return rather than the return itself that is the document of title.[590] Moreover, as with all documents of title the retention period imposed for tax documentation is irrelevant. These records must be preserved for whatever period is necessary for title investigation and, in the case of leases, throughout the entire lifetime of the lease; and

- in addition, the lack of finality and retrospective nature of much of the tax have important implications for exemptions. For example, when dealing with a rent review this relates retrospectively to the original calculation as does the situation concerned with holding over. In consequence, a rent review of land that was within a disadvantaged area at the time the lease was granted may be eligible for exemption from stamp duty land tax notwithstanding that the relief has ceased to exist. Similarly, the special rules for the computation of tax in relation to dealings between partners and connected persons[591] will potentially apply to a review or variation of a lease notwithstanding that there have been changes in the partnership in the intervening period. The reduction for the sum of the lower proportions will be measured by reference to the circumstances at the time the lease was granted and not by reference to the circumstances as they exist at the time of the variation. This possibility of exemption will, of course, enlarge the scope of documents of title since these will be necessary in order to determine what exemptions if any were available at the time the lease was granted. Conversely, exemptions that are, *prima facie*, available at the time of the subsequent event will be irrelevant because the conditions for the exemption were not satisfied when the lease was granted. For example, A Limited grants a lease to its subsidiary company C Limited with a rent review after 5 years. This lease is, *prima facie*, eligible for relief from stamp duty land tax.[592] After the expiration of 3 years but before the first review arises A Limited disposes of the share capital of B Limited. It would seem that the rent review is exempt from stamp duty land tax because it relates back to the original grant of the lease when the landlord and the tenant were members of the same stamp duty land tax group. Conversely, where the lease is granted to C Limited before it becomes a subsidiary of A Limited and subsequently A Limited acquires the shares of C Limited any rent review during the first 5 years of any lease granted to C Limited will not be eligible for exemption because at the time A Limited and C Limited were not appropriately associated.

---

[588]   FA 2003, s 106(3).
[589]   Ibid, s 100(7) or receivers s 106(4).
[590]   A print of the page could be useful.
[591]   FA 2003, Sch 15, Part 3.
[592]   Ibid, Sch 7, Part 1.

General principles

5.188 The basic principles for dealing with variable payments are contained in FA 2003, s 51, and these provisions are applied, subject to certain modifications,[593] with variations to variable payments, such as annuities,[594] and other periodical payments, such as mining and similar royalty payments,[595] as well as lease premiums and rent although separate rules apply to variable rents.[596] However, although the principles applicable to the original provisional tax computation and subsequent events vary depending upon whether the original chargeable transaction is the grant of an agreement for a new lease or some other dealing in land, there are many situations where the detailed application of the general principles to particular situations is far from clear.

Types of variable consideration

5.189 The basic position depends upon whether the variable consideration is 'contingent' or is 'uncertain' or 'unascertained'. This determines the method of computation and the nature and consequences of subsequent events. However, it has to be remembered that there are certain fundamental differences in the application of these principles to the original chargeable transaction and subsequent dealings in the interests whether by way of assignment, variation or otherwise.

5.190 It is necessary to determine at the outset whether the consideration is contingent or uncertain since this affects the calculation of the stamp duty land tax payable initially and the notification obligations at the time and in the future and the ability to apply for permission to defer payment of the estimated or provisional element in the tax. There is a definition:

- 'Contingent' The consideration is 'contingent' if it is to be paid or provided only if some uncertain future event occurs or if it is to cease to be paid or provided if some uncertain future event occurs.[597] This seems to focus the contingency on the uncertainty of the event rather than the amount. As will be seen in relation to the definition of 'uncertain' which links to the uncertainty of the amount, so that it would seem clear that this definition of 'contingency' is intended to apply only to a fixed sum that may or may not become payable or where a price that is paid is to be reduced by a specified amount in relation to some future event or the non-occurrence of a future event.[598] This provision will apply where, for example, there is a sale of land for a basic price with an undertaking to pay an additional fixed sum if planning permission is subsequently obtained.

  It is also intended to apply to situations where there is a basic price but which will reduce by a fixed amount in the future. It is important to note that the reduction is by reference to a fixed amount rather than a reduction by reference to a variable amount. For example, where there is a transfer for a consideration of £X but this is to be reduced if the expected planning permission or the receipt of rents falls below certain predicted figures this is, *prima facie*, within this provision but, for example, if the reduction in the price is not a fixed sum but is a multiple of the

---

[593] Ibid, s 52.
[594] Ibid, s 52(3); see **5.120**.
[595] Ibid, s 52(6).
[596] Ibid, Sch 17A, paras 7 and 8.
[597] Ibid, s 51(3).
[598] On the issue of potential VAT where there may not be a transfer of a going concern see **5.130**.

shortfall in the profit projections it will be outside these provisions and will be an 'uncertain' consideration. It does not apply, therefore, to a situation where an amount is linked to the rents or profits exceeding a particular figure even where this is a maximum or cap. Thus, a payment that is to be 5 per cent of the excess over £x but which is not to exceed £y would not be a 'contingent' sum for these purposes.

- *'Uncertain'* 'Uncertain' consideration is defined[599] as meaning consideration the amount or value of which depends on certain future events. This would appear to include the whole range of variables, ie the event may or may not happen and the amount to be paid may vary. Thus the situation of additional consideration being provided if certain targets are met, whether capped or uncapped, will be 'uncertain'. This will apply to the vast majority of variable consideration. It will apply to earnouts and overages such as where the price is linked to the onward sale of the property or to the number of houses sold in excess of a particular figure.[600]

- *'Unascertained'* There is no definition of 'unascertained' consideration.[601] By elimination of the other types of taxable consideration it would appear to mean consideration which has not been finally determined but all of the factors relevant to its calculation are available on the effective date. This appears to differ from the two preceding types of variable consideration by referring to prior events rather than future events. Thus this would appear to be the situation of a payment by reference to 'market value' as at the effective date or earlier. Here, all the factors are fixed but the calculation has not been made. Other situations would be somewhat unusual. The sale of a building by reference to the net lettable area where the building is completed but has not been measured would be a situation where the price depends upon data already available and would appear to be a matter for the transaction to be treated as involving 'unascertained' consideration. Another situation, although this is not quite so clear-cut, would be where a landlord is selling a freehold interest that is subject to a lease and there is a rent review in progress. In this situation the price may vary depending upon the outcome of the rent review. It appears to be the view of HMRC Stamp Taxes that where there is a rent review in progress the rent has become 'ascertained' rather than 'unascertained'. This is disputed but it is a circumstance where all of the data relating to the rent review is past data ie the market rent as at a particular date and this is just a matter of sorting out and agreeing the data. In that situation all of the data that is relevant for the adjustment in the consideration for the purchase of the reversionary interest is also past data. On this view of HMRC Stamp Taxes the consideration for the purchase of the reversion would be 'unascertained', the consideration may have ceased to be 'uncertain', but it is not 'ascertained'. It is considered that where there is a rent review in progress, although this relates to previous circumstances, the rent is not 'ascertained' until such time as the parties or their representatives have agreed.[602] This may be a situation where it can be

---

[599] FA 2003, s 51(3).

[600] But note the potentially adverse taxation consequences of such an arrangement that links the payment to events after the development has commenced as in *Page v Lowther* [1983] STC 799. This could be important given the difference in the rates applicable to capital gains tax and the taxation of income and profits in the current regime.

[601] FA 2003, s 51(3). This is unfortunate since there are many provisions relating to consideration becoming 'ascertained'. This can apply, for example, to variable rents during the first five years of the term (FA 2003, Sch 17A, paras 7 and 8) and the date at which new rents are 'ascertained' is a key factor in reporting and payment.

[602] It is important to note that it is the date of the agreement that fixes the tax events not the date when the

argued that the consideration is 'uncertain' within the above definition because it depends upon the outcome of a future event namely the agreement of the parties or their advisers as to the rents for the lease.

- *Value Added Tax* A key area in this debate is the question of VAT in relation to transactions that are treated by the parties as transfers of going concerns. In this situation a fixed sum will become payable should the transaction not be a transfer of a going concern for the purposes of VAT; namely the amount of VAT calculated by reference to the price at the rate in force on the date of the tax point for the purposes of VAT. There is, therefore, a fixed sum that is payable if certain conditions are not satisfied. It is the view of HMRC Stamp Taxes that this consideration is 'unascertained'. It is clear that the payment of the VAT is part of the consideration since the contract will usually contain a provision that if the transaction is not a transfer of a going concern there will be an obligation to make an additional payment. This is clearly a consideration and not a 'condition'.[603] This will obviously affect the computation of the tax payable and the rate applicable to the basic consideration. It is also a question as to whether the payment of the stamp duty land tax in respect of the potential VAT is a tax charge that can be deferred. The contrary view that it is a fixed sum payable upon a contingency ie the delivery by the vendor of a VAT invoice is, therefore, important because of the ability to postpone tax on contingent payments. It is considered that the analysis of HMRC Stamp Taxes is fundamentally flawed since it assumes that the effective date for stamp duty land tax will be the same as the tax point for the purposes of determining the status of the transaction for VAT and it ignores the possibility that the eligibility for treatment as a transfer of a going concern depends upon the purchaser continuing to carry on the sale business after the tax point as that that was prior to the tax point carried on by the vendor. In consequence, all of the relevant data will not necessarily be available as at the effective date for stamp duty land tax. There may, however, be issues as to the precise status of the payment where circumstances have changed and the VAT point coincides with subsequent completion which, in the view of HMRC Stamp Taxes, is a separate chargeable event.[604] This clearly illustrates some of the problems with unascertained consideration and the tax dates for the purposes of stamp duty land tax. A payment that may be uncertain at the time of substantial performance may have become 'unascertained' at the time of completion and this raises the question as to whether subsequent completion after substantial performance is a separate chargeable event requiring a reanalysis of the situation. It should, however, be noted that the relevant date is the 'effective date' which may not be the same as the date fixed for ascertaining consideration for the purposes of the contract, usually completion. There may, in many cases, be significant differences between the time when the transaction is 'substantially performed' and when it is finally completed and the valuation date arises. In this situation, since the valuation at substantial performance, ie the effective date, will be an amount dependent upon future events, ie movements in the market between the effective date and the contractual completion date, the consideration will be 'uncertain' rather than 'unascertained'.

---

parties approach their lawyers for the endorsement of a memorandum upon the lease. The rent becomes 'ascertained' at the time of the agreement not at the time of the endorsement which, if left, could mean that the parties are in default with their stamp duty land tax obligations and subject to interest and penalties for failure to file and pay on time.

[603] *Eastham v Leigh, London and Provincial Properties Limited* [1971] 2 All ER 887.
[604] FA 2003, s 44(8).

For these purposes it must be noted that the nature of the consideration may change between substantial performance and completion so that the status of the consideration may change from, for example, uncertain consideration to unascertained consideration should HMRC Stamp Taxes be correct in their view that there are two effective dates where there is a separation between substantial performance and completion.[605]

Special cases involving variable consideration and rent

5.191 Particular rules apply to certain types of variable payments, which either wholly or partially take them out of the basic regime. These include the following:

Annuities and periodical payments

5.192 Whilst these are taxed by reference to the initial reasonable estimate, the subsequent reporting and payment regime does not apply.[606]

Indexation

5.193 It is specifically provided[607] that, in relation to rents, the fact that the rent is linked to the Retail Price Index is to be ignored and this does not make the rent uncertain for these purposes. However, linking to other forms of indices such as interest rates or stock exchange indices or even a modified Retail Price Index, which excludes or includes items other than the official index, does not qualify for the benefit of this treatment. The exclusion for the variable consideration also does not apply where the link to the Retail Price Index is merely one of the variables. Thus, where the rent is to be increased by indexation or 5 per cent, whichever is the greater, the rent will be variable and so within the provisions of FA 2003, s 51.

Computation and variable payments other than rent

Initial transaction and retrospective review

5.194 Where there is a variable consideration there will be, at least, two sets of calculations. The nature of the initial filing and dealing with subsequent events depends upon the nature of the consideration as at the effective date.[608] The essence of the arrangement is that there will be an initial payment and self-assessment based upon 'guestimates'. The retrospective element gives rise to numerous important practical implications. For example, because the subsequent crystallisation of the tax liability relates back to an earlier event the question of whether there is an exemption or relief is to be tested by reference to the original circumstances and not by reference to the circumstances as they exist as at the date of the subsequent event that triggers the liability.[609] In addition, there may not be just one subsequent event. There may be many situations where part of the additional consideration becomes 'ascertained' this requires separate reporting and payment for each time part of the consideration becomes crystallised.[610] For example, a developer may enter into the acquisition of land upon the

---

[605] Ibid, s 44(8); Sch 17A, para 12A.
[606] Ibid, s 52(7); see **5.121**.
[607] Ibid, Sch 17A, para 7(5).
[608] Or the last or latest effective date where there is more than one; FA 2003, s 44(8), Sch 17A, para 12A; see **7.25**.
[609] See **5.198** and **5.205**.
[610] FA 2003, s 80.

basis that he will pay an additional consideration in respect of each house sold above a particular price. In this situation each sale of a house will be an event that 'ascertains' part of the consideration. There will, therefore, be an obligation to pay and file a return in respect of each house sale, at least where this produces additional taxation. On the other hand, where there is a purchase by a developer for a consideration that refers to the overall disposal proceeds or profits of the development since these can be ascertained only on one occasion namely after the development is completed and sold or leased there will be only one further retrospective reporting obligation.

5.195 The issue, as with all variable consideration, is the amount that may become payable if the event happens or does not happen; it is not a question of the likelihood of the event happening. There are two potential issues when preparing the initial self-assessment:

- how likely is it that any payment will be made; and

- if payable what is the likely amount.

The first issue appears to be irrelevant – the legislation requires a reasonable estimate of the amount potentially payable. It seems that HMRC Stamp Taxes require 'reasonable' to include an assumption that the event had happened. Taxpayers who prepare their land transaction return (both SDLT 1 and 4 will be required) on the basis that they have no immediate plans to seek planning permission will be submitting an incorrect return with the consequent risk of penalties. A taxpayer who prepares return upon the basis that it is unlikely that the payment will made is preparing an incorrect return.[611] The return is, *prima facie*, negligent and potentially fraudulent if the taxpayer does not genuinely believe that no payment will be made. Penalties could arise and there will be issues as to interest upon tax that should have been paid because it was not declared and postponed. In this situation preparation of the return is not a major problem since the amount of the additional potential payment is fixed. There is no need for estimates as to the amount. In consequence, there must be a return that includes the total potential payment ie the basic price plus the fixed amount. Any return not prepared upon this basis will, *prima facie*, be negligent.

Contingent consideration

5.196 Where the whole or part of a chargeable consideration for a transaction is contingent, the amount or value of the consideration is determined for the purposes of stamp duty land tax on the assumption that the outcome of the contingency will be such that the consideration is payable or, as the case may be, does not cease to be payable.[612] The chargeable consideration is, therefore, the amount paid as actual consideration plus the amount of the contingent sum.[613] Where the contingency arrangement is for the consideration to be reduced then stamp duty land tax is paid upon the actual consideration moving. There is no deduction in relation to the computation and information required in the return by reference to substantial performance or completion by reference to the contingent nature of the sums in question.[614]

---

[611] Ibid, Sch 10, para 8.
[612] Ibid, s 51(1)
[613] Deferment may be possible: FA 2003, s 90; see **16.34**.
[614] Ibid, s 51(1).

5.197 The tax must be calculated upon the maximum figure. This means that the rate must be fixed by reference to the total amount. In consequence, where there is a sale for a basic price of £250,000 with a further contingent payment of £1,000,000 the chargeable consideration this will produce an overall rate of 4 per cent. Although it may be possible to defer the payment of the tax in respect of the contingent sum the rate of tax applicable to the initial price of £250,000 is 4 per cent. Should the event in question not happen the consideration will reduce to £250,000 and there will be an entitlement to a refund of the additional tax paid because of the reduction in the rate of 4 per cent to 1 per cent.

It is possible to defer the payment of tax upon the contingent sum.[615]

5.198 Where the contingency subsequently occurs or it becomes clear that it will not occur then the parties have to revisit the transaction and any transaction in relation to which it is a linked transaction, since this may require adjustment that could affect the availability of lower rates of stamp duty land tax and other matters.[616] If the effect of the new information is that a transaction becomes notifiable or chargeable or that additional tax is payable in respect of a transaction or that tax is payable where none was previously payable, the purchaser must make a return to HMRC Stamp Taxes within 30 days, which must contain a self-assessment of the tax chargeable in respect of the transaction on the basis of the information contained in the return. The tax so chargeable is to be calculated by reference to the rates in force at the effective date of the transaction, not the date on which the contingency occurs or ceases to be relevant. The return must be accompanied by payment of the tax or additional tax payable.[617] If the tax has been dealt with initially by declaring the amount and postponing the tax[618] the additional tax will be payable but without interest or penalty. On the other hand, if the tax has not been properly dealt with by reference to the initial filing there will have been an underpayment of tax as at the filing date ie 30 days after the effective date so that interest will arise from 30 days after the effective date and there may be questions as to penalties for filing a negligent or improper return. If the effect of the new information is that tax is payable in respect of the transaction, ie the contingent event reduces the consideration, the amount overpaid shall on a claim by the purchaser[619] be repaid together with interest as from the date of payment.[620] The return required by these provisions must comply with and be subject to all of the sanctions imposed by FA 2003, Sch 10.[621]

Unascertained consideration

5.199 Where the whole or part of the chargeable consideration for the transaction is unascertained, its amount is to be determined for the purposes of stamp duty land tax on the basis of a reasonable estimate.[622] Failure to carry out appropriate steps to determine what is a 'reasonable' estimate will undoubtedly be regarded as producing a negligent return and may even be viewed by HMRC Stamp Taxes as fraud in extreme cases. In these circumstances because the parties are dealing with previous data there

---

[615] See **16.34**.
[616] FA 2003, s 80(1).
[617] Ibid, s 80(2).
[618] See **16.34**.
[619] Prepared presumably in accordance with FA 2003, Sch 11A.
[620] Ibid, s 80(4).
[621] Ibid, s 80(3).
[622] Ibid, s 51(2); see ibid, s 90 for deferment.

should be a reasonable view as to the likely level of payment. The parties may not have concluded their negotiations or valuation processes but these will be in progress and there will be upper and lower parameters which should give a reasonable guide to the figure.

5.200 Tax has to be paid on the total amount including the amount estimated for the unascertained consideration. This will be the figure taken into account in determining the rate. It may be that the estimated figure is above a particular threshold. The rate will be fixed by reference to that figure. If the subsequent events produce a figure below the estimated figure and below the relevant threshold there will be a situation of tax having been overpaid because of the excessive rate and the excessive estimate and appropriate refunds will be available. There is no power to postpone the tax in relation to unascertained consideration.

5.201 Where an originally unascertained amount of consideration or any instalment thereof becomes 'ascertained' and the effect of the new information is that a transaction becomes chargeable and/or notifiable (eg because it takes the consideration over the nil rate threshold in force for the type of property at the time) or additional tax becomes payable in respect of a transaction or that tax is payable where none was payable before, then the purchaser must make a return to HMRC Stamp Taxes within 30 days, which must contain a self-assessment of the stamp duty land tax chargeable on the basis of the information contained in the return. If the amount including the initial return on the 'guestimated' basis is below the final figure additional tax will be payable together with interest from 30 days after the effective date. Conversely, if the amount was initially overestimated there will be an entitlement to a tax refund together with interest. In the event of an underestimate HMRC Stamp Taxes may wish to claim that the return was improperly prepared and therefore potentially subject to penalties.[623]

5.202 The tax so chargeable is to be calculated by reference to the rates in force at the effective date of the transaction, not the date on which the new information and the adjustment arises. The subsequent return must be accompanied by a payment of the tax or any additional tax payable. The return must comply with the requirements of, and is subject to the sanctions contained in FA 2003, Sch 10.[624]

Uncertain consideration

5.203 Where the chargeable consideration is 'uncertain' in whole or in part the tax is calculated by reference to an estimated figure, ie the aggregate of the basic or initial price, if any, plus a reasonable estimate of the uncertain amount. No guidance is provided as to how to estimate the impact of future events although interest for late payment and possibly penalties may become payable if the estimate, although 'reasonable' is below the final figure.[625] Professional advisers are justifiably reluctant to become involved in seeking to estimate the reasonable impact upon valuation of obtaining planning permission at some uncertain time during the following 80 years.

---

[623] Ibid, s 80(4).
[624] Ibid, s 80(3).
[625] Moreover, unless there is clear contemporaneous evidence of the steps taken the return may be subject to the extended discovery period of 21 years on the basis that it was prepared negligently. For the ease with which HMRC Stamp Taxes can establish a discovery see *Langham v Veltema* [2004] STC 544. Compare the unhelpful comments on a similar situation by Russell LJ in *Crane Fruehauf v IRC* [1975] STC 51 that the parties must do the best they can.

5.204 Having 'reasonably' estimated the total consideration, tax has initially to be calculated (ie the rate to apply) by reference to the total estimated figure; but any payment of tax is to be made upon the initial, basic or any fixed consideration and it is possible to apply to postpone the payment of the tax on the uncertain figure.[626] This process of 'guestimating' future values might appear to be a totally impossible exercise since no-one can predict future movements in value and to expect a 'reasonable estimate' of the likely impact of obtaining planning permission some 70 or 80 years into the future and allowing for the effects of price inflation is clearly nonsense. Nevertheless, HMRC Stamp Taxes are committed to this view[627] and expect some attempt to be made.[628] Contrary to advice that is frequently provided by the so-called Helpline, it is not proper to ignore the possibility of the additional payment and 'sort it out later'. This is advice provided by HMRC Stamp Taxes in order to enable them to maximise interest and penalties for failure to comply with the requirements. A reasonable estimate must be made. Whilst there are particular difficulties in relation to variable rents[629] in relation to lump sum payments the position is less onerous. It is possible to postpone the tax upon the uncertain payment.[630] In consequence, the process is one designed to avoid the potential exposure of the taxpayer to potential charges for interest for underestimating and penalties for negligent returns. In consequence, it is a prudent course to over 'guestimate' the potential payment. If payment is postponed, the client does not have to make any payment on account of tax and so is not out of pocket and is not prejudiced by the fact that the parties have made a generous estimate of his ultimate potential liability. Should the parties under guestimate then should the event happen the tax underestimated will be subject to interest and there may be questions as to whether the underestimate was negligent for the purposes of penalties. However, it is only the excess over the estimated figure that will bear the penalty.

5.205 Where all or any instalment of the uncertain consideration[631] becomes 'ascertained' a further return is required retrospectively recalculating the tax on the basis of the updated information.[632] The tax postponed or part thereof becomes payable, but no interest is chargeable if paid within the 30 days. If the original estimate was below the final figure interest is payable upon the deficit, such interest runs from 30 days after the initial effective date. In consequence, since there is the possibility of deferring without payment of interest a basic defensive strategy is for the 'reasonable' estimate to err on the high side.

Exit strategy

5.206 A key factor for any purchaser entering into an acquisition for a variable consideration is the prudent requirement for including a mechanism for disposing of the property in due course which deals with the outstanding contractual liability to pay the

---

[626]　FA 2003, s 90; Stamp Duty Land Tax (Administration) Regulations 2003, SI 2003/2837, Part 4; see **16.34**.

[627]　Which is an unsatisfactory attempt to bring the benefits of enhanced tax on artificial and unrealistic figures proceeded by the alleged contingency principle from stamp duty into a statutory form that is inappropriate to a tax imposed at very high rates.

[628]　Failure to deal with this issue in preparing the initial land transaction return (SDLT 1) is likely to be regarded as negligence and incur penalties pursuant to FA 2003, Sch 10, para 8.

[629]　See **7.161**.

[630]　FA 2003, s 90; Stamp Duty Land Tax (Administration) Regulations 2003, SI 2003/2837, Part 4; see **16.34**.

[631]　These filing problems appear to differ as regards variable rent when, for example, changes in the rate of VAT upon the rent may not have to be returned with the expiration of the fifth year of the term; FA 2003, Sch 17A, para 8(1)(b) which requires the rent for the first 5 years to become certain during the first 5 years which cannot be the case where VAT is involved since rates may change at any time so that a return is not required until after the fifth year.

[632]　FA 2003, ss 80 and 87.

additional consideration and which, in consequence, cancels the related stamp duty land tax liability and will entitle the taxpayer to reclaim any tax paid because the variable consideration had the effect of requiring the tax to be paid at a rate higher than would have applied to the basic or initial consideration.[633] The essence of such an exit strategy is an in-built novation arrangement whereby the original purchaser is released from the contractual liability to pay any additional consideration which will cancel the related stamp duty land tax liabilities because the consideration ceases to be payable, provided that he produces a suitable instrument from the next purchaser undertaking to pay the additional consideration if the conditions are satisfied. This releases the first purchaser from any additional tax, although the second or subsequent purchaser has to deal with the problems of agreeing to pay a variable consideration notwithstanding that the payment is to be made to a third party (ie the original vendor) and not the direct seller to him.

Deemed consideration

General principles

5.207   In some situations there is a deemed consideration usually by reference to market value. This usually overrides the actual consideration. In these circumstances there will be some interesting opportunities for debate of general principles with HMRC Stamp Taxes such as where the actual consideration includes some form of overage or clawback payment and how this hope value can be turned into market value.[634] HMRC Stamp Taxes will be faced with a difficult problem of arguing that as a matter of general principle a fiscal valuation should include some form of overage payment when determining the market value. This requires them to establish that the market value is not a once-for-all exercise but is a hypothetical commercial negotiation and since the professional advisers of vendors may be required to use reasonable endeavours to obtain some form of overage or clawback payment.[635] It is, however, an intriguing exercise as to the taxation consequences of a hypothetical consideration and whether this can include an element of variable consideration with all the long-term consequences for the taxpayer. This is an unresolved issue of valuation and the principles to be applied in the rather loosely drafted legislation referring to 'market value'.[636]

Connected companies

5.208   Particular problems arise when the person acquiring the interest or being treated as acquiring an interest such as in respect of certain lease variations,[637] is a company that is connected with the other party to the transaction or where some or all of the consideration for the transaction consists of the issue or transfer of shares in a company with which the person disposing of the interest is connected, because there is a deemed consideration of not less than the market value.[638] In this situation the legislation merely

---

[633]   The right to reclaim the tax overpaid arises because the higher rate of tax no longer applies because the additional consideration is no longer payable.

[634]   HMRC Stamp Taxes are faced with the problem of determining market value (a once-for-all payment) when the market (*Akazuc Enterprises v Farmar* [2003] PL SCS 127) works upon deferred consideration and are left with the problem whether the initial price passing is the market value which reflects the 'hope value' or this is displaced by the overage or other payment which substitutes for the hope value.

[635]   See *Akazuc Enterprises v Farmar* [2003] PL SCS 127.

[636]   See **Chapter 27**.

[637]   FA 2003, s 43(3)(d); Sch 17A, para 15A.

[638]   Ibid, s 53(1).

substitutes a minimum chargeable consideration.[639] It appears that if the actual consideration exceeds the market value this will prevail and be the chargeable consideration. There is no guidance as to how this provision is to operate where the actual consideration includes some variable element. As indicated above[640] there is no guidance as to whether the 'market value' must relate to a fixed price at the effective date taking into account 'hope value' or can include a variable element where this would be a routine commercial matter so that there will, however, be questions as to whether the land transaction return has to be prepared upon the basis of the market value rather than the actual consideration, initial or basic, plus the estimate of the additional consideration; but it seems that market value may not override the variable consideration rules and the initial or basic price will frequently be the current use value of the land ie its market value if the specified events do not occur. Since the market value will include immediate payment and take into account the risks that the event in question may not happen it is likely that the potential consideration will exceed the market value. It is thought that in these circumstances the land transaction return has to be prepared upon the basis of the estimated figure and not the current market value of the land including any hope or expectation since this estimated, rather than the ultimate consideration, exceeds the current market value. As indicated above, the variable consideration has to be prepared upon the basis that the event will happen which is likely to be significantly higher than the market value which may be prepared upon the basis that the event may not happen. In the latter case the likelihood of the additional payment being made is a factor which is not a permissible element when computing the liability to stamp duty land tax for variable payments.

5.209 This is a wide-ranging provision. Connected companies can include corporate trustees,[641] groups of companies,[642] and the incorporation of businesses[643] Including partnerships. Dividends and distributions *in specie* are exempt[644] unless the company making the distribution received the property pursuant to an acquisition exempted by Finance Act 2003, Sch 7, Part 1, in the 3 years preceding the distribution. Appointment and advancements by trustees to corporate beneficiaries may be within the charge.

Partnerships

5.210 A special regime based upon market value rather than the actual consideration applies to dealings between partners, partnerships and connected persons.[645]

Employees

Leases to employees

5.211 Where a land transaction is entered into by reason of the purchaser's employment or that of a person connected with him and this arrangement would give

---

[639]   The draftsman has not addressed the issues of lack of finality and retrospection which he has made fundamental to the structure and day-to-day operation of the tax so that the impact of the connected company provisions upon transactions with retrospective effect such as where the initial transaction involved a connected company but the company is not connected at the time of any relevant subsequent events and vice versa.

[640]   See **5.207**.

[641]   But note the exemptions in ibid, s 54.

[642]   These transactions may be exempt pursuant to ibid, Sch 7, Part 1, but have to be notified.

[643]   But note the exemption for limited liability partnerships: FA 2003, s 65.

[644]   Ibid, s 54.

[645]   Ibid, Sch 15, Part 3; see **Chapter 13**.

rise to a charge to tax under the Income Tax (Earnings and Pensions) Act 2003 as a benefit in kind, there is a deemed rent payable by the employee or tenant equal to the cash equivalent chargeable as the benefit in kind.[646] Care may be needed in calculating the tax since such a lease may be for an indefinite term and so have to be treated initially as a 12-month lease;[647] but it must be noted that such leases 'grow'. If the employee remains employed and in continuation of the occupation after the expiration of the first year he will be deemed to be a tenant of a 2 year lease or a 3 year lease and so on. Whilst this means that there may be no tax payable in respect of the rent plus benefit in kind in the first year because of the threshold of £125,000 (or temporarily £175,000) the benefit and rent will increase over the years so that the net present value may eventually exceed the relevant nil rate threshold for the rent and tax become payable. Fortunately, if the employment continues for a sufficiently long period and the employee becomes entitled to a lease for 7 years or longer there is no obligation to notify simply because of the length of the lease. The notification and payment obligations arise only if tax becomes payable for the first time or tax having already become paid further tax is due. The effect is that once tax becomes payable there will be an annual obligation to pay and file. If the transaction would give rise to a charge but for the fact that the accommodation is provided for the performance of duties,[648] the chargeable consideration is the actual consideration, if any. In any other case, ie where there is no taxable benefit in kind or the accommodation is not provided for the performance of duties, the consideration for the transaction is not less than the market value of the subject-matter of the transaction as at the effective date of the transaction.[649] As the value of the benefit in kind will vary because of the formula to be applied to it in each year, then, where the transaction falls under the first of these charging provisions (ie a taxable benefit in kind) it would seem that there is an uncertain rent and that the employee will be required to report this transaction and pay any additional tax that may be due after 5 years.[650]

Transfers to employees

5.212 If the transaction with the employee would be subject to income tax but for the accommodation being supplied for the performance of duties[651] the charge is upon the actual consideration, if any. In other cases where there is no benefit in kind or accommodation for the performance of duties, the consideration is taken to be not less than the market value of the property.[652] This could represent a potentially large charge to tax where the employee receives a chargeable interest as some form of bonus payment in kind.

Partnerships

5.213 Actual consideration other than rent, if any, is largely ignored in transactions between partners, partnerships and connected persons[653] and tax is charged by reference to market value. However, where there is an overlap between the 'vendors' and

---

[646]   Ibid, Sch 4, para 12(1)(a).
[647]   Ibid, s 120(2); Sch 7A, para 4.
[648]   Income Tax (Earnings and Pensions) Act 2003, s 99.
[649]   FA 2003, Sch 4, para 12(1)(c).
[650]   Ibid, s 51, Sch 17A, paras 7 and 8.
[651]   Pursuant to Income Tax (Earnings and Pensions) Act 2003, s 90.
[652]   FA 2003, Sch 4, para 12(1)(c).
[653]   Ibid, Sch 15, Part 3; see **Chapter 13**.

'purchasers' ie the same persons are involved on both sides of the transaction, the chargeable consideration may be reduced from the full market value by the sum of the lower proportions.

Non-chargeable consideration[654]

5.214 It is provided that certain types of consideration for a transaction are not chargeable.[655] It is important to note that this is a situation that differs from a transaction being relieved from taxation. In the latter case, the transaction is chargeable but the rate of tax is, in effect, reduced to nil. The consideration, therefore, remains chargeable and the transaction is notifiable. Indeed, many of the provisions relating to non-notification refer to a transaction having chargeable consideration above the appropriate threshold but not having to pay tax because of some relevant exemption. The current set of provisions operate in a different way, they state that the chargeable consideration for the transaction is to be treated as 'nil' or 'exempt' or is somehow otherwise to be 'ignored'. In these situations the transaction is for no chargeable consideration so that, *prima facie*, it falls within FA 2003, Sch 3, para 1. This produces an 'exempt transaction' which not only does not attract tax but is also non-notifiable.[656] It is, therefore, important to pay careful attention to the wording of the legislation that provides for the exemption for relief in question since this may affect the compliance obligations.

Obligations under a lease[657]

5.215 In the case of a grant of a lease, the following are not chargeable considerations:[658]

- any undertaking by the tenant to repair, maintain[659] or insure the demised premises;

---

[654] See **Chapter 11**.

[655] This may take many forms such as the actual consideration being ignored or disregarded or no account being taken of it, or being treated as exempt or nil. Unfortunately, the 'subtleties' if not 'crudity' of the drafting lease open potential differences that are likely to be exploited as traps for taxpayers by HMRC Stamp Taxes when they read the legislation closely and realise its potential for causing confusion and treating the various terms as having different meanings as appears to be the case with 'disregarded' which does not mean the transaction is deemed not to exist and has no consequences; but does have consequences and even tax liabilities.

[656] FA 2003, s 77A.

[657] Other arrangements in connection with a lease may be non-chargeable such as certain surrenders and regrants of leases, rent credits, and certain sale and leaseback and PFI projects (FA 2003, Sch 17A, paras 9, 16 and 17 and s 57A).

[658] Ibid, Sch 4, para 13; these may become relevant in valuations: ibid, Sch 15, para 38.

[659] This is interesting drafting. There is a possible interpretation that the undertaking by the tenant to 'repair' the premises is to 'keep in repair'; but the tenant is also under an obligation to 'maintain' which presumably includes an obligation to 'keep in repair'. It is, therefore, arguable that the obligation of the tenant 'to repair' includes an obligation on the initial grant of the lease to put in repair ie to repair and put right the dilapidations and other defects in the premises. This could be a key issue as regards certain activities. It is provided (FA 2003, Sch 4, para 10) that works, which includes repairs, can constitute chargeable consideration ie a premium for the grant of the lease. There is an exemption for works to be carried out on the land to be acquired provided that these are carried out after the effective date. This will, probably, take out from charge many of the obligations imposed upon the tenant to put the premises into an acceptable state of repair. However, in those cases where this exemption does not apply an appropriately drafted undertaking to put in repair may fall within this exclusion from chargeable consideration.

- any undertaking by the tenant to pay any amount in respect of services, repairs, maintenance or insurance or the landlord's costs of management;

- any other obligation undertaken by the tenant that is not such as to affect the rent that the tenant would be prepared to pay in the open market;[660]

- any guarantee of the payment of rent or the performance of any other obligation of the tenant under the lease;

- any penal rent or increased rent in the nature of penal rent and payable in respect of a breach of any obligation of the tenant under the lease.

5.216 Any payment in respect of such obligations or the assumption or release of any such obligation in relation to the assignment or surrender of the lease is not chargeable consideration. However, two points should be noted:

- if the sum is drafted as part of the rent or as additional rent and not separately apportioned then it may be chargeable as rent notwithstanding this exemption;[661]

- payments made in respect of a breach of any of these obligations are, *prima facie*, not chargeable but, as indicated by *Banning v Wright*,[662] where there is a payment of compensation for breach of covenant this may operate as some form of release or variation[663] which HMRC Stamp Taxes may wish to claim is a chargeable transaction.[664]

However, this is dependent upon the drafting of the lease. It is provided that 'rent' includes all sums described as rent unless separately apportioned.[665] In consequence, for example, where service charges are included within the rent they will be taxable as rent;

---

[660] This is a bizarre provision that raises a huge list of problems. In a sense every obligation or covenant in a lease is likely to affect the value or rent of the lease. The point is not immediately obvious since the initial response of the valuers or advisers in relation to the property will make certain assumptions as to the likely covenants in the lease and therefore the negotiations will be conducted upon the basis of assumed standard conditions whether or not these may affect the value ie that is to say the arm's length negotiation between the parties is carried out, at least initially, upon the basis of certain assumptions and these assumptions may affect the value. It is only if there are any unusual provisions in the lease that emerge on title investigation and due diligence that these issues will surface. The fact that the parties do not negotiate a separate price or rent because there are non-standard provisions in the lease will probably arise. It is, therefore, a major trap because parties will not be aware that there may be covenants in the lease that do affect the rent because they are standard and the rent is fixed upon the basis of standard conditions. A lease upon different terms might justify a different rent. It is provided by FA 2003, s 48(1)(b) that obligations affecting the value of land can be chargeable interests. This suggests, when viewed in the context under discussion, that covenants by tenants in favour of landlords are potentially chargeable interests in their own right constituting separate consideration. The effect would be that every lease is some form of land exchange. This issue has been put to HMRC Stamp Taxes but there has been no public response to this fundamental question. It is, therefore, assumed that HMRC Stamp Taxes do not intend to take the point and even where there is a covenant by a tenant that could affect the value of rent so that this is not the creation of a new chargeable interest that converts the lease into a land exchange.

[661] FA 2003, Sch 17A, para 10.

[662] 48 TC 421.

[663] The charging provisions in that case also referred to 'waiver'; it remains to be seen whether this will be accepted as a valid distinction since 'waiver' and 'disclaimer' are not referred to in the relevant legislation.

[664] FA 2003, s 43(3) and Sch 17A, para 15A.

[665] Ibid, Sch 17A, para 6.

but if they are separately apportioned sums, although described as 'additional rent' or enforceable as if they were rent, they will be separate payments and eligible for this exemption.

Reverse premium payments[666]

5.217 In general, the property interest and the consideration move in opposite directions but in spite of this it is expressly provided[667] that 'reverse premiums' in relation to the grant, assignment or surrender of leases are not chargeable consideration. However, this raises unanswerable questions as to when two items moving in the same direction can be chargeable consideration. It appears from the debate on the FA 2003 that there is an official view that, for example, works carried out by a landlord are consideration for the grant of a lease to a tenant in addition to any payment or rent payable by the tenant. It remains to be seen how this bizarre view is applied in practice by HMRC Stamp Taxes.

Reverse payments (ie cash payments that move in the same direction as the land) paid in respect of transactions involving leases are not chargeable consideration. These are:

- a payment moving from the landlord to the tenant in relation to the grant of the lease;

- a payment moving from the assignor to the assignee in relation to the assignment of a lease; and

- a premium or payment moving from the tenant to the landlord in relation to the surrender of a lease.[668]

These provisions raise interesting questions of whether they are intended to operate as some form of self-serving basis for argument for potentially bizarre theories of HMRC Stamp Taxes. A reverse payment ie one that moves in the same direction as the property would not normally be chargeable consideration. The consideration is the sum provided by the transferee rather than the sum provided by the transferor.[669] It is probable that HMRC Stamp Taxes inserted these provisions in order to provide justification for a bizarre argument that reverse consideration is taxable. It is unclear precisely where HMRC Stamp Taxes intend to take this argument that payments by the seller can form part of the consideration upon which the purchaser pays tax but this legislation provides the basis for such an argument. On general principle the argument would have no validity whatsoever but HMRC Stamp Taxes have set up the situation under which they can point to legislation that indicates that such reverse payments would otherwise be taxable. To challenge this view would involve the argument that the legislation in question was unnecessary and redundant. It is most unlikely that the current judiciary, with their lack of technical skills in this area, would accept such an argument of redundant legislation.

---

[666] See **2.3** and **5.91**.
[667] FA 2003, Sch 17A, para 17; see also Sch 4, para 16.
[668] Ibid, Sch 17A, para 17.
[669] See **5.91**. In this context HMRC Stamp Taxes have sought to argue that inducements offered by a landlord to a tenant such as the payment of removal expenses, stamp duty and legal fees, is not within these provisions but also operates to increase the market value of the land rather than being an indication that the price at which the property is offered is in excess of the market value ie it is a disguised attempt by the developer to reduce the price of the land.

Indemnity given by purchaser[670]

5.218 Where the purchaser agrees to indemnify the vendor in respect of liability to a third party arising from breach of an obligation owed by the vendor in relation to the land that is the subject of the transaction, neither the agreement nor any payment made in pursuance of it counts as chargeable consideration.[671] It should be noted that this indemnity is limited to situations of breaches of obligations owed by the vendor. In consequence, other forms of 'indemnity' may have stamp duty land tax implications. For example, to indemnify in relation to the transfer of property subject to a charge in respect of the mortgage payments would involve the assumption of the liability so that the mortgage became part of the chargeable consideration.[672] Whilst in some situations an agreement to indemnify the vendor will be some form of compensation or damages payment, an undertaking to indemnify may amount to the assumption of the vendor's obligations such as the obligation to pay the debts of the business. This may become important where the property is transferred with the benefit of planning permission and there are obligations upon the relevant party in the 'Section 106 Agreement'. In this case the indemnity may amount to some form of obligation to carry out the works or make payments to the local authority as part of the planning consent. In this situation the arrangement is not an indemnity but is a positive obligation upon the purchaser and therefore part of the consideration. It may have the effect of brining the obligations under the planning agreement into the realm of chargeable consideration with a charge upon any cash payments to be made or any works to be carried out upon land not being acquired such as building a new school upon land retained by the local authority.

5.219 Similarly, undertakings by an assignee of a lease to pay future rent and observe the covenants are ignored.[673] However, this is a somewhat strange provision and raises numerous questions. It was well established for stamp duty, and as a matter of general principle, that where there was a liability that was inherent in the property this would not form part of the consideration for the transfer of the property notwithstanding that the transferee became liable in respect of that obligation.[674] However, this may be another illustration of the intention of HMRC Stamp Taxes to introduce self-serving legislation that enables them to put forward bizarre arguments upon the basis that the legislation provides for relief for particular situations and therefore other situations may be taxable otherwise the relief which they introduced would not have been necessary. The contrary argument that the provision was unnecessary means that the taxpayer will have to argue that the legislation is effectively redundant which is not an argument likely to commend itself to the current judiciary who are reluctant to take the view that Parliament have been badly advised and have been wasting their time in enacting the relevant legislation. Moreover, the provision is overridden in certain circumstances. The grant of certain leases will be exempt from stamp duty land tax and since this offers the opportunity of mitigating stamp duty land tax there are specific provisions[675] to the effect that where a lease that was exempt within the appropriate categories when granted is assigned the assignee is treated as acquiring a new lease. The new lease will be granted for a premium equal to any lump sum being paid by the assignee for the grant of the lease plus the undertaking to pay the future rent. In effect, the assignee will be treated as being granted a lease for any cash sum plus the future rent. There is no obligation or tax charge in respect of the rent between the original grant and the assignment. It is,

[670] See also **5.138**.
[671] Ibid, FA 2003, Sch 4, para 16.
[672] Ibid, Sch 4, paras 8 and 8A.
[673] Ibid, Sch 17A, para 10; but note the special charge pursuant to para 11; see **7.241**.
[674] See, for example, *Swayne v IRC* [1900] 1 QB 172.
[675] FA 2003, Sch 17A, para 11.

nevertheless, a situation where an assignee may be taken by surprise in having to pay tax upon the future rent. In this situation the assignee may seek to have some form of indemnity or tax sharing operation or indemnity with the assignor. The current categories affected by this arrangement are leases to charities, leases granted as part of a sale and leaseback exercise where the leaseback is exempt,[676] leases granted in connection with company reconstructions and reorganisations,[677] and leases granted between members of the same group.[678] The Treasury are given power to extend this list.[679]

Value Added Tax[680]

5.220 The fact that VAT may arise as a result of the exercise of the option to tax after the effective date of the transaction is not regarded as chargeable consideration for the initial transaction;[681] however, the reaction of HMRC Stamp Taxes to the changes in the rate of VAT and rents raises the question as to whether they may seek to treat the consideration as variable where the option to tax may exist. Fortunately, the legislation[682] refers to VAT actually chargeable and the option to tax relates merely to VAT potentially chargeable. This will almost frequently arise in relation to leases where the lease is exempt when granted but the landlord reserves an option to charge VAT[683] which, it seems, makes the rent 'variable'.[684] However, this does not mean that the exercise of the option to tax can be ignored. For example, it is the view of HMRC Stamp Taxes that there are two effective dates where there is substantial performance of the agreement followed at some later time by completion between the same parties.[685] In consequence, the exercise of the option to tax between substantial performance and formal completion between the same parties may result in the VAT charge arising by reason of the exercise of the option to tax is now chargeable consideration. In addition, since HMRC Stamp Taxes take the view that a variation in the rate of VAT means that the rent is both variable and has been varied both for the purposes of the first 5 years of the term and for the purposes of any question of abnormal rent increases after the expiration of the fifth year of the term[686] the exercise of the option to tax represents an increase in the rent. Where the rent was initially exempt but is made subject to the rate of VAT in force at the time, this may well represent a substantial proportion of the 20 per cent per annum that is allowed before a rent increase becomes abnormal.

Chargeable consideration reduced to nil[687]

5.221 The FA 2003 contains an unusual form of relieving provision by stating that certain consideration is 'non-chargeable'. As only 'chargeable consideration' is within the computational provisions,[688] this has the effect of excluding non-chargeable consideration from the tax. However, the reason why there is not a charge to stamp duty

676 Ibid, s 57A.
677 Ibid, Sch 7, Part 2.
678 Ibid, Sch 7, Part 1.
679 Ibid, Sch 17A, para 11(3)(c) and s 123(3).
680 See also **5.126**.
681 FA 2003, Sch 4, para 2.
682 Ibid, Sch 4, para 2.
683 Ibid, Sch 4, para 2.
684 See **7.68**.
685 FA 2003, s 44(8); Sch 17A, para 12A.
686 Ibid, Sch 17A, paras, 7, 8, 14 and 15.
687 See **Chapter 11**.
688 FA 2003, s 55(1).

land tax or why it is restricted needs to be understood since this may affect the reporting obligations, which vary depending upon whether there is 'chargeable consideration'[689] which may arise where, *inter alia*, there is other consideration or it is 'exempt' for certain specific reasons.[690] The non-chargeable consideration includes the following:

Third party inducements[691]

5.222 Unless otherwise expressly provided, chargeable consideration has to be provided directly or indirectly by the purchaser or a person connected with him.[692] Subject to the issue of what is meant by the 'purchaser' indirectly providing the consideration[693] and the difficulties of identifying 'the purchaser',[694] this may mean that payments by third parties are not within the charge to tax,[695] and may mean that although there is a dual consideration there is no charge to tax because such consideration is not 'chargeable'.[696]

Exchanges involving non-major interests

5.223 It is provided[697] that as regards the acquisition of a non-major interest as part of a land exchange in certain cases the chargeable interest disposed of as part of the exchange is not within the chargeable consideration.[698]

Partition

5.224 It is provided[699] that upon a partition of jointly owned land the mutual exchange of the undivided interests in the property does not involve chargeable consideration.[700]

Works

5.225 Certain works carried out by the person acquiring upon the land being acquired are not chargeable consideration.[701]

Surrender and regrant

5.226 Where there is a surrender and grant of a new lease, the grant of the new lease and the surrender of the existing lease are not chargeable consideration for each other.[702]

---

[689] Ibid, s 77(2) and (4).
[690] Ibid, s 77(3).
[691] See **5.99**.
[692] FA 2003, Sch 4, para 1.
[693] See **5.103**.
[694] See **Chapter 14**.
[695] See **5.106**.
[696] FA 2003, Sch 3, para 1.
[697] Ibid, Sch 4, para 5(4).
[698] Ibid, Sch 4, para 5(4); see **5.161**.
[699] Ibid, Sch 4, para 6.
[700] Ibid, Sch 4, para 5; see **5.150**.
[701] Ibid, Sch 4, para 10(2); see **Chapter 8**.
[702] Ibid, Sch 17A, para 16; see also para 9 for a possible rent relief (see **7.86**).

Rent

5.227 In certain cases where there is a premium and rent for the grant of the lease, the rent may not rank as chargeable consideration. This applies, for example, to leases of residential land in a disadvantaged area.[703]

PFI projects

5.228 Certain land exchanges are ignored when part of a project involving a public body;[704] but this exemption of the actual consideration from the scope of chargeable consideration does not apply for the purposes of notification,[705] so that notwithstanding there may be no chargeable consideration should there be actual consideration above the relevant amount the transaction is notifiable although no tax may be payable.

---

[703]   Ibid, Sch 6, paras 5(4), 6(5) and (6), 9(3) and 10(5).
[704]   Ibid, Sch 4, para 17.
[705]   Ibid, Sch 4, para 17(4A).

Chapter 6

SUBSALES, ASSIGNMENTS AND SIMILAR ARRANGEMENTS[1] – INCLUDING LEASES

INTRODUCTION

6.1 There are many 'triangular' or tripartite arrangements where land is involved where, in essence, A enters into a contract or other arrangement with B, who enters into an arrangement with C and the eventual 'completion' is between A and C;[2] such as:

- subsales;

- grants of leases to third parties ie where the original party to the agreement to grant the lease directs the landlord to grant the lease to a third party;[3]

- assignments of contractual rights;

- novations and similar arrangements;[4]

- guarantees of debts and obligations;[5]

- mortgages;

- indemnities and assumption of obligations where a person becomes directly or indirectly responsible for obligations owed by one person to a third party;

- the relationship of landlord and tenant where there are assignments of leases or agreements for lease or reversions;

---

[1] For the transitional provisions relating to subsales etc, entered into before 1 December 2003, see **1.18**.

[2] Unless such situations are properly dealt with in the legislation there is a tax cascade effect which distorts the price of assets such as increasing the cost of new houses for first time buyers, which gave rise to problems in the planning of turnover taxes such as VAT because of the distorting effect of vertical integration as tax mitigation.

[3] See the analysis of such arrangements in *Attorney General v Brown* (1849) 3 Exch 662.

[4] This is a key issue for the current fashion for very long-term arrangements for 'clawback', ie the obligation to pay additional consideration should planning permission etc be obtained which leaves the purchaser/taxpayer with an open contractual and unresolved stamp duty land tax position with which to annoy his personal representatives or liquidators. The manner in which they are initially established or dealt with on subsequent sales raises many tax issues; see **6.57** and **7.235**.

[5] Note, for example, the position of guarantees of leases FA 2003, Sch 17A, para 9(1)(d).

- co-operation arrangements such as 'section 106 agreements' whereby local authorities assist developers in acquiring and developing land such as utilising the powers of compulsory acquisitions in order to obtain title to and vacant possession of the site;[6]

- third parties providing inducements in order to persuade potential vendors or purchasers to enter into the transaction;[7]

- third parties who acquire property and enter into the main contract;[8] and

- any exit strategy where clawback or similar consideration is involved.[9]

6.2   Each of these arrangements which, *prima facie*, involve two or more potentially chargeable transactions and consideration raising particular issues for stamp duty land tax. In certain cases such as the grant of leases directly to third parties at the direction of the original tenant[10] the rules are highly technical and some sophisticated due diligence will be required in order to identify the problems and to protect the interests of the client. Moreover, in some cases the analysis and consequences will depend upon prior contractual arrangements which will have been entered into without the professionals having considered the long-term taxation position of the client. The planning to deal with such situations and to retrieve a potentially serious problem for the client will not be straightforward. For example, where a person has purchased land with a clawback provision and has created problems for variable consideration, the terms of the original contractual obligations and any provisions regulating the manner in which this is to be dealt with in an onward sale will be a major factor in the structuring of the onward sale arrangements.[11]

6.3   Each of the above list of situations requires detailed consideration of the numerous and different technical and practical issues involved in each case and these are dealt with in various parts of this book. The current chapter deals with the initial acquisition and subsequent onward sales including existing leases or grants of new leases of interests to third parties. Surprisingly many solicitors still regard these arrangements in stamp duty terms on the basis that no charge to tax arises until the land is conveyed or leased. This is fundamentally wrong because of the transaction nature of stamp duty land tax.[12] In addition transactions are still being incorrectly reported to the evident annoyance of HMRC Stamp Taxes.[13] Apart from such omissions to report and pay stamp duty land tax there are many cases where taxpayers have not been properly advised and, in consequence, have not been able to take advantage of the reliefs available to them.[14]

6.4   Special provisions apply to one particular set of 'triangular relationships' described as subsales, assignments or 'transfers of rights' (but these rules are

---

[6]   For relief see FA 2003, s 60; see also FA 2003, ss 44A and 45A.

[7]   See, for example, *Central and District Properties v IRC* [1966] 2 All ER 433.

[8]   *Crane Fruehauf v IRC* [1975] STC 51.

[9]   See **5.206**.

[10]   FA 2003, Sch 17A, para 12B.

[11]   See further **5.206**.

[12]   See **3.7**.

[13]   Exposing the parties and their advisers to long-term exposure to discovery assessments for negligence and, possibly, fraudulent returns.

[14]   Note the possible actionable breach of duty by the advisers in not drawing the attention of the client to possible benefits; *BE Studios v Smith and Williamson* [2006] STC 358.

subordinated to the special rules dealing with grants of new leases to third parties[15] and the reliefs are not available where a person agrees to acquire property with a view to granting leases to third parties) because he is not disposing of the entire interest which he is acquiring. There are differences in tax consequences where there are plans to sell on the entire property albeit in parcels to several subpurchasers and acquiring property with a view to creating part-interests such as leases or subleases in relation to the property such as buy-to-let arrangements, nor do the reliefs apply to situations where a person acquires the property and at the same times is acquiring a lease with a view to granting subleases. The relief may be available where the purchaser is intending to enter into a sale and leaseback transaction in order to raise the funds to finance the transaction.[16] There are complex anti-avoidance dealing with these and other arrangements[17] which are designed to prevent persons from resting on contract and not taking a conveyance or lease[18] but also providing very restricted reliefs seeking to limit the cascade effect of a transaction-based tax and the double or multiple taxation of the same transaction.[19] Moreover, since the stamp duty land tax charge arises upon the earlier of 'substantial performance'[20] or completion[21] this effectively precludes the obtaining of an exemption equivalent to the subsale relief from stamp duty[22] for many *bona fide* commercial arrangements and by taxing every stage in the transaction, the costs of the parties increase significantly, thereby putting up prices for new dwellings for first time buyers.[23] This has significant implications for the costs of new developments,[24] especially housing and new office and retail developments, particularly in the context of the much-enlarged charge to stamp duty land tax where building and other works are involved.[25] Representations on the impact have been generally rejected by the Government, which, from the drafting of the Finance Act 2002, Sch 36 and the original cl 45 of the Finance Bill 2003, and the defects in the equivalent provision for leases,[26] does not appear to understand either the mechanics of subsale relief or the economic justification for an arrangement that has been regarded as essential since 1782 or thereabouts. In particular, the legislation fails to provide for relief where A sells to B who proposed to grant a lease to C which attracts multiple full charges to stamp duty land tax.

6.5   However, an extremely limited relief is available[27] where there is a subsequent transaction which, in effect, brings in a third party[28] after the making of a contract but

---

[15]   FA 2003, Sch 17A, para 12B; see **6.57**.
[16]   See also FA 2003, s 57A (as much amended).
[17]   FA 2003, s 45.
[18]   Although this is effectively limited by the fact that the charge is triggered by substantial performance: FA 2003, s 44. See **Chapter 14**.
[19]   But note the limited relief for multiple taxation of the same transaction: FA 2003, Sch 10, para 33; but it seems that this is intended to be restrictively applied by HMRC Stamp Taxes on the basis that transaction means chargeable transaction and not the commercial transaction. Since the single commercial transaction can include more than one chargeable transaction (see, eg, FA 2004, Sch 17A, para 12A) this is a significant reduction in the benefit of this provision.
[20]   FA 2003, s 44(4); but with a further charge upon completion.
[21]   Ibid, s 44(8).
[22]   Such a relief is feasible as in stamp duty: FA 1999, Sch 13, para 7.
[23]   VAT avoids this compounding or cascade effect with its disturbing effect on the economy in promoting vertical integration by generally allowing the recovery of input tax, ie the tax paid upon the acquisition of the asset or service. This is not done for stamp duty land tax but was done by Stamp Act 1891, s 58(4) in the case of stamp duty.
[24]   Which makes the protection of the exemption for works being carried out on the land and the exclusion of building works from the chargeable consideration very important; see **Chapter 8**.
[25]   FA 2003, Sch 4, para 10; see **Chapter 8**.
[26]   Ibid, Sch 17, para 12A.
[27]   The structure of this relief favours speculators rather than developers and attempts to keep costs under

before it is substantially performed completed in the traditional sense of a conveyance, lease or similar deed being executed to pass or perfect title. This relief is really effective only where the original contract has not been substantially performed;[29] but is available where the two or other contracts in the chain are substantially performed or completed at the time same. It is now possible to obtain the relief where there are two simultaneous completions[30] providing there has been no prior substantial performance. These provisions also apply where there is a chain of subsales and assignments[31] or subsale or assignment dealing with a part of the land.[32] Unfortunately the restrictions upon this relief, and in particular the impact of substantial performance of the original contract, are such that it is unlikely to prove of benefit in the most important situations in practice; namely, the construction of new dwellings for first time buyers and even where the relief is, *prima facie*, available the general anti avoidance provisions[33] are intended to apply.[34]

6.6 Although superficially simple, this relief, which applies to a wide range of transactions, is inevitably complex and applied strictly by HMRC Stamp Taxes so that its impact in different situations can be different. A consequence of the 'one-size-fits-all' drafting principles used in the FA 2003, is that it is often difficult to make sense of provisions that are structured upon a particular type of transaction but are designed to apply to a wide range of transactions that are technically very different.[35] This is particularly acute in the area of arrangements that are not traditional subsales. The special non-plain English usage of much of the legislation, arising from the need to make the 'conveyance on sale' drafting fit other chargeable transactions, means that it is necessary to seek to apply these provisions to arrangements whereby third parties become interested in transactions. This applies, for example, where a developer, having entered into an agreement for lease with the freeholder[36] directs the latter to grant the lease to a third party with whom the developer had entered into an agreement for the disposal of the interest.[37] This issue was not initially considered by the draftsman but the wording of FA 2003, s 45, was applicable to such situations. There are many

---

    control have been attacked by provisions such as FA 2003, ss 44A, 45A and 75A–75C. It is potentially available to a person who acquires an interest intending to turn the contract before he has to perform or pay; the relief is not available to a person who is acquiring the land with a view to developing it by constructing houses or flats on the land and then selling since he will have performed his contract and so be outside the scope of the relief.

28   Or a fourth or fifth party, and so on. The relief is available where A sells to B who on-sells to C who on-sells to C or where A sells to B who sells part to C, part to D, part to E and possible keeps part for himself. There are, of course, dozens of variations on these basic themes. A key issue in relation to the latter illustration namely where B on-sells to part to C, D and E is that these are, *prima facie*, unlinked transactions and therefore eligible for their own lower rates of tax as appropriate provided that C and D etc. are not connected persons which could operate to re-link the transactions; see **5.58**.

29   See the discussion and illustration at **6.38**.

30   Which possibility of a double completion removes many of the difficulties of dealing with standard conditions prohibiting subsales and conveyances to third parties; but inevitably creates problems when dealing with certain Land Registries who are somewhat over zealous in their obsequiousness to HMRC Stamp Taxes and are content to downgrade themselves to tax collectors.

31   FA 2003, s 45(4).

32   Ibid, s 45(5).

33   Ibid, ss 75A–75C.

34   See the illustrative list where these provisions 'may' apply in FA 2003, s 75A(3).

35   The original Finance Bill and the explanatory notes thereto made it clear that multiple charges and double taxation of the third party were intended. Fortunately this has been modified to a limited extent; but the double charge has been overlooked in the amendments in FA 2003, Sch 17A, para 12B.

36   A senior member of HMRC recruited into its expert team for the negotiations relating to the stamp duty land tax legislation described this subsale relief as fraud and a criminal offence notwithstanding that the legislation had been in place for two centuries indicating the quality of officers of HMRC generally.

37   See the different analyses possible, as in *Att-Gen v Brown* (1849) 3 Exch 662.

problems in applying this so-called relief to leases. Special provisions have been introduced[38] which are obscurely drafted but are intended to override the subsale principles in the case of new leases at least in part and contain the potential for additional taxation for third parties.[39] Moreover, where the specific provisions do not apply the general provisions of s 45 remain relevant and on a strict reading of the legislation the latter will frequently produce a more efficient result. It is, however, not easy escape from the special provisions for agreements for lease in order to apply the provisions of s 45.

6.7   It is, therefore, first necessary to determine into which category of transfer of right the transaction falls since this may affect both the legal machinery involved and the liability to stamp duty land tax. Three transactions are involved, namely:

- a subsale where A enters into a contract to sell to B who agrees to sell the property to C;

- an assignment where A enters into a contract with B who transfers the benefit of the contract to C ie B sells the contract which carries with it the right to call for the land but does not acquire the land and on-sell; and

- 'other' arrangements. These are not specified in the legislation and because of the fundamental differences between a subsale and an assignment it is not possible to make use of the *ejusdem generis* principles of statutory construction. In consequence, it may include situations such as novations where A enters into a contract with B and as part of a tri-partite arrangement A releases B in consideration of C taking on the responsibility to acquire the land, but this is not clear in law or practice. These uncertainties are not assisted by the extension of the concept of 'acquisition' to releases, surrenders and variations and it remains to be seen whether the involvement of such steps in a larger arrangement may be eligible for the benefit of the relief.

All of these three categories of transactions may be covered by the provisions in FA 2003, s 45 although as a matter of legal analysis they are fundamentally different. It is, therefore, a question of stretching the legislation designed on the basis of one variation of the above but intended to apply to all three and possibly other 'transfer of rights'. Within each of these variations are different steps possible:

- there is the contract between A and B for the sale, assignment or surrender of A's interest;

- there is an arrangement or contract between B and C; and

- there is substantial performance or completion of the arrangement or arrangements between A and C, or between A and B and B and C.[40]

---

[38]   FA 2003, Sch 17A, para 12B.
[39]   See ibid, Sch 17A, para 12B; see **6.57**.
[40]   Unlike the former stamp duty relief, the relief is available notwithstanding that B receives a transfer from A, but it is necessary to organise the completion arrangements with great care in order to meet the stringent conditions. It is potentially available in those cases where standard conditions prohibit subsales or completion with any person other than the original purchaser.

This is relatively straightforward in a subsale or assignment situation but other cases such as novations if within these provisions raise detailed technical issues. These steps or stages are the basis upon which the relief has been drafted but as indicated above the legal forms involved can differ significantly.

THE RELIEVING OR 'DISREGARDING' PROVISIONS

6.8   It is provided by FA 2003, s 45 that:

- where there is a contract for a land transaction (between A and B) (which applies to any transaction falling within the scope of stamp duty land tax, not just contracts for the sale of land), and it will, subject to the overriding provisions relating to agreements for lease,[41] apply to agreements to grant leases not falling within the specific provisions for agreements for lease[42] or the surrender of leases or to grant options or to grant or release restrictive covenants, rights of way or to exercise powers of appointment;[43]

- which is to be completed by a 'conveyance' which is essentially any form of writing[44] that passes title or possibly control over title[45] (which will include a lease or other deed such as a release or variation of rights);[46]

- there is an assignment, subsale or other transaction involving the chargeable interest by B to C, whether relating to the whole or part of the subject-matter of the original contract; and

- as a result a person ('C') other than the original purchaser ('B') becomes entitled to call for a 'conveyance' or lease to him or any other deed in his favour (whatever that may mean in technical terms),

then

- where the contract between A and B is subject to stamp duty land tax if substantially performed or completed; and

- where the contract between A and B has not been substantially performed or completed at the relevant time:
    - the third party, C (eg the subpurchaser or assignee), is not regarded as entering into a land transaction by reason of the contract for the assignment, subsale or other arrangement with the original 'purchaser' (ie as between B and C the contract is not itself a chargeable transaction);
    - there is deemed to be a contract for a land transaction, but the parties to this deemed or 'secondary' contract may differ from those who are parties to the actual contract. For subsales and assignments the secondary contract is

---

[41]   FA 2003, Sch 17A, para 12B; see **6.57**.
[42]   Ibid, Sch 17A, para 12A. These are limited provisions which are the primary relief for leases; ibid, Sch 17A, para 12A; but such are the limitations on this relief s 45 has a potentially extensive residual role.
[43]   Assuming that such arrangements are not tainted as frauds on a power.
[44]   FA 2003, s 44(1)(b) and (10)(b).
[45]   See *Diplock v Hammond* (1854) 5 De GM & G 320; *Roddick v Gandell* (1852) 1 De G M & G 763; *West London Syndicate Ltd v IRC* [1898] 2 QB 507.
[46]   See **2.1**.

between B and C except where groups of companies are involved[47] when it is between A and C. Where agreements for lease are involved it appears to be between A and C. These subtle changes in personnel can have significant impacts upon the taxation of the transaction and the compliance regime;

- the deemed chargeable consideration for that deemed secondary contract is:
    - the balance of the unpaid consideration,[48] if any, under the original contract (ie between A and B) which is usually the balance of the price after deducting any deposit or other payments made which is to be paid by the third party, or a person connected with him;[49] plus
    - the consideration paid by C to B, the original purchaser for the subsale, assignment or other arrangement;[50]

- the fact that substantial performance or completion of the original contract between A and B occurs at the same time as the substantial performance or completion of the deemed contract between A and C is ignored,[51] provided also that the completion of the second contract is in connection with completion of the first contract ie the fact that the contract between A and B is substantially performed or completed at the same time as, and possibly also by reason of, the substantial performance of the deemed contract between A and C is ignored[52] and does not give rise to a chargeable or notifiable transaction.[53] It must, however, be noted that if the original contract between A and B has previously been substantially performed, this will have already triggered a charge to stamp duty land tax upon B, but the actual completion of that contract by reason of the transfer from A to C is ignored and there is no further obligation upon B to pay any additional tax because this charge[54] applies only where there is a completion between 'the same parties' and to make further notifications as such.[55] C is, of course, liable to stamp duty land tax upon the deemed consideration for the secondary contract.

6.9   The effect of the provisions is that where A enters into a contract for the acquisition of a chargeable interest in B and B subsells or assigns the chargeable interest or the benefit of the contract to C the transaction with B will be 'disregarded'[56] provided that the contract between A and B and the contract between B and C are either substantially performed at the same time or are completed at the same time or one is completed and the other is substantially performed at the same time. A key issue is that the various contracts in the chain have to substantially perform or complete 'at the same

---

[47]   For situations where the alternative finance regime is applicable see FA 2003, ss 71A–73B.
[48]   Which avoids a possible double charge upon the deposit paid by B to A.
[49]   See **14.11** and **15.11**.
[50]   Essentially B's profit on turning the contract but C may be paying a sum to reimburse B for the deposit and other sums paid.
[51]   FA 2003, s 45(3).
[52]   Unfortunately the outside experts 'consulting' with HMRC Stamp Taxes have failed to address themselves to issues such as where, by reason of the funding arrangements, the secondary contract is technically substantially performed before the primary contract between A and B is either substantially performed or completed.
[53]   But this depends upon the effect of the word 'disregarded'; see **6.10**.
[54]   FA 2003, s 44(8) and (10)(a).
[55]   However, B may have to notify and pay in certain cases such as where the original contract between A and B involved an uncertain consideration within FA 2003, s 51, and the completion of the deemed contract between A and C triggers a payment within s 80 thereof.
[56]   FA 2003, s 45(3).

time'. This in the practice of HMRC Stamp Taxes is a matter of seconds rather than minutes. The completion arrangements will be crucial.

6.10   The relief is also available where the transactions are completed simultaneously. It is therefore possible for B to obtain the relief where, for example, A delivers a Land Registry transfer to B who at the same time delivers a Land Registry transfer to C. This 'double completion' will be a potentially frequent occurrence and was a difficulty in relation to stamp duty because subsale relief[57] was not available where the intermediate party received a 'conveyance'. In some situations the first purchaser may be obliged to take a transfer because of the terms of the contract. It is not unusual and appears in many standard conditions that the vendor will be required to convey only to the purchaser and cannot be required to convey to a third party and there may be restrictions upon subsales.[58] Similarly, B may be making a substantial profit on turning the contract and would not wish a direct transfer from A to C which could disclose the profit that he is making to A and C. Relief is now potentially available in these circumstances providing that the two contracts are performed and/or completed at the same time. The difficulty with the multiple completion route is dealing with the Land Registry. This will frequently produce situations where the parties to the stamp duty land tax documentation may differ from those appearing on the Land Registry documentation or where there is a double completion there may not be an Inland Revenue Certificate (SDLT 5) to support the first transfer from A to B. Section 45(3) provides that B's transaction is to be 'disregarded' provided that the conditions are satisfied. This, *prima facie*, suggests that the transaction is to be ignored ie did not take place for the purposes of stamp duty land tax.[59] Insofar as 'disregarded' can mean that there is no chargeable transaction for the purposes of stamp duty land tax B is under no obligation to notify.[60] However, there may be practical difficulties in dealing with the Land Registry in these circumstances without the production of an Inland Revenue Certificate (SDLT 5) because they do not accept that 'disregarded' does not bear its obvious plain English meaning of not being treated as a notifiable transaction by or on behalf of B. It may, therefore, in practice be essential for B to file a Land Transaction Return (SDLT 1) claiming the exemption 'O' for 'other' in order to produce a certificate in order to enable C to register his transfer. C should be aware of the potential difficulties with the Land Registry since it may be necessary to provide in the contract that not only the appropriate and fully executed Land Registry Transfer is delivered but also a Land Transaction Return (SDLT 1) relating to the first or any relevant prior transactions is delivered at completion so as to be available for production to HMRC Stamp Taxes so that an Inland Revenue Certificate (SDLT 5) can be generated as soon as possible so that the registration process in favour of C can proceed. There may be difficulties where C does not stipulate for the production of the necessary documentation from B in order to pacify the Land Registry since there is no statutory obligation to do so and it may be stretching the frontiers and meaning of 'further

---

[57]   Stamp Act 1891, s 58(4) and (5).

[58]   These may interfere with the treatment of the transaction as a transfer of a going concern; see *Kwik Save Group v Customs and Excise* VTD 12749; although there is no indication in the general law as to how this standard condition is to apply where the first purchaser subsells without disclosing this transaction to the original seller and takes a transfer at the closing of this agreement but pursuant to earlier arrangements with the third party immediately on-sells the property to a third party.

[59]   However, it may be that 'disregarded' has to have a particular meaning since it is extensively used in connection with the general anti-avoidance provisions pursuant to FA 2003, ss 75A–75C. In the case of the general anti-avoidance provisions 'disregarded' clearly cannot mean that the transactions are to be ignored and any tax paid is to be refunded nor taken to mean that the transactions never took place. It is, therefore, a bizarre use of the terminology and difficult to reconcile FA 2003, s 45 with ss 75A–75C.

[60]   FA 2003, ss 77 and 77A.

assurances' and the obligations imposed upon persons conveying with full title guarantee. Moreover, even if there are obligations to produce the necessary documentation, if these are not produced at completion there may be difficulties in tracing the intermediate seller or sellers should the necessary paperwork be required by the Land Registry.[61]

6.11   The compliance issues arise in relation to the identification of the deemed secondary contract. The terms of the contract are specified but it is not made clear as to who are the parties to the contract. The general provisions[62] which include amendments designed to 'clarify' the situation indicate that the secondary contract is between the first purchaser and the subpurchaser. Unlike the provision dealing with the direction to grant a lease to a third party pursuant to FA 2003, Sch 17A, para 12B, where there is a form of statutory novation, there is no indication that the original seller becomes a party to the secondary contract in general. In consequence, when reporting the transaction the seller should be identified as the first purchaser and not the original seller. This may lead to discrepancies between the stamp duty land tax documentation since if the transaction is properly reported by the subpurchaser the Inland Revenue Certificate (SDLT 5) should identify the first purchaser as the seller[63] whereas the transfer may be directly from the original owner to the subpurchaser. There is a mismatch between the stamp duty land tax documentation and the Land Registry documentation.[64] The Land Registry may require some form of clarification as to this discrepancy. Ideally, this documentation should be available at completion so that as soon as the appropriate Inland Revenue Certificates (SDLT 5) are produced, the registration can proceed without too much risk of Land Registry delaying matters to the annoyance of mortgagees.

Anti-avoidance and relief for transfers of rights

6.12   There are numerous provisions restricting the relief pursuant to FA 2003, s 45, apart from the highly technical and difficult conditions of s 45 itself. There are restrictions in relation to transactions involving groups of companies[65] and where the transaction involves steps in connection with the alternative finance regime[66] and subsale arrangements are expressly targeted by the general anti-avoidance provisions.[67]

Subsales appear in the illustrative list of transactions that 'may' be within the general anti-avoidance provisions have to be satisfied namely:

- the lower tax condition; and

- the requirement that the scheme transactions have to be involved in connection both with the disposal by V ('A') and the acquisition by P ('C').

In most cases the general anti-avoidance provisions will not apply because C will be paying a full market value for the property so that the lower tax condition[68] will not be satisfied and the provisions cannot apply. However, there will be situations where, as a

---

[61]   See further **Chapter 22**.
[62]   FA 2003, s 45(5A)(b).
[63]   Stamp Duty Land Tax (Administration) Regulations 2003, SI 2003/2837, reg 5(7).
[64]   See further **Chapter 22**.
[65]   FA 2003, s 45(5A)(a); Sch 7, Part 1.
[66]   Ibid, ss 75A–75C.
[67]   Ibid, ss 71A–73C.
[68]   Ibid, s 75A(1)(c).

result of the actions of B, C may be paying a lower price than the open market value of the property when it was disposed of by A so that the lower tax condition might be satisfied,[69] such as where B develops the land and grants a lease at a substantial premium to C so that the value of the freehold is included when sold to C subject to the lease so that In this situation there will be questions as to whether the transaction between A and B is involved in connection with the transaction between B and C.[70] Without this involvement and connection the disposal by A and the acquisition by C will not be the notional transaction within the charge pursuant to the general anti-avoidance provisions.

6.13   This limited relief extends:

- to a series of assignments or subsales or other third party transactions such as A to B to C to D etc;[71] in this situation the relief applies in a sequence. The substantial performance or completion of the secondary contract ie the deemed contract between the various subsellers and subpurchasers arising from an earlier transfer of rights at the same time as and in connection with the substantial performance or completion of the secondary contract arising from a subsequent transfer of rights is disregarded. Any intermediate subseller is, therefore, potentially eligible for the relief;[72] and

- to situations where part[73] only of the property under the original or earlier contract is subsold or assigned, such as where A agrees to sell to B, who agrees to sell part to C, part to D, and so on, including cases where B having on-sold much of the land retains a part for himself.[74] In this situation there is a question of how much tax is to be charged upon the substantial performance or completion of the part of the property retained by the first purchaser. It is provided[75] that where a transfer of rights (or several transfers of rights) relates to part only of the subject-matter of the original contract the provision for the charge on a conveyance is applied as if the reference to the amount of tax chargeable on that contract is to an appropriate proportion of that amount. There is no definition of appropriate proportion of the consideration;[76] but it would seem that the principles that were applied as a matter of general law in the absence of statutory definition in relation to stamp duty in *Maples v IRC*[77] apply to stamp duty land tax.[78] This is to the effect that the charge is not upon the balance of the consideration but upon a proportion of the consideration by reference to the original contract price and the land area. In the *Maple* case[79] it was argued that because the subpurchasers had paid a substantial part of the consideration directly to the original vendor only the balance outstanding was chargeable in respect of the transfer to the first purchaser. This is to the effect that if the

[69]   Ibid, s 75A(1)(c).
[70]   Ibid, s 75A(1)(b).
[71]   Ibid, s 45(4).
[72]   Ibid, s 45(4).
[73]   There must be a whole disposal of the interest in a physical part of the property; the relief does not apply to a part-disposal such as the grant of a lease ie a sale of the entire interest or the grant of a lease of a physical part of the property and as the grant of a lease. There is an important difference between a disposal of part and a part disposal.
[74]   FA 2003, s 45(5).
[75]   Ibid, s 45(5) (as amended).
[76]   Ibid, s 45(5)(a).
[77]   [1914] 3 KB 303.
[78]   FA 2003, s 45(5)(a) (as amended).
[79]   [1914] 3 KB 303.

consideration were 100 and purchasers of two-thirds of the land had paid 90 per cent of the price the first purchaser was taxable only upon 10. However, the Court took the view that this was not the appropriate method of proceeding and the first purchaser was taxable upon one-third of the price. This is, of course, a difficult test to apply since not all parcels of land are of equal value and there may be 'work' to be carried out on the various parcels to apply the charge by reference to the proportion of the geographical area may mean that the purchaser is paying a lower charge to tax in that he may be retaining the land that is worth 75 per cent of the value. However, this argument may be available on the basis of the 'appropriate proportion' and it may be that the ultimate test will be influenced by the level of consideration being paid by the subpurchasers who are acquiring less valuable parts of the land.

Linked transactions and part subsales[80]

6.14   Where there is a subsale situation there will be two separate contracts namely the original contract between the original vendor and the first purchaser and the subsale between the first purchaser and the second purchaser. These will be separate contracts and will not be aggregated so that, *prima facie*, the linked transaction rules are not applicable. There may be no arrangement for the onward sale but where there is such an arrangement or scheme within FA 2003, s 108 the parties will, *prima facie*, be different.[81] The position will be complicated where the first purchaser and the second purchaser are connected parties.[82] In some situations a person may acquire a property or several properties under a single contract which would clearly be a single transaction for the purposes of computing the rates of the purchaser but he intends to subsell them in parts. In this case the individual subpurchasers will, *prima facie*, be entitled to their own appropriate lower rates of tax because they will be different parties from the original parties to the transaction. Obviously, where the subpurchasers are connected persons or connected with the first purchaser there may be an issue as to whether their individual purchases are part of a single scheme so that their transactions are linked by reason of the commercial negotiations.

6.15   This leaves the question of the rate of tax applicable to a transaction where the first purchaser subsells part of the property but completes in respect of the balance.[83] The legislation dealing with this[84] is suitably ambiguous. It refers to an appropriate proportion of the tax that would be chargeable on the main contract. This does not refer to the amount of chargeable consideration but to the amount of tax. This would suggest that the rate is fixed by reference to the total consideration for the entire properties and having applied the rate of, for example, 4 per cent this rate is applied to the balance of the transaction. In consequence, where B agrees acquire property for a consideration of £1,000,000 from B and subsells 80 per cent of the property he will, *prima facie*, but not necessarily where special circumstances affect separate parts of the land so that the 'proportions' may not be simply arithmetic, be chargeable by reference to £200,000 as the appropriate consideration but this will be taxed at 4 per cent and not 1 per cent.

---

[80]   See **5.51**.
[81]   But, in practice, certain bizarre views have been taken by HMRC Stamp Taxes simply because certain parties are connected.
[82]   However, where the parties are connected and there are questions as to the level of consideration HMRC Stamp Taxes may be tempted to ignore the linked transaction rules and apply the general anti-avoidance provisions pursuant to FA 2003, ss 75A–75C.
[83]   See FA 2003, s 45(5) (as amended).
[84]   Ibid, s 45(5)(a).

Problem of s 44A

6.16 These rules for series and part-disposals also apply to assignments and subsales of contracts to convey to third parties within FA 2003, s 44A.[85]

FA 2003, s 44A, introduces a new area of charge to stamp duty land tax,[86] but which because of the manifest inadequacies of the drafting and the fact that it has its own subsale provisions[87] and is based upon legislation that refers to what are standard subsale provisions, which are inappropriate to the mitigation arrangements which it was intended to attack, has created considerable confusion in practice as to the scope of the basic subsale relief.

This special anti-avoidance charge[88] applies where:

- the initial contract is

- a contract whereby a chargeable interest

- is to be conveyed

- by one party to the contract ('A') at the direction of the other party ('B') either:
  - a third party ('C') who is not a party to the contract; or
  - to B or to C.

This situation does not necessarily involve a contract by B to acquire a chargeable interest from A but a charge to tax is imposed where any contract gives B power to direct a conveyance. It is the power to direct the conveyance or lease not the actual events.

Substantial performance of this contract by B, whatever that may mean in this context,[89] is deemed to be a chargeable transaction.[90] Since this terminology effectively reflects most contracts which expressly or impliedly permit subsales there is doubt as to whether it cancels the subsale relief pursuant to s 45 because of B's simultaneous substantial performance of both the contract with A and the contract between B and C. It is, however, generally considered that it does not repeal or modify s 45 by implication since s 44A does not involve a contract to acquire a chargeable interest and will, hopefully, be construed in a workable fashion even by the current judiciary.

6.17 There is a specific subsale relief for transactions within FA 2003, s 44A applies where there is a contract between A and B and B has power to direct a conveyance to C and there is a further transaction including an assignment whereby a fourth party ('D') becomes entitled to exercise the power of direction conferred initially upon B (ie C subsells or assigns or otherwise 'transfers his rights' whatever that may mean in this context to D).[91] In this case, D is not regarded as entering into a land transaction simply

---

85   Ibid s 45A.
86   See **3.23**.
87   FA 2003, s 45A.
88   Which is made specifically notifiable, FA 2003, s 77(1)(c).
89   It is difficult to apply FA 2003, s 44 to this situation, and as there cannot be taking possession of the land since there is no acquisition, as required by this charge.
90   For more details on FA 2003, s 44A; see **3.24** and **5.184**.
91   FA 2003, s 45A.

by reason of the arrangements between B, C and D. Instead D is treated as entering into a deemed contract (the secondary contract) which is in the same terms as the initial contract between A and B but with the substitution of D as a party in place of B. This drafting suggests that the secondary contract is deemed to be between A and D,[92] which differs from the analysis of the basic subsale provisions. The identification of the parties to the deemed secondary contract will have an important bearing upon the availability of exemptions and reliefs and the details of who has to be identified as 'vendor' in the land transaction return (SDLT 1 and SDLT 2).

6.18   The chargeable consideration under the secondary contract due from D is so much of the consideration to be provided pursuant to the initial contract referable to the subject-matter of the transfer of rights directly or indirectly by D or a person connected with him (broadly the balance of the purchase price after allowing for any deposit or stage payment made by the original purchaser, and the consideration provided for the transfer of rights to D (in the agreement between B and D).

6.19   Substantial performance of the original contract is 'disregarded', ie B and presumably C are not taxable if either:

- it occurs at the same time as,[93] and in connection with, the substantial performance of the secondary contract; or

- it occurs after the transfer of rights, ie after the agreement between B and D.

6.20   There is clearly considerable doubt as to the scope of the intended application of this provision and its impact on subsale relief. It is clearly aimed at transactions where X enters into an agreement whereby Y is to carry out construction works upon the land (but without Y agreeing to acquire an interest in the land) in consideration of a share of the sale proceeds.[94] However, the wording is wide enough to apply to standard contracts to purchase a chargeable interest in land where there is an express or implied power to subsell or assign. It is considered that in practice, at present, the HMRC Stamp Taxes will not seek to apply the new provision in such cases, so as to defeat subsale relief pursuant to the FA 2003, s 45(3); the special relief will override the general charging anti-avoidance provision.

TRANSFERS OF RIGHTS – TRANSACTIONS COVERED

6.21   The categories of transactions likely to be affected by these rules dealing with a contract that does not fit the model of a contract for the acquisition of a chargeable interest and relies upon certain deeming provisions include the following:

---

[92] But note the view of HMRC Stamp Taxes in relation to subsales and assignments within ibid, s 45 as evidenced by the changes to that section, that the secondary contract was between B and C or B and D; see **6.8** and **6.11**.

[93] HMRC Stamp Taxes take a strict view of this time factor. In particular their approach is that this is a matter of seconds, minutes or hours.

[94] Apart from the new provision such a transaction would not be within the charge to stamp duty land tax because there is no arrangement for Y to acquire a chargeable interest.

Subsale

6.22   A subsale arises where A contracts to sell land to B, who then contracts to sell the land to C, and A transfers the land to C. A similar situation arises where B subsells in part by contracting to sell parts of the land to D, E and F. The chain of transactions may be longer; the provisions are not limited to two sales.

Assignment

6.23   An assignment arises where A contracts to sell the land to B, who agrees to sell the benefit of the contract to C. The effect of these arrangements is that B disappears from the transaction but the original contract remains in place as if it were between A and C.[95]

Other transactions

6.24   It remains to be seen quite what HMRC Stamp Taxes regards as falling within this term particularly since the definition of 'acquisition' includes a wide range of transactions but which may form part of a larger arrangement where interests may be being created, varied or released and there may be a subsale or assignment at the ultimate completion stage. Much depends upon whether 'other transaction' is to be construed as *ejusdem generis* with subsale or assignment. However, as these latter two transactions do not have any common characteristics for the purposes of the *ejusdem generis* principle of statutory construction and it is specifically stated that all that is required is that a third party becomes entitled to call for a conveyance there does not appear to be any obvious restrictions on the meaning of 'other transaction' as between B and C. It is considered that it includes at least the following.

Novations

6.25   A novation is a tripartite arrangement whereby A agrees to sell land to B. Subsequently, usually in consideration of a payment by C to B, the latter releases A from the original contract and, in consideration of such release by B and of the payment by C, A agrees to sell the land to C. Ultimately A transfers the land to C. There are, however, special problems in this situation. It is provided[96] that where a contract which B may escape tax because his contract is not completed but may be 'rescinded' or not otherwise substantially performed has been substantially performed and is after the effective date rescinded or annulled, or is for any other reason not carried into effect, the stamp duty land tax paid at substantial performance can be recovered.[97] There will,

---

[95]   There is an underlying issue with assignment as to whether the assignor and the assignee are to be regarded as the 'same person' for the purposes of stamp duty land tax. As drafted, there is a potential ambiguity; it may mean either: the same physical person or legal entity so that when B assigns to C they are different persons and not the same; or the parties to the same agreement so that, notwithstanding the assignment, C is a party to the same agreement as B and is, in effect, C is substituted for B and so B and C, being the contracting parties in the same status in the same contract, are the same person. The former is considered to be the correct analysis and the meaning intended by the draftsman; otherwise FA 2003, s 45 would be differently structured. The fact that the transfer is pursuant to the 'same agreement' does not make them the same parties.

[96]   FA 2003, s 44(8).

[97]   It appears that the reference in FA 2003, s 44(8) to sub-s (3) thereof means that there can be no recovery where the contract has been 'completed' nor is there apparently any refund if there is a claim for damages which would, in effect, reduce the amount consideration or cash paid out by the purchaser. However, whilst there are difficult questions as to whether a damages claim operates as some form of reduction of the chargeable consideration the position may be slightly more favourable to the taxpayer where there is some

therefore, be difficult questions as to whether the cancellation of a contract by mutual agreement after the equitable interest may have passed is a rescission, or is a 'release' and a re-conveyance of the equitable interest to the original seller, although, arguably, as the consideration is provided by C and not by A (who would, *prima facie*, be the purchaser), this may mean that it is not chargeable consideration.[98]

Third party leases

6.26   As illustrated above, A may agree to grant a lease to B, who enters into an arrangement with C for a consideration pursuant to which B directs A to grant the lease to C. Subject to FA 2003, Sch 17A, para 12B,[99] this would appear to fall within the scope of FA 2003, s 45. It is unlikely that this was intended but it appears to be an inevitable consequence of 'one size fits all' drafting. However, the fact that the legislation was not drafted with this not-infrequent type of transaction in mind means that it may create more problems than it solves by reason of the deemed consideration provision, which does not seem to fit easily with certain types of consideration such as rent. To some extent these issues have been dealt with by specific relief[100] which overrides the subsale provisions[101] but since this does not appear to be comprehensive this original relief continues to apply to third party leases not within the new relief and, in some cases, may be more generous than the new relief. However, it seems that the provisions do not apply where A agrees to sell land to B who directs A to grant a lease to C. There is no general relief for B in such cases since he does not part with the entire interest in all or a physical part of the chargeable interest. However, subsale relief would appear to be available in situations where B is entering into a sale and leaseback transaction possibly in order to fund the acquisition of the land. Relief would be available in such cases and there may be the relief for the leaseback where this is part of a fundraising exercise.[102] There are certain reliefs in relation to alternative finance arrangements introduced for the benefit of persons whose religion or otherwise contains restrictions upon usury and the lending and paying of interest.[103] In relation to such arrangements there can be a sale and saleback within the relieving provisions or a sale and leaseback provided that the purchaser is a suitable finance company. However, subsale relief is restricted in the case of the sale and saleback[104] but may be available in relation to the sale and leaseback arrangements. This may offer an alternative to the relief available for sale and leaseback transactions but there is a considerable overlap and the availability of subsale relief may be a key factor in the choice of an alternative financing structure.

THE CHARGES AND RELIEFS

6.27   In this context there are the problems of charges and reliefs in relation to the following transactions.

---

price adjustment mechanism in the warranties and indemnities. This may mean that the consideration is variable (FA 2003, s 51) this would mean that the consideration would be under review (FA 2003, s 80) this would automatically give effect to any downward price adjustments; see **5.187**.
[98]   FA 2003, Sch 4, para 1.
[99]   See **6.57**.
[100]   FA 2003, Sch 17A, para 12B; see **6.61**.
[101]   Ibid, Sch 17A, para 12B(1).
[102]   Ibid, ss 57A and 71A–73C.
[103]   Ibid, s 71A–73B.
[104]   Ibid, s 45(3) (as amended).

The original contract between A and B

6.28 There will be a charge to stamp duty land tax if B completes substantially performs this contract prior to substantial performance of the secondary contract; but there will be no further charge or obligation to notify the transaction when the subsale or assignment is completed between A and C because it is not completion between the same parties.[105]

6.29 Where the contract has not been substantially performed, B is not liable in respect of the stamp duty land tax upon this contract.[106] In addition, no charge arises when the agreement between B and C is substantially performed or completed.[107] In consequence, B escapes liability in this situation but there is a question whether B's 'disregarded' transaction is notifiable.[108] Arguably it is not notifiable but this means that in the case of a double completion B's Land Registry Transfer will be unsupported by an Inland Revenue Certificate (SDLT 5) and in the case of a direct transfer from A to C there will be a mismatch between the Land Registry Transfer and the Inland Revenue Certificate (SDLT 5) which is required to identify the parties, who are the parties to the secondary contract.[109] The transferor and the vendor will be different parties. Moreover, since the relief is available notwithstanding that B receives a Land Registry Transfer from A which is not notifiable, C will be faced with the problem of presenting two transfers but only one Inland Revenue Certificate. In both these cases it will be necessary to produce suitable explanatory covering letters to the Land Registry and subpurchasers and assignees may find it prudent to require provisions in their contract that such letters will be produced by B at completion so that they and their mortgagees can proceed to registration. In practice it seems that frequently the 'local discretion' within the Land Registry requires B to file a Land Transaction Return (SDLT 1) showing nil tax and claiming the benefit of the 'other exemption'. This produces an Inland Revenue Certificate (SDLT 5) but gives HMRC Stamp Taxes power to enquire into what might be a non-notifiable transaction.

The transaction between B and C – 'the secondary contract'

6.30 It is provided[110] that, in general, there is no chargeable transaction between B and C where they are merely entering into the contract.[111] In addition the actual contract between B and C is replaced by a statutory agreement. This statutory arrangement is variously described as 'the transfer of rights' or 'the secondary contract'. In effect, the stamp duty land tax that would otherwise be paid is collected at completion or substantial performance of the secondary or deemed agreement between A and C which includes in the chargeable consideration an amount equal to the consideration provided by C to B.[112]

---

[105]   Ibid, s 44(1)(a).
[106]   Ibid, s 45(3). This is not regarded as substantial performance or completion of the original contract between A and B.
[107]   Ibid, s 44(1)(a).
[108]   Ibid, ss 77 and 77A; see **Chapter 18**.
[109]   Stamp Duty Land Tax (Administration) Regulations 2003, SI 2003/2837, reg 5.
[110]   FA 2003, s 45; this is merely an illustration of the general principle that merely entering into a contract is not itself a chargeable transaction; ibid, s 43.
[111]   This is merely a restatement of a general principle; FA 2003, s 44(2).
[112]   FA 2003, s 45(3)(b)(ii).

In the case of subsales

6.31   This is the contract whereby B agrees to sell the chargeable interest (e g the land) to C; no charge arises upon entry into the contract.

In the case of assignment

6.32   This is the contract whereby B disposes of the benefit of the contract with A and, in effect, C steps into B's place as the original purchaser under the original contract; no charge arises upon entry into the contract.[113]

In the case of novation

6.33   The position may be more complicated in the case of novation ie broadly a tripartite arrangement whereby A releases B from liability to a pre-existing obligation in consideration of which C agrees to perform the contract with A with arrangements.[114] It would seem that merely entering into the contract is not a chargeable transaction[115] notwithstanding that this involves the 'release' of B.[116] Similarly, it would seem that entering into the novation contract, under which the first purchaser is released from liability, would not be a chargeable transaction. However, there are difficult questions as to whether releasing a contract to acquire a chargeable interest in land is itself the 'acquisition' ie the release of a chargeable interest. However, there may be a movement of a chargeable interest in land where the situation may have arisen under which some form of equitable interest has passed to B.[117] Alternatively, since a contract to acquire a chargeable interest is itself probably a chargeable interest there is a release of a chargeable interest back to the original vendor. This will obviously be substantially performed or completed when the release takes effect or the vendor receives the relevant consideration from the third party which will be regarded as consideration for the release. Whilst no charge may have arisen in respect of the first purchaser's contract, since he will not have substantially performed his contract, there is no indication in the legislation that the release of this contract back to the original seller is not to be taxable. The relief would not obviously apply to that situation. It could be stretched to deal with the situation upon the basis that the reacquisition of the interest or the release of the original contract to the seller is followed by a contract to resell the property to the third party. In that situation the use of the words 'other arrangements' might be stretched to cover the situation of the original seller in a novation and there would be relief provided that all of the contracts are substantially performed or completed at the same time.

The transaction between A and C

6.34   In the case of a subsale there will be no direct contract between A and C. However, A may, at the direction of B, convey directly to C and C may, at the direction of B, pay monies direction to A.[118] This will be the performance of A's contract with B and the performance of B's contract with C. The secondary contract will be between B

---

[113]   Ibid, s 44(2) and 45(2).

[114]   See **6.41**.

[115]   FA 2003, s 44(2).

[116]   Ibid, s 43(3).

[117]   See, for example, *Re Kidner* [1929] 2 Ch 121; but note *Musselwhite v Musselwhite* [1962] 1 Ch 210; *Michaels v Harley House (Marylebone) Ltd* [1999] 3 WLR 229.

[118]   Such direct transfers and payments between A and C may be key issues as to whether the various steps ('scheme transactions' are involved in connection with the disposal by V and the acquisition by P for the purpose of the general anti-avoidance rules pursuant to FA 2003, ss 75A–75C; see **2.19**.

and C. However, where there is an assignment by B to C this will transfer the contract and substitute C for B so that there will be a direct contractual relationship between A and C. In the case of a novation, the contract between A and B will have been cancelled and a new direct contract between A and C will arise. These situations, although legally very different, have to be fitted within the relieving provisions as being 'transfers of rights'.

6.35   Apart from transactions where B and C are members of the same stamp duty land tax group[119] there is no transaction between A and C. Although the legislation is obscure it seems that the secondary contract is deemed to be between B and C, and that B is the 'vendor' to C which must be reflected in the land transaction return and the related Inland Revenue Certificate (SDLT 5)[120] which is likely to produce a mismatch between the stamp duty land tax documentation and the Land Registry documentation.[121] This is the view of HMRC Stamp Taxes in practice and subsequent legislation has been drafted on this basis.[122] This appears even where there is an assignment so that the primary contract is between A and B, notwithstanding the general law of contract for the purposes of stamp duty land tax the chargeable transaction is between B and C.

Subsales

6.36   Where B has contracted to sell the property, or part thereof, to C, the latter will be subject to stamp duty land tax:

- upon substantial performance of the deemed contract which will be substantial performance of the actual contract between B and C; or

- upon completion, which will, in practice, be the likely form of tax trigger and will be completion of the actual contract between B and C.

If there has been substantial performance of the subsale contract without completion, a further payment and notification obligation arises upon completion.

6.37   In the case of a chain of subsales (ie A sells to B, who sells to C, who sells to D), C will be in the same position as B – namely, if he has not substantially performed he will not become liable to the tax and notification upon substantial performance or completion by D. C will, of course, be liable if he substantially performs. However, it seems that if there are any defects in the implementation of the later subsales B and other prior purchasers will not forfeit the relief in respect of their contracts[123] although other participants in the chain may not be eligible for the relief. Suitable indemnities may be prudent for subvendors where the sub-subpurchasers etc wish to have the power to subsell or assign included in the contract because someone may default and a breach of contract does not excuse the parties from the need to perform or complete at the same time.[124]

---

[119]   FA 2003, Sch 7, Part 1; see **Chapter 12**.
[120]   Stamp Duty Land Tax (Administration) Regulations 2003, SI 2003/2837, reg 5.
[121]   See **Chapter 22**.
[122]   There is a special provision for the interaction of subsale relief and intra-group relief; see FA 2003, s 45(5A).
[123]   FA 2003, s 45(4).
[124]   The first purchaser should consider whether his claim for damages should include the stamp duty land tax which he has to pay but which would not have been due if the subpurchaser had performed on time.

Subsales of part

6.38   Where B subsells separate parcels of land to C, D, E etc, the subpurchasers of each part have their own secondary contract and be taxable on whatever deemed chargeable consideration they are providing to B. Notwithstanding that there is a single vendor whose acquisition may be a single transaction or several acquisitions which are linked transactions in these cases where the subpurchasers are unconnected, the unconnected subpurchasers' contracts will not be linked transactions entitled to whatever lower rates may be appropriate. The status of the original purchaser's contract or contracts does not taint the position of the third parties.

Subsale – retention of part

6.39   Where B does not subsell or assign the whole of the chargeable interest but retains part of his own benefit the charge on the conveyance is restricted to an appropriate proportion of the overall contractual consideration. If the original purchaser subsells only part of the land and takes a transfer of the balance remaining, this is treated as a separate contract so that substantial performance of this part subsale contract and its completion will not trigger a tax charge in respect of the entire original purchase contract, but only upon the that part of the consideration attributable to the part of the land. In consequence the subpurchaser pays tax only upon his consideration and the original purchaser pays tax only upon that part of his original consideration as is properly allocated to the balance of the land transferred to the original purchaser.[125] No statutory guidance is provided on how to determine what proportion is appropriate. In relation to stamp duty[126] the charge was determined by applying the geographical percentage of the whole land of the part retained to the original contract price. It may be, however, that HMRC Stamp Taxes will be looking to determine the charge by reference to relative market values of the part retained and the parts subsold.[127]

Assignments

6.40   Where B has assigned the benefit of the contract to C, C will be liable to stamp duty land tax and to notify upon substantial performance and completion of the deemed secondary contract between B and C, which will, in effect, be the substantial performance or completion of the contract to assign. This may or may not be the same as substantial performance of the agreement with the original seller by C who is now a party to that contract. For example, B may agree to assign the benefit of the contract to C for a cash sum. C may pay that cash sum before the time for completion of the main sale agreement. In this situation there will be separate chargeable events in respect of the contract to assign and the performance and completion of the main contract. The deemed secondary contract[128] would be identified as being a deemed contract between B and C which would be based largely upon the actual terms of the contract to assign.

Novations

6.41   In the case of a novation, this is the cancellation of the existing contract between A and B, a totally new contract between A and C, and possibly a contract between B

---

[125]   FA 2003, s 45(5)(b); see Sch 4, para 4.
[126]   *Maples v IRC* [1914] 3 KB 303.
[127]   See also **6.13**.
[128]   FA 2003, s 45(3).

and C providing the inducement for B to rescind his contract with A, giving rise to a separate chargeable transaction taxable in its own right. Where there is a contract between A and B and subsequently the contract between B and C is one whereby B agrees to give up the contract with A for a consideration provided by C, it is arguably a contract between B and A for the release[129] of a chargeable interest for a consideration, it seems, with A as the 'purchaser' because A 'acquires' the interest released and so is a party to the transaction releasing the interest, although he does not provide the consideration.[130] This analysis will not matter if HMRC Stamp Taxes accept that novations are 'other arrangements' within s 45 of the FA 2003, since these involve a 'transfer of rights' not subject to charge. However, the point will become important if s 45 does not include novations. In that case another important argument is that the consideration provided by C is not 'chargeable consideration' because it is not provided directly or indirectly by the purchaser as required by para 1 of Sch 4 to the FA 2003. This, however, is a difficult issue and much depends upon how the word 'indirectly' is applied and the precise limits applied to the scope of para 1 for consideration other than money or money's worth.

THE EFFECT OF THE LEGISLATION

6.42   If the conditions outlined above are satisfied the person described as 'B' ie the original purchaser does not enter into a chargeable transaction. His transaction is 'disregarded' so that he is not liable to tax and may not have to notify.[131] Should his contract be cancelled there is, *prima facie*, no chargeable transaction to be notified but this analysis is unclear.

6.43   If satisfied, the conditions of FA 2003, s 45, produce the tax liabilities as follows.

The original purchaser

6.44   If the original purchaser has substantially performed but not completed the agreement he will have become liable for the stamp duty land tax arising and, having substantially performed but not completed, he may be able to reclaim the stamp duty land tax already paid upon the basis that the contract has been rescinded or annulled or has not been carried into effect.[132] However, if he has not substantially performed, the payment of the outstanding balance of the purchase price or taking a transfer by the third party does not amount to substantial performance[133] and he is not liable to stamp duty land tax. Moreover, the receipt of a transfer by B because his contract with A precludes subsales or assignments does not make B liable to the tax provided that he has not previously substantially performed his contract with A and the transfer is delivered at the same time as the contract between B and C is substantially performed or completed.[134]

---

[129]   There is an important issue of principle whether this is a genuine rescission or a 're-sale' of the interest of the first purchaser for a consideration, whether in the form of the return of the original purchase price or deposit and/or any consideration provided by C for B agreeing to terminate the original agreement.

[130]   FA 2003, s 43(5).

[131]   See **6.10** and **2.25** on the compliance issues and registration problems and see **Chapter 22**.

[132]   FA 2003, s 44(9).

[133]   Ibid, s 45(3).

[134]   The legislation does not deal with the situation where the contract between B and C is substantially performed before performance of the contract between A and B. Technically the relief is not available.

6.45   If there is a chain of subsales or assignments it seems that the conditions of simultaneous completion apply to all transactions in the chain if all subpurchasers are to qualify for the relief. An error in implementing one of those transactions will not, it seems, cancel the relief for all preceding and subsequent subsales. It may cause a loss of reliefs for the immediate transactions but not necessarily affect the relief as regards prior or later transactions. For example, if A sells to B who sells to C who sells to D who sells to E. D may default in relation to his transaction with C. However, if A, B and C complete their contracts simultaneously it would seem that B would be eligible for the relief although C will not be liable because he does not simultaneous complete his transaction with D. As regards transactions between D, E and F if these are simultaneously but albeit later completed then E will be eligible for the relief although D will have had to pay tax. There will be potential questions as between C and D as to the damages for D's breach of contract and whether these can include compensation for the stamp duty land tax that C has to pay but would not have paid had D performed on time.

6.46   However, if novations are not within FA 2003, s 45, there will be the issue outlined above as to whether the original purchaser's agreement to release the original disposer is a release or re-conveyance of a chargeable interest in consideration of the repayment of any money already paid.[135]

The third party (eg subpurchaser or assignee (other than a lessee))

6.47   The entry into the contract between the original purchaser and the third party is not a chargeable transaction.[136] The actual contract is replaced by the secondary contract.[137] However, the secondary contract is between the same parties namely the original purchaser and the third party and would appear to be upon identical terms as the actual contract except for the modification as to the consideration being provided for the purposes of the charge to stamp duty land tax. The person becoming entitled under the subsale or assignment is treated as if he were a party to a transaction for which the consideration is the consideration given or pursuant to the contract between the third party and the original purchaser, together with the balance outstanding under the original contract. He is liable to stamp duty land tax.

Illustrations

6.48   The effect of the legislation in relation to certain basic types of transaction appears to be as follows.

Subsale

6.49   The effect of the arrangement in a simple subsale would be:

- A contracts to sell land to B for £100;

---

[135] Different issues can arise where there are sales or assignment of leases where the initial transaction involved variable consideration such as an overage payment, a clawback or a turnover rent or even a reasonable rent. There is an outstanding tax liability which may or may not pass to the next owner of the chargeable interest. In some cases the original contract may contain provisions for the liability of the original party to cease provided that the liability is assumed by the purchaser. This is a form of novation but the arrangements will not fall within these provisions; see **6.25**.

[136] FA 2003, s 45(2).

[137] Ibid, s 45(5) (as amended).

- B pays a deposit of £10; leaving a balance of £90;

- B agrees to subsell to C for £120;

- C pays a deposit of £12 to B;

- At completion:
    - C pays £18 to B;
    - C pays £90 to A; and
    - A, at the direction of B, transfers the land directly to C.[138]

6.50   The stamp duty land tax situation is as follows, either:

- B is not liable to stamp duty land tax. By merely paying the deposit[139] he will not have substantially performed the agreement and the payment of the balance by C to A is not to be treated as substantial performance of B's contract with A;[140]

- C pays tax upon £120 (ie £90 to A; £30 (being £12 + 18) to B) upon substantial performance of the contract with B who are usually the parties to the secondary contract;[141] or

- alternative double completion:
    - C pays B who pays A;
    - A transfers the land to B;
    - At the same time and in connection with the completion of the contract between A and B, B transfers the land to C.

The technical position is that notwithstanding receipt of a conveyance B is eligible for subsale relief and C is taxable upon the consideration which he pays.

6.51   In a similar situation:

- A contracts to sell land to B for £100;

- B pays a deposit of £10;

- before completing the contract B enters onto the land in order to build houses;

- B sells the land and houses to C for £500;

- At completion:
    - C pays £410 to B and £90 to A;

---

[138]   The relief is also available where A transfers to B and B transfers to C. The double completion is no longer incompatible with the availability of subsale relief (FA 2003, s 45(3)). There are, however, issues as to the notification by B of his transaction and what documentation will be required by the Land Registry before they will accept the Land Registry transfer from A to B (FA 2003, ss 79(1) (as amended) and 77A). See **6.10**. This means that the inconvenience caused by conditions in the contract prohibiting or restricting subsales or limiting the ability of the purchaser to direct a conveyance to some third party are no longer an obstacle to obtaining stamp duty land tax relief.

[139]   Assuming that he has not gone into possession or otherwise substantially performed the agreement with A.

[140]   FA 2003, s 45(3).

[141]   See **6.11**.

–   A conveys the land to C at the direction of B.

The effects appear to be:

*   B, having substantially performed by going into possession, is liable to stamp duty land tax on £100;

*   no charge to stamp duty land tax arises in relation to the transaction between B and C;

*   C is liable to stamp duty land tax upon £500 (ie £90 outstanding to A; £410 to B).

Assignment

6.52   In this situation:

*   A contracts to sell to B for £100;

*   B pays £10 deposit;

*   B contracts to assign[142] the contract to C for £30;

*   A transfers the land to C for the payment of the outstanding £90.

The stamp duty land tax situation is:

*   B is not liable to stamp duty land tax so long as he has not substantially performed the contract with A, and the payment of the balance by C does not amount to substantial performance by B; but

*   C is liable to stamp duty land tax upon £120 (ie £90 to A; £30 to B).

Special situations

Linked transactions and subsales

6.53   In situations where A has contracted to sell several properties to B who contracts to sell the individual properties to C, D etc, B's acquisition from A will be a single purchase of multiple properties and the total consideration for all of the properties will be aggregated in order to determine the chargeable amount and the rate. The individual subsales by B to C, D etc are not linked simply because B's power to sell derives from a larger single scheme involving several linked contracts between A and B. Each of the

---

[142]   There is a technical question as to how far B and C can proceed with their contract. Technically where there is the assignment of the benefit of a contract should this be a land transaction it will be completion and therefore a chargeable event. In this context it should be noted that directions by B to A to convey to C on notification of the assignment would itself be an assignment or conveyance. Fortunately, FA 2003, s 45 states that the contract between B and C to assign the benefit of the contract with A is not a 'land transaction'. It would seem, therefore, that completion of this contract by means of an assignment prior to completion of the arrangements between A and C is not a chargeable event and does not jeopardise the availability of the relief for B. A similar issue arises in relation to situations where a party to an agreement for lease wishing to take advantage of the equivalent relief for leases (FA 2003, Sch 17A, para 12B) 'assigns' his right to call for the lease at an early stage in the transaction.

individual contracts between B and C, D etc. will depend upon their own circumstances. Therefore, if C is buying two properties from B it will be necessary to investigate the facts as to whether there was a single arrangement for a sale of the two properties for a larger deposit in which case these transactions will be linked. However, the transactions between B and D will not be linked necessarily with C because, *prima facie*, they are between separate parties. However, the transaction between B and C and between B and D will be linked if C and D are connected parties and there is something in the background to these arrangements that links them. Parties acting for C will need to investigate details of any other purchasers where there are multiple sales from a single vendor.[143]

6.54 The subpurchaser or assignee of part will be subject to stamp duty land tax upon his deemed consideration for that part of the land: completion of the subsale of that part does not operate as substantial performance of the whole of the original contract. If the original purchaser takes a transfer of the balance of the chargeable interest the stamp duty land tax is chargeable upon an appropriate proportion of the original consideration, and this charge applies notwithstanding substantial performance of the subsale or assignment contracts by the third party.[144]

Groups of companies

6.55 Subsale relief is modified in relation to transactions where the final contract is between members of the same stamp duty land tax group so that intra-group relief is not intended to be available where the original seller was not a member of the stamp duty land tax group.[145] On the basis of the view of HMRC Stamp Taxes that the secondary contract was between the first purchaser and the subpurchaser it was possible for company B to agree to agree to acquire property from A and for company B to sell the property its subsidiary company C. In this situation if the other conditions of FA 2003, s 45 were satisfied then B would be exempt from duty and the performance of the secondary contract between B and C would be eligible for relief for intra-group transactions.[146] In order to defeat such mitigation arrangements s 45 was amended[147] to the effect that in relation to transactions where the parties were seeking group relief the references in relation to any subsale to the 'vendor' for the purposes of the secondary contract were to be treated as references to the vendor under the original contract. In this situation the contract that was being completed for the purposes of intra-group relief would be the contract between the outside original seller and the subsidiary company. In consequence, there was not a transfer between associated companies.

Alternative finance

6.56 Because of the rules prohibiting usury and borrowing or lending at interest, in certain communities, reliefs have been introduced to permit providers of funds to acquire an interest in the relevant property. For certain types of purchaser a loan supported by a mortgage is not possible. It is necessary for the provider of funds to acquire an interest in the property and derive some form of profit or income from the property that, although in substance interest, is not technically interest. Reliefs have

---

143   See **5.60**.
144   FA 2003, s 45(5); compare *Maples v IRC* [1914] 3 KB 303.
145   Ibid, s 45(5A); compare *Escoigne Properties Ltd v IRC* [1958] AC 549.
146   Ibid, Sch 7, Part 1; see **12.60**.
147   Ibid, s 45(5A)(a).

been introduced to treat such arrangements as if they were mortgages and exempt.[148] One area of relief for such alternative finance arrangement applies where property is sold by an individual to a relevant financial institution which resells the property to the individual on particular terms. In this situation the alternative finance arrangements may be part of some larger arrangement whereby A agrees to sell property to B who enters into a sale and resale operation for the purposes of the alternative finance relief. In this situation B is not entitled to subsale relief.[149] This restriction upon subsale relief applies to transactions within FA 2003, s 73(3).[150]

LEASE TO THIRD PARTY

6.57   A frequent situation arising in practice is a freeholder agreeing to grant a lease to a developer, who at some stage directs the freeholder to grant a lease of the whole or part of the property to a third party, who not only assumes the outstanding liabilities in respect of the lease (such as paying the balance of any unpaid premiums[151] or the future rent)[152] but also provides consideration to the developer.[153] This has the potential for producing a substantial number of charges to stamp duty land tax.

6.58   There is, however, a potential problem of multiple taxation where there has been substantial performance of the agreement for lease and the lease is granted to a third party. This can arise, for example, where a developer takes an agreement for lease from the freeholder, carries out building works, enters into an arrangement with a third party for a consideration and directs that the lease be granted directly to the third party. In this situation there are potential charges in respect of the substantial performance of the agreement for lease and in respect of the grant of the lease to a third party, probably as part of some arrangements for the satisfaction of the liability for any funding arrangements provided where there is an assignment of a lease of a completed building taxable upon the full amount. Given the one-size-fits-all drafting of the legislation, it is possible to bring such arrangements into subsale relief but this requires giving the words some unusual meanings and, because it is an attempt to distort a concept to apply it to a somewhat unusual situation notwithstanding it falls within the basic concept, difficulties arose where the first agreement has been substantially performed, the developer will be liable to tax.[154] The arrangement might be regarded as an assignment of the benefit of the agreement to grant the lease[155] or as some form of 'other arrangement' analogous to a subsale. It is an arrangement under which some person other than the original tenant becomes entitled to call for a conveyance or lease to him. In this situation, there would appear to be multiple charges to stamp duty land tax:

---

[148]   Ibid, ss 71A–73B.

[149]   Ibid, s 45(3) (as amended).

[150]   See **11.50**.

[151]   But note FA 2003, Sch 17A, para 12.

[152]   Ibid, Sch 17A, para 17.

[153]   There is a slight question as to what is the chargeable consideration since, pursuant to FA 2003, Sch 4, para 1, the consideration to be chargeable must be provided by the person acquiring the chargeable interest or a person connected with him (see **5.99**). However, under normal circumstances the third party will be making a payment for the grant of the lease and so would appear to be 'the purchaser' for these purposes.

[154]   These issues of substantial performance and 'effective date' are important not merely for the purposes of triggering liabilities to notify and pay tax but it is also relevant to questions of valuation and, in the context of lease, the very important question as to whether the agreement for lease has been substantially performed so that any subsequent works carried out upon the land by the tenant at his own cost are to be included within, or excluded from, the charge to stamp duty land tax. FA 2003, Sch 4, para 10.

[155]   *Att-Gen v Brown* (1849) 3 Exch 662.

- the developer is liable upon the substantial performance of his agreement for lease.[156] The situation would, therefore, be potentially available for relief but issues and charges arose including the fact that in this situation the developer would be liable for tax upon any premium payable to the landlord for the grant of the lease plus tax in respect of any rent. In these situations the premium and the rent may be variable so that the developer will, *prima facie*, be subject to ongoing long-term obligations to deal with the situation initially upon a provisional or estimated basis and to make retrospective adjustments in this position as and when the relevant consideration or rent is finally determined or treated as being settled for the purposes of stamp duty land tax;[157]

- the grant of the lease by the freeholder to the third party would not operate as a 'completion' of the original agreement for lease[158] since it is not between the same parties; in consequence, the original tenant (the developer) would not be required to deal with the possible additional tax arising and, in any event, the reporting obligations;[159]

- as regards the third party, he is liable for stamp duty land tax upon the consideration provided to the developer for presumably directing the grant of the lease. This will be regarded as the purchase of a lease. *Prima facie*, the third party will not be subject to tax in respect of the rent[160] but the transaction is likely to be regarded as a sale of the lease with a completed building so that the third party will be subject to tax upon the building work.

THE RELIEFS

Default relief

6.59   Fortunately, because of the structure of the drafting so that the provisions applicable to sales also apply to leases, it seems that inadvertently the HMRC Stamp Taxes originally introduced a form of subsale relief for leases such as where A agrees to grant a lease to B for a premium and a ground rent and B, before having constructed a block of flats, directs A to grant separate leases of each of the flats to C, D, E, and so on, who pay a premium plus a ground rent[161] and service charges.[162] Technically, it seems that such an arrangement is the assignment or other transaction involving the 'sale' of the agreement for lease between A and B from B to C for the consideration paid by C[163] and so falls within these provisions. FA 2003, s 45, provides that where a

---

[156]   For the problems relating to the amount of chargeable consideration in the context of building operations, see **Chapter 8**.

[157]   See, for example, FA 2003, ss 51, 80, 81A, Sch 17A, para 12; Stamp Duty Land Tax (Administration) Regulations 2003, SI 2003/2837, Part 4.

[158]   FA 2003, s 44(7) and (9); the modification by s 45(3) would not appear to apply.

[159]   The obligations in FA 2003, s 44(8) do not apply.

[160]   FA 2003, Sch 17A, para 17.

[161]   Different considerations may apply where B directs A to grant what are in effect subleases of the completed building at a commercial rent to third parties prior to the grant of the lease. This could arise where B is to construct a retail development and enters into various pre-lets in order to fund the development before finally directing the grant of what is at the time a headlease to X, who is acquiring B's interest in the development.

[162]   On service charges, see **7.138**.

[163]   *Att-Gen v Brown* (1849) 3 Exch 662. Inherent liabilities such as any future rent are to be ignored in computing the stamp duty land tax, notwithstanding FA 2003, Sch 4, para 8; *Swayne v IRC* [1900] 1 QB 172; but not it seems if FA 2003, Sch 17A, para 12B applies.

contract is entered into which is to be completed by a 'conveyance', which must include a lease,[164] and there is an assignment[165] or 'other transaction'[166] as a result of which some person 'other than the original purchaser', which must include a lessee, becomes entitled to call for a 'conveyance' (ie a lease) to him, then:

- there is no charge to stamp duty land tax upon the transaction between the original 'purchaser' and the third party; and

- there is deemed to be a land transaction where:
  - the third party is the 'purchaser'; and
  - the consideration for that transaction is so much of the consideration under the original transaction which is to be satisfied by the third party or a person connected with him, which will usually be the outstanding balance after payment of the deposit or any instalment, plus the consideration paid by the third party to the original party. The latter payment will usually include the reimbursement of the deposit plus any term or profit which the original party is making, but the structure of this section avoids a double charge upon the deposit and any other monies paid by the original party which is reimbursed by the third party.[167]

This would appear to mean that the third party is liable for stamp duty land tax upon the rent payable under the lease since this remains to be paid or provided. The position is obscure, since it requires the application of provisions drafted to deal with assignments and subsales but not this type of arrangement. It seems that FA 2003, s 45, applies whether or not the original agreement for lease has been substantially performed. In the circumstances under discussion that will almost certainly be the case. The consequence appears to be:

- the original developer will be liable to stamp duty land tax upon substantial performance, probably going onto the land to begin development;

- there will be no charge to stamp duty land tax upon the agreement between the developer and the third party;

- the third party will be liable to stamp duty land tax on the grant of the lease in respect of the consideration paid to the developer and the balance of the consideration outstanding on the original contract.[168] It is expected that this will include any outstanding premium, but where there is rent it seems likely, although the position is obscure, that the grantee is taxable only upon the rent in excess of that upon which the original party paid tax.[169]

6.60 In consequence, the original party will escape stamp duty land tax upon his transaction provided that he has not substantially performed the original contract. In the context of building arrangements, the question of whether entering upon the land to be leased in order to carry out the works amounts to taking 'possession' will be

---

[164] FA 2003, s 45(7).
[165] See the analysis in *Att-Gen v Brown* (1849) 3 Exch 662.
[166] It is difficult to stretch the word 'subsale' to fit the present illustration notwithstanding the verbal contortions that are required to make the basic model of the legislation fit leases.
[167] See the further discussion of subsales etc in **Chapter 6**.
[168] FA 2003, s 45.
[169] See ibid, Sch 17A, para 17.

important. There is no guarantee that the HMRC Stamp Taxes would not take this double charge and, until the position has been clarified, in practice it would seem prudent (and almost certainly cheaper) for the original agreement for lease to be completed by a grant to the developer, who then enters into an assignment to the third party. In this situation, the possible double charge upon the rent would be avoided.[170] Therefore, whilst it was possible with a certain amount of distortion of the words used in the legislation to make the subsale relief fit this type of transaction it was not particularly easy. In consequence, a specific relief has been provided[171] which overrides the relief provided by FA 2003, s 45; but the latter relief remains available in cases where the specific relief for agreements for lease is not available but the conditions of s 45 can be satisfied.

Specific relief for agreements for lease

6.61 Where:

- an agreement for lease has been entered into;

- before the agreement is substantially performed;

- the original party 'assigns';

- his interest as lessee under the agreement for lease,

the agreement for lease is deemed to have been made between the landlord and the assignee and the original party will not be liable for tax. The drafting of this provision leaves much to be desired and means that a detailed investigation of a vendor's stamp duty land tax position is essential for the protection of the third party who may find it prudent to require an indemnity against any increase in his anticipated tax liability by reason of the original party seeking to escape tax on his transaction. In some situations this can have the impact of increasing the taxation liability of the third party. For example, the grant of the lease is regarded as the completion of an agreement between the landlord and the third party as tenant. This will being into charge the rent reserved by the lease although a person who takes the assignment of a lease normally does not expect to pay tax in respect of the rent.[172] For non-residential property there may be an additional problem since there is a restriction upon the nil rate premium where the rent exceeds £1000.[173] In this situation the person taking a lease in these circumstances, in addition to any problems concerned with the rent, may find that although the sum that he is paying to the original party to the lease, such as the developer, is below the nil rate threshold it is taxable at 1 per cent. Where the provision applies, the provisions relating to substantial performance and completion[174] which are, *prima facie*, applicable because in these situations the agreement for lease will contemplate completion by a 'conveyance' ie a grant of the lease. This puts the arrangement into the special provisions for the effective date.[175] The provisions for substantial performance and completion apply as if the agreement for lease had been made between the landlord and

---

[170] Ibid, Sch 17A, para 17.
[171] Ibid, Sch 17A, para 12B.
[172] See ibid, Sch 17A, para 17; but note the provision overriding this in relation to certain leases that were exempt when granted pursuant to Sch 17A, para 11.
[173] Ibid, Sch 5, paras 9 and 9A.
[174] Ibid, s 44.
[175] Ibid.

the assignee; the assignor is removed from the scene. The consideration for the deemed agreement 'includes' any consideration given by the third party for the assignment.[176]

Problems

6.62   For example, the draftsman has utilised the word 'assigns' which has a specific, longstanding technical meaning which does not include an agreement to assign. It seems, therefore, that HMRC Stamp Taxes are entitled to insist upon the execution of a suitable written instrument formally transferring the relevant interest.[177] It is believed that HMRC Stamp Taxes will not accept as effective an agreement between the original party and the third party to the effect that the original party will direct the grant of the lease to the third party. Such an arrangement is not necessarily an 'assignment' even in plain English.[178] Regrettably this will be the standard situation because, in practice in general, the third party will not wish to take the lease unless and until the building is complete. Here there cannot be an 'assignment' because nothing is to be transferred or granted until the conditions precedent are satisfied.[179] This is a key issue of the interpretation of the legislation since the various provisions related to the arrangement refer to events taking place before or after 'the assignment'. In a strict sense, where there is an agreement to procure the grant of the lease to the third party when the building is completed there will be a contract that may rank as a contract to 'assign' but there will have been no 'assignment' which means, in general terms, the actual completion by some formal instrument of transfer of the relevant interest. Whilst a direction by the developer to the landlord to grant the lease to the third party may operate as an assignment,[180] this will normally emerge as a document or transaction only at the final stages of the transaction which will, inevitably, after the commencement of the building works and after the developer has taken possession of the land.[181] The strict interpretation of the legislation relating to the meaning of 'assigns' and 'assignment' would mean that the relief is very limited. It would apply, essentially only, to speculators who enter into agreements to take leases of several flats hoping to turn the contract before they are required to pay and take the conveyances. Even here, however, there would be difficulties because they are unlikely to be able to 'assign' in the sense of conveying their interests prior to completion which would also be substantial performance in most cases.

6.63   This also raises an issue in relation to the taxation of the building works in situations where the original agreement for lease is with a developer who hopes to enter into arrangements with some funding institution that will provide the finance for the development and take the grant of the lease in due course. In the basic situation the developer will pay tax upon the agreement for lease including any premium or rent but, probably, not the cost of the building works[182] because he will be building upon the land

---

[176]   Ibid, Sch 17A, para 12B(1) and(2).
[177]   Written notice of the assignment would also appear to be necessary from the assignee to the landlord in order to perfect the title: Law of Property Act 1925, s 136.
[178]   But note *Diplock v Hammond* (1854) 5 De GM & G 320.
[179]   Note *Warmington v Miller* [1973] 2 All ER 372.
[180]   See, for example, *Diplock v Hammond* (1854) 5 De GM & G 320.
[181]   Note also the possible implications of FA 2003, s 44A which is intended to apply to situations where there are building agreements and the person who contracts to construct the building has a 'power to direct a conveyance'. This converts certain building contracts into chargeable transactions and may be applicable here, as with many forms of subsale arrangement; see **Chapter 8**.
[182]   Which are likely to be part of the consideration see *Eastham v Leigh, London and Provincial Properties Limited* [1971] 2 All ER 887.

to be acquired.[183] There will be further charges when the lease is granted to the third party since this will be completion of the agreement to procure the grant of the lease in satisfaction of the debt. The debt will include the value of the land plus the cost of the building works and therefore the purchaser will be paying tax upon the building works. In some situations it is possible to avoid the charge to tax upon building works where there are separate contracts for the transfer of the land and the construction of the building at the cost of the purchaser.[184] If there is an arrangement to transfer the interest in the land and a separate agreement to construct and not a single agreement for the transfer of the land and the building is constructed only the land price will attract stamp duty land tax.[185] In the situation of the developer completing the works and directing the landlord to grant the lease directly to the third party FA 2003, Sch 17A, para 12B provides an opportunity for mitigating these arrangements but this depends upon the meaning of the words 'assignment'. If before having entered onto the land or carried out any other acts that might constitute substantial performance the developer enters into an agreement to 'assign' his interest as lessee to the institute providing the funds and enters into a separate agreement to build then, when the lease is granted, the institution as the grantee of the lease will be paying tax upon the rent and any premium plus any sums paid to the developer for the benefit of the land.[186] However, the building works will escape the charge to tax that might otherwise apply.[187] It would seem that in order to qualify for the purposes of the 'sublease' relief for the developer there must be some form of formal 'assignment' of his interest. In relation to stamp duty it was accepted that where there is a conveyance before the building works are commenced or completed this excluded the building works from the charge to tax.[188] It would seem that similar reasoning has been adopted by HMRC Stamp Taxes in relation to this amendment to the legislation. Provided that this minefield can be negotiated the third party may pay tax upon the rent but he may escape a much higher charge to tax upon the costs of the building works.

6.64 The draftsman has also failed to explain what he means by 'interest as lessee under' the agreement for lease. Frequently there will be building obligations in the original agreement[189] which have to be satisfied before the lease can be granted. It is unclear whether the assignee has to take over these obligation since they are an integral part of the right or interest as lessee pursuant to the agreement. Third parties will, unsurprisingly, be reluctant to take on these obligations merely to enable the original party to escape a charge to stamp duty land tax.

6.65 A major problem is the chargeable consideration. Since the deemed contract aggregates the consideration for the original agreement for lease, which is the whole

---

[183] FA 2003, Sch 4, para 10(2).

[184] See **7.74** and **8.9**.

[185] See, for example, *Prudential Assurance Co Ltd v IRC* [1992] STC 863 which HMRC Stamp Taxes have accepted applies to stamp duty land tax. There is a reference in the exclusion for works to be carried out on land to be acquired but this does not apply where it is a 'term of the arrangement' that the works will be constructed by the landlord or vendor. However, this means that the building works by the landlord or vendor must be part of the contract for the disposal of the land. Where they are in separate agreements they are not 'terms' of the arrangement for the building works.

[186] Care may be needed in order to avoid multiple charges upon any deposit or other payments made by the developer.

[187] Compare *Attorney General v Brown* (1849) 3 Exch 662.

[188] Statement of Practice SP 10/89 and 8/93; *Cory & Son Ltd v IRC* [1965] AC 1088.

[189] Which may form part of the chargeable consideration; see *Eastham v Leigh, London and Provincial Properties Limited* [1971] 2 All ER 887; and these may fall to be taxed on the third party because the draftsman has not dealt with the interaction of these provisions and the relief for building works.

amount thereof and not the balance outstanding[190] for the premium plus the rent reserved and the consideration for the assignment the assignee faces some surprising additional charges to tax; for example:

- he will be taxable upon the rent which assignees do not normally have to pay;[191]

- the consideration for the agreement for lease may include building works[192] and it is unclear whether the entry upon the land by the original party to carry out the works will be regarded by HMRC Stamp Taxes as substantial performance by the assignee/third party sufficient to offer the exemption for the costs of works effected after the effective date for the agreement for lease *prima facie*, in relation to the original agreement for lease the entry by the developer onto the land to commence building works will constitute substantial performance and this will potentially exclude from the charge to tax the cost of the building works that will be upon land that is to be acquired pursuant to the arrangement. This clearly would not be the case where the lease is granted to the third party since only at this stage will there have been 'substantial performance'. However, where there is the assignment of the right to the interest within the terms of FA 2003, Sch 17A, para 12B, prior to the developer entering upon the land to commence works ie before he substantially performs so that para 12B applies, the contract is deemed to have been made with the third party. In consequence, the building obligations, if they are part of the consideration, will be building obligations to be provided by the third party. In this situation the third party will be commissioning building to be carried out upon the land that he is to acquire. In these circumstances, the third party by entering into the building agreement and 'licensing' the developer to go upon the land in order to carry out the building works that are part of his original agreement for lease mean that the third party is taking possession of the land and therefore substantially performing his statutory agreement for lease and therefore the works would be carried out after the effective date of his statutory agreement. They would, therefore, appear to qualify for the exclusion from charge; and

- there is, in effect, a risk of a double charge upon any deposit.[193] It is probable that the original party may have paid a deposit towards the premium. When he 'assigns' the lease the consideration for the assignment will include not merely the costs of the building works but also reimbursement of prior expenses. However, the assignee is treated as paying the deposit so that it falls into tax twice.[194]

In these cases C may find it prudent to seek to obtain an indemnity from B against any enhanced stamp duty land tax liability.

6.66   If the assignment takes effect after the original party has substantially performed the agreement for lease the assignment is treated as a chargeable transaction.[195] The original party is taxable in respect of the agreement for lease and the third party is

---

[190]   Compare FA 2003, s 45(3)(b)(i).
[191]   FA 2003, Sch 17A, para 17; but note para 11 (see **7.241**).
[192]   Ibid, Sch 4, para 10; *Eastham v Leigh, London and Provincial Properties Limited* [1971] 2 All ER 887.
[193]   Note *George Wimpey Ltd v IRC* [1975] 2 All ER 45 on the double charge upon an option premium and the strike price unless carefully drafted.
[194]   This appears to be another case where those advising HMRC Stamp Taxes are not as expert in tax and conveyancing as the situation requires.
[195]   FA 2003, Sch 17A, para 12B(3).

taxable in the normal way on the acquisition of the lease. Where the substantial performance occurs after the assignment but before the grant of the lease, the former rules apply and the original party is not chargeable.

Default relief

6.67   It will have been noted that the specific relief is fraught with difficulties of interpretation and serious problems for third parties. Until such time as it has become clear how aggressive HMRC Stamp Taxes intend to be in this context third parties may find it prudent not to co-operate with the original party's tax saving in the absence of suitable indemnities, or the parties agree to work on the basis of the standard subsale relief. Unfortunately this route will not be effective where the original party is to develop the land.

SPECIFIC RELIEF FOR SUBSALES ETC

6.68   Exchanges, including part-exchanges, ie transactions where the properties are not of equal value and a cash or other equity adjustment is made, are taxable by reference to market value.[196] However, certain reliefs which operate as a highly restricted form of subsale relief are available. Current experience in practice indicates that HMRC Stamp Taxes intend to take a very hard line on these reliefs and taxpayers selected for an Enquiry should expect a difficult time in defending their decision to utilise these and similar reliefs when making the initial self-assessment.

Part-exchanges of new houses

6.69   Two areas of relief are available.

Acquisition by builder

6.70   FA 2003, Sch 6A, para 1, provides that an acquisition is exempt from stamp duty land tax where:

- there is the acquisition of a new dwelling by an individual (whether alone or with other individuals) from a house building company.[197] A building is a new dwelling if it has been constructed for use as a single dwelling and has not been previously occupied or it has been adapted for use as a single dwelling and has not been occupied since its adaptation.[198] The acquisition of the old dwelling is an acquisition by way of transfer of a major interest in the dwelling. The individual must, therefore, transfer the whole of his interest in the existing dwelling. Acquisition of the new dwelling may be by way of grant or transfer of a major interest in the new dwelling;

---

[196]   Ibid, s 47; Sch 4, para 5; see **5.158**.

[197]   It will need to be noted that the terms of the various reliefs relating to residential property in FA 2003, Sch 6A are somewhat restricted. The reliefs may be available only for certain categories of party. The relief for part-exchanges of new dwellings is available only to a house building 'company'. It will not apply, therefore, to arrangements entered into where the builder is an individual or a partnership including a limited liability partnership. Other reliefs may be limited to partnerships that consist solely of companies or similar arrangements.

[198]   FA 2003, Sch 6A, para 7(1) and (2).

- the acquisition is in consideration of the transfer of an existing dwelling which includes land occupied and enjoyed with the dwelling as its garden or grounds. Since the relief requires a 'transfer' the relief is not available where the individual grants a lease or a mortgage to the house building company or merely hands over a power of attorney to sell;

- the existing dwelling is acquired by a house building company which is defined as a company that carries on the business of constructing or adapting buildings or part of buildings for use as dwellings. The relief is available only to companies and not to individual builders or partnerships;

- the acquisition is from an individual (whether alone or with other individuals)[199] but not from other persons;

- the individual occupied the old dwelling as his only or main residence at some time in the period of 2 years ending with the date of the acquisition of the existing dwelling by the house building company. A separate relief is available for dealings with executors and administrators;

- the individual intends to occupy the new dwelling as his only or main residence. This is a major problem in practice require suitable due diligence and safeguards obtained by the developer's advisors. There can be problems, for example, where the arrangement is part of a divorce or similar settlement and either the individual receiving the new property is not the sole or even joint owner of the existing property. It seems, however, that there must only be an intention to occupy the new premises. There does not appear to be any clawback of the relief should the individual not go into occupation of the premises. Unfortunately the house building company appears to be on risk that HMRC Stamp Taxes may utilise hindsight to claim that the relief was not available should the individual not enter into possession but pass the property over to his ex-spouse or children. There will no doubt be an emerging debate with HMRC Stamp Taxes over the next few decades as to whether the house builder has not been sufficiently diligent in allowing the individual to make misleading statements in order to obtain the relief or whether such arrangements amount to a conspiracy to defraud HMRC;

- the area of land acquired by the house building company does not exceed the permitted area, which means that the land occupied and enjoyed with the dwelling as its garden or grounds does not exceed an area of 0.5 of a hectare, inclusive of the site of the dwelling, or such larger area as is required for the reasonable enjoyment of the dwelling as a dwelling having regard to its size and character.[200] Given the current heavy dependence of HMRC Stamp Taxes upon the capital gains technical division for advice and support it is expected that adopting the criteria published by the capital gains specialists will ultimately provide a reasonably practical solution to these issues. For these purposes, the permitted area is taken to consist of that part of the land that would be the most suitable for occupation and enjoyment with the dwelling as its garden or grounds if the rest of

---

[199]   It seems that the individuals who dispose of the property need not be identical with those who acquire the new property. It appears to be sufficient that there is one individual who appears in both situations. It would seem, therefore, that a disposal of an existing dwelling by A and B will be eligible for the relief notwithstanding that the acquisition of the new dwelling from the developer is by A and C.

[200]   FA 2003, Sch 6A, para 7(3).

the land were separately occupied.[201] If the condition as to permitted area is not satisfied the chargeable consideration for the acquisition by the house building company is the amount calculated by deducting the market value of the permitted area from the market value of the old dwelling.[202]

Acquisition by property trader

6.71 A separate relief is provided[203] where there is a form of part-exchange of an existing house by a company whether or not it is connected with a new house building company. Whilst the conditions for this relief are in many respects the same as those for acquisition by the house builder and will be applied in the same way as set out above, there are, unfortunately, certain important distinctions and these provide traps for the unwary to the potential benefit of HMRC Stamp Taxes who can be expected to take a strict line on meeting the conditions, given their current practice in these areas. This relief applies:

- where a dwelling including land occupied and enjoyed with the dwelling as its garden or grounds[204] is acquired by way of transfer of a major interest in the dwelling so that the individual must dispose of his entire interest in the existing house to a property trader defined as a company, a limited partnership or a partnership whose members are all either companies or limited liability partnerships that carries on the business of buying and selling dwellings. This relief is, therefore, not available to individuals;[205]

- it is acquired from an individual, whether alone or with other individuals. In consequence, the acquisition of a residential property from trustees who have been allowing a beneficiary to occupy the premises will not be eligible for this relief;

- the individual, whether alone or with other individuals,[206] acquires, whether by way of grant or transfer, a major interest in a new dwelling from a house building company. New dwellings are buildings or part of a building that have been constructed for use as a single dwelling and have not been previously occupied or have been adapted for use as a single dwelling and have not been occupied since the adaptation;[207]

- the individual occupied the old dwelling as his only or main residence at some time in the period of 2 years ending with the date of his acquisition;

- the acquisition is made in the course of a business that consists of or includes acquiring dwellings from individuals who acquire new dwellings from house building companies;

---

[201]   Ibid, Sch 6A, para 7(4).
[202]   Ibid, Sch 6A, para 1(4).
[203]   Ibid, Sch 6A, para 2.
[204]   Ibid, Sch 6A, para 2(2)(e).
[205]   Ibid, Sch 6A, para 8(1).
[206]   It seems that these need not be the same individuals as those who are disposing of the existing dwelling. Provided that there is at least one individual in common between those disposing of the property and those acquiring the new property the relief should be available.
[207]   FA 2003, Sch 6A, para 7(2).

- the acquisition of the new dwelling is from a house building company which is a company that carries on the business of constructing or adapting buildings or parts of buildings for use as dwellings;[208]

- the individual intends to occupy the new dwelling as his only or main residence;

- the property trader does not intend to spend more than £10,000 or 5 per cent of the consideration for the acquisition of the dwelling, whichever is the greater, but subject to an overall maximum of £20,000[209] on the refurbishment of the existing dwelling. 'Refurbishment' means the carrying out of works that enhance or are intended to enhance the value of the dwelling but does not include cleaning or works required solely for the purpose of ensuring that the dwelling meets the minimum safety standards, the cost of which is not, apparently, included in the permitted amount for refurbishment;[210]

- the property trader does not intend to grant a lease or licence of the old dwelling other than a licence to the individual for a period not exceeding 6 months. Care may be needed where there are deferred completions, such as where the transaction for the acquisition of the existing dwelling of the individual is acquired before the new dwelling is available for occupation. This may occur where, for example, there is a divorce arrangement and it is necessary for the existing property to be sold in order to generate the cash to provide appropriate Court order benefits for the maintenance of the former spouse. In this situation the deferred completion may require some form of licence to occupy the property and it is important that this does not exceed 6 months. Essentially, this requires an onward sale of the property with vacant possession;

- the property trader does not intend to permit any of its principals or employees or any persons connected with any of its principals or employees to occupy the old dwelling. This means that a company director or member of a limited liability partnership or a director of a company who is a member of a partnership cannot occupy the premises. If this is done, the relief is clawed back;

- the area of land acquired by the property trader does not exceed, including the site of the dwelling, an area of 0.5 of a hectare or such larger area as is required for the reasonable enjoyment of the dwelling as a dwelling having regard to its size and character.[211] The permitted area is taken to consist of that part of the land that would be the most suitable for occupation and enjoyment of the dwelling as its gardens or grounds if the rest of the land were separately occupied. If the area of land acquired by the property trader exceeds the permitted area the chargeable consideration for the acquisition is taken to be the amount calculated by deducting the market value of the permitted area from the market value of the old dwelling.[212]

This relief is available only to a 'property trader' which is limited to a company or a limited liability partnership or a partnership whose members are all either companies or limited liability partnerships that carry on the business of buying and selling

---

[208] Ibid, Sch 6A, paras 1(4) and 2(4).
[209] Ibid, Sch 6A, para 9(2).
[210] Ibid, Sch 6A, para 9.
[211] Ibid, Sch 6A, para 7(3).
[212] Ibid, Sch 6A, para 2(3).

dwellings.[213] The relief will not be available where there is a limited partnership established under the Limited Partnerships Act 1907 even where all of the partners are themselves bodies corporate, unless HMRC Stamp Taxes are prepared to apply a degree of fiscal transparency.

Forfeiture of relief

6.72   The relief available to a property trader acquiring an existing dwelling in these circumstances is withdrawn[214] if the property trader spends more than the allowed amount upon the refurbishment of the existing dwelling or grants a lease or licence of the old dwelling or permits any of its principals or employees to occupy the dwelling.

Acquisitions from personal representatives

6.73   The acquisition of a dwelling is exempt from stamp duty land tax[215] where:

- it is acquired by way of transfer of a major interest in the dwelling, ie the entire interest must be acquired by a property trader, ie a company, a limited liability partnership or a partnership whose members are all either companies or limited liability partnerships that carries on the business of buying and selling dwellings;[216]

- the acquisition is made in the course of a business that consists of or includes acquiring dwellings from the personal representatives of deceased individuals;

- the acquisition is made from the personal representatives of a deceased individual;

- the deceased individual occupied the dwelling as his only or main residence at some time in the period of 2 years ending with the date of death;

- the property trader does not intend to spend more than £10,000 or 5 per cent of the consideration for the acquisition of the dwelling, whichever is the greater, but subject to an overall maximum of £20,000,[217] on the refurbishment of the dwelling, which means the carrying out of works that enhance or are intended to enhance the value of the dwelling, but does not include cleaning the dwelling or works required solely for the purpose of ensuring that the dwelling meets minimum safety standards;[218]

- the property trader does not intend to grant a lease or licence of the dwelling, but presumably intends to dispose of the entire interest acquired and not hold it as an investment;

- the property trader does not intend any of its principals or employees[219] to occupy the dwelling;

---

213   Ibid, Sch 6A, para 8(1).
214   Ibid, Sch 6A, para 11(2).
215   Ibid, Sch 6A, para 3.
216   Ibid, Sch 6A, para 8(1).
217   Ibid, Sch 6A, para 9(2).
218   Ibid, Sch 6A, para 9(1).
219   Ibid, Sch 6A, para 8(2).

- the area of land acquired, inclusive of the site of the dwelling, occupied and enjoyed with the dwelling as its garden or grounds does not exceed 0.5 of a hectare or such larger area as is required for the reasonable enjoyment of the dwelling as a dwelling having regard to its size and character. The permitted area is taken to consist of that part of the land that would be the most suitable for occupation and enjoyment with the dwelling as its garden or grounds if the rest of the land were separately occupied.[220] Where the area of land acquired exceeds the permitted area, the chargeable consideration for the acquisition is the amount calculated by deducting the market value of the permitted area from the market value of the dwelling.

Forfeiture of relief

6.74 The relief upon the acquisition from personal representatives is withdrawn if the property trader spends more than the allowed maximum on the refurbishment of the dwelling or grants a lease or licence of it or permits any of its principals or employees or any person connected with any of them to occupy the dwelling.[221]

Chain-breaker acquisitions

6.75 The acquisition of an existing dwelling is exempt from stamp duty land tax[222] where:

- it is acquired by way of transfer of a major interest in the dwelling by a property trader which is a company or a limited liability partnership or a partnership whose members are all either companies or limited liability companies that carries on the business of buying and selling dwellings;

- the acquisition is from an individual, whether alone or with other individuals;[223]

- the individual has made arrangements to sell the existing dwelling and to acquire another dwelling, whether new or existing;

- the arrangements to sell the old dwelling fail;

- the acquisition of the old dwelling is made for the purpose of enabling the individual's acquisition of the second dwelling to proceed, whether by way of grant or transfer of a major interest in that dwelling;

- the acquisition is made in the course of a business that consists of or includes the acquisition of dwellings from individuals in such chain-breaking circumstances;

- the individual occupied the old dwelling as his only or main residence some time in the period of 2 years ending with the date of its acquisition;

- the individual intends to occupy the second dwelling as his only or main residence;

---

[220] Ibid, Sch 6A, para 7.
[221] Ibid, Sch 6A, para 11(3).
[222] Ibid, Sch 6A, para 4.
[223] This, like other reliefs, is not available where the acquisition is from trustees who have permitted an individual beneficially to occupy the dwelling in question pursuant to provisions in the trust.

- the property trader does not intend to spend more than £10,000 or 5 per cent of the consideration for the acquisition of the dwelling, whichever is the greater, but subject to a maximum of £20,000 on the refurbishment of the old dwelling, which means the carrying out of works that enhance or are intended to enhance the value of the dwelling but does not include cleaning the dwelling or works required solely for the purpose of ensuring that the dwelling meets minimum safety standards, which are, it seems, additional to these permitted sums;

- the property trader does not intend to grant a lease or licence of the old dwelling, other than a licence to the individual for a period not exceeding 6 months. Essentially he must intend to dispose of the entire interest being acquired;

- the property trader does not intend to permit any of its principals, ie directors of the relevant companies, or employees or any person connected with any of its principals or employees to occupy the old dwelling – if this or the preceding condition is subsequently broken the relief is clawed back;

- the area of land acquired being the land occupied and enjoyed with the dwelling as its garden or grounds does not exceed 0.5 of a hectare, inclusive of the size of the dwelling, or such larger area as is required for the reasonable enjoyment of the dwelling as a dwelling having regard to its size and character. This area is taken to consist of that part of the land that would be the most suitable for occupation and enjoyment of the dwelling as its garden or grounds if the rest of the land is separately occupied. Where the land exceeds the permitted area, a chargeable consideration for the acquisition is taken to be the amount calculated by deducting the market value of the permitted area from the market value of the dwelling.

Forfeiture of relief

6.76   Relief in respect of chain-breaker transactions is withdrawn if the property trader spends more than the allowed maximum on the refurbishment of the old dwelling or grants a lease or licence of the old dwelling or permits any of its employees or principals or any person connected with any of them to occupy the old dwelling.[224]

Relocation of employees

6.77   Two reliefs are available for the acquisition of a dwelling from an employee entered into for the purposes of assisting him in changing the place of his employment.

Acquisition by employer

6.78   The acquisition of a dwelling from an employee is exempt from stamp duty land tax[225] where:

- the acquisition is from an individual, whether alone or with other individuals;

- the acquisition is by his employer;

---

[224]   FA 2003, Sch 6A, para 11(4).
[225]   Ibid, Sch 6A, para 5.

• the acquisition is by way of transfer of a major interest, ie the entirety of the employee's interest, in the dwelling;

• the individual occupied the dwelling as his only or main residence some time in the previous 2 years ending with the date of acquisition;

• the acquisition is made in connection with a change of residence resulting from relocation of employment.[226] Relocation of employment means a change of the individual's place of employment due to his becoming an employee of the employer, an alteration of the duties of his employment with the employer or an alteration of the place where he normally performs his duties. The change of residence results from such relocation if the change is made wholly or mainly to allow the individual to have his residence within a reasonable travelling distance of his new place of employment and his former residence is not within such a reasonable distance;

• the consideration for the acquisition must not exceed the market value of the dwelling. This is likely to prove a major obstacle in practice since the employee will normally require this type of assistance only where his existing dwelling is not selling rapidly at the offer price. There is, therefore, a risk that HMRC Stamp Taxes will challenge the relief if for any reason the subsequent resale of the property is at a price lower than that paid to the employee or there is a delay in selling on the property. In such circumstances, the suggestion that the employee was 'over-paid' for his house will be made and it will be necessary to have very strong contemporaneous evidence of an independent professional nature[227] as to the market value at the time of the acquisition from the employee, plus supporting evidence to indicate that there has been a downturn in the market in the intervening period;

• the area of land occupied and enjoyed with the dwelling as its garden or grounds does not exceed the area, inclusive of the size of the dwelling, of 0.5 of a hectare or such larger area as is required for the reasonable enjoyment of the dwelling as a dwelling having regard to its size and character. This area is taken to consist of that part of the land that would be the most suitable for occupation and enjoyment with the dwelling as a garden or grounds if the rest of the land were separately occupied. Where the area of land exceeds this area, the chargeable consideration for the acquisition is taken to be the amount calculated by deducting the market value of the permitted area from the market value of the dwelling.

Relocation and other companies

6.79   An alternative form of relocation relief is provided[228] where:

• a dwelling;

• is acquired by way of transfer of a major interest in the dwelling;

---

[226]   Whether by a change of employer or a change of location with the same organisation.
[227]   The usual average of three separate estimates should be *prima facie* evidence of the market value but may not be conclusive.
[228]   FA 2003, Sch 6A, para 6.

- from an individual, whether alone or with other individuals;

- by a property trader which is a company, a limited liability partnership or a partnership whose members are all either companies or limited liability partnerships that carries on business of buying and selling dwellings;

and:

- the acquisition is made in the course of a business that consists of or includes acquiring dwellings from individuals in connection with a change of residence resulting from a relocation of employment. The relocation of employment means a change of the individual's place of employment due to his becoming employed by a new employer, an alteration of the duties of his employment or an alteration of the place where he normally performs those duties. The change must be due to the fact that it is made wholly or mainly to allow the individual to have his residence within a reasonable daily travelling distance of his new place of employment and his former residence is not within such a reasonable distance;

- the individual occupied the dwelling as his only or main residence at some time in the period of 2 years ending with the date of acquisition;

- the acquisition is made in connection with a change of residence resulting from relocation of employment;

- the consideration for the acquisition does not exceed the market value of the dwelling. This is likely to prove a major obstacle in practice since the employee will normally require this type of assistance only where his existing dwelling is not selling rapidly at the offer price. There is, therefore, a risk that HMRC Stamp Taxes will challenge the relief if for any reason the subsequent re-sale of the property is at a price lower than that paid to the employee or there is a delay in on-selling the property. In such circumstances, the suggestion that the employee was 'over-paid' for his house will be made and it will be necessary to have very strong contemporaneous evidence of an independent professional nature[229] as to the market value at the time of the acquisition from the employee plus supporting evidence to indicate that there has been a downturn in the market in the intervening period;

- the property trader does not intend to spend more than £10,000 or 5 per cent of the consideration for the acquisition of the dwelling whichever is the greater subject to an overall maximum of £20,000 upon the refurbishment of the dwelling. This includes the carrying out of works that enhance or are intended to enhance the value of the dwelling, but does not include cleaning the dwelling or works required solely for the purpose of ensuring that the dwelling meets minimum safety standards;

- the property trader does not intend to grant a lease or licence of the dwelling other than a licence to the individual for a period not exceeding 6 months. The trader must intend to dispose of the entire interest being acquired;

---

[229] The usual average of three separate estimates should be *prima facie* evidence of the market value but may not be conclusive.

- the property trader does not intend to permit any of its principals or employees or any person connected with any of its principals or employees, such as directors of any companies involved, to occupy the dwelling;

- the area of land to be acquired being the land occupied and enjoyed with the dwelling as its garden or grounds must not exceed an area, inclusive of the site of the dwelling, of 0.5 of a hectare or such larger area as is required for the reasonable enjoyment of the dwelling as a dwelling having regard to its size and character. This area is taken to consist of that part of the land that would be the most suitable for occupation and enjoyment with the dwelling as its garden or grounds if the rest of the land were separately occupied. If the area of land exceeds this extent the chargeable consideration for the acquisition is the amount calculated by deducting the market value of the permitted area from the market value of the dwelling.

Forfeiture of relief

6.80   The clawback relief for property traders in relation to relocation relief is withdrawn if the property trader spends more than the permitted maximum on the refurbishment of the dwelling or grants a lease or licence of it or permits any of its principals or employees or any person connected with any of them to occupy the dwelling. Further returns and payment of the tax are required.[230]

---

[230]   FA 2003, s 81 (as amended).

Chapter 7

LEASES

INTRODUCTION

Transitional arrangements

7.1   The continuing nature of leases and their virtually perpetual involvement in stamp duty land tax has given rise to fundamental transitional issues; namely:

- where a lease is granted on or after 1 December 2003 whether it is subject to stamp duty[1] because it is pursuant to an agreement entered into prior to 1 December 2003. In many cases completion of such agreements remains subject to stamp duty or eligible for stamp duty reliefs such as disadvantaged land notwithstanding the lapse of time[2] and for many transactions such as holding over the lease remains outside stamp duty land tax and not eligible for stamp duty land tax reliefs such as the rent credit on surrenders and regrants;[3] but the more favourable treatment for stamp duty is dependent upon the agreement[4] not having been varied. The transitional relief applies to agreements[5] entered into before any relevant date that were still conditional agreements[6] on 1 December 2003 and it is clear that becoming unconditional after that date is not a 'variation' of the agreement so stamp duty remains the appropriate tax. However, any other form of modification cancels this benefit. In the view of HMRC Stamp Taxes, any variation other than something that is perhaps *de minimis* such as change in the colour of paint, is sufficient to cancel the transitional benefit and bring the lease into stamp duty land tax. In this situation the parties may find it more efficient to complete the agreement for lease and pay the stamp duty and then enter into a deed of variation which may attract little or no stamp duty land tax.[7] In many cases the aggregate of stamp duty plus stamp duty land tax on the variation is likely to be less than the stamp duty land tax on the grant of the lease and may mean that the subsequent events relating to the lease also fall outside the stamp duty land tax regime such as holding over. It also means that there are less onerous compliance obligations and the lease, being a stamp duty lease, will be outside many of the stamp duty land tax provisions such as rent reviews.[8] The position is not wholly beneficial and a stamp duty lease may be at a disadvantage. For example, the rent credit for

---

1   Although it may be related but not linked transaction with stamp duty land tax implications; see FA 2003, Sch 19, paras 7(1), 7A and 8.

2   FA 2003, Sch 19 (as amended); see **Chapter 1**.

3   Ibid, Sch 17A, para 9(1); see **7.193**.

4   Primarily 11 July 2003.

5   But special arrangements apply to options; FA 2003, Sch 19, para 9; as to 'related' as opposed to 'linked' transactions, see para 7.

6   But note cases such as *Eastham v Leigh, London and Provincial Properties Limited* [1971] 2 All ER 887 on the fine but vital line between condition and consideration and permission and obligations; see also *GUS Merchandise v Customs and Excise* [1981] 1 WLR 1309.

7   FA 2003, s 43(3)(d) and Sch 17A, para 15A.

8   But note the abnormal rent increase charges FA 2003, Sch 17A, para 14(4A).

surrenders and regrants[9] is not available for stamp duty leases; surrenders and regrants of such leases should, therefore, be avoided if at all possible; and

- whether, since many of the applications of the stamp duty land tax provisions to leases are of a retrospective[10] nature any changes or transactions relating to a 'stamp duty lease' ie one granted within the previous stamp duty regime, do not give rise to a charge to stamp duty land tax. For example, certain rent reviews relate back to the original return requiring that to be adjusted. In other situations, the tax event in question may be dependent upon certain prior events which are relevant in relation to the computation of the tax on that event.[11] However, because of specific legislation this benefit does not apply to abnormal rent increases notwithstanding that the chargeable amount is dependent upon what was returned as the relevant rent in respect of the grant of the lease or prior reviews.[12]

Those provisions imposing charges upon events affecting leases after their grant such as rent reviews, renewals, holding over and variations may refer to a prior effective date which cannot apply to stamp duty leases or to previous charges to stamp duty land tax. These, *prima facie*, do not affect leases that were subject to stamp duty when granted, including those leases granted on or after 1 December 2003 but protected from stamp duty land tax by the FA 2003, Sch 19. There is no general principle and it seems to be a matter of detailed construction of the particular legislation in each case to provide a context for the potential application of the charging provisions. There may be express provisions, although these can be bizarre, such as the recent changes to abnormal rent increases,[13] some of which apply expressly to leases granted on or after 1 December 2003, regardless of whether they are stamp duty or stamp duty land tax leases,[14] a very arbitrary choice of provisions given that there are no adjustments for the treatment of contingent rents and stamp duty. In other cases the position will have to depend upon what is understood to be the practice from time to time of HMRC Stamp Taxes[15] which, although as usual, lacking in consistency, seems in general to be that in the majority of cases to be the charging provisions of the new regime do not apply to stamp duty leases. This is also not consistent with the legislation which would appear to be applicable to such leases in the absence of contrary express or implied provisions would apply to such leases.

Strategic planning

7.2   Although the rate of tax has been changed from those rates applicable for stamp duty, this has been utilised to increase the tax charge significantly because of the method used to calculate the amount upon which the tax is calculated.[16] In broad terms the

---

9   FA 2003, Sch 17A, para 9(1)(a).
10   Ibid, Sch 17A, paras 7 and 8.
11   Ibid, Sch 17A, paras 14 and 15.
12   Ibid, Sch 17A, paras. 13, 14 and 15.
13   Ibid, Sch 17A, paras 14 and 15; see **7.180**.
14   Ibid, Sch 17A, para 14(4).
15   Such as holding over; see **7.123**.
16   FA 2003, Sch 5. The then Chancellor of the Exchequer when challenged on this charge as a stealth increase claimed that there was no increase in the tax because the rate had been reduced, unsurprisingly totally missing the point, because of lack of his technical competence, that there had been a fundamental change in the calculation of the chargeable consideration from average rent to a form of aggregate rent over the term of the lease. The charge is not upon average rent but the aggregate rent. A similar method was proposed in the discussion document issued by HMRC Stamp Taxes '*Stamp Duties, the Scope for Reform*' in the

stamp tax cost of leases of commercial premises has risen by between 500 and 1000 per cent. Commercial tenants, particularly those involved in the retail trade, need to review their whole strategy of leasing and lease renewals and indeed whether High Street sites are really necessary unless the landlord is prepared to discuss lower rents or other arrangements to mitigate the increased costs imposed upon the tenants. Valuers may need to consider the impact in the next few years of the new tax on valuations as stamp duty leases terminate and the probable impact upon rents as tenants become aware of the stamp tax costs of renewal, especially where VAT is involved with a potential 4 per cent charge,[17] and constitutes a variable rent with all of the related problems[18] and the special charge upon future rents could arise.[19] The basic planning strategy for leases is to operate upon the basis of short-term leases, possibly with options to renew in an attempt to maximise the benefit of the nil rate slice[20] and defer the payment of tax without interest or penalty.[21] Such options are ignored in determining the term of the lease[22] and the short term will mean in many cases that the amount by reference to which the stamp duty land tax is to be charged will fall within the nil rate band; but the existence of specific anti-avoidance provisions, such as successive linked leases[23] and the general anti-avoidance provisions,[24] have to be noted since these may apply to strategies based upon mitigating the tax by a series of short leases where the nil rate slice for the rent is a significant amount.

Background

7.3   Leases are clearly within the charge to stamp duty land tax although the legislation, being modelled and drafted upon the basis of 'sales', may have to be 'stretched' in order to fit leases into the regime and it is important to note that the charge will apply to leases other than tenancies at will.[25] They are estates in land[26] and are treated as major interests[27] with their own charging provisions[28] and reporting obligations.[29] An interest is 'acquired' by the tenant in the general meaning of the words, but a lease will also be included by reason of the express provisions dealing with leases and because of the extension of 'acquired' to include the 'creation' of a chargeable interest.[30]

---

mid-1980s but was instantly rejected as inappropriate, crude and based upon the false premise that a lease at a full rent somehow operated to pass value to the tenant in the same way that a sale or a lease at a premium did. The current policy advisers to HMRC Stamp Taxes have rejected this approach and see the taxation of leases simply as a money raising exercise rather than as a tax on transfers of valuable interests in land. This has given rise to a crude system that involves onerous and expensive compliance and payment obligations where the taxpayer cannot safely reply upon the advice from the so-called 'helpline'.

17   See **5.126**.
18   FA 2003, Sch 17A; ss 51 and 80.
19   Ibid, Sch 17A, para 11 which overrides para 17 thereof.
20   But see successive linked leases **5.72**, **7.102** and **7.105**.
21   See **16.32**.
22   FA 2003, Sch 17A, para 2.
23   Ibid, Sch 17A, para 5.
24   Ibid, ss 75A–75C.
25   Ibid, s 48(2)(c)(i); but entry pursuant to a tenancy at will may be substantial performance (FA 2003, s 44(5) and (6)(b)) but not holding over as a tenant at will (FA 2003, Sch 17A, para 3(1)(b)).
26   Ibid, s 48(1).
27   Ibid, s 117.
28   *J&P Coats Ltd v IRC* [1897] 2 QB 427 to the effect of computational provisions and reliefs clearly indicate a liability to the tax.
29   FA 2003, ss 77 and 77A.
30   Ibid, s 43.

The charges potentially apply throughout the entire life of leases, including any reincarnation arising by reason of exercises of options to extend or renew[31] and holding over, whether under statutory provision or otherwise.[32] The charge begins with agreements for lease, and continues through grants of leases, variations, assignments and termination as well as extensions and renewals will be within the charge and it will be important to bear in mind that an agreement for lease is not the grant of a lease[33] so that there will be multiple reporting and payment obligations[34] where, for example, an agreement for lease is substantially performed and when the lease is formally 'granted'.[35]

'Grant' of leases

7.4   Whilst there is no charge to tax as such on the making of an agreement for lease[36] or the agreement becoming an unconditional actions involving both substantial performance of the of the agreement for lease and the grant of leases will be subject to stamp duty land tax by reference to both premium and rent.[37] The word 'grant' has a technical meaning of long standing[38] and drafting errors in the original legislation that failed to deal with the many differences between agreement for lease and grant and substantial performance of the agreement and grant has produced problems. Amending legislation dealing not only with the immediate problem but using the problem requiring amendment as a springboard for further stealth charges has produced its own set of difficulties that need to be considered in each case where taking possession (including possibly entry to carry out fitting out works) and formal grant do not coincide in time.[39]

Substantial performance and subsequent grant

7.5   The basic position is that a charge arises upon substantial performance with further issues upon completion or grant.[40]

Detailed rules apply to situations where there is substantial performance of an agreement for lease followed by completion by writing between the same parties.[41] It must, however, be noted that for these purposes 'completion' means completion of the land transaction proposed between the same parties in substantial conformity with the contract.[42] Two sets of provisions apply to this situation.[43] However, there are many variations where there are completions between persons other than the parties to the

---

[31]   Ibid, Sch 5, para 6(4).
[32]   See **7.195**.
[33]   *City and Permanent Building Society v Miller* [1952] Ch 840.
[34]   FA 2003, ss 44(8), 51, 77 and 80.
[35]   Ibid, ss 44(8) and 77(2); Sch 17A, para 12A.
[36]   Ibid, s 44(2).
[37]   Ibid, Sch 5, para 9.
[38]   *City and Permanent Building Society v Miller* [1952] Ch 840.
[39]   FA 2003, Sch 17A, para 12A; see **7.25**.
[40]   See further **Chapter 14**.
[41]   FA 2003, s 44(8) and (1)(a) and Sch 17A, para 12A.
[42]   Ibid, s 44(10)(a). The draftsman has failed to appreciate the technical issues arising and the impact of previous practice by HMRC Stamp Taxes where a contract is assigned rather than the property subsold; see **Chapter 6**.
[43]   None of these terms is defined but the general technical (ie non-plain English) meaning of these terms means that the relief may be virtually useless in practice if strictly applied by HMRC Stamp Taxes.

original agreement for lease, such as subsale,[44] and leases are frequently granted to third parties at the direction of the original party.[45] This involves numerous important practical issues:

- the consequences of the grant to a third party on general principles;[46]

- the special relief where leases are granted to third parties;[47] and

- the residual reliefs for leases to third parties.[48]

7.6   In consequence, the arrangements for the grant of a lease involves the following stages:

- the agreement for lease, which is not as such subject to stamp duty land tax;[49]

- substantial performance of the agreement for lease, which is deemed to be a grant of the lease[50] and triggers the basic tax charge;[51]

- the grant of the lease by execution of the deed required by Law of Property Act 1925, s 52,[52] which triggers what HMRC Stamp Taxes consider to be a separate second chargeable transaction with its own notification and payment obligations.[53] This stage requires payment only of any additional tax; there is a form of 'credit' for the stamp duty land tax paid upon the substantial performance of the agreement,[54] but this credit applies only in a limited respect to the rent.[55] This operates on the basis that the notional lease arising on substantial performance is treated as if it were surrendered but it is not expressed to be some form of surrender in consideration of the grant or regrant of a lease so that the deemed surrender does not give rise to a land exchange and it is considered that there is no deemed premium or other value for the transaction.[56] This might be a situation where should HMRC Stamp Taxes seek to charge upon any premium for the actual grant as well as any premium in respect of the deemed grant upon substantial performance the taxpayer could object because he would be subject to tax twice in respect of the same transaction.[57] However, it is provided[58] that, if

---

44 See **Chapter 6**.
45 See, eg, *Att-Gen v Brown* (1849) 3 Exch 662 on which current legislation appears to be based albeit on the basis of a superficial understanding of the issues involved.
46 See further **Chapter 6**.
47 FA 2003, Sch 17A, para 12B; see **6.57** and **7.14**.
48 Ibid, s 45 (as amended); see **Chapter 6**, especially **6.59**.
49 Ibid, s 44(2); but the grant of an option for the entry into an agreement for lease may be taxable initially (FA 2003, s 46) with problems for linked transaction when the option is exercised, the agreement is substantially performance and the lease finally granted.
50 Ibid, Sch 17A, para 12B(2).
51 Ibid, s 44(4); see **7.22** and **7.29**; see also **Chapter 14**.
52 *City Permanent Building Society v Miller* [1952] Ch 840.
53 FA 2003, Sch 17A, para 12A(3) and ss 44(8) and 77; which raises potential problems where the rate of VAT on rent is increased between substantial performance and grant.
54 It does not appear, if the tax is lower at this stage, that there is a right to repayment.
55 The legislation is unclear but the basic interpretation suggests the two stages do not involve mutual consideration so that the deemed surrender is not deemed consideration for the grant etc and the land exchange rules do not apply to impose market value charges upon both the landlord and the tenant; see FA 2003, Sch 17A, paras 9A and 16.
56 Compare FA 2003, Sch 17A, para 16.
57 FA 2003, Sch 10, para 33.
58 Ibid, Sch 17A, para 12A(3)(b).

there were some form of surrender and regrant, this is for the purpose of deeming the arrangement to fall within the provisions providing for a rent credit in respect of the rent that has borne tax upon substantial performance. However, it is specifically provided that the deemed lease upon substantial performance and the actual lease are not to be treated as a single lease.[59] This means that because the terms of the lease etc differ there is likely to be a difference in the calculations of the net present values of the rents at the various stages. The actual lease will be for a shorter period with fewer rental periods to be taken into account but there will be a reduced impact of the discounting. In addition, the rate of VAT charged upon the rent may have increased between substantial performance and completion so that there is an issue whether this produces an additional tax charge. However, it is likely that HMRC Stamp Taxes would take the view that the deemed grant upon substantial performance and the actual grant are linked transactions since they are pursuant to the same agreement[60] and therefore there will be only one nil rate slice in respect of the rent but the deemed lease and the actual lease are not to be treated as a single lease.[61] the effect of this is not to amalgamate the two leases into a single lease, but this would not appear to be intended to treat them as two separate leases with two nil rate slices for the rent.[62] It will be rather perverse if HMRC Stamp Taxes having enacted anti-avoidance legislation were to accept that both the substantial performance and the actual grant qualified or unlinked transactions providing something in the order of £300,000 nil rate slice in respect of the rents;

- further reporting and payment, including retrospective recalculations such as where FA 2003, ss 51, 80 and 90, apply;[63] or

- the tenant holds over or renews or extends the tenancy.

The effect of the lack of finality in relation to stamp duty land tax[64] means that certain aspects of the stamp duty land tax history of the chargeable interest have to be preserved and are the equivalent of documents of title. This is particularly so in the case of leases because it is specifically provided that the assignee of the lease takes over certain of the outstanding tax obligations of the assignor.[65] In addition, the position of an assignee of the lease may be dependent upon the tax position of the assignor such as in relation to certain rent reviews or holding over. An assignee of a lease will need to carry out appropriate due diligence to discover whether there are any of these open or transferable taxation issues and require the assignor to produce appropriate records and information that will enable the assignee to deal with the taxation position that is forced upon him by legislation.[66]

---

[59] Ibid, Sch 17A, para 12A(3) (as amended); but this is not the same as the issue as to whether they are separate chargeable transactions but linked which may affect the nil rate for premiums and rents.
[60] FA 2003, s 108.
[61] Ibid, Sch 17A, para 12A.
[62] This suggests that when determining the 'amount' of the rent previously taxed this may have to make an allowance for the possible double nil rate slice.
[63] See **16.3** and **16.34**.
[64] See **2.14**.
[65] FA 2003, s 81A and Sch 17A, para 12.
[66] See **7.235**.

Payment and reporting[67]

7.7   This regime of deemed grant and regrant produces at least two events requiring payment and notification obligations and, in the view of HMRC Stamp Taxes, two separate chargeable transactions each with their own separate effective dates[68] for the creation of most leases; namely:

- substantial performance of the agreement for lease;[69] and

- the subsequent grant thereof.[70]

This analysis of HMRC Stamp Taxes is supported by other legislation. Certain provisions are based upon the principle of two separate chargeable events,[71] ie the legislation deals with some but not all of the consequences of two separate chargeable transactions as opposed to a two-stage, single chargeable transaction.[72]

It would appear from the legislation that the stamp duty land tax has to be recalculated at the time of the grant by reference to the rent and other (ie non-rent) consideration, ie any premium payable or provided in kind at that time. It appears from the provision[73] that the grant of the lease (ie completion) is a separate notifiable transaction.[74] It seems, therefore, for example, that although the rent review arrangements are to be ignored upon substantial performance of the agreement for lease,[75] if there has been a review and increase of rent in the intervening period or the rate of VAT had been reduced, the increased and reduced rent is taken into account on calculating the second payment of the stamp duty land tax. This does not relieve from the 5-year revision.[76] Specific provisions[77] apply to this situation with a limited credit mechanism; but this credit mechanism applies only in respect of the rent. Other potential problems are not considered in the legislation. For example:

- although the deemed lease is treated as surrendered it is not made clear that the provisions dealing with the retrospective adjustment of the rents during the first 5 years of the term or less if the interval between substantial performance (or deemed grant) and actual grant is less than 5 years; but it seems that the recalculation may have to be made;

---

[67]   In Scotland the line between an agreement for lease and a lease differs from England and special rules apply: FA 2003, Sch 17A, para 19. Where tax has been paid in respect of a land transaction that involves missives of let that constitute a lease and subsequently a lease is granted which either is in conformity with the missives of let or relates to substantially the same property and period as the missives of let, the stamp duty land tax that is chargeable upon the grant of the lease is reduced by the amount of tax paid in respect of the missives of let.

[68]   Since the effective date for any lease is a crucial factor in many of the tax charges affecting that lease the need to know the relevant effective date is a crucial issue for title investigations and tax compliance.

[69]   See FA 2003, s 44 and Sch 17A, para 12A; **7.22**.

[70]   Ibid, Sch 17A, para 12A; *City and Permanent Building Society v Miller* [1952] 2 All ER 621.

[71]   Ibid, Sch 4, para 10 and Sch 17A, para 12A(3) (as amended).

[72]   See **7.25**.

[73]   FA 2003, s 44(8).

[74]   But see also ibid, s 77(2).

[75]   Ibid, Sch 17A, paras 7 and 8.

[76]   Ibid.

[77]   Ibid, Sch 17A, para 12A.

- the relevant date for calculating the term of the lease will have to be revised and become the date of the grant rather than the date of substantial performance.[78] This will fix the term of the lease for the purpose of calculating the net present value of the rent;

- there may have been changes in the rent in the intervening period such as changes in the rate of VAT or the exercise of the option to tax by the landlord.[79] It would seem that these changes will form part of the rent and have to be taken into account in determining the 'rent credit' available for the actual lease;

- the tenant may have commenced building works, which may have been the taking of possession that constituted the act of substantial performance. It is, fortunately, provided that these works will qualify for the exemption in respect of the lease[80] notwithstanding that they precede the effective date for the actual lease. The works will be exempt both in respect of the agreement for lease and the lease itself;

- there are reliefs for rent reviews falling within the last quarter of the first 5 years of the term[81] but these are based upon the fact that the term commencement date does not precede the effective date by more than 3 months. This may be appropriate in relation to substantial performance of the agreement for lease but where there is a significant delay between substantial performance and the grant, such as may occur where there are building obligations and the lease is to be granted only when the building is completed, any backdating of the term commencement date prior to the commencement of the building works will mean that rent reviews that would have fallen outside the 5-year period may now be within the first 5 years of the lease term and so make the rent variable subject to all of the estimation and reporting obligations;

- it seems to be the position that the availability of any relief or exemption from stamp duty land tax has to be separately assessed for both the substantial performance of the agreement for lease and the actual grant of the lease. There may be no automatic carry forward of reliefs from substantial performance to completion nor any automatic carry back of reliefs from completion to substantial performance of the agreement for lease because eligibility is tested at the relevant effective date;[82]

- it would seem that where there are any reliefs available that are subject to clawback such as intra-group transactions or leases to charities, the 3 year clawback period having commenced in relation to substantial performance will be cancelled and will restart by reference to the date of the actual grant;

- the nature of the premiums and/or the rent may have changed in the intervening period.[83] For example, where there is an agreement to grant a headlease that is

---

[78]   See **7.25**.
[79]   But note the problem arising because FA 2003, Sch 4, para 2 stating that exercises of the option to tax after the effective date are to be ignored, but should there be two or more effective dates the exercise of the option to tax may be before the second effective fate. There may also be problems where there are subsequent variations which are chargeable events in their own right with their own effective dates and the exercise of the option to tax precedes the deemed subsequent effective date.
[80]   FA 2003, Sch 4, para 10.
[81]   Ibid, Sch 17A, para 7A.
[82]   See **7.25**.
[83]   However, much of the initial calculation of the tax is provisional and estimated which has to be

subject to an existing lease which is shortly to be subject to a rent review ie the review date has not yet arrived, but the premium for the new headlease is to be adjusted in accordance with the outcome of the rent review, at this stage of substantial performance of the agreement for lease, the premium will be uncertain,[84] however, the rent review may have been initiated at the time when the lease is granted and it may be that in this situation HMRC Stamp Taxes would regard the adjustment in the consideration, although relating to the future outcome of the rent review, as being 'unascertained'. All of the data is available and the final figure is simply awaiting the outcome of negotiations, valuations and so on. In that situation there would have to be an estimate and payment in full of the consideration and any deferral of the uncertain consideration at the time of substantial performance would be cancelled.[85]

7.8   In Scotland, this distinction between an agreement for lease and a lease is less clear, and as usual, English draftsmen use their own terminology with a few minor concessions in the legislation expecting advisers north of the border to translate undiluted both technical and plain English terms into a totally different legal regime with its own specialised technical vocabulary.[86] It is provided that, where stamp duty land tax has been paid in respect of a land transaction that involves missives of let that constitute a lease and subsequently a lease is granted which either is in conformity with the missives of let or relates to substantially the same property and period as the missives to let, the stamp duty land tax chargeable in respect of the grant of the lease is reduced by the amount of stamp duty land tax paid in respect of the missives to let.[87]

7.9   It must not, however, be assumed that there will be only two reporting and payment obligations so that there is the possibility of avoiding or deferring the payment of stamp duty land tax by delaying the 'grant' of the lease. Although certain rent increases linked to the Retail Price Index (RPI) are to be ignored in computing stamp duty land tax,[88] it appears that, if there has been a rent review between the date of substantial performance of the agreement for lease and the date of the grant, the increased rent may need to be included in the second-stage calculation, or take account of the exercise of the option to tax for the purposes of VAT or require a complete readjustment of the first 5 years of the term of the lease for rent reviews during and

---

retrospectively adjusted by reference to subsequent events when the eligibility for relief will be determined by reference to the appropriate effective date ie the like of substantial performance of the agreement for lease and the actual grant of completion. Since the deemed lease arising upon substantial performance of the agreement for lease is deemed to be surrendered, the retrospective adjustments do not apply to the deemed lease which it seems may deprive the tenant/taxpayer of possible reclaims for overpaid tax in respect of the initial estimated self-assessment.

[84]   FA 2003, s 51.

[85]   Ibid, ss 51, 80, 87 and 90.

[86]   The writer once attended a lecture given by Lord Evershed where he extolled uncritically the virtues of the English common law because it had been 'adopted' by many countries in the Empire and other parts of the world; 'some of them adopting it voluntarily'! This view has not been adopted by the draftsman who appears anxious to avoid recognising the existence of basic United Kingdom laws.

[87]   FA 2003, Sch 17A, para 19(1).

[88]   Ibid, Sch 17A, para 7(5). This exclusion of index-linked leases from the variable rent regime is largely pointless since the rents will be subject to VAT in most cases and so variable upon that basis and there is the question of whether any VAT payable upon any RPI increase in the rent is taxable or is to be ignored or is within the restriction to actual VAT as at the effective date pursuant to FA 2003, Sch 4, para 2.

after that date. The provisions on this need to recalculate at 'completion', ie 'grant' and the 5-year review for variable rents[89] have not been harmonised by the amending regulations.[90]

Recalculation of the tax – retrospection

7.10   It appears from the legislation[91] that the recalculation of the tax and additional notification of the transaction is required when the lease is granted[92] and any additional tax is payable. This would seem to require the recalculation by reference to the circumstances such as the rent level applying at the date of the grant, since it seems that this is a new chargeable transaction, the effective date of the transaction for these purposes is not substantial performance of the agreement for lease, if earlier but the actual grant.[93] Unfortunately HMRC Stamp Taxes by, in their view, creating two effective dates, created a situation where the tax consequences can depend upon the frequently arbitrary circumstances of whether and, if so, when the formal lease was executed and delivered.[94]

BASIC ISSUES

7.11   There are several fundamental problems with the structuring of the legislation including the following:

'Leases'

Licence and tenancy at will

7.12   Licences to use or occupy land[95] and tenancies at will are not chargeable interests,[96] which is an important point when dealing with holding over and continuation in occupation after the termination of a lease.[97]

However, licences and tenancies cannot be totally ignored in relation to stamp duty land tax. There is, of course, the fundamental question as to whether the transaction involves a 'lease' or a 'licence' and there is a question whether what is described as a licence such as a mineral licence is, in law, some other form of chargeable interest.[98] Where a transaction involves the granting of a licence, no stamp duty land tax arises in respect of that transaction, but the granting of a licence to enter on to land such as permitting a prospective tenant to enter the land as licensee to fit out, may amount to 'substantial performance' of some other contract giving rise to an effective date and a trigger for tax, reporting and other obligations.[99] It seems that this is a matter that will be governed by

---

89   FA 2003, Sch 17A, paras 7 and 8.
90   Particularly where the lease is granted after the expiration of the fifth year of the deemed lease granted on substantial performance.
91   FA 2003, Sch 17A, para 12A; see also s 44(8)(b) and (10).
92   Ibid, ss 44(8)(a) and 77(2).
93   This appears to be additional to the review after the fifth year; FA 2003, Sch 17A, paras 7 and 8.
94   See **7.25**.
95   It is unclear whether HMRC Stamp Taxes intend to place emphasis on these words and, if so, what restrictions they may seek to impose.
96   FA 2003, s 48(2)(b).
97   Ibid, Sch 17A, paras 3 and 4; see **7.123**.
98   See, for example, *T&E Homes Limited v Robinson* [1979] STC 4351.
99   FA 2003, s 44(5)(b).

the general law. The cases, which are many, on the question of lease or licence will be relevant. Some guidance as to the approach of HMRC Stamp Taxes can be found from a discussion of the detailed issues in *Addiscombe Garden Estates Ltd v Crabbe*.[100] The drafting of the terms of the arrangement will be important and this is likely to give rise to problems were there are 'informal arrangements' ie the parties do not record their arrangements in writing. In the absence of a written instrument it will be difficult to establish the terms of the arrangement. Certain factors are important such as whether there is 'exclusive possession',[101] references to arrangements being non-exclusive is helpful since this avoids the need for the landowner to 'reserve' a right of entry which points to exclusive possession and a tenancy. Although not conclusive a statement that the parties do not intend to create a tenancy may help to tip the balance in borderline cases.[102]

Temporary rights and interest in land

7.13   As part of this exercise 'lease' is defined, at least for England and Wales and Northern Ireland. It is provided[103] that 'lease' means:

- an interest or right in or over land for a term of years (whether fixed or periodic); or

- a tenancy at will[104] or other interest or right in or over land determinable by notice at any time.

It is unclear whether the draftsman intended this as some form of plain English explanation of what is a lease or whether it was intended to apply to any arrangement whereby a chargeable interest in land such as an easement is acquired for a limited period in connection with the development of adjacent land. This would be an interest in land for a term of years. To add to the confusion, elsewhere in defining a major interest in land a lease is defined as a term of years absolute[105] which has longstanding technical meaning.[106] It is, however, unlikely that the payments made for that right, such as royalty arrangements, would be 'rent'[107] and so for the purposes of computation they are governed by the rules relating to periodical payments and not rent,[108] but, in relation to the notification obligations, they are to be treated as leases.[109] Nevertheless, this

---

[100]   [1957] 3 All ER 563.
[101]   See, for example, *Street v Mountford* [1985] 1 AC 809; although it should be noted that this case has been subsequently treated as being limited to residential property and Rent Acts and similar areas of social legislation.
[102]   In commercial situations the position appears to be less in favour of tenancies if the wish of the parties is to leave their relationship as a licence; see *Ogwr v Dykes* [1989] 2 All ER 880 where it is suggested that a specific statement that the parties do not wish to create a tenancy whilst not conclusive may tip the balance in favour of a licence where the factors are otherwise equally balanced; for a supporting principle see *Massey v Crown Life* [1978] 2 All ER 576; *Ready Mixed Concrete (South East) Limited v Minister of Pensions* [1968] 1 All ER 433.
[103]   FA 2003, Sch 17A, para 1.
[104]   However, tenancies at will are not chargeable interests: FA 2003, s 48(2)(c)(i).
[105]   FA 2003, s 117(2)(b).
[106]   See, eg, Law of Property Act 1925, ss 1 and 205(1)(xxvii).
[107]   Note *T&E Homes Limited v Robinson* [1979] STC 4351; *Lowe v JW Ashmore* [1970] 46 TC 597; see **7.98**; but the drafting may be crucial; see **7.138**.
[108]   FA 2003, s 52.
[109]   Ibid, s 77(2).

fundamental question affects the manner of the reporting and the computational rules which apply differently to 'leases' and minor interests.[110]

Grant of leases to third parties[111]

7.14   From time to time leases are granted directly to a third party at the direction of the original party to the agreement for lease such as a lease of a flat purchased from plan or the lease of a development when the buildings have been completed.[112] Specific provisions deal with this situation:[113]

- if the original tenant has substantially performed before he assigns his interest as lessee under the agreement for lease the assignee is taxable in respect of that transaction and the third party is taxable upon the consideration paid to the original tenant;[114] but he is not liable to tax on the future rent;[115]

- if the assignment of the interest under the agreement as lessee takes place before substantial performance of the agreement the original contract is cancelled and replaced by a contract, on statutory terms, between the landlord and the third party.[116] The original tenant is not subject to tax and the assignee is taxable not only upon the consideration paid to the original party but also the consideration provided by that original party including rent, deposit and building works;[117] and

- in any other case there may be a form of subsale relief for the original tenant pursuant to the FA 2003, s 45 (as amended).[118]

Where there is an agreement for lease entered into between A and B, and B assigns his interest[119] to C without the agreement for lease having been substantially performed, the charge applies as if the contract were made between A and C and the consideration included any consideration given for the assignment.[120] It seems that this provision (ie no charge falling upon B) also applies where B assigns the right to call for the lease and then substantially performs the original contract.[121] This may occur where there is a difference in the consideration passing from B to A and that passing from C to B between such as the performance of building obligations by B and the payment of cash by C. Where the agreement for lease has been previously substantially performed by B,

---

[110]   Ibid, s 77A.
[111]   See further **Chapter 6**.
[112]   See the stamp duty equivalent in *Attorney General v Brown* (1849) 3 Exch 662.
[113]   FA 2003, Sch 17A, para 12B.
[114]   Ibid, Sch 17A, para 12B(3).
[115]   Ibid, Sch 17A, para 17.
[116]   Ibid, Sch 17A, para 12B(2).
[117]   Which may be consideration: *Eastham v Leigh, London and Provincial Properties Limited* [1971] 2 All ER 887; there are difficulties in applying the relief pursuant to FA 2003, Sch 4, para 10(2) (as amended).
[118]   See **Chapter 6**.
[119]   See further **Chapter 6**.
[120]   FA 2003, Sch 17A, para 12B(2).
[121]   Where B has entered into arrangements with C for the eventual grant of the lease by A to C before commencing building operations there are complex technical and therefore drafting issues arising from the overlooked problem of whether the building or other works undertaken by B remain part of the consideration for the lease (ie a taxable premium) for the tax on which C may be responsible or are separate non-taxable works between B and C. The omission of those experts 'consulting with' HMRC Stamp Taxes to address these and other obvious problems has left taxpayers with a set of problems of great complexity when seeking to interpret the legislation in a context of self-assessment now that HMRC Stamp Taxes are consistently refusing to give advance clearances because the legislation is more than 2 years old.

the assignment to C is a separate chargeable transaction.[122] This latter will be the usual situation in practice for developers who will frequently take possession of the premises to be demised in order to commence the construction works. In consequence the timing of and structuring of any funding arrangements or onward sales from plan will have a considerable impact upon the tax charge. The person likely to be the principal beneficiary of the new rules will be the speculator who is merely acquiring the agreement for lease to sell on at a profit as quickly as possible.

7.15   This legislation is unbelievably defective, particularly in the context of technical property law and commercial and conveyancing practice. In particular, there is no explanation of what the draftsman or those advising or consulting with him meant by 'assign'. It is frequently the case that the contract between the developer and the third party refers to a power for the developer to direct the grant of the lease to the third party at the appropriate stage in the development. It is questionable where, even if the directions to grant the lease to the third party are in writing,[123] such directions can constitute an assignment.[124] There will also be issues whether these provisions can apply where there are restrictions in the building contract and agreement for lease restricting the ability of the developer or first tenant to deal with the right to the lease until the building works are completed or the agreement for lease provides that the lease is not to be granted until practical completion of the works which raises the question of what, if any, right exists which can be 'assigned' and whether such direction to grant the lease to a third party may not operate as an assignment[125] until the conclusion of the work.

7.16   Also undefined is the expression 'interest as lessee under an agreement for lease'. Frequently this interest will be dependent upon the completion of building works which are likely to be regarded by HMRC Stamp Taxes as part of the consideration (ie taxable premium) for the lease. The third party will not be willing to take a transfer of the right to call for the lease until the building conditions have been fully satisfied and the landlord will insist upon the satisfactory practical completion of the works and payment before recognising the 'assignment'. The right to call for the lease is dependent upon satisfactory conclusion of the works and the third party will not accept a transfer of rights that might expose him to risk of having to carry out the works or have these regarded as taxable consideration as far as he is concerned.

7.17   The problems of multiple taxation are obvious. The third party is taxable upon future rent which would not normally arise[126] And in the case of non-residential property should the rent exceed £1000 there will be no nil rate for the premium.[127] Since he is substituted for the original party, the developer, in the original contract, the third party will, *prima facie*, be taxable upon the whole of the chargeable consideration including works that are not protected by the exemption for works to be constructed on the land to be acquired[128] or where, when taking the assignment, the parties separate the transfer of the lease and the building contract.[129] Also he will be taxable in respect of any deposit paid by the original developer notwithstanding that the chargeable

[122] FA 2003, Sch 17A, para 12B(3).
[123] See Law of Property Act 1925, ss 53 and 136; but there may be issues whether assignment has to be a legal or an equitable assignment, where the question of appropriate notice to the landlord by the third party may be crucial.
[124] See *Attorney General v Brown* (1849) 3 Exch 662.
[125] See *Diplock v Hammond* (1854) 5 De GM & G 320.
[126] FA 2003, Sch 17A, para 17; but see para 11 thereof.
[127] Ibid, Sch 5, paras 9 and 9A.
[128] Ibid, Sch 4, para 10(2) (as amended); see **Chapter 8**.
[129] See *Prudential Assurance Co Ltd v IRC* [1992] STC 863.

consideration includes sums paid to the original tenant which will inevitably include the reimbursement of the deposit. Since this sum will also include reimbursement of the development costs which may be chargeable consideration for the grant of the lease, the third party will be paying tax twice, namely upon the sums paid to the third party and those parts of the payment that represent reimbursement of the taxable consideration under the original agreement unless the payments and cash movements are carefully structured and drafted.[130] Since HMRC Stamp Taxes originally sought to introduce such multiple taxation in the subsale provisions in the Finance Bill 2003 but were forced to back down it is expected that they will exploit the multiple taxation opportunities of these provisions which were not spotted by those groups 'consulting' with HMRC Stamp Taxes.

Residual relief for leases to third parties

7.18   Where the above specific provisions do not apply, the general subsale provisions[131] apply. This can be, for example, because there has not been an 'assignment' of the right, or the right assigned is not the right as lessee pursuant to the agreement.[132] These considerations may apply notwithstanding that there has not been substantial performance so that the general relief pursuant to FA 2003, s 45, may assist the parties mitigating the tax charge, and this general relief may be more generous than the specific relief.

7.19   There is, in consequence, a problem, *inter alia*, where there has been substantial performance of the agreement for lease and the lease is granted to a third party. This can arise, for example, where a developer takes an agreement for lease from the freeholder, carries out building works, enters into an arrangement with a third party for a consideration[133] and directs that the lease be granted directly to the third party. If the developer has, by going on to the land (ie going into possession), substantially performed the contract, he will be liable to stamp duty land tax upon the rent and any other consideration.[134] However, the lease will be granted to a third party and there is a question of how the third party tenant is to be taxed in respect of the premium and/or rent, ie whether the lease is regarded as completing the original contract with the developer (which appears to be unlikely) or completes the contract between the developer and the third party or completes or substantially performs a deemed contract between the landlord and the third party 'assignee'.[135] There does not appear to be any exclusion for the fact that the original tenant (ie the developer) will also be liable in respect of the stamp duty land tax for the rent.[136]

7.20   If the developer has not substantially performed[137] the agreement for lease,[138] but the specific relief does not apply because, for example, the arrangements do not involve the 'assignment of the right to the lease' pursuant to the agreement, the truncated

---

[130]   Compare *George Wimpey Ltd v IRC* [1975] 2 All ER 45.
[131]   FA 2003, s 45; see **Chapter 6**.
[132]   See **Chapter 6**.
[133]   This transaction is not taxable: FA 2003, s 45(2).
[134]   Which may include works to be carried out: ibid, Sch 4, para 10.
[135]   Compare *Attorney General v Brown* (1849) 3 Exch 662.
[136]   FA 2003, s 45, but see ibid, Sch 17A, para 17 for possible exclusions.
[137]   Although this is unlikely to be the case because of taking possession.
[138]   Which will be difficult because of taking possession before commencing the building works which will be necessary to avoid the risk of the costs of such works being taxable consideration; much will depend upon the drafting and structuring of the building arrangements; *Eastham v Leigh, London and Provincial Properties Limited* [1971] 2 All ER 887; *Prudential Assurance Co Ltd v IRC* [1992] STC 863.

subsale provisions pursuant to FA 2003, s 45, will apply. In consequence, the third party will be liable for stamp duty land tax upon the consideration provided to the developer for directing the grant of the lease, and so much of the consideration under the original agreement for lease as remains to be paid or provided.[139] This would appear to mean that the third party is liable for stamp duty land tax upon the rent payable under the lease since this is consideration in the original agreement for lease that remains to be paid or provided.

Agreements for lease

7.21   Entering into an agreement for lease is not, as such, a chargeable transaction.[140] Although there is no tax upon entering into agreements for lease,[141] the grant of an option to enter into or to renew a lease is a chargeable transaction in its own right;[142] but this specific charge on options does not apply to impose a separate charge where a lease contains an option to renew the lease or acquire the reversionary interest. Although there is no charge as such upon the exercise of the option, substantial performance of the agreement for lease arising upon the exercise and the grant of any lease pursuant thereto after its exercise may involve a 'linked transaction'.[143] There is also an issue of whether the existence of an option in a lease is sufficient to link the second lease arising pursuant to its exercise with the original lease, which has to be aggregated and its tax position recalculated.[144]

Substantial performance of agreement for lease

7.22   The stamp duty arrangement of resting upon the agreement for lease[145] in order to avoid a possibly higher charge upon the grant[146] will not work in cases where the rent is 'uncertain'. The attempt to prevent taxpayers from avoiding or delaying the payment of tax by relying solely upon contract and not completing the trigger event for stamp duty land tax depends upon certain actions of the parties, which depend in turn upon the drafting of the completion provisions of the agreement for lease. Except in relation to certain types of rent review or indexation where the rent is uncertain, such as a turnover rent or a review to marker rent, the rules as to uncertain consideration apply[147] so that:

- on the effective date, the stamp duty land tax has to be paid upon the basis of a reasonable estimate;[148] and

---

[139]   FA 2003, s 45(3)(b).
[140]   Ibid, s 44(2).
[141]   Ibid.
[142]   Ibid, s 46.
[143]   Ibid, ss 46(1) and 108; Sch 17A, para 5.
[144]   Ibid, Sch 17A, para 5; see **7.105**.
[145]   Which may benefit from the transitional arrangements pursuant to FA 2003, Sch 19.
[146]   This may, however, mean that title to the new lease cannot be granted and may lead to a higher charge if the lease is ultimately granted to secure registration because of the problem of two effective dates; see **7.25**.
[147]   FA 2003, Sch 5, para 4(2).
[148]   Ibid, s 51(2).

- subsequently, on or before the end of the fifth year of the term of the lease when the rents for all of the first 5 years becomes ascertained,[149] the rent position has to be reviewed taking into account the actual rent paid.[150]

7.23   Postponing the grant of the lease does not alter this and may have adverse effects because the date of the grant (ie completion) is fundamental to many long-term issues.[151] For example, it starts a totally new 5-year period for these purposes, affects the term of the lease, for determining the net present value of the rent and a new discounting regime starts so that rent previously discounted loses that benefit and is brought into charge with a lower discount and may bring VAT into charge[152] or increase the tax charge where the rate of VAT has been increased between substantial performance and the grant[153] and may involve higher rents in the calculation of net present value and there is the immensely complicated issue of how to calculate the rent credit for the new lease[154] provided by FA 2003, Sch 17A, para 12A.[155]

7.24   Where the agreement for lease is substantially performed and subsequently a lease is granted, further obligations to report, self-assess the tax again and pay any additional tax and late payment interest arise.[156] On the other hand, should the agreement for lease be substantially performed but not be completed because the agreements, rescinded or otherwise, are not carried into effect the tax is refunded.[157] Such tax must be reclaimed by amendment.[158]

Two effective dates?[159]

7.25   There was a very obvious fundamental drafting error in the original notification obligations relating to leases which produced a manifest absurdity with two totally different regimes for substantial performance of agreements for lease and the subsequent grant of the lease. However, rather than simply amend the compliance regime and maintain a consistent single effective date for all commercial transactions HMRC Stamp Taxes utilised the opportunity to introduce legislation which introduced a double charge upon leases which causes enormous practical problems and which on the advice of those 'experts' with whom HMRC Stamp Taxes 'consults' will be the basis for introducing a double charge to tax upon almost all transactions, disrupting a reasonably workable system[160] and producing many problems in practice.[161] For example:

---

[149]   However, because HMRC Stamp Taxes have taken the view that changes in the rate of VAT or possible changes therein makes the rent variable it seems that no rent can be ascertained until the expiration of the fifth year of the term; see **7.166**.

[150]   FA 2003, Sch 17A, paras 7 and 8; see **7.147**.

[151]   See **7.25**.

[152]   Although FA 2003, Sch 4, para 2 states that the exercise of the option to tax after the effective date may be ignored this may not apply because it precedes the 'new' or second effective date on the grant of the lease and so its 'actual VAT' at that date.

[153]   There is no suggestion of a refund where the rate of VAT has been reduced in the intervening period.

[154]   See **7.30** and **7.86**.

[155]   See also **7.29**.

[156]   FA 2003, ss 44(8) and 77(2); Sch 17A, para 12A; see **Chapter 14**.

[157]   Ibid, Sch 17A, para 12A(4).

[158]   Ibid, Sch 17A, para 12A(4); see **16.30**.

[159]   See **Chapter 14**.

[160]   Eg this approach will ultimately lead to problems because of FA 2003, s 44(8), which refers to any additional tax being payable, a drafting issue which has given rise to considerable difficulties of statutory interpretation given the extensive provisions dealing with variable consideration.

[161]   Similar issues will arise should HMRC Stamp Taxes press their argument that FA 2003, s 44(9) produces two separate chargeable transactions for transactions not involving leases.

- should there be two effective dates for a lease the availability of any exemption will have to be tested at both dates. There will be no automatic carry over of reliefs from substantial performance to 'completion' because these are separate taxable events. The situation has to be completely reassessed as at completion when the change of circumstances may cancel the relief. Thus, the substantial performance of an agreement for lease may occur at a time when there is no arrangement that the lessee company will cease to be a member of the group. Several years later when the lease is granted that condition may not be satisfied and the relief will not be available;

- timing will also be important for clawback of reliefs. Should a wholly owned subsidiary company substantially perform the agreement for lease at a time when the relief for intra-group transactions is available[162] but the lease is not granted until, say, 5 years later shortly before the sale of the subsidiary company when the title is tidied up, unfortunately the 3-year clawback period will be renewed and the relief will not be available for several obvious reasons;[163]

- although the rent may have been exempt from VAT at substantial performance that tax will be chargeable if the option to tax the rent has been exercised in the intervening period before the second effective date when the lease is granted since notwithstanding the exclusions of the exercise of the option to tax for VAT pursuant to FA 2003, Sch 4, para 2 this will not apply because the exercise of the option to tax will precede the effective date for the grant of the lease and so be actual VAT at the effective date. Since the formal grant of the lease is frequently arbitrary because for most purposes 'an agreement for lease is as good as a lease' this delay can represent a serious risk of extra tax;[164]

- should the rate of VAT chargeable upon the rent have increased or reduced the calculation of the net present value will differ and the rent credit computation will be more complicated but the reduction in the rate of VAT cannot reduce the taxable rent after credit below zero;[165]

- the calculation of the net present value of the rent will be different because the term of the lease on grant will be shorter;[166]

---

[162] FA 2003, Sch 7, Part 1; see **Chapter 12**.

[163] It will not be possible in such circumstances to avoid the clawback or non-availability of the relief because of arrangements for the degrouping of the lessee arguments by not completing the lease prior to the sale so that there is no clawback of the relief available upon substantial performance (because there is a totally new chargeable transaction). The relief may not be available initially, but more importantly a totally new 3-year period will commence notwithstanding that the original clawback period had long expired and HMRC Stamp Taxes have officially accepted that in such circumstances the transaction is not excluded from the relief because it is not 'tax avoidance'. Although by not completing there will not be a clawback event within the prescribed period, the subsequent chargeable transaction arising upon the grant of the lease will be with a company that is no longer a member of the stamp duty land tax group so that the relief is no longer available.

[164] For the next few years it may be possible to claim the benefit of the major transitional provisions for the changeover from stamp duty to stamp duty land tax; but these are not a comprehensive protection: FA 2003, Sch 19.

[165] FA 2003, Sch 17A, paras 12AC, 12A and 9(5).

[166] This point is apparently not widely understood within HMRC Stamp Taxes who have occasionally advised that as no additional tax can arise the taxpayer can present the lease for registration unsupported by a self-certificate (SDLT 65). This is clearly incorrect and it may be prudent to submit a formal return (SDLT 1) and invite an Enquiry to reduce the risk of penalties.

- a new 5-year period for the relief from the rent review provisions will start upon grant and this will almost inevitably refer to a quarter day that is more than 5 years before the first review date;[167]

- there will be a new commencement date for the first 5 years of the term for variable rents,[168] with consequent knock-on effects for all subsequent chargeable transactions for dealings in relation to the lease such as abnormal increase arising upon subsequent rent review or turnover calculations;[169]

- clawback of relief for charities will have a different start date.[170]

7.26   Numerous other potential traps for unwary taxpayers exist, many of which are specific to particular types of transaction; but, unfortunately, the important argument that there is only one chargeable transaction for each commercial arrangement has been undermined by subsequent legislation which makes sense only on the basis that there are two effective dates, ie two separate chargeable transactions.[171] For example:

- the relief for building works carried out after the effective date is expressly extended so that works carried out after the substantial performance of the agreement for lease but before the grant of the lease which would lose the exemption and be a chargeable premium because they are carried out before the effective date for the grant of the lease. Relief is expressly provided in this case; but the important general point is that the relief would not be necessary if there were only one effective date;

- similarly, it is provided that the successive linked leases rules do not apply in this context, ie the deemed lease and the actual lease are not to be treated as a single lease pursuant to FA 2003, Sch 17A, para 5, suggesting that they are not linked which relief presupposes that there are two separate leases.[172] This would not be necessary if the transaction involved the same lease. However, since the possibility of two separate leases opens the possibility of the nil rate slice for the rents it is possible that HMRC Stamp Taxes may wish to argue that the leases are linked on general principles requiring apportionment of the nil rate slice[173] between the two leases. However, the consequential problems arising for such treatment[174] are so complex that it would prove to be unworkable in practice.

7.27   These and other consequential problems of the double chargeable event for leases and the absence of clear relief means that taxpayers may have to develop the provision which states that a taxpayer can resist being taxed twice in respect of the same transaction.[175] However, although the legislation refers to the same 'matter', it is understood that HMRC Stamp Taxes intend to take the position that 'matter' means chargeable transaction and not commercial arrangement so that, in their view, the double tax relief does not apply to relieve the problems produced by the double charge

---

[167]   FA 2003, Sch 17A, para 7A.
[168]   Ibid, Sch 17A, paras 7 and 8.
[169]   Ibid, Sch 17A, paras 14 and 15.
[170]   Ibid, Sch 8, para 2.
[171]   See also **14.7**.
[172]   FA 2003, s 108, Sch 17A, paras 5 and 12A.
[173]   Ibid, Sch 5, para 2.
[174]   See, for example, **7.103**.
[175]   FA 2003, Sch 10, para 33.

upon the same lease.[176] Although there is a single contract there are, on this view, two separate chargeable transactions, ie two 'matters'.

7.28   In practice, the key date will be 'substantial performance'.[177] Particular rules[178] apply to agreements for lease such that the agreement for lease is substantially performed when either of the following events precedes the formal grant of the lease; namely:[179]

- the purchaser takes possession of the whole or substantially the whole of the subject-matter of the contract; or

- a substantial amount of the consideration, ie premium is paid or provided; or

- the first actual payment of rent is made.[180]

If the parties have substantially performed and the agreement is subsequently rescinded or not carried into effect, the tax is refundable although the claim must be made by amendment to the return.[181]

Substantial performance of an agreement for lease is now treated as the 'grant' of the lease.[182]

Subsequent completion

7.29   Where there has been substantial performance of the agreement for lease, the subsequent grant is treated as a surrender of the deemed lease and the grant of a new lease.[183] As the legislation does not refer to the deemed surrender being in consideration of the grant of the deemed new lease, it is considered that the land exchange rules and the exemptions and special rules in relation thereto do not apply so that there is no charge upon the land exchange element and any premium having been taxed upon the deemed grant at substantial performance is not also taxable on the actual grant[184] but there is the benefit of a specific relief that is specialised and potentially complex to the point of unworkability in practice in the form of rent credit mechanism.[185] It is provided[186] that the surrender is considered to be consideration for the purpose of a grant but only for the purposes of determining the rent credit pursuant to para 9. Since it is deemed to be a surrender and regrant for a specific purpose this indicates that the draftsman took the view that the transaction was not to be treated as a surrender and regrant by operation of the legislation for all purposes. In consequence, the transactions will not be land exchanges and it will not be necessary to refer to the conditions of FA 2003, Sch 17A, para 16 for determining whether there is any exemption.

---

[176]   The relief will, of course, be of no real benefit for linked transactions which will undoubtedly be regarded as different 'matters'.

[177]   See further **Chapter 14**.

[178]   FA 2003, s 44(4)–(7).

[179]   Ibid, s 44(7).

[180]   For a further discussion of these issues see **Chapter 14**.

[181]   FA 2003, Sch 17A, para 12A(4).

[182]   Ibid, Sch 17A, para 12A.

[183]   Ibid.

[184]   But note the possible relief pursuant to FA 2003, Sch 17A, para 16; but this merely excludes the value from land exchange rules, it does not cancel any premium.

[185]   FA 2003, Sch 17A, paras 12A, 9 and 16.

[186]   Ibid, Sch 17A, para 12A(3).

Rent credit[187]

7.30 The credit for the rent operates by reducing the rent reserved by the actual lease by the amount of the rent that would have been payable under the deemed lease for the period from the actual grant of the lease until the contractual termination date for the deemed lease. For these purposes the rent taken into account for the old lease is the amount taken into account in determining the stamp duty land tax chargeable in respect of the old lease.[188] This will not be the same as the passing rent.[189] It will be the discounted amount and the assumed rent for all years after the fifth year of the term of the deemed lease. Where there has been a delay between substantial performance and the actual grant the discounting effect will significantly reduce the amount of old 'rent' to be deducted from the new rent increasing the amount of tax payable. Where the rent is variable the new lease rent will have to be calculated on ordinary principles, ie initially on an estimated basis with a revision at some stage during or, more likely where VAT is involved, immediately upon the expiration of the first 5 years which will involve utilising estimated rents for the old lease.[190] Strictly the rent for the old lease should be calculated for each year of the lease but it may be that for a relatively straightforward calculation HMRC Stamp Taxes will accept a computation based upon the deduction of net present value of the two rents, but recalculating the net present value of the old rent from the date of the grant made with that rent being calculated for the discounted amount. The original net present value for the rent of the deemed lease will not be the correct figure to deduct.

Exemptions and reliefs

7.31 A problem has arisen in relation to reliefs for the deemed and actual grants. Since these are, apparently, two separate chargeable transactions there is a question as to the availability of exemptions or reliefs where the circumstances change between the two events. For example, the agreement for lease may be entered into between members of the same group so that substantial performance of the deemed grant would, *prima facie*, be within the relieving provisions of FA 2003, Sch 7, Part 1.[191] However, the lessee may have ceased to be a member of the stamp duty land tax group at the time when the lease is granted.[192] Since the subsequent grant is, on HMRC Stamp Taxes' practice, a separate chargeable transaction it appears to be necessary to determine whether the conditions for the relief can be satisfied at the date of the grant. It seems, therefore, that there is no automatic carry forward of an exemption in relation to substantial performance over to any later completion. It may be that the circumstances have not changed but the relief would be available in relation to the grant by reason of its own circumstances and not by carrying forward the relief from substantial performance. Conversely, it seems that any relief that may be obtained at the time of completion is not to be carried back to the time of substantial performance. For example, A Limited may be a shareholder in a

---

[187] For further issues and problems in related areas see also **7.86** and **7.130**.

[188] HMRC Stamp Taxes have not given formal public statements of whether they intend these provisions to be applied on a strict basis or a simpler process is to be adopted. Given the self-induced pressure to maximise the stamp tax yield in promises to ministers a hard line can be expected.

[189] Which means that documentation relevant to the calculation will now be part of the extra documents of title; see **2.15**.

[190] It appears from this structuring that HMRC Stamp Taxes do not regard the variable rent for the deemed lease as becoming ascertained at nil by reason of the surrender; but the interaction of these various provisions is uncertain.

[191] See **7.251** and **12.60**.

[192] This will need to be at least three years after the date of substantial performance since any relief obtained in respect of substantial performance will be subject to clawback where the degrouping is within the three year period; FA 2003, Sch 7, para 3.

joint venture company, B Limited, but does not have sufficient shares for B Limited to be a member of the same stamp duty land tax group. As part of the joint venture arrangements it may enter into an agreement for lease with B Limited which enters upon the land, commences operations and substantially performs the agreement for lease. Subsequently, but prior to the grant of the lease, A Limited may acquire the interests of the other participants of the joint venture or sufficient of them for B Limited to become a member of the same stamp duty land tax group as A Limited. In these circumstances the grant of the lease would appear to be eligible for relief pursuant to the intra-group provisions.

LEASES – THE CHARGES

7.32   Stamp duty land tax is charged at both of the stages outlined above subject to credit upon both premium and rent in certain cases.[193] Rents are taxed on a different basis from the premiums and may affect assignees of the lease differently[194] and may affect assignees of the lease differently[195] and there are certain provisions dealing with the interaction of the two sets of charges in order to prevent the parties obtaining two nil rate reliefs namely one in respect of the premium and another in respect of the rent. The major interactive provision is that relating to non-residential property to the effect that where the rent exceeds £1000 a year there is no nil rate band for the premium. The tax upon the premium at the rate of 1 per cent will start at £1 and not £150,000.[196] Where there is a variable rent such as a stepped ground rent or one which doubles every 25 years, it seems that HMRC Stamp Taxes regard this as producing a high ascertainable rent which should exceed £1000 albeit many years into the future the nil rate for the premium will not be available.[197] The stamp duty land tax is charged upon the net present value of the rent[198] where this exceeds £125,000 (or the temporary £175,000)[199] for residential property or £150,000 for non-residential or mixed property. The differential treatment of rent and other consideration and, in particular, the rates mean that the structuring of the premium and rent may have significant taxation consequences. For example, whilst variations of rent are not surrenders and regrants[200] many other forms of variation can operate as a surrender and regrant.[201] Special rules apply to variations of rent[202] but a surrender and grant of a new lease or regrant of a lease of the same premises is, *prima facie*, a land exchange[203] but the charge upon the market values of the lease surrender and the new lease granted[204] is relieved in certain cases provided that various conditions are satisfied.[205] although the introduction of stamp duty land tax has been designed to produce a dramatic increase in the tax upon rents, these are substantially more tax efficient than premiums. In general, a 7 year lease for a premium of £7,000,000 will attract tax of £280,000; the same lease for a rent of

---

[193]   See, for example, FA 2003, Sch 17A, paras 12A, 9, 9A and 16.
[194]   Ibid, s 81A; Sch 17A, para 12.
[195]   Ibid.
[196]   Ibid, Sch 5, paras 9 and 9A.
[197]   See the views of HMRC Stamp Taxes at **5.24**.
[198]   See **7.108**.
[199]   Expected to terminate on 31 December 2009.
[200]   *Gable Construction v IRC* [1968] 1 WLR 1426.
[201]   *Friends Provident Life Office v British Railways Board* [1996] 1 All ER 336.
[202]   See, for example, FA 2003, Sch 17A, paras 7, 8, 13, 14 and 15.
[203]   FA 2003, s 47.
[204]   Ibid, Sch 4, para 5.
[205]   Ibid, Sch 17A, para 16.

£1,100,000 per annum[206] will attract tax upon a significantly lower sum, namely the discounted net present value of £7,700,000 (approximately £5,500,000) less £150,000 at the lower rate of 1 per cent (approximately £53,500).[207] Although the tax upon premiums and rent is calculated upon different bases the tax liability is an aggregate of the two taxes which although individually shown in different places in the land transaction return have to be combined when showing the tax chargeable and payable.[208] This seems odd since the tax payable boxes precede the rent calculation provisions in the structure of the current returns form.

There are also numerous cases of tax calculated by reference to market value plus the net present value of the rent. Although the parties will frequently be required to prepare their self-assessment upon the basis of a reasonable estimate of future market rent the market value charges do not apply to such rent, the market value charge is based upon a notional premium which has to be determined by reference to the actual terms of the lease, including, *inter alia*, the actual rent.[209]

'Premiums' – consideration other than 'rent'

7.33   The consideration for the grant of a lease other than any 'rent' (hereinafter for convenience called the 'premium') is defined basically in terms of chargeable consideration so that the rules considered elsewhere for determining both what is and the level of chargeable consideration will apply to substantial performance agreements for lease and the grant of the lease.[210] This means that a wide range of considerations will be subject to stamp duty land tax notwithstanding that these were not subject to traditional stamp duty.[211] Many routine transactions have become taxable. Moreover, the general principles for the computation of the tax apply so that where the new lease is part of a land exchange transaction not within any of the reliefs available the stamp duty land tax will be charged on the market value of the lease. Additionally, the special basis of open market cost will apply to many building leases[212] unless the transaction is carefully organised to take the benefit of the relief from such charges.

Linked leases

7.34   There are various situations where transactions involving leases may be linked transactions.[213] These include:

---

[206]   The slightly higher rent is to provide a form of interest for the deferred payment; compare *Vestey v IRC* [1965] 1 All ER 917.

[207]   However, such a route for mitigating the tax needs to be carefully considered because of the rule that the highest rent during the first 5 years provides the basis for calculating the net present value of the rent for the remainder of the term. Such front-end loading can actually increase the overall tax charge and the tenant will almost certainly be subject to the inconvenience of multiple reporting because the rent is likely to be subject to VAT and so variable FA 2003, Sch 17A, paras 7 and 8; see **7.147**.

[208]   But see FA 2003, Sch 5, paras 2(5) and (6), 9 and 9A. For shared ownership arrangements see FA 2003, Sch 9, para 2(4A).

[209]   See **Chapter 27**.

[210]   See mainly **Chapter 5**.

[211]   For an important illustration of situations where new tax charges arise see *Yaxley v Gotts* [1999] 2 WLR 1217 where there was no written agreement and the consideration was the performance of services. FA 2003, s 42(2)(a) and Sch 4, paras 10 and 11.

[212]   Note *Eastham v Leigh, London and Provincial Properties Limited* [1971] 2 All ER 887 and *GUS Merchandise v Customs and Excise* [1981] 1 WLR 1309 on what appears to be a condition is in law the performance of the consideration.

[213]   FA 2003, s 108.

- the situation where there are leases of several different properties that are granted between the same parties or connected persons as a result of a single commercial negotiation. This can arise where members of the same family agree to take several leases of industrial units in a single development;[214]

- leases linked or unlinked by legislation. There may be deemed linked transactions such as arise in relation to certain variations of leases;[215] but in some situations the transactions may not be treated as linked;[216] and

- there may be a renewal of an existing lease relating to the same or substantially the same premises and this may be a successive linked lease.[217]

Where the transaction, ie the grant of the lease for a rent or a variation of a lease, is a linked transaction with another transaction such as the grant of several leases of different premises for the purposes of FA 2003, s 55, then no account is taken of the rent in determining the relevant consideration[218] but the premium payments, including any deemed premium, are aggregated for the purposes of determining the rate of tax. This is subject to the £1000 for non-residential property restricting the nil rate premium,[219] which will, it seems, involve the aggregate ground rents for all linked leases;[220] whether the lower rates apply is determined solely by the aggregate premiums; but there are special rules for allocating the nil rate slice to the rents of the various linked leases.[221]

7.35 A premium includes everything other than rent[222] that falls within the general definition of 'chargeable consideration' contained primarily in FA 2003, Sch 4. It is a fundamental question as to what is consideration for the lease[223]. As *Eastham v Leigh, London and Provincial Properties Limited*[224] clearly shows it is not always obvious what is 'consideration'. In that case what was described as a 'condition' was in fact the consideration for the grant of the lease.[225]

7.36 Although Sch 4 is drafted in terms of sales, it also applies for the computation of the tax upon a lease premium. In consequence, a premium will include:

- VAT actually chargeable on any lump sums payable.[226] It seems that HMRC Stamp Taxes at present do not regard the rare possibility of a subsequent effective exercise of the option to tax ie an exercise after the effective date or completion for the purposes of stamp duty land tax producing an actual charge to VAT since FA 2003, Sch 4, para 2, excludes from the tax calculation VAT arising from certain exercises of the option to tax after the effective date[227] as making the consideration variable pursuant to FA 2003, s 51, but their reaction to the change

---

214 See **5.113** and **7.102**.
215 FA 2003, Sch 17, para 14(5)(b).
216 Ibid, Sch 17A, para 12A(3).
217 Ibid, Sch 17A, para 5.
218 Ibid, Sch 5, para 2(5) and (6) (as amended).
219 Ibid, Sch 5, para 9A which may affect notification ss 77 and 77A.
220 Including the retrospective effect of successive linked leases even where these relate to different premises.
221 FA 2003, Sch 5, para 2(5) and (6).
222 Ibid, Sch 5, paras 9 and 9A.
223 See **5.90** and **5.96**.
224 [1971] 2 All ER 887.
225 See also *GUS Merchandise v Customs and Excise* [1981] 1 WLR 1309.
226 FA 2003, Sch 4, para 2.
227 See **5.126**.

of rates of VAT and rents suggests that there may be possible attacks on this basis particularly where there are several effective dates since the exercise of the option to tax may precede some of the later chargeable events,[228] although it seems that the exercise of the option to tax is not necessarily a chargeable event in its own right;[229]

• consideration in money or money's worth, including surrenders of existing leases or sales and leaseback arrangements.[230] These are land exchanges[231] but there are significant reliefs albeit of a highly restricted nature;[232]

• leases granted in satisfaction of indebtedness;[233]

• leases granted subject to the assumption or deemed assumption of liability in respect of a mortgage;

• leases granted where there are related obligations[234] to carry out works, whether upon the leased land or other land;[235] or possibly conditions in the planning permission that might involve the assumption of a liability to pay money[236] or to carry out works which could constitute chargeable consideration for the acquisition of the chargeable interest.[237] There are exemptions for works to be carried out by the tenant upon the land to be acquired[238] and there are exclusions for the giving of covenants to repair and maintain property as long as any sums paid in respect thereof.[239] Since this refers to both 'repair' and 'maintain' it may be possible to argue that the covenant to put the property into a good state of repair although consideration for the grant of the lease is not taxable works but is exempt by reason of these provisions. In relation to stamp duty HMRC Stamp Taxes published Statements[240] which stated that where the VAT in respect of rent was not reserved as rent as such it would be treated as a premium payable periodically. However, this point was rarely taken in practice and where the parties included the VAT in their 'PD form' as rent and paid tax upon it as rent, which usually produced a lower figure than being taxed as a premium, they were not challenged by HMRC Stamp Taxes. It would seem that the same argument is available to HMRC Stamp Taxes in relation to stamp duty land tax. Since the VAT in relation to rent will not be 'rent' but will be a sum separately apportioned and therefore outside the definition of 'rent' HMRC Stamp Taxes could raise the point that it is consideration other than rent and therefore a premium payable periodically. However, it seems that this point is not taken in practice and taxes

228 See, for example, **5.220**, **7.9** and **7.23**.
229 Should HMRC Stamp Taxes take the position that the exercise of the option to tax for VAT is a chargeable increase in the rent pursuant to the terms of the lease or otherwise (note FA 2003, Sch 17A, para 13). It may, of itself, produce an abnormal increase in the rent for FA 2003, Sch 17A, paras 13–15.
230 FA 2003, Sch 4, para 1, but see Sch 17A, para 16.
231 Ibid, s 47; Sch 4, para 5.
232 Ibid, Sch 17A, para 16; see **7.224**.
233 Ibid, Sch 4, para 8.
234 *Eastham v Leigh, London and Provincial Properties Limited* [1971] 2 All ER 887.
235 FA 2003, Sch 4, para 10; see **7.70** and **Chapter 8**.
236 Ibid, Sch 4, para 8 (as amended).
237 See **7.70** and **8.9**.
238 FA 2003, Sch 4, para 10.
239 Ibid, Sch 17A, para 10(1).
240 Statements of Practice 6/91 and 11/91. The first version 6/91 was withdrawn because the top management and policy section of the then Stamp Office were required to change their policy by the lowest grade of collection employees whi disagreed with the policy.

accepted and returns do not appear to have been challenged simply on the grounds that the VAT was treated and computed as if it were rent. The Guidance Note in relation to the impact of the reduction of the rate of VAT[241] simply refers, rather ambiguously, to situations where the VAT is part of the rent. This could mean situations where the rent is a single sum including the VAT or it could mean that where the VAT is treated as rent notwithstanding it is separately apportioned. There is, therefore, no indication in the Guidance Note as to when VAT is rent and crucially whether the apparent current practice[242] is likely to change;

- the provision of services;[243]

- sums payable 'periodically'.[244] This would appear to apply to VAT payable in respect of the rent where this is not reserved as part of the rent but is separately apportioned.[245] This treatment of reserved VAT as a premium is consistent with the former Statements of Practice of the Stamp Office but at present is rarely taken in practice. Where this arises the 'premium' is a crude capitalisation of the periodical payment. It is the amount payable over the life of the lease or 12 years whichever is the shorter. For example, should VAT be treated as a periodical premium in the case of a 7 year lease, the tax will be charged upon 7 years VAT without any discounting. On the other hand, where the lease is for 25 years the charge will be upon 12 years VAT, again without any discounting. There are likely to be practical problems as to whether payments are premiums or rent and drafting will be crucial;[246]

- leases granted with related loans,[247] but there is no refund of tax if the loans are subsequently repaid.[248]

Particular problems for premiums

7.37 There are, however, the same types of problem for lease premiums as for sales in relation to the following situations, and many of these obligations are dealt with initially by the original tenant on a provisional, estimated basis with obligations to deal with the open position subsequent including, it seems, not merely reporting the transaction but also the payment of tax,[249] many of which, by statute, pass to the assignee.[250]

---

[241] See HMRC Guidance Note 30 Jan 1009 STI 2009, p 460.

[242] In the case of widely known practices unsupported by written public statements senior officers of HMRC Stamp Taxes have repudiated land standing operating practices as 'mistakes' which do not bind them and stating HMRC Stamp Taxes do not have 'practices'.

[243] FA 2003, Sch 4, para 11.

[244] Ibid, s 52; see *Quietlece Ltd v IRC* [1984] STC 95.

[245] See **7.138**, **7.64**, **5.125** and **5.126**.

[246] See **5.121**.

[247] FA 2003, Sch 17A, para 18A; see **7.95**.

[248] Ibid, s 80(4A).

[249] Although the assignee of the lease (including the assignee of the assignee etc) takes over the open or provisional tax position of the original tenant it is not clear whether he is liable for penalties should there be relevant defects in the original self-assessment returns or whether he is on risk for a 21-year discovery assessment because the initial return prepared by the original tenant was negligent because he relied upon advice from the so-called helpline as to the treatment of rent reviews which advice is usually incorrect. It seems arguable that the penalties remain with the person signing the declaration, but since the substantive liabilities pass to the assignee he is tainted by the original tenant's negligence or fraud. The assignee is personally liable not only for any tax underpaid by the original tenant and the late payment interest thereon, which cannot be mitigated. As there is no statutory indemnity assignees of leases will undoubtedly rely upon their advisers to obtain the necessary indemnities and other contractual protection.

[250] FA 2003, s 81A; Sch 17A, para 12.

'Backdated rent'

7.38   Sums paid as 'rent' for periods prior to the grant of the lease are not rent but, presumably, are to be taxed as a premium[251] This may increase the charge to tax because of the 4 per cent rate applicable to premiums and there is no discounting. The charge to tax upon premiums will probably be higher than the charge upon the rent because the rent will, at least, qualify for the benefit of discounting. Moreover, a charge of 1 per cent upon the amount of rent for part of a year may be significantly lower than the charge upon the premium particularly where the rent is significant. In addition, in relation to leases of non-residential property where the rent for which a special relief may be available exceeds £1000[252] there is no nil rate band for the premium.[253] This means that even a small amount of 'backdated rent' will attract tax at the rate of 1 per cent without the benefit of the nil rate slice for rent except in holding over situations.[254] It may also affect the reporting obligation because it influences the amount to be included for the purposes of the nil rate threshold.[255] Notwithstanding that the amount of 'backdated rent' is small, the lease will not be within the nil rate threshold relief and may, subject to the £40,000 threshold, be notifiable notwithstanding it is a lease for a term not exceeding 7 years.[256]

7.39   It seems that substantial performance of an agreement for lease is a deemed grant so that only the 'rent' paid prior to the effective date is not rent,[257] but this may arise in relation to the holding over or continuation in occupation after the expiration of the contractual term where a new lease may be granted backdated to the contractual termination date although various reliefs and rent credits may be available.[258] Obviously, this cannot apply to 'rent' actually paid since actual payment of the rent will be substantial performance of the agreement for lease.[259] It must refer to sums paid and described as rent for the period prior to effective date but this may include rent paid after substantial performance of the agreement for lease and the term commencement date refers to a date prior to the grant because of the two effective dates for leases.[260]

7.40   However, it has to be noted that there are, in the intention of HMRC Stamp Taxes, two 'effective dates' in relation to many leases.[261] There will be an effective date in respect of substantial performance of the agreement for lease creating a deemed grant and a different effective date in respect of the formal grant of the lease.[262] Obviously, as indicated, in relation to substantial performance of the agreement for lease any sums paid as 'rent' prior to that date will be a potential premium.[263] This, however, leaves open the question of whether sums paid as 'rent' in the period between the deemed

---

[251]   Ibid, Sch 5, para 1A but note the reliefs in FA 2003, Sch 17A, paras 9 and 9A.
[252]   On calculating the £1000 see **5.24**.
[253]   FA 2003, Sch 5, paras 9 and 9A.
[254]   Ibid, Sch 17A, para 9A; see **7.39** and **7.195**.
[255]   Ibid, s 77.
[256]   Ibid, ss 77 and 77A.
[257]   And this applies notwithstanding that the agreement for lease is conditional. There will, therefore, be potential risks of attack upon Enquiry or discovery by HMRC Stamp Taxes, where a developer involved in a building or s 106 planning arrangement where the lease is dependent upon satisfactory practical completion of the works, that any fees paid for the period during which he is allowed onto the land albeit as licensee are 'rent', ie deemed premium for the lease.
[258]   See FA 2003, Sch 17A, paras 9 and 9A.
[259]   Ibid, s 44(7).
[260]   See **7.25**.
[261]   See s 44.
[262]   FA 2003, Sch 17A, para 12A; see **7.25**.
[263]   This is a different problem for the calculation required when dealing with rent after the effective date. In

grant arising upon substantial performance and the actual grant are rent for the deemed lease or premium for the actual lease or ate taxed twice. However, it should be noted that where FA 2003, Sch 17A, para 9A applies there is a backdating of the effective date for the lease which appears to overcome some of these problems since the payments were made or deemed to be made after the relevant date; but since this relief appears to be designed to deal with certain types of holding over rather than actual or deemed surrenders and regrants[264] and applies to the grant of leases only by express statutory provisions.[265] It is far from obvious that this treatment of previous rent could apply to the situation of rent paid between deemed grant and actual grant because there will not have been a taxable continuation in occupation after the expiration of a lease as required by para 9A.

7.41   As regards the latter effective date upon actual grant, rent paid pursuant to the substantially performed agreement for lease will be consideration paid for the grant of the lease prior to the effective date. In consequence, there is a *prima facie* situation of sums taxed as rent for the purposes of the deemed lease will be potential premium for the actual lease. In relation to the double charge[266] on substantial performance and the grant of the lease there is a credit or reduction in the rent for the new lease in relation to the rent subject to charge to tax in respect of the deemed lease.[267]

7.42   Moreover, this credit or relief only applies in respect of the 'overlap period' ie the period representing the unexpired term of the deemed lease after the effective date for the grant of the lease. It does not specifically deal with the situation between the effective date in relation to substantial performance and the date of the actual grant. This applies only in relation to the rent payable after the date of the grant of the lease. Any sums described as 'rent' for the new lease in respect of the occupation prior to the date of the grant will, *prima facie*, subject to FA 2003, Sch 17A, para 9A where there has been a holding over, be taxed as a premium for which no credit is allowable notwithstanding that the sums have been taxed as actual rent for the deemed lease arising upon substantial performance of the agreement for lease.[268] There will also be a potential problem where there is a holding over by operation of law[269] and, in particular, pursuant to the Landlord and Tenant Act 1954[270] where there will be a deemed extension and the existing lease for periods of 1 year which will overlap in whole or in part with the term for any new lease granted.[271] This will be crucial in contexts such as holding over where the sums in question are taxed as 'rent' for the statutorily enlarged term of the expired lease.[272] In these situations where there is some form of holding over or continuation in occupation while the parties negotiate for a new lease to replace the one where the contractual term has expired, the new lease will be 'backdated' in the sense that its term commencement date will be referred to as being the time of the

---

broad terms FA 2003, Sch 17A, para 9 deals with the rent credit for future rent. Para 9A deals with the past namely rent paid in respect of the holding over period and whether this is to be taxed as a premium pursuant to FA 2003, Sch 5, para 1A.

[264]   On which see FA 2003, Sch 17A, para 9(1)(c).
[265]   Ibid, Sch 17A, para 12A(3)(b).
[266]   Ibid, Sch 17A, para 12A.
[267]   Ibid, Sch 17A, para 12A(3)(b).
[268]   Where there is a holding over the rent payable will have been taxed on a yearly basis. Where the new lease is granted part way through the year the credit is available only for that part of the year prior to the grant, there is no credit available for rent paid after grant notwithstanding that this rent has already borne tax as rent for the holding over.
[269]   FA 2003, Sch 17A, para 3.
[270]   Specifically referred to in FA 2003, Sch 17A, para 9.
[271]   FA 2003, Sch 17A, para 9 which also applies for the future overlap for surrenders and regrants.
[272]   FA 2003, Sch 17A, para 3.

expiration of the previous lease. Sums paid in respect of the intervening period may well be described in the lease as 'rent' as consideration for the grant of the lease.[273] In some situations there is a rent credit available and it is important that any sums paid as consideration for the grant of the lease are treated as 'rent' for these purposes; but such rent credit is normally only for a period after the grant of the new lease; it does not deal with sums paid in respect of the intermediate period outside para 9A that would appear to be within the definition of 'premium'. The backdated rent does, therefore, not appear to qualify for credit unless para 9A applies to reconvert the deemed premium into 'rent'. It is a sum taxed as rent in respect of the holding over period where there is a deemed extension of the expired lease but is a premium for the grant of the new lease.

Possible relief

7.43 There may have been a limited attempt to deal with this problem in FA 2003, Sch 17A, para 9A but this applies only for holding over not the initial grant. This provides that where a tenant has 'continued in occupation' after the expiration of a lease and is granted a new lease which is backdated, there is a rent credit payable in certain circumstances in respect of the period prior to the grant of the new lease. This provision applies[274] where a tenant under a lease continues in occupation after the contractual termination date and is subsequently granted a new lease of the same or substantially the same premises. The term of the new lease must be expressed to begin on or immediately after the contractual termination date utilisation of other term commencement dates intended to deal with the problems of rent reviews during the last quarter of the fifth year of the term[275] could mean that this treatment of the backdated or interim rents as not available. It is, however, unclear whether this will apply to rent paid in respect of the holding over of leases where there is not a holding over where the rent is subject to stamp duty land tax. The reference to taxed rent may mean that this treatment of the deemed premium as rent does not apply to rent for holding over leases within the stamp duty regime or stamp duty land tax contracted out of the Landlord and Tenant Act 1954. The scope of the provision has to be carefully considered even before the possible effect is investigated. This provision has to be considered in the context of other provisions but it seems to apply to any situation where there is a 'continuation in occupation' whether or not by operation of law. It seems that where there is a holding over by operation of law, there will be the statutory extension of the lease[276] so that rent in respect of the interim period between the contractual termination date and the actual grant of the new lease or substantial performance of the agreement to grant the new lease will be subject to tax.[277] Rent payable in such situations may be eligible for rent credit for periods after the grant of the new lease.[278] These provisions do not deal with the 'backdated rent'. However, the rent credit may not be available[279] where the holding over is not within the prescribed circumstances. Assuming that continuation in occupation includes holding over where the parties are, for example, contracted out of the Landlord and Tenant Act 1954 there will be no rent credit because the rent for the holding over will not have been 'previously taxed', but the backdating

[273] But there may be technical issues for debate with HMRC Stamp Taxes as to whether past consideration which is essentially not consideration in general law can be chargeable consideration; see **3.42**.

[274] FA 2003, Sch 17A, para 9A(1).

[275] Ibid, Sch 17A, para 7A.

[276] Ibid, Sch 17A, paras 3 and 4.

[277] Rent paid in respect of periods after the grant of the new lease are dealt with primarily by FA 2003, Sch 17A, para 9.

[278] FA 2003, Sch 17A, para 9(1).

[279] Ibid, Sch 17A, para 19.

may mean that the backdated rent is taxed as rent and not subject to higher tax as a deemed premium[280] and having the benefit of the nil rate slice and discounting.

7.44   In addition, it is required that the grant of the new lease must be of the same or substantially the same premises. There is the usual problem of deciding whether the premises are 'substantially the same'.[281] There is no indication in the legislation as to how 'substantial' the identification must be.[282] Importantly, the term of the new lease must begin on or immediately after the contractual termination date of the expired lease. This means that any backdating of the term commencement date to any other date will mean that the provision falls outside these provisions. In consequence, the treatment provided for by para 9A will not apply and the rent payable in respect of the period between the term commencement date and the effective date for the new lease will remain taxable as a premium and in the absence of there being some holding over by operation of law or similar arrangement falling within para 9 there will be no credit against the future rent in respect of the deemed premium for the backdated rent. This will be an important consideration when the parties are considering the term commencement date for the new lease. In practice, parties frequently relate the new lease back to the expiration of the old lease but where the backdating is to a date more than 3 months (broadly the immediately preceding quarter day) before the actual grant of the lease then the relief for rent reviews in the final quarter of the first 5 years of the term will not apply and the parties may find that rent reviews fall within the first 5 years with all the complications that ensue.[283] There are, therefore, not always benefits in backdating to the contractual termination date of the previous lease.

The new lease

7.45   Where the new lease falls within the provisions of FA 2003, Sch 17A, para 9A, and is suitably backdated to immediately after the contractual termination date of the original lease, the term of the new lease is treated for the purposes of stamp duty land tax as beginning on the date on which it is expressed to begin.[284] This would appear to have the effect that sums paid in respect of the interim period between the contractual termination date (or the new term commencement date) will be sums paid after the effective date for the new lease and so retain their character as rent. This would appear to override the provision[285] treating such backdated rent as a premium. In addition, a form of rent credit is available in that rent payable under the new lease in respect of any period falling after the contractual termination date of the old lease and before the date on which the new lease is actually granted is reduced by the amount of taxable rent that is payable in respect of the interim period otherwise than under the new lease.[286] This is a further limitation upon the provision. Rent payable in respect of the interim period would normally be subject to stamp duty land tax only where there is some form of holding over or continuation by operation of law so that there is a deemed extension or growth in the term of the lease.[287]

---

[280]   Ibid, Sch 5, para 1A.
[281]   See **7.85**.
[282]   A similar problem arises in relation to the rent credit mechanism in respect of surrenders and regrants pursuant to FA 2003, Sch 17A, para 9(1)(a); see **7.223**.
[283]   FA 2003, Sch 17A, para 7A.
[284]   Ibid, Sch 17A, para 9A(2).
[285]   Ibid, Sch 5, para 1A.
[286]   Ibid, Sch 17A, para 9A.
[287]   Ibid, Sch 17A, paras 3 and 4; see **7.115**.

7.46 The effect of this provision appears to be that whenever a tenant continues in occupation, whether pursuant to provisions such as the Landlord and Tenant Act 1954 or otherwise, he can avoid the charge to tax upon the rent for the interim period as a premium by backdating any new lease provided that this backdating of the term commencement date covers the whole of the interim period from the contractual termination date of the old lease to the actual grant of the new lease although it is a far from obvious construction of the legislation that is applies where the rent for the period between the termination of the original lease and the grant of the new lease was not subject to stamp duty land tax. This seems to be a somewhat cumbersome provision for reducing the possible charge to tax upon a premium but there will be little or no credit in respect of the taxation upon the backdated rent because unless the parties are holding over by operation of law such as pursuant to the Landlord and Tenant Act 1954, there will be no taxable rent in respect of the interim period.

Variable premiums including contingent consideration

7.47 The three types of variable consideration considered earlier[288] apply equally to lease premiums, at least as regards the characterisation thereof, although as indicated, the consequences may differ because of the statutory shifting of the liability to the assignee.[289]

It must, however, be noted that the definitions of the various types of variable premium may change in their application to the circumstances of any particular transaction because of the facts as they exist at any particular time and there are possibly two effective dates for the lease. This may affect the method by which the initial tax calculation is made and the manner with which the tax has to be dealt with and these may change as the transaction develops. For example, the parties may enter into an agreement for lease and for a building to be constructed under which the premium is to be fixed by reference to the net lettable area of the building (as defined in the agreement). Since the building works have not commenced these, if part of the chargeable consideration,[290] will be an uncertain payment ie it depends totally upon future events. Subsequently, the tenant may substantially perform the agreement after the building has been constructed by entering upon the premises in order to fit out.[291] At this stage the building, having been completed but not measured, the premium will be 'unascertained' because it relates to an existing factual situation. However, it seems that the change in the nature of the variable consideration may not be an issue in practice since the premium will be taxable as at the effective date for the substantial performance of the agreement for lease and there is, notwithstanding FA 2003, Sch 17A, para 12A, no further charge upon the premium at the effective date for the grant of the lease.[292]

7.48 Similarly, there may be an arrangement between a freeholder and a developer to grant a lease as and when the development is completed and the premium is to be some form of multiple of the value of the rent to be received from subletting. In this situation the entry upon the land in order to commence the development by the developer would, *prima facie*, be substantial performance and trigger a tax event. At this stage the premium being linked to circumstances arising after the development has taken place

[288] Ibid, s 51; see **5.187**.
[289] Ibid, s 81A and Sch 17A, para 12.
[290] Note *Prudential Assurance Co Ltd v IRC* [1992] STC 863; see **Chapter 8**.
[291] FA 2003, s 44; see **Chapter 14** and note the issues relating to fitting out costs as a potential premium pursuant to FA 2003, Sch 4, para 10; see **7.76**.
[292] But note the possible effect of FA 2003, s 44(8) in this context.

would be uncertain should the premium become chargeable at this stage rather than on substantial performance. However, it may be that when the lease is finally granted after practical completion, the formula for determining the amount to be paid by way of additional premium is related solely to past events or current market values. In these circumstances, it will cease to be 'uncertain' and will be 'unascertained'.

7.49 There may also be difficult questions of analysis, which relate largely to the right to defer the payment, where an overriding lease is granted subject to and with the benefit of an existing lease where there is an imminent rent review and the price to be paid for the grant of the new lease is dependent upon the outcome of the rent review. If the review date has not arrived then the additional premium will be uncertain. On the other hand, if the review date has passed and the review may be in progress, there will be a difficult question of analysis of the legislation as to whether, at this stage, because the outcome of the rent review depends upon past events, the additional payment is unascertained rather than uncertain. This turns upon a very difficult argument as to the difference between uncertain and unascertained. Uncertain consideration is linked to future events whereas unascertained is related to past events. There is a question as to whether a rent review by reference to a previous date is 'unascertained' because all of the facts are available but items which lack a precise and simple value, such as market rents for void premises and which depend upon the outcome of negotiations, have not been agreed or whether a third party arrangement, such as a premium by a head landlord to the freeholder, is uncertain because it depends upon the future agreements of the parties to the rent review. Interest, penalties and the right to defer payment will turn upon the answers to these very difficult questions.

7.50 The general rules for variable consideration[293] apply to lease premiums but with the additional problem that the tax issues have to be assumed by third parties without the benefit of statutory protection, indemnities or even the power to require information.[294] Where the consideration for the grant of the lease other than rent is 'unascertained' and has not been finally agreed,[295] because the premium is variable, the rent or premium will have to be returned and the stamp duty land tax paid initially upon the basis of a reasonable estimate by the tenant of what he expects to pay, with an obligation to file a further land transaction return (SDLT 1) and self-assess again when the figures are finally agreed.[296] If the original estimate was correct no further tax will be payable. If the original land transaction return prepared upon the estimated basis has proved to be too high there will be an entitlement to a tax refund together with interest. However, if the estimated figures are below the final figures there will be an obligation to pay further tax and this obligation will carry interest upon the additional tax from 30 days after the filing of the original return.[297] Also, if the figures included in the original estimated return are significantly below the final figures, HMRC Stamp Taxes may take the view that the return was prepared negligently or possibly fraudulently and seek to

---

[293] FA 2003, ss 51 and 80; see **5.187** and **Chapter 16**.

[294] Ibid, s 81A; Sch 17A, para 12.

[295] This may involve an insoluble circularity in many cases because the development costs will usually include an adjustment for stamp taxes. As a minimum level problem there may be a considerable delay whilst the stamp duty land tax is finally determined because payments are variable. However, the routine problem is that the stamp duty land tax cannot be determined until the costs have been determined but such costs cannot be determined until the stamp duty land tax has been determined. In addition, because of the provisional nature of much stamp duty land tax even if the parties have agreed a figure this remains open to challenge by discovery assessment by HMRC Stamp Taxes. It seems that if the parties amend the contract by subscribing an agreed amount this could resolve the problem; but the situation is probably best addressed by suitable drafting in the original contract.

[296] FA 2003, s 80.

[297] Ibid, s 80.

impose appropriate penalties. In the circumstances, however, it should be possible to produce a reasonably close estimate to the final figures because the information is available and the parties may have commenced their negotiations and other related activities as to valuation and measurement within the 30 days before the return and payment need to be made. There is, however, no power to apply to postpone the payment of this amount or any additional sum pursuant to FA 2003, s 90; in consequence, interest upon any further stamp duty land tax payable will begin to accrue from 30 days after the effective date.[298] There will, therefore, be strong pressure upon the parties' advisers to reach agreement on the figure as soon as possible.

7.51 Fortunately, in the case of contingent or uncertain premiums, unlike variable rents,[299] and unascertained premiums, it is possible in most cases[300] to apply for the deferment of the estimated tax upon the provisional element in the chargeable premium.[301] However, in addition to the problems that arise when dealing with such variable consideration[302] and the need for the original purchaser to provide some form of exit strategy in order to enable him to dispose of the property without leaving outstanding a long-term contractual and related stamp duty land tax liability,[303] there is the complication that pursuant to statute[304] the open tax position of the original tenant or any assignees in relation to leases of the assignor in relation to any contingent variable premium is passed to the assignee who is the current holder of the lease. This is a particularly acute problem since it provides that anything that, prior to the effective date for the assignment, was an obligation of the assignor shall, if the event giving rise to the taxation event occurs after the effective date of the assignment, be done 'instead' by or in relation to the assignee. This would seem, possibly, to relieve the assignor from liability in respect of the tax and move the position over to the assignee.[305] This raises an interesting question of statutory interpretation as to whether the provision operates as some form of statutory release from liability for the tax for the assignor as regards his tax liability notwithstanding that he may remain liable as a matter of contract or whether any assignee or successor in title is subject only to a secondary tax liability ie he is liable only if the original taxpayer should default. The legislation is, however, not consistent with the secondary liability theory so that the successor in title is primarily liable for the tax.

7.52 There is a complete transfer of the open tax position of the original tenant or any successor in title who is the assignor of the lease since it is provided that so far as necessary for giving effect to these provisions anything previously done by or in relation to the assignor shall be treated as if it had been done by or in relation to the assignee.[306] This raises the question as to whether if anything that has been done by the assignor is technically incorrect and would expose the assignor to penalties and interest the consequences pass to the assignee.[307] If the assignor has failed to make a return or has delivered an incorrect return it is an open question as to whether HMRC Stamp Taxes

---

[298]   Ibid, s 87.
[299]   See **7.147**.
[300]   But not where the premium is 'unascertained'; FA 2003, ss 15 and 90; Stamp Duty Land Tax (Administration) Regulations 2003, SI 2003/2837, Part 4.
[301]   See **Chapter 16**.
[302]   FA 2003, s 80; Stamp Duty Land Tax (Administration) Regulations 2003, SI 2003/2837, Part 4.
[303]   See **5.206**.
[304]   FA 2003, Sch 17A, para 12.
[305]   Ibid, Sch 17A, para 12(1).
[306]   Ibid, Sch 17A, para 12(2) including s 81A.
[307]   It is unclear whether FA 2003, Sch 17A, para 12 operates as some form of statutory novation so that the original party or any subsequent assignee who in turn assigns the lease is released by statute from those obligations; but compare the 'statutory novation' pursuant to FA 2003, Sch 17A, para 12A.

may seek to recover the penalties from the assignee because the actions of the assignor are deemed to be the actions of the assignee.[308] Fortunately, in certain situations the assignment of an existing lease is deemed to be the grant of a new lease.[309] This applies largely where the lease was exempt when granted because of certain specific reliefs.[310] In these situations the movement of responsibility for outstanding taxation issues does not apply to the assignee because he is for tax purposes acquiring a new lease not taking over the old lease with its outstanding tax obligations.[311]

7.53 Certain of the wider issues concerned with the due diligence, warranties and indemnities required in relation to assignments of leases are considered elsewhere[312] but in relation to variable premiums a potential assignee of a lease will be required to carry out a detailed investigation as to whether the contractual liabilities run with the lease and whether he is responsible for taking over the taxation liability of the assignor or whether there has been an adequate exit strategy or escape route that enables the assignor to cancel his taxation liability so that should any liability arise in respect of the assignment this will be a new event under the control of the assignee. It is, obviously, important to avoid any situation where the assignee is taking over the responsibilities of the assignor in circumstances where he has had no control over the negotiations and although it may be possible to protect his position by means of warranties and indemnities this may be theoretical rather than real because warranties are only worthwhile if the relevant party can subsequently be found and has the resources to meet the liability.

Contingent consideration

7.54 Where the lease premium includes a contingent element, ie a fixed sum payable if a particular event happens or does not happen, the stamp duty land tax has to be calculated upon the basis that the contingent sum is payable,[313] with a refund if the contingency does not happen.[314] For example, if a lease is granted for a basic premium plus a fixed additional sum if planning permission is obtained, the stamp duty land tax is calculated initially upon the total sum potentially payable, but it may be that such tax upon such contingent element can be deferred until the event happens or it becomes certain that it cannot happen.[315] Notwithstanding that the tax on the deferred payment can be postponed, it is still taken into account for determining:

- the rate of tax on the basic premium; and

- whether there has been substantial performance by payment of the premium.[316]

These provisions also apply where there is a basic consideration but this is to be reduced by a fixed amount if an event does or does not happen in the future.

---

[308] FA 2003, Sch 17A, para 12.
[309] Ibid, Sch 17A, para 11 (as amended).
[310] Ibid, Sch 17A, para 11(3).
[311] Ibid, Sch 17A, para 12(3).
[312] See **2.13**, **12.3**, **5.189** and **7.242**.
[313] FA 2003, s 51.
[314] Ibid, s 80, plus the possibility of paying by instalments pursuant to ibid, ss 90 and 91; which may affect the interest provisions for late payment: ibid, s 87(5).
[315] Ibid, s 90; Stamp Duty Land Tax (Administration) Regulations 2003, SI 2003/2837, Part 4.
[316] Ibid, s 44; see **Chapter 14**.

It is a consequence of this approach that the maximum potential consideration is payable that the rate will be fixed by reference to that amount notwithstanding that any sum initially payable is below the £500,000 threshold. In this situation where there is, for example, an agreement to grant a lease for a premium of £140,000 but with a contingent payment of £500,000 the entry for the chargeable consideration on the land transaction return (SDLT 1) has to be the aggregate sum of £640,000. This means that the tax payable in respect of the premium will be calculated at the rate of 4 per cent notwithstanding that the additional payment and the tax thereon have been deferred. In this situation where it becomes clear that the relevant event will not happen so that the additional consideration will not be payable the taxpayer will be entitled not merely to cancel the arrangements relating to the postponed tax but also reclaim tax at the higher rate in respect of the sums actually paid.[317] Such repayment may be eligible for an interest supplement. However, in the converse situation where the land transaction return has not dealt properly with the deferred consideration and the additional payment has not been drawn to the attention of HMRC Stamp Taxes so that the tax thereon will not have been properly deferred, should the events happen and the additional payment be made, additional tax will be required and any interest and penalties will accrue from the expiration of 30 days from the effective date, not from 30 days after the relevant event producing the liability to make the additional payment arises.[318]

Unascertained consideration[319]

7.55　Where at the relevant effective date the premium for the grant of the lease is dependent upon past events not future events it is 'unascertained'. For example, this may arise where the premium depends upon the costs of the development or where a building has been constructed and is to be let for a premium linked to the square footage of the building but it has yet to be measured, the arrangements are dependent upon past events and are therefore 'unascertained'. It is simply a matter of the parties producing the relevant data and agreeing the amounts. A similar situation may arise where there is a grant of an overriding lease which is subject to an existing lease which is in the process of having the rent reviewed and the premium for the reversion is to be adjusted dependent upon the outcome of the rent review.

7.56　n these situations of 'unascertained' premium the taxpayer must make a reasonable estimate of the amount that he expects to pay by way of premium when the relevant information has been processed and the price finally agreed. The legislation requires this estimate to be made[320] and it is an incorrect return simply to ignore the problem or to make a return only on the basis of any initial price.

7.57　The return has to be upon the basis of the estimated price and the tax is calculated accordingly. This will fix the rate and may have indications for any questions of substantial performance as to whether the payment of the initial premium represents

---

[317] Ibid, Sch 11A; see **16.26** and **17.26**.
[318] It is an open question whether the provisions of FA 2003, Sch 17A, para 12 passing the liability to deal with such situations to the assignee of the lease also carry with it the penalties that the assignor would have had to pay to the assignee.
[319] FA 2003, s 51(3).
[320] Ibid, s 51.

substantial performance in the context of 90 per cent of the chargeable consideration. There is no power to defer any part of the tax in respect of such unascertained consideration.[321]

7.58 Within 30 days of the consideration being finally agreed the taxpayer must make a further return setting out the final consideration. If the original estimate should be correct there will be no further tax to pay. If the original estimate proves excessive there will be an entitlement to a refund of the tax. If the original estimate was below the final figure there will be additional tax to pay together with interest.[322]

Uncertain consideration[323]

7.59 Where the lease premium is 'uncertain' in whole or in part, ie the amount payable and/or the time of payment depends upon future events,[324] the stamp duty land tax has to be paid upon the basis of a 'reasonable estimate' of what will ultimately be payable, with an obligation to report and pay tax (or claim a refund) as the instalments become payable.[325] This applies, for example, where the premium is a percentage of the proceeds of sale of the property in due course or is a sum linked to the actual square footage or net lettable area of the building to be constructed after the effective date as actually completed. Other situations will be involved such as where a lease is granted to a tenant upon the basis that if, during the currency of the tenancy or over a specified period, the tenant or a successor in title obtains particular types of planning permission additional consideration would be paid by reference to the increase in the market value of the lease at the time. Similarly, there may be issues where a lease is granted to a developer and there is to be a lump sum payable by reference to some amount that is calculated by reference to the 'capitalised value' of the rents received from the letting of the development when completed.[326] In these situations the initial land transaction return for the grant of the lease has to be prepared on the basis that the premium ie non-rent element includes a reasonable estimate in respect of any potential additional payment.[327] As discussed elsewhere[328] this reasonable estimate has, in the view of HMRC Stamp Taxes, to be prepared upon the basis that the relevant event has happened[329] or will happen and the amount that it is estimated will arise in consequence. It is not a proper preparation of the land transaction return to act upon the basis that it is most unlikely that the event will happen. In such a case the return will have been prepared upon a negligent basis and HMRC Stamp Taxes will, potentially, have a 21 year period to issue a discovery assessment and reopen the transaction.[330]

---

[321] Ibid, s 90.

[322] Ibid, ss 80, 87 and 90.

[323] Ibid, ss 51, 80 and 90.

[324] Ibid, s 51(3).

[325] Ibid, s 80, plus the possibility of paying by instalments pursuant to ibid, s 90.

[326] The issue may be more complicated because there may be time limits imposed and questions of how voids or non-lettings of part are to be treated. Care having been taken to avoid, so far as possible, the construction and other costs forming part of the taxable premium; FA 2003, Sch 4, para 10; see **Chapter 8**.

[327] This estimated figure may also be relevant in determining whether there has been substantial performance by payment of 90 per cent of the price (FA 2003, s 44) which HMRC Stamp Taxes appear to regard as 90 per cent of the estimated price not 90 per cent of any basis or initial price; see **Chapter 14**.

[328] See **5.187**.

[329] Which is specifically the case for contingent sums (FA 2003, s 51(1)). Other variable payments in the uncertain category are not so specifically covered; see s 51(2).

[330] FA 2003, Sch 10, para 31; *Langham v Veltema* [2004] STC 544.

Postponed payment of tax

7.60   In such a situation it may be possible to defer the payment of the tax.[331] It is necessary to pay tax upon the basic or initial consideration and it is not possible to defer and reclaim tax already paid on any contingent or uncertain consideration.[332] The tax upon such consideration will be fixed by reference to the total estimated amount of the premium. This may operate to increase the rate in respect of the initial consideration. For example, where there is a premium for £120,000 but which may, by reason of the arrangement, be estimated to increase to £750,000 the tax will be chargeable upon the actual premium at the rate of 4 per cent notwithstanding that, on its own, it is below the 1 per cent threshold. Tax on the uncertain element in the premium may be deferred where it may be payable more than 6 months after the effective date,[333] but it has to be noted that what may be uncertain consideration as at the initial effective date may be unascertained consideration as at completion when different rules for computation, payment and compliance apply although it is unclear whether its status at the date of the grant is relevant.[334] If the relevant event happens or any part of the additional consideration becomes ascertained there will be an obligation to file a land transaction return and to make a payment of any tax that is due including payment in respect of which the tax has been deferred. If the tax has been properly deferred then interest and penalties will not arise provided that the payment is made and the return filed within 30 days after the happening of the trigger event. Where the tax has not been declared on the initial land transaction return and deferred the payment will have to be made upfront before the filing date and any penalties and interests that will be calculated by reference to 30 days after the effective date for the initial transaction.

7.61   The structuring of the additional consideration can be important and may affect whether there is a single obligation to file in due course or whether there are separate obligations to pay and file in respect of individual events on numerous occasions.[335] Where tax has been paid on any initial or previous payments at a higher rate than would normally apply to a total consideration of that amount then it becomes clear that the additional consideration will not become payable the taxpayer will be entitled to claim a refund of the tax in respect of the higher rate of tax together with interest.

Instalment premiums[336]

7.62   Notwithstanding that the premium is payable by instalments, stamp duty land tax is payable upon the full amount payable.[337] There is no discount for the delay in payment, whether or not interest is payable upon the instalments. It may be that, particular where HMRC Stamp Taxes suspect rightly or wrongly that tax avoidance is involved, they may seek to challenge periodical payments as rent or premium depending upon which analysis produces the higher tax charge.

---

[331]   Ibid, ss 80, 87, 90, Stamp Duty Land Tax (Administration) Regulations 2003, SI 2003/2837, Part 4.
[332]   Ibid, s 90.
[333]   Ibid, ss 80 and 90; Stamp Duty Land Tax (Administration) Regulations 2003, SI 2003/2837, Part 4; see **16.34**.
[334]   See **7.47**.
[335]   See **5.194**.
[336]   Ibid, Sch 4, para 3; see further **5.118**.
[337]   Ibid, Sch 4, para 3; but the rules differ where the payments are not instalments but are periodic payments; FA 2003, s 52; see **5.123**.

Premiums and periodical payments[338]

7.63 Where the premium consists wholly or partly of sums payable periodically ie periodical payments,[339] other than rent,[340] the stamp duty land tax is payable upon the aggregate amount of the periodical payments, without discounting over the life of the lease, provided that the term of the lease is for a definite term not exceeding 12 years.[341] However, where the lease is for an indefinite period, or a definite period exceeding 12 years, for life or in perpetuity,[342] the taxable amount is limited to the 12 highest annual payments[343] which presumably takes into account payments that may have to be made if the arrangement will or may exceed the 12 year period.[344] Where the payments are variable, linking to the RPI is ignored,[345] but in other cases, in addition to the need to make a reasonable estimate of the 12 highest annual payments,[346] the taxpayer (ie the tenant) must make a estimate of the amounts to be payable in the relevant 12-month periods for the 12 years.[347] There is, however, no power to defer payment of the tax.[348] In these circumstances there is no obligation to adjust the original estimate should the actual payments differ from the estimated figure so that there is no need to file further returns as and when each payment is ascertained and made,[349] but if the actual payments subsequently differ significantly from the reasonable estimates in the land transaction return, the taxpayer and his advisers are likely to face allegations of negligence or even fraud in preparing the return, with consequent interest and penalties.

Value Added Tax as a periodical premium

7.64 One particularly important area of what is a 'periodical payment' as a lease premium in practice is VAT, where this is not reserved as part of the rent or additional rent. The question whether it is to be taxed as a periodical premium could significantly affect the stamp duty land tax liability[350] and if to be treated as 'rent' whether the rent is variable because of possible changes in the rate of VAT.[351]

---

[338] Ibid, s 52; see further **5.120**.

[339] Which differ from a fixed sum payable by instalments FA 2003, s 51 and Sch 4, para 3; see **5.118** and **5.123**.

[340] Ibid, s 52(6); there will, of course, be difficult questions of interpretation as to when periodical payments or instalments are rent; see, eg *Quietlece Ltd v IRC* [1984] STC 95. Considerable amounts of stamp duty land tax may turn upon the analysis, particularly as, in general, rents are more heavily taxed than premiums, especially if the restriction to 12 years' payments applies; FA 2003, s 52(2). Fortunately, the legislation makes this a question of drafting see **5.123**; also many payments of a periodical nature such as service charges are exempt from all charges to stamp duty land tax; see **7.137**.

[341] This may be a problem for life annuities and similar arrangements because there is not necessarily a cessation or termination of the arrangements since the annuitant may survive the 12 year period, but may not so survive and the legislation precludes the utilisation of actuarial and similar principles; see **10.48**.

[342] Which is unlikely as leases must have a definite or ascertainable date for termination in order to be valid: see *Lace v Chantler* [1944] 1 All ER 305.

[343] FA 2003, s 52(1) and (2).

[344] See **5.120**.

[345] FA 2003, s 52(3).

[346] Which are computed by reference to 12-monthly periods which are not necessarily the same as the periods specified for computing the payments: ibid, s 52(4).

[347] FA 2003, ss 51 and 52(5).

[348] Ibid, s 52(7)(b).

[349] Ibid, s 52(7)(a), displacing s 80 thereof.

[350] See **7.36** and **7.64**; the absence of practical problems and experience of the views of HMRC Stamp Taxes in this area may be because these issues are not being properly addressed when completing land transaction returns and hitherto these have not been randomly selected for Enquiry and properly investigated by HMRC Stamp Taxes.

[351] See **7.151**.

7.65   Numerous issues arise in relation to VAT and stamp duty land tax in the case of leases. There are questions as to whether changes in the rate of VAT or the exercise of the option to tax in relation to rent can affect the computation or give rise to a tax charge.[352] In relation to situations where the VAT is consideration other than rent and therefore not 'rent'; namely:

• the situation where a lease is granted for a premium at a time when the transaction would be exempt as far as VAT is concerned but the option to tax is exercised subsequently. This is a particular problem because of the difference between the effective date or dates for the purposes of stamp duty land tax and the tax point for VAT. These may not be identical and there are clearly likely to be issues because of the view of HMRC Stamp Taxes that there are two effective dates in relation to leases namely substantial performance of the agreement for lease and the subsequent actual grant;[353] and

• how VAT in respect of rent is to be treated where this is not reserved as part of the rent but is separately apportioned or described as additional rent.[354] HMRC Stamp Taxes officially indicated many years ago[355] that in certain situations the VAT payable in respect of rent but not part of the rent will be taxable as a periodical premium. The same legislation, or at least legislation in the same words, has been carried over into stamp duty land tax. The question is under what circumstances, if any, HMRC Stamp Taxes will regard such VAT as a premium payable periodically rather than as rent.[356] In this context HMRC Stamp Taxes have created a problem for themselves. It seems that where the parties separately reserve service charges 'as additional rent' this is regarded as making the service charge not rent (FA 2003, Sch 17A, para 6) and so taken out of charge (FA 2003, Sch 17A, para 10); but it seems that they may regard VAT reserved as 'additional rent' as being 'rent'. The obvious inconsistency in this position means that the risk of the periodical premium argument cannot be totally ignored.

7.66   Stamp duty land tax is payable upon any VAT actually chargeable,[357] other than VAT arising pursuant to the exercise of the option to tax after the effective date. Where the transaction is exempt for VAT purposes at the effective date of the transaction, the possibility that the option to tax might be subsequently exercised is ignored for lump sum payments which cannot become subject to VAT; but it seems that the existence of the option to tax may make even rent exempt from VAT variable but this applies only to the effective date for the particular transaction. While the subsequent exercise of the option to tax so that VAT becomes payable may not relate back to the original effective date there are several issues arising. There will be:

• a question whether the exercise of the option to tax is, of itself, an increase in the rent;

---

[352]   See, for example, **7.151**, **7.157** and **7.189**.
[353]   FA 2003, Sch 17A, para 12A.
[354]   Ibid, Sch 17A, para 6.
[355]   Statements of Practices SP 6/91; and SP 11/91.
[356]   The recent Guidance Note 30 January 2009, STI 2009, p 460 on the interaction of VAT and stamp duty land tax deals with the situation where the VAT is part of the rent but does not indicate when HMRC Stamp Taxes regard the VAT as being rent.
[357]   FA 2003, Sch 4, para 2; see further **5.126**.

- whether the exercise of the option to tax is within the lease pursuant to FA 2003, Sch 17A, para 7 or takes effect outside the lease pursuant to paras 13 and 14 thereof which affects how the immediate event is to be treated and may have long-term implications;[358] and

- actual VAT will have become payable prior to any subsequent chargeable transaction.

It seems that, in the view of HMRC Stamp Taxes, the actual exercise of the option to tax after the effective date is to be regarded as a variation of the rent, but it is questionable whether this is consistent with FA 2003, Sch 4, para 2, excluding the option to tax, but this should not, in general, affect the amount of the premium so that, in general, ignored and there is not such a 'variation' of the lease as to require a fresh notification and payment of additional tax in respect of the premium should it be exercised.[359]

7.67 Different issues arise in relation to changes in the rate of VAT or the exercise of the option to tax the rent[360] where this is regarded as part of the rent. The question of the impact of the option to tax upon rent in the context of FA 2003, Sch 4, para 2, is intriguing. It may be that it was inserted as clarification of the abandonment of a former stamp duty practice. It was previously the argument of HMRC Stamp Taxes that in the case of rent the existence of an option to tax by the landlord was a potential *prima facie* sum within the alleged contingency principle. In consequence, they sought tax upon the VAT that might arise upon an exempt rent if the option to tax were exercised. It seems that, at least, this principle has been abandoned by para 2. However, it does have larger implications considered elsewhere such as whether the subsequent exercise of the option to tax by the landlord is a taxable increase in the rent.[361] It would, however, seem that the effect of the exclusion of the option to tax from para 2 is that where the VAT is reserved separately from the rent and so constitutes a periodical premium the subsequent exercise of the tax is not brought into account in dealing with the premium.[362] However, as regards the variable rent regime since the revision of the assessment of the initial provisional return relates back to the original effective date any exercise of the option to tax the rent during the first 5 years will be ignored unless it is a chargeable event in its own right as an increase outside the lease.[363] The exercise will, of course, precede the effective date for any subsequent chargeable transaction. This leaves a circular problem of whether the VAT so arising is to be taken into account when determining whether there has been an abnormal increase or whether it becomes relevant only if there has been an abnormal increase on other grounds.

7.68 The main issue in practice will depend upon the drafting and whether, where the VAT is not reserved as rent or an additional rent, it is taxable as a periodical premium

---

[358] See **7.180**.

[359] But note the problem of the two charges on the grant of leases where the option to tax is exercised between the two chargeable events. It will be actual VAT and so taxable when the lease is granted.

[360] Which raises an important question as to whether the exercise of the option to tax the rent, should it be treated as any increase of rent, is an increase pursuant to the terms of the lease or is a variation taking effect outside the lease like a deed of variation. It seems that HMRC Stamp Taxes incline to the former view which is important when dealing with rent increases (FA 2003, Sch 17A, paras 7, 8, 13, 14 and 15).

[361] See **7.180**.

[362] This may also be reinforced by the fact that the periodical premium has to be dealt with on an estimated basis pursuant to FA 2003, s 52 and does not have to be adjusted in the light of subsequent variations since FA 2003, ss 80, 87 and 90 do not apply.

[363] FA 2003, Sch 17A, para 13.

pursuant to FA 2003, s 52. This issue of 'periodical premium' or 'rent' was a longstanding problem in the same context for stamp duty. HMRC Stamp Taxes stated officially[364] that VAT was to be taxed as a periodical premium; but, in practice, the point was rarely taken and such VAT was taxed as 'rent' which usually produced a more favourable result for taxpayers. In relation to stamp duty land tax there is no simple pattern and there is no consistent favourable treatment for VAT as rent. HMRC Stamp Taxes have not confirmed their position officially and the Guidance Note on changes in the rate of VAT merely refers to the situation where VAT is part of the rent without indicating when VAT might be regarded as part of the rent. There is obviously the problem that VAT is not being included in the tax computation in the land transaction return and is not being challenged; but it seems that where it is included as rent HMRC Stamp Taxes are not challenging the return in practice. Nevertheless, these are still early days for the tax and the random nature of the selection for an Enquiry means that many potentially erroneous returns are not being subject to a proper in-depth scrutiny and the errors are not being discovered. Since there are potential tax savings by structuring the VAT either as rent or premium in particular cases taxpayers might wish to investigate the alternatives and, where beneficial, include the VAT as 'rent' with separate apportionment. In other cases treatment as a separately apportioned sum taxable as a premium could be adopted.

7.69   The reduction in the rate of VAT, albeit on a temporary basis, has given rise to complications in relation to the stamp duty land tax computations and returns for leases where the rent is, or is potentially subject to, stamp duty land tax.[365] An explanatory guide has been issued by HMRC Stamp Taxes dealing with this situation.[366] Unfortunately, whilst dealing with the consequences it, as usual, ignores the underlying issue of causes. The essence of the statement is to deal with situations where the rent adjusts because the VAT is 'part of the rent'. This, unfortunately, is, as usual, at best ambiguous because it does not indicate those circumstances where the VAT will be regarded as 'part of the rent'. It may refer to situations where the rent is expressed to be an appropriate amount inclusive of VAT when the VAT is part of the rent in accordance with the statutory definition. Alternatively, it may represent a wider view such as where there is a single sum reserved as the rent and this is dealt with as being also subject to the VAT which is reserved as a separate sum as additional rent. Since it is separately apportioned it is, technically, not part of the rent;[367] but it seems that, in practice, HMRC Stamp Taxes are accepting returns prepared upon the basis that the VAT is to be included in the computation of the net present value of the rent and so on.

Works[368]

7.70   Chargeable consideration includes 'works',[369] which are not restricted to building works but include improvements, repairs[370] and other items such as fitting out costs and infrastructure costs because the charging provisions[371] refer to works of construction,

---

364   See, eg, Statement of Practice SP 11/91, para 9.
365   Such fluctuations in VAT are not within FA 2003, Sch 4, para 2, because they arise pursuant to the terms of the lease and not pursuant to the exercise of the option to tax for VAT.
366   See 30 January 2009, STI 2009, p 460.
367   FA 2003, Sch 17A, para 6.
368   Ibid, Sch 4, para 10; see also **Chapter 8**.
369   But note the limited exemption for certain PFI and similar projects; FA 2003, Sch 4, para 17 (as amended).
370   But note the exclusion for certain covenants to repair and maintain the premises pursuant to FA 2003, Sch 17A, para 10.
371   FA 2003, Sch 4, para 10(1).

improvement or repair[372] of a building or other works to enhance the value of land. This indicates that activities other than building works will be subject to stamp duty land tax; but there is an important relief for 'works' to be carried out on the land to be leased provided that these are carried out after the effective date[373] so that planning the transaction can have a significant impact on the tax costs.[374] The charge upon the works is not limited to the land to be acquired but includes works to be carried out upon land owned by the vendor or landlord or even third parties which will not be within the relief. There can be significant problems when dealing with a local authority where there will be a lease to be granted by the local authority to the developer and the grant of planning permission. It is important to avoid any terms that could make the planning obligations pursuant to a 'section 106 agreement'[375] part of the consideration for the grant of the lease.

7.71   This charge can give rise to problems where, for example, as part of some joint arrangement a charity enters into an agreement with a commercial developer in circumstances where the charity agrees to grant a lease to the developer at a peppercorn rent on terms that the developer will construct on land to be retained by the charity some form of social housing. In this situation the developer will be subject to stamp duty land tax upon the costs of the works to be carried out on the land being retained by the charity. He will, *prima facie*, be exempt from stamp duty land tax upon the works to be carried out on the land that he is acquiring.

7.72   There will also be questions as to the types of 'works' that are brought within the charge. Clearly works of construction, improvement or repair will be fairly obvious particularly since they relate only to the 'repair' of 'a building'. There may be some doubts on the fringes of this charge as to what is a 'building' since there may be arrangements concerned with other types of facilities on land such as installing pipes under the land used for the transfer of water by a water company.[376]

7.73   There is a residual provision referring to other works to enhance the value of land. It is important to note the absence of the definite article. The reference is simply to the value of land in general. In consequence, it is intended to apply to works of improvement in respect of land other than that being demised by the lease. There is the question as to whether the test for enhancement of value is objective or subjective. For example, the tenant may, as part of the consideration for the grant of the lease,[377] enter into obligations to carry out works on the land to be demised to him that may have incidental benefits for land retained by the landlord whether or not the reversion in the demised premises. There may be an agreement for the sale of land under which the seller obtains the benefit of rights to access any sewers or other facilities upon the land being sold.[378] These works are not being carried out upon the land to be acquired but they may have to enter into the consideration of the taxation issues because they could enhance the value of that land. The land may benefit from works carried out elsewhere because they improve certain aspects of the land such as the ability to be developed and link into the infrastructure upon land that has previously been sold or leased. Clearly

---

[372]   But note the exemption for covenants to 'repair' and maintain the building pursuant to FA 2003, Sch 17A, para 11. Since this refers to 'repair' and 'maintain' it is arguable that a covenant in a lease to put the premises into repair is a chargeable event.

[373]   FA 2003, Sch 4, para 10(2); see **Chapter 8**.

[374]   See **Chapter 8**.

[375]   Or equivalent provisions such as Highways Act 1980, s 278.

[376]   On the problems of the effective date for such works see **Chapter 14**.

[377]   See *Eastham v Leigh, London and Provincial Properties Limited* [1971] 2 All ER 887.

[378]   Note FA 2003, s 48(1)(b); see **1.6** and **4.39**.

these works will be carried out with a view to enhancing the value of the land being acquired not with the sole or main object of enhancing the value of the land being retained by the landlord. The legislation refers to the construction of works to enhance the value of the land. This suggests that there must be a subjective element that the disposal of the land and the obligation to carry out the construction works is intended to benefit the other land. The mere fact that the works are being carried out and have the effect of enhancing the value of the land does not bring them into charge.

Two sets of charges

7.74   Two areas of charge now exist, namely:

- *Landlord as builder*
  Works to be carried out by the landlord on the land to be leased at the expense of the tenant. In this situation the same principles apply as in relation to sales and these are considered in detail elsewhere.[379] HMRC Stamp Taxes believed that they had overcome the basic techniques of stamp duty mitigation where, provided the parties entered into two separate contracts for the sale of the land and the construction of the building, tax was charged only upon the land. HMRC Stamp Taxes were looking to find what was, in effect, a single arrangement for the sale or lease of the completed building so that the building costs could be included in any stampable premium. They were, however, generally unsuccessful in these arguments[380] and they have been forced to accept that their attempts to reverse these earlier decisions by the FA 2003 have been unsuccessful. HMRC Stamp Taxes now accept that the former stamp duty practices remain effective for the mitigation of stamp duty land tax. In consequence, where A and B enter into an arrangement under which A is to grant a lease to B and a separate building agreement under which A is to construct a building upon the land to be demised at the cost of B, the building costs will only form part of the stampable premium where there is a single contract for the lease of the land together with the building. Provided that the two are separate contracts the charge is limited to the land price only.[381] The question was the construction of the contract in each particular case and these problems will continue into the current stamp duty land tax regime.[382] In addition, the linked transaction rules, since these can relate only to land prices, cannot be used by HMRC Stamp Taxes to aggregate the separate land price and the building costs. The amount of stamp duty land tax chargeable in respect of the land transaction will be governed upon the consideration allocated thereto by the parties, provided that such consideration has been allocated on a just and reasonable basis;[383] and

- *Tenant as builder*
  Works, including fitting out, to be carried out by the tenant whether on the land to be acquired or other land; but with any problem of the exemption for works constructed upon the land to be demised at the cost of the tenant provided that

---

[379] See **Chapter 8**.

[380] See, for example, *Prudential Assurance Co Ltd v IRC* [1992] STC 863.

[381] See, for example, *Prudential Assurance Co Ltd v IRC* [1992] STC 863; *Kimbers & Co v IRC* [1936] 1 KB 132; *Paul v IRC* [1936] SC 443.

[382] It should be noted that there are provisions in relation to the general anti-avoidance provisions indicating that the segregation of land and building contracts is not to be regarded as a tax avoidance scheme for these purposes; FA 2003, ss 75A–75C.

[383] FA 2003, Sch 4, para 4.

there is no term of the transaction making use of the landlord or anyone connected with the landlord as a builder.[384] This restriction where the landlord is the builder is the ineffective attempt by HMRC Stamp Taxes to counter stamp duty decisions such as *Prudential Assurance Co Ltd v IRC*.[385] However, the restriction refers to the relief not being available where it is a 'condition of the transaction' that the works are carried out by the landlord.[386] It is rather odd that HMRC Stamp Taxes chose to use the word 'transaction' with the related word 'condition' rather than something that is 'part of the arrangement'. In consequence, where the works are to be carried out by the landlord the relief will only not be available where the landlord's involvement as builder is part of the land contract. 'Transaction' must refer to the land transaction and not to the commercial transaction since this inevitably involves the landlord as builder. In consequence, if the land transfer or lease does not refer to the building arrangements or to a contract with the landlord for building works then this restriction will not apply and the tenant will, *prima facie*, be eligible for the exemption from the charge to tax upon his costs.

There is an exclusion[387] from charge for the tenant's own works; but this is available only where he is acquiring a major interest[388] and these take place after 'the effective date', ie only those works constructed after the effective date of the deemed grant of the lease[389] if appropriate will qualify for the exemption. Works carried out on the land to be demised before the effective date will be taxable where the carrying out of the works is part of the chargeable consideration.[390] To avoid some of the worst consequences of the double effective date rules currently applied by HMRC Stamp Taxes to new leases it is provided that the relief also applies to works carried out before the effective date for the grant of the lease where these works were also carried out after the effective date for the substantial performance of the agreement for lease.[391] The scope and problems of this relief are considered elsewhere.[392]

This means that as well as the question of whether the works are 'consideration' (ie a premium) for the lease[393] the issue of 'substantial performance' of the agreement for lease will be crucial. In particular, whether the entry onto the land by the builder for the purpose of carrying out the works before the right to call for the lease becomes 'unconditional' will be treated as taking 'possession' will have important consequences, but it may be prudent to recognise the need to insert artificial steps such as the payment of £1 'rent' to generate substantial performance prior to commencing the works. Clearly, organisation of these arrangements will require considerable delicacy and prudence.

7.75 The charge to tax in both cases is by reference to the 'open market cost' of the works.[394] This is defined[395] as being the amount that would have to be paid in the open market for carrying out of the works in question. This raises questions since many

---

[384] Ibid, Sch 4, para 10(2).

[385] [1992] STC 863 which makes the effective date crucial; see **7.76** and **Chapters 8** and **14**.

[386] FA 2003, Sch 4, para 10(2)(c).

[387] Ibid, Sch 4, para 10(2); see further **Chapter 8**.

[388] Ibid, Sch 4, para 10(3)(a).

[389] The rules have been amended so that works undertaken after the effective date for the agreement for lease are also exempt notwithstanding that they have been carried out before the actual grant.

[390] As in *Eastham v Leigh, London and Provincial Properties Limited* [1971] 2 All ER 887.

[391] FA 2003, Sch 4, para 10(2) (as amended).

[392] See **Chapter 8**.

[393] *Eastham v Leigh, London and Provincial Properties Limited* [1971] 2 All ER 887.

[394] FA 2003, Sch 4, para 10; see further **Chapter 8**.

[395] Ibid, Sch 4, para 10(3)(b).

construction contracts will not be on a fixed price basis but may be on the basis of costs plus a profit element and may be carried out by the taxpayer utilising his own in-house workforce. In these cases the 'costs' would be uncertain and the 'cost' of utilising an employed workforce may be very different from those that would arise in relation to the utilisation of subcontractors. In the latter case there will be a charge upon a profit element, in the former case there would be no profit element. The costs are the basic salary costs. Obviously, the internal costs would differ from the price that would be charged if the taxpayer were tendering for work in the open market when he would include a profit element. It would seem, therefore, that because this has to be looked at in the context of the open market there must be some form of profit element or other arrangements that would arise. Since this is a fiscal valuation, albeit on a somewhat novel basis, it would seem that the 'open market cost' would be fixed. It is an intriguing if not impossible concept, to approach the matter on the basis that the 'open market cost' could be on a variable price basis. It seems, however, that HMRC Stamp Taxes take the view that this reference to the open market means that they can look at the terms of actual contracts since the 'actual open market' as opposed to the 'hypothetical fiscal open market' does include variable prices. In consequence, whilst the taxpayer may have to prepare his return upon the basis of an estimated premium trying to 'guestimate' the open market costs he will be entitled to defer the payment.[396] The tax will have to be paid upon any cash premium paid but it seems that the tax can be deferred in respect of the estimated open market costs. However, it is part of the conditions for the postponement of the tax upon such variable costs[397] that the application for the postponement is accompanied by a projected timetable indicating when costs are likely to become 'ascertained' and when HMRC Stamp Taxes can expect to receive some form of payment of tax on account.

Fitting out

7.76   The fitting out of premises by a tenant could be regarded as 'works' that relate to the improvement or enhancement of the value of land. They are, therefore, potentially 'works' within the charge to tax. This means that two issues can arise where there is a lease of retail premises or commercial premises to a tenant who wish to fit out which need to be dealt with in order to avoid a possible charge of 4 per cent upon the costs of the fitting out works. These are:

- *Fitting out as consideration*
  Whether the arrangements relating to the fitting out are 'consideration' for the grant of the lease. In many cases the arrangement will be that the tenant may have permission to go upon the land to fit out if he so desires. In this situation, there being no obligation upon the tenant to enter upon the land, it is difficult to see that there is 'consideration'. The tenant is not 'earning' the lease by means of the fitting out works and any other arrangements. However, not all situations are so straightforward and there may be cases where the landlord is making a contribution towards the fitting out or the tenant is to be entitled to some form of rent holiday if he carries out the fitting out works. In these situations it is probable that the arrangements relating to the fitting out are obligations imposed upon the tenant in that he will 'earn' the right to the lease only if he carries out the works in

---

[396]   Ibid, ss 51, 80, 90 and Stamp Duty Land Tax (Administration) Regulations 2003, SI 2003/2837, Part 4.
[397]   Stamp Duty Land Tax (Administration) Regulations 2003, SI 2003/2837, Part 4, regs 13 and 14.

accordance with the agreement.[398] Where there is some form of commitment to carry out the works then it is likely that they will be potentially chargeable consideration or premium for the lease; and

- *Fitting out and relief*
  Where there is a risk that the fitting out works could form part of the consideration for the grant of the lease it is important to ensure that the fitting out works themselves take place in the circumstances where the tenant can claim the benefit of the exclusion for works to be carried out upon the land to be acquired as a major interest and the works carried out after the effective date.[399] Clearly, where the tenant is trying to earn a lease by the fitting out works he will be dealing with a major interest.[400] The question is whether there has been substantial performance or completion so that there has been an effective date before the works are carried out or before substantial expenditure is incurred. It is also important to ensure that the arrangements relating to fitting out do not involve the landlord as the person to carry out the fitting out works as part of the land arrangements since this would mean that the exemption is not available.[401] It may be that the landlord will be prepared to grant the lease and the tenant be prepared to accept the lease before the fitting out works commence[402] or the parties may begin to pay rent so that there is some element of substantial performance.[403] In other cases, the parties may have to rely upon the fact that the entry of the tenant upon the land in order to commence the fitting out works is taking possession of the whole or substantially the whole of the land. In these circumstances where the lease has not been granted the tenant's entry may be as some form of licensee or tenant at will. Fortunately, entry as a tenant at will or licensee or under some other temporary arrangement can operate as substantial performance.[404] Although HMRC Stamp Taxes start from the basic proposition that if the tenant obtains the keys to the premises this is obtaining possession this may be an overstatement of the arrangements since the keys may be provided on a temporary basis or the tenant may only be allowed in during certain permitted hours. There may be cases where the tenant is allowed in whilst the landlord and his construction teams are still on the premises so that there will be difficult issue as to whether there can be 'joint possession' for these purposes. Restricted access to the premises may be incompatible with 'possession' should HMRC Stamp Taxes decide to mount a campaign against the availability of this relief.
  In addition, apart from the question of whether there is a taking of 'possession' there may be questions as to whether that possession extends to substantially the whole of the premises. No guidance has been issued by HMRC Stamp Taxes on an official basis as to what percentage of the land will be regarded as 'substantial' for these purposes. In consequence, restricted access to the premises may mean that there has not been substantial performance. For example, there may be a situation of an agreement for lease for three floors in an office building and the tenant is allowed in initially only in respect of one of the three floors with the

---

[398] *Eastham v Leigh, London and Provincial Properties Limited* [1971] 2 All ER 887. Note the sort of issues that can arise in relation to tenants earning benefits in relation to leases and VAT as in *Ridgeons Bulk v Customs and Excise* [1994] STC 427.

[399] See **8.15**.

[400] FA 2003, Sch 4, para 10(2)(a).

[401] Ibid, Sch 4, para 10(2)(c); see **5.77**.

[402] Note *Cory Brothers v IRC* [1965] AC 1082 on early completion and stamp duty suggesting that early completion would exclude subsequent building works from the dutiable consideration.

[403] FA 2003, s 44; see **Chapter 14**.

[404] Ibid, s 44(6); see **14.17**.

understanding that he will be permitted to fit out the other floors as the construction work on these parts of the premises continues. In this situation in the initial phase there may be a taking of possession, if the facts justify an argument that there is possession, of only one-third of the premises to be demised. It is unlikely that HMRC Stamp Taxes would accept that this is substantially the whole of the premises.[405]

Land exchanges involving leases, including surrenders and regrants

7.77   Land exchanges are widely defined.[406] It applies in any situation where, as part of the consideration for entry into a land transaction, the party is to enter into another land transaction. It can, therefore, apply to straightforward situations that parties would regard as exchanges such as where A agrees to transfer a freehold interest to B in consideration of B granting a lease back to A. However, it may extend further such as where A transfers land to B and part of the consideration is B entering into a lease with A's subsidiary C.[407] In this situation A may not be entering into a land exchange nor will C but B may be. The consequence is that many transactions relating to dealings involving leases, although not regarded as exchanges, will be such within the definition and since this involves potential double charges to tax an awareness of the risks and the computation provisions is essential.

Leases can be part of many forms of land exchange, such as:

- sale and lease back;[408]

- lease and underlease back;

- surrenders and regrants including certain deeds of variation;[409]

- surrender of a lease for the grant of a lease of other premises;

- mutual transfers of leases such as where tenants of flats exchange garages.

Where the grant of the lease is part of a land exchange[410] such as a sale and leaseback there is, in effect, a deemed premium equal to the market value of that lease (depending upon the rent and the covenants because the charge arises upon the market value of the lease received by the tenant[411]) but many situations have exemptions.[412]

---

[405]   This line of argument would help HMRC Stamp Taxes reject the rent credit for surrenders and regrants which requires substantial identity of the premises; see FA 2003, Sch 17A, para 9.

[406]   FA 2003, s 47; see **5.150**.

[407]   Such a triangular arrangement would be outside the relief for sale and leaseback FA 2003, s 57A (as much amended); see **10.54**.

[408]   This point does not appear to have been fully appreciated by the draftsman of the relief in FA 2003, s 57A notwithstanding the many amendments thereto. Note also the problems of the special charge upon an assignee of the leaseback for which he may require an indemnity or reverse payment pursuant to FA 2003, Sch 17A, para 18.

[409]   *Friends Provident Life Office v British Railways Board* [1996] 1 All ER 336.

[410]   FA 2003, s 47.

[411]   Ibid, Sch 4, para 5 but see **Chapter 27** on whether this relates to the value of a lease granted hypothetically to a third party or the price which the actual tenant would obtain on an onward sale to a hypothetical party.

[412]   See, for example, FA 2003, Sch 17A, para 16.

Exchanges as premium

7.78   Routine exchanges of leases will attract the double charge on market value of the lease being received.[413] However, the definition of exchange, as illustrated, takes the scope of the charge on these premiums beyond these arrangements. Thus a transfer in consideration of the grant of lease back would be a land exchange. This can arise in a variety of situations and can provide a trap. For example, where tenants in a block of flats are proposing to enfranchise their interests[414] they may agree to acquire the freehold from the existing landlord intending to vest this in some form of management company owned by the tenants intending to transfer and receive back from the management company leases in a more acceptable modernised form including extended terms. In this situation although the tenants may be entitled to subsale relief in respect of their acquisition of the land from the landlord by transmitting it simultaneously to the management company, they will be embarking upon a land exchange in respect of which they will be subject to tax upon the market value of the leases back which will reflect the full value of the flats in the block without any credit for the value of the leases of those flats which have been surrendered.[415] However, although there are reliefs in relation to the land exchange rules for certain surrenders of leases and grants of new leases and these extend to the surrender of leases that were granted within the stamp duty regime[416] there is a major disadvantage, apart from the charge upon the rent for the new lease without any form of credit. Many of the problems of stamp duty land tax do not apply to leases granted in the stamp duty regime such as holding over and the issues of successive linked leases.[417] By entering into some form of surrender and regrant after 1 December 2003 the tenant may be subjected to considerable additional tax costs as well as the costs of complying with the new regime. It may also be possible to mitigate the hardship of the double charge for sale or lease and leaseback transactions by carving the leaseback out for the benefit of the vendor prior to the sale of the reversionary interest.

Leases, exchanges and reliefs

7.79   *Prima facie*, therefore, such a surrender would produce substantial charges to stamp duty land tax:

•   the landlord is, *prima facie*, subject to stamp duty land tax upon the market value of the existing lease that is being surrendered;

•   the tenant is liable to stamp duty land tax upon both:
   –   the market value of the lease being granted; and
   –   the net present value of the rent of the new lease.

There are numerous reliefs from the exchange charges such as those for surrenders and grants of leases[418] whether relating to the same or different premises so that there might

---

[413]   FA 2003, Sch 4, para 5; equality payments are irrelevant in this context, see **5.151**.

[414]   Note that where there is some form of collective enfranchisement there may be a special rate FA 2003, s 74 (as amended by FA 2009) removing the need for right to enfranchise companies; see **10.44**.

[415]   If the tenants arrange for the freehold to be transferred to the management company and take the benefit of subsale relief paying stamp duty land tax in the company they will then be able to surrender and regrant their leases (ie vary them) and take the benefit of the relief from the land exchange rules pursuant to FA 2003, Sch 17A, para 16. Considerable tax saving can be obtained by avoiding a transfer and leaseback.

[416]   But not in respect of the rents for the new lease; FA 2003, Sch 17A, para 9.

[417]   But note FA 2003, Sch 19, paras 7, 8 and 9.

[418]   FA 2003, Sch 17A, para 16.

be the opportunity for reducing the overall tax charge by seeking to restructure exchanges involving leases into some form of lease variation or surrender and regrant. A surrender and regrant is technically an exchange of major interests,[419] ie there is a surrender of the existing lease and grant of a new lease even where this occurs by operation of law such as a deed of variation enlarging the term of the lease. However, these reliefs are narrowly defined[420] so that care is needed to avoid multiple charges and to bring the transaction within the various reliefs. For example, whilst a surrender and regrant may be eligible for relief but a transfer and leaseback is not.

Leases and nominees

7.80 There may be advantages in structuring the transaction by carving out the leaseback prior to the arrangement. For example, a person proposing to enter into some form of sale and leaseback arrangement as part of some joint venture or other arrangement may, rather than transfer and take a grant of the lease, initially grant the lease to a subsidiary company or to a nominee which may or may not be a connected company.[421] This leaseback may be on advantageous terms. There may be little or no charge to tax upon the grant of this lease by reason of the exemptions for intra-group transactions[422] and dealings with nominees are usually tax neutral[423] although there may be complications where the connected companies charge applies[424] or because certain dealings between the nominee and the beneficial owner are deemed to take effect at full market value or upon the actual consideration involved.[425] Where the charge upon the dealing with the nominee does not take place at market value but upon the actual consideration there may be benefits where the lease is being granted on favourable terms such as at a peppercorn rent or at a low rent. These arrangements may be quite useful where a person who has acquired property with the benefit of a mortgage and having spent money upon the improvement of the property wishes to increase the mortgage in order to cover the costs of the refurbishment. In these situations banks may refuse to provide additional finance supported by a mortgage because they tend to look at the historic cost of acquisition. They may require the landowner to grant a lease to himself at a rent which will support a charge upon the property and an increase in the amount of the borrowing. However, this may well attract a full charge to stamp duty land tax. It may be necessary to investigate whether it is possible to grant the lease to a nominee in circumstances where a full charge can be avoided because of the rules relating to the dealings with nominees[426] but which satisfy the requirements of the bank.

Reliefs from double charges

7.81 This treatment on land exchanges with charges upon market value would, of course, represent a very substantial charge to tax where, for example, a tenant was

---

419 Ibid, s 47.
420 Ibid, Sch 17A, paras 9 and 16.
421 There are many issues arising around the choice of route and vehicle, such as the availability of intra-group relief and possible clawback or the special charge on assignment of the lease or the special provisions dealing with leases to nominees and the connected company charge; see FA 2003, s 53; Sch 17A, para 11; Sch 16, para 3; Sch 15, paras 10 and 18.
422 FA 2003, Sch 7, Part 1; but note the potential charge to tax upon any subsequent assignment pursuant to FA 2003, Sch 17A, para 11.
423 Ibid, Sch 16, para 3 (as amended).
424 Ibid, ss 53 and 54; although it may be possible to restrict these problems where the nominee is not a connected company.
425 Ibid, Sch 16, para 3 (as amended).
426 Ibid, Sch 16, para 3; see **Chapter 9**.

merely wishing to enlarge the term of a lease of a flat. If it were technically possible for a tenant to extend his lease in the flat by means of a reversionary lease to commence at some stage in the future there would be a potential charge to stamp duty land tax but this would be restricted to the rent arising in the future.[427] Where there is simply an agreement for a reversionary lease and the prospective tenant is in occupation as tenant under the existing lease there will be no charge to tax until the current lease expires. The agreement for a reversionary lease will be chargeable only if there is substantial performance prior to the grant but since the prospective tenant is in occupation as tenant under an existing lease his occupation of the premises cannot be taking possession for the purposes of the reversionary lease. However, if there is a formal grant of the reversionary lease HMRC Stamp Taxes claim, probably incorrectly, that the lease is taxable in respect of the rent and that the first year of the rent calculation is brought forward from the date when the lease is intended to take effect in possession to the period of the grant. It appears to be their contention that where there is a grant of a reversionary lease to commence in 10 years time the rent for year 1 is not zero but the rent that would be payable in year 10 ie the first year in which the lease begins to operate.

7.82 However, for technical reasons of conveyancing where there is not a contract to grant a reversionary lease to take effect in possession at some time in the future, the arrangement has to take effect by way of surrender and regrant.[428] In consequence, there is the *prima facie* cancellation of a lease that has already borne substantial stamp duty land tax including rent payable in respect of periods after the deemed surrender and the grant of the new lease which will be attracting tax in respect of the rent periods after grant and prior to the former contractual termination date for the surrendered lease. There is, therefore, a potential element of double taxation for rent paid in respect of the 'overlap period' ie the period between the date of the surrender and the contractual termination date for the existing lease and the effective date for the grant or deemed grant of the new lease and what would have been the contractual termination date for the existing lease. This means that there are considerable disadvantages in relation to arrangements where the proposal involves a surrender of a lease that was granted within the stamp duty regime.[429] In consequence two reliefs have been introduced:

- Essentially, surrenders and regrants of leases of substantially the same premises or the grant of new leases of different premises from those being surrendered such as where the landlord is seeking to persuade the tenants to relocate, are removed from the land exchange provisions so that the charge to tax will not arise on the market value of the interest being treated as acquired by either party.[430] In consequence, where a new lease is granted, apparently whether of the same or other premises, in consideration of the surrender of an existing lease the surrender

---

[427]   There is currently a dispute with HMRC Stamp Taxes in relation to grants of reversionary leases.
[428]   *Friends Provident Life Office v British Railways Board* [1996] 1 All ER 336.
[429]   Which can include certain leases granted on or after 1 December 2003 where this is pursuant to an agreement before July 2003 and in other circumstances (FA 2003, Sch 19). There are considerable advantages in avoiding the termination of a stamp duty lease where this would involve the 'acquisition' of a lease within the stamp duty land tax regime. There are the additional tax charges which are usually significantly greater than those that would be payable in the stamp duty regime, the fact that there are more chargeable situations such as holding over in relation to stamp duty land tax leases and the compliance arrangements involve considerable extra cost.
[430]   FA 2003, Sch 17A, paras 9 and 16.

is not a premium of the grant of the new lease and the new lease is not consideration for the surrender.[431] This appears to apply even where the lease surrendered is a stamp duty lease.

- The rent reserved by the new lease is reduced by reference to the rent that would have been payable under the old lease; but this relief applies only where the old lease is a stamp duty land tax lease[432] and the new lease is between the same parties and relates to the same or substantially the same premises.[433] In consequence, whilst the relief is likely to be available where the surrender and regrant occurs because of a variation in the terms of the lease, the issue of substantial identity of the premises will be a key problem when the deed of variation changes the scope of the demised premises.

7.83 The relief from the land exchange rules for surrenders and regrants being available in relation to any new lease in respect of the premium[434] would also appear to be available where tenants in a block of flats where the lease includes a lease of a garage enter into arrangements to exchange their garages[435] because the exemption applies to situations where the consideration includes grants of a lease of different premises. Should the parties enter into a deed of variation of the lease there will be a surrender and regrant. In this situation, *prima facie*, regardless of whether the original lease of the flat was granted within the stamp duty or the stamp duty land tax regime there will be an exemption in respect of the capital values and the land exchange rules.[436] However, there may be a question as to whether there is relief in respect of any rent adjustments between the parties. The relief in respect of the rent will be available only where the varied lease was a stamp duty land tax lease but in these situations of leases of flats the rent is likely to be a ground rent and therefore the rent for the new lease is unlikely to attract stamp duty land tax.[437] Modification of the terms of the lease to change the demised premise for each lease by varying the garage attributable to each flat will not relate substantially to the same premises, but this does not appear to matter as regards any 'premium'; provided it is granted to the same persons stamp duty land tax will not be chargeable on the 'premium' but there will be full tax upon the allocated rent although this is likely to be within the nil rate slice where residential properties are involved. The value of any interest surrendered or the market value of the interest being granted will be ignored. For these purposes, it would seem that the 'premium' that attracts the tax will be any lump sum paid by the tenant for the variation of the lease. For example, where the tenant pays the landlord £50,000 for the increase in the length of

---

[431] This means that in routine transactions the landlord is not entering into a chargeable transaction because there will normally be no chargeable consideration (FA 2003, s 77A and Sch 3, para 1) so he does not have to notify HMRC Stamp Taxes.

[432] FA 2003, Sch 17A, para 9.

[433] See **7.259**.

[434] FA 2003, Sch 17A, para 16.

[435] Such arrangements for exchanges of part of the demised premises can involve complex conveyancing issues with related complications for stamp duty land tax because such partial exchanges may involve not merely exchanges but surrenders and regrants of the balance of the demised premises not within the relief because they do not relate to substantially (i e substantial proportions of) the same premises.

[436] FA 2003, Sch 17A, para 16.

[437] The former problem of there not being a nil rate for the premium in respect of any actual consideration provided by the tenant to a landlord for the extended term where the ground rent exceeded £600 has been removed by the FA 2008.

the lease from 65 years to 150 years, the new lease will be treated as being granted for a premium of £50,000.[438] There will be no hidden premium by reason of the surrenders.

7.84   Stamp duty land tax is still payable upon the net present value of the rent reserved by the new lease, whether a commercial rent or ground rent in connection with the lease of a flat.[439] However, a limited credit is available where the new lease is between the same parties and relates to the same or substantially the same premises,[440] and the old lease was chargeable to stamp duty land tax.[441] The problem will be not so much the absence of rent credit because the rents in relation to residential property, being essentially ground rents, are unlikely to produce a situation where the net present value of the rent exceeds the nil rate threshold for the time being in force.

Substantially the same

7.85   However, where there are significant rents, such as non-residential property, or there are potential difficulties because of the absence of the nil rate relief for premiums where the rent exceeds £1000 per annum, there may be difficulties because of the requirement that the property relates to the same or substantially the same properties. Unfortunately, there is no guidance in the legislation as to when the premises demised by the old lease and the premises demised by the new lease are 'substantially the same'. In most cases where there is a surrender and regrant arising because the parties are enlarging term, the premises will be identical. The major practical problem will be where there is a surrender and regrant because the parties are enlarging or reducing the scope of the demised premises. Since the charge arises by reason of the variation in the premises included within the lease there will, inevitably, be a major question as to whether the old lease and the new lease relates to the same premises or whether the variation in the demised premises means that they are no longer 'substantially' the same. Again, the draftsman appears to have operated on a two-dimensional basis and failed to provide any guide as to changes in the demised premises by reason of extensions such as where there is an extension of the demised premises on the ground which permits an extension over many floors producing a substantial increase in the volume of the buildings.

Rent credit[442]

7.86   Where the existing lease that is being surrendered or varied is for a fixed rent, the charge to stamp duty land tax upon the new lease in respect of rent will be given credit for the amount of rent due in respect of the surrendered years of the existing lease. This superficially appears to operate on the basis that the rent during the initial years of the new lease will be reduced by the amount of the fixed rent that would have been payable under the existing lease, for example, where a tenant of a flat has a lease with 65 years unexpired at a ground rent of £1,000 and enters into an arrangement whereby upon consideration for payment of £50,000, the lease is regranted as a term of 150 years at a ground rent of £1,500. In addition to the question of the premium being taxable, it

---

[438]   Which is no longer taxable because the £600 rent restriction for residential property has been removed; FA 2003, Sch 5, para 9 (as amended); also note the special rate for collective enfranchisement FA 2003, s 74 (as amended).

[439]   Although, in practice, such rents are likely to be below the nil rate threshold for lease rents.

[440]   FA 2003, Sch 17A, para 9.

[441]   This relief will therefore be irrelevant in practice for many years.

[442]   Notwithstanding that the lease in question has obtained the benefit of this type of rent credit, it is ignored when determining the assumed rent after the expiration of the fifth year of the term; FA 2003, Sch 17A, para 7(3).

might be thought that the calculation of the net present value of the rent will be simply that for the first 65 years the ground rent will be reduced from £1,500 by the £1,000 per annum payable or reserved by the existing lease. In consequence, for the first 65 years the net present value of the rent will be determined on the basis of a rent of £500 per annum. It will, for the balance of the term, rise to £1,500.

7.87 However, the calculation of the rent credit in this and other areas is potentially a far more complex exercise[443] because the legislation is ambiguous and does not make clear whether it is the actual rent reserved by the lease (ie the actual rent prior to discounting etc) or the artificial rents taken into account and whether discounting applies. The legislation provides that the rent payable under the new lease is treated as reduced by the 'amount of the rent' that would have been payable in respect of the overlap period under the old lease. This is a problem of determining the rent that would have been payable under the old lease ie there is an issue whether this refers to the contractual rent, the discounted rent or the artificial rent for years after the expiration of the fifth year of the term and how the taxpayer is to deal with a variable rent. Even where the legislation refers to the base rent as being the rent previously subject to stamp duty land tax it retains its ambiguity. The reference would suggest that it is the amount of rent taken into account in computing the charge to tax. This would indicate that it is the artificial or assumed rent where the overlap period relates to periods after the expiration of the fifth year of the term of the old lease. This is, in one sense, the rent that was brought into the charge to tax. However, the 'amount of rent' that was actually subject to tax will be the figure for each year suitably discounted.[444] It is a question whether HMRC Stamp Taxes may wish to take the point that the amount of rent actually brought into charge is the discounted figure rather than accept the argument that the rent brought into charge is the assumed rent figure and it is the amount of tax in respect of that rent that is adjusted by reason of the discounting. The amount to be deducted is the amount of the rent for the old lease taken into account in calculating the stamp duty land tax on that lease, ie it will involve the assumed rent for all years after the expiration of the fifth year of the term and the figures will be brought in at their discounted amount. Theoretically this requires a calculation of the discounted deemed rent for every individual year that both leases overlap. This requires an unreasonably complex calculation,[445] because it would require each year of the old lease and each year of the new lease in the same period to be compared and the different amount calculated by deducting the discounted rent in respect of the old lease from the discounted rent for the new lease both of which may be artificial rents once the relevant 5-year periods, which would be different for both leases, have expired. An alternative approach would be to compare the net present value of the rent for the relevant period under the old lease compared with the net present value for the same period of the new lease taking into account the period of the old lease which has expired ie the discounting takes account of the previous years of the lease. This would not necessarily be a straightforward calculation and would probably be provisional only because the new lease may be for a variable rent. In addition, it would be necessary to enter into complex calculations in order to determine the relevant net present value in respect of the old lease. This would, *prima facie*, be the original net present value for the lease originally calculated as at the effective date for the lease or substantial performance of any agreement plus any retrospective adjustments of that lease by reference to rent reviews

---

[443] See also **7.200**.

[444] And there may be problems with the availability of two nil rate reliefs but the two transactions are unlikely to be linked transactions.

[445] Especially since it may initially be provisional or estimated and the calculation would have to be repeated on review of the new rent during or at the end of the first 5 years of the new lease.

during or at the expiration of the fifth year of the term. It would then be necessary to deduct from this figure the net present value of the rents for the first period of that lease from the effective date to the date of the surrender and regrant. This may also be a provisional figure because the arrangement may take effect during the first 5 years of the term. However, there would be the utterly unsolvable problem of dealing with the situation of the net present value for the original lease not being reviewed because the lease would have ceased to exist before the first review date. The legislation is somewhat less than clear as to how this situation is to be dealt with. There would, therefore, be a question of determining the rent credit in the context of the base rent being a provisional figure that is potentially subject to retrospective review but the event giving rise to the retrospective review cannot take place. This discounting will leave a taxable difference because the rent reserved by the old lease will have qualified for substantial discounting over time but the new lease rent will have only recently started discounting. It is hoped that HMRC Stamp Taxes will not pursue this technical point in pursuit of extra revenue and treat the rent subject to tax as being the undiscounted amount. It will, however, not necessarily involve the passing rent but relate to the assumed or other artificial rent for lease for years after the expiration of the fifth year of the term.[446] It is hoped that HMRC Stamp Taxes would in practice accept a calculation based upon the deduction of the relevant part of the net present value of the original rent from the net present value of the new rent. Unfortunately, although this seems to produce the correct arithmetic result it is probable that HMRC Stamp Taxes will take the point that the return has not been properly prepared.

Deemed premium

7.88 Although, in general, stamp duty land tax works upon the basis of the actual consideration there are numerous situations where the actual consideration is ignored and either treated as nil in which case the transaction may be for no chargeable consideration and so not notifiable;[447] or the chargeable consideration may represent consideration in kind which has to be valued[448] or it may provide for the consideration to be some different item such as in relation to lease premiums that are part of a land exchange when the consideration is not what is provided but what is received[449] or it may replace the actual consideration by consideration of market value or not less than market value such as in relation to dealings with connected companies.[450] Where there is a deemed consideration to market value there will be considerably complex issues of fiscal valuation.[451]

Deemed different consideration

7.89 There are certain provisions, such as those relating to land exchanges (e g surrenders and regrants or sale and leaseback) where the actual consideration may

---

[446] Also the credit mechanism fails to deal with a routine problem of where the rent taxable or reserved by the old lease includes a high or artificial rent during the overlap period of the first 5 years of the term of the new lease. Where this is carried over into the new lease it merely reduces the rent to nil and does not produce a negative figure. More importantly it may produce an artificially high rent as the basis for the assumed rent for all years after the fifth year of the new lease and give only limited credit because it was not the assumed rent for the old lease.

[447] FA 2003, Sch 3, para 1; s 77A.

[448] Ibid, Sch 4, paras 1 and 7.

[449] Ibid, s 47; Sch 4, para 5; but note the reliefs pursuant to FA 2003, Sch 17A, para 16 – see **7.224**.

[450] Ibid, s 53; see **5.208**.

[451] See **Chapter 27**.

have to be ignored[452] or where a different consideration is substituted[453] when computing the tax. Fortunately at present the situations where deemed consideration applies are few,[454] but apply to leases.

Connected companies

7.90   Where a lease is granted to a connected company for a consideration which consists solely of or includes rent the tax is charged upon what can be regarded as a deemed premium not less than the market value of the lease (ie the value of a lease at that rent, if any, because the rent is below the market rent for a lease on these terms) plus the net present value of the actual rent reserved.[455] In this situation where there is the charge effectively upon the greater of the actual consideration or the market value taking into account the rent reserved. It seems, however, that the market value has to be treated in the context of the actual terms of the lease. Although fiscal valuation normally requires certain assumptions as to the nature of the interest being provided and whether some alternative arrangement might produce a higher figure[456] this may not apply in all situations for the purposes of valuations and stamp duty land tax. In consequence, where there is a lease at a rent there will be a charge by reference to the actual rent level and the market value charge will be attributed to a notional premium which would be the market value of the lease taking into account the terms of the lease and, in particular, the level of the rent. Unfortunately, the provisions dealing with leases and valuation in general refer to the market value of the interest. This is ambiguous since it is unclear whether it refers to the value of the actual lease that a landlord might expect to receive if granted to a different tenant such as a special tenant ie what a third (hypothetical) party would pay as a premium for the actual lease (rather than a hypothetical lease on different terms),[457] or what the actual tenant (the connected company) could expect to receive if he sold the lease in the open market[458] ie whether it is the market value of the interest received by the tenant and the amount that he would receive should he sell the lease in the open market including a sale to a special purchaser. There may be considerable differences between the premium level for a lease granted and a premium value for a lease to be assigned.[459]

Inadvertently because of the 'one size fits all' approach to the tax, reliefs have been made available for leases where:

---

[452] Except perhaps to the extent that it may provide some evidence as to market value.
[453] FA 2003, Sch 4, para 5.
[454] See **Chapter 5**.
[455] FA 2003, s 53.
[456] See, for example, *Duke of Buccleuch v IRC* [1967] AC 506; but see Taxation of Chargeable Gains Act 1992, s 242(2) and **7.213**.
[457] The charging provisions would appear to require valuation of the actual lease rather than a different transaction.
[458] There will, therefore, be some important issues of principle to be debated with HMRC Stamp Taxes relating to the actual covenants and conditions in the lease such as restrictions upon use or restricting assignment and subletting. Break clauses may be an issue since these are, at least to some extent, to be of 'no account' (FA 2003, Sch 17A, para 2(b)) or options to renew but such clauses may have implications for the general anti-avoidance provisions (FA 2003, s 75A(3)). To some extent HMRC Stamp Taxes may have utilised their own argument by enacting special provisions for lease valuation (FA 2003, Sch 17A, para 10; Sch 15, paras 15 and 14(5)).
[459] See further **Chapter 27**.

- the lease or agreement is with a corporate trustee[460] and immediately after the transaction the corporate trustee holds the property as trustee in the course of a business carried on by it that includes or consists of the management of trust; or

- immediately after the transaction the corporate trustee holds the property as trustee and the lessee is connected with the corporate trustee only by reason of being the settlor.

The rules for trustees are modified where there is a bare trustee or nominee.[461]

Partnerships[462]

7.91   Partnerships are subject to two regimes; namely:-

- normal dealings in leases with unconnected parties such as leases granted by third party landlords;[463] and

- a special regime based upon market values where the dealings in the lease are between partners, the partnership and connected persons.[464]

In general, in the latter case, the acquisition, in the form of the grant of a lease, is charged upon market values reduced by the sum of the lower proportions.[465] Special rules apply to leases where the tax includes the actual rent reserved by the lease, although this net present value is reduced by the sum of the lower proportions.[466]

7.92   The rent will be taxable upon normal principles and the market premium, if any, will be the appropriate value whether in respect of the grant or the hypothetical assignment of the lease by reference to the rent reserved and any other terms of the lease that may have a bearing upon its value. However, the chargeable rent and the actual or deemed premium will be reduced for the purpose of computing the tax by reference to the sum of the lower proportions to the extent that there is an overlap between the persons granting the lease and the partners receiving the lease, at least to the extent that the partners in the firm receiving the lease are individuals connected with the landlord.[467]

7.93   Similar rules apply to leases granted by partnerships to persons connected with the partnership such as leases to current or certain former partners or members of their family.[468] Similar issues to those mentioned previously in relation to connected companies[469] arise so that there will be a charge by reference to the actual rent reserved and a possible market value premium where the rent is below the market rent.[470] There are provisions for reducing the market value charge and the charge upon the rent by

---

[460]   The position is obscure where there are both corporate and individual trustees. It is thought that the charge is not intended to apply in such cases.
[461]   FA 2003, Sch 16, para 3 (as amended); see **Chapter 9**.
[462]   See further **Chapter 13**.
[463]   FA 2003, Sch 15, Part 2; see **13.22**.
[464]   Ibid, Sch 15, Part 3, paras 10 and 18; see **13.25**.
[465]   See **Chapter 13**.
[466]   FA 2003, Sch 15, paras 11 and 19; see **13.31**.
[467]   FA 2003, Sch 15, para 20.
[468]   FA 2003, Sch 15, para 18.
[469]   See **7.90**.
[470]   See on valuations and partnerships *Walton v IRC* [1996] STC 68; *IRC v Gray* [1994] STC 360.

reference to the sum of the lower proportions to the extent that the partnership and the lessees are connected persons[471] although, in the case of leases by a partnership to connected persons, there may be restrictions in the sum of the lower proportions where the chargeable interest was acquired in circumstances where *ad valorem* stamp duty or stamp duty land tax was not payable.[472]

Where there is a lease between partnerships there is a further special regime. In this situation the lease between the partnerships may be taxed as a lease to a partnership with all the related rules or a lease being granted out of a partnership to connected persons. The charge is whichever produces the higher amount of tax.[473]

Employees

7.94 Where a lease is granted to an employee or a person connected with an employee by reason of his employment and the transaction is not a taxable benefit for income tax purposes, the lease is deemed to be granted for a premium not less than the market value (taking into account any actual rent payable which will also be taxable).[474]

Leases, loans and deposits

7.95 Where in connection with[475] the grant[476] or assignment of a lease the lessee or a person connected with him[477] pays a deposit[478] or makes a loan[479] to any person and the repayment of all or part of the deposit or loan is contingent on anything done or omitted to be done by the lessee on his death, the amount of the deposit or loan is taxed as a premium for the lease.[480] Similarly where there is an assignment of a lease and such a deposit or loan is made by the assignee or a person connected with him the loan or deposit is taxable as consideration for the assignment.[481]

7.96 The legislation refers to a 'deposit' or a 'loan'. These terms will raise considerable difficulties since they have special meanings. A 'deposit' in general law[482] is limited to 5 or 10 per cent of the contract price; anything in excess of these thresholds falls into a different category and in the context of the legislation a 'deposit' may include a sum of money 'deposited' with a bank as security for payment or the performance of contractual obligations. A 'loan' refers to a cash advance and not an unpaid consideration, including a deferred or contingent payment. This type of arrangement could raise potential difficulties for certain types of funding arrangements in connection with development of property. This is, of course, a problem in addition to the questions as to whether the building works will form part of the taxable premium for any lease to

---

[471] FA 2003, Sch 15, para 20.

[472] Ibid, Sch 15, para 21; see **13.49**.

[473] Ibid, Sch 15, para 23.

[474] Ibid, Sch 4, para 12.

[475] On the width of these words see, eg, *Clarke Chapman – John Thompson Ltd v IRC* [1975] STC 567.

[476] Which probably includes the deemed grant accruing on substantial performance of the agreement for lease FA 2003, Sch 17A, para 12A.

[477] Income and Corporation Taxes Act 1988, s 839.

[478] On what is a 'deposit' see *Workers Trust and Merchant Bank Ltd v Dojap Investments* [1993] 2 All ER 370 any extra may be part payment or non-loan, non-deposit element outside these provisions.

[479] On the issue of 'loan' or 'debt' see **13.36** and note the drafting trap of *Coren v Keighley* 48 TC 370.

[480] FA 2003, Sch 17A, para 18A(1).

[481] Ibid, Sch 17A, para 18A(2).

[482] *Workers Trust and Merchant Bank Ltd v Dojap Investments* [1993] 2 All ER 370.

be granted[483] and whether the developer can take advantage of the 'subsale' relief for grants of new leases pursuant to FA 2003, Sch 17A, para 12B. In these situations the developer may enter into an agreement for lease with the freeholder which may be a local authority[484] and at the same time enter into some form of funding arrangement with the potential user of the business. This may involve some arrangement for the developer to 'assign his right' under the agreement to the lease and to direct the actual grant of the lease to the funding institution when the building is practically completed. In the meantime the funding institution will by way of loan cover the costs. This may be a 'soft loan' which is on the basis that it will not bear interest which has the advantage that there is no rolled-up interest in the arrangement.[485] There is a risk that, in this situation, FA 2003, Sch 17A, para 18A may operate to convert this loan into some form of chargeable premium which could cause significant difficulties where the funding and the building arrangements are separated in that the developer and the funding institution have entered into one arrangement for the disposal of the land and a separate building contract in an attempt to reduce the tax charge upon the building works.[486] The arrangement is apparently a 'loan' although the arrangement will be that the lease will be granted in discharge of the relevant part of the indebtedness. Paragraph 18A could be a problem since the effects of an assignment pursuant to para 12B is to novate the agreement for lease to the funding institution so that it becomes the 'lessee' as a party potentially within para 18A. In some situations rather than making a 'soft loan' to a developer who is to procure the grant of a lease for a third party to the person providing the funding,[487] the person may make an advance payment,[488] which may have other stamp duty land tax advantages.[489] However, the subsequent repayment or discharge of the loan does not cancel the charge to stamp duty land tax and any tax paid is not repayable.[490]

7.97 These charges do not apply if the amount of the deposit or loan does not exceed twice the maximum rent payable during the first 5 years of the lease or twice the rent payable within the 12 months following the assignment. The tax upon such arrangements cannot be postponed[491] and there is no repayment of any part of the tax paid should the deposit or loan be repaid.[492] These arrangements would not appear to be within these anti-avoidance changes, but genuine funding arrangements and pre-sales or pre-lets will require investigation whether there is a risk of a tax charge.[493]

[483] FA 2003, Sch 4, para 10; see **Chapter 8**.
[484] In which case there may have to be considerable care in order to avoid converting any of the planning arrangements pursuant to a section 106 agreement or its equivalent under other legislation into the taxable consideration for the grant of the lease.
[485] Which may raise other problems; see, for example, *EuroHotel (Belgravia)* [1975] STC 682; and note *Chevron Petroleum v BP* [1981] STC 689.
[486] See **Chapter 8**; *Prudential Assurance Co Ltd v IRC* [1992] STC 863.
[487] *Attorney General v Brown* (1849) 3 Exch 662; FA 2003, Sch 17A, para 12B.
[488] *Faith Construction v Customs and Excise* [1989] STC 539.
[489] Such as excluding buildings works from the chargeable consideration; see *Prudential Assurance Co Ltd v IRC* [1992] STC 863; or excluding fitting out works from the charge to tax; FA 2003, Sch 4, para 10; see **Chapter 8**.
[490] FA 2003, Sch 17A, para 18A(1) and (2) and s 80(4A).
[491] Ibid, s 90.
[492] Ibid, s 80(4A).
[493] See, for example, **2.2** on a potential trap for collective enfranchisement of flats.

'Rent'

General

7.98 Stamp duty land tax is charged upon the net present value of 'rent' in excess of a specified amount[494] at all stages including lease renewals and holding over usually retrospectively, with the potential for multiple obligations to report and pay (or possibly reclaim) extra stamp duty land tax.

7.99 Stamp duty land tax is generally charged at 1 per cent of the net present value of the rent payable over the term of the lease.[495] The treatment of rents differs from premiums and purchase sums. It is provided[496] that the first £125,000 (or temporarily £175,000) for residential property or £150,000 for non-residential property[497] or mixed property (such as leases of shops with flats) of the net present value of the rent[498] is subject to tax at the nil rate[499] but this nil rate slice is apportioned and subject to retrospective re-appointment where there are linked leases of different properties or successive linked leases of the same property.[500] It is only the excess of the net present value of the rent over these figures that attracts the charge to tax at 1 per cent. Also it is not possible to defer payment of the tax charge upon the estimated figures for any variable rents[501] and the liability for this open tax position passes by statute to the assignee of the lease.[502] As there are no statutory indemnities available for the protection of the assignee he is left to the skill of his advisers in both identifying the area of potential risk during title investigation and in producing adequate warranties, indemnities and undertakings, including obligations to notify of notifiable and taxable transaction affecting the assignee where he is not a party to the transaction, in the contract and assignment documentation.[503] In addition, the assignee's tax liability as regards the future rent is dependent upon the assignor's tax position[504] so that a full stamp duty land tax history of the rent reserved by the lease from the exchange of the original agreement for lease is a fundamental part of the title documentation and due diligence required by assignees.[505]

Side effects of rent

7.100 It must also be remembered that the making of a payment described as 'rent' may indicate that the relationship is a tenancy rather than a licence[506] and the first

---

[494] FA 2003, Sch 5, para 2 (as amended).

[495] Ibid, Sch 5, para 2(2); see **5.126**.

[496] Ibid, Sch 5 (as amended).

[497] Ibid, Sch 5, para 2.

[498] Depending upon whether the property is residential or non-residential and whether or not in a disadvantaged area.

[499] For these purposes, the £1000 rent for non-residential property override does not apply; its effect is limited to the question of whether any premium is entitled to be taxed at nil per cent. FA 2003, Sch 5, paras 9 and 9A. The application of the rent override for non-residential property will affect the question as to whether the lease is reportable, since the premium even on a lease for a term not exceeding 7 years will be taxed at the rate of 1 per cent: FA 2003, s 77A.

[500] FA 2003, Sch 5, para 2; Sch 17A, paras 5 and 12 and s 81A; see **7.235**.

[501] Ibid, s 90(7).

[502] Ibid, s 81A; Sch 17A, para 11; see **7.241** and **15.40**.

[503] There are, of course, the issues of protecting or securing the payment of monies etc. by the assignor given that these problems can in theory run throughout the life of a lease for 999 years.

[504] See **7.235**.

[505] See **2.15**.

[506] *Addiscombe Garden Estates Ltd v Crabbe* [1957] 3 All ER 563.

actual payment of 'rent' can operate as a trigger for substantial performance[507] and the creation of an effective date in respect of the agreement for lease, with all the related consequences of payment, reporting and valuation.[508] In addition, becoming entitled to the right to receive and actually receiving rents and profits will involve 'possession' of the land,[509] which constitutes substantial performance of a dealing in an interest reversionary upon a lease,[510] which may be either the freehold or a head lease. This triggering of an effective date in relation to an agreement for lease does not mean the end of the problems, since the actual grant of the lease is also a notifiable event[511] where additional tax may be payable,[512] and pending the formal grant of the lease which appears to supplant the lease and all its outstanding obligations[513] which refers to the deemed lease arising upon substantial performance as being 'surrendered' ie ceasing to exist. In consequence, any obligations to deal with reviews cease to be relevant and the agreement for lease ceases to be relevant for the purposes of any charges that may arise in the event of holding over or a successive linked lease or other matters.

7.101 There are also, potentially, notification and payment obligations in relation to variations of rent.[514] Although the Government has indicated that fundraising and securitisation based upon rents are not intended to be subject to the tax, the legislation does not support this view and any attempts to use the rental flow as a basis for raising money may be a taxable dealing in a chargeable interest.[515]

Linked leases and rent

7.102 The availability of the nil rate to the threshold for the rent depends upon whether there are 'linked transactions'.[516] The introduction of a slice system so that the first £125,000 (temporarily £175,000) or £150,000 of rent is subject to nil rate tax has caused problems in relation to linked transactions. Where there are several leases granted as part of a linked transaction, such as where a landlord grants leases of a chain of shops to a single tenant or a person negotiates for the leases of several units such as warehouses or factories in a development, it is necessary to apportion the nil rate band of stamp duty land tax in respect of the rent reserved by those leases. This apportionment is done between the leases on the basis of their proportionate net present value of the rent calculated in accordance with the formula set out below. It would seem that this amount of nil rate band will be carried forward for any future computations of stamp duty land tax upon the lease, such as upon any 5-year review. It must, however, be noted that there are two distinct regimes for linked leases and the nil rate or lower rate bands but both of these affect assignees in a variety of ways. The two areas are:

- the initial grant of several leases for different properties.[517] This will arise where, for example, there is an arrangement under which a single tenant or various

---

[507] FA 2003, s 44(7).
[508] Ibid, s 44(6)(b); Sch 17A, para 12A; see **7.25**.
[509] Ibid, s 44(6)(a) (as amended).
[510] Ibid, s 44(6)(a).
[511] Ibid, ss 44(8) and 77.
[512] Ibid, ss 44(8) and 80.
[513] Ibid, Sch 17A, para 12A; see **7.25**.
[514] See **Chapter 17**.
[515] *Re Whiting* (1879) 10 Ch D 615; see also *John Lewis Properties v IRC* [2000] STC Sp CD 494; [2003] STC 157 (on appeal) [2003] STC 117.
[516] The assignee of a lease becomes responsible for making any notifications and adjustments that are required in relation to the subsequent adjustment of the nil rate band allocated to the lease assigned to him; ibid, s 81A.
[517] FA 2003, Sch 5, para 2(5) and (6).

connected persons as tenants agree to take leases of several warehouses or factory units from a developer as part of a single commercial arrangement. In this situation there is the question of a possible provisional payment of tax and subsequent retrospective adjustment since these leases may not be granted simultaneously and the linked transaction principles operate retrospectively. In consequence there will be retrospective adjustments in relation to the allocation of the various lower rates for premiums and nil rate slice for the rents.[518] Assignees can become closely involved in these arrangements[519] notwithstanding that they may not be parties to the subsequent arrangements[519] since assignees or, *prima facie*, not the same parties for the purposes of the linked transaction rules;[520] and

- successive linked leases relating to the same, or substantially the same premises.[521] This is anti-avoidance legislation introduced at a late stage by HMRC Stamp Taxes. It was intended to prevent parties entering into short leases where the net present value of the rent did not exceed the nil rate slice threshold and then renewing the lease which would itself qualify for a further nil rate slice in respect of the rent and so on. This set of provisions applies to the additional grant of a lease in respect of specific premises (whether or not linked with leases of different premises) which is renewed. In this situation the leases that HMRC Stamp Taxes would be seeking to link will relate to the same premises, other leases of different property with which it is linked and will affect not only that lease[522] but will essentially start only where the first lease has terminated and is renewed in some way whether by exercise of the option or negotiation.

There is also a related area since a successive linked lease can relate back and affect the tax upon linked leases relating to different properties.

7.103 This section is concerned with the grant of linked leases in the sense of several leases for different premises but granted as part of a single arrangement or scheme. Successive linked leases are dealt with elsewhere.[523] This requires[524] that the transactions form part of 'a single scheme' arrangement or series of transactions between the same lessor and lessee as persons connected with either of them,[525] such as where a person enters into leases for several units on a new industrial or retail development. There will clearly be problems where, for example, a retail chain enters into several leases of premises in different parts of the country with the same landlord; these will almost certainly be regarded as 'linked' by HMRC Stamp Taxes,[526] or because on a change of landlord existing leases may be renegotiated involving surrenders and regrants as a single commercial exercise.

Where there are linked transactions involving the related grant of leases of different premises, the relevant net present value of the rent is the total of the net present values

[518] Ibid, s 81A.
[519] Ibid, s 81A; Sch 17A, para 5.
[520] Ibid, s 108.
[521] Ibid, Sch 17A, para 5.
[522] There may be issues where there are variations between the deemed premises.
[523] See **7.121**.
[524] FA 2003, s 108; see **5.37**.
[525] See **7.58**.
[526] There may be considerable practical problems where the client is instructing several firms of solicitors established in different parts of the country who may not always be aware of their mutual involvement in the transaction.

of the rent payable over the terms of all those leases that are linked and apportioned between them[527] by reference to their proportion of the net present value. There is a formula for this allocation:

$$\frac{NPV}{TNPV}$$

Where

- NPV is the net present value of the rent for one of the leases; and

- TNPV is the total net present value for all of the leases.

This applies to both linked leases of different premises that are granted and later linked leases of any one of those properties[528] since these are treated as a retrospective extension of the original lease requiring a retrospective reallocation of the nil rate slice. The problem will also arise in relation to a situation where there are linked leases of different premises and there are one or more successive linked leases of those linked leases. As it is possible for a later lease, including, it seems, the renewal of a lease pursuant to the exercise of an option,[529] or by reason of negotiation, exercise of options to renew or pursuant to a court order, particularly where the leases being renewed, to be linked with the initial grant, it would appear to be the case that a subsequent lease may be linked with the grant of the original leases.[530] Since a successive linked lease requires the original lease to be treated as 'growing' and be for an enlarged term, it is necessary that there will be a retrospective recalculation of the net present[531] value of the renewed lease upon the basis that it is a lease for the aggregate term retrospectively increasing the net present value for the original lease requiring the stamp duty land tax paid on the original land transaction return and any subsequent payments upon rent reviews or turnover charges to be recalculated on the basis of the longer term. There will be only

---

[527] FA 2003, Sch 5, para 2(5)and (6) (as amended).

[528] Ibid, Sch 17A, para 5.

[529] Similar linked transaction issues may arise where the lease continues an option for the tenant to acquire the landlord's reversion. On the interaction of linked transactions, rents and lump sums see FA 2003, Sch 5, para 9(5). The failure to deal with all consequential changes means that the reference to 'that' section should refer to FA 2003, s 55.

[530] FA 2003, s 81A.

[531] It is highly likely that HMRC Stamp Taxes will regard the decisions to take and grant new leases as part of a linked transaction, producing successive linked leases, especially where the landlord and tenant are connected parties. Certain officers in HMRC Stamp Taxes appear to be of the view that the linked transaction rules apply automatically where the parties are connected. The legislation (FA 2003, s 108) requires a scheme or arrangement between the same parties or parties connected with either of them. HMRC Stamp Taxes do not regard the reference to connected persons as being prefaced by the requirement for a scheme or arrangement. In their view it is enough that the parties are connected and there is no scheme or arrangement. For example, there would be a successive linked lease were A grants a lease to X, a totally unconnected party, and at some stage X assigns the lease to Y Limited and in a further unconnected transaction A acquires the share capital of Y Limited. A negotiated lease renewal in this situation may be regarded by HMRC Stamp Taxes as a successive linked lease because the parties to the new lease are the same as the parties to the old lease at the time of its expiration. There can, in these circumstances, be no scheme or arrangement and therefore the basic condition for the application of the linked transaction rules cannot apply. This, however, does not appear to deter HMRC Stamp Taxes who have taken the view that, in relation to land exchanges, if the parties were connected this would enable them to aggregate transactions in opposite directions for the purposes of determining the rate. This particular point has been dealt with by legislation which is an exercise in self-serving by HMRC Stamp Taxes since the legislation is drafted upon the basis that the bizarre view of HMRC Stamp Taxes was good law and could only be dealt with by way of amending legislation rather than the obvious route of accepting that the basic construction of HMRC Stamp Taxes was fundamentally wrong.

one nil rate slice of rent but there are tax-saving advantages for a tenant to argue for a successive linked lease such as discounting the rent and will produce a lower tax figure than a new lease should the rent reserved by the latter exceed the benefit of the nil rate slice for the rent. The extra tax will have been deferred without interest or penalty. Taxpayers may be tempted to argue for linking and the more aggressive HMRC Stamp Taxes are on the general principles the easier it may be for tenants to reduce their tax burden. Much will depend upon how HMRC Stamp Taxes seek to develop the concept of linked transactions over the next few years;[532] but their current starting point that simply because the same parties are involved, although wrong in principle, is a point helpful to tenants renewing their leases in the longer term should the point be pressed by HMRC Stamp Taxes. This will feed back into the formula determining the fraction for allocating the nil rate slice between the leases by reference to their proportion of the net present value. In consequence, there will be an adjustment in respect of the tax allocated to each of the linked leases of different premises including linked leases yet to be granted which will themselves require a readjustment of the net present values and their proportions. Moreover, this retrospective reallocation between the linked leases already granted and those to be granted can affect assignees of leases who may find that, by reason of circumstances beyond their control and as a result of transactions to which they are not parties, they have incurred a taxation problem which may affect their immediate tax position and their long-term tax position such as where they hold over pursuant to the Landlord and Tenant Act 1954. These linked transaction principles require retrospective revision of the stamp duty land tax the nil rate slice will have to be reallocated because of the retrospective change in relative net present values. This means that tax was initially underpaid for the other leases but there is no clear machinery for dealing with this although it seems clear that the linked transaction rules[533] require the current tenants to report the linked renewal and pay the additional tax arising. The current tenant will also be carrying forward a different, probably reduced, nil rate amount for any rent reviews and other subsequent events giving rise to a charge to tax. This will arise every time there is a linked transaction by renewal of any of the leases concerned. An assignee of any of those leases will need to know the amount of nil rate relief that has been allocated to the lease that he is acquiring. It would also appear to be necessary for him to require information of any adjustments made by the assignor or any third assignees of any of the leases as a result of linked transactions, since the obligation to make further returns in respect of land transactions attaches to the lease and passes to the assignee.[534]

7.104 The issues that need to be considered in this context include:

- HMRC Stamp Taxes have already introduced anti-avoidance legislation relating to lease renewals by amendments prior to the commencement of the tax;[535] and

- break clauses are frequently less tax efficient than options and are particularly identified as targets for the general anti-avoidance provisions.[536] When determining the length of the lease break clauses are ignored and the rent is taxed by reference to the maximum duration of the lease. There is no refund should the break clause be exercised. Short leases with options to renew may be more

---

[532] It is also possibly that they may seek to apply the general anti-avoidance provisions but this is unlikely to produce any additional tax in the situation under discussion.
[533] FA 2003, s 81A and Sch 17A, para 12.
[534] Ibid, Sch 17A, para 5.
[535] See **7.121**.
[536] FA 2003, ss 75A–75C.

efficient, particularly if, as expected, HMRC Stamp Taxes take an aggressive, short-sighted approach to linked transactions.[537] This offers potential simple tax savings; but without regarding it as deferred or instalment consideration and allowing for an interest element.[538] The discounting is to take account of inflation and is not adjusted by HMRC Stamp Taxes as far as the formula is concerned as interest rates vary.

The position will depend upon the circumstances and whether the original parties remain landlord and tenant since the linked transaction rules do not apply where options to renew leases are exercised by assignees.[539] However, there are potentially considerable advantages or possibly even relatively minor advantages for taxpayers if the level of rents is appropriate. For example, where there is a lease for 15 years with a provision for breaks at five and 10 years there will be a charge to tax upon 15 years net present value rent and no refund should the break clause be exercised ie tax is wasted.[540] However, where the parties enter into a lease for 5 years with an option to renew for 5 and a further option to renew for 5 years.[541] There is only one lease and no other leases with which it can be linked either at the same time or as successive linked leases. There will, therefore, be a nil rate slice in respect of the rent and tax to pay only upon the net present value of 5 years' rent. When the lease is renewed either:

- there will be a new lease for a term of 5 years. This will attract tax upon a higher level of rent but will be eligible for a new nil rate slice in respect of the net present value of the rent. To some extent the tax paid at this stage will represent the tax that would have arisen in respect of a 10 year lease but this proportion of the tax has been deferred without the payment of interest or penalty; or

- HMRC Stamp Taxes successfully establish that the two leases are linked successively. There will be tax upon the basis of a 10 year lease. This means that there will not be a new nil rate slice but the rent will be suitably discounted and will, *prima facie*, be the assumed rent and not the passing rent reserved by the new lease. There will, therefore, be the postponement of tax that would have been paid for a period of 5 years without interest or penalty; and

- similar consequences would apply where there is a further renewal after 10 years. Should HMRC Stamp Taxes successfully establish that all three leases are linked the stamp duty land tax would be the same as that which would have been paid in respect of a 15 year lease with break clauses but substantial parts of the tax will have been postponed for a significant period without interest or penalty. On the other hand, if HMRC Stamp Taxes cannot establish that there is the scheme or arrangement necessary to link the transactions there will have been tax upon higher rents but with the benefit of three nil rate slices in respect of the rent and

[537] See **Chapter 5**.
[538] Compare *Vestey v IRC* [1965] 1 All ER 917.
[539] See **7.107**.
[540] FA 2003, Sch 17A, para 2(6). There is, however, a major problem of principle where the original lease reserves a variable rend and the lease is terminated during the first 5 years of the term so that the rent becomes ascertained at nil for certain years (FA 2003, s 80). This is a wide-ranging problem for all terminations during the first 5 years especially since the reaction of HMRC Stamp Taxes to changes in the rate of VAT means that virtually all leases are for a variable rent.
[541] Taking care to avoid the perpetually renewable leases problems; Law of Property Act 1925, s 149(3); although such provisions are ignored when determining the length of a lease for the purposes of stamp duty land tax. FA 2003, Sch 17A, para 4(2) has the effect that such a lease will be for its original term and grow as appropriate.

deferral of the payment of tax upon part without any interest or penalty charges. Should the tenant not renew there will not be any tax to pay thereby saving the tax that would have been paid and lost with the exercise of a break clause.

Successive linked leases – options to renew – anti-avoidance

7.105 For certain relatively small rent leases there is an obvious stamp duty land tax strategy of short-term leases with an option to renew on one or more occasions, seeking to obtain the benefit of several nil rate slices for the rent and deferring the payment of stamp duty land tax without interest or penalty. For example, a lease of retail premises for 7 years at an annual rent of £50,000 will attract a stamp duty land tax charge upon £100,000 approximately (ie the net present value of the rent as discounted less the £150,000 nil rate slice). However, a lease of the same premises for 3 years and 6 months with an option to renew for a similar term will be, broadly, tax free since the net present value of the rents with discounting will not exceed the nil rate threshold on either occasion.[542] In order to counteract this possible mitigation technique HMRC Stamp Taxes might seek to contend that they are 'successive linked leases', ie lease renewals which form part of a single scheme or arrangement with the original lease which is difficult for them to establish since they will not have the relevant evidence; their attack will have to be based upon presumptions and inferences which they may find difficult to substantiate or because their approach could imply a fraudulent or negligent return, they may be faced with a heavy burden of proof.[543] Therefore, an issue remains to be resolved is whether a lease which arises by reason of the exercise of an option to renew an existing lease is a linked transaction. The same principles apply as for other linked transactions[544] requiring a pre-arranged scheme or understanding that the lease would be renewed. This may be difficult for HMRC Stamp Taxes to establish where the term of the lease is a reasonable duration such as 5 years or longer, because there must be an element of commercial uncertainty as to whether the renewal will necessarily be implemented. The longer the lease the more difficult it may be to establish an arrangement for renewal.

7.106 HMRC Stamp Taxes may have scored an impressive own goal because the more they press for transactions to be linked the greater the opportunity for stamp duty land tax mitigation for leases for larger rents. Should the leases be 'unlinked' there will be a nil rate slice against the new rent. However, for larger commercial leases the nil rate slice of £150,000 is likely to be insignificant when set against the discounting of the rent over time. For example, on a lease for a rent of £1,000,000 per annum the tax saved by discounting on a linked successive lease, together with the cash flow benefit of deferring interest without penalty free the payment of substantial tax will inevitably be greater than the benefit of an additional nil rate slice. This benefit arises because of the differences in treatment of new leases and successive linked leases, namely:

- a new lease pays tax on the passing rent after deducting the nil rate slice and starts the discounting afresh;

---

[542] The position for commercial arrangements is even more efficient should the parties elect to proceed by way of a licence (totally tax free). Unfortunately, solicitors have advised potential lenders to the business that such an arrangement may not, for reasons which they usually refuse to explain, provide adequate security. It is, of course, the role of those advising mortgagees or lenders to raise problems and not to co-operate in the search for a solution that might be beneficial to all parties to the transaction.

[543] *Re Wragge* [1897] 1 Ch 796.

[544] See **5.113**.

- a successive linked lease pays delayed tax on the notional rent which is likely to be less than the passing rent and has the benefit of accrued discounting reducing the chargeable rent even further.

Assignees of leases and linked transactions

7.107 The linked transaction rules apply only to transactions between the same parties or persons connected with them.[545] This might suggest that, where the lease or the freehold reversion has been assigned, the exercise of the option to renew is not between the same parties. However, it has from time to time been the view of HMRC Stamp Taxes that where a contract is assigned, the original party/assignor and the assignee are to be treated as the same person.[546] In consequence, there is a risk that, for example, the exercise of an option to renew the lease by a purchaser of the lease will be regarded as a linked transaction attracting a higher rate of stamp duty land tax upon the new lease and a recalculation of the stamp duty land tax upon the original lease. The assignee of a lease may be adversely affected where a subsequent linked lease between other parties reduces the amount of the nil rate slice allocated to the lease.[547] It is hoped that these huge problems are inadvertent and HMRC Stamp Taxes will not be aware of and take the points in order to impose serious penalties upon taxpayers who do not link all three transactions, but merely charge the original lease retrospectively, particularly as the taxpayer will not be the 'purchaser' of that lease in a general sense and it seems harsh to tax someone retrospectively where he has technically ceased to own the property, and the new lease did not exist at the time of the exercise of the option to renew.

7.108

Net present value of 'rent'

The formula for determining the amount of the rent upon which the stamp duty land tax is to be charged[548] is:

$$v = \sum_{i=1}^{n} \frac{r_i}{(1+T)}$$

where:
   'v is the net present value of the rent, ie the chargeable amount;
   'Σ' is the generally accepted mathematical symbol for the sum of a series of numbers between an upper and a lower limit which limits are respectively denoted by the terms above and below the symbol in the formula. In this case the range is from 1 to the contractual or other deemed termination date for the lease;

---

[545] Ibid, s 108; see **Chapter 5**.
[546] On the ambiguity in relation to assignments see **Chapter 6**.
[547] FA 2003, Sch 5, para 2(5) and (6) (as amended).
[548] This appears to assume that there is judicial notice or a rule of statutory interpretation whereby certain mathematic symbols and conventions do not require explanation or definition.

'ri' is the rent payable in respect of[549] year 'i';[550]

'i' is first, second, third etc years of the term;[551]

'n' is the term of the lease, ie the number of years up to contractual or other deemed termination date for the lease; and

'T' is the temporal discount rate, currently 3.5 per cent but subject to change by statutory instrument.[552] This produces a denominator of 1.035. Because the low number in the range is '1' discounting is available for the first year's rent regardless of whether it is paid in advance or in arrears. Given the importance of the effective date as regards the charging provisions, it appears that when, for example, a subsequent notification and self-assessment is required in relation to an uncertain rent pursuant to FA 2003, Sch 17A, paras 7 and 8, the temporal discount rate to be inserted as 'T' is the rate in force on the original effective date and not the rate in force at the date of the later rent payment.

The detailed calculation involved in this formula is, in effect, a document of title and should be retained for the life of the lease.[553]

7.109 The formula is essentially an attempt to 'capitalise' the rent by aggregating the rent payable, suitably discounted, over the term of the lease, ie a bizarre concept of turning rent into a purchase price paid by instalments but taxed in a particular way. HMRC Stamp Taxes have provided an online facility in order to enable solicitors and other professional advisers to calculate the tax.[554] In consequence, for short leases at relatively low rents, the shorter the lease, the more likely it is to qualify for the nil rate band of stamp duty land tax.[555] It will, however, be an essential requirement for the protection of the client that appropriate calculations are carried out prior to entering into any agreements for lease in order to discover the term which produces the most reasonable result consistent with the overall commercial wishes of the landlord and the tenant. However, it is fundamental to the operation of these provisions that, as regards the early land transaction returns, the key factors in the equation will have to be prepared upon an estimated basis. For example, when investigating the amount of 'rent' to be inserted in the formula it is necessary to take into account that the rent may be variable during the first 5 years of the term. This will almost inevitably be the case since only rents that are linked to RPI are regarded as not variable rents,[556] but since such rents will almost inevitably be subject to VAT for commercial premises the rents remain variable and there is the question of whether VAT in respect of any RPI increase, is also

---

[549] Which may not be the same as rent paid during the year.

[550] As amended by FA 2006, s 164(2) (amending Sch 5) presumably intended, *inter alia*, to prevent parties mitigating tax by separating the dates for contractual payment and actual payment or converting premiums into rent payments over several years.

[551] There are certain issues in relation to the tax treatment of the rent since this may be expressed as rent 'for' the year, rent paid in a year, or rent paid in respect of or in relation to a year. HMRC Stamp Taxes appear, in practice, to attach great significance to their perception of the subtle differences in the drafting.

[552] It should be noted that a simple indexation of rents is ignored (FA 2003, Sch 17A, para 7(5)) so that an increase in rent if solely by reference to the Retail Prices Index (RPI) does not attract stamp duty land tax and such increases are to be ignored in determining whether there is an abnormal increase in rent. The draftsman has, unsurprisingly, failed to deal with the consequential problem of whether, because RPI increases are to be ignored, any VAT arising upon the RPI increase is also to be ignored. It seems, however, such VAT on the RPI is an increase in the rent as far as HMRC Stamp Taxes are concerned. It is understood that the temporal discount rate is also intended to allow for inflation by reducing the chargeable amount for future rents. However, HMRC Stamp Taxes have not complied with the legislative policy by adjusting the temporal discount rate in line with inflationary trends.

[553] See **2.15**.

[554] A print out of this page has, in effect, become a document of title.

[555] But there may be issues of linked transactions and options to renew; see **7.105**.

[556] FA 2003, Sch 17A, para 7(5).

to be ignored. Tenancies within the agricultural holdings and similar legislation have been brought within the variable rents charge[557] and the changes in the rate of VAT have highlighted the fact that even where the rent appears to be fixed for the first 5 years of the term it is technically variable where it is subject to VAT because the rate of VAT may vary.[558] Similarly, although the term of the lease, for the purposes of the calculation, is fixed by reference to the period between the effective date for the lease[559] and the contractual termination date, there are many situations such as holding over pursuant to the Landlord and Tenant Act 1954 requiring a retrospective recalculation of the tax by reference to a lease for a longer term. Moreover, since the linked transaction rules and the successive linked transaction rules[560] operate on a retrospective basis and apply to assignees of leases[561] the calculation may require adjustment in the light of circumstances taking effect outside the scope of the lease itself.[562] The initial application of the formula is, therefore, initially provisional on a 'guestimated' basis requiring adjustment and the obligation to adjust may affect the assignee of the lease.[563]

7.110 There are certain key elements in the application of the formula to determine the net present value of the rent. This requires a detailed understanding of the precise meanings of the factors in the equation and how they apply to the facts of each case. These are as follows.

Temporal discount rate

7.111 The temporal discount rate is, initially, 3.5 per cent producing a current denominator of 1.035; but this is variable to such other rates as may be specified by regulations made by the Treasury pursuant to FA 1989, s 178.

7.112 Although not specifically stated, it appears from the general computational provisions in relation to the 'effective date', which appear to apply to only one date,[564] that the temporal discount rate at the effective date applies to all subsequent computations which 'relate back' to the initial computation of the stamp duty land tax as at the effective date such as the first rent review or holding over pursuant to the Landlord and Tenant Act 1954. In consequence, the original rate applies to any recalculation of the stamp duty land tax upon the grant of the lease or where an uncertain rent becomes less uncertain and further notification and calculation is required,[565] notwithstanding that the temporal discount rate may have been changed by regulations in the intervening period.

---

[557] Ibid, Sch 17A, para 7(4A).
[558] See **7.150**.
[559] FA 2003, Sch 17A, para 12A.
[560] Ibid, s 108; Sch 5, para 2(5) and (6) and Sch 17A, para 5.
[561] Ibid, s 81A; Sch 17A, para 12.
[562] Such as, perhaps, the exercise by the landlord of the option to tax the rent to VAT; see **7.151**.
[563] The assignee of a lease may not have to take over the open tax position of the assignor but his tax position may be affected by the tax position of the assignor such as the rent for the lease years outside the first 5 years of the term. Without knowledge of the assignor's tax position the assignee will not be in a position to deal with his own tax position satisfactorily; see **7.235**.
[564] Ie, the relevant effective date, see **7.25**.
[565] Persons seeking to utilise the promised online facility for calculating the stamp duty land tax may need to investigate whether the rate has been changed and that they are accessing the correct facility. Unless HMRC Stamp Taxes preserve the existing facility, notwithstanding the introduction of new rates, the facility will rapidly become useless. Nevertheless, as the point may be overlooked in the updating process, the appropriate due diligence will be required.

The term of the lease

7.113 A key factor in determining the net present value of the rent is the term of the lease. This involves a multi-stage process. The initial return requires certain assumptions to be applied;[566] but these are provisional and the initial assumed term has to be revisited and retrospectively revised in the light of subsequent events such as holding over[567] and certain renewals.[568] These issues as to the provisional nature of the term pass to assignees of the lease.[569]

It is important to remember that there are at least six important dates in relation to the length of a lease. These are:

- the date from which the term is to be computed (referred to as 'the contractual term'),[570] which may frequently be earlier than any agreement for lease, substantial performance or the actual grant. This is usually described as the 'term commencement date';

- the date of the agreement for lease;

- the date of the substantial performance of the agreement for lease;

- the date of the grant of the lease itself;

- the effective date of a previous or expired lease where there is a holding over or successive linked lease or other circumstance where an existing lease 'grows' for the purposes of stamp duty land tax; and

- the contractual termination date of an expired lease where there has been a backdating of a new lease.[571]

7.114 Four of these are important in relation to stamp duty land tax:

- the 'term commencement date', ie the date from which the term of the lease is calculated as the contractual term, which is frequently a date prior to the effective date and the grant of the lease,[572] is important usually in determining the 5-year period for rent reviews[573] where the rent credit for holding over is available[574] and for the application of the different notification obligations when the lease is 'granted' which depend upon the meaning of a 7-year term;[575]

---

[566]   FA 2003, Sch 17A, para 3.
[567]   Ibid, Sch 17A, para 5.
[568]   See, for example, FA 2003, Sch 17A, paras 2, 3 and 4.
[569]   For example, FA 2003, Sch 17A, para 12; see **7.235**.
[570]   FA 2003, s 77; *Alan Estates Ltd v WG Stores Ltd* [1981] 3 All ER 481.
[571]   Ibid, Sch 17A, paras 9 and 9A.
[572]   Note the issues for 'backdated rent' as a taxable premium; FA 2003, Sch 5, para 1A; see **7.38**.
[573]   See **7.134** and **7.162**.
[574]   FA 2003, Sch 17A, para 9A.
[575]   Ibid, ss 44(8) and 77.

- the date of substantial performance,[576] ie the effective date which starts certain of the notifications and payment provisions[577] and may be the relevant date for fixing the term in calculating the stamp duty land tax[578] at least on a provisional basis pending the formal grant of the lease;[579]

- the date of the actual grant of the lease, which is a transaction which has to be notified and additional tax may be payable,[580] being the date from which the 30-day notification and payment provisions run;[581]

- the termination date of a prior or surrendered lease for calculating the rent credit for new leases[582] and whether backdated rent is rent or premium.[583]

Moreover, these dates for one lease may be important for another lease such as for a successive linked lease which is aggregated with the earlier lease,[584] or for holding over arrangements pursuant to Landlord and Tenant Act 1954 (as amended) where the original lease is deemed to be extended by 1 year.[585]

Term of the lease for rent duty calculation

7.115 Certain provisions in the original FA 2003 set out a procedure for calculating the term by identifying the start date for stamp duty land tax purposes.[586] These were repealed before the legislation took effect and have not been expressly replaced. However, it seems that in practice the effective date will be the start date from which the term of the lease will be calculated for these purposes;[587] but it has to be noted that in many cases the initial calculation merely provides only a provisional term since it will be replaced by the grant of the lease[588] and even this term may have to be revised retrospectively from time to time for situations where lease 'grow' such as periodic tenancies[589], holding over by operation of law[590] and certain lease renewals.[591]

Fixed terms[592]

7.116 A lease granted for a fixed term is treated for this purpose as a lease for a definite term equal to the fixed term[593] But even this simple situation is not specific as to the

---

[576] Ibid, s 44(3); see **Chapter 14**.
[577] Ibid, s 77 and Sch 17A, para 12A.
[578] Ibid.
[579] Ibid, Sch 17A, para 12A; see **7.235**.
[580] Ibid, Sch 17A, para 12A; see also s 44(8)(b).
[581] Ibid, Sch 5, para 6(2), but not replaced by ibid, Sch 17A.
[582] Ibid, Sch 17A, para 9.
[583] Ibid, Sch 17A, para 9A.
[584] Ibid, Sch 17A, para 9A.
[585] Ibid, Sch 17A, paras 3 and 9.
[586] Ibid, Sch 5, para 6(3).
[587] The current official interpretation of FA 2003, Sch 17A, para 12A as creating two separate chargeable transactions means that the date for the purposes under discussion may change depending upon the hitherto random nature of the formal grant of the lease. This practice of treating the formal grant as a matter of convenience may have to change dramatically in order to protect clients.
[588] FA 2003, Sch 17A, para 12A.
[589] See ibid, Sch 17A, para 4; see **7.119**.
[590] Ibid, Sch 17A, para 3; see **7.123**.
[591] Ibid, Sch 17A, para 5; see **7.105**.
[592] The term of the lease is relevant when determining whether an alternative finance bond is exempt from stamp duty land tax (FA 2009, Sch 61, para 6).
[593] FA 2003, Sch 17A, para 2.

start date. It does not deal with the situation of where the term of the lease is backdated to a previous quarter day ie whether the term is the contractual term from the term commencement date or is a term from the effective date. In that situation the term of the lease is measured from the term commencement date as a matter of contract; but it seems that the term of the lease for stamp duty land tax is from the effective date where these differ, and will be the later effective date of the actual grant of the lease where this differs from substantial performance[594] so that the effective date and initial terms at substantial performance must be regarded as provisional.

Special provisions apply to a lease for a fixed term that may continue beyond the fixed term by operation of law.[595] In this case, basically, the lease is retrospectively treated as 'growing' by 1 year. There is, therefore, a retrospective readjustment in relation to the initial return by reference to the deemed longer term. Initially such leases are unlikely to give rise to a tax charge because of the rent level, but the net present value will grow as the lease 'grows' and notification will be required when tax becomes payable. However, there is no obligation to notify simply because a lease becomes a deemed lease for 7 years or longer.[596]

Break clauses etc

7.117 When seeking to determine the length of a lease for a fixed term,[597] no account is taken of any contingency as a result of which the lease may determine before the end of the fixed term or the right of either party to determine the lease or to renew it such as by notice to quit, forfeiture or otherwise nor is an option to renew taken into account.[598] In other words, provisions for serving a notice to quit or a break clause or an option to renew or extend are ignored.[599] In this situation the lease is for the maximum term and there is no readjustment of the tax in the form of repayment where the lease is terminated by the exercise of a break clause. The initial tax and any subsequent re-self-assessment will have had to be made on the basis of the potential length of the term, ignoring the break clause. The exercise of the break clause, or any other procedure for terminating the lease such as forfeiture for breach, will shorten the term, which shorter term, had it applied originally would have meant a lower charge to stamp duty land tax. There does not appear to be any machinery for the tenant to take advantage of the early termination of the lease to recalculate the stamp duty land tax and reclaim excess tax paid on the basis of the longer term; except perhaps where the break clause is exercised during the first 5 years of the term with a variable rent when it is arguable that the rent becomes ascertained at nil so there may be a repayment claim; but the attitude of HMRC Stamp Taxes is unknown. However, where the lease has the benefit of an option to renew the lease this may extend the term of the lease requiring retrospective additional tax to be payable where the exercise of the option to renew produces a successive linked leases.[600]

---

[594] Ibid, Sch 17A, para 12A.
[595] Ibid, Sch 17A, para 3(1)(b).
[596] Ibid, Sch 17A, paras 3(5) and 4(4A).
[597] The existence of a break clause and the likelihood of its exercise are, however, potentially significant issues in valuation such as where there is an issue of a market value premium.
[598] FA 2003, Sch 17A, para 2.
[599] Which would appear to be different concepts: see *Baker v Merckel* [1960] 1 QB 657.
[600] FA 2003, Sch 17A, para 5; see **7.102**.

Holding over

7.118 In the case of a lease which was subject to stamp duty land tax on the effective date[601] for a fixed term and thereafter until determined or a lease for a fixed term which may continue beyond the fixed term by operation of law[602] such as, presumably, a 'shorthold tenancy', a lease within the Landlord and Tenant Act 1954[603] or the Agricultural Holdings Act 1986 where there is a statutory tenancy or extension of a stamp duty land tax lease in the holding-over arrangements, the lease is initially treated as if it were a lease for the original fixed term.[604] If the lease continues after the end of the initial fixed term, it is treated as if it were a lease for a fixed 1 year longer than the original fixed term. If the lease continues beyond the extension up to expiration of the fixed term, this is retrospectively treated as a lease for a fixed term 2 years longer than the original fixed term, and so on in the third, fourth and subsequent years.[605] This requires a retrospective recalculation of the original tax as this will have been affected by any subsequent retrospective adjustments for rent reviews. Returns are required and tax may have to be paid. This is an obligation that runs with the lease[606] so that any assignee of the lease will require a full stamp duty land tax history in order to have the original information (and any variations thereof) so that he can perform the retrospective recalculation in order to determine his liability.

Leases for indefinite terms[607]

7.119 A lease for an indefinite term[608] such as a periodic tenancy or other interest or right[609] terminable by a period of notice,[610] a tenancy at will or any other interest or right terminable by notice at any time,[611] is treated initially as if it were a lease for a fixed term of 1 year.[612] If it continues after the end of the year, it is treated as a lease for a fixed term of 2 years. Continuation beyond the second year retrospectively produces a

---

[601] As this provision applies only to leases that may continue by operation of law, it will not apply to leases where there is an option to renew, which option is on general principle ignored, at least until such time as it is exercised; FA 2003, Sch 17A, para 4.

[602] FA 2003, Sch 17A, paras 3(1) and (2)(a).

[603] There are at present unanswered questions of whether these rules apply to contracted out tenancies. The problem lacks practical experience since HMRC Stamp Taxes currently treat stamp duty leases as outside these provisions and few, if any, stamp duty land tax leases have expired so as to become held over.

[604] FA 2003, Sch 17A, paras 3 and 4.

[605] On holding over generally see **7.195**.

[606] FA 2003, s 81A; Sch 17A, para 12.

[607] Other than, presumably, a lease for a fixed term with a break clause: see FA 2003, Sch 17A, para 2(b).

[608] It has to be noticed that leases for indefinite terms may be void for uncertainty such as *Lace v Chantler* [1944] KB 368. The concept in the legislation must, therefore, bear a narrow meaning such as periodic tenancies or leases for a fixed term and thereafter initial termination by notice which is in effect a special form of periodic tenancy.

[609] See **7.13** on whether temporary interests other than leases are 'leases' such as a right of way granted but limited to the duration of the development. This legislative 'explanation' of an indefinite term by referring to interest etc would appear to support an argument by HMRC Stamp Taxes that a right having a limited duration is taxable as a 'lease'.

[610] FA 2003, Sch 17A, para 4(5). No clear transitional provisions are made for leases for an indefinite term which commenced prior to 1 December 2003. It seems that HMRC Stamp Taxes may be prepared to treat such tenancies as not falling into stamp duty land tax no matter how long they continue. Unfortunately, this is not necessarily supported by the legislation. This possible practice may not be adopted and continued by HMRC Stamp Taxes because it offers significant opportunities for avoidance.

[611] Ibid, Sch 17A, para 4(1)(a).

[612] Ibid, Sch 17A, para 4(3)(a). It is important to note that these provisions apply only for the purposes of calculating the tax upon the rent; it does not deem the lease to have that term for valuation purposes. Thus a lease for 7 years with an option to renew is taxed as a lease for 7 years although any deemed market value premium will take into account the existence of the option to renew and the possibility that it will be exercised.

lease of a fixed term for 3 years, and so on.[613] These provisions override any legislative provisions relating to leases for indefinite terms such as the provision in the Law of Property Act 1925[614] dealing with leases for life or perpetually renewable leases.[615]

7.120 If the deemed lease for 1 year meets the conditions of having a sufficiently high rent,[616] it has to be notified and tax paid.[617] If it is not initially notifiable because the rent or premium falls below the threshold for leases for less than 7 years[618] but the effect of the continuation beyond the deemed fixed term for 1 year (or deemed 2- or 3-year terms as a result of continuation of the lease) means that the transaction subsequently becomes notifiable or tax becomes payable for the first time because the retrospectively recalculated net present value of the rent exceeds the nil rate threshold, the tenant must deliver a return in respect of the transaction before the expiration of 30 days after the end of the initial term or the deemed second or third-year term. If the transaction was previously notifiable or tax has previously been paid, then a further return is required and additional tax will be payable on an annual basis because the net present value of the rent, having previously exceeded the nil rate slice, the inclusion of an additional year's rent will inevitably increase the taxable amount.[619] Any such return or further return must include the usual self-assessment of tax chargeable, but such tax is calculated by reference to the rates and the nil rate slice[620] in force at the effective date of the transaction, which appears to be the date of substantial performance or the grant of the initial lease or tenancy.[621] The return no longer needs to be accompanied by the payment of any tax or additional tax payable;[622] but the tax must be paid within the 30 day period. Such returns are fully within FA 2003, Sch 10.

Options to renew and similar arrangements

7.121 It is provided that the existence of an option to renew, and presumably an option to extend,[623] are to be ignored[624] in determining the length of the term when calculating the stamp duty land tax,[625] but this position may have to be retrospectively revised in the light of subsequent developments.[626] Where 'successive leases' are granted or treated as granted, of the same or substantially the same premises[627] and those grants are 'linked transactions', the series of leases is treated as if it were a single lease which was granted at the time of the grant of the first lease in the series, for a term equal to the aggregate of the terms of all the leases in the series and in consideration of the rent payable under all

---

[613] It is a retrospective adjustment to the lease not the grant of a deemed new lease.

[614] Section 149 and Law of Property Act 1922, s 8.

[615] FA 2003, Sch 17A, para 4(2).

[616] Allowing for the fact that discounting applies to the first year.

[617] FA 2003, ss 77 and 77A.

[618] See ibid, s 77A.

[619] Ibid, s 77.

[620] It seems that since the provision operates on a retrospective basis there will be no recognition of the fact that the nil rate slice for rent has been charged since the relevant effective date for the lease. Tax will be payable and notifiable notwithstanding that the net present value of the rent is below the nil rate slice at the time of the relevant 'extension' of the term; the measure is the nil rate slice of the relevant effective date.

[621] FA 2003, Sch 17A, para 12A.

[622] Ibid, s 76(3)(b) (repealed).

[623] Which would appear to be different concepts: see *Baker v Merckel* [1960] 1 QB 657; FA 2003, Sch 5, para 6(5).

[624] Ibid, Sch 5, para 6(5).

[625] Ibid, Sch 17A, para 2.

[626] Ibid, Sch 17A, para 5. On the possible benefits of options and their comparison with break clauses see **7.104**.

[627] Where there are differences in the demised premises which arise by reason of the negotiations of the parties as a consequence of the development of the property during the currency of the original lease it will be difficult for HMRC Stamp Taxes to argue for a linked lease.

of the leases[628] although the relevant 'rent' to be included in the formula for determining the net present value will be the assumed rent where the lease is extended after or 'grows' into a lease beyond the fifth year of the deemed term. In consequence, where there is an exercise of an option to renew a lease if this forms a linked transaction with the lease which is being renewed, then the actual leases arising pursuant to the exercise of the option are ignored and the renewed lease is treated as if it were part of the original lease which is 'extended' to a term equal to the aggregate of the two separate terms. In consequence, there has to be a recalculation of the tax due[629] in respect of the first lease in the series upon the basis that it is the lease for a term equal to the aggregate of the terms of the original lease and the renewed lease, and the rent formula is applied in respect of the rent payable under the new deemed lease. This will be the rent with the benefit of reliefs and discounting from the effective date for the original lease and with the benefit of the variable rent rules such as the rent for all years after the fifth year of the original lease (ie the assumed rent)[630] being applied to the new aggregate lease.[631]

7.122 The difficult question which will only be effectively answered in practice as HMRC Stamp Taxes reveal their overall policy is when the successive leases are vulnerable to claims that they are 'linked transactions' particularly as it will sometimes be beneficial for the tenant to argue that the two leases are linked.[632] If HMRC Stamp Taxes does not take the point that the successive leases are linked then the new lease will be eligible for a further slice of nil rate rent. Two basic conditions need to be satisfied before transactions can be 'linked',[633] namely:

• all of the transactions need to be between the same parties or persons connected with them. In consequence, it would seem that where a lease with an option to renew is assigned to an assignee who is unconnected with the original tenant, any exercise of the option to renew by the assignee will not be a linked transaction for these purposes; and

• there must be a single scheme, arrangement or series of transactions.[634] Moreover, as FA 2003, s 46(1), merely provides that options and the transaction arising from the exercise of the option only 'may' be linked transactions, it would seem that this provision will only apply where there is a pre-arranged plan between the same landlord and tenant (or persons connected with them) that the option will be exercised. If at the time the lease is granted there are no 'side arrangements' or understandings between the parties that the option will be exercised and there are commercial possibilities that it may or may not be exercised in due course, the transactions will not be linked.[635] Clearly, when the lease has a substantial term it is less likely that HMRC Stamp Taxes will be able to establish that there is a linkage between the grant of the lease initially and its renewal by the exercise of an

---

[628] FA 2003, Sch 17A, para 5; see further **7.105**.

[629] This may also mean that any original relief, such as disadvantaged land, is available for the new lease; see **Chapter 11**.

[630] See **7.164**.

[631] FA 2003, Sch 17A, para 5.

[632] See **5.37** and **5.113**.

[633] FA 2003, s 108.

[634] See **5.43**.

[635] HMRC Stamp Taxes may have to decide their view on situations where the parties having discussed a lease with break clauses decide to proceed on the basis of a renewable lease in the expectation that the lease is likely to be renewed if circumstances are favourable. Whilst there is a high probability that the lease will continue there is a lack of certainty so that the previous commercial negotiations for a longer lease will not, of themselves, link the leases.

option. It does, however, mean that there are difficult questions that the person completing the form has to answer concerning the commercial background to the grant of the initial lease.

Strict theory would suggest presumptions that apart from leases for very short terms (broadly 3 years or less) lease renewals are not linked because of the commercial uncertainties making 'a' scheme in the sense of a firm pre-ordained understanding an unlikely scenario. However, given HMRC Stamp Taxes' suspicion that short leases will be adopted in order to maximise the number of nil rate slices may lure them into being basically aggressive on linked transactions generally, which is already beginning to emerge as a basic approach, and so facilitate the ability of tenants to exploit the successive linked lease rules to their advantage.[636]

Holding over

7.123 It frequently happens that a tenant may continue in occupation of the premises notwithstanding that the contractual termination date for the lease has passed. In this situation the tenant will usually be either a licensee (which is not a chargeable interest for the purposes of stamp duty land tax)[637] or a tenant at will (which is also not a chargeable interest for the purpose of stamp duty land tax) or a trespasser. In consequence, the basic position would appear to be that where a tenant continues in occupation there will be no stamp duty land tax obligations arising. It may be that the arrangement produces some form of informal common law periodic tenancy which may depend upon the arrangements for the payment of 'rent'. However, even if there should be such a common law tenancy it is unlikely to give rise to stamp duty land tax charges and notification obligations because the rent will not necessarily exceed £150,000. As the arrangement involves a tenancy for 1 year with rent below the nil rate threshold, there will be no notification obligations.[638] Obviously, if the continued occupation in the form of periodic tenancy continues beyond a year then the lease will grow and the size of the net present value of the rent over the longer term will also increase so that, eventually, there may be an obligation to file and pay tax. This will become an annual event once rent has first become taxable for so long as the lease continues.

Holding over pursuant to leases granted within the stamp duty land tax regime

7.124 Whether this consequence arises depends upon the obscure meaning of 'a lease for a fixed term but may continue beyond the fixed term by operation of law'.[639] It appears that this is intended to mean holding over after the contractual termination date within some statutory provision such as the Landlord and Tenant Act 1954 or the Agricultural Holdings Act 1986.[640] It would not appear to apply to holding over in respect of expired leases that were contracted out nor to tenancies not within these provisions. There has been a certain amount of confused advice from HMRC Stamp Taxes in relation to situations where the tenant continues in occupation not pursuant to

---

636 It remains to be seen in practice whether HMRC Stamp Taxes can find any advantage (i e additional stamp duty land tax) by applying the general anti-avoidance provisions (FA 2003, ss 75A–75C) to these arrangements.

637 But see licences as substantial performance at **14.16**.

638 FA 2003, s 77A.

639 These rules do not apply to a lease for a fixed term and thereafter until determined because in such cases the same lease continues and does not expire so that there is no holding over.

640 Compare the provisions in FA 2003, Sch 17A, para 9A which refer to 'continues in occupation' which differs from 'operation of law' and the Landlord and Tenant Act 1954 (see para 9 thereof) but also may require the continuation in occupation to produce taxable rent (see para 9A(3) and (4)).

statutory provisions such as holding over a lease that is contracted out of the Landlord and Tenant Act 1954. However, it seems that this is not regarded as being 'by operation of law' notwithstanding that it may give rise to a common law yearly tenancy, particularly since such a common law tenancy is a new tenancy and not a continuation of the old tenancy but a new tenancy would not be a holding over; it is a new event and it would require an in-depth investigation for little, if any, benefit to HMRC Stamp Taxes since rents rarely exceed £150,000 per annum in such situations. It seems that the basic position of HMRC Stamp Taxes is to regard these provisions as applying only where the tenant is exercising some statutory right. However, this position is not entirely clear since FA 2003, Sch 17A, para 9A refers to the situation where a tenant continues in occupation after the expiration of the term of a lease. This provision is concerned with the charging of the rent upon any new lease granted to the tenant where, as is frequently the case, the new lease is backdated to the contractual termination date of the expired lease. This provision assumes[641] that in some situations the continuation in occupation can give rise to a charge to stamp duty land tax.[642] There is a rent credit since this refers to the rent that was previously subject to stamp duty land tax. However, *prima facie*, it is only where the holding over is by operation of law that the rent in respect of the holding over will be subject to stamp duty land tax. It is assumed, therefore, that this provision is designed to complement the rent credit in para 9. This latter provision applies to give a credit for the rent in respect of an overlap period where there is holding over under the Landlord and Tenant Act 1954.[643] This, however, is dealing with the rent that arises after the grant of the new lease. Para 9A appears to be designed to deal with the situation of sums being paid for the intervening period between the contractual termination date of the old lease and the grant of the new lease but only where para 9A appears to be dealing with the situation prior to the grant of the new lease.[644] It seems that this may resolve the problem of backdated rent as a premium[645] by recreating the effective date so that the rent or the overlap period is not prior to the actual grant and so remains rent.[646]

7.125 Where these provisions apply the effect of the holding over is deemed to extend the term of the lease by a period of 1 year. This extension is by 2, 3 or 4 years as appropriate depending upon the length of the holding over.[647] This provision can apply only to leases granted subject to stamp duty land tax because it requires the assessment on the deemed extension to be carried out by reference to the effective date,[648] ie the original grant of the lease or substantial performance thereof. It requires a recalculation of the tax but unless tax is payable there is no obligation to notify the holding over simply because the deemed aggregate term of the lease becomes 7 years or longer.[649] Recalculations may be required where orders for interim rents or similar arrangements are entered into, but this will be rare and will require an exceptionally large increase in the rent.[650] Normally the rent for the holding over period will be the assumed rent for all

---

[641]   FA 2003, Sch 17A, para 9A; **7.139**.

[642]   See FA 2003, Sch 17A, para 9A(2) and (3).

[643]   But no other statutory provisions are referred to.

[644]   It may also mean that the backdated rent is not to be taxed as a premium pursuant to FA 2003, Sch 5, para 1A; see **7.139**.

[645]   Ibid, Sch 5, para 1A.

[646]   However, the draftsman makes certain assumptions as to 'consideration' in this situation where the parties are deeming, in effect, the payments to consideration or rent.

[647]   FA 2003, Sch 17A, paras 3 and 4.

[648]   Where there is a lease granted before 1 December 2003 or after that date but pursuant to an earlier agreement for lease that has paid stamp duty where the contractual term expires thereafter and a period of holding over begins, this will not be within the above regime of FA 2003, Sch 17A, para 3, since there will be no effective date.

[649]   Ibid, Sch 17A, paras 3(5) and 4(4A) (as amended).

[650]   Ibid, Sch 17A, paras 14 and 15 (as amended).

years after the fifth year of the term, ie the highest rent paid during the first 5 years, and not the passing rent. It will also qualify for a suitable level of discounting. Since the holding over may be by the assignee of a lease he will require delivery at completion of the assignment a full stamp duty land tax history of the lease in order to be able to calculate his tax liability that may arise where he or a subsequent assignee holds over.[651]

7.126 Where a new lease is granted during the deemed extension of a lease by reason of a holding over pursuant to the Landlord and Tenant Act 1954, ie the new lease is entered into part of the way through the 1 year stamp duty land tax extension, there is a double charge upon the rent for the period after the grant of the new lease and the expiration of the stamp duty land tax extension. In consequence, it is provided that a deduction in the rent of the new lease is available. The new rent is reduced by the amount of rent brought into charge to tax under the extended term provisions.[652] Since this refers to the effective date for stamp duty land tax, the credit cannot be available in respect of holding over and renewals of leases within the stamp duty regime.

Holding over on 1 December 2003[653]

7.127 No specific provision is made for the situation where, as will be common in relation to agricultural holdings, the tenant is already holding over on 1 December 2003, whether pursuant to statute or otherwise. It is considered that this is not within the provisions of FA 2003, Sch 17A, para 3, so that no charge arises.[654] However, in practice, many tenancies may be varied in some way, particularly agricultural tenancies. These may relate to the premises to be included within the demise. Unless carefully structured, such arrangements will involve a surrender and regrant.[655] In consequence, there will be the grant of a new lease within the stamp duty land tax regime which will be subject to tax notwithstanding that the original lease was subject to stamp duty. It is, as a practical exercise, usually beneficial to the taxpayer to stay within the stamp duty regime and to avoid any event such as a surrender and regrant which would cancel that benefit.

Renewed lease

7.128 Should the parties negotiate a new lease this will, *prima facie*, take effect from its own effective date in respect of substantial performance of the agreement for lease or grant of the lease. This will have two areas for investigation in relation to stamp duty land tax:

- there is a, *prima facie*, double taxation of the rent. The holding over when by operation of law, will have given rise to a lease that grows by 1 year and stamp duty land tax will have been paid in respect of 1 year's full rent. The new lease may be granted part-way through this statutory extension of 1 year or any subsequent

---

651   See **7.235**.

652   Ibid, Sch 17A, para 9; on the difficulties involved in calculating the credit see **7.193** and **7.198**.

653   Tenants should exercise prudence when holding over such leases since any agreements to modify the situation may operate as the surrender of the stamp duty lease and its replacement by a new lease within the stamp duty land tax regime with the loss of the benefits currently applied in practice to such leases. This appears, in the writer's experience, to be a major practical issue for agricultural leases because of the 'relaxed' approach of farmers and their reluctance to obtain appropriate advice before discussing their tenancies with the managing agent.

654   Although it remains to be seen, in practice, whether HMRC Stamp Taxes intend to exploit the transitional provisions for connected transactions pursuant to FA 2003, Sch 19, paras 7, 8 and 9. There is no evidence of any interesting issues being raised by HMRC Stamp Taxes at present.

655   *Friends Provident Life Office v British Railways Board* [1996] 1 All ER 336.

deemed extension where the holding over continues for more than 1 year.[656] The period from the grant of the new lease to the expiration of the statutory extension of 1 year is known as the 'overlap period' and the rent credit may be available;[657] and

- the new lease may be 'backdated' in the sense that the term commencement date for the new lease is either the contractual termination of the old lease being held over or the quarter date immediately preceding the grant of the new lease or agreement to grant the lease which is substantially performed. This may 'deem' certain transactions to have been on the basis that the new lease had been retrospectively in place. This could raise questions of double taxation of the rent in respect of the period between the backdating or the term commencement date for the new lease and the extension of the expired lease. In many situations there will have been no tax in respect of the holding over but where there is such a charge to tax in respect of the backdating period there is a rent credit[658] and the question is whether payments in the nature of rent for the overlap period do not qualify for the rent credit and are taxable as a premium[659] or whether this provision reconverts the payments into rent.

For the period between the date of the grant of the new lease and the expiration of the statutory extension for the expired lease a special treatment is expressly available where there is an arrangement pursuant to the Landlord and Tenant Act 1954.[660]

7.129 The relief is also available where there has been a surrender and regrant such as where a lease term is extended when the overlap period and the consequent computation of the rent credit may extend over many years if not decades such as the enlargement of a lease with 60 years unexpired into a lease for 150 years. This may also apply where there is some holding over by operation of law[661] not within the specific reference to the Landlord and Tenant Act 1954 since by reason of the statutory extension of the expired term there will be some unexpired period to the end of the year so that[662] there may be some form of deemed surrender for the purposes of stamp duty land tax in respect of the balance of the deemed term where the new lease starts part way through the deemed year[663] extension. In consequence, there may be a partial credit in respect of the rent for the other period on the basis of deemed surrender and overlap.[664]

'Rent credit'[665]

7.130 The amount of previously paid rent to be deducted from the new rent is the amount that was taken into account in determining the liability to stamp duty land tax in respect of the continuation in occupation of the old lease. This is subject to the

---

[656] FA 2003, Sch 17A, para 3.
[657] There is, in a sense, a deemed surrender and regrant but the effect is only for the overlap period.
[658] FA 2003, Sch 17A, paras 9 and 9A.
[659] Ibid, Sch 5, para 1A.
[660] Ibid, Sch 17A, para 9(1)(b); see also **7.124** and **5.177**.
[661] Ibid, Sch 17A, paras 3 and 9.
[662] Ibid, Sch 17A, para 9(2).
[663] Or a longer future period where there is a surrender and regrant of a lease with a long expired term; see FA 2003, Sch 17A, para 9.
[664] Ibid, Sch 17A, para 9. Where the holding over is pursuant to statute such as the Landlord and Tenant Act 1954 and the new tenancy relates back, there will be an overlap period providing for credit on the rent.
[665] See also **7.30** and **7.198**.

uncertainties as regards the drafting of the legislation mentioned above[666] namely whether the reference to taxed rent means that notwithstanding there may be no rent available for credit the rent for the period in question is taxed as rent and is not a deemed premium, and whether it is the passing rent or, where the first 5 years of the term have expired, it is the assumed amount of rent and there is the unresolved question as to whether this amount of assumed rent has to be discounted or whether it refers to the rent taken into account during the first 5 years of the term which have not been retrospectively adjusted because the adjustment date has not arrived. There will, however, be little practical difficulty in determining the rent for the new lease in most cases. Being in respect of a backdated period, the rent will be fixed in some form. It may be unascertained at the date of the grant of the new lease such as where it is related to turnover and the turnover figures have yet to be agreed. However, the information all being past data, there will not be problems in relation to variable future rents. Obviously, where the continuation in occupation has not been pursuant to the operation of law or has not had any stamp duty land tax consequences, so that the lease has not been extended or any rent subject to stamp duty land tax, there will have been no rent taken into account in determining the tax liability so that deduction would be nil.

7.131 Where this provision applies[667] to the future rents payable under the new lease in respect of the period between the grant of the new lease and the contractual termination date of the old lease or, presumably, in relation to leases arising in respect of holding over pursuant to the Landlord and Tenant Act 1954 the deemed contractual termination date by reason of the statutory extension for a whole year of the lease[668] is treated as reduced by the amount of the rent that would have been payable in respect of that period under the old lease.[669] The rent that would have been payable under the old lease is the amount taken into account in determining the stamp duty land tax chargeable in respect of the acquisition of the old lease.[670]

7.132 Unfortunately, but unsurprisingly, there are considerable problems with this legislation.[671] This is not stated to be a calculation by reference to the net present value which would have produced the rent subject to tax ie the proportion of the actual or deemed passing rent subject to tax adjusted for discounting or other factors but by reference to the amount of the rent subject to tax. It would have been a relatively simple matter for the legislation to provide that the net present value of the rent payable under the new lease is to be reduced by the amount of net present value attributable to the rent under the old lease. The calculation is by reference to 'rent payable' as complicated by being subject to stamp duty land tax. Unfortunately, this is not simply comparing contractual or passing rents. Under the old lease it is the amount of rent taken into

---

[666] See **7.30** and **7.86**.
[667] See also **7.198**. The treatment is also available on the termination of a head lease where a subtenant is granted a new lease of the same or substantially the same premises as those comprised in his original lease in pursuance of an order of a Court on a claim for forfeiture against re-entry or forfeiture or in pursuance of a contractual entitlement arising in the event of the head lease being terminated or where a lease is granted of the same or substantially the same premises as a lease that has been terminated to a guarantor in pursuance of the guarantee (FA 2003, Sch 17A, para 9(1)(c) and (d).
[668] FA 2003, Sch 17A, para 9(3).
[669] The rent would have borne stamp duty land tax notwithstanding that it has not been paid since the tax applies by reference to future rents.
[670] FA 2003, Sch 17A, para 9(4). It is for this reason that holding over stamp duty leases would appear to fall outside the holding over regime for stamp duty land tax. However, where there is a surrender and a regrant or a situation where the statutory regime applies the rent credit may be available but since the previous arrangement will not have been within the stamp duty land tax regime there will be a nil rent to deduct from the new rent.
[671] See further **7.198**.

account in calculating the stamp duty land tax. This may be a variable rent and there may be a situation where the new lease is granted in respect of the period before the rent is reviewed or adjusted. This is unlikely to be the situation in the case of a holding over where any rent reviews will have been completed or lapsed as at the contractual termination date of the old lease. It will, therefore, be a calculation that involves the assumed rent where the fifth year of the term of the old lease has expired. This will be not the passing rent but the highest rent paid in any 12 calendar months during the first 5 years of the term,[672] but ignoring any rent credit that may have been taken into account.[673] Obviously this will be a key piece of information that all assignees will require when taking on a lease where they expect to hold over and renew the lease pursuant to the Landlord and Tenant Act 1954. However, those responsible for preparing the tax have not made clear whether the 'rent' taken into account is the basic assumed figure or is that figure as discounted for the year or years in question. At present the difference may be relatively small but over time, as the longer leases expire and new leases are granted, the rent taken into account in respect of the old or expired lease will have been considerably discounted and could be significantly below the level of the assumed rent. To take the assumed rent without discounting will, therefore, increase the amount of the rent credit.

7.133 In addition to the problem of dealing with the amount of rent subject to tax to be deducted from the new rent there is the question of the new rent which may well be variable or subject to review during the first 5 years of the term. Clearly there may be some estimated rental figures involved. Where there is a holding over pursuant to the Landlord and Tenant Act 1954 there will be less than 1 year of overlap rent credit; but in other cases the overlap period may be substantial such as where there is a surrender and regrant of a lease with a reasonable number of years unexpired. It is probable that where there is holding over pursuant to the Landlord and Tenant Act 1954 the rent for the first year of the new lease will be fixed so that it is easy to find the rent figure from which the deduction is to be made. However, there may be some form of rent holiday for the new lease in which case the deduction of the old rent is likely to produce a negative figure. However, it is provided[674] that there cannot be a negative rent. The effect of a rent holiday would be that the taxable rent would be nil.

Term commencement date issues[675]

7.134 There are numerous issues concerning the effect of backdating the term commencement date such as the adjustment for rent reviews in the first quarter of the fifth year[676] and other matters such as treating the rent paid for the prior or intermediate period as rent.[677] This can include the possibility that the rent payable in respect of the backdated period is a premium and not rent.[678] There may also be issues as to whether that sum is otherwise taxable as rent.[679] To a limited extent a relief in respect of the rent payable in the backdated or 'overlap' period is available.[680] The conditions are, however, stringent and, on the basis of traditional practice, will be strictly and narrowly applied by HMRC Stamp Taxes. Where the tenant continues in occupation after the date on

---

[672] FA 2003, Sch 17A, para 7(3).
[673] Ibid, Sch 17A, para 7(3).
[674] Ibid, Sch 17A, para 9(5).
[675] See also **7.114**.
[676] FA 2003, Sch 17A, para 7A.
[677] See ibid, Sch 5, para 1A; see **7.38**.
[678] Ibid, Sch 5, para 1A.
[679] Ibid, Sch 5, para 1A and Sch 17A, para 7.
[680] Ibid, Sch 17A, para 9A.

which the original lease terminates and he is granted a new lease of the same or substantially the same premises[681] and the term of the new lease is expressed to begin on or immediately after the contractual termination date of the old lease there is a rent credit. However, it has to be noted that this relief is available only where the backdating is to the contractual termination date of the old lease.[682] Where there is backdating of the commencement of the new lease to another date such as the immediately preceding quarter date[683] the rent payable in respect of the backdated period ie the period after the contractual termination date and before the date on which the new lease is actually granted is reduced by the amount of rent that was payable in respect of the backdated period otherwise than under the new lease. In this context the term of the new lease is treated as beginning on the date on which it is expressed to begin ie on the contractual termination date or the immediately following quarter date.[684] This would mean that any 'rent' paid in respect of the backdated period would not be sums paid before the grant of the lease and would therefore retain its character as rent and not be a premium.[685]

'Rent'

7.135 The charge is by reference to the 'rent' and a figure that has to be included in respect of any year[686] in the formula for net present value.

This section deals with the basic principles of the charge to stamp duty land tax and the question of what constitutes 'rent' for the purposes of deferring the date to be inserted in the formula for determining the net present value of the rent at the various times when returns have to be filed in relation to chargeable transactions such as the initial return and related retrospective return. The issue of how the taxable amount of 'rent' is to be calculated, particularly where it is variable or uncertain (eg turnover rents) or it is reviewable is considered later.[687] In some situations there is a deduction in the 'rent' or credit for rent previously taxed; some of these are considered elsewhere.[688]

7.136 'Rent' is not, as such, defined[689] and so it would appear that the normal meaning of the term is applicable[690] although the legislation indicates[691] that any sum described as rent is taxable as rent unless it is separately apportioned from the true rent and perhaps separately described as 'additional rent' or as being enforceable as if it were rent.

Rent and drafting issues

7.137 FA 2003, Sch 17A, para 6, provides that for the purposes of calculating the stamp duty land tax upon 'rent', a single sum expressed to be payable either:

- in respect of rent; or

---

[681] See **7.44** and **7.85** on the issue of when premises are 'substantially' the same.
[682] FA 2003, Sch 17A, para 9A(1)(c).
[683] The significance of which see FA 2003, Sch 17A, para 7A.
[684] FA 2003, Sch 17A, para 9A(2).
[685] Ibid, Sch 5, para 1A.
[686] See ibid, Sch 5, para 3.
[687] See **7.147**.
[688] See, for example, **7.30**, **7.86** and **7.198**.
[689] FA 2003, Sch 17A, para 6, merely includes certain payments; the basic term is not defined.
[690] See, eg, *T&E Homes Limited v Robinson* [1979] STC 4351; broadly a sum paid on a periodical basis as consideration for the utilisation of the land; see also *Lowe v JW Ashmore* [1970] 46 TC 597.
[691] FA 2003, Sch 17A, para 6.

- in respect of rent and other matters but not separately apportioned,[692]

is to be treated entirely as 'rent'.[693] This suggests that the reservation of various items as 'rent' in order to provide the landlord with possible additional powers in relation to the enforcement of the covenant to pay the rent may have adverse effects upon the tenant, such as converting exempt items[694] such as service charges into taxable rent or possibly sufficient in some cases to make the proposed lease commercially unattractive because of the stamp duty land tax charge. The problem will turn upon the effect HMRC Stamp Taxes give to the words 'as additional rent'. This will raise issues as to whether there is a single specific sum or item specified as 'rent', or whether there is a sum reserved as 'rent', plus some other item such as a service charge or VAT, which is reserved in 'additional rent' and is to be separately calculated.[695] The key question is whether the segregation in this way will be regarded as sufficient 'apportionment' so that it is a separate item and is not to be treated as 'rent'. It seems that in practice HMRC Stamp Taxes accept that such drafting excludes the relevant items from the charge to stamp duty land tax as rent.

'Additional rent', service charges etc[696]

7.138 This can be important as a drafting exercise since sums, frequently described as 'rent' such as VAT and service charges and other similar payments are not taxable as rent and, apart from VAT, may not be taxable[697] if not reserved as part of the rent they are excluded from stamp duty land tax.[698] Insofar as service or other charges are reserved as a single sum with the rent they will be taxable accordingly. If they are reserved as a separate item and separately apportioned they will not be subject to the charge, but there is an obligation to apportion consideration between the rent and the services or other items on a just and reasonable basis.[699] The problem is that whilst HMRC Stamp Taxes appear to accept that service charges and other payments reserved as 'additional rent' are not rent and so exempt,[700] should they consistently treat VAT reserved as 'additional rent' in the same way ie not as rent it will convert the VAT into a periodical premium.[701] It may be that the effect of FA 2003, Sch 17A, para 6 is that, where the VAT and the rent are not expressed as a single sum but are reserved as two separate items, the VAT is not 'rent'. In this case it would seem that the VAT not being reserved as 'rent' may constitute a periodical premium as was the official position for stamp duty,[702] where the lease is for a term exceeding 12 years the stamp duty land tax is

---

[692] On a just and reasonable basis: FA 2003, Sch 5, para 4(1).

[693] Where the sum is apportioned between various items such apportionments must be made on a 'just and reasonable' basis: ibid, Sch 4, para 4; see **5.110**.

[694] FA 2003, Sch 17A, para 10.

[695] HMRC Stamp Taxes have not as yet addressed the problem of should they treat VAT reserved as additional rent rather than a periodical premium then strict consistency means that service charges etc within FA 2003, Sch 17A, para 10, are also rent. This would put HMRC Stamp Taxes into revising their original position (SP 9/11) that VAT is not rent but is a periodical premium (see **7.138**). There is, however, no evidence in practice that HMRC Stamp Taxes intend to treat VAT otherwise than as rent with all of the problems for variable rent; see **7.64**.

[696] See also **7.213**.

[697] FA 2003, Sch 17A, para 10; see **7.213**.

[698] Ibid, Sch 17A, para 10; see **7.213**.

[699] Ibid, Sch 17A, paras 7 and 8, but note para 10. Since the service element, if included for stamp duty land tax purposes in the rent, is likely to vary, this will make the rent 'uncertain' within s 51(2) of the FA 2003 so that, *prima facie*, the initial self-assessment of the stamp duty land tax payable will have to be based upon a reasonable estimate of the amount or value, with additional notification and payment at the end of the fifth year of the lease.

[700] Ibid, Sch 17A, para 10.

[701] Ibid, s 52 and Sch 17A, para 6; see **7.137**.

[702] See SP 9/11, para 9; but this point was rarely raised in practice in relation to stamp duty. The cases where it

charged upon the basis of a 12-year[703] annual payment.[704] There is no provision for leases not exceeding 12 years but it would seem to be the intention of the legislation that the stamp duty land tax is charged upon the aggregate VAT over the life of the lease and the charge to stamp duty land tax may be significantly higher than that upon VAT as 'rent'.[705] Fortunately, at present, HMRC Stamp Taxes seem to be willing to accept returns and payments made on the basis that the VAT is treated as rent, although in many cases this will produce a lower tax charge. However, treating the VAT as part of the rent would make the rent 'variable' with all the problems associated with such rent[706] because the rate of VAT may change during the life of the lease[707] and HMRC Stamp Taxes have taken this approach although their Guidance Note[708] merely refers to where the VAT is included in the 'rent' without providing guidance as to when it is 'rent'.[709]

Credited 'backdated' rent[710]

7.139 In addition, where there is rent 'backdated' ie a sum is payable as rent in respect of a period prior to the grant of the lease (which, presumably, includes periods prior to the deemed grant of the lease upon substantial perform of the agreement for lease) this is treated as consideration other than rent ie is treated as a premium.[711] This will frequently produce a higher charge to tax where the amounts are substantial and in relation to non-residential property where the rent exceeds £1000 there will be no nil rate in respect of the premium including any deemed premium arising from any such backdated rent. However, where the backdating occurs in the context where there is an existing lease which has expired and the tenant has continued in occupation which may include situations where there is a holding over whether by operation of law or otherwise. In this situation where the tenant is granted a new lease of the same or substantially the same[712] premises and the term commencement date for the new lease is the contractual termination date or immediately following that subject to the 'backdating' of the term commencement date for the expired lease any sum payable as rent in respect of the backdating period is treated as rent.[713] This arises because the new lease is deemed to commence on the term commencement date so that it is not 'backdated rent' as being paid in respect of a period prior to the effective date.[714] In this case this backdated rent is reduced by the amount of rent that was taxable in respect of the backdated or 'overlap'[715] period.[716] However, not all such continuations in

---

appeared to be taken were those where the parties were seeking to argue that stamp duty should not be paid upon VAT notwithstanding the decision in *Glenrothes Corporation v IRC* [1993] STC 74. It may also be that the question of stamp duty upon rent was rarely drawn to the attention of HMRC Stamp Taxes because it was not included in the appropriate part of the stamp duty 'PD form'.

[703] The annual amount is not necessarily related to the rent charged; it is calculated in 12-month periods starting from the effective date of the transaction: FA 2003, s 52(4). There are issues about rent paid 'in respect of particular periods'; see, for example, FA 2003, Sch 5, para 3.

[704] Ibid, s 52(2).

[705] Stamp Act 1891, s 56.

[706] See **7.188**.

[707] See **7.188**.

[708] 30 January 2009, STI 2009, p 460.

[709] See **7.64**.

[710] See **7.198**.

[711] FA 2003, Sch 5, para 1A.

[712] On the problems of the possible meaning of 'substantially the same' see **7.85**.

[713] FA 2003, Sch 17A, paras 9 and 9A.

[714] Ibid, Sch 17A, paras 9 and 9A; Sch 5, para 1A; see **7.130**.

[715] Ie either the period between the expiration of the contractual term of a lease that is deemed to grow and the grant of the new lease or the period between the grant of a new lease and the future extension of the old lease ie future period or unexpired term of the existing lease and the period between the grant of the new lease and that future expiration date.

occupation will have given rise to rents subject to stamp duty land tax although rent may have been paid because it is not taxable there will be a nil deduction. The credit will not be available in cases where there is the grant of a new lease but it is not backdated to the contractual termination date of the old lease but to some other intermediate quarter day. It will also not be available where there is the grant of a completely new lease without any preceding lease and sums payable prior to grant are taxable as rent. It would seem that where there is a backdating of the new lease to some intermediate quarter day then the backdated amount is not reconverted into rent and therefore there will be no credit against the sum so backdated in respect of any rent that was taxable in respect of the holding over period such as where there is holding over pursuant to the Landlord and Tenant Act 1954.[717]

Service charges

7.140 Service charges and similar payments are exempt from stamp duty land tax provided that they are separately apportioned and not reserved as part of the rent.[718]

Deemed rent

Market value transactions

7.141 There are certain chargeable transactions liable to stamp duty land tax involving leases where the chargeable consideration is deemed to be market value or not less than market value such as leases to connected companies[719] or from connected persons to partnerships[720] or by partnerships to connected persons.[721] In such situations the relevant legislation states that there is a charge upon the actual rent, if any, and the market value element is taxed as a deemed premium, usually a sum equal to the price which the actual lease at that rent would obtain if sold in the open market.[722] In this situation there is no attempt to tax future market rent[723] HMRC Stamp Taxes have abandoned their previous attempt to tax market rents as such and have focussed on market value premiums. Nevertheless, the fundamental question for a possible undervalue is whether the actual rents are below market rents. However, market rents are a function of the market and parties deal with the markets in a variety of way such as rent reviews, rent holidays,[724] turnover or profit sharing arrangements or the covenants in the lease affect the market rent.[725] There will, therefore, be an initial problem of whether the rents are below the market rent in all the circumstances. In consequence, the taxpayer in these, but not other circumstances required to estimate future rents although such estimates may be crucial in determining the current premium. There is, therefore, a major commercial or valuation problem for new leases in this situation where there is a potential market value premium. This depends upon the rent and whether it is a market rent since a market rent will indicate that there is no

---

[716] FA 2003, Sch 17A, para 9A; see **7.130**.

[717] It should be noted that the rent credit in FA 2003, Sch 9 is related to rent arising after the date of the grant of the new lease.

[718] FA 2003, Sch 17A, paras 5 and 10(1).

[719] Ibid, ss 53 and 54; see **5.208** and **7.90**.

[720] Ibid, Sch 15, Part 3 (as amended).

[721] Ibid, Sch 15, para 18.

[722] But note the problems of determining market value in this context; see, for example, **7.90** and **Chapter 27**.

[723] Unlike the rules for taxing variable rents which frequently require attempts at determining future market rents; see **7.161**.

[724] HMRC Stamp Taxes have, from time to time, taken the position that a rent holiday is not commercial and, therefore, the rent is not a market rent; clearly a misconceived argument.

[725] See FA 2003, Sch 17A, para 10(1)(c).

undervalue in the lease.[726] There are, therefore, problems in dealing with the situation since the taxpayer will have to estimate future rents for the net present value and determine whether future rents for deciding whether there is an undervalue should the estimate of future rents no necessarily reflect expected market rents because, for example, the rent reserved is a turnover or profit rent and not reviewed to market rent. The taxpayer will also be required to estimate future rents when preparing the land transaction return.[727] There will be a major difference between dealing with variable rents for the purposes of the filing of the initial self-assessment return which will be retrospectively adjusted,[728] and estimating future rent movements insofar as these are a key element in the debate with HMRC Stamp Taxes on whether there is a 'low rent' which is a major issue as to whether the lease has a deemed value for the purposes of market value and deemed overlap charges. The lease will usually be taxable upon the actual rent and the market value will be attributed to a premium for a lease at that rent ie whether the rent is below market rent so that it has a 'capital value'.[729]

Employees[730]

7.142 Where a lease[731] is granted in consideration of a person's employment or the employment of a person connected with him, and the arrangement is such that it generates a benefit in kind within Chapter 5 of Part 3 of the Income Tax (Earnings and Pensions) Act 2003, there is a charge to stamp duty land tax upon an amount equal to the cash equivalent of the benefits chargeable under that Act as if it were a sum of rent.[732] Where rent is actually payable the amount of the rent is increased by the amount of the benefit in kind. As this charge is based upon a notional rent equal to the cash equivalent charged to income tax and that cash equivalent is variable,[733] this notional rent would appear to be 'uncertain' within FA 2003, s 51, so that the initial payment of stamp duty land tax will be based upon two 'guestimates' namely:

- a reasonable estimate of the amount of the chargeable consideration, ie the estimated notional rent;

---

[726] But note the views of HMRC Stamp Taxes as set out in the legislation on valuation of leases, rent and covenants such as their definition of 'market value leases' pursuant to FA 2003, Sch 15, para 15; but this is excluded for certain purposes by Sch 15, para 38, and note the approach to covenants pursuant to Sch 17A, para 10(1) especially covenants that may affect the rent in the open market (para 10(1)(c)).

[727] FA 2003, s 51; see **7.157**.

[728] Ibid, Sch 17A, paras 7 and 8.

[729] This issue of rent below current rates for determining market values contains a stealth trap although it seems that at present HMRC Stamp Taxes are unaware in practice of their powers to make a discovery (compare *Langham v Veltema* [2004] STC 544) where there is a dealing in a lease between rent review dates and the current passing rent may be below current market rates ie there is a limited accepted value because the current rent is below market rent and there is a benefit between the effective date for the chargeable transaction and the next rent review ie an assignee may be prepared to pay a 'premium' for the assignment because of the benefit of the current low rate. Conversely, there are the issues of reverse payments (FA 2003, Sch 17A, para 18) where the passing rent exceeds current market rents.

[730] See also **6.77**.

[731] These issues do not arise where the interest of the employee is a 'licence to occupy' which will usually be the case since such licenses are not chargeable interests (FA 2003, s 48).

[732] See the Income Tax (Earnings and Pensions) Act 2003.

[733] Or possibly a claim for repayment of overpaid tax.

- and the term of the lease which will be initially a lease for 1 year but which lease grows should the employment continue.[734] There may therefore be obligations to notify, recalculate the tax and payment of additional tax[735] if the lease continues for more than a year.[736]

Depending upon the level of 'rent', it will be necessary to review the situation annually as the employment continues so as to extend the deemed term of the lease and the rent may eventually exceed the nil rate threshold.[737] It is likely that the level of the notional rent, even when combined with any actual rent, will not exceed the nil rate threshold so as to give rise to a positive charge to tax, so that notification and payment will not be required even where the deemed term of the lease converts the arrangement into a deemed lease for more than seven years;[738] but once tax has been payable the inevitable increase in the net present value will require annual payment and filing.

7.143 Hopefully this provision is unlikely to have a significant impact in practice since, in general, the interest of the employee is likely to be an exempt interest as a licence[739] or as a tenancy at will,[740] but represents a stealth trap where the circumstances differ. In addition, the term of the lease will be uncertain in many cases. It may be that the employee has a fixed-term contract in which case the lease may, by implication, be for a similar term. However, the arrangement may be ongoing so that the lease to employee will be a periodic tenancy or for an uncertain term[741] start for 1 year and will continue growing as each year of the employment continues. Should the employee survive to be awarded his gold watch or other long service award then he may, eventually, be the deemed tenant of a very long lease.

Increase or reduction of rent?

7.144 Unfortunately, but unsurprisingly, although there are many situations where charges may arise where rent is varied ie increased or reduced[742] whether by agreement outside the lease,[743] such as by a deed of variation[744] or pursuant to the terms of a lease on a rent review or separate negotiation or pursuant to the terms of the lease which provide for an automatic increase, and where a landlord may change the rent basis from a turnover or similar rent to a market rent subject to periodic reviews, the draftsman has not provided comprehensive guidance as to how to determine whether there has been an increase or reduction. Broadly, there is no general formula or definition for finding the base rent ie original rent being adjusted and the new rent so that a comparison can be

---

[734] FA 2003, Sch 17A, para 4.
[735] It may be necessary to investigate and keep copies of Form P11D or its equivalent.
[736] FA 2003, s 48(1)(b).
[737] Notification is not required simply because the lease to the employee becomes a deemed lease for 7 years or longer: FA 2003, Sch 17A, paras 3(5) and 4(4A) (as amended).
[738] FA 2003, Sch 17A, para 3(5) and 4(4A) and s 77.
[739] Ibid, s 48(1)(c)(i).
[740] Ibid, s 77(2)(b)(ii).
[741] Ibid, Sch 17A, para 4.
[742] There are many technical issues of statutory construction on 'increase' etc. This may depend upon whether there is a subjective or objective element in the adjustment. There is a key legislative difference between rent which 'increases' and which is 'increased'. The former situation implies a subjective operation such as a rent review; the latter implies an objective situation such as where the amount of the rent variation takes effect automatically such as where rather than a rent review based upon agreement the increase is a specified or stepped amount.
[743] See, for example, FA 2003, Sch 17A, para 13.
[744] Which is not a surrender and regrant *Gable Construction v IRC* [1968] 1 WLR 1426.

made to determine whether there has been an increase or a reduction.[745] Whilst there are provisions which indicate how to determine the base rent in some cases,[746] it is unclear how the new rent is to be determined particularly where it is a variable rent such as where there is a change from a turnover to a market rent or an alteration in the rent review date.[747] In such cases it is difficult to determine the base rent, ie the old rent, in the absence of special provisions. Fortunately, the changes to the abnormal increase regime will apply to most cases where the lease is at least 5 years old; new leases retain the difficulty for variations otherwise than pursuant to the lease and there will be difficulties in deciding whether there is a reduction in the rent where the abnormal increase rules do not apply.

7.145 There is no explanation of how to determine the new rent and whether this is related to a comparison of the net present values, or whether it relates to the actual passing rents, or deemed rents or the rents as discounted for the relevant years when the lease was initially taxed. In many cases the tax is effectively unworkable and the prudent approach would seem to be a comparison of the net present value of the old rent as passing or the assumed rent net as discounted and the net present value of the new rent as estimated. This seems to provide a workable basis for determining whether there is an increase or a reduction. Having discovered this the different calculations required will have to be applied to determine the tax charge, if any.

7.146 A reduction of rent, if made for a chargeable consideration provided by the tenant such as a commutation payment, will be a chargeable transaction.[748] It is a variation of the lease within the basic definition of 'acquisition' and related definitions.[749]

Variable or uncertain rents including rent reviews

General principles

7.147 Few leases, it any, will be for a fixed rent for the entire term of the lease because of possible changes in the rate of VAT[750] and most leases contain a rent that will or may change at some stage,[751] whether by reason of rent review or because they are linked to some form of turnover or participation figure in relation to subrents received or potential changed in the rate of expenditure from time to time. Even ground rents for flats may be subject to increase such as stepped rents which increase to specified amounts or double every 25 years.[752] The new tax becomes immensely complicated in relation to compliance, if not calculation, in relation to such leases in that there are five sets of problems, namely:

- what are variable rents;

---

[745] There has also been a failure to address the similar situation of how to compute rent credits for overlap periods in these and similar situations; see **7.198**.

[746] Such as abnormal increases; FA 2003, Sch 17A, paras 13–15.

[747] Compare the similar problems for the rent credit mechanism; see **7.30** and **7.86**.

[748] FA 2003, s 45(3)(d) and Sch 17A, para 15A.

[749] Ibid, s 43(3)(d).

[750] See **7.188**; but note the limited exclusion for rents linked solely to RPI, FA 2003, Sch 17A, para 7(5); see **7.154**.

[751] FA 2003, Sch 17A, paras 7 and 8.

[752] Any linkage to RPI is to be ignored; FA 2003, Sch 17A, para 7(5).

- how such rents are to be taxed on the effective date as at substantial performance;[753]

- how such rents are taxed where the effective date changes from substantial performance by reason of a grant of a lease;[754]

- whether any variation in the rent subsequently gives rise to either a liability to pay further tax or a refund of overpaid stamp duty land tax and/or an obligation to notify HMRC Stamp Taxes of the variation;[755] and

- as a result of various changes including the FA 2006 the basic provisions calculating the tax initially depend essentially upon whether the rent may change during the first 5 years of the term; subsequent changes do not affect these provisions but have their own charging provisions as 'abnormal increases'.[756]

'Variable rent' defined

7.148 A variable rent is any rent other than a fixed rent or a rent deemed to be fixed such as a rent solely linked to the Retail Prices Index.[757] However, whilst the indexation may be ignored the rent is likely to be variable because of potential fluctuations in the rate of VAT,[758] and the draftsman has failed to deal with the question of whether any VAT payable in relation to the proportion of the rent linked to the RPI is to be taxed as VAT or ignored as RPI. This area of variable rents has been extended by legislation which has brought in to charge to tax rents that may be varied under the provisions of the various Agricultural Holdings Acts and related legislation,[759] and by the fact that HMRC Stamp Taxes have, possibly contrary to expectation, taken the view that where VAT forms part of the rent the fact that the rate of VAT may change during the relevant period means that the rent is 'variable'.

Fixed rents

7.149 Basically 'fixed rents' are regarded as those rents that do not change during the entire term of the lease.[760] This depends upon whether the rent varies in accordance with the provisions in the lease[761] or is contingent, unascertained or uncertain. There is a reference to a 5-year period[762] in relation to such rents.[763] This is, however, not part of the definition of whether the rent is 'variable' but is part of the mechanics for determining the amount of tax payable in respect of rents that may vary even after the expiration of the fifth year of the term. The possibility of a variation after the fifth year of the term, such as a stepped rent as a ground rent for the lease of a flat which double every 25 years are variable rents,[764] means that the rent is variable, since although the

[753] FA 2003, Sch 17A, para 12A.
[754] Ibid, Sch 17A, para 12A.
[755] Ibid, Sch 17A, para 8.
[756] Ibid, Sch 17A, paras 14 and 15; see **7.180**.
[757] Ibid, Sch 17A, para 7(5).
[758] See **7.188**.
[759] FA 2003, Sch 17A, para 7(4A).
[760] A point that may become important in practice should HMRC Stamp Taxes seek to exploit the double charging provisions pursuant to FA 2003, Sch 17A, para 12A when the 5-year period moves forward.
[761] FA 2003, Sch 17A, para 7(1)(a).
[762] Subject to rent reviews during the last quarter; FA 2003, Sch 17A, para 7A.
[763] FA 2003, Sch 17A, para 7(2) and s 51.
[764] Ibid, Sch 17A, para 7(1)(a). Such rents are unlikely to constitute a problem in practice because as ground

amount of such rent is fixed in advance, it changes in accordance with the terms of the lease.[765] Fortunately, at least initially, the possibility of a variation outside the fifth year of the term is ignored and certain assumptions are made as to the rent after the expiration of the fifth year of the term.[766] Such rents are rare in practice and since most rents are subject to VAT in some form the fact that the rate of VAT may change as well as the widespread existence of rent review and similar arrangements there will be extremely few fixed rents in practice.

Types of variable rent

7.150 Rent variations may take many forms including increases and reductions and may be pursuant to terms of the lease such as stepped ground rents or by reason of external agreements or other external factors such as rent reviews or changes in the rate of VAT or variations in the tenant's turnover or profits which form the basis for calculating the rent for any particular rent period. There is a definition of variable rents as being:

- rents that change pursuant to the terms of the lease such as stepped rents; or

- rents that are contingent, unascertained or uncertain;[767]

but in practice virtually every rent will be variable for these purposes. It is usually, but not invariably, clear when rent is variable; but it is not always clear when the rent is varied nor by how much the rent is increased or reduced. Some alterations in rent are less obvious than changes in rent because of changes in turnover. Even simple exercises such as a change of a review date which may include an agreement to cancel or defer or postpone a rent review[768] because of the recession.[769] However, the mere fact that a review is cancelled does not mean it may have the effect of varying the rent nor is the case where the landlord has a power to change the rent computation basis. For example, the lease may be initially granted on the basis that the landlord is entitled to a rent calculated by reference to the 'profits' received by the tenant or a percentage of turnover but with a power exercisable from time to time to change the basis of rent to a market rent subject to review. Other leases may be upon the basis that the tenant is subject to repairing obligations and can deduct the cost of these repairs is to be deducted when calculating the 'landlord's share' of the rents received by or turnover of the tenant. In such a situation the parties may adjust the repairing obligations or make other alterations to the formula for calculating the landlord's share of the rent as the passing

---

rents they are unlikely to exceed the nil rate threshold for rent and for residential property no longer affect the nil rate threshold for lease premiums because of the abolition of the £600 rent limit (FA 2003, Sch 5, paras 9 and 9A) see the views of HMRC Stamp Taxes on such rents set out at **5.24**.

[765]   FA 2003, Sch 17A, para 7(1)(a); see **7.150**.

[766]   Ibid, Sch 17A, para 7(3).

[767]   Ibid, Sch 17A, para 7(1).

[768]   There are key issues for stamp duty land tax in this context. The cancellation of a rent review suggests that the current rent will continue for the next 5 years. The deferral of a review implies that the review will be carried out at a later date but the revised rent will be payable from the originally agreed review date and not from the later review date. A postponed review implies that there will be a later rent review and that the new rent will be payable from the later review date and not retrospectively from the original review date ie within the term of the charging provisions in FA 2003, Sch 5 (as amended). The rent is payable 'in respect of' an earlier year from that in which it is actually paid or payable.

[769]   In some case there may be a negotiated reduction in the rent, this may not be taxable as there is no chargeable consideration (FA 2003, Sch 17A, para 15A(1)) and it seems that this will be taken into account for the variable rent provisions enable the tenant to reclaim tax paid on the basis of an estimated higher rent; FA 2003, Sch 17A, para 8(5).

rent reserved by the head lease. Since, in these situations, both the original rent and the new rent are likely to be variable or uncertain figures it is difficult to determine whether the rent has increased or reduced[770] or been increased or been reduced which might occur where the landlord has the repairing and maintenance obligations and the parties agree to transfer these to the tenant upon the basis that the tenant can deduct any actual expenditure when calculating the rent to be paid to the landlord.

7.151 For such leases it is the initial rent for the first 5 years which forms the basis of the calculation; the subsequent increases are ignored when making the initial calculation;[771] but certain assumptions are made.[772] The statutory provisions applying during the first 5 years for variable rents also affect those leases which are within the stamp duty land tax regime where the rent varies in accordance with the provision in the lease,[773] which excludes arrangements where outside the terms of the lease the landlord and the tenant enter into a deed of variation affecting the rent where special provisions apply,[774] or the rent is contingent, uncertain or unascertained.[775] They will include not merely turnover and similar profit-sharing rents, but also standard rent reviews to market rent whether upwards only or to market rent including reductions or a power of the landlord to change the rent basis. The lease may be granted originally upon the basis of profit-share such as where the landlord is to receive either a premium that is a multiple of the rents from the letting of the property or is a specified percentage of the rents received or receivable by the tenant from the occupying subtenants[776] but with a power for the landlord to change the rent to a share of the gross turnover or to market rent. Whilst these basic definitions of the types of variable consideration generally apply to rents the consequences of their application differ in relation to the variation of rents taking effect outside the lease.[777] A deed increasing or reducing the rent is not a surrender and regrant.[778] The effect of such a deed of variation as a rent variation[779] and the reference to the rent varying in accordance with the lease[780] means that the provisions apply where the change is 'objective' ie the rent is 'increased' by an amount possibly fixed in advance within the terms of the lease such as where a ground rent may double after 25 years. In other situations where there is a 'subjective element' such as the decision whether to implement a rent review the rent will be within the category of 'uncertain' rent. It would seem that possible changes in the rate of VAT would mean that where the VAT is part of the rent calculation the rent will be variable for these purposes and it seems that where the landlord had not exercised the option to tax for the purposes of VAT but has the power to do so in the lease the exercise of the power will mean that the rent is initially 'uncertain'[781] and therefore within the variable rent provisions. The exclusion of the exercise of the option to tax for VAT pursuant to FA 2003, Sch 4, para 2, only applies to exercises after the effective date. This would, *prima facie*, means

---

[770] FA 2003, Sch 17A, paras 15A(1) and 13.

[771] It seems that this also forms the basis for deciding whether the average annual rent exceeds £1000 for the availability of the nil rate band for the premium for non-residential leases: FA 2003, Sch 5, paras 9 and 9A; see **5.24**. The alternative would be to make a manual calculation for each individual year of the lease, since the official calculator is not designed for such a calculation.

[772] FA 2003, Sch 17A, para 7(3).

[773] Ibid, Sch 17A, para 7(1)(a).

[774] See, for example, ibid, Sch 17A, paras 13 and 15A.

[775] Ibid, Sch 17A, para 7(1)(b); see s 51 and **5.187**.

[776] But, no doubt, provision calculating payments to the net rent at market value where there are 'voids' such as parts of the property being unoccupied by subtenants at the relevant time.

[777] FA 2003, Sch 17A, paras 15A(1), 13 and 14.

[778] *Gable Construction v IRC* [1968] 1 WLR 1426.

[779] Which is not a surrender and regrant; *Gable Construction v IRC* [1968] 1 WLR 1426.

[780] FA 2003, Sch 17A, paras 13 and 15A(1).

[781] Ibid, s 51; see **5.187**.

that since the variable rent regime relates back to the original effective date an exercise of the option to tax is, *prima facie*, ignored. However, events subject to exercise may have their own effective date of the exercise of the option to tax[782] should the exercise of the power be a tax event it will mean that the rent has, perhaps, become 'certain' or 'ascertained' rather than 'unascertained' and therefore there may be filing and payment obligations. Where the power is exercised outside the 5-year period the impact of the increase in the rent by reference to the rate of VAT may be a factor to be taken into account in determining whether there has been an abnormal increase in the rent over the relevant period,[783] although there is the question of whether the exercise of the option to tax, which will be before the effective date for the deemed new lease, is to be taken into account in determining whether there has been an abnormal increase ie helps to trigger the effective date or its operation only after there has been an abnormal increase for other reasons. It seems that HMRC Stamp Taxes will seek to include the VAT in determining whether there has been an abnormal increase because the exercise precedes the effective date.[784]

7.152 This may mean even more returns and possible payments or claims for refunds where the rate of VAT drops below that taken into account on the initial calculation. The difficulty arises because the calculation for stamp duty land tax is based upon rent years but VAT will adjust by reference different periods. For example, a lease may be granted with a term commencement date for 25 March. The rate of VAT may be changed on 1 April and may be changed in the opposite direction on 1 April the following year. This means that the first quarter's rent for the year from 25 March will be at the original rate of VAT. The rent for the periods June, September and December will be at the new rates as will the rent for the period from March; but the possible changes in the rate if announced in advance will have to be taken into account when making the necessary estimates. The position would be more complicated where the rate changes as of 1 December. Rent periods for March, June and September would be at appropriate rates, there would then be different rates applicable.

Agricultural tenancies

7.153 Included by statute[785] within the category of variable rents are tenancies where there is a possibility of a variation pursuant to:

- Agricultural Holdings Act 1986, s 12, 13 or 33;

- Agricultural Tenancies Act 1995, Part 2;

- Agricultural Holdings (Scotland) Act 1991, s 13, 14, 15 or 31; and

- Agricultural Holdings (Scotland) Act 2003, s 9, 10 or 11.

---

[782] See **5.220**, **7.65** and **7.189**.
[783] FA 2003, Sch 17A, paras 14 and 15.
[784] Ibid, Sch 17A, paras 14 and 15.
[785] Ibid, Sch 17A, para 7(4A).

Indexation

7.154 It is provided[786] that no account is to be taken for the purposes of computing stamp duty land tax upon rent of any provision for the rent reserved to be adjusted in line with the RPI.[787] Again there is a doubt from the drafting as to whether an upwards-only increase is within this provision but, for the reasons set out above in relation to market rent, it is considered that such rents are not to be treated as 'uncertain'. It must, however, be noted that this exclusion applies only where the rent adjustment is 'in line with' the retail prices index. This leaves open an argument that an increase of 50 per cent of the change in RPI is 'in line with' the index and so a 'fixed rent'; but such rents are unlikely to be fixed since they will usually be subject to VAT. Adjustments related to a modified version of the index may not be accepted as excluded by HMRC Stamp Taxes. Linking to other indices will render the rent 'uncertain',[788] and rent reviews linked to some other factor such as movements in interest rates are not covered by these provisions. This creates a significant compliance problem for finance leases, ie leases granted as part of a sale and leaseback that is essentially a fundraising transaction involving financial considerations rather than simply property factors,[789] *inter alia*, where the rent is linked to movements in interest rates, which is likely to be the case where there are sale and leaseback and similar arrangements intended as fundraising exercises. The legislation fails to deal with the question of whether an increase in the amount of VAT arising because of a rent increase by reason of RPI is also to be ignored. It seems that, *prima facie*, such an increase in the VAT upon the RPI increase is a taxable increase in the rent and has to be taken into account in determining whether there has been an abnormal increase in the rent.[790]

Alternative variables

7.155 However, this treatment of index linked rents as fixed rents[791] does not apply where the review to market rent or the index linking is merely one of several contingencies. It is possible that the rent review provisions may provide for increase in the rent to the higher of the market rent or the RPI or by a minimum specified percentage. Such alternative or multiple variation contingencies, if the alternatives are limited to the higher of market rent or index linking, may arguably be exempt, but there is an argument that such an arrangement does not satisfy either requirement and so the rent is to be treated as uncertain. If there is a possible fixed percentage alternative increase or a linking to interest rates, these exclusions do not apply. This, however, is no longer an issue of multiple possible methods of charging tax. The regime at present ultimately focuses on the actual rent paid for the relevant period rather than any particular alternative.[792] When making a return the taxpayer has, in a sense, to ignore the theoretical basis for the rent computation and to estimate what is likely to be paid given the several bases for computation. The process is not a choice between different bases but the amount that the various rent formulae are likely to produce as actual rent. Obviously, when carrying out the subsequent retrospective recalculation, the possible

---

[786] Ibid, Sch 17A, para 7(5).
[787] But such rents may nevertheless be variable where they are subject to VAT, the rates of which may vary.
[788] See **7.155**.
[789] Note the relief for a leaseback pursuant to FA 2003, s 57A (as much amended).
[790] FA 2003, Sch 17A, paras 14 and 15.
[791] Which is currently of little compliance benefit. Although to some extent this may reduce the tax charge the tenant for the time being still has to deal with the issue of a variable rent since apart from residential property the rent will be variable because of possible changes in the rate of VAT; see **7.188**.
[792] As was the case with the alleged contingency principle for traditional stamp duty.

bases become irrelevant since the computation involves the actual sums paid once these have been agreed by the landlord and tenant.

Variable rents and stamp duty

7.156 It is important to note that these provisions[793] in general apply only to leases granted on or after 1 December 2003 which fall into charge to stamp duty land tax.[794] Leases where rents vary in accordance with these provisions but which were subject to stamp duty are in general unaffected by them, at least until holding over or variations involving surrender and regrant or other similar arrangements apply to deem new leases to come into existence for the purposes of stamp duty land tax. Sometimes this is express as with abnormal rent increases,[795] in other cases it is dependent upon whether the relevant provision refers to an effective date or some other terminology that has a special stamp duty land tax meaning inappropriate for stamp duty.[796]

Multi-stage process – 'guestimates' and retrospection

7.157 The effect of the legislation[797] is that where the rent is contingent, unascertained or uncertain (but not otherwise variable)[798] there is, at least,[799] a two-stage process in relation to the determination of the amount of stamp duty land tax chargeable upon rent that either varies in accordance with the provisions in the lease or is contingent or uncertain or unascertained[800] or subject to VAT;[801] but there is no power to postpone the payment of the tax upon rent which is available for certain other types of variable purchase price or premium.[802] Where the rent may vary during the first 5 years of the lease,[803] for example, a turnover rent, two calculations are in theory required and almost certainly four in practice. These provisions will not apply where there is a fixed reviewable rent and the first review is after or shortly before the end of the fifth year of the lease.[804] In such a case, the initial rent is treated as being provisionally the rent for the whole term); but such leases will be rare in practice because where the rent includes VAT the possible variation of the rate of VAT during the first 5 years means that the rent is variable so that such a rent cannot become 'certain' at any time during the first 5 years of the term.[805] HMRC Stamp Taxes have taken the position that the possible change of rate of VAT of itself makes the rent variable. This is unclear where the rent is

---

[793] FA 2003, Sch 17A, para 7(1).
[794] Certain provisions relating to abnormal increases in rent apply to all leases granted after 30 November 2003 even where these are leases within the stamp duty regime. FA 2003, Sch 17A, para 14(7)(a).
[795] Ibid, Sch 17A, para 14.
[796] See **7.2**.
[797] FA 2003, ss 51, 80, 87 and 90; Sch 17A, paras 7, 8, 13, 14 and 15.
[798] Ibid, Sch 17A, paras 7(1) and 8(1). It is, however, uncertain where the lease is exempt for the purpose of VAT but contains a power for the landlord to exercise the option to tax the rent.
[799] There may be a minimum of three or four-stage process where there is substantial performance of the agreement for lease, subsequent completion (FA 2003, Sch 17A, para 12A) and a rent review etc. (FA 2003, Sch 17A, para 8 and s 80).
[800] As generally defined FA 2003, s 51. See **5.187**.
[801] See **7.188**.
[802] FA 2003, s 90(7).
[803] Currently not properly defined, but it is believed to be 5 years after the effective date for the lease, not, as the legislation suggests, 5 years from the term commencement date.
[804] However, reviews taking place in the last quarter of the 5 years after the effective date are ignored to allow for the traditional backdating of the term commercial date to the preceding quarter date: FA 2003, Sch 17A, para 7A. However, the limited backdating is unlikely to apply where the lease is granted after substantial performance because the grant is more than 3 months after the term commencement date such long review periods may be subject to tax as abnormal rent increases: FA 2003, Sch 17A, paras 14 and 15.
[805] FA 2003, s 80 and Sch 17A, paras 8(1)(b) and (2)(b).

exempt although the landlord is able to exercise the option to tax. It is an open question whether the specific reference to ignoring the option to tax in FA 2003, Sch 4, para 2, means that actual VAT arising upon the rent pursuant to the exercise of the option to tax means that such exercise is not an increase in the rent whether pursuant to the terms of the lease or otherwise.[806] The change of rate in VAT is an actual variation in the rent and so may be the exercise of the option to tax the rent producing an abnormal increase in the rent.[807]

Contingent rent

7.158 It is unlikely that there will be a contingent rent, ie a rent that increases or reduces by a fixed amount if something happens or does not happen;[808] but in such a case the initial calculation is on the basis that the full contingent amount is payable but this is subject to review if the contingency occurs or ceases to be relevant during the first 5 years[809] of the term.[810] If no such event has occurred during the first 5 years the rent is reassessed at the end of the fifth year on the basis of the rent actually payable which also provides the basis for the rent for the balance of the term.[811] This can lead to an artificially high tax charge if the rent is to reduce if the event happens. The initial high rent will be the basic rent notwithstanding the contingent reduction remains applicable at the end of the fifth year and there is no reduction in the tax paid if the contingency occurs to reduce the rent after the end of the fifth year of the term.

Unascertained rent

7.159 There are likely to be numerous situations where the rent may be 'unascertained' ie the rent calculation is dependent upon past data which has to be processed and agreed by the parties. HMRC have indicated that their view, almost certainly erroneous as a general principle, that the rent changes character where a rent review date has passed converting the rent from 'uncertain' to 'unascertained' regardless of whether there has been the actual initiation of the rent review procedure by either party.[812] However, the legislation relating to such payments[813] refers to 'ascertained'. In other cases the issues are less clear cut such as where the rent reserved is linked to the rents to be received from underlettings or is a fixed figure as a multiple of the rents receivable or a multiple of the area of the building. For unascertained rent the initial calculation has to be on the basis of a reasonable estimate of the probable rent. This is adjusted as and when the rent is finally ascertained. The area where this is most likely to arise in practice is during rent reviews whilst the parties are negotiating the new rent.

Uncertain rent

7.160 This arises where the consideration, in this case the rent, will or may fluctuate by reference to factors arising in the future ie after the effective date for the chargeable

---

[806] Ibid, Sch 17A, paras 13, 14, 15 and 15A; see **7.188**.

[807] Ibid, Sch 17A, paras 13, 14 and 15.

[808] An increase of rent of RPI or 6 per cent whichever is the greater is not within these provisions. Stepped rents are outside these arrangements since the increase is automatic upon the expiration of time not dependent upon other events outside the lease.

[809] FA 2003, Sch 17A, para 7A.

[810] Assuming that at this stage the rent becomes 'ascertained' notwithstanding the possibility that the rent includes VAT and the rate may change during the remainder of the first 5 years.

[811] FA 2003, Sch 17A, para 7.

[812] See **7.171**.

[813] FA 2003, s 80 and Sch 17A, para 8(2).

transaction in question which is either the deemed grant upon substantial performance or the subsequent actual grant[814]. This will apply to most rents since it includes situations where the rent will fluctuate in accordance with future events, most rent reviews, possible changes in the rate of VAT,[815] and turnover rents.

Variable rents and calculation procedures

7.161 The process for dealing with variable rents that are contingent, unascertained or uncertain,[816] is initially[817] a two-stage process. It requires an initial calculation and a subsequent adjustment. The initial calculation is, usually, prepared upon the basis of estimated figures. These estimated figures which have to be prepared on a 'guestimated basis' since there is no machinery or guidance provided in the legislation as to how future events are to be treated for this purpose have to be revised in the light of subsequent events. The process is retrospective. Frequently the later recalculation involves returning to the original estimated return and adjusting this in the light of the subsequent events. It seems that the process is required even where there are no changes after the expiration of the fifth year of the term. The subsequent changes are, however, ignored at this stage in the process.[818] There will be a fixed rent for the first 5 years of the term and the actual rents for the balance of the term are ignored and the rent for the entire term of the lease will be the initial contractual rent. The alternative view is that where the rents are fixed in advance[819] then it is necessary to carry out a separate calculation that will not be within the scope of the on-screen calculator inserting the actual rent for each year on some form of arithmetic basis or making use of a computer-based spreadsheet system. Fortunately, many of the situations where there will be stepped rents will be residential properties for low ground rents and therefore unlikely to produce a situation where the net present value of the rents, even taking into account the increases in the future, will, after discounting, exceed the nil rate threshold. There may be, however, an obligation to notify because the leases will be for more than 7 years.[820]

The two-stage charge upon the creation of leases, namely substantial performance and grant, means that this process has to be repeated on the grant of the lease with a rent credit for the rent taxed at substantial performance. This figure will differ from that involved in the initial calculation in respect of the agreement for lease because the first 5 years of the term will have changed and the term of the lease will be shorter so that the discounting for certain of the rents will be significantly lower producing higher figures to go into the calculation.

---

[814]   Ibid, Sch 17A, para 12A.

[815]   At least until the review date arrives when in the current view of HMRC Stamp Taxes the rent becomes 'unascertained'.

[816]   FA 2003, Sch 17A, para 8(2).

[817]   But other long-term consequences exist.

[818]   This ill-considered legislation can have seriously disadvantageous and very expensive consequences for tenants who may be severely penalised by half-baked understanding of the issues by those advising HMRC Stamp Taxes. Certain leases such as mineral arrangements may produce particularly high rents during the first 5 years of the term but the nature of the arrangements means that these rents will not be repeated in subsequent years. Nevertheless, they are the basis of the taxable rent for all years after the expiration of the fifth year of the term notwithstanding that it is manifestly clear that commercially the tax figures are nonsensical. It is crucial, therefore, that solicitors discuss with clients the anticipated rent pattern for the first 5 years of the term because that can distort the tax position. An exceptional year, such as 2012, which provides a basis for ripping off visitors or persons in hotels can generate a high and unrealistic tax liability to find the cost overrun for the Olympics.

[819]   Ie in accordance with the terms of the lease pursuant to FA 2003, Sch 17A, para 7(1)(a).

[820]   FA 2003, ss 77 and 77A.

Initial calculation – the first 5 years[821]

7.162 To the extent, if any, that the rent is known for the first 5 years of the lease, these figures must be included in the formula set out above[822] for the relevant years. Insofar as the rent during the 5 years is not certain, the tenant must insert a reasonable estimate for the rent for those 5 years. This estimate will usually include VAT at the current rate at the effective date unless there has been an announcement that the rate is to change on a specific date when it will be necessary to take into the estimate the projected rate of VAT. This applies whether all or part of the rent is fixed such as a base rent subject to review or wholly variable such as a turnover rent.

Making the estimate

7.163 There is no guidance in the legislation as to how the estimate of an uncertain payment should be made other than it must be 'reasonable'. HMRC Stamp Taxes have frequently given the unhelpful and incorrect advice that the parties can ignore the impact of rent reviews and rent changes and file the return upon the basis that the initial or basic rent applies for the whole term of the lease and deal with the situation as and when the circumstances arise at the end of the first 5 years of the term. However, it seems that HMRC Stamp Taxes will not allow reliance upon this advice as a means for mitigating any penalties that arise because the return is 'negligent' ie no attempt has been made to arrive at a 'reasonable estimate' and reliance on their advice is not an attempt to make a reasonable estimate. In addition, HMRC Stamp Taxes cannot mitigate the interest cost that would arise by reason of the late payment.

The parties must, therefore, make an attempt to predict future rent movements such as predictions of the impact of the first rent review or guestimated turnover figures, rents potentially receivable or the relevant cash for determining the rent received or receivable net of expenses is the turnover figure for a business. Unfortunately, this is not an area where flexibility is involved because there is no ability to defer the payment of tax upon estimated or guestimated rents.[823] If the amount is underestimated so that additional tax becomes payable after the review or other event then interest will be payable on the amount of the underestimated tax.[824] The only guidance that has been provided by HMRC Stamp Taxes in this context is a brief comment dealing with the changes in the rate of VAT.[825] It is the official policy that where a temporary reduction in the rate of VAT has been announced for a specified period and the rate is to be increased then when making the estimate for the purpose of the return in respect of a lease granted during the period of the temporary reduction in the rate of VAT, the rate of VAT is the rate currently in force for the overlap period between the grant of the lease and the date when the rate of VAT will increase, for periods after that the rental payments have to

---

[821] This may require two full stamp duty land tax returns, namely substantial performance of the agreement for lease and the actual grant thereof.
[822] See **7.108**.
[823] FA 2003, s 90(7).
[824] Ibid, Sch 17A, para 8(3).
[825] See **7.188**.

include the estimated amount of the increase in the rate of the VAT[826] for the period after the expected increase in the rate of VAT.[827]

7.164 As regards the rent for the balance of the term after the fifth year of the lease, this is an assumed rent equal to the reasonable estimate of the highest rent payable or estimated to be payable in any 12 consecutive (apparently) calendar months.[828] This is a practical problem since most rents are payable quarterly not monthly and the years for the lease will not be the same as the quarterly rent periods ie the 12 month period may straddle 2 years of the lease term. This assumed rent is applied for all years after the fifth year which can be a major cost to tenants where, during the first 5 year period, there is a period of 12 months when the rent is above normal such as a mineral rent or some event such as the Olympics in 2012 which increases turnover or hotel rates but only for a limited time. Tax upon this exceptional rent is payable for the balance of the term notwithstanding the inevitable fall in the rent during the remainder of the first 5 years or the balance of the term.

7.165 Notwithstanding that the amounts are variable, the ability to postpone the payment of tax on variable payments does not apply to rents[829] so that full tax is payable on both of these returns, notwithstanding that they are based upon unscientific 'guestimates'.[830] There are also sanctions for guestimates as to future movement in rents[831] with obligations to pay any tax underestimated[832] with interest[833] or an ability to reclaim tax[834] with interest[835] if there has been an overestimate and possible penalties if HMRC Stamp Taxes can establish a negligent guestimate. This applies even where the parties have made a reasonable attempt to estimate the unpredictable where, whether in reliance upon advise from the so-called Helpline or otherwise, no attempt to deal with future rent movements are made interest and penalties begin to accrue immediately[836] without any mitigation for penalties for relying upon the 'advice' of HMRC Stamp Taxes.

---

[826] It remains to be seen how HMRC Stamp Taxes will react to a situation where the rate of VAT is increased above the estimated rent. In this situation it is considered that because the rate of VAT may change subsequently during the first 5 years of the term then the rent does not become 'certain' for these purposes and the increase can be ignored in the sense that a return does not have to be filed. However, it would mean that any estimated figure will be low and therefore additional tax will become payable together with interest. It may be questionable whether this is a situation where the parties should consider making a payment on account or some adjustment on account in order to minimise the question of interest and penalties in the future (FA 2003, s 87(6)).

[827] For the practical problems because VAT periods, rent periods and stamp duty land tax and years of the lease which rarely coincide see **5.130**.

[828] Not rent periods linked to quarter days.

[829] FA 2003, ss 80 and 90; see **16.32**.

[830] Compare the relief for premiums for loans FA 2003, ss 51, 80, 87, 90 and Stamp Duty Land Tax (Administration) Regulations 2003, SI 2003/2837, Part 4; see **Chapter 16**.

[831] FA 2003, ss 52, 87 and 90.

[832] Ibid, Sch 17A, para 8(3).

[833] Ibid, s 87(3)(c).

[834] Ibid, Sch 17A, para 8(5).

[835] Ibid, s 89(2).

[836] Ibid, Sch 17A, paras 8(3) and (4).

Retrospective revised calculation during the first 5 years

7.166 Where the rent is contingent, uncertain or unascertained[837] or it is varied in accordance with the terms of the lease,[838] such as turnover rents or rent review or changes in the rate of VAT during the first 5 years so that the rent for the balance of the 5 years becomes certain, a further return and tax payment may be required.[839] However, the attitude of HMRC Stamp Taxes to variations of the rate of VAT as this affects rent suggests that most rents[840] are and remain variable during the balance of the first 5 years and do not become 'ascertained' until the possibility of changes ceases at the end of the first 5 years of the term so that the number of land transaction returns (SDLT 1) required to be filed during the first 5 years of the term will be significantly less than HMRC Stamp Taxes are expecting because most such returns will relate to future uncertain events. In particular the return by reference to any rent review during the first 5 years may not be necessary. Where the rent becomes 'certain', it is necessary to recalculate the net present value of the rent retrospectively as at the appropriate date and report and pay (or reclaim) tax, as appropriate.[841] This involves revisiting the original land transaction return and substituting the actual figures for the guestimate. It is, therefore, a retrospective amendment of the original return. This is a somewhat ambiguous provision in several respects since it refers to the amount of rent payable in respect of the first 5 years of the term of the lease ceasing to be 'uncertain'. This refers to the rent payable in respect of a year which may not be the same as the rent paid for any year it would also seem to be the situation of the rent for balance of the 5 years ceasing to be 'uncertain' not the situation of the rent for part of the period becoming uncertain. In consequence, it seems that the obligation to deal with the situation would arise only where the rent for the balance of the first 5 years of the term becomes fixed and non-variable. The provisions may not apply where there is a potentially temporary variation in the rent such as where there is a declaration that the rate of VAT is to be reduced for a limited period. In this situation the rent for the limited period becomes 'certain' but it remains 'uncertain' because the rent may change further within the balance of the 5 years period or there may be a further change in the rent when that period expires. This may, however, depend upon the timing of the VAT reduction. For example, where the lease has been recently granted and the variation takes place within the first year or two then the rates of VAT for the future will mean that the rent remains uncertain for the balance of the term after the expiration of the reduced rates period. On the other hand, where the variation is expressed to be for 1 year and commences in the fourth year of the term of the lease then the rate will be fixed for the balance of the period and beyond the expiration of the fifth year. In this situation the rent will become certain. However, the variations in the rate of VAT will rarely, if ever, coincide with the dates for the payment of rent which usually are linked traditionally to quarter days rather than dates that apply generally for stamp duty land tax purposes or to create tax

---

[837] See **5.187** for a discussion of these terms.

[838] For rent variations outside the terms of the lease such as deeds of variation and possibly the exercise of the VAT option to tax the rent see **7.188**.

[839] FA 2003, Sch 17A, para 8.

[840] However, it is considered that if the taxpayer can establish that genuine and realistic attempts have been made to receive up-to-date, independent professional advice based upon properly drafted valuation instructions, HMRC Stamp Taxes may find it difficult to persuade even the current judiciary that there has been negligence in the preparation of the land transaction return (SDLT 1).

[841] FA 2003, s 52; Sch 17A, para 8; s 80 of the FA 2003 is removed from variable rents. In consequence, it seems that it will not be necessary to report each time rent is ascertained and paid; see **Chapter 16**.

points for the purposes of VAT.[842] It is obviously an irritating question of fact and highly technical legal analysis to be applied in any particular case for the changes pursuant to the VAT changes.

7.167 For these purposes the amount of rent ceases to be 'uncertain' in specific but not necessarily all cases. It is important to note that there is a double use of the word 'uncertain' in this context. It is used in the technical sense as defined by FA 2003, s 51(1) and it is used in the general sense of relating to 'variable rents' for the purposes of Sch 17A, para 7 thereof. In order to clarify this double use of the word 'uncertain' it is provided[843] that the rent ceases to be 'uncertain' where, in the case of contingent rent, the contingency occurs or it becomes clear that it will not occur and in relation to uncertain or unascertained rent the amount becomes 'ascertained'. As indicated above, it seems that this requires that the rent becomes certain and not subject to further possible variation during the balance of the 5 year term. This certainty is unlikely to arise in most cases since the rent in non-residential property cases will be subject to VAT and where rent includes VAT HMRC Stamp Taxes have indicated that, in their view, the rent is 'uncertain' in the technical sense and because the rate may fluctuate it has not become 'ascertained'. Therefore, notwithstanding that there has been a completed rent review, the rent has not been 'ascertained' for the remainder of the first 5 years of the term since the new rent is potentially uncertain if only because the rate of VAT may change.

7.168 This would apply, for example, to a lease with an initial 6 month rent holiday with a review to market rent thereafter every 5 years.[844] In such a case, the net present value of the rent would have been calculated by reference to the initial low rent for the first 6 months with a reasonable estimate of the rent for the remaining 4½ years as affected by the possible review. The assumed rent for the balance of the term ie for all years after the expiration of the fifth year of the term, would be the equivalent of 1 year's estimated rent after the review date. Unfortunately the draftsman has based this computation upon monthly calculations although many rents are paid on a quarterly basis. Moreover, the draftsman fundamentally overlooked the fact that 12 calendar months, even where by concession HMRC Stamp Taxes accept when the review occurs the rent becomes certain subject, *inter alia*, to VAT rate changes until the next review day and so the rent may be known for the first 5 years. Within 30 days of the rent being agreed the tenant must recalculate the rent duty upon the basis of the initial rent for the first 6 months plus the reviewed rent for balance of the 4½ years to the expiration of the fifth year of the term. The assumed rent will be 'certain', ie 1 year's rent after the review. However, this process of requiring reviews, returns and payments to be made after the first rent review may now be incorrect. HMRC Stamp Taxes have indicated that where the rent includes VAT this makes the rent 'uncertain'. In consequence, since the rate of VAT may change during the first 5 years of the term or the balance thereof after the first review, the rent remains 'uncertain' notwithstanding the rent review. It is 'uncertain' in both sense of the term:

- it is 'uncertain' for the purposes of the application of FA 2003, Sch 17A, para 7; and

---

[842]   Value Added Tax Act 1994, s 6.

[843]   FA 2003, Sch 17A, para 8(2).

[844]   Note the technical issues in computing rent review dates; FA 2003, Sch 17A, para 7A.

- it is 'uncertain' in the strict technical sense imposed by s 51 thereof. In consequence, where the rent includes VAT the rent will never become 'certain' within this definition until the expiration of the fifth year of the term.[845]

HMRC Stamp Taxes have, from time to time, indicated that where there is a rent review the taxpayer is required to deliver a return within 30 days of the rent review date. However, this is considered to be incorrect because the rent will only become 'certain'[846] when the parties agree the new rent. *Prima facie*, therefore, no return is required until 30 days from the agreement of the parties or their advisers as to the new rent. It is important to note at this stage that it is not 30 days from the endorsement of the new rent by way of memorandum upon the lease. It is 30 days from the agreement because stamp duty land tax is a transaction tax not a documentation tax a major trap for clients who do not regard rent reviews as a matter for legal advice and reply upon valuers etc who are unaware of the technicalities and subtleties of stamp duty land tax.

7.169 There will be questions as to whether the rent has become 'certain' at this stage. It would seem that where there are no further reviews or adjustments in the rent and the rent is exempt from VAT and the landlord has covenanted not to exercise the option to tax then the rent may become 'certain' because there are no possibilities within the terms of the lease that the rate of VAT could change and therefore the rent cannot change. However, this will be a rare situation. The review for the balance of the term will, therefore, really produce a further uncertain rent. It is, however, the view of HMRC Stamp Taxes that the rent becomes sufficiently 'certain' and that the variation in the rate of VAT may make the rent 'certain' at least for part of the term or the first 5 years of the term and require appropriate adjustments to be made. In a press release[847] HMRC Stamp Taxes indicated that the parties might become entitled to immediate refunds in view of the reduction in the rate of VAT on a temporary basis from 17½ per cent to 15 per cent. However, this may only apply where the fifth year of the term expires during the period of the VAT reduction. In those situations where the 5 years will not expire because the current projection is that the rate of VAT will increase at the end of the temporary relief period, the rent will be and remain uncertain. Even when the new rate is specified, because that rate may itself be varied in the future, the rent continues uncertain for the balance of the 5 years of the term. There are clearly significant technical issues that need to be investigated in order to save the parties from the need to file several returns where the period of any temporary VAT rate adjustment falls into more than 2 years of the lease.[848]

7.170 In addition to the question of whether the potential movements in the rates of VAT mean that the rent has not become 'certain' for the balance of the first 5 years, there will be difficulties in presenting the return within 30 days of the review date. HMRC Stamp Taxes take the view that this is a situation where the rent becomes 'ascertained' because the rent depends upon previous data namely market rents as at the review date sand will not change by reason of future events such as changes in the rate of VAT. However, this will be a situation where it is 'unascertained' because it has not been processed. It is clear to everyone other than HMRC Stamp Taxes that in the context of their legislation consideration or rent is 'unascertained' where it relates to

[845] HMRC Stamp Taxes do not appear to understand the technical issues involved since their press release suggests that the change does make the rent 'certain' but this applies only for part of the term i e until there are further VAT rate changes.
[846] FA 2003, Sch 17A, para 8 and s 80.
[847] See Guidance Note 30 January 2009, STI 2009, p 460.
[848] See **7.188**.

previous rates yet to be agreed which makes the sums or rent 'unascertained' and this becomes 'ascertained' only when agreed. It is, therefore, not 'certain' within the statutory definition.[849]

Deferred and postponed reviews – issues for the recession

7.171 Moreover, there may be a delay in the implementation of the review, particularly where there is a recession or there have been circumstances where the general level of market rents may not have increased. In these circumstances the parties may either not immediately implement the rent review procedures[850] or may positively agree to cancel or postpone the review. The implications of such an arrangement relating to the deferral of the rent review depend upon the circumstances. If the parties merely agree to postpone the review for a specified period upon the basis that when the review is carried out it will relate back to the review date, then the rent remains uncertain because it is subject to review during the current period albeit there will be a retrospective adjustment. In this situation there will be no 'certain' rent requiring a filing.[851] On the other hand, the parties may agree to cancel the current review either permanently or agree to create a new review date some time in the future but the review will take effect only as at that date. In this situation, because there is no rent review procedure potentially applicable either currently or retrospectively, the rent will, perhaps, have become 'certain' subject, of course, to the question of possible changes in the rate of VAT and how this affects the 'certainty' of rent. In this situation, where the review is cancelled because the current market rents are not expected to have increased, then as the parties may have prepared their initial return on the basis of an increase in the rents the estimated figures taken into account will be excessive and therefore there may be an eligibility for a repayment claim.[852] However, there may not be an obligation to pay and file because the rent for the balance of the first 5 years of the term has not become 'ascertained'.

Negotiated reductions

7.172 During the recession the parties may negotiate a rent reduction which will be by deed of variation and not pursuant to the terms of the lease.[853] The reduction itself will not be taxable since it is not for a chargeable consideration. However, a reduction does not produce a tax reclaim and the question is whether this can be regarded as falling within FA 2003, paras 7 and 9. In those cases where the rent is uncertain, contingent or unascertained[854] the downward negotiations of the rent during the first 5 years is to be taken into account for the variable rent provisions and since this is likely to be a rent below the original 'guestimated' figure the tenant may be entitled to a refund with interest.[855]

---

849   FA 2003, Sch 17A, para 8(2); but see s 80.
850   Subject to the provisions of the lease and the questions as to whether time is of the essence in these arrangements.
851   It is uncertain whether the rent review removes sufficient uncertainty to require a retrospective revision of the original guestimate and a new filing. It is considered that this is not a valid analysis because the rent is not 'certain' and this is not an error in the return requiring prompt correction pursuant to FA 2003, Sch 10, para 8.
852   FA 2003, Sch 11A.
853   Ibid, Sch 17A, para 15(1).
854   Ibid, Sch 17A, para 7(1)(b).
855   Ibid, s 88 and Sch 17A, para 8(5); see **7.190**.

7.173 If the rent remains uncertain throughout the first 5 years, such as a turnover rent or subject to the possibility of changes in the rate of VAT,[856] which means that few, if any, rents will become 'certain' for the purposes of FA 2003, Sch 17A, para 8,[857] so that a rent review during the first 5 years will not terminate the provisional nature of the tax return[858] and will postpone the possibility of claiming a refund of the overestimated figure where the rate of VAT has been temporarily reduced or the recession means that the initial 'guestimate' of the impact of a rent review was optimistic and the rent review produces a lower rent than the estimated figure or the rent review is cancelled, the recalculation and reporting obligation arises at the end of the fifth year.[859] The tenant (or assignee) has to recalculate the rent duty. This will involve including in the formula the actual rent paid for each of the first 5 years. For the balance of the term, the rent is assumed to be the highest rent actually paid in any 12 consecutive (apparently) calendar months during the first 5 years. The stamp duty land tax has to be calculated and, if necessary, a return made and tax paid (or reclaimed) within 30 days after the expiration of the fifth year of the term. The legislation specifies a 30 day period[860] but this is unrealistic in practice in many cases since the parties may have to agree turnover figures, market rents for voids, the tenant's deductions etc. The figures for the final years may not be available for some time. It seems probable that HMRC Stamp Taxes will take the position that the rent is at this stage 'unascertained' ie all relevant data is available; but such a provisional estimated return should be filed and tax paid; but this is not entirely consistent with the legislation. There will be the technical question of whether a reduction in the rent during the recession which, because of the terms of the rent review which permit any upwards reviews and had to be effected by a deed of variation,[861] ie whether it is included in FA 2003, Sch 17A, paras 7 and 8 because it is not pursuant to the terms of the lease and the possibility of such a reduction does not make the rent 'uncertain'. The position may be more helpful to the taxpayer where the rent is 'uncertain' for other reasons such as VAT changes.

7.174 Assignees of leases, in addition to the need to deal with the first rent review of the expiration of the fifth year of the term,[862] become responsible for carrying out the second and later review of the rent for abnormal increases. Information will be required from the assignor, and arrangements may be necessary to deal with any overpayments or underpayments of tax made on an earlier filing that is retrospectively adjusted as between assignor and assignee.

7.175 At this point the calculation of the initial rent duty is completed, but the problems of subsequent abnormal rent increases and other rent variations after the expiration of the fifth year of the term remain.[863]

---

[856] See **7.188**; Guidance Note 30 January 2009, STI 2009, p 460.
[857] See **7.166**.
[858] See **7.171**.
[859] FA 2003, Sch 17A, paras 8 and 15.
[860] FA 2003, Sch 17A, para 8(3)(a).
[861] Which is not a surrender and regrant; *Gable Construction v IRC* [1968] 1 WLR 1426.
[862] FA 2003, Sch 17A, para 8; s 81A; Sch 17A, para 12.
[863] Ibid, Sch 17A, paras 14 and 15.

Retrospective recalculation of the end of fifth year

Rent increases not pursuant to the terms of the lease during the first 5 years of the term

7.176 Major changes were made[864] to the situation where the parties agree to increase the rent otherwise than pursuant to a provision in the lease, such as where the landlord agrees to take over the tenant's repairing obligations for a higher rent. Such a transaction is taxed as the grant of a new lease if entered into during the first 5 years of the lease.[865]

Deed varying the rent during the first 5 years[866]

7.177 Not all variations take effect pursuant to the terms of the lease. There may also be a situation where a lease is varied by deed such as where a landlord makes a payment to a tenant to increase the rent in order to enhance the value of the freehold reversion or to purchase the benefit of the tenant's improvements or the tenant may take over the landlord's repairing or other obligations so that there is an enhanced cost for the tenant which is to be included in the formula for determining the landlord's share of turnover or rents received. Specific provisions deal with such increases or reductions in rent; but do not set out the interaction of these provisions with those relating to variable rents whether during the first 5 years or afterwards.[867]

7.178 It is provided[868] that where a lease is varied during the first 5 years of the term so as to increase the amount of the rent reserved by the lease,[869] otherwise than in pursuance of a provision already contained in the lease,[870] the variation is treated as if it were the grant of a new lease in consideration of the additional rent made payable by it.[871] It does not require a re-self-assessment of the rent pursuant to the original lease. In consequence, there will be a deemed lease for the amount of the increased rent but no guidance is provided on whether the new lease is for a term equal to the unexpired term of the existing lease or only for a term equal to the period for which the increase may apply which is not necessarily the unexpired term of the lease. Thus, if the rent is increased only to the next rent review date, there will be a fairly short lease. On the other hand, if the rent operates to increase the minimum rent for the whole of the term unexpired the new lease will be treated as being for that unexpired term.

7.179 Where there is a deed reducing the rent whether during the first 5 years or subsequently the tenant is deemed to acquire chargeable interests.[872] This will be chargeable upon any chargeable consideration provided by the tenant such as a

---

[864] FA 2006, Sch 25, para 6.

[865] Ibid, Sch 25, para 7.

[866] FA 2003, Sch 17A, paras 15A and 13. Such increases after the expiration of the fifth year of the term are now taxed pursuant to the abnormal increase regime, as amended by the FA 2006. The broad effect is that the increase is not abnormal if it does not exceed an average 20 per cent of the rent previously taxed per annum.

[867] See **7.173**.

[868] FA 2003, Sch 17A, para 13(2) which does not deal with the length of the deemed new term.

[869] For reductions see FA 2003, Sch 17A, para 15A(1).

[870] See FA 2003, Sch 17A, para 13.

[871] See **7.188** on the impact of the exercise of the VAT option to tax the rent.

[872] FA 2003, Sch 17A, para 15A(1).

commutation payment. There is, however, no express guidance as to how such a reduction interacts with the retrospective review and self-assessment for variable rents at the end of the first 5 years of the term.[873]

Rent variations after the fifth year of the term

7.180 The provisions relating to rent increases after the expiration of the fifth year of the term have been fundamentally revised by FA 2006[874] and it has been officially stated that further changes in the legislation are intended because the current legislation does not work in the manner in which HMRC Stamp Taxes intended notwithstanding several previously unsuccessful attempts.

The current position is that if at any time after the end of the fifth year of the lease, the rent is increased whether in accordance with the terms of the lease such as a rent review or increase in turnover[875] or by provisions or agreements outside the lease such as a deed of variation,[876] such that the new rent exceeds the old rent by an 'abnormal' amount determined by a three-step calculation process or there is a deemed new lease[877] for a rent equal to the difference between the new rent and the rent which was previously taken into account for the purposes of calculating the stamp duty land tax.[878] There is a question of whether the exercise by the landlord of the option to tax the rent for VAT is, notwithstanding the exclusion of the option to tax by FA 2003, Sch 4, para 2,[879] an increase in the rent for these purposes.[880] Should this be the case at current rates of VAT this may produce an abnormal increase in the rent.

7.181 Tenants or lessees will have to carry out an investigation at each review or in relation to turnover or other alteration in the rent after each year's rent is paid to determine whether this represents an abnormal increase in rent previously payable which is not the same as the rent payment for the previous year; artificial figures intrude into the calculation. It should be noted for these purposes that the base rent for making comparison is not necessarily the passing rent but is the rent that was previously subject to stamp duty land tax.[881] Where, as will usually be the case, the parties have had to prepare the relevant tax return upon the basis of the assumed rent, namely the highest amount of rent paid in any 12 calendar months during the first 5 years of the term, this will initially form the basis of the test for abnormality.[882] Assignees will require full disclosure of the tax history of the lease.[883] Tenants may wish to investigate whether some protection against or compensation for the tax charge can be obtained from the

---

[873] See **7.166**.

[874] There have been adverse comments in relation to the effectiveness of these provisions and it has been announced that further changes are to be introduced.

[875] It is the view of HMRC Stamp Taxes that these provisions apply to such rents but the contrary view that they do not apply is not unarguable.

[876] Which is not a surrender and regrant by operation of law; see *Gable Construction v IRC* [1968] 1 WLR 1426.

[877] FA 2003, Sch 17A, paras 14 and 15.

[878] Ibid, Sch 17A, para 7(3).

[879] See **7.188**.

[880] See **7.164**.

[881] FA 2003, Sch 17A, para 14(4) and (4A) and note para 14(4B) but note also para 15(1) Step 3 'R'.

[882] In future where there has been an abnormal increase in the rent then the rent that forms the abnormal rent will be the base rent carried forward against subsequent reviews or other rent increases, including changes in the rate of VAT. Since this figure will be part of the initial tax computations the information used to produce the assumed rent will be a key issue of title.

[883] See **7.235**.

landlord. Assignees of leases will require information as to the stamp duty land tax calculation, since the tax may have been based upon an assumed rent rather than the actual rent passing at any time.

7.182 These provisions apply where a lease is deemed to be extended beyond the 5-year period such as holding over pursuant to the Landlord and Tenant Act 1954. The excess rent is the difference between the new rent and the rent previously taxed[884] and the rent is variable, in addition to the need for annual reviews as the lease is extended during the first 4 years, there will be a need for the review at the expiration of the fifth year of the term.[885] Reassessments will be required in subsequent years as the term is deemed to extend. These provisions apply not just to stamp duty land tax leases but to all leases granted on or after 1 December 2003 including leases subject to stamp duty.[886] The regime will apply, therefore, to leases granted after that date but which are subject to stamp duty because they were pursuant to agreements for lease entered into prior to that date.[887]

In consequence this provision implies that a rent increase outside the lease is not part of the deemed rent after the expiration of the fifth year of the term. This may mean that a rent reduction during the recession is excluded from the calculation at the end of the fifth year cancelling any refund.

'Abnormal increases'

7.183 To determine whether the increase[888] is abnormal[889] it is necessary to apply the formula:

$$\frac{R \times Y}{5}$$

where:

- R is the rent previously taxed; and

- Y is the number of whole years elapsed between the start date and the date of the rent increase.

---

[884] See **7.130**, **7.197** and **7.198** on the problems of determining the 'rent previously taxed' and issues such as the effect of discounting and the assumed rent for years after the expiration of the fifth year of the term such as whether the rent previously taxed is the artificial rent with or without discounting. It seems that an order for interim rents may be part of an abnormal increase.

[885] FA 2003, Sch 17A, para 14.

[886] Ibid, Sch 17A, para 14(7)(a) and Sch 19.

[887] Ibid, Sch 17A, paras 14(7)(a) and Sch 19.

[888] A major problem is to determine where the variation in the rent is an increase. The draftsman has at least provided a base figure ie the rent previously taxed although this is not necessarily an issue free from doubt (see **7.185**); but there is no express guidance on how to determine the new rent especially where this is variable or subject to VAT.

[889] FA 2003, Sch 17A, para 15.

In broad terms, the effect is that a rent increase averaging in excess of 20 per cent per annum from the relevant start date is abnormal.[890]

As this is a form of averaging it is necessary to determine the time span, namely 'Y'. This means that it is first necessary to find the start date which sets up the period over which the size of the increase has to be measured, ie the interval between the start date and the new rent being fixed. The start date is:

• if the rent is within the variable rent regime,[891] the date on which during or at the end of the 5-year period when the assumed rent for all years after the expiration of the first 5 years of the term is determined. This will usually be the rent review date or the end of the period for turnover or rent sharing arrangements;

• if there has been an increase in the rent otherwise than pursuant to a provision in the lease such as a deed of variation,[892] during the first 5 years of the term the date of the variation or the last such variation; and

• in all other cases,[893] the beginning of the term of the lease. This is ambiguous but it is thought to refer to the effective date for the lease which is the start date for the term of the lease for the purposes of stamp duty land tax.[894] or stamp duty; not the term commencement date.

It is then necessary to find the number of whole years between the start date and the date of the increase.

7.184 The other factor is 'R' ie the rent previously taxed. This is:

• where the rent is variable[895] the rent assumed to be payable for all years after the expiration of the fifth year of the term, ie the highest rent paid during any 12 consecutive months during the first 5 years of the term;

• where the rent has been varied during the first 5 years of the term. This is an extremely significant provision since it suggests two major issues of principle:
  – variation of rent otherwise than pursuant to the terms of the lease are not taken into account for variable rents and the 5 year adjustment;
  – the deemed new lease of FA 2003, Sch 17A, para 13 is not consolidated or merged with the actual lease for all purposes during the first 5 years of the term, the rent payable as a result of the variation or the last such variation;

• where there has been a previous abnormal increase, the rent payable as increased by the previous application of the abnormal increase provisions; and

• in all other cases[896] the rent payable under the lease without the increase.

---

[890] This would now appear to include changes in the rate of VAT over the relevant period and the effect of a landlord exercising the option to subject the rent to VAT. The latter could have a major impact upon whether the 20 per cent threshold average has been exceeded.
[891] FA 2003, Sch 17A, para 7.
[892] Ibid, Sch 17A, para 13.
[893] Which presumably includes stamp duty leases granted after 1 December 2003.
[894] On the vexed question of the effective date for leases see **7.25**.
[895] FA 2003, Sch 17A, para 7.
[896] Which presumably includes stamp duty leases granted after 1 December 2003.

Where there has been a lease granted with a credit for rent payable in respect of an earlier lease,[897] the credit is ignored in determining the rent previously taxed,[898] because the entire rent will have been taxed albeit in two stages namely the original rent providing the credit and the new rent in excess of the credited amount.

7.185 'R', ie the rent previously taxed, is potentially ambiguous.[899] It can mean the amount of rent taken into account or the amount of that rent after discounting. Whilst the latter is the obvious and generally applied meaning of the term it seems that in this particular context it is the nominal amount not the discounted amount that is the relevant base figure. However, the amount of the abnormal increase brought into charge will begin to qualify for discounting.

7.186 Having not dealt fully with the issue of the base rent ie the rent previously taxed,[900] the draftsman assumes that the new rent will be easy to ascertain, ie it is a fixed amount. Unfortunately, this will not invariably be the case. The draftsman has provided the formula for deciding base rent and to some extent has defined the two key factors in the formula; namely 'R' and 'Y'. Unfortunately, when deciding whether there is an increase and if so whether abnormal it is necessary to have the number to which the product of the formula is to be applied. Since this does not appear in the formula it seems the draftsman has overlooked the need for a vital component in the calculation. Indeed, it is a vital component in two calculations; namely:

- whether the arrangement represents an increase in the rent;

- whether it is 'abnormal'; and

- the rent brought into the charge to tax in relation to the deemed new lease that arises.

Obviously the key calculations were in respect of the latter. The problem is that this is not a straightforward case of a deemed new lease for the revised rent with a new rent credit for the rent previously taxed. It is a deemed new lease for a deemed rent equal to the difference between the rent previously taxed and the rent for the new lease. It may be that HMRC Stamp Taxes will take the view that the 'rent previously taxed' is the relevant proportion of the net present value determined when the lease was originally granted deducted from the net present value of the new rent being the increased amount. However, this is not necessarily consistent with the legislation. Moreover, it introduces many practical problems such as since the deemed new lease does not appear to be absorbed into the existing lease for future rent calculations[901] there will be the question as to whether the deemed new lease must continue in existence for the purposes of the calculation of stamp duty land tax for variable rents after the expiration of the deemed first 5 years of the deemed lease. This may mean that the charge in respect of the abnormal increase is a variable factor that has to be retrospectively adjusted at the end of 5 years.[902] In practice, although the variable rents may be subject to review during the first 5 years of the term because of the approach of HMRC Stamp Taxes to changes

---

[897] FA 2003, Sch 17A, para 9.
[898] Ibid, Sch 17A, para 14(4A) and (4B).
[899] Compare the issue of similar ambiguity when determining rent credits such as FA 2003, Sch 17A, paras 9 and 9A; see **7.198**.
[900] Ibid, Sch 17A, para 14(3).
[901] Ibid, Sch 17A, para 15, Step 1(c).
[902] Ibid, Sch 17A, paras 7 and 8.

in the rate of VAT, it seems that the rent for deemed new lease will not be 'certain' until the first 5 years of the deemed term have expired. There will, therefore, be numerous problems in the debate with HMRC Stamp Taxes as to how the new rent to which the fraction produced by the algebraic formula is to be applied. Most of the possible solutions are effectively unworkable when dealing with variable rents or rents subject to VAT or rent reviews or turnover rents which is likely to be the case because the absence of certainty means that the deemed new lease must continue in existence for at least 5 years in order to bring back the calculation of the new 'rent' in the revised computation. This would mean that the due diligence required by any potential assignee of the actual lease need significant information concerning potential deemed new leases or actual deemed new leases for the purposes of dealing with his own rent variations in the future. Without the information and upon the basis that there are at least two leases namely the actual lease and the deemed new lease in existence for the purposes of stamp duty land tax computations the position will be difficult to estimate his own potential tax liabilities in the future. It is provided that when looking at subsequent rent increases after there has been an abnormal increase the base rent is the rent that was treated as the new rent for the previous abnormal increase. However, until the position of the new rent is determined there is no certainty that there has or has not been an abnormal increase. The estimated figures may produce a potential abnormal increase but if these are subject to the 5 year adjustment they may reduce and fall below the estimated figures so that the increase is not abnormal and the charge is potentially retrospectively cancelled. A deemed new lease may retrospectively collapse with a refund claim. The issue is not simplified by the fact that it is provided[903] that the assumption[904] that the rent does not change after the expiration of the fifth year of the term of the lease does not apply for the purposes of dealing with abnormal rent increases and the charge looks to any actual increase; but the base rent is the assumed rent and rent credits are ignored.[905] However, it is implicit[906] that the future rent is not uncertain since the deemed lease is granted in consideration of the 'excess rent' ie the amount of the immediate increase. Any possible changes in that rent are, it seems, to be ignored.

Computation provisions

7.187 Where there is an abnormal increase in the rent there is the deemed grant of a lease for the excess rent ie the difference between the base rent and the new rent. The deemed new lease is treated as being made on the date on which the increased rent first becomes payable. It is for a term equal to the unexpired part of the original lease and is not limited to any lesser period where the rent increase is purely temporary, such as a freak year in relation to turnover as may occur in relation to the Olympics. Any reduction in the rent previously taxed in respect of overlap periods such as for holding over and similar arrangements is ignored.[907] This recognises that notwithstanding that there may have been a reduction in the rent for the lease charged to tax the credit is available only where the deduction itself had borne stamp duty land tax. This avoids a charge upon certain earlier rents which would have been part of the base rent were it not for the deduction or rent credit. It seems that the provision will apply notwithstanding that the abnormal increase is of a temporary nature such as a fluctuation in turnover in any particular year. This odd result of a freak year in the rents will continue for the

---

[903] Ibid, Sch 17A, para 14(6).
[904] Pursuant to FA 2003, Sch 17A, para 7(3).
[905] Ibid, Sch 17A, paras 14(4A), 14(6) and 7(3).
[906] Ibid, Sch 17A, para 14(2).
[907] Ibid, Sch 17A, paras 9(2) and 9A(3); para 14(4B).

remainder of the life of the lease,[908] notwithstanding that it is perfectly obvious that this abnormal rent level cannot continue for more than the relevant year or for a few years thereafter. The deemed lease is also treated as being linked with the grant of the original lease and with any other transaction with which the grant of the original lease is itself linked. This will apply where there are successive linked leases of the same premises[909] or where there are linked leases relating to different properties.

VAT problems

7.188 A key problem that has emerged is the impact of VAT. It would seem that HMRC Stamp Taxes are totally of the view that changes in the rate of VAT are changes in the rent.[910] It would seem that on normal drafting principles any fluctuation in the rent by reason of changes in the rate of VAT whether up or down will be variations pursuant to the terms of the lease. They will not, therefore, fall within the separate charging provisions of FA 2003, Sch 17A, para 15A(1). Such variations in the rate of VAT will not necessarily of themselves produce an abnormal increase but will no doubt be factors to be taken into account when comparing the base rent with the new rent however that is determined. It will also mean that the problems of determining the 'new rent' or the rent for the deemed new lease will almost inevitably be variable rents with the problems of administration the tax mentioned above.

7.189 The major problem will be the exercise of the option to tax. It may be that the lease is granted for base rent and by reason of FA 2003, Sch 4, para 2 the initial charge is limited to the base rent since the potential for VAT to apply to the rent will be excluded since it is provided that the exercise of the option to tax after the effective date is to be ignored. However, should there be an exercise of the option to tax which is ignored during the first 5 years or which takes place after the expiration of the fifth year of the term these will be events prior to a situation producing an abnormal increase. They will, therefore, *prima facie*, not be excluded by Sch 4, para 2.

There will, of course, be the question of whether the exercise of the option to tax during the first 5 years of the lease is a variation pursuant to the terms of the lease and therefore dealt with by the adjustments required by FA 2003, Sch 17A, paras 7 and 8 or whether it is an increase in the rent taking effect outside the terms of the lease and therefore within para 13 thereof.

7.190 This raises numerous technical issues such as whether any variation of the rent within para 13 is taken into account during the review at the end of the fifth year of the term for the purposes of para 7 and so forms part of the assumed rent for years after the expiration of the fifth year of the term that provides the basis for the abnormal rent increase formula. Certain aspects of the provisions relating to the abnormal increase provisions suggest that any provision or any variation of the rent within the para 13 is not included in the assumed rent but it may be a factor to be taken into account in deciding whether there is an abnormal increase.[911] Should the exercise of the option to tax in the first 5 years form part of the review provisions because it is pursuant to the terms of the lease then the VAT arising will have been part of the rent previously subject

---

[908]   Ibid, Sch 17A, para 14(5)(b).
[909]   Ibid, Sch 17A, para 5.
[910]   Guidance Note, 30 January 2009, STI 2009, p 460.
[911]   FA 2003, Sch 17A, para 15, Step 1(c) which determines the start date for the abnormal increases this rent will have been taxed pursuant to para 13 but not it seems paras 7 and 8 giving the implication that it is not part of the variable rent review provisions.

to tax. However, if it is not consolidated and is regarded as being some operation outside the terms of the lease then it will not form part of the base rent being carried forward and so may itself constitute an increase of the rent. This is not a major issue for exercise of the option to tax during the first 5 years since these are specifically incorporated into the base rent but only for the purposes of determining the start date. Indeed, it would seem that they cannot be incorporated into the base rent because this is actual VAT arising after the effective date and therefore excluded from the operation of the retrospective provisions of para 7 by FA 2003, Sch 4, para 2.

7.191 However, the main issue will be where the option to tax is exercised so as to subject the rent to VAT after the expiration of the fifth year of the term. There will be the question as to whether, should the exercise of the option to tax increase the rent by an appropriate amount so as to produce an abnormal increase in its own right, this is a chargeable event. In this situation the exercise of the option to tax will produce actual VAT and will take place as at the effective date ie the exercise of the option to tax which takes the rent increases through the abnormal threshold. It will, therefore, *prima facie* not be excluded by FA 2003, Sch 4, para 2. Similarly, where the exercise of the option to tax does not increase the rent by the relevant proportion it will, it seems, nevertheless provide a factor in determining whether any future changes in the rent when combined with the increase in the VAT charge from zero to something approaching 20 per cent will produce a movement through the threshold. This will be particular unfortunate if the exercise of the option to tax coincided with a rent review which increased the rent upwards so that the increased rent plus the addition of the VAT would clearly exceed the 20 per cent threshold, although, hopefully, the averaging effect of the formula over the review period would keep the average increase below the 20 per cent target figure.

Renewal of leases

7.192 Where a lease has expired the parties may, after a period of holding over whether by operation of law pursuant to statutory provisions or informally[912] and negotiation for a possible new lease[913] enter into an agreement for a new lease or the grant of a new lease. There are issues as to whether the holding over or continuation in occupation itself possibly gives rise to chargeable transactions.[914] *Prima facie*, this lease will be a stamp duty land tax event with the tax being calculated upon any rent or premium as appropriate.[915] In particular, the tenant of the new lease may be entitled to a nil rate slice in respect of the rent[916] notwithstanding that he or his predecessor in title qualified for the nil rate in relation to the expired lease.[917] However, there are numerous special provisions dealing with the renewal of leases largely of an anti-avoidance nature designed to prevent parties entering into a succession of short leases where the net present value of the rent never exceeds the nil rate threshold. The main area is concerned with successive linked leases, which treats certain lease renewals as being part of the linked transaction regime for the purposes of calculating the stamp duty upon the rent,[918] by being a successive linked lease requiring retrospective recalculation of the tax upon the rent[919] with a consequential adjustment in the allocation of the nil rate slice

---

[912] See **7.195**.
[913] See **7.128**.
[914] FA 2003, Sch 17A, para 3 which refers to 'operation of law'; see **7.124**.
[915] See **7.37** for premium and **7.98** for rent.
[916] But note the impact upon the nil rate slice for non-residential property; FA 2003, Sch 5, paras 9 and 9A.
[917] But see FA 2003, Sch 17A, para 5.
[918] Ibid, Sch 17A, para 5.
[919] Ibid, Sch 17A, para 5.

upon linked leases of other premises[920] notwithstanding that these leases may have been assigned to third parties unconnected with either the landlord or the tenant.[921]

Since the renewal of a lease may be related to another transaction such as where there is some form of surrender and regrant then there may be a rent credit.[922] In broad terms, the rent reserved by the new lease is reduced in respect of any relevant rent for any overlap period paid in respect of the previous lease.[923]

Rent credit[924]

7.193 In certain situations the amount of the chargeable rent is reduced by reference to taxed rent for other leases but with considerable problems in computing the relief. The situations where this applies are as follows.

Surrender and regrant

7.194 Where there is a surrender and regrant of a lease whether by way of a formal surrender and regrant or by operation of law such as where there is a deed of variation affecting either the term of the lease or the extent of the demised premises[925] there may be overlapping terms because the existing lease is surrendered partway through it contractual term. Where A surrenders an existing lease to B and, in consideration of that surrender, B grants a lease to A of the same or substantially the same premises, A will have paid stamp duty land tax[926] upon the rent reserved by the original lease.[927] Part of the rent taken into that initial calculation will represent the period for which the existing lease is surrendered. For example, where A originally has a 99-year lease of a flat and when the term has 65 years unexpired he approaches the landlord for an extension of the term to 150 years, there will be a surrender and regrant. The new lease will take effect immediately but A will have borne stamp duty land tax upon the unexpired 65 years' residue of the surrender term. There is, therefore, an element of double taxation. At present the arrangements are likely to affect short leases and holding over where there is a deemed extension of a lease[928] so that where there is a new lease there is a potential surrender of a deemed lease for part of the year in consideration for the grant of the new lease.

Holding over – renewed lease

7.195 There are two regimes for the taxation of new leases granted after a period of holding over. These issues are complex in that certain holding over arrangements produce a stamp duty land tax event;[929] in other cases the holding over is not a chargeable transaction:

---

[920] Ibid, Sch 5, para 2.
[921] Ibid, s 81A, Sch 17A, para 12, s 108.
[922] There are also certain specific and limited exclusions for the land exchange rules; FA 2003, s 47; Sch 4, para 5; Sch 17A, para 16.
[923] Ibid, Sch 17A, paras 9 and 9A.
[924] See also **7.198**.
[925] *Friends Provident Life Office v British Railways Board* [1996] 1 All ER 336; but not rent; *Gable Construction v IRC* [1968] 1 WLR 1426; see **5.154** and **7.79**.
[926] FA 2003, Sch 17A, para 9.
[927] Or the Business Tenancies (Northern Ireland) Order 1996, SI 1996/725.
[928] FA 2003, Sch 17A, para 3.
[929] Ibid, Sch 17A, paras 3 and 4, for credits and reliefs see paras 9 and 9A.

- one regime deals with rent arising after the grant of a new lease. This applies where a tenant holds over premises within Part II of the Landlord and Tenant Act 1954 (as amended),[930] where there may be an overlap because there is a statutory extension of the expired term of the existing lease by 1 year.[931] This will attract stamp duty land tax in respect of a whole year's rent, as discounted. The new lease may be granted part-way through that year. That will attract stamp duty land tax in respect of the period from the grant and there will be an element of double taxation in respect of the period between the grant of the new lease and the expiration of the statutory 1 year extension of the lease being held over. A credit for the period is available;[932]

- the other regime deals with the situation of rent arising in respect of the period between the termination of the existing lease and the grant of the new lease ie in respect of the parties' treatment of the rent during the holding over period which is potentially taxable as a premium without credit.[933] This deals with prior matters in respect of the 'backdating period' between the contractual termination date and the actual grant of the new lease. The FA 2003[934] provides an additional regime for the 'backdating of leases'. Where a tenant continues in occupation after the expiration of the lease and is granted a new lease of the same or substantially the same premises[935] and the term commencement date for the new lease is expressed to be on or immediately after the contractual termination date of the old lease, the term of the new lease is treated as beginning on the term commencement date. The rent payable in respect of the period between the contractual termination date and the date when the new lease is granted[936] is reduced by the amount of the rent taken into account for tax during that interim period;[937] but this applies only for rent expressed to be payable for the period prior to the lease. It would seem that where the provision applies since the new lease is deemed to commence on the expiration of the old lease, the sum paid in respect of that period between the contractual termination date and the effective date for the new lease whether in the form of substantial performance of the agreement for lease or the actual grant of the lease will be a sum payable as consideration for the grant of the lease but after the deemed relevant effective date. It would seem, therefore, that in this situation the sum will not be treated as a deemed premium,[938] because it is deemed to be paid after the grant of the lease.[939] However, this treatment is not available when backdating the term commencement date to any intermediate date such as the quarter day immediately preceding the grant of the new lease[940] will fall outside

---

[930] Ibid, Sch 17A, para 9(4).
[931] Ibid, Sch 17A, para 3(1)(b).
[932] Ibid, Sch 17A, para 9.
[933] Ibid, Sch 5, para 1A.
[934] Ibid, Sch 17A, para 9A.
[935] On the problems of substantial identity see **5.177** and **7.85**.
[936] Which presumably includes the deemed grant on substantial performance of the agreement for lease.
[937] On problems of calculating the credit see **7.198**. This presumably overrides the provision treating backdated rent as a premium; see **7.38**.
[938] FA 2003, Sch 5, para 1A.
[939] Ibid, Sch 17A, para 9A(2).
[940] Which is relevant for determining whether certain rent reviews fall within the first 5 years of the term (FA 2003, Sch 17A, para 7A) but unless the provisions of FA 2003, Sch 17A, para 9A operate to backdate the lease so that the computation of the term commencement date and the relevant 3 month period condition for excluding certain rent reviews applies.

this treatment and the backdated rent may remain taxable as a premium with the problems of the absence of a nil rate slice for non-residential property where the rent exceeds £1000 per annum.[941]

New sublease on forfeiture

7.196 The rent credit is available to a person claiming relief against re-entry or forfeiture who is granted a new lease by the court.[942]

Lease to guarantor

7.197 There are complex principles of general law whereby a person who guarantees a debt may, if payment has to be made, the guarantor is entitled to an indemnity from the principal debtor although the fact that he has been called upon to pay usually indicates that the indemnity is worthless.[943] Alternatively he may be entitled to be subrogated to the position of the creditor which may be of limited benefit if the creditor has taken security for the loan or debt.[944] Where a guarantor[945] of a lease that is terminated is granted a lease of the same or substantially the same premises pursuant to the guarantee he is taxable in respect of that lease but the rent reserved by the new lease in respect of the period between the grant of the new lease to the guarantor and what would have been the date for the termination of the old lease is reduced by the rent payable in respect of that period as taken into account in determining the tax in respect of the original lease.[946]

Calculation of the rent credit[947]

7.198 The rent credit is expressed[948] as a reduction in the chargeable rent in the new lease by the amount[949] of the rent that would have been payable in respect of the overlap period under the old lease ie the period from the commencement of the new lease to what would have been the contractual termination date of the existing lease being surrendered or deemed to be surrendered. The old or deductible rent is defined as the 'amount' taken into account in determining the stamp duty land tax[950] chargeable upon the old lease. It is possible that the draftsman intended the reference to the 'amount' of the rent brought into charge to be the net present value of the rent, but this could have been more clearly expressed. Moreover, it is difficult to justify this global treatment of the rent since for certain purposes the effect of the rent credit on certain years' rent has

---

[941] FA 2003, Sch 5, paras 9 and 9A.
[942] Ibid, Sch 17A, para 9(1)(c).
[943] There are fundamental questions of whether the giving of guarantees is a proper exercise of power or is a breach of duty by persons in fiduciary positions such as company directors and trustees because the risk outweighs the reward even in those cases where the prudent or well-advised guarantor insists upon a fee for entering into the guarantee; Companies Act 2006, ss 170–181; *Rolled Steel Products Ltd v British Steel Corporation* [1985] 3 All ER 52.
[944] Such guarantees if corporate debt frequently involve the shareholders giving a charge by way of security over their homes. Such guarantee mortgages are frequently and wrongfully omitted when dealing with FA 2003, Sch 4, para 8 (as amended).
[945] On guarantees see FA 2003, Sch 17A, para 10(1)(d).
[946] On calculation of the credit see also **7.198**.
[947] See also **7.30** and **7.86**.
[948] FA 2003, Sch 17A, para 9(2).
[949] Which is ambiguous such as, *inter alia*, the actual rent (or deemed rent) the discounted figure or the net present value. The reference to 'amount' rather than the rent raises considerable issues of interpretation.
[950] This means the rent credit is not available where the old lease was subject to stamp duty.

to be ignored[951] and since this has to be the rent for the relevant period it may imply that each year's rent may have to be considered separately. This may, however, be possible where the rent credit, however computed, can be easily ignored,[952] but this requires a separate complex calculation to determine the proportion of the net present value of the old rent for the relevant part of the term. The old rent is, therefore, based upon the taxable rent, not the actual rent, but the assumed rent for all years after the fifth year of the term. The reference to the 'amount' of the rent suggests that it is subject to the relevant temporal discount for that rent for each individual year which, in theory, has to be separately calculated. This is likely to be onerous where, for example, there is an enlargement of a lease of a flat with an unexpired term (ie overlap period) of 80 years. Eighty years of rent credit has to be calculated with two sets of rent actual or assumed and both being discounted on a different time basis. For holding over pursuant to the Landlord and Tenant Act 1954 the overlap period will be less than 1 year subject to possibly longer periods where FA 2003, Sch 17A, para 9A applies.[953]

7.199 It is also necessary to determine the rent reserved by the new lease. This is not defined but it is likely to be interpreted as the amount of the rent brought into charge for the new lease. This means that where there is a variable rent, even if only because the rent is subject to VAT, the credit calculation will have to be carried out on at least two occasions during the first 5 years of the new term, and on two other occasions to cope with the double charge where there is a delay between substantial performance and grant in respect of the new lease because of the double charge. This latter situation requires a calculation for the old lease giving a credit for the new deemed lease at substantial performance and a new calculation when the lease is granted because the credit is in respect of the rent taxed in respect of the deemed lease. How these two credits for the same lease interact has not been clarified but technically it is only the net rent (ie after credit) for the agreement for lease that is subject to tax within the wording of the credit. However, it is hoped that HMRC Stamp Taxes will allow the aggregate credit.

Some problems for rent credit computation

7.200 The calculation of the credit is not a simple process because there is a lack of detailed rules for dealing with, *inter alia*, variable rents whether as the old rent and/or the new rent. Whilst there is some limited guidance for the base rent, ie the original rent as taken into account for calculating the tax on the original lease but without any explanation of how, for example, any discounting is to be taken into account or ignored, there is no guidance as to how the new rent is to be identified. Subject to the possibility that 'amount of the rent' refers to the relevant proportion of the net present value previous taxed, the legislation does not set out a simple process of deducting net present value for the relevant period of the old lease from net present value of the rent for the overlap period of the new lease; nor of deducting rent whether actual or deemed or assumed from rent for each and every year of the lease with an obligation to revise the rent credit when dealing with the rules for variable rents reserved by the new lease during and at the expiration of the first 5 years of the term of the new lease.

7.201 For example, the effect of the variable rents provision, the assumed rent after year five and the effect of discounting mean the passing rent will inevitably differ from

---

[951] FA 2003, Sch 17A, para 14(4B).
[952] However, this could give rise to problems where the old or base rent qualified for substantial discounting because it was reserved by a lease for a long term.
[953] See **7.128** and **7.139**.

the rent brought into account in the original self-assessment and any subsequent adjustments thereof.[954] The 'taxed rent' may be the assumed rent for all years after the fifth year of the term or the basic rent ignoring the effect of discounting or rent reviews after the expiration of the fifth year of the term unless treated as an abnormal increase. It will be less than the current passing rent because of the effect of discounting whereas the new rent will not necessarily qualify for significant discounting because it is reserved by an actual or deemed new lease.

7.202 Additionally there is no indication how variable rents in the new lease are to be approached although it seems probable that these rents as adjusted are subject to the basic principles relating to the first 5 years of the new term ie these are to be adjusted. In consequence, should there be a rent credit it will be a factor in the initial provisional self-assessment with further involvement in any subsequent retrospective recalculation of the rent duty[955] nor is there any indication as to whether this arrangement has to be carried out on a year-by-year basis ie the new rent for any particular year has to be treated separately and the amount of rent for that year under the old lease deducted from it. This may be something of a difficult problem because the rent years for the actual or deemed new leases may differ. The original lease may have been backdated to the March quarter day whereas the new lease may be granted with a term commencement date of 25 December. The rent years will, therefore, not correspond exactly. To deduct one from the other would be rather difficult unless even more arithmetic calculations are required to deal with part years and then adjusting every other year in the overlap period on to an artificial year basis. Moreover, there is the question of whether the new rent has to take into account some form of discounting for a relevant year for each year of the overlap period.[956] However, since the legislation refers to the 'amount' of rent brought into the tax computation, rather than the amount of rent actually charged, it is arguable that it is the nominal figure for the relevant rent, such as the assumed rent without discounting. The amount of rent charged could be the nominal amount of rent inserted in the formula with the discounting being part of the calculation of the tax. Alternatively, HMRC Stamp Taxes may wish to argue that since the reference is to the 'amount' of the rent charged to tax not to the 'rent' as such the discounting has to be taken into account otherwise there would be a serious tax-free discrepancy between the two rents after a full credit and tax previously paid. Similarly, the new rent would be the rent as ascertained for the first 5 years and as assumed for periods thereafter without discounting. It would also seem that where the new rent is a variable rent it has to be retrospectively revised during the first 5 years of the term or the expiration thereof, the rent credit will have to be taken into account as the new rent will require to be adjusted. Assignees of leases would seem interested in having this initial calculation made available to them so that they can recalculate the tax taking into account any credit that was available since this may be relevant when calculating their taxation liability when holding over or renewing the lease or varying the terms of their lease.[957]

7.203 Whilst a treatment of deducting an appropriate proportion of the net present value of the old rents from the net present value of the new rents for the overlap period would recognise the effect of discounting as a factor in net present value; but this method does not necessarily produce the correct result (but seems likely to do so in the

---

[954] See FA 2003, Sch 17A, paras 9 and 9A on the interaction of rent credit and holding over.
[955] Subject to the special provisions for abnormal rent increases; FA 2003, Sch 17A, para 14(4B).
[956] See **7.201**.
[957] FA 2003, Sch 17A, para 7(3).

vast majority of cases) it has the advantage of relative simplicity and perhaps might be accepted in practice by HMRC Stamp Taxes; however, this has not been publicly agreed by them.

7.204 For example, where a tenant having a lease of a flat at a ground rent of £1,000 per annum with 65 years unexpired extends the term to 150 years, it might appear that the rent for the first 65 years of the new tenancy will be reduced by £1,000. For the balance of the term, the rent will be the rent reserved by the new lease or deemed new lease. Unfortunately the credit mechanism requires the calculation to include the amount of the taxed rent which may not be the same as the actual rent, or assumed rent possibly as suitably discounted for each year.[958] This is deducted from the rent reserved by the new lease or deemed lease on a year-by-year basis.[959] The provision is also virtually unworkable where either or both of the rents reserved is variable so that there is no certain sum to be deducted except to the extent that the discounted assumed rent for years after the expiration of the fifth year of the term can be relied upon in whole or in part.

7.205 This appears to operate on the basis that the rent during the initial years of the new lease will be reduced by the amount of the fixed or assumed rent that would have been payable under the existing lease, for example, where a tenant of a flat has a lease with 65 years unexpired at a ground rent of £1,000 and enters into an arrangement whereby in consideration of a payment of £50,000, the lease is varied or regranted as a term of 150 years at a ground rent of £1,500. In addition to the question of the premium being taxable,[960] the calculation of the net present value of the rent will be that for the first 65 years the ground rent will be reduced by deducting from the discounted portion of the £1,500 by the suitably discounted proportion of the £1,000 per annum payable or reserved by the existing lease. In consequence, for the first 65 years the net present value of the rent will be determined on the basis of a reduced rent. It will, for the balance of the term, rise to £1,500. The problem is that the draftsman has failed to deal with the 'amount' of the rent to be brought into charge to tax either as regards the new lease rent or the rent in respect of the old lease. The opportunity to provide expressly for a comparison between the net present values of the old and the new lease rents has been rejected. The issue is, therefore, the general one of whether the deductible rent is, as the legislation suggests, the artificial discounted amount of the rent taken into the many computations of the rent for the old lease[961] the base figure which will produce a different deductible amount for each year of the overlap period, ie the period between the commencement of the new lease[962] and the termination date or deemed termination date[963] of the existing or statutorily extended expired lease, the legislation also suggests that the deduction has to be made for each relevant overlap year for the new lease before

---

[958] It is, however, arguable that the 'rent' brought into charge to tax is the undiscounted figure ie the whole rent is taxed the discount goes to the tax computation not to the amount of rent brought into the calculation; but this may be a difficult technical argument to develop.

[959] Regrettably those responsible for the structuring of the tax have not made it clear whether the deduction of the old rent as adjusted and discounted is deducted before or after the newly started discounting machinery has been applied to the new rent.

[960] It seems likely that the credit will be available only in respect of those leases which have borne stamp duty land tax upon the rent, and so surrenders and regrants of leases that have borne stamp duty will be taxable to stamp duty land tax in full upon the rent reserved without credit.

[961] Crucially HMRC Stamp Taxes have failed to provide clear legislation on the question of how the old rent is to be assessed in those cases where the tax assessment is not final at the relevant date such as where the relevant event precedes the first rent review or is within the first 5 years of the term.

[962] Note, for example, FA 2003, Sch 17A, para 9A.

[963] See, for example, ibid, Sch 17A, paras 3 and 4.

determining the discounted amount to be included in the calculation of the net present value of the rent reserved by the new lease.[964]

7.206 This credit only applies in respect of stamp duty land tax paid upon the original lease.[965] It does not provide any form of credit for stamp duty paid upon the lease surrendered.[966] The provision does not, however, have the effect of treating the new rent as being a negative amount such as may occur during the recession. There is no reduction of the rent below nil where the rent under the new lease is lower than the rent brought into charge to tax under the original lease.

EXCLUSIONS FROM THE CHARGE ON PREMIUMS

7.207 Various items of consideration are excluded from the scope of chargeable consideration other than rent.

Reverse premium

7.208 On general principle, a reverse premium such as a sum paid by a landlord to induce the tenant to take the lease or by a tenant as an inducement for the landlord to accept early termination of the lease would not rank as chargeable consideration because it is not being provided directly by the person acquiring the interest or a person connected with him as required by FA 2003, Sch 4, para 1.[967] It is a sum provided by the 'vendor', ie the person 'disposing' of the interest. In order to constitute consideration, the payment and the property interest must be moving in opposite directions or at least from the purchaser albeit to a third party. However, a reverse payment follows and moves in the same way as the property. The reverse payment by a tenant moves from the tenant to the landlord in the same way that the surrender goes from tenant to landlord. It is, therefore, impossible upon any general principle of law or statutory construction to regard a payment by a vendor or landlord to the purchaser or tenant as consideration provided by the tenant for the acquisition of the chargeable interest. Nevertheless those advising HMRC Stamp Taxes on the legislation appear to have given bizarre advice to the contrary thereby requiring unnecessary legislation which merely adds to the confusion and problems for other professional advisers who understand the basic issues helping their clients on a proper basis. There is, therefore, a bizarre theory of 'reverse consideration'.[968] It is difficult to see the benefits of this; nevertheless there is some self-serving legislation introduced by HMRC Stamp Taxes which would assist them in promoting this bizarre theory. This is the theory of statutory construction that amending legislation would not be necessary if there were not the problem.[969] In consequence, by referring to the provisions dealing with reverse payments HMRC Stamp Taxes have provided support for their own bizarre theories that 'reverse

---

[964] See also **7.108**.
[965] See **7.2**.
[966] Note the complications for post 1 December 2003 stamp duty leases for abnormal increases in rents; FA 2003, Sch 17A, para 15, Step 1(a); see **7.183**.
[967] FA 2003, Sch 17A, para 18.
[968] See **5.91**.
[969] See **2.3**.

consideration' is chargeable consideration.[970] In specified situations, payment of a reverse sum does not count as chargeable consideration,[971] namely:

- a payment by the landlord to the tenant in connection with the grant of a lease;

- a payment by the assignor to the assignee upon the assignment of a lease such as where there is an onerous rent or dilapidations are a potential cost to the assignee.[972] This exemption may also be helpful to assignees of those leases which were exempt when granted but attract an special charge upon assignment[973] as if they were the grant of new leases. Such a person may wish to have some contribution from the original taxpayer since he is bearing the cost of that other person's exemption; and

- a payment by the tenant to the landlord to accept an early termination by taking the surrender of a lease.

'Reverse payment'

7.209 Nevertheless, where there are wider arrangements such as the surrender of one lease and a related grant of another lease, whether of the same or different premises, there will be a very difficult question of whether the payment is a reverse payment. Thus, for example, where the tenant is making a payment to the landlord there will be a difficult issue of whether the payment is a reverse premium for accepting the surrender or a premium for the grant of a new lease particularly if HMRC Stamp Taxes take the view that the arrangement is simply a sophisticated device to commute the rent without a charge to tax.[974] Where the landlord is making a payment as an inducement to the tenant to move premises, it may be appropriate, subject to other taxation and commercial considerations, to apportion and allocate the payment between the various items in order to compute the payment, such as compensation for disturbance to business, damage to goodwill, removal expenses and so on, so as to reduce the amount, if any, attributable to the surrender of the existing lease. It may be easier to argue that these payments are inducements to take the new lease rather than an incentive to surrender the old lease taking the benefit of the exemption.

Rent holidays, reverse premiums and rent

7.210 A reverse premium in the form of an inducement to the tenant to take the grant of the lease normally means that the rent reserved by the lease, at least during the period to the first review date, will be higher than might otherwise be payable. In consequence, there will be a liability for the tenant to stamp duty land tax upon the higher rent which is likely to produce a substantial charge by reason of the increased charges upon rent.[975] In such circumstances, a rent holiday rather than a reverse premium with a higher rent

---

[970] There have been difficulties in practice with inducements offered by developers to pay the costs of the purchaser or tenant since HMRC Stamp Taxes regard this as enhancing rather than reducing the market value of the property.
[971] FA 2003, Sch 5.
[972] This should also exempt any indemnities given by the assignor to the assignee in respect of any underpaid tax on the initial return.
[973] FA 2003, Sch 17A, para 11; see **7.241**.
[974] Ibid, Sch 17A, para 15A(1).
[975] Ibid, Sch 17A, paras 7 and 8.

will almost certainly prove to be more stamp duty land tax efficient because there is a lower amount of rent for the relevant period to be included in the computation of the tax.

Indemnities given by tenants[976]

7.211 Where a tenant agrees to indemnify the landlord in respect of liabilities to a third party arising from breach of an obligation owed by the landlord in relation to the land that is the subject-matter of the transaction, neither the agreement nor any payment made in pursuance of it counts as chargeable consideration.[977] There are practical problems as to whether this relief extends to situations such as where the tenant agrees to indemnify the landlord or to carry out obligations imposed by a section 106 agreement[978] since there has been no prior breach of the agreement. It is believed that HMRC Stamp Taxes intend to include indemnities in respect of breaches committed by the assignee after the assignment at least in those cases where the assignor is potentially liable for the breach by the assignee but this has not been officially confirmed.[979]

7.212 Undertakings by an assignee of a lease to the assignor to pay rent and observe the covenants are ignored in calculating the tax, as are any payments made pursuant to such undertakings.[980] However, this relief does not take into account those situations where the assignment of a lease is taxed as the deemed grant of a new lease[981] where the assignee becomes liable for the stamp duty land tax upon the future rent. The relief also ignores the fact that assignees of leases are by statute made responsible for the open tax position of the assignor including compliance and payment so that they will be responsible for the tax upon future rent reviews and abnormal rent increases.

---

[976]   Specialised indemnities may be required because of the statutory transfer of the open tax liabilities in relation to leases pursuant to FA 2003, s 81A and Sch 17A, para 12.

[977]   FA 2003, Sch 17A, para 17. There are many theoretical questions concerning the nature of indemnities and stamp duty land tax. The legislation is ill-prepared. In some situations an indemnity may be the assumption of a liability that constitutes chargeable consideration pursuant to the FA 2003, Sch 4, paras 8 and 8A. In other situations the indemnity may be some form of reverse payment which is excluded from tax (FA 2003, Sch 17A, para 18) alternatively it may be some form of damages which would not normally be regarded as consideration (*Western United Investment Co v IRC* [1958] 1 All ER 257; *Photo Productions Ltd v Securicor Transport Ltd* [1981] 2 WLR 283 which indicates that damages deal with the area of secondary liability not the primary liability to perform the contract. There are also the questions of indemnities where there are inherent liabilities such as *Swayne v IRC* [1900] 1 QB 172 but the self-serving legislation dealing with such payments (FA 2003, Sch 17A, para 18) is simply further evidence of HMRC Stamp Taxes seeking to use odd legislation in order to provide support for their bizarre theories.

[978]   See **8.32**.

[979]   However, to the extent that HMRC Stamp Taxes regard the indemnity as chargeable consideration it may be possible to counter-argue that it is 'uncertain' consideration which can be postponed if the parties apply in time; see **16.34**.

[980]   FA 2003, Sch 17A, para 10. However, any undertaking by the tenant to pay to the assignor any overpaid tax that he recovers would seem to be regarded by HMRC Stamp Taxes as additional consideration subject to tax. Technically this makes the consideration uncertain and has to be factored into the initial calculation and an application to postpone submitted at the same time as the return, ie within the 30-day period.

[981]   Ibid, Sch 17A, para 11; see **7.241**.

Miscellaneous obligations under the lease[982]

7.213 It is provided[983] that the following do not count as chargeable consideration provided that they are separately apportioned from the rent:[984]

- any undertaking by the tenant to repair, maintain or insure the demised premises or, in Scotland, the leased premises. This does not necessarily mean that such undertakings by the tenant can be totally ignored for the purposes of the tax. For example, the lease may be granted upon the basis that the rent reserved by the landlord is the 'landlord's share' or specified percentage of the 'net' rents received by the tenant ie after the deduction of certain specified expenses of managing the properties. The expenses may include such items.[985] This is an intriguing form of drafting which suggests that there may be a significant exclusion from the charge to tax that would otherwise arise pursuant to the provisions dealing with the costs of works.[986] It would be usual to refer to an obligation to 'keep in repair' the premises but, to a large extent, given the plain English assumptions of the legislation the obligation to 'maintain' would appear to include routine repair. This would appear to include the covenant and related costs to 'put' as opposed to 'keep' the premises in repair such as where there are arrangements relating to previous dilapidations whether by the current tenant under a previous lease or a previous tenant.[987] In many situations the covenant to repair would clearly be part of the chargeable consideration but it will, *prima facie*, relate to land to be acquired and therefore potentially excluded from charge.[988] However, this requires the works to be carried out after the effective date for the transaction. This requires[989] the investigation of complex issues such as whether the person is acquiring possession of the whole or substantially the whole of the land or entering into some other arrangement that constitutes substantial performance. It would seem that this argument to the effect that 'repair' means 'put in repair' will be a supplementary argument for such taxes where there are difficulties in establishing substantial performance and only limited access is given to effect the repairs before the tenant can obtain full 'possession'; but would not include fitting out;

- a tenant's undertaking tenant to pay any amount in respect of services, repairs, maintenance or insurance or the landlord's costs of management.[990] This provides that if a single sum is expressed to be payable by way of rent then it should be treated as entirely rent even though it may relate to other matters such as services. The benefit of this exclusion of a charge to services from duty as a premium may

---

[982] There may, however, be valuation issues associated with the presence of such provisions in the lease especially where partnerships are involved: FA 2003, Sch 15, para 38.

[983] This needs to be considered in connection with the provisions of FA 2003, Sch 17A, para 6.

[984] Ibid, Sch 17A, para 6; see **7.137**.

[985] However, in such cases the need to agree the deductions and amount of expenses together with the need to agree a market rent for any voids ie premises unlet at the relevant time means that the tenant may have difficulty in complying with the filing and payment requirements within the specified period of 30 days after the expiration of the fifth year of the term pursuant to FA 2003, Sch 17A, para 8(1)(a); see **7.176**.

[986] FA 2003, Sch 4, para 10; see **Chapter 8**.

[987] In some situations the repairing obligation in this situation might be covered by some form of reverse premium or other inducement by the landlord for the tenant to take the lease. Such an arrangement would be outside the charge to stamp duty land tax; FA 2003, Sch 17A, para 18.

[988] Ibid, Sch 4, para 10.

[989] See **Chapter 14**.

[990] Without this provision the charge upon services pursuant to FA 2003, Sch 4, para 11 would include a charge to stamp duty land tax upon the market cost of obtaining a third party guarantee on the tenant's obligations.

be lost if the payment of rent wraps up the service charges into a single unapportioned sum. In consequence, it is necessary for this provision to apportion any obligations in relation to services or contributions to the landlord's costs as a separate sum. The fact that this may be referred to as 'additional rent' does not make it rent since this is separately apportioned[991] and so remains within the exemption.[992] The legislation does leave open an intriguing question in relation to certain types of rent arrangements. For example, a landlord may grant a lease to a developer reserving a rent that is related to the rents received from occupational subtenants.[993] This may be a share of the gross rents received or a share of the net rents. There may be other situations referring to the rents 'receivable' ie the contractual payment not the actual receipt. Where the arrangement is on a 'net' basis, the landlord's share of the relevant rent figure, in the hands of the tenant ie the amount which the tenant has to pay may include a deduction for the costs of management incurred by the tenant, including costs of repairs. It would seem that such undertaking to pay the costs of such repairs or maintenance may be regarded as a possible contribution towards the landlord's cost of management. Obviously, much will depend upon the drafting and structuring of the arrangements as to situations where the repair or maintenance obligations are undertaken by the landlord so that there is no deduction, as such, in computing the payment paid by the tenant. However, if the rent is not reduced because the landlord is bearing the costs then part of the rent will be a contribution towards the landlord's costs of repairs and management. Not being separately apportioned, these contributions will be chargeable as rent. However, if the rent is drafted upon the basis that the landlord's share is determined after the tenant has made the appropriate contribution to the landlord's costs of management, there may be significant tax saving for the tenant;

• any other obligation undertaken by the tenant that is not such as to affect the rent that a tenant would be prepared to pay in the open market.[994] This is an obscure charging provision since not only is it indirect by excluding something from a relief and thereby treating it as chargeable, it means that any covenant by a tenant which affects the rent is taxable. Thus a covenant in a lease by the tenant to manage the property the costs of which are deducted when calculating the landlord's share of the rents received clearly affects the rent and so is a chargeable transaction although it will normally be part of the original lease. The drafting of this provision is based upon a misunderstanding. Normally properties will be advertised or offered for leasing upon certain assumptions. The initial valuation will usually be carried out upon the basis that the 'standard conditions'[995] apply because there are certain routine arrangements and a degree of standard form documentation. It would seem that any initial advice as to valuations and rents will be upon the basis that the routine situation exists ie there are no unusual conditions or covenants in the lease will apply but which will take into account the effect of such covenants upon the rent. Every covenant, even routine covenants, have some effect upon the rent in the market. The question of whether negotiations are required to adjust the figures will depend upon whether there are

---

[991] On a just and reasonable basis FA 2003, Sch 4, para 4.
[992] But note the problems for VAT; see **7.188**.
[993] Complications will arise in relation to the taxation of these issues because frequently there will be assumptions as to the rent that would be received where the premises are not occupied. The assumption as to 'voids' can affect the amount of tax in the short and the longer term.
[994] Note the equivalent provisions in FA 2003, s 48(1)(b); see **4.39**.
[995] There may, however, be difficulties in deciding whether there are 'standard conditions' in a technical sense; *Sweet & Maxwell v Universal News Services* [1964] 3 All ER 30; *Scammell v Ouston* [1941] AC 251.

any 'unusual' or non-routine covenants and arrangements. Therefore, for HMRC Stamp Taxes to take the position that covenants do not affect the value is based on a false assumption namely that the covenants do not affect the value. The correct analysis would appear to be that the value makes certain assumptions as to the covenants which may be changed. The value is fixed by reference to the impact of the covenants that it is assumed would be applicable. This view, of course, means that on a strict analysis every covenant affects the value of the lease but this is not obvious because of the assumptions that are made in routine transactions;

- any guarantee of the payment of rent or performance of any other obligation of the tenant under the lease;[996]

- any penal rent,[997] or increased rent in the nature of penal rent, payable in respect of any breach of an obligation of the tenant under the lease.

7.214 The exclusion from charge applies not merely to assuming the obligation such as by way of novation or indemnity but also any payment made in discharge of the obligation.[998] Similarly, the assumption or release of any such obligation does not count as chargeable consideration in relation to the assignment or surrender of the lease.[999] Unfortunately those responsible for the structuring of the tax and those with whom they consult have not addressed the issue of whether a payment of 'compensation' or damages for breach of one of the relevant covenants is exempt pursuant to these provisions or is taxable as a payment by the tenant for a variation or release in whole or in part of the underlying exempt covenant.[1000] It is understood that HMRC Stamp Taxes intend to exploit this defective drafting in any Enquiry and do not regard the specific exempting provisions as modifying the general charging provisions involved in the definition of 'acquisition'. Where there is a payment of damages or compensation in connection with a breach of covenant such as failure to repair, there is also the question of whether there is a variation of the covenant which has been broken that constitutes a chargeable transaction.[1001]

VARIATIONS OF LEASES OTHER THAN RENT

Background

7.215 It is provided that 'acquisition' of an interest includes the 'variation' of a chargeable interest. In such a case the 'purchaser' will, *prima facie*, be the person providing the consideration and whose interest in the land is benefitted by the transaction.[1002] In consequence, *prima facie*, any form of variation of a lease for a consideration (other than provisions relating to rent where specific provisions are made) originally ranked as a chargeable transaction giving rise to obligations to report and pay tax regardless of whether the payment was by the landlord or the tenant. The original legislation created many problems in practice if only because certain key variations

---

[996] FA 2003, Sch 17A, para 10; for the relief for guarantors receiving a lease see FA 2003, Sch 17A, para 9 and **7.197**.

[997] *Weston v Metropolitan Asylum District Managers* (1882) QBD 404; *Moss Empires Ltd v Olympia (Liverpool) Ltd* [1939] AC 544.

[998] FA 2003, Sch 17A, para 10(2).

[999] Ibid, Sch 17A, para 17.

[1000] See, eg, *Banning v Wright* 48 TC 421.

[1001] FA 2003, s 43(3)(b).

[1002] Ibid, s 43(4).

operate as surrenders and regrants.[1003] In consequence, there have been several subsequent attempts by HMRC Stamp Taxes[1004] involving amending legislation to deal with variations of leases.

Current position

7.216 The current position is that variations of the terms of leases are not taxable unless the variation either:[1005]

- the variation takes effect as the grant of a new lease by general law;[1006] or

- is deemed by the legislation to take effect as the grant of a new lease;[1007] or

- the arrangement otherwise falls within FA 2003, Sch 17A, para 15A.[1008]

This means that many chargeable variations will be 'hidden' in the legislation by reason of the need to find arrangements that are deemed to be new leases[1009] or there are variations of rent for which specific provisions are made. Paragraph 15A specifies three situations where the variation of a lease is chargeable and does not involve the deemed grant of a new lease. These are:

- where the variation reduces the amount of the rent;[1010]

- where there is a variation of a lease other than a variation in the amount of the rent or the term of the lease, and consideration is given in money or money's worth other than an increase of rent by the lessee;[1011] and

- the lease is varied so as to reduce the term.

The problem is that certain of the variations, such as the reduction in the term but not the variation in the rent,[1012] will operate as a surrender and regrant, so that it will be covered by the first part of the charging provisions but there cannot be defective or redundant or meaningless legislation. It is difficult to see[1013] there being such a variation which is not the grant of a new lease when a lease is varied so as to reduce the term without a surrender and regrant since even if a variation involves the insertion of a break clause or similar provision[1014] for termination prior to the contractual termination

---

[1003] *Friends Provident Life Office v British Railways Board* [1996] 1 All ER 336; *Gable Construction v IRC* [1968] 1 WLR 1426.

[1004] FA 2003, s 43(3)(d).

[1005] Ibid, s 43(3)(d) (as amended).

[1006] See, for example, ibid, Sch 17A, paras 13 and 14(2).

[1007] And, therefore, an acquisition of a major interest for notification purposes pursuant to FA 2003, s 77.

[1008] Which may involve the deemed acquisition of a chargeable interest rather than the creation of a major interest so that it is uncertain whether it is notifiable but the result of the unsatisfactory drafting appears to create a notifiable transaction.

[1009] *Friends Provident Life Office v British Railways Board* [1996] 1 All ER 336.

[1010] FA 2003, Sch 17A, para 15A(1).

[1011] Ibid, Sch 17A, para 15A(1)(a).

[1012] *Gable Construction v IRC* [1968] 1 WLR 1426.

[1013] FA 2003, s 43(3)(d)(i).

[1014] Although potentially not taxable as such the insertion of a break clause may be regarded by HMRC Stamp Taxes as a 'scheme transaction; for the purposes of the general anti-avoidance provisions (FA 2003, ss 75A–75C) since certain issues of break clauses are included as specific targets in the illustration list to which the legislation 'may' apply.

date this does not, as such, reduce the term and the legislation provides that when looking at the term of a lease any provisions for termination are to be ignored.[1015] It is also difficult to regard a formal surrender (ie early termination) of a lease as a shortening of the term since the legislation appears to presuppose the existing lease continuing but for a reduced term. Nor would the exercise of a break clause to the delivery of an effective notice to quit seem to be within these provisions since the term 'ends' rather than continues as 'shortened'.

7.217 The broad effect of the legislation is, therefore, that a potential charge to stamp duty land tax under a notification obligation arises where either:

- the variation involves a surrender and regrant;[1016]

- there is specific provision for a charge such as certain increases in rent during the first 5 years of the term,[1017]

- there are provisions dealing with abnormal increases after the fifth year of the term,[1018]

- there is a reduction of the rent at any time;[1019]

- there is a reduction of the term of the lease that is not a surrender and regrant, if this is possible in law;[1020] or

- any variation of a lease other than the rent or the term paid for by the tenant otherwise than by an increase in the rent.[1021] Variations where the consideration is provided by the landlord or a third party are not taxable unless falling within the above list.

There are many drafting deficiencies and structural defects in the current legislation such as fundamental problems of how to determine whether the 'rent' is increased or reduced which is not obvious because of the prevalence of variable rents. Notwithstanding that different regimes apply to the increases[1022] and the reduction[1023] of rent and may depend upon whether the increases take effect pursuant to the terms of the lease or by reason of arrangements outside the lease at least during the first 5 years.[1024] This also means that there are potential multiple and complex compliance and payment obligations by landlords and tenants which might simply be regarded as part of some job creation scheme by HMRC Stamp Taxes.

[1015] FA 2003, Sch 17A, para 2.
[1016] See **7.194** and **7.223**.
[1017] FA 2003, Sch 17A, para 13.
[1018] Ibid, Sch 17A, paras 13 and 14 (as amended).
[1019] Ibid, Sch 17A, para 15A(1); see **7.144**.
[1020] Ibid, Sch 17A, para 15A(2). See **7.194**.
[1021] Ibid, Sch 17A, para 15A(1A).
[1022] Ibid, Sch 17A, paras 7 and 13.
[1023] Ibid, Sch 17A, para 15A(1).
[1024] Ibid, Sch 17A, paras 7(1)(a) and 13; see **7.144** and **7.151**.

'Variation' and other 'acquisitions'

7.218 There are specific provisions dealing with the variation of leases other than rent,[1025] but it is not provided that these are the sole provisions affecting the changes in the covenants or conditions in a lease, particularly when it is noted that the extended definition of 'acquisition' includes 'release' of rights in or over land,[1026] and there has been no attempt to deal with the overlaps in terms such as 'variation' or 'release'. There is a perennial problem of the possibility of two or more charging provisions applying to the same event. For example, a landlord may pay a tenant to agree to the inclusion of a covenant restricting the use of the premises because this may make neighbouring property more attractive for other traders. If treated as a 'variation' this will not be taxable because the payment is made by the landlord;[1027] however, it will be a chargeable transaction involving the 'creation' of a new chargeable interest, ie an obligation affecting the value of an estate or interest in land[1028] or a covenant affecting the amount of the rent[1029] and taxable notwithstanding that the payment is provided by the landlord whose reversionary interest benefits from the transaction.[1030] It is expected that HMRC Stamp Taxes will begin to exploit these areas of double charging provisions in the future, because of their potential ability to chose between the various heads or charging provisions.

7.219 Variations of leases may, therefore, be vulnerable because they are both variations and releases of covenants and it may be that HMRC Stamp Taxes may be able to choose between several simultaneous applicable charging provisions notwithstanding that one or more of these may be exempt from charge.[1031]

Additionally, however, stamp duty land tax applies not merely to obvious situations such as deeds expressly varying the terms of a lease where, for example, the landlord agrees to the modification of a covenant restricting the user of the demised premises in consideration of a payment by the tenant. There may be situations that are not so obviously a 'variation'. For example, it is provided by FA 2003, Sch 17A, para 10(1)(a). that any undertaking by the tenant to repair or maintain the premises is not chargeable consideration,[1032] and by para 10(2) thereof a payment made in discharge of such an obligation is also not chargeable consideration.[1033] However, in *Banning v Wright*[1034] where payment was made to a landlord as part of a compromise of litigation whereby the landlord sought forfeiture of the lease in consequence of a breach of covenant by the tenant, the payment was held to be a sum for the waiver, release or variation of a term of the lease.[1035] This will mean that disputes between the landlord and tenant and the settlement thereof by agreement, particularly those relating to dilapidations or

---

[1025] Ibid, s 43(3)(d) and Sch 17A, para 15A (as both amended).

[1026] *Gable Construction v IRC* [1968] 1 WLR 1426.

[1027] FA 2003, Sch 17A, para 15A(1A).

[1028] Ibid, s 48(1)(b).

[1029] And, in consequence, excluded from the exemption for certain covenants given by tenants pursuant to FA 2003, Sch 17A, para 10; see **7.213**.

[1030] FA 2003, s 43; see **Chapter 3**.

[1031] However, should HMRC Stamp Taxes take this approach there is a counter principle that the alternative heads of charge principles do not apply where one charge is general and another is specific. In such a case the specific provision prevails over the general provision.

[1032] Although the draftsman has failed to deal with the situation of such a covenant affecting the market rent pursuant to FA 2003, Sch 17A, para 10(1)(c).

[1033] See **7.213**.

[1034] It may be important to note the possibly wider drafting at the charging provisions relevant in that case: e g 'waiver'.

[1035] (1978) 48 TC 421.

change of user covenants, may need to be carefully considered in the context of this particular issue in view of the restrictions contained in para 10(3) which provides, *inter alia*, that the release of such an obligation does not count as consideration in relation to the assignment or surrender of the lease. This suggests that such an arrangement is chargeable consideration in other cases.

7.220 Far more subtle and challenging issues arise such as whether a change of rent review dates can operate as an increase or reduction in rent,[1036] or is merely a variation of the lease. The satisfaction of a claim made against the tenant for a breach by the landlord may involve a chargeable transaction. The question will be whether HMRC Stamp Taxes would wish to apportion the payment[1037] in some way on a just and reasonable basis[1038] between that which was paid in respect of the breach and so outside the scope of stamp duty land tax and the balance, if any, which was paid on the release or variation of the section or covenant for the future which would seem to be subject to tax.

7.221 Apart from the conceptual difficulties and legislative deficiencies involved in such routine practical problems, there are also major problems of principle because of the different ways in which variations of leases are taxed sometimes as deemed new leases, sometimes as deemed acquisitions of chargeable interests of an unspecified nature and sometimes as other forms of 'acquisition'. It is necessary to understand the nature of the transaction as this is treated by the stamp duty land tax legislation because the nature of the transaction may dictate the consequences. In some cases the transaction is taxed as the deemed grant of a new lease to the tenant;[1039] in others the rent variation is the chargeable event. In other cases such as where there is a variation in the lease for a consideration provided by the tenant there is the acquisition of an undescribed and unspecified chargeable interest by the tenant.[1040] Since some transactions might fall into both categories, such as a change in the rent review pattern which may be regarded by HMRC Stamp Taxes as either a rent increase or a lease variation, the approach to be adopted by HMRC Stamp Taxes is crucial. For example, an acceleration of rent review dates for a payment by the landlord is not taxable if treated merely as a variation of the lease but is taxable upon the tenant if regarded as an increase in the rent. No official guidance has been provided on these major practical problems to assist taxpayers.

7.222 Each of these situations in the list of chargeable variations requires detailed examination because the nature of the deemed chargeable transaction (usually badly drafted and undefined) differs and the consequence computation of tax related filing obligations also differ.

Surrender and regrant

7.223 Variations that expressly or by operation of law[1041] involve a surrender and regrant are technically exchanges[1042] of major interests,[1043] ie there is a surrender of the

---

[1036] See **7.144** on the possible impact of such changes in the rent review pattern on the variable rent regime.
[1037] FA 2003, Sch 17A, para 14.
[1038] Ibid, Sch 4, para 4; see **5.109**.
[1039] See, eg, ibid, Sch 17A, para 14(2); and note the difference in the treatment of rent variations, ibid, Sch 17A, paras 14 and 15A which makes the absence of adequate machinery for determining whether the rent has been increased or reduced is a major problem in a self-assessment regime.
[1040] Ibid, Sch 17A, para 15A(1A) and (2).
[1041] *Friends Provident Life Office v British Railways Board* [1996] 1 All ER 336; *Gable Construction v IRC* [1968] 1 WLR 1426.
[1042] FA 2003, s 47.

existing lease and the grant of a new lease, each being land transactions entered into as consideration. *Prima facie*, therefore, if the parties do not arrange matters so that they fall within the reliefs,[1044] such a surrender would produce substantial charges to stamp duty land tax:

- the landlord is, *prima facie*, subject to stamp duty land tax upon the market value of the existing lease that is being surrendered;

- the tenant is *prima facie* liable to stamp duty land tax upon both:
  - the net present value of the rent of the new lease; and
  - the market value of the lease being granted taking into account the rent reserved.

This would, of course, represent a very substantial charge to tax where, for example, a tenant was merely wishing to enlarge the term of a lease of a flat[1045] but reliefs may be available,[1046] as set out in the following paragraphs.

Capital amounts or premium reliefs for surrender and grant of new lease

7.224 Essentially, certain surrenders and regrants[1047] are to be removed from the land exchange provisions so that the charge to tax will not arise on the market value of the interest being treated as acquired by either party provided that the old lease and the new lease are between the same parties. Contrary to the views of certain solicitors, the reference to the parties refers to the current parties not merely the original parties to the lease so that a successor in title to the landlord's reversion and an assignee of the lease would be the parties for the purposes of this relief.[1048] In consequence:

- the new lease is not consideration for the surrender so that the landlord is not chargeable unless he provides other consideration to the tenant;[1049] and

- the surrender is not consideration for the grant of the new lease, ie it is not a taxable premium or part of any premium.

Importantly the relief applies whether the new lease is of the same or different properties. For example, the relief for the premium would also appear to be available where tenants in a block of flats where the lease includes a lease of a garage enter into arrangements to exchange their garages. A straightforward exchange of the two garages

---

[1043] Ibid, s 117.
[1044] See **7.78**.
[1045] Notwithstanding that the premium ie the payment for the extended term, is small it may not qualify for the nil rate of tax should the rent exceed £1000.
[1046] FA 2003, Sch 17A, paras 9 and 16 (as amended).
[1047] It is important to note that this relief does not apply to a transfer and leaseback.
[1048] It seems that these criteria will be satisfied where the current relationship arose between parties who where head landlord and subtenant and the intermediate lease has been surrendered or otherwise terminated.
[1049] See FA 2003, s 47; Sch 4, para 5 and Sch 17A, paras 9 and 16. Previously the landlord could deal with the Land Registry upon the basis that the transaction was for no chargeable consideration and therefore could be supported by a self-certificate (SDLT 60) unless the landlord paid the tenant for the surrender such as where there may be a dispute with HMRC Stamp Taxes as to the nature of any 'compensation' involved in the relocation of the tenant. Given the 'local discretion' of the Land Registry it remains to be seen how they will deal with these arrangements particularly since there are difficulties with certain Land Registries in persuading them as to the correctness of the self-certificate under the previous regime.

would involve a double charge;[1050] but restructuring as some form of surrender and regrant, if the landlord can be persuaded to co-operate, may be more tax efficient. Modification of the terms of the lease to change the demise by varying the garage attributable to each flat will not relate substantially to the same premises, but this does not appear to matter as regards any 'premium'. The value of any interest surrendered or the market value of the interest being granted will be ignored. For these purposes, it would seem that the 'premium' will be any lump sum paid by the tenant for the variation of the lease. For example, where the tenant pays the landlord £50,000[1051] for the increase in the length of the lease from 65 years to 150 years, the new lease will be treated as being granted for a premium of £50,000.[1052] There will be no hidden premium or value shifting by reason of the surrenders.

Rent credit for surrenders and regrant

7.225 Stamp duty land tax is still payable upon the net present value of the rent reserved by the new lease, whether a commercial rent or ground rent in connection with the regrant lease of a flat. However, a limited credit is available where the new lease relates to the same or substantially the same premises and the lease in question was granted on or after 1 December 2003 and subject to stamp duty land tax.[1053] Where the existing lease that is being surrendered or varied is for a fixed rent, the charge to stamp duty land tax upon the new lease in respect of rent will be given credit for the amount of rent due in respect of the surrendered years of the existing lease.

Reduction of the term of the lease

7.226 A variation that reduces[1054] the term of a lease is chargeable;[1055] but the scope of this provision is completely uncertain. An early termination of the lease thereby reducing its term will usually be taxable as a surrender and not as a variation since the lease ends and does not continue in a changed form which the concept of 'variation' appears to require. If there is a variation changing the length of the term the shortening of the term is a surrender and regrant[1056] governed by its own regime.[1057] The provision is aimed at a change in a continuing lease such that there is no chargeable transaction upon basic principles. It may have been aimed at the insertion of break clauses, but such a change does not, of itself, shorten the term of the lease.[1058] When exercised the

---

[1050] Assuming that there is not a further set of charges because the exchange is so drafted as to involve a change in the demised premises thereby producing two surrenders and regrants; but this may have problems where the landlord is a party and the deemed new leases will be outside the relief because the old and the new lease will not be between the same parties.

[1051] The lease will be notifiable because the premium exceeds £40,000; FA 2003, ss 77 and 77A.

[1052] The nil rate band may not to be available for non-residential premises (FA 2003, Sch 5, paras 9 and 9A) and dealing separately with garages may not be a dealing in residential property; see FA 2003, s 116; see **5.23** and **5.30** if the rent exceeds the threshold of £1000.

[1053] The relief is not available where the lease being surrendered was within the stamp duty regime notwithstanding that it was granted on or after the implementation date.

[1054] The legislation appears to require an actual reduction in the term rather than an arrangement which potentially reduces the term; on break clauses see *Kushner v Law Society* [1952] 11 KB 244.

[1055] FA 2003, Sch 17A, para 15A.

[1056] *Friends Provident Life Office v British Railways Board* [1996] 1 All ER 336.

[1057] FA 2003, s 47, Sch 4, para 5 and Sch 17A, paras 9 and 16.

[1058] Moreover, it is not, currently, a surrender and regrant to insert such a provision; see the comments in *Friends Provident Life Office v British Railways Board* [1996] 1 All ER 336 on the current scope of variations of leases as surrenders and regrants; see also *Gable Construction v IRC* [1968] 1 WLR 1426. Also such arrangements may be regarded by HMRC Stamp Taxes as being scheme arrangements within the general anti-avoidance provisions of FA 2003, ss 75A–75C. The provisions dealing with the term of a lease require break clauses to be ignored when determining the basic term of a lease so that the variation of a lease by

determination notice terminates and does not vary the lease. It is therefore difficult to identify any routine transactions likely to fall within this charge. It may, however, be not a case of legislation being prepared upon the basis of inadequate technical knowledge or bad advice from outside advisory and consultancy bodies but a deliberate policy which is intended to override the rules relating to surrenders and regrants specifically contained in the legislation. Given the potential inconsistency in the numerous provisions in the legislation dealing with this type of situation HMRC Stamp Taxes may have in mind some attempt to attack what they regard as potential avoidance and mitigation arrangements so that notwithstanding that there is a deed of variation shortening the term of the lease this is not to be treated as a surrender and regrant within the relieving provisions but is to be subject to a charge to tax. In this situation the variation of a lease that shortens the term is not to be taxed as a surrender and regrant with the credits that are available[1059] but that it remains taxable as a land exchange upon the basis that the lessor is acquiring a chargeable interest.[1060] This might be aimed at a potential mitigation device whereby a tenant enters into a lease for a lengthy term at a rent which is taxable at the rate of 1 per cent upon a heavily discounted figure. A deed or variation entered into subsequently would not qualify for any credit in respect of the tax paid for rent after the deed of variation reducing the scope of the term. However, it is possible that HMRC Stamp Taxes may have been supplied with information which suggests that, in this type of situation, the tenant could, effectively, provide a premium in the form of rent for a relatively short lease that is taxable at 1 per cent rather than 4 per cent. Since there is a specific charging provision there will be a question as to whether, in this type of situation, the mitigation arrangements are effective or the reliefs for surrenders and regrants also applies to override them. There is a fundamental question of statutory interpretation as to whether FA 2003, Sch 17A, para 15A(2) prevails over paras 9 and 16 thereof or vice versa. In addition, arrangements involving the insertion of a break clause into an existing lease followed by an exercise of the provisions could be regarded as 'scheme transactions' for the purposes of the general anti-avoidance provisions.[1061] Where there is such a transaction it is taxed as the acquisition of a chargeable transaction by the landlord.[1062] The nature of the chargeable interest is not defined so that if it is not the acquisition of a freehold or leasehold, it will be the acquisition of a minor interest not requiring notification unless the consideration exceeds the nil rate threshold;[1063] but the contrary position ie the variation of a lease is a variation of a major interest and has to be treated as an 'acquisition' of a major interest.[1064]

Variations paid for by the tenant

7.227 Any variation of a lease (other than a variation involving a change in the rent[1065] or a variation in the term where the lessee[1066] gives consideration in money or money's

---

inserting a break clause cannot in any way affect the term of the lease (FA 2003, Sch 17A, para 2(b)); even the current judiciary would find it intellectually difficult to challenge this obvious interpretation of the legislation.
[1059] FA 2003, Sch 17A, paras 9 and 16 unless HMRC Stamp Taxes have in mind some bizarre interpretation of FA 2003, s 43(3)(d)(i) overriding the general land law principles relating to surrenders and regrants.
[1060] Ibid, Sch 17A, para 15A(2).
[1061] Ibid, ss 75A–75C; see **2.19**.
[1062] Ibid, Sch 17A, para 15A(2).
[1063] Ibid, s 77A.
[1064] Ibid, ss 43 and 117.
[1065] Ibid, Sch 17A, para 15A(1).
[1066] But there may be charges upon the landlord because there is a release or surrender or other acquisition of a chargeable interest arising by reason of the changes in the term of the lease; see FA 2003, ss 43, 47, Sch 17A, para 15A.

worth other than an increase in the rent) is taxed on the acquisition of a chargeable interest by the tenant.[1067] Variations such as a reduction in the rent in consideration of a commutation payment or the variation reduces the term are dealt with separately.[1068] This charge pursuant to FA 2003, Sch 17A, para 15A(1A) will apply to any modifications of the covenants. As the deemed acquisition does not involve the acquisition of a freehold or a leasehold the transaction may involve a minor interest and is notifiable only if the chargeable consideration exceeds the nil rate threshold[1069] but since it is a variation of a major interest it is, arguably, more likely to be an 'acquisition' of a major interest,[1070] although variations of leases are excluded from this charging provision. The point may mean that many lease variations are not notifiable;[1071] but the provisions excluding dealings in major interests from notification set out in FA 2003, s 77A, whilst referring to assignments and surrenders of leases, do not refer to variations of leases thereby failing to provide a clear answer to the problem.

TERMINATION OF LEASES

Lapse of time

7.228 *Prima facie* the termination of a lease by lapse of time is not subject to stamp duty land tax. This does not involve a release or surrender and, in general, there will be no consideration where the lease expires.[1072] This does not mean that no payments will be made. For example, the tenant may be making payments to the landlord in respect of dilapidations or the landlord may be making payments to the tenant by way of compensation pursuant to the Landlord and Tenant Act 1954 (as amended). Many such payments, such as the payment of compensation, will not be chargeable consideration, since they are not the price being paid for the termination of the lease but are being paid pursuant to statute or as compensation for breach of an obligation. In addition, FA 2003, Sch 17A, para 10 provides that both entering into covenants to repair premises and payments made in pursuant of such a covenant, and possibly as damages for breach,[1073] do not count as chargeable consideration.

7.229 However, the termination of the contractual term may mean that the tenant remains in occupation holding over in some capacity,[1074] whether pursuant to statute or at common law, which may produce either a deemed extension of the lease or a deemed grant of a new lease or may possibly have no consequences.[1075]

[1067] See **7.218**.

[1068] FA 2003, Sch 15A, paras 1 and 2.

[1069] Ibid, s 77 (as amended).

[1070] Ibid, s 43(3)(c).

[1071] Ibid, ss 77(1)(b) and 77A.

[1072] Payments of statutory compensation because the lease renewal or other protection or security of tenure legislation is not applicable are not, generally, regarded as consideration for the 'surrender' of a statutory right to a new tenancy. It is assumed that the tenant deciding not to take the benefit of the statutory protection may not be dealing in a chargeable interest in land (but see FA 2003, s 48(1)(b)) and statutory compensation is not consideration.

[1073] *Western United Investment Co v IRC* [1958] 1 All ER 257; see also *Photo Productions Ltd v Securicor Transport Ltd* [1981] 2 WLR 283; but see *Banning v Wright* 48 TC 421 on whether the payments relate to something other than damages.

[1074] Which may have implications for the taxation of the rent reserved by the new lease; FA 2003, Sch 5, paras 9 and 9A; see **7.225**.

[1075] See **7.123**.

Notice to quit and break clauses

7.230 Similarly, termination by notice to quit or the operation of a break clause would not seem to be within the charge to stamp duty land tax[1076] even though the landlord giving the notice to quit may be required to pay some form of compensation either under the terms of the lease or otherwise.[1077] A surrender and a notice to quit are different forms of legal operation[1078] and so termination by notice to quit cannot be included under a 'surrender' or 'release', since these require the participation of the tenant whereas a notice to quit or 'break the lease' is a unilateral action of the landlord or the tenant. Moreover, the giving of the notice to quit is not the shortening of the term of the lease[1079] but the defining of the term by powers contained in the lease.[1080]

7.231 The existence of a break clause is ignored in determining the term of a lease[1081] so that tax on the rent is calculated upon the maximum possible term. However, there is no readjustment or repayment of tax if the break clause is exercised and the lease is terminated early.[1082]

Surrenders

7.232 A surrender of a lease whether by operation of law[1083] or by deed by a tenant in consideration of a payment or other property or services by the landlord[1084] gives rise to a charge to stamp duty land tax in respect of which the landlord is the 'purchaser'. Where the tenant makes a payment to the landlord as an inducement to accept the surrender and early termination, the reverse payment is not taxable.[1085]

7.233 In some cases, where the lease of one set of premises is being surrendered in return for the grant of a new lease of other premises which is *prima facie* not subject to tax in respect of the land exchange rules[1086] but since the premises do not relate to 'substantially' the same premises the relief for rent will not be available[1087] and the landlord is making a payment to the tenant in addition to the exchange of leases there are possibly charges to stamp duty land tax. There may be a cash payment by the landlord to the tenant. It may be important whether this payment is regarded as consideration for the surrender, when it appears to be taxable, or a reverse premium or inducement to take the new lease, when it is not taxable.[1088] Alternatively the payment may be a contribution to removal expenses, disturbance of business or to fitting out, when it appears to be outside the scope of stamp duty land tax.

[1076] Subject to the problem potentially arising pursuant to the general anti-avoidance provisions set out in FA 2003, ss 75A–75C.

[1077] Statutory compensation for such an event would not appear to be consideration for this purpose.

[1078] *Barrett v Morgan* [2000] 1 All ER 481.

[1079] FA 2003, Sch 17A, para 15A(2).

[1080] Also break clauses are to be ignored for many purposes of stamp duty land tax; FA 2003, Sch 17A, para 2(b).

[1081] Ibid, Sch 17A, para 2(b).

[1082] In such situations tenants may find that shorter leases with options to renew are a far more tax efficient vehicle; see **7.122** and **7.192**.

[1083] Ie without a document but nevertheless a chargeable transaction, FA 2003, ss 42(2)(a) and 43(2).

[1084] A payment by the tenant as an inducement to the landlord to accept the early termination of the lease is not taxable; FA 2003, Sch 17A, para 18(2)(a).

[1085] FA 2003, Sch 17A, para 18(2)(c).

[1086] Ibid, Sch 17A, para 16.

[1087] Ibid, Sch 17A, para 9(1)(a).

[1088] Cf *Swayne v IRC* [1900] 1 QB 172.

Forfeiture

7.234 Forfeiture of a lease for breach of covenant will usually be a transaction for no chargeable consideration and so exempt and non-notifiable.[1089]

ASSIGNMENTS OF LEASES

7.235 The assignment of an existing lease is an acquisition by the assignee of a chargeable interest. There are, however, several aspects to this problem including:

- the tax charge on the assignment;

- the responsibility of the assignee for the open tax liability of the original tenant or assignor,[1090] and whether the statutory provisions release the assignor from liability and create some form of joint or several liability; and

- the information that the assignee will require from the assignor in order to deal with his own future tax liabilities which may depend upon the tax position of the assignor and which may, in turn, be required for the same reason by any person to whom he may assign the lease.

Tax is chargeable upon any consideration provided by the assignee but not in respect of that part of the consideration that is properly apportioned between 'fixtures' and other items that have retained their character as chattels.[1091] Where there is a rent reserved by the lease, the undertaking by the assignee to pay all future rent is, in general, not chargeable consideration.[1092]

7.236 Where the assignor makes a payment to the assignee as an inducement to take the assignment, described by the FA 2003[1093] as a 'reverse premium', it is specifically provided that such a payment is not chargeable consideration.[1094] As the payment is moving in the same direction as the lease, it is difficult to see how on general principles the making of the payment is consideration for the assignment since, on general principles of the law of contract, the consideration for the acquisition of property moves from the transferee or a third party; it is money or money's worth being provided by the assignee and not consideration moving from the transferor of the property. Nevertheless, it was felt to be necessary to introduce this exemption into the legislation so that this exemption may be an indication that certain types of 'reverse consideration' are chargeable consideration.[1095]

7.237 As a basic principle, upon the assignment of a lease the assumption by the assignee of any obligation to pay rent or perform covenants under the lease is not chargeable consideration for the assignment.[1096] In addition, any reverse premium paid by the assignor to the assignee, such as to cover outstanding dilapidations, or to

---

[1089] FA 2003, Sch 3, para 1; ss 77 and 77A.
[1090] Ibid, s 81A and Sch 17A, para 12.
[1091] See **4.10**.
[1092] FA 2003, Sch 4, para 15(1) and (2)(b); see also *Swayne v IRC* [1900] 1 QB 172.
[1093] Ibid, Sch 17A, para 17.
[1094] FA 2003, Sch 17A, para 18.
[1095] See **5.91**.
[1096] FA 2003, Sch 17A, para 17; but see para 11.

compensate for the rent being above market rent or to contribute towards the stamp duty land tax issues passing to the assignee, is not subject to tax.[1097]

Special situations for assignment of lease

7.238 Much of stamp duty land tax operates on a provisional basis with the initial land transaction return having to be filed upon a provisional and estimated basis[1098] but which require retrospective adjustment in the light of subsequent events.[1099] This applies to both rent and premiums such as where there is a long lease with a clawback provision or variable rents,[1100] and these can pass to the assignee.[1101] This open tax position on lease premiums has caused problems where the property is transferred. Leases are particularly vulnerable to variable payments such as premiums and rent or situations where retrospective adjustment of tax or special charges affected by history arise. Detailed rules have been made[1102] but the consequences of these have not been adequately thought through by those responsible for the tax. Significant changes in conveyancing practice are required when dealing with the acquisition of existing leases and planning exit strategies will be required in relation to the grant of new leases.[1103]

Transferred liability

7.239 The assignee of a lease becomes responsible for the obligations to the assignor in a variety of circumstances.[1104] The assignee of a lease becomes responsible for any event being a chargeable or notifiable transaction that but for the assignment would be required or authorised to be done by or in relation to the assignor[1105] where, after[1106] the effective date for the assignment:

- there is adjustment required in relation to a contingent or uncertain or unascertained consideration[1107] whether of premium or rent;[1108]

- the obligations arise in consequence of later linked transactions;[1109] since it is considered that assignees are not affected by the linked transactions unless connected with the original parties[1110] this is a particularly harsh obligation since the assignee of a lease is made responsible for reporting and paying tax in respect of transactions after his assignment and to which he is not a party;[1111]

[1097] Ibid, Sch 17A, para 18.

[1098] FA 2003, s 51.

[1099] See, for example, rent reviews FA 2003, Sch 17, para 7.

[1100] See **2.14**.

[1101] FA 2003, s 81A; Sch 17A, para 12.

[1102] Ibid, s 81A; Sch 17A, para 12.

[1103] See, for example, **5.206**.

[1104] FA 2003, s 81A, Sch 17A, para 12; but this does not apply where the assignment of the lease is treated as the grant of a new lease pursuant to FA 2003, Sch 17A, paras 11, 12(3).

[1105] However, two points require notice: (i) there is no suggestion in the legislation that the assignor is relieved from his tax and compliance obligations or that this is some form of joint and several liability; and (ii) there is no statutory right to any indemnity or to demand information from the assignee.

[1106] There is no limitation period for this transferred liability so that the assignee remains liable indefinitely such as the balance of the 80 year period for the normal clawback premium.

[1107] FA 2003, s 80.

[1108] Ibid, Sch 17A, para 8.

[1109] Ibid, s 81.

[1110] See **5.53**

[1111] Unless HMRC Stamp Taxes intend to press the argument that an assignee is the same person as the assignor; see **5.55**.

- the making returns where leases for indefinite periods continue and reporting becomes necessary.[1112]

It will be noted that this applies to any assignee not merely the first assignee. It is, therefore, a long-term risk that continues throughout the term of the lease and beyond since it has implications for holding over and lease renewals that are successive linked leases.[1113] Since this requires the assignee or a successor assignee to carry out all actions for which the assignor was liable he will have to calculate the tax and pay any additional tax personally. Should he require an indemnity for such tax he must include it in the contract; there is no statutory indemnity. Any payment under the indemnity will be exempt as a reverse premium.[1114] The provisions appear to require the assignee to bear the late payment interest cost,[1115] but there is an open question as to whether the assignee is regarded by HMRC Stamp Taxes as being liable for any penalties that could be imposed upon the original taxpayer for filing an erroneous return or even whether the original taxpayer is released by the assignment. The assignee will, it seems, be liable for penalties and interest if he is late in filing his return for the assignor's linked transaction because he was not aware that it had occurred.[1116]

7.240 The obligation to deal with later linked transactions[1117] is particularly onerous since it is not limited to transactions to which the assignee is a party.[1118] Indeed, if the view expressed elsewhere,[1119] to the effect that the assignees are not the same party for the purposes of the linked transaction rules be correct, the obligation can only mean that the assignee has to report transactions between other persons of which he may not have notice and he should consider whether the assignment should for his own protection contain undertakings by the assignor to supply relevant information.[1120] Assignees cannot simply ignore this risk because later linked transactions can significantly affect their tax position even though they are not parties to them. For example, where there are linked leases of separate properties and successive linked leases of the same property,[1121] the nil rate slice for the rent has to be allocated, and if necessary, subsequently reallocated for later linked transactions *pro rata*. The nil rate slice for each lease will, in consequence, subsequently reduce so that tax on each lease

---

[1112] FA 2003, Sch 17A, paras 3 and 4.

[1113] See **5.73**.

[1114] Where the assignor requires payment of any overpaid tax received by the assignee this is likely to be treated by HMRC Stamp Taxes as additional chargeable consideration exposing the assignee to extra cost with an increased stamp duty land tax liability.

[1115] It is specifically provided (FA 2003, Sch 17A, para 12(2)) that 'so far as necessary' anything previously done by the assignor is treated as having been done by the assignee. It remains to be seen whether HMRC Stamp Taxes treat this as entitling them to recover penalties from the assignee. However, it is considered that such an argument would be of doubtful validity.

[1116] There will be interesting debates as to breach of contract and the quantification of damages where the assignee has secured appropriate covenants in the contract to provide information and indemnities for additional tax, interest and penalties should the assignor fail to provide the necessary details.

[1117] FA 2003, s 81A and Sch 17A, para 12.

[1118] Indeed any transaction to which the assignee is a party may not be linked because it will not be between the same parties as the original transaction.

[1119] See **5.53** and **5.55**.

[1120] There is a fundamental flaw in the linked transaction provisions that have escaped the attention of those with whom HMRC Stamp Taxes 'consult', namely, although linked transactions apply only as between the same parties these provisions do not address the problem of third parties who are by statute made responsible or are adversely affected by transactions to which they are not direct parties but hold a chargeable interest that when acquired by a predecessor in title was actually linked with concurrent or previous chargeable transactions or was potentially linked with subsequent transactions which have come to pass and where there are express provisions imposing reporting obligations or retrospectively modifying the stamp duty land tax history of the chargeable interest to their disadvantage.

[1121] For illustrations where linked leases may arise see **7.102**.

even if held by an assignee has been underpaid and the figures required for later transactions affecting the rent may be lower than originally expected. In consequence, failure to deal with linked transactions will expose the assignee and his successors in title to penalties for negligently prepared returns.

These situations may require indemnities such as:

- an indemnity from the assignor should the assignee be subjected to tax in respect of the assignor's open tax position such as rent reviews or clawback provisions; and

- an indemnity from the assignee in respect of any windfall tax repayment for tax overpaid or overestimated by the assignor.

Assignment as a deemed new lease

7.241 In certain cases the assignment of a lease is not taxed as an assignment but it is treated as if it were the grant of a new lease to the assignee.[1122] The new lease is for the unexpired term of the assigned lease and for the current rent at the time of the assignment and is deemed to be granted by the assignor. In consequence, the assignee is taxable not only upon any consideration that he pays to the assignor as purchase price but also upon the future rent notwithstanding the general relieving provisions for covenants by assignees to pay the future rent.[1123] Where the rent is variable the normal rules for adjustments during the first 5 years apply. Where the assignee pays a consideration to the assignor this is taxed as a premium for the deemed new lease. As the assignee is, contrary to the provisions of the FA 2003, Sch 17A, para 17, made liable for tax on the future rent, assignees may think it prudent to investigate the stamp duty land tax history and whether there was a relevant exemption. This does not apply if the exemption in the above list has been clawed back pursuant to the 3-year provisions. This occurs where the initial grant of the lease was exempt from stamp duty land tax because it was:

- part of a sale or lease and leaseback arrangement;[1124]

- acquired in connection with an intra-group transaction, or company reconstruction or reorganisation relief;[1125]

- granted to a public body falling within the prescribed list;[1126]

- granted initially to a charity;[1127] or

- pursuant to regulations issued by the Treasury.[1128]

[1122] But this may not be an assignment exposing the assignee to the obligations for subsequent transactions pursuant to FA 2003, s 81A and Sch 17A, para 12.
[1123] FA 2003, Sch 17A, para 11.
[1124] Ibid, s 57A (as much amended).
[1125] Ibid, Sch 7, Parts 1 and 2.
[1126] Ibid, s 66; see **10.65**.
[1127] Ibid, Sch 8.
[1128] Ibid, Sch 17A, para 11(3)(e); pursuant to FA 2003, s 123(3) designed to deal with unusual historic exemptions from stamp duty; see **11.51**.

Title issues – due diligence

7.242 The above two situations mean that assignees have to investigate the assignor's tax position in considerable depth and there are other areas where they require detailed information because, although they do not as such have to assume liability for the assignor's tax, their tax position can be dependent upon the assignor's tax position. This has changed the whole concept of contract terms and completion arrangements since it may be necessary for a purchaser or assignee of a lease to seek additional information and comfort in the form of warranties, indemnities for additional tax charges and undertakings.[1129]

Open tax liability

7.243 In certain situations, such as where the first rent review has not been carried out or a potential later linked transaction or an open overage or clawback consideration incorporated in the premium where there is a direct obligation[1130] upon the assignee to deal with the situation so that he will require an undertaking to disclose all information relating to such potential future events, and will require a detailed history for actual events. In other situations the tax computation by the assignee of the lease will possibly be retrospective to the original tax return of the assignor such as in holding over pursuant to the Landlord and Tenant Act 1954.[1131]

Tax computation issues

7.244 Also the third party's taxation liability may be dependent upon the taxation history of the lease prior to his acquisition. For example, a tenant may not be able to deal with the question whether there has been an abnormal increase in the rent after the expiration of the fifth year of the term[1132] without details of the assumed rent taken into account by the original tenant in making his computation where the lease was for a term exceeding 5 years.[1133] In situations where the original lease was for less than 5 years so that there was no need for the original tenant to take into account the assumed rent for all years after the expiration of the fifth year of the term[1134] it will be necessary for the assignee who is holding over pursuant to the Landlord and Tenant Act 1954,[1135] or who has negotiated a new lease[1136] to have complete details of the assignor's calculations including any turnover or other relevant data and rent credits that the assignor would have required had his lease been for a term exceeding 5 years so that he can project what would have been the rent taken into account for all years of the term or deemed term after the expiration of the fifth year of the term had this been necessary for the original tenant. In these circumstances, delivery of a completed land transaction return (SDLT 1 to SDLT 4) will be virtually useless because these deal in global figures and not in terms of the detailed figures for each year's rent.[1137] Without the relevant information such as the figure included for assumed rent after the expiration of the fifth year of the term the assignee will not be in a position to determine whether there is a liability nor to compute

---

[1129] See also **2.13**.
[1130] FA 2003, s 81A; Sch 17A, para 12.
[1131] Ibid, Sch 17A, paras 3, 4, 9 and 9A.
[1132] Ibid, Sch 17A, paras 14 and 15.
[1133] Ibid, Sch 17A, paras 13, 14 and 15.
[1134] Ibid, Sch 17A, para 7(3).
[1135] Ibid, Sch 17A, para 3.
[1136] Ibid, Sch 17A, paras 9 and 9A.
[1137] A print of the on-line calculator calculation of the net present value of the rent could be a key document of title in this context.

the amount of tax payable. Since an abnormal increase in the rent leads to the deemed grant of a new lease for the balance of the term at the 'excess rent' ie the difference between the previously taxed rent and the new rent. Where the rent is subject to VAT it may be necessary to investigate whether the rent was subject to VAT *ab initio* or as a consequence of the subsequent exercise of the option to tax since this may, *inter alia*, affect the treatment of rent reviews pursuant to FA 2003, Sch 17A, paras 7, 8, 14 and 15.[1138]

Lease granted to third parties

7.245 Assignees of agreements for lease or purchasers from a developer who is able either to take the grant of the lease or to procure the grant of the lease to a third party[1139] need to investigate whether the original agreement has been substantially performed prior to the 'assignment' since this fundamentally affects his liability[1140] such as a liability for the future rent, any premium paid by the initial tenant[1141] and the loss of a nil rate for any consideration below the nil rate threshold where the premises are non-residential and the rent exceeds the £1000 threshold.[1142]

Loans and deposits

7.246 Where in connection with the assignment of a lease the assignee or a person connected with him provides a deposit[1143] or makes a loan the repayment of which, whether in whole or in part, is contingent upon anything done or to be done by the assignee or on the death of the assignee the deposit or loan is treated as chargeable consideration for the assignment.[1144] However, this charge does not arise if the amount of the loan or deposit does not exceed twice the highest rent payable during the first 5 years of the term of the lease.[1145]

EXEMPTIONS FOR LEASES

7.247 As the legislation is drafted upon the basis that conveyances and leases are the same, ie are 'acquisitions' the full range of basic exemptions will apply to both[1146] although there may have to be some distortion in the construction of the legislation since this is drafted upon the basis of sale. Unlike stamp duty, where there were separate exemptions for conveyances and leases, the structure of the legislation is that the exemptions for conveyances have been inadvertently extended to leases. In consequence, the following reliefs are available:

[1138] See **7.147**.
[1139] Note the analysis of such arrangements in *Attorney General v Brown* (1849) 3 Exch 662; see **6.57**.
[1140] FA 2003, Sch 17, para 12B; see **Chapter 6**.
[1141] Because he becomes the party to the agreement for lease; see **6.61**.
[1142] FA 2003, Sch 5, paras 9 and 9A.
[1143] But note the limits upon what is a 'deposit'; see *Workers Trust and Merchant Bank Ltd v Dojap Investments* [1993] 2 All ER 370; on loans and prepayments see *Faith Construction v Customs and Excise* [1989] 2 All ER 938 on loan or debt see *Coren v Keighley* 48 TC 370, and **7.96**.
[1144] FA 2003, Sch 17A, para 18A.
[1145] See further **7.95**.
[1146] See **Chapter 11**.

General reliefs[1147]

Gifts[1148]

7.248 A grant of a lease for no chargeable consideration ie for no premium and a peppercorn rent[1149] is exempt unless made to a connected company[1150] or to a partnership.[1151] However, the exemptions from that charge in FA 2003, s 54, apply to leases[1152] and the market value and other charges for partnerships may be reduced to nil by the availability of a 100 per cent deduction for the sum of the lower proportion. This may mean that the lease may not be notifiable.[1153] It is, however, important to note that a peppercorn is not regarded as chargeable consideration but a token rent of £1 is a chargeable rent. There are, therefore, important compliance issues between such rents where no premiums are involved.

Matrimonial breakdown[1154] *and civil partnership breakdown*[1155]

7.249 A lease granted in relation to a divorce or judicial separation may be exempt. This has been extended to transactions in connection with the breakdown of civil partnerships. It should be noted that in these cases there needs to be an order of the Court pursuant to which the property settlement is dealt with. Relief is available if the chargeable transaction is pursuant to:

–   an order of the Court made in respect of the parties granting a decree of divorce, nullity of marriage or judicial separation or for the dissolution or annulment of a civil partnership or judicial separation of civil partners;

–   an order of the Court made in connection with the dissolution or annulment of a marriage or the parties judicial separation or the dissolution or annulment of a civil partnership or their judicial separation at any time after the granting of an order for dissolution, annulment or judicial separation;

–   a Court order made pursuant to Matrimonial Causes Act 1973, ss 22A, 23A or 24A or the Family Law (Scotland) Act 1985, s 8(2) or their equivalent provisions pursuant to the Civil Partnership Act namely Sch 5 or the Family Law (Scotland) Act 1985, s 14; or

–   at any time in pursuance of an agreement of the parties made in contemplation or otherwise in connection with the dissolution or annulment of the marriage, judicial separation or the making of a separation order or the dissolution or annulment of a civil partnership or judicial separation or making of a separation order in respect of the parties. It should be noted that this provision[1156] although expressed to be pursuant to an agreement must be made in contemplation of or in

---

[1147]   See further **Chapter 11**.

[1148]   FA 2003, Sch 3, para 1.

[1149]   A lease reserving a rent of £1 is not for no chargeable consideration (it seems that a rent of 99p or less is not chargeable consideration.

[1150]   FA 2003, s 53.

[1151]   Ibid, Sch 15, Part 3.

[1152]   Ibid, s 53.

[1153]   Ibid, s 77 and 77A but note FA 2003, s 53(4); Sch 15, para 25(1).

[1154]   Ibid, Sch 3, para 3; see **Chapter 11**.

[1155]   Ibid, Sch 3, para 3A.

[1156]   Ibid, Sch 3, para 3(d) and 3A(d).

connection with some Court decision. It seems that an agreement by the parties to separate and to deal with their property for their voluntary separation would not be eligible for relief.

Variations of estates of deceased persons[1157]

7.250 There would seem to be no reason why the 'exemption' for certain variations of the estates of deceased persons should not extend to a lease granted as part of those arrangements provided that the other conditions are satisfied.

Corporate reorganisations[1158]

Intra-group transactions[1159]

7.251 The relief for intra-group transactions applies to leases since it relieves the 'acquisition' (eg creation) of a chargeable interest (eg a lease); but with a clawback of the relief in the form of a special charge upon any subsequent assignment of the lease.[1160]

Reconstructions and reorganisations of companies[1161]

7.252 The relief for reconstruction and reorganisation of companies[1162] may have been inadvertently enlarged to exempt leases as land transactions entered into for the purposes of or in connection with[1163] the transfer of the undertaking.[1164] Subject to whether there is an 'undertaking' acquired where a lease is granted, it may no longer be necessary to transfer the entire land interests of the company whose business is being transferred in order to qualify for the relief. Granting a lease of the premises utilised or occupied for the purpose of carrying on the activities may now be eligible for relief. This may be helpful where the purpose of the reorganisation is to separate the trading activities of the company from its land such as where a company owns the land upon which it carries on business and it is decided for commercial reasons that it is appropriate to separate the ownership of the land from the business activities so that the freehold interest will be transferred to one new company and the businesses, goodwill and their assets and liabilities will be transferred to another company. As part of the arrangements (ie arguably in connection with) the company receiving the freehold interest is to grant a lease to the new trading vehicle. Since there is an overall plan it is considered that the granting of the leases are potentially eligible for the exemption. However, there is likely to be considerable debate with HMRC Stamp Taxes as to whether the transfer of the freeholds to the new property holding vehicle involves the transfer of an 'undertaking' for the purposes of the relief[1165] or the transfer is in connection with the transfer of the undertaking to the other vehicle company within the terms of the relief.

[1157] Ibid, Sch 3, paras 4 and 3A; see **Chapters 10** and **11**.
[1158] See further **Chapter 12**.
[1159] FA 2003, Sch 7, Part 1; see **Chapter 12**.
[1160] Ibid, Sch 17A, para 11.
[1161] Ibid, Sch 7, Part 2.
[1162] See **12.15**.
[1163] See *Clarke Chapman – John Thompson v IRC* [1975] 3 All ER 701 and **12.17**.
[1164] The general anti-avoidance provisions are also relaxed to some extent in this context; FA 2003, ss 75A–75C, especially 75C(3).
[1165] See *E Gomme v IRC* [1964] 3 All ER 497.

Specific reliefs for leases

7.253 There are certain reliefs that are available only for transactions involving leases. Although not necessarily expressed as some form of relief for leases the terms of the relief is such that they are not generally available and would not be available to conveyances or other forms of chargeable transaction. These include:

Rent credits

7.254 In some situations a lease may be granted that overlaps with a period of another lease which has already borne stamp duty land tax. In these situations such as surrenders and regrants and grants of new leases pursuant to holding over similar arrangements.[1166] In these situations there is a rent credit which, broadly, takes the effect of a reduction in the chargeable amount of rent for the new lease which is usually calculated by reference to the rent that was brought into charge to tax for the overlapped lease.[1167]

Land exchanges

7.255 There is an exemption from the land exchange rules[1168] where there is the surrender of a lease in consideration of the grant of a new lease between the same parties.[1169] It should be noted that this relief is limited to surrenders and regrants; it will not apply to a situation where there is a transfer of a freehold and the grant of a lease back or the transfer of an existing lease with the grant of an underlease back. These will be eligible for relief only if they fall within the alternative finance arrangements[1170] or partial relief pursuant to the sale and lease back provisions.[1171]

In addition to avoid the exchange charging provisions the lease must be between the same parties as the original lease although it need not relate to the same or substantially the same premises.[1172]

Subsales and assignments[1173]

7.256 It seems, as described elsewhere,[1174] that where a lease is granted to a third party the original party to the agreement for lease may be exempt from stamp duty land tax. Two areas of possible relief are available:

–   where the original party assigns his right as lessee pursuant to the agreement before he has substantially performed the contract, the agreement for lease is deemed to be between the lessor and the assignee.[1175] This is not always beneficial for the taxpayer so that it may be better to avoid this relief by subtle planning; and

---

[1166] FA 2003, Sch 17A, paras 9 and 9A.
[1167] See **7.198**.
[1168] FA 2003, s 47; Sch 4, para 5; see **5.150**.
[1169] Ibid, Sch 17A, para 16; see **7.79**.
[1170] Ibid, ss 71A–73C.
[1171] Ibid, s 57A.
[1172] Ibid, Sch 17A, para 16.
[1173] Ibid, s 45.
[1174] See **Chapter 6**.
[1175] FA 2003, Sch 17A, para 12B; see **Chapter 6**.

– in situations where the preceding relief does not apply the original party may be entitled to 'subsale relief'.[1176] This latter relief appears to be more generous than the former in many cases and is not subject to such stringent conditions.

Alternative finance

7.257 There is an expanding area of relief aimed primarily, but not exclusively, at benefitting persons, who are, by reasons of their religion or otherwise, restricted in relation to the funding of the transaction by the principles of usury prohibiting the lending or borrowing of money and the payment of interest or the receipt of interest. In order to enable such persons to 'borrow' money on terms equivalent to a person who is entitled to borrow and mortgage the property and pay interest, reliefs are available[1177] for such transactions. The relief is necessary because in order to evade the restrictions upon interest it is necessary for the provider of funds to acquire an interest in the property. There would, therefore, be a risk of some form of land exchange or a charge upon what is essentially a mortgage by reference to the value of the interest being acquired. One variation of the relief[1178] applies where there is a sale to a financial institution and a leaseback. This relief has been extended from 'individuals' to 'persons' and includes both residential and non-residential property. Where the conditions are satisfied[1179] the leaseback is exempt from tax. To a limited extent this residual relief may be more favourable, where the conditions as to financial institution etc can be satisfied, than traditional sale and leaseback arrangements[1180] or even in equity release schemes. This arises because where there is this type of fundraising exercise both the sale and the leaseback are exempt. There are alternative reliefs involving a sale and saleback but there are significant restrictions upon subsale relief such as where the person raising the funds is acquiring the property and is selling and leasing back or selling and buying back instead of mortgaging the property.[1181] It seems that the relief may be available where there is a lease and underlease back in which case both lease and underlease will be exempt.[1182]

PFI and similar projects[1183]

7.258 Certain PFI projects involving public or educational bodies that involve the grant or assignment of a lease by a qualifying body to a non-qualifying body is exempt where the consideration or part of the consideration for the transfer of the interest or grant of the interest is a grant by the non-qualifying body to the qualifying body of a lease or underlease of the whole or substantially the whole of the land in question and B undertakes to carry out works or to provide services to the qualifying body. It is also required that some or all of the consideration given by the qualifying body to the non-qualifying body for the carrying out of those works or the provision of the services

---

[1176] Ibid, s 45 (as amended); see **Chapter 6**.
[1177] Ibid, ss 71A and 73B.
[1178] Ibid, s 71A.
[1179] See further **10.57**.
[1180] Ibid, s 57A (as much amended).
[1181] FA 2003, s 45(3) (as amended).
[1182] Ibid, s 71(1)(a) referring to the 'purchase of a major interest'. Major interest includes both freeholds and leaseholds and includes the creation of new interests such as the grant of a lease.
[1183] Ibid, Sch 4, para 17; such arrangements may be notifiable notwithstanding that there is no or little chargeable consideration; FA 2003, Sch 4, para 17(4A).

is consideration in money.[1184] It is irrelevant whether or not there is also a transfer or grant or assignment of a lease of any other land by the qualifying to the non-qualifying body. Qualifying bodies include:

-       public bodies;[1185]

-       educational institutions within the Further and Higher Education Act 1992, ss 17, 90, 91 and 482; or

-       their Scottish equivalent funded by the Scottish Further Education Funding Council or the Scottish Higher Education Funding Council.[1186]

The consideration for the transfer, grant or assignment of a lease by the qualifying body in this context is not for a chargeable consideration where this includes, or to the extent that this includes, the leaseback, the carrying out of building works[1187] or the provision of services.[1188] The leaseback is also eligible for relief since the chargeable consideration for the leaseback does not include the main transfer, the transfer of any surplus land or any consideration in money paid by the qualifying body for the building works or other services.[1189] However, the treatment of the various leases back or payments as non-chargeable consideration is to be disregarded for the purpose of determining whether the transaction in question is notifiable,[1190] the notification obligation relates to the actual consideration and this may not be the same as the consideration that would have been the chargeable consideration but for the relief. For example, as there will be land exchanges the chargeable consideration will be the value of the chargeable interest received whereas the actual consideration with the interest disposed of. It may, however, be that HMRC Stamp Taxes regard para 17(4A) as merely reinstating the chargeable consideration for the purposes of notification. It seems that the effect of this provision is that where these are the only consideration, the transaction will not be for a non-chargeable consideration and so exempt pursuant to FA 2003, Sch 3, para 1 and that these amounts of consideration have to be taken into account in determining whether the relevant threshold of £40,000 or the nil rate threshold pursuant to FA 2003, s 77A is exceeded.

Sale and leaseback arrangements[1191]

7.259   Sale and leaseback relief pursuant to FA 2003, s 57A, has been enlarged to apply on a wider basis so as to include residential property. A lease granted as part of a sale and leaseback arrangement is exempt when granted, but the first assignment of such a lease is taxed as on the grant of a new lease.[1192] It is frequently overlooked that a sale and leaseback is a land exchange pursuant FA 2003, s 47.[1193] The 'sale' is, therefore, strictly taxable upon the market value of that interest rather than the cash being provided. HMRC Stamp Taxes are currently beginning to accept the argument that the market value has to be determined taking into account the obligation to grant the lease

---

[1184]   Ibid, Sch 4, para 17(1)(d).
[1185]   Listed in FA 2003, s 66.
[1186]   FA 2003, Sch 4, para 17(2).
[1187]   Ibid, Sch 4, para 10.
[1188]   Ibid, Sch 4, para 11.
[1189]   Ibid, Sch 4, para 17(4).
[1190]   Ibid, Sch 4, para 17(4A).
[1191]   Ibid, s 57A.
[1192]   Ibid, Sch 17A, para 11; see **7.143**.
[1193]   See **Chapter 5**.

back and as part of this process appear to accept that where the parties are acting at arm's length and possibly with the benefit of independent professional advice the actual cash consideration specified in the documentation will, prima facie, be regarded as the market value of the property in the particular circumstances of the case. The relief is no longer restricted to non-residential property; it will be available for equity release schemes for homeowners and similar arrangements, but many of the arrangements eligible for this relief will not qualify for the favourable inheritance tax arrangements and vice versa.

The relief is available in respect of the leaseback, but not in respect of the sale element,[1194] where:

-   A transfers to B a major interest in the land. The new relief is, in consequence, available for lease and leaseback transactions where the parties wish to retain the capital allowances;

-   out of that interest B grants a lease or underlease back to A. Presumably 'grant'[1195] includes 'deemed grant' pursuant to FA 2003, Sch 17A, para 12A; but whether the actual lease would be exempt if granted to B but not if granted to some third party at the direction of B;[1196]

-   the lease must be of the same or possible part of the same premises as those that were the subject-matter of the sale. The reference to 'same premises' does not have any qualifying adjective such as 'substantial' so the leaseback must be of identical premises;

-   the leaseback is granted only to A (since there is no reference to a person connected with A);

-   the consideration for the sale and presumably the grant of the head lease does not consist of or include anything other than the payment of money, whether in sterling or other currency, or the assumption, satisfaction or release of a debt, which means an obligation, whether certain or contingent, to pay a sum of money either immediately or at a future date;

-   the sale (or new lease) must be entered into wholly or partly in consideration of the leaseback;

-   the only consideration for the sale other than the leaseback is the payment of money or the assumption, satisfaction or release of a debt; and

-   the sale transaction is not a subsale or other transfer of rights within FA 2003, s 45 or s 45A[1197] the parties to the transaction must not be members of the same stamp

---

[1194] Special arrangements are made for certain sale and leaseback arrangements in relation to residential property: FA 2003, s 72.

[1195] *City and Permanent Building Society v Miller* [1952] 2 All ER 621.

[1196] Because of the two effective dates principle; see **7.25**.

[1197] There is no reference to FA 2003, Sch 17A, para 12B but this would mean that the lease would be granted to the wrong person.

duty land tax group within Sch 7, Part 1.[1198] Group relief would normally be available, but the conditions for this relief differ and it is subject to possible clawback.

Collective enfranchisement

7.260 A special rate applies where tenants combine to enfranchise their interests. This is linked to the average price.[1199]

Reliefs not available for leases

7.261 Certain reliefs are not available for leases, namely:

• lease of the existing house in a part-exchange of new houses;[1200]

• lease of the employee's existing house in relation to relocation relief;[1201]

• certain exemptions involving compulsory purchase,[1202] reorganisations of public bodies[1203] and parliamentary constituencies[1204] appear to require outright transfers so that the grant of a lease would seem to be an unlikely event and may not be exempt. The exemption for land transactions in compliance with planning obligations may include the grant of leases.

[1198] See **12.60**.
[1199] FA 2003, s 74 (as amended).
[1200] Ibid, Sch 6A, paras 1 and 2; see **Chapters 10** and **11**.
[1201] Ibid, Sch 6A, paras 3 and 4; see **Chapters 10** and **11**.
[1202] Ibid, s 66.
[1203] Ibid, s 67.
[1204] Ibid, s 61.

Chapter 8

BUILDING AGREEMENTS

INTRODUCTION

8.1   There has been a considerable extension from the former charge to stamp duty where there are single or related separate agreements relating to the sale or lease or other disposal and acquisition of chargeable interests[1] in land and contracts relating to building and other works connected with the land transaction which are now taxable even where these are to be carried out by the purchaser or tenant at his own expense. The charge to tax has been extended in a major fashion and the early indications on practice are that HMRC Stamp Taxes intend to exploit the new charging provisions to their maximum potential no matter how poor the quality of their argument[2]; but it is thought that HMRC Stamp Taxes may not seek to apply the new anti-avoidance provisions[3] in order to combine separate land and building contracts into a single contract for the sale or lease of the completed building.

Stamp duty land tax involves building and other works in many ways, namely:

- the situation where a landowner enters into an agreement to sell or lease land to a person and at the same time the parties enter into a contract for the construction of a building upon that land or to perform certain fitting out. The construction is to be carried out by the landowner or a company connected with him but at the cost of the tenant. The issue is whether the chargeable consideration includes the cost of the building work.[4] HMRC Stamp Taxes have officially accepted that in this situation nothing has changed from the former stamp duty position;[5]

- the situation of a person acquiring land where, as part of the arrangement, he is to carry out works ie the building for other works, which can include fitting out, whether upon that land, land owned by the vendor or lessor or some third party's land.[6] Here the scope of the tax has been significantly enlarged[7] and can apply to the costs of the purchaser or tenant in carrying out the building works. Relief is available for works to be carried out on the land to be acquired but it should be

---

[1]   But the relief mentioned below is limited to acquisitions of major interests.

[2]   This aggressive attitude by HMRC Stamp Taxes has been carried over into an attempt to frustrate the reliefs available to local authorities and registered social landlords such as FA 2003, ss 60 and 61 and the restrictions upon the reliefs for charities and registered social landlords who are not being publicly funded where their activities involve joint arrangements involving commercial developers contained in FA 2003, Sch 8 (see **11.41**) notwithstanding that their approach will increase the cost of important social and affordable housing because of the cascade effect of stamp taxes.

[3]   FA 2003, s 73A.

[4]   Ibid, Sch 4, para 10, *Eastham v Leigh, London and Provincial Properties Limited* [1971] 2 All ER 887.

[5]   IR Statement, April 2004; see **8.8**.

[6]   On the question of what may be consideration see *Eastham v Leigh, London and Provincial Properties Limited* [1971] 2 All ER 887.

[7]   FA 2003, Sch 4, para 10 subject to the relief for reverse payments which might include contributions by the landlord towards building, repairs or fitting out costs; FA 2003, Sch 17A, para 18.

noted that there is also an exclusion from chargeable consideration for a covenant by a tenant to 'repair' the premises.[8] Since this would appear to apply to a tenant agreeing to 'put into repair' this may provide some form of relief or benefit where the main exclusion for building upon the land to be acquired is not available and the current approach of HMRC Stamp Taxes is to seek to restrict wherever possible the relief for works to be carried out on the land to be acquired.[9] There are likely to be considerable arguments in Enquiries as to the effect in general law as to whether such arrangements constitute consideration. The question of the 'costs' as chargeable consideration[10] and, in particular, whether the actions of the taxpayer have been sufficient to produce a situation where the open market costs of the fitting out etc are exempt from tax because his actions constitute substantial performance;

- in some situations, in order to maximise the possible benefit for building upon the land to be acquired after the effective date,[11] parties may enter into an arrangement under which the whole interest of the landowner is transferred to the developer for a consideration that includes the developer agreeing to provide one of the houses or one of the flats for the vendor either free of charge or upon reasonable terms. This, being an exchange of major interests, may give rise to two potential areas of stamp duty land tax:

  - the arrangement for the transfer of the newly constructed house or grant of the lease of a new flat constitutes a land exchange[12] so that the developer has to pay stamp duty land tax upon the market value of the land being acquired;[13]

  - the transfer of the new house or grant of the lease of a new flat is not a gift since it is in consideration of the agreement by the vendor to transfer the land upon which the development is to be carried out. This is a chargeable transaction in its own right and is a land exchange taxable upon the value of the property received. This would seem to be the open market value of the new house or flat which, broadly, could probably be taken as being the asking price at which the properties were being offered to the public.

- the provision of services is now made chargeable consideration.[14] This imposes a charge to tax where a chargeable interest is acquired in return for services with the tax being computed upon the cost of the services in the open market (which raises difficult issues of whether cost includes VAT and how far the true nature of the transaction has to be taken into account for a hypothetical fiscal valuation).[15] This would include situations where a person agrees to market the properties in return

---

[8]   Ibid, Sch 17A, para 10(1).
[9]   Ibid, Sch 4, para 10(2).
[10] Ibid, Sch 4, para 10(3)(b).
[11] Ibid, Sch 4, para 10(2); but note the problems of Sch 8, paras 2(1) and 3(2)(b) for charities wishing to embark on joint developments.
[12] Ibid, s 47.
[13] Ibid, Sch 4, para 5; but in this situation, subject to any cash adjustments between the parties, the land may have a significant reduced market value because the benefit of the arrangements may take time and the value of land yet to be developed, whether with merely hope value or the benefit of existing planning permission, will be significantly below the price which the land might be expected to realise on a sale when the development is completed.
[14] FA 2003, Sch 4, para 11; see also s 44A.
[15] See **Chapter 27**.

for the acquisition of one of the properties or, as in *Yaxley v Gotts*[16] a person agrees to carry out works in connection with the development of the property in return for an interest in the property.

In these circumstances, there are references to 'costs' and it is provided that where the costs are 'uncertain'[17] the taxpayer may defer the payment of any tax arising in respect of such costs until they are ascertained. This requires the taxpayer to declare the estimated amount of the costs upfront and to provide a timetable for anticipated payments.[18]

8.2 As part of the arrangements it may be that the vendor or lessor of the land will grant certain rights to the developer to construct infrastructure works over land retained by the vendor or will grant to the vendor easements or similar rights by way of access to any services either on the land owned by the vendor or lessor or owned by a third party but access to these is only over or under the land retained by the vendor or lessor. This will involve the acquisition of rights by the developer over the land of the vendor or lessor but, *prima facie*, stamp duty land tax will be by reference to the consideration being provided for the land acquisition as a whole.

- the stamp duty land tax is charged on the basis of 'open market cost'[19] but with power for the taxpayer to apply to defer payment of the tax where the open market cost is uncertain;[20] and

- the extent and nature of the consideration is significantly changed. It now includes 'works' and 'services'. An agreement to transfer land to a person in return for services including construction services is now taxable.[21]

There is a charge to stamp duty land tax where there is an acquisition of a chargeable interest where the consideration provided by the taxpayer consists of 'works'[22] and/or 'services'.[23] The tax is charged upon the 'open market cost' of such works[24] or services but with power to apply to defer the payment of tax where the costs are uncertain.[25] The application must be accompanied by detailed information such as a timetable indicating when HMRC Stamp Taxes can expect payment. This application must be made within 30 days following the effective date.[26] It is, however, available only for larger projects because the postponement applies only where the final costs will be known more than 6 months after the effective date.

---

16   [1999] 2 WLR 1217.
17   But not 'unascertained'; FA 2003, s 51; see **5.189**.
18   FA 2003, ss 80 and 90; Stamp Duty Land Tax (Administration) Regulations 2003, SI 2003/2837, Part 4, especially regs 13 and 14.
19   Ibid, Sch 4, paras 10 and 11.
20   Ibid, s 80; Stamp Duty Land Tax (Administration) Regulations 2003, SI 2003/2837, Part 4.
21   *Yaxley v Gotts* [1999] 2 WLR 1217 would now be a transaction subject to stamp duty land tax. There are also problems about whether the provision of a guarantee by an associated company is part of the chargeable consideration and, if so, the chargeable amount in respect thereof. This is, of course, a very different problem from those arising in connection with the sale of land interests together with the benefit of related contractual arrangements such as guarantees. In the latter case the issue is whether the contractual rights are chargeable interests; in the former case the issue is whether the rights are the creation of chargeable interests for a consideration.
22   FA 2003, Sch 4, para 10 (as amended).
23   Ibid, Sch 4, para 11.
24   Ibid, Sch 4, para 11(1).
25   Ibid, s 80; Stamp Duty Land Tax (Administration) Regulations 2003, SI 2003/2837, regs 13 and 14.
26   HMRC Stamp Taxes claim that they have no power to extend this time limit; but see FA 2003, s 97.

8.3   It is provided[27] that where the whole or part of the consideration[28] for a land transaction consists of the carrying out of works of construction, improvement or repair[29] of a building or other works to enhance the value of land then the value of the works is taken into account or included as the whole or part of the chargeable consideration in the computation.[30] Various points require to be noted in this charging provision.

8.4   It is fundamental to this charging provision that the works in question may be carried out not only on land being acquired but also other land apparently whether owned by the vendor/lessor or a third party. This is not restricted to land being acquired under the transaction since it applies to other land owned by the vendor or landlord. For example, where a purchaser already owns land acquired from a third party and it is part of the arrangement that the purchaser will construct works, *inter alia*, upon the land already owned which will be sold or leased to the vendor, the works are likely to form part of the chargeable consideration for the acquisition of the land but, because they are works to be carried out on land already owned, they should fall within the exemption. Obviously the question of whether the works are part of the consideration for the chargeable interest being acquired is likely to prove a difficult one where third parties are involved. This may be an acute issue in relation to 'section 106' and similar planning agreements with a local authority.[31] Where the local authority is not contributing any land to the arrangements, any conditions or undertakings upon the developer will not be consideration for the acquisition of the chargeable interest in the land but part of the arrangements for the obtaining of the planning consent.[32] The charge to stamp duty land tax would appear not to apply in relation to the works involved because there is no chargeable transaction.[33] However, if the local authority is contributing land to the development such as granting a lease to the developer of all or any part of the land to be developed it may prove more difficult to convince HMRC Stamp Taxes that the arrangements relating to the works are not part of the consideration attributable to the acquisition by the developer of the land interest.

8.5   Traditional stamp duty had many problems in relation to contracts for sale or lease of land and related contracts for carrying out of building works largely because the charge to stamp duty was limited to 'sales' and certain deemed sales and the carrying out of building works was not a type of consideration with the scope of stamp duty as well as the problem for HMRC Stamp Taxes of the promise to build and the land transfer or lease moving in the same direction and so incapable of constituting

---

27   FA 2003, Sch 4, para 10.
28   On the issue of whether the works are consideration see **8.16**.
29   But see the exclusion for leasehold covenant to 'repair' pursuant to FA 2003, Sch 17A, para 10(1).
30   There are, however, fundamental issues of principle in debate with HMRC Stamp Taxes as to whether in such cases the land exchange principles prevail over the charge on the building costs.
31   See further **5.138**.
32   Such stipulations may be important because of the narrow view of the reliefs for land acquired by local authorities in planning matters and are strenuously seeking to restrict the reliefs pursuant to FA 2003, ss 60 and 61. There is also a relief in such contexts for PFI-type projects pursuant to FA 2003, Sch 4, para 17 (as amended). The cascade effect of stamp duty land tax in such cases makes the obtaining of the reliefs essential in order to avoid multiple charges to tax increasing the cost of social housing and social facilities such as new schools.
33   The position may be more complex where the land is being acquired from a third party who may also be a party to the planning agreement. Since it is a requirement of consideration as a matter of contract that it moves from the promisee not necessarily to the promisor an undertaking to carry out works on the land of a third party who is unconnected with the vendor may nevertheless form part of the consideration for the land transfer.

'consideration' for the land. In consequence, the basic issue was[34] whether the price paid for the building works was 'really' the purchase price of the land. The case law and the various statements of practice indicate that HMRC Stamp Taxes were almost entirely[35] unsuccessful in their claims. The new tax has attempted, unsuccessfully, to reverse the stamp duty land tax and, regrettably successfully, to bring into charge a wide range of building contracts. This successful attack takes two forms:

- an agreement to carry out building works is made a chargeable consideration; and

- building or other works carried out by the tenant/purchaser at his own expense are now *prima facie* taxable.

8.6   In certain cases related building contracts could form part of the stampable consideration.[36] This charge is much enlarged by FA 2003, Sch 4, para 10 (as amended) in several ways. In particular it applies to works, not limited to building works, and so will include improvement or repair[37] of a building or works enhancing the value of land which will include works carried out on other land such as infrastructure works which benefit the main development land. More importantly, it applies to works carried out on land other than that involved in the transaction such as where, as part of a larger arrangement, the tenant of land agrees to carry out certain building or infrastructure works on land being retained by the landlord. For example, a local authority may enter into a development agreement with a developer and as part of this the local authority[38] may grant a chargeable interest such as a long lease at a turnover rent. As part of the arrangements,[39] the developer may be required to make payments to the local authority and there will be questions as to whether such cash payments are part of the premium. In addition, the developer may be required to construct new buildings or social housing upon land retained by the local authority. In this situation there will be a land exchange.[40] Similarly, a person may agree to acquire land from a golf club and as part of the arrangement the purchaser is to construct a new clubhouse with access facilities. In this situation the construction of the new clubhouse and related facilities will be part of the consideration and being works or services will be taxable by reference to open market cost.[41]

8.7   This issue of the taxation of the cost of works is clearly a significant issue for arrangements built into planning agreements with local authorities. For example, it may be part of the arrangement for obtaining planning permission for private residential development, possibly including commercial development that the developer agrees to

34   And still is for completion of transactions where the contract was entered into prior to 1 December 2003 subject to the complex and retrospective provisions of FA 2003, Sch 19 (as amended).
35   The apparent single victory in *M'Innes v IRC* [1934] SC 424 is to be noted since shortly thereafter in *Paul v IRC* [1936] SC 443 the judges involved in both cases effectively stated that their earlier decision was unsatisfactory.
36   See, eg, *McInnes v IRC* [1934] SC 424.
37   But note the relief for covenants to 'repair' premises to be leased; FA 2003, Sch 17A, para 10.
38   Possibly having acquired the land with the benefit of stamp duty land tax relief for chargeable interests acquired under threat of compulsory powers pursuant to FA 2003, s 60; see **11.31**.
39   Usually in a 'section 106' planning agreement; see also **5.138**.
40   On the question of whether the arrangements are consideration see *Eastham v Leigh, London and Provincial Properties Limited* [1971] 2 All ER 887; but since it is an integral part of the agreement for lease that the developer 'earns' the right to the lease by constructing the new school it will be difficult to argue that the arrangements are not part of the consideration.
41   See **8.30**; FA 2003, Sch 4, para 11(1); ss 51, 80 and 90; Stamp Duty Land Tax (Administration) Regulations 2003, SI 2003/2837, Part 4, regs 13 and 14.

construct social housing or other facilities for the local authority.[42] There will be a fundamental question in each case of whether the stipulations imposed are simply conditions for implementing the planning permission or are consideration for land acquired from the local authority. If no such land is acquired, the stipulations cannot be consideration for the land acquisition. An indemnity to a seller of land who has entered into such an agreement is not subject to tax.[43] The open market cost of this social housing will *prima facie* form part of the taxable consideration for the acquisition of the other land from the local authority.[44] The same problems will apply where there is a construction of a new bus station or a school or the provision of recreational facilities such as swimming pools and libraries or the relocation of a waste disposal unit.[45] Since the charge applies to 'works' which are more widely defined and not limited to 'building works', this type of exercise will attract a considerable charge to stamp duty land tax. There is an exemption for transfers and leases of land where there are works and services in connection with projects involving certain public bodies and education bodies[46] or the land is acquired in connection with compulsory powers as part of a development[47] or as part of a section 106 agreement.[48]

RELATED LAND AND BUILDING CONTRACTS – VENDOR/LESSOR AS BUILDER[49]

8.8   In certain cases, contracts for the sale or lease of land are combined with other arrangements, such as an agreement by the seller or landlord to construct a building on the land at the cost of the tenant[50] and a question arises whether the consideration for the other arrangements is or is not part of the price of the sale or premium for the lease

---

42   The reliefs for acquisitions by registered social landlords (FA 2003, s 71) or by housing associations and other bodies that are charities (FA 2003, Sch 8) do not apply since they are the recipients of building services and not 'purchasers' acquiring chargeable interests in land.

43   FA 2003, Sch 4, para 16. This covers prior breaches and if well prepared the section 106 agreement will contain provisions whereby a party to the agreement is not to be liable for breaches of the planning obligations during such terms as he is not interested in the land thereby removing the need for indemnities.

44   There are other potentially different but equally technical issues where the planning agreement (section 106 agreement) requires the party obtaining the benefit of the planning permission to make a payment to the local authority as a contribution to other related activities; this could easily be regarded as a cash payment for the acquisition of the land.

45   But note the possible relief for PFI projects pursuant to FA 2003, Sch 4, para 17 (as amended).

46   FA 2003, Sch 4, para 17; see **Chapter 11**.

47   Ibid, s 60.

48   Ibid, s 61.

49   For the new regime where the taxpayer is taxed upon his costs of building upon his own land and other land see **8.15**.

50   Major issues of liability may depend upon whether the building costs are to be paid for by the tenant so as to constitute some form of 'premium' or are reimbursed to the developer as deferred payment in the form of rent. There may also be difficult questions as to where the tenant is paying or a contributing to the costs of fitting out or including certain equipment within the building. There may be questions as to whether such payments are for chattels or are part of the price being paid for the land as a 'completed building'. There is no charge to stamp duty land tax in respect of agreements to acquire chattels, this may be important where HMRC Stamp Taxes seek to apply the general anti-avoidance provisions pursuant to FA 2003, ss 75A–75C because the rules relating to 'incidental transactions' indicate that the segregation of the acquisition of land and related building contracts which, presumably, would also extend to the acquisition of chattels which are attached to the land, are not to be included as part of the scheme transactions and the consideration subject to charge upon the notional transaction. There are also important issues of principle which will frequently operate to the disadvantage of taxpayers where a developer enters into a building lease and funds the building arrangements by a loan from a third party who agrees to take the grant of the lease in full or partial satisfaction of the indebtedness arising from the funding agreement; see FA 2003, s 45 (as amended); Sch 17A, para 12B; *Att-Gen v Brown* (1849) 3 Exch 662; para 18A and **7.14** and **Chapter 6**.

of the land. For instance, if land is purchased and at the same time money is paid to a builder who has built a house on it representing payment for the building of the house, the question arises whether the payment to the builder is part of the chargeable consideration.[51] A partial answer to this question is that it is clearly part of the consideration if the building is complete before there is any contract to buy the land.[52] Conversely if the land is conveyed before the building contract is entered into, the building payment is not part of the chargeable consideration in relation to the land.[53]

8.9   There have been and continue to be major problems with HMRC Stamp Taxes involving where the land contract and building agreement are entered into more or less simultaneously.[54] However, it is clearly established and accepted by HMRC Stamp Taxes, that the mere fact that the two contracts coincide in time does not, of itself, bring the building costs into the charge to tax.[55] The fact that either or both of the parties would not enter into one contract unless all contracts are executed and exchanged at the same time is irrelevant[56] and cannot in general law, of itself, convert two independent contracts into a single contract for the sale or lease of the completed building thereby making the building costs taxable. This is particularly so where the building agreement is expressed to be conditional upon completion of the land contract since the existence of such a condition is a conclusive indication that there are two contracts and not one,[57] or the land may be conveyed before completion of the building.[58] Similarly, the mere fact that the vendor (or lessor) of the land and the builder are one and the same person is not conclusive that there is merely one contract for the acquisition of the land and the completed building,[59] even though commercially the parties would not have signed one agreement unless the other agreement were also signed.

8.10   HMRC Stamp Taxes have upon advice been compelled to accept that the stamp duty position continues to apply to stamp duty land tax; namely[60] that the amount payable for building operations after the date of the contract will be regarded as part of the consideration in respect of which stamp duty was and now stamp duty land tax is payable only if the following two conditions are both satisfied:[61]

---

[51]   In such cases if the site has been purchased before 'works' have commenced the property will under normal circumstances be 'non-residential' with the benefit of the slightly higher nil rate threshold.

[52]   *M'Innes v IRC* [1934] SC 424. Any attempt in such a situation to enter into separate contracts for the land and for the building would be a pretence that there was no building and so be fraud.

[53]   *Kimbers v IRC* [1936] 1 KB 132; *Cory Brothers v IRC* [1965] AC 1082.

[54]   See Press Release SP 8/93, 12 July 1993.

[55]   *The Prudential Assurance Co Ltd v IRC* [1993] 1 WLR 211.

[56]   HMRC Stamp Taxes at one stage suggested that the linked transaction rules would enable them to aggregate the land and the building contracts and treat the building price as part of the land price. However, they now, albeit reluctantly, accept that the linked transaction rules apply only to link land contracts. The rules cannot be applied to aggregate the price being paid for land and the price being paid for non-land assets. HMRC Stamp Taxes cannot aggregate the land price, the building price simply to produce a higher rate of tax for the land transaction. Nor can they seek to apply the linked transaction legislation so as to produce a single contract for the sale or lease of the completed building. The linked transaction rules are concerned simply with the rates applicable to land, they are not some form of basic anti-avoidance provision, provided, of course, that the parties allocate the consideration between the land and the building works upon a just and reasonable basis as required by FA 2003, Sch 4, para 4.

[57]   *Kimbers v IRC* [1936] 1 KB 132.

[58]   *Cory & Son Ltd v IRC* [1965] AC 1088.

[59]   Ibid.

[60]   *Paul v IRC* [1936] SC 443; *Kimbers & Co v IRC* [1936] 1 KB 132; *Prudential Assurance Co Ltd v IRC* [1992] STC 863.

[61]   *Paul v IRC* [1936] SC 443 at 452. This case is confusing to an English reader because the contracts in the case are referred to as 'missives' and the conveyances as 'feu contracts'; but the principles for all jurisdictions are clearly in favour of the taxpayer.

(1)   the superior (ie landowner or the seller) and the building contractor are one and
       the same person, or perhaps[62] one is the agent or nominee of, or is connected with,
       the other; and

(2)   the contracts (for sale and for building) are so interlocked that if default is made
       on either, the other is not enforceable by either side.[63] This usually requires either
       that the contracts are expressed to be interlinked in some way or that the overall
       transaction is to be completed only when the works are finished, for example,
       upon the issue of a certificate of practical completion.

In other words, if the purchaser of the land is entitled to a conveyance upon payment of
the land price regardless of the state of the building works, payments in relation to the
building costs are not part of the land price for the purposes of stamp duty land tax and
the conveyance is subject to tax only upon the land price. There are two separate
contracts: one for the land and one for the construction of the building.[64] This argument
against liability upon the construction works is reinforced where the land transaction is
completed before the building works commence or progress too far.[65]

8.11   The first two of these conditions is not satisfied merely because the
vendor/landowner and the builder are working in collaboration with one another,[66] but
if the landowner has agreed to sell his land to the builder, or his agent or nominee, then
the conveyance direct from landowner to ultimate purchaser is incidentally the
completion of a subsale by the builder[67] (or his agent or nominee) and the first
condition is satisfied.

8.12   Following the taxpayer's comprehensive victory in the *Prudential* case,[68] a revised
Statement of Practice was issued, which was considerably shorter than its two
predecessors and was basically flawed. It states that each case will clearly depend upon
its own 'facts', but the cases referred to in the immediately preceding paragraphs
indicate that the true issue is the construction of the contract or contracts in question –
whether there is a single contract for the sale or lease of the completed building or two
independent contracts for the sale or lease of the land and the construction of a
building, respectively.[69] For these purposes, it seems that it does not, of itself, matter
whether the arrangements are contained in one or two instruments.[70] Nor is it relevant
that as a commercial matter the parties would not have signed one contract unless both

62   Cf *M'Innes v IRC* [1934] SC 424, but comments in both *Paul v IRC* (above) and *Kimbers v IRC* (above) cast
      doubt on the correctness of that decision in its reliance on this factor.
63   This condition is too widely stated by Lord Normand in *Paul v IRC* (above) having regard to the case of
      Kimbers v IRC (above) at 137. This condition may be no more than that the contracts must be so interlocked
      that if the purchaser defaults on the building contract, he cannot enforce the contract for the sale of the
      land: see *Paul v IRC* (above) at 453.
64   *Kimbers v IRC* (above); *Prudential Assurance Co Ltd v IRC* [1993] 1 WLR 211, [1992] STC 863, ChD; *Cory
      Brothers v IRC* [1965] AC 1082.
65   *Cory & Son Ltd v IRC* [1965] AC 1088.
66   *Re Cary-Elwes' Contract* [1906] 2 Ch 143.
67   Cf *Att-Gen v Brown* (1849) 3 Ex 662.
68   [1992] STC 863; although the case could have been avoided by the taxpayer referring in early correspondence
      to specific provisions in the then current Statements of Practice which would have precluded HMRC Stamp
      Taxes from putting forward their arguments.
69   *Kimbers v IRC* [1936] 1 KB 132.
70   But note the comments of Scarman LJ in *Crane Fruehauf v IRC* [1975] STC 51 on whether there is a single
      contract or two separate contracts which cannot be converted into a single contract simply because the
      parties cannot enter into one contract unless both were signed and exchanged.

were signed at the same time.[71] Regrettably HMRC Stamp Taxes did not give any guidance on its view of the factors which point to one or two contracts (other than where one contract is so drafted that it cannot be completed if there is a default on the other, which merely recites earlier judicial statements).

8.13 The cost of the building works is not liable to stamp duty land tax where there are two separate contracts. In this context the words imposing a charge where the use of the vendor/lessor as the builder is a 'condition of the transaction' are to be construed as part of the overall commercial transaction or arrangement. Obviously, cross-considerations such as the building works being conditional upon some aspect of the land transaction or vice versa could bring this condition into operation so that the building costs become subject to stamp duty land tax.

8.14 It seems that where such construction work attracts VAT, stamp duty land tax, if chargeable, will be claimed upon that VAT.[72]

WORKS AS CONSIDERATION – TENANT OR PURCHASER AS BUILDER

8.15 The major question arises where a purchaser or a tenant agrees to carry out building works as part of the arrangements. Such undertakings are likely to form part of the consideration[73] particularly where the works are to be carried out by the purchaser/tenant upon land owned by the vendor or landlord and not included in the sale or lease[74] and are now made taxable as consideration for the acquisition of the chargeable interest.[75] Being consideration for the grant of the lease other than 'rent' the open market costs of the works will be taxable as a premium for any leases involved.[76] These provisions are of considerable importance in practice because 'works' include fitting out by prospective tenants. There are, therefore, major issues for advisers as to whether their drafting has produced a contract or agreement for lease where the fitting out obligations of the tenant are consideration (ie a premium) for the lease ie in a sense the tenant is 'earning'[77] the right to the lease by fitting out or building and if so whether the implementation of these fitting out arrangements can be brought within the exemption for works carried out after the effective date.[78]

Consideration

8.16 There is a preliminary issue as to precisely what is 'consideration' in this area and whether it is 'chargeable' although certain covenants by tenants to 'repair' the premises are not chargeable.[79] Frequently the arrangements may be expressed as being a condition. It must be shown that the building or fitting out works are the consideration or part thereof for the acquisition of the chargeable interest. It might seem odd that

---

71   *Prudential v IRC* [1992] STC 863.
72   See **5.126**.
73   *Eastham v Leigh, London and Provincial Properties Limited* [1971] 2 All ER 887.
74   But note the exemption for leasehold covenants by tenants to 'repair' premises which may include an initial covenant to put the demised premises into a proper state or repair; FA 2003, Sch 17A, para 10(1)(a).
75   Ibid, Sch 4, para 10.
76   See **8.26**.
77   Note the approach for the purposes of VAT in *Ridgeons Bulk v Customs and Excise* [1994] STC 427.
78   FA 2003, Sch 4, para 10(2) (as amended).
79   Ibid, Sch 17A, para 10.

works to be carried out by a tenant at his own expense could be consideration for his acquisition especially where he is employing independent third party contractors. However, what appears to be a condition may be consideration.[80] As regards sales or leases where there is an overage payment the vendor may impose obligations on the purchaser to carry out the works expeditiously to accelerate the payment of the additional consideration. This may make the works part of the consideration. Similarly landlords may make fitting out obligatory so as to ensure that the tenant enters into trading operations quickly so that any extra turnover rent is payable as soon as possible. Obviously there are many variations on this theme and each case is likely to turn upon its own particular circumstances and especially the drafting of the contract. For example, a landowner may agree to grant a lease of premises to a developer that is expressed to be conditional upon the construction of a building by the prospective tenant to an appropriate standard. However, it is important to note that in *Eastham v Leigh, London and Provincial Properties Limited*[81] such an arrangement was held not to be a condition but was part of the consideration for the grant of the lease.[82] Parties must, therefore, not be misled by the terminology of the documentation in future since the building or other operations to be carried out must, under penalty, be included in the computation of the stamp duty land tax.

8.17 There are likely to be some very difficult technical issues around this area such as whether the 'works' are consideration where the facts are not identical with *Eastham v Leigh, London and Provincial Properties Limited*.[83] For example, where a person acquiring land from A agrees with B, an adjoining landowner, to construct works on B's land in consideration of B releasing a restrictive covenant, such an agreement will be consideration for the 'acquisition' of the restrictive covenant but it will *prima facie* not be consideration for the acquisition of the land from A notwithstanding that such agreement is conditional upon B entering into the appropriate arrangements. There will be consideration involving chargeable interests and so a land exchange with two potential charges.[84]

8.18 It will be immediately obvious that there are likely to be problems of considerable complexity where, for example, the acquisition is made in the context of a 'section 106 agreement' where the original grantee of the planning permission requires indemnities should the terms of the planning agreement not be observed. It is now a vitally important issue for negotiation because of the legislation which provides that a section 106 agreement can be made on terms that it is not to be enforceable against persons in respect of breaches during periods when they are not owners of the property. Indemnities for prior breaches are potentially exempt,[85] but undertakings to carry out the terms of the section 106 agreement will cause potential tax charges for the purchaser even where these are not necessary to protect the vendor or there is an earnout or fitting out obligation and the seller/landlord insists upon imposing obligations upon the taxpayer so as to ensure that matters proceed expeditiously and the seller/landlord receives his payment at the earliest possible date. Such arrangements are rarely in the

---

[80]   See, eg, *Eastham v Leigh, London and Provincial Properties Limited* [1971] 2 All ER 887.

[81]   [1971] 2 All ER 887.

[82]   On the other hand, an agreement where the grant of the lease is dependent upon obtaining planning consent will be a conditional contract and the obtaining of the planning consent will not be regarded as part of the chargeable consideration; but where there is an acquisition of land with the benefit of planning permission the undertakings or indemnities required by the vendor from the purchaser or tenant may be chargeable consideration; see **8.18**.

[83]   Above.

[84]   FA 2003, s 47; Sch 4, para 5.

[85]   Ibid, Sch 4, para 16.

best interests of the taxpayer either in relation to the initial transaction or subsequent dealings in the land. Such arrangements raise a wide range of issues. In a sense, it may be said that the benefit of the planning agreement runs with the land but this carries with it the inherent obligations. In general, inherent liabilities are not part of the consideration;[86] however, HMRC Stamp Taxes have, by self-serving legislation,[87] provided a specific exemption for certain types of inherent liability which suggests that they have in mind a bizarre argument that an inherent liability where the transferee has no choice but to accept and be burdened by the liability, is consideration rather than a limitation upon the property that is being acquired. In consequence, there may, therefore, be an issue as to whether the obligations contained in the planning agreement, whether in the form of payments of cash to the local authority or to carrying out building works upon land acquired by the local authority, are automatically part of the consideration even though there is no specific reference to the performance of these obligations in the purchase from the landowner. It may be that the vendor would require some form of indemnity.[88] However, such indemnities will relate to the breach of the obligations and are dependent upon the vendor of the land being held liable to compensate the local authority. In this situation, since these are sums payable in the event of breach, they are, *prima facie*, not consideration.[89] However, the vendor may require a positive commitment from the developer to carry out the works. In this situation there is a grave risk that the negotiating position of the vendor has converted what is merely a 'permission' which can be acted upon albeit at a price into a positive obligation as part of the land transaction. The effect is, *prima facie*, to make all the obligations or conditions in the planning agreement part of the consideration for the transfer of the land. Therefore, although the purchaser may be exempt from stamp duty land tax in respect of the works that he will be carrying out on the land that he is acquiring, he is exposed to the risk that HMRC Stamp Taxes will take the view that because these are positive obligations, they are part of the chargeable consideration and he will be exposed to tax upon any cash payments to be made to the local authority plus any works to be carried out on land other than that being acquired.

8.19   On the other hand, where there is a transfer of land by A to B in consideration, *inter alia*, of the construction by B of a building upon land owned by A there will be a liability upon B to stamp duty land tax upon the open market cost of constructing the building. For example, where A, a golf club, agrees to sell land to B for a cash sum plus an undertaking to build a new clubhouse and access road B will be subject to stamp duty land tax upon both the cash sum and the open market cost of the new clubhouse and access road. This simple situation is, of course, merely an indication of the complex problems of arrangements involving local authorities where the overall arrangements for development with social housing or new schools being required as part of the price for the planning permission.[90] There are many variations on this theme each with its own particular set of tax consequences.[91]

---

86   *Swayne v IRC* [1900] 1 QB 172.
87   FA 2003, Sch 17A, para 17.
88   Ibid, Sch 4, para 16; Sch 17A, para 17.
89   See, for example, *Western United Investment Co v IRC* [1958] 1 All ER 257; *Photo Productions Ltd v Securicor Transport Ltd* [1981] 2 WLR 283.
90   Note the limited reliefs in FA 2003, Sch 4, para 17.
91   These situations differ fundamentally from those where there is to be a transfer or lease of property subject to an obligation to grant a lease or sublease of part of the premises when the construction works are completed. This may be relatively straightforward such as where A transfers a freehold to B for a cash sum and the grant of a lease of one of the flats to be constructed on the land. Other situations are more complex, such as where a charity enters into an arrangement with a developer for the construction of certain commercial premises such as a supermarket on the ground floor with related offices on the first floor and affordable housing in the airspace above the first floor commercial development. There may be major

Practical problem

8.20   This new charge to tax is a major problem for builders of new houses and commercial properties. Hitherto such parties would have been able to control this aspect of their costs by careful use of the stamp duty subsale relief[92] but the new version of subsale relief[93] is so structured that this method of mitigating the tax is not available to most developers, because it is dependent upon the builder or developer not substantially performing the contract and this will almost inevitably occur when he commences building operations since this will usually constitute taking possession. Moreover, attempts to produce an equivalent relief for new dwellings and first time buyers have already been subjected to anti-avoidance provisions.[94] A limited relief is available[95] which if carefully observed may go some way towards replacing the removal of subsale relief,[96] by excluding the charge upon certain aspects of the building works; but not the land price.

8.21   However, there may be an opportunity to mitigate the multiple charges upon the land price where the arrangement involves an agreement for lease where the developer assigns his right to the lease[97] under the terms of the agreement to the third party who enters into a separate building agreement. In this situation the developer may be able to take advantage of the exemption for situations where there are early assignments of agreements for lease before substantial performance occurs.[98] In addition, by assigning the right and entering into a separate building agreement the third party has an argument that he is taxable only upon the price that he pays for the land and any other consideration attributable to his notional agreement pursuant to FA 2003, Sch 17A, para 12B.[99] In this situation, although the third party may be subject to a higher charge to tax in respect of the land price than would have been the case had the developer taken the lease and assigned it, the third party will benefit because the cost to the developer would be reduced by the stamp duty land tax saved and the building works will fall out of charge to tax.[100] Additionally, the third party should be able to claim the benefit of the exemption for works to be carried out on the land since he is incurring the costs of building upon the land that he is to acquire and he will take possession of the demised premises when the builder, as his agent, enters onto the land in order to commence the building works.

---

differences in the stamp duty land tax liability of both parties. (It may be that the charity is exempt in respect of any interests which it acquires as part of the arrangements; but the arrangements themselves may mean that charitable relief is not available for any land acquisitions by the charity or where such relief has been obtained it ceases it ceases to be available because, technically, the land creases to be held for permitted charitable purposes and the relief is clawed back or any assignment of leasehold interests is subject to the special charge on assignments of leases by charities. The scope of the two very different reliefs for charities where development is involved must be properly investigated.) Ideally, and subject to other tax and commercial considerations, the parties should consider whether it is possible to be stamp duty land tax efficient by taking steps to convert the arrangements for the flats or social or affordable housing into obligations to build in the appropriate 'airspace' rather than lease and underlease back. In the former situation that charge is *prima facie* limited to the building works, although this can be a difficult issue because of the additional costs of installing foundations suitable for a tower block rather than a supermarket. A simple grant of a lease plus a sublease back will be a land exchange with charges upon non-charitable land owners.

92   Stamp Act 1891, s 58(4) and (5) (as amended).
93   FA 2003, s 45 (as amended); Sch 17A, para 12B; see **Chapter 6**.
94   Ibid, ss 44A and 45A; see **3.24**.
95   Ibid, Sch 4, para 10(2).
96   See ibid, Sch 17A para 12B and 7.12 and **Chapter 6**.
97   However, the clawback provisions for the exemption for charities need to be noted for joint developments; FA 2003, Sch 8, paras 2 and 3(4).
98   Ibid, Sch 17A, para 12B.
99   See **6.61**.
100 See, for example, *Prudential Assurance Co Ltd v IRC* [1992] STC 863.

8.22 Attempts to mitigate this additional cost of new housing by means of profit sharing or similar arrangements have already been attacked by anti-avoidance legislation.[101] For developers of commercial leasehold property where leases are involved it may by careful structuring and timing of the onward transmission of the property be possible to obtain relief[102] but at the risk of extra stamp taxes for the person to whom the lease is to be granted.[103]

8.23 Such reliefs as are available are dependent upon the effective date. For example, certain building works or fitting out commenced after the effective date are free of tax. Other cases such as subsale relief depend upon events happening before or at the same time as the effective date.[104] Substantial performance is, therefore, a key concept in this context.

8.24 Substantial performance involves taking possession of the whole or substantially the whole of the land involved.[105] This involves two factors 'possession' and 'substantially the whole of the land' for present purposes.[106]

Possession

8.25 It should also be noted that HMRC Stamp Taxes take the view that where there is any licence to enter upon land to carry out building works or fitting out and under the terms of the licence the licensor, ie the freeholder, is permitted to enter upon the land in question in order to ensure that the building works are progressing satisfactorily, this is an indication that the licence confers exclusive possession upon the developer and may amount to some form of tenancy.[107] Although this is merely an indication of tenancy, it is not conclusive but, as the reporting obligations and self-assessment system impose penalties, the point will, nevertheless, need to be thought through.

The charge upon 'works'

The charge upon works by purchaser or tenant

8.26 There is a charge upon works carried out by a purchaser or tenant as part of the consideration subject to a limited relief where the works are to be carried out on the land being acquired.[108] The charge includes:

- *'Works'*
  The charging provision extends beyond building works. It now extends to construction, improvements or repair[109] or other works to enhance the value of the land. It will be interesting to see whether HMRC Stamp Taxes will understand

---

[101]   FA 2003, ss 44A and 45A; see **3.24** and **6.16**.
[102]   Ibid, Sch 17A, para 12B.
[103]   See **6.61**.
[104]   But see **Chapter 14**.
[105]   See further **14.12**.
[106]   Other actions can constitute 'substantial performance'; see **Chapter 14**.
[107]   See the comments in *Street v Mountford* [1985] 1 AC 809 and *Addiscombe Garden Estates Ltd v Crabbe* [1957] 3 All ER 563; but note the decision in *Ogwr v Dykes* [1989] 2 All ER 880 where there is the suggestion that the inclusion of a provision in the agreement that the arrangement is not intended to create the relationship of landlord and tenant may be effective to prevent the creation of a tenancy.
[108]   FA 2003, Sch 4, para 10.
[109]   But note the exemption for, *inter alia*, leasehold covenants by the tenant to 'repair' the deemed premises pursuant to FA 2003, Sch 17A, para 10.

the problem of demolition. Frequently, demolishing buildings upon land does not enhance the value of the land. It may be a step towards the enhancement of its value but since there is no longer a worthwhile income-producing asset on the land its value may have dropped because of the delay and costs in reinstating the land and the building. The provision would also seem to apply to construction of extensions, refurbishment programmes and similar matters.

- *Other works to enhance the value of land*
  The question of enhancing the value of land is important. It would appear that it is not limited to enhancing the value of land owned by the vendor or a lessor or some other third party. It appears to apply to works carried out to enhance the value of the land being acquired, ie the person is paying stamp duty land tax upon the works for which he is paying for his own benefit; but there may be questions as to where the works, either by intention or as an incidental consequence, enhance the value of land. For example, there may be arrangements for the sale of land with the 'reservation' of rights to the vendor to access or otherwise exploit the benefit of works being carried out upon the land being sold by the purchaser.[110] This will raise issues of consideration and whether it is a chargeable cost but within the benefit. However, there may be questions of incidental benefit to the land. It would seem that because the enhancement of the value of land is part of the consideration, then it must be an obligation to carry out the works and the fact that the parties thought it necessary to include an obligation to carry out the works would be an indication that the vendor, at least, thought that these would enhance the value of the land that he is retaining. In addition, although there may be the enhancement of the value of other land, because the works are being carried out on the land being acquired, the exemption would appear to be available.
  Presumably, this issue of enhancing the value of the land is intended to operate on a subjective basis. It would appear, although it is by no means conclusive, that the charge will only apply where it is the intention of the parties that the works carried out are done with a view to enhancing the value of the land.[111] If works are carried out not with a view to enhancing the value of the land but for some other purpose then, arguably, there is no charge to stamp duty land tax simply because the value of land might be increased. For example, the charge applies whether the works are carried out on the land being acquired or other land. In consequence, there would be a charge where a developer who has entered into an agreement for the lease of a particular plot of land which he intends to develop needs to carry out certain works upon land retained by the freeholder by way of infrastructure. The value of such works such as access roads, drains and other facilities may have the effect of enhancing the value of the land held by the landlord but that may not be the intention of the parties. Alternatively there may be a development of commercial premises to be leased to the developer with flats above them which are to be retained by the freeholder. In such cases it is arguable that the infrastructure and foundation works may be more elaborate than those required for the ground floor commercial premises but they are constructed to enable the commercial development to proceed rather than to enhance the landlord's airspace/flats.[112]

---

[110]   There may be questions as to whether the vendor is creating a problem for himself by creating some form of chargeable interest and producing a land exchange; see **5.151**.

[111]   There may be questions of enhancing value where the works are essentially demolition especially where the demolition relates to buildings where the vendor/landlord's land is not included in the transaction.

[112]   Unfortunately in most such situations the terms of the contract will be such that the additional infrastructure costs are made part of the consideration.

It may be a consequence that the land is enhanced in value but the intention of the parties is to carry out works that will enable the development of the land being leased to be carried out. However, as the charging provision is not obviously restricted to the enhancement of the value of the land upon which the works are carried out, the intention that these infrastructure works should assist in the development of other land, the value of which may be 'indirectly' enhanced, would appear sufficient to bring such works into charge if the test is applied on an objective basis; but since this requires the works to be part of the consideration and be to enhance the value of land, this points to a subjective construction of the legislation. Plain English drafting has not helped solve this problem since, as indicated above, the drafting means that the enhancement can be indirect enhancement of the value of the land being acquired and it will always be the intention to improve the value of that land.

- *Infrastructure issues*
  The construction of infrastructure works upon land being retained by the seller in order to link the land being acquired to services or roads would be chargeable consideration because it is being undertaken to enhance the value of the land being acquired. The exemption for works on the person's own land[113] could not apply because that is limited to works on the land owned or to be acquired by the person carrying out the works. In such situations there are also likely to be problems of liability to stamp duty land tax in relation to any easements or other rights granted over the adjoining land upon which the works are carried out as regards rights of way over service or site roads or other access for the long-term utilisation of the works when constructed.

- *Exchange issues*
  Large-scale developments, particularly where local authorities and section 106 agreements are involved, have to be carefully investigated since there will frequently be aspects of the overall transaction which are land exchanges with their own special computational rules.[114] This may involve transfers of land and leases back,[115] or interim arrangements such as the grant of a right of way over land retained by the vendor during the course of the development. Here land interests may be moving in opposite directions where there is an as yet unresolved dispute whether the land exchange rules applying the market value rules to the undeveloped land prevail over the charge upon the purchase price of the land plus, where appropriate, the building costs. Whilst it is considered that the former represents the correct charge to tax and is likely to assist the taxpayer in most cases, HMRC Stamp Taxes appear to incline towards the latter higher tax position, because the purchase price, particularly where it includes an element of overage, is likely to reflect an element in relation to the profit that will arise upon the future disposal of the developed property. In the case of an exchange where the market value is important, whilst there are key issues as to who are the parties to the notional sale[116] the value of the land may be depressed because of the costs of the proposed development and the fact that it may be several years before the

---

[113] FA 2003, Sch 4, para 10(3)(b); see **7.75**.
[114] Ibid, s 47; Sch 4, para 5; see **5.150**.
[115] But note the possible reliefs such as FA 2003, s 57A (as much amended) but since this is intended to apply to fundraising there may be debates with HMRC Stamp Taxes in this type of context because the consideration may not be solely cash or debt (FA 2003, s 57A(3)(b)); Sch 4, para 17 (as amended).
[116] See **Chapter 27**.

existing site is cleared of its current occupants and the buildings demolished[117] and the fact that it will be several years before the project can be realised and the benefits received.

Rights of vendor/lessor

8.27 In some situations the person disposing of the land may require access to the land being sold or to the infrastructure works, such as rights of way or easements. Here the stamp duty land tax may depend upon the structure of the documentation. For example:

- the seller may 'except and reserve' the appropriate rights from the conveyance. In this case, although the rights reserved are likely to be chargeable interests, there should not be any charge to stamp duty land tax since they are 'retained' by the person and are not acquired by 'creation'. Subsequent dealings in such rights will potentially be taxable. However, HMRC Stamp Taxes are currently insisting that 'exception and reservation' can operate only by way of transfer and regrant so that the land exchange principles will be applied to impose two market value charges;[118]

- the seller may transfer the land and the purchaser grants the rights in question back to the vendor. Here there would appear to be an 'acquisition'. This will involve a land exchange because part of the consideration for the transfer of the freehold is the grant of the new rights. The computation of the stamp duty land tax will be by reference to the market value of the various interests since, of the notional two transactions: one is for the acquisition of a major interest;[119] the other is for the acquisition of a non-major interest,[120] ie a major for non-major exchange.[121]

8.28 It is a not unusual arrangement which occurs frequently in joint developments between commercial developers and local authorities[122] or registered social landlords[123] or charities[124] whereby part of the property is to be developed for commercial use and the balance for social or affordable housing (such as a ground floor commercial development with flats above). An obvious structure is for a lease to the developer who grants an underlease to the registered social landlord of the relevant part of the land[125] which may be eligible for exemption.[126] There is a theoretical problem for the developer because two charging provisions apply to his acquisition:

---

[117] In many situations HMRC have argued that the costs of construction are not expenditure on improving the value of land and are therefore not allowable in certain circumstances such as capital gains tax; see Taxation of Chargeable Gains Act 1992, s 38(2).

[118] FA 2003, s 48(1)(b); see **4.39**.

[119] Ibid, Sch 4, para 5(3).

[120] Ibid, Sch 4, para 5(4).

[121] See **5.160**.

[122] FA 2003, ss 60 and 61 and Sch 4, para 17.

[123] Certain of the participants in such arrangements are charitable bodies. However, there have been difficulties with the Government and the basic relief for charities because they are not regarded as acquiring the land solely for charitable purposes; an alternative form of relief has been introduced for charities that may be helpful in particular cases; FA 2003, Sch 8 (as amended); see **11.42**.

[124] But note the problems for charities pursuant to FA 2003, Sch 8, paras 2 and 3(2)(b).

[125] This may also be a key factor in depressing the market value of the main interest because of the obligations to carry out the works in question.

[126] FA 2003, s 71.

- it is an exchange taxable upon market value;[127] or

- it is an acquisition in consideration of building works which is likely to be the costs of the social housing.

It is considered that the former applies and is likely to be applied by HMRC Stamp Taxes, but since it is arguable that because the developer retains a reversionary interest in the land underleased back the works are carried out on the land he is acquiring and retains, the exemption is available as regards the latter charge. Moreover, there may be issues for the registered social landlord or charity involved. In some situations the registered social landlord can acquire land free of stamp duty land tax[128] but in many cases, particularly where it is not being publicly funded, it may have to rely upon the charity exemption. Difficulties arise in relation to the preservation of the charitable exemption where the land is acquired with a view to participating in some form of joint development which is to commence within 3 years of the land.[129]

8.29 An alternative is for the developer to be granted a lease of the commercial property and to agree to construct works on the land retained. Here there is no exchange because only one land transaction occurs. However, whilst the developer is not taxable in respect of the building works on the land to be leased to him, he remains vulnerable to a claim that the works constructed on the land retained by the registered social landlord are taxable consideration for his acquisition, unless the building arrangements are a separate contract and not part of the consideration for the grant of the lease – a possible drafting issue. Moreover, where the building works are not being carried out at something like the open market cost, it will be virtually impossible to persuade HMRC Stamp Taxes and the current judiciary that the arrangements relating to the building works without a full charge was not part of the arrangement for making the other land available to the developer, particularly where the land is transferred to him for a token consideration or is leased without premium (other than possibly the building works) and a peppercorn rent. Indeed, to suggest that transactions at below the market value were not related to the building or other works would, *prima facie*, produce a situation where the charity might be accused of disposing of its land for non-charitable purposes or otherwise than in accordance with the rules for disposal at a property value.[130]

Open market cost

8.30 The chargeable consideration in relation to the works is the amount that would have to be paid on the open market for the carrying out of the work in question.[131] This looking at the cost of the works rather than the value of the benefit[132] raises some novel valuation issues not covered by existing case-law.

8.31 Clearly, since the open market cost of using an independent contractor to carry out the works would include some element of profit, the figure cannot be limited necessarily to the actual cost to the person carrying out the works such as where a

---

[127] This being determined at an early stage in the development may be slight; but the implications of the double charge on leases pursuant to FA 2003, Sch 17A, para 12A need to be considered; see **7.25**.

[128] FA 2003, s 71.

[129] Ibid, Sch 8, para 2; see **11.41**.

[130] See, for some of the problems involving charities and developments, *Re Rosemary Simmons Memorial Housing Association* [1988] 1 WLR 1440; *Marson v Marriage* 54 TC 59.

[131] FA 2003, Sch 4, para 10(3)(b).

[132] Compare Income and Corporation Taxes Act 1988, s 209.

developer with his own workers and equipment is to carry out works on the vendor's land and the actual costs will be further reduced since he will have the necessary men and equipment on or near the site. Insofar as the person acquiring the interest carries out the works using his own labour force he will be incurring costs ie cost of materials plus his payroll costs. This will, however, be different from the price that he would have charged had he tendered for the work against competitors. There may be some guidance in relation to the open market cost where subcontractors are employed and materials are purchased from a third party supplier, since these will be charging an open market figure for their services and materials which will include a profit element. Presumably, upon the basis that fiscal valuations are always intended to work on the extreme, ie the highest value that a seller would receive, then there is an argument that the open market cost is the lowest price that a consumer would pay for the services.[133] However, the concept of hypothetical open market tendering where competitors jealously guard their cost figures from the competition will provide district valuers and the courts with some interesting technical issues, because the alternative suppliers in the open market will be anxious to avoid revealing their profit margins.

Planning agreements – social housing etc

Exemption for works[134]

8.32 Relief is available for works to be carried out by the purchaser or tenant.[135] The relief is, however, limited to the construction of works upon the major interest to be acquired. In the circumstances under consideration, the developer is acquiring the land, intending to obtain planning permission, demolish the existing buildings upon the site[136] and carry out works at his own expense. Traditionally, in stamp duty,[137] the construction of works upon land acquired or to be acquired at the purchaser or tenant's own expense was not subject to stamp duty.[138] However, such works are subject to stamp duty land tax if they are part of the chargeable consideration for the sale or lease[139] unless:[140]

- the interest acquired must be a major interest. The provision restricting the interests in land to major interests applies only for the purposes of making the limited exemption available. It does not apply to limit the charge in any other respect but it is unlikely that there will be relevant consideration for the release of the right of way. It states that acquisition of land means the acquisition of a major interest.[141] These words appear only in relation to the very limited relief for works

---

[133] A key issue frequently overlooked in fiscal and similar valuations is that a willing seller is looking for the highest price whereas a willing purchaser is looking for the lowest price; *Re Brian Pierson* [1999] BCLC 26; *Scottish Co-operative Wholesale Society v Meyer* [1958] 2 All ER 66.

[134] Other exemptions, whole or partial, may be available for providers of dwellings such as registered social landlords (FA 2003, s 71), charities (FA 2003, Sch 8) and certain PFI projects (FA 2003, Sch 4, para 17).

[135] Works carried out by third parties engaged by the purchaser or tenant are unlikely to be chargeable consideration. Although they may be consideration (*Eastham v Leigh, London and Provincial Properties Limited* [1971] 2 All ER 887) they are likely to be works or fitting out on the land to be acquired and will not be a condition involving the vendor/landlord as builder.

[136] The impact of the time of the demolition upon the exemptions and reliefs for disadvantaged land is an important issue where the existing buildings, although unoccupied, are suitable for use as 'dwellings'. Planning around the nil rates and 'linked transactions' will also be important.

[137] See Statement of Practice SP 8/93, 12 July 1993.

[138] This was upon the basis either that the carrying out of such works was not consideration (but see *Eastham v Leigh, London and Provincial Properties Limited* [1971] 2 All ER 887) or, if consideration, it was not the type of consideration that was subject to conveyance on sale duty.

[139] See *Eastham v Leigh, London and Provincial Properties Limited* [1971] 2 All ER 887; and see **8.17**.

[140] FA 2003, Sch 4, para 2.

[141] Ibid, s 117.

carried out on land to be acquired by the builder. In other cases, the terminology is that of a land transaction so that the charge will apply in relation to construction works related to non-major interests. It seems that this is intended to prevent the relief being available to persons who as developer who acquires only a limited right of way over the land where the works are to be constructed.

- the works are carried out after the effective date of the transaction;[142]

- the works are on land acquired or to be acquired under the transaction or on other land held by the purchaser or tenant or a person connected with him; and

- it is not a condition of the transaction that works are carried out by the vendor, lessor or a person connected with him.[143]

In effect, this excludes from the charge building works and related operations carried out by the purchaser or tenant on the land a major interest in which has been or is to be acquired by him but, as indicated above, not necessarily in relation to works upon other land intended to improve the land being acquired.

8.33 The problem with this relief is that the works have to be carried out after the effective date of the transaction. This will give rise to problems for so-called 'conditional' obligations which may be consideration.[144] The vital issue will be whether there has been substantial performance at a particular point of time. The effective date is not 'completion' in the strict sense but in such cases, assuming that the transaction is to be completed by way of conveyance or lease, it is the date of substantial performance. This is defined[145] where the purchaser takes possession of the whole or substantially the whole of the subject-matter or a substantial amount of consideration is paid or provided. Obviously, the latter is unlikely to be satisfied if the consideration includes the building works, especially if the threshold is set in practice at 90 per cent of the total open market cost[146] or there is some overage arrangement.[147] Frequently, in such situations, the developer may be allowed onto the land ahead of completion in the technical sense of taking the transfer or lease but the question is whether going into such occupation as licensee is sufficient to constitute taking 'possession' and so be substantial performance. This may be a problem where, for example, there is to be a phased development and the land is released or made available to the developer only in stages. There will be questions as to when the stamp duty land tax charge is triggered, and the extent to which the cost of the building works prior to that date are within the amount chargeable to tax.

---

142 The relief is extended for leases in order to deal with the situation of the double charge upon agreements for lease (FA 2003, Sch 17A, para 12A). Works carried out after the effective date for the agreements for lease are exempt notwithstanding that on the legislation they precede the effective date for the actual grant of the lease.

143 FA 2003, Sch 4, para 10(2).

144 *Eastham v Leigh, London and Provincial Properties Limited* [1971] 2 All ER 887.

145 FA 2003, s 44(4); see **Chapter 14**.

146 Which is something of a problem since the building works will be exempt only if these are not part of the chargeable consideration but the exclusion of the consideration depends upon the exemption being available ie there may not be payment of sufficient consideration to constitute substantial performance so that ensuring that the developer takes 'possession' of the whole or substantially the whole of the land will be a crucial factor in structuring the transaction.

147 See **8.39**.

8.34   It is provided that a purchaser or lessee takes possession if he receives or becomes entitled to receive rents and profits and it is immaterial whether the purchaser takes possession under the contract or under a licence or lease of a temporary character.[148] This leaves open the question as to whether going into 'occupation' in order to carry out building works as part of the satisfaction of the conditions or provision of the consideration is taking 'possession'. It seems that 'occupation' as licensee under a building arrangement may be sufficient to constitute substantial performance but as a matter of prudence it may be appropriate also for any cash consideration, such as purchase price or premium to be paid. Where the arrangement involves the agreement to grant a lease for a rent, albeit a rent agreement linked to turnover, it is provided by FA 2003, s 44(6)(b), that if the only consideration is rent then the contract is substantially performed when the first payment of rent is made. If the consideration includes both rent and other consideration, which is likely to be the case if the building obligation is part of the consideration, then the contract is substantially performed when the first payment of rent is made if this precedes the provision of the whole or substantially the whole of the consideration other than rent.

8.35   It must not be a 'condition of the transaction' that the works are to be carried out by the vendor or lessor or a person connected with such parties, such as a subsidiary or associated company. The question is the precise meaning of 'condition of the transaction'. Looked at technically, this has a very narrow meaning. In the context of the legislation, 'the transaction' is in general clearly limited to the specific land transaction, ie the contract for the 'acquisition' or purchase or lease of a major chargeable interest in the land, and a condition of that transaction would be a specific term of the land contract. Obviously it cannot refer to a condition of the building contract since the vendor/landlord will be a party to the contract. This clearly indicates the term of the land contract are the controlling factors on this issue. Upon this analysis, the old stamp duty position in which there were two independent contracts would appear to have continued. Moreover, it appears that HMRC Stamp Taxes upon advice accept this analysis and so do not intend to seek to develop the view that the transaction is 'the commercial transaction', although this would not appear to have any justification in terms of the legislation, and a condition of that transaction would be the commercial circumstance that the parties would not sign the land contract unless the building contract was signed more or less simultaneously. This approach is not justified upon normal principles of statutory construction, but the type of conditions such as appeared in *Kimbers v IRC*,[149] which indicated that there were two separate contracts, would no doubt be attacked by HMRC Stamp Taxes as being part of an arrangement under which the transactions were commercially linked in the sense that both contracts would have to be signed although technically legally independent of each other.[150]

---

[148]   FA 2003, s 44(5).
[149]   [1936] 1 KB 132.
[150]   This argument was convincingly rejected in *Prudential Assurance Co Ltd v IRC* (above); see also *Kimbers & Co v IRC* (above), where a similar view was put forward with equal lack of success. The effect of *Cory & Son v IRC* [1965] AC 1088 would also appear to be reversed, ie the fact that the building works were to be carried out after the land transaction had been substantially performed or even completed by a conveyance or the grant of a lease meant that no stamp duty was payable in respect of the 'building contract'; upon the view of the potential stamp duty land tax position expressed in the text, the fact that the land transaction had been perfected would also be irrelevant and the land transaction return would have to refer to the building costs. There is also the question as to whether the open market cost of the building works is 'an uncertain figure' even though there is a fixed priced contract, because the parties may change the building specifications and adjust the price accordingly. The parties must also not simply put in the contract price as the consideration as part of the land transaction return. There would need to be appropriate contemporaneous evidence to resist any allegation by HMRC Stamp Taxes that the prices had been manipulated and artificial figures for the building works had been included. Whilst the contractual figure as

SITE ASSEMBLY

8.36   A key factor in the price of newly constructed residential accommodation usually for first time buyers is the stamp duty land tax cost of 4 per cent for builders and developers acquiring the site.[151] The effective removal of subsale relief from such transactions[152] makes an unavoidable and accelerated cascade cost which can easily be increased from 4 per cent of the land price to include 4 per cent of most if not all of the works to be carried out in developing the land. This additional taxable amount is not limited to the infrastructure costs but also the costs of implementing planning agreements with the local authority such as social housing or swimming pools and schools and the cost of the new dwelling being constructed by the developer for his own resale, although with a little care in most cases this last tax charge should be easily avoidable.

8.37   The problem is to identify the amount of such stamp duty land tax which, as indicated above, is not limited to the 4 per cent charge upon the cost of purchasing the land or any premium paid for the lease. The previous stamp duty device of resting on contract and dealing with the matter by way of subsale is no longer a realistic option in most cases. Although there is a form of relief for subsales and assignments,[153] this relief is not available where the first purchaser has substantially performed the contract, ie has either provided about 90 per cent of the consideration or has gone into possession, or where the interest being acquired by the developer in a long lease has begun to pay a rent, even if this is only a temporary £1 rent during the development phase.[154] This will either mean pressure upon the developer's costs and reduced profits or an increase in price to new homeowners who will be paying tax upon the increased price.[155] It is difficult to believe that it will be possible to organise a transaction in such a way that the developer who needs to enter upon the land to be acquired in order to construct the building is not taking 'possession'. It is assumed that 'possession' has a wide meaning notwithstanding some inadequacies in the drafting.

8.38   There are also complex drafting and structuring problems where it is necessary to provide rights in relation to access to the land or adjoining land and/or rights to link into services and/or to construct infrastructure works such as services or site rights on the land or adjoining land. The arrangements relating to these may easily be drafted in such a way as to create additional consideration for the land acquisition, as well as long-term problems where these rights require modification subsequently as the development progresses and problems emerge. Insofar as these rights are in favour of the seller of the land, it may be possible to escape a charge to tax by arranging for the relevant right to be excepted and reserved from the conveyance to the developer so that

---

between the parties might be useful evidence as to the open market cost, the special relationship of the parties as part of the overall transaction may mean that HMRC Stamp Taxes may not be prepared to accept it as being the open market figure: cf *Lap Shun Textiles Industrial Co v Collector of Stamp Revenue* [1976] AC 530.

[151]   Subject to the availability of the nil rate band because the various properties being acquired (whether freehold or leasehold) are below the relevant threshold which differs where the property is not suitable for use as a dwelling at the time it is acquired, a charge to stamp duty land tax has to be factored into the cost to the developer. The developer may wish to arrange for demolition of any existing residential property before he agrees to acquire the property to exploit the difference in the threshold levels (FA 2003, s 55).

[152]   It is virtually inevitable that there will be substantial performance and a total tax charge upon the developer when he enters upon the land to begin construction: FA 2003, s 44(4) and (8); see Sch 6.

[153]   FA 2003, s 45.

[154]   Ibid, s 44.

[155]   See **6.4** on the cascade effect of stamp taxes.

there is no acquisition or creation of new rights.[156] Where this is not possible and the land has to be conveyed and new rights granted by the developer back to the seller, there is clearly the creation of a new chargeable transaction and a land exchange whereby a major interest is exchanged for a non-major interest, giving rise to two chargeable transactions taxed separately at market value.[157] It must also be noted that in some contexts mere contracts that are not interests in land can be chargeable interests in their own right because they affect the value of land.[158]

Overage and similar arrangements[159]

8.39 Development arrangements frequently include provisions under which the vendor or lessor is to receive additional consideration linked to the sale proceeds or profits of the development or where there are 'clawback' arrangements (such as where the purchaser or lessee agrees that if planning permission for the land is obtained within a specified period he will make an additional payment equal to a specified percentage of the increase in the market value of the land).[160] There may also be arrangements under which the consideration is to vary depending upon the nature of a planning consent and, in particular, the density achieved. Any such arrangements make the consideration 'uncertain',[161] in which case the developer will be required to make a reasonable estimate of the amount that he expects to pay when making the initial return on the transaction,[162] with obligations to submit fresh returns and new self-assessments and payments as and when each instalment becomes ascertained.[163] In relation to a residential development such as the construction of numerous houses or blocks of flats, this reporting and payment obligation can become rather tedious. For example, depending upon the terms of the overage arrangements, as and when each house is sold or each flat let[164] and an instalment of the additional or overage consideration can be calculated and becomes due and payable, the developer will be required to make a fresh return, recalculate the tax and file and pay accordingly[165] and there will be the need to apply to defer payment of the stamp duty land tax in respect of such instalments,[166] otherwise interest for late payment runs from the effective date of the original transaction.[167] Where there is a significant development over a period of time, this can prove a rather costly exercise.[168]

---

[156] See further **3.19**.

[157] See further **5.160**.

[158] FA 2003, s 48(1)(b); see **4.39**.

[159] See further **5.188**.

[160] Solicitors acting for the vendor may be under a duty to try for such arrangements on behalf of their clients – see *Akazuc Enterprises v Farmar* [2003] PL SCS 127.

[161] FA 2003, s 51.

[162] Ibid, s 51.

[163] Ibid, s 80; but there may be a right to apply to postpone the payment of tax in respect of such overage elements pursuant to FA 2003, s 90 thereof: see Stamp Duty Land Tax (Administration) Regulations 2003, SI 2003/2837, Part 4. It must be noted that unless an application to defer payment in respect of the 'uncertain' element is made pursuant to FA 2003, s 80, the interest upon any stamp duty land tax paid upon subsequent instalments runs from the effective date of the transaction, not from the date of the instalment falling due: see FA 2003, s 87(5).

[164] It is not the sale or lease itself which triggers the reporting and payment obligations, but it is in fact the determination of the price, which may operate to make all or part of the uncertain amount 'ascertained'.

[165] FA 2003, s 80.

[166] Ibid, s 90.

[167] Ibid, s 87(5).

[168] There are, at present, no arrangements for making periodical returns in these circumstances; each transaction must be separately reported and paid for.

Chapter 9

TRUSTS AND ESTATES

GENERAL

9.1   *Inter vivos* and testamentary trusts and the estates of deceased individuals are affected by stamp duty land tax in numerous ways. There will be the normal rules applicable where the trustees buy land from third parties as an investment and personal representatives[1] may be faced with the problems of paying any outstanding stamp duty land tax such as where the deceased failed to deal with the tax on his acquisitions correctly or there are open tax issues such as rent reviews or holding over any business tenancies and issues of postponed or retrospective tax on a variable consideration where the deceased had entered into a contract acquiring land with some form of overage or clawback arrangement and whether the deceased had built in an effective exit strategy.[2] In addition, there will be the problems of stamp duty land tax arising in connection with the administration and management of the trust such as allocation of assets between the beneficiaries, exercises of powers of appointment or advancement and so on. Trustees are the persons responsible for paying the tax and for making any returns that are necessary.[3] Similarly, variations of estates including the appropriation of assets in satisfaction of liabilities or more substantial variations are potentially chargeable transactions although there may be reliefs available provided the conditions are specified.[4]

9.2   Whilst this Chapter, within the terms of reference for the book, focuses on stamp duty land tax, it has to be noted that stamp duty and stamp duty reserve tax issues can arise because trusts and estates can include assets such as shares and marketable securities and interests in partnerships.[5] Whilst there are certain reliefs for stamp duty there are no exemptions for stamp duty reserve tax; the principal charge to the latter tax is, however, cancelled where stamp duty has been paid.[6] This cancellation applies even where the transfer attracts only the fixed duty, or is certified pursuant to the Stamp Duty (Exempt Instrument) Regulations 1987[7] or is exempt.[8] It is, therefore, necessary to structure the transaction and, in particular, execute documentation that attracts an appropriately small or nil amount of stamp duty in order to save a 0.5 per cent charge. When arranging the variation of a trust or estate where stamp duty land tax arises it must not be overlooked that other assets in the instrument many not only be 'chargeable consideration' for the variation of the interest in the land, but also the land may be

---

1   FA 2003, s 106(3); but see Sch 10, para 31(4).
2   See **2.16** and **5.206**.
3   FA 2003, Sch 16, paras 4–6; see **9.9** and **Chapter 16**.
4   Ibid, Sch 3, paras 3A and 4; Sch 4, paras 8 and 8A.
5   See **Chapter 1**.
6   FA 1986, s 92; but it seems that in many cases the exemption from stamp duty for transactions below £1000 may not, in practice, be available because stock transfer forms duly certified will not be executed producing a fixed £5 charge.
7   SI 1987/516.
8   Such as pursuant to FA 1985, ss 82 and 84.

'consideration' for the variation of the other assets consisting of shares potentially attracting a 0.5 per cent charge which has to be reported[9] and paid promptly, unless appropriate stamp duty planning is implemented.[10]

TERMINOLOGY

9.3   Two types of trust situation exist, namely:

- a bare trust or nominee arrangement; and

- a settlement.

The definitions are limited. It is stated[11] that a 'settlement' means a trust that is not a bare trust. This throws the emphasis upon a 'bare trust' which means[12] a trust under which property is held by a person as trustee either for a person who is absolutely entitled as against the trustee or who would be so entitled but for being a minor or other person under a disability or for two or more persons who are or would be jointly so entitled. This follows the definition for capital gains tax[13] and the related practices and case law[14] will no doubt be followed by HMRC Stamp Taxes. For these purposes a person is absolutely entitled to property as against the trustee in cases where the person has the exclusive right, subject only to satisfying any outstanding charge, lien or other right of the trustee, to resort to the property for the payment of duty, taxes, costs or other outgoings or to direct how the property is to be dealt with.[15] It will be noted that this definition is somewhat similar to that in relation to trusts and capital gains tax[16] and presumably the various cases upon 'absolutely entitled' etc will have a direct applicability when seeking to apply this legislation.

Nominee situations

9.4   Subject to certain important exceptions[17] the existence of a bare trust or nominee is ignored and all transactions in relation to the land are treated as having been performed by the beneficial owner.[18] In consequence, most transactions involving nominees, such as a change of nominee, do not incur any liability to stamp duty land tax. It also means that when completing the land transaction return (SDLT 1) the person to be identified as seller or purchaser will be the beneficial owner. He will be the person responsible for the payment of the tax and signing the appropriate declaration as purchaser. However, in practice, HMRC Stamp Taxes have produced a bizarre interpretation of the legislation. Since the actions of the nominee are deemed to be the

---

[9]   Stamp duty reserve tax is self-assessed and has to be notified, under penalty, within very few days; Stamp Duty Reserve Tax Regulations 1986, SI 1986/1711, reg 4.

[10]   Payment of the former fixed duty of £5 or even no stamp duty can cancel the *ad valorem* stamp duty reserve tax charge provided the necessary 'conveyance' exists.

[11]   FA 2003, Sch 16, para 1(1).

[12]   Ibid, Sch 16, para 1(2).

[13]   Taxation of Chargeable Gains Act 1992, ss 60 and 68. This differs from 'settlement' etc for other purposes.

[14]   See, for example, *Kidson v Macdonald* [1974] STC 54; *Crowe v Appleby* [1995] STC 502; *Jerome v Kelly* [2002] STC 609; *Pogson v Lowe* [1988] STC 365; *Bentley v Pike* [1981] STC 360; *Harthan v Mason* [1980] STC 94; *Booth v Ellard* [1980] STC 555; *Hoares Trustees v Gardner* [1978] STC 89.

[15]   FA 2003, Sch 16, para 1(3).

[16]   Taxation of Chargeable Gains Act 1992, s 60.

[17]   See FA 2003, Sch 16, para 3 (as amended); see **9.6**.

[18]   This may be a technical problem for foreign estates where there is some form of universal succession.

actions of the beneficial owner[19] the signature of the nominee on the declaration has been treated as a signature by the taxpayer in the return accepted as valid. Unfortunately owing to obvious defects in the drafting of the original FA 2003, Sch 4, para 8, and the subsequent extensive anti-avoidance provisions technically a change of trustee in the strict sense of a settlement or a nominee or bare trustee there is a full charge to stamp duty land tax where the trust assets consist of or include land which is subject to a mortgage or charge or lien. In the view of HMRC Stamp Taxes this applies even where the new trustees enter into a without or limited recourse arrangement and no personal covenant is given by the new trustees, ie the incoming trustees give a routine recognition that the property is mortgaged but insist that their liability is limited to the extent of the trust funds under their control. Even where solicitors acting for mortgagees understand the technical issues and practical importance of these restrictions upon the security issues and the fact that their client is not exposed to an additional risk their previous actions which require the outgoing trustees to require indemnities from the incoming trustees and that such new trustees give probably unnecessary security to their client the mortgages have given HMRC Stamp Taxes the opportunity to claim large amounts of tax. Currently, however, HMRC Stamp Taxes have informally indicated that in routine transactions such as normal retirement and appointment of trustees they will not pursue their claim; but they have refused to produce amending or 'clarifying' legislation so that they are free to attack transactions where they believe that there may be tax avoidance especially where corporate trustees are involved.[20]

9.5   The existence of a nominee as holder of the legal title[21] could mean that there would be a discrepancy between the stamp duty land tax documentation and the names appearing on the Land Registry documentation. In this situation it seems that the Land Registry will usually be prepared to act on the basis of an explanatory letter plus any appropriate supporting documentation. It may, however, be necessary to persuade them that the person on the register is merely a nominee and not a person acting in some other capacity. The parties will frequently choose a body corporate as a nominee. This, *prima facie*, raises issues in relation to the connected company charge since holding property in a fiduciary capacity is still within the charge, subject to the exceptions for commercial trustees.[22] However, it appears that as regards bare trustees or nominees HMRC Stamp Taxes are prepared to accept the argument that, because the transaction vests the property in the beneficial owner, no value can be attributed to the land acquired by the nominee company and no charge to tax arises. However, other issues may arise so that it may be prudent to make use of a body corporate as nominee and ensure that it is not connected.

Dealings between nominee and beneficial owner

9.6   In general, transactions between the beneficial owner and the nominee are ignored.[23] However, these principles, which mean that no tax arises, do not apply in relation to the grant of the lease[24] which will, presumably, include the deemed grant of a lease arising upon substantial performance of the transaction. Where a lease is granted to a person as a bare trustee, he is treated for the purposes of stamp duty land tax as if

---

[19]   FA 2003, Sch 16, para 3(2) to (4).
[20]   Ibid, ss 53 and 54; but note Sch 15, para 12(3) and 20(3); see also *Jasmine Trustees Ltd v Wells & Hind* [2007] STC 660.
[21]   Although it may be necessary to have 2 nominees in order to satisfy the requirements of the Law of Property Act 1925, s 26.
[22]   FA 2003, ss 53 and 54; see **5.208**.
[23]   Ibid, Sch 16, para 3(1).
[24]   Ibid, Sch 16, para 3(2).

he were the purchaser of the whole of the lease interest acquired. There is deemed to be a full transaction. Similarly, where a lease is granted by a person as bare trustee, he is to be treated as the vendor of the whole of the interest disposed of.[25] It will be noted, however, that there is no specific market value provision.[26] The transaction is taxed by reference to the actual terms since these anti-avoidance rules do not prescribe a special chargeable consideration. In consequence, it would seem that where a lease is granted to a nominee he will be taxable only upon the actual consideration, if any, whether premium or rent so that where the lease is for a nil premium at a peppercorn rent there will be no charge to tax and no notifiable transaction.[27] However, it seems that in this situation the connected company charge by reference to not less than the market value[28] would apply emphasising the need to avoid connected companies as corporate nominees.[29]

9.7 Subject to the questions of leases, the use of nominees may have certain advantages.[30] In some situations a person may wish to transfer land or to sell land but to except and reserve various interests to himself. As described elsewhere,[31] HMRC Stamp Taxes take the view that there is very little scope for excepting and reserving as a means of retaining interest in the land; in their view there has to be a full transfer with the regrant of the rights in question which produces a potential chargeable interest[32] and a possible land exchange imposing a charge to market value upon both of the parties.[33] In these situations the parties, subject to the conveyancing requirements, may find that there are fewer problems and may be able to avoid market value issues by granting the rights, initially to a nominee for the vendor, and having carved out the interest to be retained transfer the property subject to existing interests held by the nominee for the vendor.

9.8 On the other hand, where bare trustees are involved, the 'purchaser' or 'vendor' is the beneficial owner, and the beneficial owner is the only person who can sign the declaration on the land transaction return or self-certificate. There can be no secrecy, such as a person acting as agent for an undisclosed principal; but HMRC Stamp Taxes have accepted the unusual argument that since the acts of the nominee are the acts of the beneficial owner the signature of the declaration by the nominee is deemed to be the signing by the beneficial owner.[34] This does not mean that a person can hide behind a nominee since it does not relieve the person signing from identifying and disclosing

---

[25] Ibid, Sch 16, para 3(3) and (4).

[26] Particular other provisions such as FA 2003, ss 53 and 54 may apply.

[27] FA 2003, s 77A and Sch 3, para 1.

[28] Ibid, s 53; see **5.208**.

[29] These provisions apply to transactions after 16 March 2005.

[30] However, since nominees tend to be utilised where there are joint ventures (which might be more efficiently carried on through a company) and the land, if held for the various participants by a bare trustee, may be more tax efficient should the joint venture and the nominee not involve a partnership.

[31] See **3.19**.

[32] FA 2003, s 48.

[33] Ibid, s 47; Sch 4, para 5; see **5.150**.

[34] This will only apply to nominees, i e persons holding the legal title; it does not apply to agents in general who are governed by a separate regime; FA 2003, ss 81B and 106; and there is a revised SDLT1 permitting agents to sign as to the effective date provided that the 'purchaser' signs the declaration for all other matters included in the land transaction return. HMRC have also not officially confirmed that the nominee or agent signing the form is not also severally liable for any penalties and interest, upon both late payment of interest and penalties, imposed upon but not paid by the beneficial owner especially where the latter is bankrupt or in insolvent liquidation and any indemnities are valueless.

details of the actual vendors and purchasers on SDLT 2. It will be necessary when completing the return to determine the capacity of the persons apparently acting as vendor/landlord and purchaser/tenant.

9.9 On the other hand, where there is a 'settlement', whether *inter vivos* or testamentary, although the beneficiaries have or are deemed to have chargeable interests where the trust investments include land in the United Kingdom,[35] the trustees are treated as the 'purchaser' making the acquisition,[36] and are made responsible for payment and compliance,[37] and signing the declaration.[38] It is, therefore, necessary to be able to recognise which situation is in operation at the relevant time.

CHANGE OF STATUS

9.10 It is important for trustees and personal representatives to note that their status may change to that, for example, in the case of a nominee where interests change, such as where a trustee becomes a bare trustee because a person becomes absolutely entitled on attaining a specified age, or on the death of the life tenant, or where a power of appointment or advancement is exercised but the legal title is not immediately transferred. Appropriation by executors may have similar consequences. There may also be major technical problems where a person beneficially entitled re-settles his interest on the property held by the legal owner. This affects the question of whether the beneficial owner is a major or minor interest.[39] Similarly there may be technical issues where personal representatives are to be trustees of the estate and have completed the administration by paying off or providing for creditors.[40]

TRUST INTERESTS AS CHARGEABLE INTERESTS

9.11 It appears to be the assumption of the draftsman that equitable interests in trusts, where the trust fund includes land in the United Kingdom, can be chargeable interests in the land held as part of the trust assets.[41] In consequence, a life tenant or a remainderman in a trust governed by the laws of England and Wales or Northern Ireland which includes land in its investments will, on this basis, have a chargeable interest; but a discretionary or similar interest where there is no equitable interest in the trust assets,[42] nor is the involvement as a possible recipient of assets as a consequence of powers to appoint or advance trust assets.[43]

---

[35] FA 2003, Sch 16, para 2.
[36] Ibid, Sch 16, para 4; and presumably the 'vendor' for the purposes of completing SDLT 1 and 2.
[37] FA 2003, Sch 16, para 5.
[38] Ibid, Sch 16, para 6.
[39] The question is whether the interest of the beneficiary is a 'major interest' since it is neither a leasehold nor a freehold interest in equity but is a limited interest. It is considered that trust interests are minor interests so that the status of the legal owner or executor as trustee or nominee will be crucial to the analysis and tax charge. This will be important in relation to the rules for calculating the tax upon exchanges of interests and reporting obligations.
[40] Which may be a key issue in deciding whether the estate is solvent or insolvent and whether the beneficiaries have an interest in the assets currently forming part of the estate.
[41] See **4.41**.
[42] *Gartside v IRC* [1968] AC 553; *Holmden v IRC* [1968] AC 685.
[43] But note FA 2003, Sch 16, para 7, where an object of a power 'buys his way in'.

A key issue is the nature of the interest of the beneficiary. It appears to be the assumption in the legislation that there is not a single chose in action such as a single right as against the trustee but a collection of individual interests in each of the separate investments held by the trustees in any particular time.[44] In consequence, for the purposes of stamp duty land tax, the person will be regarded as having interests in land and interests in shares. However, the opposite position has been taken in relation to stamp duty and, in particular, stamp duty reserve tax. In general, the beneficiary is treated is having a single interest which is not an interest in shares and therefore not a chargeable security.[45] This means that many transactions involving a variation of trusts that hold shares will not be sales notwithstanding that the person surrendering one interest receives shares as compensation.[46] The effect of having a collection of interests means that any variation of trusts will involve the mutual transfer of equitable interests in a variety of assets. This may mean that there are exchanges of interests in land, which will usually be minor interests, but other interests will be transferred in return for interests in other items of property which could constitute chargeable consideration. This could produce immensely complicated computations and returns.[47]

FOREIGN ELEMENTS

9.12   Foreign factors intrude in many ways such as having foreign settlors, overseas beneficiaries and the termination of interests, individuals as well as trusts and estates governed by foreign law and the holding of foreign assets which may have to be valued.

As usual the draftsman has assumed that foreign legal systems including Scotland are identical with English law and failed to provide diluted legislation to deal with fiduciary, agency or mandate arrangements including universal succession arising under overseas jurisdictions. The charge to stamp duty land tax applies to such structures where these have chargeable interests in United Kingdom land and has been extended to beneficiaries involved in such arrangements. There will, therefore, be difficult questions of determining the rights and liabilities of the parties involved in such structures and whether these equate to trusts, settlements or merely contractual or *in personam* arrangements in English law.

9.13   This wide-ranging charging provision emerges indirectly from the rules dealing with certain types of trust. It is provided that although foreign trusts, including trusts governed by the laws of Scotland, may differ from English trusts in the sense that the beneficiaries may not have some form of equitable interest in the underlying property, i e a proprietary interest that may entitle them to trace the property to a certain extent, but have merely a personal right against the trustees to compel proper administration of the trust and to sue for breach (but without any rights of a proprietary nature in relation to the underlying property),[48] the fact that the foreign law merely gives an *in personam*

---

[44]   It is interesting to compare this with the general approach of HMRC Stamp Taxes which was to treat interests in partnerships as being a single separate item of property and not a collection of individual interests in each of the assets of the partnership business.

[45]   FA 1986, s 99 (as much amended).

[46]   Note the discussion in *Oughtred v IRC* [1960] AC 206 where the beneficiaries were exchanging their various interests in shares. Also note the limitations imposed upon this decision by *Neville v Wilson* [1997] Ch. 144 which allows oral arrangements to prevail so that s 53(2) of the Law of Property Act 1925 appears to take precedence over s 53(1)(c) thereof.

[47]   See **9.29**.

[48]   See *Garland v Archer-Shee* 15 TC 693; *Archer-Shee v Baker* (1928) 15 TC 1.

right is overridden by legislation[49] so that interests in foreign trusts are treated as though the trust was governed by English law and life interests and remainders in foreign trusts are effectively converted into chargeable interests.[50] Thus, if English law would give the beneficiary some form of proprietary interest in the underlying property then, notwithstanding that the trust is governed by foreign law and administered by trustees outside the United Kingdom, the interest of the beneficiary, who may be non-resident, is a chargeable interest and dealings in that interest for consideration are subject to stamp duty land tax.[51]

9.14 Whatever regime applies the fragmentary nature of the actual or deemed interests of beneficiaries for the purposes of stamp duty land tax can be important. It will help to define such interests as being minor interests because, although they may subsist in relation to freehold or leasehold interests, they will be limited interests and will not, in themselves, represent the fee simple or the term of years absolute.[52]

9.15 This can have important issues for the computation of the charge since exchanges of minor interests are taxable only upon any equality adjustment[53] and would be important in relation to valuation. It should be noted that even where there is a nominee situation, such as a statutory trust for joint owners, which is treated as a bare trust for stamp duty land tax[54] each of the parties may be entitled to some form of discount for his interest. For example, it seems that, in many cases in practice, HMRC Share Valuation Division will accept that where land is jointly held in equal shares then one of the participants will be entitled to a 10-15 per cent discount. This discount can increase where the person's interest is significantly less than 50 per cent.[55]

ACQUISITIONS OF LAND BY TRUSTEES

Ordinary purchasers

9.16 Acquisitions of land by trustees from third parties will be subject to stamp duty land tax in the normal way. They will be responsible for notifying the transaction and for paying any tax that is due.[56] They will, in consequence, also be responsible for dealing with any rent reviews or abnormal increases in the rent or any charges that arise by reason of the holding over of the lease or subsequent linked transactions.

Settlement of land

9.17 In many cases the trustees may acquire land from a connected person as settlor. This will usually be by way of gift and will be a transaction for no chargeable

---

[49] FA 2003, Sch 16, para 2.
[50] Such interests will normally be minor interests which is important when varying trusts and estates (FA 2003, Sch 4, para 5). Many problems remain where the status of interests in English law remain unresolved such as annuities and discretionary participation; but note FA 2003, Sch 16, para 7.
[51] The assumption of the draftsman that the tracing remedy of beneficiaries under English trusts is an interest in land in the general sense is questionable, but the legislation having been prepared on the basis that it is a chargeable interest it will be difficult to persuade the current judiciary that the legislation was prepared on a false premise. The argument will be that, by necessary implication for the purpose of stamp duty land tax, the interest of the beneficiary is a chargeable interest.
[52] FA 2003, s 117.
[53] Ibid, Sch 4, para 5 and may not have to be reported (see s 77(1)(b)); see **Chapter 18**.
[54] FA 2003, Sch 16, para 3.
[55] *Re Wight* [1982] 2 EGLR 236.
[56] FA 2003, Sch 16, paras 4–6.

consideration[57] so that no charge to tax will arise and the transaction will not be notifiable.[58] However, the connected companies charge by reference to not less than the market value of the property[59] can apply to gifts or undervalue transactions with trustees. *Prima facie*, a transfer by a corporate trustee would be vulnerable to the charge because trustees and the settlor are connected persons.[60] However, there are exceptions for certain corporate trustees contained in FA 2003, s 54. These are:

- where immediately after the transaction the company holds the property as trustee in the course of a business carried on by it that consists of or includes the management of trusts; or

- where immediately after the transaction the company holds the property as trustee and the vendor is connected with the company only because of the Income and Corporation Taxes Act 1988, s 839(3); or

- where the vendor is a company and the transaction is or is part of a distribution of the assets of that company (whether or not in connection with its winding-up) and the interest in question or an interest from which it is derived was not acquired by reason of an intra-group transaction within the preceding 3 years. This is useful in that it enables trustees to hold assets through other companies and to liquidate such companies or return capital *in specie* without the market value charge applying.

Since these fall within the exclusion pursuant to FA 2003, s 54, they are considered to be non-notifiable notwithstanding s 53(4) which applies only to transactions within s 53 and s 54(1) provided that s 53 does not apply to specified exclusions.

9.18 Where the trustees enter into the acquisition of a chargeable interest for a variable consideration, they will be responsible for dealing with the situation and this will have to be taken into account when they are disposing of the property such as appointing the land in question to a beneficiary.[61] The fact that the overage or clawback arrangements[62] have to be renegotiated may mean that the transaction is not one for which there is no chargeable consideration but where there is an assumption of liability or an undertaking to pay money, albeit of a contingent nature, so that the beneficiary is providing some form of chargeable consideration which will have to be estimated and dealt with in the usual way,[63] and dealing with any exit strategy established by the purchasers on the initial acquisition or negotiating a suitable arrangement.[64]

---

57   Ibid, Sch 3, para 1.
58   Ibid, Sch 3, para 1.
59   Ibid, ss 53 and 54.
60   Income and Corporation Taxes Act 1988, s 839.
61   On appointments and advancements or transactions for no chargeable consideration see FA 2003, Sch 3, para 1; see **11.8** and **9.26**.
62   Which may have security arrangements that are chargeable interests pursuant to FA 2003, s 48(1)(b); see **4.39**.
63   FA 2003, ss 51, 80 and 90; Stamp Duty Land Tax (Administration) Regulations 2003, SI 2003/2837, Part 4.
64   See **5.206**.

DEALINGS IN EQUITABLE INTERESTS

9.19 Since the interests of beneficiaries can be chargeable interests where the trust holds land in the United Kingdom, the trustees may find it helpful to hold such land through a company assuming there are no other adverse taxation consequences. This would mean that dealings in relation to beneficial interests will not be chargeable interests.

9.20 However, where there is a direct holding of land by the trustees, the acquisition of a person's beneficial interest will, *prima facie*, be a chargeable transaction unless there is no chargeable consideration such as where a beneficiary settles his interest upon another trust or makes a gift of his interest. A person who purchases an interest in a trust will be potentially subject to stamp duty land tax upon an apportioned part of the consideration.[65] The main area of difficulty will be variations of trusts where there are exchanges of interests which are either exchanges of minor interests and land exchanges or will be transfers of chargeable interests for a consideration in kind.

9.21 However, one particular area of variation of chargeable interests as a taxable transaction qualifies for a limited relief. This relates to the allocation of assets by the trustees.[66] It seems that the consent by a beneficiary to the allocation of assets may be regarded as bringing about some form of contractual arrangement for which there is chargeable consideration.[67] In order to provide relief from mere allocation of assets which requires the co-operation of beneficiaries producing a charge, it is provided[68] that where the trustees of a settlement reallocate trust property in such a way that a beneficiary acquires an interest in certain trust property and ceases to have an interest in other trust property and, however, this merely relieves the giving of consent.[69] It would seem that the allocation of assets can still be for a chargeable consideration. It seems that the intention is that, if the trustees are given the power to allocate assets without the consent of the beneficiaries, no charge will arise because there is no 'contract'. This is to deal with those situations where the co-operation of the beneficiaries is necessary and the contract might otherwise arise. Other forms of variation of interest that are not the allocation of assets will remain unaffected by this relief.

9.22 As a consequence of this, variations of trusts or other arrangements involving disposals of a beneficial interest where the trust assets include land will involve potentially chargeable transactions if done for a consideration or deemed consideration such as where the beneficiary is a body corporate,[70] notwithstanding that the trust assets are held by non-resident trustees and the beneficiaries are resident offshore, holding under a trust governed by foreign law with a foreign settlor. Direct investment in the United Kingdom is, therefore, potentially unattractive and inappropriate for foreign trustees and individuals and their executors holding interests in the United Kingdom

---

[65] Any advance of land to such a person may incur a special charge; FA 2003, Sch 16, para 7; see **9.26**.
[66] FA 2003, Sch 16, para 8.
[67] Compare the position in relation to the administration of estates as in *Jopling v IRC* [1940] 2 KB 282 and those cases where the power to appropriate was based upon statue (Administration of Estates Act 1925, s 40) and did not require consent so that no 'sale' would arise.
[68] FA 2003, Sch 16, para 8 with effect from 19 July 2006.
[69] Compare *Jopling v IRC* [1940] 2 KB 282; Administration of Estates Act 1925, s 44.
[70] FA 2003, ss 53 and 54; see **5.208**.

through companies formed[71] outside the United Kingdom holding through a partnership is less efficient because of the special charges that may apply.[72]

9.23 Since 'acquisition' includes not merely assignments but also the creation of interests as well as releases and surrenders, but not disclaimers and possibly waivers and renunciations,[73] many dealings in interests in trusts will be subject to stamp duty land tax if done for a consideration.[74] For example, an assignment by a life tenant of all or part of his interest for a consideration will require the purchaser of that interest to pay stamp duty land tax and make a return. Similarly, the release of a life interest, if done for consideration, will be chargeable, as will a surrender of an interest if done for consideration.

9.24 Frequently there will be consideration since the adjustment in the rights of beneficiaries will be part of a variation of the trust under which interests are 'exchanged', such as where a life tenant and remainderman agree to exchange part of their respective interests so as to become 'absolutely entitled' in order to partition the fund; the arrangements are likely to be a surrender of an interest in consideration of the release or the 'acquisition' of one area of participation in the investments another party which is, *prima facie*, a land exchange; as such market values will be involved.[75] This arrangement will not qualify for the special treatment for partitions, since the interest will not be jointly owned, ie the parties are not joint tenants or tenants in common but have interests in succession.[76] In such a situation, the life tenant and remainderman will be 'exchanging' chargeable interests in land so that charges to stamp duty land tax will arise.[77] However, as this will be an exchange of minor interests, only any equality adjustment will be taxable.[78] Where there is an exchange of an interest in land for an interest in other property there will be an acquisition for the value of the other property.[79]

Discretionary trusts

9.25 Discretionary and similar trusts do not have interests in the underlying property as far as the beneficiaries are concerned.[80] The interests of discretional beneficiaries are merely personal rights against the trustees for proper administration.[81] In consequence,

---

[71] In general, for UK stamp taxes incorporation in the United Kingdom is a bad decision but incorporation abroad and residence in the United Kingdom is usually stamp tax efficient. Sale of shares in such companies is almost invariably a much more attractive transaction to purchasers whether United Kingdom or overseas. Failure to investigate these issues is likely to prove an expensive error for the average client.

[72] FA 2003; Sch 15, Part 3, especially paras 10 and 14; see **Chapter 13**.

[73] See **3.21** although these may be more relevant for the administration of estates; *Re Paradise Motors Ltd* [1968] 1 WLR 1125.

[74] Assuming that such exercises are not tainted as frauds on the power.

[75] It is essential to note that where it is the value of the interest received that is taxable, the fact that it merges with other interests is irrelevant. Actuarial principles will be fundamental in this context. Thus the fact that life interest may combine with a remainder to become an unencumbered freehold is irrelevant; the interest involved will remain a minor interest so that the exchange rules do not apply and any market value will depend upon he statistical life expectancy of the life tenant.

[76] FA 2003, s 121.

[77] Ibid, s 47.

[78] See **5.151**.

[79] Where the other property consists of or includes shares or marketable securities there may be a charge of 0.5 per cent on the value of stamp duty reserve tax, but since the consideration for that interest is land the transfer will be subject only to the fixed stamp duty of £5. Payment of this fixed stamp duty cancels the *ad valorem* stamp duty reserve tax: FA 1986, s 92; see *Oughtred v IRC* [1960] AC 206.

[80] See, eg, *Gartside v IRC* [1968] AC 553; *Holmden v IRC* [1968] AC 685.

[81] Other interests may be vulnerable to or dependent upon the activities of the trustees or other persons such as

in general, dealings in such interests are not dealings in chargeable interests even if done for a consideration. However, it is specifically provided[82] that where a chargeable interest is acquired pursuant to the exercise of a discretion or power of appointment vested in the trustees of a settlement, the acquisition is treated as being made for a sum equal to any consideration that was given for the person in whose favour the appointment or discretion was exercised before becoming an object of the power or discretion. Therefore, if a person pays a sum of money, whether to the trustees or to the settlor or to any other party, in order to be included within the class of discretionary beneficiaries or appointees, that money will rank as chargeable consideration in respect of any land transferred to him out of the trust.[83]

Powers of appointment and advancement

9.26   Chargeable interests include powers over land,[84] and there is no reason why this should not include powers of appointment or advancement exercisable by trustees. Given the general exemption for gifts[85] except where connected companies or partnerships are involved,[86] the normal exercise of power by trustees is unlikely to give rise to a charge to stamp duty land tax. However, where consideration is provided so that the asset is effectively sold to the appointee, assuming that this does not constitute some type of fraud on a power, or where the property appointed is subject to a mortgage,[87] then, insofar as the property appointed or advanced out of the settlement includes land, there will be a chargeable transaction as far as the appointee is concerned because he is not providing consideration. Also, where a chargeable interest is acquired by virtue of the exercise of a power of appointment, which would normally be non-taxable[88] and non-notifiable[89] if any consideration was given by the person in whose favour the appointment is made before becoming an object of the power, the appointment shall be treated as being the acquisition of the interest or right for a consideration equal to the amount that was paid for becoming an object of the power.[90]

COMPUTATIONAL ISSUES

9.27   Two areas of computational problems arise because of these principles charging consideration in kind and it will rarely be the case that the trust fund consists solely of land. In consequence the trusts interests involved in the variation are likely to be packages of interests in a variety of property; namely:

---

trusts where there are powers of appointment or advancement. The exercise of such powers can defect or create trust interests and effectively change ownership of all or part of the underlying chargeable interests held by the trustees. There will, therefore, be a movement of property interests which are potentially taxable since such interests are treated as interests are regarded as chargeable interests so that, eg, the exercise of a power of appointment not only may terminate or 'vary' an existing interest but 'create' new interests. Normally such exercise of power by trustees will not be taxable because there will not be any chargeable consideration (FA 2003, Sch 3, para 1); but special provisions may apply such as exchanges and partitions and certain specific anti-avoidance provisions.

82   FA 2003, Sch 16, para 7.
83   Assuming that the exercise is not tainted as a fraud on a power or similar breach of trust.
84   FA 2003, s 48(1)(a).
85   Ibid, Sch 3, para 1.
86   Ibid: the previous stamp duty exemption for distribution out of trusts contained in FA 2000, s 120 has not been continued in relation to stamp duty land tax.
87   FA 2003, Sch 4, para 8.
88   Ibid, Sch 3, para 1.
89   Ibid, s 77A.
90   Ibid, Sch 16, para 7(a).

Apportionment

9.28 Insofar as the trust fund consists of a mixture of investments including both shares and land and the consideration for the variation of the chargeable interest consists solely of property not including land so that there is an acquisition for value and not a land exchange, the whole of that consideration will be within the tax charge. Presumably where the interest varied is itself a mixture of land and other assets it will be necessary to apportion any cash consideration paid upon an assignment of the interest or allocated to or vested in the other party between the interest in the land and the interest in the other assets being varied on a just and reasonable basis.[91] Only the consideration apportioned to the former would appear to be within the charge to stamp duty land tax.

'Exchanges'

9.29 More frequently, however, the arrangement will involve mutual transfers of beneficial interests which may include land on one side or both. The computation rules will differ depending upon whether there is an exchange of interests in land or there is only one interest in land and the property being received does not include any land interest, such as where a life tenant agrees to transfer the interest, including the interest in any land held in the trust by the remainderman, in consideration of becoming absolutely entitled to shares held by the trustees.

9.30 Where the interests being exchanged or varied both involve interests in land, the land exchange rules[92] which do not deal with the issue of exchanges of mixed assets will apply. The interest of the beneficiary in a trust is only a limited interest in such land and, *prima facie*, would appear not to be a 'major interest'.[93] In consequences where the exchange does not involve the acquisition of a major interest on either side, then the chargeable consideration is the amount or value of any consideration provided other than the disposals that are given.[94] This would appear to limit the charge to any consideration that represents equality or other adjustments. The value of the interests in land being mutually exchanged is ignored. There is no guidance from HMRC Stamp Taxes as to how they expect taxpayers to cope with two routine situations:

- a trust interest in land is 'exchanged' for an equitable interest in a package of mixed interests including land; and

- an equitable interest in a mixed package including land is 'exchanged' for a similar mixed package of interests.

The tax liability will differ significantly depending upon whether HMRC Stamp Taxes accept this as an exchange of minor interests with an equality adjustment or as two separate acquisitions for full chargeable consideration.

---

91   See ibid, Sch 4, para 4.
92   Ibid, s 47.
93   Ibid, s 117; see **5.151**.
94   Ibid, Sch 4, para 5(4)(a) and (b); but see ibid, Sch 16, para 8; and **9.21**.

ESTATES OF DECEASED PERSONS

Compliance

9.31   The personal representatives of a deceased person become liable for any unpaid stamp duty land tax owed by the deceased.[95] This will include deferred and other liabilities in respect of variable consideration pursuant to the FA 2003, ss 51 and 80. The administration of the estate cannot be completed until this outstanding liability has been resolved in some way. Where the land is sold by the personal representatives, unless the deceased included a suitable exit strategy in the purchase agreement,[96] they will have to take appropriate action to deal with this open provisional tax liability, and make any necessary returns and payments to HMRC Stamp Taxes and to deal with any situation where there is any outstanding postponed tax agreement with HMRC Stamp Taxes. Where the property is retained within the estate the personal representatives will be required to carry out any obligations that would have applied to the deceased such as filing returns and paying tax where the consideration becomes certain in whole or in part. They will also have to deal with the open provisional tax position when assenting or appropriating the land to the beneficiaries.[97] Returns will be required if the chargeable interest is a lease where there is a variable rent or the terms are varied. This may be a problem where the deceased disposed of the chargeable interest during his lifetime but failed to secure a release and pass on the liability to the next party in cases where the statutory provisions, which are limited to variable premiums and rent, do not apply to pass on the liability to the assignee of the lease.

9.32   It would seem interests in the estates of deceased individuals which hold chargeable interests are within the tax, if only indirectly because exemptions for certain types of transactions are provided. These exemptions would not be necessary unless HMRC Stamp Taxes believed that they had created wide-ranging charging provisions.[98] In consequence, interests of devisees and residuary beneficiaries in the estates of deceased persons can be chargeable interests.[99] It also seems that trusts created by the wills of deceased persons even where the deceased was domiciled abroad and the will or estate is governed by a foreign law are governed by the basic trust regime set out above, although there may be some questions dependent upon the foreign law as to when the land ceases to form part of the estate of the deceased person or becomes trust property or the personal representatives become nominees[100] with all of the compliance issues related to the change of status, and whether an assent or other appropriate vesting arrangement has been entered into by the executors, particularly where these are the same persons as the trustees of the testamentary settlement.

9.33   This question of interests in land held by testamentary trusts and the related issue of the interests of the legatees and devisees therein will also be important in relation to the interests of the devisees and others and at some stage the personal representatives may become trustees. In English law[101] a residuary legatee has no interest in the underlying property during the course of the administration; his rights are limited to a purely *in personam* claim against the executors for proper administration. This is

---

[95]   Ibid, s 106(3); Sch 12, para 31(4).

[96]   See **5.206**.

[97]   They will, of course, have to deal with any contractual or other issues still outstanding with the vendor or landlord.

[98]   FA 2003, Sch 3, paras 3A and 4.

[99]   But there are issues as to when the legatees 'acquire' chargeable interests; see **4.50**.

[100]   Ibid, Sch 16, para 1; *Re King's Will Trust* [1964] Ch 542.

[101]   *Commissioner of Stamp Duties (Queensland) v Livingston* [1964] 3 All ER 692.

because, until the administration is complete, or the creditors have been paid or property provided for, there is no certainty whether the particular asset will be available for legatees or will need to be sold in order to provide for the interest of creditors. Similar issues may also apply to the interests of specific devisees where the estate is heavily burdened with debt. It appears that HMRC Stamp Taxes intend to take a similar approach to all devisees so that even a specific devisee has no chargeable interest until the administration of the estate is complete or, at least, all creditors have been satisfied or otherwise provided for. It is unclear, at present, whether HMRC Stamp Taxes will wish to take any points concerning the time at which the interest of a particular beneficiary under a will or an intestacy ceases to be a purely *in personam* right and becomes a chargeable interest. Once the interest has become a chargeable interest, then the dealings by the interested beneficiary will be subject to stamp duty land tax as far as the person acquiring that interest for a consideration is concerned. It may also affect the question of who is the relevant party for the purposes of the completion of the land transaction return even where, as will usually be the case, the executors are the vendors.

Appropriations

9.34   However, persons other than specific devisees of land may be affected by stamp duty land tax. For example, a pecuniary legatee may enter into an arrangement with the personal representatives that a particular parcel of land be appropriated to him in satisfaction in whole or in part of his right to the pecuniary legacy or possibly other property.[102] Relief is provided where property is 'acquired' in or towards satisfaction of his entitlement under or in relation to a will or an intestacy.[103] The relief is not available if the person gives any consideration for the appropriation other than the assumption of secured debt such as where the property is subject to a mortgage.[104] Therefore, where that consideration consists of the assumption of a liability for a debt or obligation[105] to pay money in the future which immediately after the death was secured on the property, the chargeable consideration does not include the liability in respect of the mortgage.[106] Where there is consideration, other than the assumption of a secured liability, the chargeable consideration for the appropriation does not include the amount of the secured debt.[107] This means that when determining the availability of the nil or lower rates of stamp duty land tax, the mortgage is to be ignored. In consequence, where the property is subject to a charge of £500,000 but the beneficiary pays a £100,000, the chargeable consideration is only £100,000 and so within the nil rate band.

9.35   This relief appears to apply where the matrimonial home[108] is appropriated towards the interests of the surviving spouse.

---

[102]   When issues of transfers in satisfaction of a debt or consideration in kind or an exchange may arise; FA 2003, s 47; Sch 4, paras 5, 8 and 8A.

[103]   FA 2003, Sch 3, para 3A(1).

[104]   Ibid, Sch 3, para 3(2); presumably this means consideration other than the acceptance in satisfaction of the legacy (compare *Jopling v IRC* [1940] 2 KB 282).

[105]   Including contingent obligations such as guarantees.

[106]   FA 2003, Sch 4, para 8A.

[107]   Ibid, Sch 4, para 8A(1).

[108]   On the approach of HMRC Stamp Taxes to the nil rate band arrangements for the matrimonial home for inheritance tax see Guidance Note 12, November 2004; but the inheritance tax planning in this context has moved on so that the stamp tax issues may be different from those set out in the Guidance Note.

Variation of estates

9.36 It is not unusual for the persons interested in an estate of a deceased person, whether on intestacy or where there is a will, to enter into arrangements to vary the dispositions arising by reason of the death, otherwise than by appropriations of property. Insofar as at the time[109] the interest of any of the parties to such a transaction is a chargeable interest then such an arrangement will, *prima facie*, give rise to a charge to stamp duty land tax if done for a consideration. Much may depend upon the circumstances of the arrangement. For example, a disclaimer of a legacy which would usually be without consideration should not give rise to a charge to stamp duty land tax even though the interest vests in some other person because a disclaimer is not an 'acquisition'.[110]

9.37 As with trusts, mentioned above, there may be some form of disposition, whether a release, surrender or otherwise, in return for some reciprocal arrangement or the payment of consideration directly. Insofar as the consideration for the disposal of the chargeable interest in land consists of consideration other than entering into another land transaction within the land exchange provisions,[111] the stamp duty land tax upon the person acquiring the interest will be by reference to the amount or value of the consideration provided. However, where there is some form of reciprocal arrangement whereby interests in one property are released or surrendered in consideration of other interests being released or surrendered, so that the parties are in effect exchanging interests in land, then the land exchange provisions will apply.[112] In this situation, the question as to whether the particular devisee has a major or non-major or a non-chargeable interest will be important.[113] For example, where there is a specific devise of a freehold interest to A it would seem that, *prima facie*, A has a major interest albeit his interest subsists in equity.[114] However, where the interest is part of some form of testamentary trust, or a limited interest is granted such as a right to occupy for life, the interest may not be a major interest.[115] This affects the computation and notification obligations.

9.38 Insofar as there is an exchange involving one or more major interests, such as where one beneficiary is exchanging the freehold land left to him for freehold land devised to some other beneficiary, then there will be two charges to stamp duty land tax based upon the market value of the interest being acquired. Any equality adjustment would appear to be ignored.[116] However, where the transaction involves 'exchanges' of interests, none of which are major interests, the mutual exchange of interests is ignored in determining the extent of the chargeable consideration, which is limited to any other consideration provided such as any equality payment or other consideration.[117]

---

[109] See **4.50**.
[110] *Re Paradise Motors Ltd* [1968] 1 WLR 1125.
[111] FA 2003, s 47.
[112] Ibid, Sch 4, para 5.
[113] In this context the apparent view of HMRC Stamp Taxes that the beneficiaries in an estate have no interest in the assets until the administration is complete (ie they have no chargeable interest) will mean that many such variations will not be chargeable or notifiable even where there is consideration. It may, however, not be prudent to rely too heavily upon this analysis since it is not unknown for HMRC Stamp Taxes to change their practices or as they tend to express it 'cease to make mistakes'.
[114] FA 2003, s 117.
[115] Assuming that this is some form of licence to occupy rather than a lease for life. It may also be a question of construction whether such an arrangement involves a life interest in a settlement which would be a non-major interest.
[116] FA 2003, Sch 4, para 5(3).
[117] Ibid, Sch 4, para 5(4).

Relief for variations of estates

9.39 There is a limited exemption from stamp duty land tax in respect of certain variations of the estates of deceased persons.[118] It is provided[119] that no charge to stamp duty land tax arises in respect of the variation of an estate of a deceased person, provided that:

• the deceased was competent to dispose of the chargeable interest in question. This means that the deceased was not acting as trustee or had a special power of appointment over the property. It would seem that where the deceased had a general power of appointment over the property, whether exercisable by deed or will, he is to be regarded as competent to dispose for these purposes;

• the transaction is carried out within the period of 2 years after the death;

• no consideration in money or money's worth other than the making of a variation of another such disposition is given for the variation; and

• it is immaterial whether or not the administration of the estate is complete or the property has been distributed in accordance with the original dispositions.[120]

9.40 Where there is consideration other than the making of such other variations, for example, such as where the taxpayer provides cash from his own resources to produce equality the chargeable consideration does not include the making of that other variation such as where cash to balance the interest is paid by the beneficiary from resources outside the estate. Only the equality adjustment is taxable; but since the interests in the estate are not part of the chargeable consideration, the availability of the lower rates of stamp duty land tax will be tested against the amount of the outside consideration, in this case it seems that if the property is subject to a charge and the liability is assumed by the taxpayer the amount of the secured debt is included in the charge,[121] where HMRC Stamp Taxes are prepared to accept the argument that assuming the liability in respect of the mortgage is not money or money's worth.[122]

---

[118] This exemption is also important in relation to notifiable transactions: FA 2003, s 77(3).

[119] Ibid, Sch 3, para 4.

[120] Ibid, Sch 3, para 4(3).

[121] It may be possible to avoid this charge where the taxpayer accepts the property subject to the charge but does not assume the liability such as by giving a personal covenant to repay the debt; see **9.34**. This is subject to anti-avoidance imposing a charge if the terms of the mortgage are subsequently changed in connection with this variation: FA 2003, Sch 4, para 8 (as amended); see **5.140**.

[122] See *Secretan v Hart* 45 TC 701.

Chapter 10

RESIDENTIAL MATTERS

BACKGROUND

Limited special regime

10.1 In the discussion documentation leading to the somewhat truncated and unsatisfactory so-called 'consultation process' (which was essentially a fishing process by HMRC Stamp Taxes to get certain tax practitioners to reveal client confidential information[1] involving stamp tax efficiency so as to enable HMRC Stamp Taxes to identify technical weaknesses in the arrangements and to design a tax to block tax-efficient arrangements)[2] it was suggested that there might be effectively a different regime for residential and non-residential property, which might be reflected in the form of different compliance regimes such as different land transaction return forms and far less complicated charging provisions. Although a distinction is drawn between residential and commercial transactions, the promise of a simplified regime has not been delivered as such so that a sale of a house with a paddock where the vendor requires an 80-year clawback[3] should planning permission for a building be obtained[4] is governed by the same computation and compliance regime as a sale of land for £100 million with a clawback if a super casino is built within one mile during the following 80 years. In effect, the legislation is designed to deal with complex transactions with huge anti-avoidance provisions with a compliance regime that is appropriate for large and complex transactions so it is necessary to work backwards from the complex commercial regime to the residential regime and see how to make the provisions fit transactions for which they were not really designed. The effect is that significant changes arc rcquircd in relation to contractual terms, title investigations and completion arrangements. There is a tendency for solicitors to try to process residential conveyancing and to use non-qualified employees for this process but given the traps built into the complex transactions which inevitably apply to routine residential matters, require investigation and monitoring of the actions of the parties between contract and

---

[1]   Which approach led to a complete breakdown of the initial process when certain 'experts' invited by HMRC Stamp Taxes walked out of the process.

[2]   Apart from basic issues of client confidentiality and questions of the propriety of disclosing such information to HMRC Stamp Taxes in return for an early disclosure of the draft legislation which might be useful when advising clients as to the timing of transactions ahead of time, the writer is aware of 'position papers' prepared for HMRC Stamp Taxes by professionals involved in the so-called consultation process that were effectively verbatim copies of his advice to lay clients. As a practical matter advisers need to be aware of these issues since they may fundamentally affect their dealings with other advisers acting for other parties and whether it is worthwhile giving stamp tax efficient advice to their clients because of the risk that it will be rapidly disclosed to HMRC Stamp Taxes and possibly attacked before it can be implemented even where the arrangements do not fall within the disclosure of tax schemes regime see **2.29**.

[3]   Note the major tax problems that arise where payment is made out of the sale proceeds as in *Page v Lowther* [1983] STC 799.

[4]   Based upon the possible application of perpetuity rules.

completion which may have tax disadvantages;[5] or possible benefits[6] and which raise similar problems even for routine residential conveyancing this is a high risk strategy.

There are also significant problems with the Land Registry where there are differences between the paperwork for a properly reported transaction for stamp duty land tax and the Land Registry forms[7] and the timetables differ.

10.2 Simple matters such as the purchaser obtaining the keys before completion could be regarded by HMRC Stamp Taxes as substantial performance of the contract so that two returns might be required, one in respect of delivery of the keys, the other at formal completion. A solicitor who completes a land transaction return upon the basis that the effective date is simply at completion will be submitting an incorrect return and may be exposed to penalties if failure to carry out the appropriate investigations is 'knowledge' of an impropriety.[8] There have even been questions of goodwill in relation to the sale of residential property where persons such as dentists or accountants have practised from home and whether any arrangements relating to the business could be regarded as extra value embedded in the land[9] or purchasers of leases from plan through a speculator hoping to turn his contract,[10] or the investigations needed before signing off a return upon the basis that it is not a linked transaction[11] in order to avoid being involved in fraud.[12] The absence of a separate regime means that even routine single purchase residential transactions have to be approached with caution.

10.3 Having made a distinction between 'residential' and other property[13] there is little recognition of the need for special arrangements for social and affordable housing and for first-time buyers who tend to be the victims of anti-avoidance legislation aimed at major commercial transactions. In addition, the proposal for different regimes has been only partially carried through in that there are a few differences between residential and commercial and non-residential property, namely:

- the nil rate band for stamp duty land tax is much lower for residential property (£125,000, temporarily for 2009 at £175,000) than for non-residential property (£150,000);[14]

- the nil rate threshold for residential property in a disadvantaged area was £150,000;

- there are certain highly restricted exemptions available for residential property that are not available for non-residential property;[15]

---

[5] Such as by accelerating the effective date and producing two chargeable events and two chargeable transactions.

[6] Such as protecting the costs of building upon the land or fitting out (FA 2003, Sch 4, para 10); see **Chapter 8**.

[7] See **Chapter 22**.

[8] See FA 2003, ss 96 and 95 and note *Slattery v Moore Stephens* [2003] STC 1379 on the importance of asking the right questions when completing a tax return.

[9] See **1.5**.

[10] FA 2003, Sch 17A, para 12B; see **Chapter 6**.

[11] Ibid, s 108; see **5.42**.

[12] Ibid, ss 95 and 96; *Saunders v Edwards* [1987] 2 All ER 651.

[13] See, for example, FA 2003, s 116; see also s 55 (rates of tax); Sch 6 (disadvantaged land); SDLT 4 filing requirements.

[14] FA 2003, s 55(2) but see Sch 9, para 2(4A) for nil rates and shared ownership and residential properties.

[15] See, eg, part-exchanges involving new houses in ibid, Sch 6A, paras 1 and 2; and relocation relief for employees in ibid, Sch 6A, paras 5 and 6; right-to-buy and similar transactions in ibid, s 70; certain dealings by registered social landlords in ibid, s 71; enfranchisement by leaseholders and crofters in ibid, ss 74 and 75.

- the proposed intentions by HMRC Stamp Taxes for a different percentage of transactions to be reviewed by means of Enquiry for residential property, which is currently expected to be around 3 per cent of all residential property transactions; but hitherto there has been no indication that this target is regarded as applicable;

- SDLT 4 is not usually required;
  - the nil for small premiums for residential property is no longer subject to the £600 restriction by reference to the rent; the restriction remains for non-residential property so that the nil rate premium is not available where the rent for non-residential property exceeds £1000 per annum;[16]
  - there are slightly favoured regimes for shared ownership and similar transactions;[17] and
  - the disclosure of tax scheme requirements are not so severe in relation to residential property.[18]

There is, at present, no separate compliance regime nor different return forms for residential transactions although SDLT 4 is not intended to apply to normal purchases of houses and flats, but all other forms (SDLT 1 to 3) strictly apply. Since many residential properties are purchased in joint names and full details of the true beneficial vendors and purchasers are required,[19] SDLT 2 will frequently be required.[20] However, current indications are that it is intended that at least 3 per cent of all single residential transactions are to be the subject-matter of Enquiries.[21] This is somewhat less than the 100 per cent Enquiry level intended for larger, more complex transactions, but since the Enquiries are essentially based upon random selection many perfectly straightforward single residential purchases will be subjected to investigation[22] which will provide additional costs for taxpayers which do not necessarily lead to additional tax receipts for HMRC Stamp Taxes,[23] whilst more aggressive tax mitigation arrangements will not be called in for scrutiny.[24]

---

[16] FA 2003, Sch 5, paras 9 and 9A (as amended). For the position in relation to shared ownership transactions see FA 2003, Sch 9, para 2(4A).

[17] Ibid, Sch 9.

[18] See **2.34**.

[19] FA 2003, s 103.

[20] This will require detailed technical analysis where parents make a 'contribution' towards a purchase to be taken in the name of one of their children. If they are joint purchasers rather than donors or lenders there will be taxpayers requiring an SDLT 2.

[21] See **Chapter 19**.

[22] This may make it important how Box 59 on the land transaction return (SDLT 1) is completed since this might be utilised by HMRC Stamp Taxes as one of the addresses to which the letter initiating the Enquiry is addressed notwithstanding that the taxpayer is no longer a client of the firm. It is better to rely upon Box 56 (telephone communications relating to the return).

[23] It seems that a key trigger for residential Enquiries will be transactions at the rate thresholds in order to investigate whether the apportionment to chattels has been made on a fraudulent basis (*Saunders v Edwards* [1987] 2 All ER 651). Another trigger seems to be the filing of several land transaction returns (SDLT 1) on the same day which is taken as an indication that there are linked transactions.

[24] But note the obligation to file a special land transaction return where the general anti-avoidance provisions apply, although whether they apply is virtually the decision of the taxpayer; FA 2003, ss 75A–75C and 77 (as amended).

SPECIAL RELIEFS FOR CERTAIN RESIDENTIAL TRANSACTIONS

10.4   Reliefs for certain transactions relating solely to residential property have been introduced, namely:

• part-exchanges of new houses,[25]

• relocation of employees;[26]

• chainbreaker companies;[27]

• acquisition by property traders from personal representatives of deceased persons;[28]

• variations of leases such as enlarging the term[29] or enfranchising;[30]

• acquisitions by charities[31] which can include registered social landlords where the special relief for publicly funded transactions does not apply;[32]

• certain tenancies granted by registered social landlords;[33] and

• right to buy and shared ownership transactions.[34]

However, these do not necessarily apply to all transactions since, for example, certain of them do not apply to leases.[35]

GENERAL PRINCIPLES FOR RESIDENTIAL PROPERTIES

'Residential property'

10.5   Residential property is defined[36] as meaning:

• a building that is used or suitable for use as a dwelling;

• a building that is in the process of being constructed or adapted for use as a dwelling;[37]

---

[25]   FA 2003, Sch 6A, paras 1 and 2; see **10.22**.
[26]   Ibid, Sch 6A, paras 5, 6 and 11; see **10.35**.
[27]   Ibid, Sch 6A, para 4; see **6.75**.
[28]   Ibid, Sch 6A, para 3; see **6.73**.
[29]   See ibid, Sch 17A, paras 9 and 16; **7.194**.
[30]   Ibid, s 74; see **10.42**.
[31]   Ibid, Sch 8 (as amended); see **11.28**.
[32]   Ibid, s 71; see **11.9** and **11.28**.
[33]   See ibid, Sch 3, para 2; see **11.20** and **11.28**.
[34]   Ibid, s 70 and Sch 9 (as amended); see **10.67**.
[35]   See **7.261**.
[36]   FA 2003, s 116.
[37]   A key issue is whether as at the effective date any building operations have been commenced on the site. This is fundamental to numerous issues such as whether the property is residential or non-residential and

- land that is or forms part of a garden or grounds of a building that is used or is suitable for use or is being constructed or adapted for use as a dwelling; or

- an interest in or right over land that subsists for the benefit of a building or land suitable for use with a dwelling.

Use as a dwelling

10.6 In addition to the normal situation of a house or a flat, the definition requires the existence of 'a building' which is a 'dwelling' and which is treated as used as a dwelling when used as:

- residential accommodation for school pupils;

- residential accommodation for students other than accommodation as a hall of residence for students in further or higher education;

- residential accommodation for members of the armed forces;

- an institution that is the sole or main residence of at least 90 per cent of its residents and which is not used as:
  - a home or other institution providing residential accommodation for children;
  - a hall of residence for students in further or higher education;
  - a home or other institution providing residential accommodation with personal care for persons in need of personal care by reason of old age, disablement, past or present dependence on alcohol or drugs or past or present mental disorder. This, it seems, would not necessarily cover the provision of hostel accommodation for unemployed or other homeless persons;
  - a hospital or hospice. This would seem to be limited to hospices providing accommodation with some form of medical treatment;
  - a prison or similar establishment;
  - a hotel, inn or similar establishment.[38] As hotels and inns are run for providing temporary accommodation on a profit-making basis, it is considered that 'similar establishments' will not extend to hostels and similar accommodation for homeless and other persons.

---

significantly whether the developer has substantially performed his contract to acquire the land triggering the charge to tax and probably increasing his costs and the price of new housing to first time buyers.

[38] FA 2003, s 116(2) and (3); however, the progress of the building may change the analysis. This definition requires a building as at the effective date of the transaction. In consequence, where there is a purchase of property from plan, the transaction will not, at least initially, be one involving residential property. This means that the property may not be residential property at the time of certain actions of the parties. This may offer the opportunity of entering into separate contracts for the acquisition of the land and for the construction of a building on the land. If suitably structured (see **Chapter 8**) there will be the purchase of non-residential property which will be subject to stamp duty land tax and a separate non-taxable building contract. Such arrangements have been accepted as effective by HMRC Stamp Taxes and in most situations such arrangements will fall outside the general anti-avoidance provisions (FA 2003, ss 75A–75C, especially 75B(3)(a)) there is power to amend by statutory instrument in s 116(8)(a).

Current actual use and future intentions

10.7   Where at the effective date the building is actually being used for any of the institutional purposes that are not regarded as the provision of dwellings, it is that actual use or the state of building works that is taken into account and the fact that it is suitable for any other use is to be ignored.[39]

10.8   Where the building is not in use at the relevant date but is suitable both for a purpose that is to be treated as use as a dwelling and at least one of those purposes that is not to be regarded as use as a dwelling (such as a hall of residence for students in further or higher education) then, if there is one such use for which it is more or most suitable, it is that use taken into account when deciding whether it is a dwelling or not;[40] but otherwise the building is to be treated as suitable for use as a dwelling.[41]

10.9   The effect of the legislation would seem to be that the policy is to make as much property residential even though it may be unfit for human habitation at the time (ie taxed slightly more) as possible, and it is likely that in any borderline cases HMRC Stamp Taxes will seek to argue that the property is to be regarded as a 'dwelling'.

10.10   It would seem that it is the actual use or suitability for use at the time of the transaction ie the effective date not the contract date which governs the status of the property as residential or non-residential. The future use of the property does not appear to be a relevant consideration. This may mean that the timing of the entering into and implementation of and the structure of transactions could be important. For example, where there is the acquisition of commercial property with a view to redevelopment as residential, such as the conversion of a hotel into flats, then its non-residential status at the effective date of the acquisition will be the factor governing the liability or level of the nil rate for stamp duty land tax for that transaction; the future intended use will not be appropriate. On the other hand, if the property acquired consists of several dwellings and does not meet the relief for six or more dwellings acquired under a single transaction,[42] notwithstanding that the dwellings are empty and acquired with vacant possession and are about to be demolished it seems that the property is to be regarded as residential and the fact that the existing buildings are to be converted into non-residential property is irrelevant.

Mixed property

General purchases

10.11   For these purposes, 'building' includes part of a building[43] so that issues will arise where there is a sale of a single structure with mixed use, such as a shop with a flat above or a public house with accommodation or a building combining commercial properties such as a supermarket with dwellings. There is no general principle setting out specific procedure for dealing with such mixed-use structures which affects, *inter alia*, the rate

---

[39]   FA 2003, s 116(4).
[40]   Ibid, s 116(5)(a).
[41]   Ibid, s 116(5)(b).
[42]   Ibid, s 116; see **10.13**.
[43]   Ibid, s 116(6).

structure, where there is a single transaction that includes such a structure, it will be treated as one that is for 'mixed property' for which the special tables of rates apply the nil rate band[44] for non-residential property.

Lease premium

10.12 The issue of mixed property also arises in relation to the rate applicable to lease premiums. Where the relevant land is entirely non-residential property the nil rate band for the premium does not apply if the relevant rent is at least £1000.[45] However, where the relevant land is partly residential and partly non-residential it is necessary to apportion the relevant rent on a just and reasonable basis between the various categories of property.[46] Where the relevant rent apportioned to the non-residential property is at least £1000 the transaction is treated as two separate transactions or two sets of linked transactions, one relating to residential property, the other relating to non-residential property.[47] There will be no rent restriction in respect of the residential property[48] but since the relevant rent apportioned to the non-residential property exceeds £1000 per annum[49] there will be no nil rate applicable to the lease premium. This restriction will also apply where there are linked leases of non-residential property and the relevant rent which appears to be the aggregate rent for all of the linked leases for the linked transactions of £1000.

Six or more properties

10.13 It is specifically provided that, where there is a single transaction involving the transfer of major interests in or the grant of a lease over six or more separate dwellings, those dwellings are treated as not involving residential property;[50] but with the abolition of disadvantaged land relief, the taxpayer will almost certainly be better off by seeking to organise the acquisition as numerous independent unlinked transactions[51] which can apply notwithstanding there are several sellers to a single purchaser each with their own nil rate threshold rather than seeking to produce a single transaction simply to secure the tax on £125,000 (or temporarily £175,000), especially since the individual properties are likely to be below the £500,000 threshold and the transactions are likely to be unlinked because the vendors may be unconnected parties.[52] Unfortunately should there be a desire to produce a single purchase, there is no explanation of what is a 'single transaction' for these purposes. It is obviously not the same as a 'linked transaction'.[53] Transactions are linked if they form part of a 'single scheme, arrangement or series of transactions' between the same vendor and purchaser or persons connected with either of them, ie they are separate transactions not a single transaction. There is no general provision which means that linked transactions are to be a single transaction although this may be the effect of the retrospective nature of the legislation relating to successive

---

[44] Ibid, s 55(2), Table B; but note the restriction upon the availability of the nil rate band for non-residential property where the annual rent exceeds £1000, such as in ibid, Sch 5, paras 9(2) and 9A.
[45] Ibid, Sch 5, para 9A(2).
[46] Ibid, Sch 5, para 9A(3).
[47] Ibid, Sch 5, para 9A(4).
[48] For transactions with an effective date on or after 12 March 2008.
[49] Defined in FA 2003, Sch 5, para 9A(6); see **5.25**.
[50] Ibid, s 116(7).
[51] See **5.37**.
[52] This will apply notwithstanding that the contracts contain clauses to the effect that any one transaction will not complete unless all of the related transactions complete at the same time. This may link the transactions commercially but they may be 'unlinked' because there are different, unconnected, sellers.
[53] FA 2003, s 108; see **4.37**.

linked leases.[54] This gives rise to difficult issues which, if the legislation is applied literally, will frustrate part of the purposes of the relief. The purpose is clearly to provide relief from stamp duty land tax for persons acquiring blocks of property for the purposes of redevelopment.[55] As it is likely that, for example, a person proposing to redevelop by acquiring several adjacent properties with a view to demolition and construction of new premises or the refurbishment of existing premises will be dealing with separate vendors then, technically, this would be several separate transactions and not a single transaction. The property will not be non-residential[56] and any relief from stamp duty land tax will depend upon each of the properties being acquired for a consideration below the £150,000 threshold. Since there are different vendors who are not connected with each other, the transactions will not be linked.[57] On the other hand, if the purchaser acquires seven houses in a single contract in separate parts of the country from the same vendor, the relief would appear to be available but this will not be as beneficial as the transaction being so structured as to qualify for several unlinked transactions each with their own separate nil rate relief. However, the abolition of disadvantaged area relief means that there are complex issues for a small amount of tax which can easily be exceeded by the costs involved in debating the issues with HMRC and the tax bill can be reduced by other means.

Non-occupation interests – share in freehold

10.14 One unresolved problem is the status of reversionary interests upon leases and tenancies of residential property and whether these interests in a dwelling are residential property although not being interests for physical occupation. This may occur where a tenant enfranchises his lease or a third party such as a management company purchases the freehold subject to the residential tenancies. Similar issues could arise in relation to interests in trusts.[58] The draftsman assumes that a beneficiary in a trust, although having only a minor interest, nevertheless has a chargeable interest should the trust assets include land in the United Kingdom. The trustees may own a residential property which they permit one of the beneficiaries to occupy pursuant to powers to contained in the trust deed. There is an unresolved issue as to whether the interests of the beneficiaries are interests in residential property which could be significant where there is a variation of trusts and the rate may differ depending upon whether the property is residential or non-residential. It is also a subsidiary but deeply vital question as to whether the interest of the life tenant occupying the premises is residential, whereas the interest of the remainderman is to be regarded as non-residential. Fortunately, given the trivial differences between the residential and the non-residential regimes these are, at present, unlikely to be issues involving significant amounts of tax. Indeed, apart from the temporary increase in the rate of tax for residential property, taxpayers will have the incentive of arguing for the interests behind the trust to be non-residential because this does give a slightly higher nil rate threshold.

Should the issue be significant in any rare case, at present, it is considered that the physical building is a 'dwelling' although the interest being acquired does not confer vacant possession and the chargeable interest itself is not suitable for use as a dwelling the transaction involves acquiring residential property. However, the issues are far from

---

54   Ibid, Sch 17A, para 5; see **7.105**.
55   The fact that the implementation of the proposals for disadvantaged areas has been totally misdirected and includes relief for areas that have already been developed should not affect the approach to the legislation.
56   The test is applied to the property as at the date of the acquisition. The intended future use is irrelevant.
57   FA 2003, s 108.
58   See **Chapter 9**.

straightforward but HMRC Stamp Taxes are likely to contend that as the interest acquired is an interest in a building that is physically a dwelling, the acquisition is of residential property notwithstanding that it is being acquired as an investment rather than a residence. The official interpretation is not known but will probably seek to extend the yield from the tax by enlarging the meaning of 'residential property' to include reversions. The position is, however, even more confused where the interest includes the common parts of a block of flats which, *prima facie*, would not appear to be 'residential'.

ROUTINE RESIDENTIAL COMPLETION ARRANGEMENTS

Effective date – contract to completion

10.15 The important practical issue is the question of the 'effective date' of the transaction.[59] This is particularly important for solicitors who take advantage of electronic filing[60] and the ability to file and pay separately[61] because they may intend to rely upon the provisions for signing by an agent[62] because it means that they have to monitor the actions of the client between contract and completion or face penalties for being involved in a negligent return.[63] For routine single purchase residential property transactions the basic principle of the effective date being completion will, in general, apply.[64] However, it is dangerous to make this assumption since routine residential transactions include provisions for completion by 'conveyance'.[65] The vendor is required to deliver an appropriate Land Registry transfer form. In consequence, the arrangements are subject to special provisions namely that the effective date is the earlier of substantial performance or completion.[66] In a strict sense, therefore, the fact that completion is the effective date is technically accidental or a coincidence; it is not something that can be relied upon. The parties may enter into arrangements between contract and completion and these may affect the tax analysis and failure to investigate them may expose the professional adviser to penalties for not signing the declaration as to the correct effective date when preparing the land transaction return (SDLT 1).[67]

10.16 The new principles as to the effective date mean that events occurring between contract and completion can affect the timing of the tax charge and may create the obligation to file two complete land transaction returns (SDLT 1)[68] which have to be separately prepared and signed at the cost of the taxpayer. The normal rules as to the effective date apply[69] and since HMRC Stamp Taxes are firmly committed to the view that mere receipt of the keys of itself constitutes taking 'possession'[70] it is obvious that the interval between contract and completion needs careful monitoring. Since the charge

---

[59]   FA 2003, ss 119 and 44.
[60]   Stamp Duty Land Tax (Electronic Communications) Regulations 2005, SI 2005/844; see also FA 2003, s 81B on filing by agents.
[61]   FA 2003, s 76(3)(b) having been repealed; see Stamp Duty Land Tax (Administration) Regulations 2003, SI 2003/2837, reg 4.
[62]   FA 2003, Sch 10, para 1A.
[63]   Ibid, Sch 10, para 8; *Slattery v Moore Stephens* [2003] STC 1379.
[64]   Ibid, s 119(1)(a).
[65]   Ibid, ss 119(1) and 44.
[66]   Ibid, ss 119(1)(b) and (2) and 44.
[67]   *Slattery v Moore Stephens* [2003] STC 1379.
[68]   Where, as will usually be the case for routine single residential property transactions, the completion is between the same parties; FA 2003, s 44(8).
[69]   See **Chapter 14**.
[70]   An extremely dubious view and one that can probably be defeated by careful planning in advance.

can arise even where the contract is conditional,[71] the activities of the purchaser can create problems although the tax charge may be cancelled if the contract is rescinded or otherwise aborts because of the failure of the condition.[72] Moreover, it is immaterial whether he takes possession under the contract or under a licence or lease of a temporary character.[73] Thus a purchaser or tenant who is allowed to enter into 'possession' in whatever capacity will trigger a tax charge and reporting obligation.[74] Therefore, there may be dangers in purchasers going into possession prior to payment of the purchase price or conveyance, or pending the grant of probate. This may give rise to difficulties and, with careful planning, possible benefits where there is a lease and the tenant is allowed into occupation of the land for the purpose of carrying out fitting out or repairs or redecoration prior to actual completion in the sense of payment.[75] Most transactions will involve a contract that contemplates completion by a written instrument such as a conveyance or lease between the vendor or the purchaser[76] so that the effective date will be the earlier of substantial performance or completion.[77] In practice these two events are likely to be the same (as at present), namely when the parties deliver the appropriate lease or Land Registry transfer and receive payment of the balance of the purchase price after allowing for the deposit.[78]

However, it is necessary to bear in mind that this basic structure will not always operate, particularly where the parties may be paying the price but deferring the taking of the transfer.[79] However, such an arrangement of resting on contract is of no taxation benefit because there is no subsale relief available[80] since stamp duty land tax would be payable at the effective date, ie substantial performance of the contract.[81]

---

[71] But see *Eastham v Leigh, London and Provincial Properties Limited* [1971] 2 All ER 887; *Errington v Errington & Woods* [1952] 1 KB 290; *GUS Merchandise v Customs and Excise* [1981] 1 WLR 1309 as illustrations on what is a condition and what is consideration.

[72] FA 2003, s 44(9).

[73] Ibid, s 44(6).

[74] Ibid, s 44; see **Chapter 14**.

[75] But this may be beneficial for certain taxpayers where fitting out or construction operates are involved because of the relieving provisions in FA 2003, Sch 4, para 10 (as amended); see **Chapter 8**.

[76] The fact that the purchaser may have a power to direct a subsale transfer would not affect this practice, but such a power is unlikely to have any significant stamp duty land tax benefit because of the reduction in the scope of subsale relief by FA 2003, s 45; see **Chapter 6**.

[77] FA 2003, s 44(3) and (4). It must be noted that stamp duty land tax is chargeable upon the full amount of the chargeable consideration notwithstanding that this is not due at the date of substantial performance. As the tax must be paid not later than 30 days after the date of substantial performance, taxpayers should arrange to have sufficient funding in place to meet this liability, although there may be difficulties in providing adequate security at this stage. It must also be noted that, although the completion and final payment are to be effected within a short time after substantial performance, the 30 days for payment still run from substantial performance and not the later completion, notwithstanding that this is itself a notifiable transaction (ibid, s 44(8)) with its own 30-day time limit.

[78] Ibid, s 44(3).

[79] Issues have arisen in practice with HMRC Stamp Taxes and 'delayed completed' such as whether the arrangement cancels the special reliefs for residential property pursuant to FA 2003, Sch 6A (see **10.22** and following) and, on occasions, whether the arrangement permitting the vendor to remain in occupation of the premises is the grant of a new chargeable interest producing a land exchange – a view strongly expressed by a former solicitor to HMRC Stamp Taxes although almost certainly incorrect.

[80] FA 2003, s 45.

[81] Ibid, s 44(4).

Effective date for residential conveyancing

A substantial amount of consideration is paid or provided

10.17 The normal rules for the effective date apply.[82] There is no difference between the effective date for a sale of a single flat or for the sale of the entire block of offices or a factory. It is, however, necessary to seek out and identify possible areas that could operate as traps for the unwary conveyancer who signs off the land transaction return as to the effective date.[83] Payment of a 'substantial amount of the consideration', not the whole of it, is sufficient to constitute substantial performance.[84] For these purposes, if none of the consideration is rent, ie the consideration is the purchase price or a premium for a lease, the consideration is substantially provided where the whole or substantially the whole of the consideration is paid or provided.[85] Safe harbour guidelines indicate that[86] 'substantial amounts' of consideration will under normal circumstances be regarded as 90 per cent[87] of the amount or estimated amount[88] where there is a clawback arrangement[89] for the consideration in the contract.[90] In consequence, the payment of a normal deposit of 5 or 10 per cent[91] will not amount to substantial provision of the consideration. However, where there are building or other arrangements[92] involving stage payments then this question will have to be considered more closely. Obviously, the first few stage payments will not amount to 'substantially the whole' of the price, but subsequent stage payments may take the aggregate over the operating threshold applied by HMRC Stamp Taxes from time to time. This may become a complex issue where the payments are for or include an element for 'extras'. Where these are fixtures not chattels then these will form part of the chargeable consideration and count towards the 90 per cent threshold. All payments between contract and completion require monitoring. In consequence, where the developer enters into some form of pre-sale or pre-let as a means of financing the arrangement, then the contract may have been substantially performed.[93] Similarly, where a prospective purchaser or tenant, as part of the financing arrangements and in order to reduce the costs, agrees to make a loan to the developer on favourable terms,[94] there will be questions as to whether the provision of such a 'soft loan' or a guarantee of any loan

---

[82] See **Chapter 14**.

[83] FA 2003, Sch 10, para 1A.

[84] Note the limitations upon constructive trusts and the need for payment as in *Michaels v Harley House (Marylebone) Ltd* [1999] 3 WLR 229; *Musselwhite v Musselwhite* [1962] 1 Ch 210; *Langen and Wind Ltd v Bell* [1972] Ch 685; compare *Parway Estates Ltd v IRC* 45 TC 135; *Re Kidner* [1929] 2 Ch 121.

[85] FA 2003, s 44(7)(a).

[86] But these may not apply where tax avoidance is involved.

[87] There is, of course, a fundamental issue whether these guidelines will be applied when they are relied upon purely as part of a tax avoidance arrangement as it is not unlikely that there will be anti-avoidance concepts developed.

[88] This includes any 'guestimated' consideration where there is an overage or clawback arrangement FA 2003, s 51; see **5.188**.

[89] See **5.187**.

[90] See **5.206**.

[91] But note *Workers Trust and Merchant Bank Ltd v Dojap Investments* [1993] 2 All ER 370, PC to the effect that a payment in excess of 10 per cent is not a 'deposit' but may be a 'penalty' and unprotected for the vendor and some other payment that does not protect the vendor who may have to prove actual damage rather then 'forfeit' the payment. Parties seeking to exploit the substantial payment rules may have to organise a *bona fide* deposit and a part-payment. This principle may be important in relation to the special charge upon lease premiums and assignments where a 'loan' is involved pursuant to FA 2003, Sch 17A, para 18A; see **7.95**.

[92] Which, if suitably structured, may mean that the land is non-residential but the price for the building works escape the charge to tax, see **7.74** and **8.10**.

[93] But note the benefits of selling from plan offered by FA 2003, Sch 17A, para 12B; see **8.21**.

[94] Cf the VAT position of *Faith Construction v HM Customs and Excise* [1989] STC 539.

taken out by the developer from a bank might amount to 'indirect provision of the consideration' within the view of HMRC Stamp Taxes.[95] These may be quite rare in relation to single dwelling transactions but where the residential construction is part of a larger project involving, for example, social housing or affordable housing with a local authority or housing association, such financing may be more common. The implications for the timing of any transactions will be an important part of the structuring of such arrangements.

10.18 If the consideration consists of or includes rent substantial performance occurs when the first actual payment of rent is made if there has been no other act of substantial performance.[96]

Subsequent conveyance or lease

10.19 Where there has been substantial performance without a completion, such as where a purchaser goes into possession before receiving a Land Registry Transfer, albeit as a licensee or a tenant who is party to an agreement for lease, starts paying rent before the lease is granted, and the contract is subsequently completed by a written instrument between the same parties[97] in substantial conformance with the contract,[98] both the contract and the transaction effected on completion are notifiable transactions.[99] Tax is chargeable on the completion to the extent that the amount of tax chargeable on it is greater than the amount of tax chargeable on the contract. Such further tax is unlikely to arise unless perhaps there has been a change in the rate of VAT in those rare occasions where the residential transaction is subject to VAT. The problems are interest for late payment of the tax and penalties.[100]

EXCHANGES AND PART-EXCHANGES OF HOUSES, FLATS AND GARAGES

10.20 Land exchanges, which include variations of leases, are subject to a special onerous regime of both sides being subject to a full charge to tax; but although there are reliefs these are subject to stringent conditions which will be strongly applied by HMRC Stamp Taxes.

Developers may enter into part-exchange arrangements for their new dwellings such as where they accept as all or part of the consideration the purchaser's existing dwelling. Cash may be paid for equality. This is a taxable land exchange.[101] *Prima facie*, the exchange or part-exchange of residential property will be subject to the basic rules of stamp duty land tax[102] but basic subsale relief[103] will not usually be available.[104] This will apply to straightforward exchanges of property or part interests therein whether

---

[95]   Such arrangements may also fall foul of the treatment of loans and deposits as taxable premiums or taxable consideration for the assignment see FA 2003, Sch 17A, para 18A where leases are involved.

[96]   FA 2003, s 44(7)(b) and (c).

[97]   These rules do not apply where subsales are involved; but note FA 2003, s 45(5) (as amended).

[98]   FA 2003, s 44(10)(a).

[99]   Ibid, s 44(8).

[100]   Ibid, s 87; Sch 10, paras 8 and 25.

[101]   Ibid, s 47, Sch 4, para 5.

[102]   Ibid, s 47, Sch 4, para 5.

[103]   Ibid, s 45 (as amended).

[104]   See **Chapter 6**.

geographical or part estates or interests such as where tenants in a block of flats exchange garages, surrenders and regrants when leases of flats are enlarged,[105] or there are transfers and leaseback as part of an equity release scheme[106] as well as purchases of new houses and flats. The consequences, where A agrees to exchange land with B who may or may not pay a sum by way of equality because such an exchange will inevitably involve an exchange involving at least one major interest in land[107] are:

- A will pay stamp duty land tax upon the market value of the property being acquired from B;

- B will pay stamp duty land tax upon the market value of the land being acquired from A;[108] and

- any equality payment is ignored.

The transaction being one involving the exchange of major interests in land,[109] the full double charge will apply.[110] The same rules would apply where one side of the transaction was the grant of a new lease which is a transaction involving a major interest in consideration of the transfer of the freehold or leasehold of the other house. Insofar as the lease is granted as a rent (whether with or without a premium), the rent will form part of the consideration for the acquisition[111] in addition to the deemed or hidden premium equal to its market value.

Market value

10.21 Exchanges or part-exchanges have many issues and reliefs, such as they are no longer linked transactions.[112] However, exchanges involve market value charges.[113] Such charges are rare in stamp duty land tax[114] but it has to be noted that HMRC Stamp Taxes take the view that arm's length sales are not necessarily at market value. In consequence sales at a discount for bulk purchases from plan or for a speedy completion are not at market value as may be the case when buying from an executor.[115]

Reliefs for residential property

Part-exchanges of new houses[116]

10.22 There is a limited relief for part-exchanges of residential properties which is available where numerous conditions have been satisfied. These two reliefs for

---

[105] But see **7.77** for possible reliefs.
[106] But see **10.48** and FA 2003, s 57A (as much amended).
[107] FA 2003, s 117.
[108] Ibid, Sch 4, para 5(3).
[109] Ibid, s 117.
[110] Ibid, Sch 4, para 5(3).
[111] Ibid, Sch 4, para 5(3)(b)(ii).
[112] Ibid, s 47(5) (as amended).
[113] See **5.153**.
[114] See **Chapter 27**.
[115] See, for example, *Lap Shun Textiles Industrial Co v Collector of Stamp Revenue* [1976] AC 530; *Cowan de Groot Properties Ltd v Eagle Trust plc* [1991] BCLC 1045.
[116] The original drafting meant that the relief was only available for 'trading-up'; this no longer appears to be necessary.

acquisitions of property in a part-exchange by new house builder companies or financing companies have been described in detail earlier.[117]

Surrenders and regrants

10.23 A surrender and regrant is a form of exchange of major interests and can arise where there is an enlargement of the term of a lease even when taking effect as a deed of variation.[118] The tenant is actually or by operation of law surrendering his existing lease in consideration of the grant of a new lease. This means that there is a transaction in which land is part of the consideration on both sides.[119] However, this would impose multiple charges upon market values. Fortunately, limited reliefs are available; but it is important to note the restrictions upon these reliefs. For example, the relief is not available where there is a transfer and leaseback.[120] It is provided[121] that where there is a surrender of a lease and the grant of a new lease between the same parties of the same or possibly different property, the land exchange rules do not apply. This arises because the surrender of the old lease is not consideration or premium for the grant of the new lease and the grant of the new lease is not consideration provided by the landlord for the surrender or the existing lease.[122] However, this is unlikely to be of any great significance in practice for residential property. This arises because:

- the relief for rent[123] arises only where the original lease has been subject to stamp duty land tax.[124] Many of the residential leases being enlarged or modified will have been granted within the stamp duty regime so that the relief for the rent under the new lease will not be available; but

- residential property at a ground rent is unlikely to produce a sufficiently large rent to exceed the nil rate slice threshold for the purposes of taxation upon rent.

Exchanges – not linked

10.24 It is not unusual for residential property to be involved in routine exchanges such as where a mother with a large house enters into some form of exchange with a daughter who has a small flat.[125] This is a straightforward land exchange subject to a potential double charge to tax depending upon the values of the properties.[126] However, it is now provided[127] that such exchanges do not involve linked transactions notwithstanding that the parties are connected persons.[128] Each party will pay at the rate of tax appropriate to

---

[117]   FA 2003, Sch 6, paras 1 and 2. See **5.164** and **5.167**.
[118]   *Friends Provident Life Office v British Railways Board* [1996] 1 All ER 336.
[119]   FA 2003, s 47.
[120]   This can cause problems where tenants in a block of flats seek to modernise their leases when dealing with the freehold interest.
[121]   FA 2003, Sch 17A, para 16.
[122]   There is also a very limited relief in respect of rents; FA 2003, Sch 17A, para 9.
[123]   FA 2003, Sch 17A, para 9(1).
[124]   And relates to substantially the same land; FA 2003, Sch 17A, para 9.
[125]   Different issues and reliefs apply where this is part of the variation of the estate of a deceased individual; see FA 2003, Sch 3, paras 3A and 4; and **Chapter 9**.
[126]   But such transactions are no longer linked; FA 2003, s 108(4) and 47(1) (as amended).
[127]   FA 2003, 47(1).
[128]   Ibid, ss 108(4) and 47(1) (as amended). However, this may be a case of self-serving legislation. HMRC Stamp Taxes pretending that there is a problem which requires amending legislation so that they can apply the rather dubious principles elsewhere. Their argument is that the amending legislation would not have been necessary if there had not been a real problem initially. This is a somewhat inappropriate argument for

the value of the property they are acquiring.[129] It is no longer necessary to aggregate the two values in order to determine the rate applicable to both parties.

Exchanges – an illustrative problem

10.25 The structuring of transactions involving property exchanges relating to residential property the existence of basic charges upon land exchanges[130] and the availability of reliefs for certain limited types of transaction mean that structuring is important and can affect the chargeable amount of the tax. There may be a variety of ways of implementing a transaction and the taxation consequences can be enormously different. For example, the tenants of a block of flats may be hoping to enfranchise the entire block.[131] They may also wish to use this as an opportunity to 'modernise' their leases and increase the terms. Obviously, the latter exercise involves the question of surrender and regrant. In some situations the tenants have acquired the freehold themselves from the existing outside landlord but this leaves the problem of flying freeholds and dealing with common parts. They may then enter into a transaction with a management company[132] transferring the freehold and granting new leases back of the individual flats which are varied from the existing leases because they need to take account of the new management structure as well as enlarging the terms. In this situation there is a danger that not only will the tenants have to pay their share of the stamp duty land tax in respect of the acquisition cost but there will be a land exchange in the dealings with the management company. There will be a transfer of a freehold in consideration of the grant of the leases back. This is a land exchange but not being a surrender and regrant will not be eligible for relief. In consequence, the management company will be subject to tax upon the market value of the land that it is acquiring which will, *prima facie*, be the price paid to the landlord for those interests and the tenants will be subject to tax upon the entire market value of the new leases of their flats,[133] not merely the extra value generated by the arrangement.

Other illustrative problems

10.26 Other forms of exchange may occur in relation to residential property where there are various routes of differing stamp tax efficacy. For example, tenants of flats wish to exchange their garages. In these situations, the tenants may enter into some form of deed of exchange of the relevant parts of the leases. This will, *prima facie*, be subject to tax upon the market value of the leases of the two garages but since the new leases relate to different properties the rent credit will not be available.[134] In practice, these leases may be below the nil rate threshold for both the premium and the rent although there may be some interesting questions with HMRC Stamp Taxes as to whether the properties are residential or non-residential.[135] Indeed, this may be a situation where, if the values are particularly low, there may not even be a notification obligation.[136] However, this may produce somewhat messy titles and the parties may enter into slightly

---

public bodies to take since it requires the taxpayer to persuade the current judiciary that tax legislation is redundant and unnecessary which is unlikely to commend itself as an argument to the courts.

[129] FA 2003, Sch 4, para 5.
[130] See **5.150**.
[131] On collective enfranchisement see FA 2003, s 74 (as amended); and see **10.44**.
[132] The funding of such arrangements need to be monitored because of FA 2003, Sch 17A, para 18A; see **7.95**.
[133] Note also the funding arrangements may produce a lease premium pursuant to FA 2003, Sch 17A, para 18A; see **7.95**.
[134] FA 2003, Sch 17A, para 9.
[135] See **10.14**.
[136] FA 2003, s 77A.

more complicated arrangements with a view to keeping the title simple. The parties may prefer to enter into some form of variation of the demised premises within their leases requiring the participation of the landlord. This would, *prima facie*, involve a surrender and regrant;[137] but the exemption might be available. In this situation the new leases ie the exchanged garages would relate to different property but the leases would be between the same parties ie the landlord and the relevant tenant as were parties to the original leases of the garages being disposed of.[138] Obviously, in this type of situation where there are groups of interests, the values of the properties may exceed the nil rate threshold. In these cases where the market values are not within the nil rate threshold the relief for surrenders and regrants may mean that it is more stamp duty efficient to vary the leases themselves rather than to exchange[139] Interests in the land. There are certain reliefs for a limited range of surrenders and regrants.[140] Moreover, the exchange of part of the demised premises (where the exchanged property is not part of a separate lease) the variation itself may amount to a surrender and regrant as well as an exchange because of the variation in the demised premises.[141]

ROUTINE SITUATIONS

Putting matrimonial homes into joint names

10.27 As there is no general exemption from stamp duty land tax for inter-spouse dealing,[142] putting property such as the matrimonial home into joint names can be expensive. Where, as will usually be the case, there is an inter-spouse gift (ie a transaction for no chargeable consideration), no charge arises[143] and it is not notifiable.[144]

10.28 However, there is a chargeable transaction for stamp duty land tax where the property transferred is subject to a mortgage,[145] which includes contingent debts such as a charge by way of guarantee of the debts of a company of which the transferor may be a shareholder or director.[146] Various concessions operated in this area in relation to stamp duty.[147] It was a longstanding practice that where only part of the property was transferred, stamp duty was charged upon only that proportion of the mortgage. This concession is continued into stamp duty land tax on a statutory basis. It is now provided[148] that where there is a debt charged on the property and the liability is assumed and either:

---

137 *Friends Provident Life Office v British Railways Board* [1996] 1 All ER 336.
138 FA 2003, Sch 17A, para 15A; see **7.218**.
139 Ibid, s 47, Sch 4, para 5.
140 Ibid, Sch 17A, paras 9 and 16; see **7.194**.
141 *Friends' Provident Life Office v British Railways Board* [1996] 1 All ER 336.
142 There are special rules for certain transactions between parties to a failed marriage or civil partnership (FA 2003, Sch 3, paras 3 and 3A) and such person are connected for the purpose of stamp duty land tax. Cohabiting persons may not be eligible for the breakdown reliefs but are not connected persons for special charges.
143 FA 2003, Sch 3, para 1; and it is a non-notifiable transaction (FA 2003, s 77A).
144 Ibid, s 77A.
145 These rules do not apply to appropriations of property by personal representatives in satisfaction of legacies; FA 2003, Sch 3, para 3A; Sch 4, para 8A; see **Chapter 9**.
146 Ibid, Sch 4, para 8.
147 Statement of Practice 6/90.
148 FA 2003, Sch 4, para 8(1B).

- immediately before the transaction there are two or more persons holding individual shares;[149] or

- immediately after the transaction there are two or more persons[150] holding an individual share,

the amount of secured debt brought into charge is the proportion of the debt corresponding to his undivided share of the property at that time. It seems that the former relief is intended to apply to taking property out of joint names and putting it into a single name;[151] the latter applies to taking the property out of a single name and putting it into two or more names. In consequence, where the mortgage is less than £250,000 (or temporarily £350,000),[152] a transfer of a one-half share in the house will be taxable upon one-half ie a sum of less than £125,000 (temporarily £175,000) so that the parties can take advantage of the nil rate of stamp duty land tax.[153]

10.29 It was the practice in stamp duty that if the transferor agreed to indemnify the transferee against liability upon the mortgage, no tax charge arose.[154] This has been continued into stamp duty land tax expressly in the legislation. Before the mortgage becomes part of the chargeable consideration the transferee must assume personal liability for the debt secured on the transferred property. If the transferee simply accepts the property subject to the charge but does not either give a personal covenant to pay (ie on a without recourse basis) or indemnifies the transferor there is no assumption of liability so that the mortgage is ignored in computing the tax charge regardless of the amount. However, anti-avoidance legislation[155] provides that where a debt is charged on the land immediately before and immediately after the transaction and the rights or liabilities in relation to that date are changed as a result of or in connection with the transaction there is deemed to be an assumption of the debt by the purchaser and the tax is increased accordingly. This means that where the liability is not assumed by the purchaser any subsequent dealings in relation to the mortgage may attract a tax charge. It must, however, be noted that the subsequent variation must be causally related to the transfer is 'as a result of or in connection with' the transaction.[156]

10.30 Frequently when property is put into joint names the parties take the opportunity to refinance the mortgage. In this situation it seems that HMRC Stamp Taxes start from the position that notwithstanding that the old mortgage is redeemed and a totally new loan is obtained from a different lender there is an assumption of a liability. This will be the appropriate proportion, but the proportion is applied to the old mortgage not the new mortgage.

---

[149] Ie the parties are joint tenants or tenants in common; it does not apply where the parties are entitled in succession such as A for life remainder to B.

[150] This does not appear to require more than one person on both sides of the transaction at all times, there can be one to two or two to one.

[151] See also the relief for matrimonial breakdown FA 2003, Sch 3, paras 3 and 3A.

[152] Until 31 December 2009.

[153] The transaction may alternatively be exempt if effected in connection with matrimonial breakdown; FA 2003, Sch 3, para 3; see **10.47, 11.22** and **7.249**.

[154] Statement of Practice 6/90, para 8; this may represent the correct law for the purposes of stamp duty land tax rather than a concession which was necessary for stamp duty since Stamp Act 1891, s 57 imposed a liability simply by reason of the existence of the charge and did not require the personal assumption of the liability which was a consequence of a longstanding campaign see *Chandos v IRC* 6 Exch 464; *Mortimore v IRC* 2 H&C 838.

[155] FA 2003, Sch 4, para 8(1A).

[156] These are, however, words of wide application; see, eg, *Clarke Chapman – John Thomspon Ltd v IRC* [1975] STC 567.

Estates[157]

10.31 Residential property will frequently cause problems in relation to the administration of the estates of deceased individuals whether testate or intestate. The problems are many and it is possible only to give an indication of the sort of areas that require investigation and the potential consequences.

10.32 The potential problems start at the *inter vivos* stage. There is a fundamental and important question as to whether an arrangement between an elderly person who owns a house or a flat and a younger relative which is entered into upon the basis that if the younger person cares for the older person the former will be entitled to the property on the death of the latter. This raises numerous issues as to whether there is a chargeable transaction, and, if so, when it arose and the chargeable amount. There will, therefore, be questions as to whether entering upon the premises to care for the current owner is taking some form of 'possession' should HMRC Stamp Taxes seek to put forward the argument that there can be 'joint possession'. Notwithstanding that this arrangement is oral, it probably has sufficient equitable principles applicable to it so that the absence of writing is irrelevant. In *Yaxley v Gotts*[158] Walker LJ stated that equitable notions of constructive trust or proprietary estoppel could override the statutory requirement of a need for detailed writing before there could be a valid contract between the parties.[159] Obviously, there will be certain fundamental questions as to whether there was the intention to create legal relations[160] although the serious nature of the transaction means that this is unlikely to be regarded as a conditional gift not binding upon the elderly person.[161] Moreover, arrangements such as that whereby the owner of property which is subject to a charge indicates that if the occupier of the property pays off the mortgage the property will belong to him.[162] Clearly, in these situations a property interest will pass at some stage.[163] Similarly, informal arrangements whereby property is transferred from A to B upon the basis that B will provide certain benefits to C can be sufficient to create interests in residential property.[164] There is, therefore, ample authority that an informal or unwritten arrangement between the parties can provide some form of equitable arrangement pursuant to which property will pass from one person to another as part of an *inter vivos* arrangement and will not form part of the estate. Indeed, attempts to deal with the situation as part of the estate of the deceased 'donor' is likely to be regarded by HMRC Stamp Taxes as a fraud because by treating the property as passing through the estate there may be an attempt to take advantage of the exemptions available for the reorganisation and appropriation of assets within the administration of the estate.[165]

10.33 The basic problem in this situation, to which there is no simple answer, is not so much whether a tax charge accrued but when it accrued ie when was the effective date of the transaction. It may be possible for the parties to argue that the concept of caring for the landowner is not chargeable consideration because it is not money or money's

---

[157] See also **Chapter 9**.
[158] [1999] 2 WLR 1217.
[159] Compare *First Post Homes v Johnson* [1995] 4 All ER 355; but note the fact that options may be exercised orally pursuant to *Spiro v Glencrown Properties Ltd* [1991] 1 All ER 600.
[160] Compare *Parker v Clark* [1961] All ER 93.
[161] See *GUS Merchandise v Customs and Excise* [1981] 1 WLR 1309.
[162] *Errington v Errington & Woods* [1952] 1 KB 290.
[163] Creating problems for identifying the effective date; FA 2003, s 119 and **Chapter 14**.
[164] See, for example, *Binnions v Evans* [1972] Ch 359.
[165] See, for example, FA 2003, Sch 3, paras 3A and 4.

worth[166] but services, undefined, are now specifically made chargeable consideration.[167] This charge is by reference to the 'open market cost' of the service and it will probably be the key argument in relation to many domestic arrangements concerned with residences that the actions undertaken in reliance upon the promise although giving rise to equitable obligations upon the promisor, did not have a value or cost because the equivalent services were not available in the open market.[168] However, much will depend upon the precise circumstances of any particular case and where the arrangement is not the provision of carer services but discharging the mortgage or spending money on the property, then it will be less straightforward to argue that there is no chargeable consideration that has a value or cost.

10.34 Having analysed and resolved the many issues arising[169] from such lifetime arrangements involving the deceased[170] including the identification of deferred tax issues such as overages and clawbacks which may not have been correctly dealt with initially[171] or no exit strategy has been set out in the documents so not included in the original transaction,[172] it will be necessary to administer the estate.[173] Frequently, the terms of the will or the statutory regime on intestacy will not be satisfactory to the parties and there will be alterations in the *prima facie* situation. There are, however, important reliefs that could assist in dealings with residential property within the estate. There are reliefs for the appropriation of chargeable interests by personal representatives in satisfaction of legacies[174] and it seems that this is regarded by HMRC Stamp Taxes as applying where there is an appropriation of the matrimonial home to the widow in satisfaction of the statutory legacy on intestacy. Similarly, there are reliefs for variations of the estate within 2 years following the death of the individual provided that certain conditions are satisfied.[175] These reliefs have been amended from time to time in order to deal with the situation of where the assets in the estate are not sufficient to compensate persons giving up their interest in the residential property or the residential property is subject to a charge. The fact that there is consideration arising from outside the estate ie is not the giving up or transfer of an interest in property within the estate but involves a payment of, for example, cash that is borrowed from a bank or the person taking the property enters into some arrangement with the bank concerning the cancellation of the existing mortgage and the grant of a new mortgage.[176] Given that the residential property is likely to represent the bulk of the estate the costs of ensuring that any dealings in relation to that property is part of the administration of the estate are likely to be disproportionate.[177]

---

[166] Services are not normally regarded as money's worth because they cannot be sold notwithstanding the comments in *Secretan v Hart* 45 TC 701.

[167] FA 2003, Sch 4, para 11.

[168] Ibid, Sch 4, para 11(1).

[169] Including the problem with such domestic arrangements as to whether there is the necessary intention for the arrangements to be legally binding.

[170] Which may be complex, given the current extent of the usage of clawback and overage arrangements in relation to residential property; see **5.187**.

[171] See **5.187**.

[172] See **5.206**; FA 2003, s 81A; Sch 17A, para 12.

[173] See **4.50** on the problems of when the interests of the beneficiaries become chargeable interests.

[174] FA 2003, Sch 3, para 3A; see **11.26**.

[175] Ibid, Sch 3, para 4; see **11.23** and **9.36**.

[176] Ibid, Sch 3, para 4; Sch 4, paras 8 and 8A; see **5.134**.

[177] Note also the guidance issued by HMRC Stamp Taxes in relation to nil rate discretionary trusts for the purpose of mitigating inheritance tax. The stamp duty costs in such situations frequently exceeded the potential inheritance tax saving. See also **10.48**.

Employees

Occupation of premises

10.35 Special rules apply to employees who obtain or occupy property by reason of their employment. It is provided[178] that where a land transaction is entered into by reason of the taxpayer's employment or the employment of a person connected with him, then, if the transaction gives rise to a taxable benefit in kind,[179] he is treated as paying rent equal to the benefit in kind in addition to any rent actually payable. As this has to be a chargeable transaction this provision will apply only where there is a lease or tenancy; no charge arises where there is a licence or a tenancy at will.[180] This is a long-term problem since it is unlikely that the net present value of the aggregate of the actual and the deemed rent will initially exceed the nil rate slice of £125,000 (or the temporary £175,000). However, it is probable that if the occupation is related to employment, the tenancy, if any, will be of a periodic or indeterminate nature. In consequence, although taxed as a lease for one year,[181] if it continues for more than one year the lease term increases by one year on an annual basis. The stamp duty land tax position will have to be reviewed annually if there is any risk that the net present value of the actual and deemed rent could become taxable. Land transaction returns will be required annually once the rent is taxable, although because the rent is variable after the retrospective review on the expiration of the fifth year of the term the taxable rent will be the assumed rent ie the highest deemed rent payable during any 12 consecutive months in the 5-year period. If the occupation is by reason of employment but is exempt because the accommodation is provided for the performance of duties[182] the chargeable consideration is limited to the actual consideration.

Benefits or payment in kind

10.36 From time to time and for a variety of reasons some of which may be related to tax and national insurance mitigation an employee may be remunerated or given a bonus payment in kind, which includes interests in land. If the transaction is entered into by reason of the employment of the person or a person connected with him but does not fall within the income tax regime referred to in the preceding paragraph the transaction is chargeable upon a consideration that is taken to be not less than the market value of the subject-matter of the transaction[183] on the effective date.[184] This charge is, of course, not limited to the vesting by the company in the employee of any residential property occupied by him.

Relocation of employees

10.37 Two areas of relief are available for acquisition of residential property from employees by either their employer or a relocation company in connection with certain changes of employment or workplace,[185] namely:

---

[178]   FA 2003, Sch 4, para 12.
[179]   Pursuant to the Income Tax (Earnings and Pensions) Act 2003.
[180]   These are not chargeable interests; FA 2003, s 48.
[181]   FA 2003, Sch 17A, para 4; see **7.119**.
[182]   Income Tax (Earnings and Pensions) Act 2003, s 99.
[183]   Which is wider than the chargeable interest; FA 2003, s 43(6).
[184]   FA 2003, Sch 4, para 12(1)(c).
[185]   Ibid, Sch 6A, paras 5 and 6.

The acquisition of the property by the employer.

10.38 In times of recession where companies may be reorganising and there is a certain amount of mobility and relocation of employees and there are difficulties for relocating employees in disposing of property, arrangements to provide an employee with funds to acquire property at the new location will become important because the transaction is likely to involve some form of land exchange or a subsale. Essentially, the employer will agree to acquire the employee's existing property from him in order to provide the funds for the employee to acquire property at his new location. The employer will, if possible, wish to avoid increasing the costs of this arrangement by not having to pay stamp duty land tax. A limited form of subsale relief is available.[186] This applies where a dwelling is acquired from an individual (whether alone or with other individuals) by his employer. The employer's acquisition is exempt from the charge to stamp duty land tax provided that the individual occupied the dwelling as his only or main residence at some time in the period of 2 years ending with the date of the acquisition by the employer:

- the acquisition is made in connection with a change of residence by the individual resulting from relocation of employment;

- the consideration for the acquisition does not exceed the market value of the dwelling;

- the area of the land does not exceed the permitted area.[187] For these purposes the permitted area in relation to a dwelling means land occupied and enjoyed with the dwelling as its garden or grounds provided that it does not exceed an area of 0.5 of a hectare (which 0.5 includes the site of the dwelling) or such larger area as is required for the reasonable enjoyment of the dwelling as a dwelling having regard to the size and character. This is very similar to the exemption from capital gains tax for the principal private residence[188] and given the reliance of HMRC Stamp Taxes upon the Capital Gains Tax section of the Revenue for technical advice and assistance, it is likely that the criteria applied for capital gains tax will also be applied in this situation. When determining the permitted area, because the area exceeds the 0.5 of a hectare, the area to be taken into account is that part of the land that would be the most suitable for occupation and enjoyment with the dwelling as a garden or grounds if the rest of the land were separately occupied.[189] Where the land exceeds the permitted area but the other conditions for the relief are satisfied, the chargeable consideration for the acquisition is taken to be the amount calculated by deducting the market value of the permitted area from the market value of the dwelling.[190] An individual is relocated as regards his employment where there is a change of place of employment due to either his becoming an employee or the employer (ie is moving between employers) or an alteration of the duties of his employment with the same employer or an alteration of the place where he normally performs those duties.[191] It is necessary to show that the change of residence is one that results from the relocation of the employment. For these purposes the relocation results from the change, if the change is made wholly or mainly to allow the individual to have his residence

---

[186] Ibid, Sch 6A, para 5.
[187] Ibid, Sch 6A, para 7(3).
[188] Taxation of Chargeable Gains Act 1992, s 222.
[189] FA 2003, Sch 6A, para 7(4).
[190] Ibid, Sch 6A, para 5(3).
[191] Ibid, Sch 6A, para 5(4).

within a reasonable daily travelling distance of his new place of employment and his former residence is not within a reasonable travelling distance of that place.[192] The new place of employment for the individual means the place where the individual normally performs or is normally to perform the duties of his employment after the relocation; and

- the acquisition must be of a major interest in the dwelling and consist of a 'transfer'. Notwithstanding the ambiguities in the plain English legislation, it appears that in this situation 'transfer' means that the employee disposes of the whole of his existing interest in his residence to the employer. The relief does not include the grant of a lease by the employee to the employer.[193]

The market value of the dwelling and of the permitted area are references to the market value of the major interest in the dwelling and of that interest so far as it relates to the permitted area.[194] An individual's employer includes a prospective employer.[195]

Acquisition by relocator companies

10.39 Employers may not be willing to take on the responsibility for dealing with or becoming the owners, even temporarily, of the employee's existing residence and so may enter into a contract with a company to acquire the property. In order to reduce the costs to the employer it is important that the relocator company does not incur stamp duty land tax on the acquisition of the employee's existing premises, although it is inevitable that the employee will have to pay stamp duty land tax upon the acquisition of his new residence at his new place of employment.

A relief is available where a dwelling is acquired by a property trader from an individual, whether alone or with other individuals,[196] provided that:

- the acquisition is made in the course of a business that consists of or includes acquiring dwellings from individuals in connection with a change of residence resulting from the relocation of employment;

- the individual occupied the dwelling as his only or main residence at some time in the period of 2 years ending with the date of the acquisition;

- the acquisition is made in connection with a change of residence by the individual resulting from relocation of employment;

- the consideration for the acquisition does not exceed the market value of the dwelling;

- the property trader does not intend to spend more than the permitted amount on the refurbishment of the dwelling. This involves two hurdles that have to be crossed. It is limited to 'refurbishment' which means the carrying out of works that enhance or are intended to enhance the value of the dwelling but does not

---

[192]   Ibid, Sch 6A, para 5(5).
[193]   Ibid, Sch 6A, para 5(6)(a).
[194]   Ibid, Sch 6A, para 5(6)(b).
[195]   Ibid, Sch 6A, para 5(6)(c).
[196]   Ibid, Sch 6A, para 6(1).

include either cleaning the dwelling or works required solely for the purposes of ensuring that the dwelling meets minimum safety standards.[197] Also the amount that can be expended on the enhancement of the value of the dwelling must be not more than £10,000 or 5 per cent of the consideration for the acquisition of the dwelling whichever is the greater but this cannot exceed a maximum of £20,000;[198]

- the property trader must not intend to grant a lease or licence of the dwelling by acquiring it and reselling it;[199] or permit any of its principals or employees or any person connected with any of its principals or employees to occupy the dwelling; but this does not apply to the grant of a lease or licence to the individual who is being relocated provided that this lease or licence does not exceed a period of more than 6 months;

- the area of the land acquired must not exceed the permitted area.[200]

The conditions relating to relocation of employment, permitted area, change of residence resulting from employment are the same as those considered above in relation to the relief provided for employers.[201]

10.40 The relief granted to a property trader, which is a company or a limited liability partnership or a partnership whose members are all either companies or limited liability partnerships that carry on the business of buying and selling dwellings.[202] The relief is withdrawn if the property trader spends more than the permitted amount on the refurbishment of the dwelling or grants a lease or licence of the dwelling other than to the individual limited to a period of 6 months or permits any of its principals or employees or any person connected with any of its principals or employees to occupy the dwelling.[203]

Market value problem

10.41 The practical difficulty both of these situations is persuading HMRC Stamp Taxes that the price paid to the individual does not exceed the market value.[204] This has given rise to difficulties in the past particularly in relation to the restriction introduced in relation to subsale relief that the subsale must be at not less than the market value of the property. Certain officers in HMRC Stamp Taxes and employees of the District Valuer have, from time to time, subscribed strongly to a theory that property prices cannot go down. This means that where the price paid to the employee exceeds the price ultimately obtained on the resale of the property, HMRC Stamp taxes have taken the point that the employee was overpaid and received more than the market value. Dealing with this is a particularly difficult problem since employees are likely to become involved in the relocation reliefs only where they are having difficulties selling their property at the price they hope to receive within an acceptable timeframe to enable them to fund the purchase of their new dwelling. This means that the employer will be under pressure, either personally or through pressure upon the relocator company, to allow a purchase which

---

[197] Ibid, Sch 6A, para 9(1).
[198] Ibid, Sch 6A, para 9(2).
[199] Ibid, Sch 6A, para 6(2)(e)(ii).
[200] Ibid, Sch 6A, para 6(2)(f).
[201] Ibid, Sch 6A, para 6(3), (4) and (5).
[202] Ibid, Sch 6A, para 8(1).
[203] Ibid, Sch 6A, para 11(5).
[204] Ibid, Sch 6A, paras 6(2)(d) and 5(2)(c).

may produce a loss. The starting point of HMRC Stamp Taxes and the District Valuer is, of course, fundamentally flawed since it does not depend upon the state of the recession and the property market at any particular time. It does, however, mean that if the parties are anxious to avoid a protracted and pointless but nevertheless expensive dispute with HMRC Stamp Taxes that they take proper steps by means of an appropriate number of valuers with weighted average figures in order to arrive at the price to be paid to the employee. Fortunately, HMRC Stamp Taxes tend to be extremely reluctant at certain levels to take on independent professional valuers and provided that an appropriate up-to-date certificate of figures and values is presented to them prepared by correctly instructed independent professional advisers they may well accept the numbers. However, where the parties are seeking to justify their decision by hindsight, which is weakened by the fact that the price for the resale is lower, they are likely to encounter a degree of stubbornness by HMRC Stamp Taxes who are well aware of the blackmail power they exercise because the amount of tax involved is small relative to the costs.

ENFRANCHISEMENT AND SIMILAR OPERATIONS

10.42 Residential tenants frequently seek to increase the length of their tenancy.[205] This may take the form of an acquisition of all or part of the reversionary interest whether the freehold or head leasehold interest or an extension of the terms of their lease which involves a surrender and regrant.[206]

10.43 The acquisition by the tenant of the reversionary interest upon his lease for a consideration is subject to stamp duty land tax at least where the consideration exceeds the nil rate threshold for the time being in force even where this is effected pursuant to any statutory provisions enabling the tenant to acquire the landlord's interest.[207] The lease and the reversionary interest may subsequently be merged, but the merger operation of itself is not taxable since there is no 'acquisition' as the 'transaction' involves only one person;[208] the tax will have been paid in acquiring the various interests that are merged.

---

[205] On the increase of the term of a lease see **7.223** and **9.30**; on lease renewals see **7.121**. On the reduction of the term of a lease see FA 2003, Sch 17A, para 15A(2); see **7.226**.

[206] *Friends Provident Life Office v British Railways Board* [1996] 1 All ER 336.

[207] The charge to stamp duty land tax arises where the transaction is under any statutory provision: FA 2003, s 43(2). This assumes that HMRC Stamp Taxes intend the legislation to mean a transaction that arises where a person exercises a statutory power, which may be a transaction arising 'by operation of law' rather than where the completion takes effect under a statutory provision. There is a fundamental defect in the drafting because of the ambiguity of key provisions. It is unclear whether the legislation is intended to apply where the transaction arises by operation of law or pursuant to statutory provision or whether the transaction is simply completed by operation of law or statutory provision. The legislation is not consistent on this point. It is, however, assumed that the tax is intended to apply where the transaction itself arises not by reason of the contractual negotiation but a form of deemed contract arising because some person exercises a statutory power. However, as the amendments in relation to the variations of estates (FA 2003, Sch 3, para 4) and those dealing with the allocation of assets by trustees without consent (FA 2003, Sch 16, para 8) indicate that this is regarded as being a potential problem where a power is exercised which produces a change in property interests but which is not chargeable because there is no consent.

[208] It is not possible to 'acquire' from or to 'transfer' to oneself; see, for example, *Rye v Rye* [1961] 2 All ER 146, a point consistently accepted by HMRC Stamp Taxes for the purposes of stamp duty. A person cannot convey to himself even where he may be acting in a different capacity. This was, in effect, accepted by the Special Commissioners for the purposes of stamp duty reserve tax (*Save and Prosper Securities Ltd v IRC* [2000] STC SpC 38) and was applied by HMRC Stamp Taxes even where there was a change of nominee holder of the legal title transferring to himself for the purpose of redesignating the account because there had been an unstamped transfer of the beneficial interest behind the legal title. It is unclear how far this

Collective enfranchisements[209]

10.44 Special rules originally applied where a chargeable transaction is entered into by an RTE company[210] in pursuance of a right of collective enfranchisement but the legislation creating RTE companies has not been implemented.[211] In consequence, the provisions were amended.[212] The relief has been revised because of the non-existence of RTE companies is now currently available[213] where the chargeable transaction is entered into by a person or persons nominated or approved by tenants of flats in premises who are entitled either to a right of first refusal pursuant to Landlord and Tenant Act 1987, Part 1, or to collective enfranchisement pursuant to Leasehold Reform, Housing and Urban Development Act 1993, Part 1, Chapter 7 as these terms and conditions are defined by these Acts. In these cases the chargeable consideration is not adjusted but special rules apply when determining the rate. The transaction is broken down to some extent for the purposes of possibly obtaining the lower rates of stamp duty land tax. It is provided[214] that the rate of tax is to be determined by reference to the fraction of the relevant consideration produced by dividing the total amount of the consideration by the number of qualifying flats (as defined by the two above Acts) in the premises. The tax chargeable is then determined by applying that rate to the chargeable consideration for each individual transaction even where the relevant consideration exceeds the threshold.[215]

TENANT COMPANIES

10.45 For convenience in the management and maintenance of common parts the ultimate reversionary interest may be vested in a company owned by the tenants or freeholders.[216] The acquisition of the freehold by a tenant or by a management company[217] owned by the tenants of a block of flats to hold the common parts and to deal with services and similar matters, is a chargeable consideration subject to stamp duty land tax upon the consideration provided.

10.46 Various technical issues might arise in such transactions with management companies, which will require to be investigated: for example, where a developer has constructed a block of flats and granted leases to the tenants at a premium and for a ground rent, whether or not uncertain by reason of service and other charges being included therein,[218] the value of the freehold interest is likely to be relatively small. This may be transferred to a management company. Parties might be tempted to think that

---

principle has been affected by the provisions dealing with nominees and beneficial owners pursuant to FA 2003, Sch 16, para 3 (as amended). Certain aspects of these provisions may not have been necessary if the persons responsible for the legislation had worked upon the basis that there cannot be a transfer to oneself even in a representative capacity.

[209] A similar relief applies to transactions involving crofts in Scotland: FA 2003, s 75.

[210] 'Rights to enfranchise' company as defined by Leasehold Reform, Housing and Urban Development Act 1993, s 4A.

[211] *Elizabeth Court (Bournemouth) Ltd v HMRC* [2008] SCT (SCD) 366.

[212] FA 2009, s 80.

[213] FA 2003, s 74 (as amended by FA 2009, s 80).

[214] Ibid, s 74(2).

[215] There does not appear to be any application of the linked transaction rules where any of the qualifying tenants are connected persons.

[216] On estate rent charges see **4.55**.

[217] It may be helpful to organise such a company so that it qualifies for the special rate for collective enfranchisement FA 2003, s 74 (as amended).

[218] See **7.138**.

the actual consideration being small, there may be little or no stamp duty land tax to pay.[219] This, however, could be extremely deceptive. For example:

- the consideration will be the aggregate consideration and not separate acquisitions for the purchases provided by the individual tenants. This is a case of a single collective acquisition not separate acquisitions where the linked transaction principles might apply unless the revised collective enfranchise relief[220] is available;

- the management company may be subject to the charge to stamp duty land tax upon market value for dealings involving connected companies.[221] This will require the parties to take appropriate steps to justify the market value figure included in the land transaction return;[222]

- where there is an acquisition of the reversionary interest or a freehold of the common parts, the tenants may take the opportunity to vary their leases.[223] Where these are merely modifications of the general covenants it is unlikely that any consideration provided by the tenants will exceed the nil rate threshold but should it do so tax will be payable.[224] Modifications of the ground rent will be subject to the general rules for increases and reductions of rent.[225] Frequently this will include an increase in the term of the existing lease. This will be a surrender and regrant for which reliefs are available[226] so that no charge will arise upon the management company as landlord and the tenant will be taxable only in respect of the rent for the increased term but with a possible credit for stamp duty land tax paid on his existing lease;

- in some cases the tenants may enter into a subsale arrangement pursuant to which they may agree to purchase the head interest and agree to transfer this to the management company.[227] There are numerous possible variations on this theme but have certain common issues that should be investigated. The tenants may wish to structure the transaction so as to obtain subsale relief.[228] If the transfer to the management company is part of the arrangements for the variations of the existing leases, this is likely to be a land exchange as far as the management company is concerned[229] subjecting it to a market value charge. Fortunately HMRC Stamp Taxes are beginning to accept the argument that the market value has to be determined taking into account the contractual obligations to grant the lease back which can substantially depress the market value but this clearly indicates that the leaseback has the full market value. As regards the tenants this transaction may not qualify as a surrender and regrant so that the reliefs may not be available, unless the contracts specifically arrange for the existing leases to be surrendered as part of the arrangements;

---

[219] It is unclear whether the interest, being reversionary, is residential or non-residential property for a nil rate.
[220] FA 2003, s 74; FA 2009, s 80.
[221] Ibid, s 53.
[222] Where the management company is 'connected' with the tenants there may be linked transactions affecting the rates particularly the availability of the lower rates for the management company.
[223] It must be noted that the funding of the management company may produce a taxable premium; see FA 2003, Sch 17A, para 18A.
[224] FA 2003, Sch 17A, para 15A (as amended).
[225] Ibid, Sch 17A, paras 14 and 15 (as amended by FA 2006 so that these provisions will not normally apply where the lease was granted before 1 December 2003); Sch 19; see also **7.1**.
[226] See **7.223**.
[227] See further **10.23**.
[228] FA 2003, s 42; see **Chapter 6** but note FA 2003, ss 75A–75C (the general anti-avoidance provisions).
[229] Ibid, s 47; see **5.150**.

- where the acquisition of the freehold is made either directly or indirectly by the new management company it will be necessary to fund the purchase price. The tenants may be willing to contribute an appropriate amount of share capital to the management company which should be essentially neutral as far as charges to stamp duty land tax are concerned. Alternatively, they may enter into some arrangement under which, when their leases are modernised, there will be a contribution to the landlord that could be a potentially stampable premium for the new leases whether arising by transfer of the freehold in consideration of the grant of a new lease back plus the adjustment or by means of some more efficient version of surrender and regrant for a small cash payment.[230] This will avoid the charge that might otherwise arise upon the full market value of the new leases of the flats. Alternatively, the tenants may prefer to have the mortgages and interest charges at their personal level rather than have some form of collective mortgage at the management company level. In this situation there may be some form of loan or debt arising whereby money is owed by the management company to the tenants. In this situation the anti-avoidance provisions of FA 2003, Sch 17A, para 18A need to be noted. These deal with the situation of where there is a loan in relation to the grant of a lease. In this situation the loan may constitute some form of stampable premium but without any possibility of refund if and when the loan is repaid.[231]

MATRIMONIAL AND CIVIL PARTNERSHIP BREAKDOWN

10.47

(a) The breakdown of a marriage or civil partnership will frequently result in mutual adjustments of property interest, including interest in land such as the former matrimonial home. Unlike other taxes, there are no general exceptions, as with other taxes, for dealings between spouses or civil partners. Stamp duty land tax applies in full to any such dealings.[232] There is, however, a limited exemption from stamp duty land tax in relation to a transaction between one party to a marriage and the other where it is effected:

- in pursuance of an order of a court made on granting a decree of divorce, nullity of marriage or judicial separation of the parties;
- in pursuance of an order of a court made in connection with a dissolution or annulment of the marriage or the parties' judicial separation, at any time after the granting of such a decree;
- in pursuance of an order of a court made under Matrimonial Causes Act 1973, s 22A, s 23A or s 24A or Family Law (Scotland) Act 1985, ss 8(2) and 14;
- at any time in pursuance of an agreement between the parties made in contemplation of or otherwise in connection with[233] the dissolution or annulment of the marriage, their judicial separation or the making of a separation order in respect of them.[234]

---

[230] FA 2003, Sch 17A, paras 9 and 16; see **7.194**.
[231] See **7.95**.
[232] For putting the matrimonial home into joint names where there is a mortgage on the property, see **5.143** and **10.27**.
[233] These are words of the very widest application and can apply to subsequent transactions that have a link in a business sense with the original agreement: *Clarke Chapman – John Thompson v IRC* [1975] STC 567.
[234] FA 2003, Sch 3, para 3.

It will be noted that directly or indirectly some form of Court order is required so that the property is made pursuant to such an order or in contemplation of an order being made. Other arrangements may be taxable should they involve mutual transfers of property which may be land exchanges or transfers of chargeable interests for a consideration in kind, subject to the relief for transferring property into a single name pursuant to FA 2003, Sch 4, para 8 (as amended).

(b) The relief has been extended to civil partnerships.[235] There is an exemption from stamp duty land tax in respect of a transaction between one party to a civil partnership and another provided that it is effected:

- in pursuance of an order of a Court made on granting in respect of the parties an order or decree for the dissolution or annulment of the civil partnership or their judicial separation;
- in pursuance of an order of a Court made in connection with the dissolution or annulment of the civil partnership, or the parties judicial separation, at any time after the granting of such an order or decree for dissolution, annulment or judicial separation;
- in pursuance of an order of a Court made at any time under the provisions of the Civil Partnership Act 2004, Sch 5,[236] or an incidental order of the Court made under any provisions of the Civil Partnership Act 2004;[237]
- at any time in pursuance of an agreement of the parties made in contemplation of or otherwise in connection with the dissolution or annulment of the civil partnership, their judicial separation or the making of a separation order in respect of them.

HOME ANNUITY, REVERSION AND SIMILAR SCHEMES

General principles

10.48 There are many arrangements designed to enable people to maintain their standard of living by freeing up the capital locked in their home. Many of these have potential long-term problems such as rolled up interest and although such an arrangement might appear to be effective to mitigate stamp duty land tax in the short term the longer-term costs are significantly greater. These can vary from straightforward mortgages, which are exempt interests,[238] to variations upon sale and leaseback and the grant of annuities. There are many variations on the theme and it is possible only to illustrate a few as a means of indicating the types of problem area that may arise, as set out in outline below. These arrangements may involve several movements of chargeable interests because of the conveyancing issues involved or in order to provide the parties with reasonable security. However, each such movement of land interests is potentially taxable and such property movement may involve multiple charges to tax upon market value[239] because there is a land exchange involved.[240] HMRC Stamp Taxes are anxious

---

[235] Ibid, Sch 4, para 3A.
[236] Which correspond to the provisions in the Matrimonial Causes Act 1973, s 22A, 23A or 24A.
[237] Corresponding with Family Law (Scotland) Act 1985, s 82 by virtue of s 40(1) thereof.
[238] FA, s 48(2)(a) and (3)(a) but foreclosure and other enforcement measures may give rise to a charge to stamp duty land tax; see ibid, Sch 4, para 8; see **5.134**.
[239] Fortunately, HMRC Stamp Taxes are, albeit reluctantly, beginning to accept the argument that where property is transferred subject to an obligation to grant back rights to the transferor or, possibly, third parties the value of the interest being transferred can be depressed by reference to the impact of the rights to be regranted. The property is to be valued upon the basis that it is acquired subject to the existing rights and therefore at a lower value than the unencumbered freehold would attract on a sale in the open market. This

to exploit conveyancing consequences in order to increase the tax charge.[241] Movements of land interests are now more likely to be subject to stamp duty land tax, so that a sale and leaseback will *prima facie* be subject to double taxation as a land exchange[242] subject to a relief for the leaseback which now applies to residential property[243] and the alternative finance regime may be more beneficial should the transaction meet the necessary conditions.[244] Structuring the arrangements in a suitable fashion can mitigate the potential stamp duty land tax costs. For example, there can be a significant tax difference between the sale of a partial interest in consideration of the grant of an annuity and a part sale for cash which is applied in the purchase of an annuity.[245] Without prudent investigation of the issues the stamp duty land tax costs can make substantial inroads into the amount of cash available to the land owner.

10.49 Insofar as it is possible to create the relevant property structure without involving transfers and retransfers or regrants of freehold or leasehold interests,[246] and moving only non-major interests in the land, then the charging provisions may operate on a less onerous basis. It is provided that where there are exchanges of non-major interests on both sides of the transaction, the stamp duty land tax is chargeable only upon any consideration other than the property interests moving, such as the cash being paid. There is a potentially large charge where there is a transfer of land in consideration of the grant of an annuity. There are certain arbitrary rules concerned with the valuation of annuities which, broadly, mean that the chargeable consideration is the amount of the annuity payable over 12 years. This arbitrary period of 12 years applies regardless of the life expectancy of the transferor of the land who is the annuitant.[247] There is a potentially large difference between market value, deemed consideration and actuarial values which may provide a basis for planning the arrangement so as to mitigate stamp taxes. Indeed, the parties may feel that it is cheaper to transfer the interest or part interest in the land for a cash sum, which cash sum is separately applied in purchasing the annuity.[248] The cash sum being related to the market value of the land interest being acquired and the actuarial value of the annuity is likely to produce a lower chargeable consideration than the arbitrary rules for capitalising annuities in FA 2003, s 52 where the chargeable interest is transferred as the purchase consideration for the grant of the annuity. This may produce a much lower chargeable consideration than the rules relating

---

is particularly important where HMRC Stamp Taxes challenge the argument that the words 'excepting and reserving' restrict the interest being transferred and so affect its value by pressing their argument that little or nothing can be excepted and reserved and there has to be a transfer of the unencumbered interest with the grant back of the appropriate rights. Fortunately, the obligation to grant back the rights is now recognised as affecting the market value. Compare *Park v IRC* [1970] 1 All ER 611 and [1972] 1 All ER 394.

[240] FA 2003, s 47; Sch 4, para 5 but reliefs such as sale and leaseback (FA 2003, s 57A) or even alternative finance relief (FA 2003, ss 71A and following) may provide surprisingly useful areas of relief.

[241] But note the comments against undue reliance by HMRC on conveyancing requirements in order to create tax liabilities which would not arise if the conveyance principles did not compel the parties to adopt a particular route in *Sargaison v Roberts* [1969] 3 All ER 1072.

[242] FA 2003, s 47; see **5.150**.

[243] Ibid, s 57A (as amended); see **7.259**; but this may not be compatible with inheritance tax arrangements.

[244] FA 2003, ss 71A–73B.

[245] See ibid, s 52.

[246] Note the special rules for leases for life; FA 2003, Sch 17A, para 4(2).

[247] See ibid, s 52; see **5.192**.

[248] There is, however, the possibility that notwithstanding the general principle that where there are a choice of routes available to a taxpayer choosing the route which is perceived to be more tax efficient is not tax avoidance (*Willoughby v IRC* [1995] STC 143; *Sherdley v Sherdley* [1987] STC 266) provided, at least, that the taxpayer is not abusing that choice by seeking to make use of the particular structure for purposes which the judiciary believe Parliament did not intend to be available in the circumstances, it is theoretically possible that HMRC Stamp Taxes might seek to apply the general anti-avoidance provisions pursuant to FA 2003, ss 75A–75C; see **2.19**.

to the calculation of duty upon annuities as consideration. Similarly, if it is possible to deal in limited or equitable interests which, *prima facie*, would not be major interests so that the land exchange rules apply on a limited basis charging only any equality payment, then there will be only one chargeable transaction subject to duty upon its actual consideration.[249]

10.50 The different possible structures have widely different stamp duty land tax consequences which require investigation in each case. Similarly, a transfer of the freehold interest in consideration of a leaseback will, *prima facie*, be a land exchange[250] with potential double charges.[251] In consequence, the company providing the funds will be taxed upon the market value of the land being received. This will, *prima facie*, be the open market value of the land, which is not necessarily the same as the sum being paid to the life tenant; but it will be a value that is subject to the obligation to grant the leaseback to the lessee/person realising the equity value. In this situation HMRC Stamp Taxes will not necessarily be prepared to accept the price being paid since there are special circumstances which may mean that the actual circumstances cannot be regarded as a transaction between a willing buyer and a willing seller.[252] However, it is usually possible to persuade them to accept that the market value is reduced by the obligation to grant the leaseback. The leaseback itself will be taxed upon market value which will be calculated by reference to the rent. However, in this situation it is necessary to put the argument to HMRC Stamp Taxes that the market value of the leaseback has to be determined upon an actuarial basis. The stamp duty land tax legislation provides[253] that a lease for life is not to be treated in accordance with the provisions of the Law of Property Act 1925[254] but as being a lease for 1 year which 'grows' for each year that the tenant remains in occupation. However, the growing of the lease relates to the taxation of the rent and not to the market value of the premium. There will, therefore, be questions as to whether the premium has to be determined in the context of the actuarial value of the leaseback. Since this is a valuation of the freehold interest and not the valuation of the leaseback it should not be affected by the notional rules of a lease for 1 year; similarly, because the transaction looking at the price in the open market, the fact that the lease is deemed to be for 1 year should not affect the basic valuation principles which may be linked to actuarial factors although the potential increase in the liability for stamp duty land tax that would be incurred by any assignee[255] may be factors that can be taken into account to depress the value of the leaseback.

Mortgage

10.51 The raising of cash by borrowing secured by a charge on the land is free of tax[256] and special reliefs are available for fundraising by means of the alternative finance regime.[257]

---

[249]   FA 2003, Sch 4, para 5(4).
[250]   Ibid, s 47.
[251]   Ibid, Sch 4, para 5.
[252]   See *Lap Shun Textiles Industrial Co v Collector of Stamp Revenue* [1976] AC 530; *Cowan de Groot Properties Ltd v Eagle Trust plc* [1991] BCLC 1045.
[253]   FA 2003, Sch 17A, para 4(2).
[254]   Section 149.
[255]   FA 2003, s 81A; Sch 17A, para 12.
[256]   See **3.30**.
[257]   FA 2003, ss 71A to 73B; FA 2009, Sch 61.

Purchases of part interest

10.52 A purchase of a part interest in the property will attract stamp duty land tax upon the purchase price. This applies whether it is a sale of a current interest so that the parties became tenants in common or it is a purchase of a reversion on the life of the current owner. These will be taxable upon the actual consideration. The taxpayer will be the institution providing the funds, but there may be a slight tax saving if the stamp tax costs are excluded from the purchase price. Obviously the funding institution will be anxious to pass these costs to the vendor, but the manner of so doing may increase the tax such as if the vendor agrees to indemnify the purchaser out of the sale proceeds rather than the purchaser reducing the price and bearing the stamp duty land tax costs.

Creating a trust

10.53 There are potential long-term issues to be noted. A sale of a current interest creating a tenancy in common will mean that there are two owners of the property for future transactions and the compliance rules for joint owners[258] will apply but the fact that there are joint owners, the interests of the beneficial interest may not be valued as a simple proportion of the whole market value but the individual interests may qualify for a minority interest discount.[259] A sale of a future interest may take effect by creating some form of trustee when the rules for trustees of a settlement will apply[260] and transfers in consideration of the grant of annuities are subject to tax upon the capitalised value of the annuity. The rules for calculating this amount have eased somewhat,[261] albeit they remain rather crude in their operation where the annuity is variable.[262]

Sale and leaseback

10.54 It is possible to fund the purchase of an interest in land about to be acquired by an onward sale of all or part of the land to be acquired[263] for a cash sum and a leaseback. There may be an arrangement under which there is a sale, probably for an amount significantly below the market value of the property, because of the amount of cash being raised and the terms of the leaseback. Such a transaction can arise where the person is granted some form of lease or underlease, whether for life or a fixed term, at a rent significantly below the market rent being, in effect, some form of interest cost on the amount of cash paid for the freehold interest. It is, in substance, a loan at interest dressed up as a lease at a rent but it is not treated as a mortgage. Such a transaction will fall into the land exchange rules,[264] since it will be part of the arrangement that the homeowner agrees to sell the part interest in the house in consideration of the funding institution entering into the leaseback, ie another land transaction. In such a situation, since there are dealings in freehold and leasehold interests, there will be an exchange of

---

[258] Ibid, s 103; Sch 16, para 3 (as amended).

[259] *Re Wight* [1982] 2 EGLR 236.

[260] FA 2003, Sch 16 (as amended); see **Chapter 9**.

[261] Ibid, s 52; see **5.192**.

[262] Ibid, s 52(7).

[263] Care my be needed in order to reduce the costs of the transaction by making use of the limited subsale relief pursuant to FA 2003, s 45; see **Chapter 6**.

[264] FA 2003, s 47, Sch 4, para 5; see **5.150**; but many practitioners appear to ignore these technical issues and report the transaction as a sale.

major interests within the charging provisions,[265] and both parties will have to produce separate land transaction returns as they are separate transactions.[266] In consequence:

- the funding institution will be liable to report and to pay stamp duty land tax upon the market value of the land being acquired,[267] not merely that part interest in the land for which it is paying. This will be the value as encumbered by the leaseback, contrary to the traditional view of HMRC Stamp Taxes; but since the leaseback will be at a full rent the freehold will inevitably have a major value;

- the homeowner will be liable to report and to pay stamp duty land tax upon:
  - the market value of the lease being acquired which will be a substantial value depending upon the level of the rent. However, because this is now based upon market value, it will be the actuarial value of the interest. However, it should be noted that leases for life and similar arrangements are leases for indefinite terms[268] but when calculating the stamp duty such leases are treated as leases for a term of one year but are deemed to extend if the tenancy continues for more than one year. This should not affect the market value of the leaseback which is the actuarial value, but it will affect the rent and reporting and payment obligations in respect thereof as the tenancy continues;[269] plus
  - the net present value of the rent, albeit reduced.

  In these situations the landowner may be eligible for relief for the leaseback pursuant to FA 2003, s 57A.

10.55 Relief may be available for sale and leaseback or lease and underlease back[270] where:[271]

- A transfers or grants a major interest to B;

- out of that interest B grants a lease to A;[272]

- the consideration provided by B for the sale or grant of the lease is wholly or partly the grant of the leaseback or underlease back;

- the only other consideration, if any, provided by B is the payment of money or the assumption by B of a debt or the satisfaction or release of a debt or a combination thereof. For these purposes it is irrelevant whether the money is in sterling or some other currency. The type of 'debt' to be assumed is an obligation, whether certain or contingent, to pay a sum of money either immediately or at a future date.[273]

---

[265] Ibid, Sch 4, para 5(3).
[266] Ibid, s 47.
[267] It seems that HMRC Stamp Taxes are beginning in practice to accept that the market value of the land being so acquired is reduced, if appropriate, because of the obligation to grant the lease back.
[268] FA 2003, s 120 (as originally enacted but repealed).
[269] Ibid, Sch 17A, para 4.
[270] It must, however, be noted this relief from stamp duty land tax may not be compatible with reliefs from inheritance tax.
[271] FA 2003, s 57A (as amended); see further **7.239**.
[272] There are no connected party provisions for a leaseback to a subsidiary company.
[273] FA 2003, s 57A(4).

The relief is not available, for current purposes, where it is part of a subsale transaction[274] or where A and B are members of the same corporate group for stamp duty land tax purposes.[275]

Transfer for annuity

10.56 It is provided that where the chargeable consideration for a land transaction consists of an annuity, then, *prima facie*, the consideration is the aggregate amount payable pursuant to the annuity. This appears to apply only where the annuity is for less than 12 years, and different rules apply where the annuity is for life, in perpetuity, for an indefinite period or for a definite period exceeding 12 years. In these cases the consideration is the aggregate amount payable in respect of the 12 annual payments.[276] Provision is made for variable annuities, although for these purposes, index linking providing for adjustment in line with the RPI, but no other form of indexation is ignored,[277] the annuity is not treated as variable. In other cases where the amount of the annuity is variable, the charging and computation provisions in the legislation it is uncertain, and provisions requiring a reasonable estimate of the amount to be paid, presumably over the relevant 12-year period, apply.[278] However, this initial reasonable estimate of the amount to be paid appears to be final, since the provisions for adjustment where the consideration becomes ascertained and the right to pay by instalments does not apply.[279] HMRC Stamp Taxes are unlikely to object where there is an overestimate and it appears that it will be difficult to amend the land transaction return or reclaim overpaid tax;[280] but if there is an underestimate it is most probable that allegations of fraud and/or negligence will be made.

Alternative finance arrangements[281]

10.57 Since certain persons are prohibited by usury rules from either lending or borrowing money and paying or receiving interest the funding of property transactions to such person could prove rather expensive for stamp duty land tax. In order to evade the restrictions upon interest payments and receipts it is necessary for the party to acquire an interest in the property which generates an income that substitutes for interest. This would create an interest in land within the charge to stamp duty land tax and possible land exchanges rather like a sale and leaseback. Reliefs are provided in this situation.[282] Reliefs are provided so that such form of sale and saleback or sale and leaseback transactions are, broadly, equated with mortgages and outside the charge to stamp duty land tax. However, since the relief cannot be restricted to persons within a particular religious community the relief is available to other persons and may, in suitable circumstances, be helpful in relation to equity release schemes. These may be more useful than the sale and leaseback provisions[283] because the latter impose a charge upon the transfer of the freehold and exempt the lease with a potential trap upon the

---

[274] Ibid, s 57A(3).
[275] Ibid, s 57A(4); Sch 7, Part 1; *Escoigne Properties Ltd v IRC* [1958] AC 549.
[276] Ibid, s 52(2).
[277] Ibid, s 53(2).
[278] Ibid, ss 52(5) and 51.
[279] Ibid, s 52(7).
[280] Such mistakes in 'guestimates' are unlikely to be accepted as error or mistake arrangements; see FA 2003, Sch 10, para 34.
[281] See also **7.257**.
[282] FA 2003, ss 71A–73B (as amended).
[283] Ibid, s 57A.

assignment of the lease where a special charge applies to the assignee.[284] For the alternative finance relief both the sale and the leaseback or other arrangements are exempt from charge, although the reliefs are not so widely available because the person providing the funds has to be a financial institution.[285]

FINANCING HOUSE PURCHASES

Mortgages

10.58 The acquisition of a house by means of a loan secured by a mortgage is subject to stamp duty land tax as a purchase or lease of the house but no additional stamp duty land tax arises in respect of the mortgage arrangements since grants of mortgages are not chargeable transactions. They are exempt and not chargeable interests[286] but it should be noted that, although most forms of enforcing the security such as appointing a receiver or exercising the power of sale will not give rise to a charge upon the mortgage,[287] foreclosure of the security in the event of default will be a chargeable transaction being in satisfaction of the mortgage debt.[288]

10.59 Other forms of financing such as sale and leaseback or other exercises may have two consequences:

- they may give rise to chargeable transactions in their own right, as with the case of home annuity schemes considered above;[289]

- the funding operation may amount to a provision of the substantial amount of the consideration required for substantial performance and so trigger the tax charge,[290] as considered below.

Alternative finance[291]

10.60 Special financing does, however, qualify for a limited form of relief in one narrow area designed to cope with problems of financing where parties are restricted by rules against usury or the taking of interest and the financing must take the form of some form of participation in the profits or gains of the property. It should be noted that although these reliefs are intended for the benefit of certain groups in society they are not limited to such persons. Anyone is entitled to obtain the benefit of these reliefs even though they are not subject to restrictions upon their borrowing powers. Two areas of relief are available and these reliefs are being both gradually enlarged and subjected to increasing anti-avoidance rules.

---

[284]   Ibid, Sch 17A, para 11.
[285]   See ibid, s 71A(1).
[286]   Ibid, s 48(2)(a).
[287]   It is important to identify who is the 'vendor' of the interest being sold, for compliance purposes.
[288]   FA 2003, Sch 4, para 8.
[289]   See **10.48**.
[290]   FA 2003, s 44(3)–(7).
[291]   The reliefs are made available in Scotland with suitable modification for Scottish conveyancing principles;
        FA 2003, ss 72 and 72A.

Sale and leaseback arrangements

10.61 Where, pursuant to an arrangement between a person[292] and the financial institution being a bank,[293] a building society[294] or wholly owned subsidiary of either or consumer credit company whereby the financial institution acquires a major interest in land and grants a lease or sublease out of that interest to the person or a company with a consumer credit licence[295] and enters into an arrangement under which the person has a right to require the transfer of the major interest purchased by the reversioner:

- there is an exemption for the transfer of the interest to the financial institution from stamp duty land tax if the vendor under the first transaction is the person or another financial institution by whom the interest was acquired under arrangements similar to those currently being entered into;

- the leaseback is exempt if the acquisition of the major interest by the institution is itself exempt under these provisions provided that any tax chargeable is paid;[296] and

- the re-transfer of the freehold or head leasehold interest to the person originally entitled is exempt from charge provided that the initial acquisition of the major interest and the leaseback is exempt and at all times between then and the transfer of the reversionary interest the interest purchased by the institution is held by it and the lease or sublease granted is held by the person.[297]

Sale and resale

10.62 Where arrangements are entered into between a financial institution and an person[298] pursuant to which the institution (ie a bank or building society as above) purchases a major interest in land and sells that interest to the person, and the person grants the institution a legal mortgage over that interest,[299] then the acquisition of the major interest by the institution is an exempt charge if the vendor is the person concerned or another financial institution which acquired the interest under arrangements similar to those under discussion. The sale to the person is exempt if the financial institution complies with its obligations relating to the first transaction, including the payment of any tax chargeable which would arise where the land is acquired from a third party.

Right to buy

10.63 The stamp duty relief in relation to the right to buy and shared ownership transactions is carried forward into stamp duty land tax.[300]

---

292 This relief was extended to 'persons' and include bodies corporate by FA 2006, s 168 and personal representatives of deceased individuals.
293 Income and Corporation Taxes Act 1988, s 840A.
294 Building Societies Act 1986.
295 FA 2005, s 46.
296 FA 2003, s 71A(3).
297 Ibid, ss 71 and 71A (as amended).
298 Which includes his personal representatives after his death: FA 2003, s 73(6).
299 For definition of legal mortgage, see ibid, s 73(5)(b).
300 Ibid, s 70; Sch 9 (as amended).

10.64 A right to buy transaction is either:

• a sale of a dwelling at a discount or the grant of a lease of a dwelling at a discount by a relevant public sector body; or

• the sale or grant of a lease or dwelling in pursuance of a 'preserved' right to buy ie:
    − if:
      (a) the vendor is either:
          (i) in England and Wales, a person against whom the right to buy under Part 5 of the Housing Act 1985 is exercisable by virtue of that Act s 171A, or
          (ii) in Scotland, a person against whom the right to buy under Housing (Scotland) Act 1987, s 61 is exercisable by virtue of that Act s 81A,
      (b) the purchaser is the qualifying person for the purposes of the preserved right to buy, and
      (c) the dwelling is the qualifying dwelling-house in relation to the purchaser.

10.65 The relevant public bodies are:

• *Government*
    − A Minister of the Crown
    − The Scottish Ministers
    − A Northern Ireland department

• *Local government*
    − A local housing authority within the meaning of the Housing Act 1985
    − A county council in England
    − A council constituted under Local Government etc (Scotland) Act 1994), s 2, the common good of such a council or any trust under its control
    − A district council within the meaning of the Local Government Act (Northern Ireland) 1972

• *Social housing*
    − The Housing Corporation
    − Scottish Homes
    − The Northern Ireland Housing Executive
    − A registered social landlord
    − A housing action trust established under Part 3 of the Housing Act 1988

• *New towns and development corporations*
    − The Commission for the New Towns
    − A development corporation established by an order made, or having effect as if made, under the New Towns Act 1981
    − A development corporation established by an order made, or having effect as if made, under the New Towns (Scotland) Act 1968
    − A new town commission established under New Towns Act (Northern Ireland) 1965, s 7
    − An urban development corporation established by an order made under Local Government, Planning and Land Act 1980, s 135
    − The Welsh Development Agency

- *Police*
  - A police authority within the meaning of Police Act 1996, s 101(1)
  - A police authority within the meaning of Police (Scotland) Act 1967, s 2(1) or 19(9)(b)
  - The Northern Ireland Policing Board

- *Miscellaneous*
  - An Education and Libraries Board within the meaning of the Education and Libraries (Northern Ireland) Order 1986[301]
  - The United Kingdom Atomic Energy Authority
  - Any person mentioned in Housing (Scotland) Act 1987, s 61(11), paras (g), (k), (l) or (n)
  - A body may be prescribed for the purposes of this relief by Treasury order
  - NHS foundation trusts.[302]
    The Treasury may also prescribe transactions by value. They have done so for certain transactions pursuant to Energy Act 2004, s 38.[303]
    The relief also extends to transactions within School Standards and Framework Act 1998, Sch 22, paras 23(2), 4(2), 5(4B) and 8(2)(b)[304] where public bodies are involved.

10.66 In relation to such a transaction any consideration that would be payable on a contingency is ignored and the rules as to variable consideration are disapplied as regards contingent consideration.[305] Any grant pursuant to Housing Act 1996, s 20 or 21 relating to a purchase at a discount involving registered social landlords is not part of the chargeable consideration where the vendor in the chargeable right to buy transaction is a registered social landlord.[306]

Shared ownership leases

10.67 Relief is available where:

- there is the grant of a lease which gives the lessee or lessees exclusive use of a dwelling;

- the lessee is given the right to acquire the reversion;

- the lease is granted partly in consideration of rent and partly for a premium calculated by reference to the market value of the dwelling, which market value is the sum calculated by reference to that value as set out in the lease;

- the lease is granted by a qualifying body or in pursuance of a preserved right to buy.

A qualifying body is:

- a local housing authority within the Housing Act 1985;

---

[301] SI 1986/594.
[302] FA 2003, s 66 (Prescribed Persons) Order 2005, SI 2005/83.
[303] FA 2003, s 66 (Prescribed Transactions) Order 2005, SI 2005/648.
[304] FA 2003, s 66 (Prescribed Provisions) Order 2005, SI 2005/1388.
[305] FA 2003, Sch 9, para 1.
[306] Ibid, Sch 9, para 1(5).

- a housing association within either:
  - the Housing Associations Act 1985; or
  - the Housing (Northern Ireland) Order 1992, Part 2;[307]

- a housing trust established pursuant to the Housing Act 1988, Part 3;

- the Northern Ireland Housing Executive;

- the Commission for New Towns;

- a development corporation pursuant to the New Towns Act 1987

- a local housing authority within the Housing Act 1985;

- a housing association within either:
  - the Housing Associations Act 1985; or
  - the Housing (Northern Ireland) Order 1992, Part 2;[308]

- a housing trust established pursuant to the Housing Act 1988, Part 3;

- the Northern Ireland Housing Executive;

- the Commission for New Towns;

- a development corporation pursuant to the New Towns Act 1981.

The preserved right to buy means a lease is granted in pursuance of the right to buy if the vendor is a person against whom the right to buy pursuant to Part 5 of the Housing Act 1988 is exercisable[309]and the lessee and the dwelling qualify.[310]

10.68 In such a case the purchaser elects for the chargeable consideration for the grant of the lease in the amount of the market value of the dwelling or the sum calculated by reference to that value stated in the lease. The election, which is irrevocable, must be included in the land transaction return.[311] Where an election has been made and the stamp duty land tax, if any, has been paid the acquisition of the reversion is exempt from charge.[312]

10.69 Relief is also available for rent to shared ownership arrangements.[313] This is a scheme or arrangement where a qualifying body[314] grants an assured shorthold tenancy within Housing Act 1988, Part 1, of a dwelling to the tenant or tenants and subsequently there is a grant of a shared ownership lease of the dwelling or another dwelling to one or more of the tenant the grant of the assured shorthold tenancy, the shared ownership lease and any other land transaction between the parties as part of the

---

[307] SI 1992/1725.
[308] Ibid.
[309] Section 171A.
[310] FA 2003, Sch 9, para 5.
[311] Ibid, Sch 9, para 2(3).
[312] Ibid, Sch 9, para 3.
[313] Ibid, Sch 9, para 13.
[314] See **10.65**.

scheme are not linked transactions,[315] and taking possession pursuant to the shorthold tenancy is not substantial performance of the share ownership lease.[316]

10.70 Similar treatment is extended to arrangements involving shared ownership trusts[317] in relation to land in England or Wales that is a dwelling and one or more of the beneficiaries is to have the exclusive use of the trust property as the only or main resident of the beneficiary provided that he makes rent-equivalent payments and entitling him to make additional payments to the social landlord to acquire additional equity in the property. The documents must specify the market value to calculate the initial capital sum. The purchaser (beneficiary) must make the election for the treatment in the land transaction return and cannot revoke it. Any staircasing transaction is exempt provided that the election is made and all appropriate tax has been paid.

Staircasing[318]

10.71 Relief is available where a lease is granted[319] by a qualifying body[320] giving the lessee exclusive use of a dwelling. The lease must be granted partly in consideration of rent and partly in consideration of a premium calculated by reference to the premium obtainable in the open market for a lease on the same terms; but the minimum rent payable under the lease is substituted. The lease must contain a statement of the minimum rent and the open market premium or the sum calculated by reference thereto. The terms of the lease must provide[321] that the lessee may upon payment of a sum require the rent to be reduced. In such circumstances the taxpayer may elect for the tax to be chargeable upon the minimum rent stated in the lease and the amount stated in the lease as being calculated by reference to the open market value.[322] Any such election which is irrevocable must be included in the land transaction return.[323]

10.72 Where the tenant exercises the right to reduce the rent and acquires an additional interest calculated by reference to the market value of the dwelling and is expressed as a percentage of the dwelling or its value, the acquisition is exempt from stamp duty land tax if the election has been exercised and any tax chargeable upon the grant has been paid, or immediately after the acquisition the total share of the dwelling held by the lessee does not exceed 80 per cent.

Rent to mortgage

10.73 Where there is a rent to mortgage transaction (ie the transfer or lease of a dwelling to a person pursuant to his exercise of the right to acquire under Part 5 of the Housing Act 1985), the chargeable consideration is equal to the price pursuant to s 126 of that Act on a transfer or lease in accordance with the exercise of the power.[324]

---

[315] FA 2003, Sch 9, para 13(3).

[316] Ibid, Sch 9, para 13(4).

[317] This relief may apply to stamp duty leases; see FA 2003, Sch 19, para 7(2).

[318] FA 2003, Sch 9, paras 7 to 12.

[319] Which presumably includes a deemed grant arising upon substantial performance of an agreement for lease.

[320] FA 2003, Sch 9, para 5(2).

[321] Problems have arisen because the original lease has been lost and the parties are, *prima facie*, unable to prove that the relevant statements were made. It is hoped that HMRC Stamp Taxes will accept an office copy of the lease from the Land Registry as sufficient proof on this technical issue.

[322] FA 2003, Sch 9, para 4.

[323] Ibid, Sch 9, para 4(3).

[324] Ibid, Sch 9, para 6.

10.74 Equivalent relief is provided for Scottish transactions pursuant to Housing (Scotland) Act 1987, Part 3 and s 62.

Chapter 11

EXEMPTIONS AND RELIEFS – GENERAL

'RETROSPECTIVE RELIEFS'

11.1   Much of stamp duty land tax is dealt with on a provisional or guestimated basis[1] to be retrospectively revised by a subsequent adjustment by reference[2] to later events which relate back to the original relief. In consequence a later chargeable event may be entitled to relief by reference to the law applicable at the original effective date notwithstanding intervening changes in circumstances which would mean that if it were a chargeable event in its own right the relief would not be available. Although there is possibly no general 'wait-and-see principle'[3] the fact that much of the tax is provisional to be retrospectively adjusted in the light of subsequent events means that any initially available reliefs or exemptions or special rates remain available for the later adjustments. This is, however, a different principle from that applying where by reason of the separation of substantial performance and completion there may, in the view of HMRC Stamp Taxes, be two separate effective dates and chargeable transactions.[4] Should there be two such chargeable transactions each has to be separately reviewed for relief. There is no automatic carry forward of a relief from substantial performance to completion nor vice versa.

11.2   In addition, the absence of any clear wait-and-see general principle raises fundamental problems for reliefs namely the conditions for the relief may not be satisfied as at the effective date particularly where this is substantial performance but the conditions are likely to be satisfied at completion, at least if the parties carry out the terms of the contract precisely.[5] Also the chargeable consideration (which may differ from the actual consideration) may be provisional as at the effective date and not meet the conditions for the relief but these may be satisfied by reason of any retrospective adjustments. The former is illustrated by a routine problem such as on a reconstruction; the charge may arise but there may be a delay before the consideration shares are technically 'issued',[6] for example, where the effective date may precede formal completion. The question is whether there is a right to 'wait-and-see'; but fortunately HMRC Stamp Taxes have not hitherto taken this type of point in practice. The latter issue would be the question of some contingent additional consideration being involved. Here HMRC take the point that such potential consideration destroys the eligibility for

---

[1]   The legislation refers to reasonable estimates but fails to address the issue of how a taxpayer is to make a reasonable estimate of future variables.

[2]   FA 2003, s 48.

[3]   See **5.83**.

[4]   FA 2003, s 44(8) and Sch 17A, para 12A; but not relieved by FA 2003, Sch 10, para 33 (relief against double taxation of the 'same transaction' whatever that may mean).

[5]   See **11.1** and **12.62**.

[6]   FA 2003, Sch 7, Part 2; *Oswald Tillotson v IRC* [1933] 1 KB 134; *Brotex Cellulose Fibres Ltd v IRC* [1933] 1 KB 158; *Murex v IRC* [1933] 1 KB 173; see **12.30**, **12.48** and **14.27**.

the relief and do not appear to regard the relief arising, subsequently, although this approach of HMRC Stamp Taxes is very debatable in the provisional retrospective structure of stamp duty land tax.

'EXEMPT'

11.3   The bizarre drafting of the FA 2003 is particularly significant, raising acute problems in relation to questions of reliefs from stamp duty land tax and the related scope of the obligations to notify.[7] There is a variety of ways in which a transaction is relieved in whole or in part from the charge to tax and, because of the strange ie 'plain English' and inappropriate terminology adopted, the precise nature of the relieving provision will have to be carefully noted as it may have other implications, particularly in relation to the reporting obligations. In addition, even where a transaction is specifically made 'exempt', certain provisions apply only where the 'exemption' is available for particular reasons and may be subject to forfeiture or clawback. To some extent this can be dealt with by referring to those transactions that fall outside the tax altogether and are non-notifiable as 'exempt' and other transactions where no tax is payable but the transaction is notifiable as being 'relieved', but in order to produce this result it is necessary to investigate the legislation to determine why no tax is payable and because 'exempt' is utilised in several ways in the legislation such as exempt transaction,[8] exempt interest and exempt consideration.[9] It is not always possible to take this approach so that detailed scrutiny of the legislation is required in every case to avoid traps and to avoid unnecessary costs and tax charges for clients by reporting or paying tax when not required by the legislation or risking penalties where reporting is required notwithstanding that no tax is payable.

11.4   A major problem in seeking to understand the tax is the variety of 'plain English' ways reliefs may be made available. There is no single term for relief and words that imply some form of relief are frequently utilised in special ways and not with any degree of consistency. This means that certain words in the legislation have to be approached with a degree of caution not only because their direct effect as to whether the transaction may or may not be subject to some reduction or relief from the tax but also whether the form in which it is expressed means that the transaction qualifies for other benefits such as being non-notifiable.[10] The key words and indications of their potential meanings and consequences include:

- *Exempt*
  The word 'exempt' is used in a variety of contexts:

---

[7]   Certain acquisitions of major interests are not notifiable if they are 'exempt' for certain specified reasons (FA 2003, s 77A). However, one of these exemptions refers to transactions for 'no chargeable consideration' (ibid, Sch 7, para 1). In consequence, many transactions such as some, but not all, of those relating to disadvantaged land (ibid, Sch 6), may have actual consideration which for one reason or another is not 'chargeable' within the list in ibid, Sch 4 (see **Chapter 5**) and may be 'exempt' for these purposes. Close study of the badly drafted legislation is needed in each case in order to avoid exposing clients to unnecessary costs by incurring expenditure in preparing returns or tax computations that are not required. In other cases detailed amendments mean that transactions that superficially are exempt and not notifiable are taken out of the general principles and expressly made notifiable notwithstanding that no tax is payable; such as dealings with connected companies, partnerships and PFI projects.

[8]   FA 2003, Sch 7, para 1(1).

[9]   Such as nil consideration FA 2003, Sch 4, para 18.

[10]   FA 2003, Sch 3, para 1; s 77A.

- it may refer to the nature of a particular item of property such as an 'exempt interest'[11] which means that there is no chargeable transaction because there is no dealing in a chargeable interest;[12]
- it may also refer to a transaction being eligible for a particular relief;
- it may also be used in the context of consideration being treated as 'exempt'. This last usage of the term will usually mean that there is no chargeable consideration[13] which has the effect that the transaction is 'exempt' for the purposes of FA 2003, Sch 3, para 1, with the benefits attaching to that form of relief;[14] such as no obligation to notify;[15]

- *Consideration to be treated as 'nil'*
  This has the effect that there is no chargeable consideration and therefore the transaction falls within FA 2003, Sch 3, para 1, and is therefore, *prima facie*, not a notifiable transaction;[16]

- *'Does not count as chargeable consideration'*[17]
  This appears to be the equivalent of a transaction having its consideration adjusted. Where the relevant consideration is the only consideration, the transaction will be 'exempt' in the strict sense of FA 2003, Sch 3, para 1. In other cases the effect is to reduce the amount of the consideration upon which the chargeable consideration is to be calculated;

- *'Does not include'*
  This is the equivalent of the preceding point that the chargeable consideration is different from the actual consideration by certain items being excluded;[18]

- *No account*
  It is stated that 'no account' is to be taken of certain matters. Some of these are essentially of an administrative nature.[19] However, it seems that it may have the effect of excluding transactions from the tax regime or taking amounts of consideration out of the computation;[20]

- *Disregarded*
  It is stated that certain transactions shall be 'disregarded' for the purposes of stamp duty land tax. This can apply to certain aspects of subsales[21] or the general anti-avoidance provisions.[22] However, whilst the normal use of the word 'disregarded' means that the transaction is to be treated as though it never happened for the purpose of the tax, it seems that this is not the particular meaning given by the legislation. For example, it is the view of HMRC Stamp Taxes that notwithstanding the first purchaser in a chain of subsales has his

---

[11] Ibid, s 48(2).
[12] Ibid, s 43(1).
[13] Ibid, Sch 3, para 1.
[14] Ibid, s 77A; subject to various exclusions where transactions for no chargeable consideration are nevertheless notifiable.
[15] Ibid, s 77A.
[16] Ibid.
[17] See, for example, FA 2003, Sch 17A, para 16.
[18] See, for example, FA 2003, Sch 4, para 17.
[19] Such as FA 2003, s 110(4).
[20] See, for example, FA 2003, s 75C(4).
[21] FA 2003, s 45(3).
[22] Ibid, s 75A(4)(a).

transaction 'disregarded' there is nevertheless still a notifiable transaction notwithstanding that his acquisition is 'disregarded' and because the consideration may be below the threshold, he still has to notify. Similarly, in relation to 'scheme transactions' within the general anti-avoidance provisions although these are 'disregarded' it seems that there is no refund of the taxation in respect of those transactions and that the 'disregarding' takes the form of a credit for the tax against the charge arising upon the notional transaction pursuant to FA 2003, s 75A(5);

This is, however, a somewhat cryptic treatment of transactions namely certain transactions are to be 'disregarded'.[23] This word appears in various context dealing with situations where tax may not arise; for example:

- subsales;[24]
- zero carbon homes;[25]
- general anti-avoidance principles;[26]
- certain PFI projects;[27]
- lifting the veil of corporate partnerships;[28]
- successive linked leases;[29]
- transitional provisions.[30]

In general 'disregarded' means that the event is deemed not to have occurred or to have had not relevant consequences. However, it seems that HMRC Stamp Taxes have a different set of interpretations; for example:

- notwithstanding that certain arrangements in relation to subsales are to be 'disregarded' and no tax arises HMRC Stamp Taxes[31] maintain that the 'disregarded' events are to be 'regarded' as having taken place and filing of land transaction returns is required;

- in relation to the general anti-avoidance provisions the 'disregarded' scheme transactions are 'regarded' as having taken place as chargeable transactions so that they have to be reported and tax paid and the 'disregarding' is limited to the tax payable upon such disregarded transactions being available as a credit for the person ultimately identified as the offending purchaser 'P'.

Clearly there will need to be much debate with HMRC Stamp Taxes about the scope of 'disregarding' and exemption or relief.

- *Credit*

There is a form of relief within the stamp duty land tax regime by way of a 'credit' in respect of tax upon previous transactions having been paid.[32] The credit

---

23 Note the utilisation of the same word for stamp duty such as, for example, FA 1958, s 34 certificates of rates; FA 1973, Sch 19, para 10; FA 1986, s 88; FA 1991, s 113; FA 1999, Sch 13, para 6; FA 2000, Sch 34, para 4; FA 2001, Sch 30; FA 2003, s 195.
24 FA 2003, ss 45(3) and (4), 45.
25 Ibid, s 58(2).
26 Ibid, ss 75A–75C.
27 Ibid, Sch 4, para 17.
28 Ibid, Sch 15, para 2.
29 Ibid, Sch 17A, para 5.
30 Ibid, Sch 19, para 1.
31 And it seems certain employees of the Land Registry.
32 This appears to be different from the protection for taxpayers against being taxed twice in respect of the same transaction pursuant to FA 2003, Sch 10, para 33 although there is it seems considerable potential for debate given the limited views of HMRC Stamp Taxes as to what is a 'transaction' for these purposes since this does not, in their view, extend to situations where the events in question are stages in an overall commercial transaction but are technically separate 'chargeable transactions' for the purpose of stamp duty land tax.

mechanism, which is usually available in relation to rents,[33] has not been thoroughly prepared and there are considerable technical issues as to how the credit is to be calculated.[34]

11.5 Notwithstanding these numerous variations on the issue and/or type of 'relief' the word 'exempt' itself is ambiguous[35] in the context of stamp duty land tax namely is not taxable such as exempt interests[36] or exempt transactions[37] and is not notifiable or is not taxable but is notifiable and, in consequence, has to be subdivided in order to make sense of the legislation. It has given rise to problems in relation to stamp duty over many years. On a broad view, a transaction is 'exempt' if it is not liable to the tax, ie either because there was a specific provision cancelling or modifying a charge or because it did not fall within the charging provisions.[38] However, it was the view of HMRC Stamp Taxes for many years that in order to be a transaction or instrument that was 'exempt' from stamp duty or was not a chargeable security for the purposes of stamp duty reserve tax,[39] it had to be an instrument that fell within the charge to tax and was specifically taken out because of a relieving provision.[40] The wider view of 'exempt' as meaning not being liable because the transaction did not fall into charge at all was strenuously rejected by HMRC Stamp Taxes so that a transaction entirely outside the scope of stamp duty could have significant stamp tax implications. It is likely that, given the multitude of relieving structures in stamp duty land tax illustrated above, and the variety of ways in which a transaction does not bear an actual charge to tax (which includes many of the transactions falling with the nil rate band[41]) similar issues will arise so that transactions excluded from the charge to stamp duty land tax may, in the current approach of HMRC Stamp Taxes, have wide-ranging implications for the tax and compliance regimes that are more onerous than, for example, those transactions that are *prima facie* taxable but relieved by FA 2003, Sch 3 (as amended); and parties completing land transaction returns will need to bear the terminology in mind precisely, if only to be able to meet the confusing compliance obligations.

---

[33] See, for example, FA 2003, Sch 17A, para 9, 9A and 12A.
[34] See, for example, **7.198**.
[35] Which is highlighted because the draftsman left his notes in the text to become part of the legislation; FA 2003, s 49(2).
[36] FA 2003, s 48(2) (as indirectly amended).
[37] Ibid, Sch 3.
[38] However, even this apparently obvious proposition has ambiguities. Eg the transaction may not be taxable because it does not relate, in part, to exempt interests or property that is not within the charge; also there is a theoretical difference between a contract that includes a sale of equipment that has retained its character as chattels, ie can never be a chargeable interest, and a contract that includes the sale of the benefit of a licence, ie an interest that is *prima facie* a chargeable interest but which like tenancies at will and mortgages is excluded from the definition of chargeable interests. In a broad sense one contract is outside the scope of the tax; the other is within the charge to tax but is specifically taken out of charge. Many consequences for computation and compliance turn upon this point such as the possible impact of the linked transaction principle.
[39] FA 1986, s 99 (as much amended).
[40] But see *IRC v Ansbacher* [1963] AC 191.
[41] See, eg, FA 2003, s 77 (as amended) and 77A.

GENERAL PRINCIPLES

11.6   Reliefs from stamp duty land tax take a variety of forms. For example:

- the property involved may have nothing to do with land;[42]

- the transaction may be stated to be non-chargeable;

- the interest in land may be non-chargeable or is an exempt interest;[43]

- consideration may be stated to be non-chargeable or nil or reduced or adjusted,[44] ignored or disregarded. This applies, *inter alia*, to partitions[45] and exchanges[46] including certain surrenders and regrants where the actual consideration is ignored (including any equality payment) in whole or in part and specific deemed consideration may be applied so that any actual consideration is ignored;[47]

- the transaction may be *prima facie* relieved by various provisions such as acquisitions by charities[48] or registered social landlords;[49]

- the rate of tax may be reduced for the particular transaction;[50] and

- the transaction may be 'disregarded'.[51]

11.7   It is important to note that the form the relief takes may be important in relation to other aspects of stamp duty land tax, particularly the compliance procedures. For example:

- the grant of a lease for a term of less than 7 years, which is taxable at the rate of 1 per cent in the case of rents and 1 per cent or higher in relation to premiums,[52] is notifiable, even where it is a lease which would have been so taxable but for a 'relief';[53] such as where the lease is granted to a charity;

---

[42]   But note the special notification obligations for disadvantaged and PFI projects (FA 2003, Sch 6, para 13 and Sch 4, para 17 respectively).

[43]   Ibid, ss 43(1), 48(1) and (2) and 73B; such transactions are outside the scope of stamp duty land tax and do not require notification to HMRC Stamp Taxes or SDLT 5 for entries in the land register.

[44]   See, eg, the part-exchange of new dwellings in ibid, Sch 6A, para 1 where the land exceeds the 'permitted area'.

[45]   Ibid, Sch 4, para 6.

[46]   Ibid, Sch 4, para 5.

[47]   See, eg, ibid, Sch 17A, para 9.

[48]   Ibid, Sch 8.

[49]   Ibid, s 71.

[50]   Ibid, Sch 7, Part 2, para 8.

[51]   See, for example, ibid, s 45(3) and s 75A(4)(a) and see **11.4**.

[52]   In this context it is important to bear in mind that the limitation upon the 1 per cent rate for premiums is enlarged where the property is non-residential and the annual rent exceeds £1000; see FA 2003, Sch 5, paras 9(2) and 9A.

[53]   Ibid, s 77(1)(b); see also s 77A(2) thereof for non-major interests.

• other acquisitions of major interests are notifiable unless they are exempt, but only by reason of FA 2003, Sch 3[54] or the thresholds imposed by FA 2003, s 77A, even where the actual transaction is relieved from tax such as an intra-group lease.[55]

The nil consideration issue[56]

11.8   A key issue, but not the sole criterion for 'exemption', is the treatment of the consideration. A transaction for no chargeable consideration is 'exempt'[57] and is not notifiable[58] because it falls within Finance Act 2003, Sch 3.[59] This relaxation of the compliance regime[60] applies not only to transactions where there is no actual consideration[61] but does apply to most cases where there is actual consideration which is deemed to be nil.[62] There is a different regime where the consideration is ignored, treated as nil or is otherwise 'exempt' from that applying where the relief, in effect, takes the form of the rate of tax being reduced to nil. In the former case there is no chargeable consideration so that the transaction falls within FA 2003, Sch 3, para 1, and so subject to certain exclusions[63] it is not notifiable,[64] as the taxable consideration is calculated in a particular way so that the chargeable amount is nil such as partnerships because there is a 100 per cent reduction in the charge for the sum of the lower proportions,[65] or the market value of the property is nil such as the assignment of a lease at a full reviewable rack rent. There are problems for notification of certain transactions that fall within FA 2003, Sch 3, para 1. It is provided that certain transactions have to be notified notwithstanding the absence of chargeable consideration, but there is the question of whether they are taken out of the notification regime because the chargeable consideration falls below the £40,000 or nil rate threshold for notification.[66] For example, the notification rules for partnerships are subject to the specific requirements of notification pursuant to FA 2003, Sch 15, para 31,[67] and special rules apply to alternative finance arrangements.[68] In other cases the provisions of the specific reliefs

---

[54]   Ibid, s 77(3).
[55]   Ibid, Sch 7, Part 1.
[56]   There is also the practical problem that HMRC Stamp Taxes' systems frequently have difficulties in giving immediate effect to land transaction returns showing zero chargeable consideration in Box 10.
[57]   FA 2003, Sch 3, para 1.
[58]   But note the current aggressive posture of HMRC Stamp Taxes in relation to both the definition of 'land' and 'chargeable interests'. The former issues related to, *inter alia*, embedded goodwill and fixtures or chattels; the latter includes issues of contractual restrictions upon development of the land that is not a restrictive covenant, contractual arrangements that may involve an opportunity to re-purchase the land, and possibly overage and clawback provisions that may affect the price for the onward sale of the land because the next purchaser has to give a fresh overage or clawback consideration. The initial structuring of such arrangements and the contractual provisions for an automatic novation may have long-term stamp duty land tax implications and possible benefits.
[59]   FA 2003, s 77(3).
[60]   Ibid, s 77(3) (as amended).
[61]   Unless some market value rules apply such as connected companies and the special partnership regime.
[62]   Close study of the badly drafted legislation is needed in each case in order to avoid exposing clients to unnecessary costs by incurring expenditure in preparing returns or tax computations that are not required. There are also significant problems as to whether such non-taxable consideration is the same as non-chargeable consideration for the purposes of linked transactions (see **5.38**).
[63]   Connected companies (FA 2003, ss 53 and 54), PFI projects (FA 2003, Sch 4, para 17).
[64]   Ibid, s 77A.
[65]   Ibid, Sch 15, Part 3; but these may be notifiable see Sch 15, para 31.
[66]   Ibid, s 77A(1), points 3, 4 5 and 5; see further **Chapter 17**.
[67]   See **11.8** and **11.18**; FA 2003, s 77(2)(b).
[68]   FA 2003, s 77(2)(a).

need to be considered since these raise the problems of construing the exclusion because of non-chargeable consideration arising by reason of another 'relief'.[69]

PARTIAL EXEMPTION

11.9 A key practical problem is whether relief is available upon a partial basis such as where a charity and a commercial developer jointly[70] acquire land for development which includes a substantial benefit to the charity or registered social landlord namely whether stamp duty land tax is not payable upon the part of the consideration provided by the charity but is taxable on the part of the price paid by the other party although there may be issues whether the charity is acquiring its interest in the land solely for charitable purposes within the terms of the relief.[71] Similar issues arise where there is a transfer of land to joint purchasers one or more but not all of whom are stamp duty land tax subsidiaries of the vendor. There may be longer term issues as regards exemptions for rent in the cases of acquisitions of leases some of which are eligible for reliefs because the tenants include a subsidiary company, for the time being.[72] Obviously there are technical issues of construction of the legislation and whether 'chargeable interest' includes 'part of a chargeable interest' or whether the acquisition has to be solely for charitable purposes. Since the rent is taxed up front this should not provide HMRC Stamp Taxes with any useful ammunition in this debate and there is the consequential issue as to where this applies. The developer is entitled to the benefit of the lower rates of tax because his part of the chargeable consideration falls below a threshold notwithstanding that the total consideration including the charity's contribution exceeds the rate threshold.

11.10 HMRC Stamp Taxes in a change from the practice which they had to some extent adopted in relation to stamp duty reliefs are adamant in their view that relief is an all or nothing exercise.[73] Thus on the above facts relief would be totally refused and the registered social landlord would be denied relief. This question of partial relief is of major practical importance where partnerships or joint ventures are involved and connected with the taxpayer or charities have an interest in the project. This created problems because the initial relief for acquisitions by charities required the intention to utilise the chargeable interest solely for charitable purposes.[74] To deal with this particular problem a limited relief, subject to stringent conditions, was introduced;[75] but the manner of its introduction was no doubt intended by HMRC Stamp Taxes to provide indirect support for their main argument against partial relief. Group structures are particularly vulnerable so that relief is likely to be refused by HMRC Stamp Taxes where a joint venture[76] involving a subsidiary company and a third party is dissolved and the land transferred to another subsidiary company. HMRC Stamp Taxes have strongly indicated that no relief is available in respect of the part interest in the property

---

[69] Ibid, ss 77(2) and 77A(3).
[70] And whether it matters whether the acquisition was as equitable joint tenants or tenants in common.
[71] FA 2003, Sch 8, para 1(2); but note the alternative relief pursuant to para 3.
[72] Note the special charge for leases upon assignment FA 2003, Sch 17A, para 11.
[73] Unless perhaps the transaction was publicly funded pursuant to FA 2003, s 71.
[74] Ibid, Sch 8, para 1(2).
[75] Ibid, Sch 8, para 3.
[76] This may be even more complicated and expensive should the joint venture be regarded as a partnership by HMRC Stamp Taxes because special rules apply pursuant to FA 2003, Sch 15, Part 3; see **Chapter 13** and there are difficult inconsistencies in practice by HMRC Stamp Taxes on the question of whether partnerships can affect group structures and the notional ownership of shares and assets for the purposes of intra-group relief.

that is transferred from one subsidiary company to another where the entire interest is transferred because of the outside involvement.[77] On the question of groups and partial relief there are changes in the legislation. Stamp duty relief required acquisition of 'a' not 'the' beneficial interest which arguably include a partial interest whether joint or successive.[78] All that stamp duty land tax requires is 'a transaction;'[79] no mention being made of the nature of the transaction or the nature or extent of the interest being acquired. Careful structuring of such arrangements, such as separate sales or leases of part interests so that there is a single whole acquisition so as to avoid claims for partial relief would seem to be prudent. Although the definition of 'chargeable interest' includes partial interests in property[80] it may be worthwhile dealing with such interests on a separate basis rather than a global transfer of the entire equitable interest for the time being.

PROCEDURE AND SELF-ASSESSMENT ISSUES – 'CLAIMING RELIEF'

11.11 It is important to note that, unlike for stamp duty where adjudication is frequently required in order to obtain an exemption or mitigation of a charge in respect of a particular instrument, there is no similar specific procedure for establishing eligibility for relief from stamp duty land tax and, in practice, there is little possibility of obtaining helpful guidance from HMRC Stamp Taxes who have refused to help because the questions are 'too difficult'. As the tax is based upon self-assessment,[81] the taxpayer and his advisers must take a reasonable and reasoned view of the transaction[82] and decide whether the relief is available.[83] The taxpayer will then complete the return and take this view into account by not accounting for tax in whole or in part. It will be necessary to make the entry in the appropriate box on the land transaction return that the self-assessment has been made on the basis that an exemption is available. It is expected that the indication that the relief has been taken will inevitably mean that a notice initiating an Enquiry into the transaction[84] will be issued and that the taxpayer will be put to considerable expense in defending the entries in the return.[85]

---

[77] This attitude on these facts seems bizarre because a separate intra-group transfer would, *prima facie*, be eligible for relief.

[78] There are also unresolved issues as to the 'beneficial ownership' of land since the cases are predominantly concerned with shares.

[79] FA 2003, Sch 7, para 1(1).

[80] Attempts to deal with equitable joint tenancies may raise separate issues.

[81] FA 2003, s 76(3)(a).

[82] And it will be important to keep records of the discussions and advice received concerning the issue of the availability of the exemption. Failure to keep such records will mean that there will not be any contemporaneous evidence either that the issues were considered or of the basis for the decision being taken which will mean that there is a significant risk in a claim for penalties in respect of the submission of a negligent return being made. It will be necessary to establish that such a review took place and to show that the issues were fully and properly considered. The absence of contemporaneous records will make it extremely difficult to substantiate these points in practice.

[83] It may be possible to apply for a refund of tax paid since a relief might be available as an error or mistake claim (FA 2003, s 34) but there is a 6 year limitation period. It may be necessary to make a formal claim for relief pursuant to FA 2003, Sch 11A, since amendments are limited to 12 months; FA 2003, Sch 10, para 6.

[84] Pursuant to FA 2003, Sch 10. There is, however, an increasing body of evidence that hitherto the vast majority of cases which have been made the subject-matter of an Enquiry are those where professional advisers lacking the courage of their technical skills have advised clients to submit a covering letter explaining the background to the land transaction return. Whilst this seems to be recommended as a means of escaping allegations of fraud and penalties, given the difficulties in this situation for HMRC Stamp Taxes in establishing fraud (the criminal law rules apply; *Re Wragge* [1897] 1 Ch 796) it seems that the main

11.12 Attempts to obtain comfort in the form of an advance ruling or clearance are generally pointless even where there are specific anti-avoidance provisions within the relief.[86] No clearance procedure is provided. Such rulings, if they are given, are not regarded as binding by HMRC Stamp Taxes[87] unless stringent, if not impossible, conditions are satisfied,[88] and there are indications that reliance upon a non-binding ruling will not be regarded as the basis for mitigating any penalties for filing an erroneous return.[89] Moreover, on occasions, such pre-transaction rulings have been refused[90] because the issues were too difficult for HMRC Stamp Taxes.

11.13 In some situations the relief may be dependent not only upon the interpretation of the law but also upon the interpretation of the facts such as whether the company reconstruction is to be carried out for a *bona fide* commercial purpose and not with a tax avoidance motive[91] or the intention of the party acquiring the chargeable interest such as a charity[92] which requires both an absence of tax avoidance purposes[93] and an intention to utilise the land solely for charitable purposes.[94] In some cases this will prove a difficult matter to establish and HMRC Stamp Taxes are likely to challenge the evidence supplied by the taxpayer in an Enquiry. Certain advance clearances are available on some of these issues from other divisions of HMRC such as capital gains tax.[95] HMRC Stamp Taxes usually accept such clearance although they strongly prefer those obtained for capital gains tax. However, as is sometimes the case, there may be a clearance for capital gains tax but a refusal of the clearance for income tax.[96] In such a case HMRC Stamp Taxes usually adopt the capital gains tax clearance and ignore the problems for income tax. Unfortunately HMRC Stamp Taxes are beginning to form their own views of what is tax avoidance[97] and what is a transaction undertaken primarily for a commercial reason and not as part of some tax avoidance purpose[98] HMRC Stamp Taxes are reluctant to assist on these matters in advance although they may be prepared to rely upon formal clearances in relation to capital gains tax.[99] In this situation the taxpayer's advisers have the difficult task of predicting the likely response of HMRC Stamp Taxes which, as described later, has produced some challenging interpretation of both the facts and the legislation.

11.14 In this context of taking a relief, it is vital to be aware and to notify clients that the issue by HMRC Stamp Taxes of a certificate (SDLT 5) required to permit

---

function of such a letter is to significantly increase the risk of an Enquiry being launched with large additional costs simply to establish the obvious entitlement to the relief.

[85] This is, of course, a key factor in the lack of finality as regards stamp duty land tax.

[86] See, for example, FA 2003, Sch 7, paras 2(4A), 7(5) and 8(5B).

[87] See *J Rothschild Holdings v IRC* [1989] STC 435.

[88] Note the comments of Lord Nolan in *R v IRC ex parte Matrix Securities Ltd* [1993] STC 774.

[89] It will be questionable whether such reliance will mean that there is no negligence entitling HMRC Stamp Taxes to extend the period for Discovery Assessments from 6 to 21 years pursuant to FA 2003, Sch 10, para 31(2).

[90] But note Code of Practice CoP 10.

[91] FA 2003, Sch 7.

[92] Ibid, Sch 8.

[93] Ibid, Sch 8, para 1(3).

[94] Ibid, Sch 8, para 1(3).

[95] See, for example, Taxation of Chargeable Gains Act 1992, ss 137 and 139.

[96] Income and Corporation Taxes Act 1988, s 707.

[97] Assisted by certain 'experienced' employees of the Land Registry who insist they have a statutory duty to report tax mitigation arrangements and refuse registration of the transaction notwithstanding that there is a Revenue Certificate (SDLT 5).

[98] See **12.12**.

[99] But note that these may not be in terms helpful for stamp taxes and may be utilised against the taxpayer as in *Swithland Investments v IRC* [1990] STC 448.

registration[100] is not conclusive that the relief or exemption is available either at all or to the extent claimed.[101] It must also be pointed out in many cases that the relief may be provisional because the relief, even though properly claimed, is potentially vulnerable to clawback[102] or forfeiture[103] and may create problems for a purchaser.[104]

11.15 As regards the basic entitlement to the relief, the parties, having taken the relief, are on risk that HMRC Stamp Taxes will test the availability of the exemption (ie the correctness of the return) on a subsequent Enquiry but any subsequent challenge by HMRC Stamp Taxes[105] does not jeopardise the registration of title pursuant to the certificate issued and any security interest is protected.[106] There appears to be no procedure at present for obtaining a definitive post transaction ruling,[107] as with stamp duty adjudication, shortly after the transaction. There is no procedure for submitting a letter claiming the relief asking for a decision although it is possible to file a return and temporarily depositing tax with HMRC Stamp Taxes,[108] on account as a means of seeking to avoid the running of interest and liability to penalties.[109] However, this does not produce a correct return and the best that can be hoped for is a speedy response by HMRC Stamp Taxes in launching an Enquiry. The parties must submit the return upon the basis that they think the relief is available and take their chances with Enquiries and penalties for incorrect returns in due course. The important principle to bear in mind is that it is essential to have well-documented records of the steps taken to decide upon the availability of the relief. Having taken such steps, it will be more difficult for HMRC Stamp Taxes to establish the return was negligent, although incorrect,[110] or even fraudulent, which may be important in deciding whether a discovery assessment can be issued by HMRC Stamp Taxes for up to 21 years.[111] Moreover, should HMRC Stamp Taxes successfully attack any such claim for relief, all taxpayers are subject to an obligation under a tax-related penalty to rectify the 'error' in the initial return claiming the relief[112] and deciding not to rectify the error may be attacked by HMRC Stamp Taxes as a conspiracy to defraud them.

---

[100] FA 2003, s 79.

[101] The mere fact that the self-assessment of the transaction indicates that stamp duty land tax is not payable does not necessarily make the transaction non-notifiable, since the fact that no tax is payable does not make the transaction 'exempt' or within the nil rate band for the purposes of the exclusions from filing the land transaction return: ibid, s 77.

[102] See, for example FA 2003, Sch 7, paras 3 and 9.

[103] See, for example, FA 2003, Sch 6A, para 11.

[104] See, for example, FA 2003, Sch 17A, para 11.

[105] Assuming that the Land Registry, in the exercise of their local discretion, do not challenge the Inland Revenue Certificate (SDLT 5) on the basis that the employee in question believes in their evidence that the relief is not available as happens from time to time.

[106] See **22.09**.

[107] Application for a post-transaction and post-filing ruling is treated by HMRC Stamp Taxes as an order to initiate full Enquiry with related costs.

[108] FA 2003, s 87(6).

[109] There is a risk that if the parties submit a return (SDLT 1) on the basis that the transaction is taxable together with a claim for a post-transaction ruling that in their current approach HMRC Stamp Taxes may refuse to repay the tax on the basis that an error or mistake claim is not effective because either there was no error but a deliberate decision to pay the tax or the return was submitted on the basis of the generally understood practice at the time (FA 2003, Sch 10, para 34). Advisers who propose such a course of action rather than returning as an exempt transaction and asking for an Enquiry may be on significant risk.

[110] Not every error is negligence but note that failure to ask the right questions when completing the return is negligence; *Slattery v Moore Stephens* [2003] STC 1379.

[111] It is important to note the argument that, provided the taxpayer has taken proper advice, he may not be 'negligent' even if the advice may be wrong, so that the 9-month period for opening Enquiries is not capable of extension up to 21 years.

[112] FA 2003, Sch 10, para 8; note also the power to amend a land transaction return by the taxpayer during an Enquiry or to deal with a determination by filing a return where no tax return has been previously filed; see FA 2003, Sch 10, paras 18 and 27.

11.16 This problem of having to take the relief and take the risk has increased because of the attitude of the Land Registry to transactions presented to them as non-notifiable and, therefore, not in need of an Inland Revenue Certificate (SDLT 5).[113] Their suggestion is to file a land transaction return showing that no tax is payable and claiming 'other' relief. However, it must be noted that although HMRC Stamp Taxes have no power to Enquire into non-notifiable transactions[114] they can Enquire into any transaction where a land transaction return has been filed.[115] Complying with the suggestion of the Land Registry will, therefore, enlarge the powers of HMRC Stamp Taxes and expose the taxpayer to the risks of costs in dealing with a legally unnecessary Enquiry. Moreover, this problem with the Land Registry has been enlarged because certain employees claim in the exercise of their 'local discretion' they can scrutinise applications presented to them even where supported by an Inland Revenue Certificate (SDLT 5) because they believe that the claimed exemption is not available, although they are unlikely to have sufficient, if any, information on this point or they believe that there has been what they regard as 'tax avoidance' involved in the transaction.[116]

EXEMPT PROPERTY

11.17 It is specifically provided[117] that the tax applies only where there is the acquisition of a chargeable interest.[118] The definition of chargeable interest provides for 'exempt interests', ie those interests in property which are not subject to the charge. These are:

- any security interest, which means an interest or right (other than a rent charge)[119] held for the purpose of securing the payment of money or the performance of any other obligation;[120]

- a licence to use or occupy land;[121]

- in England and Wales or Northern Ireland, a tenancy at will, an advowson, franchise or manor;[122]

- land held by a financial institution as part of an alternative finance arrangement;[123] and

---

[113] Ibid, s 79(1) (as amended).
[114] Ibid, Sch 11 (as amended).
[115] Ibid, Sch 10, para 12(1).
[116] See **Chapter 22**.
[117] FA 2003, s 49(1).
[118] Ibid, s 43(1).
[119] Which appears to include estate rent charges and raises various fundamental problems such as: whether the creation of a rent charge or the assumption of liability for an existing rent charge issuing out of the chargeable interest constitutes chargeable consideration; whether a rent charge is a chargeable interest; in which case if it cannot be reserved but takes effect as a regrant, the transaction will be an exchange and since rent charges can be sold they may have a market value which may be quite small should there be interest obligations to expend money on services etc; where there is a chargeable transaction when a rent charge is sold should it be a chargeable interest.
[120] FA 2003, s 48(2)(a) and (3)(a).
[121] Ibid, s 48(2)(b).
[122] Ibid, s 48(2)(c).
[123] Ibid, s 73B.

- certain asset backed loans that form the basis of the income flow as disguised interest to satisfy the ethical requirements of alternative finance.[124]

'EXEMPT TRANSACTIONS'

11.18 Two levels of exempt transactions exist, namely:

- those exempt transactions within FA 2003, Sch 3, which are also generally[125] exempt from notification obligations; and

- those transactions (sometimes described as 'exempt') which are 'relieved' from a positive charge to stamp duty land tax, but which are notifiable.[126]

It seems that transactions falling outside the scope of stamp duty land tax altogether although not taxable are not regarded as 'exempt transactions'; but will not be notifiable transactions because these are not 'land transactions' which are the only transactions that are notifiable.[127]

Exemptions not requiring notification[128]

Transactions where there is no chargeable consideration[129]

11.19 The basic relief is in respect of gifts and certain dealings involving partnerships where there is a 100 per cent reduction for the sum of the lower proportions.[130] It is, however, a wide exemption, since it would appear to apply where there is actual consideration but which by reason of the legislative drafting is not 'chargeable consideration', such as in relation to PFI projects, or where the reduction in the market value charge upon acquisitions or disposals between partners, partnerships and connected persons by the sum of the lower proportions (SLP) produces a nil consideration because the SLP equals 100.[131] The relief is basically available for, *inter alia*:

- gifts;

- dividends *in specie*, subject to the charge upon connected companies where the distributing company acquired the property within the preceding 3 years by means

---

[124] Ibid, s 73C; FA 2009, Sch 61.

[125] Ibid, s 77A; but see ibid, Sch 6, para 13 (disadvantaged land); Sch 4, para 17 (PFI projects); Sch 15, para 31 (partnerships) and s 53(4) (connected companies); but Sch 3, para 1 applies to transactions within the exclusions from the connected company charge pursuant to s 54 thereof.

[126] Ibid, s 77(2), (3) and (4).

[127] Ibid, s 77(1) (as amended).

[128] But see, on agreements for lease, ibid, s 77(2) and (3); it is necessary to work 'backwards' in this case since exemption from notification of the substantial performance stage does not, of itself, relieve from the notification obligation of the 'grant' stage: see s 77(2) where the exclusion from notification differs significantly.

[129] Ibid, s 77A and Sch 3, para 1.

[130] But it must be noted that there are market value charges upon transactions involving connected companies; FA, ss 53 and 54; Sch 15, Part 3.

[131] FA 2003, Sch 15, Part 3; see **Chapter 13**.

of an exempt intra-group transfer.[132] However, the imposed charge may be eligible for intra-group relief in appropriate circumstances;

- distribution in the course of a winding-up, subject to the charge upon connected companies where the distributing company acquired the property within the preceding 3 years by means of an exempt intra-group transfer.[133] However, the imposed charge may be eligible for intra-group relief in appropriate circumstances;

- distributions by trustees and personal representatives to beneficiaries who are absolutely entitled where no actual consideration or no deemed consideration[134] passes. This includes appropriations to specific and residuary devisees;[135]

- changes of trustee or nominee;[136]

- possibly distribution *in specie* by trustees of a unit trust scheme;[137]

- certain dealings in relation to certain PFI and PPP projects where certain parts of the consideration are ignored;[138]

- surrenders and regrants of leases[139] and deeds of variation.

Land transactions involving leases granted by registered social landlords

11.20   Leases granted by registered social landlords[140] are exempt if granted to one or more individuals for an indefinite term or terminable by notice of a month or less pursuant to arrangements between a registered social landlord and the housing authority under which the landlord provides for individuals nominated by the authority in pursuance of its statutory housing functions temporary rented accommodation which the landlord has obtained on a short-term basis, ie the accommodation is leased to the landlord for a term of 5 years or less.

11.21   A housing authority is a principal council within the meaning of the Local Government Act 1972 or the Common Council of the City of London, a council constituted under Local Government etc (Scotland) Act 1994, s 2, or the Department for Social Development in Northern Ireland or the Northern Ireland Housing Executive.[141]

---

[132]   Ibid, ss 53 and 54.
[133]   Ibid.
[134]   Ibid, Sch 16, para 3; Sch 3, para 1; see **9.26**.
[135]   But see **9.33**.
[136]   At present HMRC Stamp Taxes do not take any point where there is a mortgage secured on the trust assets notwithstanding FA 2003, Sch 4, para 8, but reserve the right to attack such transactions if they believe that tax avoidance is involved. In general dealings involving nominees are ignored (FA 2003, Sch 16, para 3) except for leases (see **Chapter 9**).
[137]   But see also FA 1999, Sch 19 for the possibility of charges to stamp duty reserve tax.
[138]   FA 2003, Sch 4, para 17 (as amended); but although exempt these transactions may have to be notified para 17(4A).
[139]   Ibid, Sch 17A, para 16.
[140]   Ibid, s 71, provides for relief upon acquisitions by registered social landlords who may also be eligible for the relief for acquisitions by charities; FA 2003, Sch 8.
[141]   Ibid, Sch 3, para 2.

Transactions in connection with matrimonial breakdown and civil partnerships[142]

11.22 There is no general stamp duty land tax relief for transactions between married persons or persons in a civil partnership such as transferring property into joint names although in these situations, unlike people who are cohabiting, the parties are 'connected' which may affect the stamp duty land tax issues. Marriage or civil partnership offers no tax relief in general for dealings between the parties and only narrow specific reliefs are available[143] but the taxpayers are well served on divorce. However, it should be noted that there is no equivalent relief for the separation of cohabiting couples. A transaction between one party to a marriage[144] or a civil partnership[145] and the other[146] is exempt from stamp duty land tax if it is effected:

- in pursuance of an order of a court made on granting in respect of the parties a decree of divorce, nullity of marriage or judicial separation;

- in pursuance of an order of a court made in connection with the dissolution or annulment of the marriage or the parties' judicial separation at any time after the granting of such a decree;

- in pursuance of an order made at any time under Matrimonial Causes Act 1973, s 22A, s 23A or s 24A or Family Law (Scotland) Act 1985, ss 8(2) and 14(1) or the Civil Partnership Act 2004, Sch 5;

- at any time in pursuance of an agreement of the parties made in contemplation of or otherwise in connection with the dissolution or annulment of the marriage, their judicial separation or the making of a separation order in respect of them.

It will be noted that a Court order at some stage of the transaction is required. The transaction must be pursuant to an order or an agreement made in contemplation of an order. The relief is not available for parties separating without any Court intervention.

Variation of estates of deceased persons[147]

11.23 The interests of beneficiaries in the estate of a deceased individual can be chargeable interests[148] so that dealings in such interests or any chargeable interests held as part of the estate are potentially taxable. This emerges if only because there are reliefs in relation to estates which would not be necessary unless charges arose.

An initial problem is to determine when the interest of the beneficiary becomes a chargeable interest.[149] It is long-established[150] that the interest of persons entitled to the residue, are not proprietary interests and there may be similar problems as regards the

---

[142] It should be noted that there is no general exemption from stamp duty land tax for transactions between spouses or parties to a civil partnership.

[143] See, for example, FA 2003, Sch 4, para 8.

[144] Ibid, Sch 3, para 3.

[145] Tax and Civil Partnership Regulations 2005, SI 2005/3229, reg 174; FA 2003, Sch 3, para 3A.

[146] The relief is not available where children or other dependents are involved in the transaction.

[147] See also **9.39**.

[148] Although this is potentially a difficult area, the current views of HMRC Stamp Taxes appear to be helpful to the taxpayer but not necessarily consistent with the legislation. See **Chapter 9**.

[149] This is a different issue from that of whether a person is entitled to an asset owned by the deceased but

interests of even specific legacies and devisees. It seems that HMRC Stamp Taxes may regard the principle of no proprietary interest extends beyond residuary interests and insolvent estates and all assets may have to be sold leaving nothing for the beneficiaries or even where the estate is 'solvent' ie there are sufficient assets to discharge the liabilities and land that has been specifically divided but is vulnerable to the principles of abatement or the needs of the personal representative to sell the land to meet the claims of creditors. In consequence, there may not be chargeable interests until the property has been specifically appropriated to the devisee. It is, however, difficult to reconcile this with HMRC Stamp Taxes' own legislation relieving variations of estates[151] where the estate is insolvent.

11.24 There is an exemption from stamp duty land tax in respect of a transaction following a person's death that varies any disposition, whether effected by will or intestacy or otherwise, of property of which the deceased was competent to dispose, provided that:

- the transaction is carried out within a period of 2 years after the person's death; and

- no consideration in money or money's worth other than the making of a variation of another such disposition is given for it. The relief is *prima facie* not available where in order to balance the values one of the parties provides consideration or there is an acceptance of a property subject to a charge. However, it is now provided[152] that where there is consideration other than the variation of another disposition, the relief remains partially available and the charge does not apply to the consideration provided by way of making the variation and only the outside cash is taxable.

Since much of the actual consideration is to be ignored, the availability of the lower rates of tax will be tested solely by reference to the outside consideration. It also seems that where any particular item that is appropriated is subject to a mortgage the normal rules[153] do not apply so that the amount of the mortgage is not added to the chargeable consideration.[154]

11.25 This relief applies whether or not the administration of the estate is complete or the property has been distributed in accordance with the original dispositions.[155] It remains to be seen whether HMRC Stamp Taxes will be prepared to accept the argument that the satisfaction of a legacy is the variation of a disposition of the will or the rights in an intestacy, in which case this relief will be important in practice as an alternative relief where there are appropriations which may not be eligible for relief[156] and provides a possible counter to claims for stamp duty land tax by HMRC Stamp Taxes in relation to, *inter alia*:

---

pursuant to arrangements taking effect outside the will, such as where the deceased promised that the person concerned would have the house if he or she cared for the deceased (see **3.46**) or other equitable principles apply (see *Binnions v Evans* [1972] Ch 359).

[150] *Commissioner of Stamps v Livingston* [1964] 3 All ER 692 (PC).
[151] See **9.39**.
[152] FA 2003, Sch 4, para 8A(2).
[153] Ibid, Sch 4, para 8.
[154] Compare the exclusions of mortgages for appropriations by personal representatives to beneficiaries pursuant to FA 2003, Sch 4, paras 8 and 8A.
[155] Ibid, Sch 3, para 4.
[156] Ibid, Sch 3, paras 3A and 4; see also **9.34** and **9.36**.

- appropriations by a surviving spouse of the matrimonial home in satisfaction of the statutory legacy upon an intestacy; and

- appropriations by personal representatives whether with or without consent or pursuant to Administration of Estates Act 1925, s 41 of land in full or partial satisfaction of pecuniary legacies.[157]

Appropriations by personal representatives[158]

11.26 An appropriation in or towards the satisfaction of a legatee or devisee's entitlement in the estate of a deceased person, whether testate or intestate, is exempt. This applies whether the appropriation is with the consent of the beneficiary or is without consent pursuant to statutory or other power.[159]

11.27 No charge to tax arises notwithstanding that the property appropriated is subject to a mortgage and the legatee accepts the charge;[160] but the provision of any other consideration, such as where the value of the property exceeds the entitlement of the beneficiary or there are insufficient assets in the estate to compensate the other beneficiaries so that the person to whom the property is appropriated has to contribute cash from his or her own assets by way of equality, makes the transaction taxable but with a tax charge only upon such other consideration.[161] In this situation the amount of the chargeable consideration does not include the mortgage so that the unavailability of the lower rates of stamp duty land tax will be determined solely by reference to the amount of the outside consideration.

Exemptions not relieved from notification[162]

Registered social landlord[163]

11.28 Acquisitions of a chargeable interest in land is relieved[164] from charge where either:

- the person making or deemed to be making the acquisition is a registered social landlord[165] which is controlled by its tenants, and

---

[157] On the importance of consent see FA 2003, Sch 15, para 8; see **9.21**.

[158] A similar relief applies to the 'reallocation' of trust assets by trustees as between beneficiaries (FA 2003, Sch 16, para 8); but this states that the mere giving of consent is not chargeable consideration so that if there is no other chargeable consideration for the transaction it will be exempt pursuant to FA 2003, Sch 3, para 1 and so not notifiable.

[159] Administration of Estates Act 1925, s 41; *Jopling v IRC* [1940] 2 KB 282; see also FA 2003, Sch 16, para 8 dealing with reallocation of assets of a trust with consent and **9.21**.

[160] FA 2003, Sch 3, para 3A(2).

[161] Ibid, Sch 4, para 8A(1).

[162] Disadvantaged land relief was abolished by FA 2005 subject to transitional relief and the exemption for the initial establishment of unit trusts (FA 2003, s 64A) was abolished by FA 2006.

[163] FA 2003, s 71. Such bodies may also be exempt as charities (FA 2003, Sch 8 (as amended)), but their intentions to deal in leases or participate in joint development may affect the relief and produce the possible clawback thereof.

[164] This relief may be more useful to a registered social landlord than the relief for charities to which it may be entitled because there are fewer restrictions upon the relief and no clawback, nor is the assignment of any lease granted within the relief subject to the special charge upon assignment pursuant to FA 2003, Sch 17, para 11.

[165] Registered social landlords may also be eligible for one of the two reliefs for charities but unlike those reliefs the relief in the text is not subject to clawback. Other relief is available for acquisitions from such landlords; see **11.20**.

- the vendor is a qualifying body; or

- the transaction is funded with the assistance of a public subsidy; or

- the purchaser is a profit making registered provider of social hosing if the transaction is funded with the assistance of a public subsidy.[166]

A body is controlled by its tenants if the majority of its board of members are tenants occupying properties owned or managed by it. A board member means:

- a director of the company;

- if it is a body corporate whose affairs are managed by its members, a member;

- a trustee if it is a body of trustees;

- or a member of the committee of management or other body to which is entrusted the direction of its affairs in any other case.[167]

11.29 There is also an exemption where the purchaser is a profit making registered provider of social housing if the transaction is funded with the assistance of a public subsidy.[168]

A qualifying body for the purpose of being the 'vendor' means:

- a registered social landlord;

- a housing action trust under Part III of the Housing Act 1988;

- a principal council with the Local Government Act 1972;

- the Common Council of the City of London;

- the Scottish Ministers;

- a council established under Local Government etc (Scotland) Act 1994, s 2;

- Scottish Homes;

- the Department for Social Development in Northern Ireland;

- the Northern Ireland Housing Executive.

The relief also extends to a land transaction pursuant to which the purchaser (which should include a lessee) is a profit-making provider of social housing provided that the transaction is funded with the assistance of a public subsidy.[169]

---

[166]　FA 2009, s 81(3).
[167]　FA 2003, s 71(2).
[168]　Ibid, s 71(A1).
[169]　Ibid, s 71(A1).

11.30 A public subsidy is a grant or other financial assistance:[170]

- made or given by way of distribution under the National Lottery Act 1993, s 25;

- under the Housing Act 1996, s 18;

- under the Housing Grants, Construction and Regeneration Act 1996, s 126;

- under the Housing (Scotland) Act 1988, s 2; or

- under the Housing (Northern Ireland) Order 1992,[171] art 33.

Compulsory purchase facilitating development

11.31 A compulsory purchase facilitating development is exempt from stamp duty land tax.[172] It is an acquisition of a chargeable interest in respect of which the person acquiring the interest has made a compulsory purchase order for the purpose of facilitating development[173] by another person;[174] but it does not matter how the acquisition is effected so that the relief applies where the acquisition is effected by agreement[175] in England and Wales or Scotland. In Northern Ireland the reference is to a vesting order.[176] Development by the local authority itself does not qualify for the relief; only development by some other person is within the conditions for the relief. Notwithstanding that since the relief is designed as a form of subsale relief, ie there must be two acquisitions – by the local authority and by the developer from the local authority, although it seems that a lease or sublease to the developer by the local authority will probably be regarded as being sufficient to satisfy the condition for development by someone other than the local authority so that the relief to apply by HMRC Stamp Taxes. It does not matter how the acquisition is made, so that the relief applies where the acquisition is effected by agreement or vesting order[177] provided that compulsory purchase orders have been made. HMRC Stamp Taxes are taking a strict line in relation to this relief. The project must constitute 'development' as defined by the planning legislation so that a project of acquisition of development property for refurbishment may not be eligible for this relief.

11.32 It is an open question how far the negotiations between the local authority and the developer need to have progressed so that the 'purpose test' can be satisfied but it seems that there must be reasonably firm arrangements in place between the local authority and the developer for the compulsory acquisition to be for the purpose of the development.[178] HMRC Stamp Taxes are reluctant to grant the relief where there is a possibility that the development may not take place so that the local authority escapes the charge to tax. Anything less than a conditional contract[179] in place as at the effective

---

170 Ibid, s 71(4).
171 SI 1992/1725.
172 FA 2003, s 60.
173 Defined by reference to Town and Country Planning Act 1990, s 55; Town and Country Planning (Scotland) Act 1997, s 26; Planning (Northern Ireland) Order 1991, SI 1991/1220 (NI 11), art 11.
174 FA 2003, s 60(2).
175 Ibid, s 60(3).
176 Ibid, s 60(2)(b) and (4).
177 Ibid, s 60(3) and (4).
178 Note the unsatisfactory analysis of Vinelott J in *Combined Technologies plc v IRC* [1985] STC 348.
179 But see **8.18** and **8.32** on the problems arising from dealings in land where there is a section 106 agreement in place at the time.

date of the compulsory acquisition is on risk of the relief not being available and it will not be granted retrospectively if the development actually proceeds.

11.33 This makes the effective date of the compulsory acquisition crucial. In practice HMRC Stamp Taxes have suggested that the effective date is the making of the compulsory purchase order but this does not meet any of the criteria for 'completion' ie legal title does not pass nor is payment made or for substantial performance since there is no payment nor is possession taken.[180] In consequence, this is considered to be incorrect and, *prima facie*, the conveyance of the land or the general vesting declaration seems to represent the basic date.[181] However, because there will be completion by 'conveyance' a special rule applies on general principles where there is a contract the effective date will be substantial performance such as the taking of possession, payment of a substantial proportion of the compensation price or the making of the vesting order;[182] but many of these issues may depend upon a variety of factors such as appeals, decisions of the Lands Tribunal and negotiations in general before the landowner is deprived of his land.

Compliance with planning obligations

11.34 There is an exemption from stamp duty land tax in respect of a transaction which is entered into in order to comply with a planning obligation[183] or modification[184] of a planning obligation, provided that:

- the planning obligation or modification is enforceable against the vendor;

- the person making the acquisition is a public authority; and

- the transaction takes place within a period of 5 years beginning with the date on which the planning obligation was entered into or modified.[185]

It is also the view that the land acquisition must be included within the section 106[186] or section 229A agreement so as to comply with s 106(9) thereof for the relief to be available.

Certain PFI and similar projects

11.35 A limited relief arises for certain PFI projects because it is provided that certain types of actual consideration in the form of land interests or services do not count as chargeable consideration. This may also mean that if the relevant items represent the whole of the consideration the transaction *prima facie* is for no chargeable consideration

---

[180]   FA 2003, s 44.
[181]   Compare ibid, s 69(4).
[182]   Ibid, s 44(3).
[183]   Town and Country Planning Act 1990, s 106(9) or 229A(2); Town and Country Planning (Scotland) Act 1997, ss 75 and 246; Planning (Northern Ireland) Order 1991, SI 1991/1220 (NI 11) art 40.
[184]   Town and Country Planning Act 1990, s 106A(1); Planning (Northern Ireland) Order 1991, SI 1991/1220 (NI11), art 40.
[185]   FA 2003, s 61.
[186]   Town and Country Planning Act 1990 or the equivalent in Scotland in Town and Country Planning (Scotland) Act 1997, ss 75 and 246, or para 10 of the Planning (Northern Ireland) Order 1991 (1991/1220 (N 11)).

and so 'exempt' pursuant to FA 2003, Sch 3, para 1, but the transaction remains notifiable.[187] Where a transfer of a freehold or the grant or assignment of a lease is made:[188]

- by a qualifying body,[189] ie:
    - bodies within FA 2003, s 66, set out above;[190]
    - institutions within the further or higher education sectors;[191]
    - persons who undertake to establish and maintain and carry on or provide for the carrying on of an Academy;
    - Scottish institutions funded by the Scottish Further Education Funding Council or Higher Education Funding Council;

- to a non-qualifying body;

- for a consideration which consists:
    - in whole or in part of the grant of a lease or underlease of the whole or substantially the whole of the land; and
    - the carrying out of works or the provision of services by the non-qualifying body to the qualifying body;

then:

- the consideration for the transfer, assignment or lease is not chargeable[192] to the extent that it consists of
    - the leaseback;
    - the carrying out of the works; or
    - the performance of the service;

- the consideration for the leaseback is not chargeable[193] to the extent that it consists of
    - the transfer, assignment or lease;
    - any consideration in money paid by the qualifying body to the non-qualifying body for the building works; or
    - the provision of services.

The relief applies notwithstanding that 'surplus land' is involved.[194] This is land which is not included within the project. The transfer of such land is exempt from tax and it does not constitute chargeable consideration for the grant of the leaseback to the qualifying body.[195]

11.36 Notwithstanding that the effect of excluding various parts of the consideration may be to reduce the chargeable consideration to nil the transactions are made fully

---

[187] FA 2003, Sch 4, para 17(4A).
[188] Ibid, Sch 4, para 17 (as amended).
[189] Ibid, Sch 4, para 17(2).
[190] See **10.67**.
[191] Further and Higher Education 1992, ss 91, 17 and 90.
[192] FA 2003, Sch 4, para 17(3).
[193] Ibid, Sch 4, para 17(4).
[194] Ibid, Sch 4, para 17(1) (as amended).
[195] Ibid, Sch 4, para 17(3) and (4).

notifiable[196] if the actual consideration that would otherwise be chargeable exceeds any relevant threshold.[197] This notification obligation is based upon the actual consideration not being treated as chargeable consideration,[198] so that it seems that the transaction is notifiable if, apart from these provisions, there would have been a chargeable consideration in excess of the notification threshold[199] such as where the actual consideration would have been chargeable consideration apart from this relief. The £40,000 notification threshold applies in theory but it is unlikely that the actual consideration will be below this figure.

Transfers involving public bodies

11.37 There is an exemption from stamp duty land tax in respect of a transaction entered into on or in consequence of or in connection with a reorganisation effected by or under statutory provision involving the establishment, reform or abolition of one or more public bodies listed above[200] or the creation, alteration or abolition of functions to be discharged by them.[201]

Reorganisation of parliamentary constituencies

11.38 There is a relief where an order in Council is made and there is a transfer of chargeable interests in land from an existing local constituency association to a new association that is its successor.[202]

Acquisitions by bodies established for national purposes

11.39 A land transaction is exempt if the person making the acquisition is:

- a Historic Buildings and Monuments Commission for England;

- the National Endowment for Science, Technology and the Arts;

- Trustees of the British Museum;

- Trustees of the National Heritage Memorial Fund; or

- Trustees of the National History Museum.[203]

---

[196] Ibid, Sch 4, para 17(4A).
[197] Ibid, Sch 4, para 17(4A).
[198] Ibid, Sch 4, para 17(4A).
[199] Ibid, s 77A.
[200] Defined ibid, s 66(4); see **10.67**.
[201] Ibid, s 66.
[202] Ibid, s 67.
[203] Ibid, s 69.

Incorporation of a limited liability partnership[204]

11.40 The transfer[205] of a chargeable interest to a limited liability partnership in connection with[206] its incorporation is exempt provided that:

- the effective date of the transaction is not more than 1 year after the date of incorporation of the limited liability partnership;

- the transferor is, at the time when he acquired the interest if he acquired the interest after the incorporation, or, in any other case, immediately before the incorporation, a partner in a firm comprising all of the persons who are or are to be members of the limited liability partnership and no other person is a partner. If the transferor holds the interest as a nominee he must hold for one or more of the partners in such a partnership;

- the proportions of the persons who are partners in the existing (ie the incorporating) partnership in the property immediately before the transfer are the same as those to which they were entitled immediately before the incorporation or immediately after the incorporation or, if there are differences in the proportions, these do not arise as part of a scheme or arrangement of which the main or one of the main purposes is the avoidance of liability to any duty or tax.

Charities

11.41 Two areas of relief are available for charities depending upon whether or not the land is initially acquired with intention of using it solely for charitable purposes. The initial intention is important since there are certain differences in the subsequent circumstances giving rise to the loss of the relief ('clawback').

Acquisitions wholly for charitable purposes

11.42 Acquisitions by charities or a charitable trust[207] are exempt from stamp duty land tax, provided that:[208]

- the acquisition is for a qualifying charitable purposes, ie either:
    - for the purposes of the charity or another charity; or
    - as an investment, the proceeds of which are applied solely for the purposes of the charity acquiring the chargeable interest; and

- the acquisition is not made as part of a tax avoidance arrangement, ie the charity is not renting out its exemption from stamp duty land tax in order to assist other parties to acquire the land free from the charge to tax.

---

[204] There being no reliefs for the incorporation of a business partners requiring only limited liability may find this a useful arrangement for achieving this status. See also **Chapter 13**.

[205] Which suggests that the exemption is not available for leases or surrenders or other forms of 'acquisition'.

[206] On the scope of these words see *Clarke Chapman John Thompson Ltd v IRC* [1975] STC 567.

[207] FA 2003, Sch 8, para 4 (as amended).

[208] Ibid, Sch 8, para 1.

Traditionally HMRC have allowed reliefs only where the charity is formed or established in the United Kingdom and this has judicial support. However, this approach is debatable[209] and it is unclear whether HMRC Stamp Taxes intend to allow the relief for acquisitions by foreign charities.

The scope of the relief, which has been extended to charitable trusts,[210] has given rise to problems where the property, when acquired, was not intended to be utilised solely for charitable activities such as providing accommodation for the homeless or as a hospice for the terminally ill or as a school but the acquisition of a lease of premises intended to operate as a charity shop since trading is not a charitable activity. After a certain amount of hesitation HMRC Stamp Taxes now appear to accept that provided the entirety of the income from the 'commercial activity' is applied for charitable purposes the relief is available. Charity shops are exempt whether they deal in donated goods or goods which they have bought in for onward sale. This means that the concept of an 'investment' will be important such as where part of the use of the premises includes letting out the premises on commercial terms in order to generate income.[211] It is thought that, depending upon the precise facts, HMRC Stamp Taxes are unlikely to be sympathetic to the argument that this is utilising the property as an investment. The requirement of use solely for charitable purposes gives rise to problems where the charity is involved in acquiring land, possibly jointly with a developer, in order to enlarge the area of land already held by the charity as part of a project for development involving the developer constructing buildings for the charity[212] whilst constructing commercial premises or non-social housing for his own profit.[213] This means that the land will not be wholly utilised for charitable purposes notwithstanding that the development furthers the charity's activities[214] on favourable terms and it is not an investment because it does not generate a commercial income or rent. Moreover, the apparent absence of partial relief,[215] at least in the view of HMRC Stamp Taxes, means that in such situations there is no relief where the land is acquired jointly with the developer. However, an alternative form of relief may be available.

Anti-avoidance for basic relief for charities and charitable trusts

11.43 In addition to the requirement that there is no tax avoidance motive in the charity's acquisition, ie where there is a joint arrangement the attempt to acquire all of the land by the charity and enter into a tax efficient arrangement with the developer so that the charity is, in effect, 'selling' it exempt status there are two situations where the relief is vulnerable to subsequent attack, namely:

---

[209] This restriction of the relief applied in practice by HMRC Stamp Taxes may be improper as discrimination within the European Union.

[210] FA 2003, Sch 8, para 4.

[211] It seems that HMRC Stamp Taxes are taking a strict line on this and the other conditions so that the land must produce a reasonable income to qualify as an investment (see *Marson v Marriage* 54 TC 59) so that an intention to enter into a joint venture involving a lease to a third party on favourable terms such as being the beneficiary of building works which may be a premium for tax purposes and a peppercorn rent will be outside this particular relief because the income return is not a commercial rate notwithstanding the benefit of the works as a lump sum and may have to reply upon the alternative relief below.

[212] Which may be chargeable consideration imposing additional tax upon the developer should any land be transferred or leased by the charity to the developer; FA 2003, Sch 4, para 10.

[213] Where possible it is probably preferable to utilise the relief for acquisitions by Registered Social Landlords pursuant to FA 2003, s 71; see **11.20**.

[214] Note the comments on charities and developments in *Re Rosemary Simmons Memorial Housing Association* [1988] 1 WLR 1440.

[215] See **11.9**.

Clawback

11.44 Where the land is acquired with the sole intention that it is to be utilised solely for eligible charitable purposes the relief is forfeited and stamp duty land tax becomes payable equal to the tax that would have been payable on the original transaction, or a proportion thereof where only part of the land is affected by the change of use and reportable within 30 days if, while the charity still retains the land, within a 3-year period it ceases to be utilised for the purposes of the charity or held as an investment or the acquirer ceases to be a charity. Thus, for example, if a religious charity acquires premises for utilisation as a place of worship or as a residence for its religious leader or minister, the initial acquisition will be exempt, and a subsequent sale of the land because the premises are no longer required will not involve a clawback. Where only part of the land ceases to be so utilised the relief is partially withdrawn.[216] However, a change of use of the premises to an activity that is not accepted as either a charitable activity or exploiting the asset as an investment such as where the land is utilised for a joint development with a commercial developer who is to receive an interest in the land or part thereof in return for carrying out building works to be used for the purposes of the charity produces a liability to notify and pay the stamp duty land tax.[217] Alternatively, if rather than selling or assigning the chargeable interest the charity grants a lease at a premium at a token rent it will be subject to clawback because whilst the charity retains the reversionary interest it is no longer an investment because, in the view of HMRC Stamp Taxes, it does not produce sufficient income.[218] The fact that there is a chargeable premium[219] because the tenant is to construct buildings upon the charity's land for use as part of the charity's activities is not sufficient. The charity may be receiving value but this is a disposal and not an investment ie a receipt of income, the grant of a lease rather than an outright sale means that the charity is using the land for non-charitable purposes.

Subsequent assignment of lease to charities

11.45 Where the property is leased to a charity within the exemption a subsequent assignee of the lease is taxed as if he were receiving the grant of a new lease.[220] In consequence he pays tax not only on any consideration he pays for the lease but also by reference to the net present value of the current passing rent on the basis of a new lease for the unexpired term of the lease.[221] This raises a problem for charity finances. A potential assignee may require a reverse payment to cover his additional tax costs. Such a payment is exempt[222] but means that the asset has a negative value for the charity since the purchaser may be able to acquire the lease of nearby premises without the extra tax charge.[223] This charge on assignees does not apply if the relief has been clawed back or there has been a prior chargeable transaction that is not exempt.

---

[216] FA 2003, Sch 8, para 2(1).
[217] Ibid, Sch 8, para 2; s 81(1)(c).
[218] See *Marson v Marriage* 54 TC 59.
[219] FA 2003, Sch 4, para 10.
[220] Ibid, Sch 17A, para 11.
[221] This arises notwithstanding the usual exemption for undertakings by the assignee to pay the future rent; ibid, Sch 17A, para 17.
[222] Ibid, Sch 17A, para 18(2)(b).
[223] Ibid, Sch 17A, para 17.

Other charitable acquisitions

11.46 Where land is acquired by a charity or a charitable trust[224] but the charity does not intend to hold the land solely for charitable purposes so that the previous relief is not available but instead intends to hold the greater part of the subject-matter of the transaction for qualifying charitable purposes the relief is initially available. Qualifying charitable purposes are the purposes of the charity or another charity or holding the chargeable interest as an investment the proceeds of which are applied solely for the purposes of the charity making the acquisition. The greater part in the debatable view of HMRC Stamp Taxes is represented by a 51 per cent economic interest; it is not as such directly related to the geographical area. This will be important in relation to vertical developments such as ground floor commercial premises with social housing above because the draftsman has overlooked the three-dimensional nature of land and airspace.

Clawback

11.47 The relief is lost if within 3 years after the effective date[225] either:

- whilst still in the ownership of the charity the land ceases to be utilised for a qualifying charitable purpose or the acquirer ceases to be a charity. Where only part of the land is involved there is a partial clawback;[226] or

- the charity otherwise than in the furtherance of its charitable purposes either:
    - transfers a freehold in the whole or part of the land.[227] There is no restriction upon any 'part' of the land which appears to be a reference to a physical part of the land rather than a successive interest or lease. It seems that even a transfer of 1 per cent of the land produces a clawback; or
    - grants a lease of the whole or part of the land for a premium and a low rent, ie a rent, if any, which does not exceed £1000 per annum.[228]

By reason of the absence of legislative clarification there is a question of whether the grant of a lease to a developer who agrees to construct buildings upon the land retained by the charity for its purposes is a disposal or utilisation of the land in furtherance of its charitable purposes ie is a payment for the works for its benefit by the charity to the developer.

It should be noted that in these cases there may be the grant of a lease to a developer at a low rent but on terms that it will carry out certain works for the benefit of the charity possibly upon the land retained by the charity which will constitute chargeable consideration other than rent.[229] The extent and cost of these works may influence the rent level but the statutory threshold has to be noted.

---

[224] Ibid, Sch 8, para 3.
[225] Note the problems of two effective dates for leases; Ibid, Sch 17A, para 12A; see **7.25**; delay in executing the lease can extend the clawback period.
[226] Ibid, Sch 8, para 2(1).
[227] Ibid, Sch 8, para 3.
[228] Ibid, Sch 8, para 3(3)(b) (as amended); Sch 5, para 9A.
[229] Ibid, Sch 4, para 10; see **Chapter 8**. Attempts to escape from the charge upon the works by the developer taking a lease of the entire land to be developed for the charity so that he is carrying out the works on his own land with an obligation to sublease the relevant part back to the charity produces a land exchange (FA 2003, s 47) but the charity *prima facie* will not be subject to tax on its lease, but with a potential problem should it assign the lease to a non-charity (FA 2003, Sch 17A, para 11). Although this arrangement is not so

There is a 'premium' if there is any consideration other than rent which will include all chargeable premiums such as certain backdated rent,[230] building works,[231] transfers and leasebacks[232] and there is no express suggestion in the legislation that these provisions for clawback of relief do not apply although as indicated elsewhere[233] a simple reference to 'consideration' is to 'chargeable consideration' so that, on this interpretation of the legislation, there is no clawback where the buildings works as premium for the lease are not taxable pursuant to FA 2003, Sch 4, para 10(2)[234] which could be a key factor for joint developments between charities and commercial developers.

Charitable trading subsidiaries[235]

11.48 Attempts to deal with this situation by forming a subsidiary company to which the property is transferred and which agree to transfer are likely to involve substantial charges to stamp duty land tax. Notwithstanding that all of the profits are to be passed over to the charity the charitable exemption is not available for direct acquisitions of chargeable interests where the charity owns the land but may have tax difficulties because its utilisation of the land. The transfer to the company is within the connected company charge.[236] However, this charge is likely to be supplanted by the provision that, where a lease was granted to a charity with the benefit of the exemption, any assignment of the lease will be treated as a fully taxable deemed grant of a new lease to the assignee.[237] Even where the charity is a body corporate it is questionable whether the relief for intra-group transfers is available pursuant to FA 2003, Sch 7, Part 1, because it is doubtful whether charitable companies are the beneficial owners of the shares in their subsidiary companies but in practice hitherto HMRC Stamp Taxes have not relied upon this point.

Consideration reduced to nil or ignored

11.49 Other exemptions are less explicit. For example, in certain situations it is provided that any actual consideration is to be treated as if it were nil or not 'chargeable consideration' or 'exempt'. This has three consequences:

(1)   the actual consideration must be ignored in self-assessing the liability to stamp duty land tax. The failure to appreciate the difference between actual and chargeable consideration will result in an unnecessary charge to stamp duty land tax for clients;

(2)   there may be a situation where there is no other chargeable consideration, so that the transaction is 'exempt' pursuant to FA 2003, Sch 3, para 1, which may avoid the need to notify the transaction[238] and so reduce the compliance costs for taxpayers significantly;

---

favourable for non-exempt bodies, such as local authorities, it takes place at market value (FA 2003, Sch 4, para 5) and not for the building works so that it may assist the developer in reducing his tax charge.

[230]   Ibid, Sch 5, para 1A; Sch 17A, paras 9 and 9A; see **7.38**, **7.130** and **7.139**.

[231]   Ibid, Sch 4, para 10.

[232]   Ibid, s 47; Sch 4, para 5; Sch 17A, para 16.

[233]   See **16.26**.

[234]   See **Chapter 8** and **7.70**.

[235]   There may be significant company law and trust issues in such activities see, eg, *Re Rosemary Simmons Memorial Housing Association* [1988] 1 WLR 1440.

[236]   FA 2003, s 53.

[237]   Ibid, Sch 17A, para 11(2)(d).

[238]   Ibid, s 77.

(3)   the actual consideration is ignored for the linked transaction rules.

This applies mainly in relation to transactions involving PFI projects.[239] The area most likely to be encountered in practice involves surrenders and regrants such as increasing the term of a lease of a flat.[240]

Other specialised reliefs

11.50 Highly focused and specialised reliefs, which are described in more detail in relevant paragraphs, are available for:

* right to buy and shared ownership;[241]

* intra-group transactions;[242]

* company reconstructions and reorganisations;[243]

* demutualisations of insurance companies[244] and building societies;[245]

* transfers involving certain public bodies,[246] and the reorganisation of parliamentary constituencies.[247] The utilisation of the word 'transfer' may restrict the scope of this relief;

* certain alternative finance arrangements for land acquisition where lending at interest may not be allowed.[248] Although intended to benefit persons whose principles prohibit usury this relief is available to all taxpayers. The relief has been extended to certain fundraising instruments;[249]

* the crofting communities' right to buy;[250]

* acquisition of residential property in connection with the relocation of employees;[251]

* acquisition of residential property in consideration of exchanges and part-exchanges for newly constructed dwellings;[252]

* acquisitions by chainbreaker companies of residential property;[253]

---

[239] Ibid, Sch 4, para 17 (as amended).
[240] See **7.223**.
[241] FA 2003, s 70, and Sch 9 (as amended); see **10.67** and following.
[242] Ibid, Sch 7, Part 1; see **Chapter 12**.
[243] Ibid, Sch 7, Part 2.
[244] Ibid, s 63.
[245] Ibid, s 64.
[246] Ibid, s 66.
[247] Ibid, s 67.
[248] Ibid, ss 71–75B; see **6.56**.
[249] FA 2009, Sch 61; see **3.30**.
[250] FA 2003, s 75; see **5.35**.
[251] Ibid, Sch 6A, paras 5 and 6; see **10.37**.
[252] Ibid, Sch 6A, paras 1 and 2; see **6.69** and **10.20**.
[253] Ibid, Sch 6A, para 4; see **6.75**.

- acquisitions of dwellings of deceased individuals from personal representatives.[254]

Historic hangovers

11.51 Regulations[255] issued pursuant to FA 2003, s 123(2), bring forward certain specialised reliefs from stamp duty in old legislation into stamp duty land tax, usually by inserting relieving provisions into the relevant legislation namely exemptions pursuant to:

- Inclosure Act 1845, s 163A;

- Metropolitan Commons Act 1866, s 33;

- Chequers Estate Act 1917, s 3A;

- Finance Act 1931, s 28(3), including land transaction returns within the list of instruments;

- Chevening Estate Act 1959, s 2A;

- Finance Act 1960, s 74A (visiting forces);

- Friendly Societies Act 1974, s 105A (amalgamations);

- Welsh Development Agency Act 1975, Sch 1, para 20;

- National Health Service (Scotland) Act 1978, ss 12DA and 104A;

- National Heritage Act 1980, s 11A;

- Industry Act 1980, s 2A;

- Highways Act 1980, s 281A;

- Airports Act 1986, s 76A;

- Building Societies Act 1986, s 109A (mergers pursuant to sub-ss 93 and 94);

- National Health Service and Community Care Act 1990, s 61A;

- Ports Act 1991, s 36A;

- Water Resources Act 1991, Sch 3, paras 8(3)–(5);

- Further and Higher Education Act 1992, s 88A;

- Further and Higher Education (Scotland) Act 1992, s 58A;

---

[254] Ibid, Sch 6A, para 3; see **6.73**.
[255] Stamp Duty Land Tax (Consequential Amendment of Enactments) Regulations 2003, SI 2003/2867.

- Friendly Societies Act 1992, s 105A;

- Museums and Galleries Act 1992, s 8;

- Finance Act 1994, s 254(4);

- Health Authorities Act 1995, Sch 2, para 5(2A)–(2C);

- Merchant Shipping Act 1995, s 221(2A);

- Broadcasting Act 1996, Sch 7, para 25;

- Education Act 1997, s 53A;

- Regional Development Agencies Act 1998, s 39A;

- School Standards and Framework Act 1998;

- Access to Justice Act 1999, s 34A;

- Criminal Justice and Court Services Act 2000, s 19;

- Learning and Skills Act 2000, s 94A;

- Transport Act 2000, Sch 26, para 40A;

- Communications Act 2003, Sch 3, para 5A; and

- Ports (Northern Ireland) Order 1994, art 23A.[256]

Since these exemptions are issued pursuant to the powers in FA 2003, s 123, the first assignment of any lease granted within the exemption in the list is subject to tax as the deemed grant of a new lease.[257]

---

[256]　SI 1994/2809 (NI 16).
[257]　FA 2003, Sch 17A, para 11.

Chapter 12

EXEMPTIONS – CORPORATE REORGANISATIONS AND INTRA-GROUP TRANSACTIONS

PART I – CORPORATE REORGANISATIONS

INTRODUCTION

12.1 Companies[1] are both 'vendors' and 'purchasers' for the purposes of stamp duty land tax. They are liable to tax upon their acquisitions as other taxpayers with slight modification of the compliance regime.[2] Acquisitions made from connected persons take place at not less than the market value,[3] subject to certain limited exclusions[4] and acquisitions for no chargeable consideration such as where the property is a lease at a full reviewable rack rent and so has no market value, may have to be notified;[5] but there are issues whether the notification thresholds of £40,000 or the nil rate threshold apply to override this.[6] In consequence, dealings where connected companies are involved will, *prima facie*, attract a high charge to tax. This will apply to, *inter alia*:

- incorporations of businesses. Since there is an acquisition by the existing owners of the business who will receive the shares the connected company charge will almost inevitably apply. There is no general relief for converting a sole trader or a partnership into a company unlike conversions into a limited liability partnership (LLP).[7] There are many issues as to the possible effective date for such transactions;[8]

- companies[9] are both 'vendors' and purchasers' for the purposes of stamp duty land tax. They are liability to tax upon their acquisitions as other taxpayers with slight modification of the compliance regime.[10] Acquisitions made from connected

---

1   Defined for stamp duty land tax by FA 2003, s 100; but note that although limited liability partnerships (LLPs) are bodies corporate their corporate personality is ignored, at least for certain purposes; see FA 2003, Sch 15, para 2.
2   FA 2003, s 100(2); see **15.28**.
3   Ibid, s 53.
4   Ibid, s 54.
5   Ibid, s 53(4); see **9.17** and **11.19**.
6   Ibid, ss 77 and 77A; see **Chapter 17**.
7   Ibid, s 65; see **11.40**.
8   See **Chapter 14**.
9   Defined for stamp duty land tax by FA 2003, s 100; but note that although Limited Liability Partnerships (LLPs) are bodies corporate their corporate personality is ignored, at least for certain purposes, see FA 2003, Sch 15, para 2.
10   Ibid, s 100(2); see **15.28**.

persons take place at not less than the market value,[11] subject to certain limited exclusions[12] and acquisitions for no chargeable consideration such as where the property is a lease at a full reviewable rack rent and so has no market value may have to be notified,[13] but there are issues whether the notification thresholds of £40,000 or the nil rate threshold apply to override this.[14] In consequence dealings where connected companies are involved will *prima facie* attract a high charge to tax. This will apply to, *inter alia*;

- incorporations of businesses. Since there is an acquisition from the existing owners of the business who will receive the share the connected company charge will almost inevitably apply. There is no general relief for converting a sole trade or a partnership into a company unlike conversion into a limited liability partnership (LLP).[15] There are many issues as to the possible effective date for such transactions[16] because of the various steps in the process of subscribing for or being issued with shares as consideration[17] and the company may take 'possession' of the land before issue of the shares or execution of the conveyance so that the former subsale relief is not possible;[18]

- dealings with companies as sellers contains problems since, for example, where there is an assignment of a lease which qualified for the relief for intra group exemptions,[19] notwithstanding the exclusion from chargeable consideration for assignments of leases in general[20] this assignment is subject to a special charge.[21]

Two areas of highly specialised relief and the inevitably related complex long-term anti-avoidance legislation are available in relation to corporate reorganisations involving the 'acquisition' of chargeable interests in land, namely:

- total exemption for a limited range of corporate reconstructions;[22] and

- a reduced rate of 0.5 per cent for certain types of corporate reorganisations,[23] described as 'acquisitions relief'.

12.2 There is also a relief for intra-group transactions which applies to all dealings in chargeable interests but is subject to very restrictive conditions and clawback provisions.[24]

In this context the issue of 'partial relief' may be crucial. HMRC Stamp Taxes are firmly of the view that partial relief is not available.[25] There are, therefore, difficulties where the

---

[11] Ibid, s 53.
[12] Ibid, s 54.
[13] Ibid, s 53(4).
[14] Ibid, ss 77 and 77A; see **Chapter 17**.
[15] Ibid, s 65; see **11.40**.
[16] See **Chapter 14**.
[17] See **1.27** and **14.27**.
[18] FA 2003, s 45; see **Chapter 6**.
[19] Ibid, Sch 7, Part 1; see **12.60**.
[20] Ibid, Sch 17A, para 17.
[21] Ibid, Sch 17A, para 11.
[22] Ibid, Sch 7, para 7.
[23] Ibid, Sch 7, para 8.
[24] Ibid, Sch 7, para 1; see also **12.102**.
[25] See **11.9**.

transaction involves the acquisition of a part interest in property such as where the company being reconstructed, or acquiring the chargeable interest being transferred intra-group, has only a part interest such as a tenant in common. In the view of HMRC Stamp Taxes regardless of whether the transferor had only a part interest in the property and is passing the whole of that interest, or whether the transferor has the entire interest which is being joint acquired by a relevant company and on outsider, this outside involvement precludes the availability of the relief notwithstanding that only the part interest is being acquired and there is no acquisition from or transfer by the other co-owner. These problems of partial relief apply across the whole spectrum of exemptions and reduced rates of stamp duty land tax such as where a registered social landlord and a commercial developer jointly acquire land with the intention of constructing a block whereby the first two floors are commercial property and the remaining 18 floors are social housing, or a company transfers land into a corporate joint venture or partnership involving outside participants. In these cases although the land is to be in part applied for charitable purposes or is retained within the stamp duty land tax group HMRC Stamp Taxes are, in practice, adamant in their view[26] that the exemptions do not apply in part so that charities or the group company are not entitled to any relief whatsoever.[27] It is considered that the definition of 'chargeable interest' which includes part interest in property is incompatible with the view of HMRC Stamp Taxes as currently applied but, in practice, alternative methods of dealing with the land acquisition may be prudent for the time being. There are more problems where the reorganisation or intra-group transfer involves the entire interest in the property including the other party's interest. HMRC Stamp Taxes are firmly of the view that a transfer by joint owners cannot qualify for any exemptions whatsoever notwithstanding that there is an effective acquisition of a separate chargeable interest acquired from a suitable party.[28] Two transactions seem to be prudent for the time being.[29]

Due diligence – 'time bombs' etc

12.3   Although the major stamp tax issues relating to shares and marketable securities are outside the scope of this book, it has to be noted that, although there is not, as such, a charge to stamp duty land tax upon share transactions,[30] movements involving shares can have stamp duty land tax implications. There are issues for share sales[31] but there are important issues of due diligence and new types of title problems for persons purchasing or leasing land from companies considered in this Chapter. For example,

---

[26]   Which is not consistent with the position which applied in practice in the later days of traditional stamp duty.

[27]   There may be issues as to whether the land is to be utilised solely for the relevant charitable purpose pursuant to FA 2003, Sch 8.

[28]   There may be issues as to the nature of the consideration provided in such cases unless there is a separate allocation and separate contract for the acquisition, but HMRC Stamp Taxes do not proceed to such detailed issues because even though there may be separate contracts they take the position that such joint involvement is incompatible with the exemptions or reliefs.

[29]   The linked transaction principles do not apply to reconvert two separate transfers into a single transaction for the purposes of the relief; they merely aggregate chargeable consideration; but HMRC Stamp Taxes may seek to apply the general anti-avoidance provisions pursuant to FA 2003, ss 75A–75C; see **2.19**.

[30]   A senior member of HMRC boasted that he had solved the problem of 'land rich companies' for these purposes but nothing to justify his boasting has appeared in the legislation and these principles have been withdrawn as ineffective in other parts of the world.

[31]   Note the importance of timing share sales for the purposes of the general anti-avoidance provisions; FA 2003, s 75C(1).

- an acquisition of a chargeable interest in consideration of the issue of shares is a taxable transaction with important problems in determining the effective date;[32]

- transactions involving shares can constitute scheme transactions for the purposes of the general anti-avoidance provisions,[33] but transfers of shares are ignored if they would otherwise have been the first scheme transaction.[34]

Also a purchaser of shares acquires not only the company but all of the stamp duty land tax problems of that company. In consequence, the question of investigations, warranties and indemnities as well as the adequacy of any disclosure letter will need to take this tax and its general lack of finality into account.

12.4 It is no longer sufficient to ask whether the target company's documents have been 'duly stamped'. The lack of finality in stamp duty land tax[35] and the plethora of anti-avoidance measures requires a wholly different approach to contracts. The structure of warranties, indemnities and due diligence in relation to share transactions has changed enormously. The areas for investigation are:

- whether the share transaction itself will have any stamp duty land tax consequences, such as the clawback of intra-group relief;[36]

- whether the share sale is a scheme transaction for the purposes of the general anti-avoidance provisions;[37]

- whether the company is up-to-date as regards its compliance;

- whether there are any risks of future Enquiries and investigations by HMRC Stamp Taxes or the making of discoveries etc[38] which is a particular problem in relation to self-assessment and retrospective investigation rather than immediate approval or objection to the documentation;

- whether the event rather than stopping a time relief from running and producing clawback means that a new time clock commences;

- whether the company has any long-term problems such as leases subject to rent review or land purchased subject to some form of overage or clawback or other variable consideration[39] which will continue whilst the company owns the property and possibly beyond;

- whether deferred or postponed tax, such as that dealing with rent reviews and clawbacks, has been properly dealt with so that the company will not be exposed to interest or penalties.

---

[32] See **1.27** and **Chapter 14**.
[33] FA 2003, ss 75A–75C.
[34] Ibid, s 75C(1).
[35] See **2.14**.
[36] FA 2003, Sch 7, Part 1.
[37] Ibid, s 75C(1).
[38] Ibid, Sch 10, para 31; which can arise over 21 years.
[39] Note that the company may be subject to such obligations notwithstanding it was not a party to the original transaction (FA 2003, s 81A; Sch 17A, para 12).

These are issues relating solely to the shares in the company: they are an entirely separate set of problems from those involved in transferring property to a company or purchasing or leasing property from a company. However, these special charges could be relevant in relation to the purchase of shares. Although the liability for dealing with the special charge upon land falls upon the assignee or purchaser of the property he may require some form of indemnity or comfort against any additional tax that arises because he is being penalised for the fact that the vendor obtains some form of relief from stamp duty land tax. This could produce a potential liability for the company and may, on certain views, produce a lease with a negative value. The obtaining of these reliefs or their equivalent for stamp duty[40] in relation to share transactions affecting companies which have benefited from intra-group and other relief[41] may be relevant in deciding whether there is to be an immediate clawback of any intra-group relief or either of the reconstruction reliefs obtained within the preceding 3 years or longer where the clawback event, although happening outside the 3-year period, takes effect in connection with arrangements entered into during the 3-year period.[42]

12.5 There are also long-term issues for purchasers of assets from companies since, for example, it is provided[43] that where a lease has qualified, *inter alia*, for relief in these areas the first assignment of that lease that is not 'exempt' is taxable as if it were the grant of a new lease, ie there is, *inter alia*, a tax on the future rent.[44] A purchaser of a business from a company, therefore, runs the risk that he has to pay stamp duty land tax not only upon the apportioned part of the consideration allocated to land[45] but also the future rent and faces the usual problems of long-term reporting and payment obligations for variable rent since a new 5-year period commences. Well-advised purchasers may seek indemnities against such additional tax since they are being forced to subsidise the vendor's tax emption. Unlike the basic clawback with a 3-year time limit, this special charge on future rent applies no matter how long the interval between grant and assignment and notwithstanding these two events are totally unconnected and not part of any 'arrangements'. Companies and their auditors may need to consider whether the accounts should recognise that either there is a deferred tax liability or the lease may have a 'negative value' because of the risk that indemnities on future sale may be a substantial amount where thee is a long lease at a full rent with a high net present value.

12.6 In consequence, when planning a reconstruction of a company or a group and the possible utilisation of these reliefs, it is now necessary to consider whether the proposed transaction will either:

- trigger a clawback of previously obtained reliefs;[46] or

---

[40] The clawback and exclusion events will be related to share transactions and so within the realms of stamp duty and its reliefs, such as s 42 of FA 1930 and ss 75 and 77 of FA 1982. As the clawback is related to a company leaving the group or a change of control, the relieving events from the clawback will be linked to the share transfers. Both sets of relieving provisions must, therefore, be noted.

[41] See FA 1930, s 42 and FA 1986, s 75.

[42] FA 2003, Sch 7, paras 4 and 9. There is no benefit to be obtained by entering into negotiations but deferring the completion date until after the 3-year period has expired.

[43] Ibid, Sch 17A, para 11; see **7.232**.

[44] These provisions override the exclusion from charge of the usual covenants to pay future rent pursuant to ibid, Sch 17A, para 17.

[45] Including, in the view of HMRC Stamp Taxes, the embedded goodwill of the business; see **1.5**.

[46] Including a relief from stamp duty obtained within the preceding 2 or 3 years (depending upon the date of the instrument for which the relief was obtained) since such relief remains subject to clawback: see FA 2003, Sch 19, para 6.

- set up a new 3-year period in relation to land in the United Kingdom involved in the reconstruction;[47] or

- involve a roll-over of previously obtained relief so that the clawback risk passes into the new group for the balance of the 3-year period;[48] or

- require the potential impact upon the proposed arrangements to be investigated possibly where there are plans for the liquidation of any company which may become liable directly or indirectly for the clawback amount.[49] This will involve a need for careful planning of any arrangements to fund any stamp duty land tax[50] actually clawed back since this may involve a payment in cash as part of the reconstruction, which is not permitted by the terms of the section granting the relief intended to be relied upon, thereby destroying the exemption being sought; or the possible roll-over of the clawback into the new group will also need to be investigated where the particular stage is merely one step in a much larger reconstruction involving onward movement of shares which may be inconsistent with the roll-over treatment of the clawback; or

- create long-term valuation issues because of the charge upon future rents should certain leases be granted as part of the arrangement where purchasers will justifiably seek some form of indemnity against the increased tax charge on acquiring the leases; or

- whether there is land with an open stamp duty land tax position such as rent renewals or the contract for the acquisition of the land contain an open overage or clawback payment. This existence of such a consideration may inhibit the reconstruction because the proposed reconstruction is incompatible with the formula for calculating the additional consideration as there may be no effective exit strategy.[51]

Warranties

12.7 A sale of shares[52] in a company is likely to involve a degrouping or change of control[53] which may operate to trigger a clawback event so that whenever shares are acquired it will be necessary to investigate whether there has been an acquisition within a relieving provision and to take appropriate warranties and indemnities. It will also be necessary to ensure that the company complies with its obligations to notify the clawback and pay the stamp duty land tax within the prescribed 30-day period.[54] There are also fundamental warranties required to the effect that the company has preserved

---

[47]   FA 2003, Sch 7, paras 3 and 9.
[48]   See, eg, FA 2003, Sch 7, para 4(6) and (7).
[49]   On the recovery of clawback liabilities from associated companies see FA 2003, Sch 7, paras 5 and 12.
[50]   Or stamp duty from the previous regime FA 2003, Sch 19, para 6.
[51]   See **5.206**; FA 2003, s 81A; Sch 17A, para 12.
[52]   Transactions other than the transfer of shares (such as the issue of new shares or the creation of certain types of loan capital or pre-emptive rights) may cause the clawback provision to apply and the subscribers may find it prudent to seek indemnities against loss arising from the company's liability to stamp duty land tax because the new issue of shares affects 'control'.
[53]   It may also affect the question as to whether the arrangement is a scheme of reconstruction for the purposes of certain reliefs; see, for example, *Crane Fruehauf v IRC* [1975] STC 51; *Snell v HMRC* [2006] STC (SCD) 295. This could be particularly important in relation to reorganisations of companies in the recession because of the need for new monies or the desire to dispose of non-core businesses.
[54]   FA 2003, Sch 7, paras 3 and 9.

all appropriate records so that the company (ie effectively the purchaser of the shares) can carry out any subsequent tax obligations including providing the necessary information to purchasers of chargeable interests held by the company in due course.[55] Certain documentation is required in order to enable the company to deal with its own position but subsequent purchasers of the property may require certain information so that they have the basis for calculating their tax liability such as in relation to holding over or rent reviews after the expiration of the fifth year of the term of the lease. Also there are many long-term risk situations ('time bombs') where a company is a taxpayer with an open stamp duty land tax position such as leases with variable rents,[56] and the long-term risk of abnormal rent increases,[57] later linked transactions[58] including lease renewals[59] and challenges by discovery assessments for up to 21 years.[60] Notwithstanding that the proposed transaction involves only the shares in the company, the fact that it owns interests in land requires in-depth investigation to discover that, if any, problems exist such as whether the company has made any acquisitions for a variable consideration, and whether these include an acceptable exit strategy[61] or has a lease that attracts a special charge upon assignment where provision for indemnities on sale may be required, or has claimed reliefs subject to clawback, where there is a base rent for the purposes of subsequent rent reviews and abnormal increases in rent, or obligations to make overage or clawback payments.

Associated companies – secondary liabilities

12.8   It is necessary to apply the warranties not merely to the company whose shares are being acquired and any subsidiary companies that are being acquired with it and to companies being retained by the vendor. There may be potential liabilities for the unpaid tax of other companies. For example, where an associated company has obtained the benefit of relief pursuant to FA 2003, Sch 7 but has not paid the tax arising upon a subsequent clawback event or there is power to recover the clawback amount from other companies in the same group as the acquiring company or lessee body corporate,[62] so that it is necessary to take protection against this contingent liability. This warranty will need to cover not only a liability to pay the clawback which has already occurred but also a liability which may arise if a clawback event occurs in the future in respect of transactions which have occurred prior to the share sale. For example, the subsequent sale of the transferee or lessee company may, if the stamp duty land tax is not paid, result in the target company in the current transaction having to pay the tax with little hope of recovering from the relevant company, such as where that company is insolvent.

PROCEDURE FOR RELIEF

12.9   There is no formal procedure for 'claiming' the relief. The parties simply take the relief by making appropriate entries in the land transaction tax return and not self-assessing any tax or paying the lower amount of stamp duty land tax and hoping

---

[55]   Ibid.
[56]   Ibid, Sch 17A, paras 7 and 8.
[57]   Ibid, Sch 17A, paras 13, 14 and 15.
[58]   Ibid, ss 81A, 108 and Sch 17A, para 11.
[59]   Ibid, Sch 17A, para 5.
[60]   Ibid, Sch 10, para 31; note also para 12(2A).
[61]   See **5.206**.
[62]   FA 2003, Sch 7, para 5.

that any subsequent HMRC Stamp Taxes Enquiry agrees with their views.[63] The usual range of penalties and interest will apply if the interpretation adopted by the parties proves to be incorrect, but, provided that the parties have considered all relevant matters properly and can prove this by having made and returned contemporaneous written records, they may not be subject to the additional penalties or extended discovery periods for 'negligence' or 'fraud'.

RECONSTRUCTIONS AND DEMERGERS – RELIEFS

12.10 FA 2003, Sch 7, para 7 provides for relief[64] on a provisional basis ie subject to clawback[65] from stamp duty land tax for chargeable transactions in land entered into pursuant to a scheme of reconstruction. This relief is total and applies to all forms of chargeable transactions. It is not limited to sales but includes the grant, surrender or variation of leases, grants or options and pre-emption rights, restrictive covenants and other chargeable interests.

12.11 There is a total relief[66] where:

- pursuant to;[67]

- a scheme for reconstruction;[68]

- which is entered into for *bona fide* commercial purposes and not for tax avoidance;[69]

- of a body corporate;[70]

- whereby another body corporate acquires the whole or part of the undertaking[71] of the company; and

- pursuant to or in connection[72] with the transfer of the undertaking;

- a land transaction[73] is entered into;

- the consideration for the acquisition consists either:

---

[63] See **11.11**.
[64] The transaction nevertheless remains notifiable: FA 2003, s 77.
[65] See **12.51** and **12.103**.
[66] The transaction is a chargeable transaction but, in effect, the tax rate is reduced to nil.
[67] This differs significantly from the equivalent relief from stamp duty which was available for transfers 'in connection with' a reconstruction see *Dobush v Greater Winnipeg Water District* [1945] 2 WWR 371; *Baker v Provident Accident and White Cross Insurance Co Ltd* [1939] 2 All ER 690.
[68] See **12.15**.
[69] See **12.93**.
[70] Company includes body corporate; FA 2003, s 100(1).
[71] See **12.21**.
[72] *Clarke Chapman – John Thompson Ltd v IRC* [1975] STC 567, holding that these are wide words including matters not directly part of the scheme; compare the construction of 'for the purpose of' in *Combined Technologies plc v IRC* [1985] STC 348.
[73] See **3.1**.

- wholly of the issue[74] of non-redeemable shares[75] in the company acquiring the undertaking to either:
- the company whose undertaking is being acquired; or
- all or any of that company's shareholders; or
- partly of the issue of non-redeemable shares and the assumption or discharge of the liabilities[76] of the company whose undertaking is being acquired;

- so that after[77] the acquisition:
  - each shareholder of each of the companies is a shareholder of the other company; and
  - the proportion of shares of each of the companies held by any shareholder is the same or as nearly may be the same as the proportion of shares held by that shareholder in the other company.

Motive or purpose condition

12.12 The acquisition must be effected for *bona fide* commercial reasons and not form part of a scheme of arrangement the main purpose or one of the main purposes of which is the avoidance of liability to stamp duty, income tax, corporation tax, capital gains tax or stamp duty land tax. These are two separate disqualifying conditions and have to be analysed and applied separately. In most cases the transaction will be one where the parties are seeking clearances from other divisions of HMRC. This is important since HMRC Stamp Taxes have not introduced a specific clearance procedure and either refuse to give advance clearances because the issues are too difficult for them and they do not have the ability to ensure that they have asked the appropriate questions to ensure that they have all appropriate information from the perspective of their current bizarre interpretations of the legislation and there is no express statutory duty to provide any form of pre or post transaction ruling; and a request for guidance after the event is effectively a trigger for HMRC Stamp Taxes to launch a full, expensive and time consuming Enquiry and any 'formal rulings' whether pre or post transaction do not bind HMRC Stamp Taxes and are not regarded by them as a basis for mitigating penalties[78] or seek to renege where they have given a clearance.[79] In practice, however, a clearance for the purposes of capital gains tax[80] will usually be accepted as sufficient to satisfy this condition.

12.13 However, this comfort may be diminishing since in practice where there is not or cannot be a clearance for other taxes HMRC Stamp Taxes are taking an extremely aggressive line. Although it applies in the context of corporate reconstructions this approach is particularly important in the context of intra-group transactions where a

---

[74]   See **1.27**.

[75]   See **12.30**.

[76]   See **12.25**.

[77]   Which appears to mean 'immediately after' the effective date, although arrangements for the onward movement of the consideration or other shares may affect the conditions requiring a 'reconstruction' or the 'true nature' of the consideration: see, eg, *Crane Fruehauf v IRC* [1975] STC 51; compare *Snell v HMRC* [2006] STC (SCD) 295.

[78]   Also there are no powers to mitigate interest even where the late payment is a direct consequence of bad advice from HMRC Stamp Taxes.

[79]   HMRC Stamp Taxes have refused advance clearances because they find the question both difficult and, for example, on one occasion reneged on a clearance on the basis that the draft documents involved assets in the name of the beneficial owner whereas the final documents were in the name of a nominee which was not a point relevant to whether the conditions for the relief had been satisfied.

[80]   Taxation of Chargeable Gains Act 1992, ss 137, 138 and 139.

similar qualifying condition applies[81] where there are extremely few situations where a clearance can be obtained for the taxes so that HMRC Stamp Taxes are left to their own assessment of the situation. There is a more detailed discussion below of the current practical problems in the context of intra-group transactions but the comments are also relevant in this context.[82]

12.14 Various aspects of these conditions raise highly technical issues, as follows.

'Reconstruction'

12.15 A scheme of reconstruction requires that an existing company transfers its undertaking to another company which carries on substantially the same activities and that both companies are owned by substantially the same shareholders. The reference is to 'a' scheme and this can be a key factor. There will be a fundamental difference between a single overall scheme which proceeds by stages and several separate transactions or schemes notwithstanding that these produce the same end result. For example, there may be a difference between a company reconstruction that is followed by a separate sale of the consideration shares[83] and a single agreement to reorganise the companies and sell the shares.[84] However, these cases suggest that the issue may not be capable of final resolution at the time of registering the shares issued as consideration[85] but may, contrary to long-standing practices and understanding, include possible onward sales of the shares or outside investment in the acquiring company.

12.16 Since there are requirements for total identity of members,[86] there is a tendency to regard the word 'reconstruction' in the qualifying conditions as being redundant but this is not correct although there is a tendency for many aspects of the construction of these two terms to overlap.[87] Notwithstanding that total shareholder identity[88] is an express condition for this relief and the general law test for reconstruction required is only 'substantial identity', merely satisfying the former condition is not necessarily sufficient to satisfy this test although this would satisfy the substantial identity definition of 'reconstruction'. There may be situations where, notwithstanding that the mirror share capital condition is satisfied, there may not be a scheme of reconstruction and the relief is not available. For example, where there are plans for the onward movement of the shares in the acquiring company to a third party which have become so integrated into the contracts that they are part of 'the scheme', the onward sale can affect what is the consideration[89] and/or whether there is the necessary shareholder identity.[90] This can include provisions in the company's articles of association creating pre-emptive rights which commit the party to offer or dispose of the shares in a particular way; such provisions become part of the scheme where the articles of association are altered or the company is initially incorporated with such provisions in its articles of association so that the terms on which the consideration shares are issued

---

[81]   See **12.36** and **12.93**.
[82]   See **12.93**.
[83]   Although in certain cases this may raise questions as to whether the relief is clawed back because of a change of control.
[84]   See, for example, *Crane Fruehauf v IRC* [1975] STC 51; *Snell v HMRC* [2006] STC (SCD) 295.
[85]   *Crane Fruehauf v IRC* [1975] STC 51.
[86]   FA 2003, Sch 7, para 7(4).
[87]   For the interaction of this requirement and the provisions referring to 'after' the transaction see **12.11** and **12.15**.
[88]   Allowing for rounding of share issues in situations where the entitlement is to partial interests in shares.
[89]   *Crane Fruehauf v IRC* [1975] STC 51.
[90]   *Central and District Properties v IRC* [1966] 2 All ER 433; *Crane Fruehauf v IRC* [1975] 1 All ER 429.

must be part of the scheme notwithstanding that those rights are not referred to in the main contracts. Such contracts will refer to the issue of the consideration shares which will be issued or allotted on the terms and conditions set out in the articles of association or the resolution creating the relevant class of share capital with the restrictions inherent in the shares so that the scheme involving the issue of shares must include the terms of those shares and their rights and restrictions as part of the reconstruction. Hitherto HMRC Stamp Taxes do not appear to have spotted this obvious basis of attack but it must only be a matter of time before they do and transactions including past transactions are subject to Enquiries or discovery assessments. Where there are plans for the injection of fresh outside capital into the acquiring company, the documentation relating to and the timing of such contributions can affect whether there is a scheme of reconstruction.[91] The word therefore raises a larger range of issues in testing for the entitlement to the exemption.

12.17 It is first necessary to identify the scheme which will depend upon a variety of factors. This depends upon a variety of factors such as the original intentions and possible modifications as problems emerge[92] and how these modifications change on the target shareholders or the banks change their views during the process. For example, in *Crane Fruehauf v IRC*,[93] there was a proposal for the acquisition of the whole of the issued share capital of the target company. In order to maintain its shareholding position, one of the participants in the target company required other shareholders to enter into an arrangement pursuant to which the shares which they received under the terms of the offer were to be sold to it for a cash consideration. Although this was an arrangement involving third parties, it was held that on the facts of the case the step formed part[94] of the overall scheme and had to be taken into account in determining whether there was a 'scheme of reconstruction'. Normally, it seems the scheme ends when the consideration shares are registered but in that case the terms of the scheme ie the overall contractual situation required further movement of the shares.[95] In this case, because there was a movement of the consideration shares as an integral part of the overall arrangement, this meant there was a significant change in the shareholder proportions so that there was not a scheme of reconstruction.[96]

12.18 It was accepted in practice by HMRC Stamp Taxes that, notwithstanding decisions such as *Crane Fruehauf v IRC*,[97] provided the inducement of an onward sale or other benefit from a third party[98] or arrangement with the third party constituted an independent contract[99] and was not a term of the scheme, it could be ignored for the purposes of testing both whether there was a reconstruction and the nature of the consideration. In other words, provided that the onward movement of the shares was not integrated into the reconstruction arrangements, such as where the terms of the offer imposed an obligation on the target company shareholders to sell all or part of the

---

91   See the discussion in *Crane Fruehauf v IRC* [1975] 1 All ER 429.
92   See, for example, *Clarke Chapman John Thompson Ltd v IRC* [1975] STC 567.
93   [1975] 1 All ER 429; see also *Central and District Properties Ltd v IRC* (above).
94   There is an important difference between 'part of' the scheme and an element in a larger arrangement of which the scheme itself is merely a part. The drafting of the documentation is crucial.
95   See also *Snell v HMRC* [2006] STC (SCD) 295.
96   There were also questions as to whether the benefit of the option arrangements or the cash received pursuant thereto was part of the 'consideration' to be taken into account in determining whether the consideration consisted of relevant qualifying consideration or included too much cash.
97   [1975] STC 51.
98   *Central and District Properties v IRC* [1966] 2 All ER 433.
99   Which, it seems, can include an agreement to buy and sell the shares which is expressed to be conditional upon the reorganisation taking place. The condition creates two separate contracts; see *Kimbers & Co v IRC* [1936] 1 KB 132.

consideration shares, or by being underwritten by the acquiring company or by being supported by some form of warranty or other arrangement from the acquiring company that the third party would meet its obligations pursuant to the contract, then the onward movement of the shares was ignored and the test as to whether there has been substantial shareholder identity and substantial continuity of the business could be tested simply by reference to the moment at which the shares were entered on the register of the company making the acquisition. It would seem that this type of structuring will be important for stamp duty land tax in exactly the same way as for stamp duty. Moreover, the onward movement of the consideration shares will need to be considered in the context of whether there is a change of control or related event giving rise to a clawback of the relief.[100]

12.19 It appears that a liquidation of the target is not an essential requirement. There may, therefore, be a reconstruction where there is a demerger by some form of distribution of shares from a new company by way of an indirect dividend *in specie*.[101]

Reconstruction of a company – foreign companies

12.20 There is no special definition of 'company' for the purposes of this relief although there is a long tradition of HMRC Stamp Taxes seeking to treat the word 'company' as being restricted to companies incorporated under the United Kingdom companies legislation,[102] leaving the words 'body corporate' to include foreign vehicles. This may depend upon the context in which the words appear in the legislation. In consequence, the general definition for stamp duty land tax of a company includes any body corporate or unincorporated association other than a partnership including a limited liability partnership.[103] The reference to 'body corporate' is sufficiently wide to include companies incorporated outside the United Kingdom and this has recently been put on a statutory basis in other contexts.[104] It would seem, therefore, that the relief will now be available where one or even both of the companies involved in the reconstruction is not incorporated or resident in the United Kingdom.[105] The major difficulty would be that concerning the issue of the appropriate form of shares to the relevant members and recording these in such a way that satisfies the need to 'issue' the shares and the production of appropriate share capital structures and membership entries on the register.[106]

---

[100]   FA 2003, Sch 7, para 9.

[101]   See the comments on 'sideways distributions' or disguised dividends in *Aveling Barford v Perrion* [1989] BCLC 626 and *Barclays Bank plc v British and Commonwealth Holdings plc* [1995] BCC 19; affd [1995] BCC 1059.

[102]   See, for example, *Nestle v IRC* [1953] 1 All ER 1388; *Chelsea Land v IRC* [1978] 2 All ER 113.

[103]   FA 2003, s 110.

[104]   FA 2006, s 169.

[105]   There are considerable opportunities for the mitigation of stamp taxes in the short and the long-term where the acquiring company is incorporated outside the United Kingdom particularly in the context of listed companies. Residence in the United Kingdom is not relevant since the charge attaches to companies incorporated in this country. Unfortunately, listing on the London Stock Exchange and dealings through CREST can be an expensive disincentive especially for smaller investors.

[106]   Technically there would seem to be problems where the shares in question are bearer shares. This point has never been satisfactorily addressed by HMRC Stamp Taxes in relation to stamp duty relief, since bearer securities are 'issued' in one sense but not 'registered'. The point has not been of a great practical significance, since bearer securities are relatively rare as far as UK companies are concerned, but may become more of a problem where the relief is sought in relation to foreign incorporated entities.

Acquisition of undertaking

12.21 There must be the acquisition of the whole or part of an undertaking.[107] The cases dealing with this issue have not always segregated the issue of whether there is a 'business' for the purposes of whether there is a reconstruction and whether the assets being acquired are sufficiently a business so as to amount to an undertaking.[108] Also since the relief from stamp duty land tax contains the possibility that there may be leases granted as part of the arrangement, the legislation indicates that it may not be necessary that the transferee carries on the business on precisely the same basis as the existing or target company. There will be a key issue at some stage whether the segregation of the business from the land upon which the business is carried on affects the question of what is an 'undertaking' for the purposes of this legislation. Certain basic but rather limited principles emerge from the cases:

- not every single asset of a company can be regarded as 'part of an undertaking', particularly where only part of the assets of the relevant company are involved such as where the assets and activities of the existing company are partitioned amongst several new companies. Although the holding of investments such as holding land and receiving the rent can itself constitute a business[109] and can be an undertaking, peripheral or 'trade' investments not part of the main business structure may not be qualifying assets.[110] This may be a matter of fact and degree.[111] For example, where the company is transferring 5 out of 50 hotels or 10 acres out of 500 acres of agricultural land, this, *prima facie*, is unlikely to be accepted by HMRC Stamp Taxes as part of an undertaking. However, if the five hotels concerned have been operated as a separate division (such as under a particular name) and there is some related goodwill with specific employees, the argument that there is a separate business which is an undertaking in its own right improves. On the other hand, where the disposing company has only one hotel so that the entirety of its assets and liabilities is passing, the argument that this must be an undertaking is very forceful;

- the assets transferred must constitute a 'business' or 'part of a business' of the transferring or target company. It is implicit in the concept of an undertaking that there is some form of business being carried on.[112] There is, accordingly, a question of fact in each case whether the assets concerned formed part of a business or were mere investments not constituting a business as such.[113] This requirement has frequently given rise to difficulties with HMRC Stamp Taxes in practice where the assets involved are land or shares. There is a tendency for HMRC Stamp Taxes to regard the holding of land as an investment receiving the rent as not being a business;

- it is the view of HMRC Stamp Taxes put forward from time to time, but not consistently, that it is not sufficient that what is transferred must constitute a

---

[107] See also *R v Industrial Dispute Tribunal, ex p Courage and Co Ltd* [1956] 1 WLR 1062.
[108] The related nature of the two arguments was commented upon by Plowman J in *Baytrust Holdings Ltd v IRC* [1971] 1 WLR 1333.
[109] See, eg, *IRC v Tyre Investment Ltd* [1924] 12 TC 646.
[110] See, eg, *Baytrust Holdings Ltd v IRC* [1971] 1 WLR 1333.
[111] There may be similar issues as to whether there is a real partnership or an acquisition for the business of a partnership on the facts relating to the acquisition of the land and its utilisation as well as the intentions of the parties and partners.
[112] See also *E Gomme Ltd v IRC* [1964] 1 WLR 1348.
[113] *Baytrust Holdings Ltd v IRC* [1971] 1 WLR 1333.

business or going concern of the disposing company – the transferred activity must be carried on substantially unchanged by the acquiring company.[114] This is not justified by the legislation on this point. The relief merely requires that the disposing company has an undertaking. Some support for the view can be found in the requirements for substantial identity of interest in substantially the same business on the question of what is a reconstruction.[115] On this view, even though the assets concerned undoubtedly formed part of the basic structure of the business of the target company, relief will not be granted if the assets when transferred do not themselves constitute the same business of the acquiring company. Thus, a company that wishes to segregate its real property from its trading activities, such as where it occupies land as its office buildings and factory premises and intends to transfer the land interests to another company which will lease[116] the land to the company carrying on the trading activities, may find itself in some difficulty in obtaining this relief. The relief would be refused on the basis that, although the letting and management of land may be a business and so is an undertaking carried on by the acquiring company, this is not the same business as that of the disposing company, and, additionally, although the property formed a fundamental part of the structure of the business of the acquiring company, it was not carried on by that company as a separate business. It is, however, difficult to accept the correctness of this view of HMRC Stamp Taxes. There would seem to be no reason in principle why a company should not be entitled to the relief where it acquires assets constituting a trade or business of the disposing company and absorbs them into its own distinct trading activities, with the effect that the business acquired may change substantially or lose its identity[117] and qualify for this relief by using them for a somewhat different type of trading activity, particularly now that the one-size-fits-all plain English drafting appears to grant the relief to leases granted in connection with the disposal of a trading operation or business. There may also be issues where, as part of the reconstruction during a recession, the existing company not only transfers part of its assets to a new company but closes down its remaining activities and disposes of the surplus assets in the course of a general winding-up. Alternatively the acquiring company may, immediately upon the acquisition, rationalise and restructure the business that is had acquired closing down certain activities and disposing of certain of the assets required. HMRC Stamp Taxes may seek to attack the relief on the basis that the same business is not involved on both sides of the transaction; but it is considered that this argument is unconvincing because the reference to part of the undertaking and that it is sufficient that the assets were part of the transferor's undertaking including part of its capital structure and do not need to constitute an undertaking in their own right and are the same activity to be carried on by the acquiring company. This suggests that the relief may be available where freehold interests in factories or warehouses are transferred in isolation from the main business which is transferred to another company and the land is leased to the company acquiring the main trading operation. The land was part of the original undertaking and is put to a business usage by a company which is essentially carrying on a property business. However, HMRC Stamp Taxes are likely to be

---

114 HMRC Stamp Taxes' view appears to be based on *Melon v Hector Powe Ltd* [1981] 1 All ER 313, HL, a case decided on the meaning of 'transfer of a business' within Redundancy Payments Act 1965, s 13(1)(a) and so of extremely doubtful utility in relation to the interpretation of the legislation discussed in the text, but this may be a key issue for treatment as a Transfer of a Going Concern for VAT which can easily cause a loss of the relief from stamp taxes; see **12.26**.

115 See **12.15**.

116 Since the reliefs now apply to all 'acquisitions', the granting of a lease is *prima facie* eligible for the relief.

117 See, eg, *Falmers Jeans Ltd v Rodin* [1990] STC 270.

extremely provoked by the suggestion that a company acquiring the property of a trading operation separately from the main trade is acquiring part of an undertaking indicates that total identity of activity is not required. There may also be issues as to whether the immediate disposal of the assets acquired means that they are utilised in such a way that a business has been acquired[118] ie whether the fact that the vendor disposed of a business or undertaking means that the purchaser has acquired an undertaking or carried on a business for these purposes,[119] because the ownership of the assets was too brief to permit significant business operations to be carried on.

The consideration – shares and liabilities – inducements etc

12.22 It is not always easy to identify what is the consideration in corporate restructuring, particularly where larger arrangements are involved. As the decisions in *Crane Fruehauf v IRC*,[120] and *Central and District Properties Ltd v IRC*[121] clearly indicate, arrangements relating to the possible sale of the shares may affect the question of whether the consideration consists solely of shares or includes the cash from the onward sale.[122] This depends upon the very fine line between arrangements that are part of the scheme of reconstruction itself and arrangements that, although related to the scheme, are not part of it.[123] If the acquiring company contracts in effect to procure the provision of consideration by a third party, that agreement is consideration provided by the acquiring company.[124] On the other hand, where there is a separate and independent offer by a third party to purchase the consideration shares from the original vendors, this cash will not form part of the consideration since it is not imposed by the acquiring company, nor does that company guarantee that the cash will be forthcoming.[125] Following the decision in *Crane Fruehauf v IRC*,[126] HMRC Stamp Taxes formally indicated that they would grant the relief where the arrangement for the onward sale of the shares was independent of the reconstruction as a matter of law. This position has not been officially confirmed for the purposes of stamp duty land tax but, as the legislation on the point is substantially the same as that for the previous reliefs and the practice represented the correct law, it is assumed that HMRC Stamp Taxes will, at least for the time being, continue to operate in accordance with its previous stated practice but this has not been officially confirmed and this may change after the decision in *Snell v HMRC*.[127]

12.23 It must be noted that the consideration for these purposes will include not only the chargeable consideration for the land but also consideration for other assets. Any attempt to insert cash into the transaction by purporting to purchase non-land assets for cash and allocating only shares to the land is unlikely to be successful since HMRC Stamp Taxes have power to reallocate the consideration to some extent.[128] Moreover,

---

[118] *Kwik Save Group v Customs and Excise* VTD 12749.
[119] And whether his onward disposal means the third party has acquired a business or undertaking.
[120] [1975] 1 All ER 429.
[121] [1966] 1 WLR 1015.
[122] This may also be relevant on the question of whether there is a scheme or reconstruction (see **12.15**) and whether the conditions for 'after' the transaction have been satisfied (see **12.17**).
[123] Cf *Shop and Stores Developments Ltd v IRC* [1967] 1 All ER 42.
[124] *Central and District Properties Ltd v IRC* [1966] 1 WLR 1015 at 1074.
[125] See *Crane Fruehauf v IRC* [1975] 1 All ER 429 and *IRC v Kent Process Control Ltd* [1989] STC 245; cf *Shop and Stores Developments Ltd v IRC* [1967] 1 All ER 42.
[126] [1975] 1 All ER 429.
[127] [2006] STC (SCD) 295.
[128] FA 2003, Sch 4, para 4.

attempts to deal with this by two separate transactions runs a serious risk that HMRC Stamp Taxes will successfully argue that the land was not acquired as part of the undertaking or business part of an undertaking as required by the relief.

Non-redeemable shares

12.24 It is necessary to show that the consideration for the acquisition (except such part as consists of the assumption of or discharge by the acquiring company of liabilities of the target company[129]) consists solely of the issue of non-redeemable shares[130] in the acquiring company to all of the shareholders of the target company.[131] This is presumably to prevent parties including a cash element indirectly by having redeemable shares which, having been issued, are immediately redeemed.[132]

Liabilities

12.25 Consideration consisting in the assumption or discharge of the debts of the existing company is permitted. This includes actual payment of the debts of the company whose undertaking is acquired as well as simply giving indemnities and agreeing to discharge such debts. It also means that the relief is available where the property is subject to a mortgage which is taken over by the acquiring company. Bizarrely, however, refinancing in the sense of the acquiring company acquiring free from the mortgage and paying cash generated by a loan from a bank which receives a new charge over the land is likely to preclude the availability of the relief because paying cash in order to enable the transferor company to pay off its mortgage debts will distort the consideration.[133] This can include the indemnity for the vendor's taxation liabilities,[134] but not the immediate liability to VAT should the transaction not be a transfer of a going concern[135] and there is some form of deferred payment linked to future transactions where the deferred payment obligations are not 'cash payments'.

No cash – VAT traps

12.26 This limitation on the type of consideration permitted means that it is important to ensure that the transfer of the undertaking escapes the charge to VAT because it is a transfer of a going concern within regulations of the Value Added Tax Special Provisions Order.[136] Should there be a payment of cash as VAT, which will form part of the consideration in the view of HMRC Stamp Taxes, this cash will take the reconstruction outside the scope of the exemption from stamp duty land tax. This will apply even where the VAT is allocated to non-land assets such as where the land has not

---

[129] Which may include tax liabilities *Re Hollebone* [1959] 2 All ER 152; *Ponsonby v Customs and Excise* [1988] STC 28.
[130] FA 2003, Sch 7, para 7(2).
[131] Ibid.
[132] The provision does not, as such, prevent a subsequent purchase of own shares by the acquiring company; but presumably if these arrangements are in place it is possible that HMRC Stamp Taxes may contend that the cash received on the share buyback was 'really' part of the consideration for the chargeable transaction. Such a buy-back of own shares attracts a stamp duty charge; FA 1986, s 66.
[133] Acquiring companies must also be aware of the risks involved in acquiring land subject to a charge in order to meet this condition and then embarking upon a refinancing exercise intended to relieve the transferor company from its liability in respect of the mortgage because this is apparently regarded by HMRC Stamp Taxes as a variation in the mortgage taxable pursuant to FA 2003, Sch 4, para 8, which provision retrospectively cancels the overall relief.
[134] *Ponsonby v Customs and Excise* [1988] STC 28.
[135] See **12.26**.
[136] Value Added Tax (Special Provisions) Order 1995, SI 1995/1268, reg 5.

been opted to tax. The consideration is in the view of HMRC Stamp Taxes the overall package not that part allocated to the chargeable interest but this view has not been tested against appropriately drafted agreement with apportioned consideration. Unfortunately this provides HMRC Stamp Taxes with an argument that there are two separate acquisitions jeopardising the taxpayer's argument that there is an undertaking or part of an undertaking which is fundamental to the relief.

12.27 The relief may be at risk where the company issues shares to the net value of the business and agrees to pay cash to the disposing company in order to enable it to have the funds available to pay the VAT arising or to discharge its mortgages.[137] In the former case, where the parties believe that the transaction involves a transfer of a going concern, but make the usual provision that, should the transaction not qualify as a transfer of a going concern, the purchaser will pay the VAT upon delivery of an appropriate tax invoice, such payment in cash must inevitably exceed the permitted 10 per cent limit. There is little evidence of the approach of HMRC Stamp Taxes in practice probably because the relief is little used and the parties incorrectly fail to report the transaction properly because they take the view that VAT will not be payable so that probably taxpayers and their advisers did not comply with their obligations to make full disclosure to HMRC Stamp Taxes which on the legislation requires the taxpayer to assess the amount of possible consideration upon the basis that it is payable and not take into account the likelihood that a payment will be required. Insofar as extra consideration is required, it should consist of an obligation to issue further shares, but this still leaves liquidity problems and is vulnerable to the well-known contention of HMRC Stamp Taxes that an undertaking, albeit contingent, to issue further shares is not the 'issue' of share and as it is a consideration consisting of a separate *chose in action,* ie a right to the allotted shares which is neither the issued shares nor an immediate payment of cash or the assumption of liabilities is not a consideration eligible for the various reliefs in this area. The most prudent course is to provide that the consideration consisting of the issue of shares is inclusive of VAT, if any, payable. This avoids the possibility that HMRC Stamp Taxes might refuse the relief upon the ground that, where there is an obligation to issue further shares if VAT is chargeable, the obligation to issue shares in VAT was not an issue of shares within the relieving provisions but was merely an undertaking to issue shares if necessary. It is to be hoped that, since the relief requires a transfer of an undertaking, the transaction may qualify for exclusion from VAT as a transfer of a going concern. In relation to stamp duty land tax, the issue raises somewhat different problems from stamp duty, being a transaction-based and not a document-based tax and the issues of 'wait-and-see' may be very different. There is a risk that, although the relief is taken, the subsequent payment of VAT will retrospectively invalidate the original self-assessment. There may be no true general principle of 'wait-and-see' for stamp duty land tax,[138] HMRC Stamp Taxes, carrying forward the bizarre once and for all concepts and principles of traditional stamp duties such as the up-front contingency principle unless there is specific provision to the contrary, have indicated that unless the conditions as to the consideration can be satisfied as at the effective date which may not be 'completion'[139] the relief will not be available notwithstanding that subsequent events are consistent with the conditions for the exemption to have applied retrospective operations unilaterally in favour of HMRC Stamp Taxes. This raises a fundamental timing issue in that everything necessary must be done to comply with the conditions for the relief as at the effective date, leaving

---

[137]   However, it seems that a direct payment of the mortgage can be within the relief because it is the assumption or discharge of liabilities.

[138]   See also **5.84**.

[139]   See **Chapter 14**.

matters to formal completion could prove to be an expensive error. It is prudent to avoid the arguments on these technical issues by making the share consideration initially provided the sole VAT inclusive consideration.

Shareholder identity – 'Mirror share capital'

All of the members

12.28 There are many technical points for the eligibility for the relief relating to the identity of the members but 'own shares' held by the company are to be ignored.[140] These relate to questions such as who are the members which may affect both the general definition of reconstruction[141] and statutory requirements[142] these issues are, essentially, related to the state of share registers before and immediately 'after' the transaction;[143] but there are indications in other tax areas that wider arrangements may be relevant.[144] It is necessary for the shares to be 'issued' which means registered in the correct names[145] rather than merely the subject of a resolution to allot or a full allotment without registration.[146] There are also issues as to the comparison of the share registers in deciding whether there is a scheme of reconstruction.[147] There is also a condition that the consideration shares are issued to all of the members so that each of them receives at least one share. It is not necessary that the consideration shares are issued *pro rata*; it is sufficient that, at the relevant time, the shares are registered in the correct proportions.

Same proportions

12.29 It is necessary that each shareholder appears in the members' registers of both companies holding shares in the same proportion or as near thereto as is possible. This means that there must be a correct entry upon the register in order to maintain the proportions. It is not necessary that the consideration shares are issued *pro rata*; what matters is the correct proportion on the share register 'after' the transaction.[148] This raises two important points that have caused considerable difficulty in practice[149] these are:

- shares must be issued to 'all' of the members;[150] and

- ultimately the shares must be held in the same proportions.

---

[140] FA 2003, Sch 7, para 7(5A).
[141] See **12.15**.
[142] FA 2003, Sch 7, para 7(4).
[143] *Crane Fruehauf v IRC* [1975] STC 51.
[144] *Snell v HMRC* [2006] STC (SCD) 295.
[145] From time to time the judiciary who are inexperienced in this area of tax have suggested that registration in the correct names is not sufficient and the relief is not available where there are changes in beneficial ownership behind the register. HMRC Stamp Taxes have hitherto rejected this attempt by the judiciary inciting them to argue that there is not a scheme of reconstruction etc; but this longstanding practice may change since HMRC Stamp Taxes proudly proclaim that they do not have practices that can be relied upon by taxpayers – they have merely made the same mistakes over decades.
[146] See **1.27**.
[147] See **12.15**.
[148] See **12.18**.
[149] Although on many unreported occasions it is possible for the author to correct the situation by arranging for an application to the Court to rectify the share registers of the various companies involved pursuant to Companies Act 2006, s 125; see **12.5**.
[150] Ie the registered shareholders.

As regards the requirement of 'issue' of shares to all of the members, it is not sufficient that all of the members appear on the register[151] of the acquiring company if for some technical reason shares were not issued to such members. It is not sufficient that the proportions are correct at the end of the transaction[152] if in the process of arriving at the correct position 'after' the transaction shares have not been issued. For example, problems arose and relief was refused in a case where the new company acquiring the undertaking was formed with s capital having shares of £1 par value. The company whose undertaking was being acquired had shares of nominal value 10p. A person who is a shareholder with a small number of shares in a sister company may become the subscriber or one of the subscribers[153] in the acquiring company but may be adversely affected by changes to the arrangement because of the difference in the nominal value of the shares in the two companies. The particular person may be entitled to a fairly small number of shares by way of consideration and during the arrangements the share capital of the acquiring company may be converted into shares of 10p nominal value. As a consequence of this the subscriber in the new company who originally took 1 share of £1 by reason of the subdivision into 10 shares, will hold more than the number of shares than he would be entitled to by way of consideration. In these circumstances in order to maintain the proportionate shareholding relationships no consideration shares can be issued to this person. In consequence, because no shares would be issued the relief would not be available. Conversely, if even one share is issued to this person it is likely to affect the proportions and therefore the relief would not be available. These are very small points of detail but they are regarded by HMRC Stamp Taxes as absolutely fundamental and they will use the slightest deviation from either of the requirements as a justification for challenging the availability of the relief.[154] This has been modified by requiring the proportions to be 'the same or as nearly as may be the same'. This will allow for rounding up or down and avoid arguments such as arose in practice where differences emerged at the seventh decimal place. The fact that there is no change in the underlying beneficial ownership of the company does not matter since registration in the names of different nominees is not within the relief notwithstanding that the beneficial owners remain unchanged. It is the proportion upon the share register immediately after the reconstruction that controls the availability of the exemption. Problems can easily arise, such as where the subscriber shares in the new company acquiring the undertaking are not properly organised and the relevant number of consideration shares is not appropriately adjusted to take account of this. Failure to deal with these may mean that the final share register is not as nearly as may be to the correct figures. Failure to make the adjustments needed will still cause a loss of the relief. For example, where A legally owns one share and B holds one share as nominee for A, an allotment of 98 shares to allow for the two subscriber shares as to 97 to A and one to B[155] may reflect the true ownership of the company but it is not an issue as nearly as may be to the 50/50

---

[151] In traditional stamp tax terms certain judges with no experience in this area have expressed views totally inconsistent with the general principles and commonsense such as Russell and Stamp LJJ in *Crane Fruehauf v IRC* [1975] STC 51. The rules relate to the register and charges behind the register are irrelevant unless these attack conditions as to 'control'.

[152] This is the effective date but there are major issues of principle where all of the conditions have not been satisfied on the effective date because there is no express statutory wait-and-see; see **5.84**.

[153] But note the limitation on the number of shareholders required to be involved in companies pursuant to Companies (Single Member Private Companies) Regulations 1992, SI 1992/1699 which in some respects simplifies these issues.

[154] Previously HMRC Stamp Taxes refused the relief where the divergence emerged at the seventh decimal place making it difficult to deal with rounding!

[155] It will be necessary to allot to B otherwise the condition requiring the issue of shares to all of the members will not be satisfied. It is essential to remember that there are at least two conditions to be satisfied namely: an issue to all of the members; and the correct proportions on the register thereafter. It is not always possible to satisfy both of these conditions.

registration required. The recent amendment dabbles with decimal points but not the substantive issues.[156] Although there is no change in the underlying ownership, the share registration does not reflect the correct proportions. The shares must be issued 50 to A and 50 to B in order to obtain the relief. This can provide something of a trap where the company making the acquisition has subscriber shares in issue.[157] The existence of such shares can easily upset the arithmetic proportions of the registration of the consideration shares. It is possible to reduce the number of shares to be issued to any of the subscribers so that after the transaction the correct proportions are maintained. On the other hand, since, subject to the general anti-avoidance provisions[158] it may be possible to reorganise the relevant share capital by resolution without transfers or moving existing shares into the names of nominees with *ad valorem* duty[159] so that the share register can be in appropriate names.

'Issue' of shares

12.30	The consideration shares must be 'issued' to the right persons ie by reference to the share register. The word 'issue' has a precise and limited meaning in relation to this type of operation. The word 'issue' means put upon the register of the relevant company. Simply allotting shares to the correct person is not sufficient; the shares must be registered in the correct name.[160] Since the test is likely to be applied in relation to registration, this point on 'issue' is important.

Timing factors

12.31	There is a fundamentally important timing aspect to the eligibility for this relief: namely the effective date may precede the formal completion arrangements[161] so that, for example, final registration of the consideration shares may be sometime after the directors of the company resolved to allot the consideration shares (ie provide the whole of the consideration) for the purposes of substantial performance, or takes possession before the register of members is made up. This is a fundamental issue of principle as to whether there is any form of wait-and-see arising because of the charge to a transaction-based tax.[162] This has the potential for creating chaos in this context as well as many others. The tax charges may arise because of the linking of the effective date to substantial performance rather than final completion,[163] the effective date is, *inter alia*, where the company takes possession of the land, receives a transfer or the board of directors resolve to allot the consideration shares.[164] This frequently precedes the formal registration which as an administrative rather than substantive step is frequently dealt with in a relaxed fashion. In consequence, as at the effective date the conditions for the relief will not have been satisfied. It may be that when the land is formally conveyed and the transaction is 'completed' between the same parties there may be a secondary chargeable event[165] and at that stage the conditions may be satisfied because the shares may be registered at that time. However, it is the view of HMRC Stamp Taxes that where

156	See **12.28**.
157	But see Companies (Single Member Private Companies) Regulations 1992, SI 1992/1699.
158	FA 2003, ss 75A–75C.
159	But note FA 1965, s 90.
160	*Oswald Tillotson Ltd v IRC* [1933] 1 KB 134; *Brotex Cellulose Fibres Ltd v IRC* [1933] 1 KB 158; *Murex Ltd v IRC* [1933] 1 KB 173; *National Westminster Bank v IRC* [1994] STC 580.
161	See **12.31**, **Chapter 14**, **12.27** and **1.27**.
162	See **3.7**.
163	FA 2003, ss 119 and 44(4).
164	See **14.27**.
165	FA 2003, s 44(8).

there are two separate chargeable events such as occur in relation to substantial performance of an agreement for lease and the subsequent grant of a lease[166] the eligibility for the relief has to be tested independently at both stages so that relief cannot be carried forward from substantial performance to completion and the relief available at completion cannot be carried back to the effective date. This potential fundamental flaw in the legislation was never applied by HMRC Stamp Taxes in relation to the equivalent stamp duty reliefs and instruments could be adjudicated as exempt notwithstanding that the shares were not registered until some time after the execution of the instrument and its submission for adjudication. Unfortunately, it seems that this practice may not have been brought forward from stamp duty into stamp duty land tax since it is understood that HMRC Stamp Taxes are considering exploiting this issue so that it is, for the time being, prudent to ensure that allotment and registration procedures for the consideration shares are implemented immediately upon substantial performance or, better, ensuring that there is no earlier substantial performance or subsequent transactions and that everything is dealt with precisely and exactly as required at the same time at completion. Subsequent satisfaction of the conditions if attacked by HMRC Stamp Taxes does not provide a retrospective re-instatement of the relief. The solution to these problems is not assisted by the fact that it is unclear whether there is any form of wait-and-see in relation to stamp duty land tax. Such a treatment was not applied for stamp duty nor was it applied to capital duty notwithstanding that this was a transaction based tax based upon European law.[167] Since there does not appear to be a general wait-and-see provision[168] and none or the arrangements for dealing with deferred considerations appear to be appropriate[169] there is a potential risk if the paperwork is not up-to-date for any transaction. This is, of course, essentially the same as the problem relating to the uncertainty surrounding the treatment of a transaction as a transfer of a going concern for the purposes of VAT where it does not appear to be possible as a general principle to wait-and-see although the rules for variable consideration might help in that case.

Issue to the members

12.32 The registration ie issue of the consideration shares[170] must be in the correct names and in the correct proportions at the right time but the reference here to 'shareholders' or 'members' rather than to 'holders of shares' is probably not a significant variation likely to produce a change of practice and the term would seem to be taken in the case of registered shares to refer to those persons on the register of the target company.[171] The relief will not be available if the shares are issued to the beneficial owner where the shares were held in the name of the nominee in the original company. Similarly, issuing shares into the name of a nominee, albeit for the same beneficial owner as appears on the register of the existing company, will not satisfy this condition. The fact that there may be a change in the beneficial ownership behind the register at some stage during the course of the reorganisation will not, of itself, cause difficulties provided that the shares are registered in the same name. There may be a question as to whether such a change in the underlying beneficial ownership that is not

---

[166]   Ibid, Sch 17A, para 12B; see **7.22**.

[167]   *Rothschild v IRC* [1988] STC 645 (on appeal [1989] STC 435).

[168]   See **3.7**.

[169]   FA 2003, s 51.

[170]   And of any earlier shares which may have to be put into the appropriate names as a preliminary planning stage.

[171]   The legislation fails to deal with bearer shares which are not 'registered' and so may not be 'issued'. However bearer shares may have to be registered initially before conversion (Companies Act 2006, s 779) which if properly observed may avoid technical problems in relation to the relief.

reflected in the register affects the question of whether there is a scheme of reconstruction as discussed above. Notwithstanding certain wild and ill-considered judicial utterances to the effect that if there was a change of underlying beneficial ownership the former stamp duty relief would not be available, this point was never taken seriously and was at one stage repudiated by HMRC Stamp Taxes. If the change in beneficial ownership of the shares is not an integral part of the arrangements then it should not affect the question of whether there is a scheme of reconstruction.

After the transaction

12.33 Certain conditions have to be satisfied 'after' the transaction and it seems that this must refer to immediately after the transaction.[172] However, as with the related question of whether larger events affect the question of whether there is a scheme of reconstruction this condition depends upon defining the scope of the transaction. Should there be an arrangement for reorganisation of the company and the disposal of some or all of the shares in the company it will be crucial to this condition, as to others, whether the onward sale of the shares is simply part of the transaction or whether the reorganisation is simply part of a larger transaction which the onward sale is one of the stages.[173] Much will, therefore, depend upon the drafting of the documentation and the structuring of the arrangements in order to isolate various stages and convert them from a single large transaction into several separate smaller transactions.

PARTITIONS AND REORGANISATIONS – REDUCED RATE

12.34 A reduced rate of stamp duty land tax of 0.5 per cent (but without any adjustment to the amount of the chargeable consideration) is available where a company acquires the whole or part of the undertaking of another company for an issue of shares.[174] This relief is being subjected to an increasing number of conditions that have to be satisfied and anti-avoidance rules as well as clawback.

12.35 This reduced rate is available where there is:

- an acquisition;

- which is undertaken for *bona* fide commercial reasons and not for tax avoidance;

- by one company;

- from another company;

- of the latter's undertaking or part thereof;[175] but

---

172 *Crane Fruehauf v IRC* [1975] STC 51.
173 Ibid.
174 FA 2003, Sch 7, para 8.
175 HMRC Stamp Taxes have problems in practice of recognising a 'part' of an undertaking even where this consists of a separate business.

- that undertaking or the part thereof being acquired must not have as its main activity the carrying on of a trade that consists wholly or mainly of dealing in chargeable interests;[176]

- the consideration must consist either:
  - wholly in the issue;
  - of non-redeemable shares in the acquiring company; or
  - partly in the issue of non-redeemable shares in the acquiring company, and partly in either the assumption or discharge of liabilities of the disposing company, and/or cash not exceeding 10 per cent of the nominal value of the non-redeemable shares issued as part of the consideration;

  such consideration shares being issued either:
  - to the company whose undertaking is being acquired; or
  - to all or any of the shareholders in the company whose undertaking is being acquired; and

- the acquiring company must not be associated with another company that is a party to arrangements with the company whose undertaking is being acquired which relate to shares issued by the company in connection with the transfer of the undertaking or part.

Motive test

12.36 The acquisition must be effected for *bona fide* commercial reasons and not form part of arrangements the main purpose or one of the main purposes is the avoidance of liability to tax (ie stamp duty, income tax, corporation tax, capital gains tax or stamp duty land tax).[177] These are treated by HMRC Stamp Taxes as two separate conditions and have been known to refuse to give pre-transaction guidance because they find the technical questions too difficult and are not sufficiently trained and experienced in the factual background of commercial motives to deal with the issues involved within a commercially acceptable timeframe. This issue of motive or purposes will in many cases be covered by a clearance from the capital gains tax division of HMRC but these are not always available and the overall correspondence prepared by persons not aware of the subtleties of stamp duty land tax may contain comments potentially dangerous to the stamp duty land tax relief[178] and may not necessarily be conclusive in the light of current HMRC Stamp Taxes practice.[179] These issues are described elsewhere[180] but there is a particularly acute potential problem of whether a transaction or step in a transaction is *bona fide* commercial there it is entered into for the benefit or in the interests of the members such as where there may be inheritance tax or foreign tax benefits is not *bona fide* commercial. HMRC Stamp Taxes take the view that a transaction benefitting individuals is 'personal' and not 'commercial' This potential problem arises because the type of corporate reorganisation being described is frequently entered into because the shareholders who are usually the directors have fallen out and the only way to resolve the issue is to partition the company's business. This, in the view of HMRC Stamp Taxes, is not 'commercial' but a domestic issue of the

---

[176] FA 2003, Sch 7, para 8(5A).
[177] Ibid, Sch 7, para 8(5B) and (5C).
[178] As in *Swithland Investments v IRC* [1990] STC 448.
[179] See **12.73**.
[180] See **26.5**.

individuals. Fortunately, HMRC Stamp Taxes generally accept the 'commerciality' of such arrangements if this can be supported by a clearance from HMRC Stamp Taxes in relation to capital gains if available.

12.37 Each of these conditions requires considerable expansion and comment. It is important to note that this reduced rate relief is more generous than the total relief previously considered,[181] although many of the terms have the same meaning and there is an increasing body of anti-avoidance legislation. For example, the reduced rate does not require:

- a scheme of reconstruction or shareholder identity. This means that the reduced rate may be available where the company is being partitioned between different groups of shareholders;[182]

- a total absence of cash consideration.

The fact that these particular restrictive conditions do not apply means that the reduced rate relief is useful in a variety of circumstances where the total relief or reconstructions might not be available. For example, the reduced rate relief may be available in relation to certain types of restructuring involved in establishing a joint venture company. There may be arrangements between A Ltd and B Ltd pursuant to which they intend to form C Ltd as a jointly owned subsidiary company and intend to contribute their various relevant undertakings into that company for the purpose of the joint venture.[183] Clearly the relief for company reconstructions would not be available since the shares were issued to the company transferring the undertaking not to the members. However, the reduced rate may be available but the clawback and anti-avoidance provisions, such as those triggered by changes of control etc, may need to be carefully considered because of joint venture agreements may provide for disposal of shares should one of the parties seek to terminate the agreement.[184]

12.38 The reduced rate would, subject to the operation of the disqualifying conditions concerning arrangements relating to shares in the acquiring company and the clawback provisions, seem to be available for many forms of company reorganisations (such as partitions between various shareholders,[185] or demergers, or putting trades and assets into joint venture) provided that the other conditions of the section are satisfied.

12.39 This provision merely reduces the rate; it does not reduce or modify the extent of the chargeable consideration. Whilst in determining the eligibility for the reduced rate the assumption or discharge of liabilities is to be ignored,[186] this does not mean that, even where the relief is appropriate, the extent of the liabilities taken over is to be ignored in computing the amount of duty. FA 2003, Sch 4, para 8, will apply with full force and effect so that, although the stamp duty land tax will be charged at the lower

---

[181]   FA 2003, Sch 7, para 7.
[182]   As in *Brooklands Selangor Holdings Ltd v IRC* [1970] 1 WLR 429.
[183]   This may be more efficient than establishing a partnership notwithstanding the reduction in the market value by reason of the sum of the lower proportions since it seems that HMRC Stamp Taxes may be challenging whether joint ventures are, in law, partnerships and there are numerous anti-avoidance provisions intended to cancel the SLP reduction; but see FA 2003, Sch 7, para 8(5A).
[184]   On the implications of which see *Steele v EVC* [1996] STC 785.
[185]   Cf *Brooklands Selangor Holdings Ltd v IRC* [1970] 1 WLR 429.
[186]   FA 2003, Sch 7, para 8(3).

rate, it will be calculated by reference to the value of any shares issued,[187] cash paid and the face value of the liabilities taken over as apportioned on a just and reasonable basis to the chargeable interest acquired.

12.40 Notwithstanding the reduced number of qualifying conditions, numerous other conditions apply, some of which are similar to those in relation to the relief previously considered and there are different conditions which together raise a significant number of technical issues. The conditions may be divided into two categories for the purposes of understanding the manner in which they operated. There are the qualifying conditions which set out the circumstances in which the relief is, *prima facie*, available and there are disqualifying conditions which operate on the basis that the relief being otherwise available is to be denied in certain circumstances. There are also separate conditions cancelling the relief should certain events, whether or not connected with the original reorganisation, occur. The various conditions are as follows:

Qualifying conditions

'Company'

12.41 The target vehicle must be a 'company'.[188]

Acquires

12.42 This drafting of the legislation must mean that the relief applies the relief to all forms of 'acquisition' as defined by FA 2003, s 43,[189] of assets forming part of an undertaking and raises the question of whether the relief applies to the grant of a lease where the company transferring its undertaking retains the reversionary interest and grants a lease to the acquiring company which may be a key part of the establishment of a joint venture company. There will be disputes with HMRC Stamp Taxes as to whether carving a lease out of a freehold, for example, means that the lease is the acquisition of part of an undertaking notwithstanding the original company owned the freehold. In such situations it is probable that HMRC Stamp Taxes will seek to argue that to acquire part of an undertaking requires the acquisition of the whole of the interest of the transferor in the chargeable interest and a carve out of a partial interest is not acceptable. However, it seems that this argument may not be sustainable since the undertaking is, essentially, the business and the capital infrastructure this does not necessarily mean that the assets have to be precisely the same.

The whole or part of an undertaking

12.43 The basic meaning of 'undertaking' or part thereof has been considered above,[190] but this relief is subject to a restriction as to the type of undertaking that can be acquired.[191] The undertaking or the part undertaking being acquired must have as its main activity the carrying on of a trade that does not consist wholly or mainly of dealing in chargeable interests. This raises numerous technical problems for the interpretation and implementation of the relief that will cause significant problems in

---

[187] Ibid, Sch 4, paras 1 and 7.
[188] See ibid, s 100 and see **12.63** and **13.12**.
[189] See **3.14**.
[190] See **12.21**.
[191] FA 2003, Sch 7, para 8(5A).

practice for commercial transactions unless these restrictions on the relief are applied in a reasonable fashion by HMRC Stamp Taxes which seems an unlikely eventuality.

12.44 The first problem is that the undertaking must involve a 'trade' as defined for the purposes of the Income and Corporation Taxes Act 1988.[192] This means that a company carrying on an investment activity is not eligible for the relief.[193] For example, a company whose main activity is investment in subsidiary companies is not eligible for the relief as regards the transfer of its offices. Clearly a land investment company will not have an appropriate undertaking for the purposes of the relief; even though it is taxed as if its income were a trade this is not treated as a trade for all purposes. A rationalisation of a company designed to separate its trading activities from its property will not apparently qualify for the relief. The transfer of the land to a separate company from that receiving the trading activities will be vulnerable to claims by HMRC Stamp Taxes that the land is not a part undertaking[194] or if it should be an undertaking it will not be a trade or is a non-qualifying undertaking. Moreover, the structure of the arrangement means that the extraction of the freehold or head leasehold interests which are then leased or underleased back will not themselves form part of the undertaking of the company. They are part of its capital structure but may not constitute the carrying on of a business.[195] However, if it can be established that this extraction of the major freehold interests and leasehold interests into a property vehicle is the acquisition of part of an undertaking the restriction may not apply because the company's 'trade' will not be a property dealing trade. It will be the essential commercial activity which is carried on from the property but the dealing in the property is part of the capital arrangements of the business not part of its trading activities.

12.45 There is also uncertainty as to what is meant by 'dealing' in land for the purposes of the restriction. Since this is in the context of a trade this would appear to involve acquisitions and disposals and not merely acquisitions of land for use in the business such as holding offices or a factory as a long-term investment.[196] Many genuine commercial reorganisations will not be eligible for the reduced rate because they hold land. Farming and manufacturing companies are likely to experience considerable difficulties in this context should it be necessary to reorganise them when the family fall out amongst themselves or wish to reduce their involvement in the enterprise in order to have the cash to pursue other interests. There is a significant risk that, although such companies are not in the property dealing business, HMRC Stamp Taxes will take the technical point that the company by entering into liquidation or an agreement to dispose of the business means that it has ceased to trade and so is in the property investment business.[197] This will be a key issue when a company begins to rundown its

---

[192] There is an important distinction for other land taxes between carrying on a 'trade' and holding land as an investment or Schedule A business which may be taxed as if it were a trade but which does not thereby become a 'trade'. This distinction is likely to become a key issue for stamp duty land tax reliefs.

[193] But note *IRC v Tyre Investment Ltd* [1924] 12 TC 646.

[194] Although many such arrangements are likely to be 'reconstructions' within FA 2003, Sch 7, para 7 this type of rationalisation is also vulnerable to this point that what is being acquired is not an undertaking, ie a business or a part thereof being carried on by the existing company. There must be an element of business on both sides although it is not necessary that identical activities are carried on by both companies.

[195] Compare the comments in *Baytrust Holdings Ltd v IRC* [1971] 1 WLR 1333.

[196] The intention of the parties to the joint venture to retain the property and not to charge participants may influence the decision whether to make an election pursuant to FA 2003, Sch 15, para 12A; see **13.25** and **13.62**.

[197] Compare the cases on 'business' and temporary changes in the asset structure for the purposes of inheritance tax such as where a major asset or a large proportion of trading stock is sold leaving the company cash rich for a short time Inheritance Tax Act 1984, s 112; see *Barclays Bank Trust Co Ltd v IRC* [1998] STC (SCD) 125; *American Leaf Blending v Director General* [1978] STC 561.

activities or closes down activities carried out upon the land which is to be retained for development or sold to a third party as land rather than as part of a business or where a farming company sets aside part of the farmland or applies for planning permission to develop part of its land or sell the land for development rather than continuing its farming activities. It seems that HMRC Stamp Taxes are anxious to exploit such temporary situations to refuse the relief for any reorganisations that may be entered into in order to facilitate the beneficial disposal of land that has become superfluous to requirements albeit temporarily. The facts of each case will require detailed investigation if this less than meritorious but technically potentially quite convincing to the current judiciary is to be defeated.

Consideration

Shares, liabilities and cash

12.46 The consideration must consist predominantly of the issue of non-redeemable shares. Where shares are not the sole consideration (ignoring liabilities), the relief is available only if the remainder of the consideration consists of cash not exceeding 10 per cent of the nominal value of the consideration shares. 'Cash' would seem to be limited to actual payment of money; deferred payments are probably debts and not cash for this purpose.[198] This restriction to nominal value may be important where the consideration shares are being issued at a premium. Any consideration other than shares, cash and liabilities (such as the issue of loan notes) totally precludes the availability of the reduced rate. The issues concerning the identification of the consideration, particularly where third parties are involved, have been considered above.[199]

12.47 The problem arising in relation to VAT when the transaction is not a transfer of a going concern has been set out above.[200] This remains a problem notwithstanding that there is a permitted cash amount since this is only 10 per cent and VAT is likely to be charged at a higher rate.[201] However, the cash amount[202] may not exceed the limit for stamp duty land tax relief, especially where the land component is an exempt interest for the purposes of VAT. In consequence, it may be possible to include cash payments for the VAT when not all of the assets are subject to that tax such as where a major part of the undertaking in land which has not been opted to tax. However, this route will require very careful calculations and valuations in order to ensure that if the figures are challenged for the purposes of VAT the 10 per cent stamp duty land tax threshold will not be exceeded.

Issue of shares to company or members

12.48 The consideration shares must be 'issued' either to the target company or to all or any of its members (ie its shareholders). In consequence, it will be necessary to 'issue' its shares by placing the target company or its registered shareholders on the register of

---

[198] But note the rules of set-off which equate debt with cash as in *Coren v Keighley* 48 TC 370.
[199] See **12.17** and **12.22**.
[200] See **12.26**.
[201] Although there are significant technical issues where not all of the assets might be subject to VAT should the arrangement not be a transfer of a going concern.
[202] Which appears to apply to the overall cash payment is not related to the land interests or because other assets do not attract VAT the relevant payment overall falls within the 10 per cent limitation.

members of the acquiring company. The giving of renounceable letters of allotment,[203] or the entering of nominees on the register, or the entry of beneficial owners who were not on the target company register in place of mere nominees will not be sufficient.[204] This has been considered above.[205]

Disqualifying conditions

'Arrangements'

12.49   The relief is not available unless the acquiring company is not associated[206] with another company that is a party to arrangements with the target company, relating to shares of the acquiring company issued in connection with the transfer of the undertaking or part of an undertaking.[207] This provision is aimed at transactions where the acquiring company is an existing subsidiary of another company and there are 'arrangements'[208] whereby the transferor company is to dispose of the consideration shares to a purchaser company thereby enabling the latter company to acquire the land at the reduced rate. This is likely to cause problems for establishing joint ventures where for other tax reasons it may be more efficient to establish a new company into which the trades and assets are transferred since there are likely to be pre-emptive or similar rights created between the parties.[209] Such transactions are clearly on risk although not within the mischief intended to be blocked. It remains to be seen how aggressive HMRC Stamp Taxes intend to be where *bona fide* commercial arrangements and normal commercial protection provisions of this nature are involved.

12.50   This change of control condition does not apply where the relevant arrangements are not with a body corporate but with individuals or possibly partnerships, even where these include corporate partners.[210] It must, however, be noted that limited liability partnerships are, in general law, bodies corporate[211] and arrangements with these may fall within this restriction upon the relief. This restriction should, therefore, not operate to disapply the relief where there is a plan to put the company into liquidation and to transfer its undertaking to two or more new companies, each of which issues shares to some of the members in the company which is being wound up. Technically, such issue of shares to the members is an arrangement in respect of which HMRC Stamp Taxes may not wish to take any points although under normal circumstances, both companies will be 'associated'.

---

[203]   *Oswald Tillotson Ltd v IRC* [1933] 1 KB 134; *Brotex Cellulose Fibres Ltd v IRC* [1933] 1 KB 158; *Murex Ltd v IRC* [1933] 1 KB 173. See also *National Westminster Bank v IRC* [1994] STC 580. This point was, however, left open by Lord Hanworth MR in *Oswald Tillotson Ltd v IRC* (above).

[204]   Where an incorrect entry has been made in the register of the acquiring company it may be possible to obtain the benefit of the reduced rate if a court order rectifying the register is obtained under Companies Act 2006, s 125.

[205]   See **12.28**.

[206]   For these purposes, companies are 'associated' if one has control of the other or both are controlled by the same person or persons as defined by Income and Corporation Taxes Act 1988, s 416.

[207]   FA 1986, s 76(3A).

[208]   Since it has been argued that 'arrangements' can include the articles of association or shareholders' agreements even routine commercial arrangements will not qualify for the relief.

[209]   Even if not offending arrangements; but see *Steele v EVC* [1996] STC 785; *Irving v Tesco Stores (Holdings) Ltd v IRC* [1982] STC 881, to the effect that shareholder agreements and the articles of association of a company may be 'arrangements'. In addition, the implementation of such rights could result in a clawback of the relief.

[210]   But note *Jasmine Trustees Ltd v Wells & Hind* [2007] STC 660 on whether trustees are 'individuals'.

[211]   But note the fiscal transparency for stamp duty land tax pursuant to FA 2003, Sch 15, para 2; but note the possible limitations on this transparency – see **13.14**.

CLAWBACK OF THE RELIEF FOR CORPORATE RECONSTRUCTION AND REORGANISATIONS

12.51 Where relief has been obtained pursuant to either of the above two relieving provisions, the relief or an appropriate proportion of it is withdrawn and stamp duty land tax becomes chargeable[212] and the event giving rise to the forfeiture of the relief is notifiable on a full land transaction return (SDLT 1) within 30 days where:

- control of the acquiring company changes before the end of the period of 3 years beginning with the effective date of the transaction or more than 3 years after that date where the change of control is in pursuance of or in connection with arrangements which include any scheme, arrangement or understanding whether or not legally enforceable[213] made before the end of the 3-year period.[214] It is not, for example, possible to avoid clawback where there is an independent approach for the purchase of the shares during the 3-year period but completion does not occur or is postponed until after the expiration of the basic 3-year period.[215] The clawback is linked to the effective date and should HMRC Stamp Taxes be correct in their view that there can be two effective dates[216] the commencement of the clawback period can change where there is a delay between substantial performance and completion between the same parties which is a potential trap fro advisers tidying up titles; and

- at the time of the change of control the company which acquired the land or a relevant associated company holds a chargeable interest that was acquired by the exempt transaction or is derived from an interest so acquired; and

- that interest has not subsequently been acquired at market value under a chargeable transaction in relation to which relief pursuant to either FA 2003, Sch 7, para 7 or para 8, was available but was not claimed.

There is a technical issue as yet unresolved with HMRC Stamp Taxes where a contract has been substantially performed and there is a clawback event after the expiration of the 3 year period so that there is, *prima facie*, no clawback but there is a subsequent completion taking place after the clawback event. It would seem that there may be no clawback at completion but there is the question of whether the relief would be available for the later completion should this be a separate chargeable event.

---

[212] FA 2003, Sch 7, para 9.

[213] Ibid, Sch 7, para 9(5)(a).

[214] This could apply to provisions in the company's articles of association or shareholder agreements establishing buyout options or pre-emptive arrangements producing an open-ended risk for joint venture and similar companies.

[215] It must be noted that HMRC Stamp Taxes, upon the advice of the then solicitor to the Inland Revenue and passages in *Sergeant and Sims on Stamp Duties* which strongly reflect the official line rather than the argument helpful to the taxpayer, have argued that serious negotiations for the sale of the shares falling short of options or condition contracts can strip the vendor of beneficial ownership thereby degrouping the target and possibly other companies. Whilst this argument is obviously technically incorrect it is necessary to note the views of HMRC Stamp Taxes and their former advisers in order to ensure that appropriate evidence of the course of events is preserved for utilisation in possible future Enquiries.

[216] FA 2003, s 44(8); Sch 17A, para 12A; see, for example, **7.25**.

'Control'

12.52 'Control' is defined in accordance with Income and Corporation Taxes Act 1988, s 416.[217] Control of a company changes[218] where it becomes controlled:

- by a different person;

- by a different number of persons; or

- by two or more persons, at least one of whom is not the person or one of the persons by whom the company was previously controlled.

12.53 The anti-avoidance rules merely require a 'change' of control. It does not require that the original controller loses control or passes shares to another unassociated party. It must be noted that because of the complexities of the Income and Corporation Taxes Act 1988, s 416, it is possible by reason of the application of different criteria for two or more unconnected parties to be treated as both having 'control' simultaneously. Thus the original party may retain 'control' on one basis whilst another person becomes a controller. The original controller may retain control and at the same time some other person may acquire control. Normally this would, in plain English, not be regarded as a 'change' of control but it seems from the context that the acquisition of 'control' on one basis by a particular person operates as a 'change' of control notwithstanding that the original controller is also regarded by the arbitrary nature of the drafting of the drafting of the legislation as remaining in control and has not lost his control. It is understood that HMRC Stamp Taxes will take the point that the acquisition of control by a new person is sufficient to constitute a 'change of control' notwithstanding that the original controller does not lose his control. The retention of control by the original party is not sufficient to prevent the clawback operating. There are no tie-breaker rules for such situations. In consequence of this definition of change of control, it seems that there may be a clawback where, notwithstanding that the original party retains control, another party also acquires 'control' on a different basis pursuant to a transaction unconnected with the original chargeable transaction for which the relief was claimed.

12.54 Also it is not a condition for the clawback to operate that the change of control is in any way connected with the exempt transaction. The clawback applies even though the relief was obtained in connection with a transaction that was totally unconnected with the subsequent change of control. Thus an unrelated injection of new capital from an outside source or the company making an acquisition as part of a joint venture will suffice to change control.

'Relevant associated company'

12.55 The basic clawback applies where there is a change of control of the original purchaser or lessee whilst it still owns the chargeable interest or part thereof. However, it has been extended by anti-avoidance legislation to bring into charge situations where the original transferee has passed the land to its own subsidiary company so that it itself does not own the land. The charge to clawback arises where another company leaves the group with the original transferee or lessee because, in effect, the original purchaser of the chargeable interest still owns the chargeable interest acquired with the benefit of the

---

[217] Ibid, Sch 7, para 9(5)(b).
[218] Ibid, Sch 7, para 9(5)(c).

relief is still owned indirectly. This is done by reference to 'relevant associated companies' which are companies that are controlled by the company that acquired the land pursuant to the exempt transaction immediately before the control of that company changes and of which control changes in consequence of the change of control of that company.[219] This is intended to attack situations where the acquiring company having acquired the land transfers the land down to a subsidiary company which leaves the group at the same time taking the land with it out of the group. Although the company whose share capital has been purchased and which was the original acquirer of the chargeable interest no longer owns the property the transfer of its shares effectively pass the benefit of the property because the chargeable interest or an interest derived therefrom is held by a subsidiary company of the original acquirer.

12.56 This restriction upon the relief which applies where the chargeable interest had been dropped down by the original acquirer of the chargeable interest to a subsidiary company (known as 'the double dropdown') and there were problems in relation to the 'double bounce' where the property was transferred by A Ltd to C Ltd which was a sub-subsidiary because the shares in C Ltd were owned by B Ltd which were owned by A Ltd and C Ltd, having acquired the property with the benefit of the relief, transferred the property up to its immediate subsidiary B Ltd. There was, in one sense, no change of control of C Ltd but a change of control in B Ltd which was not a party to the original transaction has not proved sufficient to prevent tax mitigation and it has in effect been extended to include within the clawback 'successive transactions'.[220] This clawback extension applies[221] where:

• there is a change of control of the purchaser;

• within the 3-year period or a longer period where there were de-grouping arrangements entered into during the 3-year period such as the grant of an option intended to be exercised outside the perpetuity;[222] and

• there have been previous transactions which:
   - were exempt as intra-group transactions[223] or company reconstructions or reorganisations;[224]
   - and the effective date occurred during the immediately preceding 3 years;
   - the chargeable interest held by the company at degrouping was originally acquired in circumstances where an exemption within Sch 7 was available; and
   - the property has not been subject to a charge to tax in the intervening period.

---

[219]   Ibid, Sch 7, para 9(4).
[220]   Ibid, Sch 7, para 4A.
[221]   Ibid, Sch 7, para 4ZA and 9(1).
[222]   It is unclear how far HMRC Stamp Taxes intend to treat a company's articles of association or a shareholders' agreement as 'arrangement' for these purposes also not necessarily connected with the relieved transaction.
[223]   Ibid, Sch 7, Part 1.
[224]   Ibid, Sch 7, Part 2.

Chargeable amount for clawback

12.57 The amount of the tax is the amount that would have been chargeable in respect of the transaction for which the exemption was obtained[225] if that had been for a chargeable consideration of an amount equal to the market value of the chargeable interest acquired together with any interest or right appurtenant or pertaining to the chargeable interest that is acquired with it or, where only a part of the transferred chargeable interest or a part interest therein is retained, an appropriate proportion of the market value. This represents a modification of the provision that would otherwise apply namely the connected company charge which specifies that the amount of consideration for tax purposes is to be not less than the market value of the property acquired. By limiting the charge to the market value there will be no charge if the transferee company 'overpaid' for the chargeable interest. Since the clawback refers to the tax that would have been chargeable on the original transaction it appears that the market value is to be determined as at the original effective date[226] and not as at the date of the event giving rise to the clawback. This could be important where the company has carried out substantial improvements in the period from its acquisition. For these purposes, appropriate proportion means an appropriate proportion having regard to the chargeable interest acquired together with any interest or right appurtenant or pertaining thereto that is acquired with it and what is held at the time of the change of control by the company that acquired the land pursuant to the original exempt transaction or, as the case may be, by that company and any company that is controlled by the company that originally acquired the land immediately before the change of the company changes and control of which changes in consequence of the change of control of the company that originally acquired the land.

EXCLUSIONS FROM CLAWBACK

12.58 The exemptions for land acquired in connection with a scheme of reconstruction or reorganisation are not withdrawn ie there is no clawback of the relief where:[227]

- the change of control arises as a result of a transaction in shares that is between one party to a marriage[228] and the other party, which is effected:
  - in pursuance of an order of a court made on granting in respect of the parties a decree of divorce, nullity of marriage or judicial separation;
  - in pursuance of an order of a court made in connection with the dissolution or annulment of the marriage, or the parties' judicial separation, at any time after the granting of such a decree;
  - in pursuance of either an order of a court made at any time under Matrimonial Causes Act 1973, s 22A, s 23A or s 24A, or an incidental order of a court made under Family Law (Scotland) Act 1985, s 8(2), by virtue of s 14(1) thereof;

---

[225] This appears to require a payment of 4.5 per cent where the acquisition relief for reorganisations is withdrawn.

[226] But where there may be two effective dates it seems that it will be the later date of completion between the same parties rather than the prior substantial performance. This will affect the chargeable amount.

[227] FA 2003, Sch 7, para 10(2).

[228] It seems that this exclusion may inadvertently not have been extended to dissolution of civil partnerships pursuant to FA 2003, Sch 3, para 3A which are not made part of the original relief.

    –   at any time in pursuance of an agreement of the parties made in contemplation or otherwise in connection with the dissolution or annulment of the marriage, their judicial separation or the making of a separation order in respect of them;[229]

- the control of the company acquiring the land changes as a result of a transaction varying a disposition following a person's death, whether that disposition is effected by will or under the laws relating to intestacy or otherwise, of property of which the deceased was competent to dispose and the transaction is carried out within a period of 2 years after the person's death and no consideration in money or money's worth other than the making of a variation of another such disposition is given for it or arrangements involve mortgages.[230] For these purposes, it is irrelevant whether the administration of the estate is complete or the property has been distributed in accordance with the original dispositions or not. Unfortunately those responsible for the tax have not provided for relief where control changes by reason of the death of the individual shareholder such as where he bequeaths sufficient shares to a person to give the latter control; changing the will may be too late even though the change is not a clawback event. The exclusion does not apply to acquisitions of control arising pursuant to an appropriation by a personal representative in satisfaction of a legacy even though such a transaction is itself exempt from tax and falls within FA 2003, Sch 3 (as amended);[231]

- the control of the company acquiring the land changes as a result of an intra-group transfer of its shares which qualifies for exemption pursuant to FA 1930, s 42,[232] or Finance Act (Northern Ireland) Act 1954, s 11.[233] However, this is not a total exemption from the clawback; it merely rolls over the charge into the new structure and clawback may arise during the balance of the 3-year period. In consequence, the clawback roll-over ceases and tax is payable where:
  - a company holding either:
    - the shares in the company which has acquired the land pursuant to the exempt transaction;
    - shares which were acquired by reason of the exemption pursuant to s 42 of the FA 1930;[234] or
    - shares which are derived from the shares for which the exemption for the transfer of shares was obtained;
  - ceases to be a member of the same stamp duty land tax group as the company from which the land was acquired by reason of the exempt transaction either:
    - before the end of the period of 3 years beginning with the effective date of the transaction for which the exemption was obtained; or
    - after the end of the 3-year period where it ceases to be a member of the group in pursuance of or in connection with arrangements made before the end of the 3-year period; and
  - at that time either:

---

229   FA 2003, Sch 3, para 3; see **11.22**.
230   Ibid, Sch 3, para 4; Sch 4, para 8A.
231   Ibid, Sch 3, para 4; see **11.26** and **Chapter 9**.
232   This will be the stamp duty relief, since the relieving event is a share transfer not a disposal of the chargeable interest.
233   FA 2003, Sch 7, para 10(4).
234   Or Finance Act (Northern Ireland) 1954, s 11.

    –   the company that acquired the land by reason of the exempt transaction; or

    –   a relevant associated company (ie a company that is controlled by the company that acquired the land immediately before the change of control of the company) changes and of which control changes in consequence of the change of control of the company that acquired the land;

holds either a chargeable interest that was transferred to the company that originally acquired the land by reason of the exempt transaction or a chargeable interest that is derived from the interest that was so transferred and that has not been subsequently transferred at market value by a chargeable transaction in relation to which relief pursuant to paras 7 or 8 of Sch 7 to the FA 2003 was available but was not claimed;

- where the control of the company acquiring the land changes as a result of transfer of shares to another company in relation to which relief from stamp duty pursuant to FA 1986, s 77, is available.[235] However, this exclusion from the clawback arrangements is not permanent; it merely carries forward the situation for the balance of the 3-year period. In consequence, it is provided that the clawback applies and the tax is payable where:

    –   control of the company acquiring the shares in the company which acquired the land changes before the end of the period of 3 years beginning with the effective date of the transaction for which the original exemption was obtained, or after the 3-year period if the change of control is in pursuance of or in connection with arrangements made before the end of the 3-year period; and

    –   at the time when the change of control occurs that company holds any shares transferred to it by the exempt transfer or any shares derived from shares so transferred;

    -     at the time of the change of control the company that acquired the land or a relevant associated company at the time of the change of control of the new parent company holds the chargeable interest that was transferred to the acquiring company by the exempt transaction or that is derived from an interest that was so transferred and has not subsequently been transferred at market value by a chargeable transaction in relation to which relief for a reconstruction or reorganisation pursuant to para 7 or para 8 of Sch 7 to the FA 2003 was available but was not claimed;

- where the change of control arises upon a technicality because a loan created acquires or ceases to have control, provided that other persons who were deemed to have control retain control.[236]

Enforcement of clawback charge

12.59 There is an obligation upon the company to notify the occurrence of the clawback event and to self-assess and pay the stamp duty land tax due.[237] This applies notwithstanding that there are new shareholders in the company and the stamp duty land tax, if not paid by the acquiring company, can be recovered from associated

---

[235]   FA 2003, Sch 7, para 10(5).
[236]   Ibid, Sch 7, para 10(6).
[237]   Ibid, s 81 and Sch 7, para 12; see **12.104**.

companies[238] and controlling directors.[239] These secondary liabilities must be considered when asking for warranties and indemnities when acquiring companies that have been members of a group.[240]

PART II – INTRA-GROUP TRANSACTIONS

INTRODUCTION

12.60 Since members of a group are almost certainly connected companies dealings between them will take place at not less than the market value.[241] This can be something of a problem since many intra-group transactions are likely to be informal and not necessarily fully documented, which may be a key issue when searching for evidence as to whether the transaction involved a tenancy or a licence. In the absence of writing it is difficult to establish what the terms of the arrangement between the parties was and therefore there is nothing to which the taxpayer can point to indicate that there was a licence which falls outside the scope of stamp duty land tax altogether.[242]

An exemption[243] from stamp duty land tax is available if the vendor/lessor/grantor etc of any type of chargeable interest and the purchaser/lessee/grantee etc acquiring a chargeable interest are both bodies corporate and members of the same stamp duty land tax group at the effective date of the transaction.[244] This need for association as at the effective date is proving to be a problem in practice because of the view of HMRC Stamp Taxes that there are two effective dates where substantial performance and completion are not simultaneous[245] especially where new leases are involved.[246] On this view there is no automatic carry over of relief from substantial performance to completion and there is no retrospective credit for completion to substantial performance.[247] In addition completion, in the view of HMRC Stamp Taxes, starts a new 3-year clawback period because it is a separate chargeable transaction and independent of any prior substantial performance. Relaxed completion of associated company transactions and reorganisations is likely to be an expensive exercise if in the future should HMRC Stamp Taxes continue to press their current interpretations of the legislation.

Scope of relief

12.61 The 'one size fits all' drafting means that the relief is available for all forms of chargeable transactions including surrenders of leases and variations of chargeable interests such as the change of the dates relating to the exercise of an option and there is no requirement that the relevant company becomes the beneficial owner of the

---

[238] Ibid, Sch 7, para 12(2)(a).
[239] Ibid, Sch 7, para 12(2)(b).
[240] See **12.99**.
[241] FA 2003, ss 53 and 54; see **5.208**.
[242] Ibid, s 48.
[243] Ibid, Sch 7, para 1(1) refers to 'exemption' but since the transaction remains notifiable this is a form of relief.
[244] Ibid, Sch 7, para 1.
[245] Ibid, s 44(8).
[246] Ibid, Sch 17A, para 12A.
[247] See, for example, **7.25** and **11.1**.

chargeable interest.[248] The relief is, in consequence, much wider than its predecessor in relation to stamp duty particularly as there are consequential changes such as there must merely be an 'acquisition', including a deemed acquisition, and this means the relief may be available notwithstanding that the beneficial ownership does not vest in the acquiring company. It is, therefore, essential that the legislation is approached without stamp duty preconceptions.

However, the relief is not available in connection with subsale arrangements.[249]

Retrospection

12.62 The scope of the relief must also be considered in the context of the temporal implications arising from the lack of finality in relation to the tax, its provisional and retrospective nature and the fact that there may not be any form of wait-and-see.[250] For example, where there is the grant of a lease with a rent review during the first 5 years of the term the initial calculation as at the effective date is on a provisional and estimated basis.[251] These provisional calculations have to be subsequently revisited or retrospectively revised[252] so that the immediate transaction is a retrospective adjustment of the initial transaction and, therefore, in consequence, it is necessary to investigate the particular transaction in the context of the original arrangements. For example, where the lease was granted within the intra-group or disadvantaged land exemption the relief in respect of the rent review is, *prima facie*, still available because the review is not a separate chargeable event but an adjustment of the original chargeable event. On the other hand, the fact that the parties are within the group relationship at the time of the rent review does not guarantee that it will be exempt. There is no carry forward of reliefs for subsequent chargeable events but since these are the same chargeable event unlike the potential separation into tax chargeable transactions for substantial performance and completion[253] the reliefs may continue to be available.[254]

'Company'

12.63 The relief is only available for companies which applies to bodies corporate[255] subject to the exclusion of partnerships[256] and unit trusts. The reference to 'body corporate' means that unlimited companies, foreign incorporations, certain local authorities, charter corporations and other bodies are within the scope of the relief.[257] However, since the structure of the group requires beneficial ownership of ordinary share capital, the relief will be available where such companies are involved only where they are the parent of the group. Whilst certain charities may be bodies corporate,[258] there is an open question as to whether they are the beneficial owner of their subsidiary

---

[248] But see **11.9** on the possibility of partial exemption.
[249] FA 2003, s 45(7)(a) compare FA 1967, s 27(7)(b) and *Escoigne Properties Ltd v IRC* [1958] AC 549.
[250] However, this means that there is, in the view of HMRC Stamp Taxes, no automatic carry forward of the relief from substantial performance to completion nor an automatic carry back.
[251] FA 2003, s 51.
[252] See, for example, ibid, Sch 17A, paras 7 and 8.
[253] Ibid, s 44(8) and Sch 17A, para 12A; see **7.25**.
[254] See **11.1**.
[255] FA 2003, s 100; but not unit trusts, s 101(7) and there are issues with limited liability partnerships (LLPs); see Sch 15, para 2.
[256] Including limited liability partnerships notwithstanding that these are in general law bodies corporate.
[257] See **12.20** on the approach of HMRC Stamp Taxes to 'company' as being limited to companies incorporated in the UK.
[258] This is not the same as a company being the trustee of a charitable trust. In such as case as it is a trustee and

companies for these purposes. It seems, however, in practice that HMRC Stamp Taxes act upon the basis that a charitable company is the beneficial owner of the shares in its subsidiary companies.

The stamp duty land tax group

12.64 In order to be a stamp duty land tax group, it is necessary that:

- the vendor is a body corporate;

- the 'purchaser' is a body corporate;

- either:
  - one body corporate which may be either the vendor or the purchaser so that the relief will be available in respect of transfers from a subsidiary to parent or from a parent to subsidiary is the 75 per cent subsidiary of the other; or
  - both are 75 per cent subsidiaries of a third company so that the relief may be available in respect of sideways movements of chargeable interests.

This means that the stamp duty land tax group may take one of two structures, namely:

- a linear group where A Ltd owns shares in B Ltd which owns shares in C Ltd etc; or

- a triangular structure or a mixture thereof where A Ltd owns shares in both B Ltd and C Ltd, and B Ltd owns shares in D Ltd and E Ltd; C Ltd may be in the same stamp duty land tax group as B Ltd, D Ltd and E Ltd.

Obviously B Ltd and D Ltd and E Ltd may constitute their own stamp duty land tax group since the stamp duty land tax group is not investigated beyond the degree necessary for the purpose of the particular chargeable transaction, which is important when investigating the clawback arrangements. The grouping test goes no further than is necessary for the particular transaction; it is not necessary to find the ultimate parent of the entire group so that in relation to a transaction between D Ltd and E Ltd it is not necessary to go beyond B Ltd the immediate common parent and this has important implications for the operation of the clawback of the relief.

The situation is, however, not entirely straightforward since there may be partnership arrangements involved in the group structure. For example, A Ltd may joint with B Ltd, an unassociated company in forming a partnership as a joint venture vehicle in which A Ltd is entitled to 90 per cent of the capital and income of the firm which owns the whole of the issued share capital of C Ltd. There are conflicting views within HMRC Stamp Taxes on two key issues namely:

- whether A Ltd is the beneficial owner of the share capital of C Ltd so that transfers between A Ltd and C Ltd are eligible for group relief; and

---

not the charity it is not the beneficial owner of the assets and in both cases the transfer may be within the connected company charge pursuant to FA 2003, s 53 unless the corporate trustee falls within the exclusions set out in s 54 thereof.

- whether a transfer of the shares in C Ltd by the partnership to D Ltd, a wholly owned subsidiary of A Ltd, is eligible for group relief because the transfer is a partnership and a body corporate unless there is some for of fiscal transparency as regards the partnership and its assets.

75 per cent subsidiary

12.65 The test for a 75 per cent subsidiary involves several stages. There is:

- an initial test of an appropriate percentage of the issued ordinary share capital; and

- if this test is satisfied it is then necessary to determine whether:
  - the parent company has an appropriate deemed economic interest in the subsidiary company;[259]
  - the control test can be satisfied.[260]

There are, however, negative conditions and anti-avoidance provisions which apply to cancel that eligibility to the relief where certain circumstances or arrangements exist.

The basic shareholding test

12.66 In order to be a 75 per cent subsidiary of another company, it is necessary that one body corporate:

- is the direct or indirect (ie through other companies);

- beneficial owner;

- of not less than 75 per cent;

- of the ordinary share capital of another body corporate.

12.67 The effect is that:

- where all the companies in the group are wholly owned by their immediate parents, then the group relationship will be 100 per cent;

- the 75 per cent can be owned directly or indirectly through another body corporate or bodies corporate.[261] The indirect shareholding is calculated in accordance with the provisions of Income and Corporation Taxes Act 1988, s 838(5)–(10). Where one or more of the companies is not wholly owned, then the shareholding relationship is based upon the relevant percentage or fraction of the particular company; where two companies are less than wholly owned, the sub-subsidiary company is beneficially owned as to a percentage of the percentage. For example, if A owns 80 per cent of B (so that they are associated for the purposes of stamp duty land tax) and B owns 80 per cent of the ordinary share capital of C (so that these are associated for the purposes of stamp duty land tax), A will be deemed to

---

[259] See **12.77**.
[260] See **12.83**.
[261] FA 2003, Sch 7, para 1(4).

own 64 per cent (ie 80 per cent of 80 per cent) of C so that A and C will not be members of the same stamp duty land tax group. However, if A owns 100 per cent of the shares in D which owns the other 20 per cent of D, A is deemed to own 84 per cent of C (ie 64 per cent through B and 20 per cent through D).

75 per cent

12.68 There is no specific statutory test as to how to determine whether there is a holding of 75 per cent of the relevant shares. There is some authority from stamp duty in *Canada Safeway v IRC*,[262] but the facts of that case limited the scope of the potential arguments. In effect, because the judge was faced with a choice between nominal value and market value, the case is no more than authority that market value is not the proper test. The emphasis in that case on nominal value was because the market value was too difficult to apply because it fluctuates from day to day. This basis has been undermined by the economic interest tests which are even more complex and largely nonsense in a transaction based tax. There can be no objection to the market value test on the grounds of difficulty when at the same time the parties have to apply a very similar economic interest test. The same comments have been made in relation to group capital gains tax and it seems, broadly, that HMRC apply the tests on a pragmatic basis; a group structure exists in practice if the facts seem to satisfy the conditions on the day and HMRC Stamp Taxes relying upon a capital gains tax advice appear to adopt a similar approach. Moreover by adopting economic tests HMRC Stamp Taxes have effectively destroyed their successful argument in the *Canada Safeway* case.[263] Moreover, the nominal value test is inappropriate to foreign companies where there are shares of no par value.[264] In such cases HMRC Stamp Taxes grant the relief where 75 per cent of the number of the shares in all relevant shares chosen is owned. In consequence, there is now considerable doubt as to the content of the 75 per cent test. Ideally, the parties have 75 per cent in nominal terms, but where this cannot be satisfied other tests may be appropriate such as the number of shares regardless of nominal value. A test related to capital contributed such as share premium account may be more suited to the situation since HMRC Stamp Taxes have consistently argued that the relief is intended to be available only where there is no change in economic ownership which suggests a test based on capital and/or net assets.

12.69 Virtually insoluble problems have arisen in practice in relation to foreign companies and 'treasury shares' ie those share in itself acquired by a company[265] and not cancelled as part of a reduction of capital[266] as a purchase or redemption of its own shares.[267] Since the shares remain in existence, they have to be included in the calculation and produce circularity problems of percentages because the company concerned is not wholly owned by its parent. Such arrangements are now permitted by United Kingdom legislation,[268] and the shares are to be ignored for certain specific stamp duty purposes.[269] It seems that the practice of HMRC Stamp Taxes to accept that an appropriate group structure exists provided that at least another 75 per cent were held by

---

[262] [1972] 1 All ER 666.
[263] Ibid.
[264] There are also problems where companies incorporated overseas own their own shares or shares in their parent company.
[265] Companies Act 2006, s 724 (FA 2003, Sch 40; Finance Act 2003, Section 195 and Schedule 40 (Appointed Day) Order 2003, SI 2003/3077.
[266] Compare FA 2003, Sch 7, para 7(7A); FA 1986, ss 75(5A) and 77(3A).
[267] Companies Act 2006, ss 690 and 709.
[268] Ibid, s 641.
[269] FA 1986, ss 75(5A) and 77(3A) and FA 2003, Sch 7, para 7(7A).

other bodies corporate. However, this has not been fully dealt with by statute[270] and such shares are ignored when calculating the 75 per cent. Virtually insolvable problems have arisen in practice in other cases and in relation to foreign companies and 'treasury shares' ie those shares in itself acquired by a company and not cancelled as part of a reduction of capital[271] or a purchase or redemption of its own shares.[272] Since the shares remain in existence they have to be included in the calculation and produce circularity problems of percentages because the company concerned is not wholly owned by its parent. It seems that the practice of HMRC Stamp Taxes is to accept that an appropriate group structure exists provided that at least 75 per cent of the outstanding shares are held by the relevant company the relief will be granted.[273]

Ordinary share capital

12.70 This test is based upon 'ordinary share capital', which is defined as all of the issued share capital of the body corporate, by whatever name known, of the company other than capital the holders of which have a right to a dividend at a fixed rate but have no other right to share in the profits of the company.[274] The reference to the absence of right to share in the 'profits' of the company is, obviously, intended to exclude fixed rate preference shares which where a problem of their own making for HMRC Stamp Taxes by reason of the limited scope of their arguments in *Canada Safeway v IRC*.[275] However, there may be fixed dividend preference shares[276] which are entitled to participate in the surplus assets in a winding-up. It seems, however, that such surplus assets although potentially representing undistributed profits are not profits[277] and in consequence such participation rights are to be ignored. HMRC Stamp Taxes have from time to time put forward the view that, where there are shares which have no dividend rights (such as deferred shares), the shares are not shares not having a dividend at a fixed rate and are, in consequence, 'ordinary share capital'.[278] It must be noted that the definition of ordinary share capital for the purposes of this test is irritatingly different from the definition for the purposes of the 75 per cent economic interest test.

Beneficial ownership of shares[279]

12.71 Whether the alleged stamp duty land tax group is linear or triangular it is necessary that the shares which form the basis of the relationship are owned or deemed to be beneficially by the parent company.[280] There is a limited provision which provides

---

270 FA 2003, Sch 7, para 7(7A). Substantial changes are made by FA 2009, Sch 9, to ICTA 1988, Sch 18 dealing with preference shares having limited dividend rights but FA 2003, Sch 7, is not expressly amended.

271 Companies Act 2006, s 641.

272 Ibid, s 724.

273 Compare FA 2003, Sch 7, para 7(5A).

274 Ibid, Sch 7, para 1(5).

275 [1972] 1 All ER 666.

276 Such shares are also a problem because such shares may be initially non-voting but carry a right to vote when their dividends are in arrears. Clearly if temporarily enfranchised by reason of such arrears they will be relevant for the control test (see **12.83**); but there is a more difficult question of whether the articles of association of the company constitute arrangements whereby control may change if, at the time, the dividends are not in arrears (compare *Irving v Tesco Stores (Holdings) Ltd v IRC* [1982] STC 881).

277 *Re Richmond Gate* [1965] 1 WLR 335.

278 See also *Syme Darby London v Syme Darby Holdings* [1975] STC 562 on shares whose dividends vary with the rate of tax. Ordinary share capital does not include certain interests in guarantee companies: see *Southshore Mutual Insurance Company Limited v Blair* [1999] STC SCD 296.

279 It is no longer necessary that the beneficial ownership in the transferred or leased or released chargeable interest passes to the 'purchaser' body corporate.

280 Compare *Rodwell Securities Ltd v IRC* [1968] 1 All ER 257.

a form of fiscal transparency in that a parent company is deemed to be the beneficial owner of shares in its subsidiary company. For example, where A owns the share capital of B which owns share capital in C, A is deemed to be the beneficial owner of the shares in C held by B; but this is different from the question of the percentage of share capital in C of which A is deemed to be the beneficial owner.[281] There is, however, unfortunately no positive definition of when beneficial ownership exists; there are merely several cases indicating when it may not exist. The existing case-law is, therefore, of a negative nature. The following paragraphs are, therefore, illustrations of where a company has lost the beneficial ownership of the share capital in question.

Contacts and options

12.72 For the purpose of the section, it is clear that a company which has entered into an unconditional contract for the sale of property is not the beneficial owner of that property,[282] and this may be so notwithstanding that the contract is conditional.[283] Beneficial ownership may not be suspended where the company has granted an option to call for sale of the shares in the subsidiary, except perhaps in those cases where the terms of the option severely restrict the company's use and enjoyment of the shares during the period until the option is exercised and the contract for the sale of the shares comes into existence.[284] It seems that the crucial test is whether the arrangement restricts the right or power of the shareholder to enjoy the benefit of dividends in respect of the shares.

Shareholder agreements[285]

12.73 Shareholder agreements, including, it seems, arrangements relating to the disposal of shares in the company contained in the articles of association may affect the

---

[281] See **12.67**.

[282] *Parway Estates Ltd v IRC* (1958) 37 ATC 164; *Baytrust Holdings Ltd v IRC* [1971] 1 WLR 1333. This is not the same issue as whether the beneficial ownership has passed to or vested in the purchaser, which may not occur until the purchase price has been paid and the contract has become specifically enforceable: see *J Sainsbury plc v O'Connor* [1991] STC 318. However, it may be open to question by reason of the numerous cases relating to the residual rights of unpaid vendors, whether such a person has, in the absence of restrictions in the contract of sale, lost beneficial ownership. The cases on the topic have been dealt with somewhat superficially and have not given adequate consideration to the issues of the rights of unpaid vendors: see, eg, *Musselwhite v Musselwhite* [1962] 1 Ch 210; *Michaels v Harley House (Marylebone)* [1999] 3 WLR 229. In such a case the purchaser is not the equitable and beneficial owner because he does not have the right to call for specific performance. As regards the position of the vendor, some interest remains and, as *J Sainsbury plc v O'Connor* (above) was concerned to reunite equitable and beneficial ownership in commercial situations (ie it was seeking to limit the principles relating to the temporary disappearance of beneficial ownership to cases where there is a special statutory regime regulating the rights of the parties such as insolvency and succession to the estates of deceased persons), it is open to argument that, in many cases, the vendor may have sufficient interest in the share capital for the purposes of satisfying these conditions, at least in those cases where the contract does not restrict the right to take dividends from the relevant company.

[283] *Brooklands Selangor Holdings Ltd v IRC* [1970] 1 WLR 429, applying *Wood Preservation Ltd v Prior* [1969] 1 WLR 1077; *IRC v Ufitec Group* [1977] 3 All ER 929. In all of these cases, restrictions upon the 'enjoyment' of the shares in question had been imposed so that, eg, no dividends could be obtained, and in *J Sainsbury plc v O'Connor* [1991] STC 318, the Court of Appeal appears to have had certain reservations as regards the precise scope of the decision in *Wood Preservation v Prior*. The reasoning would extend to an option to purchase, at least where restrictions as to dividends and use are imposed. The position remains open where no such fetters on the benefits of property are imposed (see, eg, *Thompson v ASDA-MFI plc Group* [1988] 2 All ER 722).

[284] See *J Sainsbury plc v O'Connor* (above).

[285] Shareholder agreements may also be relevant in determining whether there is control of the company (see

beneficial ownership of the share capital. This can be important when structuring joint venture arrangements. Articles of association may provide for the acquisition of the shares of one member of the company by other members in certain circumstances. These may vary from pre-emptive rights to obligations to purchase the shares. In the latter case HMRC regard this as a binding contract to sell and purchase the shares.[286] In the circumstances the beneficial ownership of the shares may have been lost.[287]

12.74 It has been held that a company is not the beneficial owner of any of its property which controlling members have agreed to procure the company to sell.[288] Whilst it was formerly thought that a party would not lose beneficial ownership in the absence of some directly enforceable fetter on his use or enjoyment of an asset or share,[289] it has been said that a company is not the beneficial owner of property that is the subject of equitable obligations[290] in favour of others.[291] The decision in *Holmleigh Holdings*[292] comes close to the proposition that a company is not the beneficial owner of property if there is a subsisting arrangement that it shall cease to be.[293] Notwithstanding the powerful judgment of the Court of Appeal in *J Sainsbury plc v O'Connor*,[294] seeking to restore the link between beneficial and equitable ownership and requiring some form of specifically enforceable relationship which would entitle the party to some form of injunction to protect his position before beneficial ownership is to be regarded as lost, HMRC Stamp Taxes have sought to develop this argument in two ways, namely:

• where there is a pre-arranged scheme which is not contractually binding but which, once commenced, commercially (but not legally) commits the parties to proceed to completion, any relevant beneficial ownership ceases to exist on the first step being taken. This type of argument was advanced in *Swithland Investments Ltd v IRC*,[295] based upon the overall scheme set out in a letter to the Inland Revenue applying for clearance under what is now Taxation of Chargeable

   Steele v EVC [1996] STC 785; Revenue Guidance December (1996) and whether there is a scheme or reconstruction *Swithland Investments v IRC* [1990] STC 448; *Snell v HMRC* [2006] STC (SCD) 295.

[286] This may also raise a question of whether the deceased was competent to dispose of the property for the purposes of the exemption from stamp duty land tax in relation to the variation of the estates of deceased persons pursuant to FA 2003, Sch 3, para 4.

[287] *Parway Estates Ltd v IRC* (1958) 37 ATC 164; but note the position where the price has not been paid as in *Musselwhite v Musselwhite* [1962] 1 Ch 210; *Michaels v Harley House (Marylebone) Ltd* [2000] Ch 104, although this may depend upon the restrictions if any upon the payment of dividends in operation at the time.

[288] *Holmleigh (Holdings) Ltd v IRC* (1958) 37 ATC 406. It would seem that the quasi-purchaser can get specific performance of such a contract: see *Elliott v Pierson* [1948] Ch 452; *Jones v Lipman* [1962] 1 WLR 832. See [1962] BTR 343; also *Swithland Investments v IRC* [1990] STC 448.

[289] Cf *Fitch Lovell Ltd v IRC* [1962] 1 WLR 1325 at 1342.

[290] It is clear that not all equitable or even legal obligations to others detract from beneficial ownership. Thus, a mortgagor is nevertheless beneficial owner: *English Sewing Cotton Co v IRC* [1947] 1 All ER 679. However, the position may be different where, instead of appointing a receiver who is treated as the agent of the mortgagor, the mortgagee actually enters into possession of the mortgaged property. See also *Parway Estates Ltd v IRC* (1958) 45 TC 135.

[291] *Leigh Spinners v IRC* (1956) 46 TC 425. It appears to be an open question whether the equitable obligations in favour of others were the rights of persons who had agreed to purchase the property concerned (as with the cases in the previous note) or the rights of persons who had the benefit of a contract that the members of a company would procure that company to sell the property concerned (see further *Nock* [1990] BTR 269 at 282).

[292] (1958) 37 ATC 406.

[293] But see *Times Newspapers Ltd v IRC* [1973] Ch 155, distinguishing *Curzon Offices Ltd v IRC* [1944] 1 All ER 606, per Goddard LJ at 607 (fuller statement of facts in 22 ATC 306).

[294] [1991] STC 318; see also *Michaels v Harley House (Marylebone) Ltd* [1999] 3 WLR 229.

[295] [1990] STC 448.

Gains Act 1992, s 135,[296] but the learned judge declined to extend the law to that extent although he indicated that the position might have been different if there had been a formal agreement binding the shareholders to carry out the scheme; and

- beneficial ownership ceases to exist when the parties reach a 'serious stage' in their negotiations for the sale and purchase of an asset. The main area of difficulty concerns potential sales of subsidiary companies where the prospective purchaser does not wish to acquire all of the assets held by the subsidiary company. This may also be complicated by the provisions that a company is not the stamp duty parent of the other company if another person has or could obtain control of the other.[297] It would seem, however, that this requires existing and enforceable rights such as options and, hopefully, will not apply to normal commercial negotiations.

Attempts by the vendor to remove the land from the subsidiary prior to a sale of the subsidiary company within the scope of this relief may encounter the claim by HMRC Stamp Taxes that the parent company had ceased to be the beneficial owner of the share capital of the subsidiary at some earlier stage.[298]

Insolvency issues

12.75 The appointment of a receiver or administrator does not affect the beneficial ownership of the company's assets including the shares in its subsidiary company;[299] nor does the fact that the company's liabilities exceed its assets.

HMRC Stamp Taxes appear to be moving towards the view that in certain circumstances the existence of a mortgage may deprive the mortgagor of beneficial ownership of the shares mortgaged.[300]

However, the appointment of a receiver or administrator will almost inevitably indicate the sale of the company's assets in due course including the shares in any subsidiary companies. In consequence, any transfer of assets down to a new subsidiary company or between subsidiaries is likely to encounter insuperable difficulties in obtaining and retaining the relief because there will be an arrangement whereby the transferee is to leave the group precluding the obtaining of the relief,[301] or there is a degrouping event on the sale of the shares in the transferee company within the 3-year period.[302] Even the liquidation or sale of the transferor company may trigger a clawback event if occurring within the relevant 3 years.[303]

---

[296] This case illustrates quite clearly the practical problem of dealing with HMRC Stamp Taxes. They require production of clearance letters dealing with the capital gains tax issues but seek to exploit such letters if ineptly drafted without these problems in mind and to deny the relief.

[297] FA 2003, Sch 7, para 2(1).

[298] The anti-avoidance provisions relating to degrouping do not apply because it is the transferor which is leaving the stamp duty land tax group but there may be a clawback of the relief if the transferee subsequently leaves the group; FA 2003, Sch 7, para 3.

[299] *English Sewing Cotton Co Ltd v IRC* [1947] 1 All ER 679.

[300] On occasion, HMRC Stamp Taxes appears to have been contending, apparently upon legal advice, that the beneficial ownership is with the mortgagee where there is negative equity and possibly the mortgagee is in possession of the property.

[301] FA 2003, Sch 7, para 2(2)(b).

[302] Ibid, Sch 7, para 3.

[303] Ibid, Sch 7, paras 4(4) and 4ZA.

Liquidations

12.76 It has been held that a company in liquidation is not the beneficial owner of its property[304] and, accordingly, the commencement of even a solvent members' voluntary winding-up means that the company in liquidation will cease to be the beneficial owner of the shares in any of its subsidiary and sub-subsidiary companies. In consequence, for example, where a liquidator is proposing to transfer assets into a newly formed subsidiary company with a view to its sale, this relief will not be available because there is no stamp duty land tax group in place.[305] However, in such circumstances, the beneficial ownership of the surplus assets will at some stage, probably after all creditors have been paid or properly provided for, vest in the members or parent company of the liquidating company and this may help to establish or preserve the necessary association, but this will lie with the parent company.

A major consequence of degrouping is the possible application of the provisions clawing back any relief obtained within the preceding 3 years.[306] However, the relief is not clawed back where the purchaser ceases to be a member of the same group by reason of anything done for the purpose of,[307] or in the course of, winding-up the vendor or another company that is above[308] the vendor in the group structure.[309]

The economic interest test

12.77 It is necessary not merely to own 75 per cent of the ordinary share capital;[310] it is also necessary for the parent company to be beneficially entitled to not less than 75 per cent of any profits available for distribution to equity holders of the company or of all of the companies involved and 75 per cent of any assets available for distribution to equity holders in a winding-up. The primary condition is ownership of 75 per cent of the relevant share capital and the 75 per cent economic interest test is then applied. It is, however, not sufficient to be entitled to a 75 per cent economic interest. There must be ownership of the requisite number of shares. These tests which are drawn from other different types of tax are impossible to apply because stamp duty land tax is a tax based essentially upon the circumstances as at the effective date but these tests are based upon annual accounts which do not refer to a particular date. Similar conceptual problems apply to corporation tax upon chargeable gains. However, it seems that the capital gains tax sections of HMRC seem to operate on an informal basis such that if the circumstances appear to be within the test the conditions are satisfied. Since HMRC Stamp Taxes appear to be dependent upon capital gains tax divisions for technical

---

[304] *IRC v Olive Mill Ltd* [1963] 1 WLR 712; see also *Pritchard v MH Builders Ltd* [1969] 1 WLR 409; *Ayerst v C & K Construction Ltd* [1975] 1 All ER 162. The first-named case was not followed in relation to a solvent company by the East African Court of Appeal in *Ruderva Estates Ltd v Stamp Duties Commission* [1966] EAR 566; and see [1968] BTR 51–56.

[305] It is thought that the appointment of a receiver does not have this effect, although in that case there may be an issue whether there is an arrangement whereby the parties are to cease to be associated within the anti-avoidance rules. This may depend upon whether at the relevant time there are or are not negotiations with prospective purchasers. In the latter case, there is merely an intention to sell but not an 'arrangement' to do so.

[306] FA 2003, Sch 7, para 3.

[307] Note the limitation on these words excluding preparatory steps as in *Combined Technologies plc v IRC* [1985] STC 348.

[308] Defined FA 2003, Sch 7, para 4(5).

[309] Ibid, Sch 7, para 4(4).

[310] See **12.66** and **12.70** on the issue of 75 per cent.

support it is probable that they will adopt the same approach of not challenging the relief if the group looks to be alright on the day.[311]

12.78 The test for economic interest applies not only to shareholders but also includes the interest of 'equity holders'. Equity holders include certain creditors and such 'equity holdings' are treated as a form of ordinary share capital.[312] In consequence, when determining whether 75 per cent or more of the available profits or available assets in a winding-up would pass to the company which it is claimed is the parent company, the appropriate proportion of assets and any interest received in respect of such non-commercial loans is treated as if it were income available for distribution by way of dividend or assets available for distribution in the winding-up. 'Equity holders' are defined[313] as a person:

- who holds ordinary shares in the company; or

- who is a loan creditor of the company in respect of a loan which is not a normal commercial loan.

Ordinary shares

12.79 'Ordinary shares' here has a slightly different meaning from the ordinary share capital test which is applied for the purposes of the 75 per cent shareholding test. It means[314] all shares other than fixed rate preference shares,[315] which are shares issued for a consideration which is or includes new consideration and which do not carry any right either for conversion into shares or securities of any other description other than conversion into shares or securities of the company's quoted parent or rights to the acquisition of any additional shares or securities and do not carry any rights to dividends other than those of a fixed amount or fixed rate percent of the nominal value of the shares. The dividend rights must also represent no more than a reasonable commercial return on the new consideration received by the company in respect of the issue of the shares. They must also on repayment not carry any rights to an amount exceeding the new consideration except insofar as those repayment rights are reasonably comparable with those generally available for fixed dividend shares listed on a recognised stock exchange.

'Loan creditors' and normal commercial loans

12.80 A 'loan creditor' is a person other than a person carrying on the business of banking[316] and lending money to a company in the ordinary course of business, who is

---

[311] There are, however, numerous published practices by HMRC intended to make Sch 18 workable for other taxes, and it has been indicated that HMRC Stamp Taxes will apply these practices of the other divisions of HMRC to the new provisions in relation to stamp duty land tax, such as the fact that the shares in the acquiring body corporate are subject to a mortgage where there is a possibility that the mortgagee may foreclose or sell pursuant to powers in the mortgage and so change the control of the company will not be taken as precluding the parties from obtaining the relief.

[312] FA 2003, Sch 7, para 1(6); FA 2009, Sch 9 has made substantial changes to the treatment of preference shares and group structures.

[313] Income and Corporation Taxes Act 1988, Sch 18.

[314] Ibid, Sch 18, para 1(2) and (3).

[315] FA 2003, Sch 7, para 1(5); FA 2009, Sch 9 has made substantial changes to the treatment of preference shares and group structures.

[316] However, certain arrangements involving banks and capital allowances may be relevant: see ibid, Sch 18, para 1(6)–(8). It is provided that where any person has directly or indirectly provided new consideration for

a creditor in respect of any debt incurred by the company for any money borrowed or capital assets acquired by the company or for any rights to receive income created in favour of the company or for consideration the value of which to the company was, at the time when it was incurred, substantially less than the amount of the debt including any premium thereon or in respect of any redeemable loan capital issued by the company.[317]

12.81 A normal commercial loan is a loan[318] of or including new consideration and which does not carry rights either to conversion into shares or securities except other non-convertible securities or shares or securities of the company's quoted parent and does not carry the right to the acquisition of any additional shares or securities. Any interest upon the loan must not depend to any extent upon the result of the company's business or any part of it or the value of the company's assets or exceed a reasonable commercial return on the new consideration lent. The amount on repayment must either not exceed the new consideration lent or be reasonably comparable with the amount of any premium on redemption generally repayable in respect of an equal amount of new consideration under the terms of issue of securities listed on a recognised stock exchange.

12.82 Other forms of non-commercial loan include loans which have limited recourse or are without recourse except in relation to a loan made to a company for the purpose of facilitating acquisition of land and none of the land to be acquired is acquired with a view to resale at a profit. The whole of the loan must be applied in the acquisition of land by the company or in meeting the incidental costs of obtaining the loan, the amount payable in connection with the loan to the person making it must be secured on the land which the loan is to be used to acquire, and no other security is to be required for the payment of any such amount.

Control test

12.83 The exemption is not available where, at the effective date of the transaction, arrangements are in place by virtue of which at that time or at a later time:

---

any shares or securities in a company and that person or any person connected with him uses, for the purposes of his trade, assets which belong to the company and in respect of which there is made to the company any first year or writing-down allowance in respect of any acquisition of plant or machinery or any expenditure incurred on research and development, then that person and no other is treated as being an equity holder in respect of those shares and securities and as being beneficially entitled to any distribution of profits or assets attributable to those shares. Where the person providing the money is a bank and the only new consideration provided by the bank for any shares or securities is provided in the normal course of its banking business by way of normal commercial loan and the cost to the company of the asset falling for the capital allowances is less than the amount of the new consideration, the equity holding in respect of the loan is restricted to such amount as is equal to the costs of the assets.

[317] Income and Corporation Taxes Act 1988, s 417(7) and (9).
[318] This gives rise to a difficult point of interpretation. The definition of 'loan creditor' refers to debt which includes unpaid consideration, such as for the acquisition of capital assets. This differs from a 'loan', which is a transaction under which cash is advanced and does not on normal principles include an unpaid consideration. This raises the question as to whether the use of the word 'loan' in the definition of normal commercial loan carries its general meaning of a liability in respect of cash advanced or is to be taken to include debts for unpaid consideration. The point could be of considerable importance where there is indebtedness in respect of unpaid consideration where there are overage or turnover payments and the amount payable is linked to the value of assets which may make it a non-commercial loan or non-commercial 'debt'. This could be particularly important where the company which is indebted is a subsidiary company. The unpaid consideration might operate as a loan which is not a normal commercial loan making the creditor or unpaid seller an equity holder in that company and so operating to degroup it for the purposes of stamp duty land tax.

- any person has or could obtain control of the acquiring company without obtaining control of the disposing company; or

- any persons together have or could obtain control of the acquiring company without obtaining control of the disposing company.[319]

12.84 'Control' is defined in terms of Income and Corporation Taxes Act 1988, s 840.[320] HMRC Stamp Taxes have indicated in relation to the equivalent provisions for relief from stamp duty that the existence of a power of sale in a mortgage over the shares in question will not be treated in practice as an offending arrangement. However, the fact that it was necessary to indicate that this situation would be ignored is a clear indication that it is intended to be applied widely. Traps may exist in relation to:

- arrangements in the articles of association or shareholder agreements relating to situations where the shares may have to be offered for sale;

- provisions in the articles of association conferring votes upon preference shares where their dividends are in arrears; and

- provisions in the articles of association dealing with pre-emptive and similar rights.

It must be noted that, because of the use of the word 'could' in relation to the acquisition of control, the word 'arrangements' must bear a different meaning from that hitherto applied in the restrictions upon the relief from stamp duty.[321] There appears to be no need for any form of causal relationship between the acquisition of the chargeable interest and the possible change of control. The fact that the control arrangement was entered into prior to and unconnected with the chargeable transaction is irrelevant. It is simply a stealth trap for the unwary.

Anti-avoidance and disqualifying conditions

12.85 This exemption is not available where the chargeable transaction is effected in pursuance of or in connection[322] with any arrangement under which either:

- the consideration, or any part of the consideration for the conveyance or transfer was to be provided or received,[323] directly or indirectly, by an outsider, ie a person other than an appropriately associated body corporate; or

- the disposing company and acquiring company were to cease to be associated by reason of either:
  - the acquiring company ceasing to be a 75 per cent subsidiary of the disposing company; or
  - ceasing to be a 75 per cent subsidiary of the third company.

---

[319] FA 2003, Sch 7, para 2(1); on other possible problems with preference shares see **12.70**.

[320] Ibid, Sch 7, para 2(5); which, irritatingly, is different from the definition of 'control' for the purposes of corporate reconstructions and reorganisations in Sch 7, Part 2.

[321] FA 1967, s 27(3); FA 1995, s 151(3).

[322] See, for example, *Clarke Chapman John Thompson Ltd v IRC* [1975] STC 567; *Dobush v Greater Winnipeg Water District* [1945] 2 WWR 371.

[323] Introduced to counteract the decision in *Shop and Stores Developments v IRC* [1967] 1 All ER 42 in FA 1967, s 27(3) but never applied in practice in relation to stamp duty.

This does not apply where the degrouping is relieved by FA 1986, s 75, involving the acquisition,[324] or there are arrangements relating to the demutualisation of insurance companies.[325]

'Arrangements'

12.86 'Arrangements' are defined as including any scheme, agreement or understanding whether or not legally enforceable.[326] This seems to be a much wider than the test for 'arrangements' in the previous stamp duty relief.[327] At present, however, it seems that in practice much of the former approach of HMRC Stamp Taxes has been carried over into the new tax. Unfortunately for the taxpayer, attempts have been made to extend these provisions. HMRC Stamp Taxes have sought to argue that intentions and expectations are sufficient and that the element of 'necessity'[328] is no longer needed to establish an arrangement. However, upon general principles for there to be an arrangement there must be some involvement with a third party.[329] There needs, in broad terms, to be at least discussions with an identified third party not a hope that a third party may emerge in the foreseeable future.[330]

The actual arrangements

Provision or receipt of the consideration

12.87 It is provided that arrangements fall within the anti-avoidance provisions if under them the vendor or the purchaser or another member of the stamp duty land tax group is to be enabled to provide any of the consideration or is to part with it by or in consequence of the carrying out of a transaction or transactions involving or any of them involving a payment or other disposition by a person other than a group company.

12.88 It is expected that the situations as illustrated in Statement of Practice SP3/98 will continue to apply and the use of loans and mortgages will not under normal circumstances such as group refinancing cause the exemption to be unavailable. However, HMRC Stamp Taxes have on several occasions taken the point that an interest-free loan or unpaid consideration means that the transaction is not entitled to relief for a variety of unconvincing reasons such as it means the transaction is not 'commercial' but is tax avoidance.[331]

12.89 The question of the 'receipt of the consideration' by a non-group company is not within the above definition and so is a matter of considerable obscurity. The question is whether the reference to arrangements to part with any of the consideration is intended to apply here. This provision copies that introduced into FA 1967, s 27(3), to counteract the decision in *Shop and Stores Developments v IRC*.[332] The difficulty is that the

---

324 FA 2003, Sch 7, para 2(1).
325 Ibid, Sch 7, para 2(3A); FA 1997, s 96.
326 Ibid, Sch 7, para 2(5).
327 FA 1967, s 27(3); *Times Newspapers v IRC* [1971] 3 All ER 98. Statement of Practice SP3/98 would appear to be irrelevant on the meaning of 'arrangements', although it may be helpful when looking at the application of the prohibited arrangements.
328 *Times Newspapers v IRC* [1971] 3 All ER 98.
329 Compare 'for the purpose of' *Combined Technologies plc v IRC* [1985] STC 348.
330 However, should such a person emerge within 3 years there is likely to be a clawback of the relief (FA 2003, Sch 7, para 3).
331 See **12.93**.
332 [1967] 1 All ER 42.

provision has, in the writer's experience, never been applied in practice even in circumstances similar to those in the *Shop and Stores* case.[333] In that case, property had been transferred in consideration of an issue of shares and the consideration shares were sold on to a third party. The House of Lords held that this was not the provision of consideration by the third party, which was the only offending arrangement relating to consideration at the time. The provision relating to parting with the consideration was introduced. This would suggest, in the context of that case, that the consideration must be received and then transferred on to the third party. This would be an important issue where, for example, a company grants a lease to an associated company seeking the exemption within these provisions and there are proposals for the transfer of the reversionary interest, which would carry with it the right to receive the rent (ie the consideration on the grant of the lease). Hitherto, HMRC Stamp Taxes have not taken this point in practice on sales of reversions on leases, and it may be that there is a convincing argument against there being any suggestion that the sale of the reversion involves the receipt of a consideration. The important wording in these provisions is that a person 'parts' with the consideration. By selling the freehold reversion, a person may part with the reversion which may carry the right to receive the rent but it is not parting with the rent having received it. It is considered that the relief should be forthcoming in this situation.[334]

Degrouping

12.90 The relief is not available if the transaction is effected in pursuance of or in connection with[335] arrangements under which the vendor/lessor/grantor and the purchaser/lessee/grantee are to cease to be members of the same group by reason of the purchaser/lessee ceasing to be a 75 per cent subsidiary of the vendor/lessor or a third body corporate.

12.91 It is important to note that the fact that the transferor or lessor is to cease to be a member of the group (ie assets are being removed from a company prior to its sale to a third party) will not fall within these provisions but the transaction must be so structured that the transferor remains beneficially owned by the relevant company so that it forms part of the stamp duty group at the time of the effective date of the transaction. Being too far into the negotiations might produce a situation where beneficial ownership of the transferor/lessor has been lost and the group does not exist but it is considered that attempts by HMRC Stamp Taxes to contend that beneficial ownership is lost by advanced negotiations falling short of a binding contract[336] are unfounded in law, particularly after the decision of the Court of Appeal in *J Sainsbury Plc v O'Connor*.[337]

Subsales

12.92 Notwithstanding that in subsales and similar situations[338] the secondary contract is between the first purchaser and the subpurchaser it is provided that where the

---

[333] Ibid.
[334] But it must be noted that there are certain cryptic and technically confusing comments in SP 3/98 suggesting that HMRC Stamp Taxes may wish to attack such arrangements because they offer a more efficient method of many routine operations such as sale and leaseback and PFI projects.
[335] *Clarke Chapman – John Thompson Ltd v IRC* [1975] STC 567.
[336] See **12.74**.
[337] [1991] STC 516.
[338] See **Chapter 6**.

chargeable transaction between the associated companies is part of a subsale arrangement the intra-group relief is not available.[339]

Motive test[340]

12.93 It is now necessary for the taxpayer to establish that the transaction:

• was effected for bona fide commercial reasons; and

• was not part of arrangements the main purpose or one of the main purposes of which is the avoidance of stamp duty, stamp duty land tax, income tax, corporation tax or capital gains tax. Arrangements includes any scheme, agreement or understanding whether or not enforceable.

There is no advance clearance procedure and HMRC Stamp Taxes have on occasion refused to give a pre-transaction ruling. As this test applies for other taxes in general a ruling obtained for capital gains tax[341] is usually acted upon by HMRC Stamp Taxes. However, since the list of taxes differs there is no guarantee that they will automatically accept such a clearance. The emphasis is upon capital gains tax clearance so if one is obtained but there is a refusal to give a clearance pursuant to Income and Corporation Taxes Act 1988, s 707, the latter is ignored.

12.94 Unfortunately whilst the types of transaction within the two company reorganisation reliefs frequently fall within a capital gains tax clearance regime there are extremely few situations where an intra-group transaction will be within such a regime. HMRC Stamp Taxes are in consequence left to apply their own experience in these areas and develop their own policies.

12.95 So far as can be ascertained in practice at the moment the approach of HMRC Stamp Taxes is to treat the test as being two separate tests so that the mere fact that there is no tax avoidance purpose does not automatically mean that the transaction is bona fide commercial. There are also current uncertainties as to whether the test applies only to the chargeable transaction itself or to the overall commercial arrangements of which the transaction itself is merely a part or one step. It seems that the tax avoidance test is applied to the overall arrangements so that even though the transaction itself does not avoid tax the relief is not available if it assists in saving some other tax. The bona fide commercial test appears to be limited to the chargeable transaction but it seems that HMRC Stamp Taxes are intending to reserve the right to investigate whether the overall arrangement is on commercial terms.[342]

---

[339] FA 2003, s 45(5A); compare *Escoigne Properties Ltd v IRC* [1958] AC 549; FA 1967, s 27(3)(b).

[340] Ibid, Sch 7, para 2(4A); see also **12.36**.

[341] Such as TCGA 1992, s 135 or 139.

[342] HMRC Stamp Taxes have also challenged the relief where the transaction involves individuals since individuals cannot have a commercial purpose!

Tax avoidance

12.96 There is an initial issue as to what is tax avoidance. Various cases indicate that merely organising a transaction in a tax-efficient manner is not tax avoidance[343] nor is setting up a structure that is intended may provide the basis for tax saving in the future.[344]

12.97 'Tax' means income tax, capital gains tax, corporation tax, stamp duty or stamp duty land tax. Only the taxes listed fall within the prohibition; seeking to save other taxes such as foreign taxes or VAT is not tax avoidance. However, seeking to save such taxes may mean that the transaction is not *bona fide* commercial. Thus HMRC Stamp Taxes declined to comment on whether a reconstruction which might mitigate inheritance tax was *bona fide* commercial.

12.98 To 'assist' taxpayers HMRC Stamp Taxes have issued some guidance on what, in their view, is not tax avoidance but have not provided any guidance on how this essentially subjective test with the difficulties of processing evidence is to interact with the essentially objective general anti-avoidance provisions designed to avoid the need for HMRC Stamp Taxes to process evidence. This guidance gives some examples of transactions where it is accepted that group relief is not denied by the FA 2003, Sch 7, para 2(4A). This states:

> It should be noted that the examples are intended only to give general guidance and do not use technical or statutory language, nor should they be interpreted as if they were a statute.

> They also assume that the transactions described do not form part of any larger scheme or arrangement which might have tax consequences.

> Anyone who wants guidance on a specific transaction is welcome to write to us under the provisions of Code of Practice 10.[345]

Examples of transactions where group relief is not denied by FA 2003, Sch 7, para 2(4A)

- The transfer of a property to a group company having in mind the possibility that shares in that company might be sold more than three years after the date of transfer
- The transfer of a property to a group company having in mind the possibility that shares in that company might be sold within three years of the date of transfer, with a consequent claw-back of group relief, in order that any increase in value of the property after the intra- group transfer might be sheltered from stamp duty land tax
- The transfer of property to a group company having in mind the possibility that either of the preceding two events might occur
- The transfer of a property to a group company prior to the sale of shares in the transferor company, in order that the property should not pass to the purchaser of the shares

---

[343] *Brebner v IRC* (1967) 43 TC 705; *Willoughby v IRC* [1995] STC 143.
[344] *Shepperd v Lyntress* [1989] STC 617.
[345] But this has not provided useful hitherto since guidance has been refused on occasions because, *inter alia*, the issues were too difficult for them and does not necessarily bind HMRC Stamp Taxes. Also as the legislation is no longer 'new' HMRC Stamp Taxes are apparently reducing the clearance procedure. Application for post transaction guidance is treated as initiating a full Enquiry.

- The transfer of property to a group company in order that commercially generated[346] rental income may be matched with commercially generated losses from a Schedule A business
- The transfer of property to a group company in order that commercially generated chargeable gains may be matched with commercially generated allowable losses
- The transfer of property to a non-resident group company in the knowledge that future appreciation or depreciation in value will be outside the scope of corporation tax on chargeable gains
- Transactions undertaken as part of a normal commercial securitisation
- The transfer of the freehold reversion in a property to a group lessee in order to merge the freehold and the lease, and thus prevent the lease being subject to the wasting assets rules as respects corporation tax on chargeable gains
- The transfer of property to a group company in order that interest payable on borrowings from a commercial lender on ordinary commercial terms may be set against commercially generated* rental income
- Borrowings on ordinary commercial terms
  - from a commercial lender, or
  - intra-group in circumstances which would have been commercial had they arisen between unconnected third parties

'Transfer' means the transfer of a freehold, in Scotland ownership of land, or the assignment, in Scotland assignation, of a lease.

Cases involving the grant of a lease will need to be considered on their facts.

12.99 It will, however, be noted that this statement is largely irrelevant in practice. Apart from the facts that the types of transaction referred to are not really tax avoidance even as that term is widely applied by the current judiciary and it does not deal with the wider issues of mitigating other taxes as not 'commercial' it is wrapped up by two conditions; namely:

- it does not apply generally to leases which have to be considered on an individual basis; and

- tax avoidance (ie other taxes than those prescribed) may exclude this White List from applying to relieve the transaction ie it means that it is not a commercial transaction.

Bona fide commercial

12.100 There is some doubt as to the intentions of HMRC Stamp Taxes as to the scope of this test, ie whether it is limited to the actual chargeable transaction for which the relief has been claimed or the overall circumstances are relevant, ie the particular transaction has to be investigated on its own merits in isolation from the remainder of the transaction, and the purposes behind the individual transaction must include its role in the larger scheme of things.

12.101 HMRC Stamp Taxes apply a variety of criteria to be satisfied. It must be shown that the chargeable transaction is on commercial terms. They have sought to refuse relief where the consideration was left outstanding as a debt not bearing a commercial rate of interest or where the consideration is obtained by means of an

---

[346] Including income, gains and losses which are generated intra-group on transactions which would have been commercial had they been entered into by unconnected third parties.

interest-free loan. Similarly where the overall arrangement is not driven by commercial but personal interests or is overall not on commercial terms their contention appears to be that this, in their view, taints the individual steps. Thus HMRC Stamp Taxes have indicated that a transfer of land as part of an overall arrangement for the mitigation of inheritance tax for the shareholders may not qualify for the relief notwithstanding that the transfer is for full value. This is because shareholder arrangements are 'domestic' and not commercial and this appears to be applied even where the shareholder dealings are for full value. The relief is more likely to be attacked if the overall transaction is not for full value. It is considered that most of this approach is misconceived and not justified by the legislation. It may be that, although capital gains tax clearances are not directly available the practices adopted by the capital gains tax clearance section in other cases where similar issues can be drawn to the attention of HMRC Stamp Taxes who may be persuaded by this advice to adopt a more reasonable approach.

CLAWBACK OF INTRA-GROUP RELIEF

The charge

12.102   The exemption obtained pursuant to FA 2003, Sch 7, para 2, is initially provisional and is withdrawn and stamp duty land tax becomes payable in whole or in part where:

- the purchaser/lessee ceases to be a member of the same stamp duty land tax group as the vendor/lessor before the end of the period of 3 years beginning with the effective date of the transaction or in pursuance of or in connection with arrangements made before the end of the 3-year period; and

- at the time the purchaser/lessee ceases to be a member of the same group as the vendor/lessor, it or a company that is a member of the same group as the purchaser/lessee immediately before the purchaser/lessee ceases to be a member of the same group as the vendor/lessor, and ceases to be a member of the same group as the vendor/lessor in consequence of the purchaser/lessee so ceasing, holds a chargeable interest that was either acquired by the purchaser under the transaction for which the exemption from stamp duty land tax was obtained or that is derived from a chargeable interest that was acquired by such exempt transaction and that has not subsequently been acquired at market value under a chargeable transaction for which the exemption from stamp duty land tax for intra-group transactions was available but was not claimed. The departure of the vendor from the group does not trigger the clawback charge but such a charge may arise upon a subsequent change of control of the transferee company.[347]

In such a case, group relief in relation to the relevant transaction is withdrawn or, where only part or a partial interest in the chargeable interest is retained, an appropriate proportion of it is withdrawn and stamp duty land tax becomes chargeable and a land transaction return has to be filed.[348] The amount of tax chargeable is the tax that would have been chargeable in respect of the transaction for which the exemption was obtained for the intra-group/lease upon the basis that the chargeable consideration for that

---

[347]   FA 2003, Sch 7, para 3.
[348]   Ibid, s 81.

transaction had been an amount equal to the market value[349] of the chargeable interest acquired by that transaction together with any interest or right appurtenant or pertaining to the chargeable interest that is acquired with it. An appropriate proportion of the tax that would have been so chargeable which is an appropriate proportion having regard to the subject-matter of the relevant transaction for which the exemption was obtained and what is held at the time of the companies ceasing to be members of the same stamp duty group by the transferee or by that company and any company that is a member of the same group as the purchaser/lessee immediately before the purchaser/lessee ceases to be a member of the same group as the vendor/lessor and ceases to be a member of the same group as the vendor/lessor in consequence of the purchaser so leaving.

Exclusions from clawback

12.103 The exemption for intra-group transactions is not withdrawn where:

- the purchaser ceases to be a member of the same stamp duty land tax group as the vendor/lessor because the vendor/lessor leaves the group.[350] The vendor/lessor is regarded as leaving the group if the relevant company ceases to be a member of the same group by reason of a transaction relating to shares in the vendor or another company that as a result of the transaction ceases to be a member of the same group as the purchaser/lessee;[351] HMRC Stamp Taxes encountered difficulty with the situation where the vendor was the first company to leave the group followed by the purchaser within the 3 year period. In consequence a special charge is applied to clawback the relief in the transferee body corporate.[352] Group relief is not withdrawn where the purchaser ceases to be a member of the same group because the vendor leaves the group by reason of a transaction in shares in:
    - the vendor; or
    - another company that:
        - is above[353] the vendor in the group structure; and
        - as a result of the transaction ceases to be a member of the same group as the purchaser.

However, should there be a change of control of the purchaser after the vendor leaves the group the clawback of the relief applies unless the departure of the transferor from the group the clawback applies upon the basis that the purchaser or lessor had creased to be a member of the same group as the vendor. In effect, the departure of the vendor is ignored and the change of control of the purchaser is a clawback event unless the change of control arises because a loan creditor acquires or loses control and the other persons who controlled the purchaser continue to have control;[354]

- the purchaser/lessee ceases to be a member of the same group as the vendor/lessor by reason of anything done for the purposes of or in the course of winding up the vendor/lessor or another company that is above the vendor/lessor in the group

---

[349] As the clawback provisions refer to the tax that would have been payable but for the relief it seems that this is the market value as at the original effective date and not the date of the event giving rise to the forfeiture of the relief.
[350] FA 2003, Sch 7, para 4(2).
[351] Ibid, Sch 7, para 4(3).
[352] Ibid, Sch 7, para 4ZA.
[353] Defined ibid, Sch 7, para 4ZA(3).
[354] Ibid, Sch 7, para 4ZA(7).

structure.[355] A company is 'above' the vendor/lessor in the group structure if the vendor/lessor or another company that is above the vendor/lessor in the group structure is a 75 per cent subsidiary of the company.[356] However, HMRC Stamp Taxes are awaiting an opportunity in an Enquiry to enforce the clawback on the basis that 'another company' means a third body corporate. In their view, which has been awaiting an opportunity to be utilised for over a decade, 'another company' does not mean any company other than the vendor/lessor, it means a third company, ie another company than the vendor or purchaser. In their view where the company above the transferor/lessor is the transferee/lessee it is not 'another company', ie it is not a company other than the transferor and transferee. In such a case the liquidation of the transferee/lessee triggers a clawback. The view is extremely dubious particularly as the legislation is taken over from stamp duty where the context was the same and there has been a long tradition of using the words 'third body corporate' to indicate a company other than the transferor and transferee indicating strongly that the use of 'another company' did not require that company to be a third body corporate. However, as this point frequently arises in connection with pre-sale and similar reorganisations, rather than face the prospect of an expensive Enquiry and litigation, the parties may find it prudent to consider alternatives where relief for intra-group transactions is not required such as a distribution in specie which is exempt as being for no chargeable consideration[357] and which is not notifiable[358] since it is specifically excluded for the connected company charges.[359]

Alternatively this apparent but probably incorrect official view means that parties have to pay close attention to other exclusions from the clawback, such as Sch 7, para 4(6);

- the purchaser ceases to be a member of the same group as the vendor/lessor as a result of an acquisition of shares by another company in relation to which the share transfer is exempt from stamp duty pursuant to FA 1986, s 75, so that the purchaser/lessee is, immediately after that acquisition, a member of the same group as the company acquiring the shares in question.[360] However, in this case, the exclusion of the clawback is not on a permanent basis and the position is merely held over for the balance of the 3-year period since if the purchaser/lessee ceases to be a member of the same group as the company acquiring the relevant shares before the end of a period of 3 years beginning with the effective date of the transaction for which the exemption for intra-group transactions was obtained (or after the end of the 3-year period if this is in pursuance of or in connection with arrangements made before the end of the 3-year period) and at the time the purchaser/lessee ceases to be a member of the same group as the company acquiring the shares, the purchaser/lessee or any company that is a member of the same group as the purchaser/lessee but ceases to be a member of the same group as the company acquiring the shares, in consequence of the purchaser/lessee ceasing to be a member of such group, holds a chargeable interest that was acquired by the purchaser under the transaction for which the exemption for intra-group transactions was obtained or which is derived from an interest so acquired but has not been subsequently acquired at market value under a

---

[355]   Ibid, Sch 7, para 4(4).
[356]   Ibid, Sch 7, para 4(5).
[357]   Ibid, Sch 3, para 1.
[358]   Ibid, s 77A; the reporting obligations in s 53(4) do not apply to transactions excluded by s 54.
[359]   Ibid, ss 53 and 54.
[360]   Ibid, Sch 7, para 4(6).

chargeable transaction for which exemption from stamp duty land tax in respect of intra-group transactions was obtained[361] but was not claimed. In such a case, the stamp duty land tax is clawed back upon the happening of the later event.

- Where there is a change of control[362] of the purchaser within the clawback period in circumstances where the basic clawback charge does not operate certain previous transactions are brought within the scope of the clawback.[363] This is intended to deal with variations on the 'double drop' arrangements such as where A Ltd owns B Ltd which owns C Ltd A Ltd transfers land to C Ltd which transfers the land up to B Ltd. In this situation the basic clawback of para 3 would not arise upon a sale or change of control in B Ltd. Other variations are affected since these provisions apply where there has been a previous transaction has been entered into within the preceding 3 years which is exempt as either an intra-group transaction[364] or a company reconstruction or reorganisation[365] and the chargeable interest acquired under the subsequent transaction is exempt as an intra-group transaction is the same as or comprises, forms part of or is derived from the chargeable interest acquired under the previous transaction. The clawback provisions apply as if the transferor in respect of the previous transaction was the vendor for the latest transaction. This charge does not apply where, between the previous or the latest transaction, the chargeable interest has been subject to a chargeable transaction.

COLLECTION OF STAMP DUTY LAND TAX IN A CLAWBACK CONTEXT

12.104   There is a detailed code for the reporting and collection of the tax due on the clawback event which is by reference to the tax that would have been chargeable on the original transaction had that been for a consideration equal to the market value of the chargeable interest plus, in the case of a lease, the rent reserved.[366] This can affect not only the purchaser but other companies so that the scope of any warranties and indemnities in any contract for the purchase of shares in a company that has been a member of a group needs to be carefully considered so that, *inter alia*, they cover such secondary liabilities.

The purchaser

12.105   The happening of a clawback event gives rise to an obligation upon the 'purchaser' to file a land transaction return, including a self-assessment and to pay the stamp duty land tax within 30 days after the clawback event.[367] Interest arises for late payment[368] and penalties are imposed for failure to notify in time. It is expected that eventually, when HMRC Stamp Taxes have finally produced a workable compliance regime and programmed their computers adequately, there is likely to be contact by HMRC Stamp Taxes at some time after the expiration of the 3-year period, requesting

---

[361]   Pursuant to ibid, Sch 7, para 1.
[362]   Ibid, Sch 7, para 4A(3) and (3A).
[363]   Ibid, Sch 7, para 4A.
[364]   Ibid, Sch 7, Part 1.
[365]   Ibid, Sch 7, Part 2.
[366]   Ibid, Sch 7, para 3(2).
[367]   Ibid, ss 81 and 86(2).
[368]   Ibid, s 87(3).

confirmation that the necessary group relationship or control is still in place. The inability to give the appropriate confirmation is likely to provoke some attempt to issue a determination or discovery assessment by HMRC Stamp Taxes.[369]

Associated companies and controlling directors

12.106 Where the clawback provision applies, cancelling the relief obtained pursuant to FA 2003, Sch 7, paras 1, 7 or 8 and the amount of tax chargeable has been finally determined[370] and the whole or part of the amount so chargeable is unpaid 6 months after the date on which it becomes payable, the tax may be recovered from:

- any company that at any time between the effective date of the relevant transaction and the change of control which gives rise to the clawback was a member of the same group as the company which acquired the land and was 'above' it in the group structure.[371] For these purposes, a company is 'above' another company in a group structure if that other company is a 75 per cent subsidiary of that company or is a company which is a 75 per cent subsidiary of another company above it in the group;[372]

- in the case of relief for intra-group transactions pursuant to Sch 7, para 1, the 'vendor' (ie the body corporate disposing of the interest is also liable for the payment of the tax);[373]

- any person who was, at any time between the effective date of the relevant transaction and the change of control giving rise to the clawback, a controlling director of the company that acquired the land or of a company having control of the company that acquired the land.[374] For these purposes a 'director' is a person within Income Tax (Earnings and Pensions) Act 2003, s 67(1) (read in conjunction with s 67(2)) and includes any person falling within Income and Corporation Taxes Act 1988, s 417(5). Such a director has control if he has a person who has control of the company pursuant to the provisions of s 416 of the Income and Corporation Taxes Act 1988.

12.107 However, before HMRC Stamp Taxes may recover tax from any person other than the company that acquired the land pursuant to the exempt transaction, it must serve a notice upon the relevant person[375] requiring him within 30 days of the service of the notice to pay the amount that remains unpaid.[376] Such a notice may be served at any time before the end of the period of 3 years beginning with the date upon which the amount of the stamp duty land tax has been finally determined.[377] The notice must specify the amount required to be paid by the person on whom it is served and such a notice is to be treated as if it were an assessment and that amount were an amount of tax due from the person upon whom the notice was served for the purposes of

---

[369] Pursuant to ibid, Sch 10, para 25 assuming that their powers to call for information and documents, enable them to make such requests and to treat the responses as a 'discovery'.
[370] This may take time since it is by reference to the market value of the actual consideration of the original transaction.
[371] FA 2003, Sch 7, para 12(2)(a).
[372] Ibid, Sch 7, para 12(4).
[373] Ibid, Sch 7, para 5(2)(a).
[374] Ibid, Sch 7, paras 5(2)(c) and 12(2)(b).
[375] Ibid, Sch 7, para 12(2).
[376] Ibid, Sch 7, para 13(1).
[377] Ibid, Sch 7, para 13(2).

recovering the tax[378] and for the purposes of appeals.[379] Any person, whether an associated company or a controlling director, who has paid stamp duty land tax pursuant to such a notice may recover the amount of the tax from the company that acquired the land pursuant to the original exempt transaction. However, as it is likely that HMRC Stamp Taxes will pursue such other persons only where the particular company is unable to pay the tax because it has been liquidated or is insolvent, this right of indemnity is likely to prove valueless in practice. No tax relief for any purpose is available in respect of any payment made pursuant to such a notice.[380]

---

[378] Ibid, Sch 12.
[379] Ibid, Sch 10, Part 7; Sch 17.
[380] Ibid, Sch 7, para 13(6).

Chapter 13

PARTNERSHIPS

BACKGROUND

13.1 Partnerships have for generations been a source of many problems for HMRC Stamp Taxes because of a fundamental failure to produce legislation that addresses the basic issues and to provide an answer that gives a workable if not entirely satisfactory answer. Even in the short life span of stamp duty land tax they have been the subject-matter of several major revisions, including the FA 2006 which has removed some of the errors of principle in the previous regimes. A further series of amendments is probably necessary because the realisation of a need to provide a framework for dealing with the fundamental issues has never been dealt with by bringing in competent advisers with experience and the defects have been dealt with on a piecemeal basis ignoring essential consequential adjustments. Moreover, since the amendments have not been drafted consistently with the pre-existing legislation[1] the latest changes mean that many fundamental defects still remain and new internal inconsistencies have emerged. The latest regime has produced many opportunities for mitigating tax which will have already been notified to HMRC Stamp Taxes pursuant to the notification legislation.[2] In consequence the FA 2006 major changes have proved short-lived and have undergone a further major revision with defects with effect from 6 December 2006 where at least one body corporate is involved at any stage in the transaction.[3] For example, it is no longer easy to incorporate a partnership without a market value charge. There have been further changes in relation to the transfer of interests in partnerships limiting those, superficially, to property investment partnerships.[4] Also it seems that HMRC Stamp Taxes are intending to attack joint venture arrangements as not being partnerships because they lack reality of business.[5] This may be helpful to taxpayers involved in joint ventures where, subject to the problems of nominee companies[6] and the connected company charge,[7] there are fewer anti-avoidance provisions than for partnerships so that it may be easier and cheaper to deal with interests and there may be reliefs such as reconstruction relief[8] when setting up the vehicles.

---

[1] Such as the question of fiscal transparency in FA 2003, Sch 15, Part 1, which was apparently overlooked when Sch 15, Part 3 was inserted and amended; see **13.14**.

[2] See **2.29**.

[3] Stamp Duty Land Tax (Variation of the Finance Act 2003) Regulations 2006, SI 2006/ 3237; FA 2003, s 73A.

[4] FA 2003, Sch 15, para 14 (as amended).

[5] However, not the problems likely to arise in challenging the concept of business or partnership where there may be a tax efficiency motive because of the comments in *Ensign Tankers (Leasing) Ltd v Stokes* [1992] STC 226 that activities may still be a trade notwithstanding tax planning.

[6] FA 2003, Sch 16, para 3; see **Chapter 9**.

[7] Ibid, s 53; see **5.208**.

[8] Ibid, Sch 7, para 8.

PROFESSIONAL FIRMS

13.2 Allegedly, the regime relating to transfers of interests in partnerships has been simplified by eliminating the charges upon transfers of shares in professional and trading firms, and limiting the charge to interests in property investment partnerships ie partnerships whose sole or main activity does not involve investing and dealing in chargeable interests (whether or not that activity involves the carrying out of construction operations on the land in question).[9] Solicitors and accountants are not for the time being necessarily faced with having to file a stamp duty land tax return on every admission to or retirement from the firm.[10] Unfortunately, owing to a stealth amendment to the legislation, whilst the direct charge upon 'transfers' of partnership interest in such firms is excluded, there has been a large extension of anti-avoidance legislation[11] some of which only applies where there is no direct charge pursuant to para 14 on the transfer of the partnership interest which, by the back door, potentially brings professional changes in all partnerships into charge unless HMRC Stamp Taxes take the unlikely position of not enforcing this indirect tax rigorously.

TWO STAGE TAX REGIMES[12]

13.3 In addition to the special regime between partners, partnerships and connected persons, partnerships are subject to the normal principles of stamp duty land tax upon their ordinary acquisitions of land such as leases of the office. The new relief from the special regime are *prima facie* intended to apply to ordinary firms such as family farming or manufacturing partnerships[13] where the holding of land is essential to its activities but the dealing therein is not its main function. However, the definitions of 'property investment partnerships'[14] and 'partnership property'[15] clearly indicates there is the potential for massive problems where, as a result of changing political policies especially in relation to agriculture and the European Union, it becomes clear that the main farming or trading activity becomes commercially inappropriate. It is generally understood that as this situation develops HMRC Stamp Taxes intend to exploit the deficiencies in the legislation such as the current indications that they may contend that a vehicle not carrying on what, in their view, is a business or assets are 'set aside' from the main or core business is either not a partnership or there has been a transfer of the land out of the partnership, notwithstanding the vehicle being registered pursuant to the Limited Partnership Act 1907 or the Limited Liability Partnerships Act 2000 and rely upon the legislation to impose charges to tax such as claiming that there is either:

---

[9] Ibid, Sch 15, para 14 (as amended); FA 2004, s 74 assuming that HMRC Stamp Taxes are prepared to accept that holding property is a 'business' and do not press their view that the vehicle for investment is not a partnership.

[10] But note the enlarged scope of FA 2003, Sch 15, para 17 which has occurred by stealth because of the narrowing of the charge pursuant to para 14 thereof.

[11] Ibid, Sch 15, para 17 and s 17A.

[12] See **13.7**.

[13] Unfortunately, considerable care is required where, as a matter of general convenience, the participants propose to hold land through nominee companies so that routine changes in partners do not require the conveyancing and Land Registry costs of changing trustees because of the old-fashioned legislation limiting the number of trustees of legal title, and the consequent problems of retirement and death.

[14] FA 2003, Sch 15, para 14(8); see **13.11**.

[15] Ibid, Sch 15, para 34(1), see also paras 35–37 and para 9.

- notwithstanding that the land is not actually transferred a deemed transfer of the land out of the partnership because it ceases to be utilised for partnership activities;[16] or

- the partnership has become a property investment partnership because it has ceased to utilise land for the purposes of its business such as where it has rationalised its business and shut down certain activities but holding the land upon which those activities were carried out to produce income pending a sale or lease at a suitable opportunity or the partnership may have technically ceased to carry on business because, for example, it may be about to liquidate or incorporate or split between different groups of partners. In consequence any dealings in which partnership interests may be involved such as changes in partners or, on HMRC Stamp Taxes' interpretations, alterations in profit or capital sharing proportions is taxable.

STAMP DUTY

13.4 Partnerships have given rise to considerable problems in relation to stamp duty because HMRC Stamp Taxes have never felt able to adopt a fixed approach to them because of the uses to which partnerships can be put and the inherent flexibility in their structuring. There is a fundamental question of fiscal transparency and whether the vehicle is to be taken into account or ignored for all or some purposes such as relief for intra-group transactions and incorporations of partnerships. Their basic position appears to be that a share or interest in a partnership is a single separate item of property and is not a collection of equitable interests in the partnership assets ie there is no general principle of fiscal transparency. They did, however, from time to time take the point that a share in a partnership was an equitable interest in its own right and therefore there could be no effective transfer of that interest in the absence of writing.[17] However, a partnership is a contractual legal relationship as regards the shares; the question is whether the share is a separate item of property or a collection of equitable interests. This revealed an internal inconsistency in the position of HMRC Stamp Taxes in that they looked to the interests in the assets rather than to the partnership interest as a separate item. Fortunately, the point related to partnership interests being equitable interests in property was rarely raised and never pursued too vigorously if suitably opposed by the taxpayer. Moreover, the point of a direct interest in the underlying assets has never been raised in relation to stamp duty reserve tax. HMRC Stamp Taxes never sought to develop a consistent argument that a partnership interest was an equitable interest in shares and therefore a chargeable interest for the purposes of stamp duty reserve tax[18] where the partnership held shares. There are also questions of fiscal transparency in relation to the intra-group relief where shares in one of the companies involved in a relevant transaction were held through some form of partnership arrangement. HMRC Stamp Taxes were inconsistent even where all of the interests in the partnership were held within the group so that the partnership was in effect itself wholly owned. However, in order to deal with the situation in relation to stamp duty land tax and stamp duty in respect of shares the approach appears to be, broadly, that

---

[16] See ibid, para 37.

[17] Pursuant to FA 2003, s 53(1)(c) relying upon *Oughtred v IRC* [1960] AC 206; although in a non-stamp duty context this decision has been effectively overruled by the Court of Appeal in *Neville v Wilson* [1997] Ch 144.

[18] FA 2003, s 99 (as much amended).

the interest of the partner is a bundle of interests in the underlying assets. However, this does not appear to have been adopted for the purposes of the principal charge to stamp duty reserve tax.

In consequence of this 'fragmentation' of partnership shares[19] transfers of interests in a partnership on sale are subject to *ad valorem* stamp duty at the rate of 0.5 per cent to the extent that the consideration is apportioned to shares and marketable securities that form part of the assets of the partnership.[20] Since it is the partnership interest which is taxed it is immaterial that the shares or marketable securities are in a company incorporated outside the United Kingdom.[21] Also because the provisions of Stamp Act 1891, s 14(4) continue to apply, it is immaterial whether the partnership is formed under the law of the United Kingdom or elsewhere.

13.5 The charge requires a written instrument of transfer or a memorandum of a transfer such as a new partnership deed giving effect to or recording previous partnership changes. It is the view of HMRC Stamp Taxes that where one partner contributes cash by way of capital and simultaneously another partner withdraws cash by way of reduction or total withdrawal of his capital, this is evidence of a possible sale from the contributing to the withdrawing partner. Obviously, if one partner contributes land and the other partner contributes cash which is in whole or in part withdrawn by the partner contributing the land, the strength of any argument that there is possibly a sale is significantly increased. Any cash received by a person in connection with his becoming a partner or increasing his capital contribution or even a straightforward sale by a partner to the firm is ignored, but if the payment of that cash is deferred so as to become, for example, a partner loan account,[22] the subsequent repayment of that unpaid consideration might be regarded by HMRC Stamp Taxes as a chargeable transaction pursuant to the FA 2003, Sch 15, para 17A. However, this view is regarded as incorrect as a general principle since it ignores the fundamentally important, well-known distinction between a 'debt' and a 'loan'.

13.6 Partnerships are subject to stamp duty or stamp duty reserve tax upon their acquisitions of shares and the acquisitions of interests in other partnerships which hold shares or marketable securities. They are also subject to stamp duty land tax upon their ordinary acquisitions of chargeable interests[23] which can be broadly described, albeit at some risk to the overall accuracy of the content, as being land dealings between the partnership and persons who are not partners or persons connected with them.

---

[19] There is an, as yet unresolved, issue of fundamental principle as to the nature of a partnership 'share' and how this differs from a partnership 'interest'.

[20] FA 2003, s 125 and Sch 15, paras 31, 32 and 33.

[21] Such shares and marketable securities are generally exempt from stamp duty land tax but remain subject to stamp duty if the jurisdictional provisions of Stamp Act 1891, s 14 are satisfied so that there is no reason to regard such shares as falling outside the special partnership regime for shares or partnership property.

[22] A potentially misleading description since it is a 'debt' rather than a 'loan' but the presentation may assist HMST to argue that because it is described as a 'loan ' there has been a set-off to convert the debt into a loan; see *Coren v Keighley* 48 TC 370.

[23] FA 2003, Sch 15, para 5; see **13.22**.

STAMP DUTY LAND TAX

Two regimes

13.7 The basic position of partnerships in relation to stamp duty land tax is, essentially, the same as for any other taxpayer. They are liable to tax upon any acquisitions of chargeable interests in land from third parties, ie otherwise than by way of contribution to capital by partners or incoming partners.[24] Notification of transactions is required.[25] For these purposes, *prima facie*, all partners are required to sign the declaration at the end of the land transaction return, although it is possible to nominate representative partners, who must be approved by and accepted by HMRC Stamp Taxes in advance, who can complete and sign the return on behalf of the partnership. Nevertheless, as all the partners will be vendors or lessors or purchasers, it would seem that all of their details will have to be disclosed upon the form (ie multiple SDLT 2), not merely that information in relation to the representative partners. However, in practice HMRC Stamp Taxes are prepared to accept a return in which the purchaser or the vendor is described by the partnership name, thereby avoiding the need to complete numerous SDLT 2s setting out the details of each partner.

13.8 There are, however, special charging and compliance regimes where:

- a partnership acquires land from a person who is a partner, or who becomes a partner, or who is connected with the existing partner;[26]

- a person who is or was a partner or is a person connected with a current or former partner acquires land from a partnership which includes mergers and demergers of partnerships;[27]

- there is a transfer of a chargeable interest between partnerships[28] such as on mergers or demergers;

- there is a 'transfer' or deemed transfer[29] of an interest (undefined) in a property investment partnership whether or not for an actual consideration;[30] and

- certain arrangements that are covered by an expanding body anti-avoidance legislation.[31]

The constitution of the partnership is important to these charges. Apart from the question of whether a pre-existing partnership agreement unrelated to the relevant land transaction is an 'arrangement' within the anti-avoidance provisions it affects whether the special regime applies, the amount of the charge because of the significant reduction where the relevant participants are 'connected' and the amount thereof. (Especially

---

[24] Ibid, Sch 15, Part 1.
[25] See **13.21**.
[26] Technically the charge is expressed in terms of 'transfers' to a partnership but since 'transfer' is defined in terms virtually identical with 'acquisition' it is convenient to continue the general usage into this area and avoid confusion with the different definition of 'transfer' for the purposes of the transfer of partnership interests.
[27] FA 2003, Sch 15, para 18.
[28] Ibid, Sch 15, para 23.
[29] Ibid, Sch 15, para 36 (as much amended).
[30] Ibid, Sch 15, para 14 (as amended).
[31] Ibid, Sch 15, paras 17 and 17A.

when any of the participants is a body corporate, when the reduction in the market value charge because of the identification of previous and current 'owners' is restricted and available only as between individuals.)[32]

Transitional trap

13.9   There was significant delay in delivering the legislation relating to the stamp duty land tax regime for partnerships. In consequence, many transactions relating to partnership acquisitions of land and dealings in partnership interest remained subject to stamp duty after 1 December 2003. Many of these were straightforward stamp duty mitigation arrangements attracting no stamp duty or, at most, the fixed duty of £5. In consequence, there are retrospective anti-avoidance provisions which affect current transactions where the land acquisition was effected around the time of the announcement of the changeover from stamp duty to stamp duty land tax for certain aspects of partnership transactions which preceded the implementation of stamp duty land tax. These provisions apply where *ad valorem* stamp duty was not paid. In broad terms, when dealing with the acquisition of land by a connected person from a partnership which acquired the land on or after 20 October 2003 there are provisions for reducing the chargeable amount by reference to the interest of the transferor's part of the transaction;[33] but there are reductions of such interests to nil, ie the partner is treated as having no prior interest whatsoever where, *inter alia*, the acquisition has not borne a full charge to stamp duty or a proper charge to stamp duty land tax.[34] This is an intentional trap for the unwary because most acquisitions of land by partnerships during the relevant period were properly stamped only with the fixed duty because they were not 'sales' within the old regime or were not stampable because the writing did not constitute a 'conveyance' whether on sale or otherwise. Payment of the correct amount of stamp duty even in routine commercial transactions leaves the parties exposed to a major charge to stamp duty land tax on a later probably unconnected transaction. Fortunately, if during the relevant period when the current rules were not published, the correct amount of stamp duty land tax was actually paid[35] even though not based upon full market value this appears to give the parties a reasonable base figure for computing the stamp duty land tax. The retrospective nature of this reduction in the relief means that details of transactions entered into around the relevant period will form key documents of title in relation to the land for the purposes of partnership dealings. Since there is no time restriction upon the anti-avoidance provisions notwithstanding they are retrospective, the original documentation and the stamp tax paid in respect thereof will have to be maintained until such time as the partnership disposes of the land which may be many decades in the future.

KEY TERMINOLOGY

13.10   As with so much of the application of the half-baked notion that 'plain English' drafting of complex tax legislation will be comprehensible in the context of longstanding legislation and general law with all of its necessary technicalities and subtleties, rather than confusing, because of the inconsistencies in terminology and

---

32   Stamp Duty Land Tax (Variation of the Finance Act 2003) Regulations 2006, SI 2006/3237.
33   FA 2003, Sch 15, paras 18 and 20.
34   Ibid, Sch 15, paras 21 and 22.
35   No payment because the parties were unaware of the complexities of the interpretation of the then rules by HMRC Stamp Taxes will leave them liable to a tax based upon a nil interest on later extractions of the land and even interests thereon, ie a full market value charge.

professional usage and practice, there are major problems because the draftsman has failed to address the need for definitions. In consequence, key concepts appear to be governed by the general law or even their non-technical general dictionary meaning with all of the complexities and uncertainties of case-law where there are already indications in practice that HMRC Stamp Taxes' policy approach is not compatible with such general principles. For example, there are major difficulties in practice already in relation to the following areas.

'Partnerships'

13.11 For the purposes of stamp duty land tax 'partnership' is widely partially defined but only by reference to other United Kingdom legislation.[36] In other jurisdictions there is legislation relating to partnerships or business vehicles which may be partnerships in UK terms but not in the foreign law.[37] This leaves open the traditional problems of whether joint ownership is a partnership, although partnerships are excluded from the definition of unit trust schemes,[38] which is a starting point before any analysis can be applied in accordance with the legislation to foreign business vehicles performing a similar but not necessarily identical function. Technically partnerships require 'businesses' and are not necessarily investment vehicles,[39] but joint ownership of one or more interests in land to be held as income-producing investments will not necessarily be a partnership.[40] Certain aspects of the stamp duty land tax legislation recognise the 'investment' nature of partnerships. There are key issues relating to 'property investment partnerships' which is defined[41] as a partnership whose sole or main activity is investing in or dealing in chargeable interests whether or not the activity involves the carrying out of construction operations on the land in question. This refers to 'investing' in land and would suggest that partnerships may possibly be an 'investment vehicle' but there may be difficult lines to be drawn in practice between activities that are merely joint ownership and those which are 'businesses'. The scale of the operations and the nature of the operations may be important as may be the fact that the activities are carried out on a business basis such as employing managers for the purposes of the business. Hitherto the practice of HMRC generally appears to be that if the parties have described themselves as a partnership this is usually accepted at face value.[42] However it is understood that HMRC Stamp Taxes are considering arguments to attack arrangements which operate to mitigate tax because of the special rules relating to the partnerships. It seems that they may be looking more closely at transactions of an investment nature in order to put forward the argument that the vehicle can be treated as not being a partnership[43] or the asset is not 'transferred' because it is not used for a

---

[36]   Partnership Act 1890, Limited Partnerships Act 1907 and Limited Liability Partnerships Act 2000.

[37]   See, **13.12**; and eg, Partnership At 1890, ss 1 and 2 setting out certain criteria which may indicate the existence of a partnership or non-partnership vehicle and which it seems have to be applied to foreign business vehicles whether locally incorporated or unincorporated which will raise problems for the definition of a company pursuant to FA 2003, s 100.

[38]   FA 2003, Sch 15, para 4.

[39]   Which may be a crucially important issue as to whether a joint venture is a partnership so as, eg, to be penalised as property investment partnership for the tax on transfers of interest.

[40]   Partnership Act 1890, s 2(1).

[41]   FA 2003, Sch 15, para 14(8).

[42]   On the other hand, the mere fact that the parties state in their documents that their arrangements are not to constitute a partnership is not conclusive but the statement may, in borderline cases, tip the balance in their favour.

[43]   This, if pressed to its conclusion, will convert many 'partnerships' into some form of joint ownership and there will be many difficult questions as to whether the winding-up of the vehicle, for example, which involves a division of a pool of jointly owned assets is some form of 'partition' where tax is charged only upon any equality adjustment FA 2003, Sch 4, para 5; see **5.169**. There is, however, a difficult question as to

business[44] or has been deemed to be transferred because it has been set aside and ceases to be utilised for the partnership 'business'.[45] This attack on the vehicle as not being a 'partnership' may be difficult for HMRC Stamp Taxes where the parties have registered themselves as a limited partnership pursuant to the Limited Partnerships Act 1907 and the Limited Liability Partnerships Act 2000 since there is a vehicle created by law that is a 'partnership'. In this situation HMRC Stamp Taxes may seek to argue that the acquisition is not for the purposes of a partnership business and therefore falls outside the legislation.[46] However, the mere fact that an activity is undertaken for some tax benefit is not inconsistent with there being some form of business or trade for tax purposes.[47] Moreover, such arrangements would not be 'shams' for general purposes since many transactions are undertaken on an artificial basis but that does not make them 'shams'.[48] Obviously, should HMRC Stamp Taxes establish that the vehicle is not a partnership then the participants will not be partners. Dealings in their interests will not be interest or shares in the partnership but will be the equity or beneficial interests of joint owners of property where there is joint tenants or tenants in common behind some form of trust.

Foreign vehicles

13.12 A partnership is expressed to include a general partnership,[49] a limited partnership[50] and a limited liability partnership,[51] as well as foreign vehicles having similar characteristics to such United Kingdom entities. The starting point for whether a foreign vehicle is a partnership is the general law of the foreign jurisdiction pursuant to which the vehicle in question was established.[52] The fact that the vehicle has a particular status for foreign tax law and it is taxed, for example, as if it were a company is irrelevant, as is the fact that a foreign company is taxed abroad as a partnership. This, however, merely sets up the attributes of the overseas vehicle and these attributes have to be tested against the implicit criteria for partnerships hidden in the amendments to the FA 2003. Obviously, the attributes of the vehicle have to be determined by reference to the foreign law of business associations but whether those attributes constitute a partnership or some other form of legal entity is to be judged by reference to the English criteria which are essentially the Partnership Act 1890 and the many cases decided without legislation. In these circumstances limited liability and corporate personality are not, as such, relevant factors.[53] Obviously corporate personality is no longer a conclusive factor because of the statutory rules lifting the corporate veil[54] and because a limited liability partnership is a body corporate.[55] Other factors in determining whether there is a body corporate such as perpetual succession are equally irrelevant. Limited or unlimited liability is no longer a feature of significance because there can be limited

---

how the liabilities of the joint activity will be regarded (FA 2003, Sch 4, paras 8 and 8A) and whether mortgages charging the property are liabilities and have to be ignored when determining the market value of the assets concerned or whether the transfer subject to a mortgage, whether or not involving an assumption of new liabilities, is some form of equality adjustment.

44   FA 2003, Sch 15, paras 35 and 34.
45   Ibid, Sch 15, paras 35, 36 and 37.
46   See, for example, FA 2003, Sch 15, paras 34 and 35; see **13.26**.
47   *Ensign Tankers (Leasing) Ltd v Stokes* [1992] STC 226.
48   *Gisborne v Burton* [1988] 3 All ER 760; *Belvedere v Frogmore* [1996] 1 All ER 317.
49   Partnership Act 1890, s 1.
50   Limited Partnership Act 1907.
51   Limited Liability Partnership Act 2000.
52   *Dreyfus v IRC* 14 TC 560.
53   FA 2003, Sch 15, para 2.
54   Ibid, Sch 15, para 2.
55   Limited Liability Partnerships Act 2000, s 1(2).

partners and unlimited companies. The requirement of at least one partner having unlimited liability is no longer a necessary feature of partnerships having limited liability. All of the former simple criteria have gone; it is likely that HMRC Stamp Taxes will attach great significance to labels and to factors such as a general unlimited partner. Situations where all participants have limited liability will be much more difficult for them, but the method of calculating their participation will be major factor. Calling these 'shares' and subdividing the participation in units of small value and uniform size like the par value of shares rather than an individual unit per participant of varying size may establish the vehicle as a company. As an additional problem to provide a 'unit' or participant that is a single right expressed as an overall percentage rather than a number of rights being a collection of units of a fixed amount may tempt HMRC Stamp Taxes generally into asserting the arrangement is a unit trust or a collective investment scheme which is usually not to the benefit of the taxpayer holding the interest. There may also be issues whether the partnership activities have commenced and whether taking steps to establish a new business means that the partnership has commenced.[56] The structure of the capital of the vehicle may be important since 'companies' tend to have capital divided into specific individual units generally described as 'shares' with a 'par value' or nominal value whereas a partnership has 'capital' which is held as a block amount with the individual partner's interest being expressed as a single overall percentage.[57] Voting rights may be important and the fact that particular investors in the vehicle may not be permitted to take part in day-to-day management or the ordinary activities of the business may point to a vehicle similar to a limited partnership act in UK law notwithstanding that it may have corporate personality under the foreign law. In consequence, even when the English definition of partnership is the test against which foreign vehicles are to be measured.

13.13 The practical problem for professional advisers is the total absence of worthwhile guidance from HMRC Stamp Taxes as to the operating dividing line between a body corporate under foreign law that is treated as a 'company' and a similar body corporate that is treated as a transparent partnership. The consequences of the difference in classification are fundamental and wide ranging[58] and involve major compliance risks and penalties where the professional advisers fail to guess in advance the attitude of HMRC Stamp Taxes. Even a successful defence of the land transaction return (SDLT 1) in an Enquiry will be expensive. HMRC generally owe no duty of care to taxpayers.

Transparency and its limitations

13.14 The legislation requires the fact that certain partnerships are bodies corporate to be ignored.[59] The problem is the extent of this disregarding of corporate personality. This lifting of the corporate veil,[60] *prima facie*, is essentially a compliance matter and

---

[56] See *Keith Spicer v Mansell* [1970] 1 WLR 333; *Kahn v Miah* [2000] 1 WLR 2123.

[57] But see **13.16** on determining a partner's share which is defined in terms of the share of the undefined income profits of the firm; see FA 2003, Sch 15, para 34(2); note also *Barclays Bank Trust v Bluff* [1982] 2 WLR 198.

[58] Eg in relation to the special regime for partnerships the problem arises on two levels in the same transaction, namely: whether the acquiring corporate vehicle is a partnership; and where the vehicle is a partnership whether the participants are themselves bodies corporate or partnerships since special principles with enhanced charges and bizarre applications of the intra-group relief apply to 'partnerships' where all of the partners are 'bodies corporate'.

[59] FA 2003, Sch 15, para 2.

[60] See *Sadler v Whiteman* [1910] 1 KB 868.

changes in the partners do not affect the continuity of the partnership.[61] In effect the partners are the vendors or the purchasers. The chargeable interest held by or on behalf of a partnership is treated as held by or on behalf of the partners, who are treated as being the persons entering into any chargeable transactions entered into for the purposes of the partnership. Originally, it seemed that this transparency did not extend beyond compliance issues and HMRC Stamp Taxes took and continue to take the point that a partnership interest was not or did not include a chargeable interest.[62] However, as from 6 December 2006 for certain transfers of partnership interests the interest is a chargeable interest[63] and there are issues for intra-group relief.[64]

'Partner'

13.15 The legislation does not define 'partner' which must depend upon the general law.[65] In consequence, there will be the usual crop of issues as to the precise status of the salaried partners,[66] persons who are remunerated by some basis related to profits of the firm,[67] partners who have not given formal notice of their retirement,[68] and persons who are held out as partners in some way.[69] Doubtless HMRC Stamp Taxes will seek to apply the widest possible definition in order to maximise the recovery of the tax and the obtaining of information.

'Partnership share' or 'interest'

13.16 The relationship of a partner to the firm and its assets is usually generally described as his 'share' although there are fundamental questions as to whether his share or interest is a separate item of property or is a collection of separate choses in action for each individual asset of the partnership. The partnership legislation has changed the definition in relation to stamp duty land tax on several occasions[70] but much of the legislation refers to 'interest' rather than the defined 'shares'[71] of partners. This can be a key problem in practice because the tax is usually charged where there is some change of 'interest' but the chargeable amount is usually fixed by reference to the partnership 'share' which is, usually, also the amount of the reduction in the market value charge on lands transferred into and out of partnerships by reference to the sum of the lower proportions.[72] No indication is given as to the different between 'share' and 'interest' or what is comprised in an 'interest' in the legislation and this issue is complicated by the anti-avoidance rules which deal with certain types of economic involvement of partners and others in the partnership without relating these to the definition of 'interest'.[73]

---

[61]   FA 2003, Sch 15, para 3; this also avoids the technical charge pursuant to para 23 that would arise upon the transfer from one partnership to another partnership on every change of partner.
[62]   See **13.18**.
[63]   FA 2003, Sch 15, para 14(9); Stamp Duty Land Tax (Variation of the Finance Act 2003) Regulations 2006, SI 2006/3237 now FA 2003, ss 75A–75C.
[64]   FA 2003, Sch 7, Part 1; see **Chapter 12**.
[65]   Partnership Act 1890, s 14.
[66]   *Stekel v Ellice* [1973] 1 All ER 465.
[67]   On the problems these raise for ascertaining a partner's 'share' see **13.16**.
[68]   *Tower Cabinets v Ingram* [1949] 1 All ER 1033.
[69]   Partnership Act 1891, s 14.
[70]   FA 2003, Sch 15, para 34.
[71]   See, for example, FA 2003, Sch 15, paras 14, 17 and importantly transfer of an 'interest' in para 36 (as much amended).
[72]   See **13.31**.
[73]   See FA 2003, Sch 15, para 17A.

Another difficulty is that the legislation generally refers to 'partnership interest' rather than 'partnership share'. Frequently the charge arises by reference to dealings in the partnership 'interest' but the chargeable consideration is measured by reference to the partnership 'share' which requires actual consideration to be ignored. Partnership 'interest' is not defined but the apparent view of HMRC Stamp Taxes is that a partnership interest is the entire economic involvement of the partner with the firm such as share of profits, capital, loan accounts and even undrawn profits. Dealings affecting any of these factors may have tax consequences.[74]

13.17 This problem emerges most obviously in the general principle that a chargeable transaction occurs where there is a dealing in a partnership 'interest'[75] but the tax charge is calculated by reference to the partnership 'share' (whatever that may mean) notwithstanding the definition of the partner in relation to the relevant asset.[76] Also there is a considerable flexibility in the undefined concept of partnership 'interest' to give HMRC Stamp Taxes scope to attack transactions involving adjustments in partnership participation, retirements and admissions which fall outside the definition of 'transfer', such as an adjustment of profit sharing ratio without consideration.[77]

Partnership share or interest as chargeable interest

13.18 A problem that has arisen from time to time is the nature of a partnership share or partnership interest and whether this is a chargeable interest in its own right. There are certain provisions providing for a form of fiscal transparency as regards partnerships.[78] These apply not merely to lifting the corporate veil where there is a partnership with corporate personality[79] but also for the purposes of collecting the tax and compliance.[80] However, notwithstanding the fiscal transparency HMRC Stamp Taxes accepted that the interest of a partner in a partnership was not a chargeable interest.[81] In consequence, the mere holding of a 'participation' in a partnership is not a chargeable interest. This may affect the structuring of arrangements so that persons may prefer to hold their interests in partnerships through a company or a trust that is formed or established abroad. Dealings in the interest in the trust would not be dealings in chargeable interests because the trust asset is the partnership interest and not the underlying land held by the partnership. This basic position of the partnership interest not being a chargeable interest is supported by legislation introduced by HMRC Stamp Taxes which treat interests in partnerships as being chargeable interests namely:

- an interest in a partnership may be a chargeable interest for the purposes of the intra-group relief;[82] and

---

[74] Ibid, Sch 15, para 14 charges transfer of interests and para 17A charges certain withdrawals of capital or loans which may be transfers of interests see para 36.

[75] FA 2003, Sch 15, para 14(1)(a).

[76] See FA 2003, Sch 15, para 14(5)(c) and (5A)(c).

[77] Unless HMRC Stamp Taxes spot the potential argument that such an adjustment may be an implied consideration consisting of agreeing to work with enthusiasm for the benefit of the partnership which may not be chargeable consideration but is actual or legal consideration; *Attorney General v Boden* [1912] 1 KB 539.

[78] FA 2003, Sch 15, para 2; see **13.14**.

[79] Ibid, Sch 15, para 2.

[80] Ibid, Sch 15, para 6.

[81] This arose in connection with the former relief for the initial seeding of unit trust schemes FA 2003, s 64A (abolished FA 2006) when HMRC Stamp Taxes took the view that where a unit trust scheme acquired an interest in a partnership it was not acquiring a chargeable interest.

[82] FA 2003, Sch 15, para 27.

- for the purposes of the general anti-avoidance provisions[83] an interest in a property investment partnership[84] is a chargeable interest insofar as it concerns land owned by the partnership.[85]

Such provisions would not be necessary should a partnership share or interest be a chargeable interest.

Partnership interest

13.19 Although the amount of the charge is measured by reference to partnership 'share' in the income profits of the firm the tax charge is triggered by a transfer of the undefined 'interest' in a partnership. Partnership 'share' is defined (as a share in income profits[86]) but there is no explanation of what is meant by a 'partnership interest'.[87] It will include the partner's share in the capital of the firm. It may also encompass variations in the participations of the partners in the firm so that adjustments in profit or capital shares or other adjustments in the participation ratios may be attacked by HMRC Stamp Taxes as transfers of interests;[88] but insofar as such adjustments do not alter the partner's income or profit share there may be a charge to tax but no amount upon which the tax is chargeable.

The interesting question is whether a partner's interest is intended to encompass the whole of the partner's economic interest in the firm such as 'loans',[89] or undrawn profits.[90] This could mean that repayment of partnership loans could produce a transfer if there is a related reduction in the 'interest'. It seems that HMRC Stamp Taxes are inclined towards a wide view of 'interest' and are likely to look to loans and similar involvement as part of the interest of a partner.[91]

Measuring 'share'

13.20 A 'partnership share' in stamp duty land tax has the very special meaning of participation in the income profits (undefined) of the firm[92] and is a crucial restriction upon the relief for the market value charge in the special regime by providing a key factor in computing the reduction for the sum of the lower proportions. Unfortunately there are two related problems which threaten to make the legislation totally unworkable; namely the absence of any explanation of what are the 'income profits' of the firm and how to deal with the computation of the amount of a partner's 'share' of those income profits in many cases because the shares may vary. These are based upon the fundamental error of those responsible for designing the tax and advising HMRC Stamp Taxes in the so-called consultation process to appreciate the incompatibility of a

---

83   Ibid, ss 75A–75C especially s 75C(8)(a).
84   Ibid, Sch 15, para 14.
85   Ibid, s 75C(8)(a).
86   On the difficulties of this see **13.20**.
87   See **13.16**.
88   Note the definition of transfer pursuant to FA 2003, Sch 15, para 36 (as amended); see **13.44**.
89   Which have a special status because there are conceptual problems about partners being their own creditors. This is part of the larger problem of whether interest on partner loans is to be taken into account in determining his 'share' in the income profits of the firm; see **13.20**.
90   Note FA 2003, Sch 15, para 17A(2) which specifically deals with these issues which, in consequence, raises questions as to the basic principles to be applied which requires this specific legislation.
91   There may also be issues as to whether a person who has a loan which is sometimes profit related, such as variable interest, is not a creditor but is a partner.
92   FA 2003, Sch 15, para 34(2).

transaction tax and the effective date for stamp duty land tax and concepts based upon arbitrary annual periods.[93] Not only is there no explanation of what are the 'income profits' of the firm such as whether interest on partnership loans is to be added back into the profits, but also there is no machinery for determining the percentage as at the effective date. Thus the amount of profits to which a partner may be entitled may include interest on his loan or a fixed amount such as a fixed share of profits (which may be regarded as a 'salary' where there are questions as to whether he is a 'partner' or an employee plus a profit share.[94] The proportion of these receipts to the total profits will not in practice be known for many months after the end of the firm's financial year (which may be over a year after the transaction), which makes it impossible to make any necessary calculations as at the effective date. HMRC Stamp Taxes will have to accept either the application some form of wait-and-see because of the variable consideration provisions[95] or a highly simplistic approach based upon the nominal percentage of profit as set out in the partnership deed without any write backs for interest on partner loans or capital or any salaries or fixed fees paid to partners which will have to be ignored for these purposes.

THE CHARGING PROVISIONS

13.21 There are, broadly, two distinct regimes for transactions involving partnerships. These are:

- normal transactions where the partnership acquires a chargeable interest from a third party who is not connected with the partnership in that he is neither a partner nor some person connected with a partner. Broadly, these are governed by the normal rules which apply to all taxpayers;[96] and

- a special regime for dealings in chargeable interests where a partnership is involved and the other party to the transaction is either a partner or a person who is connected with the partnership and as a subregime special rules for dealing in interests in certain types of partnership.

General liability – ordinary transactions

13.22 A partnership is subject to the general principles of stamp duty land tax on its ordinary acquisitions of chargeable interests ie from persons who are not connected with the partnership.[97] All of the partners are responsible[98] for the tax upon their ordinary acquisitions[99] and the responsible partners are responsible for everything that is required or authorised to be done by or in relation to the purchaser.[100]

---

[93] A similar problem exists in relation to relief for intra-group transactions pursuant to FA 2003, Sch 7, Part 1; see **Chapter 12**.
[94] Assuming, as appears to be the view of HMRC Stamp Taxes, that the fixed payment is to be included in the share of income. However, this approach has additional uncertainties where the fixed sum is payable regardless of whether there are profits or losses.
[95] FA 2003, s 51; but this is likely to be on the basis of unascertained consideration requiring immediate payment on an estimated basis.
[96] See **5.83**.
[97] FA 2003, Sch 15, Part 2.
[98] There is a difference between 'responsible partners' and 'representative partners' FA 2003, Sch 15, paras 6(2) and 8.
[99] Ibid, Sch 15, para 6(1).
[100] Ibid, Sch 15, para 6(1).

For these purposes the 'responsible partners' are the persons who are partners at the effective date of the transaction and persons who become a member of the partnership after the effective date of the transaction. This is primarily a question of liability, the question of the completion of forms etc is dealt with separately and is described below. The liability of the partners in relation to making a payment of tax or interest on unpaid tax or to deal with any assessment to recover excessive tax repaid or to any penalty or interest on a penalty is a joint and several liability. However, no payment in respect of tax or interest on unpaid tax or excessive repayment of tax can be recovered from a person who did not become a responsible partner until after the effective date of the transaction in question.[101] In addition, no penalty or interest on a penalty may be recoverable from a person who did not become a responsible partner until after a relevant time.[102] For these purposes the date at which a person becomes liable depends upon the nature of the penalty. Where the penalty is payable in respect of any day or interest on such a penalty the liability of a new partner in respect of outstanding penalties begins at the beginning of the day when he becomes a partner.[103] In relation to any other penalty or interest on a penalty his liability is only in relation to the time when the act or omission occurred that caused the penalty to become payable.[104] Although the liability is joint and several[105] there is no express statutory right to indemnity or contribution between the 'responsible' parties. The persons liable include persons who are partners as at the effective date of the chargeable transaction[106] and any person who becomes a member of the partnership after the effective date. Retirement does not discharge the partners, and since the liability is that of the partner not the partnerships they will not be protected by the limited liability of the firm itself. This liability of the partners is joint and several, as regards tax or interest on the effective date. Partners are not responsible for penalties arising from acts or omissions before they become a partner unless it is a daily penalty where they are liable for such penalties accruing after they become partners. These principles of liability will require careful analysis of the general law.

Completing the return – representative partners[107]

13.23 It is obviously cumbersome for partnerships to have to deal with the full requirements of the compliance regime by involving and disclosing details of all of the partners.[108] In practice HMRC Stamp Taxes are prepared to accept a land transaction return (SDLT 1) that identifies the vendor or the purchaser by the partnership name – full details of every partner on SDLT 2s are not required. Also rather than require all partners to sign the declaration or the land transaction return it is possible to nominate 'representative partners' to deal with stamp duty land tax matters including signing the declaration in the land transaction return.[109] These are persons nominated by a majority

---

[101]   Ibid, Sch 15, para 7(1A).
[102]   Ibid, Sch 15, para 7(2).
[103]   Ibid, Sch 15, para 7(3)(a).
[104]   Ibid, Sch 15, para 7(3)(b).
[105]   Ibid, Sch 15, para 7.
[106]   Ibid, ss 119 and 44; see **Chapter 14**.
[107]   Ibid, Sch 15, paras 6 and 8.
[108]   Technically all partners would be required to sign the land transaction return and their individual details would have to be included on numerous supplementary forms namely SDLT 2. It is possible for a taxpayer to act through an agent who is authorised in writing (FA 2003, Sch 10, para 1A and see Sch 16, para 2 on nominees; Stamp Duty Land Tax (Electronic Communications) Regulations 2005, SI 2005/844). However, HMRC Stamp Taxes appear to require a transaction specific power of attorney signed by the individual taxpayer so that there would need to be separate powers of attorney from every particular partner.
[109]   FA 2003, Sch 10, para 1(1)(c); Sch 15, para 8(2).

of the partners; the nomination has to be given to HMRC ahead of any transaction. The appointment can be revoked by advance notice.

Special transactions

13.24 Particular rules apply to compute the chargeable amount and identify the parties who are liable for paying the tax and compliance in the cases of the various chargeable transactions within the special regime for dealings between partners and partnerships. These particular transactions fall into numerous categories; namely:

- acquisitions of chargeable interests by partnerships from partners or connected persons;[110]

- acquisitions of chargeable interests from partnerships by partners and connected persons;[111]

- transfers of chargeable interests from one partnership to another such as on a merger or demerger;[112]

- transfers of interests in property investment partnerships;[113] and

- transfers of interests in all partnerships pursuant to anti-avoidance provisions.[114]

Transfers to partnerships from partners and connected persons

13.25 A special charge arises[115] where there is either:

- a transfer of a chargeable interest by a partner to a partnership; or

- a transfer of a chargeable interest by a 'person' in return for a partnership interest;[116] or

- a transfer of a chargeable interest to a partnership by a person who is connected with either a partner or with a person who becomes a partner as a result of or in connection with the acquisition.

It is irrelevant whether the transfer is in connection with the formation of the partnership or is made by an existing partnership. Where the partnership is a property investment partnership the partners may elect to disapply the charge[117] which produces a full charge upon the market value but reduces the charge upon the transfers of the partner's interest.[118]

---

[110] Ibid, Sch 15, para 10.
[111] Ibid, Sch 15, para 18.
[112] Ibid, Sch 15, para 23; see **13.45**.
[113] Ibid, Sch 15, para 14 (as amended).
[114] Ibid, Sch 15, paras 17 and 17A; see **13.35**.
[115] Ibid, Sch 15, paras 9 and 10(1).
[116] This includes contributions of capital and may extend to sales for an unpaid consideration; see **13.36**.
[117] FA 2003, Sch 15, para 12A.
[118] Ibid, Sch 15, para 14; see **13.54**.

13.26 These 'acquisitions' are defined in terms of 'transfers' which in the context of FA 2003, Sch 15, is ambiguous because of several not entirely consistent definitions. This is particularly a problem since the overall context of a stamp duty land tax 'transfer' would appear to have a basic meaning of 'transfer' rather than lease or grant, with 'conveyance' being restricted to a document that 'completes' the transaction.[119] In addition to the general definition of 'transfer' there is a special definition to the effect that there is a 'transfer' where a chargeable interest becomes 'partnership property',[120] ie it is held by or on behalf of a partnership or the members of a partnership for the purposes of the partnership business.[121] HMRC Stamp Taxes have already indicated that they intend to take a very wide view of these provisions. In their view, where a partner or a connected person grants a licence to a partnership to utilise land for partnership purposes this does not involve a transfer of a chargeable interest but because the land becomes partnership property there is a deemed transfer[122] with the consequence that the entire freehold interest in not only that part of the land over which the licence is granted, but all other land within the same title or ownership related to the licensed land is transferred to the partnership at its full market value. Fortunately in many such cases the sum of the lower proportions is likely to be a high percentage reducing the chargeable amount significantly; but it is generally thought that there are limits on the scope of HMRC Stamp Taxes' view, since the licence is the interest held for the partnership business not the land over which the licence is granted. It may, however, take time to establish this line of argument and persuade HMRC Stamp Taxes of the error of their ways.

13.27 Where there is a relevant acquisition within these provisions the actual consideration is ignored except to the extent that it consists of rent reserved by the grant of a lease.[123] Subject to the issue of rent, the actual consideration is substituted by 'market value'. This will mean that where a lease is granted it will be necessary to look at the level of rent and decide whether this is below the market rent in which case there may be a deemed premium.

Subject to the making of a para 12A election,[124] the chargeable consideration for the acquisition by the partnership where the persons interested after the transfer are or include individuals[125] is:

$$MV \times (100 - SLP)\%$$

Where:

- MV is the market value of the property; plus

- where the property is a lease the net present value of the rent and special rules apply for determining the market value;[126] and

---

[119] See ibid, s 44(4), (8) and (10).
[120] Ibid, Sch 15, para 35.
[121] Ibid, Sch 15, para 34(1).
[122] See ibid, Sch 15, para 35 compare para 9.
[123] Ibid, Sch 15, paras 10(6) and 11.
[124] Ibid, Sch 15, para 12A; see **13.62**.
[125] Ibid, Sch 15, paras 10 and 11; Stamp Duty Land Tax (Variation of the Finance Act 2003) Regulations 2006, SI 2006/3237; see *Jasmine Trustees Ltdv Wells & Hind* [2007] STC 660.
[126] FA 2003, Sch 15, para 38.

- SLP is the sum of the lower proportions.

Property investment partnerships may elect to disapply these provisions which imposes a full charge upon the market value and no reduction for the SLP.[127] This affects the computation of the chargeable amount upon dealings in interests in property investment partnerships.[128]

The charge is solely by reference to market value, and except where rent is involved,[129] actual consideration such as a purchase price is ignored.[130] An important question is the market value of that chargeable interest in the grant of a lease whether there is deemed a payment of a premium by the tenant this premium will be influenced by the amount of the rent. There is no attempt to tax by reference to market rent.

Background

13.28 However, the charge upon the market value and the net present value of the actual rent where reserved is reduced by reference to the sum of the lower proportions (SLP).[131] This is best understood in terms of the apparent policy behind the legislation although this policy is not necessarily fully carried into effect by the legislation. The broad policy is that no charge to tax should arise where the chargeable interest is regarded as being retained by the vendor and/or individuals[132] connected with him through their interests in the partnership. It is the manner in which their continuing interest in the chargeable interest is measured that causes complications, particularly as for these purposes a partnership 'share' is defined in terms of income and profits which are an annual matter inappropriate to a transaction tax rather than capital. It is vital to note that an individual's deemed interest in the land will not necessarily correspond with his capital entitlement.

Market value

13.29 There is no special machinery for determining the market value (MV) – the normal rules apply[133] with the consequent risk for taxpayers in a self-assessment system of the attempts to find market value being challenged by discovery assessments outside the basic Enquiry period[134] with a probable risk period of 21 years, because inserting the wrong market value will almost certainly be regarded by HMRC Stamp Taxes as 'negligence'[135] This arises where the correct methodology ie the undisclosed process of HMRC Stamp Taxes was not adopted by the taxpayer and his advisers. However, HMRC Stamp Taxes do not appear to have a large budget for valuation and appear to be reluctant to embark upon valuation disputes involving the Share Valuation Division and/or the District Valuer at least where the stated value in the land transaction return is of a reasonable amount[136] and can be supported by an up-to-date valuation supplied by correctly instructed independent valuers.

---

[127] Ibid, Sch 15, para 12A(2) the election must be in the return and is irrecoverable.
[128] Ibid, Sch 15, para 14; see **13.56**.
[129] See **13.30**.
[130] But leaving the price unpaid may mean that subsequent payment is taxable; FA 2003, Sch 15, para 17A.
[131] Ibid, Sch 15, paras 10 and 12.
[132] Stamp Duty Land Tax (Variation of the Finance Act 2003) Regulations 2006, SI 2006/3237.
[133] See **Chapter 27**; but there are certain comments contained in Sch 15 itself that many have implications for valuation disputes in particular cases; see paras 15, 32 (on the impact of mortgages), 33 and 38.
[134] *Langham v Veltema* [2004] STC 544.
[135] See **23.5**.
[136] There is relatively little benefit for HMRC Stamp Taxes in attacking or challenging relatively small

Rent

13.30 Where there is a lease at a rent the net present value of the rent is the tax computation with all of the problems for variable rents over the first 5 years.[137] The question of variable rent and the reduction for the sum of the lower proportions raises may interesting problems. The net present value of the rent will have to be reviewed during the first 5 years of the term if only for changes in the rate of VAT or because of a rent review. This is a retrospective adjustment of the initial calculation in the light of the subsequent events. The initial provisional calculation prepared on an estimated basis[138] is retrospectively recalculated. However, since this is a retrospective adjustment of the original calculation the reduction for the sum of the lower proportions (SLP) remains the same as that applied as at the relevant initial effective date[139] notwithstanding that there may have been changes in the parties and/or their shares of the income profits in the intervening period.[140]

Sum of the lower proportions (SLP)

13.31 Not all of the market value or premium or net present value of the rent[141] is brought into charge to tax. This is reduced by the deemed interest of the transferor or any individuals connected with the transferor.[142] This reduction is defined by reference to the individual's 'proportion' of interest in the property. Two tests are available and the amount of the reduction is by reference to the lower of the two amounts. The two amounts are:

- the amount that the parties allocate, for the purposes of stamp duty land tax, to the partner; and

- his 'share' which is his entitlement to a proportion of the income profits of the firm.[143]

For each individual his relevant proportion is the lower of the two items and for the partnership as a whole it is the aggregate of the lower proportion applied to each partner who is within the connected individual provisions. It will be seen that the basic restriction is by reference to the income share in the profits of the partner. There is a potential loss of tax if the parties decide to allocate less than his income share because the excess between the amount allocated to him and the income is not carried over to other persons and to the extent that the parties allocate a higher than income share the excess over the income share will be lost. In practice, the optimum result is almost invariably obtained by operating on the basis of the share in the income profits of the firm of the relevant partners.

---

consideration since even a large increase in the valuation is likely to produce a small tax increase unjustified in terms of the cost and time incurred by HMRC Stamp Taxes.

[137]   See also **13.33**.

[138]   FA 2003, s 51; Sch 17A, paras 7 and 8.

[139]   Taking into account the possible double effective date for agreements for lease and grants of leases pursuant to FA 2003, Sch 17A, para 12A; see **7.25**.

[140]   These changes may have given rise to charges pursuant to FA 2003, Sch 17A, paras 17 and 17A but these do not appear to be affected.

[141]   FA 2003, Sch 15, para 11.

[142]   Note *Jasmine Trustees Ltd v Wells & Hind* [2007] STC 660, and certain trust companies may be individuals see FA 2003, Sch 15, paras 12(3) and 20(3).

[143]   FA 2003, Sch 15, para 34; but see **13.20** on the problems of calculating this proportion.

13.32 To determine the SLP the transferor's interest in the property before the transaction is allocated to the transferor if he becomes or is a partner and to any other individuals[144] who are partners with whom he is connected before the acquisition. It is important to note that as a result of amendments the allocation of the partner's interest in the transferred property might only be allocated to individuals who are connected with him. This does not mean that the relief is not available where bodies corporate are involved. For example, where the transferor or lessor is itself a body corporate and it is a partner it will be on both sides of the transaction. There will, therefore, not be a question of allocating the interest of the body corporate to another body corporate but to itself and to individuals who may be shareholders or other persons within the connected persons definition.[145] The parties are free to make this allocation on whatever basis is thought by the parties to produce the most tax-efficient result. It is not limited to capital or income share. It is then necessary to determine the individual partner's or connected individual's 'share' in the property measured by reference to his share in the income profits of the firm. The lower proportion for each partner is the lower of the share allocated to him or his income share. The sum of the lower proportions is the aggregate of the lower of the allocated share or the income share for each partner. This is then utilised to reduce the proportion of the market value brought into the charge to tax. For example:

A, B and C who are individuals and connected are in partnership with D who is unconnected.[146] Capital is held 40 per cent by A, and 20 per cent each by B, C and D; profits are shared 25 per cent each. A sells land to the partnership for £600,000;[147] its market value is £1,000,000. The actual price is ignored, and the charge is based upon the market value.

An allocation of the £1,000,000 by capital share would produce the following SLP:

- A 25 per cent (income share). Although allocated 40 per cent by reference to his capital share A's lower proportion is determined by reference to his income share.

- B and C 20 per cent (allocated share).
  SLP = 65 per cent; chargeable amount £350,000. D's interest is ignored.

An allocation by income share would produce the following chargeable amount SLP:

- A, B and C 25 per cent each.
  SLP = 75 per cent; chargeable amount £250,000. D's interest is ignored.
  However, if the income share of the partners is A, C and D 20 per cent each and B 40 per cent, an allocation by income ignoring the capital share produces an SLP of 80 per cent; namely:

- A – 20 per cent

---

[144] Stamp Duty Land Tax (Variation of the Finance Act 2003) Regulations 2006, SI 2006/3237.
[145] Where the transferor is a body corporate and one or more of the partners are bodies corporate there may be questions as to whether the intra-group relief pursuant to FA 2003, Sch 7, Part 1 is available; see **12.60**.
[146] In consequence it seems immaterial whether D is an individual or a company since tax is payable.
[147] The fact of the sale is ignored as is the movement of cash. It is considered that where the cash is paid as part of the acquisition and at the same time it is ignored and the provisions of FA 2003, Sch 15, para 17A do not apply. These provisions apply only to subsequent withdrawals of money or money's worth from the firm; see **13.35**.

- B – 40 per cent

- C – 20 per cent

- D's interest is ignored because he is not a connected individual. The allocation by reference to profit share produces the optimum result.

It will be obvious that the income share is a key and frequently a limiting factor in calculating the maximum SLP.[148]

Leases and rent

13.33 Where the transaction involves the grant by a partner to a partnership of a lease at a rent, whether or not also at an actual premium, there are two stages in the tax:

- there is a charge upon the market value of the lease, ie a deemed premium if there is an element of undervalue in the actual lease; any actual premium is ignored. For these purposes[149] when determining the deemed premium any obligations undertaken by the tenant are to be ignored unless they are in the list of covenants excluded from charge pursuant to FA 2003, Sch 17A, para 10.[150] The chargeable proportion of the market value premium is reduced by (100 – SLP) per cent calculated as above; plus

- a charge on the relevant chargeable part of the net present value of the actual rent[151] or of the various rents if more than one linked lease is involved which is determined by reducing the net present value by (100 – SLP) per cent.[152]

Corporate partnerships

13.34 Formerly where the partnership consisted wholly of bodies corporate and these were so connected that the sum of the lower proportions is 75 or greater the charge was based upon the full market value without reduction for the SLP factor. As from 6 December 2006 this is repealed since now there will be a charge because of the restriction of sum of the lower proportions where companies are involved.[153] Where the transferor is both a body corporate and a partner the reduction for the SLP is available because the company is on both sides of the transaction and it is not necessary to rely upon the connected person provisions. In addition, where the transferor is connected with any of the other companies involved there may be intra-group relief available.[154]

Subsequent cash and other movements

13.35 Where there has been an acquisition of a chargeable interest in these circumstances and within 3 years beginning with the date of the land transfer (which presumably means the effective date of the acquisition rather than the date of the

---

[148] Attempts to mitigate the tax by increasing the SLP by adjusting the profit share of partners on a temporary basis may be subject to the anti-avoidance principles in FA 2003, Sch 15, paras 17 and 17A.

[149] FA 2003, Sch 15, para 38.

[150] See **7.213**.

[151] Determined on normal principles pursuant to FA 2003, Sch 5; see **Chapter 7**.

[152] FA 2003, Sch 15, para 11.

[153] Stamp Duty Land Tax (Variation of the Finance Act 2003) Regulations 2006, SI 2006/3237.

[154] FA 2003, Sch 7, Part 1; see **Chapter 12**.

conveyance), there is a withdrawal of money or money's worth from the partnership otherwise than by way of income profits (such as a return of capital, repayment of a loan, retirement or death), there is a chargeable transaction upon a chargeable consideration equal to the amount withdrawn or the market value of the chargeable interest transferred as at the effective date (as reduced by any tax previously paid) whichever is the smaller.[155] Such arrangements may also constitute a transfer of a partnership interest.[156] In such cases the charge pursuant to FA 2003, Sch 15, para 17A, is reduced by the amount chargeable in respect of the transfer.[157] This is a particularly wide-ranging provision since it applies to virtually all withdrawals of cash or assets from the partnership. It also applies where a person 'ceases to be a partner'. It would seem that this would apply to normal retirements in accordance with the partnership agreement or the death of a partner. It may also apply where there is a two partner firm and one of the partners retires so that the partnership, as such, ceases to exist and the continuing partner becomes a sole trader. There have also been difficulties in relation to the repayment of loans because it applies not only to repayment of a loan to the 'relevant partner' it extends to arrangements for the repayment of 'connected party loans' which can catch the unwary who refinance bridging and similar arrangements incurred when setting up the partnership. This includes loans involving a person who is connected with the relevant partner. It may be that a partner has, for example, a partner may contribute capital to the firm that is derived from a loan made to it by its parent company. The parent company may have borrowed this money from a bank as part of some group banking arrangements. The repayment of the loan within the 3 year period could constitute a repayment of a connected party loan and bring the anti-avoidance provisions of para 17A into operation.

13.36 The provision refers to capital and to 'loans'. There is an important general distinction between a 'loan' and a 'debt' the former relates to a cash advance, the latter relates to an unpaid consideration. It is considered that where the land was acquired for an unpaid consideration so that a 'debt' arose the subsequent payment of the outstanding purchase price would not be the repayment of a loan.[158] It is clear that these provisions can apply notwithstanding that the partnership is not a property investment partnership. Although a transfer in a non-property investment partnership is not a chargeable transaction pursuant to para 14, it is provided that where this provision applies and there is also a charge pursuant to para 14 the amount of the charge under para 17A is reduced by the amount of the charge under para 14. This envisages situations where there is a chargeable transaction within para 17A that does not fall within para 14. In consequence, it seems that the charge will apply in relation to non-property investment partnerships such as professional firms an farming partnerships.

Subsequent partnership changes

13.37 A special charge arises where there has been an acquisition of a chargeable interest pursuant to para 10 so that the above charging provisions with the benefit of the reduction in the market value charge for the sum of the lower proportions applies,[159]

---

[155] Ibid, Sch 15, para 17A.
[156] Ibid, Sch 15, paras 14 and 36.
[157] Ibid, Sch 15, para 17A(8).
[158] However, this may depend upon the drafting of the contract since in some situations the parties may convert an unpaid consideration into some form of set-off which constitutes a cash payment and a loan back of cash which would be within the provisions; see, for example, *Coren v Keighley* 48 TC 370.
[159] Note that property investment partnerships may elect to disapply these provisions so that the para 10 charge

ie where there is a market value charge with a reduction for the SLP and there is subsequently a transfer of a partnership interest[160] pursuant to arrangements in place at the time of the acquisition[161] and the transfer of the interest in the partnership is not otherwise a chargeable transaction ie is not within para 14 because the partnership is not a property investment partnership the transfer of the partnership interest is a chargeable transaction.

13.38 There is considerable scope for HMRC Stamp Taxes to cause difficulties over what is an 'arrangement' for these purposes and it is understood that HMRC Stamp Taxes are intending to take the point that a pre-existing unconnected partnership contract or agreement can constitute 'an arrangement' for these purposes.[162] Since there is no need for a causal link ie the transfer of the property need not be 'in connection with the arrangements' nor need the implementation of the 'arrangements' ie the change in the partnership be in connection with the transfer of the land. The test is purely chronological, the transfer of the land is succeeded by changes pursuant to arrangements that were entered into before the transfer of the land. It is, however, unclear whether HMRC Stamp Taxes intend to press the point that the normal forms of retirement and admission to membership and adjustments in partnership shares that are embodied in a pre-existing partnership agreement are 'arrangements'.

13.39 This provision would apply to changes in partnerships that are not property investment partnerships although the charge upon transfers of interests in partnerships are not intended to apply to professional partnerships or partnerships that have substantial interests in land such as farming partnerships or retail consortia that own premises since these are not property investment partnerships. However, the effect of these provisions[163] is that these provisions will apply where there is not a chargeable transfer pursuant to para 14.

13.40 The charge pursuant to FA 2003, Sch 15, para 14, is now limited to transfers of interests in property investment partnerships, the charge pursuant to para 17 has been indirectly or by stealth enlarged, in effect reinstating many of the charges intended to be removed by the reduction of the scope of para 14. In consequence professional firms as well as farming and manufacturing partnerships will be affected by para 17, but it seems that routine changes in partners in accordance with the partnership deed may not be regarded by HMRC Stamp Taxes as 'arrangements'.

13.41 The main safeguard is that for most professional firms there is unlikely to be the acquisition of a chargeable interest from a partner or connected person because the family element is minimal and rules restrict the right to recruit family members into the firm. Most chargeable interests will, in consequence, be acquired pursuant to the general regime and outside the special regime of FA 2003, Sch 15, Part 3. However, this will not necessarily apply to many forms of family businesses such as retail operations involving husband and wife[164] or farming businesses and many commercial joint ventures even where companies are involved because the business contributed is likely to include

---

does not apply and this may affect subsequent dealings such as the charge upon transfers of interests in such partnerships and whether the anti-avoidance provisions pursuant to para 17 apply.

[160] Undefined; see **13.16** and **13.19**.
[161] Ibid, Sch 15, para 17.
[162] Compare *Irving v Tesco Stores (Holdings) Ltd v IRC* [1982] STC 881 on the question of whether a company's articles of association are 'an arrangement'.
[163] FA 2003, Sch 15, para 17(1)(f).
[164] Or parties within a civil partnership.

chargeable interests in land together with the problems of embedded goodwill.[165] The charge is upon a proportion of the market value,[166] but it should be noted that there is no reduction in the charge for an equivalent of the sum of the lower proportions notwithstanding that the relevant parties are connected individuals and the reduction would have been available had the transferee been a partner at the time of the transfer.

13.42 The onus of paying the tax and making the necessary returns applies to those partners who were partners immediately before the transfer and who remain partners after the transfer and any person who became a partner as a result of or in connection with the transfer.[167] The chargeable consideration is a proportion of the market value as at the date of the transfer of the partnership interest. That proportion depends upon the status of the person transferring the partnership interest. If the transferor of the partnership interest is not a partner immediately after that transfer the chargeable proportion of market value of the interest is acquired by the partnership. If he remains a partner immediately after the transfer the chargeable proportion is the reduction of his partnership share as a result of the transfer.

13.43 Numerous problems exist as to the scope of these provisions which it seems, as a matter of speculation as to the policy involved, are intended to apply to situations where a partner has a high income share at the time of the acquisition of the chargeable interest in order to maximise the SLP (sum of the lower proportions) deduction from the market value or net present value of the actual rent chargeable amounts; but this profit share is to be reduced in favour of other partners who are connected for the purposes of SLP. Unfortunately this perceived policy has not been properly implemented because the special charge arises even where the transferee of the partnership interest is a connected person within the SLP reduction provisions but whose increased involvement would not have altered the original charge since the relevant party is not eligible for an SLP reduction.

13.44 The tax charge arises where there is a transfer of a partnership interest which, as mentioned above,[168] is not defined which is the chargeable transaction but the chargeable amount is based upon partnership 'shares'. The circumstances where the charge may arise are uncertain on several grounds:

- what is a 'transfer'; and

- what 'transfers' are not within the specific charging provisions for transfers.[169]

There is a definition[170] much changed[171] of 'transfer' in the context of transfer of 'partnership interest' (not transfer of 'partnership share') which formerly involved a direct assignment of an interest or a situation where one person becomes a partner and

---

[165] See **1.5**.
[166] FA 2003, Sch 15, para 17(4) and s 51.
[167] Ibid, Sch 15, para 17(7).
[168] See **13.19**.
[169] FA 2003, Sch 15, para 14; see **13.54**.
[170] Ibid, Sch 15, para 36.
[171] There are numerous problems in relation to the meaning and scope of the current definition so that a knowledge of the previous provisions whether merely amended or replaced may be helpful in trying to make reasonable commercial sense of the definition in place at the time of the relevant transaction which may not be the same as the current definition.

an existing partner reduces his interest or ceases to be a partner.[172] This definition made no specific reference to a frequent situation of one existing partner reducing his interest and another existing partner increasing his interest. This issue of reduction of interest was subsequently included but these definitions have been replaced although it is understood that HMRC Stamp Taxes may regard such a transaction as a transfer but this interpretation was not necessarily supported by the earlier legislation. Currently the definition of a 'transfer' of a partnership 'interest' applies where a person acquires a share in a partnership or increases a share in a partnership. This is a definition in terms of shares of income and not in terms of other variations of the economic involvement of the person concerned in the partnership such as variations in capital or repayments of loans.[173]

Acquisitions by partners from partnerships – disposals by partnerships

Basic charge

13.45 There is a special charge where there is a 'transfer' of a chargeable interest either:

- from a partnership to a person who is or has been a partner; or

- from a partnership to a person connected with a person who is or has been one of the partners.[174]

Different rules apply to transfers between partnerships[175] and the partners in a property investment partnership may elect to disapply these provisions in relation to movements between partnerships[176] ie where a para 10 and para 18 charge may apply[177] whichever produces the greater amount of tax.[178]

The chargeable amount is the market value or a proportion of the net present value of rent reduced by the SLP as a percentage. The policy here appears to be the same as that for putting property into partnerships; namely, the basic chargeable amount of the market value is reduced to the extent that the chargeable interest remains owned by the same persons or persons connected with them.

13.46 'Transfer' appears to bear its special contextual meaning equivalent to 'acquisition';[179] but there is also a transfer from a partnership where a chargeable interest that was partnership property, ie was held for the purposes of the partnership business,[180] ceases to be partnership property or a chargeable interest is granted or

---

[172] It would seem that this definition of 'transfer' applies rather than the much wider general definition of transfer because it is a definition of 'transfer of a partnership interest' rather than 'transfer' of a chargeable interest.

[173] This analysis is assisted by the fact that repayment of capital and loans are specifically dealt with in FA 2003, Sch 15, para 17A suggesting strongly that they are not 'shares' and the variations, in consequence, cannot be 'transfers'.

[174] FA 2003, Sch 15, para 18.

[175] See ibid, Sch 15, para 23; see also **13.52**.

[176] Ibid, Sch 15, para 23.

[177] Ibid, Sch 15, para 23(2A); see **13.52**.

[178] It seems that this is a special charging provision rather than a mere computational arrangement which has important consequential problems not addressed by the draftsman of the amendments.

[179] FA 2003, Sch 15, para 9(2) although this differs in certain key aspects from the definition of acquisition pursuant to FA 2003, s 43.

[180] Ibid, Sch 15, para 34(1).

created out of partnership property and the newly created interest is not partnership property such as the grant of a sublease.[181] However, where the partnership is being dissolved or wound up the effective date does not arise until the property is distributed.[182]

13.47 The charge is by reference to the market value[183] including a reduction for the sum of the lower proportions[184] and where the transaction involves a lease in addition to the reduction of any deemed premium equal to market value within the charge[185] the net present value of the actual rent as reduced by the SLP is included. To cover cases where the lease is on favourable terms there is a deemed premium equal to the market value generally reduced by the sum of the lower proportions for that lease.[186]

Sum of the lower proportions

13.48 Although for disposals by a partnership the same algebraic formula is utilised as that applied for acquisitions by firms there are differences in calculating 'SLP' because of the nature of the data to be inserted into the computation. This is determined by allocating the interest of the transferee in the land after the transaction amongst the partners and persons[187] connected with the transferee who are interested in the land immediately before the transaction. The transferee is a person who immediately after the transaction has an interest in the land and was a partner or connected with a partner immediately before the transaction. His interest is apportioned between himself and any persons who were connected with him. This allocation can be made on whatever basis the parties believe will produce the best result for them; the allocation need not be made on the basis of actual shares in the land but on whatever basis the parties regard as producing the lowest tax charge, it is not restricted to any person's share of capital or income. However, as described above,[188] it is almost invariably the case that the lowest tax charge will arise where the parties elect to apply the share in the income profits of the firm (whatever this term may mean in the current context)[189] because any other allocation would produce an excess figure that will be disallowed, presumably producing a loss of relief for other person's income share or reduce the maximum relief that is potentially available. However, two 'proportions' have to be ascertained for each participant so that the lower of the two can be identified and only this lower amount or percentage is taken into account. This allocation by the participants is only one of the proportions, the other is the partnership share attributable to the partner so that in effect the maximum allocation in the income share. This is because for each person it is necessary to determine his lower proportion which is the lower of the amount allocated as above or his share in the income profits of the firm.[190] His share for these purposes cannot, therefore, exceed his profit share which can usually be taken as providing the best after tax result.

---

[181] Ibid, Sch 14, para 37.
[182] Ibid, Sch 15, para 18(7). The possible extent of this provision could affect the possible application of the anti-avoidance provisions and the 3 year period pursuant to FA 2003, Sch 15, para 17A such as the repayment of capital on the death of a partner, provided that the widow is willing to co-operate.
[183] Any actual premium is ignored.
[184] FA 2003, Sch 15, paras 18(2), 20–22.
[185] On market value premium in such circumstances see **Chapter 27**.
[186] Special rules apply as to the covenants to be included when valuing the lease; FA 2003, Sch 15, para 38.
[187] Ibid, Sch 15, paras 18 and 20(1).
[188] See **13.31**.
[189] See **13.20**.
[190] See **13.9**.

Special situations

Partner's SLP 'share' as zero

13.49 However, in relation to the removal of land from a firm (ie land ceasing to be an asset utilised for the purposes of the partnership business) there is a further restriction depending upon whether the land was acquired before or on or after 20 October 2003.[191] Where the effective date for the transfer to the partnership was before that date, the starting point is his share which is measured by reference to his participation in the income profits of the firm;[192] if he became a partner on or after that date the starting point is his share on admission. The starting share is increased if there was an increase subsequently and reduced by any reductions in his share. However, increases are allowed only if full stamp duty (not a fixed duty) or stamp duty land tax was paid in respect of the increase. Where the transfer to the partnership of the relevant chargeable interest was on or after 20 October 2003 and the instrument by which the transfer was effected has not born *ad valorem* stamp duty but is either not stampable or is subject only to a fixed duty or stamp duty land tax has not been duly paid in respect of the transfer, the partner's share is deemed to be zero.[193] If the partner's share is not zero the share is determined by reference to the date when he became a partner. If he was a partner on 19 October 2003 the relevant date for determining his share is that date. If he became a partner after that date his share is the share at the date on which he became a partner.[194] Having determined the basic share it is necessary to increase his partnership share by reference to any increases in that share which occur in a period either on or after 19 October 2003 if a partner at that date or since he became a partner if he became a partner after that date.[195] However, there are restrictions upon the increases that can be taken into account. Where the increase took place on or before 22 July 2004 the increase is taken into account only if the instrument by which the transfer was effected has been duly stamped with *ad valorem* stamp duty. For these purposes payment of any fixed duty would not be appropriate notwithstanding that this was the correct amount of stamp duty and the instrument was adjudicated. If the transfer producing the increase in the partner's share took place after 22 July 2004 the increase is only taken into account any stamp duty land tax payable in respect of the transfer has been duly paid.[196] The partner's share may also be reduced by reference to any deceases in the partner's partnership share which occur in the period starting on 19 October 2003 if he was a partner at that date or the date on which he became a partner and before the chargeable transaction involving the transfer of the land out of the partnership. However, a partner's share cannot be reduced below zero by reason of such deductions.[197] Where there is a transfer to a person who was a former partner if he ceased to be a partner before 19 October 2003 and the transfer of the chargeable interest to the partnership was before 20 October 2003 his share is zero.[198] Where the transfer was on or after 20 October 2003 and the person has ceased to be a partner before that transfer to the partnership his attributable share is zero.

---

[191]   FA 2003, Sch 15, paras 21 and 22.
[192]   Ibid, Sch 15, para 34(2).
[193]   Ibid, Sch 15, para 21(3).
[194]   Ibid, Sch 15, para 22.
[195]   Ibid, Sch 15, para 22(1).
[196]   Ibid.
[197]   Ibid, Sch 15, para 22(2).
[198]   Ibid, Sch 15, para 22(3).

Leases by partnerships

13.50 Where the disposal consists of the grant of a lease by a partnership to a partner or person connected with the partner(s) which reserves a rent the general rule of the market value charge is modified in that a proportion of the net present value of the actual rent is added to the chargeable consideration of the market value premium (although this will be determined by the size of the rent reserved).[199] The chargeable consideration includes the net present value of the rent reserved reduced by the sum of the lower proportions in accordance with the formula NPV x (100 – SLP) per cent.[200] The charge is therefore on the reduced amount of the rent plus the reduced market value premium intended to reflect the continuity of ownership in the demised premises by the connected persons.

Partnerships consisting wholly of bodies corporate[201]

13.51 Where there is a transfer from a partnership consisting wholly of bodies corporate and the sum of the lower proportions is 75 per cent or more the charge is upon the market value of the lease and the net present value of any actual rent.[202] In this situation there may be relief for intra-group transactions.[203] Where this special provision could be a problem it may be possible to escape from it by including individuals in partnerships albeit for relatively small amounts.

Partnership mergers and demergers

13.52 Where there is a transfer from one partnership to another such as on a merger or demerger the transaction is treated as both an acquisition by a firm and an acquisition from a firm and the tax is the higher amounts produced by these two calculations.[204] Technically changes in the partners by way of retirement, death or admission may involve a cessation of the existing partnership and the commencement of a new partnership but this is to be ignored for certain stamp duty land tax purposes.[205] This is a difficult issue for the self-assessment since, although the mechanics for calculating the tax appear to be similar, there are major differences between the charging provisions for transfers into and out of partnerships. For example, the deduction for the SLP is wider on transfers out of a partnership since this is not restricted to connected individuals; but the partnership share of the persons involved depends upon when and how the partnership acquired the land as mentioned above.[206]

---

[199] Ibid, Sch 15, paras 19 and 38.

[200] This formula does not as such appear in the legislation but is considered to be a correct reflection of the provisions.

[201] This provision is a potentially key point in any debate concerning the taxation of the incorporation of a partnership which is an area of transactions that are totally unacceptable to HMRC Stamp Taxes; but there has not been the same carry over from transfer into partnerships of the restriction of the reliefs for the sum of the lower proportions (SLP) to 'individuals'. This restriction involves the removal of the special treatment for the relief for partnerships of bodies corporate. The consequential changes have not been carried over into transfers by or between partnerships and the retention of those provisions for partnerships of bodies corporate (which are easily avoided) are continued which would not be necessary should there be restrictions upon or transfers to bodies corporate.

[202] FA 2003, Sch 15, para 24.

[203] Ibid, Sch 7, Part 1 but note the special amendments for partnerships in Sch 15, para 27 thereof; see **13.68**.

[204] The latter basis is likely to provide the higher charge for many years because of the transitional rules which will reduce the partner's lower proportion to zero so that there is effectively no SLP.

[205] See FA 2003, Sch 15, para 3.

[206] See **13.48**.

13.53 This is a separate charge to tax. It is not a charge pursuant to para 10 or pursuant to para 18, they are relevant only for the purpose of computing the tax charge. In consequence, it is arguable that the anti-avoidance provisions of paras 17 and 17A[207] do not apply to subsequent variations in the transferee partnership since these require a specific charge under para 10.[208] However, it seems that HMRC Stamp Taxes take the view that this is a transaction which is chargeable pursuant to both provisions and they merely apply the higher charge. In consequence, where the transferee partnership is a property investment partnership it can elect to disapply the application of para 10 and since the transaction is also potentially chargeable pursuant to para 18 it can apply to disapply the para 18 charge.[209] The effect is that the chargeable consideration for the transaction is the market value of the chargeable interest transferred. It is, in consequence, treated as being an ordinary acquisition outside the scope of the special provisions.[210] The making of such an election also has important consequences for the computation of the charge upon any transfer of an interest in a property investment partnership.[211]

Transfer of interests in partnership

13.54 In addition to a charge to stamp duty[212] upon any written transfer of a share in a partnership of 0.5 per cent to the extent that the consideration is apportioned to shares or marketable securities that form part of the assets of the partnership,[213] including shares or marketable securities in companies incorporated abroad, there is a special charge to stamp duty land tax where the assets of the partnership include chargeable interests in land. It is specifically provided that a charge arises upon a transfer of a partnership interest only in the circumstances prescribed by FA 2003, Sch 15, para 14 (as amended);[214] but where there is a transfer of a partnership interest that does not fall into charge pursuant to these provisions there may be a special charge where the transfer of the interest is either part of the arrangements involving the transfer of a chargeable interest into the firm,[215] or involves a return of assets or repayment of loans.[216]

13.55 It must be noted initially that, notwithstanding the look-through provisions,[217] HMRC Stamp Taxes originally argued that a partnership interest was not itself a chargeable interest. However, notwithstanding amendments to the legislation that have made partnership interests chargeable interests this is only for limited purposes;[218] and the general proposition that a partnership interest is not a chargeable interest remains applicable. In consequence, indirect dealings in partnership interests such as shares in companies or interests in trusts holding interests in partnerships are, in general, not dealings in chargeable interests.

---

[207] See **13.35**.

[208] This is one of the reasons why the question of principle of whether these provisions are separate charging provisions or are merely computational provisions and a choice between paras 10 and 18. The answer to this question has major implications although it seems that it would be difficult for HMRC Stamp Taxes to support the argument that para 23 is not a special charging provision.

[209] FA 2003, Sch 15, para 12A.

[210] Ibid, Sch 15A, para 12A(2).

[211] Ibid, Sch 15, para 14 (as amended); see **12.58**.

[212] Fortunately the interest in a partnership is not converted into a chargeable security for the purposes of the principal charge to stamp duty reserve tax (FA 2003, ss 87 and following).

[213] FA 2003, Sch 15, paras 32 and 33 (as amended).

[214] Ibid, Sch 15, para 29.

[215] Ibid, Sch 15, para 17; see **13.37**.

[216] Ibid, Sch 15, para 17A; see **13.35**.

[217] Ibid, Sch 15, Part 1; see **13.21**.

[218] See **13.18**.

Partnerships affected

13.56 Not all partnerships are within these provisions: the charge on transfer applies only where the partnership is a 'property investment partnership';[219] but this recent limitation of the charge has by stealth increased the scope of the charge for other partnership pursuant to certain anti-avoidance provisions[220] dealing with the adjustment of partnership interests subsequent to the transfer of the land into the partnership so that farming, manufacturing and professional firms remain on risk, to some extent, when routine changes of partners take place because HMRC Stamp Taxes have, on numerous, but unofficial, occasions, indicated that, in their view, the 'arrangements' do not have to be connected with the transfer and can include pre-existing partnership agreements. In consequence, unconnected variations in the partnership structure[221] are taxable arrangements but on occasion it seems that they may be 'sympathetic' to situations where the change is 'routine' such as new appointments, regular retirements and death. A 'property investment partnership' is a partnership[222] whose sole or main activity is investing or dealing in chargeable interests, whether or not that activity involves the carrying out of construction operations on the land.[223] This will exclude most trading and professional partnerships notwithstanding that land is a major asset of the partnership. Farming partnerships will not be within the charge because the main activity is farming not land holding to produce rent.[224] However, the status of a partnership may change such as where it ceases to trade or farm but holds the land for development or letting it temporarily pending sale. HMRC generally have attacked such arrangements (albeit entered into temporarily) as changing the status of the taxpayer from trader to investor, even where only part of its assets are involved. Ownership of factories and office premises will also not bring partnerships into the charge provided that the trading activities continue and involve the utilisation of the premises, relocating a business may leave premises temporarily unused with the risks that the property is deemed to have been transferred out of the partnership and/or the partnership becomes a property investment partnership.

'Transfer'

13.57 All that is required for the charge to arise is the transfer of an interest in a property investment partnership. It is irrelevant whether there is consideration;[225] but the existence or absence of consideration may affect the computation of the charge.[226] 'Transfer' of a partnership interest is given a special meaning[227] namely a person acquires or increases a partnership share ie a participation in income profits.[228]

---

[219] Defined FA 2003, Sch 15, para 14(8).

[220] FA 2003, Sch 15, para 17 which only applies where the transfer is not otherwise chargeable ie falls outside para 14 thereof; see para 17(1)(f) whereas para 17A applies where para 14 applies should it produce a higher charge see para 17A(8).

[221] But there may be a vital distinction between situations where the event occurs by reason of negotiation of the parties or as a consequence of some pre-agreed arrangement that occurs automatically.

[222] There is, of course, the fundamental question of whether a purely investment vehicle is a 'partnership'. If not these provisions and other anti-avoidance legislation will not apply.

[223] FA 2003, Sch 15, para 14(8) (as amended); some guidance on these issues may emerge as HMRC Stamp Taxes have to deal with the restrictions upon the type of undertaking eligible for the relief for corporate reorganisations pursuant to FA 2003, Sch 7, para 8(5A).

[224] But these have become subject to different anti-avoidance rules by stealth.

[225] FA 2003, Sch 15, para 14; the original requirement for consideration pursuant to para 14(6) has been progressively repealed.

[226] Ibid, Sch 15, para 14(3A); see **13.58**.

[227] Ibid, Sch 15, para 36.

[228] Ibid, Sch 15, para 36 applied to situations where either: (a) a partner 'transfers' the whole or part of his interest as a partner to another person whether or not an existing partner. This would apply to a

Chargeable amount

13.58 Where there is a chargeable transfer of an interest in a property investment partnership the calculation of the tax payable depends upon the nature of the transfer. The charge arises simply where there is a 'transfer' of a partnership interest.[229] Consideration is no longer necessary[230] however the chargeable amount depends upon, *inter alia*, whether there is consideration. The 'purchaser' who is responsible for filing the land transaction return and paying any tax is the person who acquires an increased partnership share or becomes a partner in consequence of the transfer.[231] There are three categories of transfer each with their own computational rules:

- *Type A transfer – variation 1.*
  This arises if the transfer of a partnership interest[232] takes the form of arrangements entered into under which the whole or part of a partner's interest as partner is acquired by another person who may be an existing partner and consideration in money or money's worth is given by or on behalf of the person acquiring the interest;[233]

- *Type A transfer – variation 2.*
  This is a transfer of a partnership interest[234] that takes the form of arrangements entered into under which a person becomes a partner (as opposed to increases his partnership interest)[235] and the interest of an existing partner in the partnership is reduced or an existing partner ceases to be a partner and there is a withdrawal of money or money's worth from the partnership by the existing partner whose interest is reduced or who ceases to be a partner other than money or money's worth paid from resources available to the partnership prior to the transfer.[236] This, *prima facie*, appears to be very similar to the longstanding argument by HMRC Stamp Taxes that there was a transfer of a partnership interest where there was a contribution of cash to the partnership by one person and a simultaneous withdrawal of cash by another person. However, this provision cryptically refers to the money being withdrawn not being available from new resources. Obviously, resources not previously available would include capital contributed by a new partner or a person increasing his interest. The question is whether 'resources' would include a loan made by such a partner. Similarly, there may be questions as to whether a new banking arrangement entered into in order

---

straightforward assignment of an interest; or (b) a person becomes a partner and an existing partner reduces his interest in the partnership or ceases to be a partner. In this case the consideration is provided by the withdrawal of money or money's worth from the partnership. There does not seem to be a need for a related contribution of capital by the new partner. On the other hand there is considerable doubt whether a mere contribution of capital by a new or existing partner is a 'transfer' notwithstanding that it may operate to diminish or dilute the interests of the other partners. However, if there is a simultaneous reduction of another partner's capital this will be regarded by HMRC Stamp Taxes as a transfer. However, notwithstanding that these provisions have been repealed and replaced they are likely to provide useful material when disputing the current or any subsequent definitions with HMRC Stamp Taxes.

[229] FA 2003, Sch 15, para 36.
[230] Ibid, Sch 15, para 14(1)(b) (as amended) has been repealed.
[231] Ibid, Sch 15, para 14(3).
[232] Ibid, Sch 15, para 34(2).
[233] Ibid, Sch 15, para 14(3A).
[234] Ibid, Sch 15, para 34(2).
[235] Which may not be the same as where the partner's share 'is increased' as a consequence of arrangements built into the partnership agreement for automatic increases or productions not requiring the intervention of the parties; arrangements for 'bonus payments' increasing the take home pay can clearly give rise to serious problems in this area.
[236] FA 2003, Sch 15, para 14(3B)(e).

to provide the partnership with sufficient cash to return the capital of the retiring partner or person reducing his interest is a 'new resource'. The position becomes somewhat arbitrary if the partnership has a large working capital facility with the bank which is not fully utilised and draws upon this in order to repay the capital to the outgoing partner. This, however, assumes that HMRC Stamp Taxes intend 'resources' to include not merely assets owned by the partnership but also 'resources' in the wider sense such as banking and working capital loans. There will, therefore, be issues where an incoming partner contributes capital in kind and the outgoing partner withdraws cash where, for example, the newly contributed asset is utilised to provide security for a new borrowing which generates the cash to pay the retiring partner or person reducing his interest. The lack of precision in this legislation will offer ample opportunities for uncertainty and prolonged and expensive debates with HMRC Stamp Taxes;

- *Type B transfer.*
  A Type B transfer is any other transfer[237] ie a transfer that is not either form of a Type A transfer.[238]

13.59 The chargeable consideration for the transfer of the partnership interest is an amount equal to a proportion of the market value of the relevant property. This requires the determination of numerous factors such as:

- the existence of a transfer;[239]

- the relevant proportion;

- the relevant partnership property; and

- the market value of that property.

Chargeable proportion

13.60 The chargeable proportion of the market value depends upon whether there has been a para 12A election[240] and whether the person acquiring the interest was or was not a partner before the transfer.[241] If he was not a partner before the transfer of the partnership interest the proportion is his partnership share immediately after the transfer. This reference to partnership share means his percentage involvement in the income profits of the firm.[242] Where the person acquiring the interest was a partner before the transfer the chargeable proportion is the difference between his partnership share ie share in the income profits of the firm before and that share after the transfer.[243]

---

[237] Ibid, Sch 15, para 34(2).
[238] Ibid, Sch 15, para 14(3C).
[239] Ibid, Sch 15, para 34(2).
[240] See **13.27**.
[241] FA 2003, Sch 15, para 14(7).
[242] Ibid, Sch 15, para 34(2); see **13.16**.
[243] Ibid, Sch 15, para 14(7)(b).

Chargeable property

13.61 The charge does not arise by reference to any actual consideration for the transaction, it is necessary to determine the relevant partnership property. This depends on whether there is a Type A transfer or a Type B transfer. In relation to a Type A transfer the relevant partnership property is every chargeable interest held as partnership property immediately after the transfer of the partnership interest other than:

- any chargeable interest that was transferred to the partnership in connection with the transfer, for example, the land transferred is consideration for the share or interest;

- a lease where:[244]
    - there is no chargeable consideration other than rent given in respect of the grant of a lease;
    - no arrangements are in place at the time of the transfer of a partnership interest for any chargeable consideration other than rent to be given in respect of the lease;
    - the rent payable under the lease as granted was a market rent at the time of the grant;
    - the term of the lease is 5 years or less or if the term of the lease is more than 5 years the lease provides for the rent payable under the lease to be reviewed at least once in every 5 years of the term and the rent payable under the lease as a result of the review is required to be a market rent at the review date;
    - there has been no change to the lease since it was granted which is such that, immediately after the change has effect, the rent payable under the lease is less than the market rent which is defined as the rent which the lease might reasonably be expected to fetch at that time in the open market;[245]

- any chargeable interest that is not attributable economically to the interest in the partnership that is transferred. This is not defined but it would seem to be intended to deal with situations where the capital interest of the partners are divided into 'shares' or 'units' in some form of cell or similar structure. For example, where partner X has an 'A' share and this is defined as being related to property A, B and C then property F or G would not be economically related to the partnership interest of X.

13.62 In relation to a Type B transfer of an interest in the partnership the relevant property is every chargeable interest held as partnership property[246] immediately after the transfer of the partnership interest other than:

- any chargeable interest that was transferred into the partnership in connection with the transfer of the partnership share; a lease[247] where:
    - there is no chargeable consideration other than rent given in respect of the grant of a lease;

---

[244] Ibid, Sch 15, paras 14(5A) and 15.
[245] A review date is the date from which the rent determined as the result of the rent review is payable (FA 2003, Sch 15, para 15(7)).
[246] Ibid, Sch 15, para 34(1).
[247] Ibid, Sch 15, paras 14(5A) and 15.

– no arrangements are in place at the time of the transfer of a partnership interest for any chargeable consideration other than rent to be given in respect of the lease;

– the rent payable under the lease as granted was a market rent at the time of the grant;

– the term of the lease is 5 years or less or if the term of the lease is more than 5 years the lease provides for the rent payable under the lease to be reviewed at least once in every 5 years of the term and the rent payable under the lease as a result of the review is required to be a market rent at the review date;

– there has been no change to the lease since it was granted which is such that, immediately after the change has effect, the rent payable under the lease is less than the market rent which is defined as the rent which the lease might reasonably be expected to fetch at that time in the open market;[248]

• any chargeable interest that is not attributable economically to the interest in the partnership that is transferred. This is not defined but it would seem to be intended to deal with situations the capital interest of the partners are divided into 'shares' or 'units' in some form of cell or similar structure. For example, where partner X has an 'A' share and this is defined as being related to property A, B and C then property F or G would not be economically related to the partnership interest of X;[249]

• any chargeable interest that was transferred[250] to the partnership on or before 22 July 2004;[251]

• any chargeable interest in respect of whose transfer to the partnership an election has been made under para 12A disapplying the application of para 10 and, in appropriate circumstances, or where there is a partnership merger or demerger[252] para 18. The effect of making an election under para 12A is that the charge does not arise under para 10 but under the general provisions and the reduction from the market value of the sum of the lower proportions is not available ie the charge is upon the full market value and/or the net present value of the rent. The election must be included in the land transaction return made in respect of the transaction to which the election relates or in an amendment to the return. An election is irrevocable and a land transaction return may not be amended so as to withdraw the election.[253] It seems that where an election is not made in the land transaction return it may be made by means of an amendment to the return but it should be noted that amendments may be made to land transaction returns only within 12 months of the effective filing date.[254] Where an election is made in respect of a transaction by means of an amendment to a land transaction return the election has effect as if it had been made on the date on which the land transaction return was made and any land transaction return in respect of an affected transaction may be amended within the permitted period for amendment of that return to

---

[248] A review date is the date from which the rent determined as the result of the rent review is payable (FA 2003, Sch 15, para 15(7)).

[249] Ibid, Sch 15, para 14(5A)(c).

[250] 'Transferred' is not defined so that there may be a major problem where there was a contract before the relevant date but which was not completed before that date.

[251] FA 2003, Sch 15, para 14(5A)(d).

[252] Ibid, Sch 15, para 23.

[253] Ibid, Sch 15, para 12A(4).

[254] Ibid, Sch 10, para 6; but note the power to extend time limits for complying with obligations pursuant to ibid, s 97 or where HMRC Stamp Taxes provider otherwise.

take account of the election.[255] For these purposes an 'affected transaction' means a transaction that involves a transfer of an interest in a property investment partnership within para 14 with an effective date on or after the effective date of the transaction. In effect, the parties may make a retrospective election within a limited time and this retrospective election will also make retrospective adjustments in the calculation of the tax arising in respect of any transfer of a partnership interest between the effective date for the acquisition of the land and the making of the election by means of an amendment;

- any other chargeable transaction where the transfer to the partnership did not fall within para 10.[256]

It will be necessary to determine the market value of each of the chargeable interests that are excluded from the relevant chargeable property. This will be upon the normal principles.[257]

13.63 Where the transfer of the partnership interest is part of a land exchange transaction this is treated as an exchange of a major interest if the partnership property includes a major interest.[258] The provisions excluding partitions from the land exchange rules do not apply, so that a partition of partnership assets will be treated as an exchange.[259]

RELIEFS AND EXEMPTIONS

General

13.64 *Prima facie*, subject to a modification of the relief for transactions for no chargeable consideration[260] all other exemptions and reliefs apply to partnership transactions within the special regime; but numerous provisions are made producing consequential changes in relation to other areas of stamp duty land tax.

No chargeable consideration

13.65 There are no specific reliefs for partnership dealings and the exemption for transactions for no chargeable consideration[261] is disapplied,[262] so that even where there is no chargeable consideration the transaction is notifiable.[263] Other exemptions apply[264] but some of these are modified.[265] It should also be noted that certain transactions are

---

[255] Ibid, Sch 15, para 12A(5).
[256] Ibid, Sch 15, para 14(5A)(f).
[257] See **Chapter 27**.
[258] FA 2003, Sch 15, para 16(1); Sch 4, para 5.
[259] Ibid, Sch 15, para 16(2); Sch 4, para 6.
[260] Ibid, Sch 15, para 25(1), a matter largely related to notification than imposing a charge; see ibid, s 77A.
[261] Ibid, Sch 3, para 1.
[262] Ibid, Sch 15, para 25(1).
[263] Ibid, s 77A; but the transaction may not be notifiable upon the alternative basis that the chargeable consideration is below the £40,000 threshold; see **Chapter 17**.
[264] Ibid, Sch 15, para 25(1); see **Chapter 11**.
[265] Namely: (a) group relief FA 2003, Sch 7, Part 1 and Sch 15, paras 27 and 27A; charities, FA 2003, Sch 15, para 28; and (c) there are modifications for the relief for transactions involving land in a disadvantaged area (FA 2003, Sch 6 and Sch 15, para 26). Although abolished the lack of finality of the tax and the provisional nature of much of the tax means that the relief remains available because later events may have a retrospective effect; see **11.1**.

taxed on a provisional or estimated basis with retrospective adjustments by reference to subsequent events. Since these adjustments ate retrospective any exemptions or reliefs will be determined by reference to the original estimated filing and not by the facts and circumstances as they exist as at the 'review date'. In consequence, for example, changes in the partners should not affect the reduction for the sum of the lower proportions.[266]

It is provided[267] that the provisions relating to transfers for no chargeable consideration do not apply to transactions within the special regime.[268] It would seem that Sch 3, para 1, does not apply where there is, for example, a transfer of land into a partnership and the market value charge is reduced because there is a 100 per cent reduction for the sum of the lower proportions. This provision does not impose a charge to tax in this situation; but it would seem that the intention is that the transaction should be notifiable notwithstanding the exclusion for such transactions pursuant to FA 2003, s 77A. However, the draftsman has not dealt with the interaction of this provision and the alternative threshold for transactions where the chargeable consideration does not exceed £40,000. It is, therefore, arguable that a transaction for no chargeable consideration is not notifiable notwithstanding this provision[269] because it falls under the alternative exclusion from notification for transactions below £40,000 or the nil rate threshold where the interest in question is a minor interest.

Incorporation of limited liability partnerships

13.66 There are exemptions from stamp duty (the obtaining of which will cancel the *prima facie* liability to the principal charge to stamp duty reserve tax) and stamp duty land tax where an existing partnership is converted into a limited liability partnership and there is effectively continuity of the business and the same parties are involved.[270] There are numerous conditions before the relief is available; namely:

- the effective date of the transaction must be not more than 1 year after the date of the incorporation of the limited liability partnership;[271]

- at the time the transferor is a partner in a partnership composed of all the persons who are or are to be members of the limited liability partnership (and no-one else) or the transferor holds the interest as nominee or bare trustee for one or more of the partners in such a partnership;[272] and

- the proportions of the interest transferred to which the persons in the existing partnership are entitled immediately after the transfer are the same as those to which they were entitled at the relevant time which is where the transferor acquired the interest after the incorporation of the limited liability partnership immediately after he acquired the interest and in any other case immediately before the

---

[266] Also the change in the law of December 2006 limiting the relief to individuals will be irrelevant when calculating the tax on subsequent events that operate retrospectively.
[267] FA 2003, Sch 15, para 25(1).
[268] It seems, however, that FA 2003, Sch 3, para 1, does apply where para 17A arises but not where para 17 is involved.
[269] Ibid, Sch 15, para 25(1).
[270] Limited Liability Partnerships Act 2000, s 12; FA 2003, s 65; Tax Bulletin 50.
[271] FA 2003, s 65(2). This limitation period is linked to the incorporation of the limited liability partnership which may be an arbitrary date rather than the date of any contract or proposal to incorporate. Delays in the early stage may, therefore, jeopardise the relief.
[272] FA 2003, s 65(3).

incorporation of the limited liability partnership.[273] In practice, where there are differences in the proportions these are ignored provided that they have not arisen as part of a scheme or arrangement of which the main purpose or one of the main purposes is to avoid liability to any duty or tax. This is to deal with the situation where upon the incorporation existing partners may retire and new partners may be admitted.

Incorporation of partnerships

13.67 There is no exemption for the conversion of a partnership into a company whether or not having limited liability. Transactions to this effect, especially those seeking to rely upon capital gains tax rollover or holdover will, *prima facie*, be exposed to a full charge to tax by reason of the connected company charge upon not less than the market value,[274] because the transfer of a business or chargeable interest from land to a company upon incorporation is likely to involve connected companies.[275] This will give rise to a specific charge within the partnership regime[276] being a specific charge presumably overrides the general charge for dealings with connected companies. This imposes a charge upon the market value of the property but allows a reduction in the market value by reference to the sum of the lower proportions where the chargeable interest is transferred to a 'person' connected with the partners.[277] This would appear to deal with the situation of a transfer to a company which is a connected 'person' although it may not be an individual.[278]

Companies and groups and partnerships

13.68 Two issues arise for the interaction of the rules for partnership transactions and the relief for transactions within a group of companies; namely:

- whether a partnership in which one or more of the group companies interferes with the availability of the group relief; and

- whether the transfer of an interest in a partnership is eligible for the intra-group relief.

Special rules apply to transactions involving acquisitions by connected companies[279] but relief is provided for intra-group transactions;[280] but the fact that the parties are 'connected' does not mean that there will be a stamp duty land tax group since 'connection' is based around a 50 per cent involvement, but group relief requires a 75 per cent shareholding and economic interest. Where there is a stamp duty land tax group the charge is reduced by the sum of the lower proportions that would have

---

[273]   Ibid, s 65(4) and (5).

[274]   Ibid, ss 53 and 54.

[275]   Income and Corporation Taxes Act 1988, s 839.

[276]   FA 2003, Sch 15, para 18.

[277]   See **13.45**.

[278]   See also FA 2003, Sch 15, para 20(1); but note the problems for trustees and others in *Jasmine Trustees Ltd v Wells & Hind* [2007] STC 660.

[279]   FA 2003, ss 53 and 54; see **5.208**.

[280]   Ibid, Sch 7, para 1. There have been difficulties with HMRC Stamp Taxes and intra-group relief for many years where partnerships are involved. They have contended that partnerships mean that the partners do not beneficially own the shares in relevant subsidiaries and/or the land does not vest in the partners as such. Fortunately these views are not, hitherto, consistently pressed in practice.

applied but for the restriction of the relief to individuals.[281] The exemption for intra-group transactions may be available and the rules restricting the relief where there is outside consideration are relaxed;[282] also the clawback provisions for degrouping are modified so that if a partner ceases to be a member of the stamp duty land tax group within the 3-year period still holding the land on behalf of the partnership the relief is cancelled and tax is chargeable.[283]

13.69 Intra-group relief is available but the conditions are modified; namely:

- the anti-avoidance provision[284] relating to the provision of the consideration or part thereof by a non-associated person does not apply;

- as regards the clawback of the relief where the purchaser ceases to be a member of the same group as the vendor the clawback provision[285] applies where a partner who was at the effective date of the transaction a partner and a member of the same group as the transferor leaves the group;

- group relief is specifically applied to transactions involving a transfer to a partnership and to chargeable transactions relating to dealings in partnership interests pursuant to arrangements within FA 2003, Sch 15, para 17.[286] However, when applying these provisions the 'purchaser' is partner who was a partner as at the effective date of the relevant transaction;[287]

- the clawback of relief is modified. A normal clawback applies where the purchaser of the property ceases to be a member of the same group as the vendor and it or a relevant associated company holds a chargeable interest that was acquired under the exempt transaction or derived from that interest.[288] This is replaced by a clawback where the relevant partner ceases to be a member of the same group as the vendor and a chargeable interest is held by or on behalf of the members of the partnership and that chargeable interest was acquired by or on behalf of the partnership under the transaction for which the lease was obtained or is derived from a chargeable interest so acquired and has not subsequently been acquired at market value under a chargeable transaction for which group relief was available but not claimed.[289]

Where there is a partial clawback of the relief the relevant proportion is the proportion to which the relevant partner was entitled at the relevant time to share in the income profits of the partnership.

---

[281] FA 2003, Sch 15, para 27A; Stamp Duty Land Tax (Variation of the Finance Act 2003) Regulations 2006, SI 2006/3237.

[282] FA 2003, Sch 15, para 27A(3); Stamp Duty Land Tax (Variation of the Finance Act 2003) Regulations 2006, SI 2006/3237.

[283] FA 2003, Sch 15, para 27.

[284] Ibid, Sch 7, para 2(2)(a).

[285] Ibid, Sch 7, para 3(1)(a).

[286] Ibid, Sch 15, para 27(1).

[287] Ibid, Sch 15, para 27(2).

[288] Ibid, Sch 7, para 3(1)(b).

[289] Ibid, Sch 15, para 27(3).

Charities

13.70 Transfers of interests in partnerships to charities are exempt provided every chargeable interest held in partnership property is held for charitable purposes,[290] but is subject to clawback if the land ceases to be held for charitable purposes.

Disadvantaged land relief

13.71 Detailed provisions are made for making disadvantaged land relief available where there is a chargeable transaction relating to transfers of partnership interests which are taxable pursuant to para 14 or para 17. These provisions are of potentially limited effect but may still have some residual impact because of the transitional provisions in relation to transactions entered into before 16 March 2005.[291]

---

[290] Ibid, Sch 15, para 28.
[291] Ibid, Sch 15, para 26.

Chapter 14

TAX EVENT

14.1 Notwithstanding that the tax is charged upon any 'acquisition' of a chargeable interest and not in general,[1] by reference to the contract,[2] a tax event which triggers not merely the liability to pay but also begins the notification process, clawback periods etc[3] is not necessarily linked to the vesting or disappearance of the property whether legally or beneficially. The policy of accelerating the tax charge[4] and preventing parties from 'resting on contract' and virtually abolishing subsale relief[5] has produced a situation where a tax charge can arise before any constructive trust arises i e before any interest passes in favour of any relevant party.[6] The charge, therefore, may become effective before any property is 'acquired' within the ordinary meaning of that term since there can be a tax event even in the case of a conditional agreement, such as where a tenant enters into fit out before the relevant landlord(s)' consent, notwithstanding that no interest in the property is at that stage 'acquired' by the tenant.[7]

14.2 Since entry into contract of itself as the tax charge was too early and could produce too many claims where conditions were not satisfied in the contract otherwise terminated before completion It was considered unacceptable in practice to charge stamp duty land tax upon entering into contracts but one of the basic policies of the tax is to prevent people relying upon contracts and not taking a transfer so that an intermediate date between contract and conveyance had to be devised. The tax is transaction and not documentation based notwithstanding that completion is the basic trigger for the tax;[8] but because of the provision of numerous special rules events between contract and completion can bring the tax into operation. Detailed monitoring of such events is indispensable to the efficient management of the tax by taxpayers particularly in relation to the problem of whether the same transaction can have two effective dates especially in the case of leases.[9] However, where there has been an effective date but subsequently the contract is, to any extent, rescinded or annulled or for any other reason is not carried into effect, the tax or the appropriate part thereof is recoverable by the taxpayer,[10] except in relation to leases.[11] Similar rules apply in relation

---

[1]   But note special rules such as options and pre-emption rights FA 2003, s 46.

[2]   Ibid, s 119 and as a special rule s 44(2); see also, for example, s 45(2) and 45A(2). Note also that the tax charge may arise notwithstanding that the contract is conditional such as an agreement to assign a lease subject to obtaining the landlord's consent; see *Warmington v Miller* [1973] 2 All ER 372.

[3]   See **2.2**, **7.25** and **14.5**.

[4]   See **2.9**.

[5]   FA 2003, s 45 and attacking these transactions specifically in the illustrative list in the general anti-avoidance provisions FA 2003, s 75A; see **Chapter 6**.

[6]   Which normally applies only where the consideration has been paid or provided in full: *Michaels v Harley House (Marylebone) Ltd* [1999] 3 WLR 229; *Musselwhite v Musselwhite* [1962] 1 Ch 210; *Parway Estates Ltd v IRC* 45 TC 135; *Re Kidner* [1929] 2 Ch 121; *Langen and Wind Ltd v Bell* [1972] Ch 685.

[7]   See, eg, *Warmington v Miller* [1973] 2 All ER 372.

[8]   FA 2003, s 42(2)(a); see **3.7**.

[9]   Ibid, s 44(8); Sch 17A, para 12B.

[10]   Ibid, s 44(9).

[11]   Ibid, s 44(10); Sch 17A, paras 12A(3) and 19 (Scotland).

to substantial performance of agreements for lease[12] so that where the agreement, as a whole or in part, is substantially rescinded or annulled or is for any other reason not carried into effect, the tax paid upon substantial performance is recoverable by the taxpayer who must claim repayment by an amendment to the land transaction return (SDLT 1) filed at substantial performance. There is a technical problem in that amendments may be made only within 12 months unless otherwise provided.[13] It remains to be seen whether this claim procedure is, by implication, within the 'otherwise provided' category; but it is necessary for an 'amendment' to be accompanied by the relevant documentation,[14] as is necessary in agreements not involving leases which are rescinded or annulled. Interest is payable by HMRC Stamp Taxes upon the amount repaid.[15]

TAX CHARGE

14.3 It is provided[16] that tax is due by reference to the 'effective date'.[17] HMRC Stamp Taxes are given power to change the effective date by regulation,[18] and this is no doubt part of the power to accelerate the payment and filing obligations if e-conveyancing is introduced since HMRC may also reduce the filing and, in consequence, the payment period.[19] The 'effective date' is defined as being the date of completion.[20] However, this is expressly made subject to any special provisions of which there are many and which, in practice, apply to virtually every transaction,[21] namely:

- where there is a contract which contemplates completion in writing, the effective date is the earlier of completion or substantial performance.[22] This will apply to virtually every contract for sale or lease since standard conditions generally provide that the purchaser or lessee will receive a written instrument including a deed of release or variation at completion. This will apply notwithstanding that there is a power in the contract to subsell or assign the benefit of the contract and/or the parties themselves do not intend to complete or they intend that legal title will be granted to a third party. It is only in extremely unusual circumstances such as where the vendor agrees to hold the property on trust for the purchaser;[23]

- where there is an agreement to grant an option or pre-emptive right;[24]

- contracts providing for a conveyance to a third party;[25]

- subsale and assignment of contracts providing for a conveyance to a third party;[26]

---

[12] Ibid, Sch 17A, para 12A(4).
[13] Ibid, Sch 10, para 6(3).
[14] Ibid, Sch 10, para 6(2)(b); see further **17.26**.
[15] Ibid, s 89.
[16] Ibid, s 76.
[17] This differs from the filing date but provides the basis for calculating that date; FA 2003, Sch 10, para 2(1).
[18] Ibid, s 119(1)(b).
[19] Ibid, s 86(1) (as amended).
[20] Ibid, s 119 (as amended) to permit this to be changed by regulation.
[21] Ibid, s 119(1) and (2) (as amended).
[22] Ibid, s 44.
[23] But an undertaking to execute a declaration of trust will be a 'written completion' within the special rule.
[24] FA 2003, s 46.
[25] Ibid, FA 2003, s 119(2); s 44A(3).
[26] Ibid, s 45A(8).

- agreements for lease and subsequent grants[27] where there appears to be two chargeable transactions with two separate effective dates;[28]

- assignment of agreements for lease,[29] after the agreement has been substantially performed.[30]

14.4 Other dates may have an effect on the tax position:

- where there has been a relief which is clawed back the effective date is the date of the original transaction not the later transaction which triggers the clawback,[31] notwithstanding that the latter date established the start date for the clawback payment and compliance procedures;

- the original effective date may be relevant for the purposes of reliefs. Much of the tax is initially assessed on a provisional or estimated basis which has to be revised subsequently and frequently retrospectively.[32] This may affect the rates of tax and thresholds as well as the availability of exemptions and reliefs;

- where there is a withdrawal of money or money's worth from a partnership within the 3 years following the transfer of the land into the partnership the effective date is the date of the withdrawal;

- where there is a rent review or similar variation of the rent the effective date is the original effective date for the lease[33] not the date of the rent review (although the latter date is important for the compliance regime);[34]

- detailed rules apply for determining the 5 year period for rent reviews;[35]

- where there are subsequent linked transactions including successive linked leases the effective date for the original transaction remains unchanged although the tax has to be retrospectively adjusted, and the compliance regime commences from the effective date for the later linked transaction;

- leases that 'continue' after expiration such as by holding over retain their original effective date requiring retrospective adjustment with compliance on a potentially annual basis if the rent is or becomes taxable taking effect from the anniversary of the termination of the lease;[36]

---

27 Ibid, FA 2003, s 119(2); Sch 17A, para 12A.
28 See **7.25**.
29 Ibid, FA 2003, s 119(2); Sch 17A, para 12B; and Sch 17A, para 19(3) for Scotland.
30 Ibid, Sch 17A, paras 7 and 8.
31 Ibid, Sch 7, paras 3 and 9.
32 See **11.1**.
33 Determined pursuant to ibid, Sch 17A, para 12A.
34 FA 2003, Sch 17A, paras 7 and 8.
35 Ibid, Sch 17A, para 7A.
36 Ibid, Sch 17A, paras 3 and 4.

- where there is an assignment of a lease that was exempt for certain reasons when granted which is taxed upon assignment as the grant of a new lease the effective date appears to be the date that would apply to the effective date for the contract to assign the lease;[37]

- no special effective date is specified for the deemed grant of a new lease in respect of any increase of rent otherwise than pursuant to the terms of the lease during the first 5 years of the term.[38] On general principles this would seem to be the execution of the deed of variation (ie 'completion') unless, perhaps, there is a prior payment of the additional rent;

- where there is an abnormal increase in the rent after the expiration of the fifth year of the term there is deemed to be the grant of a new lease on the date on which the increased rent first becomes payable rather than paid. This is, presumably, the effective date. This raises a practical issue where the new rent is effectively backdated to a prior rent review date. In this situation it is a question whether the rent becomes 'payable' as from the earlier date or, as is considered to be the better view, only from the date when the new rent is finally agreed;[39]

- no express effective dates are provided for other variations of leases such as modifications of the covenant or reduction of rent.[40] Such transactions are treated as acquisitions of chargeable interests by the relevant party and presumably the special rules for contracts contemplating completion in writing apply so that the effective date is the earlier of execution of the deed of variation or substantial performance, which will usually be payment of the reduced rent or the consideration for the variation since the taxpayer will usually already be in possession under the lease so that there is no new taking of possession;[41]

- the term commencement date for leases (which will frequently be different from the date of the agreement for lease, substantial performance and the actual grant) has many implications for tax computations.[42]

Given the provisional, estimated and retrospective nature of much of stamp duty land tax subsequent events may not generate new effective dates but they do have an impact on the original self-assessment such as rent reviews during the first 5 years of the term or subsequent linked transactions which can include lease renewals or holding over. The dates of such subsequent events are important since although they may relate back to the original effective date the payment and notification procedures commence on the date of the later event.[43] The effective date is potentially a key issue for third parties, particularly assignees of leases, who may, by statute, be affected by the open tax position of the original taxpayer[44] or whose tax position may be related to that of the original taxpayer such as an assignee holding over an expired lease pursuant to the Landlord and

---

[37] Ibid, Sch 17A, para 11.

[38] Ibid, Sch 17A, para 13 (as amended); compare para 14(5)(a).

[39] And Sch 17A, para 14(5)(a), which will not necessarily be the date when a memorandum of the new rent is endorsed upon the lease.

[40] FA 2003, Sch 17A, para 15A.

[41] Ibid, s 44.

[42] See, for example, FA 2003, Sch 17A, paras 7A, 9 and 9A; see **Chapter 7**.

[43] There will, of course, be significant practical problems for dealing with such subsequent events when e-conveyancing with its instant payment requirements becomes fully operational since most of such subsequent events do not involve the Land Registry.

[44] See, for example FA 2003, s 81A; Sch 17A, para 12.

Tenant Act 1954[45] because it relates back to the original tax return. In these cases it is not necessarily prudent to assume that the date of completion as appearing and lease or conveyance is the correct date. In a sense the effective date has become an issue of title.

SIGNIFICANCE OF THE EFFECTIVE DATE

14.5 In addition to being a potential 'title' issue for third parties[46] the effective date is of wider importance than merely triggering the charge to stamp duty land tax. Numerous consequences flow by reference to the time of the effective date, namely:

- the taxpayer is required to notify the tax by filing the land transaction return before the end of the period of 30 days after the effective date;[47]

- penalties for failure to file a return run from and are graduated by reference to the time elapsed since the thirtieth day after the effective date;[48]

- the power for the taxpayer to amend a return is *prima facie* limited to the period of 12 months after the expiration of 30 days from the effective date;[49]

- the time for maintaining records is *prima facie* 6 years from the effective date;[50]

- the basic power of HMRC Stamp Taxes to issue a determination of tax due is generally for 6 years from the effective date.[51] A similar period of limitation applies to powers to assess the tax.[52] However, discovery assessments may be issued for up to 21 years;[53]

- VAT arising as a result of the exercise of the option to tax exercised after the effective date is not chargeable to stamp duty land tax[54] unless it relates to rent and operates as an increase in the rent;[55]

- where the market value of consideration in land is involved this is to be determined by reference to its value as at the effective date;[56]

- the nature of any variable consideration will be affected since this has to be judged as at the effective date and problems may arise where there is an interval between substantial performance and completion. For example, land may be sold for a consideration linked to market value as at completion. Should the purchaser take

---

[45] Ibid, Sch 17A, paras 3, 9 and 9A.
[46] See, for example, ibid, s 81A and Sch 17A, para 12; see **7.235**.
[47] Ibid, s 76(1).
[48] Ibid, Sch 10, paras 2–5.
[49] Ibid, Sch 10, para 6; but note para 7.
[50] Ibid, Sch 10, para 9. However, insofar as the records have indirectly become documents of title (see **2.15**, **7.242**) it will, in practice, be necessary to retain appropriate records (which are more extensive than the records required for tax purposes) for much longer periods.
[51] Ibid, Sch 10, para 25.
[52] Ibid, Sch 10, para 31.
[53] Ibid, Sch 10, para 31(2).
[54] Ibid, Sch 4, para 2.
[55] See **5.126**, **5.220**, **7.67** and **7.118**.
[56] FA 2003, Sch 4, para 7.

possession of the land prior to completion the consideration will be uncertain[57] when it may be possible postpone payment of the tax, but at completion it will become unascertained when the tax cannot be postponed;[58]

- the amount of any debts or liabilities assumed as part of the consideration, including outstanding interest, is determined at the effective date;[59]

- the conversion of foreign currency is at the rate of exchange on the effective date;[60]

- whether works carried out on the land to be acquired are exempt depends upon whether they are carried out before or after the effective date[61] or substantial performance where there is a later grant of the lease;

- when calculating the net present value of the rent, the length of the lease term is calculated by reference to the effective date[62] which may change where there is separate substantial performance and completion;[63]

- whether a person is entitled to subsale relief depends upon whether he has generated an effective date for his contract before or at the same time as the effective date for the subsale or assignment;[64]

- where a lease is granted to a third party at the direction of the original tenant the availability of 'subsale' relief for the original tenant and the tax liability of the third party depends upon whether the 'assignment of the right as lessee under the agreement' takes place before or after there has been substantial performance of the original agreement for lease;[65]

- it is considered that, although not stated in the legislation, the rate of tax or the temporal discount rate to be applied when calculating the net present value of the rent is the relevant rate in force at the effective date, and that these rates and not any changes in the temporal discount rate in the intervening period continue to apply where there are subsequent reporting and payment obligations of a retrospective nature in relation to the same chargeable transaction, such as subsequent payments in relation to uncertain consideration or variable rents;

- the period during which reliefs or intra-group transactions, company reconstructions and acquisition by charities are subject to clawback is calculated from the effective date;[66]

- the first instalment of any stamp duty land tax has to be paid within 30 days after the effective date;[67]

---

[57]   Ibid, s 51.
[58]   Ibid, s 90(1)(a).
[59]   Ibid, Sch 4, para 8.
[60]   Ibid, Sch 4, para 9.
[61]   Ibid, Sch 4, para 10(2)(a) (as amended).
[62]   Ibid, Sch 5, para 6 (repealed, but it is thought to represent the current view); see **7.113**.
[63]   Ibid, Sch 17A, para 12A; see **7.25** and **14.7**.
[64]   Ibid, s 45(3).
[65]   Ibid, Sch 17A, para 12B(3) and s 119(2).
[66]   Ibid, Sch 7, paras 3(1) and 9(1) and Sch 8, para 2(1).
[67]   Ibid, s 86(1).

- interest on unpaid tax generally runs from 30 days after the effective date,[68] unless the tax is declared and postponed.[69]

Effective date and notifiable transactions

14.6 There are many situations where a transaction whether or not written has to be notified within the 30 day filing period.[70] Many of these notifiable events will not be chargeable transactions in their own right and may not involve dealings with the Land Registry, but filing is required. In these cases which will frequently arise because of the lack of finality in the tax structure[71] and the effective date for the purposes of self-assessing the tax or claiming any relief will be the effective date for an earlier stage in the transaction or some other transaction. This retrospective separation of effective date and filing date has to be noted.

One effective date or two?[72]

14.7 A major issue of principle for the basic special provision for effective dates namely substantial performance[73] has arisen as a consequence of the changes made in relation to the grant of new leases. This issue is whether where there is a separation of formal completion from substantial performance or some other specified event which applies to create an effective date such as where a tenant enters into possession to fit out prior to grant there is one effective date or two, ie one or two chargeable transactions.[74]

14.8 It was originally believed that there was only one effective date and one chargeable transaction notwithstanding this temporal separation. Some doubt existed because it is provided[75] that where substantial performance of a contract contemplating completion in writing precedes actual completion the effective date is the date of substantial performance. This would suggest that there is only one effective date and all subsequent events are, in the absence of special rules, related retrospectively to that date.

14.9 Unfortunately three sets of legislation have cast doubt upon this simple and sensible principle of a single effective date; but it is crucial to note that when making a key amendment[76] the draftsman specifically refers to the relevant provisions namely FA 2003, s 44(8) and Sch 17A, para 12A[77] as creating a 'notifiable' not 'chargeable' transaction but totally misses the fundamental point that the issue is related to effective and notifiable dates. Clearly he was not properly instructed or did not understand what he was doing:

- FA 2003, s 44(8), states that where a contract is substantially performed and subsequently completed as between the same parties[78] both substantial performance and completion are 'notifiable transactions'. This is a necessary provision since notification is required in order to produce the Inland Revenue

---

[68]   Ibid, s 87(3)(c) but note s 87(5).
[69]   Ibid, s 87; Stamp Duty Land Tax (Administration) Regulations 2003, SI 2003/2837, Part 4.
[70]   See **Chapter 17**.
[71]   See **2.14**.
[72]   See also **7.25**.
[73]   FA 2003, s 44(3) and (4).
[74]   Ibid, s 44(8)(a); Sch 17A, para 12A(2) and 3(a).
[75]   Ibid, s 44(8)(b).
[76]   Ibid, Sch 4, para 10(2A).
[77]   And the Scottish equivalent provisions in FA 2003, Sch 17A, para 19.
[78]   In consequence this provision does not apply to subsales and similar arrangements.

Certificate (SDLT 5) needed for registration of title.[79] It would be inefficient where there has been substantial performance for HMRC Stamp Taxes to permit registration of the completion without a certificate since this would not provide any assurance that the prior substantial performance had taken place and the tax paid. Unfortunately those preparing the legislation go on to provide that tax is chargeable on the completion to the extent, if any, that the tax chargeable on completion between the same parties is greater than the amount of tax chargeable on the contract, ie at substantial performance.[80] The draftsman has had no difficulty in other parts of the legislation in stating whether a transaction is or is not to be treated as a chargeable transaction[81] but for some reason finds that a problem here. It is merely stated that the transaction is notifiable, not that it is a separate chargeable transaction, and merely that additional tax, if any, arising is payable. Since much of stamp duty land tax is provisional only and relates back,[82] this could merely be a reference to an amendment to or adjustment in the original return upon the basis that events taking place at completion between the same parties requires a retrospective adjustment in the return filed and tax provisionally paid as of the effective date. The problem has been an attempt to find a situation where additional tax is payable at completion that is not covered by other rules. For example, where the purchase price is related to the market value at completion the consideration will be uncertain at substantial performance and will become unascertained at completion pursuant to FA 2003, s 51 which requires adjustments to be made[83] if only because the consideration has changed from uncertain to unascertained and in the official view from time to time the estimated tax cannot be postponed any longer[84] so that in this type of situation the provisions of s 44(8)(b) thereof are redundant. Moreover to suggest that it creates a second 'chargeable' as opposed to a merely 'notifiable' transaction could create major issues of principle any reliefs available as at substantial performance will not be automatically carried forward to completion or vice versa even if there is a true wait-and-see for these purposes. Clawback dates would be brought forward, building works could become taxable but a specific relief has been introduced[85] to deal with sales and new leases. This relief is not necessary if there is only one effective date so that its enactment is an indication that there are two effective dates. However, if as the draftsman appears to believe, 'notifiable transaction' and 'chargeable transaction' are synonymous[86] there will be major issues such as where the option to tax the land for the purposes of VAT is exercised in the interval between substantial performance and completion the VAT will be subject to stamp duty land tax as actual VAT arising as at the second effective date. Any exemption

[79] FA 2003, ss 77 and 79 (as both amended).
[80] Ibid, s 44(8)(b). This overlooks the principles whereby other actions between substantial performance and completion may have produced notifiable events and situations where additional tax has become payable. It also means that no additional tax will necessarily be payable where the completion is between different parties such as on a subsale (FA 2003, s 45(2) and (3)).
[81] See, for example, ibid 2003, Sch 17A, para 13 deeming there to be a new 'grant'; Sch 15, paras 17(2) and 17A(4).
[82] See **2.14**.
[83] See also FA 2003, s 80.
[84] Ibid, ss 57, 90 and 80, but there is some doubt because s 80 refers to consideration becoming 'ascertained' whereas in the illustration in the tax the consideration becomes 'unascertained'.
[85] Ibid, Sch 4, para 10(2A).
[86] Although this raises issues as to why the particular term was utilised especially as 'notifiable transaction' would in the overall context of the legislation mean that details of chargeable transactions that have to be notified. Not all chargeable transactions are notifiable, but it seems that the draftsman is reversing the meaning so that a notifiable transaction has to be chargeable with their own effective dates; see also FA 2003, s 44(8)(a).

which was available as at substantial performance will not automatically be carried over to completion; the availability of any relief will have to be reassessed by reference to the circumstances as they exist at completion. Conversely a transaction may be entitled to a relief at completion but not at substantial performance, but whilst this means that no additional tax is payable there is no refund claim for the tax paid at substantial performance. If, as seems likely, HMRC Stamp Taxes intend to argue for two effective dates there will be a long period of uncertainty whilst the difficulties are discovered and resolved;

- a specific provision deals with substantial performance of any agreement for lease and the subsequent grant.[87] It is clearly the view of HMRC Stamp Taxes that this provision, which was needed only to amend a technical defect in the compliance regime, creates two separate chargeable transactions. The provisions dealing with events between substantial performance and grant and the rules dealing with the deemed lease and the actual lease as not being a single lease indicate two separate chargeable events.[88] In the case of leases this subsequent effective date on a separate lease means that many changes have to be made in the tax assessments for the lease. For example, the 5 years for rent reviews recommences and the time between substantial performance and grant is effectively lost for clawback provisions. The whole net present value of the rent has to be revised and the term of the lease reduced;[89] and

- there have been amendments to the relief for works carried out on the land being acquired.[90] The relief is dependent upon the appropriate works being carried out after the effective date. *Prima facie*, this would relieve any works carried out after substantial performance of the agreement for lease but as the subsequent grant of the lease is, in the view of HMRC Stamp Taxes, a separate chargeable event such works will precede the effective date for the grant of the lease and so be outside the relief in relation to the grant thereby retrospectively cancelling the relief. It is, therefore, provided[91] that works after substantial performance of the agreement for lease are not taxable in respect of the subsequent grant. This, of course, provides support for HMRC Stamp Taxes on the two effective date argument since, if there were not two effective dates, this relief would not be necessary and the current judiciary are most unlikely to accept an argument that such legislation is unnecessary or redundant.

This emerging doctrine of two separate chargeable transactions with separate effective dates and not merely a need for multiple notifications of the same chargeable transaction, will provide many potential traps for the unwary particularly in relation to leases since the date of the grant is frequently in practice rather arbitrary, being a matter of convenience rather than necessity. Unfortunately there will be great pressure to complete at substantial performance or as soon thereafter or proceed straight to completion as is possible in order to minimise the risks generated by a delay.

---

[87] Ibid, Sch 17A, para 12A; see **6.57** and **7.14**.
[88] Ibid, Sch 17A, para 12A.
[89] See further **7.25**.
[90] FA 2003, Sch 10, para 4.
[91] Ibid, Sch 4, para 10(2A).

THE GENERAL RULE – THE THEORY AND THE PRACTICE

14.10   The legislation provides a basic starting rule for determining the effective date namely 'completion'.[92] However, this is subject to other provisions one of which refers to a contract and conveyance within the terms of FA 2003, s 44.[93] Section 44 applies wherever a contract for a land transaction is entered into under which the transaction is to be completed by a 'conveyance'.[94] Since 'conveyance' includes any written instrument,[95] however one interprets the word 'conveyance' which is currently a practical problem because the word had a well established meaning in stamp duty and it is unclear how much baggage HMRC Stamp Taxes intend to bring forward into the new regime;[96] it is clear that, in practice, virtually every contract, certainly those in standard form, will contain some provision requiring the vendor, landlord, grantor or other disposing party to deliver some form of writing at completion. Moreover, it seems to be a matter of the terms of the contract not the intention of the parties. If the arrangements worked upon intention and relied upon the factual situation the tax would be virtually unworkable. For example, where a purchaser enters into a contract intending to turn the contract by means of some form of subsale these provisions would not apply notwithstanding that the contract provided that the vendor would, at completion, deliver an instrument in favour of the purchaser or as the purchaser may direct. In consequence, it must simply be a question of whether the vendor has to produce some writing. This, as indicated, is likely to apply to virtually every contract that is entered into in routine practice so that s 44 will apply.

Although described[97] as a special rule, the almost inevitable consequence of contractual drafting and practice is that FA 2003, s 44 will be the basic principle for determining the effective date for virtually all transactions. This 'special rule' provides:[98]

- if the transaction is completed[99] between the same parties in substantial conformity with the contract without previously having been substantially performed the effective date of the chargeable transaction is the date of completion; and

---

[92]   Ibid, s 119.

[93]   Ibid, s 119(2).

[94]   Ibid, s 44(1).

[95]   It will be noted that this definition in FA 2003, s 44(10)(b) but does not state that it is to be an instrument that operates to convey or transfer property. There will, therefore, be significant issues as to whether any writing that was regarded as a 'conveyance' or completion instrument for the purposes of stamp duty will be carried forward as a matter of practice into the new regime so that powers of attorney given to a purchaser may, in certain circumstances, operate as a 'conveyance' or equitable assignment. However, it seems that the nature of the instrument must be described in the contract as being the piece of paper that will be delivered at completion therefore there may be questions as to certain types of powers of attorney depending upon whether they are delivered at completion or as part of some interim arrangement or to deal with situations where the contract is not performed by the vendor; see, for example, *Diplock v Hammond* (1854) 5 De GM & G 320; *Roddick v Gandell* (1852) 1 De G M & G 763.

[96]   This issue is complicated in two ways: (i) the current staff of HMRC Stamp Taxes appear to be unaware of the traditional and general meaning of terms in stamp taxes; and (ii) in *Rothschild Holdings plc v IRC* [1988] STC 645 (on appeal on other grounds [1989] STC 435), Vinelott J bizarrely accepted that where there were different approaches between senior management and policy makers and lower grade employees the views of the lower grades had to prevail. This also emerged in relation to the statement of practice on the interaction of stamp duty and VAT. The original version had to be withdrawn notwithstanding it was issued by senior management because the lower grant employees did not like its terms. Reliance upon guidance for senior employees is therefore a waste of time.

[97]   FA 2003, s 119(2).

[98]   Ibid, s 44(3) and (4).

[99]   The key definition of the tax point, i e the effective date, is the date of 'completion'. It is explained (FA 2003,

- if the contract is substantially performed without having been previously completed the effective date of the chargeable transaction is when the contract is substantially performed.[100]

Where the effective date is substantial performance the subsequent completion between the same parties is a notifiable transaction.[101]

The general principle in conveyancing practice

14.11 Given the routine conveyancing process which almost invariably whether by standard form conditions or express terms, requires the vendor to hand over some documentary title (i.e. a 'conveyance') the normal timetable for stamp duty land tax is likely to be:

- execution or exchange of contracts, which, unless the purchaser or lessee is already in possession under some other arrangement,[102] which is replaced by the contract, such as the grant of a new lease to a tenant holding over an expired lease, should not normally trigger a charge to the tax;[103]

- possibly substantial performance, such as taking possession or paying or providing the consideration without taking a transfer, which does trigger a charge to the tax;[104] and

- completion, in the sense of taking the conveyance or lease or other deed or possibly a power of attorney,[105] whether or not accompanied by payment or possession, which does trigger a tax charge or a further tax charge and notification obligations if there has been prior substantial performance.[106]

In most cases, in practice, substantial performance and completion will coincide or the parties will proceed straight to completion without a contract,[107] which should usually mean that only one payment and notification obligation arises.[108] However, this will not always be the case, and taxpayers and their advisers need to be aware of the possible acceleration of the tax charge from 'completion' to the 'effective date'. This may require adjustments to conveyancing practice, particularly where this has been operated on a process basis. The actions of the purchaser or tenant between contract and completion may need to be monitored in order to ensure that his activities do not constitute

---

s 121) that in Scotland 'completion' means settlement of the transaction, but no other guidance is given as to what constitutes 'completion'. In consequence, the normal concept of completion of delivery of the title deeds and transfer documentation or grant of a new lease against payment apply. The main emphasis, however, is upon the delivery of the transfer or lease or other deed rather than payment.

[100] The fact that events that would constitute substantial performance such as first payment of rent occur after completion or occur at the same time as completion is irrelevant and does not produce another chargeable or notifiable event.

[101] FA 2003, s 44(8); but see **7.25**.

[102] But note the special rules for options and pre-emption rights, FA 2003, s 46.

[103] Such as where a tenant who is holding over enters into a new agreement for lease so that his status as occupier changes from licensee to prospective tenant.

[104] FA 2003, s 44(3); Sch 17A, para 12A(5).

[105] *Diplock v Hammond* (1854) 5 De GM & G 320.

[106] FA 2003, s 44(8); Sch 17A, para 12A.

[107] But there may be many cases where the parties delay completion such as a landlord refusing to agree to completion until the stipulated works by the tenant have been completed or there is a development of a phased nature where the seller will complete only against payment etc.

[108] FA 2003, s 119.

substantial performance triggering an effective date, particularly where the professional adviser is signing a split land transaction return confirming the effective date. Should the solicitor sign for the effective date as being completion when the purchaser has received the keys and entered into occupation of the land in order to carry out repairs or improvements he will be participating in an incorrect return which if he 'knows' of the error exposes him to penalty[109] to the funding arrangements so that the taxpayer is in a position to pay the tax where this is due and payable before the taxpayer is in a position to drawdown funds under the main financing agreement, and the lender may be reluctant to provide the funds because the taxpayer may not be in a position to provide satisfactory security. This will be particularly acute where the taxpayer inadvertently, or through bad advice, triggers an effective date earlier than intended, such as by going into possession. However, where the taxpayer is entering upon the land for the purposes of fitting out or commencing building operations then although there is the inconvenience of possible multiple reporting there is the potential benefit of relief from the charge to tax upon building works.[110] It may be necessary to generate an early effective date through substantial performance in order to take advantage of this relief.

The question is, therefore, in virtually every transaction whether there has been substantial performance before completion.

Substantial performance

14.12 These special provisions, as they apply in practice, mean that the basic charging provisions are in practice, therefore, based upon 'substantial performance', ie the policy is that parties can no longer rest on contract and subsell their way out of a charge to tax.[111] The question of substantial performance depends upon whether or not the transaction involves a lease. Substantial performance involves two potential events for most transactions namely:

- the purchaser either taking possession of the whole or substantially the whole of the land; or

- paying substantially the whole of the purchase price.

Both of these concepts apply to conveyances and to leases in terms of payment of the premium or taking possession of the demised premises but there are manifest difficulties in relation to easements and restrictive covenants, such as when a person who is to construct a pipeline under the land of another, can take 'possession' of a hole in the ground not yet fully constructed or even started which could mean that the entire construction costs are subject to stamp duty land tax. In addition, for leases the first actual payment of rent is an event of substantial performance. Each of these events requires further explanation.

Transactions not involving leases

14.13 For transactions not involving a lease, the contract is substantially performed when either:

---

[109]   Ibid, s 96; Sch 10, para 8; see also *Slattery v Moore Stephens* [2003] STC 1379 on completing a tax return without asking the right questions being negligence.

[110]   Ibid, Sch 4, para 10(2); see **Chapter 8**.

[111]   Note the restrictions upon the new relief; ibid, s 45 (as amended); see **Chapter 6**.

(a)   the purchaser takes possession of the whole or substantially the whole of the chargeable interest together with any other interest or right appurtenant or pertaining to the chargeable interest that is acquired with it;[112] or

(b)   a substantial amount of the consideration is paid or provided;[113]

whichever is the earlier.

14.14 In consequence, the effective date is the earliest of the following:[114]

- completion between the same parties;[115]

- payment of a substantial proportion of the consideration; or

- entry into 'possession' of the whole or substantially the whole of the property together with any other interest or right appurtenant or pertaining to the chargeable interest to be acquired.

Where completion has taken place the fact that acts which could constitute substantial performance occur at the same time or subsequently is irrelevant; such events are ignored as such for the effective date but may constitute events that are notifiable and may produce a liability to pay additional tax.

Transactions involving leases

14.15 For transactions involving a lease, the transaction is substantially performed when either:[116]

- the purchaser or a person connected with the purchaser takes possession of the whole or substantially the whole of the chargeable interest together with any other interest or right appurtenant or pertaining to the chargeable interest that is acquired with it;[117] or

- a substantial amount[118] of the consideration other than rent ie premium is paid or provided;[119] or

- the first actual payment of rent,

whichever is the earliest. For transactions involving limited interests in land such as easements where it may be difficult if not impossible to take 'possession' it may be tax

---

[112]   FA 2003, s 44(4)(b).
[113]   Ibid, s 44(4)(a).
[114]   Ibid, s 44(7), (4) and (5).
[115]   Events subsequent to completion do not affect the issue of the effective date for the basic transaction but such events may be chargeable transactions in their own right.
[116]   FA 2003, s 44(3), (4), (5) and (7).
[117]   Ibid, s 44(5)(a) (as amended).
[118]   Ibid, s 44(7)(a) and (b).
[119]   Ibid, s 44(6)(b).

efficient to convert the transaction into a lease[120] and pay rent in order to trigger substantial performance to protect construction costs.[121]

Each of these tests requires detailed investigation.

Possession

14.16 'Possession' has a technical meaning in land law[122] and it is provided that in addition to taking physical possession of the relevant proportion of the land a purchaser is to be regarded as taking possession for the purposes of stamp duty land tax if he receives or becomes entitled to receive rents and profits.[123] It is immaterial whether the purchaser takes possession under a contract or pursuant to a licence or lease or other arrangement of a temporary nature.[124]

14.17 This test of possession as physical entry into and occupation of the land gives rise to difficulties as to the typical presence upon the land that constitutes 'possession' in the physical sense, particularly as it includes possession as a licensee or tenant at will or under a temporary arrangement, which is not necessarily sufficiently exclusive to constitute a tenancy.[125] There are, however, fundamental issues how 'exclusive' the occupation must be to constitute 'possession', how temporary the occupation may be, whether there can be joint or multiple possession of the land and whether such shared possession is sufficient to constitute substantial performance. Also where there is joint occupation whether the fact that one of the joint occupiers is the owner of the land is inconsistent with other parties who are upon the land as licensees having possession. For example, where an elderly parent is living in a house and arranges with a son or daughter that if they live with him and care for him they will become entitled to the house, ie there is potentially a contract to transfer the land in consideration of the performance of services, the question is whether such joint occupation involving a licence[126] also involves the son or daughter entering into possession because the parent already has possession (ie there is the fundamental issue of principle whether two or more persons can simultaneously be in joint possession of land).[127]

14.18 Problems will frequently arise where prospective tenants are allowed to enter upon the land but only for limited purposes such as fitting out[128] or making good dilapidations prior to the grant of the lease. The official attitude as to whether such licence constitutes 'possession' remains unclear but, since such licences are not exclusive and the licensor retains stronger rights to the land, it is considered that they should not involve taking possession. Other questions of 'split occupation' or 'joint possession' can arise. For example, it is not unusual as part of a building arrangement whereby the developer or builder is to construct premises to a particular level and then step back allowing the purchaser or tenant to enter upon the land to commence the first phase of

---

[120] But note the special definition of 'lease' pursuant to FA 2003, Sch 17A, para 9(a).

[121] Ibid, Sch 4, para 10.

[122] See Law of Property Act 1925, s 205(1)(xix); this Act also draws a distinction between 'possession' and 'occupation' – see, eg, ss 14 and 51; and the VAT legislation also refers to licences to occupy which appear to be different from licences to enter upon land for a purely temporary purpose and do not give exclusive rights to a particular area of land.

[123] FA 2003, s 44(6)(a) (as amended).

[124] Ibid, s 44(6)(b) (as amended).

[125] *Street v Mountford* [1985] 1 AC 809.

[126] *Errington v Errington & Woods* [1952] 1 KB 290.

[127] The terms of the arrangement may alternatively create a settlement see *Binnions v Evans* [1972] Ch 359.

[128] FA 2003, Sch 4, para 10(2)(a); see **Chapter 8**.

fitting out operations. Once this initial fitting out has reached the specified stage the purchaser or tenant steps back and the developer re-enters the premises and completes the building and other works at which point the purchaser or tenant enters in order to complete the fitting out. It is obviously important from the tenant's point of view that the first phase of fitting out constitutes substantial performance in order to protect the costs of his fitting out works from liability to stamp duty land tax.[129] It is, of course, possible to argue that fitting out works are not part of the consideration; but in these circumstances, given the commercial pressures, it is unlikely that the tenant will be allowed to operate merely on permission and the developer or seller will wish to impose positive restrictions or obligations upon the purchaser or tenant to carry out the particular works. This means that they are likely to be part of the consideration for the arrangement and not mere permissions.[130] HMRC Stamp Taxes are firmly of the view that merely receiving the keys is sufficient to constitute possession even where the person does not make a physical entry onto the land. This is not correct as an absolute principle since 'possession' requires some degree of exclusivity. It is considered that a person does not take possession if the original owner remains in occupation and the taxpayer has only limited access[131] for a limited purpose such as being allowed onto the land only during certain hours solely to fit out the premises.

14.19 Tenants seeking to protect their fitting out costs or purchasers seeking to protect the cost of any building or infrastructure works that they are carrying out on the land from the charge to tax upon costs that form part of the consideration there are also major issues of principle yet to be resolved relating to certain types of easement or similar arrangement. For example, an oil or water company may wish to enter into an arrangement to acquire some interest in land for the purposes of laying a pipeline. Hopefully, in these situations, the documentation will be structured in such a way that the construction works will not be part of the consideration;[132] but should they be part of the consideration then it will be necessary to set up the transaction in such a way that it should be possible to acquire a major interest and trigger an effective date before substantial expenditure is incurred such as by taking a lease and paying rent rather than a different interest for a fee. There are obvious difficulties about taking possession of a hole in the ground that is yet to be constructed. Should there not be possession then effectively the whole of the costs will be subject to tax. In these situations the taxpayer may need to consider some form of revision of the arrangements such as taking a lease of the underground rights and making a payment of rent.

Substantially the whole

14.20 The possession must relate to the whole or substantially[133] the whole of the land.[134] No guidance has been provided by HMRC Stamp Taxes on this issue but it seems that significantly more than 50 per cent of the land must be occupied. This can be

---

[129] Ibid, Sch 4, para 10(2).

[130] Compare *Eastham v Leigh, London and Provincial Properties Limited* [1971] 2 All ER 887.

[131] However, limited access which contains provision for the landowner to enter to investigate progress is likely to create a tenancy; see *Addiscombe Garden Estates Ltd v Crabbe* [1957] 3 All ER 563.

[132] But see *Eastham v Leigh, London and Provincial Properties Limited* [1971] 2 All ER 887.

[133] This problem of what is 'substantial' is a major defect in the drafting of the legislation throughout. Apart from the question of substantial payment and substantial possession there are issues for the relief for surrenders and regrants as to substantial identity of the property (FA 2003, Sch 17A, para 9) and charities relief refers to the 'greater part' (FA 2003, Sch 8, para 3(1)(b)); compare Stamp Act 1891, s 77.

[134] This issue of the meaning of 'substantial' runs throughout stamp duty land tax such as the relief for surrenders and regrants pursuant to FA 2003, Sch 17A, para 9. Compare the relief for charities referring to the 'greater part' of the land; FA 2003, Sch 8, para 3(1)(b).

a problem where there is to be a staged completion such as where a developer intends to draw down one-third of the land in each of 3 successive years. The first and possibly the second years may not involve substantially the whole of the land which may bring any building costs into charge to tax as being incurred before substantial performance.[135] Similarly a person buying several flats from plan may have difficulties in taking sufficient possession of all of the flats, particularly before construction is completed. In such cases the taxpayer may find it prudent to enter into separate contracts or options relating to separate parcels of land each of which can be separately performed. Persons vulnerable to a claim that their building or fitting out obligations are consideration will need to consider not merely the quality of their occupation but also the extent thereof. Fitting out only one floor of three within the lease will not necessarily be accepted as substantial performance, particularly if the developer is still on the premises completing the building works.

14.21 These rules will apply to land exchanges so that there will be substantial performance when one party takes possession of his land. It remains an open question whether taking such possession will be regarded as the provision of the consideration by the other party thereby substantially performing the other side of the exchange. It is thought that there is no necessity for simultaneous substantial performance on both sides so that there may be different effective dates.

Non-major interests

14.22 The question of effective dates will also differ for transactions involving interest other than major interests and many types of acquisition affecting major interests.

14.23 Obviously the question of taking 'possession' of a restrictive covenant or a right to light or a right to access the main services to be constructed upon the land being sold will be manifest nonsense in many cases within the extended meaning of 'acquisition' for the purposes of determining what is a chargeable transaction. It is difficult to imagine how a person entitled to a pre-emptive right who receives a payment for variation of that right can enter into 'possession' in this sense. It is difficult to see how a tenant can enter into possession of a varied lease or a modified restrictive covenant or the cancellation of a contractual restriction upon development of land. Since such transactions will usually contain a provision in the contract for the execution of some form of deed or other instrument which may be necessary under the Law of Property Act 1925, they will be taxable upon the effective date or completion, whichever is the earlier. It is considered that the time of the effective date will be linked to substantial provision of the consideration or 'completion'.

Substantial payment or provision of consideration including lease premium

14.24 There is no specified figure as to when a substantial amount of consideration is paid or provided. The legislation[136] states that if none of the consideration is rent then a substantial amount is paid or provided where the whole or substantially the whole of the consideration is paid or provided. Guidelines have to be issued indicating that, in general, provision of 90 per cent of the consideration will be the threshold for

---

[135] FA 2003, Sch 4, para 10(2); a potential trap exists in Sch 19, para 4 for pre-1 December 2003 contracts because of the problems over effective dates and stamp duty.

[136] Ibid, s 44(5)(b).

substantial performance.[137] In consequence, the payment of normal deposits[138] will not trigger a charge to stamp duty land tax.[139] However, this will undoubtedly be subject to restriction to prevent taxpayers abusing the situation by paying a small amount of the consideration and, whilst technically leaving the balance unpaid, making the cash available to the disposing party by means of an interest-free loan.[140] Any such arrangements may involve a chargeable lease premium with no refund should the loan be repaid.[141] Two fundamental issues arise:

- there will be questions as to whether 90 per cent of any variable consideration has been provided. It seems that HMRC Stamp Taxes take the view that the 90 per cent is to be measured by reference to the estimated consideration included in the land transaction return.[142] It is not sufficient that the party pays 90 per cent or the whole of any initial price. This would seem to be technically correct and may represent a trap for persons who are relying upon payment of the basic price as a means of establishing substantial performance in order to protect subsequent costs of works where possession is not taken by reason of entry to fit out the demised premises. In this situation it may be more appropriate to rely upon taking possession of the whole or substantially the whole of the land as the trigger event which can also protect building costs from the charge to tax; and

- there is no guidance how to deal with consideration in kind such as construction works or services where the provision of non-cash consideration may extend over time. In some situations such as the allotment of consideration shares there will usually be a clear event but where the property is to be acquired in return for services[143] the issue is far from clear unless such services displace the application of FA 2003, s 44 and the situation reverts to 'completion' as the total performance of the service.

14.25 Developers and others who intend to finance the development by way of pre-sales and pre-lets[144] or soft and low interest loans from prospective purchasers or tenants[145] need to have these provisions and any guidelines in mind in order to avoid accelerating the other party's tax point and jeopardising subsale and other reliefs.[146] Persons making stage payments need to monitor the amount of payment made at any time since eventually these may cross the threshold.

14.26 There will also be questions of when the consideration is 'provided'. It may be, as illustrated by *Coren v Keighley*,[147] that the drafting may produce a situation where in law there is a set-off (ie a payment and re-lending) rather than a situation of unpaid consideration so that the consideration has been provided.[148] It remains to be seen whether HMRC Stamp Taxes will take such points during the conduct of Enquiries. It

---

[137] But these guidelines do not appear to provide measurement for possession of the land.
[138] On what is a real deposit see *Workers Trust and Merchant Bank Ltd v Dojap Investments* [1993] 2 All ER 370.
[139] But note he problem of deposits as premiums for a lease pursuant to FA 2003, Sch 17A, para 18A.
[140] Compare *Faith Construction v HM Customs and Excise* [1990] 1 QB 905.
[141] FA 2003, Sch 17A, para 18A; s 80(4A).
[142] Ibid, s 51.
[143] See, for example, *Yaxley v Gotts* [1999] 2 WLR 1217.
[144] Which may offer the possibility of mitigating the duty upon sales or leases of land with related building agreements as in *Prudential Assurance Co Ltd v IRC* [1992] STC 863; see **Chapter 8**.
[145] Note also FA 2003, Sch 17A, para 18A.
[146] Ibid, ss 45, 45A and Sch 17A, para 12B.
[147] 48 TC 370; see also *D'Arcy v HMRC* [2006] STC SCD 543.
[148] This may also create a 'loan' for other purposes such as partnerships pursuant to FA 2003, Sch 15, para 17A.

would seem that the consideration is likely to be regarded officially as having been 'provided' when it is made available or is at the disposition of the vendor.

14.27 Where the consideration consists of or includes the shares or other securities of a company,[149] the question will be whether the consideration is 'provided' when the shares or securities are 'allotted' (ie the board of directors or the shareholders take the necessary steps to create the shares and allocate them to the other parties),[150] or where they are 'issued' (ie registered in the relevant names).[151] It is not unusual for there to be delay between the resolution of the board of directors and the actual entry of names in the company's register and the issue of the certificates.[152] It is considered that, as the resolution to allot brings the share capital into existence, the consideration is provided at this point and the resolution constitutes the effective date unless the resolution has been preceded by the entry of the company into possession. It is unlikely that HMRC Stamp Taxes would be prepared without a serious challenge to allow taxpayers to defer the effective date simply by a decision to defer making up the register of members.[153]

Rent

14.28 In the case of new leases payment of rent is sufficient to constitute substantial performance.[154] This means the first actual payment of rent. There is no substantial performance where the rent day passes but no rent is paid.

Later completion – Subsequent instrument or 'conveyance'

14.29 Where a contract has been substantially performed and subsequent to that effective date it is completed between the same parties in substantial conformity[155] with the contract[156] by a 'conveyance', then both the substantial performance and the completion are notifiable transactions.[157] Moreover, stamp duty land tax is chargeable on the completion to the extent, if any, that the tax chargeable on that date is greater than the amount of tax chargeable at the effective date, ie substantial performance. It is thought that this additional tax is calculated by reference to the rate of stamp duty land tax in force on the effective date of the prior substantial performance and, where appropriate, by reference to market value etc as at that prior date,[158] but that depends upon whether the second notifiable transaction, ie completion is also a separate chargeable transaction with its own effective date.[159] In this situation where the rate of VAT has increased between substantial performance there will be a question whether that increase produces an additional liability to tax ie on the difference between the rate

---

[149]   On the various stages see **1.27**.
[150]   *Pye-Smith v IRC* [1958] 1 WLR 905; *Letts v IRC* [1957] 1 WLR 201.
[151]   *Oswald Tillotson v IRC* [1933] 1 KB 134; *Brotex Cellulose Fibres Ltd v IRC* [1933] 1 KB 158; *Murex v IRC* [1933] 1 KB 173; *National Westminster Bank v IRC* [1994] STC 580.
[152]   Which is crucial to the availability of reliefs such as reconstructions pursuant to FA 2003, Sch 7, Part 2; see **1.27** and **Chapter 12**.
[153]   Normally, however, the company will wish to begin trading which will involve taking possession of the land.
[154]   Receipt of the rent may operate to constitute possession in relation to the acquisition of the reversionary interest.
[155]   But note the modification of these rules for part subsales by FA 2003, s 45(2) and (5).
[156]   FA 2003, s 44(9)(a).
[157]   Ibid, s 44(7)(b). It is important to note that although HMRC Stamp Taxes refer to these as separate chargeable transactions, the draftsman refers to the later event merely as a 'notifiable transaction'.
[158]   Ibid, s 44(9).
[159]   See **7.25** and **14.7**.

current at substantial performance and the rate at completion.[160] In the case of agreements for lease where substantial performance occurs this is a deemed 'grant' of the lease and the subsequent actual grant is a surrender of the deemed lease of the grant of a new lease with a credit for the rent taxed at substantial performance.[161]

Rescission or cancellation after substantial performance

14.30 Since the effective date and the tax charge can arise upon substantial performance which will be prior to the passing of the equitable interest,[162] and can occur notwithstanding that the contract is still conditional,[163] it is provided that, if the contract is, to any extent, after substantial performance, rescinded or annulled or is for any other reason not carried to effect, such as because the condition is not satisfied the tax paid upon the substantial performance can be reclaimed.[164] This must be done by means of an amendment to the land transaction return made in respect of the substantial performance of the contract,[165] but 'amendments' basically may only be made within 12 months unless other provision[166] is made and it is at present uncertain whether HMRC Stamp Taxes will allow[167] a later amendment.[168] This means that:

- the taxpayer may amend the land transaction return given by him by notice to HMRC Stamp Taxes;

- the notice must be in such form and contain such information as HMRC Stamp Taxes may require;[169]

- unless special provisions provide otherwise, an amendment may not be made more than 12 months after the expiration of the last day of the period within which the return must be delivered,[170] which in this case will usually be 30 days after the effective date, ie the date of substantial performance. This would seem to raise a problem where the contract is rescinded more than 12 months after it is substantially performed, since there is no express extension of the time period permitted by Sch 10, para 6. However, it would seem that the time limit would be impliedly overruled in such a case.[171]

---

[160] There is, of course, no suggestion that unless rent is involved there is a tax refund where the rate of VAT is reduced between substantial performance and completion!

[161] FA 2003, Sch 17A, para 12A; see **7.25**.

[162] However, by allowing a purchaser into 'possession' an unpaid vendor may lose his liens or other rights and this could affect the passing of interests in the property.

[163] Such as where the parties are awaiting the landlord's consent.

[164] FA 2003, s 44(8); see Sch 10, para 6, which provides for a general limitation period of 12 months after the effective date for amending a return; presumably this time limit will be extended to allow for long completion arrangements, such as where building operations or the need for planning consent are involved.

[165] Ibid, s 44(9); Sch 10, para 2(1).

[166] Ibid, Sch 10, para 6.

[167] Ibid, s 97.

[168] But see ibid 2003, s 97. It is also uncertain whether this reference to 'amendment' precludes the making of a claim for repayment pursuant to FA 2003, Sch 11A.

[169] Note that certain amendments must be accompanied by the contract and the completion documentation if any. Since the rescission is by way of amendment these documents would be necessary (Ibid, Sch 10, para 6(2A)).

[170] Ibid, s 46(1)(b); on the nature of pre-emptive rights, see *Pritchard v Briggs* [1980] Ch 338.

[171] If not the taxpayer may have to consider some form of error or mistake claim (FA 2003, Sch 10, para 34) but this may depend upon the reasons for the rescission. Presumably the stamp duty land tax can be recovered where the contract is void for any reason such as mistake or is set aside for misrepresentation.

14.31 It is considered, however, that, if the contract has been 'completed' in the full sense of payment and delivery of the 'conveyance' or even in the limited sense that the full consideration has been paid or provided, any attempt to withdraw from the arrangement would not be a rescission or cancellation, unless this is based upon some arrangement that renders the contract voidable such as misrepresentation which is only discovered after completion, but a new chargeable transaction, the original agreement having been carried into effect, it is, *prima facie*, too late to rescind and there is a risk that HMRC Stamp Taxes may contend that there has been a resale of the interest acquired in satisfaction of the obligation to repay the consideration received unless it is established that the contract is void for mistake, voidable for misrepresentation or can be repudiated for breach of a fundamental terms. Any modifications in the amount of consideration returned by the original seller or lessor would also be an indication of a new chargeable consideration.

OPTIONS AND RIGHTS OF PRE-EMPTION

Pre-emptive rights

14.32 The acquisition of a right of pre-emption preventing the person granting the right from entering into or restricting the right of the grantor to enter into a land transaction for the disposal to a third party is a land transaction distinct from any land transaction resulting from the exercise of the pre-emptive right.[172] This produces two stages in the tax computation:

• there is a charge in relation to the creation of the pre-emptive right; and

• there is a charge in relation to the substantial performance and completion of the contract arising from the exercise of the option.

14.33 Although the grant of the pre-emptive right is expressed to be a land transaction in its own right,[173] it 'may' also become a linked transaction with any later contract arising from the exercise of the right in due course.[174]

14.34 The effective date in the case of the acquisition of a pre-emptive right is when the right is acquired as opposed to when it becomes exercisable.[175] Thus, a right of pre-emption is acquired when granted, although it is not effective unless and until the person granting the right enters into the appropriate situations concerned with a potential sale or other disposition of the relevant property.

Options

14.35 The acquisition of an option binding the grantor of an option to enter into a land transaction is a land transaction[176] distinct from any land transaction resulting

---

[172] FA 2003, s 46(1).
[173] There will also be a key question as to whether, where land is conveyed subject to a pre-emptive right, there is the creation or acquisition of a new right producing a land exchange pursuant to FA 2003, s 47 and Sch 4, para 5.
[174] Ibid, s 46(3); see **4.35** and **5.49**.
[175] Ibid, s 46(1)(a).
[176] Since an option is a chargeable interest, so that the variation of an option or its release is an acquisition pursuant to FA 2003, s 43(3) (as amended). There is a key issue as to whether where land is transferred

from the exercise of the option.[177] This would seem to be wide enough to include both put and call options so that an option whereby the grantee who owns land can require the grantor of the option to enter into a contract to buy the land will be a relevant option, as will an option whereby the grantee is entitled upon the grantor who owns the land to enter into a contract to sell the land. However, the charge will be limited since the 'exchange' of options is an exchange of non-major interests taxable only upon any equality money paid.[178] It also applies to an option binding the grantor to enter into a land transaction or to discharge his obligations under the option in some other way.[179]

14.36 The effective date of the transaction in the case of the acquisition of an option is when the right is acquired as opposed to when it becomes exercisable, such as where there is an option to acquire land if planning permission is obtained. The stamp duty land tax arises upon the grant of the option.[180] The grant of the option and the substantial performance or completion of the contract arising pursuant to its exercise are separate transactions but may be linked transactions.[181] This means that the tax upon the grant of the option premium will be on a stand alone basis and may be within the lower rates of stamp duty land tax. However, since the linked transaction rules operate retrospectively, the subsequent exercise of the option, if linked with the grant because of the facts and because it is exercised by the grantee or a connected person but not an unconnected assignee, will increase the total chargeable consideration ie the aggregate of the premium and the strike price,[182] thereby potentially retrospectively increasing the tax rate applicable to the option premium requiring a further filing separate from the land transaction return for the main contract and payment of the additional tax.[183] However, where the exercise of an option involves the renewal of a lease this may, if it is linked with the original grant of the lease,[184] produce a 'successive linked lease'.[185] There is the situation of not two leases but a single lease that is retrospectively extended by reason of the aggregation of the terms of the two or more leases involved. In this situation there will be a separate effective date in relation to the exercise of the option on the grant of the new lease but the tax computation will be carried out retrospectively by reference to the initial return in respect of the grant of the original lease.

---

subject to the grant of an option to repurchase or to put back the land there is a land exchange pursuant to FA 2003, s 47 and Sch 4, para 5. Since an option in a lease to purchase the reversion moves in the same direction as the lease this issue would not be expected to arise.

[177] Ibid, Sch 4, para 5(4). Unfortunately, the position regarding the value of the option and the chargeable consideration is not clear as regards the recalculation of the tax in respect of the contract arising. Where this involves an acquisition of a major interest it seems that the value of the option may have to be included: para 5(3).

[178] Ibid, s 46(2).

[179] Ibid, s 46(3).

[180] Ibid, s 46.

[181] Ibid, s 46(1).

[182] Note the drafting issues raised by *George Wimpey Ltd v IRC* [1975] 2 All ER 45.

[183] FA 2003, s 81A.

[184] Ibid, ss 47 and 108.

[185] Ibid, Sch 17A, para 5.

Chapter 15

THE TAXPAYER

THE PURCHASER

15.1 The legislation frequently refers to the 'purchaser' for both liability and compliance reasons. There is even a definition to the effect that a 'purchaser' includes a party to a transaction where there is no actual or chargeable transaction.[1] This is because in certain situations a transaction without actual consideration may be a notifiable transaction[2] even if not a chargeable transaction and there has to be a person to sign the declaration on the Land Transaction Return (SDLT 1) notwithstanding that tax may not be payable.[3] It does not refer to the 'taxpayer'. This failure to identify the 'taxpayer' rather than the 'purchaser' has to be noted because, for example:

- the one-size fits all style of drafting by reference to 'the purchaser' includes a wide range of persons who would not be regarded as buyers in any generally accepted or technical meaning of the word. It applies to lessees and may apply to landlords for certain dealings in leases. It includes grantees of interests such as options as well as persons benefiting from releases and variations of rights;[4] and

- the word 'purchaser' implies that the relevant person is a party to the initial chargeable transaction.[5] However, the open-ended provisional nature of much of stamp duty land tax means that the tax liability is, by statute, passed on to persons other than the original party. This is done without any definition of 'purchaser' as including successors in title. There are provisions which, for example, rather stealthily make assignees of leases liable for the open tax position of the original tenants.[6]

In consequence, the identification of the person who is, by statute, the taxpayer rather than the person who is the original purchaser[7] in any particular transaction is important since this carries with it:

- the liability to pay the tax;[8]

- the obligation to make the appropriate notification[9] by completing and filing the necessary returns;

---

[1]   FA 2003, s 43(4) and (5).

[2]   Ibid, s 77A; Sch 15, para 25(1).

[3]   Ibid, s 76 and Sch 10, para 1.

[4]   Ibid, s 43(4).

[5]   See also ibid, s 43(5).

[6]   Ibid, s 87A; Sch 17A, para 12; s 81A.

[7]   There is no express statutory indemnity in such cases to persons who are required to pay what is, in effect, another person's tax.

[8]   FA 2003, ss 85, 103(2); Sch 15, Part 2; Sch 16, para 5.

[9]   Ibid, s 76(1).

- the obligation to sign the declaration, since essentially only the purchaser can sign and, with the exception for partnerships where representative partners have been nominated and accepted by HMRC Stamp Taxes,[10] all purchasers must sign the declaration;[11]

- the obligation to maintain records and provide information.[12]

15.2   It appears from FA 2003, Sch 4, para 1 that only consideration provided by the 'purchaser'[13] is chargeable consideration, ie consideration provided by a third party who is not connected with the purchaser and which is not indirectly provided by the 'purchaser' is, *prima facie*, not within the charge to stamp duty land tax.[14]

15.3   Apart from the special provisions dealing with the clawback of the three reliefs for corporate restructuring provided by Finance Act 2003, Sch 7,[15] and certain rules affecting assignees of leases,[16] no general provision at present exists for the recovery of stamp duty land tax from other persons, such as professional parties acting in the transaction. Non-payment of stamp duty land tax is no longer the same type of title issue that applied for stamp duty.[17] Although proof of payment of the tax is, to some extent, a factor in both taxes, it is not necessary to have exemptions or valuations approved in advance of registration. Nevertheless, there may be inconvenience where the person disposing of the interest is not the registered owner and may not be able to produce the certificate required to register his interest, this does not prevent the person acquiring from him submitting his own application to the Land Registry, supported by the appropriate certificate. If the person disposing is not a necessary party to the application, because, for example, some third party executes the Land Registry transfer or the lease, his participation in the registration process may not be necessary and the register can be altered notwithstanding his non-payment of the stamp duty land tax.[18]

15.4   There are, however, wide-ranging powers to issue regulations and the provisions making certain third parties liable for the collection and payment of stamp duty reserve tax and the notification of the transaction as 'accountable persons' which do not appear in the basic legislation but only in regulations.[19] It is, therefore, possible that other persons may become 'accountable' for the tax, particularly where non-resident parties are involved where at present the only provisions relate to foreign companies[20] or when electronic conveyancing becomes operational and the filing or payment period is reduced to 'nil',[21] ie payment on the effective date or notification to the Land Registry. There are also obligations imposed upon special purchaser situations which are set out

---

[10]   Ibid, Sch 15, para 8(2).

[11]   It seems, however, that even where there are representative partners in theory all partners must be identified and their details included in the land transaction return, not merely the representative partner, whether the partnership is the disposer or the acquirer of the chargeable interest; however, it seems that in practice HMRC Stamp Taxes will accept a land transaction return in the name of the partnership and not require numerous SDLT 2 forms fro the individual partners as an effective date.

[12]   FA 2003, Sch 10, para 14; Sch 11, para 9; Sch 13, Part 1.

[13]   This is a case where the ambiguity with drafting between purchaser and taxpayer matters. It seems that in this case it means the original party to the transaction and not persons connected with a successor in title.

[14]   See **5.100** and **15.7**.

[15]   See **12.51** and **12.103**.

[16]   FA 2003, Sch 17A, para 12, which appears to impose both reporting and payment obligations.

[17]   But see **2.15** on the different issues of title and documents of title for stamp duty land tax.

[18]   See also **Chapters 16, 18** and **22**.

[19]   Stamp Duty Reserve Tax Regulations 1986, SI 1986/1711, reg 4.

[20]   FA 2003, s 100(4)(b).

[21]   Ibid, s 76(2).

below.[22] It is, therefore, possible that regulations issued will enlarge the number of persons who are personally 'accountable' although not 'liable' for the stamp duty land tax.

General position

15.5 The taxpayer is unhelpfully identified as the 'purchaser'. This must, however, be construed in the context of the legislation and the facts of each particular case. Thus, upon the grant of an option, *prima facie*, the 'purchaser' is the grantee of the option. Upon the grant of a lease, the 'purchaser' is the tenant but, upon a variation for a consideration paid to the tenant such as a payment for the tenant agreeing to change the rent review pattern, the 'landlord' is the 'purchaser'.[23]

15.6 The 'purchaser' is basically defined as the person acquiring the subject-matter of the transaction[24] who either:

* provides consideration; or

* is a party to the transaction;[25] and

is a person:

* who becomes entitled to an interest on its creation;[26] or

* whose interest is benefited or enlarged by the surrender or release of a chargeable interest;[27] or

* who benefits from the variation of a chargeable interest.[28]

However, there is a steadily increasing number of situations where persons other than the original 'purchaser' become liable for the outstanding tax on the original transaction. Obviously this will include persons who are liable in a representative capacity such as liquidators or receivers of companies and personal representatives of deceased persons,[29] but it has been extended to persons who become personally liable in their own right such as assignees of leases.[30] This deals with actual personal liability and compliance obligations not with the mechanism of merely collecting tax owed by one person from another person. Additionally, there is a wholly different set of problems for third parties whose tax position may be dependent upon the tax position of the original purchaser and his subsequent conduct such as in relation to rent reviews and abnormal increases in rent[31] where the person's liability involves a calculation which takes into account the tax computations of some other person, usually the person liable for the tax upon the initial acquisition of the land.

---

22 See **15.17** and **15.39**.
23 But no tax may arise FA 2003, s 45(3)(d) and Sch 17A, para 15A.
24 FA 2003, s 43(4).
25 Ibid, s 43(5).
26 Ibid, s 43(3)(a)(i).
27 Ibid, s 43(3)(b)(i).
28 Ibid, s 43(3)(c)(i).
29 Ibid, s 106(3).
30 Ibid, s 81A and Sch 17A, para 12; see **7.235** and **15.39**.
31 See ibid, Sch 17A, paras 14 and 15; see **7.183**.

The problem of the purchaser and the consideration

15.7 The provider of the consideration is a key issue in the identification of the 'purchaser' and the scope of charge to stamp duty land tax. Unfortunately, the process of identification is more than a little tortuous, since the consideration may not always be provided by the person who receives the benefit of the transaction. Much may depend upon the technical legal analysis of the events. For example:

- A contracts to sell land to B;

- B directs A to transfer the land to C, the trustee of a settlement.

This may need to be analysed as two transactions:

- a sale, taxable, to B who provides the consideration;[32] and/or

- a gift, non-taxable,[33] by B to C who appears to be a party to the transaction with B and/or A because he benefits by a gift from B and receives a transfer from A.

This definition of 'purchaser' applies even although there is no consideration given for the transaction.[34] However, a person is not treated as a 'purchaser' unless he has given consideration for or is a party to the transaction.[35] This raises many difficult problems of interpretation because of the use of the 'consideration' and the fact that a person may be a purchaser where there is no consideration for the transaction, for example, a donee of a gift is a 'purchaser' but such a transaction is not taxable.[36] It is, however, necessary to identify a purchaser so that there is someone who can sign the land transaction return since the reference may be to 'actual consideration' as opposed to 'chargeable consideration',[37] although the position is not clear, a donee who is a party to a transaction that is for a deemed consideration such as the connected companies charge[38] the company will be a 'purchaser' and, therefore, the person to sign the return.[39]

15.8 A standard illustration of the problem would be where there is an arrangement between a developer and a landowner[40] whereby the developer is to procure the assignment and surrender of all existing leases and subleases upon the land and to acquire the freehold or other interests in any other land owned by third parties that is relevant to the development. Such interests will vest in the landowner, who will at an appropriate stage grant a lease of the site to the developer or to such persons as the developer may direct.[41] The purchaser in this transaction is the freeholder since he is the person acquiring the subject-matter of the transaction, ie the leases of adjoining land. He will, *prima facie*, not be providing actual consideration or 'chargeable consideration',

---

32   But because there is no consideration for the transfer to C subsale relief may not be available for B, FA 2003, s 45; see **Chapter 6**.
33   Ibid, Sch 3, para 1.
34   Ibid, s 43(4).
35   Ibid, s 43(5).
36   Ibid, Sch 3, para 1.
37   There is the inherent ambiguity in relation to a person being a purchaser without providing 'consideration' because the draftsman consistently fails to specify whether he is referring to 'chargeable consideration' or 'actual consideration whether chargeable or not'. A person may provide actual consideration but this is not treated as chargeable consideration and vice versa.
38   FA 2003, ss 53 and 54.
39   Or, more accurately, an appropriate officer of the company is the person to sign the declaration.
40   Note the limited reliefs for local authorities; FA 2003, ss 60 and 61.
41   Note ibid, Sch 17, para 12B.

since the cash and other benefits being provided to the tenants derive from the developer who is not the purchaser or a person connected with the purchaser,[42] unless this is to be treated as two separate transactions,[43] namely the acquisition by the developer and a separate acquisition by the landowner pursuant to a contract with the developer, which appears to be the likely end result for stamp duty land tax. It would appear unlikely that these sums would be allowed to fall out of charge to stamp duty land tax.[44] The question, then, is who is the 'purchaser' and whether this differs in relation to the two legs of the transaction.[45]

Connected persons

15.9 The question of whether a person is 'connected' with another occurs many times in the legislation. Connected persons, as defined by Income and Corporation Taxes Act 1988, s 839 are important for a variety of reasons, including:

- the market value charge upon transfers to connected companies;[46]

- the question of whether the consideration is provided by an appropriate person to be chargeable consideration,[47] including subsales;[48]

- whether there are linked transactions for the lower rates;[49]

- reliefs for part-exchanges[50] and relocation of employees.[51]

'Connection' is not the same as being 'associated' for the purposes of group relief[52] but companies in a group are likely to be connected. Parties are 'connected' as follows.[53]

---

[42] On third party inducements as consideration see **5.222**.

[43] Which may fall within ibid, s 45; see **Chapter 6**.

[44] See **5.83** et seq.

[45] On certain variations of this type of situation there may also be issues whether there is a land exchange (FA 2003, s 47) in respect of all or some of the stages in the overall transaction. Although cross-headed 'Exchanges', the provision appears to be much wider than mere mutual exchanges between the same parties. It states that there is a chargeable transaction where a person enters into one land transaction as a purchaser and provides consideration for that transaction by entering into another land transaction as vendor. It does not appear to be a requirement that the 'purchaser' under the second contract is the same person as the 'vendor' under the first contract. In consequence, it seems that this provision will apply where A agrees to transfer land to B in consideration of B transferring other land to C, or granting a lease to D, which does not appear to be eligible for sale and leaseback relief (FA 2003, s 57A) or alternative finance relief (FA 2003, ss 71A–73C). There is no express requirement in the legislation that the parties to the two contracts are the same persons. The intriguing problem is that, although C would appear to be a purchaser in that he is a party, he is not providing the consideration, so that *prima facie* there is no charge to stamp duty land tax within FA 2003, Sch 4, para 1, which requires that chargeable consideration is provided by the purchaser or a person connected with him and the transaction is exempt pursuant to FA 2003, Sch 3, para 1.

[46] Ibid, ss 53 and 54.

[47] Ibid, Sch 4, para 1.

[48] Ibid, s 54(3)(b).

[49] Ibid, s 108.

[50] Ibid, s 58.

[51] Ibid, s 59.

[52] Ibid, Sch 7, Part 1.

[53] Income and Corporation Taxes Act 1988, s 839.

Relations

15.10 A person is connected with an individual if that person is the individual's wife or husband, or is a relative,[54] or the wife or husband of a relative, of the individual or of the individual's wife or husband.

Settlement

15.11 A person, in his capacity as trustee of a settlement, is connected with:

(a)   any individual who in relation to the settlement is a settlor;

(b)   any person who is connected with such an individual; and

(c)   any body corporate which is connected with that settlement.[55]

15.12 A body corporate is connected with a settlement if:

(a)   it is a close company (or only not a close company because it is not resident in the United Kingdom) and the participators include the trustees of the settlement; or

(b)   it is controlled (within the meaning of s 840) by a company falling within paragraph (a) above.

Partnerships

15.13 Except in relation to acquisitions or disposals of partnership assets pursuant to *bona fide* commercial arrangements, a person is connected with any person with whom he is in partnership, and with the wife or husband or relative of any individual with whom he is in partnership.

Companies

15.14 A company is connected with another company:

(a)   if the same person has control of both, or a person has control of one and persons connected with him, or he and persons connected with him, have control of the other; or

(b)   if a group of two or more persons has control of each company, and the groups either consist of the same persons or could be regarded as consisting of the same persons by treating (in one or more cases) a member of either group as replaced by a person with whom he is connected.[56]

15.15 A company is connected with another person if that person has control of it or if that person and persons connected with him together have control of it.

---

54   Ie brother, sister, ancestor or lineal descendent.
55   The terms 'settlement' and 'settlor' have the same meaning as in Income and Corporation Taxes Act 1988, Chapter IA of Part XV (see s 660G(1) and (2)).
56   See *Steele v EVC* [1996] STC 785; and Revenue Interpretation 160 (December 1996).

15.16 A person may have 'control' of a company if he exercises,[57] or is able to exercise or is entitled to acquire,[58] direct or indirect control over the company's affairs, and in particular, but without prejudice to the generality of the preceding words, if he possesses or is entitled to acquire:

(a) the greater part of the share capital or issued share capital of the company or of the voting power in the company; or

(b) such part of the issued share capital of the company as would, if the whole of the income of the company were in fact distributed among the participators (without regard to any rights which he or any other person has as a loan creditor), entitle him to receive the greater part of the amount so distributed; or

(c) such rights as would, in the event of the winding-up of the company or in any other circumstances, entitle him to receive the greater part of the assets of the company which would then be available for distribution among the participators.[59]

There are attributed to any person any rights or powers of a nominee for him, that is to say, any rights or powers which another person possesses on his behalf or may be required to exercise on his direction or behalf.

Where two or more persons together satisfy any of the above conditions they shall be taken to have control of the company.[60] Any two or more persons acting together to secure or exercise control of a company are treated in relation to that company as connected with one another and with any person acting on the directions of any of them to secure or exercise control of the company.

Particular purchasers

15.17 There are basic principles that there must be a declaration by the purchaser that the return is to the best of his knowledge correct and complete.[61] This is done by the purchaser or purchasers signing the return. This basic principle is subject to numerous special provisions.

Agents

15.18 It is obviously inconvenient for the taxpayer to have to attend a completion meeting but until there has been actual completion there may not be an effective date and as this is a key feature of the land transaction return signature by the taxpayer in advance of the completion meeting would be incorrect. There are obvious risks should there be a delay in completion such that it takes effect after the date set by the contract for 'completion'. A return signed in advance by reference to the contractual completion

---

[57] This may refer to *de facto* control by a person who is a shadow director.

[58] This includes anything which he is entitled to acquire at a future date, or will at a future date be entitled to acquire. The company's articles of association and share rights may be an issue; see *Irving v Tesco Stores (Holdings) Ltd v IRC* [1982] STC 881.

[59] This definition is of considerable importance in practice given the more or less automatic uncritical reaction of solicitors acting for certain parties such as mortgagees or vendors to 'boilerplate' or excessively protect the interests of their client, possibly unnecessarily. Such protection could be utilised by HMRC Stamp Taxes as a basis for attacking the stamp tax planning.

[60] See, for example, *Steele v EVC* [1996] STC 785; Revenue Interpretation 160 (December 1996).

[61] FA 2003, Sch 10, para 1(c).

date would be incorrect in such circumstances. Also it may be somewhat imprudent to postpone the signing of the declaration until after completion since the client may not appreciate the need for the signature and having completed the transaction and taken possession not be in a hurry to return to deal with extra paperwork[62] and any delays in processing the return, obtaining the Inland Revenue Certificate (SDLT 5) and registration of title may irritate mortgagees.

15.19 To mitigate these problems two specific solutions are provided for agents to sign.

- in addition to the specific provisions dealing with partners and trustees where not all of the relevant persons are required to sign the declaration,[63] it is permissible for an individual to appoint an agent to sign the form.[64] This must be an authorisation by way of power of attorney in writing signed by the individual. In addition, it appears that this authority must be to act on behalf of the individual 'in relation to the matters to which the return or certificate relates'.[65] This would appear to require a specific and focused power of attorney for the signing of the form. It would seem that a resolution of the board of directors or committee of any unincorporated association will be required to authorise appropriate persons to sign on behalf of the company or club. In this situation, however, it would seem that a general resolution authorising a particular person to deal with the stamp duty land tax affairs of the company or association would be sufficient and need not be a specific resolution for every property transaction; or

- where the purchaser or purchasers authorise an agent to complete the return the purchaser makes a declaration that with the exception of the effective date the information provided in the return is to the best of his knowledge correct and complete and the agent makes a declaration that the effective date provided in the return is to the best of his knowledge correct, the declaration has been properly made.[66] A special version of SDLT 1 has been issued for this purpose.

15.20 Technically nominees are agents and require appropriate authorisation to sign but in practice HMRC Stamp Taxes have accepted such signatories[67] are effective upon the basis that the acts of the nominee or the acts of the beneficial owner.[68]

Joint purchasers

15.21 The rules identify persons who are 'purchasers' where there is an acquisition by two or more persons who are or will be jointly entitled to the interest acquired,[69] ie:

---

62 Indeed, in some cases, the purchaser has 'disappeared' leaving the land transaction return unsigned. In this situation the title becomes 'blocked' in that the Land Registry will not act until the Revenue certificate (SDLT 5) is produced and HMRC Stamp Taxes will refuse to issue a certificate until they receive a properly signed stamp duty land tax return. At this point there is a hunt to find some person who can within the law execute the land transaction return to the satisfaction of HMRC Stamp Taxes. See, for example, nominees and bare trustees within FA 2003, Sch 16, para 3.
63 Although all must be identified as vendors or purchasers in order that the form can be properly completed.
64 FA 2003, s 81B.
65 Ibid, s 81B(2).
66 Ibid, Sch 10, para 1A.
67 See **15.26**.
68 FA 2003, Sch 16, para 3.
69 Ibid, s 103.

- in England and Wales, will be beneficially entitled as joint tenants[70] or tenants in common;

- in Scotland, will be entitled as joint owners or owners in common; and

- in Northern Ireland, will be beneficially entitled as joint tenants, tenants in common or coparceners,[71]

but this does not include partners[72] or trustees.[73]

15.22 In such case, if a transaction is notifiable then only a single land transaction return is required, although where there are numerous joint purchasers a supplemental SDLT 2 return to identify all relevant parties is needed; but any obligation to the purchaser in relation to the transaction is an obligation of the purchasers jointly, although it may be discharged by any of them.[74] Any liability of the purchaser in relation to stamp duty land tax, such as liability arising by reason of failure to file a return or to pay the tax, is a joint and several liability of such joint purchasers.[75]

15.23 Detailed rules are provided for joint owners in relation to:

- the giving of notices of an Enquiry and the conduct thereof;[76]

- the effectiveness of determinations or discovery assessments;[77] and

- appeals.[78]

Partnerships[79]

15.24 In relation to partnerships, which includes general partnerships,[80] limited or limited liability partnerships,[81] or a firm or entity of a similar character formed or established under the laws of a country outside the United Kingdom, the obligations are essentially those of the partners. For these purposes, in certain jurisdictions, partnerships may have separate legal identity. However, this separate legal personality or corporate status of the partnership[82] is ignored.[83] Notwithstanding the technical issues arising where there are changes in the partners which may mean a termination of one partnership and the formation of a new partnership, a partnership is treated as being the same partnership notwithstanding any changes in membership from time to time.[84] This

---

[70] On the position of joint tenants see also FA 2003, s 121; Sch 15, para 12(2).
[71] Ibid, s 121.
[72] Ibid, s 103(8); see **15.21**.
[73] Ibid; see **15.23**.
[74] Ibid, s 103(2)(a).
[75] Ibid, s 103(2)(c).
[76] Ibid, s 103(5); see **Chapter 19**.
[77] Ibid, s 103(6); see **Chapter 22**.
[78] Ibid, s 103(7); see **Chapter 24**.
[79] Ibid, Sch 15, Part 1; see **Chapter 13**.
[80] Partnership Act 1890.
[81] Limited Partnerships Act 1907; Limited Liability Partnerships Act 2000.
[82] However, a partnership is not treated as a body corporate for the purposes of stamp duty land tax; FA 2003, s 100.
[83] FA 2003, Sch 15, para 2.
[84] Ibid, Sch 15, paras 5 and 9.

can be important when dealing with the special regime for partnership sand can be utilised to avoid charges that could arise on technical grounds, such as transfers between partnerships,[85] or land ceasing to be used for the purposes of the business of the 'terminating' partnership[86]

15.25 Where a partnership incurs a liability to stamp duty land tax,[87] anything required to be done in relation to the transaction is the responsibility of the persons who were partners on the effective date of the transaction and any person who becomes a member of the partnership after the effective date.[88] However, for convenience, the partners may nominate a representative partner or partners to act on behalf of the firm, including the making of declarations and the giving of self-certificates.[89] The liability to pay the tax or any interest or penalties is a joint and several liability of the persons who were partners on the effective date and any person who subsequently becomes a partner.[90] In addition in order to avoid the need to identify a large number of individual partners on SDLT 2 HMRC Stamp Taxes have indicated that the partnership name can be utilised to identify either the vendor or the purchaser in the land transaction return and individual names and details are not required.

Nominees and bare trustees[91]

15.26 Transactions other than leases[92] between nominees and bare trustees[93] and their beneficial owners are ignored[94] and the acts of the nominee are deemed to have been carried out by the beneficial owner.[95] In strict theory this means that notwithstanding the contract is made by the nominee as undisclosed agent and he takes the transfer of the legal title without disclosing his role, the purchaser for the purposes of the land transaction return is the beneficial owner[96] who is the correct person to sign the land transaction return and appear as the purchaser. However, HMRC Stamp Taxes have accepted the bizarre argument that because the acts of the nominee are treated as the actions of the beneficial owner the nominee's signature is deemed to be the signature of the real purchaser.[97]

Trustees other than bare trustees[98]

15.27 Apart from the case of bare trustees or nominees,[99] it is the responsibility of the trustees of the settlement on the effective date and any person who subsequently

85 Ibid, Sch 15, para 21; see **13.52**.
86 Ibid, Sch 15, para 37; see **13.35**.
87 Ie other than those transactions relating to partnership land and partnership shares where stamp duty continues to apply; see **1.10**; see also **Chapter 23**.
88 FA 2003, Sch 15, para 6.
89 Ibid, Sch 15, paras 6(3) and 8.
90 Ibid, Sch 15, para 7.
91 See **Chapter 9**.
92 FA 2003, Sch 16, para 3 (as amended) see **9.4** and **9.6**.
93 See **9.3**.
94 FA 2003, Sch 16, para 3.
95 See **Chapter 9**.
96 There is a similar problem for identifying the vendor although the purchaser may find it difficult to obtain details of the beneficial owner. It remains to be seen how aggressive HMRC Stamp Taxes intend to be in relation to penalties if there has not been any attempt to discover whether the settlor is the beneficial owner.
97 This, however, may not justify the inclusion of the nominee in the body of the form as the purchaser. Since this goes to enforcement HMRC Stamp Taxes may take a stricter line.
98 See **9.16**.
99 FA 2003, Sch 16, para 3.

becomes a trustee to pay the tax.[100] A return or self-certificate in relation to a land transaction may be made by any one or more of the persons who are trustees on the effective date or who subsequently become trustees.[101]

Bodies corporate

15.28 A 'company', which for these but not for all purposes of stamp duty land tax[102] means any body corporate or unincorporated association[103] other than a partnership, may be a purchaser for a transaction.[104] Everything required to be done by such a company is to be done through the proper officer of the company or any other person for the time being having the express, implied or apparent authority of the company to act on its behalf for the purposes of stamp duty land tax.[105]

15.29 In relation to 'companies' that are not bodies corporate or are incorporated outside the United Kingdom, in addition to all other methods of recovering the tax, it may be recovered from the proper officer of the company.[106] The proper officer of the company is the secretary or a person acting as the secretary of the 'company'.[107] In relation to unincorporated associations or a company that does not have a secretary or acting secretary, the proper officer is the treasurer or the person acting as treasurer.[108] If a liquidator or administrator has been appointed for the company, then the liquidator or the administrator is the proper officer.[109] If there are two or more persons acting jointly or concurrently as administrators of the company, the proper officer is such of them as is specified in notice to HMRC Stamp Taxes for these purposes. In default of any such notification, HMRC Stamp Taxes may designate who is to be the proper officer.[110]

Unit trust schemes

15.30 For the purposes of the payment and compliance regime,[111] the trustees of a unit trust scheme are treated as a company, and the rights of unit holders are treated as shares in a company.[112] Where there is an umbrella scheme, each scheme under the umbrella is treated as a separate company and the umbrella trust is ignored.[113] In consequence, the trustees will be the purchaser liable for the tax, and the person who is the equivalent of the company secretary will be responsible for making the return.

---

[100] Ibid, Sch 16, para 5.
[101] Ibid, Sch 16, para 6.
[102] Such as in relation to the connected company rules; see ibid, s 53.
[103] Note, however, certain special provisions treating companies as 'individuals' in FA 2003, Sch 15, paras 12(3) and 20(3); see also *Jasmine Trustees Ltd v Wells & Hind* [2007] STC 660.
[104] FA 2003, s 100(1).
[105] Ibid, s 100(2).
[106] Ibid, s 100(4).
[107] Ibid, s 100(6)(a).
[108] Ibid, s 100(6)(b).
[109] Ibid, s 100(7)(a).
[110] Ibid, s 100(7)(b).
[111] But note that there is a special stamp duty and stamp duty reserve tax regime for unit trust schemes and open-ended investment companies; FA 1999, Sch 19 (as implemented by numerous regulations).
[112] FA 2003, s 101.
[113] Ibid, s 101(2) and (3).

Open-ended investment companies

15.31 Open-ended investment companies are bodies corporate, so that the 'company' will be liable for the stamp duty land tax and the administration will be the responsibility of the company secretary.[114] Regulations may be issued to assimilate such companies to the position of unit trust schemes.

Personal representatives[115]

15.32 The personal representative of a deceased individual is a person who is a purchaser or responsible for discharging the obligations of the purchaser in relation to stamp duty land tax. Personal representatives may deduct any payment made by them out of the assets and effects of the deceased person.[116]

15.33 The position of a personal representative can be particularly difficult since the deceased may have been involved in an open stamp duty land tax position such as having acquired a chargeable interest with an overage or clawback arrangement.[117] Obviously, the personal representative cannot complete the administration of the estate or even assent or appropriate assets to beneficiaries until the open tax position has been resolved. This may depend upon whether the property was a lease with a variable premium[118] or was an acquisition where there was an effective exit strategy.[119] There may also be issues as to the nature of the interests of the beneficiaries whilst such open contractual tax position continues.[120]

Minors

15.34 The parent or guardian of a minor is responsible for discharging any obligations of the minor that are not discharged by the minor himself,[121] such as where the minor has entered into a land transaction.

Receivers

15.35 A receiver appointed by a court in the United Kingdom having the direction and control of any property is responsible for discharging any obligations in relation to stamp duty land tax affecting that property as if the property were not under the direction or control of the court.[122] The appointment of a receiver or administrator does not appear to affect the beneficial ownership of the company's assets such as shares in subsidiary companies[123] so that at that stage there is no clawback of any intra-group relief. However, liquidations have more serious consequences by degrouping subsidiary companies.[124]

---

[114]   Ibid, s 100; see **15.28**.
[115]   Note also the possible relief for the acquisition of property by property traders from personal representatives pursuant to FA 2003, Sch 6A, para 3; see **6.73**.
[116]   Ibid, s 106(3).
[117]   Ibid, ss 51, 80 and 90 and Stamp Duty Land Tax (Administration) Regulations 2003, SI 2003/2837; see **16.34**.
[118]   Ibid, Sch 17A, para 12(1)(a).
[119]   See **5.206**.
[120]   See **4.50**.
[121]   Ibid, s 106(2).
[122]   Ibid, s 106(4).
[123]   *English Sewing Cotton Co Ltd v IRC* [1947] 1 All ER 679.
[124]   *Ayerst v C & K (Construction) Ltd* [1976] AC 167.

Incapacity

15.36 The person having the direction, management or control of the property of an incapacitated person, which would appear to include any person holding an enduring power of attorney,[125] is responsible for discharging any obligations in relation to stamp duty land tax to which the incapacitated person would be subject if he were not incapacitated. That person may retain out of money coming into his hands on behalf of the incapacitated person sums sufficient to meet any payment he is liable to make in respect of stamp duty land tax. Insofar as he is not reimbursed through monies received, he is entitled to be indemnified in respect of any such payment.[126]

Official Solicitor

15.37 Where the Official Solicitor is acting for any of the purchasers under a disability he may sign the declaration.[127] This requires a special form.[128]

The Crown

15.38 Stamp duty land tax applies to public offices and departments of the Crown.[129] However, any such office or department is not required to make a payment that would ultimately be borne by the Crown. There are certain exemptions from stamp duty land tax in respect of:

- a minister of the Crown;

- the Scottish ministers;

- a Northern Ireland department;

- the corporate officer of the House of Lords;

- the corporate office of the House of Commons;

- the Northern Ireland Assembly Commission;

- the National Assembly for Wales.[130]

Certain reliefs are available for public sector bodies such as public authorities.

---

[125] Note that in certain situations the grant of a power of attorney may be an equitable assignment (*Diplock v Hammond* (1854) 5 De GM & G 320; but see *Roddick v Gandell* (1852) 1 De G M & G 763), note also the principles of imperfect gifts and accidental vesting where there is an imperfect *inter vivos* gift which is perfected when the intended donee acquires the legal title as the personal representative after the death of the donor.

[126] Ibid, s 106(1).

[127] Ibid, Sch 10, para 1B(1).

[128] Ibid, Sch 10, para 1B(2).

[129] Ibid, s 107(1) (as amended).

[130] Ibid, s 107(2).

Assignment of leases — third parties as 'purchasers'[131]

15.39 Late changes in the FA 2003 by regulations inserting Sch 17A and other provisions mean that persons who were not parties to the original transaction may either be affected by the liability to pay tax in respect thereof, or have to report transactions or deemed transactions, or be affected by later transactions involving other parties. The persons at risk are assignees of leases. This includes the following situations.

- *Returns of later linked transactions*
  A purchaser, ie the original taxpayer, is required to notify and, if necessary, pay any stamp duty land tax or any additional tax arising where there is a later linked transaction,[132] which may include a later linked lease arising upon the exercise of an option to renew.[133] These obligations are transferred to an assignee of a lease.[134]

- *Returns where consideration is contingent or uncertain*
  Where, pursuant to FA 2003, s 80, a further return is required in relation to variable consideration, such as a variable premium upon the grant of a lease,[135] there is an obligation on the assignee to make the return and, it seems, to pay any additional tax[136] rather than the original taxpayer although it is not clear whether this legislation transfers the liability totally, as appears to be the case, or merely creates some form of joint and several liability. There are, however, no statutory provisions providing the assignee with an automatic right of indemnity or to call for information; these are essentially issues for the contract to acquire the property.[137]

- *Variable rents*
  Where, during the first 5 years of the term of a lease with a variable rent, it is assigned, the assignee becomes responsible for any reporting and payment[138] obligations in relation to the recalculation of the stamp duty land tax during or at the end of the fifth year of the term.[139]

- *Leases for indefinite terms, holding over etc*[140]
  Where a lease such as a periodic tenancy continues, or a holding over on the termination of the contractual term begins without creating a new lease, or any

---

[131] These are separate issues from those arising as to whether the assignee is the 'same person' as the assignor for certain purposes of the tax such as linked transactions because he is the purchaser to the original contract ie he may be a distinct person but he occupies the same place or status in the transaction since he becomes the party to the original certain purposes of the tax because he is the purchaser to the original contract ie he may be a distinct person but he occupies the same place or status in the transaction since he becomes the party to the original contract.
[132] FA 2003, s 81A.
[133] Ibid, Sch 17A, para 5.
[134] Ibid, Sch 17A, para 12(1)(b).
[135] Ibid, Sch 17A, para 12(1)(a).
[136] Conversely, subject to negotiation of the contract, the assignee would appear to be entitled to any refund of tax arising.
[137] See **7.235**.
[138] Or recovery of overpaid tax.
[139] FA 2003, Sch 17A, para 8.
[140] Ibid, Sch 17A, paras 3 and 4.

new holding over tenancy continues beyond one year, any assignee of a lease or, it seems, any deemed lease becomes responsible for any reporting or payment obligations.[141]

Assignment of relieved leases

15.40 It is provided[142] that where, *inter alia*, the agreement for lease or a lease has on substantial performance and/or grant obtained the benefit of one of the exemptions or reliefs specified in FA 2003, Sch 17A, para 11 and that agreement for lease or lease is subsequently assigned to a third party, the latter is deemed to receive the grant of a new lease which is chargeable to stamp duty land tax. This exposes the assignee to liability to tax in respect of the future rent notwithstanding that covenants to pay future rent are exempted from the tax.[143] The relevant reliefs are:

- leases to charities;[144]

- intra-group leases;[145]

- leases granted in connection with reconstructions and reorganisations;[146] and

- sale and leaseback arrangements.[147]

There is power to add to the list which may have been exercised.[148]

This will represent a trap for persons acquiring leases, including leases acquired as part of the purchase of a business as a going concern, since no tax avoidance motive is required. This deemed new lease arises even where the assignment is totally unconnected with and occurs many years after the original grant.[149] This is in addition to any liabilities for outstanding stamp duty land tax issues.[150] The deemed new lease will be for the future rent which may be viable with the inevitable 5 year reviews[151] and related consequences;[152] but also for 'premium' equal to any lump sum paid to the assignor. As this is most likely to arise in relation to non-residential property, the assignee may find that even a small premium is subject to tax at 1 per cent because the relevant rent exceeds £1000 per annum.[153]

---

[141] Ibid, Sch 17A, para 12(1)(d).
[142] Ibid, Sch 17A, para 11.
[143] Ibid, Sch 17A, para 17.
[144] Ibid, Sch 8.
[145] Ibid, Sch 7, Part 1.
[146] Ibid, Sch 7, Part 2.
[147] Ibid, s 57A (as much amended).
[148] Ibid, Sch 17A, para 11(3)(d); see also s 123(3) and **11.51**.
[149] The assignee also takes over many of the payment and compliance obligations of the assignor whether or not the latter is the original tenant.
[150] FA 2003, s 81A; Sch 17A, para 12.
[151] Ibid, Sch 17A, paras 7 and 8.
[152] Ibid, Sch 17A, paras 13, 14 and 15.
[153] Ibid, Sch 15, paras 9 and 9A.

THE VENDOR

15.41 The 'vendor' is not a person liable for the stamp duty land tax; nor is he liable to notify HMRC Stamp Taxes of the sale or lease transaction. However, the identity of the 'vendor', who can include the lessor or the grantor of a chargeable interest such as an option and the tenant where he is the party providing the chargeable interest, is important in several situations, namely:

- identifying the relevant parties for subsale and other reliefs;[154]

- intra-group relief and clawback;[155]

- whether certain transactions are linked for the purposes of the lower rates of stamp duty land tax since these rules apply only to transactions between the same vendor and same purchaser or persons connected with either of them;[156]

- whether the parties are suitably related for the charge upon transactions involving connected companies or partnerships;[157]

- in applying the land exchange provisions.[158] This appears to mean that the land exchange rules apply where A transfers land to B in consideration of B transferring other land or granting a lease to C;[159]or

- whether certain reliefs are available which depend upon the parties being the same person such as surrenders or regrants.

15.42 The 'vendor' is defined[160] as the person disposing of the chargeable interest acquired together with any interest or right appurtenant or pertaining to it that is acquired with it. It includes all transactions treated or acquisitions, namely the creation, surrender, release or variation of chargeable interests.[161] The vendor is, in consequence, the person:

- whose interest or right is subject to the chargeable interest created;[162]

- who ceases to be entitled to any interest released or surrendered;[163] or

- whose interest is subject to or limited by the variation of a chargeable interest.[164]

The rules as to nominees and bare trustees also apply to vendors[165] and, essentially, the beneficial owner is the person to be included in the return as the vendor.

---

[154] Ibid, ss 45, 45A and Sch 17A, para 12B.
[155] Ibid, Sch 7, para 3(1).
[156] Ibid, s 108(1).
[157] Ibid, s 53(1); see **5.208**; ibid Sch 15, Part 3; see **Chapter 13**.
[158] Ibid, s 47; Sch 4, para 5; see **5.150**.
[159] See **5.153**.
[160] FA 2003, s 43(4).
[161] Ibid, s 43(3).
[162] Ibid, s 43(3)(a)(ii).
[163] Ibid, s 43(3)(b)(ii).
[164] Ibid, s 43(3)(c)(ii).
[165] Ibid, Sch 16, para 3.

PREPARING LAND TRANSACTION RETURNS

15.43 It is necessary to identify the vendor and purchaser in the land transaction return form (SDLT 1 and 2). This requires the purchaser's advisers to investigate the title issues. It remains to be seen how strict HMRC Stamp Taxes will be in relation to penalties where the correct vendor is not identified particularly since the so-called 'help line' has fairly consistently advised that where the vendor reasonably refuses to disclose his address the person signing the return can include the address of the purchased premises. This need to identify the vendor who is the beneficial owner and not necessarily the legal owner or which may be a partnership which holds land through some form of nominee arrangement means that the Inland Revenue Certificate (SDLT 5) which must contain the name of the vendor[166] may differ from the person executing the land transaction return. This will be one of the situations where the Land Registry may require supplementary information in order to explain the discrepancy between the Land Registry documentation and the stamp duty land tax documentation.[167]

---

[166] Stamp Duty Land Tax (Administration) Regulations 2003, SI 2003/2837, reg 5(7)(b).
[167] See **Chapter 22**.

Chapter 16

LIABILITY AND PAYMENT

16.1 The original provisions dealing with the person liable to pay and report the tax, the obligation to pay the tax and the methods of filing and payment have been extended by FA 2003, Sch 17A, so as to make persons other than the original purchaser liable to pay tax in relation to transactions to which they were not initially parties.[1] There is no restriction upon other persons paying the tax such as a mortgagee who is anxious to obtain registration of the title. However, this question of payments by third parties and retentions by mortgagees and others until such time as the stamp duty land tax issues have been resolved is not wholly effective. HMRC Stamp Taxes have in the past refused to accept payment of tax from third parties unless they are accompanied by a properly completed stamp duty land tax return signed by the true 'taxpayer'. In this situation there is little point, as such, in a mortgagee retaining funds in order to pay the stamp duty land tax. The funds should not, in practice, be released until what appears to be an appropriately executed stamp duty land tax return (SDLT 1) has been obtained since it is generally automatic that a Revenue certificate (SDLT 5) will be issued if the form *prima facie* appears to be in order.[2] If there is not a *prima facie*, valid return payment of the tax will be rejected by HMRC Stamp Taxes. Ideally, the funds should be retained until the Revenue certificate (SDLT 5) has been obtained since at this point registration of title is automatic. The Land Registry has no power to reject an application for registration that is accompanied by an Inland Revenue Certificate (SDLT 5).

16.2 The tax is reportable and self-assessed and is transaction based. In consequence, there is a heavy burden upon taxpayers who may not be aware that their actions are taxable transactions such as holding over but they may not consult professional advisers. They will be unaware of the risks that they are running and should they seek advice on the particular transaction or some subsequent transaction or proposed transaction will be required to give the client the advice that he has at some previous date incurred a tax liability and is currently subject to interest payments and very severe penalties probably equal to the tax. Failure to deal with this situation may mean that the adviser is party to the preparation of an instrument which he 'knows' to be incorrect[3] because he has not asked the right question[4] and so is exposed to penalty.[5]

---

[1] On the 'taxpayer' see **Chapter 15**.
[2] See **Chapter 22**.
[3] FA 2003, s 96.
[4] See *Slattery v Moore Stephens* [2003] STC 1379.
[5] Note also FA 2003, s 95 on evasion and knowledge that the client does not intend to deal with the previous unpaid tax liability.

LIABILITY

The purchaser

16.3   The purchaser is liable to pay the tax.[6] The identification of the 'purchaser'[7] is not a straightforward matter.[8] It is, basically, the person acquiring (within the extended meaning of that term) the chargeable interest acquired together with any interest or right appurtenant or pertaining to it that is acquired with the chargeable interest. It is stated that this definition applies even if there is no consideration given for the transaction but a person is not treated as a 'purchaser' unless he has given consideration for, or is a party to, the transaction.[9] It must also, incidentally, be noted that the chargeable consideration for the transaction must be provided, directly or indirectly, by the purchaser or a person connected with him.[10]

Other persons

Liability[11]

16.4   No other person is initially liable or, in general, 'accountable' for the stamp duty land tax owed by the purchaser, but such tax may be provisional and/or deferred in which case assignees of a lease may subsequently become responsible for both the tax and reporting.[12] The question of whether the stamp duty land tax has been paid correctly is no longer an issue of title, and a purchaser or lessee can present his documents in evidence or for registration notwithstanding either non-payment of the tax, or the fact that HMRC Stamp Taxes have successfully challenged the amount of tax initially paid provided that the registration process does not require the participation of the person who has not paid the tax and who is an essential party in the movement of the title, ie is needed to execute the Land Registry transfer or other documentation.[13]

---

[6]   FA 2003, s 85(1).

[7]   Ibid, s 43(4).

[8]   See further **Chapter 15**.

[9]   FA 2003, s 43(5).

[10]   Ibid, Sch 4, para 1(1); see **Chapter 5**.

[11]   There is a key issue in taxation between liability for the tax and accountability. The latter is, essentially, an obligation to pay tax on behalf of another usually with a right of indemnity but this indemnity is dependent upon the solvency of the taxpayer and the ability to enforce it (but note Stamp Duty Reserve Tax Regulations 1986, SI 1986/1711, reg 7 which may be helpful since HMRC Stamp Taxes have regs 2 ('accountable persons') and 4 in mind as models for the future development of the tax.

[12]   FA 2003, Sch 17A, paras 11 and 12. In addition, a person who discovers that stamp duty land tax has not been paid in respect of the current or an earlier transaction may be required to disclose the details as money laundering.

[13]   There are numerous situations where the seller is not a party to the Land Registry application and his name does not appear on the transfer or lease documentation, such as subsales. In consequence there can be differences between the Inland Revenue Certificate (SDLT 5) and the Land Registry Transfer. In such situations the seller may be required to participate in the Land Registry application. This is frequently done not by producing an appropriate certificate since the seller may not be a purchaser in a chargeable transaction but by covering letter to the Land Registry. It is not necessary for him to prove by SDLT 5 that he has paid tax on his acquisition; he must merely explain the difference between the two sets of forms. Purchasers may find it prudent to insist that such covering letter is produced with the other completion documentation since its absence is likely to delay the application to register (and affect a mortgagee's security) if the documentation is correctly prepared for submission to HMRC Stamp Taxes who appear to be becoming irritated that many transactions are not correctly reported especially in the context of identifying vendors and purchasers.

Accountability

16.5 In general,[14] no person is accountable for the stamp duty land tax payable by another person at present (ie 'accountable' but not 'liable'; he is merely required to pay another's tax out of assets belonging to the 'true taxpayer' or with a right of indemnity); but special provisions apply to personal representatives and other 'representatives',[15] certain bodies corporate[16] and liquidators.[17] For example, currently solicitors are not responsible for the stamp duty land tax payable by their clients, nor are they required to ensure that the form is returned. However, failure to take proper steps to advise the client or continuing to act after discovery that the client does not intend to pay the tax now that it is possible to obtain a Revenue Certificate without payment[18] may mean that they are liable to imprisonment for up to 7 years and/or a fine because they are knowingly concerned in the fraudulent evasion of tax by another person.[19]

Nominees and trustees

16.6 It must not be overlooked that where there is a 'bare trust', ie a trust or nominee arrangement under which property is held by a person as trustee for a person who is absolutely entitled as against the trustee or who would be so entitled but for being a minor or other person under a disability or for two or more persons who are or would be jointly so entitled,[20] the beneficial owner is treated as the person making the acquisition.[21] In such a situation, it will be the beneficial owner rather than the nominee who is required to pay the tax; but HMRC Stamp Taxes may be prepared to accept a declaration in the land transaction return signed by a nominee.[22] This, however, appears to be modified in relation to certain leases between nominees and beneficial owners.[23] In these situations the relevant person is deemed to be acquiring the full interest and would, therefore, appear to be a purchaser for the purposes of stamp duty land tax and accountable but the transaction is not deemed to take place at anything other than the actual consideration unless the nominee is a connected company,[24] so that where, for example, the lease is at a peppercorn rent no tax will be payable.[25]

Trustees other than bare trustees

16.7 In the case of trustees other than nominees, they are treated as the purchaser of the chargeable interest for the purposes of stamp duty land tax.[26] The stamp duty land

---

[14] But note the special provisions for persons in representative provisions etc such as FA 2003, s 106 or officers or liquidators of companies such as FA 2003, s 100.
[15] Ibid, s 106.
[16] Ibid, s 100(4) and (5).
[17] Ibid, s 100(7).
[18] Ibid, s 75(3)(b) having been repealed.
[19] Ibid, s 95.
[20] Ibid, Sch 16, para 1(2).
[21] Ibid, Sch 16, para 3; see **9.4**.
[22] See **9.8** and FA 2003, Sch 10, para 1A.
[23] Ibid, Sch 16, para 3 (as amended); see **9.6**.
[24] Ibid, ss 53 and 54.
[25] Ibid, Sch 3, para 1; see **11.8** and **11.19**; see also FA 2003, s 77A.
[26] Ibid, Sch 16, para 4.

tax may be recovered from any one or more of the 'responsible trustees'[27] who are the persons who are the trustees at the effective date of the transaction and any person who subsequently becomes a trustee.[28]

Joint purchasers

16.8   Where there are two or more purchasers acting jointly, ie are acquiring as joint tenants or tenants in common in England and Wales, as joint owners or owners in common in Scotland or beneficially as joint tenants, tenants in common or coparceners in Northern Ireland[29] any obligation of the purchaser applies to them jointly but may be discharged by any of them.[30] The parties will be jointly and severally liable to pay the tax[31] although any liability arising in relation to the transaction including any liability by reason of failure to fulfil any obligation is a joint and severable liability.[32]

Partnerships[33]

Normal acquisitions[34]

16.9   Where land is acquired by a partnership from a person unconnected with the partners,[35] then anything required to be done in relation to stamp duty land tax in relation to the 'purchaser' is required to be done by or in relation to all of the persons who are partners at the effective date of the transaction and by any person who becomes a member of the partnership after the effective date of the transaction.[36] There is a provision, probably of limited effect, for fiscal transparency in relation to partnerships having corporate personality[37] this linked with provisions setting out the liability suggests strongly that limited liability is removed and, for example, the members of a limited partnership[38] or limited liability partnerships[39] (LLP), appear to be personally liable for the tax without the benefit of limited liability. The relevant partners are jointly and severally liable to make a payment of the tax or interest on unpaid tax.[40] The partners may, however, appoint a representative partner or partners who, if approved by HMRC Stamp Taxes, become responsible for the payment of the tax and general compliance therewith.[41] At present, this power of the partners to appoint representatives to do things in relation to the signing of forms and payment of the tax does not relieve from the obligation to disclose upon the form details of all of the partners or vendors or purchasers. The signing requirement does not relieve from the disclosure requirements; but, in practice, the use of the partnership name is accepted by HMRC Stamp Taxes as

---

27   Ibid, Sch 16, para 5(1)(a).
28   And this would appear to include liability for any penalties outstanding; compare FA 2003, Sch 15, para 7(2).
29   Ibid, s 121.
30   Ibid, s 103(2)(a).
31   Ibid, s 103(2)(c).
32   Ibid.
33   See further **Chapter 13**.
34   FA 2003, Sch 15, Parts 1 and 2.
35   Ibid, Sch 15, Part 2.
36   Ibid, Sch 15, para 6.
37   Ibid, Sch 15, para 2; see **13.14**.
38   Limited Partnerships Act 1907.
39   Limited Liability Partnership Act 2000.
40   FA 2003, Sch 15, para 7(1)(a).
41   Ibid, Sch 15, para 8.

sufficient disclosure[42] and it seems that it is not necessary to file a large number of forms SDLT 2 identifying and giving the national insurance number of each partner.

Special regime

16.10 There is a special and complex regime for land dealings between partnerships and persons connected with the partners and partners themselves.[43] This applies to:

- acquisitions of land from connected persons by partnerships.[44] In this situation the responsibility of the partners in relation to anything required or authorised to be done by or in relation to the purchaser is the responsibility of those who were partners immediately before the transfer and who remain partners after the transfer and any person becoming a partner as result of or in connection with the transfer;[45]

- transfers of chargeable interests from a partnership to connected persons.[46] No specific provisions are provided but it would seem that the person acquiring the property from the partnership will be the 'purchaser' who is responsible for the payment of the tax and filing relevant documentation;

- transfers between partnerships.[47] In this situation HMRC Stamp Taxes may choose to treat the transaction either as an acquisition by the partnership or an acquisition from the partnership whichever produces the higher rate of tax taking into account the modifications to the relevant provisions.[48] No specific provision is set out for liability and notification. It is assumed that the transferee partnership will be the 'purchaser' for these purposes and the responsibility will be upon the basis of the provisions relating to acquisitions when the responsibility lies with those who were partners immediately before the transfer and who remain partners after the transfer and any person who becomes a partner as a result of or in connection with the transfer[49] but since HMRC Stamp Taxes must apply either of this or the preceding bullet point on demergers and mergers of partnerships it is unclear how these rules are intended to operate in such cases. Also these provisions are not necessarily appropriate where the partnerships are not or do not involve connected parties;

- transfers of interests in property investment partnerships.[50] The person responsible for the tax, ie the purchaser under the transaction, is the person who acquires an increased partnership share or, as the case may be, becomes a partner in consequence of the transfer;[51]

- anti-avoidance provisions relating to arrangements to change the partnership.[52] In this situation the partners are the purchasers under the transaction responsible for

---

42 Whether the partnership is technically the 'purchaser' or the 'vendor'.
43 FA 2003, Sch 15, Part 3; see **Chapter 13**.
44 Ibid, Sch 15, paras 10 and following.
45 Ibid, Sch 15, para 10(7).
46 Ibid, Sch 15, paras 18 and following.
47 Ibid, Sch 15, para 23.
48 See **13.52**.
49 FA 2003, Sch 15, para 10(7).
50 Ibid, Sch 15, para 14 (as amended).
51 Ibid, Sch 15, para 14(3).
52 Ibid, Sch 15, para 17; see **13.37**.

dealing with the tax.[53] However, it is provided that the partners responsible for dealing with the situation are those who were partners immediately before the transfer and who remain partners after the transfer and the person becoming a partner as a result of or in connection with the transfer;[54]

- withdrawals or repayments of capital and loans within 3 years of an acquisition by a partnership from a connected person.[55] In this situation the partners are taken to be the purchasers under the transaction;[56] but the partners who are responsible for dealing with the tax are the persons who are partners at the effective date of the transaction and any person who becomes a member of the partnership after the effective date of the transaction,[57] although these matters may be dealt with by representative partners where they exist.[58]

Companies and bodies corporate[59]

16.11 Everything required to be done by a company, including making payment of the tax, is to be done by the company acting through the proper officer of the company or unincorporated association or any other person for the time being having the express, implied or apparent authority of the company to act on its behalf, such as a person nominated by the board of directors, unless a liquidator has been appointed.[60] In particular, the tax due from an unincorporated association in the United Kingdom or elsewhere or from a company that is incorporated under the laws of a country outside the United Kingdom may, without prejudice to any other method of recovery, be recovered from the proper officer of the company[61] but such officer may retain out of any money coming into his hands on behalf of the company sufficient sums to indemnify him.[62] The proper officer of a body corporate is the secretary or the person acting as secretary;[63] in relation to an unincorporated association or company not having a secretary, the proper officer is the treasurer or person acting as treasurer[64] unless a liquidator or administrator has been appointed. Where a liquidator or administrator has been appointed then the liquidator or the administrator is the proper officer.[65]

Unit trusts and open-ended investment companies

16.12 In relation to unit trust schemes, the trustees are treated as if they were a company for these purposes.[66] Regulations may be issued to deal with the position of open-ended investment companies[67] but this power has not yet been exercised.

---

53   Ibid, Sch 15, para 17(3).
54   Ibid, Sch 15, para 7.
55   Ibid, Sch 15, para 17A.
56   Ibid, Sch 15, para 17A(5).
57   Ibid, Sch 15, para 17A(6) and para 7.
58   Ibid, Sch 15, para 17A(6) and para 8.
59   Ie bodies corporate or unincorporated associations, but not partnerships: FA 2003, s 100(1).
60   Ibid, s 100(2); there may be interesting questions of personal liability where the company is insolvent; but note the special rules for liquidators, receivers and administrators; FA 2003, s 100(7).
61   Ibid, s 100(4).
62   Ibid, s 100(5).
63   Ibid, s 100(6)(a).
64   Ibid, s 100(6)(b).
65   Ibid, s 100(7).
66   Ibid, s 100(1).
67   Ibid, s 102.

Incapacity

16.13 The responsibility for the payment of stamp duty land tax owed by a person who is incapacitated lies upon the person having the direction, management or control of the incapacitated person's property,[68] such as a person holding an enduring power of attorney. He is entitled to reimburse himself out of money[69] coming into his hands and to be indemnified in respect of any payment of stamp duty land tax.[70]

Minors

16.14 The parents or guardians of a minor are liable for the stamp duty land tax that is not paid by the minor.[71]

Deceased persons

16.15 The personal representatives of a deceased person who is a 'purchaser' for the purposes of stamp duty land tax are responsible for paying the tax.[72] They are entitled to reimbursement out of the assets of the deceased,[73] if any.[74] However, such personal representatives are faced with many technical problems such as where the deceased has failed to pay the tax or has been involved with negligent advice or the preparation of a negligent return[75] or even where the deceased has dealt properly with the acquisition of land and may have deferred any variable tax liability[76] but has not included a reasonable exit strategy in the contract for the acquisition of the property or the grant of the lease in question.[77]

Receivers

16.16 Court-appointed receivers are responsible for the payment of stamp duty land tax in respect of any property over which they have the direction and control in the same way as if they had not been appointed by the court.[78]

NOTIFICATION AND SELF-ASSESSMENT

16.17 The purchaser, including the persons listed above plus any person who is deemed to acquire a chargeable interest[79] and in certain situations, third parties who are affected by the open tax liability of the original taxpayer,[80] is required to deliver a return of every notifiable transaction,[81] which return must include a self-assessment of the stamp duty land tax chargeable in respect of the transaction calculated on the basis of the

---

[68] Ibid, s 100(1)(a).
[69] But not, it seems, other assets.
[70] FA 2003, s 106(1)(b).
[71] Ibid, s 106(2).
[72] Ibid, s 106(3)(a); see also **5.206** for problems of open tax positions such as earnouts and clawbacks.
[73] Ibid, s 106(3)(b).
[74] No special rules for priority are provided.
[75] FA 2003, Sch 10, para 8.
[76] Ibid, ss 51, 89 and 90; Stamp Duty Land Tax (Administration) Regulations 2003, SI 2003/2837, Part 4.
[77] Ibid, s 81A; Sch 17A, para 12.
[78] Ibid, s 106(4).
[79] See, for example, ibid, Sch 17A, paras 14, 15 and 15A.
[80] For example ibid, s 81A; Sch 17A, para 12.
[81] Ibid, s 76(1); see **Chapter 22**.

information contained in the return.[82] It is, however, no longer necessary for there to be simultaneous payment and filing.[83] This requires the taxpayer to decide whether the transaction is notifiable requiring a land transaction return (SDLT 1) or is not a chargeable transaction and subject to difficulties with the Land Registry,[84] not requiring any filing whatsoever.[85] It must also be noted that the self-assessment process is required each time a notification or land transaction return is required, such as in relation to variable rents[86] or the clawback reliefs (e g intra-group transactions and acquisitions by charities).[87]

16.18 Taxpayers must take reasonable steps to check the accuracy of the information in the form,[88] including 'market cost' of services and construction works, the impact of rent reviews and turnover and anticipated future levels of service charges where these are reserved as rent not apportioned;[89] and they must take a considered view as to whether to 'take' any reliefs or exemptions,[90] ie calculate the tax that would be payable and adjust that by treating the transaction or relevant part of the transaction as relieved and declaring the tax as nil or appropriately reduced in the land transaction return and inserting the reference the relief relied upon. Self-assessment involves a massive risk-shifting exercise and calculating the tax chargeable upon the correct chargeable consideration as calculated by the taxpayer.

16.19 In consequence, any errors in the self-assessment or in the preparation of the information used to complete the return will mean that an incorrect return has been filed,[91] with the consequent tax-related penalties[92] if completed fraudulently or negligently,[93] or if not corrected without unreasonable delay once an error has been discovered by the taxpayer.[94] The error may also extend the periods during which HMRC Stamp Taxes can reopen a transaction on the basis of a 'discovery' from 6 years to 21 years,[95] or demand documents or information from third parties beyond 6 years with the consent of the General or Special Commissioners.[96] Many such areas of self-assessment will require the making of difficult judgments. Mere disagreement with HMRC Stamp Taxes will not necessarily produce a negligent or fraudulent return

---

[82]   Ibid, s 76(3)(a).
[83]   Ibid, s 76(3)(b) (as amended), although certain failure to deal with the consequentials of these amendments are not complete but it seems that and Inland Revenue Certificate (SDLT 5) can be issued notwithstanding that payment has not been received; note the apparently unamended provisions of Stamp Duty Land Tax (Administration) Regulations 2003, SI 2003/2837, reg 4(5).
[84]   See **Chapter 22**.
[85]   Such as transactions where a party is eligible for subsale relief or a surrender and regrant where the landlord may not be providing 'chargeable consideration' (FA 2003, s 45 (as amended); Sch 17A, paras 9 and 16). These may require explanatory letters to the Land Registry.
[86]   FA 2003, s 80.
[87]   Ibid, s 81.
[88]   Their advisers may be negligent if they do not ask the right questions to produce the right answers; *Slattery v Moore Stephens* [2003] STC 1379; and failure to process the data in the correct way such as adopting an incorrect valuation procedure (see *Langham v Veltema* [2004] STC 544) so that the information may be incorrect.
[89]   See **5.215** and **7.138**.
[90]   See **11.11**.
[91]   On the duty of professional advisers see *Slattery v Moore Stephens* [2003] STC 1379.
[92]   Ie a sum not exceeding the amount of unpaid tax; FA 2003, Sch 10, para 8(2).
[93]   FA 2003, Sch 10, para 8(1)(a).
[94]   Ibid, Sch 10, para 8(1)(b).
[95]   Ibid, Sch 10, para 31(2).
[96]   Ibid, Sch 13, para 24.

attracting penalties, although late payment interest charges will arise and the taxpayer may be put to considerable cost to justify the figures included in the land transaction return.

16.20 This self-assessment requirement consequently applies to a whole range of actual and deemed transactions,[97] such as where:

- an exemption or relief is clawed back in relation to intra-group transactions and company reorganisations and charities;[98]

- new information emerges in relation to contingent or uncertain or unascertained consideration within FA 2003, s 51;[99]

- the '5-year review' of uncertain rent;[100]

- the notification of clawback of reliefs;[101]
    - whether the new anti-avoidance rules apply since these do not require a tax avoidance motive.[102] This is in addition to any land transaction return required for the actual acquisition by 'P';
    - whether the deemed new lease rules apply to an assignment.[103]

- later linked transactions,[104] such as leases granted pursuant to the exercise of an option to renew;[105]

- deemed extensions of leases where the holding over rules apply;[106]

- continuations of periodic and similar tenancies, such as assured shorthold tenancies which continue;[107]

- deemed grants of new leases.[108]

In many cases, the self-assessment process will be relatively straightforward, ie applying the relevant percentage to the cash sum payable. However, in other cases the issue may not be quite so simple. For example:

---

[97] Ibid, s 81A.
[98] Ibid, s 81(2)(a).
[99] Ibid, s 80(2)(b).
[100] Ibid, Sch 17A, paras 7 and 8.
[101] Ibid, Sch 8, para 2; Sch 7, paras 3 and 9.
[102] Ibid, ss 73A and 77; Stamp Duty Land Tax (Variation of the Finance Act 2003) Regulations 2006, SI 2006/3237.
[103] Ibid, Sch 17A, para 11.
[104] Note also the fact that the filing of a later return relating to the same land may empower HMRC Stamp Taxes to launch an Enquiry into an earlier return or earlier stage in the transaction notwithstanding that the statutory limited period of 9 months has expired; FA 2003, Sch 10, para 12(2A) and they may issue a discovery assessment notwithstanding that here has been a previous full Enquiry; FA 2003, Sch 10, para 30(3).
[105] Ibid, s 81A; Sch 17A, para 12.
[106] Ibid, Sch 17A, para 3(1)(b).
[107] Ibid, Sch 17A, para 4.
[108] Ibid, Sch 17A, paras 13 and 14(2).

- the taxpayer is required to apply the formula for determining the net present value of the rent correctly which requires many detailed issues of 'guestimating' future rent, adjusted rental payments from a yearly to a monthly basis in order to find the assumed rent for years after the expiration of the fifth year;[109]

- the taxpayer must apply the correct rules for determining the annual rent[110] for the £1000 rent threshold for nil rate premiums for leases of non-residential property;[111]

- the taxpayer is required to apply the correct formula for calculating the stamp duty land tax upon the rent. As the temporal discount rate will vary, it is important to note that, it seems that where, for example, there is a variable rent which requires subsequent notification, the formula to be applied is that in force at the time of the effective date of the transaction, not the date of the variation. It will be necessary to check that the historic formula is still provided online by HMRC Stamp Taxes and/or that it is correctly applied;

- the taxpayer is required to understand the difference between a contingent sum and uncertain and unascertained consideration, including uncertain rent.[112] The latter requires the taxpayer to make a reasonable estimate of the amount of chargeable consideration, including, where appropriate, future service charges that will actually be payable in the future. This would appear to require tenants who are paying some form of variable rent (which may include service charges and guesses as to future changes in the rate of VAT) to make a reasonable prediction of the level of passing rent in the future over the life of the lease[113] in order to have reasonable sums to include in the rent formula;

- the taxpayer will be required to make reasonable estimate of market value, probably upon the basis of independent professional advice for most forms of consideration in kind;[114]

- the taxpayer must take reasonable steps to determine the open market cost of works and services;[115]

- appropriate steps are required to determine anticipated levels of taxable benefits in kind for service tenancies and deemed rents;[116]

- the taxpayer must be able to justify his view that land in excess of 0.5 hectares is appropriate to the residential property included in any land exchange or relocation arrangement eligible for relief;[117]

---

[109] Ibid, Sch 17A, para 7(3) which is inappropriate for most leases paying rent on a quarterly basis, and where rent may be paid initially on an estimated basis in advance to be adjusted later such as many turnover rents.
[110] See **5.24**.
[111] FA 2003, Sch 5, paras 9 and 9A.
[112] Ibid, s 51.
[113] Pursuant to ibid, Sch 6A, paras 1–7.
[114] Ibid, Sch 4, para 7.
[115] Ibid, Sch 4, para 11(1).
[116] Ibid, Sch 6A, para 7(3).
[117] Pursuant to ibid, Sch 4, para 14.

- the taxpayer must be able to support the argument that, upon a surrender and regrant where relief has been taken,[118] the old and the new lease are 'substantially' the same; and

- the taxpayer must be able to produce suitable evidence that he had reasonable grounds for taking the benefit of any exemption or relief, such as where the transaction was in connection with a scheme of reconstruction that qualified for relief pursuant to FA 2003, Sch 7, Part 2 or that such a scheme will be regarded by HMRC Stamp Taxes as being *bona fide* commercial and not for tax avoidance.[119]

These obligations may also apply to assignees of leases,[120] who also is responsible for the self-assessment of his own tax but this may depend upon the tax position of the assignor so that the assignee's self-assessment depends upon the self-assessment of the assignor and challenges thereto by HMRC Stamp Taxes including successful challenges and assessments many years after the assignment.

16.21 Self-assessment involves the calculation of the amount of stamp duty land tax to be paid on the transaction. This involves, broadly, four steps:

- being aware that the transaction is taxable in its own right and is an event that requires a filing and retrospective adjustment of a previous transaction such as a rent review or holding over or the postponement of a rent review or a change in the rate of VAT. In many of these situations the taxpayer will not necessarily seek professional advice at all or until too late to avoid problems. These issues and the related lack of finality as regards most of the tax in practice place a heavy burden upon solicitors to ensure that they give appropriate advice to clients as to their future liabilities and potential risks from certain possible future actions;

- calculating the amount of chargeable consideration;[121]

- applying the appropriate rate to the chargeable amount; and

- deducting the amount of tax paid in respect of any previous land transaction returns for the same chargeable transaction such as variable rents.

Only the excess over tax previously paid is payable. Since the land transaction return can be applied to several acquisitions with the same effective date and includes both sales and leases, there will be calculations involving purchase prices, lease premiums and rent which have different principles and rate structures. These sums and the tax due in respect thereof have to be aggregated for inclusion in the land transaction return.

The chargeable amount

16.22 The reference in the return to the consideration is to the chargeable consideration not the actual consideration, another problem for the taxpayer. In most cases this is a simple process as the chargeable consideration or the rent will be cash. However, stamp duty land tax has introduced a wider range of chargeable consideration based upon

---

[118] See **7.85**.
[119] See **Chapter 12**.
[120] FA 2003, s 81A; Sch 17A, para 11; see **7.235**.
[121] See **Chapter 5**.

market or projected future values or costs. It is the taxpayer's obligation to prepare these figures and produce a market value,[122] which can be challenged by HMRC Stamp Taxes.[123] HMRC Stamp Taxes can challenge the return for up to 21 years if the valuation is negligent or fraudulent or if the methodology adopted and the factors taken into account are inappropriate and negligent.[124] Appropriate advice would seem to be essential and full records of the advice and the basis upon which it was prepared should be obtained and prepared and retained since these may, in effect, become documents of title as they are essential for successors in title sealing with how own tax position because this relates back to prior events[125] or he has become responsible for the open tax position of some predecessor in title.[126]

16.23 The greatest practical difficulty in self-assessment is dealing with variable consideration[127] where the taxpayer is required to make reasonable estimates of the amount[128] of future overage or clawback payments or of the effect of future rent reviews. Professional advice is difficult to obtain because advisers are not fortune tellers. The so-called 'help-line' is, in general, advising taxpayers to ignore this aspect of the consideration initially and to deal with the problem when the certainties eventually emerge. Unfortunately this exposes taxpayers acting on this basis to an interest charge backdated to 30 days after the effective date, which can be easily avoided by making an estimate and applying to postpone the payment.[129] In addition there may be penalties associated with the preparation of an incorrect return.[130] In the unhelpful words of Russell LJ in *Crane Freuhauf v IRC*[131] when dealing with difficult issues of share valuations 'the parties must do the best they can' and take the risk of penalties and interest if they get it wrong.

16.24 It will become an important issue of principle for debate with HMRC Stamp Taxes across the whole range of their enforcement powers as to whether the parties when they have made a mistake or have provided a value with which HMRC Stamp Taxes disagree have necessarily been negligent. Provided the taxpayer has taken proper advice and can show from written contemporaneous records that the proper factors have been taken into account it may be difficult for HMRC Stamp Taxes to establish 'negligence' in the preparation of the self-assessment.

Rate

16.25 It needs to be noted that the rate[132] applied may be only provisional because there may be changes in the rate of VAT or sums do not become payable or there are

---

122 See **Chapter 27**.
123 Note the ease with which HMRC were able to issue a discovery assessment challenging market values in *Langham v Veltema* [2004] STC 544. The subsequent publication by HMRC of the practices which they intend to apply in the future does not bind HMRC Stamp Taxes who are not parties to it.
124 FA 2003, Sch 10, para 31.
125 See, for example, ibid, Sch 17A, para 3.
126 See, for example, ibid, s 81A; Sch 17A, para 12.
127 See **5.187** and **7.113**.
128 This return must reflect the possible sum not the likelihood of its becoming payable; see **5.195**.
129 See FA 2003, ss 80 and 90; Stamp Duty Land Tax (Administration) Regulations 2003, SI 2003/2837, Part 4. There are also suggestions that HMRC Stamp Taxes may refuse to mitigate penalties even where the taxpayer's claim for relief was based upon incorrect or inappropriate advice from the so-called 'help-line'.
130 FA 2003, Sch 10, para 8.
131 [1975] STC 51.
132 See **Chapter 5**.

later linked transactions not necessarily relating to the same property[133] requiring adjustment and new returns.[134] Where the consideration is variable the rate of tax has to be applied to the estimated figure in the land transaction return. For example, where the parties believe their transaction is a transfer of a going concern for the purposes of VAT but include the usual provision to deal with the situation should a HMRC Customs and Excise disagree the rate of tax will be determined by reference, initially, to the basic price plus the potential VAT. This may push the transaction through a particular threshold. Similarly, where there is some form of clawback or uncertain consideration the rate of tax will be determined by reference to the total estimated consideration which again may push the transaction through a particular threshold that would have otherwise applied to the initial or basic price. These requirements as to the rate apply notwithstanding that the actual tax upon the deferred or VAT element is deferred.[135] Obviously, should the additional consideration not become payable then the taxpayer will, *prima facie*, be entitled to a refund of tax arising in relation to the initial or basic price because of the reduction in the rate applicable to the final consideration.[136]

Previous tax and repayment claims

16.26 Much of stamp duty land tax is initially self-assessed on a provisional basis requiring later returns and retrospective re-self-assessment.[137] Although not obvious from the land transaction return (SDLT 1) the entry for the consideration,[138] which refers to chargeable consideration not actual consideration, refers to the total or aggregate estimated consideration as at the date of the return. This is utilised to calculate the total tax for the chargeable transaction to date;[139] but the entry for the amount of tax paid[140] is to the net balance after deducting tax previously paid from the total tax. There is no obvious machinery for making this deduction clear since unless HMRC Stamp Taxes, in their uncertain and variable practice, are prepared to accept and an amendment where the circumstances can be set out in the relevant letter, a completely new return is required with its own numbers or bar codes and there is no facility for cross-referencing to previous returns. It would seem that where the return involves a repayment of tax this may be dealt with by means of an amendment provided that this is within 12 months of the effective date.[141] Where this does not apply there is a procedure for making claims[142] introduced some time after the commencement of the tax by what is now FA 2003, Sch 11A.[143] The difficulty is, however, that whilst the land transaction return is adequate to deal with the situation where no additional tax is payable there is no provision in the return for a situation where the subsequent event establishes that too much tax was paid and there is a negative figure. The taxpayer is, in effect, asking for a repayment of tax overpaid. In this situation the taxpayer may have to submit a return in respect of the latest transaction showing no additional tax payable and making a claim in respect of any tax overpaid on a previous occasion.[144]

---

133 Because there are two distinct linked transaction regimes for leases namely FA 2003, Sch 5, para 2(5); Sch 17A, para 5; see also s 81A and Sch 17A, para 12.
134 FA 2003, s 87A.
135 Stamp Duty Land Tax (Administration) Regulations 2003, SI 2003/2837; FA 2003, ss 90 and 80.
136 See **5.198**, **5.201** and **5.**205; see also FA 2003, Sch 7, para 8.
137 On the title issue and records required see **2.15**.
138 SDLT 1 Box 10.
139 SDLT 1 Box 14.
140 SDLT 1 Box 15.
141 FA 2003, Sch 10, para 6.
142 Which may relate to an error or mistake claim FA 2003, Sch 10, para 34 with its own limitation period.
143 See **17.26**.
144 Taxpayers such as purchasers of leases who may be involved in a situation of having to assume the responsibilities and liabilities of the original taxpayer may require indemnities against additional tax but the

Payment

General points

16.27 The stamp duty land tax must be paid within 30 days of the effective date[145] for the transaction or the clawback date or where the relevant information for the uncertain consideration emerges or a payment is made. If the cheque is paid on first presentation, payment is treated as made on the day on which the cheque was received by HMRC Stamp Taxes,[146] which may be relevant for computing interest.[147] It is no longer necessary that payment must be made together with the delivery of the land transaction return.[148] It is now possible to obtain an Inland Revenue Certificate (SDLT 5) notwithstanding that tax has not been paid.[149] Payment may be made by cheque. It is recommended that the transaction reference number (bar code) that appears on any payment slip or land transaction return should be set out upon the cheque. It is important to have this referencing since even where the cheque accompanies the land transaction return it is not unusual for HMRC Stamp Taxes to lose track of the cheque and the taxpayer may find it difficult to prove that he has actually made payment. When utilising forms available electronically,[150] it is vital that the necessary steps are taken to ensure that the document identification number appears on the return,[151] any supplemental forms, for example, SDLT 4, the payslip, the cheque and any plans required by the land transaction return. This requires steps other than merely calling up the form within the solicitor's own system. Now that there is a separation of the requirements for filing and payment other forms of payment are possible, but there is a risk that, if the cheque or other form of payment does not accompany the land transaction return, HMRC Stamp Taxes may not be able to match the payment with the land transaction return for the purpose of acknowledging receipt of payment in order to issue the Revenue certificate (SDLT5)for the purposes of the Land Registry.

Special situations and forfeiture of reliefs

Clawback of reliefs

16.28 Where a relief or reduced rate has been made available in respect of intra-group transactions, company reconstructions or reorganisations[152] or in respect of acquisitions by charities,[153] and that relief is clawed back, as a result of the withdrawal of the relief, the tax must be paid within 30 days of the clawback event,[154] together with the required

---

original taxpayer may require some form of counter-indemnity whereby the assignee of the lease will be required to account for any windfall repayment that he may receive.

[145] Note the power of HMRC to reduce the payment period from 30 days; FA 2003, s 76(2).
[146] Ibid, s 92.
[147] Ibid, s 87.
[148] Ibid, ss 76(3)(b) and 86(1) (as amended).
[149] The regulations relating to the contents of an Inland Revenue Certificate (SDLT 5) refers to payment having been made but this is, it seems, an oversight in dealing with the consequential amendments required for the separation of filing and payment.
[150] Stamp Duty Land Tax (Electronic Communications) Regulations 2005, SI 2005/844; see **17.30**.
[151] There may also be issues as to whether such forms incorporate the necessary declaration signed by the taxpayer (FA 2003, Sch 10, paras 1(a), (c); 1A; Stamp Duty Land Tax (Administration) Regulations 2003, SI 2003/2837, reg 4(3)(b)).
[152] FA 2003, Sch 7.
[153] Ibid, Sch 8.
[154] Ibid, ss 81 and 86.

land transaction return.[155] Similar returns are required where any of the special reliefs for residential property pursuant to FA 2003, Sch 6A are forfeited.[156]

Variable consideration

16.29 Where the consideration including rent is contingent, unascertained or uncertain,[157] but not an uncertain annuity,[158] the taxpayer is required to notify HMRC Stamp Taxes and make any appropriate payment of additional tax when the sum becomes 'ascertained' including all or any part of tax the payment of which has been postponed[159] whenever new information arises that makes the transaction either notifiable initially or indicates that additional tax is payable in respect of that which was originally paid. The purchaser[160] must make a return within 30 days of the receipt of the new information, which return must contain a self-assessment of the tax and must be accompanied by payment of the tax or any additional tax payable.[161] If the effect of the new information is that less tax is payable than has already been paid, the amount overpaid may be reclaimed by the purchaser, together with interest from the date of payment.[162]

Amended returns[163]

16.30 The taxpayer is empowered to amend a land transaction return, although, in general, an amendment may not be made more than 12 months after the expiration of the 30 days from the effective transaction[164] or is obliged to make a further return because, for example, uncertain consideration becomes more certain.[165] It seems that 'amendment' does not require the taxpayer to retrieve the original form and physically alter the entries. Amendment is to be made by notice in a form to be prescribed by HMRC Stamp Taxes[166] and must contain the information which they require. It seems that at present an explanatory letter setting out the adjusted information and a recalculation of the tax is accepted by HMRC Stamp Taxes as an effective 'amendment'.[167] Where an amendment is made before the expiration of the 30 days after the effective date, then the date for payment of the additional tax becoming due is the

---

[155] Ibid, s 81(1).

[156] Ibid, Sch 6A, para 11.

[157] Ibid, s 51; see **5.188**.

[158] Ibid, s 52(5); see **5.121**.

[159] Ibid, ss 80 and 90; Stamp Duty Land Tax (Administration) Regulations 2003, SI 2003/2837, Part 4.

[160] Which includes an assignee of a lease; FA 2003, s 87A; Sch 17A, para 12.

[161] Ibid, s 80(2).

[162] Ibid, s 80(4).

[163] See also **17.26**; and FA 2003, Sch 10, para 18 and Sch 11A, para 4.

[164] It seem that is some situations where a second or subsequent land transaction return is required within 12 months of the original filing date HMRC Stamp Taxes may be prepared to accept 'an amendment' to the return rather than requiring a separate land transaction return. This would seem to be a convenient procedure where it is permitted since the amendment would take the form of an explanatory letter setting out all the circumstances and appropriate cross-referencing. Where a full return is required by HMRC Stamp Taxes there will still need to be an explanatory letter setting out why no tax is payable and, even more significantly, why the taxpayer is expecting a repayment, provided that he encloses the contract and conveyance and other relevant documentation; FA 2003, Sch 10, para 6(2A).

[165] Ibid, Sch 10, para 6.

[166] At present it seems that HMRC Stamp Taxes may be prepared to act on the basis of a letter.

[167] This procedure may be adopted as part of a process of reclaiming overpaid tax; but note the restrictions on error and mistake claims in FA 2003, Sch 10, para 34; see also ibid, Sch 11A.

thirtieth day after the effective date.[168] Where tax becomes payable as a result of an amendment to a return made after the thirtieth day has passed, the tax must be paid forthwith.

Determinations and assessments

16.31 Where the stamp duty land tax is due pursuant to a determination[169] or assessment made by HMRC Stamp Taxes, the tax is payable within 30 days[170] after the issue of the determination or assessment.

Deferment of payment of tax

16.32 Since the stamp duty land tax regime has tried to adopt the apparent benefits of the alleged stamp duty contingency principle of producing artificially high tax charges and produced a system working on 'guestimates' and lack of finality there has had to be a limited modification of the hardships of the regime and to a limited extent tax on estimated figures may be postponed but importantly not in the expensive area of rents which at present are virtually all variable and have to be returned on an estimated basis under penalty if the estimate is low. This deferment is virtually automatic since HMRC Stamp Taxes have very limited powers to refuse the application to postpone tax.[171]

Variable consideration

16.33 The taxpayer may apply to HMRC Stamp Taxes for the deferment of payment of tax in a case where the amount of the chargeable consideration at the effective date of the transaction is contingent or uncertain[172] and falls to be paid or provided on one or more future dates, of which at least one falls or may fall more than 6 months after the effective date of the transaction.[173] Regulations have been published to establish this facility.[174] These regulations indicate that this postponement facility is also available where tax is charged by reference to costs such as building works and services.[175] In this latter case the application for postponement must include a detailed timetable of proposed payments and other matters.

Procedure for deferment

16.34 Where the consideration is variable namely the consideration is contingent or uncertain[176] and may be paid or provided on one or more future dates of which at least one falls or may fall more than 6 months after the effective date of the transaction the taxpayer may apply to postpone the tax, the taxpayer may apply to defer the tax on the variable element.[177] However, the application must be made on or before the last day of the filing period relating to the transaction in question.[178] HMRC Stamp Taxes have

---

[168] Ibid, s 86(3).
[169] Ibid, Sch 10, Parts 4 and 5; see **17.35** and **23.2**.
[170] Ibid, s 86(4).
[171] Stamp Duty Land Tax (Administration) Regulations 2003, SI 2003/2837, Part 4, reg 17; see **16.35**.
[172] But not 'unascertained' nor rent; FA 2003, s 90(1) and (7).
[173] FA 2003, s 86(4).
[174] Stamp Duty Land Tax (Administration) Regulations 2003, SI 2003/2837, Part 4.
[175] FA 2003, Sch 4, paras 10 and 11; Stamp Duty Land Tax (Administration) Regulations 2003, SI 2003/2837, reg 13.
[176] FA 2003, s 51.
[177] Ibid, s 90.
[178] Stamp Duty Land Tax (Administration) Regulations 2003, SI 2003/2837, reg 11.

proved difficult in relation to the extension of the 30 day period claiming that they have no powers of care and management[179] nor do they have power to extend the tax notwithstanding the clear wording of FA 2003, s 97. It is, however, possible to apply even before contracts are entered into or before completion in order to ensure that the actions of the parties may not produce an effective date earlier than the parties are planning and so cause the 30 day period to run from an earlier date that anticipated. This is recognised by the land transaction returns which refer to permission to postpone having been already obtained. The application must be in writing setting out all the facts and circumstances relevant to it and, in particular, must set out:

- the consideration to which it relates;

- the respects in which the consideration is contingent or uncertain. This is important since it is necessary to identify the consideration as being contingent or uncertain since 'unascertained' consideration cannot be postponed and there is no power to postpone the tax upon variable rents;[180] and

- the events on the occurrence of which the whole or any part of the consideration will either cease to be contingent or become ascertained.[181]

Additional information is required where the consideration consists of works or services.[182] In this situation the application to defer the tax must contain, in addition to the above information, a scheme for payment of tax setting out a proposal for payment of the tax in respect of the consideration or element of the consideration consisting of the carrying out of such works or the provision of services but in 30 days after the carrying out or provision is substantially completed. If the carrying out of such works or the provision of such services is expected to last for more than 6 months, proposals for a scheme of payment of tax at intervals of not more than 6 months must be included.[183] HMRC Stamp Taxes are given power to deliver a written notice requiring a person by whom an application to defer payment of tax has been made to provide such information as they may reasonably require for the purpose of determining whether to accept the application. This notice must specify the time during which the applicant must comply with it; but this must not be less than 30 days from the date of the issue of the notice.[184] Failure to provide the information required by HMRC Stamp Taxes is a reason for refusing the application for deferring the tax.[185]

16.35 The ability to postpone the tax is virtually automatic, provided that the appropriate letter is sent to Birmingham Stamp Office within the prescribed time limit and the payments may exceed a period of 6 months. HMRC Stamp Taxes have very limited power to reject the application.[186] These are:

- the conditions for making an application set out in s 90 are not satisfied;

---

[179] But see FA 2003, s 42(3).
[180] FA 2003, s 90(1) referring only to contingent and uncertain consideration and (7).
[181] Stamp Duty Land Tax (Administration) Regulations 2003, SI 2003/2837, reg 12(2); see also s 80.
[182] Chargeable pursuant to FA 2003, Sch 4, paras 10 and 11.
[183] Stamp Duty Land Tax (Administration) Regulations 2003, SI 2003/2837, reg 13(2).
[184] Ibid, reg 14.
[185] Ibid, reg 17(e).
[186] Ibid, reg 17.

- the application does not set out the information required. This means that it is important to set out all relevant and required information in the initial letter or application;

- there are tax avoidance arrangements in relation to the transaction.[187] For these purposes arrangements are tax avoidance if one of their main objects is to enable payment of tax payment in respect of the transaction to be deferred or to avoid the amount or value of the whole or part of the chargeable consideration for the transaction being determined in accordance with the provisions of FA 2003, s 51, which deals with variable consideration.[188] It must also be noted that the power to defer the payment of tax does not apply where the tax has been paid so that it is not possible to reclaim tax paid upon variable consideration.

Prima facie, where an application has been made or an appeal has been entered against the refusal to grant the application the tax remains due and payable as if there had been no application or appeal.[189] However, payment of tax which would not be due and payable if the application were to be accepted is to be postponed pending the reaching of the decision on the application. If the application is refused and there is no appeal then the tax is due and payable as if it were tax due by reason of an assessment issued by HMRC Stamp Taxes ie from the date on which the application notice is refused.[190]

16.36 Should HMRC Stamp Taxes reject the application on the limited grounds available to them, they must give written notice to the person by whom the application is made and the grounds for the refusal and the amount of tax payable in consequence of the refusal. However, where HMRC Stamp Taxes accept an application they must issue a written notice to the taxpayer setting out the terms on which the application has been accepted including, in particular, any tax payable in accordance with the land transaction return relating to the transaction in question, the nature of any relevant events whereby the consideration will be regarded as ceasing to be contingent or uncertain and the dates of any such events, if known.[191] The notice must also state that tax is payable within 30 days after the occurrence of one of these trigger events.[192] Further information is required in a return where the deferred consideration consists of works or services.[193]

The advantage in making the deferment application having declared the relevant amount in the land transaction return is that interest in respect of the tax that is deferred accrues only from 30 days after the relevant event triggering the liability to account for the tax.

Appeals

16.37 Where there is an appeal against amendment of a self-assessment or against a conclusion stated or amendment made in a closure notice or a discovery assessment or

---

[187] It is difficult to see how HMRC Stamp Taxes might at this stage have evidence to suggest that there is, what the might regard as, 'tax avoidance' under the regulation require the taxpayer to set out purposes and motives.
[188] Stamp Duty Land Tax (Administration) Regulations 2003, SI 2003/2837, reg 18.
[189] Ibid, reg 15.
[190] Ibid, reg 15(3) and (4).
[191] Ibid, reg 16(2).
[192] Ibid, reg 4(2).
[193] Ibid, reg 27.

an assessment to recover excessive repayment of tax, the tax in question remains due and payable as if there had been no appeal.[194] However, parties may agree that payment of an amount of tax should be postponed pending the determination of an appeal;[195] or the taxpayer who has grounds for believing that he was overcharged tax may by written notice apply to the Commissioners for a direction that payment of an amount of tax should be postponed pending the determination of the appeal. The amount, if any, of the tax postponed may be reviewed if there is a change of circumstances. Either party may apply for such a review.[196]

Interest on unpaid tax[197]

Basic position

16.38 Interest is payable on the amount of any unpaid stamp duty land tax from the expiration of 30 days after the effective date until the tax is paid,[198] at the rate fixed from time to time pursuant to the powers contained in s 178 of the FA 1989.[199] It is possible to avoid or reduce the interest charge by depositing an amount with HMRC Stamp Taxes. In such a case, interest is charged only upon any stamp duty land tax payable on the excess, if any, of the amount over the sum deposited.[200]

Clawback and forfeiture of reliefs

16.39 In a case where relief from tax has been obtained because of group transactions[201] or company reconstructions[202] or reorganisations[203] or charitable relief,[204] but such relief is forfeited, interest runs from 30 days after the clawback event that gives rise to the cancellation of the relief.[205]

Instalments

16.40 In a case of deferred payment where the consideration is contingent or uncertain, interest runs from 30 days after the date when the deferred payment is due.[206] If the payment is not deferred for such contingent or uncertain consideration, interest upon tax paid upon subsequent adjustments pursuant to FA 2003, s 80, runs from the effective date of the transaction.[207] Where the amount deferred is lower than the final tax charge because, for example, the original estimates were below the final figures, the excess bears interest from 30 days after the effective date.

---

[194] FA 2003, Sch 10, paras 39 and 40.
[195] Ibid, Sch 10, para 40.
[196] Ibid, Sch 10, para 39.
[197] Whilst HMRC Stamp Taxes have power to mitigate penalties, they do not have power to relieve from the liability to pay interest.
[198] FA 2003, s 87(1).
[199] Ibid, s 87(7).
[200] Ibid, s 87(6).
[201] Ibid, Sch 7, Part 1.
[202] Ibid, Sch 7, Part 2, para 7.
[203] Ibid, Sch 7, Part 2, para 8.
[204] Ibid, Sch 8.
[205] Ibid, s 87(3)(a).
[206] Ibid, s 87(3)(b).
[207] Ibid, s 87(5).

16.41 Where there has been a postponement of tax pending the determination of an appeal such deferment of the tax does not affect the date from which the interest is payable, ie it continues to run from 30 days after the effective date.

Forfeiture of residential reliefs

16.42 Where the relief granted for residential property pursuant to FA 2003, Sch 6A,[208] is forfeited pursuant to para 11 thereof, interest runs from 30 days after the event giving rise to the forfeiture.[209]

COLLECTION OF TAX

16.43 Where tax is due and payable, a collector may make a demand for the sum charged from the person liable to pay it.[210] On payment, the collector is required to give a receipt if so requested.[211] If the person neglects or refuses to pay, HMRC Stamp Taxes may recover the tax:

- by distraint in England and Wales or Northern Ireland;[212] or

- by diligence in Scotland;[213] or

- an amount not exceeding £2,000 due by and payable by way of tax may be recoverable as a civil debt or proceeding in England and Wales or Northern Ireland in a magistrates' court or court of summary jurisdiction;[214] and

- proceedings for the recovery of tax as a debt due to the Crown may be brought in a county court or in a sheriff court,[215] or in the High Court or in the Court of Session (in Scotland).[216]

SELF-ASSESSMENT[217]

Duty to calculate the tax

16.44 The taxpayer has a duty to self-assess the tax and there is no automatic scrutiny of the information set out in the return nor the processing of the materials necessary to produce that data such as the methodology adopted for determining market value or estimating future values.[218] Since the risks of detection of errors or fraud is random at present it is necessary to have suitably severe sanctions where 'errors' are detected and HMRC Stamp Taxes can establish that the return is incorrect. This is set out in FA 2003,

---

[208] See **Chapter 10**.
[209] FA 2003, s 87(3)(c) and (4)(za).
[210] Ibid, Sch 12, para 1(1).
[211] Ibid, Sch 12, para 1(2).
[212] Ibid, Sch 12, para 2.
[213] Ibid, Sch 12, para 3.
[214] Ibid, Sch 12, para 4.
[215] Ibid, Sch 12, para 5.
[216] Ibid, Sch 12, para 6.
[217] For recovery of overpaid tax see also **Chapter 23**.
[218] Note *Langham v Veltema* [2004] STC 544.

Sch 10, para 8 which, *inter alia*, provides that a person who fraudulently or negligently delivers a land transaction return is liable to a tax related penalty.[219]

'Negligence'

16.45 It is, however, highly probable that HMRC Stamp Taxes will be prepared to penalise taxpayers, not because they do not agree with the figures, but because in their view the taxpayer has not taken what they regard as appropriate steps to produce a reasonable figure. As it is unlikely that HMRC Stamp Taxes will have conducted an independent valuation exercise before opening an Enquiry, their obvious approach would be to require production of the information upon which the figures inserted in the land transaction return were based. The absence of any independent professional advice and written records of the instructions to the professional advisers and of their report will be taken as a clear invitation to challenge the value included in the return and claim that the return was prepared 'negligently'.[220] In other words, the failure to obtain appropriate contemporaneous advice[221] duly recorded will be an almost irrebuttable presumption of negligence.[222]

16.46 Moreover, if the parties include a very low figure, this may be open to challenge as fraud, as will the inclusion of an artificial figure not representing the real consideration for the purposes of obtaining a mortgage, or artificially depressing the basic figure upon part-exchange of land.[223]

Professional advisers

16.47 Professional advisers are likely to find themselves under attack from taxpayers who have been penalised for incorrect returns where they did not complete the form but failed to indicate in writing to the taxpayer the type of professional or other advice that should be sought before the form is signed and delivered to HMRC Stamp Taxes. This will include negligence by the professional adviser in not asking the right questions of the client when completing the return[224] or advising on the completion of the return.

16.48 At present, professional advisers are not responsible to HMRC Stamp Taxes for the tax but they may incur penalties where they 'assist' in the preparation of certain incorrect returns. Moreover, where HMRC Stamp Taxes are assessing a penalty, they are unlikely to mitigate that penalty if they believe that the taxpayer is entitled to an indemnity or to compensation from his professional advisers.[225]

---

[219] FA 2003, s 99 and Sch 10, para 4.
[220] Advice obtained upon the basis of hindsight is unlikely to impress either HMRC Stamp Taxes or any tribunal to which an appeal against the penalty is taken.
[221] *Lap Shun Textiles Industrial Co v Collector of Stamp Revenue* [1976] AC 530, on arm's length negotiations being merely 'evidence' of value, not conclusive.
[222] *Saunders v Edwards* [1987] 2 All ER 651.
[223] FA 2003, ss 95 and 96.
[224] *Slattery v Moore Stephens* [2003] STC 1379.
[225] But see *Mrs S Moores v Customs and Excise* VAT Decision 19024.

Chapter 17

NOTIFIABLE TRANSACTIONS AND LAND TRANSACTION TAX RETURNS

CERTIFICATES

17.1   Where there is a notifiable transaction, the taxpayer is required under penalty[1] to file a land transaction return (SDLT 1 to 4)[2] and in view of the attitude of certain employees with the various local officers in the Land Registry in practice it may be necessary to file an unnecessary Land Transaction Return (SDLT 1 to 4) and produce a technically unnecessary Revenue certificate (SDLT 5) before they will process a non-notifiable transaction presented to them. Apart from the question of avoiding penalties,[3] it is a pre-condition to effect changes in the registration of notifiable transactions to obtain the issue of the Inland Revenue Certificate (SDLT 5) which states[4] that a land transaction return (SDLT 1) has been delivered and a certificate (SDLT 5) obtained.[5] No certificate is required in cases where there is no chargeable or notifiable transaction or does not relate to a chargeable interest;[6] because problems may arise as a consequence of the changes in FA 2008 in practice where a transaction is presented to the Land Registry as non-notifiable without the support of an official certificate[7] because the SDLT 60 has been abolished and the certificates in relation to the exemption from the fixed stamp duty[8] have been removed from the Land Registry standard forms.[9]

Limitations of effect of Revenue certificate

17.2   The certificate issued by HMRC Stamp Taxes (SDLT 5) for the purposes of enabling entries to be made at the relevant Land Registry[10] is merely a certificate that the obligations to make a return, to self-assess the tax in accordance with that return and to make payment have been satisfied;[11] but the requirement in the regulations appears to be redundant as a result of an oversight in making the consequential changes arising from the removal of the condition that payment accompanies the land transaction return. The issue of the Inland Revenue Certificate (SDLT 5) is not the

1	FA 2003, s 76.
2	Stamp Duty Land Tax (Administration) Regulations 2003, SI 2003/2837, Part 1 and Schedules 1 to 4 (as amended).
3	FA 2003, Sch 10, paras 3–5.
4	See **Chapter 22**.
5	FA 2003, s 79(3)(a) and detailed regulations to be published pursuant to s 79(4).
6	Ibid, s 79(1) (as amended); see **Chapter 22**.
7	See **Chapter 22**.
8	Stamp Duty (Exempt Instrument) Regulations 1985, SI 1985/1688.
9	But see FA 2008, Sch 32, para 22.
10	Ibid, s 79; see **Chapter 22**.
11	Stamp Duty Land Tax (Administration) Regulations 2003, SI 2003/2837, reg 4(5); but this appears to be a drafting oversight when dealing with consequential changes since filing and payment are no longer required to take effect together; FA 2003, s 76(3).

equivalent of stamp duty adjudication and is not conclusive that the correct amount of stamp duty land tax has been calculated and paid. Unfortunately it is not a final sign-off by HMRC Stamp Taxes that the correct tax has been paid; it is nothing more than an acknowledgement that a land transaction return in some form has been received and accepted by HMRC Stamp Taxes. It is no guarantee that HMRC Stamp Taxes accept that either the amount paid or the data on the form is correct. The self-assessment is open to review upon an Enquiry by HMRC Stamp Taxes[12] and vulnerable to discovery assessments.[13]

17.3   For routine conveyancing in principle the Land Registry cannot challenge an SDLT 5 because they suspect that either insufficient tax may have been paid or there may have been what they regard as tax avoidance, or the forms are being utilised incorrectly; nevertheless they are closely involved in passing information to HMRC Stamp Taxes and certain officers have claimed they are entitled to pass on information where they, in their extensive practical tax experience, believe that tax mitigation is involved. In consequence of the provisions of FA 2003, s 79(1) (as amended) they cannot reject an application supported by an appropriate certificate, but they do so.

17.4   However, problems have arisen in practice following the abolition of the self-certificate (SDLT 60) and converting those transactions into non-notifiable transactions.[14] The difficulty is that the Land Registry are unpredictable as to how they may react to situations such as where there is documentation presented to them upon the basis that the transaction is non-notifiable. Whilst the Land Registry cannot, in principle,[15] challenge the transaction because they believe that an exemption or relief has been improperly claimed and they cannot investigate whether the amount shown as chargeable consideration in the land transaction return (SDLT 1) is the correct amount, since this is not a document of title within their powers to scrutinise, difficulties have arisen, in practice, in numerous cases because of the actions of individuals acting within their perception of a 'local discretion' where, for example, there is no equivalent of a self-certificate or even a certificate pursuant to the Stamp Duty (Exempt Instruments) Regulations 1987[16] indicating the transaction is not subject to stamp duty because it falls within an exemption, which has been removed from Land Registry forms, which usually overlapped with those situations where there was no chargeable consideration or the transaction was otherwise 'exempt' in the basic sense of not taxable and not subject to notification for the purposes of stamp duty land tax.

Also, in principle, they cannot change the registration where a subsequent Enquiry establishes that insufficient tax has been paid.[17] Titles are secure once an Inland Revenue certificate (SDLT 5) is produced to the Land Registry.

17.5   Whilst there is currently a potentially complex issue with the Land Registry as to their powers to investigate transactions that are presented to them as non-notifiable and where they have claimed a statutory duty to reject any application that is presented to them when supported by an Inland Revenue Certificate (SDLT 5) where their experience

---

[12]   Ibid, Sch 10, para 12 et seq; see **Chapter 19**.
[13]   Ibid, Sch 10, para 28.
[14]   Ibid, ss 79 and 79A (as amended).
[15]   However, it seems that certain officers of the Land Registry claim that their 'local discretion' requires them to challenge transactions where they believe that tax avoidance is involved and that they are required to pass information to HMRC in general; see **Chapter 22**.
[16]   SI 1987/516; see also SI 1985/1688.
[17]   See **22.9**.

suggests there has been or may have been 'tax avoidance'. They have no power to question whether the certificate was properly obtained in the sense that the taxpayer may have claimed a relief or calculated the tax on a basis that is not correct; but this does not appear to restrict certain individuals from passing the file over to HMRC Stamp Taxes for comment.[18] The fact that HMRC Stamp Taxes successfully subsequently challenge the land transaction return and the included self-assessment is not a matter that the Land Registry can rely upon to defer the registration process. This ability to 'compel' registration where there is an Inland Revenue Certificate (SDLT 5) is a key issue for mortgages and others.

OBLIGATION TO NOTIFY

17.6 The taxpayer must deliver a land transaction return whether hard copy or electronic before the expiration of 30 days from the effective date of the transaction in respect of every 'notifiable transaction'.[19] It must be noted that notifiable transaction is not the same as a transaction where the Land Registry may become involved. There are many situations where HMRC Stamp Taxes expect to receive a land transaction return and produce an Inland Revenue certificate although there is nothing to register such as substantial performance of a contract to purchase land.[20] Similarly, where beneficial holders behind some form of trust reorganise their interests without intending to change the legal title which is registered in the name of the nominees or trustees there will be a chargeable transaction[21] requiring notification which will produce a Inland Revenue Certificate (SDLT 5) but this will not be relevant to the Land Registry because there is nothing in relation to the transaction that they will be required to register. It may be that the parties might wish to provide some form of notification on the register[22] as to their involvement such as a restriction against the title to the effect that no dealing may be made in relation to the legal title without the consent or participation of certain specified individuals such as themselves. It seems that such restrictions upon dealing with the title are not matters that require to be supported by a certificate. Other matters may be registered without a certificate and provision is made for the insertion of certain entries on the register without the need for an Inland Revenue Certificate (SDLT 5).[23] The need to produce an Inland Revenue Certificate (SDLT 5) does not apply in respect of the entry of a notice under the Land Registration Act 2002, s 34[24] where the land transaction in question is the variation of a lease.[25] The requirement for an Inland Revenue Certificate (SDLT 5) also does not apply where the entry is required to be made without any application or so far as the entry relates to an interest or right other than the chargeable interest acquired by the purchaser under the land transaction which gives rise to the application.[26]

---

[18] Note FA 2003, s 78A; FA 2005, s 47.
[19] Ibid, s 76(1).
[20] Ibid, s 44(4) and s 79(2)(a). Such contracts are registerable against the title without any form of certificate; see **Chapter 22**.
[21] Ibid, Sch 16; see **Chapter 9**.
[22] But note ibid, s 79(2) on entries on the register without a certificate.
[23] Ibid, s 79.
[24] Or Land Registration Act (Northern Ireland) 1970, s 38.
[25] FA 2003, s 79(2A).
[26] Ibid, s 79(1).

TIMETABLES

17.7 However, the stamp duty land tax timetable is fundamentally irrelevant in the practical world. The relevant timetable is not that of HMRC Stamp Taxes, but that of the Land Registry whose deadlines really matter on issues of title and priority. The Inland Revenue certificate (SDLT 5) must be obtained sufficiently early to permit appropriate registration which is likely to be a significant issue for mortgagees worried about their security.[27] The fact that the certificate may not be received from HMRC Stamp Taxes within time to permit registration or protection of interests has been recognised by the Land Registry in Bulletin Number 8, which provides for protection on an interim basis where there are delays by HMRC Stamp Taxes in processing the land transaction return. This temporary concession is being continued for the time being because of the delays being encountered in the issue of the Inland Revenue Certificate (SDLT 5).

NOTIFICATION OBLIGATIONS

17.8 The regime relating to filing land transaction returns ie dealing with notifiable, non-notifiable and other transactions was fundamentally revised by the FA 2008.[28] This abolished the ability to make use of self-certificates for non-notifiable transactions and provided a basic structure whereby, essentially, all dealings in major interests are notifiable unless they fall within certain exclusions and dealings in minor interests are not required for notification unless tax is payable or would be payable but for an exemption; but has removed the facility for surplus dealings for non-notifiable transactions which have caused problems with the Land Registry although senior employees deny that there are such difficulties because these are dealt with at a certain level below their pay grade.

'Major interest'

17.9 A special regime is applied to transactions involving a major interest which is defined[29] as being:

- for land in England and Wales and Northern Ireland, an estate in fee simple absolute or a term of years absolute[30] whether subsisting in law or equity in either case;

- for land in Scotland, the interest of an owner of land or the right of a tenant over property subject to a lease.

Notification

17.10 The notification obligation arises in relation to a chargeable transaction including an 'acquisition' and so will be linked to:

---

[27]   See **22.12**.
[28]   See FA 2003, ss 77 and 77A.
[29]   Ibid, s 117.
[30]   Note that this differs significantly from the definition of 'lease' contained in FA 2003, Sch 17A, para 1; see **7.13**.

- all forms of 'acquisition' such as variations and surrenders[31] and deemed acquisitions;

- substantial performance of the contract; and

- any completion by 'conveyance'[32] or any written instrument other than the grant or deemed grant of a lease covered by specific provisions mentioned above.

There are, however, situations where the person is deemed to acquire a chargeable interest such as certain variations of leases.[33] In some situations there may be a statement that the taxpayer is deemed to acquire a new lease[34] in this situation the term of the deemed new lease will be as specified in the legislation or, usually, the unexpired term of the existing lease. However, no guidance in provided in relation to the deemed acquisition of other interests. It is, therefore, difficult to determine whether the deemed interest being acquired is a major or a minor interest. This will be particularly so where transactions involve variations of leases which give rise to a deemed acquisition of a new chargeable interest. HMRC Stamp Taxes have not made clear in the legislation whether, because the variation or other chargeable event relates to a major interest, it is a variation and therefore an acquisition of a major interest. Whilst this may not affect the amount of tax involved it does relate to the notification obligation because, for example, of the different thresholds[35] and it may be prudent to operate upon the basis that the transaction relates to a major interest and may have to be notified until such time as HMRC Stamp Taxes have clarified their position rather than embark upon technical arguments on the legislation with a risk of penalties for not filing a return where appropriate.

17.11 It must not be overlooked that, because the effective date is not necessarily the same as 'completion'[36] in the traditional sense, there are separate notifications required for both substantial performance and completion[37] (ie execution of any relevant deeds), except in relation to subsales,[38] because 'completion' refers to completion between the same parties which will not apply to subsales where the transfer will not necessarily be between the original parties.[39] Some transactions such as leases with variable rents or sales with an overage or clawback payment give rise to multiple notification obligations. Assignees of leases may be required to notify certain transactions.[40]

NOTIFIABLE TRANSACTIONS

17.12 There are significantly different notification thresholds depending upon the nature of the transaction in addition to the numerous rules requiring notification and payment for transactions other than purchasers and leases:

---

[31] Ibid, s 43(3) (as amended).
[32] See also ibid, s 44(8).
[33] See ibid, Sch 17A, para 15A.
[34] See, for example, ibid, Sch 17, paras 14 and 15.
[35] Ibid, s 77A.
[36] See ibid, s 44(10)(a) and s 121 (Scotland).
[37] Ibid, s 44(8); Sch 17A, para 12A.
[38] Ibid, s 45(3).
[39] However, this will depend upon the structure of the transaction since subsale relief is available where the initial purchaser receives a Land Registry transfer but this is not 'completion' requiring notification; see **Chapter 6**.
[40] FA 2003, Sch 17A, para 12.

Major interests

17.13 For transactions with an effective date on or after 12 March 2008 the land transaction is notifiable if it is the acquisition of a major interest in land (ie a freehold or leasehold[41]) unless it is:[42]

- exempt from charge pursuant to Sch 3 to the FA 2003. This exempts:
  - transactions for no chargeable consideration such as gifts or other transactions where the stamp duty land tax legislation treats the transaction as being for no chargeable consideration.[43] Certain transactions for no chargeable consideration are notifiable notwithstanding that there is no chargeable consideration; but it is an open question whether the notification threshold of £40,000 overrides the exclusion from Sch 3;
  - transactions in connection with matrimonial[44] and civil partnership[45] breakdown;
  - certain transactions involving registered social landlords;[46]
  - variations of the estates of deceased persons and appropriations by personal representatives of deceased individuals;[47]

- an acquisition other than the grant, assignment or surrender of a lease where the chargeable consideration for that acquisition together with the chargeable consideration for any linked transactions is less than £40,000;

- the grant of a lease for a term of 7 years or more where the chargeable consideration other than the rent (ie premium) is less than £40,000 and the relevant rent is less than £1000;[48]

- the assignment or surrender of a lease where the lease was originally granted for a term of 7 years or more and a chargeable consideration for the assignment or surrender other than rent is less than £40,000 and the relevant rent is less than £1000;

- the grant of a lease for a term of less than 7 years where the chargeable consideration does not exceed the zero-rate threshold;[49] and

- the assignment or surrender of a lease where the lease was originally granted for a term of less than 7 years and the chargeable consideration does not exceed the zero-rate threshold.

---

[41]   Ibid, ss 117 and 77(1)(a).
[42]   Ibid, ss 77 and 77A; see **Chapter 18**.
[43]   This is different from the transaction being relieved from tax.
[44]   FA 2003, Sch 3, para 3; see **11.22**.
[45]   Ibid, Sch 3, para 3A; see **11.22**.
[46]   Ibid, Sch 3, para 2; see **11.20**.
[47]   Ibid, Sch 3, paras 3A and 4; see **11.23** and **11.26**.
[48]   Which may affect change in tax upon premiums for leases of non-residential property; FA 2003, Sch 5, paras 9 and 9A.
[49]   But note that in certain situations relating to non-residential property where the rental amount is treated as exceeding £1000 the nil rate threshold does not apply; see FA 2003, Sch 5, paras 9 and 9A.

Minor interests

17.14 The acquisition of a chargeable interest other than a major interest in land is notifiable where the chargeable consideration in respect of which tax is chargeable at a rate of 1 per cent or higher or would be so chargeable but for a relief.[50] The chargeable consideration does not exceed the zero-rate threshold if it does not consist of or include any amount in respect of which tax is chargeable at a rate of 1 per cent or higher or would be so chargeable but for some relief or exemption.

Special situations

17.15 Certain situations are selected for special notification namely:

- a land transaction that falls within the terms of s 44A(3) of the FA 2003 namely the situation where a person enters into a contract relating to a chargeable interest and acquires a power to direct a conveyance;[51] and

- the notional transaction deemed to arise pursuant to the general anti-avoidance provisions.[52] This need to notify the notional transaction[53] appears to be in addition to the obligation to notify the actual acquisition of the chargeable interest.

New leases

17.16 Particular rules apply to substantial performance of agreements for lease and the grants of leases. The grant of a lease including the deemed grant of a lease on substantial performance of the agreement for lease[54] is notifiable when:

- the proposed lease is for a term of 7 years or more and is granted for chargeable consideration for a premium of £40,000 or higher and the rent exceeds £1000.[55] HMRC Stamp Taxes have confirmed that a peppercorn rent is not a chargeable consideration but £1 if demanded is a chargeable rent. In certain situations such as surrenders or existing and grants of new leases where the legislation treats the actual consideration as nil or non-chargeable. Such situations will be non-notifiable where there is no other chargeable consideration;

- the proposed lease is for a term of less than 7 years and either the chargeable premium exceeds the nil rate threshold and/or the rent does not exceed the nil rate slice.

In relation to leases granted between partners and partnerships and connected persons which fall into charge pursuant to FA 2003, Sch 15, paras 11 and 19, the relevant rent is the chargeable proportion of the annual rent (ie the rent as reduced by the sum of the lower proportions).

---

[50] Ibid, s 77(1)(b).
[51] Ibid, s 77(1)(c); see **3.24**.
[52] Ibid, ss 75A–77C; see **2.19**.
[53] Ibid, s 75A(5).
[54] Ibid, Sch 17A, para 12A.
[55] It has to be noted that the nil rate threshold is not available for lease premiums where deemed premises are non-residential and the average annual rent exceeds £1000; FA 2003, Sch 5, paras 9 and 9A.

Term of seven years

17.17　The reporting provisions originally referred to the contractual terms of the lease, ie from the term commencement date. This has been amended to refer to a term related to 7 years but no clear definition of the term of the lease has been included. It appears that HMRC Stamp Taxes intend to apply the effective date of the lease as the date from which the term is calculated, although it is difficult to justify this on the amended legislation. However, the position has been clarified in relation to the assignment of leases. The term of the lease as to 7 years or longer or shorter is determined by reference to the term of the lease at the time of the actual grant. In consequence, a lease for more than 7 years at grant will always remain a lease for a term exceeding 7 years for the purposes of charges upon assignment and so on.[56]

Non-major interests

17.18　An acquisition[57] of a 'non-major interest', such as the grant, variation, assignment or surrender of an option, easement, profit à prendre, interests in settlements holding land, a restrictive covenant or, possibly, certain variations of leases where these are not taxed as the deemed grant of a new lease, is notifiable if there is chargeable consideration in respect of which tax is chargeable at the rate of 1 per cent or higher or where tax would be chargeable at such a rate but for a relief.[58] There is, therefore, no obligation to notify in respect of variations of leases or restrictive covenants where the consideration is below £125,000 (or temporarily £175,000), or £150,000. There is also no obligation to notify in respect of gifts of such interests or where there is a release for no consideration.[59]

OTHER NOTIFIABLE TRANSACTIONS

17.19　In addition to the specific notification required for two areas of anti-avoidance legislation,[60] notification is also required largely in the form of retrospective adjustment[61] of earlier returns, in a variety of situations such as:

- clawback of exemptions for charities;[62]

- clawback of relief for intra-group transactions;[63]

---

[56]　Ibid, s 77A.

[57]　Which presumably includes a deemed grant which takes two forms, namely: the deemed grant of a lease upon the substantial performance of an agreement for lease where there is a real lease in place; and the deemed grant of a lease on certain variations and assignments where there are tax leases in place ie the original lease and the deemed lease where the latter is not reflected by a real lease. It is unclear how far HMRC Stamp Taxes intend to press this messy situation of two leases one of which does not exist for all transactions after the deemed grant so that a subsequent rent review affects both leases. The taxpayer's argument that this could involve double taxation of the same event pursuant to FA 2003, Sch 10, para 33 will not be accepted by HMRC Stamp Taxes because two separate chargeable transactions are involved (ie a real lease and the subsequent deemed lease).

[58]　FA 2003, s 77(1)(b).

[59]　Ibid, Sch 3, para 1; s 77 (as amended).

[60]　Ibid, s 77(1)(c) and (d) relating to contracts with a power to direct a conveyance (FA 2003, ss 44A and 45A) and the general anti-avoidance provisions (FA 2003, ss 75A–75C).

[61]　This does not appear to be a case where the earlier initial return can be 'amended', particularly because of the constraints upon amendments pursuant to ibid, Sch 10, para 6; see **17.26**.

[62]　FA 2003, Sch 8; s 81.

[63]　Ibid, Sch 7, Part 1; s 81.

- clawback of relief for company reconstructions and reorganisations;[64]

- where a contingent sum becomes payable or ceases to be payable;[65]

- where an uncertain sum becomes ascertained,[66] such as:
  - variable rents;[67]
  - the costs of services and works,[68] because on the effective date the costs may be uncertain;[69]

- later linked transactions;[70]

- recalculation of variable rent;[71]

- deemed grant of a new lease for abnormal rent increase;[72]

- deemed grant of a new lease where rent increased;[73]

- deemed new lease on assignment of certain leases exempt on grant;[74]

- forfeiture of the special residential reliefs.[75]

Notification is required and produces an SDLT 5 notwithstanding that in these cases there will frequently be no dealings with the Land Registry.

RETURN

17.20 The taxpayer is under an obligation to deliver a land transaction return before the expiration of 30 days after the effective date of the transaction or the date of the event giving rise to the obligation to notify such as a clawback of a relief, abnormal rent increase or the uncertain consideration becomes certain.[76]

17.21 Complex provisions are set out for the land transaction return and the related obligations.[77] Regulations set out the form and the information that is required. There is power to issue a variety of forms dealing with different situations.

---

[64] Ibid, Sch 7, Part 2; s 81.
[65] Ibid, s 51(1); s 80.
[66] Ibid, s 71(2); s 80.
[67] Ibid, s 51; s 80 (but not variable annuities: ibid, s 52).
[68] Ibid, Sch 4, para 10.
[69] Ibid, s 51.
[70] Ibid, s 81A; Sch 17A, para 12.
[71] Ibid, Sch 17A, paras 7, 8 and 12.
[72] Ibid, Sch 17A, paras 14 and 15.
[73] Ibid, Sch 17A, para 13.
[74] Ibid, Sch 17A, para 11.
[75] Ibid, Sch 6A, para 11.
[76] Ibid, s 76.
[77] Ibid, Sch 10, para 1.

CONTENTS OF THE LAND TRANSACTION RETURN

17.22 The contents of the land transaction return are prescribed by regulations.[78] These require details of all vendors and purchasers, being the 'true' parties such as the beneficial owners, not nominees,[79] and details of the property and the consideration.

17.23 The land transaction is a lengthy document but much of the information required is not directly relevant to stamp duty land tax. The two key areas are:

- self-assessment;

- the declaration that the return is correct.

Parties using electronic forms need to ensure that the bar code or reference number is recorded on the form, payslip, cheque and any plan attached.

Self-assessment

17.24 The land transaction return must include a self-assessment of the tax calculated on the basis of the information contained in the return but no longer has to be accompanied by the payment of the amount of tax chargeable as shown by the return.[80] Two entries regarding the tax payment are required. One refers to the total tax for the transaction, the other refers to the tax payable at the current stage taking credit for tax already paid upon prior returns.

Declaration – 'signature'

17.25 The form contains a declaration that the information is true and correct. The declaration has to be signed by all of the true purchasers,[81] except in the case of partnerships where representative partners have been nominated and accepted by HMRC Stamp Taxes or other special provisions apply.[82]

Amendments[83]

17.26 The taxpayer is given power to amend a return on notice to HMRC Stamp Taxes and certain situations are required to be dealt with by way of amendment; but, in general, such an amendment may not be made more than 12 months after the filing date, which is 30 days after the effective date.[84] It seems that 'amendment' does not involve retrieving the original land transaction return from HMRC Stamp Taxes and physically altering the data included. The amendment must be in such form and contain such information as HMRC Stamp Taxes require.[85] No forms appear to have been prescribed although the amendment, which is presumably included in a letter setting out the revised date, must be accompanied by documentation if there is a claim for a tax

---

78 Stamp Duty Land Tax (Administration) Regulations 2003, SI 2003/2837.
79 FA 2003, Sch 16, para 3 (as amended).
80 Ibid, s 76(3).
81 On the identification of the 'purchaser' see **Chapter 15**; and on dealings by agents, nominees etc see **15.17**.
82 See **Chapter 14**.
83 Note the obligation of the temporarily open-ended obligation to 'rectify' errors in the return which came to his attention within a reasonable time or face a tax related penalty; FA 2003, Sch 10, para 8.
84 Ibid, Sch 10, para 6.
85 Ibid, Sch 10, para 6.

repayment.[86] There appears to be no power to amend a return after the 12 months have expired so that presumably a letter explaining the problem will suffice, although where tax is payable HMRC Stamp Taxes may also require a completely new land transaction return.

Revenue correction of return

17.27 HMRC Stamp Taxes, after a brief scrutiny of the return probably by way of computer scan intended to spot any manifest errors such as incorrect calculation of the tax or application of an incorrect rate, are required to issue a certificate (SDLT 5)[87] that a land transaction return has been delivered, which will enable the parties to make whatever entries may be required in the Land Registry in the relevant jurisdiction.[88] This is not conclusive that the tax has been correctly self-assessed and paid. The real challenge to the return is intended to be made by an Enquiry.[89]

17.28 HMRC Stamp Taxes are given power to amend the return so as to correct 'obvious' errors or omissions in the return by giving notice to the taxpayer, but this power is limited and cannot amount to a power to challenge the land transaction return such as questioning the eligibility for the relief claimed[90] but no such correction may be made more than 9 months after the date on which the return was delivered or, if the correction is required in consequence of an amendment made by the taxpayer, 9 months after the day on which the amendment was made.[91] The taxpayer may challenge the correction and it is of no effect if he amends the return so as to reject the correction; or, if it is too late to amend the return, he may reject the correction within 3 months from the date of the issue of the notice by HMRC Stamp Taxes.[92] HMRC may specify other persons such as the various land registrars in the various jurisdictions as persons who may exercise the power to correct land transaction returns.[93] However, this power if created would not give rise to a power for officers of the Land Registry to conduct their own form of Enquiry in relation to the land transaction return.[94] Moreover, consequent upon the abolition of the self-certificate (SDLT 60) the present regime is such that the Land Registry will not see the land transaction return (SDLT 1); their involvement will be limited to either a transaction supported by an Inland Revenue Certificate (SDLT 5) or a transaction presented to them as being non-notifiable. Moreover, such persons to whom the power is delegated, as with HMRC Stamp Taxes, are limited so they may correct only 'obvious errors or omissions' in the return whether errors or principle, arithmetical mistakes or otherwise. It seems reasonable to expect HMRC Stamp Taxes to deal with obvious errors such as arithmetic and omissions in the return such as the failure to include the relevant postcode. However, even these powers are limited since it is provided that HMRC Stamp Taxes may amend a land transaction return; it does not enable them to demand that the taxpayer corrects the return. It may be that, in practice, HMRC Stamp Taxes will be in a position to contact the taxpayer or his advisers who

---

[86] Ibid, Sch 10, para 6(2A).
[87] Stamp Duty Land Tax (Administration) Regulations 2003, SI 2003/2837, Part 1.
[88] FA 2003, s 79; see **Chapter 22**.
[89] See **Chapter 19**.
[90] FA 2003, Sch 10, para 7(2).
[91] Ibid, Sch 10, para 7.
[92] Ibid, Sch 10, para 7(4).
[93] Ibid, Sch 10, para 7(1A).
[94] Moreover, any such power created would be less extensive that the power currently claimed by certain Land Registry officers to investigate transactions in depth and even to challenge Inland Revenue Certificate (SDLT 5) where they believe the insufficient tax has been paid or although tax has been paid there has been 'tax avoidance' as defined by the Land Registry.

have indicated that they are 'agents' for the purposes of the return and request them to supply information that is left off the return rather than sending the return back for the relevant information to be completed. However, it is difficult to see how HMRC Stamp Taxes can correct a return for an obvious error of 'principle'. There may be errors of principle such as a party claiming relief for a company reorganisation where, on a strict analysis, the conditions of FA 2003, Sch 7, Part 2 are not satisfied. However, this would not necessarily be an 'obvious error' since the return will not contain the information required for determining whether the conditions have been satisfied. Similarly, there may be errors of principle in relation to the valuation techniques involved in determining the amount to be included as consideration in kind or the market value of the interest being acquired for the purposes of land exchange. These errors will not be 'obvious' from the face of the return. In practice, HMRC's realistic power to challenge the return is in the form of an Enquiry.[95]

17.29 However, although HMRC Stamp Taxes may have made corrections or have accepted the form and issued the certificate, it is not conclusive that the return is correct, and it may be challenged by HMRC Stamp Taxes upon an Enquiry[96] or upon a discovery assessment[97] which itself may be made notwithstanding that there has previously been an Enquiry. The issue of a certificate or the absence of correction is not like adjudication for stamp duty purposes.

Disclosure and confidentiality

17.29A Any information contained in a land transaction return may be disclosed to or is available for use by:[98]

- listing officers;[99]

- is evidence in an appeal as to value pursuant to Local Government Finance Act 1988, Sch 11;[100]

- the Commissioner for Valuation for Northern Ireland;[101] and

- any other person specified by regulations.

---

[95]   This would clearly cast considerable doubt upon the claims by certain officers of the Land Registry to be under a statutory duty to investigate the land transaction return, the presentation of documents for registration upon the basis that they are not notifiable since there is no obligation to deliver a land transaction return and therefore nothing for HMRC Stamp Taxes to investigate or correct. These provisions indicate that the powers or duties claimed by the Land Registry are greater than those conferred upon HMRC Stamp Taxes.

[96]   See **Chapter 19**.

[97]   FA 2003, Sch 10, para 38; see **Chapter 23**.

[98]   Ibid, s 78A.

[99]   Local Government Finance Act 1992, s 20.

[100] Ibid, s 24.

[101] Rates (Northern Ireland) Order 1977.

ELECTRONIC FILING

17.30 Regulations have been introduced[102] permitting land transaction returns to be filed electronically.[103] The regulations relate to the delivery of a land transaction return to HMRC or to the Keeper of the Registers of Scotland by means of the ARTL system[104] and the making of any payment or repayment of tax or other sums in connection with the delivery of a land transaction return.[105]

Electronic communications may be utilised by HMRC only if the recipient has indicated that he consents to the Board using electronic communications in connection with the transmission of land transaction returns or payments or repayments of tax and HMRC have not been notified that consent has been withdrawn.[106]

The taxpayer may only use electronic communications provided that:

- the person is, for the time being, permitted to use electronic communication by authorisation given by a director of the Board;

- he uses an approved method for authenticating the identity of the sender, an approved method of electronic communication and an approved method for authenticity in England;[107] and

- the person must maintain such records in written or electronic form as may be specified in a general or specific direction of the Board.

Directions under reg 3 of the SDLT (Electronic Communications) Regulations, SI 2005/844

Returns under Part 1 of Schedule 10 to the Finance Act 2003

17.31 The Commissioners for Her Majesty's Revenue and Customs ('the Commissioners') direct that, on and after 13 July 2005, a person who is required to deliver a land transaction return under Part 1 of Schedule 10 to the Finance Act 2003 ('the relevant information') is authorised to do so over the Internet.

The Commissioners further direct that:

(*a*) the methods approved by them for —
  (i)   authenticating the identity of the person sending the relevant information,
  (ii) delivery of the relevant information, and
  (iii) authenticating the relevant information; and

(*b*) the form approved by them in which the relevant information is to be delivered; are the methods and form set out, at the time of, and for the purposes of, the delivery of the relevant information, in the terms and conditions for use of the

---

102 Stamp Duty Land Tax (Electronic Communications) Regulations 2005, SI 2005/844.
103 With effect from 11 April 2005.
104 Requirements of Writing (Scotland) Act 1995, s 12(1).
105 Stamp Duty Land Tax (Electronic Communications) Regulations 2005, SI 2005/844, reg 2.
106 Ibid, reg 3(1).
107 Ibid, reg 3.

Stamp Taxes Online Land Transaction Return on the website of Her Majesty's Revenue and Customs (www.hmrc.gov.uk).

Agents acting on behalf of purchasers – returns under Part 1 of Schedule 10 to the Finance Act 2003

17.32 The Commissioners for Her Majesty's Revenue and Customs further direct that, on and after 13 July 2005, an agent who delivers information on behalf of a person who is required to deliver the relevant information is authorised to do so over the Internet provided that the following conditions are met.

The first condition is that:

(a) the agent makes a copy of the relevant information before it is sent; and

(b) the person, who is required to deliver the land transaction return, makes a declaration to the agent, before the return is sent, that either
   (i) the relevant information contained is correct to the best of his knowledge and belief; or
   (ii) the relevant information, with the exception of the effective date, is correct to the best of his knowledge and belief.

The second condition is that the agent completes the appropriate declaration within the Stamp Taxes Online computer application.

The Commissioners further direct that —

(a) the methods approved by them for —
   (i) authenticating the identity of the person sending the relevant information;
   (ii) delivery of the relevant information; and
   (iii) authenticating the relevant information; and

(b) the form approved by them in which the relevant information is to be delivered; are the methods and form set out, at the time of, and for the purposes of, the delivery of the relevant information, in the terms and conditions for use of the Stamp Taxes Online Land Transaction Return on the Inland Revenue website (www.hmrc.gov.uk).

Scotland

17.33 The Keeper of the Registers is empowered to receive on behalf of the Board land transaction returns in respect of ARTL transactions, payments of any stamp duty land tax in respect of ARTL transactions and transmitting to the Board those land transaction returns and payment of stamp duty land tax in respect of the ARTL transactions to which they relate.[108] If a land transaction is returned to the Keeper in connection with an ARTL transaction by means of the ARTL system it must be accompanied by an appropriate declaration by the person completing the return that the information has been approved by the purchaser and a digital signature.[109]

---

[108]   Ibid, reg 4A with effect from 31 January 2007.
[109]   Ibid, reg 4B.

The effects of electronic filing

17.34 The information delivered electronically is treated as having been delivered in the manner required by the legislation and the Stamp Duty Land Tax (Land Transaction Returns) Regulations 2003 and it is treated as having been delivered on the day on which all the conditions are satisfied.[110]

Where information is delivered electronically through the ARTL system to the Keeper of Registers in Scotland this is to be treated as having been delivered to HMRC on the date on which it is delivered to the Keeper. However, the Board may make changes as to the date or a different date.

A document certified by an officer of the Board to be a printed out version of any information delivered by means of electronic communication is to be evidence, unless the contrary is proved, that the information was delivered by means of a electronic communications on that occasion and constitutes the entirety of what was delivered on that occasion[111] except where it is a communication to the Keeper of the Registers in Scotland when it is assumed, unless the contrary is proved, that the information was delivered on the relevant occasion and constitutes to entirety of what was delivered on that occasion in connection with the document.[112]

REVENUE DETERMINATION IN DEFAULT OF A RETURN

17.35 HMRC Stamp Taxes are given power to make a determination of what they believe to be the amount of stamp duty land tax due where no land transaction return has been filed[113] by the expiration of the thirtieth day after the effective date or other date upon which a return is required to be filed (such as in relation to clawback of exemptions), HMRC Stamp Taxes may determine to the best of their information and belief the amount of tax chargeable in respect of the transaction within 6 years after the effective date.[114] Notice must be served on the purchaser[115] and has the effect as if it were a self-assessment by the purchaser.[116]

17.36 If, after a determination has been made, a purchaser delivers a land transaction return, the self-assessment included in that return supersedes the determination, provided that the return is delivered not more than 6 years after the day on which the power to make the determination first became exercisable, or not more than 12 months after the date of the determination, whichever is the later. Where proceedings have begun for recovery of the tax, these proceedings may continue for the purposes of recovering such part of the self-assessment as has not been paid.[117]

---

[110] Ibid, reg 5(1) and (2).
[111] Ibid, reg 6(1).
[112] Ibid, reg 6(1A).
[113] FA 2003, Sch 10, para 25; see **Chapter 22**.
[114] Ibid, Sch 10, para 31.
[115] Ibid, Sch 10, para 25.
[116] Ibid, Sch 10, para 26.
[117] Ibid, Sch 10, para 27.

PENALTIES

Failure to deliver a return

17.37 A wide range of penalties (to some extent cumulative) is imposed for failure to deliver a return, namely.

Flat rate penalty

17.38 There is a flat-rate penalty if a return is not delivered within the 30-day period. This penalty is:

- £100 if the return is delivered within 3 months after the expiration of the relevant 30-day period; and

- £200 in any other case.[118]

Tax-related penalty

17.39 A purchaser who fails to deliver a return within 12 months after the expiration of the 30-day period is liable to a tax-related penalty not exceeding the amount of tax chargeable in respect of the transaction.[119] This penalty is chargeable in addition to the flat-rate penalty above.[120]

Daily penalty

17.40 If it appears to HMRC Stamp Taxes that a purchaser has failed to deliver a land transaction return within the prescribed period, they may issue a notice requiring him to deliver a land transaction return and, if the purchaser does not comply with that notice within the period specified in the notice, HMRC Stamp Taxes may apply to the General or Special Commissioners for an order imposing a daily penalty not exceeding £60 for each day in which the default continues after the day on which the Commissioners direct that he is liable to penalties.[121] This is in addition to any flat-rate or tax-related penalty.[122]

These rules are modified for partnerships.[123]

Incorrect returns

17.41 The taxpayer who either:

- fraudulently or negligently[124] delivers an incorrect land transaction return; or

---

[118] Ibid, Sch 10, para 3.
[119] Ibid, Sch 10, para 4.
[120] Ibid, Sch 10, para 4(1).
[121] Ibid, Sch 10, para 5.
[122] Ibid, Sch 10, para 5(5).
[123] Ibid, Sch 15, para 7; see **Chapter 13**.
[124] It must be noted that a return subsequently successfully challenged by HMRC Stamp Taxes is not automatically 'negligent' especially where the taxpayer and his advisers gave reasonable consideration to the issue.

- discovers that a land transaction return already delivered is incorrect and does not remedy the error without unreasonable delay, whether or not the original return was delivered neither fraudulently nor negligently,

is liable to a tax-related penalty not exceeding the amount of the tax understated in the return,[125] and professional advisers may be subject to penalties.[126]

---

[125] Ibid, Sch 10, para 8.
[126] Ibid, ss 95 and 96.

Chapter 18

NON-NOTIFIABLE TRANSACTIONS

REGISTRATION OF TITLE

18.1 It is necessary apart from certain specific situations[1] and non-notifiable transactions[2] to produce an appropriate certificate from HMRC Stamp Taxes (SDLT 5) for notifiable transactions to the relevant Land Registry in the appropriate jurisdiction in order to effect certain changes to the register.[3] Following the changes made by the FA 2008[4] this obligation to produce an Inland Revenue Certificate (SDLT 5) is limited to 'notifiable transactions'. The former regime dealing with certain non-notifiable transactions which could be registered only if supported by a self-certificate (SDLT 60) has been abolished, together with the power of HMRC Stamp Taxes to enquire into non-notifiable transactions.[5] This has been combined with a major restructuring of the fixed duties in relation to stamp duty including some of those relating to land, although it appears that certain of the fixed duties may be retained.[6] Recently the Land Registry has redesigned the forms and removed the panel dealing with stamp duty and containing the certificates for exemption from the fixed duty pursuant to the Stamp Duty (Exempt Instruments) Regulations 1987[7] which, in theory, means that a wide range of transactions can now be presented to the Land Registry without any form of certification whatsoever. This absence of any formal machinery for indicating the nature or category of the transaction in an official document including the Land Registry forms, has given rise to a significant practical problem. This is the issue of how to deal with the Land Registry in relation to transactions that are perceived to be non-notifiable by the taxpayer and the person who is likely to be presenting an application to the Land Registry for registration. There is an issue as to how far the Land Registry are under what certain employees claim to be a statutory duty[8] to investigate transactions presented to them not supported by a form of certificate.[9] There is no consistent policy and it seems that senior employees of the Land Registry are not prepared to issue a guidance note because there is no consistency of approach nor understanding of the day-to-day issues arising and the matter is a matter of 'local discretion' for the individual officers in the different Land Registries. These are issues concerned with the obtaining of registration of title and the consequential potential impact of this upon documents of title, contractual arrangements relating to the information that a purchaser may require from a vendor at completion and the possible methods of dealing

---

[1]   FA 2003, s 79(2).

[2]   Ibid, s 79(1) as amended by removal of references to self-certificates; see also ss 77 and 77A.

[3]   Ibid, s 79(1) (as amended); see **Chapter 22**; the rules relating to PD forms are amended by Stamp Duty Land Tax (Consequential Amendment of Enactments) Regulations 2003, SI 2003/2867, reg 4.

[4]   See now FA 2003, ss 77 and 77A.

[5]   See ibid, s 79(1) (as amended) and Sch 11 (as amended).

[6]   FA 2009, Sch 32, para 21; see **Chapter 22**.

[7]   SI 1987/516.

[8]   Presumably in their view pursuant to FA 2003, s 79(1) (as amended); see **Chapter 5**.

[9]   For other issues in relation to the current claims for power by the Land Registry see **Chapter 22**.

with the Land Registry. These issues are considered later.[10] The current chapter is concerned with the basic issue of which chargeable land transactions do not require to be notified to HMRC Stamp Taxes. The issues arising from the absence of any formal notification are dealt with later.

NON-NOTIFIABLE TRANSACTIONS

18.2   The restructuring of the notification regime by the FA 2008 has produced a basic list of non-notifiable transactions. The starting point as regards dealings involving major interests is that all such dealings are notifiable[11] unless excluded. These include in relation to 'acquisitions' of major interest:

- an acquisition which is exempt from charge under Sch 3 to the FA 2003; namely
  - acquisitions where there is no chargeable consideration for the transaction.[12] However, certain transactions that for various reasons may be technically for no chargeable consideration are still notifiable. For example, a transfer by a connected person to a partnership may be for no chargeable consideration because the reduction in the market value charge by reference to the sum of the lower proportions (SLP) is 100 per cent. Similarly, transactions involving connected companies may be at not less than the market value; but certain interests in land may have no market value such as an assignment of a lease at a full reviewable market rent. Also certain land exchanges involved in the range of exempt PFI projects[13] are to be ignored so that there may be actual but no chargeable consideration. In these cases because they may involve substantial amounts of legislation they may require certain of the transactions to be disclosed. For example:
    - in relation to partnerships FA 2003, Sch 3, para 1 is suspended;[14]
    - transactions involving connected companies are notifiable since FA 2003, Sch 3, para 1 is suspended[15] however, this suspension of Sch 3, para 1 applies only to transactions within s 53. It would seem there is no notification where the exclusion from s 53 contained in s 54 thereof applies;
    - in relation to the PFI projects within the relief it is provided that the provisions suspending the treatment of the consideration as being chargeable does not apply for the purposes of notification;[16]
    - transactions involving disadvantaged land;[17]

- grants of leases of dwellings where granted by registered social landlord to one or more individuals in accordance with arrangements between a registered social landlord and a housing authority under which the landlord provides for individuals as nominated by the authority in pursuance of its statutory housing functions, temporary rented accommodation which the landlord itself has obtained on a short-term basis;[18]

---

10   See **Chapter 22**.
11   FA 2003, s 77; see **17.9**.
12   Ibid, Sch 3, para 1; see **11.8** and **11.19**.
13   Ibid, Sch 4, para 17.
14   Ibid, Sch 15, para 25(1) and 30.
15   Ibid, s 53(4).
16   Ibid, Sch 4, para 17(4A).
17   Ibid, Sch 6, para **13**.
18   Ibid, Sch 3, para 2; see **11.20**.

- transactions between one party to a marriage and the other party effected in connection with divorce, nullity or judicial separation or pursuant to a Court order made under the Matrimonial Causes legislation or in connection with certain agreements between the parties related to the divorce or separation;[19]

- acquisitions of property by a person in or towards satisfaction of an entitlement under or in relation to the will of a deceased individual or on the intestacy of a deceased individual;[20]

- a transaction between one party to a civil partnership and the other in pursuance of an order for the dissolution or annulment of the civil partnership or for judicial separation;[21]

- transactions in a variation of the estate of a deceased individual, whether dying testate or intestate, within 2 years of the death;[22]

- an alternative property finance transaction which is a transfer of the property to a person exercising his right to reacquire the property provided that certain conditions are met;[23]

- any transaction falling within the alternative finance relief is not notifiable unless the transaction involves the transfer to the person of the whole of the interest purchased by the institution under the acquisition from the person so far as not transferred by a previous further transaction;[24]

- in relation to certain alternative property finance transactions in Scotland the transfer of the person pursuant to the exercise of his right to reacquire the property which is exempt from charge[25] is not notifiable unless the transaction involves the transfer to the person of the whole of the interest purchased by the financial institution under the initial acquisition of the major interest in the land so far as not transferred by a previous similar transaction;[26]

- transactions involving the transfer of interests in property investment partnerships[27] or transactions within the anti-avoidance provisions of para 17[28] is notifiable only if the consideration for the transaction exceeds the nil rate threshold;[29]

- an acquisition of a major interest other than the grant, assignment or surrender of a lease where the chargeable consideration for that acquisition together with the chargeable consideration for any linked transactions is less than £40,000. This raises the question as to whether transactions that *prima facie* fall within FA 2003, Sch 3, para 1 the listed transactions set out above, are, *prima facie*, notifiable

---

[19] Ibid, Sch 3, para 3; see **11.22**.
[20] Ibid, Sch 3, para 3A; see **11.26**.
[21] Ibid, Sch 4, para 3A (it will be noted that there are two paragraphs 3A in Sch 3); see **11.22**.
[22] Ibid, Sch 3, para 4; see **11.23**.
[23] Ibid, s 71A(4).
[24] Ibid, s 71A(7).
[25] Ibid, s 72A(4).
[26] Ibid, s 72A(7).
[27] Ibid, Sch 15, para 14.
[28] Ibid, Sch 15, para 17; see **13.37**.
[29] Ibid, Sch 15, para 30; see **18.2**.

notwithstanding they are within para 1. Subject to specific legislation where transactions are notifiable notwithstanding that they are for no chargeable consideration they will also be for a consideration that is less than £40,000 and so not notifiable. In consequence, it would seem owing to an oversight in the dealing with the consequential provisions, those transactions that are notifiable notwithstanding the fact they fall within Sch 3, para 1, are non-notifiable transactions by reason of this provision;[30]

- the grant of a lease for a term of 7 years or more where the chargeable consideration other than rent is less than £40,000 and the relevant rent is less than £1000.[31] It should be noted that the rent threshold of £1000 is significant since where the relevant rent exceeds £1000 there is no nil rate threshold for the premium and the premium of less than £40,000 would be chargeable and the transaction notifiable.[32] The question arose as to leases for terms initially less than 7 years but where by reason of holding over or other provisions the term of the lease could grow and might exceed the 7 year threshold. This could apply to leases for a fixed term where the parties might hold over by operation of law and certain periodic tenancies.[33] It is provided that such leases may produce a notifiable transaction. This arises where tax becomes payable for the first time or additional tax is payable by reason of the inclusion of the extra period within the term of the lease increasing the net present value of the rent.[34] It is, however, specifically provided that such a lease does not become notifiable where granted for a short term and becomes a deemed lease for 7 years or longer unless tax becomes payable or additional tax is payable.[35] In consequence, the mere fact that a lease becomes a deemed lease for 7 years such as a periodic tenancy continuing or a holding over pursuant to the Landlord and Tenant Act 1954 there is no obligation to notify. The question is the level of rent not the length of the extension of the term;

- the assignment or surrender of a lease where the lease was originally granted for a term of 7 years or more and the chargeable consideration for the assignment or surrender is less than £40,000.[36] It seems that it is irrelevant that at the time of the assignment or surrender the unexpired term of the lease is less than 7 years. If the original term is 7 years or longer notification will be required;

- the grant of a lease for a term of less than 7 years where the chargeable consideration does not exceed the zero-rate threshold for the time being. This will include the deemed grant of a lease by substantial performance of the agreement for lease.[37] It will be noted that this refers to the chargeable consideration and does not differentiate between rent and consideration other than rent. In consequence it is necessary to note that in relation to non-residential property where the relevant rent exceeds £1000 there is no nil rate for the premium.[38] In consequence there will be a notifiable transaction notwithstanding the premium is below the relevant threshold;[39]

---

[30] Ibid, s 77A(1), point 2.
[31] Ibid, s 77A(1), point 3.
[32] Ibid, Sch 5, paras 9 and 9A; s 77A(3).
[33] Ibid, Sch 17A, paras 3 and 4.
[34] Ibid, Sch 17A, paras 3(3) and 4(3).
[35] Ibid, Sch 17A, paras 3(5) and 4(4A).
[36] Ibid, s 77A(1), point 4.
[37] Ibid, Sch 17A, para 12A.
[38] Ibid, Sch 5, paras 9 and 9A; see **Chapter 5**.
[39] Ibid, s 77A(1), point 5.

- the assignment or surrender of a lease where the lease was originally granted for a term of less than 7 years and the chargeable consideration for the assignment or surrender does not exceed the zero-rate threshold.[40]

  It will be noted that although leases are separated the provisions refer only to the grant, assignment or surrender of a lease, they do not refer to other forms of 'acquisition' such as 'variation'. It would seem that the variation of a major interest which is likely to be only the variation of a lease as it is difficult to vary a freehold the only other form of major interest (a lease)[41] is to be treated as the acquisition of a major interest;

- acquisitions of minor interests are not notifiable where the chargeable consideration for the transaction does not exceed the zero-rate threshold ie the transaction would not be chargeable at a rate of 1 per cent or higher.[42] This would seem to apply to all forms of acquisition of minor interests including surrenders, releases and variations. In consequence, for example, a variation of an option to acquire land would not be notifiable unless the consideration for the variation exceeded the relevant nil rate threshold for that option;

- non-chargeable transactions such as mortgages, licences and tenancies at will;

- the grant or deemed grant[43] of a lease for a contractual term of 7 years or more[44] where there is no chargeable consideration,[45] which is an exempt transaction within FA 2003, Sch 3, para 1. It seems that where there is no chargeable consideration,[46] substantial performance of such an agreement for lease does not involve notification. It will, however, be necessary to keep both sets of exclusions from the notification requirements under constant scrutiny in each individual case in order to ensure that, notwithstanding the overlapping provisions, there may be differences in the drafting which affect the reporting requirements;[47]

- the grant of a lease for a contractual term of less than 7 years[48] where the nil rate of stamp duty land tax applies,[49] otherwise than by reason of some relief or exemption.[50]

18.3 The limit of exclusion from notification must be noted. Exemption otherwise than pursuant to the provisions of Sch 3 mentioned above does not relieve from the obligation to report. It would seem that there are obligations to notify in respect of transactions where the nil rate band applies because the consideration is below the relevant threshold of £125,000 (or the temporary £175,000 threshold) or £150,000, or

---

[40] Ibid, s 77A(1), point 6.
[41] Ibid, s 117.
[42] Ibid, s 77(1)(b).
[43] Ibid, Sch 17A, para 12A.
[44] On the term, see **7.113**.
[45] FA 2003, s 77(2)(a); a peppercorn rent is not chargeable consideration but a nominal £1 per annum 'if demanded' is chargeable rent and this small drafting point puts the lease into a totally different compliance regime ie a full land transaction return (SDLT 1) and any necessary ancillary returns) is required; see **11.18**.
[46] FA 2003, s 77(3), Sch 3, para 1.
[47] Ibid, s 77(3), applying, *inter alia*, Sch 3, para 1 thereto.
[48] On the term of the lease, see **7.113**.
[49] But note the restriction upon the nil rate band for lease premiums of non-residential property where the rent exceeds £1000; see **5.25**.
[50] FA 2003, s 77(2)(b).

even where the transaction consists of non-residential property in a disadvantaged area, acquisition by charities,[51] or a transaction falling within the corporate reconstruction reliefs.[52]

COMPLIANCE

Records and non-notifiable transactions

18.4   Notwithstanding that the transaction is not notifiable it is necessary to keep certain records that are necessary to establish that the transaction is not notifiable[53] unless the transaction is:[54]

- a transaction arising by reason of substantial performance of a contract or arising in connection with a subsale arrangement unless it is a transaction taking place on a contract that is substantially performed without having been completed[55] or in relation to substantial performance as modified for the purposes of subsales and transfers of rights[56] or involves the assignment of an agreement for lease prior to substantial performance by the original party;[57]

- substantial performance of a contract whereby the party has a right to direct a conveyance[58] or any subsale arrangements of such a contract[59] the deemed grant of a lease upon substantial performance of the agreement for lease[60] or any transaction relating to an increase of rent outside the terms of the lease;[61] or

- a reduction of the rent or the terms of the lease on a chargeable variation.[62]

18.5   In this situation the purchaser must keep such records for a period of 6 years after the effective date of the transaction.[63] The records required to be kept and preserved include relevant instruments relating to the transaction and, in particular, any contract or conveyance and any supporting maps, plans or similar documents and records of any relevant payments, receipts and financial arrangements.[64] This is, however, merely an illustrative list and is not exhaustive and records should also include any advice as to value or cost of the consideration, any court orders or deeds of variation of the will, or advice as to why the transaction is not notifiable by means of a land transaction return.

18.6   However, it may not be necessary to preserve the documents as such since it is provided[65] that the obligation may be satisfied by the preservation of the information

---

51   Exempt pursuant to either of the two reliefs within ibid, Sch 8; see **11.41**.
52   Ibid, Sch 7; see **Chapter 12**.
53   Ibid, Sch 11, para 4 (as amended).
54   Ibid, s 79(2).
55   Pursuant to ibid, s 44(4).
56   Pursuant to ibid, s 45.
57   Pursuant to ibid, Sch 17A, para 12B.
58   Pursuant to ibid, s 44A(3).
59   Pursuant to ibid, s 45A.
60   Pursuant to ibid, Sch 17A, para 12A(2) or para 19(3) as applied in Scotland.
61   Ibid, Sch 17A, para 13.
62   Ibid, Sch 17A, para 15A.
63   Ibid, Sch 11, para 4(1).
64   Ibid, Sch 11, para 4(3).
65   Ibid, Sch 11, para 5(1).

contained in the records and where any information is so preserved a copy of any document forming part of the records is admissible in any evidence before the General or Special Commissioners as if they were the records themselves.[66]

Penalties

Record-keeping

18.7   Records for non-notifiable transactions must be preserved for at least 6 years,[67] or copies or other records rather than the original records themselves[68] may be acceptable. A person who fails to keep the records is liable to a penalty not exceeding £3000 unless he can show to the satisfaction of HMRC that any facts that they reasonably require to be proved and would have been proved by the records are proved by other documentary evidence provided to HMRC Stamp Taxes.[69]

ENQUIRIES INTO NON-NOTIFIABLE TRANSACTIONS

18.8   Along with the removal of the ability of taxpayers to use self-certificates (SDLT 60) to facilitate their dealings with the Land Registry, the power of HMRC Stamp Taxes to investigate non-notifiable transactions has also been restricted. It would seem, therefore, that HMRC Stamp Taxes have no power to enquire into a non-notifiable transaction.[70] However, HMRC Stamp Taxes have power to enquire into a land transaction return.[71] The filing of the return which is technically unnecessary such as pursuant to pressure from the Land Registry refusing to recognise a non-notifiable transaction, will, in consequence, confer power upon HMRC Stamp Taxes to enquire into a non-notifiable transaction.

---

[66]   Ibid, Sch 11, para 5(2).
[67]   Ibid, Sch 11, para 4(2).
[68]   Ibid, Sch 11, para 5.
[69]   Ibid, Sch 11, para 6.
[70]   Ibid, Sch 11, Part 3 (repealed).
[71]   Ibid, Sch 10, para 12. It will be noted that para 12(1) refers to a land transaction return not into a notifiable transaction. In consequence, it seems that HMRC Stamp Taxes can enquire into any situation where a land transaction has been returned to them and it seems that this power applies even though the land transaction return may have been filed notwithstanding there was no notifiable transaction involved such as where the Land Registry are proving difficult in relation to accepting.

Chapter 19

HMRC STAMP TAXES ENQUIRIES

ENQUIRIES INTO LAND TRANSACTION RETURNS

No adjudication – an Enquiry

19.1   The issuing of an Inland Revenue Certificate (SDLT 5) is not conclusive that the correct amount of stamp duty land tax has been paid since the land transaction return is subject to only minimal scrutiny because at this stage HMRC Stamp Taxes will not have any worthwhile evidence on which to challenge the return notwithstanding that they are, in theory, entitled to correct a land transaction return for 'obvious' errors of principle. However, in the absence of evidence it is difficult to see how most 'errors' will be 'obvious'.

19.2   In addition, there has been an attempt to ease the problems arising with registration of title and the payment of stamp taxes. Under the stamp duty regime, as it continues to apply to shares, it was necessary to resolve any outstanding stamp duty issues before the document could be stamped and registered.[1] The position is now modified but not totally remedied. It is now possible to pay a provisional amount of stamp duty land tax and provided that the land transaction return appears to be in order[2] in these circumstances, particularly given the limited power for HMRC Stamp Taxes to intervene in the correctness of the land transaction return[3] the parties are usually in a position to obtain an Inland Revenue Certificate (SDLT 5) fairly quickly and proceed to registration. Under this regime the issue of the correctness of the tax paid is dealt with behind the title. The fact that the party may be incorrectly claiming an exemption which was formerly challenged by an adjudication for stamp duty purposes prior to stamping, is now reversed and the party can take the benefit of the exemption and dispute its applicability which HMRC Stamp Taxes in an Enquiry. The obstacle to the smooth operation of this revised process in relation to stamp duty land tax is the removal of the self-certificate and the problems now arising in practice with the Land Registry when dealing with transactions presented to them on the basis that they are not notifiable and there is no need to produce an Inland Revenue Certificate (SDLT 5).[4] However, HMRC Stamp Taxes have only limited powers to correct or challenge the land transaction return when originally filed[5] so that the Inland Revenue Certificate is little more than[6] an acknowledgement that a land transaction return that appears to be in order has been received. It no longer operates as a receipt or proof of payment[7] has been paid. The challenge to the correctness of the return is primarily the Enquiry.

---

[1]   Stamp Act 1981, s 17.
[2]   See on correction of land transaction returns **17.27**.
[3]   FA 2003, Sch 10, para 7; see **17.27**.
[4]   Ibid, s 79(1); see **Chapter 22**.
[5]   Ibid, Sch 10, para 7; see **17.27**.
[6]   SDLT 1 Box 15.
[7]   FA 2003, s 76(3)(b) (as amended); but note Stamp Duty Land Tax (Administration) Regulations 2003, SI 2003/2837, reg 4(5), not properly amended.

HMRC Stamp Taxes is given power to enquire into a land transaction return upon giving notice of its intention to do so to the purchaser before the end of the Enquiry period.[8] It is no longer possible to submit documents for adjudication.[9] This is replaced by self-assessment and the subsequent in-depth investigation of the facts on an Enquiry. This will extend beyond the documents into the facts and circumstances relating to the transaction including prior and subsequent events.[10]

Enquiries into non-notifiable transactions

19.3 Consequent upon the abolition of self-certificates (SDLT 60) and the repeal of substantial parts of FA 2003, Sch 11 HMRC Stamp Taxes have no power to launch an Enquiry into non-notifiable transactions. However, their power is not limited to Enquiries into notifiable transactions, it is a power to enquire into land transaction returns filed with them. In consequence, there is an indirect power to enquire into non-notifiable transactions where the parties unnecessarily file a land transaction return.[11] It is this area of the lack of co-operation by the Land Registry when they refuse to accept a transaction as non-notifiable and effectively for the person seeking registration to files an unnecessary return where the person can be exposed to additional and unnecessary costs and delay.

ENQUIRY PERIOD

19.4 The Enquiry period in relation to a land transaction return is:

- the period of 9 months after the filing date if the return was delivered on or before that date;

- 9 months after the date on which the return was delivered, if the return was delivered late;

- where the return was amended, 9 months after the date of the amendment; and

- where a later return is required.[12]

Discovery

19.5 HMRC Stamp Taxes must give a notice of their intention to enquire into a land transaction return to the purchaser before the end of the enquiry period.[13] If HMRC

8   Ibid, Sch 10, para 12, Sch 11, para 7.
9   On the potential problem with pre- and post-transaction rulings see, for example, **11.13** and **14.10**.
10   It is possible that an Enquiry into one return may produce information that enables HMRC Stamp Taxes to issue a discovery assessment in relation to other returns whether or not relating to the same chargeable interest. Also an adverse outcome to an Enquiry may require the taxpayer to disclose similar 'errors' in other returns (FA 2003, Sch 10, para 8). It is understood that HMRC Stamp Taxes intend to take stamp objections pursuant to Stamp Act 1891, s 14(4) where the Enquiry produces inadequately stamped documents (see *Parinv v IRC* [1998] STC 305).
11   But this may be 'necessary' in the sense that the Land Registry are proving difficult in treating the transaction on a non-notifiable basis notwithstanding that this is a manifestly correct approach to the transaction; see **Chapter 22**.
12   FA 2003, Sch 10, para 12(2A).
13   FA 2003, Sch 10, para 12(1).

Stamp Taxes give notice within the 9 month period of their intention to enquire into a land transaction return delivered in respect of transactions where there has been an adjustment in the variable consideration[14] a land transaction return filed where there has been an clawback of reliefs previously obtained[15] or a return filed in consequence of a later linked transaction[16] and it appears necessary to them to give a notice in respect of an earlier land transaction return in respect of the same land transaction they may launch an Enquiry into the earlier return notwithstanding that the 9 month period in relation to that return has expired.[17] This enables them to investigate whether the original return was properly prepared and the tax correctly paid.

19.6 However, HMRC Stamp Taxes are given wide powers to deal with situations where no land transaction return is filed and they make a discovery. They are given powers to assess tax that they believe is due notwithstanding that the 9 month Enquiry period has expired.[18] It is possible for HMRC Stamp Taxes to issue a discovery assessment notwithstanding that there has been a formal Enquiry which has closed.[19] The basic period for issuing a discovery assessment is 6 years but this is extended to 21 years where there is negligence or fraud.[20] The question is whether, as at present constituted, HMRC Stamp Taxes have sufficient resource to enquire into other arrangements and make a discovery. It seems that once their enquiry powers have expired after the 9 month period they may not be in a very strong position to launch what would be, in effect, a fishing expedition in order to find evidence to justify a discovery.

Amendment of return

19.7 If HMRC Stamp Taxes during an Enquiry form the opinion that the self-assessment in the land transaction return is in sufficient and tax may be lost if the return is not immediately amended they may issue a written notice amending the return.[21] In this case the tax is payable forthwith.[22]

The taxpayer may amend the return during an Enquiry[23] but this does not restrict the scope of the Enquiry. The amendment does not affect the tax payment during the Enquiry and operate sonly when the Enquiry is closed unless HMRC Stamp Taxes state in the closure notice taking the amendment into account or that the amendment is wrong.[24]

---

[14] Ibid, s 80; see **16.34**.
[15] Pursuant to ibid, s 81; see **16.20**.
[16] Ibid, s 81A; see, for example, **5.71** and **7.102**.
[17] Ibid, Sch 10, para 12(2A).
[18] Ibid, Sch 10, para 25.
[19] Ibid, Sch 10, para 30(3).
[20] Ibid, Sch 10, para 31(2).
[21] Ibid, Sch 10, para 17.
[22] Ibid, s 86(3).
[23] Ibid, Sch 10, para 18.
[24] Ibid, Sch 10, para 18(3).

RESTRICTIONS UPON ENQUIRIES

19.8   A return which has been the subject of one Enquiry may not be the subject of another, except in the case of a return that has been amended by the taxpayer;[25] but the completion or closure of an Enquiry does not prevent the subsequent issue of a subsequent discovery assessment and there are express limits as to what knowledge is to be attributed to HMRC Stamp Taxes at the end of an Enquiry.[26] It appears, however, that HMRC Stamp Taxes can issue a late Enquiry notice in relation to earlier returns filed for the same chargeable transaction where the earlier returns have been the subject-matter of an Enquiry.[27]

SCOPE OF ENQUIRY

19.9   An Enquiry extends to anything contained in the return or required to be contained in the land transaction return that relates either to the question of whether the transaction to which the land transaction return relates is chargeable or to the amount of tax chargeable.[28] If the notice of Enquiry is given as a result of an amendment to a land transaction return by the taxpayer and the Enquiry period relevant to that return has expired, or after an Enquiry into the return has already been completed, the new Enquiry is limited to matters to which the amendment relates or to matters that are affected by the amendment.[29]

Information powers[30]

19.10   HMRC Stamp Taxes may give notice in writing to the purchaser who has filed a land transaction return to produce to them such documents in his possession or power and to provide such information in such form as they may reasonably require for the purposes of the Enquiry.[31] The notice must specify the time within which the purchaser is to comply. Such compliance may be satisfied by the giving of copies of documents[32] unless HMRC Stamp Taxes require the original to be produced.[33] However, this should be compared with the provision relating to the preservation of records.[34] It is provided by para 10(1) of Sch 10 to the FA 2003 that the duty to preserve records may be satisfied by preservation of the information contained in them.[35] Moreover, no penalty is incurred if HMRC Stamp Taxes are satisfied that any facts that they reasonably require to be proved and would have been proved by the records are proved by documentary evidence provided to them.[36]

25   Ibid, Sch 10, para 12(3).
26   Ibid, Sch 10, para 30(3)(b).
27   Ibid, Sch 10, para 12(2A) and (3); relating to returns involving FA 2003, ss 80, 81 and 81A.
28   Ibid, Sch 10, para 13.
29   Ibid, Sch 10, para 13(2).
30   See further **Chapter 21** on the power to obtain documents and/or information from persons other than the taxpayer.
31   Ibid, Sch 10, para 14(1) and (2).
32   Ibid, Sch 10, para 14(3)(a).
33   Ibid, Sch 10, para 14(3)(b).
34   Ibid, Sch 10, paras 9 and 10.
35   See **Chapter 20**.
36   FA 2003, Sch 10, para 11(2).

19.11 There is a right of appeal to the Commissioners against a notice requiring the taxpayer to produce documents or provide information.[37] A person who fails to produce documents or information as required is liable to a penalty of £50. Where the default continues after a penalty is imposed, the person is also liable to a daily penalty of £30 if the penalty is determined by HMRC Stamp Taxes and £150 if the penalty is determined by the court.[38] If, during an Enquiry into a return, HMRC Stamp Taxes form the opinion that the amount stated in the self-assessment is insufficient and that, unless the assessment is immediately amended, there is likely to be a loss of tax, they may by written notice amend the assessment and make good the deficiency.[39]

HMRC generally have acquired extensive information powers and these have been extended by FA 2009, s 96 where they have been made applicable to stamp duty land tax.[40]

Appeals

19.12 At any time when an Enquiry into a return is in progress, any question arising in connection with the subject-matter of the Enquiry may be referred to the Special Commissioners for their determination.[41] The determination of a question is binding on the parties and has to be taken into account by HMRC Stamp Taxes in reaching their conclusions.

COMPLETION OF ENQUIRY – CLOSURE NOTICES

19.13 An Enquiry is completed when HMRC Stamp Taxes deliver a notice informing the purchaser they have completed their enquiries and stated their conclusions. Such closure notice must state whether in the opinion of HMRC Stamp Taxes no amendment of the return is required, or make such amendments to the return as may be necessary, or state that the self-certificate was correct; and, if not correct, whether the transaction to which it relates was chargeable or notifiable.[42]

Order to close Enquiry[43]

19.14 Except where a referral of a question has been made to the Special Commissioners for their determination, the purchaser may apply to the General or Special Commissioners for a direction that HMRC Stamp Taxes give a closure notice within a specified period. Such notice must be given unless the General or Special Commissioners are satisfied that HMRC Stamp Taxes have reasonable grounds for not giving a closure notice within a specified period.[44]

---

[37]   Ibid, Sch 10, para 15; Sch 11, para 10.
[38]   Ibid, Sch 10, para 16; Sch 11, para 11.
[39]   Ibid, Sch 10, para 7.
[40]   FA 2009, s 96.
[41]   FA 2003, Sch 10, para 19; Sch 11, para 12; subject to First Tier Tribunal charges.
[42]   Ibid, Sch 10, para 23; Sch 11, para 16.
[43]   Subject to the First Tier Tribunal charges.
[44]   FA 2003, Sch 10, para 24; Sch 11, para 17; see decisions on equivalent provisions for other taxes such as **21.20**.

Chapter 20

RECORDS

OBLIGATION TO KEEP RECORDS

Records and title

20.1   The stamp duty land tax legislation imposes, under a range of penalties and sanctions, obligations upon the taxpayer or a non-taxpayer who is a party to a non-notifiable transaction to preserve certain records. However, this is merely the tip of the iceberg of problems for the taxpayer and other parties.

20.2   As regards the 'purchaser' he has three areas of difficulty in practice; namely:

- the records that he needs to preserve for dealing with HMRC Stamp Taxes;

- the documents or records he will, by contract, require the vendor to produce at completion in order to obtain registration of title and deal with his own tax liabilities in the future; and

- the records that he needs to preserve in order to provide a satisfactory 'title' to potential purchasers or lessees of the land.[1] Much of stamp duty land tax is dealt with on a provisional or estimated basis requiring retrospective adjustment by reference to subsequent events such as later rent reviews. This means that in certain circumstances a third party actually becomes responsible for the original taxpayer's outstanding tax liability.[2] The purchaser will require full details of the tax situation to date. In addition, the purchaser may enter into chargeable transactions such as holding over or rent reviews which are taxable in their own right but the calculation of the tax depends upon previous tax computations including those entered into by the seller.[3] He will require a fall tax history. In these situations simply delivering a copy of the land transaction return and Revenue Certificate (SDLT 1 to 5) will be inadequate because these deal in global figures whereas the information required relates to individual events and circumstances such as the rent for any particular year.[4] Moreover, since this information is effectively part of the title of the vendor, it is necessary to preserve the documents beyond the statutory recordkeeping period in many cases. This may extend beyond the term of the lease because if the information is relevant for holding over or certain lease renewals.[5]

---

[1]   See **2.13**.
[2]   FA 2003, Sch 17A, para 12.
[3]   Ibid, Sch 17A, paras 3 and 9.
[4]   A print out of the Revenue online calculator could be a key document in this context.
[5]   FA 2003, Sch 17A, para 3; see **7.115**.

Third parties such as the vendor or estate agents or mortgagees are not, as such, required to preserve 'records' but they may be required by HMRC Stamp Taxes to provide 'information'.[6] Such persons may find it prudent to 'record' data for a reasonable time in order to provide contemporaneous evidence in support of the 'information' which they may be asked to supply.

The taxpayer

Notifiable transactions

20.3 A taxpayer[7] who delivers a land transaction return[8] must:

- keep such records as may be needed to enable him to deliver a correct and complete return or formerly to deliver a correct and complete self-certificate.[9] This clearly requires all relevant records (not merely the conveyance, lease or deed of grant or variation of rights) such as the essential advice as to matters requiring a judgment (eg the market value or other items) upon which the stamp duty land tax is calculated; and

- preserve those records for a period of 6 years after the effective date of the transaction or possibly until a later date on which any Enquiry into the return or self-certificate is completed or, if there is no such Enquiry, HMRC Stamp Taxes no longer have power to enquire into the certificate or return.[10] The power to Enquire into the return[11] or self-certificate[12] runs for the period of 9 months:
    - after the filing date, if the return was delivered on or before that date;
    - after the date on which the return was delivered, if the return was delivered after the expiration of the 30-day time limit;
    - after the date on which the amendment was made, if the return is amended by the taxpayer;
    - in relation to self-certificates, after the date on which the self-certificate was produced.

However, the practical scope of the obligation to keep records both as to the time for preservation and the persons who may find it prudent to keep records has to be considered in the context of the powers of HMRC Stamp Taxes to demand 'information' which can extend for 21 years after the effective date.[13]

Non-notifiable transactions

20.4 Notwithstanding the abolition of self-certificates (SDLT 60) the purchaser must keep and preserve for 6 years such records as may be necessary to prove that the transaction was not notifiable.[14]

---

6   Ibid, Sch 13, Part 2; see **Chapter 21**.
7   This will include all persons who are treated as taxpayers such as personal representatives who have to preserve the deceased's records.
8   FA 2003, Sch 10, para 9.
9   For returns: FA 2003, Sch 10, para 9(1)(c); note the need to ask the right questions when preparing or assisting in the preparation of the return *Slattery v Moore Stephens* [2003] STC 1379.
10   If the 9-month period has expired.
11   FA 2003, Sch 10, para 12(2).
12   Ibid, Sch 11, para 7(2).
13   See **Chapter 21**.
14   FA 2003, Sch 11, para 4.

THE RECORDS

20.5 Although separate regimes for notifiable and non-notifiable transactions are imposed, they are very similar in detail. The provisions of the FA 2003[15] give an indication of the records that are required to be maintained to support the return or non-notification are relevant instruments relating to the transaction, such as any contract or conveyance, any supporting maps, plans or similar documents, records of relevant payments, receipts and financial arrangements. However, this list is merely 'inclusive' and it is illustrative and not definitive. Other records will, in practice, be required in order to have evidence that may be acceptable to HMRC Stamp Taxes. Failure to keep records of any steps taken to arrive at the open market cost of works or the market value of any consideration in kind or the reasonable amount expected to be produced by an uncertain consideration may make it difficult to resist allegations that the land transaction return was prepared negligently or fraudulently.[16] The obtaining and preservation of contemporaneous written reports of appropriate professional advisers, although costly, will in most cases prove to be a prudent move for taxpayers and will certainly be more effective than subsequently seeking expert evidence to establish that the figures inserted were correct which are likely to be resisted by HMRC Stamp Taxes as being prepared with hindsight and therefore less persuasive although they continually base the valuation arguments with the benefit of hindsight.

20.6 The obligation to preserve records may be satisfied by the preservation of the information contained on them.[17] Where information is so preserved, a copy of any document forming part of the records is admissible in evidence in any proceedings before the General or Special Commissioners[18] to the same extent as the records themselves.[19]

PENALTIES

20.7 A person who fails to comply with the record-keeping obligation is liable to a penalty not exceeding £3,000.[20] However, no penalty is incurred if HMRC Stamp Taxes are satisfied that any facts that they reasonably require to be proved and that would have been proved by the records are proved by other documentary evidence produced to them.[21]

OTHER PARTIES

20.8 Assignees of leases are forced to take over the open tax position of the original tenant.[22] Such assignees will require access to the original taxpayer's records since they may be obliged to produce them to HMRC Stamp Taxes when their own returns are

---

[15] Ibid, Sch 10, para 9; Sch 11, para 4.
[16] But note *Re Wragge* [1897] 1 Ch 796 on the burden of proof on HMRC Stamp Taxes.
[17] FA 2003, Sch 10, para 10(1); Sch 11, para 5(1).
[18] Subject to the First Tier Tribunal charges.
[19] FA 2003, Sch 10, para 19(2); Sch 11, para 5(2).
[20] Ibid, Sch 10, para 11(1); Sch 11, para 6(1).
[21] Ibid, Sch 10, para 11(2); Sch 11, para 6(2).
[22] Ibid, s 81, 81A and 82; Sch 17A, para 12; see **7.238**; note also the different principles of the special charge upon assignees of exempt leases pursuant to ibid para 11.

being prepared or enquired into or challenged.[23] There is no statutory power for assignees to demand access to such documents so that it is matter of contractual negotiation or replying upon provisions in the contract to provide further assurances or the obligations to assist the purchaser implied by selling with absolute title guarantee to ensure that appropriate protection is obtained.

20.9 Although there is no statutory obligation imposed upon other persons to maintain records a wide range of persons involved in the transaction are subject to obligations to supply documents and information.[24] Such persons may find it prudent to maintain records so as to be in a position to support by written evidence any answers they give when questioned by HMRC Stamp Taxes.

---

23 See **7.239**.
24 FA 2003, Sch 13, Part 2.

Chapter 21

INFORMATION POWERS

DUTY TO SUPPLY INFORMATION

21.1   In addition to the specific powers to require the taxpayer[1] to provide documents and information in connection with an Enquiry,[2] HMRC Stamp Taxes are given extensive powers to call for documents or information from a variety of persons, not merely the taxpayer, and such persons may be subject to a penalty for failure to comply.[3] Subject to certain limited restrictions as to the qualifying level of officer of the Board of Inland Revenue[4] or with judicial authority,[5] or with the consent of the Special of General Commissioners,[6] HMRC Stamp Taxes may demand the production of such documents as are in the possession or power of third parties[7] such as the vendor or persons advising the vendor, including any estate agent who may have been approached to give a valuation prior to sale but whose advice was not accepted and who was not retained for the purposes of sale. Parties acting for a landlord whose sole role is the giving of a licence to assign or lawyers or valuers acting for a potential mortgagee are within the range of persons who may be called upon to produce details of their advice and other matters such as correspondence. Although only peripherally involved in the main chargeable transaction and somewhat remote from the actual taxpayer and not subject to any statutory duty to preserve records, such persons may find it prudent to preserve records of their advice if only to defend allegations of being parties to conspiracies to defraud[8] HMRC Stamp Taxes when the amount of the consideration allocated to carpets or kitchen units was possibly excessive. In such cases, HMRC Stamp Taxes, with the co-operation of the Special or General Commissioners, may require the production of documents more than 6 years old;[9] but the 6 year limitation period applies in relation to deceased taxpayers.[10]

---

[1]   Which would appear to include assignees of leases because FA 2003, Sch 17A, para 12 requires the assignee to do whatever the assignor is required to do, but this would seem to be stretching the legislation unreasonably far since the assignee may not have the information.

[2]   FA 2003, Sch 10, para 14; see **19.10**.

[3]   Note also the extended powers to demand information etc conferred upon HMRC Stamp Taxes by FA 2009, s 96.

[4]   FA 2003, ss 42(3); 113, Sch 13, paras 1(1), 6(1), 14(1), 28(1).

[5]   Ibid, Sch 13, paras 16 and 32.

[6]   Ibid, Sch 13, paras 2 and 7.

[7]   But the recordkeeping obligations are not applied to such persons; see **Chapter 20**; but prudence suggests that details are preserved as a matter of self-protection.

[8]   In *Saunders v Edwards* [1987] 2 All ER 651 the Court of Appeal indicated that such conduct could be a conspiracy which, of course, subject to the charges for First Tier Tribunals etc requires 'conspirators' such as vendors who agree to the improper price allocation and the parties' advisers who also face allegations of professional misconduct as regards their participation in preparing the documentation on the basis of false statements as to the price.

[9]   FA 2003, Sch 13, para 24.

[10]   Ibid, Sch 13, para 6(4).

21.2 The power to call for documents or information supported by a variety of sanctions exists in relation to:

- enquiries into a land transaction return;[11]

- where HMRC Stamp Taxes are seeking information relevant to the liability to taxation and the amount of such stamp duty land tax of any person;[12]

- where there are reasonable grounds for suspecting that an offence involving serious fraud in relation to stamp duty land tax has been or is about to be committed.[13]

21.3 There was also power to obtain a warrant permitting entry, if necessary by force, in search of evidence of a serious tax fraud.[14]

PERSONS LIABLE TO SUPPLY INFORMATION

21.4 The persons who may be called upon to produce documents and/or information include the following.

The taxpayer and assignees

21.5 There are two sets of powers to demand documents and/or information from the taxpayer, which duplicate each other to a significant extent save that certain powers may be exercised only during the course of an Enquiry.

During Enquiries into returns or claims

21.6 HMRC Stamp Taxes may give written notice during the course of an Enquiry into a land tax return[15] or an Enquiry into a claim for repayment of tax[16] requiring the taxpayer to produce to it such documents in his possession or power and/or to provide it with such information as it may reasonably require for the purposes of the Enquiry. The notice must specify a time being not less than 30 days after the service of the notice within which the taxpayer has to comply.[17] HMRC Stamp Taxes is empowered to take copies of documents.[18]

Restrictions

21.7 There are restrictions upon the power to call for documents or information; namely:

---

[11]   Ibid, Sch 10, para 14. The equivalent obligations for non-notifiable transactions have been removed consequent upon the abolition of self-certificates.
[12]   Ibid, Sch 13, paras 1, 14, 28.
[13]   Ibid, Sch 13, para 32.
[14]   Ibid, Sch 13, para 43; see FA 2007, s 84.
[15]   Ibid, Sch 10, para 14(1).
[16]   Ibid, Sch 11A, para 8.
[17]   Ibid, Sch 10, para 3(2); Sch 11A, para 8(2).
[18]   Ibid, Sch 10, para 14(4); Sch 11A, para 8(4).

- the taxpayer cannot be compelled to produce documents or information relating to either the conduct of any appeal by him[19] or the conduct of any question referred to the Special Commissioners[20] which is still pending during an Enquiry;[21]

- the power to call for documents does not apply to documents or information that are personal records[22] or journalistic material.[23]

21.8 There are no specific provisions dealing with documents held by the taxpayer for which legal privilege might be claimed.[24]

Sanctions

21.9 Failure to produce the documents or supply copies[25] or to supply the information attracts a penalty of £50.[26] However, if the default continues after the imposition of the £50 penalty, a further penalty is imposed on a daily basis. The amount of the daily penalty is:

- £30 if determined by an officer of the Board of HMRC; or

- £150 if determined by the court.[27]

No penalty may be imposed in respect of a failure at any time after the failure has been rectified.[28]

Appeals

21.10 It is possible to appeal against a notice to produce documents or to supply information during an Enquiry into a land transaction return[29] or a claim.[30] The notice of appeal must be:

- in writing;

- served within 30 days after the notice demanding the document or information was issued;[31] and

- served on the officer of the Board of HMRC issuing the demand.

---

[19] Ibid, Sch 10, para 14(5); Sch 11A, para 8(5).
[20] Pursuant to ibid, Sch 10, para 19; Sch 11A, para 9.
[21] Ibid, Sch 10, para 14(5)(b).
[22] Police and Criminal Evidence Act 1984, s 12; Police and Criminal Evidence (Northern Ireland) Order 1989, SI 1989/1341 (NI 12), art 14.
[23] Police and Criminal Evidence Act 1984, s 13; Police and Criminal Evidence (Northern Ireland) Order 1989, SI 1989/1341 (NI 12), art 15.
[24] Although his advisers may claim privilege; see **21.19**. This also has important practical application in relation to the notification of tax schemes, see **Chapter 17**.
[25] FA 2003, Sch 10, para 14(3); Sch 11A, para 8(3).
[26] Ibid, Sch 10, para 16(1)(a); Sch 11A, para 10(1)(a).
[27] Ibid, Sch 10, para 16(1)(b); Sch 11A, para 10(1)(b).
[28] Ibid, Sch 10, para 16(3); Sch 11A, para 10(2).
[29] Ibid, Sch 10, para 15(1).
[30] Ibid, Sch 11A, para 9.
[31] Note: not 30 days from when the demand was received.

The demand is to be set aside if it appears to the General or Special Commissioners that the documents or information are not reasonably required for the purposes of the Enquiry; but otherwise it must be confirmed.[32] The decision of the Special or General Commissioners is final.[33]

No Enquiry in progress

General powers

21.11 Where no Enquiry in a land transaction return (SDLT 1) is in progress or there is no current Enquiry into a claim after giving the taxpayer a reasonable opportunity to produce documents or information and he has failed to produce them, an appropriately authorised officer of the Board of HMRC may with the consent of the General or Special Commissioners by notice in writing require a person to deliver such documents as are in that person's possession or power which, in the officer's reasonable opinion, contain or may contain information relevant to any tax liability to which that person may be subject and the amount of any such liability or to provide him with any such information as he may reasonably require as being relevant to any such liability.[34] This problem, in practice, is that although this appears to give HMRC Stamp Taxes wide-ranging powers to embark upon a fishing expedition, those powers may be restricted in that the authorised officer of the Board must have a reasonable opinion that the documents contain information, which means that he must have some evidence that reasonably suggests facts which point to a liability to tax. In addition, the General and Special Commissioners may only consent if they are satisfied, in all circumstances, that the Board are justified in proceeding. Although the record of the Commissioners on such cases does not inspire confidence, the law indicates that any consent where there is reasonable evidence and not unsubstantiated suspicion of HMRC who will be faced with the problem of producing evidence that indicates facts to support their claim for tax lost.

21.12 The notice must specify or describe the documents or information required and specify a period within which they are to be provided.[35] This period must be not less than 30 days after the date of the notice.[36]

21.13 HMRC Stamp Taxes must give a written summary of their reasons for applying to the General or Special Commissioners for consent to the notice to the taxpayer provided that this does not require the disclosure of information or identify any person who has provided HMRC Stamp Taxes with information or if the Commissioners direct that such information should not be disclosed.[37]

Special powers

21.14 The Board, as opposed to an officer of the Board, and apparently without the consent of the Commissioners, may by notice in writing require a person to deliver to a named officer of the Board such documents as are in that person's possession or power and which in the Board's reasonable opinion contain or may contain information

---

[32]   FA 2003, Sch 10, para 15(4); Sch 11A, para 9(4).
[33]   Ibid, Sch 10, para 15(6); Sch 11A, para 9(6).
[34]   Ibid, Sch 13, para 1.
[35]   Ibid, Sch 13, para 3(1).
[36]   Ibid, Sch 13, para 3(2).
[37]   Ibid, Sch 12, para 4.

relevant to any tax liability of that person or the amount of any such liability, or to provide such information.[38] The notice must specify the documents as information to which it relates and require the documents or information to be produced within the time specified in the notice.[39] Notice may not be given unless the Board has reasonable grounds for believing that the person to whom it relates may have failed or may fail to comply with any provisions relating to stamp duty land tax and that any such failure is likely to have led, or to lead, to serious prejudice to the proper assessment or collection of tax.[40]

Restriction

21.15 This power does not extend to documents that are personal records or journalistic material but is otherwise unrestricted.[41] Again there is no specific reference to legal privilege[42] whether of the taxpayer or other parties.

Third parties

General powers

21.16 After giving any person a reasonable opportunity to deliver or make available documents[43] which HMRC Stamp Taxes believe are in that person's possession or power[44] and contain or may contain information relevant to any tax liability or the amount of any such liability of any taxpayer, including a company which has been dissolved or struck off or an individual who has died,[45] an officer of the Board of HMRC authorised for that purpose[46] may, with the consent of the General or Special Commissioners as required for the giving of such notice,[47] give a notice in writing requiring delivery of such documents. Such consent may not be given unless the General or Special Commissioner is satisfied that in all the circumstances the authorised officer of the Board of HMRC is 'justified' in seeking to exercise this power.[48] The notice must specify the documents to which it relates and the time, being not less than 30 days after the date of notice, within which they must be produced.[49] A copy of the notice must be given to the taxpayer to whom it relates[50] unless the General or Special Commissioner directs otherwise upon the basis that HMRC has reasonable grounds for suspecting the taxpayer of fraud.[51] The taxpayer must also be supplied with a summary of the reasons of HMRC Stamp Taxes in applying for consent of the Commissioners to the notice[52] unless this might lead to the identification of persons supplying information for HMRC,

---

[38] Ibid, Sch 13, para 28(2).
[39] Ibid, Sch 13, para 29.
[40] Ibid, Sch 13, para 28(2).
[41] Ibid, Sch 13, para 31; Police and Criminal Evidence Act 1984, ss 12 and 13; Police and Criminal Evidence (Northern Ireland) Order 1989, SI 1989/1341 (NI 12), arts 14 and 15.
[42] See **21.19**.
[43] FA 2003, Sch 13, para 6(8).
[44] Note the similar issues in *Lonrho v Shell* [1980] 1 WLR 627.
[45] FA 2003, Sch 13, para 6(4), but limited to a 6-year period after the death of an individual. There is no express time-limit in relation to companies but, given the problems of pursuing the assets of dissolved companies and the possible need to re-vivify such companies or to enforce any claim for stamp duty land tax, the Companies Act 2006, s 1029 may operate in practice to restrict the scope of this power.
[46] FA 2003, Sch 13, para 6(1) and (2).
[47] Ibid, Sch 13, para 7.
[48] Ibid, Sch 13, para 7(2).
[49] Ibid, Sch 13, para 8.
[50] Ibid, Sch 13, para 9(1).
[51] Ibid, Sch 13, para 9(2) and (3).
[52] Ibid, Sch 13, para 10(2).

and the General or Special Commissioners are satisfied that the authorised officer has reasonable grounds for believing that any such disclosure would prejudice the assessment and collection of stamp duty land tax,[53] or it has been approved that information need not be disclosed nor a copy be given to the taxpayer.[54]

Unnamed taxpayer

21.17 After giving a person a reasonable opportunity to deliver or make available documents in his possession or control,[55] an officer authorised by the Board of HMRC may, with the consent of a Special Commissioner,[56] give a notice requiring the production of documents without naming the taxpayer,[57] provided that the Commissioner is satisfied that the taxpayer's identity is not known to the officer or there is a class of taxpayer whose individual identity is not so known[58] and there are reasonable grounds for believing that the taxpayer or any class of taxpayers may have failed or may fail to comply with the provisions relating to stamp duty land tax.[59] It must also be shown that any such failure is likely to have led or to lead to serious prejudice of the proper assessment or collection of tax[60] and the information in the documents is not readily available from other sources.[61] The person is given 30 days to object to the notice on the ground that it will be onerous for him to comply with it.[62] If the parties cannot resolve the issue of the onerous nature of the obligation by agreement, the matter is referred to the Special Commissioners.[63]

Restriction

21.18 The power of demand for information or documents does not extend to personal records or journalistic information,[64] nor to the delivery of documents relating to the conduct of a pending appeal by the taxpayer;[65] but although barristers, advocates and solicitors are given limited protection[66] no specific reference is made to legal privilege[67] of the third party.

Professional advisers

21.19 Professional advisers may be required to disclose documents and/or information, with only limited privilege for lawyers.[68]

---

[53] Ibid, Sch 13, para 10(2) and (3).
[54] Ibid, Sch 13, para 10(2)(b) and (4).
[55] Ibid, Sch 13, para 11(34).
[56] Ibid, Sch 13, para 11(1).
[57] Ibid, Sch 13, para 11(1).
[58] Ibid, Sch 13, para 11(2)(a).
[59] Ibid, Sch 13, para 11(2)(b).
[60] Ibid, Sch 13, para 11(2)(c).
[61] Ibid, Sch 13, para 11(2)(d).
[62] Ibid, Sch 13, para 11(4).
[63] Ibid, Sch 13, para 11(5).
[64] Ibid, Sch 13, para 20(1) and (2).
[65] Ibid, Sch 13, para 21(2).
[66] Ibid, Sch 13, paras 22 and 25.
[67] Compare ibid, Sch 13, para 35.
[68] Ibid, Sch 13, para 22. There are, of course, wider issues as to whether advisers other than lawyers who give tax and legal advice are entitled to claim legal privilege since it is the advice not the adviser that is privileged. There may be distorted competition issues to be addressed. Lawyers, especially barristers, contend that the

Legal advisers

21.20 Notices may be given to barristers, advocates or solicitors but only by the Board of Inland Revenue.[69] Such a notice does not oblige the barrister, advocate or solicitor to deliver or make available without his client's consent any document in respect of which a claim to legal privilege could be maintained.[70] Legal privilege is specifically defined as being:[71]

- communications between a professional legal adviser and his client or probably any person representing his client in connection with the giving of legal advice to the client;

- communications etc made in connection with or in contemplation of legal proceedings and the purposes of such proceedings;

- items enclosed with or referred to in such communication made in connection with the giving of legal advice or in contemplation of legal proceedings for the purposes of such proceedings.

21.21 A special procedure has been established (but it seems only in relation to the obtaining of legal privilege in respect of documents pursuant to an order by a relevant judicial authority by HMRC Stamp Taxes) by regulations for the purpose of determining whether a document or part of a document is subject to legal privilege.[72] It would appear that this restriction is an oversight in the drafting of the legislation and that the special procedure should apply generally, but the official view of HMRC Stamp Taxes remains unknown at present.

Legal advisers and other professionals may have to participate in the notification of tax schemes.[73]

Auditors and tax advisers

21.22 The powers do not require disclosure of documents by a person who has been appointed as an auditor where the documents are his property and created by him or on his behalf in connection with the performance of his functions, and do not oblige a tax adviser to deliver or make available documents that are his property and consist of communications between the tax adviser and the taxpayer and any other tax adviser of the taxpayer for the purpose of giving or obtaining advice about any of the tax affairs of the taxpayer.

---

privilege is restricted to lawyers but this is probably incorrect since privilege has been extended to other advisers. Moreover, should their advice be possibly correct it may infringe competition and discrimination rules of the European Union.

[69] Ibid, Sch 13, para 22; but the limits may be unlawful discrimination.
[70] Ibid, Sch 13, para 25.
[71] Ibid, Sch 13, paras 25(2) and 35.
[72] Ibid, Sch 13, para 36; Stamp Duty Land Tax (Administration) Regulations 2003, SI 2003/2837, Part 5.
[73] FA 2004, s 306; see **2.29**. Stamp Duty Land Tax Avoidance (Prescribed Descriptions of Arrangements) Regulations 2005, SI 2005/1868; Tax Avoidance Schemes (Information) (Amendment) Regulations 2005, SI 2005/1869; Tax Avoidance Schemes (Information) Regulations 2004, SI 2004/1864; Income and Corporation Taxes Act 1988, ss 209A(4) and 840A.

Documents more than six years old

21.23 Documents which were created more than 6 years before the notice may be required for production only with an order of the Commissioners because there is suspected fraud; but there is no time-limit upon requests for information.[74]

Tax accountants

21.24 Where a person who has stood in relation to others as a tax accountant is convicted of an offence relating to tax before any court in the United Kingdom or has a penalty imposed upon him for assisting in the preparation of an incorrect stamp duty land tax return[75] and no appeal against the conviction or penalty is outstanding,[76] and that person has first been given a reasonable opportunity to deliver documents requested but has failed to do so, HMRC Stamp Taxes may, with consent of a circuit judge or a sheriff or a county court judge in the relevant jurisdiction,[77] deliver a written notice requiring that tax accountant to deliver such documents as are in his possession or power and which in the officer's reasonable opinion contain information relevant to a tax liability to which any client of his is, or has been, or may be or may have been, subject or to the amount of any such liability. The notice must specify or describe the documents to which it relates and the time within which they are to be delivered, being not less than 30 days after the delivery of the notice.[78]

Restrictions

Personal records and journalistic material

21.25 Documents that are personal records[79] or journalistic material[80] are not subject to these powers.[81]

Pending appeals

21.26 The notice cannot require the production of any documents relating to the conduct of a pending appeal against tax by the client.[82]

---

[74] There are certain time limits upon the power to demand information in relation to deceased individuals; FA 2003, Sch 13, para 6(6).
[75] Pursuant to FA 2003, s 96.
[76] Ibid, Sch 13, para 15.
[77] Ibid, Sch 13, para 16.
[78] Ibid, Sch 13, para 17.
[79] Police and Criminal Evidence Act 1984, s 12; Police and Criminal Evidence (Northern Ireland) Order 1989, SI 1989/1341 (NI 12), art 14.
[80] Police and Criminal Evidence Act 1984, s 13; Police and Criminal Evidence (Northern Ireland) Order 1989, SI 1989/1341 (NI 12), art 15.
[81] FA 2003, Sch 13, para 20.
[82] Ibid, Sch 13, para 21(3) and (4).

FRAUD INVESTIGATIONS

Powers with order of judicial authority

21.27 Where there are reasonable grounds[83] for suspecting that an offence involving serious fraud[84] in connection with or in relation to stamp duty land tax has been or is about to be committed and that documents that may be required as evidence for the purposes of any proceedings in respect of any such offence are or may be in the power or possession of any person,[85] the Board may apply to a circuit judge, sheriff or a county court judge in the relevant jurisdiction[86] for an order requiring a person who appears to have the authority to have in his possession or power the documents specified to deliver them to an officer of HMRC within 10 working days after the notice of the order is served on him or such shorter time as is specified in the notice. The person is entitled to receive notice of an intention to apply for an order against him[87] and to appear and be heard at the hearing of the application[88] unless the judicial authority is satisfied this would seriously prejudice the investigation of the offence.[89]

21.28 An offence is regarded[90] as involving serious fraud[91] if its commission has led or is intended or likely to lead either to substantial financial gain to any person or to serious prejudice to the proper assessment or collection of the tax.[92]

21.29 A person who is being given notice of an intention to apply for an order must not, except with the leave of the appropriate judicial authority or the written permission of an officer of the Board, conceal, destroy, alter or dispose of any document to which the application relates or disclose to any other person information or other matter likely to prejudice the investigation of the offence[93] – unless the application has been dismissed or abandoned or the order has been complied with.[94]

Sanctions

21.30 Failure to comply with an order is treated as a contempt of court.[95]

---

[83] This suggests a degree of objectivity in the test so that the views of the relevant officer of HMRC Stamp Taxes should be subject to the scrutiny of the Courts.

[84] This may impose a significant burden of proof upon HMRC when defending their view; *Re Wragge* [1897] 1 Ch 796.

[85] Ibid, Sch 13, para 32.

[86] Ibid, Sch 13, para 32(3).

[87] Ibid, Sch 13, para 33(1)(a).

[88] Ibid, Sch 13, para 33(1)(b).

[89] Ibid, Sch 13, para 33.

[90] This definition applies apparently only for the purposes of obtaining a warrant to enter premises (ibid, Sch 13, para 43), but this may be yet another drafting error so that it is likely to apply for the purposes currently under discussion.

[91] It must not be overlooked that allocation of the consideration between those items subject to stamp duty land tax and those items not so subject to tax may be fraudulent and professional misconduct (*Saunders v Edwards* [1987] 2 All ER 651); whether this fraud is 'serious' or not may be only a matter of the amount of stamp duty land tax involved.

[92] FA 2003, Sch 13, para 44.

[93] Ibid, Sch 13, para 34.

[94] Ibid, Sch 13, para 34(2).

[95] Ibid, Sch 13, para 40.

21.31 HMRC are given wide powers to make regulations as to the procedures for applying for an order and the persons to make the application,[96] and the contents and service of the notice.[97] No regulations have yet been issued.

Entry upon premises

21.32 These powers have been repealed but equivalent powers[98] have been extended to stamp taxes by the FA 2009.[99] Formerly an officer of the Board might[100] apply to a circuit judge, a sheriff or a county court judge in the relevant jurisdiction for the issue of a written warrant authorising an officer of the Board to enter upon premises, if necessary by force, at any time within 14 days from the time of the issue of the warrant and to search them where information is supplied on oath that there is reasonable grounds for suspecting that an offence involving serious fraud in connection with or in relation to tax is being, has been or is about to be committed and that evidence of it is to be found on premises specified in the information supplied.[101] The application may only be made if there are reasonable grounds for believing that an application for delivery of documents pursuant to judicial authority might seriously prejudice the investigation.[102] The officer must also confirm that he is acting with the approval of the Board in relation to the particular case.[103]

21.33 An officer entering the premises under authority of a warrant might take with him such other persons as may be necessary – but must disclose to the occupier of the premises, if present, a copy of the warrant or, if not present, to such other persons as may be appropriate or display it prominently – seize or remove things found there that he has reasonable cause to believe may be required as evidence. There are also powers to search any person found on the premises whom he has reasonable cause to believe to be in possession of items that may be required as evidence.[104] Items that are the subject of legal privilege as specially defined might not be seized.[105]

CRIMINAL OFFENCES

21.34 A person commits an offence if he intentionally[106] falsifies, conceals, destroys or otherwise disposes of or causes or permits the falsification, concealment, destruction or disposal of a document where a notice has been delivered requiring its production or to make it available for inspection unless such destruction, falsification etc is with the written permission of the Commissioners or an officer of the Board of HMRC or a copy has been delivered or the document itself inspected.[107] A person guilty of an

---

[96] Ibid, Sch 13, para 32(4).
[97] Ibid, Sch 13, para 32(4).
[98] Ibid, Sch 36.
[99] Section 96.
[100] But see the repeals etc in FA 2007, s 84.
[101] Ibid, Sch 13, para 43.
[102] Ibid, Sch 13, para 45(1).
[103] Ibid, Sch 13, para 45(2).
[104] Ibid, Sch 13, para 47(2)(c).
[105] Ibid, Sch 13, paras 35 and 37.
[106] The need for intent will probably protect the postman who folds the land transaction return form contrary to the instructions whilst it is in transit!
[107] FA 2003, Sch 13, para 53.

offence is liable on summary conviction to a fine not exceeding the statutory maximum. On conviction on indictment he is liable to imprisonment for a term not exceeding 2 years or a fine or both.[108]

21.35 FA 2008, Sch 36 contains extensive powers for HMRC to obtain information. These have been increased even further pursuant to FA 2009, s 95 and Sch 47. These powers now apply to stamp duty land tax and stamp duty reserve tax.[109]

---

[108] Ibid, Sch 13, para 53(6).
[109] FA 2009, s 96.

Chapter 22

REGISTRATION ISSUES

GENERAL BACKGROUND

22.1   Certain dealings in land require returns to both HMRC Stamp Taxes and the Land Registry and there are overwhelming indications in practice that the Land Registry:

- routinely and voluntarily pass information to HMRC Stamp Taxes;

- rely totally upon HMRC Stamp Taxes for advice on the tax and their own powers of registration;

- appear to be handing over the files and correspondence with solicitors obtained under the guise of requisitions and investigations of title; and

- they also challenge transactions presented to them as non-notifiable where, upon the basis solely of the documents filed in accordance with routine practice and not disclosing anything 'unusual' where the particular officer suspects either:
  - the transaction is technically notifiable; or
  - there may have been, what he regards as, tax avoidance without seeking any evidence since this would be beyond their statutory powers and duties and notify HMRC Stamp Taxes.

Dealings with the Land Registry have therefore changed from dealing with an ally in clarifying in title to a potential opponent who has evolved into a tax auditor and collector of taxes on behalf of HMRC Stamp Taxes. This presents an emerging major problem for those firms of solicitors who process their conveyancing and property practices and utilise unqualifieds who are not trained to be aware of tax problems and who may fail to spot major traps for the client,[1] or do not point out possible benefits.[2]

REGISTRATION REQUIREMENTS

22.2   A land transaction or any document effecting or evidencing a notifiable land transaction[3] must not be:

- registered;

- recorded; or

---

[1]   Note *Slattery v Moore Stephens* [2003] STC 1379 on liability for failing to ask the appropriate questions.
[2]   *BE Studios v Smith and Williamson* [2006] STC 358.
[3]   FA 2003, ss 77 and 77A; see **Chapters 17** and **18**.

- otherwise reflected in an entry;

- in a register maintained by:
  - the Chief Land Registrar in England and Wales;
  - the Keeper of the Registers of Scotland; or
  - the Land Registry or Registry of Deeds in Northern Ireland,

unless either:

- a certificate in the prescribed form is produced;[4] or

- it is within the prescribed list of transactions for which no certificate is required.[5]

However, other more fundamental changes in registered conveyancing practice are emerging as the new stamp duty land tax regime develops such as new essential techniques for investigation of title,[6] and recognising what are now fundamental documents of title which, although essentially tax records, are essential for successors in title and in the absence of which the property is strictly unsaleable, documentation required at completion[7] even in simple single residential property purchases or leases, actions of clients between contract and completion or conveyance and timetables.[8] These areas do not all require dealings with the Land Registry but require dealings with HMRC Stamp Taxes. These complications have increased as a result of changes made by reason of the removal of self-certificates (SDLT 60) by the FA 2008. Self-certificates together with the certificates for the exemption from the fixed stamp duties,[9] now removed from the Land Registry forms,[10] were formerly the supporting evidence for non-notifiable transactions. However, such transactions no longer require the support of any form of certificate. The difficulty of dealing with routine conveyancing in practice was predicting the possible reaction of the Land Registry which is based upon the local discretion of the individual employee in relation to a transaction that is presented to them for registration upon the basis that it is not notifiable and therefore not supported by a certificate.[11] There appears to be a local discretion in the various Land Registries as to which transactions they may wish to challenge where there is not an Inland Revenue Certificate (SDLT 5). Certain officers claim that there is a statutory duty to investigate all such transactions, although s 79(1) (as amended) does not impose any penalty or sanction where a title is registered incorrectly.[12] It is obviously time consuming to dispute their powers with Land Registry employees and debating the technical issues of non-notifiable transactions particularly since there is evidence in practice that such matters are referred by the Land Registry to HMRC Stamp Taxes for 'advice'. There is, therefore, a practical issue of how to present such transactions. Perversely, it seems that this should the person presenting the documentation produce some form of covering letter explaining the situation, this may be regarded by certain officers in the Land Registry as an indication that the transaction is 'unusual' and therefore should be

---

4   Ibid, s 79(1) (as amended).
5   Ibid, s 79(2) (as amended).
6   See, for example, **7.242** and **2.15**.
7   See **2.15**.
8   See **Chapter 10**.
9   Stamp Duty (Exempt Instruments) Regulations 1987, SI 1987/516.
10   Although it seems that certain fixed duties have been returned for land transactions pursuant to FA 2008, Sch 32, para 22.
11   They may be given power to correct returns FA 2003, Sch 10, para 7(1A).
12   Unlike the token penalty imposed by Stamp Act 1891, s 47; but also note that an incorrectly registered title is effective to pass legal title; *Re Nisbet v Shepherd* [1994] 1 BCLC 300.

investigated in depth. In some situations the Land Registry may suggest that the position is resolved by discussions with HMRC Stamp Taxes or the filing of a land transaction return indicating that no tax is payable and the transaction is 'exempt' for 'other' reasons. However, whilst HMRC Stamp Taxes do not have power to launch an Enquiry into a non-notifiable transaction they have power to enquire into a land transaction return.[13] It seems this power is available to them notwithstanding that the return was strictly unnecessary because the transaction was not notifiable. The Land Registry are, therefore, potentially increasing the costs and problems for persons involved in non-notifiable transactions.[14]

In addition, there is a mismatch between the limitation for the time for filing the tax and the Land Registry forms. A key practical area for registration is the change in the timetable. It is necessary to ignore the 30 day filing timetable for HMRC Stamp Taxes and act speedily to avert delays in obtaining the necessary certificate in time to meet the more important time limits for the Land Registry.

NO CERTIFICATE REQUIRED

22.3 Subject to the possible exercise of the uncertain local discretion by an employee of the Land Registry, registration may proceed without either a Revenue certificate (SDLT 5) where[15] either the transaction is not notifiable;[16] or[17]

- the entry is required to be made without any application; or

- the entry relates to an interest or right other than a chargeable interest acquired by the taxpayer under the land transaction that gives rise to the application; or

- the entry relates to a contract for a land transaction which is to be completed by a 'conveyance', ie any written instrument. This will permit the entry of a reference to a contract for sale or agreement for lease. Since the charge to stamp duty land tax does not arise at the contract stage,[18] no certificate can be produced if a purchaser wishes to include the appropriate entry in the register to protect his interest as a mere contractual purchaser or lessee; or

- the land transaction is itself a contract for the assignment of a land contract, or the assignment thereof, or a subsale contract or a similar arrangement within FA 2003, s 45.[19] These transactions do not give rise to a charge to stamp duty land tax so that no certificate could be produced if the subpurchaser or assignee wishes to protect his position by entering his contract in the register.[20]

---

[13] FA 2003, Sch 10, para 12(1).

[14] It might have been possible to deal with many of these situations had the fixed duties retained for land applied generally and the panel dealing with the certificates pursuant to the Stamp Duty (Exempt Instruments) Regulations 1987, SI 1987/1688 since these were some form of official document in support of an application and the Land Registry could investigate these or require the document to be adjudicated pursuant to Stamp Act 1891, s 17. It may be that some comfort in dealing with the Land Registry can be obtained by including the certificates within the continuation panels on the Land Registry documentation.

[15] FA 2003, s 79(1).

[16] See **Chapter 18**.

[17] FA 2003, s 79(2) (as amended).

[18] Ibid, s 44(2).

[19] See **Chapter 6**.

[20] However, if property reported by the subpurchaser or assignee there will be differences between the land

22.4 Transactions involving land that are not land transactions or contracts that do not involve the acquisition of a chargeable interest are not notifiable. This excludes the need for a certificate contracts relating to:

- grants of licences to use or occupy land;

- mortgages and other security interests;

- advowsons, manors and franchises;[21]

- certain interests held in connection with alternative financing arrangements which are 'exempt interests';[22]

- interest in certain alternative finance loan interests.[23]

REVENUE CERTIFICATES – SDLT 5

22.5 Registration requires a certificate issued by the Inland Revenue to the effect that a land transaction return has been filed but notwithstanding the unamended provisions of the Stamp Duty Land Tax (Administration) Regulations 2003[24] it is no longer necessary to pay the tax at the same time as filing the return,[25] the regulations relating to certificate still refer to the amount of stamp duty land tax self-assessed thereon having been paid[26] (SDLT 5) HMRC Stamp Taxes are entitled to inspect any certificates produced to the relevant Registrar and in his possession.[27] Arrangements may also be made in order to enable HMRC Stamp Taxes to obtain any other information and facilities for verifying that the requirements of the stamp duty land tax legislation has been satisfied.[28]

SECURITY OF TITLE

22.6 The new regime differs fundamentally from the stamp duty regime which it replaces so that the former practices relating to title, security, retention of funds and completion are no longer totally appropriate and it is necessary to reconsider what documentation is required from vendors or transferors at completion.

---

transaction return and Inland Revenue Certificate (SDLT 5) and the Land Registry documents such as TR1. The former deal with the beneficial owner (FA 2003, Sch 16, para 3) or the deemed 'seller' or 'purchaser'; the latter deal with the legal title. Although certain parties involved may not have to produce an Inland Revenue Certificate they may have to produce a covering letter to the Land Registry explaining the differences between the two sets of forms.

21 FA 2003, s 48.
22 Ibid, s 73B.
23 FA 2009, Sch 61.
24 SI 2003/2837, Part 1, reg 4(5); presumably another oversight in relation to the consequential changes.
25 FA 2003, s 76(3)(b) (repealed).
26 See **Chapter 15**.
27 FA 2003, s 79(6)(a).
28 Ibid, s 79(6)(b).

22.7 The most important change from stamp duty is that the documents are not subject to a full scrutiny by HMRC Stamp Taxes[29] before the tax is paid. The system is designed to avoid the former delays that might have occurred where the stamp duty had to be definitely denoted on the instrument before registration[30] and either adjudication was required or there was a dispute with HMRC Stamp Taxes as to the stamp duty payable or the valuation of the land. This no longer occurs[31] since HMRC Stamp Taxes have, in practice, no power to challenge the land transaction return on substantive grounds;[32] they may only challenge for minor errors and omissions such as arithmetic and post codes. They may also challenge a land transaction on 'principle'[33] where there is an 'obvious' error of principle, but it is difficult to see, on current practices and the resources available to HMRC Stamp Taxes, how they can claim to have evidence proving the facts to show that there is an 'obvious error'. The legislation does not extent to suspicion of error and cannot so extend because the error must be 'obvious' not 'suspected' or 'possible'. Since they have not seen the documentation and have no evidence as to the transaction they are not in a position to mount a serious challenge to the return.[34] As the whole process is intended to be by computerised scanning of the forms the only real question is whether the land transaction return appears to have been properly completed. In practice, therefore, the return should produce an Inland Revenue Certificate more or less automatically.

22.8 Moreover, the Land Registry have no power to reject an application supported by an appropriate certificate simply because they may suspect that the correct amount of stamp duty land tax has not been paid although certain officers of the Land Registry claim to be entitled to reject applications supported by a certificate because they suspect, without evidence, that there may have been tax avoidance (on their own definition of concept) which is claiming a greater power of initial scrutiny of the transaction than that conferred upon HMRC Stamp Taxes who refuse to give advance clearance on whether tax avoidance is involved in relation to certain reliefs.[35] They will not have the necessary evidence even for a *prima facie* case on the basis of the documents, assuming that this mitigation or tax efficiency is a title issue within their jurisdiction, although they may request a covering letter explaining any difference between the SDLT 5 and the registration documents and confirming that they relate to the same transaction.

22.9 Moreover, once registered the title cannot be challenged[36] or the entry removed. Neither HMRC Stamp Taxes nor the Land Registry can alter the register, notwithstanding that upon a subsequent Enquiry or discovery assessment HMRC Stamp Taxes establish that a larger amount of stamp duty land tax should have been paid or an exemption has been wrongly claimed. In relation to stamp duty the

---

[29] Note the limited powers for HMRC Stamp Taxes to correct land transaction returns; FA 2003, Sch 10, para 7(1).

[30] Stamp Act 1891, s 17.

[31] There are, of course, the inevitable administrative delays whilst HMRC Stamp Taxes process the forms etc; but to cope with the routine problems, the Land Registry have continued their temporary practice of giving provisional protection where nothing has been received from HMRC Stamp Taxes within 20 days following the lodging of the SDLT 1.

[32] They have power to correct errors of principle (FA 2003, Sch 10, para 7(1)) but, at this stage, they have no information or evidence upon which to base a challenge.

[33] FA 2003, Sch 10, para 7(1).

[34] Nevertheless the Land Registry, who are in a similar position as regards evidence save that they see the documents, claim wide-ranging powers although the new tax was intended to expedite the registration process.

[35] FA 2003, Sch 7.

[36] *Re Nisbet v Shepherd* [1994] 1 BCLC 300; except perhaps under the general law of fraudulently procuring registration.

difficulties with HMRC Stamp Taxes had to be dealt with at the initial stage before registration could proceed. Now registration can proceed, assuming that the Land Registry can be satisfied in relation to non-notifiable transactions the process is now reverse registration can proceed and any disputes in relation to the stamp duty land tax are dealt with behind the title. In this situation it would be inappropriate for HMRC Stamp Taxes to be able to cancel a registration simply because they managed to establish that insufficient tax has been paid to cancel the registration would cause chaos in relation to the property. For example, where HMRC Stamp Taxes establish that a relief was not available on a transfer of a freehold to a person who has subsequently granted leases out of that freehold not only would his title collapse but those leases would also be retrospectively invalidly registered. Moreover, the cancellation would require the reinstatement of the original transferor who may have died or disappeared or not be easy to trace for the re-execution of the documentation. The alternative would be to put the documentation into suspense until such time as the correct amount of tax was paid. However, this would have no point because HMRC Stamp Taxes can sue for the tax.[37] In addition, the potential uncertainty would create a degree of nervousness amongst mortgagees.

BLOCKED TITLES

22.10   However, the converse situation can arise. It is crucial to dealing with notifiable transactions[38] that an Inland Revenue Certificate (SDLT 5) is produced to the Land Registry.[39] The obtaining of this certificate is dependent upon producing what appears to be a *prima facie* valid and correctly completed land transaction return (SDLT 1 to 4). This requires appropriate signatures by the correct 'taxpayer'. If there is a manifest defect in the return[40] it may be rejected, at least temporarily, but, subject thereto, the process with HMRC Stamp Taxes' computers is more or less automatic. A key issue that has arisen in practice is where the land transaction return has not been signed by the purchaser. This may be because, rather than taking advantage of the two-tier form which enables the taxpayer to make the declaration as regards all information in the form other than the effective date and permits some other person to sign as to the effective date, which intended that it would not be necessary for the party to return at or after completion to sign the form the taxpayer would sign the entire form but there may be a delay in dealing with this. In these situations the registration document cannot be prepared because there is not a valid land transaction return to submit to HMRC Stamp Taxes. In this situation the title becomes blocked. The Land Registry cannot alter the register because there is no Inland Revenue Certificate (SDLT 5);[41] HMRC Stamp Taxes will not issue a certificate (SDLT 5) because they have not received a valid land transaction return[42] with a properly executed declaration.[43] HMRC Stamp Taxes currently claim that they have no management discretion to permit them to enter into

---

[37]   FA 2003, Sch 12.
[38]   And possibly non-notifiable transactions when dealing with certain well-identified Land Registry officers who exercise their 'local discretion' quite aggressively.
[39]   FA 2003, s 79(1).
[40]   A major problem, in practice, is the situation where, for technical reasons, the chargeable consideration is nil but a filing is required. The computer systems of HMRC Stamp Taxes have, it seems, not been upgraded to deal with these changes.
[41]   FA 2003, s 79(1) (as amended).
[42]   It seems that, in practice, HMRC Stamp Taxes are prepared to treat certain parts of the land transaction return as not being obligatory since they are gathering information for the Government rather than dealing with the computation of the tax – but this may depend upon the computer programmes for electronic filing.
[43]   FA 2003, s 79(3).

sensible operational practices which would enable a third party such as a mortgagee to pay the tax and proceed to registration. Numerous discussions are proceeding as to a possible way of dealing with this situation to the benefit of a mortgagee.[44]

ELECTRONIC FILING

22.11 It is permitted for the land transaction return to be filed electronically.[45] However, there may be no facility for 'signing' the declaration on the return.[46] In strict theory the return may not be properly completed. It may, however, be prudent notwithstanding the 'authentication' and other procedures of the Stamp Duty Land Tax (Electronic Communications) Regulations 2005[47] dealing with the delivery of electronic land transaction returns[48] to ensure that a hard copy is taken and signed by the taxpayer and preserved as part of the records should there be an Enquiry or questions raised as to the correctness of the land transaction return if only to provide evidence that the authorised party filing the electronic return was duly authorised by the client to make the return on his behalf.[49]

MORTGAGE RETENTION

22.12 A question frequently arises as to what, if any, retentions should be made by mortgages to cover the stamp duty land tax liability. Numerous issues arise including the amount to be retained and the time for which it should be retained. The amount of the retention need not exceed the amount shown on the land transaction return; this is the correct amount of tax payable at that stage.

However, retention itself is, as such, no benefit. Payment of the tax can only be made ie will, in general, only be accepted by HMRC Stamp Taxes, where a correctly completed and signed declaration in the land transaction return has been presented. If there are defects in the form such as a failure by the 'purchaser' to sign the declaration then no return has been received and HMRC Stamp Taxes have refused to act on such a return notwithstanding that the mortgagee is willing to pay the tax. Mortgagees must insist upon correct forms, rather than seeking to retain part of the loan. Once the correctly completed forms are available the registration process becomes more or less automatic since the issue of the Inland Revenue Certificate (SDLT 5) is automatic and, notwithstanding the views of certain officers of the Land Registry, there is no power to reject an application supported by an Inland Revenue Certificate SDLT 5. It is no longer necessary for HMRC Stamp Taxes to have received payment before the issue of a certificate.[50] With electronic filing it would appear that once a *prima facie* correctly

---

44 Such as finding a person who may be an agent or nominee FA 2003, s 81B or Sch 16, para 3.
45 FA 1999, ss 132 and 133.
46 Stamp Duty Land Tax (Electronic Communications) Regulations 2005, SI 2005/844, Part 3. It may be prudent to print a copy and a signature by the taxpayer thereon.
47 SI 2005/844.
48 Including the Scottish ARTL system as defined by the Requirements of Writing (Scotland) Act 1995 and dealing with the Keeper of the Registers of Scotland.
49 Stamp Duty Land Tax (Electronic Communications) Regulations 2005, SI 2005/844, Part 3.
50 FA 2003, s 75(3)(b) repealed. The continued reference to payment in the particulars of the Revenue certificate requirements in Stamp Duty Land Tax (Administration) Regulations 2003, SI 2003/2837, Part 1, reg 4, appears to be an oversight in dealing with the consequential amendments upon the separation of payment from filing in the amendments to FA 2003, s 75.

completed land transaction return has been obtained it can be presented to HMRC Stamp Taxes and the certificate is issued more or less automatically. There is no power or basis in practice to subject it to an in-depth scrutiny[51] since this would be inconsistent with the policy of expediting registration of title which will be a key issue in electronic conveyancing should this ever be introduced and material facts would not be available. It is, therefore, usually reasonably prudent to proceed once the purchaser has signed the declaration on the land transaction return verifying the information in the form. On the other hand, if the forms are not correct no amount of retention will, of itself, rectify the situation; the forms have to be corrected before an Inland Revenue Certificate (SDLT 5) will be issued; offers of payment, of themselves, will, on current HMRC Stamp Taxes practice, achieve nothing.

22.13 There is also the question of the period for retention. Since there is, contrary to the views and practices of certain individuals within the Land Registry, no power to challenge registration there is no benefit in retaining after this date; and, in practice, the funds can in most cases be released once the Inland Revenue Certificate (SDLT 5) has been obtained.

---

[51]   Note the limited powers to 'correct' a land transaction return contained in FA 2003, Sch 10, para 7.

Chapter 23

ASSESSMENTS

23.1 The power of HMRC Stamp Taxes to enquire into a land transaction return (or formerly a self-certificate) and adjust the tax charge expires at the end of the appropriate 9-month period.[1] But in certain cases where additional returns are required for the same transaction the filing of a later return enable HMRC Stamp Taxes to open an Enquiry into any earlier returns notwithstanding the 9-month limitation period has expired.[2] However, HMRC Stamp Taxes is empowered in effect to reopen cases and to assess and collect stamp duty land tax in certain situations outside the Enquiry regime. This power to assess the stamp duty land tax differs from the power to issue determinations where no return is delivered.[3]

DISCOVERY ASSESSMENTS

23.2 HMRC Stamp Taxes may make an assessment of such amount of tax as in their opinion ought to be charged[4] where they 'discover'[5] that either:

- an amount of tax that ought to have been assessed has not been assessed; or

- an assessment to the tax has become insufficient; or

- a relief is or has become excessive; or

- where, in their opinion, an excessive amount of tax has been repaid to any person.[6]

23.3 A discovery assessment can be issued notwithstanding that there has been a previous completed Enquiry[7] and for these purposes there are restrictions upon the amount of information that HMRC Stamp Taxes are deemed to have obtained[8] so that they cannot 'discover' new information but this still leaves statutory areas of doubt and uncertainty where they can make a discovery.

Restrictions upon powers to issue discovery assessments

23.4 Obviously HMRC Stamp Taxes may issue an assessment only when they make a 'discovery'. This involves two issues namely:

---

1   FA 2003, Sch 10, para 12(2); see **19.4**.
2   Ibid, Sch 10, para 12(2A).
3   Ibid, Sch 10, para 25; see **17.35**.
4   Ibid, Sch 10, para 25.
5   See *Langham v Veltema* [2004] STC 544 on the ease of making a 'discovery'.
6   FA 2003, Sch 10, para 29.
7   Ibid, Sch 10, paras 30(2) and (3).
8   Ibid, Sch 10, para 30(4).

- what is a 'discovery' of relevant information; and

- how and when can HMRC Stamp Taxes be expected to make a discovery.

The practical problem is how HMRC Stamp Taxes will be in a position to make a 'discovery', ie under what circumstances they will be able to discover the type of new information which can constitute a 'discovery' since, in practice at present, Enquiries appear to be conducted upon the same basis as stamp duty adjudications, ie by question and answer in correspondence. It is currently difficult for them to discover unreported transactions and HMRC Stamp Taxes do not have power to conduct 'fishing expeditions'. It may be that whilst investigating a later transaction such as a linked transaction or a subsequent return for the sale with an overage payment or a lease renewal or rent review they may find information not previously revealed to them. However, outside such situations their powers for spontaneous investigations outside the Enquiry period seem to be somewhat limited for the moment.

23.5   Discovery assessments are restricted by time limits and the pre-existing knowledge of HMRC Stamp Taxes. Such assessments may only be made up to 6 years but this period is extended to 21 years where either:

- the non-payment or underpayment of tax or the excessive repayment is attributable to fraudulent or negligent conduct on the part of:
  - the taxpayer; or
  - any person acting on behalf of the taxpayer; or
  - a person who was a partner of the purchaser at the relevant time.[9]
  It must, however, be noted that 'negligence' in this context has an extended meaning. It applies not merely to negligence in applying the law to the facts such as claiming reconstruction relief for companies in the case of a partnership but also negligence in preparing the return such as adopting the incorrect principles for valuation or putting the actual consideration rather than the market value;[10] or

- HMRC Stamp Taxes, at the time they ceased to be entitled to give notice of an Enquiry into the return or had completed their enquiries into the return, could not have been reasonably expected on the basis of the information made available to them to be aware of the non-payment, underpayment or excessive repayment.[11] For these purposes, information is only regarded as made available to HMRC if:
  - it is contained in a land transaction return made by the taxpayer; or
  - it is contained in any documents produced or information provided for the purposes of an Enquiry into a land transaction return; or
  - it is information the existence and relevance of which as regards the non-payment or underpayment or excessive repayment could reasonably be expected to be inferred by HMRC Stamp Taxes from information or documents supplied to them in the return or during the Enquiry, or which had been notified in writing to them by the taxpayer or a person acting on his behalf;[12] and

---

9   Ibid, Sch 10, para 30(2).
10   Persons assisting in the preparation of the form may face penalties pursuant to FA 2003, s 95 if they know that appropriate advice as to value has not been obtained.
11   FA 2003, Sch 10, para 30; see, eg, *Cenlon Finance Co Ltd v Ellwood* [1962] 1 All ER 854.
12   Ibid, Sch 10, para 30(4).

- it relates to a mistake in a return where the return was made on the basis of the practice generally prevailing at the time when it was made.[13]

23.6 Where the purchaser has died, an assessment may be made on the personal representatives of the deceased only within 3 years after his death.[14]

23.7 An assessment to recover an excessive repayment of tax is not out of time where notice of Enquiry is given into a land transaction return provided that the assessment is made before the Enquiry is completed,[15] or, in any case, where the assessment is made within one year after the relevant repayment was made.[16]

DOUBLE ASSESSMENTS

23.8 A person who believes that he has been assessed to tax more than once in respect of the same transaction[17] can claim relief. An appeal against the decision of HMRC Stamp Taxes refusing a claim for relief can be brought to the Commissioners, who have jurisdiction to hear an appeal relating to the assessment to which the claim relates.

OVERPAYMENTS DUE TO MISTAKE IN A RETURN

23.9 A person who believes he has paid tax under an assessment that was excessive by reason of some mistake in a land transaction return may claim a repayment of the tax overpaid by notice in writing given not more than 6 years after the effective date of the transaction.[18] However, no relief can be given in respect of a mistake as to the basis upon which liability ought to have been computed when the return was in fact made on the basis or in accordance with the practice generally prevailing at the time when it was made, nor in respect of a mistake in a claim or election included in the return.[19] An appeal against HMRC Stamp Taxes' decision on the claim lies to the Special Commissioners.[20]

---

[13] Ibid, Sch 10, para 30(5).
[14] Ibid, Sch 10, para 31(4).
[15] Ibid, Sch 10, para 30(3)(a).
[16] Ibid, Sch 10, para 30(2)(b).
[17] Ibid, Sch 10, para 33.
[18] Ibid, Sch 10, para 34.
[19] Ibid, Sch 10, para 34(4).
[20] Ibid, Sch 10, para 34(6).

Chapter 24

APPEALS AND REFERRALS OF QUESTIONS

24.1   Subject to the changes being made in relation to First and other Tier Tribunals, an appeal or referral to the General or Special Commissioners may be brought against:

- a notice given in an Enquiry into a land transaction return requiring the taxpayer to produce documents or provide information;[1]

- a notice given in an Enquiry requiring the taxpayer to produce documents or to provide information;

- an amendment by HMRC Stamp Taxes of a self-assessment during an Enquiry to prevent loss of tax;[2]

- a conclusion stated or amendment made by a closure notice;

- a discovery assessment;[3]

- the imposition or amount of a penalty;[4]

- an assessment to recover excessive repayment of tax;[5]

- a decision of HMRC Stamp Taxes in relation to a claim for relief against double assessment;[6]

- HMRC Stamp Taxes' decision on a claim for relief in respect of a mistake in a return;[7]

- an assessment on the basis that it is out of time;[8]

- an order directing closure of the Enquiry[9] into a land transaction return or into a self-certificate;[10]

---

[1]   FA 2003, Sch 10, para 15.
[2]   Ibid, Sch 10, para 35(1)(a).
[3]   Ibid, Sch 10, para 35(1)(b).
[4]   Ibid, Sch 14, para 5.
[5]   Ibid, Sch 10, para 31(1)(c).
[6]   Ibid, Sch 10, para 31(1)(d).
[7]   Ibid, Sch 10, para 33(4).
[8]   Ibid, Sch 10, para 31(5).
[9]   Ibid, Sch 10, para 24.
[10]   Ibid, Sch 11, para 17.

- an equivalent to an appeal in the form of a referral to the Special Commissioners of any questions arising during the progress of an Enquiry into a land transaction return;[11] or

- referral of any question arising in connection with an Enquiry into a self-certificate.[12]

An appeal against amendment of a self-assessment return cannot be heard until the Enquiry is completed.[13]

24.2   It should also be noted that certain notices to produce documents or information may be issued only with the consent of the General or Special Commissioners or judicial authority.

24.3   Regulations controlling the jurisdiction of the General and Special Commissioners or the Lands Tribunal in relation to appeals as well as any rules and procedures that are to be observed have been issued.[14]

24.4   The basic rule is that appeals are to be made to the General Commissioners except that certain matters are reserved to the Special Commissioners:[15]

- assessments in relation to which a notice of Enquiry has been given;

- an issue has arisen once an Enquiry is in progress and the purchaser and HMRC jointly in writing refer to the Special Commissioners;[16]

- enquiries into self-certificates which are now redundant;

- the appellant may elect to transfer the case from the General Commissioners to the Special Commissioners[17] such an election must be in writing;

- questions as to the market value of the subject-matter of the land transaction is to be determined on a reference to the relevant Lands Tribunal.[18]

Detailed rules are provided for determining which body of General Commissioners has jurisdiction.[19] The basic jurisdiction appears to be the division where the subject-matter of the land is situated but there may be an election by the purchaser to have proceedings brought by him where he has his place of business or residence.[20] Where there are two or more linked transactions in a single land transaction return because they are on the

---

[11]   Ibid, Sch 10, para 19.
[12]   Ibid, Sch 11, para 12.
[13]   Ibid, Sch 10, para 35(3).
[14]   Ibid, Sch 17; Stamp Duty Land Tax (Appeals) Regulations 2004, SI 2004/1363, which adopts with amendments the General Commissioners (Jurisdiction and Procedure) Regulations 1994, SI 1994/1812 and the Special Commissioners (Jurisdiction and Procedure) Regulations 1994, SI 1994/1811 but note the possible changes pursuant to Tribunals, Courts and Enforcement Act 2007.
[15]   Stamp Duty Land Tax (Appeals) Regulations 2004, SI 2004/1363, reg 4.
[16]   FA 2003, Sch 10, para 19.
[17]   Stamp Duty Land Tax (Appeals) Regulations 2004, SI 2004/1363, reg 5.
[18]   Ibid, reg 6.
[19]   Ibid, reg 8.
[20]   Ibid.

same effective date[21] these may relate to property in different jurisdictions, the purchaser may elect.[22] However if the returns are required in respect of the clawback of reliefs pursuant to s 81 of the FA 2003 the jurisdiction is with the General Commissioners for the place where the subject-matter of the land transaction is situated.[23] Where the General Commissioners believe that, because of the complexity of the appeal or the length of time likely to be required, they may refer the matter to the Special Commissioners.[24]

---

[21] FA 2003, s 108(2) and **Chapter 14**.
[22] Stamp Duty Land Tax (Appeals) Regulations 2004, SI 2004/1363, reg 9.
[23] Ibid, reg 11.
[24] Ibid, reg 17.

Chapter 25

ADMINISTRATION

MANAGEMENT BY HMRC

25.1 Stamp duty land tax is under the care and management of the HMRC ('the Board').[1] As the Board[2] is given powers of care and management and not merely collection, this means that it has power to modify the rules by a statement of practice[3] and to come to agreements with individual taxpayers. Its powers are particularly extensive and include a huge range of regulation-making powers, which would seem to enable it to repeal the FA 2003 and replace it by a statutory instrument at least for a period of 18 months.[4] For example:

- there is power to reproduce in relation to stamp duty land tax the effect of any enactments providing for exemption from stamp duty;[5]

- regulations may adjust the thresholds for the different rates of tax;[6]

- in particular, the Treasury may (if it considers it expedient in the public interest) make provision by regulation of the variation of the provision relating to stamp duty land tax in relation to land transactions of any description including:
  - power to alter transactions that are chargeable or notifiable;
  - land transactions in respect of which tax is chargeable at any existing rate or amount.

This power virtually enables a complete rewrite of the basic legislation, although the period of such variation is a maximum of 18 months from the date on which the regulations are made.[7]

25.2 In consequence, it will be necessary for practitioners to keep a very careful eye upon statutory instruments, which are not always as widely publicised as legislation and are not subject to even the cursory and uninformed debates that normally apply to stamp duty provisions in the Finance Bill, and which can take effect instantly. The various powers conferred upon the Board are sometimes subject to restrictions including

---

[1]   FA 2003, s 42(3).
[2]   Detailed rules exist in the legislation prescribing the officers with power to act in particular circumstances.
[3]   However, there are technical issues as to how far Statements of Practice etc are lawful see *Al Fayed v Advocate General* [2002] STC 910; *R (Wilkinson) v IRC* [2002] STC 347. Many such practices are now being converted into legislation.
[4]   See, eg, FA 2003, s 109.
[5]   Ibid, s 123(3).
[6]   Ibid, s 112(1)(b).
[7]   Ibid, s 109(5).

the person by whom the power may be exercised. Given the complexity of the regime and the need to protect the client's interest, it is important to be aware of whether the power is being validly exercised.

REVENUE[8] OFFICES

Returns

25.3   It appears that a specific office is to be established to receive land transaction returns and payments made in connection therewith. This is:

Inland Revenue
Stamp Taxes/SDLT
Comben House
Farmers Way
Netherton
Merseyside
L69 1BY
Tel: 0845 6030135.
or

Inland Revenue SDLT
Netherton
Merseyside
L30 4RN
or by DX to Rapid Data Capture Centre
DX 725593
Bootle 9

The telephone number is also intended to operate as an enquiry and general help-line. However, it seems that help is to be restricted to completing the form, and advice will not be provided on the interpretation of the substantive charging provisions. Taxpayers are not protected from penalties and late payment interest simply by relying upon the 'advice' provided by the so-called helpline which frequently produces incorrect answers.

Helpline 0545 603 0735

Other offices

25.4   Other offices are established to deal with other areas of administration, namely:

---

[8]   Stamp Duty on shares is dealt with at Bush House, Strand but only by post; Stamp Duty Reserve Tax is administered from Worthing.

Customer service centre

Worthing Stamp Office
Room 35 East Block
Barrington Road
Worthing
BN12 4XJ
DX: 3799 Worthing
Tel: 01903 508962

Complex cases and enquiries and Risk analysis and analysis of transactions

Birmingham Stamp Office
5th Floor
Norfolk House
Smallbrook Queens Way
Birmingham
B5 4LA
Tel: 0121 633 3313

Internet Team

Birmingham Stamp Office
9th Floor
City Centre House
30 Union Street
Birmingham
B2 4AR
DX: 15001 Birmingham 1

Newcastle Stamp Taxes Office
5th Floor, Cale Cross House,
156 Pilgrim Street
Newcastle upon Tyne, NE1 6TF.
DX 61021 Newcastle upon Tyne 1
Tel: 0191 261 7839
Fax: 0191 261 7644

Edinburgh Stamp Taxes Office
Grayfield House, Spur X,
4 Bankhead Avenue,
Edinburgh EH11 4BF.
DX ED 543303 Edinburgh 33
Tel: 0131 442 3161
Fax: 0131 442 3038

Belfast Stamp Taxes Office
Ground Floor, Dorchester House,
52–58 Great Victoria Street,
Belfast BT2 7QE.
DX 2003 Belfast 2
Tel: 028 9050 5312
Fax: 028 9050 5318

Solicitor's Offices

Solicitor's Office
Somerset House,
Strand,
London WC2R 1LB.
Tel: 020 7438 7259

Solicitor's Office (Scotland)
Clarendon House,
114–116 George Street,
Edinburgh EH2 4LH.
Tel: 0131 473 4000
Legal Post: LP18, Edinburgh 2

FORMS AND NOTICES

Land transaction return

25.5 The land transaction return must be in a form to be prescribed by HMRC Stamp Taxes in regulations.[9] There are pressures to keep the form to as few pages as possible. In consequence, the form will be incomprehensible without the use of the guidance notes (SDLT 6), which have been published to provide some limited explanation of the questions in the form. The basic land transaction return (SDLT 1) is a minimum, since many transactions will also require the filing of the supplemental forms:

- SDLT 2, setting out details where there are more than two vendors;

- SDLT 3, setting out details where there are more than two purchasers;

- SDLT 4,[10] where there is a complicated transaction such as the sale of a lease or part of the sale of a business as a going concern.[11]

---

[9]   FA 2003, Sch 10, para 1(1); Stamp Duty Land Tax (Administration) Regulations 2003, SI 2003/2837 as amended by Stamp Duty Land Tax (Administration) (Amendment) Regulations 2004, SI 2004/3124.
[10]   Revised to correct the confusion between fixtures and chattels.
[11]   There will be issues in completing SDLT 4 where goodwill is involved; see **1.5**.

In consequence, there may be about 10 to 15 pages of returns where there is a sale of a lease by several vendors, and/or with several purchasers or lessees, or of several parcels of land.[12]

Certificates – SDLT 5

25.6   Certificates required for the purposes of entries at the Land Registry,[13] which are now limited to the Inland Revenue certificate (SDLT 5),[14] which are governed by regulations prescribing form and content.[15]

Forms, notices and related matters

25.7   Forms dealing with assessment, determination notices or other documents required to be used in assessing, charging and levying tax or determining a penalty are to be dealt with in prescribed forms.

Revenue errors

25.8   However, failure by HMRC Stamp Taxes to comply with the prescribed form or any mistake, defect or omission in the prescribed form does not affect its validity if it is substantially in conformity with the legislation and its intended effect is reasonably ascertainable by the person to whom it is directed.[16] The validity of an assessment or determination is not affected by any mistake made by HMRC Stamp Taxes in it as to the name of the person liable for the amount of tax to be charged or by reason of any variance between the notice of assessment or determination and the assessment or determination itself.[17]

SERVICE OF DOCUMENTS ON TAXPAYERS

25.9   Any notice or document to be served on a person may be delivered to him or left at his usual or last known place of abode[18] or served by post.[19] The general provisions as to service by post and addresses[20] are satisfied if the notice or other document is addressed:

- in the case of an individual, to his usual or last known place of residence or his place of business;

- in the case of a company:
    - to its principal place of business;
    - if a liquidator has been appointed, to his address for the purposes of the liquidation; or

---

[12]   Unless the parties elect to utilise a separate form (SDLT 1) for each property. There is, however, power to apply for multiple Inland Revenue certificates (SDLT 5) where several Land Registries are involved.
[13]   FA 2003, s 79(1) (as amended).
[14]   Self-certificates were abolished by FA 2008.
[15]   FA 2003, s 79(4); Stamp Duty Land Tax (Administration) Regulations 2003, SI 2003/2837.
[16]   Ibid, s 83(2).
[17]   Ibid, s 83(3).
[18]   Ibid, s 84(1).
[19]   Ibid, s 84(2).
[20]   Interpretation Act 1978, s 7.

– to such place as may be prescribed by regulations.[21]

Service of notice by HMRC Stamp Taxes

25.10 Complex provisions exist for the delivery of various notices regulating which officers of the Board are eligible to effect service of a particular notice and whether (and if so which type of) consent (such as that of the General or Special Commissioners) is needed:

- a notice requiring delivery of a land transaction return must be served by HMRC Stamp Taxes, ie any officer of the Board;[22]

- a notice of enquiry may be served by any officer of the Board;[23]

- a notice to produce documents or information for the purpose of enquiry may be served by any officer of the Board;[24]

- a notice of determination, if no return is delivered, may be made by any officer of HMRC Stamp Taxes;[25]

- an issue of an assessment may be made by any officer of HMRC Stamp Taxes;[26]

- a notice of enquiry into a self-certificate may be served by any officer of HMRC Stamp Taxes;[27]

- a notice to produce documents or information for enquiry into a self-certificate may be served by any officer of HMRC.[28]

THE INFORMATION POWERS[29]

25.11 A notice requiring delivery of documents or provision of information from the taxpayer must be served by an authorised officer of the Board.[30]

25.12 An authorised officer of the Board may give notice requiring the production of information or documents from third parties[31] but the consent of a General or Special Commissioner is required for the giving of such a notice.[32]

---

21 FA 2003, s 84(3).
22 Ibid, Sch 10, para 5(1); s 113(1).
23 Ibid, Sch 10, para 12; s 113(1).
24 Ibid, Sch 10, para 14; s 113(1).
25 Ibid, Sch 10, para 25; s 113(1).
26 Ibid, Sch 10, para 28; s 113(1).
27 Ibid, Sch 11, para 7; s 113(1).
28 Ibid, Sch 11, para 9; s 113(1).
29 See **Chapter 21**.
30 FA 2003, Sch 13, para 1.
31 Ibid, Sch 13, para 6.
32 Ibid, Sch 13, para 7.

25.13 An authorised officer of the Board may give notice requiring a tax accountant to deliver documents[33] but such notice requires the consent of the appropriate judicial authority.[34]

25.14 A notice to require a person to deliver documents or information where the Board has reasonable grounds for believing that a person may have failed or may fail to comply with the provisions relating to stamp duty land tax, and there is likely to be a serious prejudice to the proper assessment or collection of tax, must be served by the Board.[35]

25.15 Orders for the delivery of documents where there are reasonable grounds for suspecting that an offence involving serious fraud in relation to stamp duty land tax has been or is about to be committed may be made only with the consent of the appropriate judicial authority.[36]

ASSESSMENT OF PENALTIES

25.16 Various penalties are to be initially assessed by HMRC Stamp Taxes, such as:

- penalty for failure to produce documents or supply information may be assessed by an officer of the Board;[37]

- penalty for failure to produce documents or information for the purposes of any enquiry into a self-certificate may be assessed by any officer of the Board,[38] but this is limited to a penalty of £30 per day;

although these are generally subject to a right of the taxpayer to appeal against both the imposition of and the amount of the penalty.

SEARCH WARRANTS

25.17 The power to effect entry with a warrant to obtain evidence may be made by the appropriate judicial authority on the application of an officer of the Board[39] has been abolished,[40] extensive replacement powers have been conferred by FA 2009.

---

[33] Ibid, Sch 13, para 14.
[34] Ibid, Sch 13, para 16.
[35] Ibid, Sch 13, para 28.
[36] Ibid, Sch 13, para 32.
[37] Ibid, Sch 10, para 16.
[38] Ibid, Sch 11, para 11(2)(a).
[39] Ibid, Sch 13, para 43.
[40] FA 2007, s 84.

LEGAL PRIVILEGE

25.18 To some extent, documents are entitled to 'legal privilege' within the special definition for the purposes of stamp duty land tax,[41] and special procedures have been established in order to determine whether documents fall within the scope of this privilege.[42]

---

41 FA 2003, Sch 13, para 35.
42 Ibid, Sch 13, para 35; Stamp Duty Land Tax (Administration) Regulations 2003, SI 2003/2837, reg 38.

Chapter 26

DRAFTING AND STRUCTURING

26.1 It was the expressed intention of HMRC Stamp Taxes during the so-called consultation process that, being a transaction-based tax and not a documentation tax,[1] stamp duty land tax would never be affected by the drafting of the documentation and structuring of the transaction such as applied where the double charge upon land exchanges could be mitigated by drafting the transaction as a 'single sale',[2] nor in their view would there be any need to change conveyancing practice in relation to the investigation of title and the documents required to provide an effective title,[3] the preparation of routine documentation in relation to title indemnities, due diligence and share sale warranties and indemnities and the obligations of vendors at completion. Their assertion was also that the new tax would not affect the drafting of commercial documents. Unfortunately, but not unsurprisingly, the simplistic thinking behind the proposals for the tax and the lack of technical skill, sophistication and experience of those who foolishly volunteered to participate in the so-called consultation process, including those representing professional bodies, has produced a situation where there have to be major changes in conveyancing practice[4] and completion procedures[5] major drafting and structuring issues are frequently arising even in routine transactions on an almost daily basis.[6] Regrettably, the new general anti-avoidance provisions of Finance Act 2003, s 75A[7] enables HMRC Stamp Taxes to restructure a series of transactions into a single notional transaction which has to be separately notified by 'P'[8] in addition to the obligation to pay and notify in relation to the actual acquisition by 'P' which is required[9] before the general anti-avoidance provisions can be applied by HMRC Stamp Taxes. No guidance on these sections other than a list of transactions in a very unsatisfactory Technical Note such as subsales and leases with break clauses primarily targeted for attack in these provisions has been provided by HMRC Stamp Taxes. Taxpayers will have to decide for themselves when preparing the return whether their transaction is adversely affected[10] and the self-assessment regime will them seriously exposed to allegations of fraud. Fortunately the new provision requires a 'series' of transactions so that suitable drafting of a single transaction[11] that is not a step in a series will still be effective.

---

[1]   See, for example, **2.6** and **7.168**.
[2]   See *Inland Revenue Tax Bulletin*, August 1995; it has proved necessary to include specific provisions in FA 2003, s 47(1) to prevent such drafting from being effective.
[3]   See, for example, **2.17**.
[4]   See, for example, **14.11** and **22.2**.
[5]   See, for example, **6.9, 7.242, 10.1** and **10.15**.
[6]   See, for example, **10.5**.
[7]   Re-enacting Stamp Duty Land Tax (Variation of the Finance Act 2003) Regulations 2006, SI 2006/3237.
[8]   FA 2003, s 77(1)(d).
[9]   Ibid, s 77(1).
[10] Because of the need to notify FA 2003, s 77(1).
[11] But what is a 'single transaction' remains unclear since it seems that HMRC Stamp Taxes may be intending to argue that contract and completion are separate transactions for their purpose there are difficulties with options and their exercise.

26.2   However, it has to be noted that the fundamental structure of land law and the conveyancing requirements which provide the basis for the organisation of land transactions and documentation for routine or complex commercial transactions may affect the stamp duty land tax position. For example, certain variation of leases can operate only by way of surrender and regrant[12] and this land law position is adopted for stamp duty land tax. Whilst it has been judicially suggested[13] that the taxation analysis should not rely upon historic legal principles in order to increase the tax charge, thee is a longstanding practice which has been stated by senior officers as being a delight in taking advantage of such basic general law to increase tax but to challenge these when they might represent a possibility of reducing the tax. The underlying general law is, therefore, a key factor in structuring transactions and a major planning issue will be the investigation of alternative methods of proceeding with the transaction which may offer cheaper alternatives in terms of tax costs.[14]

TAX IMPLICATIONS OF DRAFTING

26.3   The drafting and preparation of documentation is, nevertheless, important in stamp duty land tax terms. For example:

•   the drafting of the document may affect the amount of tax such as whether or not service charges or VAT are reserved as part of the rent or have been separately apportioned[15] and whether or not or how they are taxable;[16]

•   the treatment of VAT may depend upon whether it is taxable as rent or as a periodical premium;[17]

•   as the tax is related to the 'creation' of chargeable interests, it seems that there will be a difference in tax consequences between:
    –   a transfer of land where the transferor 'excepts and reserves' specified rights to himself or for the benefit of land which he retains; and
    –   a transfer of land and a 'regrant' of rights over that land by the transferee in favour of the transferor.
    In the former case, the rights are not 'created' but lying dormant or latent[18] because not in practice necessary, are simply recognised and retained by the transferor.[19] They are, therefore, not involved in the taxation issues at the time of the transaction, although these are likely to be chargeable interests and subsequent dealings in them, if for a chargeable consideration, are likely to be taxable. HMRC Stamp Taxes in practice do not accept this analysis, but have hitherto failed to give a definitive view on the fundamental question of whether the utilisation of such wording as 'excepting and reserving' potentially converts such transactions into land exchanges.[20] In the latter case, the regrant of the rights will constitute

---

12   *Friends Provident Life Office v British Railways Board* [1996] 1 All ER 336.
13   *Sargaison v Roberts* [1969] 3 All ER 1072.
14   Which is not, as such, tax avoidance; *Willoughby v IRC* [1995] STC 143; *Sherdley v Sherdley* [1987] STC 266.
15   FA 2003, Sch 5, para 4(1).
16   See **7.138** and **7.140**.
17   See **7.36**, **7.64** and **7.138**.
18   Note Law of Property Act 1925, s 62.
19   Cf the cases on rights created pursuant to Law of Property Act 1925, s 62.
20   There are also outstanding questions whether HMRC Stamp Taxes intend to take the point that leasehold covenants given by a tenant which fall outside the excluding provision of FA 2003, Sch 17A, para 10 and

consideration or part of the consideration for the transfer. This produces a land exchange and, *prima facie*, being an exchange of a major interest for a non-major interest, the two transactions will be taxed upon the market value;[21]

- the effective date of the transaction may depend upon the drafting of the contract. If the contract contains a provision[22] that it is to be completed by a written instrument such as a Land Registry Transfer or a lease, the effective date is the earlier of substantial performance or compliance.[23] If there is no such provision, such as where the vendor agrees to hold on trust for the purchaser from payment,[24] the effective date is the date of 'completion', ie payment in full, not substantial performance.[25] FA 2003, s 44, applies pursuant to subs (1) thereof where there is a requirement to complete by written instrument;[26]

- the creation of or execution of a 'conveyance' where there has already been substantial performance of the contract may give rise to additional reporting and payment events;[27] however, there is no general definition of 'conveyance' although it is referred to for certain purposes as including any 'instrument'.[28] Since this is only for the purposes of that section, this leaves open the question as to whether any of the former stamp duty baggage relating to what is a 'conveyance' will be carried forward in practice into the new legislation. This included a whole range of instruments that either:
  - effectively put the property under the control of the purchaser such as a power of attorney[29] or a declaration of trust;[30] or
  - in certain circumstances, acknowledge the title of the relevant party to the property such as a written memorandum;[31]

- the drafting of arrangements may affect the availability of a form of subsale relief for parties to agreements for lease.[32] This applies where a person 'assigns his right to the lease' under the agreement before he substantially performs then his transaction is disregarded and the contract is 'novated' to the assignee of the right to call for the contract. It is unclear what, at present, constitutes an 'assignment' of

---

which can be regarded as chargeable interests as being obligations affecting the value of land which would appear to apply to every covenant within ibid, para 10(1)(c); and s 48(1)(b) converts virtually every lease into a land exchange within s 47 thereof.

[21] FA 2003, Sch 4, para 5(3); see **5.151**.
[22] It is assumed that these provisions are intended to apply on an objective basis, ie the written terms of the agreement, not a subjective basis of whether the parties intend to perform the contract strictly in accordance with its terms.
[23] FA 2003, s 44(3) and (4), with additional reporting and payment obligations where there is substantial performance followed by 'completion': s 44(8).
[24] See, for example, *Angus v IRC* (1889) 23 QBD 579; *West London Syndicate Ltd v IRC* [1898] 2 QB 507; *Peter Bone v IRC* [1995] STC 921.
[25] FA 2003, s 119.
[26] See **14.10**.
[27] FA 2003, s 44(7).
[28] Ibid, s 44(8).
[29] See, for example, *Diplock v Hammond* (1854) 5 De GM & G 320; but compare *Roddick v Gandell* (1852) 1 De G M & G 763.
[30] *West London Syndicate Ltd v IRC* [1898] 2 QB 507; *Peter Bone v IRC* [1995] STC 921; *Angus v IRC* (1889) 23 QBD 579.
[31] See, for example, *Horsfall v Hey* (1848) 2 Ex 778; *A-G v Cohen* 1 KB 478 and 490; *Cohen and Moore v IRC* [1933] 2 KB 126; *Fleetwood-Hesketh v IRC* [1936] 1 KB 351.
[32] FA 2003, Sch 17A, para 12B.

the right to call for the lease.[33] Prudence may require a close following of these words rather than relying upon the normal direction to grant the lease to the third party (assignee) at completion;

- the obligation to notify may depend upon when a lease is 'granted'[34] or deemed to be granted[35] and whether the parties intend to rely upon the agreement for lease subject to the issues of substantial performance;[36]

- a lease[37] is a chargeable interest for the purposes of stamp duty land tax, but a licence to use or occupy land is not.[38] The preparation of documents and the rights of the various parties may affect this issue,[39] and a statement that the agreement is not intended to create the relationship of a landlord and tenant or to create a tenancy may be important, particularly in marginal cases.[40] In such arrangements, the parties' professional advisers must consider whether it is necessary to make express provision or whether their drafting merely makes express what the general law may imply, which may result in unnecessary charges by creating interests.[41] This is important in relation to the lease/licence question. The specific creation of a right of the licensor to enter upon the 'licensed' land, particularly where such right is restricted, is regarded as indicating that exclusive possession has been granted to the 'licensee' and, *prima facie*, a lease granted;[42]

- the methods for computing the stamp duty land tax upon instalments and periodical payments differ, particularly where the transaction may run for more than 12 years.[43] There may, in consequence, be a significant difference between a provision for the payment of £20,000,000 by 20 equal instalments (ie a deferred payment) and a consideration of 20 annual payments of £1,000,000.[44] In the former case, the stamp duty land tax is chargeable upon £20,000,000;[45] in the latter, £12,000,000.[46] There are also significant differences in the reporting and payment obligations, since the need to make additional returns and fresh self-assessment[47] does not apply to variable periodical payments;[48]

- 'substantial performance' depends, *inter alia*, upon whether substantially the whole of the consideration has been paid or provided.[49] This may depend upon whether any consideration left outstanding is drafted as an unpaid consideration or as some form of payment and leaseback being dealt with by way of set-off. The

---

[33] But compare *Attorney General v Brown* (1849) 3 Exch. 662.
[34] See *City Permanent Building Society v Miller* [1952] Ch 840.
[35] FA 2003, Sch 17A, para 12A.
[36] Ibid, s 44(3)–(6).
[37] Other than a tenancy at will; FA 2003, s 48(2(c)(i).
[38] Ibid, s 48(2)(b).
[39] See the detailed discussion of the issues involved in *Addiscombe Garden Estates Ltd v Crabbe* [1957] 3 All ER 563.
[40] *Ogwr Borough Council v Dykes* [1989] 2 All ER 880.
[41] Cf such stamp duty cases as *Peter Bone Ltd v IRC* [1995] STC 921 where express statements of what the law implied created unnecessary charges to tax.
[42] See, eg, *Addiscombe Garden Estates Ltd v Crabbe* [1957] 3 All ER 563.
[43] FA 2003, Sch 4, para 3 and s 52.
[44] Ibid, s 52(2).
[45] Ibid, Sch 4, para 3.
[46] Ibid, s 52; see **5.123**.
[47] Ibid, ss 51 and 80.
[48] Ibid, s 52(7).
[49] Ibid, s 44(5)(b).

latter is and has for certain purposes been accepted by HMRC Stamp Taxes as a payment of cash.[50] It is likely, therefore, that upon an Enquiry they will seek to treat the arrangement as involving the provision of the whole of the consideration so as to enable them to accelerate the effective date and to impose interest and penalties upon the parties and their advisers for late payment and incorrect returns;

- the terms upon which a tenant is to fit out the premises may make their arrangements consideration[51] and the terms upon which he is allowed only the premises may affect whether he enters into sufficient possession to obtain the benefit of the exclusion from the charge to tax upon his costs pursuant to FA 2003, Sch 4, para 10;

- 'substantial performance' depends, *inter alia*, upon whether the taxpayer has taken possession of the whole or substantially the whole of the subject-matter of the transaction.[52] Where there is to be a phased acquisition of the land, such as in a development by stages, and there is a need for the building costs to be incurred after the 'effective date' in order to qualify for the exemption,[53] the question of whether there is a single contract to be completed by stages or a series of separate contracts each of which is to be fully performed separately could be important since it may be easier to satisfy the conditions relating to possession in the latter case. A series of options, including cross-options, would appear to assist the argument for separate contracts. Although such arrangements may be linked transactions, this is relevant only for the purposes of the availability of the lower rates of stamp duty land tax; it is not relevant on the question of when the effective date of each linked contract occurs;

- in relation to building work, arrangements whereby the vendor or lessor of the land or a person connected with him is to be involved in the construction may affect the level of the chargeable consideration depending upon whether these arrangements are 'a condition of the transaction'.[54] Drafting may affect this since this requires the building obligation to be included in the land contract and not as part of a separate contract;[55]

- the drafting of building contracts may enable the charge upon building works[56] to be mitigated;

- the drafting of the documentation may affect the question of whether the document in question is a contract, which does not, of itself, give rise to a charge to stamp duty land tax until it is substantially performed,[57] or is a conveyance,[58] which does;[59]

---

[50] *Coren v Keighley* 48 TC 370; see also *D'Arcy v HMRC* [2006] STC SCD 543 where drafting was significant.
[51] *Eastham v Leigh, London and Provincial Properties Limited* [1971] 2 All ER 887; *Ridgeons Bulk v Customs and Excise* [1994] STC 427.
[52] FA 2003, s 44(5)(a).
[53] Ibid, Sch 4, para 10(2)(a).
[54] Ibid, Sch 4, para 10(2)(c).
[55] Cf *Kimbers & Co v IRC* [1936] 1 KB 132; *Prudential Assurance Co Ltd v IRC* [1992] STC 863; see **Chapter 8**.
[56] FA 2003, Sch 4, para 10.
[57] Ibid, s 44(2) and (4).
[58] See, eg, *Peter Bone Ltd v IRC* [1995] STC 921.
[59] FA 2003, s 44(3) and (10).

- the form of ancillary documentation may produce a 'conveyance',[60] which may trigger notification and payment obligations and may substantially perform or complete a contract at an inappropriate stage.[61] Since 'conveyance' is defined as any instrument, it remains to be seen how much stamp duty baggage on what is a 'conveyance'[62] is brought across in practice into the new tax. Thus, a power of attorney delivered to the purchaser or tenant, being an equitable assignment,[63] may be a 'conveyance' triggering a charge or possibly precluding the availability of subsale relief,[64] which works only where a charge to stamp duty land tax has not arisen in relation to the first contract; but a power to the purchaser or lessee or other party to execute documentation only if the vendor, lessor or other party has been called upon to do so but his failure to execute the documentation within the prescribed time limits which is not a conveyance, will not of itself trigger a 'completion' for these purposes;

- there may be advantages in buying shares as the first step in the transaction.[65]

STRUCTURING ARRANGEMENTS

26.4   It is not necessarily sufficient merely to draft the documents in a manner that is intended to be stamp tax efficient, there are frequently alternative methods of implementing a commercial arrangement. The structures available may differ significantly but the end commercial result is the same. For example the parties may either enter into a contract for the sale of land with a completed building and the parties may enter into a single contract for the sale of land and a separate agreement for the construction of a building upon the land. The former attracts stamp duty land tax upon the combined price for the land and the building whereas the latter is taxable only upon the land price and this may mean the transaction falls below a rate threshold and qualifies for a lower rate of tax. It is, therefore, potentially important for the choices being made by the parties. In general, a choice of alternative methods of implementing the commercial arrangements is not tax avoidance notwithstanding that the parties choose a route that will produce what they regard as the best after tax position.[66] In consequence, the choice of possible routes there may, therefore, be considerable differences in relation to the timing of the tax and possibly the amount of tax ultimately payable depending upon whether there is an option or a conditional contract. In relation to conditional contracts although taking possession can amount to substantial performance even where the contract is conditional at the time the charge may be postponed until substantial performance or completion occurs. There is no automatic charge when the condition is satisfied. Also if the option and its exercise are separate and not linked transactions,[67] the lower rates are possibly available without aggregation of the premium and the strike price. On the other hand, an option to acquire property is taxable immediately upon the premium paid for the option.[68] There may, therefore, be a significant advantage in delaying the charge to tax upon a deposit for a conditional

---

[60]   Ibid, s 44(10)(b).
[61]   Ibid, s 44(3) and (10).
[62]   Cf the stamp duty definition in Stamp Act 1891, s 62; FA 2003, Sch 13, para 1(2).
[63]   See, eg, *Diplock v Hammond* (1854) 5 De GM & G 320.
[64]   FA 2003, s 45.
[65]   Ibid, s 75C(1).
[66]   See, for example, *Willoughby v IRC* [1995] STC 143.
[67]   FA 2003, s 46(1) indicating that they only 'may' be linked; see **5.78**.
[68]   Although the charge upon the strike or contract price will be postponed until the option is exercised and the contract is substantially performed or completed.

contract rather than entering into an option arrangement where the same amount is the premium for the grant of the option and taxable immediately.[69]

Other illustrations of the tax effects of choice of structure include:

- tenants in a block of flats may wish to enter into some form of collective enfranchisement arrangement.[70] There are numerous ways in which this arrangement can proceed:
  - the tenants may form a management company which acquires the freehold interest of the landlord.[71] The management company will pay an appropriate amount of stamp duty land tax. The tenants may then modernise their leases by some form of deed of variation which will usually operate as a surrender and regrant. There are various reliefs for surrenders and regrants although the relief in relation to rents would not be available where the lease being varied is a stamp duty lease. However, in these situations there would be a charge only[72] upon the rent which is unlikely to exceed the net present value of the nil rate slice. The land exchange rules are to be ignored;
  - the tenants may enter into an arrangement to acquire the landlord's reversion and to subsell this to the management company. Obviously, the timing and structuring of these arrangements could be important in relation to the question as to whether the tenants would be entitled to subsale relief.[73] If the tenants should subsell the land to the management company it will pay tax which will be similar to the tax that would have been paid under the previous route. The tenants are then free to modernise their leases by means of a deed of variation operating as a surrender and regrant and take advantage of the reliefs for such arrangements, so far as these are available;[74]
  - the tenants may agree to acquire the freehold interest from the landlord and enter into a single stage transaction under which they agree to subsell the land to the management company in consideration of the grant of modernised leases of their flats. In this situation they may be eligible for subsale relief.[75] However, because the transaction would not be a surrender and regrant but a transfer and a grant of a new lease the reliefs would not be available and the transaction will be a straightforward land exchange subjecting both the management company and the individual tenants to full charges to stamp duty land tax upon the market value of what they receive which will include the full open market value of each of their flats;[76]

- there may be advantages in relation to certain sale and leaseback transactions. A sale and leaseback transaction is a form of land exchange with market value

---

[69] FA 2003, s 46; see **14.35**.
[70] Note the special relief pursuant to FA 2003, s 74 (as amended).
[71] Note that there may be problems in relation to the reorganisation of the tenants' leases depending upon how the management company is funded since loans in connection with leases may constitute chargeable premium payments (FA 2003, Sch 17A, para 18A) whereas funding by way of share capital does not involved such risks.
[72] FA 2003, Sch 17A, paras 9 and 16.
[73] Ibid, s 45 (as amended).
[74] Ibid, Sch 17A, paras 9 and 16.
[75] Provided that the conditions of FA 2003, s 45 are satisfied but subject to the problems of rent for stamp duty leases being renewed.
[76] FA 2003, s 47; Sch 4, para 5.

charges upon both sides of the transaction plus a charge to tax upon the rent.[77] There is a relief for certain types of sale and leaseback transaction[78] which may be useful for certain equity release schemes;

- the reorganisation of the company may form part of a larger commercial arrangement. There may, for example, be arrangements under which a new company is to be formed acquiring control of the existing companies or businesses with arrangements for new money to be injected by an outside new investor. The structuring of the arrangements and drafting of the contract may influence the question as to whether the injection of the outside money is part of the scheme and therefore potentially jeopardises the relief or is not part of the scheme but is part of a larger arrangement of which the scheme itself is merely a part in which case the relief may be available;[79]

- as part of the pre-sale reorganisation of a company it may be necessary to form a new company which takes over the existing arrangements and assets are to be transferred to the new company. Obviously, the choice of assets to be transferred on the intra-group arrangements prior to the sale will influence the stamp tax issues. The difficulty is that there may be clawback of any reliefs that are obtained. It is, therefore, of structuring importance to avoid charges to stamp taxes wherever they are subject to clawback. For example, where a company has shares in other companies and certain assets including land it will be preferable to transfer the subsidiary companies rather than the land. There is no clawback of any stamp duty reliefs obtained in respect of the transfer of shares although there are potential clawback arrangements in relation to the transfer of land. It may, however, be possible to avoid the clawback since this applies only where the intra-group relief[80] is necessary. It is possible to effect some form of dividend in specie or return of capital such as by converting the existing company into an unlimited company which is a transfer for no chargeable consideration and therefore not taxable and not notifiable.[81] The transaction also falls outside the connected companies charge.[82] It may, therefore, avoid one particular set of charges although there may be difficulties upon the liquidation of the transferee company or any subsequent change of control of other companies by reason of the clawback arrangements. It is, however, important to minimise the number of charges given the multiplicity of steps involved;

- the appointment of a receiver or administrator does not affect beneficial ownership of a company's assets[83] whereas beneficial ownership is lost on the appointment of a liquidator.[84] This could be a key factor in insolvency planning;

- the timing of transactions may be important since certain reliefs are subject to clawback if certain events occur within a 3 year period;[85]

---

[77]   Ibid, s 47; Sch 4, para 5.
[78]   Ibid, s 57A (as much amended).
[79]   See, for example, *Crane Fruehauf v IRC* [1975] STC 51; but note *Snell v HMRC* [2006] STC (SCD) 295.
[80]   FA 2003, Sch 7, Part 1.
[81]   Ibid, s 77A and Sch 3, para 1.
[82]   Ibid, ss 53 and 54.
[83]   *English Sewing Cotton Co Ltd v IRC* [1947] 1 All ER 679.
[84]   *Ayerst v C & K (Construction) Ltd* [1976] AC 167.
[85]   FA 2003, Sch 7, paras 3 and 9; Sch 8, para 2; Sch 15, para 17A.

- it may be important to complete a transaction as soon as possible to reduce the risk of clawback or restarting the clawback period;

- in relation to certain types of development arrangement a developer may enter into an agreement for lease with the freeholder pursuant to which he is to become entitled to a lease subject to the construction of the building.[86] The developer may enter into some form of arrangement with a funding institution which is to take over the building as an investment when it is completed.[87] The funding arrangements may take the form of a loan which is to be satisfied and 'repaid' by the transfer of the lease at the end of the project. In this situation the developer is, *prima facie*, subject to tax in respect of the basic land arrangements such as any premium paid and any rent chargeable, although he may not be subject to tax because the building works are to be carried out on the land that is to be leased.[88] A direction to grant the lease to the funding institution will be regarded as some form of 'sale' of the interest and the institution will be subject to tax upon the amount of the consideration, including any loan written off by the arrangements. However, there is a relief for the developer pursuant to the FA 2003, Sch 17A, para 12B. Should the developer enter into the funding arrangements at a suitably early stage ie before he substantially performs the agreement for lease by taking possession to commence the building works and assigns his right to call for the lease then he will disappear from the transaction there is a form of subsale relief. In this situation the agreement for lease is deemed to be made between the landlord or freeholder and the funding institution. In this situation it may be possible for the funding institution to enter into an arrangement to acquire the lease from the developer and a separate agreement for the construction of the building works. If suitably established then, although the statutory novation may impose certain additional liabilities upon the funding institution, it should escape liability to stamp duty land tax upon the building costs.[89] By this type of structuring it is possible to avoid potentially two charges upon the land consideration (other than, perhaps, rent) and to avoid a charge upon the building costs.

ANTI-AVOIDANCE

26.5 As a transaction-based tax, stamp duty land tax may prove open to the application of anti-avoidance principles such as *Ramsay v IRC*[90] and *Furniss v Dawson*,[91] and HMRC Stamp Taxes have introduced legislation containing general anti-avoidance provisions[92] as well as inserting specific anti-avoidance provisions requiring *bona fide* commercial purposes as part of the qualifying conditions for certain reliefs[93] Correspondence between the parties' advisers,[94] or even clearance applications

---

[86] Note the question of whether the construction obligations are part of the chargeable consideration pursuant to FA 2003, Sch 4, para 10; *Eastham v Leigh, London and Provincial Properties Limited* [1971] 2 All ER 887.

[87] But note the problems of loans and deposits made in connection with leases being taxed as premiums FA 2003, Sch 17A, para 18A without relief if the loan is repaid; s 80(4A).

[88] FA 2003, Sch 4, para 10(2).

[89] Note the discussions in decisions such as *Prudential Assurance Co Ltd v IRC* [1992] STC 863; *Kimbers & Co v IRC* [1936] 1 KB 132.

[90] [1982] AC 300, [1981] 1 All ER 865, HL.

[91] [1984] 1 AC 474, [1984] 1 All ER 530, HL (but see **Chapter 2**).

[92] FA 2003, ss 75A–75C.

[93] Ibid, Sch 7.

[94] Which may not be protected by legal privilege should HMRC Stamp Taxes serve a notice demanding their

to HMRC[95] which may need to be produced upon an Enquiry, may be utilised by HMRC Stamp Taxes as a basis for attacking the land transaction return. In consequence, valuations for different amounts prepared for different purposes, such as negotiating the price and supporting an application for a mortgage, may prove embarrassing on an Enquiry.

SIDE EFFECTS

26.6 Drafting and structuring issues are not limited to the liability to tax on the original transaction: they may have long-term commercial issues. For example, although it must be noted that these incidental problems for draftsmen are not unique, difficulties arise where:

- **Clawback and overage payments**
  Where a purchaser is required by the vendor to enter into some form of overage or clawback arrangements it will be prudent to consider building in arrangements for an exit strategy dealing with the onward sale of the property or dealings with it by personal representatives of the purchaser or its liquidation or reconstruction.[96] Such forward planning may expedite those later transactions and avoid the need to return to the original vendor or his successors in title who need to co-operate in the transaction. The stamp duty land tax in such cases remains[97] with the original purchaser, because it remains part of his contractual obligations to pay the additional consideration and so his tax position remains open since he may have to pay the clawback payment. An indemnity or similar deferred consideration by the next purchaser may effectively protect the first purchaser from commercial risk but does not terminate his open stamp duty land tax position even where the tax has been postponed. In such cases it is necessary for the first purchaser to secure a release of his contractual liability which terminates his tax liability since he has no further consideration to pay. Ideally the original contract should contain a provision whereby the original purchaser will be released from his obligation to pay the deferred consideration if he obtains an appropriate covenant to pay the additional consideration from the next purchaser. The latter, of course, becomes subject to an open tax position because he will be providing a variable consideration.

- **Development cost**
  From time to time development arrangements are influenced by stamp duty land tax costs. Thus the landlord's share of the rent may be a percentage of the development costs incurred and these may include stamp taxes. Given the fact that such situations frequently involve variable rents or uncertain building costs any initial stamp duty land tax costs will be provisional only and may require adjustment over many years possibly even extending beyond the initial rent review during the first 5 years of the term. It will be necessary for the professional adviser to determine, for example, whether the deduction of the tenant's costs in

---

production: see ibid, Sch 10 and Sch 13; see **Chapter 21**; see also *Ridgeons Bulk Ltd v Customs and Excise Commissioners* [1994] STC 427 where the correspondence was used to establish the 'real bargain' between the parties.

95   *Swithland Investments v IRC* [1990] STC 448.
96   See, for example, **5.206**.
97   But note especially FA 2003, Sch 17A, para 12; see **5.73** and **5.206** on the need to build in an appropriate exit strategy.

computing the landlord's share of the net rent should include provision for any additional stamp duty land tax arising upon any rent variations or other events during the first 5 years of the term. The preparation of these documents needs to take into account the fact that the stamp duty land tax costs may not be known for some time and may themselves add to the uncertain or variable elements in the consideration or rent and so increase the problems of uncertain consideration.[98]

- **Interaction with other taxes**

  It must not be overlooked that stamp duty land tax interacts with other taxes in a variety of ways. There are situations where stamp duty land tax is chargeable upon any VAT.[99] For example, there may be issues with transfers of going concerns[100] and there are complicated issues relating to the impact of changes of rate of VAT in relation to rent.[101] It will, however, be unusual for stamp duty land tax to form part of the consideration, as such, upon which the VAT is charged. Other taxes are not dealt with in relation to the legislation. For example, stamp duty land tax will form part of the consideration paid for the acquisition of assets that may be eligible for capital allowances. Part of the consideration part for an industrial building may include land subject to stamp duty land tax and HMRC Stamp Taxes may take the view that certain items of equipment that qualify as machinery and plant are fixtures and subject to stamp duty land tax upon purchase. Similarly, stamp duty land tax will form part of the acquisition cost for the purposes of chargeable gains. Although Taxation of Chargeable Gains Act 1992, s 38, refers to stamp duty it does not refer to stamp duty reserve tax. However, it would seem that such tax will form part of the acquisition costs for capital gains tax. However, this simple statement overlooks the fact that stamp duty land tax is frequently assessed provisionally[102] so that the costs may not be settled for many years. In consequence, it may prove difficult if not impossible to produce definitive figures for the purposes of other taxes. This problem of fluctuating tax costs is recognised in relation to VAT and the Capital Goods Scheme for the purposes of capital allowances;[103] but there are no equivalent provisions for dealing with fluctuating levels of stamp duty land tax. Obviously, the level of stamp duty land tax will not fluctuate from year to year unless there are situations where the overage or additional consideration is payable on a frequent basis and the amounts become 'ascertained' so that stamp duty land tax crystallises to that extent. It does, however, nevertheless mean that a taxpayer may have underpaid tax, at least in those cases where the deferred consideration has itself been postponed and the tax itself deferred.[104] It is unclear whether auditors should insist that accounts are drawn up on a basis that recognises not only the potential liability to stamp duty land tax but also the potential impact of stamp duty land tax upon other tax computations which may affect the level of profits whether capital or income.

---

[98] There are significant risks of circularity in that the costs may not be known until the stamp duty upon the rent or building works has been determined but the rent and costs themselves require adjustment by reason of the costs which in turn may require adjustment to take account of an adjustment rent and so on.

[99] FA 2003, Sch 4, para 2; see **5.126**.

[100] See **5.130**.

[101] See **7.162** and **7.168**.

[102] See **2.14**.

[103] See Capital Allowances Act 2000, ss 234 and following.

[104] FA 2003, ss 80, 90 and Stamp Duty Land Tax (Administration) Regulations 2003, SI 2003/2837, Part 4; see **16.32**.

SHARE TRANSACTIONS

26.7   There is no charge to stamp duty land tax upon the sale of shares, at present,[105] but there are potential interactions between the sale of shares and stamp duty land tax. For example, a sale of shares is not a scheme transaction where the transfer is the first stage in the arrangement;[106] however, where this does not apply the consideration for the sale of the shares may be taken into account in computing the charge upon the notional transaction for the purpose of the general anti-avoidance provisions[107] but there is no credit against the stamp duty land tax payable for any stamp duty or stamp duty reserve tax paid in respect of the shares.[108]

26.8   More significant for the purposes of share transactions is the question of warranties and indemnities, particularly given the open-ended nature of much of stamp duty land tax. It is important that where a company is the tenant under a lease that has a variable rent or may be subject to charges and abnormal rent increases or has acquired land with some form of overage or clawback, whether or not the tax has been deferred, its net asset position will be influenced by the potential tax charges that could arise.

---

[105]   See **1.23**.
[106]   FA 2003, s 75(1).
[107]   Ibid, s 75A(5).
[108]   Ibid, s 75A(5)(a).

Chapter 27

VALUATION AND RELATED ISSUES

27.1 Valuation is a major issue for stamp duty land tax. There are many areas where consideration other than cash is chargeable with stamp duty land tax[1] and in some situations the actual consideration, if any, is replaced by market value or there is a deemed consideration.[2] In addition, there are many situations where a specious form of valuation which has more in common with fortunetelling than valuation has been imposed on the taxpayer as part of the self-assessment process. As indicated elsewhere,[3] much of stamp duty land tax is dealt with on an estimated or provisional basis. This may require the taxpayer to estimate future market values such as where there is a clawback providing for additional consideration to be paid by reference to a proportion of the market value some 80 years in the future depending upon the nature of the planning permission that might be obtained.[4] Similarly, the existence of variable rents, such as rent reviews or turnover rents or anticipated or possible changes in the rate of VAT, require the parties to make predictions as to future rents. Variable annuities require estimates of the best years.[5]

27.2 It is relatively easy for HMRC Stamp Taxes to challenge a return upon the basis of the valuation since there is little specific guidance as to the factors to be taken into account when carrying out a valuation nor is there any indication to the relative weight to be attached to the various factors; but, in practice, it may be difficult for them to 'discover' the valuation principle adopted[6] because they are not currently in a position to 'audit' land transaction returns or to become aware of transactions not reported.[7] These issues of principle are important since should HMRC Stamp Taxes spot that the valuation has been prepared on a particular basis they may be in a position to allege that the terms not correctly prepared and they have made a 'discovery' that entitles them to deal with the transaction afresh.[8] They are entitled to note that a return is incorrect because it was prepared upon the basis of an incorrect methodology adopted in relation to the valuation. Essentially, similar principles apply to the valuation of property other than land. There is basically the same market value charge but no general explanation is contained in the legislation of how the market value charge is to be applied in any particular case. There may be problems in relation to the share valuation issues because, at the time of the effective date when the market value of the consideration has to be determined, the consideration shares may not be in issue and substantial performance may produce an effective date before the commercial valuations are intended to take place or the number of shares to be issued is to be determined and the best guidance

---

[1] See FA 2003, Sch 4; see **Chapter 5**.
[2] Ibid, s 53; Sch 15, paras 10, 14 and 18.
[3] See **2.14**.
[4] FA 2003, s 51; see **5.1**.
[5] Ibid, s 52; but these are not subject to retrospective revision.
[6] See ibid, Sch 13; see **Chapter 21**.
[7] See ibid, Sch 13 and Sch 10, para 25.
[8] Ibid, Sch 10, para 28; see *Langham v Veltema* [2004] STC 544; see **Chapter 23**.

that Russell LJ could offer in the Court of Appeal in *Crane Fruehauf v IRC*[9] was the parties must do the best they can.[10] It is specifically provided[11] that for most forms of consideration in kind this is to be the open market value of the relevant assets but it may be related to open market costs.[12] There are also numerous ridiculous situations where a taxpayer is required to make a return upon the basis of a 'reasonable' estimate of future market value or rents many years in the future, where professional advisers are wisely refusing to become involved with the advice from the so-called 'help-line' to insert the current rent or value. This involves the taxpayer in making an incorrect return with the consequent risk of penalties and interest. Problems can exist in practice even where current values are involved such as where the purchase price is the market value as at completion which has not been agreed at that date. Two difficulties particularly arise in such a case:

- such consideration is 'unascertained'[13] and the return has to be prepared on the basis of a 'reasonable estimate' and tax paid on that amount. A subsequent full return is required when the figure is finally agreed; and

- HMRC Stamp Taxes can challenge that value upon Enquiry or discovery[14] since, in their view, even arm's length negotiations supported by independent professional advice is not necessarily the fiscal market value.[15] Fiscal valuations require a willing seller and a willing buyer. However, a person may technically be a willing seller in that he is prepared to sell but is under a certain pressure to sell such as a need to raise cash.[16] In such a case he is not, for fiscal valuation purposes, a 'willing seller' who is, it seems, a person prepared to wait and is in a position to wait until the right offer is received. The actual sale is, therefore, not within the scope of hypothetical fiscal sales; it can, therefore, be ignored; but HMRC Stamp Taxes are faced with the problem that there has been an actual sale or lease so that in fact the vendor is 'willing' and so is the purchaser or lessee.

In practice it seems that HMRC Stamp Taxes are not anxious to become involved in valuations because they are required to spend part of their budget on obtaining advice from the District Valuer or Share Valuation Division which also delays the negotiations. It seems that if the taxpayer can produce reasonably up-to-date advice (ie not more than a few months old) from independent professional advisers who have been properly instructed and the numbers are reasonably small they will generally be prepared to act on that advice.

27.3   The self-assessment basis of stamp duty land tax[17] and the need to avoid the problems associated with 'negligent returns',[18] or the risk of a discovery assessment[19] means that taxpayers or their advisers should take at least the following steps:

---

9   [1975] STC 51.
10   See *Holt v IRC* [1953] 1 WLR 1488.
11   FA 2003, Sch 4, para 7.
12   Ibid, Sch 4, paras 10 and 11; Stamp Duty Land Tax (Administration) Regulations 2003, SI 2003/2837.
13   See **5.187**, **26.6** and **4.3**.
14   *Langham v Veltema* [2004] STC 544.
15   *Lap Shun Textiles Industrial Co v Collector of Stamp Revenue* [1976] AC 530; *Cowan de Groot Properties Ltd v Eagle Trust plc* [1991] BCLC 1045.
16   *Cowan de Groot Properties Ltd v Eagle Trust plc* [1991] BCLC 1045.
17   See **16.17** and **16.44**.
18   See **23.4**; see also **19.8**, **21.7**.
19   FA 2003, Sch 10, para 28; *Langham v Veltema* [2004] STC 544.

- determine into which category of transaction and chargeable consideration the transaction in question falls. This frequently affects the nature of the chargeable consideration which may not be the actual consideration;

- determine what is the chargeable consideration for the transaction which involves identifying the assets to be valued, and this is not always obvious. For example, in relation to the exchange of major interests, the stamp duty land tax is charged upon the market value of the land interest being acquired,[20] not, as is usually the case, the market value of the land being disposed of as consideration;

- determine whether the chargeable consideration is charged by reference to value, cost or otherwise;

- having identified the transaction, the chargeable consideration and the basis of charge, determine whether there are any special principles concerning how the valuation or other basis of charge is to be applied;[21]

- take appropriate steps to arrive at a reasonable and defensible figure. Failure to take appropriate advice is likely to be regarded as negligent;

- consider whether allowing any part of the tax upon the chargeable consideration may be postponed and make the necessary application;[22] and

- include the figure arrived at in the computation in the land transaction return and calculate the tax accordingly.

Although apportionment of the consideration between various assets and services being acquired is frequently required this has to be on a just and reasonable basis;[23] this does not require a market value apportionment; but HMRC Stamp Taxes are attacking the arm's length allocation by the parties particularly in the context of embedded goodwill.[24]

27.4   It must be noted that these issues of valuation apply not merely to land but to other property which may constitute consideration in kind. A transfer of land to a company in consideration of the issue of shares may be taxed on either the market value of the land if the connected company charge applies[25] or the market value of the shares if that charge does not apply.[26] Share valuation issues can therefore arise.

---

[20]   Ibid, Sch 4, para 5.
[21]   See, for example, the special rules for land exchanges where the tax is upon the value acquired or the value provided as consideration (FA 2003, Sch 4, para 5) and the special rules for valuing leases where partnerships are involved (FA 2003, Sch 15, para 38 and para 15).
[22]   FA 2003, ss 80, 87 and 90 and Stamp Duty Land Tax (Administration) Regulations 2003, SI 2003/2837, Part 4.
[23]   Ibid, Sch 4, para 4.
[24]   See **1.5**.
[25]   FA 2003, ss 53 and 54.
[26]   Ibid, Sch 4, paras 1 and 7.

GAPS IN THE LEGISLATION

27.5   The only basis of charge for which any form of guidance is provided is market value[27] and cost.[28] 'Market value' is defined by reference to certain provisions in the Taxation of Chargeable Gains Act 1992.[29] In relation to the charge arising upon costs in relation to the provision of services other than works the value of the consideration is the amount that would have to be paid in the open market to obtain those services.[30] Similarly in relation to consideration that consists of the carrying out of works the value of the works is the amount that would have to be paid in the open market for the carrying out of the works in question[31] but there is no statutory guidance what principles of valuation are to be applied or the relative weight to be attached to them. This, however, merely provides the basic principles, it does not set out the rules governing the detailed process of valuation.

27.6   Guidance in other areas where similar principles for fiscal valuations exist may provide some assistance such as when the parties may be assumed to be a willing seller and a willing buyer and that the sale is in an open market so that special purchasers may be possible factors to consider, but a single special purchaser who is the only purchaser such as the owner of the dominant land benefiting from a restrictive covenant will not be an open market.

27.7   Unfortunately, most other fiscal valuations are for the purposes of deemed transactions so that numerous assumptions have to be made such as the type of purchaser and the terms of sale. In relation to stamp taxes there will usually be an actual transaction where either the value of the consideration has to be determined or there are actual terms of sale. There will in consequence need to be a preliminary debate with HMRC Stamp Taxes as to the assumptions if any to be made, and as to whether the terms of the actual transaction can be taken into account or a totally hypothetical sale on different terms has to be assumed such as the issue of whether market value includes VAT[32] where the actual seller has not opted to tax the land. There is also the identification of the seller, ie whether the sale in the open market is to be made by the actual seller or landlord to a third party or whether it is deemed to be an on-sale by the purchaser or the tenant. In either case the terms of the deemed sale will have to be agreed.

27.8   There is no guidance on other novel bases of tax such as the cost of works or services or how to arrive at a reasonable estimate of future uncertain payments or valuation for these future rents. The only guidance in the legislation is the implied scope of the requirement. Many variable payments involve two factors:

* the likelihood of the payment being made; and

* the possible amount to be paid in the event that the obligation to pay arises.

---

27   Other bases of valuation exist such as 'value' or 'fair value' which have different sets of principles applicable to them.
28   FA 2003, Sch 4, paras 10 and 11.
29   Ibid, s 118; Taxation of Chargeable Gains Act 1992, ss 272–274.
30   Ibid, Sch 4, para 11 (as amended).
31   Ibid, Sch 4, para 10(3).
32   See **5.129**.

Only the latter is relevant on the statutory provisions for stamp duty land tax. Any taxpayer who prepares his tax return on the basis that it is virtually impossible that any additional consideration will become payable because he has no intention of seeking planning permission or because he is confident that the transaction will be accepted as a transfer of a going concern for the purposes of VAT, and so does not include any references to this in the return, will be making an incorrect return and will be running risks of major penalties and interest costs in the event that his gamble proves to be incorrect. He is, for example, required to predict the impact or market value if planning permission should be obtained by a successor in title 50 years in the future.

MARKET VALUE

27.9 'Market value' in relation to any assets means the 'price' which those assets might reasonably be expected to fetch on a sale in the open market.[33] This requires a 'market' which is 'open'. There will be questions of whether there is a market where there are prohibitions upon sale.[34] Even where the asset is saleable, there may be a limited number of potential purchasers who may not be a 'market' or be too few to be an 'open market'. However, if there are no legal restrictions upon a possible sale it has to be assumed that there has been a sale no matter how unlikely it is that any person would actually bid for the asset.[35]

27.10 This open market sale is usually interpreted in the cases as being a sale on a hypothetical basis between a hypothetical willing seller and a hypothetical willing buyer and the terms and conditions the sale are also hypothetical. It is also necessary to assume that there will be sale notwithstanding that, in fact, it will be impossible or virtually impossible to make an actual sale. This does not take the matter very far since in many cases in stamp duty land tax there will be an actual transaction in the background; but there may be difficulties in identifying who is the seller and who is the buyer. For example, a market value to an actual seller may be different from the market value of the property to a purchaser. There may be situations where the price which a buyer could realise on re-sale would be greater or less than that which he is paying to the vendor or landlord.

27.11 It is assumed that the seller is a willing seller and not in a situation of a forced sale such as being under pressure from a lender or required to sell as quickly as possible or in order to finance the development he is willing to offer discounts for a quick sale HMRC Stamp Taxes have taken the point that a 'forced sale' is not at arm's length because the seller is not 'willing'. In consequence, persons who are anxious to sell, such as liquidators, receivers and personal representatives of deceased individuals, may be prepared to take a lesser price in order to be in a position to wind up the affairs of the companies or the estate.[36] In relation to stamp duty land tax there is a basic issue of principle as to who is the seller in the hypothetical transaction. There may be different issues affecting the identity of the hypothetical seller. For example, in relation to land

---

[33] FA 2003, Sch 4, para 7; Taxation of Chargeable Gains Act 1992, s 272(1).

[34] Such assets may have a value because of the possibility of some person being willing to pay to be freed from their nuisance; *Alexander v IRC* [1991] STC 112; see *Crossman v IRC* [1936] 1 All ER 762; *Stanyforth v IRC* [1930] AC 339.

[35] This is no evidence that there is no market; but may be a factor in reducing the value.

[36] See, for example, *Lap Shun Textiles Industrial Co v Collector of Stamp Revenue* [1976] AC 530; *Cowan de Groot Properties Ltd v Eagle Trust plc* [1991] BCLC 1045.

exchanges the chargeable consideration is the market value of the land received.[37] This would suggest that the hypothetical seller is the actual 'purchaser' namely the transferee or lessee of the land ie it is the value to him if he on-sold the asset rather than the sale price which the actual seller or transferor might receive should he deal with a third party. The identity of the hypothetical parties could influence the terms and conditions of the hypothetical sale and change the actual terms and produce significantly different figures. Similarly where there is some form of building arrangement the sale of the land to the potential developer with building commitments may be different from either a hypothetical sale of the land by the actual seller to a third party who may not be a builder[38] or a sale by the purchasing builder subject to arrangements relating to the building arrangements such as pre-sales or pre-lets whether with or without financing arrangements. This issue of the nature of the asset can be important in its value and there will be key issues of principle, for example, as regards the terms of a lease.[39]

27.12 From time to time the District Valuer and Shares Valuation Division refer to 'comparables' ie the prices realised in actual sales for the same type of asset.[40] However, these are of limited benefit in valuations since no two parcels of land are identical or even closely comparable. Similarly, details of other actual transactions that provide the basis of comparables may be of little benefit because of the circumstances surrounding the sale which may mean that it was not at market value even though at arm's length.[41] The development potential or planning consent may be different, the state of the title may be different and, importantly, the terms of the two sales may be different. Such approaches by the District Valuer should be resisted.

27.13 Where the property is leased on a full reviewable rack rent then clearly there is unlikely to be any value in the lease, although from time to time, the point is raised that if there is some time before the next review and market rents have increased the lease does have a small value by reference to the rent level below current market rents. As regards the value of the reversion this may be influenced by interest rates and be a multiple of the full rent payable for the lease.

Mortgages

27.14 A problem arises from time to time in relation to the valuation of property that is subject to a charge. The question is whether the value of the land is the equity of redemption or is the value of the land free from the mortgage. For many years HMRC Stamp Taxes accepted that the market value of the interest was the value of the equity of redemption ie subject to the mortgage. However, recently there have been indications that they may be revising this view and may be seeking to value the land not subject to the mortgage. It is considered that this change of practice is debatable since there is nothing in the general discussion of valuation principles to indicate that the terms of the hypothetical sale of the land being unencumbered. Clearly, the hypothetical terms cannot apply to assume that the land will not be subject to any easements or restrictive covenants that run against the land and there is no reason why a person who is not required to buy off a restrictive covenant before sale is required to discharge a mortgage.

---

[37]   FA 2003, Sch 4, para 5.

[38]   Note the potential arguments of hypothetical participants who are 'involved' because they are assumed to believe that they can turn the contract or make a profit from the onward sale to a special purchaser, and so may be prepared to pay a slightly higher price for the opportunity.

[39]   On which see FA 2003, Sch 17A, para 10; Sch 15, paras 15 and 38.

[40]   Frequently relying upon the information provided in stamp tax returns such as the 'PD' form or SDLT 1.

[41]   *Salvesen's Trustees v IRC* (1930) 9 ATC 43.

Other taxes

27.15 This legislation effectively throws the parties upon general fiscal principles. HMRC Stamp Taxes appear in practice to rely heavily upon the capital gains tax divisions of the HMRC for technical and practical support and in this, as in many other areas of stamp duty land tax, has adopted capital gains tax legislation. The provisions and assumptions to be made are contained in Taxation of Chargeable Gains Act 1992, ss 272–274. This involves totally inappropriate concepts for the hypothetical sale or lease and parties, since the value of the assets will depend for the purposes of stamp duty land tax upon the actual terms of the deal between the parties rather than the assumed terms of a hypothetical lease or sale.[42] However, little help can be expected from cases on valuation in other areas on similar legislation since those valuations are based upon hypothetical transactions; but stamp duty land tax arises in the context of actual transactions. This means that the actual terms of the sale or the covenants in the lease will be relevant. The actual terms of the real transaction are usually relevant where there is the grant of a lease for a deemed market value premium. This requires the parties to take into account the actual rent and all other terms and covenants in the actual lease. This introduces a principle that the actual transaction has to be taken into account and HMRC Stamp Taxes cannot substitute 'better' terms.[43] For example, HMRC Stamp Taxes are beginning to accept the argument that where land is transferred subject to obligations to grant rights back the existence of such rights can be taken into account when valuing the interest transferred which indicates that the sale is not entirely hypothetical and the actual terms of sale may be relevant. Once HMRC Stamp Taxes accept the actual terms of sale in one case it will become increasingly difficult for them to seek to change the actual terms of sale in other case.

Problems with actual terms

27.16 The possible but inevitable drift towards actual terms of sale rather than hypothetical sales will raise problems because of the prevalence of variable consideration in land transactions at present.[44] This will raise the question as to whether the market value has to be determined on the basis of an initial price ignoring the possible fluctuations, marriage value, changes in planning permission and development potential.[45] No doubt parties could sell for a fixed price that reflected some sort of hope value although the clawback is designed to avoid such difficulties. Similarly, it may be an obligation of trustees to seek some form of share in the profits of the proposed development.[46] If these arrangements are not properly structured, which could be especially important now that rates of income tax are far in excess of the rates applicable to capital gains tax, this might require an investigation into the intentions of the parties. For example, there may be questions as to whether the intention of one of the parties to seek planning permission and develop the land is a relevant factor. In some situations the fact that the parties may be related or have knowledge of the other party's intention

[42] See, for example, FA 2003, Sch 17A, para 10 referring a covenant affecting the rent and s 48(1)(b) referring to obligations affecting the value of land.
[43] Compare *Duke of Buccleuch v IRC* [1967] AC 506.
[44] Note the obligation of professional advisers to seek to obtain such arrangements in *Akazuc Enterprises v Farmar* [2003] PL SCS 127.
[45] There may be issues of principle because there are various reasons for such additional consideration arrangements. They may be designed to capture a share or a profit on re-sale or they may be intended to provide a machinery for coping with the problems of recognising development potential and hope value. These differences may be reflected in the mechanics for payment such as a share of the re-sale proceeds or capitalised rents or a share of the enhanced value without a sale.
[46] But note the difficulties of this as illustrated by *Page v Lowther* [1983] STC 799.

could be a factor to be taken into account in the valuation.[47] However, notwithstanding the existence of hope value, land with a development potential may have a reduced value by the time of the effective date because the deferred consideration is to be ignored. For example, even where planning permission has been obtained, it may necessary to enter upon the land, demolish the existing buildings, relocate the existing tenants, the project requires an outlay of cash and no prospect of a return for a considerable time unless the developer is in a position to dispose of the property from plan or at an early stage but in this situation he is likely to have to offer a substantial discount upon the price that he might expect to receive on a willing seller basis if he were in a position to wait until the development was completed.

Hypothetical sale terms and conditions

27.17 There are the questions of the terms of the hypothetical sale. The problems arise because of the absence of standard terms for a lease or freehold. The covenants and rights in or over the land will vary from parcel to parcel. For example, in *Duke of Buccleuch v IRC*[48] it was held that a seller could obtain a better price by selling the land in smaller parcels. There are potential discounts for jointly owned property[49] rather like minority discounts for shareholdings.[50] In consequence, when looking at potential willing sellers and willing buyers the actual buyer may be a joint owner who is prepared to pay more than the minority value for the property because he would be acquiring control of the property. On the other hand should the seller sell in the open market or the purchaser having acquired the interest to sell on the same minority interest the price would differ. This, of course, raises the question as to whether a potential 'special purchaser' exists.[51] This would raise particular problems since there may always be a particular purchaser for property. For example, in some situations a lease or interest may be effectively non-assignable but there may be a value to the person entitled to the interest because of his nuisance value as against the owner of the land.[52] The question is whether such a limited potential purchaser is a special purchaser in the open market. It would seem that one person cannot constitute a market.

27.18 The key issue in the market value process is assuming a hypothetical as opposed to an actual sale and then debating with HMRC Stamp Taxes the terms and conditions of the hypothetical sale. For example, there may be an issue as to whether the market value should be determined upon some different basis and whether it would be appropriate for HMRC Stamp Taxes to suggest that the terms of the actual lease should be ignored and a lease granted on totally different terms and covenants substituted for it as part of the valuation process. There may be advantages in selling land in small parcels rather than as a large estate.[53] A hypothetical sale might proceed on that basis; but it is questionable whether HMRC Stamp Taxes will seek to rewrite the arrangement between the parties to that extent. However, if HMRC Stamp Taxes do take it upon themselves to argue for totally different terms of sale then part of these negotiations might be the identity of the parties. Apart from the question as to whether HMRC Stamp Taxes could take into account a special purchaser who might be prepared to pay extra for the

---

47   See, for example, *Walton v IRC* [1996] STC 68; *IRC v Gray (exor of Fox)* [1994] STC 360.
48   [1967] AC 506; but see Taxation of Chargeable Gains Act 1992, s 242(2).
49   *Re Wight* [1982] 2 EGLR 236.
50   See, for example, *Re Duker, Lloyds Bank v Duker* [1987] 3 All ER 193 on the question of joint holdings and control.
51   See *Robinson Bros v Houghton* [1938] AC 371; *Glass v IRC* (1915) 52 SLR 411; *IRC v Clay* [1914] 3 KB 466; *Holt v Holt* [1990] 1 WLR 1250; *Ferguson v MacLennon* [1990] SLT 618.
52   See, for example, *Alexander v IRC* [1991] STC 112.
53   *Duke of Buccleuch v IRC* [1967] AC 506; Taxation of Chargeable Gains Act 1992, s 242(2).

property,[54] it would seem that HMRC Stamp Taxes could not contend that the actual state of the land could be ignored, for example, suggesting that where the land was affected by restrictive covenants or rights of way or other encumbrances these could be ignored. Similarly, where the land is subject to an option the terms upon which the option is exercised would clearly influence the price of the land. It would not seem appropriate to make the assumption that the seller would attempt to buy out the option in order to obtain a higher price for the land. This may influence the question of the identities of the parties to the sale. For example, there may be a difference in the terms of the hypothetical sale and potential purchaser if the vendor is the person is presumed to be selling the interest in the open market. This would obviously be a factor if, for example, HMRC Stamp Taxes sought to fragment the land and sell in numerous separate parcels. On the other hand, if the seller in the open market is the purchaser the terms of his actual purchase may differ from the terms of the hypothetical sale by the actual seller or lessor. This may become an acute issue with certain aspects of stamp duty land tax particularly in the area of exchanges and partitions since the tax is charged upon the market value of what is received. This might point towards the price that the purchaser might obtain if he sold the interests he receives rather than the price that the seller would obtain if he sold the land rather than exchanged it and dealt with a third party. Much confusion and misapplication of the legislation is, in consequence, expected in practice, and the first priority in any valuation negotiations will be to agree the terms of the hypothetical sale.

Value Added Tax

27.19 It is unclear whether, in determining the 'market value' of the asset, the question of whether or not VAT is an issue has to be taken into account.[55] The definition of market value is the 'price' in the open market which is *prima facie* the figure including VAT.[56] In some cases the vendor or landlord may not have exercised the option to tax the land. In other cases the parties may be hoping that the transaction will be accepted as a transfer of a going concern without any VAT. There is, therefore, no necessity that a sale in the open market will involve VAT. It seems that in practice HMRC Stamp Taxes do not include VAT when determining the market value of the asset.

27.20 The position is more complex when the tax is charged by reference to 'cost'. To the extent that HMRC Stamp Taxes are prepared to act on the basis of actual costs there will be an actual VAT situation. However, in these situations the actual purchaser may be entitled to some credit for the input tax, if any, charge upon his costs. The question is whether the input tax credit can be utilised to reduce the 'costs' when computing the chargeable amount but this may vary where the taxpayer is partially exempt. The issue complicates itself when HMRC Stamp Taxes look to open market costs because, for example, the taxpayer is utilising his own resources and his 'costs' are lower because they do not include the profit element that would normally be involved in an arm's length transaction. It seems that HMRC Stamp Taxes will look to the amounts actually charged but not allow any input tax credit that the taxpayer might receive. It is necessary either to ignore the VAT charged or to ignore the possible credit. Any other arrangement being a matter of tax over time, possibly 10 years, produces a situation that is unworkable for a transaction based tax.

---

54 But this might mean that the actual purchaser if aware of a special purchaser might pay a slightly higher price upon the basis he could turn the land and make a profit.
55 Cf Statement of Practice D7.
56 Value Added Tax Act 1994, s 19; *Glenrothes Development Corporation v IRC* [1994] STC 74.

General stamp duty land tax legislation

27.21 In estimating the market value of any assets, no reduction is to be made in the estimate on account of the estimate being made on the assumption that the whole of the asset is to be placed on the market at one and the same time.[57] It is difficult to see the point of this as the parties are concerned with an actual transaction where the whole of the subject-matter of the transaction is to be valued, unless the market value legislation contemplates a hypothetical onward sale or sales of the asset to be acquired by the taxpayer.[58] This, however, is a two dimensional problem in that the item to be valued may not be the land interest being acquired but the consideration in kind being provided such as a transfer of land to an unconnected company in consideration of the issue of shares.[59] The valuation is of the consideration shares which are not being on-sold or placed at arm's length and are not listed. Different principles apply to the valuation of shares where the sale in the market is almost certainly hypothetical because there will be no actual onward sale of the shares.

Minor interests

27.22 There are many situations where the market value of minor interests is an issue particularly where such interests are 'excepted and reserved' to the vendor which in the view of HMRC Stamp Taxes operates by way of transfer and regrant[60] producing a land exchange within FA 2003, s 47. It is clear that such interests are valuable[61] but they may not have a 'market value' in the terms of the legislation. This is a major principle since there is a difference between 'value' and 'market value'.[62] It is essential to recognise that there may be assets which, for technical legal reasons, cannot be sold but have a value,[63] if only a 'nuisance value', ie there is a price that one particular person may be prepared to pay in order to obtain the interest or to free his interests from the irritations and inconveniences of the existence of the interest.

27.23 Such interests give rise to many conceptual and technical analytical problems of considerable complexity. The basic question is whether the obligations or restrictions[64] in question affect the market value of other land involved. For example, land may be sold to a developer whereby additional rights over the land retained by the vendor may be granted such as rights of way during the development or access to main services upon the land retained by the vendor or 'reserving' to the vendor certain rights such as easements or rights to light over the land retained by the vendor. Such arrangements are land exchanges. Notwithstanding that the vast bulk of the consideration consists of cash, the tax is charged upon market value.[65] Fortunately, HMRC Stamp Taxes are

---

[57] Taxation of Chargeable Gains Act 1992, s 272(2); compare *Buccleuch v IRC* [1967] AC 506.

[58] See **27.11**.

[59] See also, for example, **Chapter 9** for the problems of mixed consideration in variation of trust.

[60] There is also the unanswered question whether the same principles apply to covenants given by tenants in leases so as to convert every lease into a land exchange unless the covenant falls within the exemption of FA 2003, Sch 17A, para 11. The fact that those responsible for the design and amendment of the tax thought it necessary to exclude certain covenants from the charge to tax must mean that such covenants are separate chargeable interests creating a land exchange.

[61] See, for example, *Alexander v IRC* [1991] STC 112.

[62] See *Stanton v Drayton Commercial Investment Co. Ltd* [1982] STC 585; note 'fair value' *Dean v Prince* [1954] 1 All ER 749.

[63] *Alexander v IRC* [1991] STC 112.

[64] Which may be chargeable interests; FA 2003, s 48(1)(b); see **4.39**.

[65] The practical problem is the longstanding view of HMRC Stamp Taxes that arm's length negotiations is not the market value so that the contract price is not conclusive on this issue. Current indications are that they will look to the initial offer or indicative price as the market value so that reductions in that price although

beginning to accept the argument that the market value of an interest must take into account the obligation to regrant rights over the land or chargeable interest in question. In the above illustration certain of the rights may operate to enhance the value of the land, in the latter situation it may depress the value of the land.

27.24 There will, in consequence, be an issue as to how the new right regranted or reserved is to be taxed. This will depend upon a highly complex technical analysis of the nature of the right in question. In general, minor interests such as restrictive covenants or easements can exist only as part of the dominant land. They do not exist 'in gross'. Therefore, they cannot be sold as separate choses in action but only when the dominant land is sold as part of the land. They do not have a 'market value' since as 'separate rights' they cannot be individually sold on the open market. At most they can be released to the owner of the servient land, which may be a chargeable transaction but is not a sale in the open market.[66] In consequence having no market value the 'creation' of such rights will involve the acquisition of minor interests for no chargeable consideration and so this side of the transaction will be within the non-notifiable regime.[67]

27.25 However, it is far from obvious that such rights or restrictions will necessarily qualify as restrictive covenants or easements because either there is no dominant land to be benefited or where there is land that might qualify the arrangement does not benefit it. In such cases there is a simple contractual obligation but since this may affect the value of an estate or interest in land it is a chargeable interest.[68] As a simple chose in action not depended for its existence upon dominant land it will be *prima facie* capable of separate sale and so will have a market value.[69] In consequence the parties involved in reserving such a right to what is in effect a deferred consideration may face two tax charges; namely:

- a charge upon the 'exchange' creating the chose in action in the initial transaction; and

- possibly the 'acquisition' of the right when payment is finally made. However, it seems that the point may not be technically correct since the obligation to pay the deferred consideration will have been subject to tax[70] and there is an argument that this would be to subject the same matter to double taxation.[71] It is also arguable that the discharge of an obligation does not fall into charge even on the much extended definition of acquisition. The view of HMRC Stamp Taxes on these technical issues has not been revealed in practice.

---

genuinely commercial such as a reduction in the price for early completion are to be ignored because this is not the market price (see *Cowan de Groot Properties Ltd v Eagle Trust plc* [1991] BCLC 1045).

[66] *Alexander v IRC* [1991] STC 112.
[67] FA 2003, Sch 3, para 1; s 77A; see **Chapter 18**.
[68] Ibid, s 48(1)(b).
[69] For the valuation and related issues around such choses in action see the case law developed from *Marren v Ingles* 54 TC 76 which has given rise to a large amount of complex legislation.
[70] FA 2003, s 51.
[71] Ibid, Sch 10, para 33.

Costs as taxable consideration

27.26 Where building works or services are part of the chargeable consideration[72] the tax is charge by reference to the costs of such works or services in the open market.

The question of costs is essentially a matter of fact since HMRC Stamp Taxes have introduced a regime for deferring payment of the tax upon such costs until they are 'ascertained'.[73] There needs to be a market in the services and it will be a question of looking at the open market. However, in relation to services prices will fluctuate. Third parties may be reluctant to volunteer evidence of what they would charge for such a contract. HMRC Stamp Taxes may be prepared to consider what the person would charge for those services if he were tendering for a contract. However, it is clear that the 'cost' must include a 'profit element'. In some situations a person supplying services may make use of his own labour force. This could be particularly in the case in relation to building works where a developer may have employees rather than subcontractors. In this situation the cost of the services will be related to payroll and may not include a 'cost' that is a profit element. Presumably HMRC Stamp Taxes will require some profit factor to be included.

27.27 The other question is the treatment of VAT. Many services are subject to VAT upon the contract price. This is the 'price' that is paid in the open market.[74] However, the cost to a particular person may vary depending upon whether he can recover the VAT charged to him as an input tax in whole or in part. It may be that, as with market value, HMRC Stamp Taxes may be prepared to ignore the potential impact of VAT. Since the transaction must be on a hypothetical basis it would seem that the recoverability by the particular person of any VAT that might be charged is irrelevant.

Reversions

27.28 An important issue may be the rent payable. When valuing a reversion a major factor is the number of years' purchase to be applied to the rent, possibly adjusted to take account of costs (ie the test may look to the net or profit rent). Where there is a lease at a full market reviewable rent it is unlikely under normal circumstances to have a market value.

Other related assets

27.29 Since there may be consideration in kind it is necessary to value non-land assets.[75]

Quoted securities

27.30 The provisions of s 272, with ss 273 and 274 of the Taxation of Chargeable Gains Act 1992, have effect subject to Part I of Schedule 11.

27.31 Complex provisions apply where the chargeable consideration consists of or includes shares and other securities such as assets in a unit trust scheme.

---

[72] FA 2003, Sch 4, paras 10 and 11; *Eastham v Leigh, London and Provincial Properties Limited* [1971] 2 All ER 887.
[73] Stamp Duty Land Tax (Administration) Regulations 2003, SI 2003/2837, Part 4, especially regs 13 and 14.
[74] Value Added Tax Act 1994, s 19; *Glenrothes Development Corporation v IRC* [1994] STC 74.
[75] FA 2003, Sch 4, paras 1 and 7.

27.32 The market value of shares or securities quoted in *The Stock Exchange Daily Official List* (except where, in consequence of special circumstances, prices quoted in that List are by themselves not a proper measure of market value) shall be as follows:

(a) the lower of the two prices shown in the quotations for the shares or securities in *The Stock Exchange Daily Official List* on the relevant date plus one-quarter of the difference between those two figures; or

(b) halfway between the highest and lowest prices at which bargains, other than bargains done at special prices, were recorded in the shares or securities for the relevant date,

choosing the amount under paragraph (a), if less than that under paragraph (b), or, if no such bargains were recorded for the relevant date, choosing the amount under paragraph (b) if less than that under paragraph (a). This does not apply to shares or securities for which The Stock Exchange provides a more active market elsewhere than on the London trading floor; and, if the London trading floor is closed on the relevant date, the market value shall be ascertained by reference to the latest previous date or earliest subsequent date on which it is open, whichever affords the lower market value.

27.33 In this Act 'market value', in relation to any rights of unit holders in any unit trust scheme the buying and selling prices of which are published regularly by the managers of the scheme, shall mean an amount equal to the buying price (that is the lower price) so published on the relevant date, or if none were published on that date, on the latest date before.

Unquoted shares and securities

27.34 For the purposes of a determination of the market value of unquoted shares it shall be assumed that, in the open market which is postulated for the purposes of that determination, there is available to any prospective purchaser of the asset in question all the information which a prudent prospective purchaser of the asset might reasonably require if he were proposing to purchase it from a willing vendor by private treaty and at arm's length.[76] For land valuation there will be the usual investigation of title.

Value determined for inheritance tax

27.35 Where on the death of any person inheritance tax is chargeable on the value of his estate immediately before his death and the value of an asset forming part of that estate has been ascertained (whether in any proceedings or otherwise) for the purposes of that tax, the value so ascertained shall be taken for the purposes of this Act to be the market value of that asset at the date of the death. It is difficult to see any realistic application of this provision since, at present, death and the market value of chargeable interests at the time of death has no relevance when computing the charge to stamp duty land tax.

---

[76] *Lynall v IRC* [1972] AC 680; *Caton v Couch* [1995] STC (SCD) 34; *Clark v Green* [1995] STC (SCD) 99.

Appendix 1

FINANCE ACT 2003

2003 c 14

PART 4
STAMP DUTY LAND TAX

Introduction

42 The tax

(1) A tax (to be known as 'stamp duty land tax') shall be charged in accordance with this Part on land transactions.

(2) The tax is chargeable –

    (a)   whether or not there is any instrument effecting the transaction,

    (b)   if there is such an instrument, whether or not it is executed in the United Kingdom, and

    (c)   whether or not any party to the transaction is present, or resident, in the United Kingdom.

(3) The tax is under the care and management of the Commissioners of Inland Revenue (referred to in this Part as 'the Board').

Land transactions

43 Land transactions

(1) In this Part a 'land transaction' means any acquisition of a chargeable interest.

As to the meaning of 'chargcable interest' see section 48.

(2) Except as otherwise provided, this Part applies however the acquisition is effected, whether by act of the parties, by order of a court or other authority, by or under any statutory provision or by operation of law.

(3) For the purposes of this Part –

    (a)   the creation of a chargeable interest is –

        (i)   an acquisition by the person becoming entitled to the interest created, and

        (ii)   a disposal by the person whose interest or right is subject to the interest created;

    (b)   the surrender or release of a chargeable interest is –

        (i)   an acquisition of that interest by any person whose interest or right is benefitted or enlarged by the transaction, and

        (ii)   a disposal by the person ceasing to be entitled to that interest;

    (c)   the variation of a chargeable interest other than a lease is –

        (i)   an acquisition of a chargeable interest by the person benefiting from the variation, and

      (ii)   a disposal of a chargeable interest by the person whose interest is subject to or limited by the variation.

   (d)   the variation of a lease is an acquisition and disposal of a chargeable interest only where –

      (i)   it takes effect, or is treated for the purposes of this Part, as the grant of a new lease, or

      (ii)   paragraph 15A of Schedule 17A (reduction of rent or term) applies.

(4) References in this Part to the 'purchaser' and 'vendor', in relation to a land transaction, are to the person acquiring and the person disposing of the subject-matter of the transaction.

These expressions apply even if there is no consideration given for the transaction.

(5) A person is not treated as a purchaser unless he has given consideration for, or is a party to, the transaction.

(6) References in this Part to the subject-matter of a land transaction are to the chargeable interest acquired (the 'main subject-matter'), together with any interest or right appurtenant or pertaining to it that is acquired with it.

Amendments: Finance Act 2004, ss 296, 326, Schs 39, 42.

44   Contract and conveyance

(1) This section applies where a contract for a land transaction is entered into under which the transaction is to be completed by a conveyance.

(2) A person is not regarded as entering into a land transaction by reason of entering into the contract, but the following provisions have effect.

(3) If the transaction is completed without previously having been substantially performed, the contract and the transaction effected on completion are treated as parts of a single land transaction.

In this case the effective date of the transaction is the date of completion.

(4) If the contract is substantially performed without having been completed, the contract is treated as if it were itself the transaction provided for in the contract.

In this case the effective date of the transaction is when the contract is substantially performed.

(5) A contract is 'substantially performed' when –

   (a)   the purchaser or person connected with the purchaser takes possession of the whole, or substantially the whole, of the subject-matter of the contract, or

   (b)   a substantial amount of the consideration is paid or provided.

(6) For the purposes of subsection (5)(a) –

   (a)   possession includes receipt of rents and profits or the right to receive them, and

   (b)   it is immaterial whether possession is taken under the contract or under a licence or lease of a temporary character.

(7) For the purposes of subsection (5)(b) a substantial amount of the consideration is paid or provided –

(a)   if none of the consideration is rent, where the whole or substantially the whole of the consideration is paid or provided;

(b)   if the only consideration is rent, when the first payment of rent is made;

(c)   if the consideration includes both rent and other consideration, when –

  (i)   the whole or substantially the whole of the consideration other than rent is paid or provided, or

  (ii)   the first payment of rent is made.

(8) Where subsection (4) applies and the contract is subsequently completed by a conveyance –

(a)   both the contract and the transaction effected on completion are notifiable transactions, and

(b)   tax is chargeable on the latter transaction to the extent (if any) that the amount of tax chargeable on it is greater than the amount of tax chargeable on the contract.

(9) Where subsection (4) applies and the contract is (to any extent) afterwards rescinded or annulled, or is for any other reason not carried into effect, the tax paid by virtue of that subsection shall (to that extent) be repaid by the Inland Revenue.

Repayment must be claimed by amendment of the land transaction return made in respect of the contract.

(9A) Where –

(a)   paragraph 12A of Schedule 17A applies (agreement for lease), or

(b)   paragraph 19(3) to (6) of Schedule 17A applies (missives of let etc in Scotland),

it applies in place of subsections (4), (8) and (9).

(10) In this section –

(a)   references to completion are to completion of the land transaction proposed, between the same parties, in substantial conformity with the contract; and

(b)   'contract' includes any agreement and 'conveyance' includes any instrument.

(11) Section 839 of the Taxes Act 1988 (connected persons) has effect for the purposes of this section.

Amendments: Finance Act 2004, s 296, Sch 39.

44A   Contract providing for conveyance to third party

(1) This section applies where a contract is entered into under which a chargeable interest is to be conveyed by one party to the contract (A) at the direction or request of the other (B) –

(a)   to a person (C) who is not a party to the contract, or

(b)   either to such a person or to B.

(2) B is not regarded as entering into a land transaction by reason of entering into the contract, but the following provisions have effect.

(3) If the contract is substantially performed B is treated for the purposes of this Part as acquiring a chargeable interest, and accordingly as entering into a land transaction.

The effective date of the transaction is when the contract is substantially performed.

(4) Where the contract is (to any extent) afterwards rescinded or annulled, or is for any other reason not carried into effect, the tax paid by virtue of subsection (3) shall (to that extent) be repaid by the Inland Revenue.

Repayment must be claimed by amendment of the land transaction return made in respect of the contract.

(5) Subject to subsection (6), section 44 (contract and conveyance) does not apply (except so far as it defines 'substantial performance') in relation to the contract.

(6) Where –

(a) this section applies by virtue of subsection (1)(b), and
(b) by reason of B's direction or request, A becomes obliged to convey a chargeable interest to B,

section 44 applies to that obligation as it applies to a contract for a land transaction that is to be completed by a conveyance.

(7) Section 44 applies in relation to any contract between B and C, in respect of the chargeable interest referred to in subsection (1) above, that is to be completed by a conveyance.

References to completion in that section, as it so applies, include references to conveyance by A to C of the subject matter of the contract between B and C

(8) In this section 'contract' includes any agreement and 'conveyance' includes any instrument.

Amendments: Finance Act 2004, s 296, Sch 39.

45   Contract and conveyance: effect of transfer of rights

(1) This section applies where –

(a) a contract for a land transaction ('the original contract') is entered into under which the transaction is to be completed by a conveyance,
(b) there is an assignment, subsale or other transaction (relating to the whole or part of the subject-matter of the original contract) as a result of which a person other than the original purchaser becomes entitled to call for a conveyance to him, and
(c) paragraph 12B of Schedule 17A (assignment of agreement for lease) does not apply.

References in the following provisions of this section to a transfer of rights are to any such assignment, subsale or other transaction, and references to the transferor and the transferee shall be read accordingly.

(2) The transferee is not regarded as entering into a land transaction by reason of the transfer of rights, but section 44 (contract and conveyance) has effect in accordance with the following provisions of this section.

(3) That section applies as if there were a contract for a land transaction (a 'secondary contract') under which –

(a) the transferee is the purchaser, and
(b) the consideration for the transaction is –

(i)   so much of the consideration under the original contract as is referable to the subject-matter of the transfer of rights and is to be given (directly or indirectly) by the transferee or a person connected with him, and

(ii)   the consideration given for the transfer of rights.

The substantial performance or completion of the original contract at the same time as, and in connection with, the substantial performance or completion of the secondary contract shall be disregarded except in a case where the secondary contract gives rise to a transaction that is exempt from charge by virtue of subsection (3) of section 73 (alternative property finance: land sold to financial institution and re-sold to individual).

(4) Where there are successive transfers of rights, subsection (3) has effect in relation to each of them.

The substantial performance or completion of the secondary contract arising from an earlier transfer of rights at the same time as, and in connection with, the substantial performance or completion of the secondary contract arising from a subsequent transfer of rights shall be disregarded.

(5) Where a transfer of rights relates to part only of the subject-matter of the original contract ('the relevant part') –

(a)   subsection (8)(b) of section 44 (restriction of charge to tax on subsequent conveyance) has effect as if the reference to the amount of tax chargeable on that contract were a reference to an appropriate proportion of that amount, and

(b)   a reference in the second sentence of subsection (3) above to the original contract, or a reference in subsection (4) above to the secondary contract arising from an earlier transfer of rights, is to that contract so far as relating to the relevant part (and that contract so far as not relating to the relevant part shall be treated as a separate contract).

(5A) In relation to a land transaction treated as taking place by virtue of subsection (3) –

(a)   references in Schedule 7 (group relief) to the vendor shall be read as references to the vendor under the original contract;

(b)   other references in this Part to the vendor shall be read, where the context permits, as referring to either the vendor under the original contract or the transferor.

(6) Section 839 of the Taxes Act 1988 (connected persons) applies for the purposes of subsection (3)(b)(i).

(7) In this section 'contract' includes any agreement and 'conveyance' includes any instrument.

Amendments: Finance Act 2004, ss 296, 326, Schs 39, 42; Finance (No 2) Act 2005, s 49, Sch 10.

45A   Contract providing for conveyance to third party: effect of transfer of rights

(1) This section applies where –

(a)   a contract ('the original contract') is entered into under which a chargeable interest is to be conveyed by one party to the contract (A) at the direction or request of the other (B) –

(i)   to a person (C) who is not a party to the contract, or

     (ii)   either to such a person or to B,
     and

(b)   there is an assignment or other transaction (relating to the whole or part of the subject-matter of the original contract) as a result of which a person (D) becomes entitled to exercise any of B's rights under the original contract in place of B.

References in the following provisions of this section to a transfer of rights are to any such assignment or other transaction.

(2) D is not regarded as entering into a land transaction by reason of the transfer of rights, but section 44A (contract providing for conveyance to third party) has effect in accordance with the following provisions of this section.

(3) That section applies as if –

(a)   D had entered into a contract (a 'secondary contract') in the same terms as the original contract except with D as a party instead of B, and

(b)   the consideration due from D under the secondary contract were –
     (i)   so much of the consideration under the original contract as is referable to the subject-matter of the transfer of rights and is to be given (directly or indirectly) by D or a person connected with him, and
     (ii)   the consideration given for the transfer of rights.

(4) The substantial performance of the original contract shall be disregarded if –

(a)   it occurs at the same time as, and in connection with, the substantial performance of the secondary contract, or

(b)   it occurs after the transfer of rights.

(5) Where there are successive transfers of rights, subsection (3) has effect in relation to each of them.

(6) The substantial performance of the secondary contract arising from an earlier transfer of rights shall be disregarded if –

(a)   it occurs at the same time as, and in connection with, the substantial performance of the secondary contract arising from a subsequent transfer of rights, or

(b)   it occurs after that subsequent transfer.

(7) Where a transfer of rights relates to only part of the subject matter of the original contract, or to only some of the rights under that contract –

(a)   a reference in subsection (3)(a) or (4) to the original contract, or a reference in subsection (6) to the secondary contract arising from an earlier transfer, is to that contract so far as relating to that part or those rights, and

(b)   that contract so far as not relating to that part or those rights shall be treated as a separate contract.

(8) The effective date of a land transaction treated as entered into by virtue of subsection (3) is not earlier than the date of the transfer of rights.

(9) In relation to a such a transaction –

(a)   references in Schedule 7 (group relief) to the vendor shall be read as references to A;

(b)   other references in this Part to the vendor shall be read, where the context permits, as referring to either A or B.

(10) Section 839 of the Taxes Act 1988 (connected persons) applies for the purposes of subsection (3)(b).

(11) In this section 'contract' includes any agreement.

Amendments: Finance Act 2004, s 296, Sch 39.

46 Options and rights of pre-emption

(1) The acquisition of –

  (a)   an option binding the grantor to enter into a land transaction, or

  (b)   a right of pre-emption preventing the grantor from entering into, or restricting the right of the grantor to enter into, a land transaction,

is a land transaction distinct from any land transaction resulting from the exercise of the option or right.

They may be 'linked transactions' (see section 108).

(2) The reference in subsection (1)(a) to an option binding the grantor to enter into a land transaction includes an option requiring the grantor either to enter into a land transaction or to discharge his obligations under the option in some other way.

(3) The effective date of the transaction in the case of the acquisition of an option or right such as is mentioned in subsection (1) is when the option or right is acquired (as opposed to when it becomes exercisable).

(4) Nothing in this section applies to so much of an option or right of pre-emption as constitutes or forms part of a land transaction apart from this section.

47 Exchanges

(1) Where a land transaction is entered into by the purchaser (alone or jointly) wholly or partly in consideration of another land transaction being entered into by him (alone or jointly) as vendor, this Part applies in relation to each transaction as if each were distinct and separate from the other (and they are not linked transactions within the meaning of section 108).

(2) A transaction is treated for the purposes of this Part as entered into by the purchaser wholly or partly in consideration of another land transaction being entered into by him as vendor in any case where an obligation to give consideration for a land transaction that a person enters into as purchaser is met wholly or partly by way of that person entering into another transaction as vendor.

(3) As to the amount of the chargeable consideration in the case of exchanges and similar transactions, see –

paragraphs 5 and 6 of Schedule 4 (exchanges, partition etc).

paragraph 17 of that Schedule (arrangements involving public or educational bodies)

Amendments: SI 2004/1096: Finance Act 2004, s 326, Sch 42: Finance Act 2007, s 76(1), (3).

Chargeable interests, chargeable transactions and chargeable consideration

48 Chargeable interests

(1) In this Part 'chargeable interest' means –

(a)   an estate, interest, right or power in or over land in the United Kingdom, or

(b)   the benefit of an obligation, restriction or condition affecting the value of any such estate, interest, right or power,

other than an exempt interest.

(2) The following are exempt interests –

(a)   any security interest;

(b)   a licence to use or occupy land;

(c)   in England and Wales or Northern Ireland –

(i)   a tenancy at will;

(ii)   an advowson, franchise or manor.

(3) In subsection (2) –

(a)   'security interest' means an interest or right (other than a rentcharge) held for the purpose of securing the payment of money or the performance of any other obligation; and

(b)   'franchise' means a grant from the Crown such as the right to hold a market or fair, or the right to take tolls.

(3A) Section 73B makes additional provision about exempt interests in relation to alternative finance arrangements.

(4) In the application of this Part in Scotland the reference in subsection (3)(a) to a rentcharge shall be read as a reference to a feu duty or a payment mentioned in section 56(1) of the Abolition of Feudal Tenure etc. (Scotland) Act 2000.

(5) The Treasury may by regulations provide that any other description of interest or right in relation to land in the United Kingdom is an exempt interest.

(6) The regulations may contain such supplementary, incidental and transitional provision as appears to the Treasury to be appropriate.

(7) This section has effect subject to subsection (3) of section 44A (contract and conveyance to third party) and to paragraph 15A of Schedule 17A (reduction of rent or term of lease).

Amendments: Finance Act 2004, ss 296, 297, Sch 39; Finance Act 2007, ss 73B, 75(2), (4)(a), (b).

49   Chargeable transactions

(1) A land transaction is a chargeable transaction if it is not a transaction that is exempt from charge.

(2) Schedule 3 provides for certain transactions to be exempt from charge.

Other transactions are exempt from charge under other provisions of this Part.

50   Chargeable consideration

(1) Schedule 4 makes provision as to the chargeable consideration for a transaction.

(2) The Treasury may by regulations amend or repeal the provisions of this Part relating to chargeable consideration and make such other provision as appears to them appropriate with respect to –

(a)   what is to count as chargeable consideration, or

(b)   the determination of the amount of chargeable consideration.

(3) The regulations may make different provision in relation to different descriptions of transaction or consideration and different circumstances.

51 Contingent, uncertain or unascertained consideration

(1) Where the whole or part of the chargeable consideration for a transaction is contingent, the amount or value of the consideration shall be determined for the purposes of this Part on the assumption that the outcome of the contingency will be such that the consideration is payable or, as the case may be, does not cease to be payable.

(2) Where the whole or part of the chargeable consideration for a transaction is uncertain or unascertained, its amount or value shall be determined for the purposes of this Part on the basis of a reasonable estimate.

(3) In this Part –

'contingent', in relation to consideration, means –
> (a) that it is to be paid or provided only if some uncertain future event occurs, or
> (b) that it is to cease to be paid or provided if some uncertain future event occurs; and

'uncertain', in relation to consideration, means that its amount or value depends on uncertain future events.

(4) This section has effect subject to –

section 80 (adjustment where contingency ceases or consideration is ascertained), and

section 90 (application to defer payment in case of contingent or uncertain consideration).

(5) This section applies in relation to chargeable consideration consisting of rent only to the extent that it is applied by paragraph 7 of Schedule 17A.

Amendments: Finance Act 2004, s 296, Sch 39.

52 Annuities etc: chargeable consideration limited to twelve years' payments

(1) This section applies to so much of the chargeable consideration for a land transaction as consists of an annuity payable –

- (a) for life, or
- (b) in perpetuity, or
- (c) for an indefinite period, or
- (d) for a definite period exceeding twelve years.

(2) For the purposes of this Part the consideration to be taken into account is limited to twelve years' annual payments.

(3) Where the amount payable varies, or may vary, from year to year, the twelve highest annual payments shall be taken.

No account shall be taken for the purposes of this Schedule of any provision for adjustment of the amount payable in line with the retail price index.

(4) References in this section to annual payments are to payments in respect of each successive period of twelve months beginning with the effective date of the transaction.

(5) For the purposes of this section the amount or value of any payment shall be determined (if necessary) in accordance with section 51 (contingent, uncertain or unascertained consideration).

(6) References in this section to an annuity include any consideration (other than rent) that falls to be paid or provided periodically.

References to payment shall be read accordingly.

(7) Where this section applies –

(a)   section 80 (adjustment where contingency ceases or consideration is ascertained) does not apply, and
(b)   no application may be made under section 90 (application to defer payment in case of contingent or uncertain consideration).

53   Deemed market value where transaction involves connected company

(1) This section applies where the purchaser is a company and –

(a)   the vendor is connected with the purchaser, or
(b)   some or all of the consideration for the transaction consists of the issue or transfer of shares in a company with which the vendor is connected.

(1A) The chargeable consideration for the transaction shall be taken to be not less than –

(a)   the market value of the subject-matter of the transaction as at the effective date of the transaction, and
(b)   if the acquisition is the grant of a lease at a rent, that rent.

(2) Section 839 of the Taxes Act 1988 (connected persons) has effect for the purposes of this section.

(3) In this section –

'company' means any body corporate;
'shares' includes stock and the reference to shares in a company includes a reference to securities issued by a company.

(4) Where this section applies paragraph 1 of Schedule 3 (exemption of transactions for which there is no chargeable consideration) does not apply.

But this section has effect subject to any other provision affording exemption or relief from stamp duty land tax.

(5) This section is subject to the exceptions provided for in section 54.

Amendments: Finance Act 2004, s 297.

54   Exceptions from deemed market value rule

(1) Section 53 (chargeable consideration: transaction with connected company) does not apply in the following cases.

In the following provisions 'the company' means the company that is the purchaser in relation to the transaction in question.

(2) Case 1 is where immediately after the transaction the company holds the property as trustee in the course of a business carried on by it that consists of or includes the management of trusts.

(3) Case 2 is where –

(a)   immediately after the transaction the company holds the property as trustee, and

(b)   the vendor is connected with the company only because of section 839(3) of the Taxes Act 1988.

(4) Case 3 is where –

(a)   the vendor is a company and the transaction is, or is part of, a distribution of the assets of that company (whether or not in connection with its winding up), and

(b)   it is not the case that –
(i)   the subject-matter of the transaction, or
(ii)   an interest from which that interest is derived,

has, within the period of three years immediately preceding the effective date of the transaction, been the subject of a transaction in respect of which group relief was claimed by the vendor.

Amount of tax chargeable

55   Amount of tax chargeable: general

(1) The amount of tax chargeable in respect of a chargeable transaction is a percentage of the chargeable consideration for the transaction.

(2) That percentage is determined by reference to whether the relevant land –

(a)   consists entirely of residential property (in which case Table A below applies), or

(b)   consists of or includes land that is not residential property (in which case Table B below applies),

and, in either case, by reference to the amount of the relevant consideration.

Table A: Residential

Relevant consideration	Percentage
Not more than £125,000	0%
More than £125,000 but not more than £250,000	1%
More than £250,000 but not more than £500,000	3%
More than £500,000	4%

Table B: Non-Residential or Mixed

Relevant consideration	Percentage
Not more than £150,000	0%
More than £150,000 but not more than £250,000	1%

More than £250,000 but not more than £500,000	3%
More than £500,000	4%

(3) For the purposes of subsection (2) –

(a)   the relevant land is the land an interest in which is the main subject-matter of the transaction, and

(b)   the relevant consideration is the chargeable consideration for the transaction,

subject as follows.

(4) If the transaction in question is one of a number of linked transactions –

(a)   the relevant land is any land an interest in which is the main subject-matter of any of those transactions, and

(b)   the relevant consideration is the total of the chargeable consideration for all those transactions.

(5) This section has effect subject to –

section 74 (exercise of collective rights by tenants of flats), and

section 75 (crofting community right to buy),

(which provide for the rate of tax to be determined by reference to a fraction of the relevant consideration).

(6) In the case of a transaction for which the whole or part of the chargeable consideration is rent this section has effect subject to section 56 and Schedule 5 (amount of tax chargeable: rent).

(7) References in this Part to the 'rate of tax' are to the percentage determined under this section.

Amendments: Finance Act 2006, s 162(1); Finance Act 2009, s 80(6), (7).

56   Amount of tax chargeable: rent

Schedule 5 provides for the calculation of the tax chargeable where the chargeable consideration for a transaction consists of or includes rent.

Reliefs

57   Disadvantaged areas relief

(1) Schedule 6 provides for relief in the case of transactions relating to land in a disadvantaged area.

(2) In that Schedule –

Part 1 defines 'disadvantaged area',
Part 2 relates to transactions where the land to which the transaction relates is wholly situated in a disadvantaged area,
Part 3 relates to transactions where the land to which the transaction relates is partly situated in a disadvantaged area, and
Part 4 contains supplementary provisions.

57A   Sale and leaseback arrangements

(1) The leaseback element of a sale and leaseback arrangement is exempt from charge if the qualifying conditions specified below are met.

(2) A 'sale and leaseback' arrangement under which –

    (a)   A transfers to B a major interest in land (the 'sale'), and

    (b)   out of that interest B grants a lease to A (the 'leaseback').

(3) The qualifying conditions are –

    (a)   that the sale transaction is entered into wholly or partly in consideration of the leaseback transaction being entered into,

    (b)   that the only other consideration (if any) for the sale is the payment of money or the assumption, satisfaction or release of a debt (or both),

    (c)   that the sale is not a transfer of rights within the meaning of section 45 (contract and conveyance: effect of transfer of rights) or 45A (contract providing for conveyance to third party: effect of transfer of rights), and

    (d)   where A and B are both bodies corporate at the effective date of the leaseback transaction, that they are not members of the same group for the purposes of group relief (see paragraph 1 of Schedule 7) at that date.

(4) In this section –

'debt' means an obligation, whether certain or contingent, to pay a sum of money either immediately or at a future date; and

'money' means money in sterling or another currency.

Amendments: Section inserted: Finance Act 2004, s 296, Sch 39.

58 . . .

58A   Relief for certain acquisitions of residential property

Schedule 6A provides for relief in the case of certain acquisitions of residential property.

Amendments: Section substituted: Finance Act 2004, s 296, Sch 39.

58B   Relief for new zero-carbon homes

(1) The Treasury may make regulations granting relief on the first acquisition of a dwelling which is a 'zero-carbon home'.

(2) For the purposes of this section –

    (a)   a building, or a part of a building, is a dwelling if it is constructed for use as a single dwelling, and

    (b)   'first acquisition', in relation to a dwelling, means its acquisition when it has not previously been occupied.

(3) For the purpose of subsection (2) land occupied or enjoyed with a dwelling as a garden or grounds is part of the dwelling.

(4) The regulations shall define 'zero-carbon home' by reference to specified aspects of the energy efficiency of a building; for which purpose 'energy efficiency' includes –

    (a)   consumption of energy,

    (b)   conservation of energy, and

    (c)   generation of energy.

(5) The relief may take the form of –

(a)	exemption from charge, or
(b)	a reduction in the amount of tax chargeable.

(6) Regulations under this section shall not have effect in relation to acquisitions on or after 1st October 2012.

(7) The Treasury may by order –

(a)	substitute a later date for the date in subsection (6);
(b)	make transitional provision, or provide savings, in connection with the effect of subsection (6).

Amendments: Section inserted: Finance Act 2007, s 19(1) : Finance Act 2008, s 93(1), (2), (7).

### 58C	Relief for new zero-carbon homes: supplemental

(1) Regulations under section 58B –

(a)	shall include provision about the method of claiming relief (including documents or information to be provided), and
(b)	in particular, shall include provision about the evidence to be adduced to show that a dwelling satisfies the definition of 'zero- carbon home'.

(2) Regulations made by virtue of subsection (1)(b) may, in particular –

(a)	refer to a scheme or process established by or for the purposes of an enactment about building;
(b)	establish or provide for the establishment of a scheme or process of certification;
(c)	specify, or provide for the approval of, one or more schemes or processes for certifying energy efficiency;
(d)	provide for the charging of fees of a reasonable amount in respect of services provided as part of a scheme or process of certification.

(3) In defining 'zero-carbon home' regulations under section 58B may include requirements which may be satisfied in relation to a dwelling either –

(a)	by features of the building which, or part of which, constitutes the dwelling, or
(b)	by other installations or utilities.

(4) Regulations under section 58B may modify the effect of section 108, or another provision of this Part about linked transactions, in relation to a set of transactions of which at least one is the first acquisition of a dwelling which is a zero-carbon home.

(5) In determining whether section 116(7) applies, and in the application of section 116(7), a transaction shall be disregarded if or in so far as it involves the first acquisition of a dwelling which is a zero-carbon home.

(6) Regulations under section 58B –

(a)	may provide for relief to be wholly or partly withdrawn if a dwelling ceases to be a zero-carbon home, and
(b)	may provide for the reduction or withholding of relief where a person acquires more than one zero-carbon home within a specified period.

(7) Regulations under section 58B may include provision for relief to be granted in respect of acquisitions occurring during a specified period before the regulations come into force.

Amendments: Section inserted: Finance Act 2007, s 19(1); Finance Act 2008, s 93(3)–(5), (6)(a), (b), (7).

59 . . .

60   Compulsory purchase facilitating development

(1) A compulsory purchase facilitating development is exempt from charge.

(2) In this section 'compulsory purchase facilitating development' means –

- (a) in relation to England and Wales or Scotland, the acquisition by a person of a chargeable interest in respect of which that person has made a compulsory purchase order for the purpose of facilitating development by another person;
- (b) in relation to Northern Ireland, the acquisition by a person of a chargeable interest by means of a vesting order made for the purpose of facilitating development by a person other than the person who acquires the interest.

(3) For the purposes of subsection (2)(a) it does not matter how the acquisition is effected (so that provision applies where the acquisition is effected by agreement).

(4) In subsection (2)(b) a 'vesting order' means an order made under any statutory provision to authorise the acquisition of land otherwise than by agreement.

(5) In this section 'development' –

- (a) in relation to England and Wales, has the same meaning as in the Town and Country Planning Act 1990 (c 8) (see section 55 of that Act);
- (b) in relation to Scotland, has the same meaning as in the Town and Country Planning (Scotland) Act 1997 (c 8) (see section 26 of that Act); and
- (c) in relation to Northern Ireland, has the same meaning as in the Planning (Northern Ireland) Order 1991 (1991/1220 (NI 11)) (see Article 11 of that Order).

61   Compliance with planning obligations

(1) A land transaction that is entered into in order to comply with a planning obligation or a modification of a planning obligation is exempt from charge if –

- (a) the planning obligation or modification is enforceable against the vendor,
- (b) the purchaser is a public authority, and
- (c) the transaction takes place within the period of five years beginning with the date on which the planning obligation was entered into or modified.

(2) In this section –

- (a) in relation to England and Wales –

'planning obligation' means either of the following –
- (a) a planning obligation within the meaning of section 106 of the Town and Country Planning Act 1990 that is entered into in accordance with subsection (9) of that section, or
- (b) a planning obligation within the meaning of section 299A of that Act that is entered into in accordance with subsection (2) of that section; and

'modification' of a planning obligation means modification as mentioned in section 106A(1) of that Act;

    (b)   in relation to Scotland, 'planning obligation' means an agreement made under section 75 or section 246 of the Town and Country Planning (Scotland) Act 1997;

    (c)   in relation to Northern Ireland –

'planning obligation' means a planning agreement within the meaning of Article 40 of the Planning (Northern Ireland) Order 1991 that is entered into accordance with paragraph (10) of that Article, and

'modification' of a planning obligation means modification as mentioned in Article 40A(1) of that Order.

(3) The following are public authorities for the purposes of subsection (1)(b) –

Government

A Minister of the Crown or government department

The Scottish Ministers

A Northern Ireland department

The Welsh Ministers, the First Minister for Wales and the Counsel General to the Welsh Assembly Government

Local government: England

A county or district council constituted under section 2 of the Local Government Act 1972 (c 70)

The council of a London borough

The Common Council of the City of London

The Greater London Authority

Transport for London

The Council of the Isles of Scilly

Local government: Wales

A county or county borough council constituted under section 21 of the Local Government Act 1972

Local government: Scotland

A council constituted under section 2 of the Local Government etc. (Scotland) Act 1994 (c 39)

Local government: Northern Ireland

A district council within the meaning of the Local Government Act (Northern Ireland) 1972 (c 9 (NI))

Health: England and Wales

A Strategic Health Authority established under section 13 of the National Health Service Act 2006

A Special Health Authority established under section 28 of that Act or section 22 of the National Health Service (Wales) Act 2006

A Primary Care Trust established under section 18 of the National Health Service Act 2006

A Local Health Board established under section 11 of the National Health Service (Wales) Act 2006

A National Health Service Trust established under section 25 of the National Health Service Act 2006 or section 18 of the National Health Service (Wales) Act 2006

Health: Scotland

The Common Services Agency established under section 10(1) of the National Health Service (Scotland) Act 1978 (c 29)

A Health Board established under section 2(1)(a) of that Act

A National Health Service Trust established under section 12A(1) of that Act

A Special Health Board established under section 2(1)(b) of that Act

Health: Northern Ireland

A Health and Social Services Board established under Article 16 of the Health and Personal Social Services (Northern Ireland) Order 1972 (SI 1972/1265 (NI 14))

A Health and Social Services Trust established under Article 10 of the Health and Personal Social Services (Northern Ireland) Order 1991 (SI 1991/194 (NI 1))

Other planning authorities

Any other authority that –

    (a)   is a local planning authority within the meaning of the Town and Country Planning Act 1990 (c 8), or

    (b)   is the planning authority for any of the purposes of the planning Acts within the meaning of the Town and Country Planning (Scotland) Act 1997 (c 8).

Prescribed persons

A person prescribed for the purposes of this section by Treasury order.

Amendments: Entries substituted: Government of Wales Act 2006, ss 46, 160(1), 161(4), (5), Sch 10, paras 62, 63; National Health Service (Consequential Provisions) Act 2006, ss 2, 8(2), Sch 1, paras 232, 233(a)–(e).

62   Group relief and reconstruction or acquisition relief

(1) Schedule 7 provides for relief from stamp duty land tax.

(2) In that Schedule –

Part 1 makes provision for group relief,

Part 2 makes provision for reconstruction and acquisition reliefs.

(3) Any relief under that Schedule must be claimed in a land transaction return or an amendment of such a return.

63 Demutualisation of insurance company

(1) A land transaction is exempt from charge if it is entered into for the purposes of or in connection with a qualifying transfer of the whole or part of the business of a mutual insurance company ('the mutual') to a company that has share capital ('the acquiring company').

(2) A transfer is a qualifying transfer if –

    (a)   it is a transfer of business consisting of the effecting or carrying out of contracts of insurance and takes place under an insurance business transfer scheme, or

    (b)   it is a transfer of business of a general insurance company carried on through a permanent establishment in the United Kingdom and takes place in accordance with authorisation granted outside the United Kingdom for the purposes of –

        (i)   Article 14 of the life assurance Directive, or

        (ii)   Article 12 of the 3rd non-life insurance Directive,

and, in either case, the requirements of subsections (3) and (4) are met in relation to the shares of a company ('the issuing company') which is either the acquiring company or a company of which the acquiring company is a wholly-owned subsidiary.

(3) Shares in the issuing company must be offered, under the scheme, to at least 90% of the persons who are members of the mutual immediately before the transfer.

(4) Under the scheme all of the shares in the issuing company that will be in issue immediately after the transfer has been made, other than shares that are to be or have been issued pursuant to an offer to the public, must be offered to the persons who (at the time of the offer) are –

    (a)   members of the mutual,

    (b)   persons who are entitled to become members of the mutual, or

    (c)   employees, former employees or pensioners of –

        (i)   the mutual, or

        (ii)   a wholly-owned subsidiary of the mutual.

(5) The Treasury may by regulations –

    (a)   amend subsection (3) by substituting a lower percentage for the percentage mentioned there;

    (b)   provide that any or all of the references in subsections (3) and (4) to members shall be construed as references to members of a class specified in the regulations.

Regulations under paragraph (b) may make different provision for different cases.

(6) For the purposes of this section a company is the wholly-owned subsidiary of another company ('the parent') if the company has no members except the parent and the parent's wholly-owned subsidiaries or persons acting on behalf of the parent or the parent's wholly-owned subsidiaries.

(7) In this section –

    'contract of insurance' has the meaning given by Article 3(1) of the Financial Services and Markets Act 2000 (Regulated Activities) Order 2001 (SI 2001/544);

'employee', in relation to a mutual insurance company or its wholly-owned subsidiary, includes any officer or director of the company or subsidiary and any other person taking part in the management of the affairs of the company or subsidiary;

'general insurance company' means a company that has permission under Part 4 of the Financial Services and Markets Act 2000 (c 8), or paragraph 15 of Schedule 3 to that Act (as a result of qualifying for authorisation under paragraph 12(1) of that Schedule), to effect or carry out contracts of insurance;

'insurance company' means a company that carries on the business of effecting or carrying out contracts of insurance;

'insurance business transfer scheme' has the same meaning as in Part 7 of the Financial Services and Markets Act 2000;

'the life assurance Directive' means the Council Directive of 5th November 2002 concerning life assurance (No 2002/83/EC);

'mutual insurance company' means an insurance company carrying on business without having any share capital;

'the 3rd non-life insurance Directive' means the Council Directive of 18th June 1992 on the co-ordination of laws, regulations and administrative provisions relating to direct insurance other than life insurance and amending Directives 73/239/EEC and 88/357/EEC (No 92/49/EEC);

'pensioner', in relation to a mutual insurance company or its wholly-owned subsidiary, means a person entitled (whether presently or prospectively) to a pension, lump sum, gratuity or other like benefit referable to the service of any person as an employee of the company or subsidiary.

64 Demutualisation of building society

A land transaction effected by section 97(6) or (7) of the Building Societies Act 1986 (c 53) (transfer of building society's business to a commercial company) is exempt from charge.

64A

Amendments: Repealed by Finance Act 2006, ss 166(1), (2), 178, Sch 26.

65 Incorporation of limited liability partnership

(1) A transaction by which a chargeable interest is transferred by a person ('the transferor') to a limited liability partnership in connection with its incorporation is exempt from charge if the following three conditions are met.

(2) The first condition is that the effective date of the transaction is not more than one year after the date of incorporation of the limited liability partnership.

(3) The second condition is that at the relevant time the transferor –

(a)   is a partner in a partnership comprised of all the persons who are or are to be members of the limited liability partnership (and no-one else), or

(b)   holds the interest transferred as nominee or bare trustee for one or more of the partners in such a partnership.

(4) The third condition is that –

(a)   the proportions of the interest transferred to which the persons mentioned in subsection (3)(a) are entitled immediately after the transfer are the same as those to which they were entitled at the relevant time, or

(b)   none of the differences in those proportions has arisen as part of a scheme or arrangement of which the main purpose, or one of the main purposes, is avoidance of liability to any duty or tax.

(5) In this section 'the relevant time' means –

(a)   where the transferor acquired the interest after the incorporation of the limited liability partnership, immediately after he acquired it, and

(b)   in any other case, immediately before its incorporation.

(6) In this section 'limited liability partnership' means a limited liability partnership formed under the Limited Liability Partnerships Act 2000 (c 12) or the Limited Liability Partnerships Act (Northern Ireland) 2002 (c 12 (NI)).

66   Transfers involving public bodies

(1) A land transaction entered into on, or in consequence of, or in connection with, a reorganisation effected by or under a statutory provision is exempt from charge if the purchaser and vendor are both public bodies.

(2) The Treasury may by order provide that a land transaction that is not entered into as mentioned in subsection (1) is exempt from charge if –

(a)   the transaction is effected by or under a prescribed statutory provision, and

(b)   either the purchaser or the vendor is a public body.

In this subsection 'prescribed' means prescribed in an order made under this subsection.

(3) A 'reorganisation' means changes involving –

(a)   the establishment, reform or abolition of one or more public bodies,

(b)   the creation, alteration or abolition of functions to be discharged or discharged by one or more public bodies, or

(c)   the transfer of functions from one public body to another.

(4) The following are public bodies for the purposes of this section –

Government, Parliament etc

A Minister of the Crown

The Scottish Ministers

A Northern Ireland department

The Welsh Ministers, the First Minister for Wales and the Counsel General to the Welsh Assembly Government

The Corporate Officer of the House of Lords

The Corporate Officer of the House of Commons

The Scottish Parliamentary Corporate Body

The Northern Ireland Assembly Commission

The National Assembly for Wales Commission

Local government: England

A county or district council constituted under section 2 of the Local Government Act 1972 (c 70)

The council of a London borough

The Greater London Authority

The Common Council of the City of London

The Council of the Isles of Scilly

Local government: Wales

A county or county borough council constituted under section 21 of the Local Government Act 1972

Local government: Scotland

A council constituted under section 2 of the Local Government etc. (Scotland) Act 1994 (c 39)

Local government: Northern Ireland

A district council within the meaning of the Local Government Act (Northern Ireland) 1972 (c 9 (NI))

Health: England and Wales

A Strategic Health Authority established under section 13 of the National Health Service Act 2006

A Special Health Authority established under section 28 of that Act or section 22 of the National Health Service (Wales) Act 2006

A Primary Care Trust established under section 18 of the National Health Service Act 2006

A Local Health Board established under section 11 of the National Health Service (Wales) Act 2006

A National Health Service Trust established under section 25 of the National Health Service Act 2006 or section 18 of the National Health Service (Wales) Act 2006

Health: Scotland

The Common Services Agency established under section 10(1) of the National Health Service (Scotland) Act 1978 (c 29)

A Health Board established under section 2(1)(a) of that Act

A National Health Service Trust established under section 12A(1) of that Act

A Special Health Board established under section 2(1)(b) of that Act

Health: Northern Ireland

A Health and Social Services Board established under Article 16 of the Health and Personal Social Services (Northern Ireland) Order 1972 (SI 1972/1265 (NI 14))

A Health and Social Services Trust established under Article 10 of the Health and Personal Social Services (Northern Ireland) Order 1991 (SI 1991/194 (NI 1))

Other planning authorities

Any other authority that –

(a)   is a local planning authority within the meaning of the Town and Country Planning Act 1990 (c 8), or

(b)   is the planning authority for any of the purposes of the planning Acts within the meaning of the Town and Country Planning (Scotland) Act 1997 (c 8).

Statutory bodies

A body (other than a company) that is established by or under a statutory provision for the purpose of carrying out functions conferred on it by or under a statutory provision.

Prescribed persons

A person prescribed for the purposes of this section by Treasury order

(5) In this section references to a public body include –

(a)   a company in which all the shares are owned by such a body, and

(b)   a wholly-owned subsidiary of such a company.

(6) In this section 'company' means a company as defined by section 1 of the Companies Act 2006.

Amendments: Finance (No 2) Act 2005, s 49, Sch 10, Pt 2, paras 17, 18, 22(1); Government of Wales Act 2006, ss 46, 160(1), 161(4), (5), Sch 10, paras 62, 64(a), (b); National Health Service (Consequential Provisions) Act 2006, ss 2, 8(2), Sch 1, paras 232, 234(a)–(e); SI 2009/1890.

67   Transfer in consequence of reorganisation of parliamentary constituencies

(1) Where –

(a)   an Order in Council is made under the Parliamentary Constituencies Act 1986 (c 56) (orders specifying new parliamentary constituencies), and

(b)   an existing local constituency association transfers a chargeable interest to –

(i)   a new association that is a successor to the existing association, or

(ii)   a related body that as soon as practicable transfers the interest or right to a new association that is a successor to the existing association,

the transfer, or where paragraph (b)(ii) applies each of the transfers, is exempt from charge.

(2) In relation to any such order as is mentioned in subsection (1)(a) –

(a)   'the date of the change' means the date on which the order comes into operation;

(b)   'former parliamentary constituency' means an area that, for the purposes of parliamentary elections, was a constituency immediately before that date but is no longer such a constituency after that date;

(c)   'new parliamentary constituency' means an area that, for the purposes of parliamentary elections, is such a constituency after that date but was not such a constituency immediately before that date.

(3) In relation to the date of the change –

(a)   'existing local constituency association' means a local constituency association whose area was the same, or substantially the same, as the area of a former parliamentary constituency or two or more such constituencies, and

(b)   'new association' means a local constituency association whose area is the same, or substantially the same, as that of a new parliamentary constituency or two or more such constituencies.

(4) In this section –

(a)   'local constituency association' means an unincorporated association (whether described as an association, a branch or otherwise) whose primary purpose is to further the aims of a political party in an area that at any time is or was the same or substantially the same as the area of a parliamentary constituency or two or more parliamentary constituencies, and

(b)   'related body', in relation to such an association, means a body (whether corporate or unincorporated) that is an organ of the political party concerned.

(5) For the purposes of this section a new association is a successor to an existing association if any part of the existing association's area is comprised in the new association's area.

68   Charities relief

(1) Schedule 8 provides for relief from stamp duty land tax for acquisitions by charities.

(2) Any relief under that Schedule must be claimed in a land transaction return or an amendment of such a return.

69   Acquisition by bodies established for national purposes

A land transaction is exempt from charge if the purchaser is any of the following –

(a)   the Historic Buildings and Monuments Commission for England;
(b)   the National Endowment for Science, Technology and the Arts;
(c)   the Trustees of the British Museum;
(d)   the Trustees of the National Heritage Memorial Fund;
(e)   the Trustees of the Natural History Museum.

70   Right to buy transactions, shared ownership leases etc

Schedule 9 makes provision for relief in the case of right to buy transactions, shared ownership leases and certain related transactions.

71   Certain acquisitions by registered social landlord

(A1) A land transaction under which the purchaser is a profit-making registered provider of social housing is exempt from charge if the transaction is funded with the assistance of a public subsidy.

(1) A land transaction under which the purchaser is a registered social landlord is exempt from charge if –

(a)   the registered social landlord is controlled by its tenants,
(b)   the vendor is a qualifying body, or
(c)   the transaction is funded with the assistance of a public subsidy.

(2) The reference in subsection (1)(a) to a registered social landlord 'controlled by its tenants' is to a registered social landlord the majority of whose board members are tenants occupying properties owned or managed by it.

'Board member', in relation to a registered social landlord, means –
- (a) if it is a company, a director of the company,
- (b) if it is a body corporate whose affairs are managed by its members, a member,
- (c) if it is body of trustees, a trustee,
- (d) if it is not within paragraphs (a) to (c), a member of the committee of management or other body to which is entrusted the direction of the affairs of the registered social landlord.

(3) In subsection (1)(b) 'qualifying body' means –

- (a) a registered social landlord,
- (b) a housing action trust established under Part 3 of the Housing Act 1988 (c 50),
- (c) a principal council within the meaning of the Local Government Act 1972 (c 70),
- (d) the Common Council of the City of London,
- (e) the Scottish Ministers,
- (f) a council constituted under section 2 of the Local Government etc (Scotland) Act 1994 (c 39),
- (g) Scottish Homes,
- (h) the Department for Social Development in Northern Ireland, or
- (i) the Northern Ireland Housing Executive.

(4) In this section 'public subsidy' means any grant or other financial assistance –

- (a) made or given by way of a distribution pursuant to section 25 of the National Lottery etc Act 1993 (c 39) (application of money by distributing bodies),
- (b) under section 18 of the Housing Act 1996 (c 52) (social housing grants),
- (c) under section 126 of the Housing Grants, Construction and Regeneration Act 1996 (c 53) (financial assistance for regeneration and development),
- (ca) under section 19 of the Housing and Regeneration Act 2008 (financial assistance by the Homes and Communities Agency),
- (d) under section 2 of the Housing (Scotland) Act 1988 (c 43) (general functions of the Scottish Ministers), or
- (e) under Article 33 or 33A of the Housing (Northern Ireland) Order 1992 (SI 1992/1725 (NI 15)).

Amendments: SI 2006/3337; Housing and Regeneration Act 2008, s 56, Sch 8, paras 78, 79; SI 2008/3068; Finance Act 2009, s 81(1)–(4), (8).

71A Alternative property finance: land sold to financial institution and leased to individual

(1) This section applies where arrangements are entered into between a person and a financial institution under which –

- (a) the institution purchases a major interest in land or an undivided share of a major interest in land ('the first transaction'),
- (b) where the interest purchased is an undivided share, the major interest is held on trust for the institution and the person as beneficial tenants in common,

(c) the institution (or the person holding the land on trust as mentioned in paragraph (b)) grants to the person out of the major interest a lease (if the major interest is freehold) or a sub-lease (if the major interest is leasehold) ('the second transaction'), and

(d) the institution and the person enter into an agreement under which the person has a right to require the institution or its successor in title to transfer to the person (in one transaction or a series of transactions) the whole interest purchased by the institution under the first transaction.

(2) The first transaction is exempt from charge if the vendor is –

(a) the person, or

(b) another financial institution by whom the interest was acquired under arrangements of the kind mentioned in subsection (1) entered into between it and the person.

(3) The second transaction is exempt from charge if the provisions of this Part relating to the first transaction are complied with (including the payment of any tax chargeable).

(4) Any transfer to the person that results from the exercise of the right mentioned in subsection (1)(d) ('a further transaction') is exempt from charge if –

(a) the provisions of this Part relating to the first and second transactions are complied with, and

(b) at all times between the second transaction and the further transaction –

    (i) the interest purchased under the first transaction is held by a financial institution so far as not transferred by a previous further transaction, and

    (ii) the lease or sub-lease granted under the second transaction is held by the person.

(5) The agreement mentioned in subsection (1)(d) is not to be treated –

(a) as substantially performed unless and until the whole interest purchased by the institution under the first transaction has been transferred (and accordingly section 44(5) does not apply), or

(b) as a distinct land transaction by virtue of section 46 (options and rights of pre-emption).

(7) A further transaction that is exempt from charge by virtue of subsection (4) is not a notifiable transaction unless the transaction involves the transfer to the person of the whole interest purchased by the institution under the first transaction, so far as not transferred by a previous further transaction.

(8) In this section 'financial institution' has the meaning given by section 46 of the Finance Act 2005 (alternative finance arrangements).

(9) References in this section to a person shall be read, in relation to times after the death of the person concerned, as references to his personal representatives.

(10) This section does not apply in relation to land in Scotland.

Amendments: Inserted by the Finance Act 2005, s 94, Sch 8; Finance Act 2006, ss 168(1), (2), 178, Sch 26; Finance Act 2007, s 75(3), (4)(a), (b).

72   Alternative property finance: land sold to financial institution and leased to individual

(1) This section applies where arrangements are entered into between a person and a financial institution under which the institution –

    (a)   purchases a major interest in land ('the first transaction'),

    (b)   grants to the person out of that interest a lease (if the interest acquired is the interest of the owner) or a sub-lease (if the interest acquired is the tenant's right over or interest in a property subject to a lease) ('the second transaction'), and

    (c)   enters into an agreement under which the person has a right to require the institution to transfer the major interest purchased by the institution under the first transaction.

(2) The first transaction is exempt from charge if the vendor is –

    (a)   the person, or

    (b)   another financial institution by whom the interest was acquired under arrangements of the kind mentioned in subsection (1) entered into between it and the person.

(3) The second transaction is exempt from charge if the provisions of this Part relating to the first transaction are complied with (including the payment of any tax chargeable).

(4) A transfer to the person that results from the exercise of the right mentioned in subsection (1)(c) ('the third transaction') is exempt from charge if –

    (a)   the provisions of this Part relating to the first and second transactions are complied with, and

    (b)   at all times between the second and third transactions –

        (i)   the interest purchased under the first transaction is held by a financial institution, and

        (ii)   the lease or sub-lease granted under the second transaction is held by the person.

(5) The agreement mentioned in subsection (1)(c) is not to be treated –

    (a)   as substantially performed unless and until the third transaction is entered into (and accordingly section 44(5) does not apply), or

    (b)   as a distinct land transaction by virtue of section 46 (options and rights of pre-emption).

(7) In this section 'financial institution' has the meaning given by section 46 of the Finance Act 2005 (alternative finance arrangements).

(9) References in this section to a person shall be read, in relation to times after the death of the person concerned, as references to his personal representatives.

(10) This section applies only in relation to land in Scotland.

Amendments: Finance Act 2005, ss 94, 104, Schs 8, 11; Finance Act 2006, ss 168(1), (2), 178, Sch 26; Finance Act 2007, s 75(3), (4)(a), (b).

72A   Alternative property finance in Scotland: land sold to financial institution and individual in common

(1) This section applies where arrangements are entered into between a person and a financial institution under which –

(a)   the institution and the person purchase a major interest in land as owners in common ('the first transaction'),

(b)   the institution and the person enter into an agreement under which the person has a right to occupy the land exclusively ('the second transaction'), and

(c)   the institution and the person enter into an agreement under which the person has a right to require the institution to transfer to the person (in one transaction or a series of transactions) the whole interest purchased under the first transaction.

(2) The first transaction is exempt from charge if the vendor is –

(a)   the person, or

(b)   another financial institution by whom the interest was acquired under arrangements of the kind mentioned in subsection (1) entered into between it and the person.

(3) The second transaction is exempt from charge if the provisions of this Part relating to the first transaction are complied with (including the payment of any tax chargeable).

(4) Any transfer to the person that results from the exercise of the right mentioned in subsection (1)(c) ('a further transaction') is exempt from charge if –

(a)   the provisions of this Part relating to the first transaction are complied with, and

(b)   at all times between the first and the further transaction –
 (i)   the interest purchased under the first transaction is held by a financial institution and the person as owners in common, and
 (ii)   the land is occupied by the person under the agreement mentioned in subsection (1)(b).

(5) The agreement mentioned in subsection (1)(c) is not to be treated –

(a)   as substantially performed unless and until the whole interest purchased by the institution under the first transaction has been transferred (and accordingly section 44(5) does not apply), or

(b)   as a distinct land transaction by virtue of section 46 (options and rights of pre-emption).

(7) A further transaction that is exempt from charge by virtue of subsection (4) is not a notifiable transaction unless the transaction involves the transfer to the person of the whole interest purchased by the institution under the first transaction, so far as not transferred by a previous further transaction.

(8) In this section 'financial institution' has the meaning given by section 46 of the Finance Act 2005 (alternative finance arrangements).

(9) References in this section to a person shall be read, in relation to times after the death of the person concerned, as references to his personal representatives.

(10) This section applies only in relation to land in Scotland.

Amendments: Finance Act 2005, s 94, Sch 8; Finance Act 2006, s 168(1), (2); Finance Act 2007, s 75(3), (4)(a), (b).

73   Alternative property finance: land sold to financial institution and re-sold to individual

(1) This section applies where arrangements are entered into between a person and a financial institution under which –

(a) the institution –
    (i) purchases a major interest in land ('the first transaction'), and
    (ii) sells that interest to the person ('the second transaction'), and
(b) the person grants the institution a legal mortgage over that interest.

(2) The first transaction is exempt from charge if the vendor is –

(a) the person concerned, or
(b) another financial institution by whom the interest was acquired under other arrangements of the kind mentioned in section 71A(1), 72(1) or 72A(1) entered into between it and the person.

(3) The second transaction is exempt from charge if the financial institution complies with the provisions of this Part relating to the first transaction (including the payment of any tax chargeable on a chargeable consideration that is not less than the market value of the interest and, in the case of the grant of a lease at a rent, the rent).

(5) In this section –

(a) 'financial institution' has the meaning given by section 46 of the Finance Act 2005 (alternative finance arrangements);
(b) 'legal mortgage' –
    (i) in relation to land in England or Wales, means a legal mortgage as defined in section 205(1)(xvi) of the Law of Property Act 1925 (c 20);
    (ii) in relation to land in Scotland, means a standard security;
    (iii) in relation to land in Northern Ireland, means a mortgage by conveyance of a legal estate or by demise or sub-demise or a charge by way of legal mortgage.

(6) References in this section to a person shall be read, in relation to times after the death of the person concerned, as references to his personal representatives.

Amendments: Finance Act 2005, s 94, Sch 8; Finance Act 2006, s 168(1)–(3); Finance Act 2007, s 75(3), (4)(a), (b).

73A   Sections 71A to 73: relationship with Schedule 7

Sections 71A to 73 do not apply to arrangements in which the first transaction is exempt from charge by virtue of Schedule 7.

Amendments: Inserted by Finance Act 2006, s 168(4); Finance Act 2008, s 155(1), (2).

73AB   Sections 71A to 72A: arrangements to transfer control of financial institution

(1) Section 71A, 72 or 72A does not apply to alternative finance arrangements if those arrangements, or any connected arrangements, include arrangements for a person to acquire control of the relevant financial institution.

(2) That includes arrangements for a person to acquire control of the relevant financial institution only if one or more conditions are met (such as the happening of an event or doing of an act).

(3) In this section –

'alternative finance arrangements' means the arrangements referred to in section 71A(1), 72(1) or 72A(1);
'arrangements' includes any agreement, understanding, scheme, transaction or series of transactions (whether or not legally enforceable);

'connected arrangements' means any arrangements entered into in connection with the making of the alternative finance arrangements (including arrangements involving one or more persons who are not parties to the alternative finance arrangements);

'relevant financial institution' means the financial institution which enters into the alternative finance arrangements.

(4) Section 840 of the Taxes Act 1988 applies for the purposes of determining who has control of the relevant financial institution.

Amendments: Inserted by Finance Act 2008, s 155(1), (3), (4).

73B   Exempt interests

(1) An interest held by a financial institution as a result of the first transaction within the meaning of section 71A(1)(a), 72(1)(a) or 72A(1)(a) is an exempt interest for the purposes of stamp duty land tax.

(2) That interest ceases to be an exempt interest if –

    (a)   the lease or agreement mentioned in section 71A(1)(c), 72(1)(b) or 72A(1)(b) ceases to have effect, or

    (b)   the right under section 71A(1)(d), 72(1)(c) or 72A(1)(c) ceases to have effect or becomes subject to a restriction.

(3) Subsection (1) does not apply if the first transaction is exempt from charge by virtue of Schedule 7.

(4) Subsection (1) does not make an interest exempt in respect of –

    (a)   the first transaction itself, or

    (b)   a further transaction or third transaction within the meaning of section 71A(4), 72(4) or 72A(4).

Amendments: Inserted by Finance Act 2007, s 75(1), (4)(a), (b).

73C   Alternative finance investment bonds

Schedule 61 to the Finance Act 2009 makes provision for relief from charge in the case of arrangements falling within section 48A of the Finance Act 2005 (alternative finance investment bonds).

Amendments: Inserted by Finance Act 2009, s 123, Sch 61, Pt 4, paras 24, 25.

74   Exercise of collective rights by tenants of flats

(1) This section applies where a chargeable transaction is entered into by a person or persons nominated or appointed by qualifying tenants of flats contained in premises in exercise of –

    (a)   a right under Part 1 of the Landlord and Tenant Act 1987 (right of first refusal), or

    (b)   a right under Chapter 1 of Part 1 of the Leasehold Reform, Housing and Urban Development Act 1993 (right to collective enfranchisement).

(2) The rate of tax is determined by reference to the fraction of the relevant consideration produced by dividing the total amount of that consideration by the number of qualifying flats contained in the premises.

(3) The tax chargeable is then determined by applying that rate to the chargeable consideration for the transaction.

(4) In this section –

'flat' and 'qualifying tenant' have the same meaning as in the Chapter or Part of the Act conferring the right being exercised;
'qualifying flat' means a flat that is held by a qualifying tenant who is participating in the exercise of the right.

(5) References in this section to the relevant consideration have the same meaning as in section 55.

Amendments: Inserted by Finance Act 2009, s 80(1)–(3)(a), (b), (4), (5), (7).

75   Crofting community right to buy

(1) This section applies where –

(a)   a chargeable transaction is entered into in pursuance of the crofting community right to buy, and
(b)   under that transaction two or more crofts are being bought.

(2) In that case, the rate of tax is determined by reference to the fraction of the relevant consideration produced by dividing the total amount of that consideration by the number of crofts being bought.

(3) The tax chargeable is then determined by applying that rate to the amount of the chargeable consideration for the transaction in question.

(4) In this section 'crofting community right to buy' means the right exercisable by a crofting community body under Part 3 of the Land Reform (Scotland) Act 2003 (asp 2).

(5) References in this section to the relevant consideration have the same meaning as in section 55.

75A   Anti-avoidance

(1) This section applies where –

(a)   one person (V) disposes of a chargeable interest and another person (P) acquires either it or a chargeable interest deriving from it,
(b)   a number of transactions (including the disposal and acquisition) are involved in connection with the disposal and acquisition ('the scheme transactions'), and
(c)   the sum of the amounts of stamp duty land tax payable in respect of the scheme transactions is less than the amount that would be payable on a notional land transaction effecting the acquisition of V's chargeable interest by P on its disposal by V.

(2) In subsection (1) 'transaction' includes, in particular –

(a)   a non-land transaction,
(b)   an agreement, offer or undertaking not to take specified action,
(c)   any kind of arrangement whether or not it could otherwise be described as a transaction, and
(d)   a transaction which takes place after the acquisition by P of the chargeable interest.

(3) The scheme transactions may include, for example –

(a) the acquisition by P of a lease deriving from a freehold owned or formerly owned by V;
(b) a sub-sale to a third person;
(c) the grant of a lease to a third person subject to a right to terminate;
(d) the exercise of a right to terminate a lease or to take some other action;
(e) an agreement not to exercise a right to terminate a lease or to take some other action;
(f) the variation of a right to terminate a lease or to take some other action.

(4) Where this section applies –

(a) any of the scheme transactions which is a land transaction shall be disregarded for the purposes of this Part, but
(b) there shall be a notional land transaction for the purposes of this Part effecting the acquisition of V's chargeable interest by P on its disposal by V.

(5) The chargeable consideration on the notional transaction mentioned in subsections (1)(c) and (4)(b) is the largest amount (or aggregate amount) –

(a) given by or on behalf of any one person by way of consideration for the scheme transactions, or
(b) received by or on behalf of V (or a person connected with V within the meaning of section 839 of the Taxes Act 1988) by way of consideration for the scheme transactions.

(6) The effective date of the notional transaction is –

(a) the last date of completion for the scheme transactions, or
(b) if earlier, the last date on which a contract in respect of the scheme transactions is substantially performed.

(7) This section does not apply where subsection (1)(c) is satisfied only by reason of –

(a) sections 71A to 73, or
(b) a provision of Schedule 9.

Amendments: Inserted by Finance Act 2007, s 71(1)–(3); SI 2006/3237.

75B Anti-avoidance: incidental transactions

(1) In calculating the chargeable consideration on the notional transaction for the purposes of section 75A(5), consideration for a transaction shall be ignored if or in so far as the transaction is merely incidental to the transfer of the chargeable interest from V to P.

(2) A transaction is not incidental to the transfer of the chargeable interest from V to P –

(a) if or in so far as it forms part of a process, or series of transactions, by which the transfer is effected,
(b) if the transfer of the chargeable interest is conditional on the completion of the transaction, or
(c) if it is of a kind specified in section 75A(3).

(3) A transaction may, in particular, be incidental if or in so far as it is undertaken only for a purpose relating to –

(a) the construction of a building on property to which the chargeable interest relates,

(b) the sale or supply of anything other than land, or

(c) a loan to P secured by a mortgage, or any other provision of finance to enable P, or another person, to pay for part of a process, or series of transactions, by which the chargeable interest transfers from V to P.

(4) In subsection (3) –

(a) paragraph (a) is subject to subsection (2)(a) to (c),

(b) paragraph (b) is subject to subsection (2)(a) and (c), and

(c) paragraph (c) is subject to subsection (2)(a) to (c).

(5) The exclusion required by subsection (1) shall be effected by way of just and reasonable apportionment if necessary.

(6) In this section a reference to the transfer of a chargeable interest from V to P includes a reference to a disposal by V of an interest acquired by P.

Amendments: Inserted by Finance Act 2007, s 71(1)–(3); SI 2006/3237.

75C   Anti-avoidance: supplemental

(1) A transfer of shares or securities shall be ignored for the purposes of section 75A if but for this subsection it would be the first of a series of scheme transactions.

(2) The notional transaction under section 75A attracts any relief under this Part which it would attract if it were an actual transaction (subject to the terms and restrictions of the relief).

(3) The notional transaction under section 75A is a land transaction entered into for the purposes of or in connection with the transfer of an undertaking or part for the purposes of paragraphs 7 and 8 of Schedule 7, if any of the scheme transactions is entered into for the purposes of or in connection with the transfer of the undertaking or part.

(4) In the application of section 75A(5) no account shall be taken of any amount paid by way of consideration in respect of a transaction to which any of sections 60, 61, 63, 64, 65, 66, 67, 69, 71, 74 and 75, or a provision of Schedule 6A or 8, applies.

(5) In the application of section 75A(5) an amount given or received partly in respect of the chargeable interest acquired by P and partly in respect of another chargeable interest shall be subjected to just and reasonable apportionment.

(6) Section 53 applies to the notional transaction under section 75A.

(7) Paragraph 5 of Schedule 4 applies to the notional transaction under section 75A.

(8) For the purposes of section 75A –

(a) an interest in a property-investment partnership (within the meaning of paragraph 14 of Schedule 15) is a chargeable interest in so far as it concerns land owned by the partnership, and

(b) where V or P is a partnership, Part 3 of Schedule 15 applies to the notional transaction as to the transfer of a chargeable interest from or to a partnership.

(9) For the purposes of section 75A a reference to an amount of consideration includes a reference to the value of consideration given as money's worth.

(10) Stamp duty land tax paid in respect of a land transaction which is to be disregarded by virtue of section 75A(4)(a) is taken to have been paid in respect of the notional transaction by virtue of section 75A(4)(b).

(11) The Treasury may by order provide for section 75A not to apply in specified circumstances.

(12) An order under subsection (11) may include incidental, consequential or transitional provision and may make provision with retrospective effect.

Amendments: Inserted by Finance Act 2007, s 71(1)–(3); SI 2006/3237.

Returns and other administrative matters

76 Duty to deliver land transaction return

(1) In the case of every notifiable transaction the purchaser must deliver a return (a 'land transaction return') to the Inland Revenue before the end of the period of 30 days after the effective date of the transaction.

(2) The Inland Revenue may by regulations amend subsection (1) so as to require a land transaction return to be delivered before the end of such shorter period after the effective date of the transaction as may be prescribed or, if the regulations so provide, on that date.

(3) A land transaction return in respect of a chargeable transaction must –

   (a) include an assessment (a 'self-assessment') of the tax that, on the basis of the information contained in the return, is chargeable in respect of the transaction.

Amendments: Inserted by Finance Act 2007, ss 80(1), (2), (9)(a), 114, Sch 27, Pt 4(4).

77 Notifiable transactions

(1) A land transaction is notifiable if it is –

   (a) an acquisition of a major interest in land that does not fall within one or more of the exceptions in section 77A,
   (b) an acquisition of a chargeable interest other than a major interest in land where there is chargeable consideration in respect of which tax is chargeable at a rate of 1% or higher or would be so chargeable but for a relief,
   (c) a land transaction that a person is treated as entering into by virtue of section 44A(3), or
   (d) a notional land transaction under section 75A.

(2) This section has effect subject to –

   (a) sections 71A(7) and 72A(7), and
   (b) paragraph 30 of Schedule 15.

(3) In this section 'relief' does not include an exemption from charge under Schedule 3.

Amendments: Finance Act 2004, ss 296, 298(1), (2), 326, Schs 39, 42; Finance Act 2006, s 164(1); substituted by Finance Act 2008, s 94(1), (2), (5).

77A Exceptions for certain acquisitions of major interests in land

(1) The exceptions referred to in section 77(1)(a) are as follows.

   1   An acquisition which is exempt from charge under Schedule 3.

2   An acquisition (other than the grant, assignment or surrender of a lease) where the chargeable consideration for that acquisition, together with the chargeable consideration for any linked transactions, is less than £40,000.

3   The grant of a lease for a term of 7 years or more where –
      (a)   any chargeable consideration other than rent is less than £40,000, and
      (b)   the relevant rent is less than £1,000.

4   The assignment or surrender of a lease where –
      (a)   the lease was originally granted for a term of 7 years or more, and
      (b)   the chargeable consideration for the assignment or surrender is less than £40,000.

5   The grant of a lease for a term of less than 7 years where the chargeable consideration does not exceed the zero rate threshold.

6   The assignment or surrender of a lease where –
      (a)   the lease was originally granted for a term of less than 7 years, and
      (b)   the chargeable consideration for the assignment or surrender does not exceed the zero rate threshold.

(2) Chargeable consideration for an acquisition does not exceed the zero rate threshold if it does not consist of or include –

(a)   any amount in respect of which tax is chargeable at a rate of 1% or higher, or
(b)   any amount in respect of which tax would be so chargeable but for a relief.

(3) In this section –

'annual rent' has the meaning given in paragraph 9A of Schedule 5,
'relevant rent' means –
      (a)   the annual rent, or
      (b)   in the case of the grant of a lease to which paragraph 11 or 19 of Schedule 15 applies, the relevant chargeable proportion of the annual rent (as calculated in accordance with that paragraph), and

'relief' does not include an exemption from charge under Schedule 3.

Amendments: Inserted by Finance Act 2008, s 94(1), (2), (5).

78 Returns, enquiries, assessments and related matters

(1) Schedule 10 has effect with respect to land transaction returns, assessments and related matters.

(2) In that Schedule –

Part 1 contains general provisions about returns;

Part 2 imposes a duty to keep and preserve records;

Part 3 makes provision for enquiries into returns;

Part 4 provides for a Revenue determination if no return is delivered;

Part 5 provides for Revenue assessments;

Part 6 provides for relief in case of excessive assessment; and

Part 7 provides for appeals against Revenue decisions on tax.

(3) The Treasury may by regulations make such amendments of that Schedule, and such consequential amendments of any other provisions of this Part, as appear to them to be necessary or expedient from time to time.

78A Disclosure of information contained in land transaction returns

(1) Relevant information contained in land transaction returns delivered under section 76 (whether before or after the commencement of this section) is to be available for use –

    (a)   by listing officers appointed under section 20 of the Local Government Finance Act 1992, for the purpose of facilitating the compilation and maintenance by them of valuation lists in accordance with Chapter 2 of Part 1 of that Act,

    (b)   as evidence in an appeal by virtue of section 24(6) of that Act to a valuation tribunal established under Schedule 11 to the Local Government Finance Act 1988,

    (c)   by the Commissioner of Valuation for Northern Ireland, for the purpose of maintaining a valuation list prepared, and from time to time altered, by him in accordance with Part 3 of the Rates (Northern Ireland) Order 1977, and

    (d)   by such other persons or for such other purposes as the Treasury may by regulations prescribe.

(2) In this section, 'relevant information' means any information of the kind mentioned in paragraph 1(4) of Schedule 10 (information corresponding to particulars required under previous legislation).

(3) The Treasury may by regulations amend the definition of relevant information in subsection (2).

(4) In this section 'valuation tribunal' means –

    (a)   in relation to England: the Valuation Tribunal for England;

    (b)   in relation to Wales: a valuation tribunal established under paragraph 1 of Schedule 11 to the Local Government Finance Act 1988.

Amendments: Inserted by Finance (No 2) Act 2005, s 48(1); SI 2009/2094; Local Government and Public Involvement in Health Act 2007, ss 220(1), 241, Sch 16, para 9(1)–(3), Sch 18, Pt 17; SI 2008/3110.

79 Registration of land transactions etc

(1) A land transaction to which this section applies, or (as the case may be) a document effecting or evidencing a land transaction to which this section applies, shall not be registered, recorded or otherwise reflected in an entry made –

    (a)   in England and Wales, in the register of title maintained by the Chief Land Registrar,

    (b)   in Scotland, in any register maintained by the Keeper of the Registers of Scotland (other than the Register of Community Interests in Land), or

    (c)   in Northern Ireland, in any register maintained by the Land Registry of Northern Ireland or in the Registry of Deeds for Northern Ireland,

unless there is produced, together with the relevant application, a certificate as to compliance with the requirements of this Part in relation to the transaction or such information about compliance as the Commissioners for Her Majesty's Revenue and Customs may specify in regulations.

This does not apply where the entry is required to be made without any application or so far as the entry relates to an interest or right other than the chargeable interest acquired by the purchaser under the land transaction that gives rise to the application.

(2) This section applies to every notifiable land transaction other than a transaction treated as taking place –

    (a)   under subsection (4) of section 44 (contract and conveyance) or under that section as it applies by virtue of –
        (i)   section 45 (contract and conveyance: effect of transfer of rights), or
        (ii)   paragraph 12B of Schedule 17A (assignment of agreement for lease),
    (b)   under subsection (3) of section 44A (contract providing for conveyance to third party) or under that section as it applies by virtue of section 45A (contract providing for conveyance to third party: effect of transfer of rights),
    (c)   under paragraph 12A(2) or 19(3) of Schedule 17A (agreement for lease), or
    (d)   under paragraph 13 (increase of rent) or 15A (reduction of rent or term) of that Schedule.

In this subsection 'contract' includes any agreement and 'conveyance' includes any instrument.

(2A) Subsection (1), so far as relating to the entry of a notice under section 34 of the Land Registration Act 2002 or section 38 of the Land Registration Act (Northern Ireland) 1970 (notice in respect of interest affecting registered land), does not apply where the land transaction in question is the variation of a lease.

(3) The certificate referred to in subsection (1) must be –

    (a)   a certificate by the Inland Revenue (a 'Revenue certificate') that a land transaction return has been delivered in respect of the transaction.

(4) The Inland Revenue may make provision by regulations about Revenue certificates.

The regulations may, in particular –

    (a)   make provision as to the conditions to be met before a certificate is issued;
    (b)   prescribe the form and content of the certificate;
    (c)   make provision about the issue of duplicate certificates if the original is lost or destroyed;
    (d)   provide for the issue of multiple certificates where a return is made relating to more than one transaction.

(5) Part 2 of Schedule 11 imposes a duty to keep and preserve records in respect of transactions that are not notifiable.

(6) The registrar (in Scotland, the Keeper of the Registers of Scotland) –

    (a)   shall allow the Inland Revenue to inspect any certificates produced to him under this section and in his possession, and
    (b)   may enter into arrangements for affording the Inland Revenue other information and facilities for verifying that the requirements of this Part have been complied with.

Amendments: Finance Act 2004, ss 296, 297(1), (5)–(7), 298(1), (3), Sch 39; Finance (No 2) Act 2005, s 47(2); Finance Act 2008, s 94(1), (3)–(5), Sch 30, paras 1, 2(1)–(4).

80   Adjustment where contingency ceases or consideration is ascertained

(1) Where section 51 (contingent, uncertain or unascertained consideration) applies in relation to a transaction and –

    (a)   in the case of contingent consideration, the contingency occurs or it becomes clear that it will not occur, or

(b) in the case of uncertain or unascertained consideration, an amount relevant to the calculation of the consideration, or any instalment of consideration, becomes ascertained,

the following provisions have effect to require or permit reconsideration of how this Part applies to the transaction (and to any transaction in relation to which it is a linked transaction).

(2) If the effect of the new information is that a transaction becomes notifiable, or that additional tax is payable in respect of a transaction or that tax is payable where none was payable before –

(a) the purchaser must make a return to the Inland Revenue within 30 days,
(b) the return must contain a self-assessment of the tax chargeable in respect of the transaction on the basis of the information contained in the return,
(c) the tax so chargeable is to be calculated by reference to the rates in force at the effective date of the transaction, and
(d) the tax or additional tax payable must be paid not later than the filing date for the return.

(3) The provisions of Schedule 10 (returns, enquiries, assessments and other matters) apply to a return under this section as they apply to a return under section 76 (general requirement to make land transaction return), subject to the adaptation that references to the effective date of the transaction shall be read as references to the date of the event as a result of which the return is required.

(4) If the effect of the new information is that less tax is payable in respect of a transaction than has already been paid –

(a) the purchaser may, within the period allowed for amendment of the land transaction return, amend the return accordingly;
(b) after the end of that period he may (if the land transaction return is not so amended) make a claim to the Inland Revenue for repayment of the amount overpaid.

(4A) Where the transaction ('the relevant transaction') is the grant or assignment of a lease, no claim may be made under subsection (4) –

(a) in respect of the repayment (in whole or part) of any loan or deposit that is treated by paragraph 18A of Schedule 17A as being consideration given for the relevant transaction, or
(b) in respect of the refund of any of the consideration given for the relevant transaction, in a case where the refund –
   (i) is made under arrangements that were made in connection with the relevant transaction, and
   (ii) is contingent on the determination or assignment of the lease or on the grant of a chargeable interest out of the lease.

(5) This section does not apply so far as the consideration consists of rent (see paragraph 8 of Schedule 17A).

Amendments: Finance Act 2004, ss 296, 299(1), (4), 326, Schs 39, 42; Finance (No 2) Act 2005, s 49, Sch 10; Finance Act 2007, s 80(1), (3), (9)(b).

81 Further return where relief withdrawn

(1) Where relief is withdrawn to any extent under –

(za)   paragraph 11 of Schedule 6A (relief for certain acquisitions of residential property),
(a)   Part 1 of Schedule 7 (group relief),
(b)   Part 2 of that Schedule (reconstruction or acquisition relief), or
(c)   Schedule 8 (charities relief),

the purchaser must deliver a further return before the end of the period of 30 days after the date on which the disqualifying event occurred.

(2) The return must –

(a)   include a self-assessment of the amount of tax chargeable.

(2A) Tax payable must be paid not later than the filing date for the return.

(3) The provisions of Schedule 10 (returns, assessments and other matters) apply to a return under this section as they apply to a return under section 76 (general requirement to deliver land transaction return), with the following adaptations –

(a)   references to the transaction to which the return relates shall be read as references to the disqualifying event;
(b)   references to the effective date of the transaction shall be read as references to the date on which the disqualifying event occurs.

(4) In this section 'the disqualifying event' means –

(za)   in relation to the withdrawal of relief under Schedule 6A, an event mentioned in paragraph (a), (b) or (c) of paragraph 11(2), (3), (4) or (5) of that Schedule;
(a)   in relation to the withdrawal of group relief, the purchaser ceasing to be a member of the same group as the vendor within the meaning of Part 1 of Schedule 7;
(b)   in relation to the withdrawal of reconstruction or acquisition relief, the change of control of the acquiring company mentioned in paragraph 9(1)(a) of Schedule 7 or, as the case may be, the event mentioned in paragraph 11(1)(a) or (2)(a) of that Schedule;
(c)   in relation to the withdrawal of charities relief, a disqualifying event as defined in paragraph 2(3) or 3(2) of Schedule 8.

Amendments: Finance Act 2004, ss 296, 302(5), Sch 39; Finance Act 2007, ss 80(1), (4)(a), (b), (9)(c), 114, Sch 27, Pt 4(4).

81A   Return or further return in consequence of later linked transaction

(1) Where the effect of a transaction ('the later transaction') that is linked to an earlier transaction is that the earlier transaction becomes notifiable, or that additional tax is payable in respect of the earlier transaction or that tax is payable in respect of the earlier transaction where none was payable before –

(a)   the purchaser under the earlier transaction must deliver a return or further return in respect of that transaction before the end of the period of 30 days after the effective date of the later transaction,
(b)   the return must include a self-assessment of the amount of tax chargeable as a result of the later transaction,
(c)   the tax so chargeable is to be calculated by reference to the rates in force at the effective date of the earlier transaction, and
(d)   the tax or additional tax payable must be paid not later than the filing date for the return.

(2) The provisions of Schedule 10 (returns, enquiries, assessments and other matters) apply to the return under this section as they apply to a return under section 76 (general requirement to deliver land transaction return), with the following adaptations –

    (a)   in paragraph 5 (formal notice to deliver return), the requirement in sub-paragraph (2)(a) that the notice specify the transaction to which it relates shall be read as requiring both the earlier and later transactions to be specified;

    (b)   references to the effective date of the transaction to which the return relates shall be read as references to the effective date of the later transaction.

(3) This section does not affect any requirement to make a return under section 76 in respect of the later transaction.

Amendments: Section inserted: Finance Act 2004, s 296, Sch 39; Finance Act 2007, ss 80(1), (5), (9)(d).

81B Declaration by person authorised to act on behalf of individual

(1) This section applies to the declaration mentioned in paragraph 1(1)(c) of Schedule 10 or paragraph 2(1)(c) of Schedule 11 (declaration that return is correct and complete).

(2) The requirement that an individual make such a declaration (alone or jointly with others) is treated as met if a declaration to that effect is made by a person authorised to act on behalf of that individual in relation to the matters to which the return or certificate relates.

(3) For the purposes of this section a person is not regarded as authorised to act on behalf of an individual unless he is so authorised by a power of attorney in writing, signed by that individual.

In this subsection as it applies in Scotland 'power of attorney' includes factory and commission.

(4) Nothing in this section affects the making of a declaration in accordance with –

    (a)   section 100(2) (persons through whom a company acts), or

    (b)   section 106(1) or (2) (person authorised to act on behalf of incapacitated person or minor).

Amendments: Section inserted: Finance Act 2004, s 296, Sch 39; Finance Act 2008, s 94(4), (5), Sch 30, paras 1, 3.

82 Loss or destruction of, or damage to, return etc

(1) This section applies where –

    (a)   a return delivered to the Inland Revenue, or

    (b)   any other document relating to tax made by or provided to the Inland Revenue,

has been lost or destroyed, or been so defaced or damaged as to be illegible or otherwise useless.

(2) The Inland Revenue may treat the return as not having been delivered or the document as not having been made or provided.

(3) Anything done on that basis shall be as valid and effective for all purposes as it would have been if the return had not been made or the document had not been made or provided.

(4) But if as a result a person is charged with tax and he proves to the satisfaction of the tribunal that he has already paid tax in respect of the transaction in question, relief shall be given, by reducing the charge or by repayment as the case may require.

Amendment: SI 2009/56.

82A Claims not included in returns

Schedule 11A has effect with respect to claims not i0ncluded in returns.

Amendments: Section inserted: Finance Act 2004, s 299(1), (2).

83 Formal requirements as to assessments, penalty determinations etc

(1) An assessment, determination, notice or other document required to be used in assessing, charging, collecting and levying tax or determining a penalty under this Part must be in accordance with the forms prescribed from time to time by the Board and a document in the form so prescribed and supplied or approved by the Board is valid and effective.

(2) Any such assessment, determination, notice or other document purporting to be made under this Part is not ineffective –

    (a)   for want of form, or
    (b)   by reason of any mistake, defect or omission in it,

if it is substantially in conformity with this Part and its intended effect is reasonably ascertainable by the person to whom it is directed.

(3) The validity of an assessment or determination is not affected –

    (a)   by any mistake in it as to –
        (i)   the name of a person liable, or
        (ii)   the amount of the tax charged, or
    (b)   by reason of any variance between the notice of assessment or determination and the assessment or determination itself.

84 Delivery and service of documents

(1) A notice or other document to be served under this Part on a person may be delivered to him or left at his usual or last known place of abode.

(2) A notice or other document to be given, served or delivered under this Part may be served by post.

(3) For the purposes of section 7 of the Interpretation Act 1978 (c 30) (general provisions as to service by post) any such notice or other document to be given or delivered to, or served on, any person by the Inland Revenue is properly addressed if it is addressed to that person –

    (a)   in the case of an individual, at his usual or last known place of residence or his place of business;
    (b)   in the case of a company –
        (i)   at its principal place of business,
        (ii)   if a liquidator has been appointed, at his address for the purposes of the liquidation, or
        (iii)   at any place prescribed by regulations made by the Inland Revenue.

Liability for and payment of tax

85 Liability for tax

(1) The purchaser is liable to pay the tax in respect of a chargeable transaction.

(2) As to the liability of purchasers acting jointly see –

   (a)   section 103(2)(c) (joint purchasers);
   (b)   Part 2 of Schedule 15 (partners); and
   (c)   paragraph 5 of Schedule 16 (trustees).

86 Payment of tax

(1) Tax payable in respect of a land transaction must be paid not later than the filing date for the land transaction return relating to the transaction.

(2) Tax payable as a result of the withdrawal of relief under –

   (a)   Part 1 of Schedule 7 (group relief),
   (b)   Part 2 of that Schedule (reconstruction or acquisition relief), or
   (c)   Schedule 8 (charities relief),

must be paid not later than the filing date for the return relating to the withdrawal (see section 81).

(3) Tax payable as a result of the amendment of a return must be paid forthwith or, if the amendment is made before the filing date for the return, not later than that date.

(4) Tax payable in accordance with a determination or assessment by the Inland Revenue must be paid within 30 days after the determination or assessment is issued.

(5) The above provisions are subject to –

   (a)   section 90 (application to defer payment of tax in case of contingent or uncertain consideration), and
   (b)   paragraphs 39 and 40 of Schedule 10 (postponement of payment pending determination of appeal).

(5A) The above provisions are also subject to paragraph 7 of Schedule 61 to the Finance Act 2009 (payment of tax where land ceases to qualify for relief in respect of alternative finance investment bonds).

(6) This section does not affect the date from which interest is payable (as to which, see section 87).

Amendments: Finance Act 2007, ss 80(1), (6)(a), (b), (9)(e); Finance Act 2009, s 123, Sch 61, Pt 4, paras 24, 26, 29(2)(c).

87 Interest on unpaid tax

(1) Interest is payable on the amount of any unpaid tax from the end of the period of 30 days after the relevant date until the tax is paid.

(2) The Inland Revenue may by regulations amend subsection (1) so as to make interest run from the end of such shorter period after the relevant date as may be prescribed or, if the regulations so provide, from that date.

(3) For the purposes of this section 'the relevant date' is –

   (a)   in the case of an amount payable because relief is withdrawn under –

    (ia)   Schedule 6A (relief for certain acquisitions of residential property),
    (i)   Part 1 of Schedule 7 (group relief),
    (ii)   Part 2 of that Schedule (reconstruction or acquisition relief), or
    (iii)   Schedule 8 (charities relief),
    the date of the disqualifying event;

(aa)   in the case of an amount payable under section 81A in respect of an earlier transaction because of the effect of a later linked transaction, the effective date of the later transaction.

(ab)   in the case of an amount payable under paragraph 3(3) or 4(3) of Schedule 17A (leases that continue after a fixed term and treatment of leases for an indefinite term), the day on which the lease becomes treated as being for a longer fixed term;

(b)   in the case of a deferred payment under section 90, the date when the deferred payment is due;

(c)   in any other case, the effective date of the transaction.

(4) In subsection (3)(a) 'the disqualifying event' means –

(za)   in relation to the withdrawal of relief under Schedule 6A an event mentioned in paragraph (a), (b) or (c) of paragraph 11(2), (3), (4) or (5) of that Schedule,

(a)   in relation to the withdrawal of group relief, the purchaser ceasing to be a member of the same group as the vendor (within the meaning of Part 1 of Schedule 7);

(b)   in relation to the withdrawal of reconstruction or acquisition relief, the change of control of the acquiring company mentioned in paragraph 9(1)(a) of that Schedule or, as the case may be, the event mentioned in paragraph 11(1)(a) or (2)(a) of that Schedule;

(c)   in relation to the withdrawal of charities relief, a disqualifying event as defined in paragraph 2(3) or 3(2) of Schedule 8.

(5) Subsection (3)(c) applies in a case within section 51 (contingent, uncertain or unascertained consideration) if payment is not deferred under section 90, with the result that interest on any tax payable under section 80 (adjustment where contingency ceases or consideration is ascertained) runs from the effective date of the transaction.

(6) If an amount is lodged with the Inland Revenue in respect of the tax, the amount on which interest is payable is reduced by that amount.

(7) Interest is calculated at the rate applicable under section 178 of the Finance Act 1989 (c 26) (power of Treasury to prescribe rates of interest).

Amendments: Finance Act 2004, ss 296, 302(6), Sch 39.

88 Interest on penalties

A penalty under this Part shall carry interest at the rate applicable under section 178 of the Finance Act 1989 from the date it is determined until payment.

89 Interest on repayment of tax overpaid etc

(1) A repayment by the Inland Revenue to which this section applies shall be made with interest at the rate applicable under section 178 of the Finance Act 1989 for the period between the relevant time (as defined below) and the date when the order for repayment is issued.

(2) This section applies to –

(a) any repayment of tax, and

(b) any repayment of a penalty under this Part.

In that case the relevant time is the date on which the payment of tax or penalty was made.

(3) This section also applies to a repayment by the Inland Revenue of an amount lodged with them in respect of the tax payable in respect of a transaction.

In that case the relevant time is the date on which the amount was lodged with them.

(4) No interest is payable under this section in respect of a payment made in consequence of an order or judgment of a court having power to allow interest on the payment.

(5) Interest paid to any person under this section is not income of that person for any tax purposes.

90 Application to defer payment in case of contingent or uncertain consideration

(1) The purchaser may apply to the Inland Revenue to defer payment of tax in a case where the amount payable depends on the amount or value of chargeable consideration that –

(a) at the effective date of the transaction is contingent or uncertain, and

(b) falls to be paid or provided on one or more future dates of which at least one falls, or may fall, more than six months after the effective date of the transaction.

(2) The Inland Revenue may make provision by regulations for carrying this section into effect.

(3) The regulations may in particular –

(a) specify when an application is to be made;

(b) impose requirements as to the form and contents of an application;

(c) require the applicant to provide such information as the Inland Revenue may reasonably require for the purposes of determining whether to accept an application;

(d) specify the grounds on which an application may be refused;

(e) specify the procedure for reaching a decision on an application;

(f) make provision for postponing payment of tax when an application has been made;

(g) provide for an appeal to the tribunal against a refusal to accept an application, and make provision in relation to such an appeal corresponding to any provision made in relation to appeals under Part 7 of Schedule 10 (appeals against Revenue decisions on tax);

(h) provide for the effect of accepting an application;

(i) require the purchaser to make a return or further return, and to make such payments or further payments of tax as may be specified, in such circumstances as may be specified.

(4) The provisions of Schedule 10 (returns, enquiries, assessments and other matters) apply to a return under this section as they apply to a land transaction return.

(5) An application under this section does not affect the purchaser's obligations as regards payment of tax in respect of chargeable consideration that has already been paid or provided or is not contingent and whose amount is ascertained or ascertainable at the time the application is made.

This applies as regards both the time of payment and the calculation of the amount payable.

(6) Regulations under this section may provide that where –

(a)   a payment is made as mentioned in subsection (5), and
(b)   an application under this section is accepted in respect of other chargeable consideration taken into account in calculating the amount of that payment,

section 80 (adjustment where contingency ceases or consideration is ascertained) does not apply in relation to the payment and, instead, any necessary adjustment shall be made in accordance with the regulations.

(7) This section does not apply so far as the consideration consists of rent.

Amendments: Finance Act 2004, s 296, Sch 39; SI 2009/56.

91   Collection and recovery of tax etc

(1) The provisions of Schedule 12 have effect with respect to the collection and recovery of tax.

In that Schedule –

Part 1 contains general provisions, and

Part 2 relates to court proceedings.

(2) The provisions of that Schedule have effect in relation to the collection and recovery of any unpaid amount by way of –

(a)   penalty under this Part, or
(b)   interest under this Part (on unpaid tax or penalty),

as if it were an amount of unpaid tax.

92   Payment by cheque

For the purposes of this Part where –

(a)   payment to the Inland Revenue is made by cheque, and
(b)   the cheque is paid on its first presentation to the banker on whom it is drawn,

the payment is treated as made on the day on which the cheque was received by the Inland Revenue.

Compliance

93   Information powers

(1) Schedule 13 has effect with respect to the powers of the Inland Revenue to call for documents and information for the purposes of stamp duty land tax.

(2) In that Schedule –

Part 1 confers power on an authorised officer to call for documents or information from the taxpayer;

Part 2 confers power on an authorised officer to call for documents from a third party;

Part 3 confers power on an authorised officer to call for the papers of a tax accountant;

Part 4 imposes restrictions on the powers under Parts 1 to 3;

Part 5 confers powers on the Board to call for documents or information;

Part 6 provides for an order of a judicial authority for the delivery of documents;

Part 7 provides for entry with a warrant to obtain evidence of an offence;

Part 8 relates to falsification etc of documents.

(3) A person who is required by a notice under Part 1, 2 or 3 of Schedule 13 to deliver a document or to provide information, or to make a document available for inspection, and who fails to comply with the notice is liable to a penalty not exceeding £300.

(4) If the failure continues after a penalty has been imposed under subsection (3), he is liable to a further penalty or penalties not exceeding £60 for each day on which the failure continues after the day on which the penalty under that subsection was imposed (but excluding any day for which a penalty under this subsection has already been imposed).

(5) No penalty shall be imposed under subsection (3) or (4) in respect of a failure at any time after the failure has been remedied.

(6) A person who is required by a notice under Part 1, 2 or 3 of Schedule 13 to deliver a document or to provide information, or to make a document available for inspection, and who fraudulently or negligently delivers, provides or makes available any incorrect document or information is liable to a penalty not exceeding £3,000.

94 Power to inspect premises

(1) If for the purposes of this Part the Board authorise an officer of theirs to inspect any property for the purpose of ascertaining its market value, or any other matter relevant for the purposes of this Part, the person having custody or possession of the property shall permit the officer so authorised to inspect it at such reasonable times as the Board may consider necessary.

(2) A person who wilfully delays or obstructs an officer of the Board acting in pursuance of this section commits an offence and is liable on summary conviction to a fine not exceeding level 1 on the standard scale.

95 Offence of fraudulent evasion of tax

(1) A person commits an offence if he is knowingly concerned in the fraudulent evasion of tax by him or any other person.

(2) A person guilty of an offence under this section is liable –

(a)   on summary conviction to imprisonment for a term not exceeding six months or a fine not exceeding the statutory maximum, or both;

(b)   on conviction on indictment, to imprisonment for a term not exceeding seven years or a fine, or both.

96 Penalty for assisting in preparation of incorrect return etc

A person who assists in or induces the preparation or delivery of any information, return or other document that –

(a) he knows will be, or is likely to be, used for any purpose of tax, and

(b) he knows to be incorrect,

is liable to a penalty not exceeding £3,000.

97 Power to allow further time and reasonable excuse for failure

(1) For the purposes of this Part a person shall be deemed not to have failed to do anything required to be done within a limited time if he did it within such further time, if any, as the Inland Revenue may allow.

(2) Where a person had a reasonable excuse for not doing anything required to be done for the purposes of this Part –

(a) he shall be deemed not to have failed to do it unless the excuse ceased, and

(b) after the excuse ceased, he shall be deemed not to have failed to do it if he did it without unreasonably delay after the excuse had ceased.

98 Admissibility of evidence not affected by offer of settlement etc

(1) Statements made or documents produced by or on behalf of a person are not inadmissible in proceedings to which this section applies by reason only that it has been drawn to his attention –

(a) that where serious tax fraud has been committed the Board may accept a money settlement and that the Board will accept such a settlement, and will not pursue a criminal prosecution, if he makes a full confession of all tax irregularities, or

(b) that the extent to which he is helpful and volunteers information is a factor that will be taken into account in determining the amount of any penalty,

and that he was or may have been induced thereby to make the statements or produce the documents.

(2) The proceedings to which this section applies are –

(a) any criminal proceedings against the person in question for any form of fraudulent conduct in connection with or in relation to tax;

(b) any proceedings against him for the recovery of any tax due from him;

(c) any proceedings for a penalty or on appeal against the determination of a penalty.

99 General provisions about penalties

(1) Schedule 14 has effect with respect to the determination of penalties under this Part and related appeals.

(2) The Board may in their discretion mitigate a penalty under this Part, or stay or compound any proceedings for the recovery of such a penalty.

They may also, after judgment, further mitigate or entirely remit the penalty.

(2A) Where a person is liable to more than one tax-related penalty in respect of the same land transaction, each penalty after the first shall be reduced so that his liability to such penalties, in total, does not exceed the amount of whichever is (or, but for this subsection, would be) the greatest one.

(3) Nothing in the provisions of this Part relating to penalties affects any criminal proceedings for an offence.

Amendments: Finance Act 2004, s 298(1), (4).

Application of provisions

100   Companies

(1) In this Part 'company', except as otherwise expressly provided, means any body corporate or unincorporated association, but does not include a partnership.

(2) Everything to be done by a company under this Part shall be done by the company acting through –

   (a)   the proper officer of the company, or
   (b)   another person having for the time being having the express, implied or apparent authority of the company to act on its behalf for the purpose.

Paragraph (b) does not apply where a liquidator has been appointed for the company.

(3) Service on a company of any document under or in pursuance of this Part may be effected by serving it on the proper officer.

(4) Tax due from a company that –

   (a)   is not a body corporate, or
   (b)   is incorporated under the law of a country or territory outside the United Kingdom,

may, without prejudice to any other method of recovery, be recovered from the proper officer of the company.

(5) The proper officer may retain out of any money coming into his hands on behalf of the company sufficient sums to pay that tax and, so far as he is not so reimbursed, he is entitled to be indemnified by the company in respect of the liability imposed on him.

(6) For the purposes of this Part –

   (a)   the proper officer of a body corporate is the secretary, or person acting as secretary, of the company, and
   (b)   the proper officer of an unincorporated association, or of a body corporate that does not have a proper officer within paragraph (a), is the treasurer, or person acting as treasurer, of the company.

This subsection does not apply if a liquidator or administrator has been appointed for the company.

(7) If a liquidator or administrator has been appointed for the company, then, for the purposes of this Part –

   (a)   the liquidator or, as the case may be, the administrator is the proper officer, and
   (b)   if two or more persons are appointed to act jointly or concurrently as the administrator of the company, the proper officer is –

(i)   such one of them as is specified in a notice given to the Inland Revenue by those persons for the purposes of this section, or

(ii)   where the Inland Revenue is not so notified, such one or more of those persons as the Inland Revenue may designate as the proper officer for those purposes.

101   Unit trust schemes

(1) This Part (with the exception of the provision mentioned in subsection (7) below) applies in relation to a unit trust scheme as if –

(a)   the trustees were a company, and

(b)   the rights of the unit holders were shares in the company.

(2) Each of the parts of an umbrella scheme is regarded for the purposes of this Part as a separate unit trust scheme and the scheme as a whole is not so regarded.

(3) An 'umbrella scheme' means a unit trust scheme –

(a)   that provides arrangements for separate pooling of the contributions of participants and the profits or income out of which payments are to be made for them, and

(b)   under which the participants are entitled to exchange rights in one pool for rights in another.

A 'part' of an umbrella scheme means such of the arrangements as relate to a separate pool.

(4) In this Part, subject to any regulations under subsection (5) –

'unit trust scheme' has the same meaning as in the Financial Services and Markets Act 2000 (c 8), and

'unit holder' means a person entitled to a share of the investments subject to the trusts of a unit trust scheme.

(5) The Treasury may by regulations provide that a scheme of a description specified in the regulations is to be treated as not being a unit trust scheme for the purposes of this Part.

Any such regulations may contain such supplementary and transitional provisions as appear to the Treasury to be necessary or expedient.

(6) Section 469A of the Taxes Act 1988 (court common investment funds treated as authorised unit trusts) applies for the purposes of this Part as it applies for the purposes of that Act, with the substitution for references to an authorised unit trust of references to a unit trust scheme.

(7) An unit trust scheme is not to be treated as a company for the purposes of –

Schedule 7 (group relief, reconstruction relief or acquisition relief).

Amendments: Finance Act 2006, ss 166(1), (3), 178, Sch 26.

102   Open-ended investment companies

(1) The Treasury may by regulations make such provision as they consider appropriate for securing that the provisions of this Part have effect in relation to –

(a)   open-ended investment companies of such description as may be prescribed in the regulations, and

(b)   transactions involving such companies,

in a manner corresponding, subject to such modifications as the Treasury consider appropriate, to the manner in which they have effect in relation to unit trust schemes and transactions involving such trusts.

(2) The regulations may, in particular, make provision –

(a)   modifying the operation of any prescribed provision in relation to open-ended investment companies so as to secure that arrangements for treating the assets of such a company as assets comprised in separate pools are given an effect corresponding to that of equivalent arrangements constituting the separate parts of an umbrella scheme;

(b)   treating the separate parts of the undertaking of an open-ended investment company in relation to which such provision is made as distinct companies for the purposes of this Part.

(3) Regulations under this section may –

(a)   make different provision for different cases, and

(b)   contain such incidental, supplementary, consequential and transitional provision as the Treasury think fit.

(4) In this section –

'open-ended investment company' has the meaning given by section 236 of the Financial Services and Markets Act 2000 (c 8);

'prescribed' means prescribed by regulations under this section; and

'unit trust scheme' and 'umbrella scheme' have the same meaning as in section 101.

103   Joint purchasers

(1) This section applies to a land transaction where there are two or more purchasers who are or will be jointly entitled to the interest acquired.

(2) The general rules are that –

(a)   any obligation of the purchaser under this Part in relation to the transaction is an obligation of the purchasers jointly but may be discharged by any of them,

(b)   anything required or authorised by this Part to be done in relation to the purchaser must be done by or in relation to all of them, and

(c)   any liability of the purchaser under this Part in relation to the transaction (in particular, any liability arising by virtue of the failure to fulfil an obligation within paragraph (a)), is a joint and several liability of the purchasers.

These rules are subject to the following provisions.

(3) If the transaction is a notifiable transaction, a single land transaction return is required.

(4) The declaration required by paragraph 1(1)(c) of Schedule 10 (declaration that return is complete and correct) must be made by all the purchasers.

(5) If the Inland Revenue give notice of an enquiry into the return –

(a)   the notice must be given to each of the purchasers,

(b)   the powers of the Inland Revenue as to the production of documents and provision of information for the purposes of the enquiry are exercisable separately (and differently) in relation to each of the purchasers,

(c) any of the purchasers may apply for a direction that a closure notice be given (and all of them are entitled to be parties to the application), and

(d) the closure notice must be given to each of the purchasers.

(6) A Revenue determination or discovery assessment relating to the transaction must be made against all the purchasers and is not effective against any of them unless notice of it is given to each of them whose identity is known to the Inland Revenue.

(7) In the case of an appeal arising from proceedings under this Part relating to the transaction –

(a) the appeal may be brought by any of the purchasers,

(b) notice of the appeal must be given to any of them by whom it is not brought,

(c) the agreement of all the purchasers is required if the appeal is to be settled by agreement,

(d) if it is not settled, and is notified to the tribunal, any of them are entitled to be parties to the appeal, and

(e) the tribunal's decision on the appeal binds all of them.

(7A) In a case where subsection (7) applies and some (but not all) of the purchasers require HMRC to undertake a review under paragraph 36B or 36C of Schedule 10 –

(a) notification of the review must be given by HMRC to each of the other purchasers whose identity is known to HMRC,

(b) any of the other purchasers may be a party to the review if they notify HMRC in writing,

(c) the notice of HMRC's conclusions must be given to each of the other purchasers whose identity is known to HMRC,

(d) paragraph 36F of Schedule 10 (effect of conclusions of review) applies in relation to all of the purchasers, and

(e) any of the purchasers may notify the appeal to the tribunal under paragraph 36G.

(8) This section has effect subject to –

the provisions of Schedule 15 relating to partnerships, and

the provisions of Schedule 16 relating to trustees.

Amendments: Finance Act 2008, s 94(4), Sch 30, paras 1, 4(1)–(3); SI 2009/56.

104 Partnerships

(1) Schedule 15 has effect with respect to the application of this Part in relation to partnerships.

(2) In that Schedule –

Part 1 defines 'partnership' and contains other general provisions, and

Part 2 deals with ordinary partnership transactions, and

Part 3 makes special provision for certain transactions.

Amendments: Finance Act 2004, s 304, Sch 41, paras 2(a), 3.

105 Trustees

Schedule 16 has effect with respect to the application of this Part in relation to trustees.

106 Persons acting in a representative capacity etc

(1) The person having the direction, management or control of the property of an incapacitated person –

    (a)   is responsible for discharging any obligations under this Part, in relation to a transaction affecting that property, to which the incapacitated person would be subject if he were not incapacitated, and

    (b)   may retain out of money coming into his hands on behalf of the incapacitated person sums sufficient to meet any payment he is liable to make under this Part, and, so far as he is not so reimbursed, is entitled to be indemnified in respect of any such payment.

(2) The parent or guardian of a minor is responsible for discharging any obligations of the minor under this Part that are not discharged by the minor himself.

(3) The personal representatives of a person who is the purchaser under a land transaction –

    (a)   are responsible for discharging the obligations of the purchaser under this Part in relation to the transaction, and

    (b)   may deduct any payment made by them under this Part out of the assets and effects of the deceased person.

(4) A receiver appointed by a court in the United Kingdom having the direction and control of any property is responsible for discharging any obligations under this Part in relation to a transaction affecting that property as if the property were not under the direction and control of the court.

107 Crown application

(1) This Part binds the Crown, subject to the following provisions of this section.

(2) A land transaction under which the purchaser is any of the following is exempt from charge:

Government

A Minister of the Crown

The Scottish Ministers

A Northern Ireland department

The Welsh Ministers, the First Minister for Wales and the Counsel General to the Welsh Assembly Government

Parliament etc

The Corporate Officer of the House of Lords

The Corporate Officer of the House of Commons

The Scottish Parliamentary Corporate Body

The Northern Ireland Assembly Commission

The National Assembly for Wales Commission

(3) The powers conferred by Part 7 of Schedule 13 (entry with warrant to obtain information) are not exercisable in relation to premises occupied for the purposes of the Crown.

(4) Nothing in this section shall be read as making the Crown liable to prosecution for an offence.

Amendments: Finance Act 2004, s 296, Sch 39, Pt 2, paras 21(1)–(3), 26; Government of Wales Act 2006, ss 46, 160(1), 161(4), (5), Sch 10, paras 62, 65(a), (b).

Supplementary provisions

108   Linked transactions

(1) Transactions are 'linked' for the purposes of this Part if they form part of a single scheme, arrangement or series of transactions between the same vendor and purchaser or, in either case, persons connected with them.

Section 839 of the Taxes Act 1988 (connected persons) has effect for the purposes of this subsection

(2) Where there are two or more linked transactions with the same effective date, the purchaser, or all of the purchasers if there is more than one, may make a single land transaction return as if all of those transactions that are notifiable were a single notifiable transaction.

(3) Where two or more purchasers make a single return in respect of linked transactions, section 103 (joint purchasers) applies as if –

    (a)   the transactions in question were a single transaction, and
    (b)   those purchasers were purchasers acting jointly.

(4) This section is subject to section 47(1).

Amendments: Finance Act 2007, s 76(2), (3).

109   General power to vary this Part by regulations

(1) The Treasury may if they consider it expedient in the public interest make provision by regulations for the variation of this Part in its application to land transactions of any description.

(2) The power conferred by this section includes, in particular, power to alter –

    (a)   the descriptions of land transaction that are chargeable or notifiable;
    (b)   the descriptions of land transaction in respect of which tax is chargeable at any existing rate or amount.

(3) The power conferred by this section does not, except as mentioned in subsection (2)(b), include power to vary any threshold, rate or amount specified in –

    (a)   section 55 (amount of tax chargeable: general), or
    (b)   Schedule 5 (amount of tax chargeable: rent).

(4) This section has effect subject to section 110 (approval of regulations by House of Commons).

(5) Regulations under this section do not apply in relation to any transaction of which the effective date is after the end of –

(a)   the period of 18 months beginning with the day on which the regulations were made, or

(b)   such shorter period as may be specified in the regulations.

This does not affect the power to make further provision by regulations under this section to the same or similar effect.

(6) Regulations under this section may include such supplementary, transitional and incidental provision as appears to the Treasury to be necessary or expedient.

(7) The power conferred by this section may be exercised at any time after the passing of this Act.

110   Approval of regulations under general power

(1) An instrument containing regulations under section 109 (general power to vary this Part by regulations) must be laid before the House of Commons after being made.

(2) If the regulations are not approved by the House of Commons before the end of the period of 28 days beginning with the day on which they are made, they shall cease to have effect at the end of that period (if they have not already ceased to have effect under subsection (3)).

(3) If on any day during that period of 28 days the House of Commons, in proceedings on a motion that (or to the effect that) the regulations be approved, comes to a decision rejecting the regulations, they shall cease to have effect at the end of that day.

(4) In reckoning any such period of 28 days take no account of any time during which –

(a)   Parliament is prorogued or dissolved, or

(b)   the House of Commons is adjourned for more than four days.

(5) Where regulations cease to have effect under this section, their ceasing to have effect is without prejudice to anything done in reliance on them.

As to claims for repayment, see section 111.

111   Claim for repayment if regulations under general power not approved

(1) Where regulations cease to have effect under section 110, a claim may be made to the Inland Revenue for repayment of any tax, interest or penalty that would not have been payable but for the regulations.

(2) Section 89 (interest on repayment of tax overpaid etc) applies to a repayment under this section.

(3) A claim for repayment must be made within two years after the effective date of the transaction in question.

(4) The Inland Revenue may make provision by regulations –

(a)   for varying the time limit for making a claim;

(b)   as to any other conditions that must be met before repayment is made.

Amendments: Section inserted: Finance Act 2004, s 299(1), (5).

112   Power to amend certain provisions before implementation

(1) The Treasury may by regulations amend the following provisions of this Part –

(a) Schedule 5 (amount of tax chargeable: rent);

(b) subsection (2) of section 55 (amount of tax chargeable: general) so far as relating to the thresholds at which different rates of tax become payable.

(2) The regulations may make such consequential amendments of Schedule 6 (disadvantaged areas relief) as appear to the Treasury to be appropriate.

(3) A statutory instrument containing regulations under this section shall not be made unless a draft of the instrument has been laid before and approved by resolution of the House of Commons.

(4) The power conferred by this section is not exercisable after the implementation date.

113 Functions conferred on 'the Inland Revenue'

(1) References in this Part to 'the Inland Revenue' are to any officer of the Board, except as otherwise provided.

(2) Any power of the Inland Revenue to make regulations is exercisable only by the Board.

(3) In Schedule 10 (returns, assessments and other administrative matters) –

(a) functions of the Inland Revenue under these provisions are exercisable by the Board or an officer of the Board –
   (i) paragraph 28 (discovery assessment),
   (ii) paragraph 29 (assessment to recover excessive repayment);

(b) functions of the Inland Revenue under these provisions are functions of the Board –
   (i) paragraph 33 (relief in case of double assessment),
   (ii) paragraph 34 (relief in case of mistake in return).

(3A) The following functions of the Inland Revenue under Schedule 11A (claims not included in returns) are functions of the Board –

(a) functions under paragraph 2(1) (form of claims),

(b) functions relating to a claim made to the Board.

(4) Nothing in this section affects any provision of this Part that expressly confers functions on the Board, an officer of the Board, a collector or a specific officer of the Board.

Amendments: Section inserted: Finance Act 2004, s 299(1), (6).

114 Orders and regulations made by the Treasury or the Inland Revenue

(1) Except as otherwise provided, any power of the Treasury or the Inland Revenue to make an order or regulations under this Part, or under any other enactments relating to stamp duty land tax (including enactments passed after this Act), is exercisable by statutory instrument.

(2) Subsection (1) does not apply in relation to the power conferred by –

paragraph 8 of Schedule 5 to this Act (tax chargeable in respect of rent: power to prescribe temporal discount rate),

section 178(5) of the Finance Act 1989 (c 26) (power to prescribe rates of interest).

(3) Except as otherwise provided, a statutory instrument containing any order or regulations made by the Treasury or the Inland Revenue under this Part, or under any

other enactments relating to stamp duty land tax (including enactments passed after this Act), shall be subject to annulment in pursuance of a resolution of the House of Commons.

(4) Subsection (3) does not apply to a statutory instrument made under the power conferred by –

section 61(3) (compliance with planning obligations: power to add to list of public authorities);

paragraph 1(3) of Schedule 9 (right to buy transactions: power to add to list of relevant public sector bodies);

paragraph 2(2) of Schedule 19 (commencement and transitional provisions: power to appoint implementation date).

(5) The first set of regulations under section 58B (new zero-carbon homes) may not be made unless a draft has been laid before and approved by resolution of the House of Commons.

(6) An order or regulations under this Part –

- (a) may make provision having effect generally or only in specified cases or circumstances,
- (b) may make different provision for different cases or circumstances, and
- (c) may include incidental, consequential or transitional provision or savings.

Amendments: Finance Act 2007, s 19(2).

115 ...

Amendments: Repealed by SI 2009/56.

Interpretation etc

116 Meaning of 'residential property'

(1) In this Part 'residential property' means –

- (a) a building that is used or suitable for use as a dwelling, or is in the process of being constructed or adapted for such use, and
- (b) land that is or forms part of the garden or grounds of a building within paragraph (a) (including any building or structure on such land), or
- (c) an interest in or right over land that subsists for the benefit of a building within paragraph (a) or of land within paragraph (b);

and 'non-residential property' means any property that is not residential property.

This is subject to the rule in subsection (7) in the case of a transaction involving six or more dwellings.

(2) For the purposes of subsection (1) a building used for any of the following purposes is used as a dwelling –

- (a) residential accommodation for school pupils;
- (b) residential accommodation for students, other than accommodation falling with subsection (3)(b);
- (c) residential accommodation for members of the armed forces;
- (d) an institution that is the sole or main residence of at least 90% of its residents and does not fall within any of paragraphs (a) to (f) of subsection (3).

(3) For the purposes of subsection (1) a building used for any of the following purposes is not used as a dwelling –

(a) a home or other institution providing residential accommodation for children;

(b) a hall of residence for students in further or higher education;

(c) a home or other institution providing residential accommodation with personal care for persons in need of personal care by reason of old age, disablement, past or present dependence on alcohol or drugs or past or present mental disorder;

(d) a hospital or hospice;

(e) a prison or similar establishment;

(f) a hotel or inn or similar establishment.

(4) Where a building is used for a purpose specified in subsection (3), no account shall be taken for the purposes of subsection (1)(a) of its suitability for any other use.

(5) Where a building that is not in use is suitable for use for at least one of the purposes specified in subsection (2) and at least one of those specified in subsection (3) –

(a) if there is one such use for which it is most suitable, or if the uses for which it is most suitable are all specified in the same sub-paragraph, no account shall be taken for the purposes of subsection (1)(a) of its suitability for any other use,

(b) otherwise, the building shall be treated for those purposes as suitable for use as a dwelling.

(6) In this section 'building' includes part of a building.

(7) Where six or more separate dwellings are the subject of a single transaction involving the transfer of a major interest in, or the grant of a lease over, them, then, for the purposes of this Part as it applies in relation to that transaction, those dwellings are treated as not being residential property.

(8) The Treasury may by order –

(a) amend subsections (2) and (3) so as to change or clarify the cases where use of a building is, or is not to be, use of a building as a dwelling for the purposes of subsection (1);

(b) amend or repeal subsection (7) and the reference to that subsection in subsection (1).

Any such order may contain such incidental, supplementary, consequential or transitional provision as appears to the Treasury to be necessary or expedient.

117 Meaning of 'major interest' in land

(1) References in this Part to a 'major interest' in land shall be construed as follows.

(2) In relation to land in England or Wales, the references are to –

(a) an estate in fee simple absolute, or

(b) a term of years absolute,

whether subsisting at law or in equity.

(3) In relation to land in Scotland, the references are to –

(a) the interest of an owner of land, or

(b) the tenant's right over or interest in a property subject to a lease.

Until the appointed day for the purposes of the Abolition of Feudal Tenure etc. (Scotland) Act 2000 (asp 5), the reference in paragraph (a) to the interest of the owner shall be read, in relation to feudal property, as a reference to the estate or interest of the proprietor of the *dominium utile*.

(4) In relation to land in Northern Ireland, the references are to –

    (a)   any freehold estate, or

    (b)   any leasehold estate,

whether subsisting at law or in equity.

118   Meaning of 'market value'

For the purposes of this Part 'market value' shall be determined as for the purposes of the Taxation of Chargeable Gains Act 1992 (c 12) (see sections 272 to 274 of that Act).

119   Meaning of 'effective date' of a transaction

(1) Except as otherwise provided, the effective date of a land transaction for the purposes of this Part is –

    (a)   the date of completion.

    (b)   such alternative date as the Commissioners for Her Majesty's Revenue and Customs may prescribe by regulations

(2) Other provision as to the effective date of certain descriptions of land transaction is made by –

section 44(4) (contract and conveyance: contract substantially performed without having been completed),

section 44A(3) (contract providing for conveyance to third party),

section 45A(8) (contract providing for conveyance to third party: effect of transfer of rights),

section 46(3) (options and rights of pre-emption).

paragraph 12A(2) of Schedule 17A (agreement for lease followed by substantial performance),

paragraph 12B(3) of that Schedule (assignment of agreement for lease occurring after agreement substantially performed), and

paragraph 19(3) of that Schedule (missives of let etc in Scotland followed by substantial performance)

Amendments: Section inserted: Finance Act 2004, ss 296, 326, Schs 39, 42; Finance (No 2) Act 2005, s 47(3).

120   Further provisions relating to leases

Schedule 17A contains further provisions relating to leases.

Amendments: Section substituted: Finance Act 2004, s 296, Sch 39.

121   Minor definitions

In this Part –

    'assignment', in Scotland, means assignation;

'completion', in Scotland, means –
- (a)	in relation to a lease, when it is executed by the parties (that is to say, by signing) or constituted by any means;
- (b)	in relation to any other transaction, the settlement of the transaction;

'employee' includes an office-holder and related expressions have a corresponding meaning;

'HMRC' means Her Majesty's Revenue and Customs;

'jointly entitled' means –
- (a)	in England and Wales, beneficially entitled as joint tenants or tenants in common,
- (b)	in Scotland, entitled as joint owners or owners in common,
- (c)	in Northern Ireland, beneficially entitled as joint tenants, tenants in common or coparceners;

'land' includes –
- (a)	buildings and structures, and
- (b)	land covered by water;

'registered social landlord' means –
- (a)	in relation to England and Wales, a body registered as a social landlord in a register maintained under section 1(1) of the Housing Act 1996 (c 52);
- (b)	in relation to Scotland, a body registered in the register maintained under section 57 of the Housing (Scotland) Act 2001 (asp 10);
- (c)	in relation to Northern Ireland, a housing association registered in the register maintained under Article 14 of the Housing (Northern Ireland) Order 1992 (SI 1992/1725 (NI 15));

'standard security' has the meaning given by the Conveyancing and Feudal Reform (Scotland) Act 1970 (c 35);

'statutory provision' means any provision made by or under an Act of Parliament, an Act of the Scottish Parliament or any Northern Ireland legislation;

'surrender', in Scotland, means renunciation;

'tax', unless the context otherwise requires, means tax under this Part.

'tribunal' means the First-tier Tribunal or, where determined by or under Tribunal Procedure Rules, the Upper Tribunal.

Amendments: SI 2009/56.

## 122	Index of defined expressions

In this Part the expressions listed below are defined or otherwise explained by the provisions indicated –

acquisition relief	Schedule 7, paragraph 8(1)
assignment (in Scotland)	section 121
Bare trust	Schedule 16, paragraph 1(2)
the Board (in relation to the Inland Revenue)	section 42(3)
chargeable consideration	section 50 and Schedule 4
chargeable interest	section 48(1)
chargeable transaction	section 49

charities relief	Schedule 8, paragraph 1(1)
closure notice	Schedule 10, paragraph 23(1) (in relation to a land transaction return);
company	section 100 (except as otherwise expressly provided)
completion (in Scotland)	section 121
contingent (in relation to consideration)	section 51(3)
delivery (in relation to a land transaction return)	Schedule 10, paragraph 2(2)
discovery assessment	Schedule 10, paragraph 28(1)
effective date (in relation to a land transaction)	section 119
employee	section 121
exempt interest	section 48(2) to (5)
filing date (in relation to a land transaction return)	Schedule 10, paragraph 2(1)
implementation date	Schedule 19, paragraph 2(2)
the Inland Revenue	section 113
jointly entitled	section 121
land	section 121
land transaction	section 43(1)
land transaction return	section 76(1)
lease (and related expressions)	Schedule 17A
linked transactions	section 108
main subject-matter (in relation to a land transaction)	section 43(6)
major interest (in relation to land)	section 117
market value	section 118
notice of enquiry	Schedule 10, paragraph 12(1) (in relation to a land transaction return);
notifiable (in relation to a land transaction)	section 77 (see too sections 71A(7) and 72A(7) and paragraph 30 of Schedule 15)
partnership (and related expressions)	Schedule 15, paragraphs 1 to 4
purchaser	section 43(4)
rate of tax	section 55(7)
reconstruction relief	Schedule 7, paragraph 7(1)
registered social landlord	section 121
residential property	section 116

Revenue certificate	section 79(3)(a)
Revenue determination	Schedule 10, paragraph 25(1)
self-assessment	section 76(3)(a)
settlement	Schedule 16, paragraph 1(1)
standard securitysection 121	
statutory provision	section 121
subject-matter (in relation to a land transaction)	section 43(6)
substantial performance (in relation to a contract)	section 44(5) to (7)
surrender (in Scotland)	section 121
tax	section 121
tribunal	section 121
uncertain (in relation to consideration)	section 51(3)
unit holder	section 101(4)
unit trust scheme	section 101(4)
vendor	section 43(4) (see too sections 45(5A) and 45A(9))

Amendments: Finance Act 2004, s 296, Sch 39; Finance Act 2005, s 94, Sch 8; Finance Act 2008, s 94(4), (5), Sch 30, paras 1, 5(1)–(3), (5); SI 2009/56.

Final provisions

123   Consequential amendments

(1) Schedule 18 contains certain amendments consequential on the provisions of this Part.

(2) The Treasury may by regulations make such other amendments and repeals as appear to them appropriate in consequence of the provisions of this Part.

(3) The regulations may, in particular, make such provision as the Treasury think fit for reproducing in relation to stamp duty land tax the effect of enactments providing for exemption from stamp duty.

124   Commencement and transitional provisions

Schedule 19 makes provision for and in connection with the coming into force of the provisions of this Part.

PART 5
STAMP DUTY

125   Abolition of stamp duty except on instruments relating to stock or marketable securities

(1) Stamp duty is chargeable under Schedule 13 of the Finance Act 1999 (c 16) only on instruments relating to stock or marketable securities.

(2) Section 12 of the Finance Act 1895 (c 16) (collection of stamp duty in cases of property vested by Act or purchased under statutory powers) does not apply to property other than stock or marketable securities.

(3) This section shall be construed as one with the Stamp Act 1891 (c 39).

(4) Part 1 of Schedule 20 to this Act contains provisions supplementing this section and Part 2 of that Schedule provides for consequential amendments and repeals.

(5) This section and that Schedule have effect –

    (a)   in relation to an instrument effecting a land transaction (or any duplicate or counterpart of such an instrument), if the transaction –

        (i)   is an SDLT transaction within the meaning of Schedule 19 to this Act (stamp duty land tax: commencement and transitional provisions), or

        (ii)   would be such a transaction but for an exemption or relief from stamp duty land tax;

    (b)   in relation to an instrument effecting a transaction other than a land transaction (or any duplicate or counterpart of such an instrument), if the instrument is executed on or after the implementation date for the purposes of stamp duty land tax (see paragraph 2(2) of that Schedule).

For this purpose an instrument effecting both a land transaction and a transaction other than a land transaction (or any duplicate or counterpart of such an instrument), is treated as if it were two instruments to which paragraph (a) and paragraph (b) above respectively applied.

(6) Where in the case of an instrument effecting both a land transaction and a transaction other than a land transaction the result of applying subsection (5) is that stamp duty is chargeable on either or both of the deemed instruments, the enactments relating to stamp duty have effect as if –

    (a)   there were two instruments as mentioned in the closing words of that subsection,

    (b)   the consideration had been apportioned between them in a just and reasonable manner, and

    (c)   the amount found on that apportionment to be attributable to the chargeable instrument, or (as the case may be) to each of them, had been set forth distinctly in that instrument.

(7) In subsections (5) and (6) 'land transaction' has the same meaning as in Part 4 of this Act.

(8) This section and Schedule 20 have effect subject to paragraph 31 of Schedule 15 to this Act (continued application of stamp duty in relation to certain partnership transactions).

Amendments: Finance Act 2004, ss 296, 304, Schs 39, 41.

. . .

Schedule 3

Section 49

Stamp Duty Land Tax: Transactions Exempt from Charge

No chargeable consideration

1

A land transaction is exempt from charge if there is no chargeable consideration for the transaction.

Grant of certain leases by registered social landlords

2

(1) The grant of a lease of a dwelling is exempt from charge if the lease –

(a) is granted by a registered social landlord to one or more individuals in accordance with arrangements to which this paragraph applies, and

(b) is for an indefinite term or is terminable by notice of a month or less.

(2) This paragraph applies to arrangements between a registered social landlord and a housing authority under which the landlord provides, for individuals nominated by the authority in pursuance of its statutory housing functions, temporary rented accommodation which the landlord itself has obtained on a short-term basis.

The reference above to accommodation obtained by the landlord 'on a short-term basis' is to accommodation leased to the landlord for a term of five years or less.

(3) A 'housing authority' means –

(a) in relation to England and Wales –
   (i) a principal council within the meaning of the Local Government Act 1972 (c 70), or
   (ii) the Common Council of the City of London;
(b) in relation to Scotland, a council constituted under section 2 of the Local Government etc (Scotland) Act 1994 (c 39);
(c) in relation to Northern Ireland –
   (i) the Department for Social Development in Northern Ireland, or
   (ii) the Northern Ireland Housing Executive.

Transactions in connection with divorce etc

3

A transaction between one party to a marriage and the other is exempt from charge if it is effected –

(a) in pursuance of an order of a court made on granting in respect of the parties a decree of divorce, nullity of marriage or judicial separation;
(b) in pursuance of an order of a court made in connection with the dissolution or annulment of the marriage, or the parties' judicial separation, at any time after the granting of such a decree;
(c) in pursuance of –
   (i) an order of a court made at any time under section 22A, 23A or 24A of the Matrimonial Causes Act 1973 (c 18), or

(ii)   an incidental order of a court made under section 8(2) of the Family Law (Scotland) Act 1985 (c 37) by virtue of section 14(1) of that Act;

(d)   at any time in pursuance of an agreement of the parties made in contemplation or otherwise in connection with the dissolution or annulment of the marriage, their judicial separation or the making of a separation order in respect of them.

Assents and appropriations by personal representatives

3A

(1) The acquisition of property by a person in or towards satisfaction of his entitlement under or in relation to the will of a deceased person, or on the intestacy of a deceased person, is exempt from charge.

(2) Sub-paragraph (1) does not apply if the person acquiring the property gives any consideration for it, other than the assumption of secured debt.

(3) Where sub-paragraph (1) does not apply because of sub-paragraph (2), the chargeable consideration for the transaction is determined in accordance with paragraph 8A(1) of Schedule 4.

(4) In this paragraph –

'debt' means an obligation, whether certain or contingent, to pay a sum of money either immediately or at a future date, and

'secured debt' means debt that, immediately after the death of the deceased person, is secured on the property.

Transactions in connection with dissolution of civil partnership etc

3A

A transaction between one party to a civil partnership and the other is exempt from charge if it is effected –

(a)   in pursuance of an order of a court made on granting in respect of the parties an order or decree for the dissolution or annulment of the civil partnership or their judicial separation;

(b)   in pursuance of an order of a court made in connection with the dissolution or annulment of the civil partnership, or the parties' judicial separation, at any time after the granting of such an order or decree for dissolution, annulment or judicial separation as mentioned in paragraph (a);

(c)   in pursuance of –

(i)   an order of a court made at any time under any provision of Schedule 5 to the Civil Partnership Act 2004 that corresponds to section 22A, 23A or 24A of the Matrimonial Causes Act 1973, or

(ii)   an incidental order of a court made under any provision of the Civil Partnership Act 2004 that corresponds to section 8(2) of the Family Law (Scotland) Act 1985 by virtue of section 14(1) of that Act of 1985;

(d)   at any time in pursuance of an agreement of the parties made in contemplation of or otherwise in connection with the dissolution or annulment of the civil partnership, their judicial separation or the making of a separation order in respect of them.

Variation of testamentary dispositions etc

4

(1) A transaction following a person's death that varies a disposition (whether effected by will, under the law relating to intestacy or otherwise) of property of which the deceased was competent to dispose is exempt from charge if the following conditions are met.

(2) The conditions are –

(a)   that the transaction is carried out within the period of two years after a person's death, and

(b)   that no consideration in money or money's worth other than the making of a variation of another such disposition is given for it.

(2A) Where the condition in sub-paragraph (2)(b) is not met, the chargeable consideration for the transaction is determined in accordance with paragraph 8A(2) of Schedule 4.

(3) This paragraph applies whether or not the administration of the estate is complete or the property has been distributed in accordance with the original dispositions.

Power to add further exemptions

5

(1) The Treasury may by regulations provide that any description of land transaction specified in the regulations is exempt from charge.

(2) The regulations may contain such supplementary, incidental and transitional provision as appears to the Treasury to be appropriate.

Amendments: Finance Act 2004, ss 300(1), 301(1); SI 2005/3229.

Schedule 4

Section 50

Stamp Duty Land Tax: Chargeable Consideration

Money or money's worth

1

(1) The chargeable consideration for a transaction is, except as otherwise expressly provided, any consideration in money or money's worth given for the subject-matter of the transaction, directly or indirectly, by the purchaser or a person connected with him.

(2) Section 839 of the Taxes Act 1988 (connected persons) applies for the purposes of sub-paragraph (1).

Value added tax

2

The chargeable consideration for a transaction shall be taken to include any value added tax chargeable in respect of the transaction, other than value added tax chargeable by virtue of an option to tax any land under Part 1 of Schedule 10 to the Value Added Tax Act 1994 (c 23) made after the effective date of the transaction.

Amendment: SI 2008/1146.

Postponed consideration

3

The amount or value of the chargeable consideration for a transaction shall be determined without any discount for postponement of the right to receive it or any part of it.

Just and reasonable apportionment

4

(1) For the purposes of this Part consideration attributable –

    (a)   to two or more land transactions, or

    (b)   in part to a land transaction and in part to another matter, or

    (c)   in part to matters making it chargeable consideration and in part to other matters,

shall be apportioned on a just and reasonable basis.

(2) If the consideration is not so apportioned, this Part has effect as if it had been so apportioned.

(3) For the purposes of this paragraph any consideration given for what is in substance one bargain shall be treated as attributable to all the elements of the bargain, even though –

    (a)   separate consideration is, or purports to be, given for different elements of the bargain, or

    (b)   there are, or purport to be, separate transactions in respect of different elements of the bargain.

Exchanges

5

(1) This paragraph applies to determine the chargeable consideration where one or more land transactions are entered into by a person as purchaser (alone or jointly) wholly or partly in consideration of one or more other land transactions being entered into by him (alone or jointly) as vendor.

(2) In this paragraph –

    (a)   'relevant transaction' means any of those transactions, and

    (b)   'relevant acquisition' means a relevant transaction entered into as purchaser and 'relevant disposal' means a relevant transaction entered into as vendor.

(3) The following rules apply if the subject-matter of any of the relevant transactions is a major interest in land –

    (a)   where a single relevant acquisition is made, the chargeable consideration for the acquisition is –

        (i)   the market value of the subject-matter of the acquisition, and

        (ii)   if the acquisition is the grant of a lease at a rent, that rent;

(b)   where two or more relevant acquisitions are made, the chargeable consideration for each relevant acquisition is –
(i)   the market value of the subject-matter of that acquisition, and
(ii)   if the acquisition is the grant of a lease at a rent, that rent.

(4) The following rules apply if the subject-matter of none of the relevant transactions is a major interest in land –

(a)   where a single relevant acquisition is made in consideration of one or more relevant disposals, the chargeable consideration for the acquisition is the amount or value of any chargeable consideration other than the disposal or disposals that is given for the acquisition;
(b)   where two or more relevant acquisitions are made in consideration of one or more relevant disposals, the chargeable consideration for each relevant acquisition is the appropriate proportion of the amount or value of any chargeable consideration other than the disposal or disposals that is given for the acquisitions.

(5) For the purposes of sub-paragraph (4)(b) the appropriate proportion is –

$$\frac{MV}{TMV}$$

where –

MV is the market value of the subject-matter of the acquisition for which the chargeable consideration is being determined, and

TMV is the total market value of the subject-matter of all the relevant acquisitions.

(6) This paragraph has effect subject to –

paragraph 6 of this Schedule (partition etc: disregard of existing interest)

(7) This paragraph does not apply in a case to which paragraph 17 applies.

Amendments: SI 2003/3293; Finance Act 2004, s 326, Sch 42; SI 2004/1069.

Partition etc: disregard of existing interest

6

In the case of a land transaction giving effect to a partition or division of a chargeable interest to which persons are jointly entitled, the share of the interest held by the purchaser immediately before the partition or division does not count as chargeable consideration.

Valuation of non-monetary consideration

7

Except as otherwise expressly provided, the value of any chargeable consideration for a land transaction, other than –

(a)   money (whether in sterling or another currency), or
(b)   debt as defined for the purposes of paragraph 8 (debt as consideration),

shall be taken to be its market value at the effective date of the transaction.

Debt as consideration

8

(1) Where the chargeable consideration for a land transaction consists in whole or in part of –

  (a)   the satisfaction or release of debt due to the purchaser or owed by the vendor, or

  (b)   the assumption of existing debt by the purchaser,

the amount of debt satisfied, released or assumed shall be taken to be the whole or, as the case may be, part of the chargeable consideration for the transaction.

(1A) Where –

  (a)   debt is secured on the subject-matter of a land transaction immediately before and immediately after the transaction, and

  (b)   the rights or liabilities in relation to that debt of any party to the transaction are changed as a result of or in connection with the transaction,

then for the purposes of this paragraph there is an assumption of that debt by the purchaser, and that assumption of debt constitutes chargeable consideration for the transaction.

(1B) Where in a case in which sub-paragraph (1)(b) applies –

  (a)   the debt assumed is or includes debt secured on the property forming the subject-matter of the transaction, and

  (b)   immediately before the transaction there were two or more persons each holding an undivided share of that property, or there are two or more such persons immediately afterwards,

the amount of secured debt assumed shall be determined as if the amount of that debt owed by each of those persons at a given time were the proportion of it corresponding to his undivided share of the property at that time.

(1C) For the purposes of sub-paragraph (1B), in England and Wales and Northern Ireland each joint tenant of property is treated as holding an equal undivided share of it.

(2) If the effect of sub-paragraph (1) would be that the amount of the chargeable consideration for the transaction exceeded the market value of the subject-matter of the transaction, the amount of the chargeable consideration is treated as limited to that value.

(3) In this paragraph –

  (a)   'debt' means an obligation, whether certain or contingent, to pay a sum of money either immediately or at a future date,

  (b)   'existing debt', in relation to a transaction, means debt created or arising before the effective date of, and otherwise than in connection with, the transaction, and

  (c)   references to the amount of a debt are to the principal amount payable or, as the case may be, the total of the principal amounts payable, together with the amount of any interest that has accrued due on or before the effective date of the transaction.

Amendments: Finance Act 2004, s 301(2)-(4).

Cases where conditions for exemption not fully met

8A

(1) Where a land transaction would be exempt from charge under paragraph 3A of Schedule 3 (assents and appropriations by personal representatives) but for sub-paragraph (2) of that paragraph (cases where person acquiring property gives consideration for it), the chargeable consideration for the transaction does not include the amount of any secured debt assumed.

'Secured debt' has the same meaning as in that paragraph.

(2) Where a land transaction would be exempt from charge under paragraph 4 of Schedule 3 (variation of testamentary dispositions etc) but for a failure to meet the condition in sub-paragraph (2)(b) of that paragraph (no consideration other than variation of another disposition), the chargeable consideration for the transaction does not include the making of any such variation as is mentioned in that sub-paragraph.

Amendments: Inserted by Finance Act 2004, s 301(2), (5).

Conversion of amounts in foreign currency

9

(1) References in this Part to the amount or value of the consideration for a transaction are to its amount or value in sterling.

(2) For the purposes of this Part the sterling equivalent of an amount expressed in another currency shall be ascertained by reference to the London closing exchange rate on the effective date of the transaction (unless the parties have used a different rate for the purposes of the transaction).

Carrying out of works

10

(1) Where the whole or part of the consideration for a land transaction consists of the carrying out of works of construction, improvement or repair of a building or other works to enhance the value of land, then –

    (a)   to the extent that the conditions specified in sub-paragraph (2) are met, the value of the works does not count as chargeable consideration, and

    (b)   to the extent that those conditions are not met, the value of the works shall be taken into account as chargeable consideration.

(2) The conditions referred to in sub-paragraph (1) are –

    (a)   that the works are carried out after the effective date of the transaction,

    (b)   that the works are carried out on land acquired or to be acquired under the transaction or on other land held by the purchaser or a person connected with him, and

    (c)   that it is not a condition of the transaction that the works are carried out by the vendor or a person connected with him.

(2A) Where by virtue of –

    (a)   subsection (8) of section 44 (contract and conveyance),

    (b)   paragraph 12A of Schedule 17A (agreement for lease), or

    (c)   paragraph 19(3) to (6) of Schedule 17A (missives of let etc in Scotland), there are two notifiable transactions (the first being the contract or agreement and the second being the transaction effected on completion or, as the case may be, the grant or execution of the lease), the condition in sub-paragraph (2)(a) is treated as met in relation to the second transaction if it is met in relation to the first.

(3) In this paragraph –

(a) references to the acquisition of land are to the acquisition of a major interest in it;

(b) the value of the works shall be taken to be the amount that would have to be paid in the open market for the carrying out of the works in question.

(4) Section 839 of the Taxes Act 1988 (connected persons) has effect for the purposes of this paragraph.

(5) This paragraph is subject to paragraph 17 (arrangements involving public or educational bodies).

Amendments: SI 2003/3293; Finance Act 2004, ss 296, 297(1), (8), Sch 39.

Provision of services

11

(1) Where the whole or part of the consideration for a land transaction consists of the provision of services (other than the carrying out of works to which paragraph 10 applies), the value of that consideration shall be taken to be the amount that would have to be paid in the open market to obtain those services.

(2) This paragraph is subject to paragraph 17 (arrangements involving public or educational bodies).

Amendment: SI 2003/3293.

Land transaction entered into by reason of employment

12

(1) Where a land transaction is entered into by reason of the purchaser's employment, or that of a person connected with him, then –

(a) if the transaction gives rise to a charge to tax under Chapter 5 of Part 3 of the Income Tax (Earnings and Pensions) Act 2003 (c 1) (taxable benefits: living accommodation) and –
   (i) no rent is payable by the purchaser, or
   (ii) the rent payable by the purchaser is less than the cash equivalent of the benefit calculated under section 105 or 106 of that Act,
   there shall be taken to be payable by the purchaser as rent an amount equal to the cash equivalent chargeable under those sections;

(b) if the transaction would give rise to a charge under that Chapter but for section 99 of that Act (accommodation provided for performance of duties), the consideration for the transaction is the actual consideration (if any);

(c) if neither paragraph (a) nor paragraph (b) applies, the consideration for the transaction shall be taken to be not less than the market value of the subject-matter of the transaction as at the effective date of the transaction.

(2) Section 839 of the Taxes Act 1988 (connected persons) has effect for the purposes of this paragraph.

13–15

Amendments: Finance Act 2004, s 296, Sch 42.

Indemnity given by purchaser

16

Where the purchaser agrees to indemnify the vendor in respect of liability to a third party arising from breach of an obligation owed by the vendor in relation to the land that is the subject of the transaction, neither the agreement nor any payment made in pursuance of it counts as chargeable consideration.

Purchaser bearing inheritance tax liability

16A

Where –

(a)   there is a land transaction that is –
    (i)   a transfer of value within section 3 of the Inheritance Tax Act 1984 (transfers of value), or
    (ii)   a disposition, effected by will or under the law of intestacy, of a chargeable interest comprised in the estate of a person immediately before his death,

and

(b)   the purchaser is or becomes liable to pay, agrees to pay or does in fact pay any inheritance tax due in respect of the transfer or disposition,

his liability, agreement or payment does not count as chargeable consideration for the transaction.

Amendment: SI 2006/875.

Purchaser bearing capital gains tax liability

16B

(1) Where –

(a)   there is a land transaction under which the chargeable interest in question –
    (i)   is acquired otherwise than by a bargain made at arm's length, or
    (ii)   is treated by section 18 of the Taxation of Chargeable Gains Act 1992 (connected persons) as so acquired,
    and
(b)   the purchaser is or becomes liable to pay, or does in fact pay, any capital gains tax due in respect of the corresponding disposal of the chargeable interest,

his liability or payment does not count as chargeable consideration for the transaction.

(2) Sub-paragraph (1) does not apply if there is chargeable consideration for the transaction (disregarding the liability or payment referred to in sub-paragraph (1)(b)).

Amendment: SI 2006/875.

Costs of enfranchisement

16C

Costs borne by the purchaser under section 9(4) of the Leasehold Reform Act 1967 or section 33 of the Leasehold Reform, Housing and Urban Development Act 1993 (costs of enfranchisement) do not count as chargeable consideration.

Amendment: SI 2006/875.

Arrangements involving public or educational bodies

17

(1) This paragraph applies in any case where arrangements are entered into which –

- (a) there is a transfer, or the grant or assignment of a lease, of land by a qualifying body ('A') to a non-qualifying body ('B') ('the main transfer'),
- (b) in consideration (whether in whole or in part) of the main transfer there is a grant by B to A of a lease or under-lease of the whole, or substantially the whole, of that land ('the leaseback'),
- (c) B undertakes to carry out works or provide services to A, and
- (d) some or all of the consideration given by A to B for the carrying out of those works or the provision of those services is consideration in money,

whether or not there is also a transfer, or the grant or assignment of a lease, of any other land by A to B (a 'transfer of surplus land').

(2) The following are qualifying bodies –

- (a) public bodies within section 66,
- (b) institutions within the further education sector or the higher education sector within the meaning of section 91 of the Further and Higher Education Act 1992,
- (c) further education corporations within the meaning of section 17 of that Act,
- (d) higher education corporations within the meaning of section 90 of that Act,
- (e) persons who undertake to establish and maintain, and carry on, or provide for the carrying on, of an Academy within the meaning of section 482 of the Education Act 1996, and
- (f) in Scotland, institutions funded by the Scottish Further Education Funding Council or the Scottish Higher Education Funding Council.

(3) The following shall not count as chargeable consideration for the main transfer or any transfer of surplus land –

- (a) the lease-back;
- (b) the carrying out of building works by B for A; or
- (c) the provision of services by B to A.

(4) The chargeable consideration for the lease back does not include –

- (a) the main transfer;
- (b) any transfer of surplus land; or
- (c) the consideration in money paid by A to B for the building works or other services referred to in sub-paragraph (3).

(4A) Sub-paragraphs (3) and (4) shall be disregarded for the purposes of determining whether the land transaction in question is notifiable.

(5) This paragraph applies to Scotland as if –

(a)   references to A transferring land to B were references to A transferring the interest of an owner of land to B, and

(b)   references in sub-paragraph (1) to assignment were references to assignation.

Until the appointed day for the purposes of the Abolition of Feudal Tenure etc (Scotland) Act 2000 (asp 5), the reference in paragraph (a) to the interest of the owner shall be read, in relation to feudal property, as a reference to the estate or interest of the proprietor of the *dominium utile*.

(6) In this paragraph 'under-lease' include a sub-lease.

Amendments: SI 2003/3293; Finance Act 2004, s 296, Sch 39; SI 2004/1069; SI 2004/1206.

Schedule 5

Section 56

Stamp Duty Land Tax: Amount of Tax Chargeable: Rent

Introduction

1

This Schedule provides for calculating the tax chargeable –

(a)   in respect of a chargeable transaction for which the chargeable consideration consists of or includes rent, or

(b)   where such a transaction is to be taken into account as a linked transaction.

Amounts payable in respect of periods before grant of lease

1A

For the purposes of this Part 'rent' does not include any chargeable consideration for the grant of a lease that is payable in respect of a period before the grant of the lease.

Amendments: Inserted by Finance Act 2004, s 296, Sch 39.

Calculation of tax chargeable in respect of rent

2

(1) Tax is chargeable under this Schedule in respect of so much of the chargeable consideration as consists of rent.

(2) The tax chargeable is the total of the amounts produced by taking the relevant percentage of so much of the relevant rental value as falls within each rate band.

(3) The relevant percentages and rate bands are determined by reference to whether the relevant land –

(a)   consists entirely of residential property (in which case Table A below applies), or

(b)   consists of or includes land that is not residential property (in which case Table B below applies).

Table A: Residential

Rate bands	Percentage
£0 to £125,000	*0%*
Over £125,000	*1%*

Table B: Non-Residential Or Mixed

Rate bands	Percentage
£0 to £150,000	*0%*
Over £150,000	*1%*

(4) For the purposes of sub-paragraphs (2) and (3) –

    (a)   the relevant rental value is the net present value of the rent payable over the term of the lease, and

    (b)   the relevant land is the land that is the subject of the lease.

(5) If the lease in question is one of a number of linked transactions for which the chargeable consideration consists of or includes rent, the above provisions are modified.

(6) In that case the tax chargeable is determined as follows.

First, calculate the amount of the tax that would be chargeable if the linked transactions were a single transaction, so that –

    (a)   the relevant rental value is the total of the net present values of the rent payable over the terms of all the leases, and

    (b)   the relevant land is all land that is the subject of any of those leases.

Then, multiply that amount by the fraction:

$$\frac{NPV}{TNPV}$$

where –

   NPV is the net present value of the rent payable over the term of the lease in question, and

   TNPV is the total of the net present values of the rent payable over the terms of all the leases.

Amendments: Finance Act 2006, s 162(2).

Net present value of rent payable over term of lease

3

The net present value (v) of the rent payable over the term of a lease is calculated by applying the formula:

ri is the rent payable in respect of year i,

i is the first, second, third, etc year of the term,

$$v = \sum_{i=1}^{n} \frac{r_i}{(1 + T)^i}$$

n is the term of the lease, and

T is the temporal discount rate (see paragraph 8).

Amendments: Finance Act 2004, ss 164(2), 326, Sch 42.

4–7 ...

Amendments: Finance Act 2004, s 326, Sch 42.

Temporal discount rate

8

(1) For the purposes of this Schedule the 'temporal discount rate' is 3.5% or such other rate as may be specified by regulations made by the Treasury.

(2) Regulations under this paragraph may make any such provision as is mentioned in subsection (3)(b) to (f) of section 178 of the Finance Act 1989 (c 26) (power of Treasury to set rates of interest).

(3) Subsection (5) of that section (power of Inland Revenue to specify rate by order in certain circumstances) applies in relation to regulations under this paragraph as it applies in relation to regulations under that section.

Tax chargeable in respect of consideration other than rent: general

9

(1) Where in the case of a transaction to which this Schedule applies there is chargeable consideration other than rent, the provisions of this Part apply in relation to that consideration as in relation to other chargeable consideration (but see paragraph 9A).

the average annual rent over the period for which the highest ascertainable rent is payable.

(4) Tax chargeable under this Schedule is in addition to any tax chargeable under section 55 in respect of consideration other than rent.

(5) Where a transaction to which this Schedule applies falls to be taken into account for the purposes of that section as a linked transaction, no account shall be taken of rent in determining the relevant consideration.

Amendments: SI 2003/2914; Finance Act 2008, s 95(1), (2), (2)(a), (b), (13).

Tax chargeable in respect of consideration other than rent: 0% band

9A

(1) This paragraph applies in the case of a transaction to which this Schedule applies where there is chargeable consideration other than rent.

(2) If –

    (a)   the relevant land consists entirely of land that is non-residential property, and

    (b)   the relevant rent is at least £1,000,

the 0% band in Table B in section 55(2) does not apply in relation to the consideration other than rent and any case that would have fallen within that band is treated as falling within the 1% band.

(3) Sub-paragraphs (4) and (5) apply if –

    (a)   the relevant land is partly residential property and partly non-residential property, and

    (b)   the relevant rent attributable, on a just and reasonable apportionment, to the land that is non-residential property is at least £1,000.

(4) For the purpose of determining the amount of tax chargeable under section 55 in relation to the consideration other than rent, the transaction (or, where it is one of a number of linked transactions, that set of transactions) is treated as if it were two separate transactions (or sets of linked transactions), namely –

    (a)   one whose subject-matter consists of all of the interests in land that is residential property, and

    (b)   one whose subject-matter consists of all of the interests in land that is non-residential property.

(5) For that purpose, the chargeable consideration attributable to each of those separate transactions (or sets of linked transactions) is the chargeable consideration so attributable on a just and reasonable apportionment.

(6) In this paragraph 'the relevant rent' means –

    (a)   the annual rent in relation to the transaction in question, or

    (b)   if that transaction is one of a number of linked transactions for which the chargeable consideration consists of or includes rent, the total of the annual rents in relation to all of those transactions.

(7) In sub-paragraph (6) the 'annual rent' means the average annual rent over the term of the lease or, if –

    (a)   different amounts of rent are payable for different parts of the term, and

    (b)   those amounts (or any of them) are ascertainable at the effective date of the transaction,

the average annual rent over the period for which the highest ascertainable rent is payable.

(8) In this paragraph 'relevant land' has the meaning given in section 55(3) and (4).

Amendments: Inserted by Finance Act 2008, s 95(1), (3), (13).

Schedule 6

Section 57

Stamp Duty Land Tax: Disadvantaged Areas Relief

PART 1
DISADVANTAGED AREAS

Meaning of 'disadvantaged area'

1

(1) For the purposes of this Schedule a 'disadvantaged area' means an area designated as a disadvantaged area by regulations made by the Treasury.

(2) The regulations may –

  (a) designate specified areas as disadvantaged areas, or
  (b) provide for areas of a description specified in the regulations to be designated as disadvantaged areas.

(3) If the regulations so provide, the designation of an area as a disadvantaged area shall have effect for such period as may be specified by or determined in accordance with the regulations.

(4) The regulations may –

  (a) make different provision for different cases, and
  (b) contain such incidental, supplementary, consequential or transitional provision as appears to the Treasury to be necessary or expedient.

Continuation of regulations made for purposes of stamp duty

2

Any regulations made by the Treasury –

  (a) designating areas as disadvantaged areas for the purposes of section 92 of the Finance Act 2001 (c 9) (stamp duty exemption for land in disadvantaged areas), and
  (b) in force immediately before the implementation date,

have effect for the purposes of this Schedule as if made under paragraph 1 above and may be varied or revoked accordingly.

PART 2
LAND WHOLLY SITUATED IN A DISADVANTAGED AREA

Introduction

3

This Part of this Schedule applies to a land transaction if –

  (a) the subject matter of the transaction is a chargeable interest in relation to land that is wholly situated in a disadvantaged area, and
  (b) the land is wholly or partly residential property.

Amendment: Finance Act 2005, s 96, Sch 9.

4...

Amendments: Repealed by Finance Act 2005, ss 96, 104, Schs 9, 11.

Land all residential

5

(1) This paragraph applies where all the land is residential property.

(2) If –

    (a)   the consideration for the transaction does not include rent and the relevant consideration does not exceed £150,000, or

    (b)   the consideration for the transaction consists only of rent and the relevant rental value does not exceed £150,000,

the transaction is exempt from charge.

(3) If the consideration for the transaction includes rent and the relevant rental value does not exceed £150,000, the rent does not count as chargeable consideration.

(4) If the consideration for the transaction includes consideration other than rent, then –

    (a)   if –

        (ii)   the relevant consideration does not exceed £150,000,

        the consideration other than rent does not count as chargeable consideration;

Amendments: Finance Act 2008, s 95(4)(a), (5)(a), (b), (13).

Land partly non-residential and partly residential

6

(1) This paragraph applies, where the land is partly non-residential property and partly residential property, in relation to the consideration attributable to land that is residential property.

References in this paragraph to the consideration attributable to land that is non-residential property or land that is residential property (or to the rent or annual rent so attributable) are to the consideration (or rent or annual rent) so attributable on a just and reasonable apportionment.

(4) If –

    (a)   the consideration so attributable does not include rent and the relevant consideration does not exceed £150,000, or

    (b)   the consideration so attributable consists only of rent and the relevant rental value does not exceed £150,000,

none of the consideration so attributable counts as chargeable consideration.

(5) If the consideration so attributable includes rent and the relevant rental value does not exceed £150,000, the rent so attributable does not count as chargeable consideration.

(6) If the consideration so attributable includes consideration other than rent, then –

    (a)   if –

        (ii)   the relevant consideration does not exceed £150,000,

        the consideration other than rent does not count as chargeable consideration;

Amendments: Finance Act 2005, ss 96, 104, Schs 9, 11; Finance Act 2008, s 95(4)(b), (5)(a), (b), (13).

PART 3
LAND PARTLY SITUATED IN A DISADVANTAGED AREA

Introduction

7

(1) This Part of this Schedule applies to a land transaction if –

(a) the subject matter of the transaction is a chargeable interest in relation to land that is partly in a disadvantaged area and partly outside such an area, and

(b) the land situated in a disadvantaged area is wholly or partly residential property.

(2) References in this Part to the consideration attributable to land situated in a disadvantaged area and to land not so situated (or to the rent or annual rent so attributable) are to the consideration (or rent or annual rent) so attributable on a just and reasonable apportionment.

Amendments: Finance Act 2005, s 96, Sch 9.

Land all non-residential

8...

Amendments: Repealed by Finance Act 2005, ss 96, 104, Schs 9, 11.

Land all residential

9

(1) This paragraph applies where all the land situated in a disadvantaged area is residential property.

(2) If –

(a) the consideration attributable to land situated in a disadvantaged area does not include rent and the relevant consideration does not exceed £150,000, or

(b) the consideration so attributable consists only of rent and the relevant rental value does not exceed £150,000,

none of the consideration so attributable counts as chargeable consideration.

(3) If the consideration attributable to land situated in a disadvantaged area includes rent and the relevant rental value does not exceed £150,000, the rent so attributable does not count as chargeable consideration.

(4) If the consideration attributable to land in a disadvantaged area includes consideration other than rent ('non-rent consideration'), then –

(a) if –
(ii) the relevant consideration does not exceed £150,000,
the non-rent consideration so attributable does not count as chargeable consideration;

Amendments: Finance Act 2008, s 95(4)(c), (5)(a), (b), (13).

Land partly non-residential and partly residential

10

(1) This paragraph applies where the land situated in a disadvantaged area is partly non-residential property and partly residential property, in relation to the consideration attributable to land that is residential property.

References in this paragraph to the consideration attributable to land that is residential property (or to the rent or annual rent so attributable) are to the consideration (or rent or annual rent) attributable to land in a disadvantaged area that is, on a just and reasonable apportionment, so attributable.

2 ...

3 ...

(4) If –

  (a)   the consideration so attributable does not include rent and the relevant consideration does not exceed £150,000, or

  (b)   the consideration so attributable consists only of rent and the relevant rental value does not exceed £150,000,

none of the consideration so attributable counts as chargeable consideration.

(5) If the consideration so attributable includes rent and the relevant rental value does not exceed £150,000, the rent so attributable does not count as chargeable consideration.

(6) If the consideration so attributable includes consideration other than rent, then –

  (a)   if –

    (ii)   the relevant consideration does not exceed £150,000,

    the consideration other than rent does not count as chargeable consideration;

Amendments: Finance Act 2005, ss 96, 104, Schs 9, 11; Finance Act 2008, s 95(4)(d), (5)(a), (b), (13).

PART 4
SUPPLEMENTARY

Amendments: Finance Act 2004, s 298(1), (5).

Relevant consideration and relevant rental value

11

(1) References in this Schedule to the 'relevant consideration' in relation to a transaction are to the amount falling to be taken into account for the purposes of section 55(2) in determining the rate of tax chargeable under that section in relation to the transaction apart from any relief under this Schedule (whether in relation to that or any other transaction).

(2) References in this Schedule to the 'relevant rental value' in relation to a transaction are to the amount falling to be taken into account for the purposes of paragraph 2(3) of Schedule 5 in determining the rate of tax chargeable under that Schedule in relation to the transaction apart from any relief under this Schedule (whether in relation to that or any other transaction).

Rent and annual rent

12

For the purposes of this Schedule 'rent' has the same meaning as in Schedule 5(amount of tax chargeable: rent) and 'annual rent' has the same meaning as in paragraph 9A of that Schedule.

Amendments: Finance Act 2008, s 95(6), (13).

Notification of transactions

13

For the purposes of sections 77 and 77A (which specify what land transactions are notifiable) no account shall be taken of any provision of this Schedule to the effect that consideration does not count as chargeable consideration.

Amendments: Finance Act 2004, s 298(1), (5); Finance Act 2008, s 94(4), (5), Sch 30, paras 1, 6.

Schedule 6A

Section 58A

Relief For Certain Acquisitions Of Residential Property

Acquisition by house-building company from individual acquiring new dwelling

1

(1) Where a dwelling ('the old dwelling') is acquired by a house-building company from an individual (whether alone or with other individuals), the acquisition is exempt from charge if the following conditions are met.

(2) The conditions are –

    (a)   that the individual (whether alone or with other individuals) acquires from the house-building company a new dwelling,

    (b)   that the individual –

        (i)   occupied the old dwelling as his only or main residence at some time in the period of two years ending with the date of its acquisition, and

        (ii)   intends to occupy the new dwelling as his only or main residence,

    (c)   that each acquisition is entered into in consideration of the other, and

    (d)   that the area of land acquired by the house-building company does not exceed the permitted area.

(3) Where the conditions in sub-paragraph (2)(a) to (c) are met but the area of land acquired by the house-building company exceeds the permitted area, the chargeable consideration for the acquisition is taken to be the amount calculated by deducting the market value of the permitted area from the market value of the old dwelling.

(4) A 'house-building company' means a company that carries on the business of constructing or adapting buildings or parts of buildings for use as dwellings.

References in this paragraph to such a company include any company connected with it.

(5) In this paragraph –

(a)   references to the acquisition of the new dwelling are to the acquisition, by way of grant or transfer, of a major interest in the dwelling;

(b)   references to the acquisition of the old dwelling are to the acquisition, by way of transfer, of a major interest in the dwelling; and

(c)   references to the market value of the old dwelling and of the permitted area are, respectively, to the market value of that major interest in the dwelling and of that interest so far as it relates to that area.

Acquisition by property trader from individual acquiring new dwelling

2

(1) Where a dwelling ('the old dwelling') is acquired by a property trader from an individual (whether alone or with other individuals), the acquisition is exempt from charge if the following conditions are met.

(2) The conditions are –

(a)   that the acquisition is made in the course of a business that consists of or includes acquiring dwellings from individuals who acquire new dwellings from house-building companies,

(b)   that the individual (whether alone or with other individuals) acquires a new dwelling from a house-building company,

(c)   that the individual –
  (i)   occupied the old dwelling as his only or main residence at some time in the period of two years ending with the date of its acquisition, and
  (ii)   intends to occupy the new dwelling as his only or main residence,

(d)   that the property trader does not intend –
  (i)   to spend more than the permitted amount on refurbishment of the old dwelling, or
  (ii)   to grant a lease or licence of the old dwelling, or
  (iii) to permit any of its principals or employees (or any person connected with any of its principals or employees) to occupy the old dwelling, and

(e)   that the area of land acquired by the property trader does not exceed the permitted area.

Paragraph (d)(ii) does not apply to the grant of lease or licence to the individual for a period of no more than six months.

(3) Where the conditions in sub-paragraph (2)(a) to (d) are met, but the area of land acquired by the property trader exceeds the permitted area, the chargeable consideration for the acquisition is taken to be the amount calculated by deducting the market value of the permitted area from the market value of the old dwelling.

(4) The provisions of paragraph 1(4) (meaning of 'house-building company' etc) also have effect for the purposes of this paragraph.

(5) In this paragraph –

(a)   references to the acquisition of a new dwelling are to the acquisition, by way of grant or transfer, of a major interest in the dwelling;

(b)   references to the acquisition of the old dwelling are to the acquisition, by way of transfer, of a major interest in the dwelling; and

(c)   references to the market value of the old dwelling and of the permitted area are, respectively, to the market value of that major interest in the dwelling and of that interest so far as it relates to that area.

Acquisition by property trader from personal representatives

3

(1) Where a dwelling is acquired by a property trader from the personal representatives of a deceased individual, the acquisition is exempt from charge if the following conditions are met.

(2) The conditions are –

    (a)   that the acquisition is made in the course of a business that consists of or includes acquiring dwellings from personal representatives of deceased individuals,

    (b)   that the deceased individual occupied the dwelling as his only or main residence at some time in the period of two years ending with the date of his death,

    (c)   that the property trader does not intend –

        (i)   to spend more than the permitted amount on refurbishment of the dwelling, or

        (ii)   to grant a lease or licence of the dwelling, or

        (iii)   to permit any of its principals or employees (or any person connected with any of its principals or employees) to occupy the dwelling, and

    (d)   that the area of land acquired does not exceed the permitted area.

(3) Where the conditions in sub-paragraph (2)(a) to (c) are met, but the area of land acquired exceeds the permitted area, the chargeable consideration for the acquisition is taken to be the amount calculated by deducting the market value of the permitted area from the market value of the dwelling.

(4) In this paragraph –

    (a)   references to the acquisition of the dwelling are to the acquisition, by way of transfer, of a major interest in the dwelling; and

    (b)   references to the market value of the dwelling and of the permitted area are, respectively, to the market value of that major interest in the dwelling and of that interest so far as it relates to that area.

Acquisition by property trader from individual where chain of transactions breaks down

4

(1) Where a dwelling ('the old dwelling') is acquired by a property trader from an individual (whether alone or with other individuals), the acquisition is exempt from charge if –

    (a)   the individual has made arrangements to sell a dwelling ('the old dwelling') and acquire another dwelling ('the second dwelling'),

    (b)   the arrangements to sell the old dwelling fail, and

    (c)   the acquisition of the old dwelling is made for the purpose of enabling the individual's acquisition of the second dwelling to proceed,

and the following conditions are met.

(2) The conditions are –

    (a)   that the acquisition is made in the course of a business that consists of or includes acquiring dwellings from individuals in those circumstances,

    (b)   that the individual –

(i) occupied the old dwelling as his only or main residence at some time in the period of two years ending with the date of its acquisition, and

(ii) intends to occupy the second dwelling as his only or main residence,

(c) that the property trader does not intend –

(i) to spend more than the permitted amount on refurbishment of the old dwelling, or

(ii) to grant a lease or licence of the old dwelling, or

(iii) to permit any of its principals or employees (or any person connected with any of its principals or employees) to occupy the old dwelling, and

(d) that the area of land acquired does not exceed the permitted area.

Paragraph (c)(ii) does not apply to the grant of a lease or licence to the individual for a period of no more than six months.

(3) Where the conditions in sub-paragraph (2)(a) to (c) are met, but the area of land acquired exceeds the permitted area, the chargeable consideration for the acquisition is taken to be the amount calculated by deducting the market value of the permitted area from the market value of the old dwelling.

(4) In this paragraph –

(a) references to the acquisition of the second dwelling are to the acquisition, by way of grant or transfer, of a major interest in the dwelling;

(b) references to the acquisition of the old dwelling are to the acquisition, by way of transfer, of a major interest in the dwelling; and

(c) references to the market value of the old dwelling and of the permitted area are, respectively, to the market value of that major interest in the dwelling and of that interest so far as it relates to that area.

Acquisition by employer in case of relocation of employment

5

(1) Where a dwelling is acquired from an individual (whether alone or with other individuals) by his employer, the acquisition is exempt from charge if the following conditions are met.

(2) The conditions are –

(a) that the individual occupied the dwelling as his only or main residence at some time in the period of two years ending with the date of the acquisition,

(b) that the acquisition is made in connection with a change of residence by the individual resulting from relocation of employment,

(c) that the consideration for the acquisition does not exceed the market value of the dwelling, and

(d) that the area of land acquired does not exceed the permitted area.

(3) Where the conditions in sub-paragraph (2)(a) to (c) are met but the area of land acquired exceeds the permitted area, the chargeable consideration for the acquisition is taken to be the amount calculated by deducting the market value of the permitted area from the market value of the dwelling.

(4) In this paragraph 'relocation of employment' means a change of the individual's place of employment due to –

(a) his becoming an employee of the employer,

(b) an alteration of the duties of his employment with the employer, or

(c)   an alteration of the place where he normally performs those duties.

(5) For the purposes of this paragraph a change of residence is one 'resulting from' relocation of employment if –

(a)   the change is made wholly or mainly to allow the individual to have his residence within a reasonable daily travelling distance of his new place of employment, and

(b)   his former residence is not within a reasonable daily travelling distance of that place.

The individual's 'new place of employment' means the place where he normally performs, or is normally to perform, the duties of his employment after the relocation.

(6) In this paragraph –

(a)   references to the acquisition of the dwelling are to the acquisition, by way of transfer, of a major interest in the dwelling;

(b)   references to the market value of the dwelling and of the permitted area are, respectively, to the market value of that major interest in the dwelling and of that interest so far as it relates to that area; and

(c)   references to an individual's employer include a prospective employer.

Acquisition by property trader in case of relocation of employment

6

(1) Where a dwelling is acquired by a property trader from an individual (whether alone or with other individuals), the acquisition is exempt from charge if the following conditions are met.

(2) The conditions are –

(a)   that the acquisition is made in the course of a business that consists of or includes acquiring dwellings from individuals in connection with a change of residence resulting from relocation of employment,

(b)   that the individual occupied the dwelling as his only or main residence at some time in the period of two years ending with the date of the acquisition,

(c)   that the acquisition is made in connection with a change of residence by the individual resulting from relocation of employment,

(d)   that the consideration for the acquisition does not exceed the market value of the dwelling,

(e)   that the property trader does not intend –

(i)   to spend more than the permitted amount on refurbishment of the dwelling, or

(ii)   to grant a lease or licence of the dwelling, or

(iii)   to permit any of its principals or employees (or any person connected with any of its principals or employees) to occupy the dwelling, and

(f)   that the area of land acquired does not exceed the permitted area.

Paragraph (e)(ii) does not apply to the grant of a lease or licence to the individual for a period of no more than six months.

(3) Where the conditions in sub-paragraph (2)(a) to (e) are met but the area of land acquired exceeds the permitted area, the chargeable consideration for the acquisition is taken to be the amount calculated by deducting the market value of the permitted area from the market value of the dwelling.

(4) In this paragraph 'relocation of employment' means a change of the individual's place of employment due to –

    (a)   his becoming employed by a new employer,

    (b)   an alteration of the duties of his employment, or

    (c)   an alteration of the place where he normally performs those duties.

(5) For the purposes of this paragraph a change of residence is one 'resulting from' relocation of employment if –

    (a)   the change is made wholly or mainly to allow the individual to have his residence within a reasonable daily travelling distance of his new place of employment, and

    (b)   his former residence is not within a reasonable daily travelling distance of that place.

An individual's 'new place of employment' means the place where he normally performs, or is normally to perform, the duties of his employment after the relocation.

(6) In this paragraph –

    (a)   references to the acquisition of the dwelling are to the acquisition, by way of transfer, of a major interest in the dwelling; and

    (b)   references to the market value of the dwelling and of the permitted area are, respectively, to the market value of that major interest in the dwelling and of that interest so far as it relates to that area.

Meaning of 'dwelling', 'new dwelling' and 'the permitted area'

7

(1) 'Dwelling' includes land occupied and enjoyed with the dwelling as its garden or grounds.

(2) A building or part of a building is a 'new dwelling' if –

    (a)   it has been constructed for use as a single dwelling and has not previously been occupied, or

    (b)   it has been adapted for use as a single dwelling and has not been occupied since its adaptation.

(3) 'The permitted area', in relation to a dwelling, means land occupied and enjoyed with the dwelling as its garden or grounds that does not exceed –

    (a)   an area (inclusive of the site of the dwelling) of 0.5 of a hectare, or

    (b)   such larger area as is required for the reasonable enjoyment of the dwelling as a dwelling having regard to its size and character.

(4) Where sub-paragraph (3)(b) applies, the permitted area is taken to consist of that part of the land that would be the most suitable for occupation and enjoyment with the dwelling as its garden or grounds if the rest of the land were separately occupied.

Meaning of 'property trader' and 'principal'

8

(1) A 'property trader' means –

    (a)   a company,

    (b)   a limited liability partnership, or

(c)   a partnership whose members are all either companies or limited liability partnerships,

that carries on the business of buying and selling dwellings.

(2) In relation to a property trader a 'principal' means –

(a)   in the case of a company, a director;
(b)   in the case of a limited liability partnership, a member;
(c)   in the case of a partnership whose members are all either companies or limited liability partnerships, a member or a person who is a principal of a member.

(3) For the purposes of this Schedule –

(a)   anything done by or in relation to a company connected with a property trader is treated as done by or in relation to that property trader, and
(b)   references to the principals or employees of a property trader include the principals or employees of any such company.

Meaning of 'refurbishment' and 'the permitted amount'

9

(1) 'Refurbishment' of a dwelling means the carrying out of works that enhance or are intended to enhance the value of the dwelling, but does not include –

(a)   cleaning the dwelling, or
(b)   works required solely for the purpose of ensuring that the dwelling meets minimum safety standards.

(2) 'The permitted amount', in relation to the refurbishment of a dwelling, is –

(a)   £10,000, or
(b)   5% of the consideration for the acquisition of the dwelling,

whichever is the greater, but subject to a maximum of £20,000.

Connected companies etc

10

Section 839 of the Taxes Act 1988 (connected persons) has effect for the purposes of this Schedule.

Withdrawal of relief under this Schedule

11

(1) Relief under this Schedule is withdrawn in the following circumstances.

(2) Relief under paragraph 2 (acquisition by property trader from individual acquiring new dwelling) is withdrawn if the property trader –

(a)   spends more than the permitted amount on refurbishment of the old dwelling, or
(b)   grants a lease or licence of the old dwelling, or
(c)   permits any of its principals or employees (or any person connected with any of its principals or employees) to occupy the old dwelling.

Paragraph (b) does not apply to the grant of lease or licence to the individual for a period of no more than six months.

(3) Relief under paragraph 3 (acquisition by property trader from personal representatives) is withdrawn if the property trader –

    (a)   spends more than the permitted amount on refurbishment of the dwelling, or

    (b)   grants a lease or licence of the dwelling, or

    (c)   permits any of its principals or employees (or any person connected with any of its principals or employees) to occupy the dwelling.

(4) Relief under paragraph 4 (acquisition by property trader from individual where chain of transactions breaks down) is withdrawn if the property trader –

    (a)   spends more than the permitted amount on refurbishment of the old dwelling, or

    (b)   grants a lease or licence of the old dwelling, or

    (c)   permits any of its principals or employees (or any person connected with any of its principals or employees) to occupy the old dwelling.

Paragraph (b) does not apply to the grant of lease or licence to the individual for a period of no more than six months.

(5) Relief under paragraph 6 (acquisition by property trader in case of relocation of employment) is withdrawn if the property trader –

    (a)   spends more than the permitted amount on refurbishment of the dwelling, or

    (b)   grants a lease or licence of the dwelling, or

    (c)   permits any of its principals or employees (or any person connected with any of its principals or employees) to occupy the dwelling.

Paragraph (b) does not apply to the grant of lease or licence to the individual for a period of no more than six months.

(6) Where relief is withdrawn the amount of tax chargeable is the amount that would have been chargeable in respect of the acquisition but for the relief.

Amendments: Schedule inserted: Finance Act 2004, s 296, Sch 39.

Schedule 7

Section 62

Stamp Duty Land Tax: Group Relief And Reconstruction And Acquisition Reliefs

PART 1
GROUP RELIEF

Group relief

1

(1) A transaction is exempt from charge if the vendor and purchaser are companies that at the effective date of the transaction are members of the same group.

(2) For the purposes of group relief –

    (a)   'company' means a body corporate, and

    (b)   companies are members of the same group if one is the 75% subsidiary of the other or both are 75% subsidiaries of a third company.

(3) For the purposes of group relief a company ('company A') is the 75% subsidiary of another company ('company B') if company B –

  (a)   is beneficial owner of not less than 75% of the ordinary share capital of company A,
  (b)   is beneficially entitled to not less than 75% of any profits available for distribution to equity holders of company A, and
  (c)   would be beneficially entitled to not less than 75% of any assets of company A available for distribution to its equity holders on a winding-up.

(4) The ownership referred to in sub-paragraph (3)(a) is ownership either directly or through another company or companies.

For the purposes of that provision the amount of ordinary share capital of company A owned by company B through another company or companies shall be determined in accordance with section 838(5) to (10) of the Taxes Act 1988.

(5) In sub-paragraphs (3)(a) and (4) above 'ordinary share capital', in relation to a company, means all the issued share capital (by whatever name called) of the company, other than capital the holders of which have a right to a dividend at a fixed rate but have no other right to share in the profits of the company.

(6) Schedule 18 to the Taxes Act 1988 (equity holders and profits or assets available for distribution) applies for the purposes of subsection (3)(b) and (c) above as it applies for the purposes of section 413(7)(a) and (b) of that Act, but with the omission of paragraphs 5(3) and 5B to 5E.

(7) This paragraph is subject to paragraph 2 (restrictions on availability of group relief) and paragraphs 3 and 4A (withdrawal of group relief).

Amendments: Finance (No 2) Act 2005, s 49, Sch 10.

Restrictions on availability of group relief

2

(1) Group relief is not available if at the effective date of the transaction there are arrangements in existence by virtue of which, at that or some later time, a person has or could obtain, or any persons together have or could obtain, control of the purchaser but not of the vendor.

This does not apply to arrangements entered into with a view to an acquisition of shares by a company ('the acquiring company') –

  (a)   in relation to which section 75 of the Finance Act 1986 (c 41) (stamp duty: acquisition relief) will apply,
  (b)   in relation to which the conditions for relief under that section will be met, and
  (c)   as a result of which the purchaser will be a member of the same group as the acquiring company.

For another exception to this, see sub-paragraph (3A).

(2) Group relief is not available if the transaction is effected in pursuance of, or in connection with, arrangements under which –

  (a)   the consideration, or any part of the consideration, for the transaction is to be provided or received (directly or indirectly) by a person other than a group company, or

(b) the vendor and the purchaser are to cease to be members of the same group by reason of the purchaser ceasing to be a 75% subsidiary of the vendor or a third company.

(3) Arrangements are within sub-paragraph (2)(a) if under them the vendor or the purchaser, or another group company, is to be enabled to provide any of the consideration, or is to part with any of it, by or in consequence of the carrying out of a transaction or transactions involving, or any of them involving, a payment or other disposition by a person other than a group company.

(3A) Sub-paragraphs (1) and (2)(b) do not apply to arrangements in so far as they are for the purpose of facilitating a transfer of the whole or part of the business of a company to another company in relation to which –

(a) section 96 of the Finance Act 1997 is intended to apply (stamp duty relief: demutualisation of insurance companies), and
(b) the conditions for relief under that section are intended to be met.

(4) In sub-paragraphs (2)(a) and (3) a 'group company' means a company that at the effective date of the transaction is a member of the same group as the vendor or the purchaser.

(4A) Group relief is not available if the transaction –

(a) is not effected for bona fide commercial reasons, or
(b) forms part of arrangements of which the main purpose, or one of the main purposes, is the avoidance of liability to tax.

'Tax' here means stamp duty, income tax, corporation tax, capital gains tax or tax under this Part.

(5) In this paragraph –

'arrangements' includes any scheme, agreement or understanding, whether or not legally enforceable; and
'control' has the meaning given by section 840 of the Taxes Act 1988.

Amendments: Finance (No 2) Act 2005, s 49, Sch 10; Finance Act 2006, s 167(1)–(3).

Withdrawal of group relief

3

(1) Where in the case of a transaction ('the relevant transaction') that is exempt from charge by virtue of paragraph 1 (group relief) –

(a) the purchaser ceases to be a member of the same group as the vendor –
  (i) before the end of the period of three years beginning with the effective date of the transaction, or
  (ii) in pursuance of, or in connection with, arrangements made before the end of that period,
  and
(b) at the time the purchaser ceases to be a member of the same group as the vendor ('the relevant time'), it or a relevant associated company holds a chargeable interest –
  (i) that was acquired by the purchaser under the relevant transaction, or
  (ii) that is derived from a chargeable interest so acquired,

and that has not subsequently been acquired at market value under a chargeable transaction for which group relief was available but was not claimed,

group relief in relation to the relevant transaction, or an appropriate proportion of it, is withdrawn and tax is chargeable in accordance with this paragraph.

(2) The amount chargeable is the tax that would have been chargeable in respect of the relevant transaction but for group relief if the chargeable consideration for that transaction had been an amount equal to –

(a)   the market value of the subject-matter of the transaction, and
(b)   if the acquisition was the grant of a lease at a rent, that rent,

or, as the case may be, an appropriate proportion of the tax that would have been so chargeable.

(3) In sub-paragraphs (1) and (2) 'an appropriate proportion' means an appropriate proportion having regard to the subject matter of the relevant transaction and what is held at the relevant time by the transferee company or, as the case may be, by that company and its relevant associated companies.

(4) In this paragraph –

'arrangements' includes any scheme, agreement or understanding, whether or not legally enforceable; and
'relevant associated company', in relation to the purchaser, means a company that –
(a)   is a member of the same group as the purchaser immediately before the purchaser ceases to be a member of the same group as the vendor, and
(b)   ceases to be a member of the same group as the vendor in consequence of the purchaser so ceasing.

(5) This paragraph has effect subject to paragraphs 4 and 4ZA (cases in which group relief not withdrawn) and paragraph 4A (withdrawal of group relief in certain cases involving successive transactions).

Amendments: Finance (No 2) Act 2005, s 49, Sch 10; Finance Act 2008, s 96(1), (2), (6).

Cases in which group relief not withdrawn

4

(1) Group relief is not withdrawn under paragraph 3 in the following cases.

(4) The second case is where the purchaser ceases to be a member of the same group as the vendor by reason of anything done for the purposes of, or in the course of, winding up the vendor or another company that is above the vendor in the group structure.

(5) For the purposes of sub-paragraph (4) a company is 'above' the vendor in the group structure if the vendor, or another company that is above the vendor in the group structure, is a 75% subsidiary of the company.

(6) The third case is where –

(a)   the purchaser ceases to be a member of the same group as the vendor as a result of an acquisition of shares by another company ('the acquiring company') in relation to which –
(i)   section 75 of the Finance Act 1986 (c 41) applies (stamp duty: acquisition relief), and

        (ii)   the conditions for relief under that section are met, and

    (b)   the purchaser is immediately after that acquisition a member of the same group as the acquiring company.

(6A) The fourth case is where –

    (a)   the purchaser ceases to be a member of the same group as the vendor as a result of the transfer of the whole or part of the vendor's business to another company ('the acquiring company') in relation to which –
        (i)   section 96 of the Finance Act 1997 applies (stamp duty relief: demutualisation of insurance companies), and
        (ii)   the conditions for relief under that section are met, and

    (b)   the purchaser is immediately after that transfer a member of the same group as the acquiring company.

(7) But if in a case within sub-paragraph (6) or 6A –

    (a)   the purchaser ceases to be a member of the same group as the acquiring company –
        (i)   before the end of the period of three years beginning with the effective date of the relevant transaction, or
        (ii)   in pursuance of, or in connection with, arrangements made before the end of that period,
        and

    (b)   at the time the purchaser ceases to be a member of the same group as the acquiring company, it or a relevant associated company holds a chargeable interest –
        (i)   that was acquired by the purchaser under the relevant transaction, or
        (ii)   that is derived from an interest so acquired,
        and that has not subsequently been acquired at market value under a chargeable transaction for which group relief was available but was not claimed,

the provisions of this Part relating to group relief apply as if the purchaser had then ceased to be a member of the same group as the vendor.

(8) In sub-paragraph (7) –

'arrangements' includes any scheme, agreement or understanding, whether or not legally enforceable; and
'relevant associated company', in relation to the purchaser, means a company that is a member of the same group as the purchaser that ceases to be a member of the same group as the acquiring company in consequence of the purchaser so ceasing.

Amendments: Finance (No 2) Act 2005, s 49, Sch 10; Finance Act 2006, s 167(1), (4); Finance Act 2008, s 96(1), (3)(a), (b), (6).

Group relief not withdrawn where vendor leaves group

4ZA

(1) Group relief is not withdrawn under paragraph 3 where the purchaser ceases to be a member of the same group as the vendor because the vendor leaves the group.

(2) The vendor is regarded as leaving the group if the companies cease to be members of the same group by reason of a transaction relating to shares in –

844 *Stamp Duty Land Tax*

(a)   the vendor, or
(b)   another company that –
    (i)   is above the vendor in the group structure, and
    (ii)   as a result of the transaction ceases to be a member of the same group as the purchaser.

(3) For the purpose of sub-paragraph (2) a company is 'above' the vendor in the group structure if the vendor, or another company that is above the vendor in the group structure, is a 75% subsidiary of the company.

(4) But if there is a change in the control of the purchaser after the vendor leaves the group, paragraphs 3, 4(6) and (7), 5 and 6 have effect as if the purchaser had then ceased to be a member of the same group as the vendor (but see sub-paragraph (7)).

(5) For the purposes of this paragraph there is a change in the control of the purchaser if –

(a)   a person who controls the purchaser (alone or with others) ceases to do so,
(b)   a person obtains control of the purchaser (alone or with others), or
(c)   the purchaser is wound up.

(6) For the purposes of sub-paragraph (5) a person does not control, or obtain control of, the purchaser if that person is under the control of another person or other persons.

(7) Sub-paragraph (4) does not apply where –

(a)   there is a change in the control of the purchaser because a loan creditor (within the meaning of section 417(7) to (9) of the Taxes Act 1988) obtains control of, or ceases to control, the purchaser, and
(b)   the other persons who controlled the purchaser before that change continue to do so.

(8) In this paragraph references to 'control' shall be interpreted in accordance with section 416 of the Taxes Act 1988 (subject to sub-paragraph (6)).

Amendments: Inserted by Finance Act 2008, s 96(1), (4), (6).

Withdrawal of group relief in certain cases involving successive transactions

4A

(1) Where, in the case of a transaction ('the relevant transaction') that is exempt from charge by virtue of paragraph 1 (group relief) –

(a)   there is a change in the control of the purchaser,
(b)   that change occurs –
    (i)   before the end of the period of three years beginning with the effective date of the relevant transaction, or
    (ii)   in pursuance of, or in connection with, arrangements made before the end of that period,
(c)   apart from this paragraph, group relief in relation to the relevant transaction would not be withdrawn under paragraph 3, and
(d)   any previous transaction falls within sub-paragraph (2),

paragraphs 3, 4 and 4ZA have effect in relation to the relevant transaction as if the vendor in relation to the earliest previous transaction falling within sub-paragraph (2) were the vendor in relation to the relevant transaction.

(1A) Sub-paragraph (1) has effect subject to sub-paragraph (3A)

(2) A previous transaction falls within this sub-paragraph if –

(a)　the previous transaction is exempt from charge by virtue of paragraph 1, 7 or 8,

(b)　the effective date of the previous transaction is less than three years before the date of the event falling within sub-paragraph (1)(a),

(c)　the chargeable interest acquired under the relevant transaction by the purchaser in relation to that transaction is the same as, comprises, forms part of, or is derived from, the chargeable interest acquired under the previous transaction by the purchaser in relation to the previous transaction, and

(d)　since the previous transaction, the chargeable interest acquired under that transaction has not been acquired by any person under a transaction that is not exempt from charge by virtue of paragraph 1, 7 or 8.

(3)　For the purposes of this paragraph there is a change in the control of a company if –

(a)　any person who controls the company (alone or with others) ceases to do so,

(b)　a person obtains control of the company (alone or with others), or

(c)　the company is wound up.

References to 'control' in this paragraph shall be construed in accordance with section 416 of the Taxes Act 1988.

(3A)　Sub-paragraph (1) does not apply where –

(a)　there is a change in the control of the purchaser because a loan creditor (within the meaning of section 417(7) to (9) of the Taxes Act 1988) obtains control of, or ceases to control, the purchaser, and

(b)　the other persons who controlled the purchaser before that change continue to do so.

(4) If two or more transactions effected at the same time are the earliest previous transactions falling within sub-paragraph (2), the reference in sub-paragraph (1) to the vendor in relation to the earliest previous transaction is a reference to the persons who are the vendors in relation to the earliest previous transactions.

(5) In this paragraph 'arrangements' includes any scheme, agreement or understanding, whether or not legally enforceable.

Amendments: Finance (No 2) Act 2005, s 49, Sch 10; Finance Act 2008, s 96(1), (5)(a)–(d), (6).

Recovery of group relief from another group company or controlling director

5

(1) This paragraph applies where –

(a)　tax is chargeable under paragraph 3 (withdrawal of group relief),

(b)　the amount so chargeable has been finally determined, and

(c)　the whole or part of the amount so chargeable is unpaid six months after the date on which it became payable.

(2) The following persons may, by notice under paragraph 6, be required to pay the unpaid tax –

(a)　the vendor;

(b)　any company that at any relevant time was a member of the same group as the purchaser and was above it in the group structure;

(c)   any person who at any relevant time was a controlling director of the purchaser or a company having control of the purchaser.

(3) For the purposes of sub-paragraph (2)(b) –

(a)   a 'relevant time' means any time between the effective date of the relevant transaction and the purchaser ceasing to be a member of the same group as the vendor; and

(b)   a company ('company A') is 'above' another company ('company B') in a group structure if company B, or another company that is above company B in the group structure, is a 75% subsidiary of company A.

(4) In sub-paragraph (2)(c) –

'director', in relation to a company, has the meaning given by section 67(1) of the Income Tax (Earnings and Pensions) Act 2003 (c 1) (read with subsection (2) of that section) and includes any person falling within section 417(5) of the Taxes Act 1988 (read with subsection (6) of that section); and

'controlling director', in relation to a company, means a director of the company who has control of it (construing control in accordance with section 416 of the Taxes Act 1988).

Recovery of group relief: supplementary

6

(1) The Inland Revenue may serve a notice on a person within paragraph 5(2) above requiring him within 30 days of the service of the notice to pay the amount that remains unpaid.

(2) Any such notice must be served before the end of the period of three years beginning with the date of the final determination mentioned in paragraph 5(1)(b).

(3) The notice must state the amount required to be paid by the person on whom the notice is served.

(4) The notice has effect –

(a)   for the purposes of the recovery from that person of the amount required to be paid and of interest on that amount, and

(b)   for the purposes of appeals,

as if it were a notice of assessment and that amount were an amount of tax due from that person.

(5) A person who has paid an amount in pursuance of a notice under this paragraph may recover that amount from the purchaser.

(6) A payment in pursuance of a notice under this paragraph is not allowed as a deduction in computing any income, profits or losses for any tax purpose.

PART 2

RECONSTRUCTION AND ACQUISITION RELIEFS

Reconstruction relief

7

(1) Where –

(a) a company ('the acquiring company') acquires the whole or part of the undertaking of another company ('the target company') in pursuance of a scheme for the reconstruction of the target company, and

(b) the first, second and third conditions specified below are met,

a land transaction entered into for the purposes of or in connection with the transfer of the undertaking or part is exempt from charge.

Relief under this paragraph is referred to in this Part as 'reconstruction relief'.

(2) The first condition is that the consideration for the acquisition consists wholly or partly of the issue of non-redeemable shares in the acquiring company to all the shareholders of the target company.

'Non-redeemable shares' means shares that are not redeemable shares.

(3) Where the consideration for the acquisition consists partly of the issue of non-redeemable shares as mentioned in the first condition, that condition is met only if the rest of the consideration consists wholly of the assumption or discharge by the acquiring company of liabilities of the target company.

(4) The second condition is that after the acquisition has been made –

(a) each shareholder of each of the companies is a shareholder of the other, and

(b) the proportion of shares of one of the companies held by any shareholder is the same, or as nearly as may be the same, as the proportion of shares of the other company held by that shareholder.

(5) The third condition is that the acquisition is effected for bona fide commercial reasons and does not form part of a scheme or arrangement of which the main purpose, or one of the main purposes, is the avoidance of liability to tax.

'Tax' here means stamp duty, income tax, corporation tax, capital gains tax or tax under this Part.

(5A) If immediately before the acquisition the target company or the acquiring company holds any of its own shares, the shares are to be treated for the purposes of sub-paragraphs (2) and (4) as having been cancelled before the acquisition (and, accordingly, the company is to be treated as if it were not a shareholder of itself).

(6) This paragraph is subject to paragraph 9 (withdrawal of reconstruction or acquisition relief).

Amendments: Finance Act 2007, s 74(3), (5).

Acquisition relief

8

(1) Where –

(a) a company ('the acquiring company') acquires the whole or part of the undertaking of another company ('the target company'), and

(b) all the conditions specified below are met,

the rate of tax chargeable on a land transaction entered into for the purposes of or in connection with the transfer of the undertaking or part is limited to 0.5%.

Relief under this paragraph is referred to in this Part as 'acquisition relief'.

(2) The first condition is that the consideration for the acquisition consists wholly or partly of the issue of non-redeemable shares in the acquiring company to –

(a)   the target company, or

(b)   all or any of the target company's shareholders.

'Non-redeemable shares' means shares that are not redeemable shares.

(3) Where the consideration for the acquisition consists partly of the issue of non-redeemable shares as mentioned in the first condition, that condition is met only if the rest of the consideration consists wholly of –

(a)   cash not exceeding 10% of the nominal value of the non-redeemable shares so issued, or

(b)   the assumption or discharge by the acquiring company of liabilities of the target company, or

(c)   both of those things.

(4) The second condition is that the acquiring company is not associated with another company that is a party to arrangements with the target company relating to shares of the acquiring company issued in connection with the transfer of the undertaking or part.

(5) For this purpose companies are associated if one has control of the other or both are controlled by the same person or persons.

The reference to control shall be construed in accordance with section 416 of the Taxes Act 1988.

(5A) The third condition is that the undertaking or part acquired by the acquiring company has as its main activity the carrying on of a trade that does not consist wholly or mainly of dealing in chargeable interests.

In this sub-paragraph 'trade' has the same meaning as in the Taxes Act 1988.

(5B) The fourth condition is that the acquisition is effected for bona fide commercial reasons and does not form part of arrangements of which the main purpose, or one of the main purposes, is the avoidance of liability to tax.

'Tax' here means stamp duty, income tax, corporation tax, capital gains tax or tax under this Part.

(5C) In this paragraph 'arrangements' include any scheme, agreement or understanding, whether or not legally enforceable.

(6) This paragraph is subject to paragraph 9 (withdrawal of reconstruction or acquisition relief).

Amendments: Finance (No 2) Act 2005, s 49, Sch 10.

Withdrawal of reconstruction or acquisition relief

9

(1) Where in the case of a transaction ('the relevant transaction') that is exempt by virtue of reconstruction relief or is subject to a reduced rate of tax by virtue of acquisition relief –

(a)   control of the acquiring company changes –

       (i)   before the end of the period of three years beginning with the effective date of the transaction, or

       (ii)   in pursuance of, or in connection with, arrangements made before the end of that period,

and

    (b)   at the time control of the acquiring *company* changes ('the relevant time'), it or a relevant associated company holds a chargeable interest –

       (i)   that was acquired by the acquiring company under the relevant transaction, or

       (ii)   that is derived from an interest so acquired,

and that has not subsequently been acquired at market value under a chargeable transaction in relation to which reconstruction or acquisition relief was available but was not claimed,

reconstruction or acquisition relief in relation to the relevant transaction, or an appropriate proportion of it, is withdrawn and tax is chargeable in accordance with this paragraph.

(2) The amount chargeable is the tax that would have been chargeable in respect of the relevant transaction but for reconstruction or acquisition relief if the chargeable consideration for that transaction had been an amount equal to –

    (a)   the market value of the subject-matter of the transaction, and

    (b)   if the acquisition was the grant of a lease at a rent, that rent,

or, as the case may be, an appropriate proportion of the tax that would have been so chargeable.

(3) In sub-paragraphs (1) and (2) 'an appropriate proportion' means an appropriate proportion having regard to the subject-matter of the relevant transaction and what is held at the relevant time by the acquiring company or, as the case may be, by that company and any relevant associated companies.

(4) In this paragraph 'relevant associated company', in relation to the acquiring company, means a company –

    (a)   that is controlled by the acquiring company immediately before the control of that company changes, and

    (b)   of which control changes in consequence of the change of control of that company.

(5) In this paragraph –

    (a)   'arrangements' includes any scheme, agreement or understanding, whether or not legally enforceable;

    (b)   'control' shall be construed in accordance with section 416 of the Taxes Act 1988; and

    (c)   references to control of a company changing are to the company becoming controlled –

       (i)   by a different person,

       (ii)   by a different number of persons, or

       (iii)   by two or more persons at least one of whom is not the person, or one of the persons, by whom the company was previously controlled.

(6) This paragraph has effect subject to paragraph 10 (cases in which reconstruction or acquisition relief not withdrawn).

Amendments: SI 2003/2899; Finance (No 2) Act 2005, s 49, Sch 10.

Cases in which reconstruction or acquisition relief not withdrawn

10

(1) Reconstruction or acquisition relief is not withdrawn under paragraph 9 in the following cases.

(2) The first case is where control of the acquiring company changes as a result of a share transaction that is effected as mentioned in any of paragraphs (a) to (d) of paragraph 3 of Schedule 3 (transactions in connection with divorce etc).

(3) The second case is where control of the acquiring company changes as a result of a share transaction that –

(a)   is effected as mentioned in paragraph 4(1) of Schedule 3, and
(b)   meets the conditions in paragraph 4(2) of that Schedule (variation of testamentary dispositions etc).

(4) The third case is where control of the acquiring company changes as a result of an exempt intra-group transfer.

An 'exempt intra-group transfer' means a transfer of shares effected by an instrument that is exempt from stamp duty by virtue of section 42 of the Finance Act 1930 (c 28) or section 11 of the Finance Act (Northern Ireland) 1954 (c 23 (NI)) (transfers between associated bodies corporate).

But see paragraph 11 (withdrawal of relief in case of subsequent non-exempt transfer).

(5) The fourth case is where control of the acquiring company changes as a result of a transfer of shares to another company in relation to which share acquisition relief applies.

'Share acquisition relief' means relief under section 77 of the Finance Act 1986 (c 41) and a transfer is one in relation to which that relief applies if an instrument effecting the transfer is exempt from stamp duty by virtue of that provision.

But see paragraph 11 (withdrawal in case of subsequent non-exempt transfer).

(6) The fifth case is where –

(a)   control of the acquiring company changes as a result of a loan creditor becoming, or ceasing to be, treated as having control of the company, and
(b)   the other persons who were previously treated as controlling the company continue to be so treated.

'Loan creditor' here has the meaning given by section 417(7) to (9) of the Taxes Act 1988.

Withdrawal of reconstruction or acquisition relief on subsequent non-exempt transfer

11

(1) Where paragraph 10(4) (change of control of acquiring company as a result of exempt intra-group transfer) has effect to prevent the withdrawal of reconstruction or acquisition relief on a change of control of the acquiring company, but –

(a)   a company holding shares in the acquiring company to which the exempt intra-group transfer related, or that are derived from shares to which that transfer related, ceases to be a member of the same group as the target company –

      (i)   before the end of the period of three years beginning with the effective date of the relevant transaction, or

      (ii)   in pursuance of or in connection with arrangements made before the end of that period,

    and

(b)   the acquiring company or a relevant associated company, at that time ('the relevant time'), holds a chargeable interest –

      (i)   that was transferred to the acquiring company by the relevant transaction, or

      (ii)   that is derived from an interest that was so transferred,

    and that has not subsequently been transferred at market value by a chargeable transaction in relation to which reconstruction or acquisition relief was available but was not claimed,

reconstruction or acquisition relief in relation to the relevant transaction, or an appropriate proportion of it, is withdrawn and tax is chargeable in accordance with this paragraph.

(2) Where paragraph 10(5) (change of control of acquiring company as a result of a transfer to which share acquisition relief applies) has effect to prevent the withdrawal of reconstruction or acquisition relief on a change of control of the acquiring company, but –

(a)   control of the other company mentioned in that provision changes –

      (i)   before the end of the period of three years beginning with the effective date of the relevant transaction, or

      (ii)   in pursuance of or in connection with arrangements made before the end of that period,

    at a time when that company holds any shares transferred to it by the exempt transfer, or any shares derived from shares so transferred, and

(b)   the acquiring company or a relevant associated company, at that time ('the relevant time'), holds a chargeable interest –

      (i)   that was transferred to the acquiring company by the relevant transaction, or

      (ii)   that is derived from an interest that was so transferred,

    and that has not subsequently been transferred at market value by a chargeable transaction in relation to which reconstruction or acquisition relief was available but was not claimed,

reconstruction or acquisition relief in relation to the relevant transaction, or an appropriate proportion of it, is withdrawn and tax is chargeable in accordance with this paragraph.

(3) The amount chargeable is the tax that would have been chargeable in respect of the relevant transaction but for reconstruction or acquisition relief if the chargeable consideration for that transaction had been an amount equal to the market value of the subject matter of the transaction or, as the case may be, an appropriate proportion of the tax that would have been so chargeable.

(4) In sub-paragraphs (1), (2) and (3) 'an appropriate proportion' means an appropriate proportion having regard to the subject-matter of the relevant transaction and what is

held at the relevant time by the acquiring company or, as the case may be, by that company and any relevant associated companies.

(5) In this paragraph 'relevant associated company', in relation to the acquiring company, means a company –

(a)   that is controlled by the acquiring company immediately before the control of that company changes, and

(b)   of which control changes in consequence of the change of control of that company.

(6) In this paragraph –

(a)   'arrangements' includes any scheme, agreement or understanding, whether or not legally enforceable;

(b)   'control' shall be construed in accordance with section 416 of the Taxes Act 1988; and

(c)   references to control of a company changing are to the company becoming controlled –

(i)   by a different person,

(ii)   by a different number of persons, or

(iii) by two or more persons at least one of whom is not the person, or one of the persons, by whom the company was previously controlled.

Recovery of reconstruction or acquisition relief from another group company or controlling director

12

(1) This paragraph applies where –

(a)   tax is chargeable under paragraph 9 or 11 (withdrawal of reconstruction or acquisition relief),

(b)   the amount so chargeable has been finally determined, and

(c)   the whole or part of the amount so chargeable is unpaid six months after the date on which it became payable.

(2) The following persons may, by notice under paragraph 13, be required to pay the unpaid tax –

(a)   any company that at any relevant time was a member of the same group as the acquiring company and was above it in the group structure;

(b)   any person who at any relevant time was a controlling director of the acquiring company or a company having control of the acquiring company.

(3) For the purposes of sub-paragraph (2) 'relevant time' means any time between effective date of the relevant transaction and the change of control by virtue of which tax is chargeable.

(4) For the purposes of sub-paragraph (2)(a) a company ('company A') is 'above' another company ('company B') in a group structure if company B, or another company that is above company B in the group structure, is a 75% subsidiary of company A.

(5) For the purposes of sub-paragraph (2)(b) –

(a)   'director', in relation to a company, has the meaning given by section 67(1) of the Income Tax (Earnings and Pensions) Act 2003 (c 1) (read with subsection

(2) of that section) and includes any person falling within section 417(5) of the Taxes Act 1988 (read with subsection (6) of that section); and

(b)   'controlling director', in relation to a company, means a director of the company who has control of it (construing control in accordance with section 416 of the Taxes Act 1988).

Recovery of reconstruction or acquisition relief: supplementary

13

(1) The Inland Revenue may serve a notice on a person within paragraph 12(2) above requiring him within 30 days of the service of the notice to pay the amount that remains unpaid.

(2) Any such notice must be served before the end of the period of three years beginning with the date of the final determination mentioned in paragraph 12(1)(b).

(3) The notice must state the amount required to be paid by the person on whom the notice is served.

(4) The notice has effect –

(a)   for the purposes of the recovery from that person of the amount required to be paid and of interest on that amount, and

(b)   for the purposes of appeals,

as if it were a notice of assessment and that amount were an amount of tax due from that person.

(5) A person who has paid an amount in pursuance of a notice under this paragraph may recover that amount from the acquiring company.

(6) A payment in pursuance of a notice under this paragraph is not allowed as a deduction in computing any income, profits or losses for any tax purpose.

Schedule 8

Section 68

Stamp Duty Land Tax: Charities Relief

Charities relief

1

(1) A land transaction is exempt from charge if the purchaser is a charity and the following conditions are met.

Relief under this Schedule is referred to in this Part as 'charities relief'.

(2) The first condition is that the purchaser must intend to hold the subject-matter of the transaction for qualifying charitable purposes, that is –

(a)   for use in furtherance of the charitable purposes of the purchaser or of another charity, or

(b)   as an investment from which the profits are applied to the charitable purposes of the purchaser.

(3) The second condition is that the transaction must not have not been entered into for the purpose of avoiding tax under this Part (whether by the purchaser or any other person).

(4) In this paragraph a 'charity' means a body or trust established for charitable purposes only.

Amendments: Finance Act 2004, s 302(3).

Withdrawal of charities relief

2

(1) Where in the case of a transaction ('the relevant transaction') that is exempt by virtue of this Schedule –

    (a)   a disqualifying event occurs –
        (i)   before the end of the period of three years beginning with the effective date of the transaction, or
        (ii)   in pursuance of, or in connection with, arrangements made before the end of that period,
        and
    (b)   at the time of the disqualifying event the purchaser holds a chargeable interest –
        (i)   that was acquired by the purchaser under the relevant transaction, or
        (ii)   that is derived from an interest so acquired,

charities relief in relation to the relevant transaction, or an appropriate proportion of it, is withdrawn and tax is chargeable in accordance with this paragraph.

(2) The amount chargeable is the amount that would have been chargeable in respect of the relevant transaction but for charities relief or, as the case may be, an appropriate proportion of the tax that would have been so chargeable.

(3) For the purposes of this paragraph a 'disqualifying event' means –

    (a)   the purchaser ceasing to be established for charitable purposes only, or
    (b)   the subject-matter of the transaction, or any interest or right derived from it, being used or held by the purchaser otherwise than for qualifying charitable purposes.

(4) In sub-paragraphs (1) and (2) an 'appropriate proportion' means an appropriate proportion having regard to –

    (a)   what was acquired by the purchaser under the relevant transaction and what is held by the purchaser at the time of the disqualifying event, and
    (b)   the extent to which what is held by the purchaser at that time becomes used or held for purposes other than qualifying charitable purposes.

(5) In this paragraph 'qualifying charitable purposes' has the same meaning as in paragraph 1.

Amendments: Finance Act 2004, s 302(4).

Cases where first condition not fully met

3

(1) This paragraph applies where –

(a)   a land transaction is not exempt from charge under paragraph 1 because the first condition in that paragraph is not met, but

(b)   the purchaser ('C') intends to hold the greater part of the subject-matter of the transaction for qualifying charitable purposes.

(2) In such a case –

(a)   the transaction is exempt from charge, but

(b)   for the purposes of paragraph 2 (withdrawal of charities relief) 'disqualifying event' includes –

   (i)   any transfer by C of a major interest in the whole or any part of the subject-matter of the transaction, or

   (ii)   any grant by C at a premium of a low-rental lease of the whole or any part of that subject-matter,

   that is not made in furtherance of the charitable purposes of C

(3) For the purposes of sub-paragraph (2)(b)(ii) –

(a)   a lease is granted 'at a premium' if there is consideration other than rent, and

(b)   a lease is a 'low-rental' lease if the annual rent (if any) is less than £1000 a year.

(4) In relation to a transaction that, by virtue of this paragraph, is a disqualifying event for the purposes of paragraph 2 –

(a)   the date of the event for those purposes is the effective date of the transaction;

(b)   paragraph 2 has effect as if –

   (i)   in sub-paragraph (1)(b), for 'at the time of' there were substituted 'immediately before',

   (ii)   in sub-paragraph (4)(a), for 'at the time of' there were substituted 'immediately before and immediately after', and

   (iii)   sub-paragraph (4)(b) were omitted.

(5) In this paragraph –

'qualifying charitable purposes' has the same meaning as in paragraph 1;
'rent' has the same meaning as in Schedule 5 (amount of tax chargeable: rent) and 'annual rent' has the same meaning as in paragraph 9A of that Schedule.

Amendments: Finance Act 2004, s 302(1); Finance Act 2008, s 95(7)(a), (b), (13).

Charitable trusts

4

(1) This Schedule applies in relation to a charitable trust as it applies in relation to a charity.

(2) In this paragraph 'charitable trust' means –

(a)   a trust of which all the beneficiaries are charities, or

(b)   a unit trust scheme in which all the unit holders are charities,

and 'charity' has the same meaning as in paragraph 1.

(3) In this Schedule as it applies by virtue of this paragraph –

(a)   references to the purchaser in paragraphs (a) and (b) of paragraph 1(2) are to the beneficiaries or unit holders, or any of them;

(b)   the reference to the purchaser in paragraph 2(3)(a) is to any of the beneficiaries or unit holders;

(c)   the reference in paragraph 3(2)(b) to the charitable purposes of C is to those of the beneficiaries or unit holders, or any of them.

Amendments: Finance Act 2004, s 302(2).

Schedule 9

Section 70

Stamp Duty Land Tax: Right To Buy, Shared Ownership Leases etc

Right to buy transactions

1

(1) In the case of a right to buy transaction –

(a)   section 51 (1) (contingent consideration to be included in chargeable consideration on assumption that contingency will occur) does not apply, and

(b)   any consideration that would be payable only if a contingency were to occur, or that is payable only because a contingency has occurred, does not count as chargeable consideration.

(2) A 'right to buy transaction' means –

(a)   the sale of a dwelling at a discount, or the grant of a lease of a dwelling at a discount, by a relevant public sector body, or

(b)   the sale of a dwelling, or the grant of a lease of a dwelling, in pursuance of the preserved right to buy.

(3) The following are relevant public sector bodies for the purposes of sub-paragraph (2)(a):

Government

A Minister of the Crown

The Scottish Ministers

A Northern Ireland department

Local Government

A local housing authority within the meaning of the Housing Act 1985 (c 68)

A county council in England

A council constituted under section 2 of the Local Government etc

(Scotland) Act 1994 (c 39), the common good of such a council or any trust under its control

A district council within the meaning of the Local Government Act (Northern Ireland) 1972 (c 9(NI))

Social housing

The Housing Corporation

Scottish Homes

The Northern Ireland Housing Executive

A registered social landlord

A housing action trust established under Part 3 of the Housing Act 1988 (c 50)

New towns and development corporations etc

The Homes and Communities Agency

A development corporation established by an order made, or having effect as if made, under the New Towns Act 1981 (c 64)

A development corporation established by an order made, or having effect as if made, under the New Towns (Scotland) Act 1968 (c 16)

A new town commission established under section 7 of the New Towns Act (Northern Ireland) 1965 (c 13 (NI))

An urban development corporation established by an order made under section 135 of the Local Government, Planning and Land Act 1980 (c 65)

Police

A police authority within the meaning of section 101(1) of the Police Act 1996 (c 16)

A police authority within the meaning of section 2(1) or 19(9)(b) of the Police (Scotland) Act 1967 (c 77)

The Northern Ireland Policing Board

Miscellaneous

An Education and Libraries Board within the meaning of the Education and Libraries (Northern Ireland) Order 1986 (SI 1986/594 (NI 3))

The United Kingdom Atomic Energy Authority

Any person mentioned in paragraphs (g), (k), (l) or (n) of section 61(11) of the Housing (Scotland) Act 1987 (c 26)

A body prescribed for the purposes of this sub-paragraph by Treasury order.

(4) For the purposes of sub-paragraph (2)(b) the transfer of a dwelling, or the grant of a lease of a dwelling, is made in pursuance of the preserved right to buy if –

  (a)   the vendor is –
        (i)   in England and Wales, a person against whom the right to buy under Part 5 of the Housing Act 1985 (c 68) is exercisable by virtue of section 171A of that Act, or
        (ii) in Scotland, a person against whom the right to buy under section 61 of the Housing (Scotland) Act 1987 is exercisable by virtue of section 81A of that Act,
     (which provide for the preservation of the right to buy on disposal to a private sector landlord),
  (b)   the purchaser is the qualifying person for the purposes of the preserved right to buy, and
  (c)   the dwelling is the qualifying dwelling-house in relation to the purchaser.

(5) A grant under section 20 or 21 of the Housing Act 1996 (c 52) (purchase grants in respect of disposals at a discount by registered social landlords) does not count as part of the chargeable consideration for a right to buy transaction in relation to which the vendor is a registered social landlord.

Amendments: SI 2005/3226; Housing and Regeneration Act 2008, s 56, Sch 8, paras 78, 80(1), (2)(a), (b); SI 2008/3068.

Shared ownership lease: election for market value treatment

2

(1) This paragraph applies where –

    (a)   a lease is granted –
        (i)   by a qualifying body, or
        (ii)   in pursuance of the preserved right to buy,
    (b)   the conditions in sub-paragraph (2) are met, and
    (c)   the purchaser elects for tax to be charged in accordance with this paragraph.

(2) The conditions are as follows –

    (a)   the lease must be of a dwelling;
    (b)   the lease must give the lessee or lessees exclusive use of the dwelling;
    (c)   the lease must provide for the lessee or lessees to acquire the reversion;
    (d)   the lease must be granted partly in consideration of rent and partly in consideration of a premium calculated by reference to –
        (i)   the market value of the dwelling, or
        (ii)   a sum calculated by reference to that value;
    (e)   the lease must contain a statement of –
        (i)   the market value of the dwelling, or
        (ii)   the sum calculated by reference to that value,
        by reference to which the premium is calculated.

(3) An election for tax to be charged in accordance with this paragraph must be included in the land transaction return made in respect of the grant of the lease, or in an amendment of that return, and is irrevocable, so that the return may not be amended so as to withdraw the election.

(4) Where this paragraph applies the chargeable consideration for the grant of the lease shall be taken to be the amount stated in the lease in accordance with sub-paragraph (2)(e)(i) or (ii).

As to the tax treatment of the acquisition of the reversion in pursuance of the lease, see paragraph 3.

(4A) Where this paragraph applies no account shall be taken for the purposes of stamp duty land tax of the rent mentioned in sub- paragraph (2)(d).

(5) Section 118 (meaning of 'market value') does not apply in relation to the reference in sub-paragraph (2)(e) above to the market value of the dwelling.

Amendments: Finance Act 2007, s 78.

Transfer of reversion under shared ownership lease where election made for market value treatment

3

The transfer of the reversion to the lessee or lessees under the terms of a lease to which paragraph 2 applies (shared ownership lease: election for market value treatment) is exempt from charge if –

(a) an election was made for tax to be charged in accordance with that paragraph, and

(b) any tax chargeable in respect of the grant of the lease has been paid.

Shared ownership lease: election where staircasing allowed

4

(1) This paragraph applies where –

(a) a lease is granted by a qualifying body or in pursuance of the preserved right to buy,

(b) the conditions in sub-paragraph (2) below are met, and

(c) the purchaser elects for tax to be charged in accordance with this paragraph.

(2) The conditions are as follows –

(a) the lease must be of a dwelling;

(b) the lease must give the lessee or lessees exclusive use of the dwelling;

(c) the lease must provide that the lessee or lessees may, on the payment of a sum, require the terms of the lease to be altered so that the rent payable under it is reduced;

(d) the lease must be granted partly in consideration of rent and partly in consideration of a premium calculated by reference to –

(i) the premium obtainable on the open market for the grant of a lease containing the same terms as the lease but with the substitution of the minimum rent for the rent payable under the lease, or

(ii) a sum calculated by reference to that premium;

(e) the lease must contain a statement of the minimum rent and of –

(i) the premium obtainable on the open market, or

(ii) the sum calculated by reference to that premium,

by reference to which the premium is calculated.

(3) An election for tax to be charged in accordance with this paragraph must be included in the land transaction return made in respect of the grant of the lease, or in an amendment of that return, and is irrevocable, so that the return may not be amended so as to withdraw the election.

(4) Where this paragraph applies –

(a) the rent in consideration of which the lease is granted shall be taken to be the minimum rent stated in the lease in accordance with sub-paragraph (2)(e), and

(b) the chargeable consideration for the grant other than rent shall be taken to be the amount stated in the lease in accordance with sub-paragraph (2)(e)(i) or (ii).

(5) In this paragraph the 'minimum rent' means the lowest rent which could become payable under the lease if it were altered as mentioned in sub-paragraph (2)(c) at the date when the lease is granted.

Shared ownership lease: treatment of staircasing transaction

4A

(1) This paragraph applies where under a shared ownership lease –

    (a)   the lessee or lessees have the right, on the payment of a sum, to require the terms of the lease to be altered so that the rent payable under it is reduced, and

    (b)   by exercising that right the lessee or lessees acquire an interest, additional to one already held, calculated by reference to the market value of the dwelling and expressed as a percentage of the dwelling or its value (a 'share of the dwelling').

(2) Such an acquisition is exempt from charge if –

    (a)   an election was made for tax to be charged in accordance with paragraph 2 or, as the case may be, paragraph 4 and any tax chargeable in respect of the grant of the lease has been paid, or

    (b)   immediately after the acquisition the total share of the dwelling held by the lessee or lessees does not exceed 80%.

(3) In this paragraph 'shared ownership lease' means a lease granted –

    (a)   by a qualifying body, or

    (b)   in pursuance of the preserved right to buy,

in relation to which the conditions in paragraph 2(2) or 4(2) are met.

(4) Section 118 (meaning of 'market value') does not apply in relation to the references in this paragraph to the market value of the dwelling.

Amendments: Inserted by Finance Act 2004, s 303(1).

Shared ownership lease: grant not linked with staircasing transactions etc

4B

(1) For the purpose of determining the rate of tax chargeable on the grant of a shared ownership lease of a dwelling, the grant shall be treated as if it were not linked to –

    (a)   any acquisition of an interest in the dwelling to which paragraph 4A applies, or

    (b)   a transfer of the reversion to the lessee or lessees under the terms of the lease.

(2) In this paragraph 'shared ownership lease' has the same meaning as in paragraph 4A.

Amendments: Inserted by Finance Act 2008, s 95(8), (13).

Shared ownership leases: meaning of 'qualifying body' and 'preserved right to buy'

5

(1) This paragraph has effect for the purposes of paragraphs 2, 4 and 4A (shared ownership leases: election as to basis of taxation).

(2) A 'qualifying body' means –

    (a)   a local housing authority within the meaning of the Housing Act 1985 (c 68);

    (b)   a housing association within the meaning of –

        (i)   the Housing Associations Act 1985 (c 69), or

(ii) Part 2 of the Housing (Northern Ireland) Order 1992 (SI 1992/1725 (NI 15));

(c) a housing action trust established under Part 3 of the Housing Act 1988 (c 50);

(d) the Northern Ireland Housing Executive;

(e) the Homes and Communities Agency;

(f) a development corporation established by an order made, or having effect as if made, under the New Towns Act 1981 (c 64);

(g) a registered provider of social housing that is not within paragraph (b) (subject to sub-paragraph (2A)).

(2A) A registered provider of social housing within sub-paragraph (2)(g) ("R") is only a qualifying body in relation to a lease of premises if the following has been funded with the assistance of a grant or other financial assistance under section 19 of the Housing and Regeneration Act 2008 –

(a) the purchase or construction of the premises by R (or a person connected with R), or

(b) the adaptation of the premises by R (or a person connected with R) for use as a dwelling.

(2B) Section 839 of the Taxes Act 1988 (connected persons) has effect for the purposes of sub-paragraph (2A).

(3) A lease is granted 'in pursuance of the preserved right to buy' if –

(a) the vendor is a person against whom the right to buy under Part 5 of the Housing Act 1985 is exercisable by virtue of section 171A of that Act (preservation of right to buy on disposal to private sector landlord),

(b) the lessee is, or lessees are, the qualifying person for the purposes of the preserved right to buy, and

(c) the lease is of a dwelling that is the qualifying dwelling-house in relation to the purchaser.

Amendments: Inserted by Finance Act 2004, s 303(2); Housing and Regeneration Act 2008, s 56, Sch 8, paras 78, 80(1), (3), (b); SI 2008/3068; Finance Act 2009, s 81(1), (2), (5), (6)(a), (b), (8).

Rent to mortgage or rent to loan: chargeable consideration

6

(1) The chargeable consideration for a rent to mortgage or rent to loan transaction is determined in accordance with this paragraph.

(2) A 'rent to mortgage transaction' means –

(a) the transfer of a dwelling to a person, or

(b) the grant of a lease of a dwelling to a person,

pursuant to the exercise by that person of the right to acquire on rent to mortgage terms under Part 5 of the Housing Act 1985 (c 68).

(3) The chargeable consideration for such a transaction is equal to the price that, by virtue of section 126 of the Housing Act 1985, would be payable for –

(a) a transfer of the dwelling to the person (where the rent to mortgage transaction is a transfer), or

(b) the grant of a lease of the dwelling to the person (where the rent to mortgage transaction is the grant of a lease), if the person were exercising the right to buy under Part 5 of that Act.

(4) A 'rent to loan transaction' means the execution of a heritable disposition in favour of a person pursuant to the exercise by that person of the right to purchase a house by way of the rent to loan scheme in Part 3 of the Housing (Scotland) Act 1987 (c 26).

(5) The chargeable consideration for such a transaction is equal to the price that, by virtue of section 62 of the Housing (Scotland) Act 1987, would be payable for the house if the person were exercising the right to purchase under section 61 of that Act.

Shared ownership trust: introduction

7

(1) In this Schedule 'shared ownership trust' means a trust of land, within the meaning of section 1 of the Trusts of Land and Appointment of Trustees Act 1996, which satisfies the following conditions.

(2) Condition 1 is that the trust property is –

    (a)   a dwelling, and
    (b)   in England or Wales.

(3) Condition 2 is that one of the beneficiaries ('the social landlord') is a qualifying body.

(4) Condition 3 is that the terms of the trust –

    (a)   provide for one or more of the individual beneficiaries ('the purchaser') to have exclusive use of the trust property as the only or main residence of the purchaser,
    (b)   require the purchaser to make an initial payment to the social landlord ('the initial capital'),
    (c)   require the purchaser to make additional payments to the social landlord by way of compensation under section 13(6)(a) of the Trusts of Land and Appointment of Trustees Act 1996, ('rent-equivalent payments'),
    (d)   enable the purchaser to make other additional payments to the social landlord ('equity-acquisition payments'),
    (e)   determine the initial beneficial interests of the social landlord and of the purchaser by reference to the initial capital,
    (f)   specify a sum, equating or relating to the market value of the dwelling, by reference to which the initial capital was calculated, and
    (g)   provide for the purchaser's beneficial interest in the trust property to increase, and the social landlord's to diminish (or to be extinguished), as equity-acquisition payments are made.

(5) Section 118 (meaning of 'market value') does not apply to this paragraph.

(6) In Condition 1 'dwelling' includes –

    (a)   a building which is being constructed or adapted for use as a dwelling,
    (b)   land which is to be used for the purpose of the construction of a dwelling, and
    (c)   land which is, or is to become, the garden or grounds of a dwelling.

(7) In Condition 2 'qualifying body' means –

    (a)   a qualifying body within the meaning of paragraph 5(2)(a) to (f), or
    (b)   a registered provider of social housing within paragraph 5(2)(g) (subject to sub-paragraph (8)).

(8) A registered provider of social housing within paragraph 5(2)(g) ('R') is only a qualifying body in relation to a shared ownership trust if the following has been or is being funded with the assistance of a grant or other financial assistance under section 19 of the Housing and Regeneration Act 2008 –

  (a) the purchase or construction of the trust property by R (or a person connected with R), or

  (b) the adaptation of the trust property by R (or a person connected with R) for use as a dwelling.

(9) Section 839 of the Taxes Act 1988 (connected persons) has effect for the purposes of sub-paragraph (8).

Amendments: Inserted by Finance Act 2007, s 77(1), (2); Finance Act 2009, s 81(1), (5), (7)(a), (b), (8).

Shared ownership trust: "purchaser"

8

For the purposes of the application of stamp duty land tax in relation to a shared ownership trust, the person (or persons) identified as the purchaser in accordance with paragraph 7, and not the social landlord or any other beneficiary, is (or are) to be treated as the purchaser of the trust property.

Amendments: Inserted by Finance Act 2007, s 77(1), (2).

Shared ownership trust: election for market value treatment

9

(1) This paragraph applies where –

  (a) a shared ownership trust is declared, and

  (b) the purchaser elects for tax to be charged in accordance with this paragraph.

(2) An election must be included in –

  (a) the land transaction return for the declaration of the shared ownership trust, or

  (b) an amendment of that return.

(3) An election may not be revoked.

(4) Where this paragraph applies –

  (a) the chargeable consideration for the declaration of the shared ownership trust shall be taken to be the amount stated in accordance with paragraph 7(4)(f), and

  (b) no account shall be taken for the purposes of stamp duty land tax of rent-equivalent payments.

(5) The transfer to the purchaser of an interest in the trust property upon the termination of the trust is exempt from charge if –

  (a) an election was made under this paragraph, and

  (b) any tax chargeable in respect of the declaration of the shared ownership trust has been paid.

Amendments: Inserted by Finance Act 2007, s 77(1), (2).

Shared ownership trust: treatment of staircasing transaction

10

(1) An equity-acquisition payment under a shared ownership trust, and the consequent increase in the purchaser's beneficial interest, shall be exempt from charge if –

(a)   an election was made under paragraph 9, and

(b)   any tax chargeable in respect of the declaration of trust has been paid.

(2) An equity-acquisition payment under a shared ownership trust, and the consequent increase in the purchaser's beneficial interest, shall also be exempt from charge if following the increase the purchaser's beneficial interest does not exceed 80% of the total beneficial interest in the trust property.

Amendments: Inserted by Finance Act 2007, s 77(1), (2); Finance Act 2008, s 95(9), (13).

Shared ownership trust: treatment of additional payments where no election made

11

Where no election has been made under paragraph 9 in respect of a shared ownership trust –

(a)   the initial capital shall be treated for the purposes of stamp duty land tax as chargeable consideration other than rent, and

(b)   any rent-equivalent payment by the purchaser shall be treated for the purposes of stamp duty land tax as a payment of rent.

Amendments: Inserted by Finance Act 2007, s 77(1), (2); Finance Act 2008, s 95(9), (13).

Shared ownership trust: declaration not linked with staircasing transactions etc

12

For the purpose of determining the rate of tax chargeable on the declaration of a shared ownership trust, the declaration shall be treated as if it were not linked to –

(a)   any equity-acquisition payment under the trust or any consequent increase in the purchaser's beneficial interest in the trust property, or

(b)   a transfer to the purchaser of an interest in the trust property upon the termination of the trust.

Amendments: Inserted by Finance Act 2008, s 95(10), (13).

Rent to shared ownership lease: charge to tax

13

(1) The chargeable consideration for transactions forming part of a rent to shared ownership lease scheme is determined in accordance with this paragraph.

(2) A 'rent to shared ownership lease scheme' means a scheme or arrangement under which a qualifying body –

(a)   grants an assured shorthold tenancy of a dwelling to a person ('the tenant') or persons ('the tenants'), and

(b)   subsequently grants a shared ownership lease of the dwelling or another dwelling to the tenant or one or more of the tenants.

(3) The following transactions are to be treated as if they were not linked to each other –

- (a) the grant of the assured shorthold tenancy,
- (b) the grant of the shared ownership lease, and
- (c) any other land transaction between the qualifying body and the tenant, or any of the tenants, entered into as part of the scheme.

(4) For the purpose of determining the effective date of the grant of the shared ownership lease, the possession of the dwelling by the tenant or tenants pursuant to the assured shorthold tenancy is to be disregarded.

(5) In this paragraph –

'assured shorthold tenancy' has the same meaning as in Part 1 of the Housing Act 1988;
'qualifying body' has the same meaning as in paragraph 5;
'shared ownership lease' has the same meaning as in paragraph 4A.

Amendments: Inserted by Finance Act 2009, s 82(1), (2).

Rent to shared ownership trust: charge to tax

14

(1) The chargeable consideration for transactions forming part of a rent to shared ownership trust scheme is determined in accordance with this paragraph.

(2) A 'rent to shared ownership trust scheme' means a scheme or arrangement under which –

- (a) a qualifying body grants an assured shorthold tenancy of a dwelling to a person ('the tenant') or persons ('the tenants'), and
- (b) the tenant, or one or more of tenants, subsequently becomes the purchaser under a shared ownership trust of the dwelling, or another dwelling, under which the qualifying body is the social landlord.

(3) The following transactions are to be treated as if they were not linked to each other –

- (a) the grant of the assured shorthold tenancy,
- (b) the declaration of the shared ownership trust, and
- (c) any other land transaction between the qualifying body and the tenant, or any of the tenants, entered into as part of the scheme.

(4) For the purpose of determining the effective date of the declaration of the shared ownership trust, the possession of the dwelling by the tenant or tenants pursuant to the assured shorthold tenancy is to be disregarded.

(5) In this paragraph –

'assured shorthold tenancy' has the same meaning as in Part 1 of the Housing Act 1988;
'qualifying body' has the same meaning as in paragraph 5;
'social landlord' and 'purchaser', in relation to a shared ownership trust, have the same meaning as in paragraph 7.

Amendments: Inserted by Finance Act 2009, s 82(1), (2).

Schedule 10

Stamp Duty Land Tax: Returns, Enquiries, Assessments and Appeals

PART 1
LAND TRANSACTION RETURNS

Contents of return

1

(1) A land transaction return must –

(a)   be in the prescribed form,

(b)   contain the prescribed information, and

(c)   include a declaration by the purchaser (or each of them) that the return is to the best of his knowledge correct and complete.

(1A) Sub-paragraph (1)(c) is subject to paragraphs 1A and 1B.

(2) In sub-paragraph (1) 'prescribed' means prescribed by regulations made by the Inland Revenue.

(3) The regulations may make different provision for different kinds of return.

(4) Regulations under sub-paragraph (1)(b) may require the provision of information corresponding to any of the particulars formerly required under –

(a)   Schedule 2 to the Finance Act 1931 (c 28) (requirement to deliver particulars of land transactions in Great Britain), or

(b)   section 244 of the Finance Act 1994 (c 9) (corresponding provision for Northern Ireland).

(5) The return is treated as containing any information provided by the purchaser for the purpose of completing the return.

Amendment: SI 2004/3208.

Declaration by agent

1A

(1) Where –

(a)   the purchaser (or each of them) authorises an agent to complete a land transaction return,

(b)   the purchaser (or each of them) makes a declaration that, with the exception of the effective date, the information provided in the return is to the best of his knowledge correct and complete, and

(c)   the land transaction return includes a declaration by the agent that the effective date provided in the return is to the best of his knowledge correct,

the requirement in paragraph 1(1)(c) shall be deemed to be met.

(2) Sub-paragraph (1) applies only where the return is in a form specified by the Inland Revenue for the purposes of that sub-paragraph.

(3) Nothing in this paragraph affects the liability of the purchaser (or each of them) under this Part of this Act.

Amendment: Inserted by SI 2004/3208.

Declaration by the relevant Official Solicitor

1B

(1) Where –

    (a)   the purchaser (or any of them) is a person under a disability,

    (b)   the Official Solicitor is acting for the purchaser (or any of them), and

    (c)   the land transaction return includes a declaration by the Official Solicitor that the return is to the best of his knowledge correct and complete,

the requirement in paragraph 1(1)(c) shall be deemed to be met.

(2) Sub-paragraph (1) applies only where the return is in a form specified by the Inland Revenue for the purposes of that sub-paragraph.

(3) Nothing in this paragraph affects the liability of the purchaser (or each of them) under this Part of this Act.

(4) In this paragraph 'the Official Solicitor' means the Official Solicitor to the Supreme Court of England and Wales or the Official Solicitor to the Supreme Court of Northern Ireland (as the case requires).

Amendment: Inserted by SI 2004/3208.

Meaning of filing date and delivery of return

2

(1) References in this Part of this Act to the filing date, in relation to a land transaction return, are to the last day of the period within which the return must be delivered.

(2) References in this Part of this Act to the delivery of a land transaction return are to the delivery of a return that –

    (a)   complies with the requirements of paragraph 1(1) (contents of return).

Amendments: Finance Act 2007, ss 80(1), (7), (9)(f), 114, Sch 27, Pt 4(4).

Failure to deliver return: flat-rate penalty

3

(1) A person who is required to deliver a land transaction return and fails to do so by the filing date is liable to a flat-rate penalty under this paragraph.

He may also be liable to a tax-related penalty under paragraph 4.

(2) The penalty is –

    (a)   £100 if the return is delivered within three months after the filing date, and

    (b)   £200 in any other case.

Failure to deliver return: tax-related penalty

4

(1) A purchaser who is required to deliver a land transaction return in respect of a chargeable transaction and fails to do so within twelve months after the filing date is liable to a tax-related penalty under this paragraph.

This is in addition to any flat-rate penalty under paragraph 3.

(2) The penalty is an amount not exceeding the amount of tax chargeable in respect of the transaction.

Formal notice to deliver return: daily penalty

5

(1) If it appears to the Inland Revenue –

    (a)   that a purchaser required to deliver a land transaction return in respect of a chargeable transaction has failed to do so, and

    (b)   that the filing date has now passed,

they may issue a notice requiring him to deliver a land transaction return in respect of the transaction.

(2) The notice must specify –

    (a)   the transaction to which it relates, and

    (b)   the period for complying with the notice (which must not be less than 30 days from the date of issue of the notice).

(3) If the purchaser does not comply with the notice within the specified period, the Inland Revenue may apply to the General or Special Commissioners for an order imposing a daily penalty.

(4) On such an application the Commissioners may direct that the purchaser shall be liable to a penalty or penalties not exceeding £60 for each day on which the failure continues after the day on which he is notified of the direction.

(5) This paragraph does not affect, and is not affected by, any penalty under paragraph 3 or 4 (flat-rate or tax-related penalty for failure to deliver return).

Amendment of return by purchaser

6

(1) The purchaser may amend a land transaction return given by him by notice to the Inland Revenue.

(2) The notice must be in such form, and contain such information, as the Inland Revenue may require.

(2A) If the effect of the amendment would be to entitle the purchaser to a repayment of tax, the notice must be accompanied by –

    (a)   the contract for the land transaction; and

    (b)   the instrument (if any) by which that transaction was effected.

(3) Except as otherwise provided, an amendment may not be made more than twelve months after the filing date.

Amendment: Inserted by SI 2004/3208.

Correction of return by Revenue

7

(1) The Inland Revenue may amend a land transaction return so as to correct obvious errors or omissions in the return (whether errors of principle, arithmetical mistakes or otherwise).

(1A) The power under sub-paragraph (1) may, in such circumstances as the Commissioners for Her Majesty's Revenue and Customs may specify in regulations, be exercised –

    (a)   in relation to England and Wales, by the Chief Land Registrar;

    (b)   in relation to Scotland, by the Keeper of the Registers of Scotland;

    (c)   in relation to Northern Ireland, by the Registrar of Titles or the registrar of deeds;

    (d)   in any case, by such other persons with functions relating to the registration of land as the regulations may specify.

(2) A correction under this paragraph is made by notice to the purchaser.

(3) No such correction may be made more than nine months after –

    (a)   the day on which the return was delivered, or

    (b)   if the correction is required in consequence of an amendment under paragraph 6, the day on which that amendment was made.

(4) A correction under this paragraph is of no effect if the purchaser –

    (a)   amends the return so as to reject the correction, or

    (b)   after the end of the period within which he may amend the return, but within three months from the date of issue of the notice of correction, gives notice rejecting the correction.

(5) Notice under sub-paragraph (4)(b) must be given to the officer of the Board by whom notice of the correction was given.

Amendments: Inserted by Finance (No 2) Act 2005, s 47(4).

8 . . .

Amendments: Repealed by Finance Act 2008, s 122(1), Sch 40, para 21(k)(ii); SI 2009/571.

PART 2
DUTY TO KEEP AND PRESERVE RECORDS

Duty to keep and preserve records

9

(1) A purchaser who is required to deliver a land transaction return must –

    (a)   keep such records as may be needed to enable him to deliver a correct and complete return, and

    (b)   preserve those records in accordance with this paragraph.

(2) The records must be preserved for six years after the effective date of the transaction and until any later date on which –

(a)   an enquiry into the return is completed, or
(b)   if there is no enquiry, the Inland Revenue no longer have power to enquire into the return.

(3) The records required to be kept and preserved under this paragraph include –

(a)   relevant instruments relating to the transaction, in particular, any contract or conveyance, and any supporting maps, plans or similar documents;
(b)   records of relevant payments, receipts and financial arrangements.

Preservation of information instead of original records

10

(1) The duty under paragraph 9 to preserve records may be satisfied by the preservation of the information contained in them.

(2) Where information is so preserved a copy of any document forming part of the records is admissible in evidence in any proceedings before the tribunal to the same extent as the records themselves.

Amendment: SI 2009/56.

Penalty for failure to keep and preserve records

11

(1) A person who fails to comply with paragraph 9 in relation to a transaction is liable to a penalty not exceeding £3,000, subject to the following exception.

(2) No penalty is incurred if the Inland Revenue are satisfied that any facts that they reasonably require to be proved, and that would have been proved by the records, are proved by other documentary evidence provided to them.

PART 3
ENQUIRY INTO RETURN

Notice of enquiry

12

(1) The Inland Revenue may enquire into a land transaction return if they give notice of their intention to do so ('notice of enquiry') –

(a)   to the purchaser,
(b)   before the end of the enquiry period.

(2) The enquiry period is the period of nine months –

(a)   after the filing date, if the return was delivered on or before that date;
(b)   after the date on which the return was delivered, if the return was delivered after the filing date;
(c)   after the date on which the amendment was made, if the return is amended under paragraph 6(amendment by purchaser).

This is subject to the following qualification.

(2A) If –

(a)   the Inland Revenue give notice, within the period specified in sub-paragraph (2), of their intention to enquire into a land transaction return delivered under section 80 (adjustment where contingency ceases or consideration is ascertained), 81 (further return where relief withdrawn) or 81A (return or further return in consequence of later linked transaction), and

(b)   it appears to the Inland Revenue to be necessary to give a notice under this paragraph in respect of an earlier land transaction return in respect of the same land transaction,

a notice may be given notwithstanding that the period referred to in sub-paragraph (2) has elapsed in relation to that earlier land transaction.

(3) A return that has been the subject of one notice of enquiry may not be the subject of another, except one given in consequence of an amendment (or another amendment) of the return under paragraph 6.

Amendment: SI 2004/3208.

Scope of enquiry

13

(1) An enquiry extends to anything contained in the return, or required to be contained in the return, that relates –

(a)   to the question whether tax is chargeable in respect of the transaction, or
(b)   to the amount of tax so chargeable.

This is subject to the following exception.

(2) If the notice of enquiry is given as a result of an amendment of the return under paragraph 6(amendment by purchaser) –

(a)   at a time when it is no longer possible to give notice of enquiry under paragraph 12, or
(b)   after an enquiry into the return has been completed,

the enquiry into the return is limited to matters to which the amendment relates or that are affected by the amendment.

Notice to produce documents etc for purposes of enquiry

14

(1) If the Inland Revenue give notice of enquiry into a land transaction return, they may by notice in writing require the purchaser –

(a)   to produce to them such documents in his possession or power, and
(b)   to provide them with such information, in such form,

as they may reasonably require for the purposes of the enquiry.

(2) A notice under this paragraph (which may be given at the same time as the notice of enquiry) must specify the time (which must not be less than 30 days) within which the purchaser is to comply with it.

(3) In complying with a notice under this paragraph copies of documents may be produced instead of originals, but –

(a)   the copies must be photographic or other facsimiles, and

(b)   the Inland Revenue may by notice require the original to be produced for inspection.

A notice under paragraph (b) must specify the time (which must not be less than 30 days) within which the purchaser is to comply with it.

(4) The Inland Revenue may take copies of, or make extracts from, any documents produced to them under this paragraph.

(5) A notice under this paragraph does not oblige a purchaser to produce documents or provide information relating to the conduct of –

(a)   any pending appeal by him, or
(b)   any pending referral to the tribunal under paragraph 19 to which he is a party.

Amendment: SI 2009/56.

Appeal against notice to produce documents etc

15

(1) An appeal may be brought against a requirement imposed by a notice under paragraph 14 to produce documents or provide information.

(2) Notice of appeal must be given –

(a)   in writing,
(b)   within 30 days after the issue of the notice appealed against,
(c)   to the officer of the Board by whom that notice was given.

(3) An appeal under this paragraph shall be determined in the same way as an appeal against an assessment.

(4) On an appeal under this paragraph that is notified to the tribunal, the tribunal –

(a)   shall set aside the notice so far as it requires the production of documents, or the provision of information, that appears not reasonably required for the purposes of the enquiry, and
(b)   shall confirm the notice so far as it requires the production or documents, or the provision of information, that appears reasonably required for the purposes of the enquiry.

(5) A notice that is confirmed by the tribunal (or so far as it is confirmed) has effect as if the period specified in it for complying was 30 days from the determination of the appeal.

(6) Notwithstanding the provisions of sections 11 and 13 of the Tribunals, Courts and Enforcement Act 2007 the decision of the tribunal on an appeal under this paragraph is final.

Amendment: SI 2009/56.

Penalty for failure to produce documents etc

16

(1) A person who fails to comply with a notice under paragraph 14 (notice to produce documents etc for purposes of enquiry) is liable –

(a)   to a penalty of £50, and

(b) if the failure continues after a penalty is imposed under paragraph (a) above, to a further penalty or penalties not exceeding the amount specified in sub-paragraph (2) below for each day on which the failure continues.

(2) The amount referred to in sub-paragraph (1)(b) is –

(a) £30 if the penalty is determined by an officer of the Board, and
(b) £150 if the penalty is determined by the court.

(3) No penalty shall be imposed under this paragraph in respect of a failure at any time after the failure has been remedied.

Amendment of self-assessment during enquiry to prevent loss of tax

17

(1) If at a time when an enquiry is in progress into a land transaction return the Inland Revenue form the opinion –

(a) that the amount stated in the self-assessment contained in the return as the amount of tax payable is insufficient, and
(b) that unless the assessment is immediately amended there is likely to be a loss of tax to the Crown,

they may by notice in writing to the purchaser amend the assessment to make good the deficiency.

(2) In the case of an enquiry that under paragraph 13(2) is limited to matters arising from an amendment of the return, sub-paragraph (1) above applies only so far as the deficiency is attributable to the amendment.

(3) For the purposes of this paragraph the period during which an enquiry is in progress is the whole of the period –

(a) beginning with the day on which notice of enquiry is given, and
(b) ending with the day on which the enquiry is completed.

Amendment of return by taxpayer during enquiry

18

(1) This paragraph applies if a return is amended under paragraph 6(amendment by purchaser) at a time when an enquiry is in progress into the return.

(2) The amendment does not restrict the scope of the enquiry but may be taken into account (together with any matters arising) in the enquiry.

(3) So far as the amendment affects the amount stated in the self-assessment included in the return as the amount of tax payable, it does not take effect while the enquiry is in progress and –

(a) if the Inland Revenue state in the closure notice that they have taken the amendments into account and that –
    (i) the amendment has been taken into account in formulating the amendments contained in the notice, or
    (ii) their conclusion is that the amendment is incorrect,
    the amendment shall not take effect;
(b) otherwise, the amendment takes effect when the closure notice is issued.

(4) For the purposes of this paragraph the period during which an enquiry is in progress is the whole of the period –

    (a)   beginning with the day on which notice of enquiry is given, and

    (b)   ending with the day on which the enquiry is completed.

Referral of questions to the tribunal during enquiry

19

(1) At any time when an enquiry is in progress into a land transaction return any question arising in connection with the subject-matter of the enquiry may be referred to the tribunal for determination.

(2) Notice of referral must be given –

    (a)   jointly by the purchaser and the Inland Revenue,

    (c)   to the tribunal.

(4) More than one notice of referral may be given under this paragraph in relation to an enquiry.

(5) For the purposes of this paragraph the period during which an enquiry is in progress is the whole of the period –

    (a)   beginning with the day on which the notice of enquiry was given, and

    (b)   ending with the day on which the enquiry is completed.

Amendment: SI 2009/56.

Withdrawal of notice of referral

20

(1) The Inland Revenue or the purchaser may withdraw a notice of referral under paragraph 19

Amendment: SI 2009/56.

Effect of referral on enquiry

21

(1) While proceedings on a referral under paragraph 19 are in progress in relation to an enquiry –

    (a)   no closure notice shall be given in relation to the enquiry, and

    (b)   no application may be made for a direction to give such a notice.

(2) For the purposes of this paragraph proceedings on a referral are in progress where –

    (a)   notice of referral has been given,

    (b)   the notice has not been withdrawn, and

    (c)   the questions referred have not been finally determined.

(3) For the purposes of sub-paragraph (2)(c) a question referred is finally determined when –

    (a)   it has been determined by the tribunal, and

    (b)   there is no further possibility of the determination being varied or set aside (disregarding any power to grant permission to appeal out of time).

Amendment: SI 2009/56.

Effect of determination

22

(1) The determination of a question referred to the tribunal under paragraph 19 is binding on the parties to the referral in the same way, and to the same extent, as a decision on a preliminary issue in an appeal.

(2) The determination shall be taken into account by the Inland Revenue –

   (a)   in reaching their conclusions on the enquiry, and
   (b)   in formulating any amendments of the return required to give effect to those conclusions.

(3) Any right of appeal under paragraph 35 (appeals against assessments etc) may not be exercised so as to reopen the question determined except to the extent (if any) that it could be reopened if it had been determined as a preliminary issue in that appeal.

Amendment: SI 2009/56.

Completion of enquiry

23

(1) An enquiry under paragraph 12 is completed when the Inland Revenue by notice (a 'closure notice') inform the purchaser that they have completed their enquiries and state their conclusions.

(2) A closure notice must either –

   (a)   state that in the opinion of the Inland Revenue no amendment of the return is required, or
   (b)   make the amendments of the return required to give effect to their conclusions.

(3) A closure notice takes effect when it is issued.

Direction to complete enquiry

24

(1) The purchaser may apply to the tribunal for a direction that the Inland Revenue give a closure notice within a specified period.

(2) Any such application is to be subject to the relevant provisions of Part 5 of the Taxes Management Act 1970 (see, in particular, section 48(2)(b) of that Act).

(3) The tribunal hearing the application shall give a direction unless satisfied that the Inland Revenue have reasonable grounds for not giving a closure notice within a specified period.

Amendment: SI 2009/56.

PART 4
REVENUE DETERMINATION IF NO RETURN DELIVERED

Determination of tax chargeable if no return delivered

25

(1) If in the case of a chargeable transaction no land transaction return is delivered by the filing date, the Inland Revenue may make a determination (a 'Revenue determination') to the best of their information and belief of the amount of tax chargeable in respect of the transaction.

(2) Notice of the determination must be served on the purchaser, stating the date on which it is issued.

(3) No Revenue determination may be made more than six years after the effective date of the transaction.

Determination to have effect as a self-assessment

26

(1) A Revenue determination has effect for enforcement purposes as if were a self-assessment by the purchaser.

(2) In sub-paragraph (1) 'for enforcement purposes' means for the purposes of the following provisions of this Part of this Act –

    (a)   the provisions of this Schedule providing for tax-related penalties;
    (b)   section 87 (interest on unpaid tax);
    (c)   section 91 and Schedule 12 (collection and recovery of unpaid tax etc).

(3) Nothing in this paragraph affects any liability of the purchaser to a penalty for failure to deliver a return.

Determination superseded by actual self-assessment

27

(1) If after a Revenue determination has been made the purchaser delivers a land transaction return in respect of the transaction, the self-assessment included in that return supersedes the determination.

(2) Sub-paragraph (1) does not apply to a return delivered –

    (a)   more than six years after the day on which the power to make the determination first became exercisable, or
    (b)   more than twelve months after the date of the determination,

whichever is the later.

(3) Where –

    (a)   proceedings have been begun for the recovery of any tax charged by a Revenue determination, and
    (b)   before the proceedings are concluded the determination is superseded by a self-assessment,

the proceedings may be continued as if they were proceedings for the recovery of so much of the tax charged by the self-assessment as is due and payable and has not been paid.

PART 5
REVENUE ASSESSMENTS

Assessment where loss of tax discovered

28

(1) If the Inland Revenue discover as regards a chargeable transaction that –

(a)   an amount of tax that ought to have been assessed has not been assessed, or
(b)   an assessment to tax is or has become insufficient, or
(c)   relief has been given that is or has become excessive,

they may make an assessment (a 'discovery assessment') in the amount or further amount that ought in their opinion to be charged in order to make good to the Crown the loss of tax.

(2) The power to make a discovery assessment in respect of a transaction for which the purchaser has delivered a return is subject to the restrictions specified in paragraph 30.

Assessment to recover excessive repayment of tax

29

(1) If an amount of tax has been repaid to any person that ought not to have been repaid to him, that amount may be assessed and recovered as if it were unpaid tax.

(2) Where the repayment was made with interest, the amount assessed and recovered may include the amount of interest that ought not to have been paid.

(3) The power to make an assessment under this paragraph in respect of a transaction for which the purchaser has delivered a land transaction return is subject to the restrictions specified in paragraph 30.

Restrictions on assessment where return delivered

30

(1) If the purchaser has delivered a land transaction return in respect of the transaction in question, an assessment under paragraph 28 or 29 in respect of the transaction –

(a)   may only be made in the two cases specified in sub-paragraphs (2) and (3) below, and
(b)   may not be made in the circumstances specified in sub-paragraph (5) below.

(2) The first case is where the situation mentioned in paragraph 28(1) or 29(1) is attributable to fraudulent or negligent conduct on the part of –

(a)   the purchaser,
(b)   a person acting on behalf of the purchaser, or
(c)   a person who was a partner of the purchaser at the relevant time.

(3) The second case is where the Inland Revenue, at the time they –

(a)   ceased to be entitled to give a notice of enquiry into the return, or
(b)   completed their enquiries into the return,

could not have been reasonably expected, on the basis of the information made available to them before that time, to be aware of the situation mentioned in paragraph 28(1) or 29(1).

(4) For this purpose information is regarded as made available to the Inland Revenue if –

(a)   it is contained in a land transaction return made by the purchaser,

(b)   it is contained in any documents produced or information provided to the Inland Revenue for the purposes of an enquiry into any such return, or

(c)   it is information the existence of which, and the relevance of which as regards the situation mentioned in paragraph 28(1) or 29(1) –

   (i)   could reasonably be expected to be inferred by the Inland Revenue from information falling within paragraphs (a) or (b) above, or

   (ii) are notified in writing to the Inland Revenue by the purchaser or a person acting on his behalf.

(5) No assessment may be made if –

(a)   the situation mentioned in paragraph 28(1) or 29(1) is attributable to a mistake in the return as to the basis on which the tax liability ought to have been computed, and

(b)   the return was in fact made on the basis or in accordance with the practice generally prevailing at the time it was made.

Time limit for assessment

31

(1) The general rule is that no assessment may be made more than six years after the effective date of the transaction to which it relates.

(2) In a case involving fraud or negligence on the part of –

(a)   the purchaser, or

(b)   a person acting on behalf of the purchaser, or

(c)   a person who was a partner of the purchaser at the relevant time,

an assessment may be made up to 21 years after the effective date of the transaction to which it relates.

(3) An assessment under paragraph 29 (assessment to recover excessive repayment of tax) is not out of time –

(a)   in a case where notice of enquiry is given into the land transaction return delivered by the person concerned, if it is made before the enquiry is completed;

(b)   in any case, if it is made within one year after the repayment in question was made.

(4) Where the purchaser has died –

(a)   any assessment on the personal representatives of the deceased must be made within three years after his death, and

(b)   an assessment shall not be made by virtue of sub-paragraph (2) in respect of a transaction of which the effective date was more than six years before the death.

(5) Any objection to the making of an assessment on the ground that the time limit for making it has expired can only be made on an appeal against the assessment.

Assessment procedure

32

(1) Notice of an assessment must be served on the purchaser.

(2) The notice must state –

    (a)   the tax due,

    (b)   the date on which the notice is issued, and

    (c)   the time within which any appeal against the assessment must be made.

(3) After notice of the assessment has been served on the purchaser, the assessment may not be altered except in accordance with the express provisions of this Part of this Act.

(4) Where an officer of the Board has decided to make an assessment to tax, and has taken all other decisions needed for arriving at the amount of the assessment, he may entrust to some other officer of the Board responsibility for completing the assessing procedure, whether by means involving the use of a computer or otherwise, including responsibility for serving notice of the assessment.

PART 6
RELIEF IN CASE OF EXCESSIVE ASSESSMENT

Relief in case of double assessment

33

(1) A person who believes he has been assessed to tax more than once in respect of the same matter may make a claim to the Inland Revenue for relief against any double charge.

(4) An appeal may be made against a decision on a claim for relief under this paragraph.

Amendments: Finance Act 2004, ss 299(1), (7), 326, Sch 42; SI 2009/56.

Relief in case of mistake in return

34

(1) A person who believes he has paid tax under an assessment that was excessive by reason of some mistake in a land transaction return may make a claim to the Inland Revenue for relief against any excessive charge.

(2) The claim must be made not more than six years after the effective date of the transaction.

(4) No relief shall be given under this paragraph –

    (a)   in respect of a mistake as to the basis on which the liability of the claimant ought to have been computed when the return was in fact made on the basis or in accordance with the practice generally prevailing at the time when it was made, or

    (b)   in respect of a mistake in a claim or election included in the return.

(5) In determining a claim under this paragraph the Inland Revenue shall have regard to all the relevant circumstances of the case.

They shall, in particular, consider whether the granting of relief would result in amounts being excluded from charge to tax.

(6) On an appeal against the Inland Revenue's decision on the claim, that is notified to the tribunal, the tribunal shall determine the claim in accordance with the same principles as apply to the determination by the Inland Revenue of claims under this paragraph.

Amendments: Finance Act 2004, ss 299(1), (8), 326, Sch 42; SI 2009/56.

PART 7
REVIEWS AND APPEALS

Amendment: SI 2009/56.

Right of appeal

35

(1) An appeal may be brought against –

    (a) an amendment of a self-assessment under paragraph 17(amendment by Revenue during enquiry to prevent loss of tax),

    (b) a conclusion stated or amendment made by a closure notice,

    (c) a discovery assessment,

    (d) an assessment under paragraph 29 (assessment to recover excessive repayment), or

    (e) a Revenue determination under paragraph 25 (determination of tax chargeable if no return delivered).

(3) If an appeal under sub-paragraph (1)(a) against an amendment of a self-assessment is made while an enquiry is in progress none of the steps mentioned in paragraph 36A(2)(a) to (c) may be taken in relation to the appeal until the enquiry is completed.

Amendment: SI 2004/3208; SI 2009/56.

Notice of appeal

36

(1) Notice of an appeal under paragraph 35 must be given –

    (a) in writing,

    (b) within 30 days after the specified date,

    (c) to the relevant officer of the Board.

(2) In relation to an appeal under paragraph 35(1)(a) –

    (a) the specified date is the date on which the notice of amendment was issued, and

    (b) the relevant officer of the Board is the officer by whom the notice of amendment was given.

(3) In relation to an appeal under paragraph 35(1)(b) –

    (a) the specified date is the date on which the closure notice was issued, and

    (b) the relevant officer of the Board is the officer by whom the closure notice was given.

(4) In relation to an appeal under paragraph 35(1)(c) or (d) –

    (a) the specified date is the date on which the notice of assessment was issued, and

(b)   the relevant officer of the Board is the officer by whom the notice of assessment was given.

(4A) In relation to an appeal under paragraph 35(1)(e) –

(a)   the specified date is the date on which the Revenue determination was issued, and

(b)   the relevant officer of the Board is the officer by whom the determination was made.

(5) The notice of appeal must specify the grounds of appeal.

(5A) The only grounds on which an appeal lies under paragraph 35(1)(e) are that –

(a)   the purchase to which the determination relates did not take place,

(b)   the interest in the land to which the determination relates has not been purchased,

(c)   the contract for the purchase of the interest to which the determination relates has not been substantially performed, or

(d)   the land transaction is not notifiable (for example, because the land transaction is exempt from charge under Schedule 3).

Amendments: SI 2004/3208; Finance Act 2008, s 94(4), (5), Sch 30, paras 1, 7; SI 2009/56.

Appeal: HMRC review or determination by tribunal

36A

(1) This paragraph applies if notice of appeal has been given to HMRC.

(2) In such a case –

(a)   the appellant may notify HMRC that the appellant requires HMRC to review the matter in question (see paragraph 36B),

(b)   HMRC may notify the appellant of an offer to review the matter in question (see paragraph 36C), or

(c)   the appellant may notify the appeal to the tribunal (see paragraph 36D).

(3) See paragraphs 36G and 36H for provision about notifying appeals to the tribunal after a review has been required by the appellant or offered by HMRC.

(4) This paragraph does not prevent the matter in question from being dealt with in accordance with paragraph 37(1) (settling of appeals by agreement).

Amendment: SI 2009/56.

Appellant requires review by HMRC

36B

(1) Sub-paragraphs (2) and (3) apply if the appellant notifies HMRC that the appellant requires HMRC to review the matter in question.

(2) HMRC must, within the relevant period, notify the appellant of HMRC's view of the matter in question.

(3) HMRC must review the matter in question in accordance with paragraph 36E.

(4) The appellant may not notify HMRC that the appellant requires HMRC to review the matter in question and HMRC shall not be required to conduct a review if –

(a)   the appellant has already given a notification under this paragraph in relation to the matter in question,

(b)   HMRC have given a notification under paragraph 36C in relation to the matter in question, or

(c)   the appellant has notified the appeal to the tribunal under paragraph 36D.

(5) In this paragraph 'relevant period' means –

(a)   the period of 30 days beginning with the day on which HMRC receive the notification from the appellant, or

(b)   such longer period as is reasonable.

Amendment: SI 2009/56.

HMRC offer review

36C

(1) Sub-paragraphs (2) to (6) apply if HMRC notify the appellant of an offer to review the matter in question.

(2) When HMRC notify the appellant of the offer, HMRC must also notify the appellant of HMRC's view of the matter in question.

(3) If, within the acceptance period, the appellant notifies HMRC of acceptance of the offer, HMRC must review the matter in question in accordance with paragraph 36E.

(4) If the appellant does not give HMRC such a notification within the acceptance period, HMRC's view of the matter in question is to be treated as if it were contained in an agreement in writing under paragraph 37(1) for the settlement of that matter.

(5) The appellant may not give notice under paragraph 37(2) (desire to withdraw from agreement) in a case where sub-paragraph (4) applies.

(6) Sub-paragraph (4) does not apply to the matter in question if, or to the extent that, the appellant notifies the appeal to the tribunal under paragraph 36H.

(7) HMRC may not notify the appellant of an offer to review the matter in question (and, accordingly, HMRC shall not be required to conduct a review) if –

(a)   HMRC have already given a notification under this paragraph in relation to the matter in question,

(b)   the appellant has given a notification under paragraph 36B in relation to the matter in question, or

(c)   the appellant has notified the appeal to the tribunal under paragraph 36D.

(8) In this paragraph 'acceptance period' means the period of 30 days beginning with the date of the document by which HMRC notify the appellant of the offer to review the matter in question.

Amendments: SI 2009/56.

Notifying appeal to the tribunal

36D

(1) This paragraph applies in a case where paragraph 36A applies.

(2) The appellant may notify the appeal to the tribunal.

(3) If the appellant notifies the appeal to the tribunal, the tribunal is to decide the matter in question.

(4) Sub-paragraphs (2) and (3) do not apply in a case where –

(a) HMRC have given a notification of their view of the matter in question under paragraph 36B, or

(b) HMRC have given a notification under paragraph 36C in relation to the matter in question.

(5) In a case falling within sub-paragraph (4)(a) or (b), the appellant may notify the appeal to the tribunal, but only if permitted to do so by paragraph 36G or 36H.

Amendment: SI 2009/56.

Nature of review etc

36E

(1) This paragraph applies if HMRC are required by paragraph 36B or 36C to review the matter in question.

(2) The nature and extent of the review are to be such as appear appropriate to HMRC in the circumstances.

(3) For the purpose of sub-paragraph (2), HMRC must, in particular, have regard to steps taken before the beginning of the review –

(a) by HMRC in deciding the matter in question, and

(b) by any person in seeking to resolve disagreement about the matter in question.

(4) The review must take account of any representations made by the appellant at a stage which gives HMRC a reasonable opportunity to consider them.

(5) The review may conclude that HMRC's view of the matter in question is to be –

(a) upheld,

(b) varied, or

(c) cancelled.

(6) HMRC must notify the appellant of the conclusions of the review and their reasoning within –

(a) the period of 45 days beginning with the relevant day, or

(b) such other period as may be agreed.

(7) In sub-paragraph (6) 'relevant day' means –

(a) in a case where the appellant required the review, the day when HMRC notified the appellant of HMRC's view of the matter in question,

(b) in a case where HMRC offered the review, the day when HMRC received notification of the appellant's acceptance of the offer.

(8) Where HMRC are required to undertake a review but do not give notice of the conclusions within the period specified in sub-paragraph (6), the review is treated as having concluded that HMRC's view of the matter in question (see paragraphs 36B(2) and 36C(2)) is upheld.

(9) If sub-paragraph (8) applies, HMRC must notify the appellant of the conclusions which the review is treated as having reached.

Amendment: SI 2009/56.

Effect of conclusions of review

36F

(1) This paragraph applies if HMRC give notice of the conclusions of a review (see paragraph 36E).

(2) The conclusions are to be treated as if they were an agreement in writing under paragraph 37(1) for the settlement of the matter in question.

(3) The appellant may not give notice under paragraph 37(2) (desire to withdraw from agreement) in a case where sub-paragraph (2) applies.

(4) Sub-paragraph (2) does not apply to the matter in question if, or to the extent that, the appellant notifies the appeal to the tribunal under paragraph 36G.

Amendment: SI 2009/56.

Notifying appeal to tribunal after review concluded

36G

(1) This paragraph applies if –

(a) HMRC have given notice of the conclusions of a review in accordance with paragraph 36E, or
(b) the period specified in paragraph 36E(6) has ended and HMRC have not given notice of the conclusions of the review.

(2) The appellant may notify the appeal to the tribunal within the post-review period.

(3) If the post-review period has ended, the appellant may notify the appeal to the tribunal only if the tribunal gives permission.

(4) If the appellant notifies the appeal to the tribunal, the tribunal is to determine the matter in question.

(5) In this paragraph 'post-review period' means –

(a) in a case falling with sub-paragraph (1)(a), the period of 30 days beginning with the date of the document in which HMRC give notice of the conclusions of the review in accordance with paragraph 36E(6), or
(b) in a case falling within sub-paragraph (1)(b), the period that –
    (i) begins with the day following the last day of the period specified in paragraph 36E(6), and
    (ii) ends 30 days after the date of the document in which HMRC give notice of the conclusions of the review in accordance with paragraph 36E(9).

Amendment: SI 2009/56.

Notifying appeal to tribunal after review offered but not accepted

36H

(1) This paragraph applies if –

(a) HMRC have offered to review the matter in question (see paragraph 36C), and
(b) the appellant has not accepted the offer.

(2) The appellant may notify the appeal to the tribunal within the acceptance period.

(3) But if the acceptance period has ended, the appellant may notify the appeal to the tribunal only if the tribunal gives permission.

(4) If the appellant notifies the appeal to the tribunal, the tribunal is to determine the matter in question.

(5) In this paragraph 'acceptance period' has the same meaning as in paragraph 36C.

Amendment: SI 2009/56.

Other interpretation

36I

(1) In paragraphs 36A to 36H –

    (a)   'matter in question' means the matter to which an appeal relates;
    (b)   a reference to a notification is a reference to a notification in writing.

(2) In paragraphs 36A to 36H, a reference to the appellant includes a person acting on behalf of the appellant except in relation to –

    (a)   notification of HMRC's view under paragraph 36B(2),
    (b)   notification by HMRC of an offer of review (and of their view of the matter) under paragraph 36C,
    (c)   notification of the conclusions of a review under paragraph 36E(6), and
    (d)   notification of the conclusions of a review under paragraph 36E(9).

(3) But if a notification falling within any of the sub-paragraphs of paragraph (2) is given to the appellant, a copy of the notification may also be given to a person acting on behalf of the appellant.

Amendment: SI 2009/56.

Settling of appeals by agreement

37

(1) If, before an appeal under paragraph 35 is determined, the appellant and the Inland Revenue agree that the decision appealed against –

    (a)   should be upheld without variation,
    (b)   should be varied in a particular manner, or
    (c)   should be discharged or cancelled,

the same consequences shall follow, for all purposes, as would have followed if, at the time the agreement was come to, the tribunal had determined the appeal and had upheld the decision without variation, varied it in that manner or discharged or cancelled it, as the case may be.

(2) Sub-paragraph (1) does not apply if, within 30 days from the date when the agreement was come to, the appellant gives notice in writing to the Inland Revenue that he wishes to withdraw from the agreement.

(3) Where the agreement is not in writing –

(a)   sub-paragraphs (1) and (2) do not apply unless the fact that an agreement was come to, and the terms agreed, are confirmed by notice in writing given by the Inland Revenue to the appellant or by the appellant to the Inland Revenue, and

(b)   the references in those provisions to the time when the agreement was come to shall be read as references to the time when the notice of confirmation was given.

(4) Where –

(a)   the appellant notifies the Inland Revenue, orally or in writing, that he does not wish to proceed with the appeal, and

(b)   the Inland Revenue do not, within 30 days after that notification, give the appellant notice in writing indicating that they are unwilling that the appeal should be withdrawn,

the provisions of sub-paragraphs (1) to (3) have effect as if, at the date of the appellant's notification, the appellant and the Inland Revenue had come to an agreement (orally or in writing, as the case may be) that the decision under appeal should be upheld without variation.

(5) References in this paragraph to an agreement being come to with an appellant, and to the giving of notice or notification by or to the appellant, include references to an agreement being come to, or notice or notification being given by or to, a person acting on behalf of the appellant in relation to the appeal.

Amendment: SI 2009/56.

Recovery of tax not postponed by appeal

38

(1) Where there is an appeal under paragraph 35, the tax charged by the amendment or assessment in question remains due and payable as if there had been no appeal.

(2) Sub-paragraph (1) is subject to –

paragraph 39 (direction by tribunal postponing payment), and

paragraph 40 (agreement to postpone payment).

Amendment: SI 2009/56.

Direction by the tribunal to postpone payment

39

(1) If the appellant has grounds for believing that the amendment or assessment overcharges the appellant to tax, or as a result of the conclusion stated in the closure notice the tax charged on the appellant is excessive, the appellant may –

(a)   first apply by notice in writing to HMRC within 30 days of the specified date for a determination by them of the amount of tax the payment of which should be postponed pending the determination of the appeal;

(b)   where such a determination is not agreed, refer the application for postponement to the tribunal within 30 days from the date of the document notifying HMRC's decision on the amount to be postponed.

An application under sub-paragraph (a) must state the amount believed to be overcharged to tax and the grounds for that belief.

(3) An application may be made more than 30 days after the specified date if there is a change in the circumstances of the case as a result of which the appellant has grounds for believing that he is overcharged to tax by the decision appealed against.

(4) If, after any determination on such an application of the amount of tax the payment of which should be postponed, there is a change in the circumstances of the case as a result of which either party has grounds for believing that the amount so determined has become excessive or, as the case may be, insufficient, he may, if the parties cannot agree on a revised determination, apply, at any time before the determination of the appeal, to the tribunal for a revised determination of that amount.

(5) An application under this paragraph is to be subject to the relevant provisions of Part 5 of the Taxes Management Act 1970 (see, in particular, section 48(2)(b) of that Act).

The fact that any such application has been heard and determined by any Commissioners does not preclude them from hearing and determining the appeal or any further application under this paragraph.

(6) The amount of tax of which payment is to be postponed pending the determination of the appeal is the amount (if any) by which it appears, that there are reasonable grounds for believing that the appellant is overcharged.

(7) Where an application is made under this paragraph, the date on which any tax of which payment is not postponed is due and payable shall be determined as if the tax were charged by an amendment or assessment of which notice was issued on the date on which the application was determined and against which there was no appeal.

(8) On the determination of the appeal –

    (a)   the date on which any tax payable in accordance with that determination is due and payable shall, so far as it is tax the payment of which had been postponed, or which would not have been charged by the amendment or assessment if there had been no appeal, be determined as if the tax were charged by an amendment or assessment –

        (i)   of which notice was issued on the date on which the HMRC issues to the appellant a notice of the total amount payable in accordance with the determination, and

        (ii)   against which there had been no appeal, and

    (b)   any tax overpaid shall be repaid.

Amendment: SI 2009/56.

Agreement to postpone payment of tax

40

(1) If the appellant and the relevant officer of the Board agree that payment of an amount of tax should be postponed pending the determination of the appeal, the same consequences shall follow, for all purposes, as would have followed if, at the time the agreement was come to, the tribunal had made a direction to the same effect.

This is without prejudice to the making of a further agreement or of a further direction.

(2) Where the agreement is not in writing –

(a)   sub-paragraph (1) does not apply unless the fact that an agreement was come
       to, and the terms agreed, are confirmed by notice in writing given by the
       relevant officer of the Board to the appellant or by the appellant to that officer,
       and
(b)   the reference in that provision to the time when the agreement was come to
       shall be read as a reference to the time when notice of confirmation was given.

(3) References in this paragraph to an agreement being come to with an appellant, and
to the giving of notice to or by the appellant, include references to an agreement being
come to, or notice being given to or by, a person acting on behalf of the appellant in
relation to the appeal.

Amendment: SI 2009/56.

Tribunal determinations

41

The determination of the tribunal in relation to any proceedings under the enactments
relating to stamp duty land tax shall be final and conclusive except as otherwise
provided in –

(a)   sections 9 to 14 of the Tribunals, Courts and Enforcement Act 2007,
(b)   the Taxes Management Act 1970 applied as modified, or
(c)   the enactments relating to stamp duty land tax.

Assessments and self assessments

42

(1) In this paragraph any reference to an appeal means an appeal under
paragraphs 33(4) or 35(1).

(2) If, on an appeal notified to the tribunal, the tribunal decides –

(a)   that the appellant is overcharged by a self-assessment; or
(b)   that the appellant is overcharged by an assessment other than a
       self-assessment,
the assessment shall be reduced accordingly, but otherwise the assessment shall stand
good.

(3) If, on appeal it appears to the tribunal –

(a)   that the appellant is undercharged to stamp duty land tax by a self-assessment;
       or
(b)   that the appellant is undercharged by an assessment other than a
       self-assessment,
the assessment shall be increased accordingly.

(4) Where, on an appeal against an assessment other than a self-assessment which –

(a)   assesses an amount which is chargeable to stamp duty land tax, and
(b)   charges stamp duty land tax on the amount assessed,

it appears to the tribunal as mentioned in sub-paragraphs (2) or (3), it may, unless the
circumstances of the case otherwise require, reduce or increase only the amount
assessed; and where an appeal is so determined the stamp duty land tax charged by that
assessment shall be taken to have been reduced or increased accordingly.

Payment of stamp duty land tax where there is a further appeal

43

(1) Where a party to an appeal to the tribunal under paragraph 35 makes a further appeal, notwithstanding that the further appeal is pending, stamp duty land tax shall nevertheless be payable or repayable in accordance with the determination of the tribunal or court as the case may be.

(2) But if the amount charged by the assessment is altered by the order or judgment of the Upper Tribunal or court –

    (a)   if too much stamp duty land tax has been paid, the amount overpaid shall be refunded with such interest, if any, as may be allowed by that order or judgment; and

    (b)   if too little stamp duty land tax has been charged, the amount undercharged shall be due and payable at the expiration of a period of thirty days beginning with the date on which HMRC issue to the other party a notice of the total amount payable in accordance with the order or judgment.

Late notice of appeal

44

(1) This paragraph applies in a case where –

    (a)   notice of appeal may be given to HMRC under this Schedule or any other provision of Part 4 of this Act, but

    (b)   no notice is given before the relevant time limit.

(2) Notice may be given after the relevant time limit if –

    (a)   HMRC agree, or

    (b)   where HMRC do not agree, the tribunal gives permission.

(3) If the following conditions are met, HMRC shall agree to notice being given after the relevant time limit.

(4) Condition A is that the appellant has made a request in writing to HMRC to agree to the notice being given.

(5) Condition B is that HMRC are satisfied that there was reasonable excuse for not giving the notice before the relevant time limit.

(6) Condition C is that HMRC are satisfied that request under sub-paragraph (4) was made without unreasonable delay after the reasonable excuse ceased.

(7) If a request of the kind referred to in sub-paragraph (4) is made, HMRC must notify the appellant whether or not HMRC agree to the appellant giving notice of appeal after the relevant time limit.

(8) In this paragraph 'relevant time limit', in relation to notice of appeal, means the time before which the notice is to be given (but for this paragraph).

Questions to be determined by the relevant Upper Tribunal

45

(1) Where the question in any dispute on any appeal under paragraphs 34(6) or 35(1) is a question of the market value of the subject matter of the land transaction that question shall be determined on a reference by the relevant Upper Tribunal.

(2) In this paragraph 'the relevant tribunal' means –

(a)   where the land is in England and Wales, the Upper Tribunal;

(b)   where the land is in Scotland, the Lands Tribunal for Scotland;

(c)   where the land is in Northern Ireland, the Lands Tribunal for Northern Ireland.

Meaning of HMRC

46

In this Schedule 'HMRC' means Her Majesty's Revenue and Customs.

Amendments: SI 2009/56; SI 2009/1307.

Schedule 11

Section 79

Stamp Duty Land Tax: Record-Keeping Where Transaction is not Notifiable

Amendments: Finance Act 2008, s 94(4), (5), Sch 30, paras 1, 11.

PART 1 . . .

Amendments: Part repealed, Finance Act 2008, s 94(4), (5), Sch 30, paras 1, 8.

PART 2
DUTY TO KEEP AND PRESERVE RECORDS

Duty to keep and preserve records

4

(A1) This paragraph applies where a transaction is not notifiable, unless the transaction is a transaction treated as taking place under a provision listed in section 79(2)(a) to (d).

(1) The purchaser must –

(a)   keep such records as may be needed to enable him to demonstrate that the transaction is not notifiable, and

(b)   preserve those records in accordance with this paragraph.

(2) The records must be preserved for six years after the effective date of the transaction.

(3) The records required to be kept and preserved under this paragraph include –

(a)   relevant instruments relating to the transaction, in particular, any contract or conveyance, and any supporting maps, plans or similar documents;

(b)   records of relevant payments, receipts and financial arrangements.

Amendments: Finance Act 2008, s 94(4), (5), Sch 30, paras 1, 9(1), (2), (3)(a), (4).

Preservation of information instead of original records

5

(1) The duty under paragraph 4 to preserve records may be satisfied by the preservation of the information contained in them.

(2) Where information is so preserved a copy of any document forming part of the records is admissible in evidence in any proceedings before the tribunal to the same extent as the records themselves.

Amendment: SI 2009/56.

Penalty for failure to keep and preserve records

6

(1) A person who fails to comply with paragraph 4 in relation to a transaction is liable to a penalty not exceeding £3,000, subject to the following exception.

(2) No penalty is incurred if the Inland Revenue are satisfied that any facts that they reasonably require to be proved, and that would have been proved by the records, are proved by other documentary evidence provided to them.

PART 3 . . .

Amendments: Part repealed, Finance Act 2008, s 94(4), (5), Sch 30, paras 1, 10.

Schedule 11A

Section 82A

Stamp Duty Land Tax: Claims Not Included In Returns

Introductory

1

This Schedule applies to a claim under any provision of this Part other than a claim that is required to be made in, or by amendment to, a return under this Part.

References in this Schedule to a claim shall be read accordingly.

Making of claims

2

(1) A claim must be made in such form as the Inland Revenue may determine.

(2) The form of claim must provide for a declaration to the effect that all the particulars given in the form are correctly stated to the best of the claimant's information and belief.

(3) The form of claim may require –

    (a)   a statement of the amount of tax that will be required to be discharged or repaid in order to give effect to the claim;

    (b)   such information as is reasonably required for the purpose of determining whether and, if so, the extent to which the claim is correct;

(c) the delivery with the claim of such statements and documents, relating to the information contained in the claim, as are reasonably required for the purpose mentioned in paragraph (b).

(4) A claim for repayment of tax may not be made unless the claimant has documentary evidence that the tax has been paid.

Duty to keep and preserve records

3

(1) A person who may wish to make a claim must –

(a) keep such records as may be needed to enable him to make a correct and complete claim, and
(b) preserve those records in accordance with this paragraph.

(2) The records must be preserved until the latest of the following times –

(a) the end of the period of twelve months beginning with day on which the claim was made;
(b) where there is an enquiry into the claim, or into an amendment of the claim, the time when the enquiry is completed;
(c) where the claim is amended and there is there is no enquiry into the amendment, the time when the Inland Revenue no longer have power to enquire into the amendment.

(3) The duty under this paragraph to preserve records may be satisfied by the preservation of the information contained in them.

(4) Where information is so preserved a copy of any document forming part of the records is admissible in evidence in any proceedings before the tribunal to the same extent as the records themselves.

(5) A person who fails to comply with this paragraph in relation to a claim that he makes is liable to a penalty not exceeding £3,000, subject to the following exception.

(6) No penalty is incurred if the Inland Revenue are satisfied that any facts that they reasonably require to be proved, and that would have been proved by the records, are proved by other documentary evidence provided to them.

Amendment: SI 2009/56.

Amendment of claim by claimant

4

(1) The claimant may amend his claim by notice to the Inland Revenue.

(2) No such amendment may be made –

(a) more than twelve months after the day on which the claim was made, or
(b) if the Inland Revenue give notice under paragraph 7 (notice of enquiry), during the period –
   (i)   beginning with the day on which notice is given, and
   (ii) ending with the day on which the enquiry under that paragraph is completed.

Correction of claim by Revenue

5

(1) The Inland Revenue may by notice to the claimant amend a claim so as to correct obvious errors or omissions in the claim (whether errors of principle, arithmetical mistakes or otherwise).

(2) No such correction may be made –

    (a)   more than nine months after the day on which the claim was made, or
    (b)   if the Inland Revenue give notice under paragraph 7 (notice of enquiry), during the period –
        (i)   beginning with the day on which notice is given, and
        (ii) ending with the day on which the enquiry under that paragraph is completed.

(3) A correction under this paragraph is of no effect if, within three months from the date of issue of the notice of correction, the claimant gives notice rejecting the correction.

(4) Notice under sub-paragraph (3) must be given to the officer of the Board by whom the notice of correction was given.

Giving effect to claims and amendments

6

(1) As soon as practicable after a claim is made, or is amended under paragraph 4 or 5, the Inland Revenue shall give effect to the claim or amendment by discharge or repayment of tax.

(2) Where the Inland Revenue enquire into a claim or amendment –

    (a)   sub-paragraph (1) does not apply until a closure notice is given under paragraph 11 (completion of enquiry), and then it applies subject to paragraph 13 (giving effect to amendments under paragraph 11), but
    (b)   the Inland Revenue may at any time before then give effect to the claim or amendment, on a provisional basis, to such extent as they think fit.

Notice of enquiry

7

(1) The Inland Revenue may enquire into a person's claim or amendment of a claim if they give him notice of their intention to do so ('notice of enquiry') before the end of the period of nine months after the day on which the claim or amendment was made.

(2) A claim or amendment that has been the subject of one notice of enquiry may not be the subject of another.

Notice to produce documents etc for purposes of enquiry

8

(1) If the Inland Revenue give a person a notice of enquiry, they may by notice in writing require him –

    (a)   to produce to them such documents in his possession or power, and
    (b)   to provide them with such information, in such form,

as they may reasonably require for the purposes of the enquiry.

(2) A notice given to a person under this paragraph (which may be given at the same time as the notice of enquiry) must specify the time (which must not be less than 30 days) within which he is to comply with it.

(3) In complying with a notice under this paragraph copies of documents may be produced instead of originals, but –

(a)   the copies must be photographic or other facsimiles, and
(b)   the Inland Revenue may by notice require the original to be produced for inspection.

A notice under paragraph (b) must specify the time (which must not be less than 30 days) within which the person is to comply with it.

(4) The Inland Revenue may take copies of, or make extracts from, any documents produced to them under this paragraph.

(5) A notice under this paragraph does not oblige a person to produce documents or provide information relating to the conduct of any pending appeal by him.

Appeal against notice to produce documents etc

9

(1) An appeal may be brought against a requirement imposed by a notice under paragraph 8 to produce documents or provide information.

(2) Notice of appeal must be given –

(a)   in writing,
(b)   within 30 days after the issue of the notice appealed against,
(c)   to the officer of the Board by whom that notice was given.

(3) An appeal under this paragraph shall be determined in the same way as an appeal against an assessment.

(4) On an appeal under this paragraph that is notified to the tribunal, the tribunal –

(a)   shall set aside the notice so far as it requires the production of documents, or the provision of information, that appears not reasonably required for the purposes of the enquiry, and
(b)   shall confirm the notice so far as it requires the production of documents, or the provision of information, that appears reasonably required for the purposes of the enquiry.

(5) A notice that is confirmed by the tribunal (or so far as it is confirmed) has effect as if the period specified in it for complying was 30 days from the determination of the appeal.

(6) Notwithstanding the provisions of sections 11 and 13 of the Tribunals, Courts and Enforcement Act 2007, the decision of the tribunal on an appeal under this paragraph is final.

Amendment: SI 2009/56.

Penalty for failure to produce documents etc

10

(1) A person who fails to comply with a notice under paragraph 8 (notice to produce documents etc for purposes of enquiry) is liable –

(a)   to a penalty of £50, and
(b)   if the failure continues after a penalty is imposed under paragraph (a), to a further penalty or penalties not exceeding £30 for each day on which the failure continues.

(2) No penalty shall be imposed under this paragraph in respect of a failure at any time after the failure has been remedied.

Completion of enquiry

11

(1) An enquiry under paragraph 7 is completed when the Inland Revenue by notice (a 'closure notice') inform the purchaser that they have completed their enquiries and state their conclusions.

(2) A closure notice must either –

(a)   state that in the opinion of the Inland Revenue no amendment of the claim is required, or
(b)   if in the Inland Revenue's opinion the claim is insufficient or excessive, amend the claim so as to make good or eliminate the deficiency or excess.

In the case of an enquiry into an amendment of a claim, paragraph (b) applies only so far as the deficiency or excess is attributable to the amendment.

(3) A closure notice takes effect when it is issued.

Direction to complete enquiry

12

(1) The claimant may apply to the tribunal for a direction that the Inland Revenue give a closure notice within a specified period.

(2) Any such application is to be subject to the relevant provisions of Part 5 of the Taxes Management Act 1970 (see, in particular, section 48(2)(b) of that Act).

(3) The tribunal shall give a direction unless satisfied that the Inland Revenue have reasonable grounds for not giving a closure notice within a specified period.

Amendment: SI 2009/56.

Giving effect to amendments under paragraph 11

13

(1) Within 30 days after the date of issue of a notice under paragraph 11(2)(b) (closure notice that amends claim), the Inland Revenue shall give effect to the amendment by making such adjustment as may be necessary, whether –

(a)   by way of assessment on the claimant, or
(b)   by discharge or repayment of tax.

(2) An assessment made under sub-paragraph (1) is not out of time if it is made within the time mentioned in that sub-paragraph.

Appeals against amendments under paragraph 11

14

(1) An appeal may be brought against a conclusion stated or amendment made by a closure notice.

(2) Notice of the appeal must be given –

    (a)   in writing,
    (b)   within 30 days after the date on which the closure notice was issued,
    (c)   to the officer of the Board by whom the closure notice was given.

(3) The notice of appeal must specify the grounds of appeal.

(5) Paragraphs 36A to 37 and 44 of Schedule 10 (settling of appeals by agreement) applies in relation to an appeal under this paragraph they apply in relation to an appeal under paragraph 35 of that Schedule.

(6) On an appeal against an amendment made by a closure notice, the tribunal may vary the amendment appealed against whether or not the variation is to the advantage of the appellant.

(7) Where any such amendment is varied, whether by the tribunal or by the order of a court, paragraph 13 (giving effect to amendments under paragraph 11) applies (with the necessary modifications) in relation to the variation as it applied in relation to the amendment.

Amendment: SI 2009/56.

15 . . .

Amendment: Paragraph repealed by SI 2009/56.

Amendments: Schedule Inserted by Finance Act 2004, s 299(1), (3), Sch 40.

Schedule 12

Section 91

Stamp Duty Land Tax: Collection And Recovery Of Tax

PART 1

GENERAL

Issue of tax demands and receipts

1

(1) Where tax is due and payable, a collector may make demand of the sum charged from the person liable to pay it.

(2) On payment of the tax, the collector shall if so requested give a receipt.

Recovery of tax by distraint

2

(1) In England and Wales or Northern Ireland, if a person neglects or refuses to pay the sum charged, upon demand made by the collector, the collector may distrain upon the goods and chattels of the person charged ('the person in default').

(2) For the purposes of levying such distress a justice of the peace, on being satisfied by information on oath that there is reasonable ground for believing that a person is neglecting or refusing to pay a sum charged, may issue a warrant in writing authorising a collector to break open, in the daytime, any house or premises, calling to his assistance any constable.

Every such constable shall, when so required, assist the collector in the execution of the warrant and in levying such distress in the house or premises.

(3) A levy or warrant to break open must be executed by, or under the direction of, and in the presence of, the collector.

(4) A distress levied by the collector shall be kept for five days, at the costs and charges of the person in default.

(5) If the person in default does not pay the sum due, together with the costs and charges, the distress shall be appraised by one or more independent persons appointed by the collector, and shall be sold by public auction by the collector for payment of the sum due and all costs and charges.

Any surplus resulting from the distress, after the deduction of the costs and charges and of the sum due, shall be restored to the owner of the goods distrained.

(6) The Treasury may by regulations make provision with respect to –

    (a)   the fees chargeable on or in connection with the levying of distress, and
    (b)   the costs and charges recoverable where distress has been levied.

Recovery of tax by diligence in Scotland

3

(1) In Scotland, where any tax is due and has not been paid, the sheriff, on an application by the collector accompanied by a certificate by the collector –

    (a)   stating that none of the persons specified in the application has paid the tax to him,
    (b)   stating that the collector has demanded payment under paragraph 1 from each such person of the amount due by him,
    (c)   stating that 14 days have elapsed since the date of such demand without payment of that amount, and
    (d)   specifying the amount due and unpaid by each such person,

shall grant a summary warrant in a form prescribed by Act of Sederunt authorising the recovery, by any of the diligences mentioned in sub-paragraph (2), of the amount remaining due and unpaid.

(2) The diligences referred to in sub-paragraph (1) are –

    (a)   an attachment;
    (b)   an earnings arrestment;
    (c)   an arrestment and action of furthcoming or sale.

(3) Subject to sub-paragraph (4), the sheriff officer's fees, together with the outlays necessarily incurred by him, in connection with the execution of a summary warrant are chargeable against the debtor.

(4) No fee is chargeable by the sheriff officer against the debtor for collecting, and accounting to the collector for, sums paid to him by the debtor in respect of the amount owing.

PART 2
COURT PROCEEDINGS

Civil proceedings in magistrates' court or court of summary jurisdiction

4

(1) An amount not exceeding £2,000 due and payable by way of tax is in England and Wales or Northern Ireland recoverable summarily as a civil debt in proceedings brought in the name of the collector.

(2) All or any of the sums recoverable under this paragraph that are –

   (a)   due from any one person, and
   (b)   payable to any one collector,

may be included in the same complaint, summons or other document required to be laid before or issued by justices.

Each such document shall, as respects each such sum, be construed as a separate document and its invalidity as respects any one such sum does not affect its validity as respects any other such sum.

(3) Proceedings under this paragraph in England and Wales may be brought at any time within one year from the time when the matter complained of arose.

(4) In sub-paragraph (1) the expression 'recoverable summarily as a civil debt' in relation to proceedings in Northern Ireland means recoverable by proceedings under Article 62 of the Magistrates' Courts (Northern Ireland) Order 1981 (SI 1981/1675 (NI 26)).

(5) The Treasury may by order increase the sum specified in sub-paragraph (1).

Proceedings in county court or sheriff court

5

(1) Tax due and payable may be sued for and recovered from the person charged as a debt due to the Crown by proceedings –

   (a)   in a county court, or
   (b)   in a sheriff court.

(3) In Northern Ireland –

   (a)   the reference in sub-paragraph (1) to a county court is to a county court held for a division under the County Courts (Northern Ireland) Order 1980 (SI 1980/397 (NI 3));
   (b)   proceedings may not be brought under this paragraph if the amount exceeds the limit specified in Article 10(1) of that Order;
   (c)   Part III of that Order (general civil jurisdiction) applies for the purposes of this paragraph; and

(d)   sections 21 and 42(2) of the Interpretation Act (Northern Ireland) 1954 (c 33 (NI)) apply as if any reference in those provisions to an enactment included this paragraph.

Amendments: Finance Act 2008, s 137(6)(a), (b), (7).

Proceedings in High Court or Court of Session

6

Tax may be sued for and recovered from the person charged –

(a)   as a debt due to the Crown, or

(b)   by any other means by which a debt of record or otherwise due to the Crown may be sued for and recovered,

by proceedings in the High Court or, in Scotland, in the Court of Session sitting as the Court of Exchequer.

Evidence of unpaid tax

7 . . .

Amendments: Repealed by Finance Act 2008, s 138(2), Sch 44, para 10.

Schedule 13

Section 93

Stamp Duty Land Tax: Information Powers

PART 1

POWER OF AUTHORISED OFFICER TO CALL FOR DOCUMENTS OR INFORMATION FROM TAXPAYER

Notice requiring taxpayer to deliver documents or provide information

1

(1) An authorised officer of the Board may by notice in writing require a person –

(a)   to deliver to him such documents as are in that person's possession or power and (in the officer's reasonable opinion) contain, or may contain, information relevant to –
      (i)   any tax liability to which that person is or may be subject, or
      (ii)   the amount of any such liability, or

(b)   to provide him with such information as he may reasonably require as being relevant to, or to the amount of, any such liability.

(2) An 'authorised officer of the Board' means an officer of the Board authorised for the purposes of this Part of this Schedule.

(3) Before a person is given a notice under this paragraph he must be given a reasonable opportunity to deliver the documents or provide the information in question.

No application for consent under paragraph 2 shall be made unless he has been given that opportunity.

Requirement of consent of the tribunal

2

(1) The consent of the tribunal is required for the giving of a notice under paragraph 1.

(2) Consent shall not be given unless the tribunal is satisfied that in all the circumstances the officer is justified in proceeding under that paragraph.

Amendment: SI 2009/56.

Contents of notice under this Part

3

(1) A notice under paragraph 1 must –

(a)   specify or describe the documents or information to which it relates, and
(b)   require the documents to be delivered, or the information to be provided, within such time as may be specified in the notice.

(2) The period specified for complying with the notice must not be less than 30 days after the date of the notice.

Summary of reasons to be given

4

(1) An officer who gives a notice under paragraph 1 must also give to the person to whom the notice applies a written summary of his reasons for applying for consent to the notice.

(2) This does not require the disclosure of any information –

(a)   that would, or might, identify any person who has provided the officer with any information which he took into account in deciding whether to apply for consent, or
(b)   that the tribunal giving consent under paragraph 2 directs need not be disclosed.

(3) The tribunal shall not give any such direction unless satisfied that the officer has reasonable grounds for believing that disclosure of the information in question would prejudice the assessment or collection of tax.

Amendment: SI 2009/56.

Power to take copies of documents etc

5

The person to whom documents are delivered, or to whom information is provided, in pursuance of a notice under paragraph 1 may take copies of them or of extracts from them.

PART 2
POWER OF AUTHORISED OFFICER TO CALL FOR DOCUMENTS FROM THIRD PARTY

Notice requiring documents to be delivered or made available

6

(1) An authorised officer of the Board may for the purpose of enquiring into the tax liability of any person ('the taxpayer') by notice in writing require any other person –

(a)   to deliver to the officer, or

(b)   if the person to whom the notice is given so elects, to make available for inspection by a named officer of the Board,

such documents as are in that person's possession or power and (in the officer's reasonable opinion) contain, or may contain, information relevant to any tax liability to which the taxpayer is or may be, or may have been, subject, or the amount of any such liability.

(2) An 'authorised officer of the Board' means an officer of the Board authorised for the purposes of this Part of this Schedule.

(3) Before a person is given a notice under this paragraph he must be given a reasonable opportunity to deliver or make available the documents in question.

No application for consent under paragraph 7 shall be made unless he has been given that opportunity.

(4) The persons who may be treated as 'the taxpayer' for the purposes of this paragraph include a company that has ceased to exist and an individual who has died.

But a notice in relation to a taxpayer who has died may not be given more than six years after his death.

Requirement of consent of the tribunal

7

(1) The consent of tribunal is required for the giving of a notice under paragraph 6.

(2) Consent shall not be given unless the tribunal is satisfied that in all the circumstances the officer is justified in proceeding under that paragraph.

Amendment: SI 2009/56.

Contents of notice under paragraph 6

8

(1) A notice under paragraph 6 must –

(a)   specify or describe the documents to which it relates, and

(b)   require the documents to be delivered or made available within such time as may be specified in the notice.

(2) The period specified for complying with the notice must not be less than 30 days after the date of the notice.

(3) Subject to paragraph 11 (power to give notice in respect of unnamed taxpayer or taxpayers), a notice under this paragraph must name the taxpayer to whom it relates.

Copy of notice to be given to taxpayer

9

(1) Where a notice is given to a person under this paragraph, the officer shall give a copy of the notice to the taxpayer to whom it relates.

(2) This paragraph does not apply if, on application by the officer, the tribunal directs that it shall not apply.

(3) Such a direction shall only be given if the tribunal is satisfied that the officer has reasonable grounds for suspecting the taxpayer of fraud.

Amendment: SI 2009/56.

Summary of reasons to be given

10

(1) An officer who gives a notice under paragraph 6 must also give to the taxpayer concerned a written summary of his reasons for applying for consent to the notice.

(2) This does not require the disclosure of any information –

(a)   that would, or might, identify any person who has provided the officer with any information which he took into account in deciding whether to apply for consent, or

(b)   that the tribunal giving consent under paragraph 7 directs need not be disclosed.

(3) The tribunal shall not give such a direction unless satisfied that the officer has reasonable grounds for believing that disclosure of the information in question would prejudice the assessment or collection of tax.

(4) This paragraph does not apply if under paragraph 9(2) a copy of the notice need not be given to the taxpayer.

Amendment: SI 2009/56.

Power to give notice relating to unnamed taxpayer or taxpayers

11

(1) If, on an application made by an officer of the Board and authorised by an order of the Board, the tribunal gives consent, the officer may give such a notice as is mentioned in paragraph 6 without naming the taxpayer to whom the notice relates.

(2) Consent shall not be given unless the tribunal is satisfied –

(a)   that the notice relates –
    (i)   to a taxpayer whose identity is not known to the officer, or
    (ii)   to a class of taxpayers whose individual identities are not so known,

(b)   that there are reasonable grounds for believing that the taxpayer, or any of the class of taxpayers, to whom the notice relates may have failed or may fail to comply with any provision of this Part of this Act,

(c)   that any such failure is likely to have led or to lead to serious prejudice to the proper assessment or collection of tax, and

(d)   that the information that is likely to be contained in the documents to which the notice relates is not readily available from another source.

(3) Before a person is given a notice under this paragraph he must be given a reasonable opportunity to deliver or make available the documents in question.

No application for consent under sub-paragraph (1) shall be made unless he has been given that opportunity.

(4) A person to whom there is given a notice under this paragraph may, by notice in writing given to the officer within 30 days after the date of the notice, object to it on the ground that it would be onerous for him to comply with it.

(5) If the matter is not resolved by agreement it shall be referred to the tribunal who may confirm, vary or cancel the notice.

Amendment: SI 2009/56.

Contents of notice under paragraph 11

12

(1) A notice under paragraph 11 must –

(a) specify or describe the documents to which it relates, and
(b) require the documents to be delivered or made available within such time as may be specified in the notice.

(2) The period specified for complying with the notice must not be less than 30 days after the date of the notice.

Power to take copies of documents etc

13

The person to whom documents are delivered or made available in pursuance of a notice under this Part of this Schedule may take copies of them or of extracts from them.

PART 3
POWER TO CALL FOR PAPERS OF TAX ACCOUNTANT

Power to call for papers of tax accountant

14

(1) Where a person who has stood in relation to others as a tax accountant –

(a) is convicted of an offence in relation to tax by or before a court in the United Kingdom, or
(b) has a penalty imposed on him under section 96 (assisting in preparation of incorrect return etc),

an authorised officer of the Board may by notice in writing require that person to deliver to him such documents as are in his possession or power and (in the officer's reasonable opinion) contain information relevant to any tax liability to which any client of his is or has been, or may be or have been, subject, or to the amount of any such liability.

(2) An 'authorised officer of the Board' means an officer of the Board authorised for the purposes of this Part of this Schedule.

(3) Before a person is given a notice under this paragraph he must be given a reasonable opportunity to deliver the documents in question.

No application for consent under paragraph 16 shall be made unless he has been given that opportunity.

When notice may be given

15

(1) No notice under paragraph 14 may be given for so long as an appeal is pending against the conviction or penalty.

(2) For the purposes of sub-paragraph (1) –

(a)   an appeal is treated as pending (where one is competent but has not been brought) until the expiration of the time for bringing it or, in the case of a conviction in Scotland, until the expiration of 28 days from the date of conviction; and

(b)   references to an appeal include a further appeal, but in relation to the imposition of a penalty do not include an appeal against the amount of the penalty.

(3) No notice may be given under paragraph 14 by reference to a person's conviction or the imposition on him of a penalty after the end of the period of twelve months beginning with the date on which the power to give such a notice was first exercisable in his case by virtue of that conviction or penalty.

Requirement of consent of appropriate judicial authority

16

(1) The consent of the appropriate judicial authority is required for the giving of a notice under paragraph 14.

(2) Consent shall not be given unless that authority is satisfied that in all the circumstances the officer is justified in proceeding under that paragraph.

(3) The appropriate judicial authority is –

(a)   in England and Wales, a circuit judge;
(b)   in Scotland, a sheriff;
(c)   in Northern Ireland, a county court judge.

Contents of notice

17

(1) A notice under paragraph 14 must –

(a)   specify or describe the documents to which it relates, and
(b)   require the documents to be delivered within such time as may be specified in the notice.

(2) The period specified for complying with the notice must not be less than 30 days after the date of the notice.

Power to take copies of documents etc

18

The officer to whom documents are delivered in pursuance of a notice under paragraph 14 may take copies of them or of extracts from them.

PART 4
RESTRICTIONS ON POWERS UNDER PARTS 1 TO 3

Introduction

19

The provisions of Parts 1 to 3 of this Schedule have effect subject to the following restrictions.

Personal records or journalistic material

20

(1) Parts 1 to 3 of this Schedule do not apply –

    (a)   to documents that are personal records or journalistic material, or

    (b)   to information contained in any personal records or journalistic material.

(2) In sub-paragraph (1) –

    'personal records' means personal records as defined in section 12 of the Police and Criminal Evidence Act 1984 (c 60) or, in Northern Ireland, in Article 14 of the Police and Criminal Evidence (Northern Ireland) Order 1989 (SI 1989/1341 (NI 12)); and

    'journalistic material' means journalistic material as defined in section 13 of that Act or, in Northern Ireland, in Article 15 of that Order.

Documents or information relating to pending appeal

21

(1) A notice under Part 1 of this Schedule does not oblige a person to deliver documents or provide information relating to the conduct of any pending appeal by him.

(2) A notice under Part 2 of this Schedule does not oblige a person to deliver or make available documents relating to the conduct of a pending appeal by the taxpayer.

(3) A notice under Part 3 of this Schedule does not oblige a person to deliver documents relating to the conduct of a pending appeal by the client.

(4) An 'appeal' here means an appeal relating to tax.

Barristers, advocates and solicitors

22

(1) A notice under Part 2 or 3 of this Schedule may not be given to a barrister, advocate or solicitor by an authorised officer of the Board but only by the Board.

(2) Accordingly, in relation to a barrister, advocate or solicitor, the references in those Parts to an authorised officer of the Board shall be read as references to the Board.

Provision of copies instead of original documents

23

(1) To comply with a notice under Part 1 or 3 of this Schedule, and as an alternative to delivering documents to comply with a notice under Part 2 of this Schedule, copies of documents may be delivered instead of originals.

(2) The copies must be photographic or otherwise by way of facsimile.

(3) If so required by the officer (or, as the case may be, the Board) in the case of any documents specified in the requirement, the originals must be made available for inspection by a named officer of the Board.

(4) Failure to comply with such a requirement counts as failure to comply with the notice.

Documents originating more than six years before date of notice

24

(1) A notice under Part 2 of this Schedule does not oblige a person to deliver or make available a document the whole of which originates more than six years before the date of the notice.

(2) Sub-paragraph (1) does not apply where the notice is so expressed as to exclude the restrictions of that sub-paragraph.

(3) A notice may only be so expressed if –

    (a)   in the case of a notice given by an authorised officer, the tribunal giving consent to the notice has also given approval to the exclusion;

    (b)   in the case of a notice given by the Board, they have applied to the tribunal for, and obtained, that approval.

(4) Approval shall only be given if the tribunal is satisfied, on application by the officer or the Board, that tax has been, or may have been, lost to the Crown owing to the fraud of the taxpayer.

Amendment: SI 2009/56.

Documents subject to legal privilege

25

(1) A notice under Part 2 or 3 of this Schedule does not oblige a barrister, advocate or solicitor to deliver or make available, without his client's consent, any document with respect to which a claim to legal privilege could be maintained.

(2) 'Legal privilege' here has the same meaning as in paragraph 35 of this Schedule.

Documents belonging to auditor or tax adviser

26

(1) A notice under Part 2 of this Schedule –

    (a)   does not oblige a person who has been appointed as auditor for the purposes of any enactment to deliver or make available documents that are his property and were created by him or on his behalf for or in connection with the performance of his functions under that enactment, and

(b)   does not oblige a tax adviser to deliver or make available documents that are his property and consist of relevant communications (as defined below).

(2) 'Relevant communications' means communications between the tax adviser and –

(a)   a person in relation to whose tax affairs he has been appointed, or
(b)   any other tax adviser of such a person,

the purpose of which is the giving or obtaining of advice about any of those tax affairs.

(3) In this paragraph 'tax adviser' means a person appointed to give advice about the tax affairs of another person (whether appointed directly by that other person or by another tax adviser of his).

(4) This paragraph has effect subject to paragraph 27 (documents belonging to auditor or tax adviser: information to be disclosed).

Documents belonging to auditor or tax adviser: information to be disclosed

27

(1) This paragraph applies where a notice is given under Part 2 of this Schedule relating to a document that falls within paragraph 26(documents belonging to auditor or tax adviser) but contains –

(a)   information explaining any information, return or other document that the person to whom the notice is given has, as tax accountant, assisted any client of his in preparing for, or for delivering to, the officer or the Board, or
(b)   in the case of a notice under paragraph 11 (notice in respect of unnamed taxpayer or taxpayers), information as to the identity or address of any taxpayer to whom the notice relates or any person who has acted on behalf of any such person,

that has not otherwise been made available to the Inland Revenue.

(2) For this purpose information is regarded as having been made available to the Inland Revenue if it is contained in some other document and –

(a)   that other document, or a copy of it, has been delivered to the officer or the Board, or
(b)   that other document has been inspected by an officer of the Board.

(3) Where this paragraph applies the person to whom the notice is given must, if he does not deliver the document or make it available for inspection in accordance with the notice –

(a)   deliver to the officer (or, as the case may be, the Board) a copy (photographic or otherwise by way of facsimile) of any parts of the document that contain such information as is mentioned in sub-paragraph (1), and
(b)   if so required by the officer (or, as the case may be, the Board), make available for inspection by a named officer of the Board such parts of the original document as contain such information.

(4) Failure to comply with any such requirement counts as a failure to comply with the notice.

PART 5
POWERS OF BOARD TO CALL FOR DOCUMENTS OR INFORMATION

Notice requiring delivery of documents or provision of information

28

(1) The Board may by notice in writing require a person –

(a)   to deliver to a named officer of the Board such documents as are in the person's possession or power and (in the Board's reasonable opinion) contain, or may contain, information relevant to –
   (i)   any tax liability to which the person is or may be subject, or
   (ii)   the amount of any such liability, or
(b)   to provide to a named officer of the Board such information as the Board may reasonably require as being relevant to, or to the amount of, any such liability.

(2) Notice under this paragraph shall not be given unless the Board have reasonable grounds for believing –

(a)   that the person to whom it relates may have failed, or may fail, to comply with any provision of this Part of this Act, and
(b)   that any such failure is likely to have led, or to lead, to serious prejudice to the proper assessment or collection of tax.

Contents of notice

29

A notice under paragraph 28 must –

(a)   specify or describe the documents or information to which it relates, and
(b)   require the documents to be delivered or the information to be provided within such time as may be specified in the notice.

Power to take copies of documents etc

30

The person to whom documents are delivered, or to whom information is provided, in pursuance of a notice under paragraph 28 may take copies of them or of extracts from them.

Exclusion of personal records or journalistic material

31

(1) This Part of this Schedule does not apply to documents that are personal records or journalistic material.

(2) In sub-paragraph (1) –

'personal records' means personal records as defined in section 12 of the Police and Criminal Evidence Act 1984 (c 60) or, in Northern Ireland, in Article 14 of the Police and Criminal Evidence (Northern Ireland) Order 1989 (SI 1989/1341 (NI 12)); and
'journalistic material' means journalistic material as defined in section 13 of that Act or, in Northern Ireland, in Article 15 of that Order.

PART 6
ORDER OF JUDICIAL AUTHORITY FOR THE DELIVERY OF DOCUMENTS

Order for the delivery of documents

32

(1) The appropriate judicial authority may make an order under this paragraph if satisfied on information on oath given by an authorised officer of the Board –

    (a)   that there is reasonable ground for suspecting that an offence involving serious fraud in connection with, or in relation to, stamp duty land tax has been or is about to be committed, and

    (b)   that documents that may be required as evidence for the purposes of any proceedings in respect of such an offence are or may be in the power or possession of any person.

(2) An order under this paragraph is an order requiring the person who appears to the authority to have in his possession or power the documents specified or described in the order to deliver them to an officer of the Board within –

    (a)   ten working days after the day on which notice of the order is served on him, or

    (b)   such shorter or longer period as may be specified in the order.

For this purpose a 'working day' means any day other than a Saturday, Sunday or public holiday.

(3) The appropriate judicial authority is –

    (a)   in England and Wales, a circuit judge;

    (b)   in Scotland, a sheriff;

    (c)   in Northern Ireland, a county court judge.

(4) Where in Scotland the information relates to persons residing or having places of business at addresses situated in different sheriffdoms –

    (a)   an application for an order may be made to the sheriff for the sheriffdom in which any of the addresses is situated, and

    (b)   where the sheriff makes an order in respect of a person residing or having a place of business in his own sheriffdom, he may also make orders in respect of all or any of the other persons to whom the information relates (whether or not they have an address within the sheriffdom).

(5) In sub-paragraph (1) an 'authorised officer of the Board' means an officer of the Board authorised by the Board for the purposes of this Part of this Schedule.

(6) The Inland Revenue may make provision by regulations as to –

    (a)   the procedures for approving in any particular case the decision to apply for an order under this Part of this Schedule, and

    (b)   the descriptions of officer by whom such approval may be given.

Notice of application for order

33

(1) A person is entitled –

(a)   to notice of the intention to apply for an order against him under paragraph 32, and

(b)   to appear and be heard at the hearing of the application,

unless the appropriate judicial authority is satisfied that this would seriously prejudice the investigation of the offence.

(2) The Inland Revenue may make provision by regulations as to the notice to be given, the contents of the notice and the manner of giving it.

Obligations of person given notice of application

34

(1) A person who has been given notice of intention to apply for an order under paragraph 32 must not –

(a)   conceal, destroy, alter or dispose of any document to which the application relates, or

(b)   disclose to any other person information or any other matter likely to prejudice the investigation of the offence to which the application relates.

This is subject to the following qualifications.

(2) Sub-paragraph (1)(a) does not prevent anything being done –

(a)   with the leave of the appropriate judicial authority,

(b)   with the written permission of an officer of the Board,

(c)   after the application has been dismissed or abandoned, or

(d)   after any order made on the application has been complied with.

(3) Sub-paragraph (1)(b) does not prevent a professional legal adviser from disclosing any information or other matter –

(a)   to, or to a representative of, a client of his in connection with the giving by the adviser of legal advice to the client, or

(b)   to any person –
       (i)   in contemplation or, or in connection with, legal proceedings, and
       (ii)   for the purposes of those proceedings.

This sub-paragraph does not apply in relation to any information or other matter that is disclosed with a view to furthering a criminal purpose.

(4) A person who fails to comply with the obligation in sub-paragraph (1)(a) or (b) may be dealt with as if he had failed to comply with an order under paragraph 32.

Exception of items subject to legal privilege

35

(1) This Part of this Schedule does not apply to items subject to legal privilege.

(2) Items 'subject to legal privilege' means –

(a)   communications between a professional legal adviser and his client or any person representing his client made in connection with the giving of legal advice to the client;

(b)   communications between a professional legal adviser and his client or any person representing his client, or between such an adviser or his client or any such representative and any other person, made in connection with or in contemplation of legal proceedings and for the purposes of such proceedings;

(c)   items enclosed with or referred to in such communications and made –

    (i)   in connection with the giving of legal advice, or

    (ii)   in connection with or in contemplation of legal proceedings and for the purposes of such proceedings,

when they are in possession of a person entitled to possession of them.

(3) Items held with the intention of furthering a criminal purpose are not subject to legal privilege.

Resolution of disputes as to legal privilege

36

(1) The Inland Revenue may make provision by regulations for the purposes of this Part of this Schedule for the resolution of disputes as to whether a document, or part of a document, is an item subject to legal privilege.

(2) The regulations may, in particular, make provision as to –

(a)   the custody of the document whilst its status is being decided,

(b)   the appointment of an independent, legally qualified person to decide the matter,

(c)   the procedures to be followed, and

(d)   who is to meet the costs of the proceedings.

Complying with an order

37

(1) The Inland Revenue may make provision by regulations as to how a person is to comply with an order under paragraph 32.

(2) The regulations may, in particular, make provision as to –

(a)   the officer of the Board to whom the documents are to be produced,

(b)   the address to which the documents are to be taken or sent, and

(c)   the circumstances in which sending documents by post complies with the order.

(3) Where an order relates to a document in electronic or magnetic form, the order shall be taken to require the person to deliver the information recorded in the document in a form in which it is visible and legible.

Document not to be retained if photograph or copy sufficient

38

Where a document delivered to an officer of the Board under this Part of this Schedule is of such a nature that a photograph or copy of it would be sufficient –

(a)   for use as evidence at a trial for an offence, or

(b)   for forensic examination or for investigation in connection with an offence,

it shall not be retained longer than is necessary to establish that fact and to obtain the photograph or copy.

Access to or supply of photograph or copy of documents delivered

39

(1) If a request for permission to be granted access to a document that –

(a)	has been delivered to an officer of the Board under this Part of this Schedule, and

(b)	is retained by the Board for the purposes of investigating an offence,

is made to the officer in overall charge of the investigation by a person who had custody or control of the document immediately before it was so delivered, or by someone acting on behalf of any such person, the officer shall allow the person who made the request access to it under the supervision of an officer of the Board.

(2) If a request for a photograph or copy of any such document is made to the officer in overall charge of the investigation by a person who had custody or control of the document immediately before it was so delivered, or by someone acting on behalf of any such person, the officer shall –

(a)	allow the person who made the request access to it under the supervision of an officer of the Board for the purpose of photographing or copying it, or

(b)	photograph or copy it, or cause it to be photographed or copied.

(3) Where a document is photographed or copied under sub-paragraph (2)(b) the photograph or copy shall be supplied to the person who made the request.

(4) The photograph or copy shall be supplied within a reasonable time from the making of the request.

(5) There is no duty under this paragraph to grant access to, or to supply a photograph or copy of, a document if the officer in overall charge of the investigation for the purposes of which it was delivered has reasonable grounds for believing that to do so would prejudice –

(a)	that investigation,

(b)	the investigation of an offence other than the offence for the purposes of the investigation of which the document was delivered, or

(c)	any criminal proceedings that may be brought as a result of –

(i)	the investigation of which he is in charge, or

(ii)	any such investigation as is mentioned in paragraph (b).

(6) The references in this paragraph to the officer in overall charge of the investigation is to the person whose name and address are endorsed on the order concerned as being the officer so in charge.

Sanction for failure to comply with order

40

(1) A person who fails to comply with an order under this Part of this Schedule may be dealt with as if he had committed a contempt of the court.

(2) For this purpose 'the court' means –

(a)	in relation to an order made by a circuit judge, the Crown Court;

(b)	in relation to an order made by a sheriff, a sheriff court;

(c)	in relation to an order made by a county court judge in Northern Ireland, a county court in Northern Ireland.

Notice of order, etc

41

The Inland Revenue may make provision by regulations as to the circumstances in which notice of an order under paragraph 32, or of an application for such an order, is to be treated as having been given.

General provisions about regulations

42

Regulations under this Part of this Schedule may contain such incidental, supplementary and transitional provision as appears to the Inland Revenue to be appropriate.

PART 7 . . .

Amendments: Part repealed by Finance Act 2007, ss 84(4), 114, Sch 22, Pt 2, paras 3, 16, Sch 27, Pt 5(1); SI 2007/3166

PART 8
FALSIFICATION ETC OF DOCUMENTS

Falsification etc of documents

53

(1) A person commits an offence if he intentionally –

    (a)   falsifies, conceals, destroys or otherwise disposes of, or

    (b)   causes or permits the falsification, concealment, destruction or disposal of,

a document to which this paragraph applies.

(2) This paragraph applies to any document that the person –

    (a)   has been required by a notice under Part 1, 2, 3 or 5 of this Schedule, or an order under Part 6 of this Schedule, to deliver, or to deliver or make available for inspection, or

    (b)   has been given an opportunity in accordance with paragraph 1(3), 6(3), 11(3) or 14(3) to deliver, or to deliver or make available for inspection.

(3) A person does not commit an offence under this paragraph if he acts –

    (a)   with the written permission of the tribunal or an officer of the Board,

    (b)   after the document has been delivered or, in a case within Part 2 of this Schedule, inspected, or

    (c)   after a copy has been delivered in accordance with paragraph 23(1) or 27(3) and the original has been inspected.

(4) A person does not commit an offence under this paragraph as it applies by virtue of sub-paragraph (2)(a) if he acts after the end of the period of two years beginning with the date on which the notice is given or the order is made, unless before the end of that period an officer of the Board has notified the person, in writing, that the notice or order has not been complied with to his satisfaction.

(5) A person does not commit an offence under this paragraph as it applies by virtue of sub-paragraph (2)(b) if he acts –

(a)   after the end of the period of six months beginning with the date on which an opportunity to deliver the document was given, or

(b)   after an application for consent to a notice being given in relation to the document has been refused.

(6) A person guilty of an offence under this paragraph is liable –

(a)   on summary conviction, to a fine not exceeding the statutory maximum;

(b)   on conviction on indictment, to imprisonment for a term not exceeding two years or a fine or to both.

Amendment: SI 2009/56.

Schedule 14

Section 99

Stamp Duty Land Tax: Determination of Penalties and Related Appeals

Determination of penalties and appeals

1

The provisions of this Schedule apply in relation to penalties under this Part.

Determination of penalty by officer of the Board

2

(1) An officer of the Board authorised for the purposes of this paragraph may make a determination –

(a)   imposing the penalty, and

(b)   setting it at such amount as in the officer's opinion is correct or appropriate.

(2) Notice of the determination must be served on the person liable to the penalty.

(3) The notice must also state –

(a)   the date on which the notice is issued, and

(b)   the time within which an appeal against the determination may be made.

(4) A penalty determined under this paragraph is due and payable at the end of the period of 30 days beginning with the date of issue of the notice of determination.

(5) Where an officer of the Board has decided to impose a penalty, and has taken all other decisions needed for arriving at the amount of the penalty, he may entrust to any other officer of the Board responsibility for completing the determination procedure, whether by means involving the use of a computer or otherwise, including responsibility for serving notice of the determination.

Alteration of penalty determination

3

(1) After notice has been served of the determination of a penalty, the determination cannot be altered except in accordance with this paragraph or on appeal.

(2) If it is discovered by an authorised officer that the amount of the penalty is or has become insufficient, the officer may make a determination in a further amount so that the penalty is set at the amount which in the officer's opinion is correct or appropriate.

(3) If in the case of a tax-related penalty it is discovered by an authorised officer that the amount taken into account as the amount of tax is or has become excessive, he may revise the determination so that the penalty is set at the amount that is correct.

Where more than the correct amount has already been paid the appropriate amount shall be repaid.

(4) In this paragraph an 'authorised officer' means an officer of the Board authorised by the Board for the purposes of this paragraph.

Liability of personal representatives

4

If a person liable to a penalty has died –

(a)   any determination that could have been made in relation to that person may be made in relation to his personal representatives, and

(b)   any penalty imposed on them is a debt due from and payable out of the person's estate.

Appeal against penalty determination

5

(1) An appeal may be made against the determination of a penalty.

(2) Notice of appeal must be given in writing to the officer of the Board by whom the determination was made within 30 days of the date of issue of the notice of determination.

(3) The notice of appeal must specify the grounds of appeal.

(4) On an appeal under this paragraph that is notified to the First-tier Tribunal, the tribunal may –

(a)   if it appears that no penalty has been incurred, set the determination aside;

(b)   if the amount determined appears to be appropriate, confirm the determination;

(c)   if the amount determined appears to be excessive, reduce it to such other amount (including nil) as appears to be appropriate;

(d)   if the amount determined appears to be insufficient, increase it to such amount, not exceeding the permitted maximum, as the First-tier Tribunal considers appropriate.

(5) The provisions of paragraphs 36A to 36I of Schedule 10 apply to appeals under this paragraph.

Amendment: SI 2009/56.

Further appeal

6

(1) In addition to any right of appeal on a point of law under section 11(2) of the Tribunals, Courts and Enforcement Act 2007, the person liable to the penalty may

appeal to the Upper Tribunal against the amount of the penalty which has been determined under paragraph (5), but not against any decision which falls under section 11(5)(d) or (e) of that Act and was made in connection with the determination of the amount of the penalty.

(1A) Section 11(3) and (4) of the Tribunals, Courts and Enforcement Act 2007 applies to the right of appeal under sub-paragraph (1) as it applies to the right of appeal under section 11(2) of that Act.

(2) On an appeal under this paragraph the Upper Tribunal has the same powers as are conferred on the First-tier Tribunal by paragraph 5(4) above.

Amendment: SI 2009/56.

Penalty proceedings before the court

7

(1) Where in the opinion of the Board the liability of a person for a penalty arises by reason of his fraud, or the fraud of another person, proceedings for the penalty may be brought –

(a)   in the High Court, or

(b)   in Scotland, in the Court of Session sitting as the Court of Exchequer.

(2) Proceedings under this paragraph in England and Wales shall be brought –

(a)   by and in the name of the Board as an authorised department for the purposes of the Crown Proceedings Act 1947 (c 44), or

(b)   in the name of the Attorney General.

Any such proceedings shall be deemed to be civil proceedings by the Crown within the meaning of Part 2 of the Crown Proceedings Act 1947.

(3) Proceedings under this paragraph in Scotland shall be brought in the name of the Advocate General for Scotland.

(4) Proceedings under this paragraph in Northern Ireland shall be brought –

(a)   by and in the name of the Board as an authorised department for the purposes of the Crown Proceedings Act 1947 as for the time being in force in Northern Ireland, or

(b)   in the name of the Advocate General for Northern Ireland.

Any such proceedings shall be deemed to be civil proceedings within the meaning of Part 2 of the Crown Proceedings Act 1947 as for the time being in force in Northern Ireland.

(5) If in proceedings under this paragraph the court does not find that fraud is proved but considers that the person concerned is nevertheless liable to a penalty, the court may determine a penalty notwithstanding that, but for the opinion of the Board as to fraud, the penalty would not have been a matter for the court.

(6) Paragraph 2 (determination of penalty by officer of the Board) does not apply where proceedings are brought under this paragraph.

(7) In relation to any time before the coming into force of section 2(1) of the Justice (Northern Ireland) Act 2002 (c 26), the reference in sub-paragraph (4)(b) to the Advocate General for Northern Ireland shall be read as a reference to the Attorney General for Northern Ireland.

Time limit for determination of penalties

8

(1) The following time limits apply in relation to the determination of penalties under this Schedule.

(2) The general rule is that –

    (a)   no penalty may be determined under paragraph 2 (determination by officer of Board), and

    (b)   no proceedings for a penalty may be brought under paragraph 7 (penalty proceedings before the court),

more than six years after the date on which the penalty was incurred or, in the case of a daily penalty, began to be incurred.

This rule is subject to the following provisions of this paragraph.

(3) Where the amount of a penalty is to be ascertained by reference to the tax chargeable in respect of a transaction, a penalty may be determined under paragraph 2, or proceedings for a penalty may be begun under paragraph 7, at any time within three years after the final determination of the amount of tax by reference to which the amount of the penalty is to be determined.

(4) Sub-paragraph (3) does not apply where a person has died and the determination would be made in relation to his personal representatives if the tax was charged in an assessment made more than six years after the effective date of the transaction to which it relates.

(5) A penalty under section 96(penalty for assisting in preparation of incorrect return) may be determined by an officer of the Board, or proceedings for such a penalty may be commenced before a court, at any time within 20 years after the date on which the penalty was incurred.

Schedule 15

Section 104

Stamp Duty Land Tax: Partnerships

PART 1
GENERAL PROVISIONS

Partnerships

1

In this Part of this Act a 'partnership' means –

    (a)   a partnership within the Partnership Act 1890 (c 39),

    (b)   a limited partnership registered under the Limited Partnerships Act 1907 (c 24), or

    (c)   a limited liability partnership formed under the Limited Liability Partnerships Act 2000 (c 12) or the Limited Liability Partnerships Act (Northern Ireland) 2002 (c 12 (NI)),

or a firm or entity of a similar character to any of those mentioned above formed under the law of a country or territory outside the United Kingdom.

Legal personality of partnership disregarded

2

(1) For the purposes of this Part of this Act –

(a)   a chargeable interest held by or on behalf of a partnership is treated as held by or on behalf of the partners, and

(b)   a land transaction entered into for the purposes of a partnership is treated as entered into by or on behalf of the partners,

and not by or on behalf of the partnership as such.

(2) Sub-paragraph (1) applies notwithstanding that the partnership is regarded as a legal person, or as a body corporate, under the law of the country or territory under which it is formed.

Continuity of partnership

3

For the purposes of this Part of this Act a partnership is treated as the same partnership notwithstanding a change in membership if any person who was a member before the change remains a member after the change.

Partnership not to be regarded as unit trust scheme etc

4

A partnership is not to be regarded for the purposes of this Part of this Act as a unit trust scheme or an open ended investment company.

PART 2
ORDINARY PARTNERSHIP TRANSACTIONS

Introduction

5

(1) This Part of this Schedule applies to transactions entered into as purchaser by or on behalf of the members of a partnership, other than transactions within Part 3 of this Schedule (transactions to which special provisions apply).

Amendments: Finance Act 2004, s 304, Sch 41.

Responsibility of partners

6

(1) Anything required or authorised to be done under this Part of this Act by or in relation to the purchaser under the transaction is required or authorised to be done by or in relation to all the responsible partners.

(2) The responsible partners in relation to a transaction are –

(a)   the persons who are partners at the effective date of the transaction, and

(b)   any person who becomes a member of the partnership after the effective date of the transaction.

(3) This paragraph has effect subject to paragraph 8 (representative partners).

Joint and several liability of responsible partners

7

(1) Where the responsible partners are liable –

(a)   to make a payment of tax or to interest on unpaid tax,

(b)   to make a payment in accordance with an assessment under paragraph 29 of Schedule 10 (recovery of excessive repayment), or

(c)   to a penalty under this Part of this Act or to interest on such a penalty,

the liability is a joint and several liability of those partners.

(1A) No amount may be recovered by virtue of sub-paragraph (1)(a) or (b) from a person who did not become a responsible partner until after the effective date of the transaction in respect of which the tax is payable.

(2) No amount may be recovered by virtue of sub-paragraph (1)(c) from a person who did not become a responsible partner until after the relevant time.

(3) The relevant time for this purpose is –

(a)   in relation to so much of a penalty as is payable in respect of any day, or to interest on so much of a penalty as is so payable, the beginning of that day;

(b)   in relation to any other penalty, or interest on such a penalty, the time when the act or omission occurred that caused the penalty to become payable.

Amendments: Finance Act 2004, s 305.

Representative partners

8

(1) Anything required or authorised to be done by or in relation to the responsible partners may instead be done by or in relation to any representative partner or partners.

(2) This includes making the declaration required by paragraph 1(1)(c) of Schedule 10 (declaration that return is complete and correct).

(3) A representative partner means a partner nominated by a majority of the partners to act as the representative of the partnership for the purposes of this Part of this Act.

(4) Any such nomination, or the revocation of such a nomination, has effect only after notice of the nomination, or revocation, has been given to the Inland Revenue.

Amendments: Finance Act 2008, s 94(4), (5), Sch 30, paras 1, 12.

PART 3
TRANSACTIONS TO WHICH SPECIAL PROVISIONS APPLY

Introduction

9

(1) This Part of this Schedule applies to certain transactions involving –

(a)   the transfer of a chargeable interest to a partnership (paragraph 10),

(b)   the transfer of an interest in a partnership (paragraphs 14, 17, 31 and 32), or

(c)   the transfer of a chargeable interest from a partnership (paragraph 18).

(2) References in this Part of this Schedule to the transfer of a chargeable interest include –

(a)   the grant or creation of a chargeable interest,
(b)   the variation of a chargeable interest, and
(c)   the surrender, release or renunciation of a chargeable interest.

Transfer of chargeable interest to a partnership: general

10

(1) This paragraph applies where –

(a)   a partner transfers a chargeable interest to the partnership, or
(b)   a person transfers a chargeable interest to a partnership in return for an interest in the partnership, or
(c)   a person connected with –
       (i)   a partner, or
       (ii)   a person who becomes a partner as a result of or in connection with the transfer,
       transfers a chargeable interest to the partnership.

It applies whether the transfer is in connection with the formation of the partnership or is a transfer to an existing partnership.

(2) The chargeable consideration for the transaction shall (subject to paragraph 13) be taken to be equal to –

$$MV \times (100 - SLP)\%$$

where –

MV is the market value of the interest transferred, and

SLP is the sum of the lower proportions.

(5) Paragraph 12 provides for determining the sum of the lower proportions.

(6) Paragraph 11 applies if the whole or part of the chargeable consideration for the transaction is rent.

(7) Paragraphs 6 to 8 (responsibility of partners) have effect in relation to a transaction to which this paragraph applies, but the responsible partners are –

(a)   those who were partners immediately before the transfer and who remain partners after the transfer, and
(b)   any person becoming a partner as a result of, or in connection with, the transfer.

(8) This paragraph has effect subject to any election under paragraph 12A.

Amendments: Finance Act 2006, ss 163, 178, Schs 24, 26: Finance Act 2008, s 97(1), Sch 31, Pt 2, para 5.

Transfer of chargeable interest to a partnership: chargeable consideration including rent

11

(1) This paragraph applies in relation to a transaction to which paragraph 10 applies where the whole or part of the chargeable consideration for the transaction is rent.

(2) Schedule 5 (amount of tax chargeable: rent) has effect with the modifications set out in sub-paragraphs (2A) to (2C).

(2A) In paragraph 2 –

   (a)   for 'the net present value of the rent payable over the term of the lease' substitute 'the relevant chargeable proportion of the net present value of the rent payable over the term of the lease', and

   (b)   for 'the net present values of the rent payable over the terms of all the leases' substitute 'the relevant chargeable proportions of the net present values of the rent payable over the terms of all the leases'.

(2B) In paragraph 9A(6) –

   (a)   for 'the annual rent' substitute 'the relevant chargeable proportion of the annual rent', and

   (b)   for 'the total of the annual rents' substitute 'the relevant chargeable proportion of the total of the annual rents'.

(2C) For paragraph 9(4) substitute –

   '(4) Tax chargeable under this Schedule is in addition to any tax chargeable under section 55 as it has effect by virtue of paragraph 10 of Schedule 15.'

(2D) For the purposes of sub-paragraphs (2A) and (2B) the relevant chargeable proportion is –

$$(100 - SLP)\%$$

where SLP is the sum of the lower proportions.

(8) Paragraph 12 provides for determining the sum of the lower proportions.

(9) This paragraph is subject to paragraph 13.

Amendments: Finance Act 2006, ss 163, Sch 24: Finance Act 2008, s 95(11)(a), (13).

Transfer of chargeable interest to a partnership: sum of the lower proportions

12

(1) The sum of the lower proportions in relation to a transaction to which paragraph 10 applies is determined as follows –

Step One

Identify the relevant owner or owners.

A person is a relevant owner if –

   (a)   immediately before the transaction, he was entitled to a proportion of the chargeable interest, and

   (b)   immediately after the transaction, he is a partner or connected with a partner.

Step Two

For each relevant owner, identify the corresponding partner or partners.

A person is a corresponding partner in relation to a relevant owner if, immediately after the transaction –

(a)   he is a partner, and
(b)   he is the relevant owner or is an individual connected with the relevant owner.

(If there is no relevant owner with a corresponding partner, the sum of the lower proportions is nil.)

Step Three

For each relevant owner, find the proportion of the chargeable interest to which he was entitled immediately before the transaction.

Apportion that proportion between any one or more of the relevant owner's corresponding partners.

Step Four

Find the lower proportion for each person who is a corresponding partner in relation to one or more relevant owners.

The lower proportion is –

(a)   the proportion of the chargeable interest attributable to the partner, or
(b)   if lower, the partner's partnership share immediately after the transaction.
The proportion of the chargeable interest attributable to the partner is –
    (i)   if he is a corresponding partner in relation to only one relevant owner, the proportion (if any) of the chargeable interest apportioned to him (at Step Three) in respect of that owner;
    (ii)   if he is a corresponding partner in relation to more than one relevant owner, the sum of the proportions (if any) of the chargeable interest apportioned to him (at Step Three) in respect of each of those owners.

Step Five

Add together the lower proportions of each person who is a corresponding partner in relation to one or more relevant owners.

The result is the sum of the lower proportions.

(2) For the purposes of this paragraph persons who are entitled to a chargeable interest as beneficial joint tenants (or, in Scotland, as joint owners) shall be taken to be entitled to the chargeable interest as beneficial tenants in common (or, in Scotland, as owners in common) in equal shares.

(3) For the purpose of paragraph (b) of Step 2 a company is to be treated as an individual connected with the relevant owner in so far as it –

(a)   holds property as trustee, and
(b)   is connected with the relevant owner only because of section 839(3) of the Taxes Act 1988.

Amendments: Finance Act 2007, s 72(1), (2), (3)(a), (b), (4), (13), (16), (17); SI 2006/3237.

Election by property-investment partnership to disapply paragraph 10

12A

(1) Paragraph 10 does not apply to a transfer of a chargeable interest to a property-investment partnership if the purchaser in relation to the transaction elects for that paragraph not to apply.

(2) Where an election under this paragraph is made in respect of a transaction –

(a)   paragraph 18 (if relevant) is also disapplied,
(b)   the chargeable consideration for the transaction shall be taken to be the market value of the chargeable interest transferred, and
(c)   the transaction falls within Part 2 of this Schedule.

(3) An election under this paragraph must be included in the land transaction return made in respect of the transaction or in an amendment of that return.

(4) Such an election is irrevocable and a land transaction return may not be amended so as to withdraw the election.

(5) Where an election under this paragraph in respect of a transaction (the 'main transaction') is made in an amendment of a land transaction return –

(a)   the election has effect as if it had been made on the date on which the land transaction return was made, and
(b)   any land transaction return in respect of an affected transaction may be amended (within the period allowed for amendment of that return) to take account of that election.

(6) In sub-paragraph (5) 'affected transaction', in relation to the main transaction, means a transaction –

(a)   to which paragraph 14 applied, and
(b)   with an effective date on or after the effective date of the main transaction.

(7) In this paragraph 'property-investment partnership' has the meaning given in paragraph 14(8).

Amendments: Paragraph inserted, Finance Act 2008, s 97(1), Sch 31, Pt 2, para 6, Pt 3, para 11.

Transfer of chargeable interest to a partnership consisting wholly of bodies corporate

13 . . .

Amendments: Paragraph repealed by Finance Act 2007, ss 72(1), (2), (5), (13), (16), (17), 114, Sch 27, Pt 4(1); SI 2006/3237.

Transfer of interest in property-investment partnership

14

(1) This paragraph applies where –

(a)   there is a transfer of an interest in a property-investment partnership,
(c)   the relevant partnership property includes a chargeable interest.

(2) The transfer –

(a)   shall be taken for the purposes of this Part to be a land transaction;
(b)   is a chargeable transaction.

(3) The purchaser under the transaction is the person who acquires an increased partnership share or, as the case may be, becomes a partner in consequence of the transfer.

(3A) A transfer to which this paragraph applies is a Type A transfer if it takes the form of arrangements entered into under which –

(a) the whole or part of a partner's interest as partner is acquired by another person (who may be an existing partner), and

(b) consideration in money or money's worth is given by or on behalf of the person acquiring the interest.

(3B) A transfer to which this paragraph applies is also a Type A transfer if it takes the form of arrangements entered into under which –

(a) a person becomes a partner,

(b) the interest of an existing partner in the partnership is reduced or an existing partner ceases to be a partner, and

(c) there is a withdrawal of money or money's worth from the partnership by the existing partner mentioned in paragraph (b) (other than money or money's worth paid from the resources available to the partnership prior to the transfer).

(3C) Any other transfer to which this paragraph applies is a Type B transfer.

(5) The 'relevant partnership property', in relation to a Type A transfer of an interest in a partnership, is every chargeable interest held as partnership property immediately after the transfer, other than –

(a) any chargeable interest that was transferred to the partnership in connection with the transfer;

(b) a lease to which paragraph 15 (exclusion of market rent leases) applies, and

(c) any chargeable interest that is not attributable economically to the interest in the partnership that is transferred.

(5A) The 'relevant partnership property', in relation to a Type B transfer of an interest in a partnership, is every chargeable interest held as partnership property immediately after the transfer, other than –

(a) any chargeable interest that was transferred to the partnership in connection with the transfer,

(b) a lease to which paragraph 15 (exclusion of market rent leases) applies,

(c) any chargeable interest that is not attributable economically to the interest in the partnership that is transferred,

(d) any chargeable interest that was transferred to the partnership on or before 22 July 2004,

(e) any chargeable interest in respect of whose transfer to the partnership an election has been made under paragraph 12A, and

(f) any other chargeable interest whose transfer to the partnership did not fall within paragraph 10(1)(a), (b) or (c).

(6) The chargeable consideration for the transaction shall be taken to be equal to a proportion of the market value of the relevant partnership property.

(7) That proportion is –

(a) if the person acquiring the interest in the partnership was not a partner before the transfer, his partnership share immediately after the transfer;

(b)   if he was a partner before the transfer, the difference between his partnership share before and after the transfer.

(8) In this paragraph –

'property-investment partnership' means a partnership whose sole or main activity is investing or dealing in chargeable interests (whether or not that activity involves the carrying out of construction operations on the land in question);

'construction operations' has the same meaning as in Chapter 3 of Part 3 of the Finance Act 2004 (see section 74 of that Act).

(9) An interest in respect of the transfer of which this paragraph applies shall be treated as a chargeable interest for the purposes of paragraph 3(1) of Schedule 7 to the extent that the relevant partnership property consists of a chargeable interest.

Amendments: Finance Act 2006, s 163, Sch 24; Finance Act 2007, ss 72(1), (2), (6), (6)(a), (b), (13), (14), (16), (17), 114, Sch 27, Pt 4(1); SI 2006/3237: Finance Act 2008, s 97(1)–(3), Sch 31, Pt 1, para 1(1), (2), (3)(a)–(c), (4).

Exclusion of market rent leases

15

(1) A lease held as partnership property immediately after a transfer of an interest in the partnership is not relevant partnership property for the purposes of paragraph 14(5) or (5A) if the following four conditions are met.

(2) The first condition is that –

(a)   no chargeable consideration other than rent has been given in respect of the grant of the lease, and

(b)   no arrangements are in place at the time of the transfer for any chargeable consideration other than rent to be given in respect of the grant of the lease.

(3) The second condition is that the rent payable under the lease as granted was a market rent at the time of the grant.

(4) The third condition is that –

(a)   the term of the lease is 5 years or less, or

(b)   if the term of the lease is more than 5 years –

    (i)   the lease provides for the rent payable under it to be reviewed at least once in every 5 years of the term, and

    (ii)   the rent payable under the lease as a result of a review is required to be a market rent at the review date.

(5) The fourth condition is that there has been no change to the lease since it was granted which is such that, immediately after the change has effect, the rent payable under the lease is less than a market rent.

(6) The market rent of a lease at any time is the rent which the lease might reasonably be expected to fetch at that time in the open market.

(7) A review date is a date from which the rent determined as a result of a rent review is payable.

Amendments: Finance Act 2008, s 97(1)–(3), Sch 31, Pt 1, para 2.

Partnership interests: application of provisions about exchanges etc

16

(1) Where paragraph 5 of Schedule 4 (exchanges) applies to the acquisition of an interest in a partnership in consideration of entering into a land transaction with an existing partner, the interest in the partnership shall be treated as a major interest in land for the purposes of that paragraph if the relevant partnership property includes a major interest in land.

(2) In sub-paragraph (1) relevant partnership property has the meaning given by paragraph 14(5) or (5A) (as appropriate).

(3) The provisions of paragraph 6 of Schedule 4 (partition etc: disregard of existing interest) do not apply where this paragraph applies.

Amendments: Finance Act 2008, s 97(1)–(3), Sch 31, Pt 1, para 3.

Transfer of partnership interest pursuant to earlier arrangements

17

(1) This paragraph applies where –

(a)   there is a transfer of a chargeable interest to a partnership ('the land transfer');
(b)   the land transfer falls within paragraph (a), (b) or (c) of paragraph 10(1);
(c)   there is subsequently a transfer of an interest in the partnership ('the partnership transfer');
(d)   the partnership transfer is made –
   (i)   if the land transfer falls within paragraph 10(1)(a) or (b), by the person who makes the land transfer;
   (ii)   if the land transfer falls within paragraph 10(1)(c), by the partner concerned;
(e)   the partnership transfer is made pursuant to arrangements that were in place at the time of the land transfer;
(f)   the partnership transfer is not (apart from this paragraph) a chargeable transaction.

(2) The partnership transfer –

(a)   shall be taken for the purposes of this Part to be a land transaction;
(b)   is a chargeable transaction.

(3) The partners shall be taken to be the purchasers under the transaction.

(4) The chargeable consideration for the transaction shall be taken to be equal to a proportion of the market value, as at the date of the transaction, of the interest transferred by the land transfer.

(5) That proportion is –

(a)   if the person making the partnership transfer is not a partner immediately after the transfer, his partnership share immediately before the transfer;
(b)   if he is a partner immediately after the transfer, the difference between his partnership share before and after the transfer.

(6) The partnership transfer and the land transfer shall be taken to be linked transactions.

(7) Paragraphs 6 to 8 (responsibility of partners) have effect in relation to the partnership transfer, but the responsible partners are –

(a)   those who were partners immediately before the transfer and who remain partners after the transfer, and

(b)   any person becoming a partner as a result of, or in connection with, the transfer.

Withdrawal of money etc from partnership after transfer of chargeable interest

17A

(1) This paragraph applies where –

(a)   there is a transfer of a chargeable interest to a partnership ('the land transfer');

(b)   the land transfer falls within paragraph (a), (b) or (c) of paragraph 10(1);

(c)   during the period of three years beginning with the date of the land transfer, a qualifying event occurs;

(d)   at the time of the qualifying event, an election has not been made in respect of the land transfer under paragraph 12A.

(2) A qualifying event is –

(a)   a withdrawal from the partnership of money or money's worth which does not represent income profit by the relevant person –
  (i)   withdrawing capital from his capital account,
  (ii)   reducing his interest, or
  (iii) ceasing to be a partner, or

(b)   in a case where the relevant person has made a loan to the partnership –
  (i)   the repayment (to any extent) by the partnership of the loan, or
  (ii)   a withdrawal by the relevant person from the partnership of money or money's worth which does not represent income profit.

(3) For this purpose the relevant person is –

(a)   where the land transfer falls within paragraph 10(1)(a) or (b), the person who makes the land transfer, and

(b)   where the land transfer falls within paragraph 10(1)(c), the partner concerned or a person connected with him.

(4) The qualifying event –

(a)   shall be taken to be a land transaction, and

(b)   is a chargeable transaction.

(5) The partners shall be taken to be the purchasers under the transaction.

(6) Paragraphs 6 to 8 (responsibility of partners) have effect in relation to the transaction.

(7) The chargeable consideration for the transaction shall be taken to be –

(a)   in a case falling within sub-paragraph (2)(a), equal to the value of the money or money's worth withdrawn from the partnership,

(b)   in a case falling within sub-paragraph (2)(b)(i), equal to the amount repaid, and

(c)   in a case falling within sub-paragraph (2)(b)(ii), equal to so much of the value of the money or money's worth withdrawn from the partnership as does not exceed the amount of the loan, but (in any case) shall not exceed the market value, as at the effective date of the land transfer, of the chargeable interest transferred by the land transfer, reduced by any amount previously chargeable to tax.

(8) Where –

(a)   a qualifying event gives rise to a charge under this paragraph, and

(b)   the same event gives rise to a charge under paragraph 14 (transfer for consideration of interest in property-investment partnership),

the amount of the charge under this paragraph is reduced (but not below nil) by the amount of the charge under that paragraph.

Amendments: Finance (No 2) Act 2005, s 49, Sch 10: Finance Act 2006, ss 163, Sch 24; Finance Act 2008, s 97(1), Sch 31, Pt 2, para 8.

Transfer of chargeable interest from a partnership: general

18

(1) This paragraph applies where a chargeable interest is transferred –

(a)   from a partnership to a person who is or has been one of the partners, or

(b)   from a partnership to a person connected with a person who is or has been one of the partners.

(2) The chargeable consideration for the transaction shall (subject to paragraph 24) be taken to be equal to –

$$MV \times (100 - SLP)\%$$

where –

MV is the market value of the interest transferred, and

SLP is the sum of the lower proportions.

(5) Paragraph 20 provides for determining the sum of the lower proportions.

(6) Paragraph 19 applies if the whole or part of the chargeable consideration for the transaction is rent.

(7) For the purposes of this paragraph property that was partnership property before the partnership was dissolved or otherwise ceased to exist shall be treated as remaining partnership property until it is distributed.

(8) This paragraph has effect subject to any election under paragraph 12A.

Amendments: Finance Act 2006, ss 163, 178, Schs 24, 26; Finance Act 2008, s 97(1), Sch 31, Pt 2, para 7.

Transfer of chargeable interest from a partnership: chargeable consideration including rent

19

(1) This paragraph applies in relation to a transaction to which paragraph 18 applies where the whole or part of the chargeable consideration for the transaction is rent.

(2) Schedule 5 (amount of tax chargeable: rent) has effect with the modifications set out in sub-paragraphs (2A) to (2C).

(2A) In paragraph 2 –

  (a)   for 'the net present value of the rent payable over the term of the lease' substitute 'the relevant chargeable proportion of the net present value of the rent payable over the term of the lease', and
  (b)   for 'the net present values of the rent payable over the terms of all the leases' substitute 'the relevant chargeable proportions of the net present values of the rent payable over the terms of all the leases'.

(2B) In paragraph 9A(6) –

  (a)   for 'the annual rent' substitute 'the relevant chargeable proportion of the annual rent', and
  (b)   for 'the total of the annual rents' substitute 'the relevant chargeable proportion of the total of the annual rents'.

(2C) For paragraph 9(4) substitute –

  '(4) Tax chargeable under this Schedule is in addition to any tax chargeable under section 55 as it has effect by virtue of paragraph 18 of Schedule 15.'

(2D) For the purposes of sub-paragraphs (2A) and (2B) the relevant chargeable proportion is –

(100 – SLP)%

where SLP is the sum of the lower proportions.

(8) Paragraph 20 provides for determining the sum of the lower proportions.

(9) This paragraph is subject to paragraph 24.

Amendments: Finance Act 2006, s 163, Sch 24; Finance Act 2008, s 95(11)(b), (13).

Transfer of chargeable interest from a partnership: sum of the lower proportions

20

(1) The sum of the lower proportions in relation to a transaction to which paragraph 18 applies is determined as follows –

Step One

Identify the relevant owner or owners.

A person is a relevant owner if –

  (a)   immediately after the transaction, he is entitled to a proportion of the chargeable interest, and
  (b)   immediately before the transaction, he was a partner or connected with a partner.

Step Two

For each relevant owner, identify the corresponding partner or partners.

A person is a corresponding partner in relation to a relevant owner if, immediately before the transaction –

(a) he was a partner, and

(b) he was the relevant owner or was an individual connected with the relevant owner.

(If there is no relevant owner with a corresponding partner, the sum of the lower proportions is nil.)

Step Three

For each relevant owner, find the proportion of the chargeable interest to which he is entitled immediately after the transaction.

Apportion that proportion between any one or more of the relevant owner's corresponding partners.

Step Four

Find the lower proportion for each person who is a corresponding partner in relation to one or more relevant owners.

The lower proportion is –

(a) the proportion of the chargeable interest attributable to the partner, or

(b) if lower, the partnership share attributable to the partner.

The proportion of the chargeable interest attributable to the partner is –

    (i) if he is a corresponding partner in relation to only one relevant owner, the proportion (if any) of the chargeable interest apportioned to him (at Step Three) in respect of that owner;

    (ii) if he is a corresponding partner in relation to more than one relevant owner, the sum of the proportions (if any) of the chargeable interest apportioned to him (at Step Three) in respect of each of those owners.

Paragraph 21 provides for determining the partnership share attributable to the partner.

Step Five

Add together the lower proportions of each person who is a corresponding partner in relation to one or more relevant owners.

The result is the sum of the lower proportions.

(2) For the purposes of this paragraph persons who are entitled to a chargeable interest as beneficial joint tenants (or, in Scotland, as joint owners) shall be taken to be entitled to the chargeable interest as beneficial tenants in common (or, in Scotland, as owners in common) in equal shares.

(3) For the purpose of paragraph (b) of Step 2 a company is to be treated as an individual connected with the relevant owner in so far as it –

(a) holds property as trustee, and

(b) is connected with the relevant owner only because of section 839(3) of the Taxes Act 1988.

Amendments: Finance Act 2007, ss 72(1), (2), (7)(a), (b), (8), (13), (16), (17); SI 2006/3237.

Transfer of chargeable interest from a partnership: partnership share attributable to partner

21

(1) This paragraph provides for determining the partnership share attributable to a partner for the purposes of paragraph 20 (1) (see Step Four).

(2) Paragraph 22 applies for determining the partnership share attributable to a partner where –

(a) the effective date of the transfer of the relevant chargeable interest to the partnership was before 20th October 2003, or

(b) the effective date of the transfer of the relevant chargeable interest to the partnership was on or after that date and –

(i) the instrument by which the transfer was effected has been duly stamped with ad valorem stamp duty, or

(ii) any tax payable in respect of the transfer has been duly paid under this Part.

(3) Where the effective date of the transfer of the relevant chargeable interest to the partnership was on or after 20th October 2003 but neither of the conditions in sub-paragraphs (i) and (ii) of sub-paragraph (2)(b) is met, the partnership share attributable to the partner is zero.

(4) The relevant chargeable interest is –

(a) the chargeable interest which ceases to be partnership property as a result of the transaction to which paragraph 18 applies, or

(b) where the transaction to which paragraph 18 applies is the grant or creation of a chargeable interest, the chargeable interest out of which that interest is granted or created.

22

(1) Where this paragraph applies, the partnership share attributable to the partner is determined as follows –

Step One

Find the partner's actual partnership share on the relevant date.

In a case falling within paragraph 21(2)(a), the relevant date –

(a) if the partner was a partner on 19th October 2003, is that date;

(b) if the partner became a partner after that date, is the date on which he became a partner.

In a case falling within paragraph 21(2)(b), the relevant date –

(a) if the partner was a partner on the effective date of the transfer of the relevant chargeable interest to the partnership, is that date;

(b) if the partner became a partner after that date, is the date on which he became a partner.

Step Two

Add to that partnership share any increases in the partner's partnership share which –

(a)   occur in the period starting on the day after the relevant date and ending immediately before the transaction to which paragraph 18 applies, and

(b)   count for this purpose.

The result is the increased partnership share.

An increase counts for the purpose of paragraph (b) only if –

(i)   where the transfer which resulted in the increase took place on or before the date on which the Finance Act 2004 was passed, the instrument by which the transfer was effected has been duly stamped with ad valorem stamp duty under the enactments relating to stamp duty;

(ii)   where the transfer which resulted in the increase took place after that date, any tax payable in respect of the transfer has been duly paid under this Part.

Step Three

Deduct from the increased partnership share any decreases in the partner's partnership share which occur in the period starting on the day after the relevant date and ending immediately before the transaction to which paragraph 18 applies.

The result is the partnership share attributable to the partner.

(2) If the effect of applying Step Three would be to reduce the partnership share attributable to the partner below zero, the partnership share attributable to the partner is zero.

(3) In a case falling within paragraph 21(2)(a), if the partner ceased to be a partner before 19th October 2003, the partnership share attributable to the partner is zero.

(4) In a case falling within paragraph 21(2)(b), if the partner ceased to be a partner before the effective date of the transfer of the relevant chargeable interest to the partnership, the partnership share attributable to the partner is zero.

(5) Paragraph 21(4) (relevant chargeable interest) applies for the purposes of this paragraph.

Transfer of chargeable interest from a partnership to a partnership

23

(1) This paragraph applies where –

(a)   there is a transfer of a chargeable interest from a partnership to a partnership, and

(b)   the transfer is both –
(i)   a transaction to which paragraph 10 applies, and
(ii)   a transaction to which paragraph 18 applies.

(2) Paragraphs 10(2) and 18(2) do not apply.

(2A) The chargeable consideration for the transaction shall be taken to be what it would have been if paragraph 10(2) had applied or, if greater, what it would have been if paragraph 18(2) had applied.

(3) Where the whole or part of the chargeable consideration for the transaction is rent –

(a)   paragraphs 11 and 19 do not apply;

(b)   the tax chargeable in respect of so much of the chargeable consideration as consists of rent shall be taken to be what it would have been if paragraph 11 had applied or, if greater, what it would have been if paragraph 19 had applied;

(c)   the disapplication of the 0% band provided for by paragraph 9A of Schedule 5 has effect if –

    (i)   it would have had effect if paragraph 11(2B) of this Schedule had applied, or

    (ii)   it would have had effect if paragraph 19(2B) of this Schedule had applied.

Amendments: Finance Act 2006, s 163, Sch 24; Finance Act 2008, s 95(11)(c), (13).

Transfer of chargeable interest from a partnership consisting wholly of bodies corporate

24

(1) This paragraph applies where –

(a)   there is a transaction to which paragraph 18 applies;

(b)   immediately before the transaction all the partners are bodies corporate;

(c)   the sum of the lower proportions is 75 or more.

(2) Paragraphs 18, 19 and 23 have effect with these modifications.

(3) In paragraph 18, for sub-paragraphs (2) and (5) substitute –

'(2) The chargeable consideration for the transaction shall be taken to be equal to the market value of the interest transferred.'

(4A) In paragraph 19(2), for 'sub-paragraphs (2) to (2C)' substitute 'sub-paragraph (2C)'.

(5) In paragraph 19, omit sub-paragraphs (2A), (2B), (2D) and (8).

(9) Paragraph 20 provides for determining the sum of the lower proportions.

Amendments: Finance Act 2006, s 163, Sch 24.

Application of exemptions and reliefs

25

(1) Where paragraph 10, 14, 17 or 18 applies, paragraph 1 of Schedule 3 (exemption of transactions for which there is no chargeable consideration) does not apply.

(2) But (subject to paragraphs 26 to 28) this Part of this Schedule has effect subject to any other provision affording exemption or relief from stamp duty land tax.

Application of disadvantaged areas relief

26

(1) Schedule 6 (disadvantaged areas relief) applies to the transfer of an interest in a partnership that is a chargeable transaction by virtue of paragraph 14 or 17 with these modifications.

(2) For paragraph 3 substitute –

'3

(1) This Part of this Schedule applies to a transfer of an interest in a partnership that is a chargeable transaction by virtue of paragraph 14 of Schedule 15 if every chargeable interest comprising the relevant partnership property is a chargeable interest in relation to land that is wholly situated in a disadvantaged area.

(2) This Part of this Schedule applies to a transfer of an interest in a partnership that is a chargeable transaction by virtue of paragraph 17 of Schedule 15 if the subject matter of the land transfer is a chargeable interest in relation to land that is wholly situated in a disadvantaged area.'

(3) In paragraph 5, for sub-paragraphs (2) to (4) substitute –

'(2) If the relevant consideration does not exceed £150,000 the transaction is exempt from charge.'

(4) For paragraph 6 substitute –

'6

(1) This paragraph applies where the land is partly non-residential property and partly residential property.

(2) The non-residential proportion of the chargeable consideration for the transaction does not count as chargeable consideration.

(3) The non-residential proportion is the proportion of the market value of the relevant property that, on a just and reasonable apportionment, is attributable to land that is non-residential property.

(4) If the relevant consideration does not exceed £150,000, none of the residential proportion of the chargeable consideration counts as chargeable consideration.

(5) The residential proportion is the proportion of the market value of the relevant property that, on a just and reasonable apportionment, is attributable to land that is residential property.'

(5) For paragraph 7 substitute –

'7

(1) This Part of this Schedule applies to a transfer of an interest in a partnership that is a chargeable transaction by virtue of paragraph 14 of Schedule 15 if –

    (a)   some (but not all) of the chargeable interests comprising the relevant partnership property are chargeable interests in relation to land that is wholly situated in a disadvantaged area, or

    (b)   any chargeable interest comprised in the relevant partnership property is a chargeable interest in relation to land that is partly situated in a disadvantaged area and partly situated outside such an area.

(2) This Part of this Schedule applies to a transfer of an interest in a partnership that is a chargeable transaction by virtue of paragraph 17 of Schedule 15 if the subject matter of the land transfer is a chargeable interest in relation to land that is partly situated in a disadvantaged area and partly situated outside such an area.

(3) In this Part –

    (a)   references to the disadvantaged area proportion are to the proportion of the market value of the relevant property that, on a just and reasonable apportionment, is attributable to land situated in a disadvantaged area;

(b)   references to the advantaged area proportion are to the proportion of the market value of the relevant property that, on a just and reasonable apportionment, is attributable to land that is situated outside a disadvantaged area.'

(6) In paragraph 8, for 'consideration attributable to the land situated in the disadvantaged area' substitute 'disadvantaged area proportion of the chargeable consideration'.

(7) In paragraph 9, for sub-paragraphs (2) to (4) substitute –

'(2) If the relevant consideration does not exceed £150,000 none of the disadvantaged area proportion of the chargeable consideration counts as chargeable consideration.'

(8) For paragraph 10 substitute –

'**10**

(1) This paragraph applies where the land situated in a disadvantaged area is partly non-residential property and partly residential property.

(2) The non-residential proportion of the disadvantaged area proportion of the chargeable consideration for the transaction does not count as chargeable consideration (subject to any election under paragraph 12A).

(3) The non-residential proportion is the proportion of the disadvantaged area proportion of the market value of the relevant property that, on a just and reasonable apportionment, is attributable to land that is not residential property.

(4) If the relevant consideration does not exceed £150,000, none of the residential proportion of the disadvantaged area proportion of the chargeable consideration counts as chargeable consideration (subject to any election under paragraph 12A).

(5) The residential proportion is the proportion of the disadvantaged area proportion of the market value of the relevant property that, on a just and reasonable apportionment, is attributable to land that is residential property.'

(9) After paragraph 11 (1) insert –

'(1A) In this Schedule –

"the land transfer" means the transaction that is the land transfer for the purposes of paragraph 17 of Schedule 15;
"the relevant partnership property" has the meaning given by paragraph 14(5) or (5A) (as appropriate) of Schedule 15;

"the relevant property" –

(a)   in the case of a transfer of an interest in a partnership that is a chargeable transaction by virtue of paragraph 14 of Schedule 15, means the relevant partnership property;
(b)   in the case of a transfer of an interest in a partnership that is a chargeable transaction by virtue of paragraph 17 of Schedule 15, means the subject matter of the land transfer.

(1B) There is a transfer of an interest in a partnership for the purposes of this Schedule if there is such a transfer for the purposes of Part 3 of Schedule 15 (see paragraph 36 of that Schedule).'

(10) Omit paragraphs 11(2) and 12.

Amendments: Finance Act 2008, s 97(1)–(3), Sch 31, Pt 1, Para 4, Pt 2, para 9.

Application of group relief

27

(1) Part 1 of Schedule 7 (group relief) applies to –

(a)   a transaction to which paragraph 10 applies, and
(b)   a transaction that is a chargeable transaction by virtue of paragraph 17,
with these modifications.

(2) In paragraph 3(1)(a), for 'the purchaser' substitute 'a partner who was a partner at the effective date of the relevant transaction ("the relevant partner")'.

(3) In paragraph 3(1), for paragraph (b) substitute –

'(b)   at the time the relevant partner ceases to be a member of the same group as the vendor ("the relevant time"), a chargeable interest is held by or on behalf of the members of the partnership and that chargeable interest –
          (i)   was acquired by or on behalf of the partnership under the relevant transaction, or
          (ii)   is derived from a chargeable interest so acquired,

and has not subsequently been acquired at market value under a chargeable transaction for which group relief was available but was not claimed,'

(4) In paragraph 3(3), for the words from 'the transferee company' to the end substitute 'or on behalf of the partnership and to the proportion in which the relevant partner is entitled at the relevant time to share in the income profits of the partnership.'

(5) In paragraph 3(4), omit the definition of 'relevant associated company'.

(6) In paragraphs 4 to 6, for 'the purchaser' (wherever appearing) substitute 'the relevant partner'.

27A

(1) This paragraph applies where in calculating the sum of the lower proportions in relation to a transaction (in accordance with paragraph 12) –

(a)   a company ('the connected company') would have been a corresponding partner of a relevant owner ('the original owner') but for the fact that paragraph (b) of Step Two includes connected persons only if they are individuals, and
(b)   the connected company and the original owner are members of the same group.

(2) The charge in respect of the transaction shall be reduced to the amount that would have been payable had the connected company been a corresponding partner of the original owner for the purposes of calculating the sum of the lower proportions.

(3) The provisions of Part 1 of Schedule 7 apply to group relief under sub-paragraph (2) above as to group relief under paragraph 1(1) of Schedule 7, but –

(a)   with the omission of paragraph 2(2)(a),
(b)   with the substitution for 'the purchaser' in paragraph 3(1)(a) of 'a partner who was, at the effective date of the transaction, a partner and a member of the same group as the transferor ("the relevant partner")', and
(c)   with the other modifications specified in paragraph 27(3) to (6) above.

Amendments: Finance Act 2007, s 72(1), (2), (9), (13), (16), (17); SI 2006/3237.

Application of charities relief

28

(1) Schedule 8 (charities relief) applies to the transfer of an interest in a partnership that is a chargeable transaction by virtue of paragraph 14 or 17 with these modifications.

(2) In paragraph 1(1), for 'A land transaction is exempt from charge if the purchaser is a charity' substitute 'A transfer of an interest in a partnership that is a chargeable transaction by virtue of paragraph 14 or 17 of Schedule 15 is exempt from charge if the transferee is a charity'.

(3) In paragraph 1(2) –

    (a)   for 'the purchaser must intend to hold the subject-matter of the transaction' substitute 'every chargeable interest held as partnership property immediately after the transfer must be held';

    (b)   in paragraphs (a) and (b) for 'the purchaser' substitute 'the transferee'.

(4) In paragraph 1(3) for 'the purchaser' substitute 'the transferee'.

(5) In paragraph 2(1), for paragraph (b) substitute –

    '(b)   at the time of the disqualifying event the partnership property includes a chargeable interest –
        (i)   that was held as partnership property immediately after the relevant transaction, or
        (ii)   that is derived from an interest held as partnership property at that time,'

(6) In paragraph 2(3)(a), for 'the purchaser' substitute 'the transferee'.

(7) In paragraph 2(3), for paragraph (b) substitute –

    '(b)   any chargeable interest held as partnership property immediately after the relevant transaction, or any interest or right derived from it, being used or held otherwise than for qualifying charitable purposes.'

(8) For paragraph 2(4) substitute –

'(4) In sub-paragraphs (1) and (2) an "appropriate proportion" means an appropriate proportion having regard to –

    (a)   the chargeable interests held as partnership property immediately after the relevant transaction and the chargeable interests held as partnership property at the time of the disqualifying event, and

    (b)   the extent to which any chargeable interest held as partnership property at that time becomes used or held for purposes other than qualifying charitable purposes.'

(9) After paragraph 2 insert –

'Interpretation

3

(1) There is a transfer of an interest in a partnership for the purposes of this Schedule if there is such a transfer for the purposes of Part 3 of Schedule 15 (see paragraph 36 of that Schedule).

(2) Paragraph 34 (1) of Schedule 15 (meaning of references to partnership property) applies for the purposes of this Schedule as it applies for the purposes of Part 3 of that Schedule.'

Acquisition of interest in partnership not chargeable except as specially provided

29

Except as provided by –

(a) paragraph 10 (transfer of chargeable interest to a partnership), or

(b) paragraph 14 (transfer of partnership interest: consideration given and chargeable interest held), or

(c) paragraph 17 (transfer of partnership interest pursuant to earlier arrangements),

the acquisition of an interest in a partnership is not a chargeable transaction, notwithstanding that the partnership property includes land.

Transactions that are not notifiable

30

(1) A transaction which is a chargeable transaction by virtue of paragraph 14 or 17 (transfer of partnership interest) is a notifiable transaction if (but only if) the consideration for the transaction exceeds the zero rate threshold.

(2) The consideration for a transaction exceeds the zero rate threshold if either or both of the following conditions are met –

(a) the relevant consideration for the purposes of section 55 (amount of tax chargeable: general) is such that the rate of tax chargeable under that section is 1% or higher;

(b) the relevant rental value for the purposes of Schedule 5 (amount of tax chargeable: rent) is such that the rate of tax chargeable under that Schedule is 1% or higher.

Stamp duty on transfers of partnership interests: continued application

31

(1) Nothing in section 125 (abolition of stamp duty except in relation to stock or marketable securities), or in Part 2 of Schedule 20 (amendments and repeals consequential on that section), affects the application of the enactments relating to stamp duty in relation to an instrument by which a transfer of an interest in a partnership is effected.

(2) In Part 1 of Schedule 20 (provisions supplementing section 125) references to stock or marketable securities shall be read as including any property that is the subject-matter of a transaction by which an interest in a partnership is transferred.(3) In their application in relation to an instrument by which a transfer of an interest in a partnership is effected, the enactments relating to stamp duty have effect subject to paragraphs 32 and 33.

Stamp duty on transfers of partnership interests: modification

32

(1) This paragraph applies where –

(a) stamp duty under Part 1 of Schedule 13 to the Finance Act 1999 (transfer on sale) is chargeable on an instrument effecting a transfer of an interest in a partnership, and

    (b)   the relevant partnership property includes a chargeable interest.

(2) The 'relevant partnership property', in relation to a transfer of an interest in a partnership, is every chargeable interest held as partnership property immediately after the transfer, other than any interest that was transferred to the partnership in connection with the transfer.

(3) The consideration for the transaction shall (subject to sub-paragraph (8)) be taken to be equal to the actual consideration for the transaction less the excluded amount.

(4) The excluded amount is a proportion of the net market value of the relevant partnership property immediately after the transfer.

(5) That proportion is –

    (a)   if the person acquiring the interest in the partnership was not a partner before the transfer, his partnership share immediately after the transfer;

    (b)   if he was a partner before the transfer, the difference between his partnership share before and after the transfer.

(6) The net market value of a chargeable interest at a particular date is –

MV SL

where –

MV is the market value of the chargeable interest at that date, and

SL is the amount outstanding at that date on any loan secured solely on the chargeable interest.

(7) If, in relation to a chargeable interest, SL is greater than MV, the net market value of the chargeable interest shall be taken to be nil.

(8) If the excluded amount is greater than the actual consideration for the transaction, the consideration for the transaction shall be taken to be nil.

(9) Where this paragraph applies in relation to an instrument, the instrument shall not be regarded as duly stamped unless it has been stamped in accordance with section 12 of the Stamp Act 1891.

33

(1) This paragraph applies where stamp duty under Part 1 of Schedule 13 to the Finance Act 1999 (transfer on sale) is, apart from this paragraph, chargeable on an instrument effecting a transfer of an interest in a partnership.

(1A) If the relevant partnership property does not include any stock or marketable securities, no stamp duty shall (subject to sub-paragraph (8)) be chargeable on the instrument.

(3) If the relevant partnership property includes stock or marketable securities, the stamp duty chargeable on the instrument shall not exceed the stamp duty that would be chargeable if –

    (a)   the instrument were an instrument effecting a transfer of that stock and those securities, and

    (b)   the consideration for the transfer were equal to the appropriate proportion of the net market value of that stock and those securities immediately after the transfer.

(3A) The 'relevant partnership property', in relation to a transfer of an interest in a partnership, is the partnership property immediately after the transfer, other than any partnership property that was transferred to the partnership in connection with the transfer.

(5) The appropriate proportion is –

(a)   if the person acquiring the interest in the partnership was not a partner before the transfer, his partnership share immediately after the transfer;

(b)   if he was a partner before the transfer, the difference between his partnership share before and after the transfer.

(6) The net market value of stock or securities at a particular date is –

MV SL

where –

MV is the market value of the stock or securities at that date, and

SL is the amount outstanding at that date on any loan secured solely on the stock or securities.

(7) If, in relation to any stock or securities, SL is greater than MV, the net market value of the stock or securities shall be taken to be nil.

(8) Where this paragraph applies in relation to an instrument, the instrument shall not be regarded as duly stamped unless it has been stamped in accordance with section 12 of the Stamp Act 1891.

(9) This paragraph shall be construed as one with the Stamp Act 1891.

Amendments: Finance (No 2) Act 2005, ss 49, 70, Sch 10.

Interpretation: partnership property and partnership share

34

(1) Any reference in this Part of this Schedule to partnership property is to an interest or right held by or on behalf of a partnership, or the members of a partnership, for the purposes of the partnership business.

(2) Any reference in this Part of this Schedule to a person's partnership share at any time is to the proportion in which he is entitled at that time to share in the income profits of the partnership.

Interpretation: transfer of chargeable interest to a partnership

35

For the purposes of this Part of this Schedule, there is a transfer of a chargeable interest to a partnership in any case where a chargeable interest becomes partnership property.

Interpretation: transfer of interest in a partnership

36

For the purposes of this Part of this Schedule, where a person acquires or increases a partnership share there is a transfer of an interest in the partnership (to that partner and from the other partners).

Amendments: Finance Act 2007, s 72(1), (10), (13, (14).

Interpretation: transfer of chargeable interest from a partnership

37

For the purposes of this Part of this Schedule, there is a transfer of a chargeable interest from a partnership in any case where –

    (a)   a chargeable interest that was partnership property ceases to be partnership property, or

    (b)   a chargeable interest is granted or created out of partnership property and the interest is not partnership property.

Interpretation: market value of leases

38

(1) This paragraph applies in relation to a lease for the purposes of this Part of this Schedule if –

    (a)   the grant of the lease is or was a transaction to which paragraph 10 applies or applied (or a transaction to which paragraph 10 would have applied if that paragraph had been in force at the time of the grant), or

    (b)   the grant of the lease is a transaction to which paragraph 18 applies.

(2) In determining the market value of the lease, an obligation of the tenant under the lease is to be taken into account if (but only if) –

    (a)   it is an obligation such as is mentioned in paragraph 10 (1) of Schedule 17A, or

    (b)   it is an obligation to make a payment to a person.

Interpretation: connected persons

39

(1) Section 839 of the Taxes Act 1988 (connected persons) has effect for the purposes of this Part of this Schedule.

(2) As applied by sub-paragraph (1), that section has effect with the omission of subsection (4) (partners connected with each other).

(3) As applied by sub-paragraph (1) for the purposes of paragraph 12 or 20, that section has effect with the omission of subsection (3)(c) (trustee connected with settlement).

Amendments: Finance Act 2007, s 72(1), (11), (13).

Interpretation: arrangements

40

In this Part of this Schedule 'arrangements' includes any scheme, agreement or understanding, whether or not legally enforceable.

Amendments: Schedule Part, substituted by Finance Act 2004, s 304, Sch 41.

Schedule 16

Section 105

Stamp Duty Land Tax: Trusts And Powers

Meaning of 'settlement' and 'bare trust'

1

(1) In this Part 'settlement' means a trust that is not a bare trust.

(2) In this Part a 'bare trust' means a trust under which property is held by a person as trustee –

(a) for a person who is absolutely entitled as against the trustee, or who would be so entitled but for being a minor or other person under a disability, or

(b) for two or more persons who are or would be jointly so entitled,

and includes a case in which a person holds property as nominee for another.

(3) In sub-paragraph (2)(a) and (b) the references to a person being absolutely entitled to property as against the trustee are references to a case where the person has the exclusive right, subject only to satisfying any outstanding charge, lien or other right of the trustee, to resort to the property for payment of duty, taxes, costs or other outgoings or to direct how the property is to be dealt with.

(4) In sub-paragraph (2) 'minor', in relation to Scotland, means a person under legal disability by reason of nonage.

Interests of beneficiaries under certain trusts

2

Where property is held in trust under the law of Scotland, or of a country or territory outside the United Kingdom, on terms such that, if the trust had effect under the law of England and Wales, a beneficiary would be regarded as having an equitable interest in the trust property –

(a) that beneficiary shall be treated for the purposes of this Part as having such an interest notwithstanding that no such interest is recognised by the law of Scotland or, as the case may be, the country or territory outside the United Kingdom, and

(b) an acquisition of the interest of a beneficiary under the trust shall accordingly be treated as involving the acquisition of an interest in the trust property.

Bare trustee

3

(1) Subject to sub-paragraph (2), where a person acquires a chargeable interest or an interest in a partnership as bare trustee, this Part applies as if the interest were vested in, and the acts of the trustee in relation to it were the acts of, the person or persons for whom he is trustee.

(2) Sub-paragraph (1) does not apply in relation to the grant of a lease.

(3) Where a lease is granted to a person as bare trustee, he is treated for the purposes of this Part, as it applies in relation to the grant of the lease, as purchaser of the whole of the interest acquired.

(4) Where a lease is granted by a person as bare trustee, he is to be treated for the purposes of this Part, as it applies in relation to the grant of the lease, as vendor of the whole of the interest disposed of.

Amendments: Finance (No 2) Act 2005, s 49, Sch 10; Finance Act 2007, s 72(12)(a), (15).

Acquisition by trustees of settlement

4

Where persons acquire a chargeable interest or an interest in a partnership as trustees of a settlement, they are treated for the purposes of this Part, as it applies in relation to that acquisition, as purchasers of the whole of the interest acquired (including the beneficial interest).

Amendments: Finance Act 2007, s 72(12)(b), (15).

Responsibility of trustees of settlement

5

(1) Where the trustees of a settlement are liable –

    (a)   to make a payment of tax or interest on unpaid tax,

    (b)   to make a payment in accordance with an assessment under paragraph 29 of Schedule 10 (recovery of excessive repayment), or

    (c)   to a penalty under this Part or to interest on such a penalty,

the payment, penalty or interest may be recovered (but only once) from any one or more of the responsible trustees.

(2) No amount may be recovered by virtue of sub-paragraph (1)(c) from a person who did not become a responsible trustee until after the relevant time.

(3) The responsible trustees, in relation to a land transaction, are the persons who are trustees at the effective date of the transaction and any person who subsequently becomes a trustee.

(4) The relevant time for this purpose is –

    (a)   in relation to so much of a penalty as is payable in respect of any day, or to interest on so much of a penalty as is so payable, the beginning of that day;

    (b)   in relation to any other penalty, or interest on such a penalty, the time when the act or omission occurred that caused the penalty to become payable.

Relevant trustees for purposes of return etc

6

(1) A return in relation to a land transaction may be made or given by any one or more of the trustees who are the responsible trustees in relation to the transaction.

The trustees by whom such a return is made are referred to below as 'the relevant trustees'.

(2) The declaration required by paragraph 1(1)(c) of Schedule 10 (declaration that return is complete and correct) must be made by all the relevant trustees.

(3) If the Inland Revenue give notice of an enquiry into the return –

(a) the notice must be given to each of the relevant trustees,
(b) the powers of the Inland Revenue as to the production of documents and provision of information for the purposes of the enquiry are exercisable separately (and differently) in relation to each of the relevant trustees,
(c) any of the relevant trustees may apply for a direction that a closure notice be given (and all of them are entitled to appear and be heard on the application), and
(d) the closure notice must be given to each of the relevant trustees.

Provided that a notice is not invalidated by virtue of paragraph (a) or (d) if it is given to each of the relevant trustees whose identity is known to the Inland Revenue.

(4) A Revenue determination or discovery assessment relating to the transaction must be made against all of the relevant trustees and is not effective against any of them unless notice of it is given to each of them whose identity is known to the Inland Revenue.

(5) In the case of an appeal arising from proceedings under this Part relating to the transaction –

(a) the appeal may be brought by any of the relevant trustees,
(b) notice of the appeal must be given to any of them by whom it is not brought,
(c) the agreement of all the relevant trustees is required if the appeal is to be settled by agreement,
(d) if it is not settled, any of them are entitled to appear and be heard, and
(e) the decision on the appeal binds all of them.

Amendments: Finance Act 2008, s 94(4), (5), Sch 30, paras 1, 13.

Consideration for exercise of power of appointment or discretion

7

Where a chargeable interest is acquired by virtue of –

(a) the exercise of a power of appointment, or
(b) the exercise of a discretion vested in trustees of a settlement,

there shall be treated as consideration for the acquisition of the interest or right by virtue of the exercise of the power or discretion any consideration given for the person in whose favour the appointment was made or the discretion was exercised becoming an object of the power or discretion.

Reallocation of trust property as between beneficiaries

8

Where –

(a) the trustees of a settlement reallocate trust property in such a way that a beneficiary acquires an interest in certain trust property and ceases to have an interest in other trust property, and
(b) the beneficiary consents to ceasing to have an interest in that other property,

the fact that he gives consent does not mean that there is chargeable consideration for the acquisition.

Amendments: Inserted by Finance Act 2006, s 165(1).

Schedule 17 . . .

Amendments: Schedule repealed by SI 2009/56.

Schedule 17A

Section 120

Further Provisions Relating To Leases

Meaning of 'lease'

1

In the application of this Part to England and Wales or Northern Ireland 'lease' means –

(a) an interest or right in or over land for a term of years (whether fixed or periodic), or

(b) a tenancy at will or other interest or right in or over land terminable by notice at any time.

Leases for a fixed term

2

In the application of the provisions of this Part to a lease for a fixed term, no account shall be taken of –

(a) any contingency as a result of which the lease may determine before the end of the fixed term, or

(b) any right of either party to determine the lease or renew it.

Leases that continue after a fixed term

3

(1) This paragraph applies to –

(a) a lease for a fixed term and thereafter until determined, or

(b) a lease for a fixed term that may continue beyond the fixed term by operation of law.

(2) For the purposes of this Part (except sections 77 and 77A (notifiable transactions)), a lease to which this paragraph applies is treated –

(a) in the first instance as if it were a lease for the original fixed term and no longer,

(b) if the lease continues after the end of that term, as if it were a lease for a fixed term one year longer than the original fixed term,

(c) if the lease continues after the end of the term resulting from the application of paragraph (b), as if it were a lease for a fixed term two years longer than the original fixed term,

and so on.

(3) Where the effect of sub-paragraph (2) in relation to the continuation of the lease after the end of a fixed term is that additional tax is payable in respect of a transaction or that tax is payable in respect of a transaction where none was payable before –

(a) the purchaser must deliver a return or further return in respect of that transaction before the end of the period of 30 days after the end of that term,

(b) the return must include a self-assessment of the amount of tax chargeable in respect of the transaction on the basis of the information contained in the return,

(c) the tax so chargeable is to be calculated by reference to the rates in force at the effective date of the transaction, and

(d) the tax or additional tax payable must be paid not later than the filing date for the return.

(4) The provisions of Schedule 10 (returns, enquiries, assessments and other matters) apply to a return under this paragraph as they apply to a return under section 76 (general requirement to deliver land transaction return), with the adaptation that references to the effective date of the transaction shall be read as references to the day on which the lease becomes treated as being for a longer fixed term.

(5) For the purposes of sections 77 and 77A (notifiable transactions) a lease to which this paragraph applies is a lease for whatever is its fixed term.

Amendments: Finance Act 2007, s 80(1), (8), (9)(g); Finance Act 2008, s 94(4), (5), Sch 30, paras 1, 14.

Treatment of leases for indefinite term

4

(1) For the purposes of this Part (except sections 77 and 77A (notifiable transactions)) –

(a) a lease for an indefinite term is treated in the first instance as if it were a lease for a fixed term of a year,

(b) if the lease continues after the end of the term resulting from the application of paragraph (a), it is treated as if it were a lease for a fixed term of two years,

(c) if the lease continues after the end of the term resulting from the application of paragraph (b), it is treated as if it were a lease for a fixed term of three years,

and so on.

(2) No account shall be taken for the purposes of this Part of any other statutory provision in England and Wales or Northern Ireland deeming a lease for an indefinite period to be a lease for a different term.

(3) Where the effect of sub-paragraph (1) in relation to the continuation of the lease after the end of a deemed fixed term is that additional tax is payable in respect of a transaction or that tax is payable in respect of a transaction where none was payable before –

(a) the purchaser must deliver a return or further return in respect of that transaction before the end of the period of 30 days after the end of that term,

(b) the return must include a self-assessment of the amount of tax chargeable in respect of the transaction on the basis of the information contained in the return,

(c) the tax so chargeable is to be calculated by reference to the rates in force at the effective date of the transaction, and

(d)   the tax or additional tax payable must be paid not later than the filing date for the return.

(4) The provisions of Schedule 10 (returns, enquiries, assessments and other matters) apply to a return under this paragraph as they apply to a return under section 76 (general requirement to deliver land transaction return), with the adaptation that references to the effective date of the transaction shall be read as references to the day on which the lease becomes treated as being for a longer fixed term.

(4A) For the purposes of sections 77 and 77A (notifiable transactions) a lease for an indefinite term is a lease for a term of less then seven years.

(5) References in this paragraph to a lease for an indefinite period include –

(a)   a periodic tenancy or other interest or right terminable by a period of notice,
(b)   a tenancy at will in England and Wales or Northern Ireland, or
(c)   any other interest or right terminable by notice at any time.

Amendments: Finance Act 2007, s 80(1), (8), (9)(g): Finance Act 2008, s 94(4), (5), Sch 30, paras 1, 14.

Treatment of successive linked leases

5

(1) This paragraph applies where –

(a)   successive leases are granted or treated as granted (whether at the same time or at different times) of the same or substantially the same premises, and
(b)   those grants are linked transactions.

(2) This Part applies as if the series of leases were a single lease –

(a)   granted at the time of the grant of the first lease in the series,
(b)   for a term equal to the aggregate of the terms of all the leases, and
(c)   in consideration of the rent payable under all of the leases.

(3) The grant of later leases in the series is accordingly disregarded for the purposes of this Part except section 81A (return or further return in consequence of later linked transaction).

Rent

6

(1) For the purposes of this Part a single sum expressed to be payable in respect of rent, or expressed to be payable in respect of rent and other matters but not apportioned, shall be treated as entirely rent.

(2) Sub-paragraph (1) is without prejudice to the application of paragraph 4 of Schedule 4 (chargeable consideration: just and reasonable apportionment) where separate sums are expressed to be payable in respect of rent and other matters.

Variable or uncertain rent

7

(1) This paragraph applies to determine the amount of rent payable under a lease where that amount –

(a)   varies in accordance with provision in the lease, or

(b)   is contingent, uncertain or unascertained.

(2) As regards rent payable in respect of any period before the end of the fifth year of the term of the lease –

(a)   the provisions of this Part apply as in relation to other chargeable consideration, and
(b)   the provisions of section 51(1) and (2) accordingly apply if the amount is contingent, uncertain or unascertained.

(3) As regards rent payable in respect of any period after the end of the fifth year of the term of the lease, the annual amount is assumed for the purposes of this Part to be, in every case, equal to the highest amount of rent payable in respect of any consecutive twelve month period in the first five years of the term.

In determining that amount take into account (if necessary) any amounts determined as mentioned in sub-paragraph (2)(b), but disregard paragraphs 9(2) and 9A(3) (deemed reduction of rent, where further lease granted, for period during which rents overlap).

(4) This paragraph has effect subject to paragraph 8 (adjustment where rent payable ceases to be uncertain).

(4A) For the purposes of this paragraph and paragraph 8, the cases where the amount of rent payable under a lease is uncertain or unascertained include cases where there is a possibility of that amount being varied under –

(a)   section 12, 13 or 33 of the Agricultural Holdings Act 1986,
(b)   Part 2 of the Agricultural Tenancies Act 1995,
(c)   section 13, 14, 15 or 31 of the Agricultural Holdings (Scotland) Act 1991, or
(d)   section 9, 10 or 11 of the Agricultural Holdings (Scotland) Act 2003.

(5) No account shall be taken for the purposes of this Part of any provision for rent to be adjusted in line with the retail price index.

Amendments: Finance Act 2006, s 164(5), Sch 25.

First rent review in final quarter of fifth year

7A

Where –

(a)   a lease contains provision under which the rent may be adjusted,
(b)   under that provision the first (or only) such adjustment –
    (i)   is to an amount that (before the adjustment) is uncertain, and
    (ii)   has effect from a date (the 'review date') that is expressed as falling five years after a specified date,
    and
(c)   the specified date falls within the three months before the beginning of the term of the lease,

this Schedule has effect as if references to the first five years of the term of the lease were to the period beginning with the start of the term of the lease and ending with the review date.

References to the fifth year of the term of the lease shall be read accordingly.

Amendments: Inserted by Finance Act 2004, s 296, Sch 39.

Adjustment where rent ceases to be uncertain

8

(1) Where the provisions of section 51(1) and (2) (contingent, uncertain or unascertained consideration) apply in relation to a transaction by virtue of paragraph 7 (uncertain rent) and –

    (a)   the end of the fifth year of the term of the lease is reached, or

    (b)   the amount of rent payable in respect of the first five years of the term of the lease ceases to be uncertain at an earlier date,

the following provisions have effect to require or permit reconsideration of how this Part applies to the transaction (and to any transaction in relation to which it is a linked transaction).

(2) For the purposes of this paragraph the amount of rent payable ceases to be uncertain when –

    (a)   in the case of contingent rent, the contingency occurs or it becomes clear that it will not occur, and

    (b)   in the case of uncertain or unascertained rent, the amount becomes ascertained.

(3) If the result as regards the rent paid or payable in respect of the first five years of the term of the lease is that a transaction becomes notifiable, or that additional tax is payable in respect of a transaction or that tax is payable where none was payable before –

    (a)   the purchaser must make a return to the Inland Revenue within 30 days of the date referred to in sub-paragraph (1)(a) or (b),

    (b)   the return must contain a self-assessment of the tax chargeable in respect of the transaction on the basis of the information contained in the return,

    (c)   the tax so chargeable is to be calculated by reference to the rates in force at the effective date of the transaction, and

    (d)   the tax or additional tax payable must be paid not later than the filing date for the return.

(4) The provisions of Schedule 10 (returns, enquiries, assessment and other matters) apply to a return under this paragraph as they apply to a return under section 76 (general requirement to make land transaction return), subject to the adaptation that references to the effective date of the transaction shall be read as references to the date referred to in sub-paragraph (1)(a) or (b).

(5) If the result as regards the rent paid or payable in respect of the first five years of the term of the lease is that less tax is payable in respect of the transaction than has already been paid –

    (a)   the purchaser may, within the period allowed for amendment of the land transaction return, amend the return accordingly;

    (b)   after the end of that period he may (if the land transaction return is not so amended) make a claim to the Inland Revenue for repayment of the amount overpaid..

Amendments: Inserted by Finance Act 2004, s 296, Sch 39; Finance Act 2007, s 80(1), (8), (9)(g).

Rent for overlap period in case of grant of further lease

9

(1) This paragraph applies –

    (a)   where A surrenders an existing lease to B ('the old lease') and in consideration of that surrender B grants a lease to A of the same or substantially the same premises ('the new lease'),

    (b)   the tenant under a lease ('the old lease') of premises to which Part 2 of the Landlord and Tenant Act 1954 or the Business Tenancies (Northern Ireland) Order 1996 applies makes a request for a new tenancy ('the new lease') which is duly executed.

    (c)   on termination of a lease ('the head lease') a sub-tenant is granted a lease ('the new lease') of the same or substantially the same premises as those comprised in his original lease ('the old lease') –

        (i)   in pursuance of an order of a court on a claim for relief against re-entry or forfeiture, or

        (ii)   in pursuance of a contractual entitlement arising in the event of the head lease being terminated,

    or

    (d)   a person who has guaranteed the obligations of a lessee under a lease that has been terminated ('the old lease') is granted a lease of the same or substantially the same premises ('the new lease') in pursuance of the guarantee.

(2) For the purposes of this Part the rent payable under the new lease in respect of any period falling within the overlap period is treated as reduced by the amount of the rent that would have been payable in respect of that period under the old lease.

(3) The overlap period is the period between the date of grant of the new lease and what would have been the end of the term of the old lease had it not been terminated.

(4) The rent that would have been payable under the old lease shall be taken to be the amount taken into account in determining the stamp duty land tax chargeable in respect of the acquisition of the old lease.

(5) This paragraph does not have effect so as to require the rent payable under the new lease to be treated as a negative amount.

Amendments: Inserted by Finance Act 2004, s 296, Sch 39.

Backdated lease granted to tenant holding over

9A

(1) This paragraph applies where –

    (a)   the tenant under a lease continues in occupation after the date on which, under its terms, the lease terminates ('the contractual termination date'),

    (b)   he is granted a new lease of the same or substantially the same premises, and

    (c)   the term of the new lease is expressed to begin on or immediately after the contractual termination date.

(2) The term of the new lease is treated for the purposes of this Part as beginning on the date on which it is expressed to begin.

(3) The rent payable under the new lease in respect of any period falling –

    (a)   after the contractual termination date, and

(b)   before the date on which the new lease is granted,

is treated for the purposes of this Part as reduced by the amount of taxable rent that is payable in respect of that period otherwise than under the new lease.

(4) For the purposes of sub-paragraph (3) rent is 'taxable' if or to the extent that it is taken into account in determining liability to stamp duty land tax.

(5) Sub-paragraph (3) does not have effect so as to require the rent payable under the new lease to be treated as a negative amount.

Amendments: Inserted by Finance Act 2006, s 164(5), Sch 25.

Tenants' obligations etc that do not count as chargeable consideration

10

(1) In the case of the grant of a lease none of the following counts as chargeable consideration –

(a)   any undertaking by the tenant to repair, maintain or insure the demised premises (in Scotland, the leased premises);

(b)   any undertaking by the tenant to pay any amount in respect of services, repairs, maintenance or insurance or the landlord's costs of management;

(c)   any other obligation undertaken by the tenant that is not such as to affect the rent that a tenant would be prepared to pay in the open market;

(d)   any guarantee of the payment of rent or the performance of any other obligation of the tenant under the lease;

(e)   any penal rent, or increased rent in the nature of a penal rent, payable in respect of the breach of any obligation of the tenant under the lease.

(f)   any liability of the tenant for costs under section 14(2) of the Leasehold Reform Act 1967 or section 60 of the Leasehold Reform, Housing and Urban Development Act 1993 (costs to be borne by person exercising statutory right to be granted lease);

(g)   any other obligation of the tenant to bear the landlord's reasonable costs or expenses of or incidental to the grant of a lease;

(h)   any obligation under the lease to transfer to the landlord, on the termination of the lease, payment entitlements granted to the tenant under the single payment scheme (that is, the scheme of income support for farmers in pursuance of Title III of Council Regulation (EC) No 1782/2003) in respect of land subject to the lease.

(2) Where sub-paragraph (1) applies in relation to an obligation, a payment made in discharge of the obligation does not count as chargeable consideration.

(3) The release of any such obligation as is mentioned in sub-paragraph (1) does not count as chargeable consideration in relation to the surrender of the lease.

Amendment: SI 2006/875.

Cases where assignment of lease treated as grant of lease

11

(1) This paragraph applies where the grant of a lease is exempt from charge by virtue of any of the provisions specified in sub-paragraph (3).

(2) The first assignment of the lease that is not exempt from charge by virtue of any of the provisions specified in sub-paragraph (3), and in relation to which the assignee does not acquire the lease as a bare trustee of the assignor, is treated for the purposes of this Part as if it were the grant of a lease by the assignor –

    (a)   for a term equal to the unexpired term of the lease referred to in sub-paragraph (1), and

    (b)   on the same terms as those on which the assignee holds that lease after the assignment.

(3) The provisions are –

    (a)   section 57A (sale and leaseback arrangements);

    (b)   Part 1 or 2 of Schedule 7 (group relief or reconstruction or acquisition relief);

    (c)   section 66 (transfers involving public bodies);

    (d)   Schedule 8 (charities relief);

    (e)   any such regulations as are mentioned in section 123(3) (regulations reproducing in relation to stamp duty land tax the effect of enactments providing for exemption from stamp duty).

(4) This paragraph does not apply where the relief in question is group relief, reconstruction or acquisition relief or charities relief and is withdrawn as a result of a disqualifying event occurring before the effective date of the assignment.

(5) For the purposes of sub-paragraph (4) 'disqualifying event' means –

    (a)   in relation to the withdrawal of group relief, the event falling within paragraph 3(1)(a) of Schedule 7 (purchaser ceasing to be a member of the same group as the vendor), as read with paragraph 4A of that Schedule;

    (b)   in relation to the withdrawal of reconstruction or acquisition relief, the change of control of the acquiring company mentioned in paragraph 9(1)(a) of that Schedule or, as the case may be, the event mentioned in paragraph 11(1)(a) or (2)(a) of that Schedule;

    (c)   in relation to the withdrawal of charities relief, a disqualifying event as defined in paragraph 2(3) of Schedule 8.

Amendments: Inserted by Finance Act 2004, s 296, Sch 39; Finance (No 2) Act 2005, s 49, Sch 10.

Assignment of lease: responsibility of assignee for returns etc

12

(1) Where a lease is assigned, anything that but for the assignment would be required or authorised to be done by or in relation to the assignor under or by virtue of –

    (a)   section 80 (adjustment where contingency ceases or consideration is ascertained),

    (b)   section 81A (return or further return in consequence of later linked transaction),

    (c)   paragraph 3 or 4 of this Schedule (return or further return required where lease for indefinite period continues), or

    (d)   paragraph 8 of this Schedule (adjustment where rent ceases to be uncertain),

shall, if the event giving rise to the adjustment or return occurs after the effective date of the assignment, be done instead by or in relation to the assignee.

(2) So far as necessary for giving effect to sub-paragraph (1) anything previously done by or in relation to the assignor shall be treated as if it had been done by or in relation to the assignee.

(3) This paragraph does not apply if the assignment falls to be treated as the grant of a lease by the assignor (see paragraph 11).

Agreement for lease

12A

(1) This paragraph applies where in England and Wales or Northern Ireland –

    (a)   an agreement for a lease is entered into, and
    (b)   the agreement is substantially performed without having been completed.

(2) The agreement is treated as if it were the grant of a lease in accordance with the agreement ('the notional lease'), beginning with the date of substantial performance.

The effective date of the transaction is that date.

(3) Where a lease is subsequently granted in pursuance of the agreement –

    (a)   the notional lease is treated as if it were surrendered at that time, and
    (b)   the lease itself is treated for the purposes of paragraph 9 (rent for overlap period in case of grant of further lease) as if it were granted in consideration of that surrender.

Paragraph 5 does not apply so as to treat the notional lease and the lease itself as a single lease.

(4) Where sub-paragraph (1) applies and the agreement is (to any extent) afterwards rescinded or annulled, or is for any other reason not carried into effect, the tax paid by virtue of that sub-paragraph shall (to that extent) be repaid by the Inland Revenue.

Repayment must be claimed by amendment of the land transaction return made in respect of the agreement.

(5) In this paragraph 'substantially performed' and 'completed' have the same meanings as in section 44 (contract and conveyance)

Amendments: Inserted by Finance Act 2004, s 296, Sch 39: Finance Act 2006, s 164(5), Sch 25.

Assignment of agreement for lease

12B

(1) This paragraph applies, in place of section 45 (contract and conveyance: effect of transfer of rights), where in England and Wales or Northern Ireland a person assigns his interest as lessee under an agreement for a lease.

(2) If the assignment occurs without the agreement having been substantially performed, section 44 (contract and conveyance) has effect as if –

    (a)   the contract were with the assignee and not the assignor, and
    (b)   the consideration given by the assignee for entering into the contract included any consideration given by him for the assignment.

(3) If the assignment occurs after the agreement has been substantially performed –

    (a)   the assignment is a separate land transaction, and

(b)   the effective date of that transaction is the date of the assignment.

(4) Where there are successive assignments, this paragraph has effect in relation to each of them.

Amendments: Inserted by Finance Act 2004, s 296, Sch 39.

Increase of rent treated as grant of new lease: in first five years variation of lease

13

(1) Where a lease is varied so as to increase the amount of the rent as from a date before the end of the fifth year of the term of the lease, the variation is treated for the purposes of this Part as if it were the grant of a lease in consideration of the additional rent made payable by it.

(2) Sub-paragraph (1) does not apply to an increase of rent in pursuance of –

(a)   a provision contained in the lease, or
(b)   a provision mentioned in any of paragraphs (a) to (d) of paragraph 7(4A).

Amendments: Finance Act 2006, s 164(5), Sch 25.

Increase of rent treated as grant of new lease: abnormal increase after fifth year

14

(1) This paragraph applies if, after the end of the fifth year of the term of a lease –

(a)   the amount of rent payable increases (or is increased), whether in in accordance with the provisions of the lease or otherwise, and
(b)   the rent payable as a result ('the new rent') is such that the increase falls to be regarded as abnormal (see paragraph 15).

(2) The increase in rent is treated as if it were the grant of a lease in consideration of the excess rent.

(3) The excess rent is the difference between the new rent and the rent previously taxed.

(4) Where the provisions of this paragraph have not previously applied to an increase in the rent payable under the lease, the rent previously taxed is –

(a)   if paragraph (b) or (c) does not apply, the rent payable under the lease without the increase referred to in sub-paragraph (1);
(b)   if the amount of rent payable under the lease is determined under paragraph 7 (variable or uncertain rent), the rent that is assumed to be payable after the fifth year of the term of the lease (in accordance with paragraph 7(3));
(c)   if there has been a variation in the lease falling within paragraph 13 (increase of rent treated as grant of new lease: variation of lease in first five years), the rent payable as a result of the variation (or, if there has been more than one such variation, the most recent one).

(4A) Where the provisions of this paragraph have previously applied to an increase in the rent payable under the lease, the rent previously taxed is the rent payable as a result of the last increase in relation to which the provisions of this paragraph applied.

(4B) In determining the rent previously taxed, disregard paragraphs 9(2) and 9A(3) (deemed reduction of rent, where further lease granted, for period during which rents overlap).

(5) The deemed grant is treated as –

(a)   made on the date on which the increased rent first became payable, and

(b)   for a term equal to the unexpired part of the original lease,

and as linked with the grant of the original lease (and with any other transaction with which that transaction is linked).

(6) The assumption in paragraph 7(3) (that the rent does not change after the end of the fifth year of the term of a lease) does not apply for the purposes of this paragraph or paragraph 15 except for the purpose of determining the rent previously taxed.

(7) The reference to a lease in sub-paragraph (1) is to –

(a)   a lease actually granted on or after the implementation date, or

(b)   a lease that is treated as existing by reason of a deemed grant under paragraph 12A(2) or 19(3) of which the effective date is on or after the implementation date.

Amendments: Finance Act 2006, s 164(5), Sch 25.

Increase of rent after fifth year: whether regarded as abnormal

15

Whether an increase in rent is to be regarded for the purposes of paragraph 14 as abnormal is determined as follows –

Step One

Find the start date.

Where the provisions of paragraph 14 have not previously applied to an increase in the rent payable under the lease, the start date is –

(a)   if paragraph (b) or (c) does not apply, the beginning of the term of the lease;

(b)   if the amount of rent payable under the lease is determined under paragraph 7 (variable or uncertain rent), the beginning of the period by reference to which the rent assumed to be payable after the fifth year of the term of the lease is determined in accordance with paragraph 7(3);

(c)   if there has been a variation in the lease falling within paragraph 13 (increase of rent treated as grant of new lease: variation of lease in first five years), the date of the variation (or, if there has been more than one such variation, the date of the most recent one).

Where the provisions of paragraph 14 have previously applied to an increase in the rent payable under the lease, the start date is the date of the last increase in relation to which the provisions of that paragraph applied.

Step Two

Find the number of whole years in the period between the start date and the date on which the new rent first becomes payable.

Step Three

The rent increase is regarded as abnormal if the excess rent (see paragraph 14(3)) is greater than:

$$\frac{R \times Y}{5}$$

where –

R is the rent previously taxed (see paragraph 14(4) or (4A)), and

Y is the number of whole years found under Step Two.

Amendments: Finance Act 2006, s 164(5), Sch 25.

Reduction of rent or term or other variation of lease

15A

(1) Where a lease is varied so as to reduce the amount of the rent, the variation is treated for the purposes of this Part as an acquisition of a chargeable interest by the lessee.

(1A) Where any consideration in money or money's worth (other than an increase in rent) is given by the lessee for any variation of a lease, other than a variation of the amount of the rent or of the term of the lease, the variation is treated for the purposes of this Part as an acquisition of a chargeable interest by the lessee.

(2) Where a lease is varied so as to reduce the term, the variation is treated for the purposes of this Part as an acquisition of a chargeable interest by the lessor.

Amendments: Inserted by Finance Act 2004, s 296, Sch 39: Finance (No 2) Act 2005, s 49, Sch 10.

Surrender of existing lease in return for new lease

16

Where a lease is granted in consideration of the surrender of an existing lease between the same parties –

(a) the grant of the new lease does not count as chargeable consideration for the surrender, and

(b) the surrender does not count as chargeable consideration for the grant of the new lease.

Paragraph 5 (exchanges) of Schedule 4 (chargeable consideration) does not apply in such a case.

Amendments: Finance Act 2004, s 296, Sch 39.

Assignment of lease: assumption of obligations by assignee

17

In the case of an assignment of a lease the assumption by the assignee of the obligation –

(a) to pay rent, or

(b) to perform or observe any other undertaking of the tenant under the lease,

does not count as chargeable consideration for the assignment.

Reverse premium

18

(1) In the case of the grant, assignment or surrender of a lease a reverse premium does not count as chargeable consideration.

(2) A 'reverse premium' means –

(a)   in relation to the grant of a lease, a premium moving from the landlord to the tenant;

(b)   in relation to the assignment of a lease, a premium moving from the assignor to the assignee;

(c)   in relation to the surrender of a lease, a premium moving from the tenant to the landlord.Provisions relating to leases in Scotland

Loan or deposit in connection with grant or assignment of lease

18A

(1) Where, under arrangements made in connection with the grant of a lease –

(a)   the lessee, or any person connected with him or acting on his behalf, pays a deposit, or makes a loan, to any person, and

(b)   he repayment of all or part of the deposit or loan is contingent on anything done or omitted to be done by the lessee or on the death of the lessee,

the amount of the deposit or loan (disregarding any repayment) is to be taken for the purposes of this Part to be consideration other than rent given for the grant of the lease.

(2) Where, under arrangements made in connection with the assignment of a lease –

(a)   the assignee, or any person connected with him or acting on his behalf, pays a deposit, or makes a loan, to any person, and

(b)   the repayment of all or part of the deposit or loan is contingent on anything done or omitted to be done by the assignee or on the death of the assignee,

the amount of the deposit or loan (disregarding any repayment) is to be taken for the purposes of this Part to be consideration other than rent given for the assignment of the lease.

(3) Sub-paragraph (1) or (2) does not apply in relation to a deposit if the amount that would otherwise fall within the sub-paragraph in question in relation to the grant or (as the case requires) assignment of the lease is not more than twice the relevant maximum rent.

(4) The relevant maximum rent is –

(a)   in relation to the grant of a lease, the highest amount of rent payable in respect of any consecutive twelve month period in the first five years of the term;

(b)   in relation to the assignment of a lease, the highest amount of rent payable in respect of any consecutive twelve month period in the first five years of the term remaining outstanding as at the date of the assignment,

the highest amount of rent being determined (in either case) in the same way as the highest amount of rent mentioned in paragraph 7(3).

(5) Tax is not chargeable by virtue of this paragraph –

(a)   merely because of paragraph 9A of Schedule 5 (which excludes the 0% band in Table B in section 55(2) in cases where the relevant rent attributable to non-residential property is not less than £1,000 a year), or

(b)   merely because of paragraph 5(4)(b), 6(6)(b), 9(4)(b) or 10(6)(b) of Schedule 6 (which make similar provision in relation to land which is wholly or partly residential property and is wholly or partly situated in a disadvantaged area).

(6) Section 839 of the Taxes Act 1988 (connected persons) has effect for the purposes of this paragraph.

Amendments: Inserted by Finance (No 2) Act 2005, s 49, Sch 10, Pt 1, paras 1, 14, 16(5), (8).

19

(1) In the application of this Part to Scotland –

(a)   any reference to the term of a lease is to the period of the lease, and

(b)   any reference to the reversion on a lease is to the interest of the landlord in the property subject to the lease.

(2) Where in Scotland there is a lease constituted by concluded missives of let ('the first lease') and at some later time a lease is executed ('the second lease') –

(a)   the first lease is treated as if it were surrendered at that time, and

(b)   the second lease is treated for the purposes of paragraph 9 (rent for overlap period in case of grant of further lease) as if it were granted in consideration of that surrender.

Paragraph 5 does not apply so as to treat the first lease and the second lease as a single lease.

(3) Where in Scotland –

(a)   there is an agreement (including missives of let not constituting a lease) under which a lease is to be executed, and

(b)   the agreement is substantially performed without a lease having been executed,

the agreement is treated as if it were the grant of a lease in accordance with the agreement ('the notional lease'), beginning with the date of substantial performance.

The effective date of the transaction is when the agreement is substantially performed.

(4) Where sub-paragraph (3) applies and at some later time a lease is executed –

(a)   the notional lease is treated as if it were surrendered at that time, and

(b)   the lease itself is treated for the purposes of paragraph 9 as if it were granted in consideration of that surrender.

Paragraph 5 does not apply so as to treat the notional lease and the lease itself as a single lease.

(5) References in sub-paragraphs (2) to (4) to the execution of a lease are to the execution of a lease that either is in conformity with, or relates to substantially the same property and period as, the missives of let or other agreement.

(6) Where sub-paragraph (3) applies and the agreement is (to any extent) afterwards rescinded or annulled, or is for any other reason not carried into effect, the tax paid by virtue of that sub-paragraph shall (to that extent) be repaid by the Inland Revenue.

Repayment must be claimed by amendment of the land transaction return made in respect of the agreement

Amendments: Finance Act 2004, s 296, Sch 39; Finance Act 2006, s 164(5), Sch 25.

Amendments: Schedule inserted by Finance Act 2004, s 296, Sch 39.

Schedule 18

Section 123

Stamp Duty Land Tax: Consequential Amendments

Provisional Collection of Taxes Act 1968

1

In section 1(1) of the Provisional Collection of Taxes Act 1968 (c 2), after 'stamp duty reserve tax,' insert 'stamp duty land tax,'.

Inheritance Tax Act 1984

2

In section 190(4) of the Inheritance Tax Act 1984 (c 51) (sale of land from deceased's estate: determination of price), after 'stamp duty' insert 'or stamp duty land tax'.

Income and Corporation Taxes Act 1988

3

(1) The Income and Corporation Taxes Act 1988 (c 1) is amended as follows.

(2) In section 209B(4) (hedging arrangements), in subsection (4) for 'or stamp duty' substitute '(including stamp duty or stamp duty land tax)'.

(3) In section 213 (exempt distributions), in subsection (11)(a) for 'stamp duty' substitute 'stamp duty or stamp duty land tax'.

(4) In section 214 (chargeable payments connected with exempt distributions), in subsection (2) for 'stamp duty' substitute 'stamp duty or stamp duty land tax'.

(5) In section 215 (advance clearance by Board of distributions and payments), in subsection (2) for 'stamp duty' substitute 'stamp duty or stamp duty land tax'.

(6) In section 827 (penalties and interest not allowed as deductions for tax purposes), after subsection (1E) insert –

'(1F) Where a person is liable to make a payment by way of –
      (a)   any penalty under Part 4 of the Finance Act 2003(stamp duty land tax), or
      (b)   interest under any provision of that Part,

the payment shall not be allowed as a deduction in computing any income, profits or losses for any tax purposes.'.

Finance Act 1989

4

In section 178(2) of the Finance Act 1989 (c 26) (power of Treasury to set rates of interest: enactments to which the section applies), after paragraph (q) add –

'(r)   sections 87, 88 and 89 of the Finance Act 2003'.

Taxation of Chargeable Gains Act 1992

5

In section 38(2) of the Taxation of Chargeable Gains Act 1992 (c 12) (incidental costs of acquisition or disposal), after 'stamp duty' insert 'or stamp duty land tax'.

Income Tax (Earnings and Pensions) Act 2003

6

In section 277 of the Income Tax (Earnings and Pensions) Act 2003 (c 1) (removal benefits and expenses: acquisition of property), in subsection (3)(e) after 'stamp duty' insert 'or stamp duty land tax'.

Schedule 19

Section 124

Stamp Duty Land Tax: Commencement And Transitional Provisions

Introduction

1

(1) Subject to the provisions of this Schedule, the provisions of this Part come into force on the passing of this Act.

(2) The following provisions have effect as regards what transactions are SDLT transactions, that is, are chargeable or notifiable or are transactions in relation to which section 79 (registration etc) applies.

(3) Nothing in this Schedule shall be read as meaning that other transactions, whether effected before or after the passing of this Act, are to be disregarded in applying the provisions of this Part.

The implementation date

2

(1) A transaction is not an SDLT transaction unless the effective date of the transaction is on or after the implementation date.

(2) In this Part 'the implementation date' means the date appointed by Treasury order as the implementation date for the purposes of stamp duty land tax.

Contract entered into before first relevant date

3

(1) Subject to the following provisions of this paragraph, a transaction is not an SDLT transaction if it is effected in pursuance of a contract entered into before the first relevant date.

(2) The 'first relevant date' is the day after the passing of this Act.

(3) The exclusion of transactions effected in pursuance of contracts entered into before the first relevant date does not apply –

(a) if there is any variation of the contract or assignment of rights under the contract on or after that date;

(b) if the transaction is effected in consequence of the exercise after that date of any option, right of pre-emption or similar right;

(c) if on or after that date there is an assignment, subsale or other transaction (relating to the whole or part of the subject-matter of the contract) as a result of which a person other than the purchaser under the contract becomes entitled to call for a conveyance to him.

Amendments: Finance Act 2004, s 296, Sch 39.

Contract substantially performed before implementation date

4

(1) This paragraph applies where a transaction –

(a) is completed on or after the implementation date,

(b) is effected in pursuance of a contract entered into and substantially performed before that date, and

(c) is not excluded from being an SDLT transaction by paragraph 3.

(2) The transaction is not an SDLT transaction if the contract was substantially performed before the first relevant date.

(3) In any other case, the fact that the contract was substantially performed before the implementation date does not affect the matter.

Accordingly, the effective date of the transaction is the date of completion.

Contracts substantially performed after implementation date

4A

Where –

(a) a transaction is effected in pursuance of a contract entered into before the first relevant date,

(b) the contract is substantially performed, without having been completed, after the implementation date, and

(c) there is subsequently an event within paragraph 3(3) by virtue of which the transaction is an SDLT transaction,

the effective date of the transaction shall be taken to be the date of the event referred in paragraph (c) (and not the date of substantial performance).

Amendments: Inserted by Finance Act 2004, s 296, Sch 39.

Application of provisions in case of transfer of rights

4B

(1) This paragraph applies where section 44 (contract and conveyance) has effect in accordance with section 45 (effect of transfer of rights).

(2) Any reference in paragraph 3, 4 or 4A to the date when a contract was entered into (or made) shall be read, in relation to a contract deemed to exist by virtue of

section 45(3) (deemed secondary contract with transferee), as a reference to the date of the assignment, subsale or other transaction in question.

Amendments: Inserted by Finance Act 2004, s 296, Sch 39.

Credit for ad valorem stamp duty paid

5

(1) Where a transaction chargeable to stamp duty land tax is effected in pursuance of a contract entered into before the implementation date, any *ad valorem* stamp duty paid on the contract shall go to reduce the amount of tax payable (but not so as to give rise to any repayment).

(2) Where the application or operation of any exemption or relief from stamp duty land tax turns on whether tax was paid or payable in respect of an earlier transaction, that requirement is treated as met if *ad valorem* stamp duty was paid or (as the case may be) payable in respect of the instrument by which that transaction was effected.

Effect for stamp duty purposes of stamp duty land tax being paid or chargeable

6

(1) ...

(2) The references in section 111(1)(c) of, and paragraph 4(3) of Schedule 34 to, the Finance Act 2002 (c 23) (which relate to the circumstances in which stamp duty group relief is withdrawn) to a transfer at market value by a duly stamped instrument on which *ad valorem* duty was paid and in respect of which group relief was not claimed shall be read, on or after the implementation date, as including a reference to a transfer at market value by a chargeable transaction in respect of which relief under Part 1 of Schedule 7 to this Act was available but was not claimed.

(3) The references in section 113(1)(c) of, and in paragraph 3(3) or 4(3) of Schedule 35 to, the Finance Act 2002 (which relate to the circumstances in which stamp duty company acquisitions relief is withdrawn) to a transfer at market value by a duly stamped instrument on which *ad valorem* duty was paid and in respect of which section 76 relief was not claimed shall be read, on or after the implementation date, as including a reference to a transfer at market value by a chargeable transaction on which stamp duty land tax was chargeable and in respect of which relief under Part 2 of Schedule 7 to this Act was available but was not claimed.

Amendments: Finance Act 2004, s 326, Sch 42.

Earlier related transactions under stamp duty

7

(1) In relation to a transaction that is not an SDLT transaction but which is linked to an SDLT transaction and accordingly falls to be taken into account in determining the rate of stamp duty land tax chargeable on the latter transaction, any reference in this Part to the chargeable consideration for the first-mentioned transaction shall be read as a reference to the consideration by reference to which *ad valorem* stamp duty was payable in respect of the instrument by which that transaction was effected.

(2) In paragraph 3 of Schedule 9 (relief for transfer of reversion under shared ownership lease where election made for market value treatment) and paragraph 4A of

that Schedule (shared ownership lease: treatment of staircasing transaction) as they apply in a case where the original lease was granted before the implementation date –

(a)   the reference to a lease to which paragraph 2 of that Schedule applies shall be read as a reference to a lease to which section 97 of the Finance Act 1980 applied (which made provision for stamp duty corresponding to that paragraph), and

(b)   a reference to an election having been made for tax to be charged in accordance with paragraph 2 or 4 of that Schedule shall be read as a reference to the lease having contained a statement of the parties' intention such as is mentioned in section 97(2)(d) of the Finance Act 1980 or, as the case may be, paragraph (d) of section 108(5) of the Finance Act 1981 (which made provision for stamp duty corresponding to paragraph 4).

(3) In section 54 (exceptions from deemed market value rule for transactions with connected company) the reference in subsection (4)(b) to group relief having been claimed in respect of a transaction shall be read in relation to a transaction carried out before the implementation date as a reference to relief having been claimed under section 42 of the Finance Act 1930 (c 28), section 11 of the Finance Act (Northern Ireland) 1954 (c 23 (NI)) or section 151 of the Finance Act 1995 (c 4) in respect of stamp duty on the instrument by which the transaction was effected.

(4) For the purposes of paragraph 5 of Schedule 17A (treatment of successive linked leases) no account shall be taken of any transaction that is not an SDLT transaction.

Amendments: Finance Act 2004, ss 296, 303(3), Sch 39.

Stamping of contract where transaction on completion subject to stamp duty land tax

7A

(1) This paragraph applies where –

(a)   a contract that apart from paragraph 7 of Schedule 13 to the Finance Act 1999 (contracts chargeable as conveyances on sale) would not be chargeable with stamp duty is entered into before the implementation date,

(b)   a conveyance made in conformity with the contract is effected on or after the implementation date, and

(c)   the transaction effected on completion is an SDLT transaction or would be but for an exemption or relief from stamp duty land tax.

(2) If in those circumstances the contract is presented for stamping together with a Revenue certificate as to compliance with the provisions of this Part of this Act in relation to the transaction effected on completion –

(a)   the payment of stamp duty land tax on that transaction or, as the case may be, the fact that no such tax was payable shall be denoted on the contract by a particular stamp, and

(b)   the contract shall be deemed thereupon to be duly stamped.

(3) In this paragraph 'conveyance' includes any instrument.

Amendments: Inserted by Finance Act 2004, s 296, Sch 39.

Stamping of agreement for lease where grant of lease subject to stamp duty land tax

8

(1) This paragraph applies where –

    (a)   an agreement for a lease is entered into before the implementation date,

    (b)   a lease giving effect to the agreement is executed on or after that date, and

    (c)   the transaction effected on completion is an SDLT transaction or would be but for an exemption or relief from stamp duty land tax.

(2) If in those circumstances the agreement is presented for stamping together with a Revenue certificate as to compliance with the provisions of this Part of this Act in relation to the grant of the lease –

    (a)   the payment of stamp duty land tax in respect of the grant of the lease or, as the case may be, the fact that no such tax was payable shall be denoted on the agreement by a particular stamp, and

    (b)   the agreement shall be deemed thereupon to be duly stamped.

(3) For the purposes of this paragraph a lease gives effect to an agreement if the lease either is in conformity with the agreement or relates to substantially the same property and term as the agreement.

(4) References in this paragraph to an agreement for a lease include missives of let in Scotland.

Amendments: Inserted by Finance Act 2004, s 296, Sch 39.

Exercise of option or right of pre-emption acquired before implementation date

9

(1) This paragraph applies where –

    (a)   an option binding the grantor to enter into a land transaction, or

    (b)   a right of pre-emption preventing the grantor from entering into, or restricting the right of the grantor to enter into, a land transaction,

is acquired before the implementation date and exercised on or after that date.

(2) Where the option or right was acquired on or after 17th April 2003, any consideration for the acquisition is treated as part of the chargeable consideration for the transaction resulting from the exercise of the option or right.

(3) Where the option or right was varied on or after 17th April 2003 and before the implementation date, any consideration for the variation is treated as part of the chargeable consideration for the transaction resulting from the exercise of the option or right.

(4) Whether or not sub-paragraph (2) or (3) applies, the acquisition of the option or right and any variation of the option or right is treated as linked with the land transaction resulting from the exercise of the option or right.

But not so as to require the consideration for the acquisition or variation to be counted twice in determining the rate of tax chargeable on the land transaction resulting from the exercise of the option or right.

(5) Where this paragraph applies any *ad valorem* stamp duty paid on the acquisition or variation of the option or right shall go to reduce the amount of tax payable on the transaction resulting from the exercise of the option or right (but not so as to give rise to any repayment).

Supplementary

10

In this Schedule 'contract' includes any agreement.

Schedule 20

Section 125

Stamp Duty: Restriction To Instruments Relating To Stock Or Marketable Securities

PART 1
SUPPLEMENTARY PROVISIONS

Reduction of stamp duty where instrument partly relating to stock or marketable securities

1

(1) This paragraph applies where stamp duty under Part 1 of Schedule 13 to the Finance Act 1999 (c 16) (transfer on sale) is chargeable on an instrument that relates partly to stock or marketable securities and partly to property other than stock or marketable securities.

(2) In such a case –

    (a)   the consideration in respect of which duty would otherwise be charged shall be apportioned, on a just and reasonable basis, as between the stock or marketable securities and the other property, and

    (b)   the instrument shall be charged only in respect of the consideration attributed to the stock or marketable securities.

Apportionment of consideration for stamp duty purposes

2

(1) Where part of the property referred to in section 58(1) of the Stamp Act 1891 (c 39) (consideration to be apportioned between different instruments as parties think fit) consists of stock or marketable securities, that provision shall have effect as if 'the parties think fit' read 'is just and reasonable'.

(2) Where –

    (a)   part of the property referred to in section 58(2) of the Stamp Act 1891 (property contracted to be purchased by two or more persons etc) consists of stock or marketable securities, and

    (b)   both or (as the case may be) all the relevant persons are connected with one another,

that provision shall have effect as if the words from 'for distinct parts of the consideration' to the end of the subsection read ', the consideration shall be apportioned in such manner as is just and reasonable, so that a distinct consideration for each part of the property transferred is set forth in the transfer relating to that part, and the transfer shall be charged with *ad valorem* duty in respect of that consideration.'

(3) If in a case where sub-paragraph (1) or (2) applies the consideration is apportioned in a manner that is not just and reasonable, the enactments relating to stamp duty shall have effect as if –

(a)   the consideration had been apportioned in a manner that is just and reasonable, and

(b)   the amount of any distinct consideration set forth in any transfer relating to a part of the property transferred were such amount as is found by a just and reasonable apportionment (and not the amount actually set forth).

(4) For the purposes of sub-paragraph (2) –

(a)   a person is a relevant person if he is a person by or for whom the property is contracted to be purchased;

(b)   the question whether persons are connected with one another shall be determined in accordance with section 839 of the Taxes Act 1988.

PART 2
CONSEQUENTIAL AMENDMENTS AND REPEALS

Removal of unnecessary references to 'conveyance'

3

In the enactments relating to stamp duty for 'conveyance or transfer', wherever occurring, substitute 'transfer'.

Finance Act 1895

4

In section 12 of the Finance Act 1895 (c 16) (collection of stamp duty in cases of property vested by Act or purchased under statutory powers) –

(a)   in paragraph (a) for 'property is' substitute 'stock or marketable securities are';

(b)   in paragraph (b) for 'property' substitute 'stock or marketable securities';

(c)   in the closing words for 'conveyance', in both places where that word occurs, substitute 'transfer'.

Finance Act 1990

5

In section 108 of the Finance Act 1990 (c 29) (transfer of securities: abolition of stamp duty), for subsections (1) to (6) substitute –

'(1) Stamp duty shall not be chargeable under Schedule 13 to the Finance Act 1999 (transfer of securities).'

Finance Act 1999

6

In paragraph 1(2) of Schedule 13 to the Finance Act 1999 (c 16) for 'conveyance on sale' substitute 'transfer on sale'.

Power to make further consequential amendments or repeals

7

(1) The Treasury may by regulations make such other amendments or repeals of enactments relating to stamp duty or stamp duty reserve tax as appear to them appropriate in consequence of the abolition of stamp duty except on instruments relating to stock or marketable securities.

(2) The regulations may include such transitional provisions and savings as appear to the Treasury to be appropriate.

(3) Regulations under this paragraph shall be made by statutory instrument which shall be subject to annulment in pursuance of a resolution of the House of Commons.

Appendix 2

STAMP DUTY LAND TAX (ADMINISTRATION) REGULATIONS 2003

SI 2003/2837

PART 1
GENERAL

1 Citation and commencement

(1) These Regulations may be cited as the Stamp Duty Land Tax (Administration) Regulations 2003 and shall come into force on 1st December 2003.

2 Interpretation

(1) In these Regulations

'the 2003 Act' means the Finance Act 2003;
'the Board' means the Commissioners of Inland Revenue;
'HMRC' means Her Majesty's Revenue and Customs;
'land transaction return' has the meaning given by section 76(1).

(2) In these Regulations, a reference to a numbered section without more is a reference to the section of the 2003 Act bearing that number.

Amendments: SI 2009/56.

PART 2
REVENUE CERTIFICATES AND SELF-CERTIFICATES

3 Interpretation of Part 2

In this Part

'the Inland Revenue' means any officer of the Board;
'Revenue certificate' has the meaning given by section 79(3)(a);
'purchaser' has the meaning given by section 43(4);
'self-certificate' has the meaning given by section 79(3)(b);
'vendor' has the meaning given by section 43(4).

4 Conditions to be met before a Revenue certificate is issued

(1) The conditions specified in paragraphs (2) to (5) must be met before a Revenue certificate is issued.

(2) The first condition is that a land transaction return in respect of the transaction must have been received by the Inland Revenue.

(3) The second condition is that the return (together with any other returns that are required) –

(a)   has been completed; and
(b)   includes any declaration required by paragraph 1(1)(c) of Schedule 10 to the 2003 Act.

(4) The third condition is that –

(a)   as required by section 76(3)(a), a self-assessment is included in the return; and
(b)   on the basis of the information contained in the return, the self-assessment appears to be correct.

(5) The fourth condition is that, as required by section 76(3)(b), payment of the amount of tax chargeable in respect of the transaction accompanies the return.

5 Form and contents of Revenue certificates

(1) A Revenue certificate must be in writing and must contain the information prescribed by paragraphs (2) to (7).

(2) The information prescribed by this paragraph is the address of the land to which the transaction relates.

(3) The information prescribed by this paragraph is any number recorded –

(a)   as the title number of the land –
       (i)   for England and Wales, in the register of title maintained by the Chief Land Registrar;
       (ii)   for Scotland, in the Land Register of Scotland maintained by the Keeper of the Registers of Scotland;
(b)   for Northern Ireland, as the folio number of the land in any registry maintained by the Land Registry of Northern Ireland.

(4) The information prescribed by this paragraph is any National Land and Property Gazetteer Unique Property Reference Number.

(5) The information prescribed by this paragraph is a description of the transaction.

(6) The information prescribed by this paragraph is the effective date in relation to the transaction (within the meaning given by section 119).

(7) The information prescribed by this paragraph is –

(a)   the name of the purchaser; and
(b)   the name of the vendor.

6 Duplicate Revenue certificates

(1) If the Inland Revenue are satisfied that a Revenue certificate has been lost or destroyed ('the original certificate'), a duplicate Revenue certificate may be issued.

(2) The duplicate Revenue certificate may be issued in the form of –

(a)   a Revenue certificate equivalent to, and replacing, the original certificate; or
(b)   a new Revenue certificate superseding the original certificate.

7 Multiple Revenue certificates

(1) This regulation applies where a land transaction return is made relating to more than one transaction.

(2) Subject to paragraph (3), the Inland Revenue shall issue one Revenue certificate in respect of the transactions to which the return relates.

(3) If the purchaser requests on the return that separate Revenue certificates be issued in respect of each of the transactions to which the return relates, the Inland Revenue may provide separate certificates in respect of any of those transactions.

8 Form and contents of self-certificate

(1) A self-certificate must be in writing and –

   (a)   on the form prescribed by Schedule 1; or
   (b)   in a form that has been approved by the Board.

(2) A self-certificate must contain the information required by the form prescribed by Schedule 1.

PART 3
LAND TRANSACTION RETURNS

9 Form and contents of land transaction return

(1) A land transaction return must be in writing and completed in black ink.

(2) A land transaction return must be –

   (a)   on the form prescribed by Part 1 of Schedule 2 together with any of the forms prescribed by Parts 2 to 4 of that Schedule which are relevant; or
   (b)   in a form that has been approved by the Board.

(3) A land transaction return must contain the information required by the forms prescribed by Schedule 2.

PART 4
DEFERRED PAYMENTS

10 Interpretation of this Part

(1) In this Part –

   'application' means an application under section 90;
   'the Inland Revenue' means any officer of the Board;
   'relevant events' has the meaning given by regulation 12(2)(c).

11 When application to be made

An application must be made on or before the last day of the period within which the land transaction return relating to the transaction in question must be delivered.

12 Form and contents of application

(1) An application must be in writing.

(2) An application must set out all the facts and circumstances relevant to it and, in particular, must specify –

  (a) the consideration to which it relates;
  (b) the respects in which that consideration is contingent or uncertain; and
  (c) the events ('relevant events') on the occurrence of which the whole or any part of that consideration will –
      (i)   cease to be contingent, or
      (ii) become ascertained.

13 Additional contents of application where consideration consists of works or services

(1) This regulation applies where the consideration to which an application relates, or any element of that consideration, consists of –

  (a) the carrying out of works of construction, improvement or repair of a building or other works to enhance the value of land; or
  (b) the provision of services (other than the carrying out of such works).

(2) The application must contain a scheme for payment of tax which must include –

  (a) a proposal for the payment of tax in respect of the consideration, or element of the consideration, consisting of the carrying out of such works or the provision of such services within 30 days after the carrying out or provision is substantially completed;
  (b) if the carrying out of such works or the provision of such services is expected to last for more than 6 months, proposals for a scheme of payment of tax at intervals of not more than 6 months.

14 Provision of information

(1) The Inland Revenue may by notice in writing require a person by whom an application is made to provide such information as they may reasonably require for the purposes of determining whether to accept the application.

(2) A notice given under this regulation must specify the time (which must not be less than 30 days from the date of issue of the notice) within which the applicant must comply with it.

15 Recovery of tax not postponed by application

(1) This regulation applies where an application has been made but has not been accepted by the Inland Revenue (including where there is an appeal under regulation 19 against the refusal of the application).

(2) The tax in respect of the chargeable consideration to which the application relates remains due and payable as if there had been no application (and, if relevant, no appeal).

This is subject to –

  (a) the following paragraphs of this regulation;
  (b) regulation 22 (direction by tribunal postponing payment); and
  (c) regulation 23 (agreement to postpone payment).

(3) Payment of an amount of such tax as would not be due and payable if the application were accepted shall be postponed pending the reaching of a decision on the application.

(4) If an application is refused by the Inland Revenue, and there is no appeal under regulation 19 against the refusal of the application, the date on which any tax the payment of which had been postponed under paragraph (3) is due and payable shall be determined as if it were charged by an assessment of which notice was issued on the date on which the Inland Revenue issues to the applicant a notice of the total amount payable in consequence of the refusal of the application.

This is subject to –

    (a)   regulation 22 (direction by tribunal postponing payment); and

    (b)   regulation 23 (agreement to postpone payment).

Amendments: SI 2009/56

16 Notice of decision on an application

(1) The Inland Revenue must give notice in writing to the person by whom the application was made of their decision whether to accept or refuse an application.

(2) Where the Inland Revenue accept an application, the notice must set out the terms on which the application has been accepted and, in particular, must –

    (a)   specify –
        (i)   any tax payable in accordance with a land transaction return relating to the transaction in question;
        (ii)   the nature of any relevant events; and
        (iii)   the dates of any relevant events (if known); and
    (b)   state that tax is payable within 30 days after the occurrence of a relevant event and in accordance with Part 4 of these Regulations.

(3) Where the Inland Revenue refuse an application, the notice must set out –

    (a)   the grounds for the refusal; and

    (b)   the total amount of tax payable in consequence of the refusal.

17 Grounds on which application may be refused

An application may be refused by the Inland Revenue if –

    (a)   the conditions for making an application specified in section 90(1) are not met;

    (b)   the application does not comply with the requirements of regulation 12 or 14;

    (c)   there are tax avoidance arrangements in relation to the transaction in question (see regulation 18);

    (d)   the application, or information provided in connection with it, is incorrect; or

    (e)   information required to be provided under regulation 14 is not provided within such time as the Inland Revenue reasonably required.

18 Tax avoidance arrangements

(1) For the purposes of regulation 17(c), arrangements are tax avoidance arrangements in relation to a transaction if their main object or one of their main objects is –

    (a)   to enable payment of the tax payable in respect of the transaction to be deferred; or

    (b)   to avoid the amount or value of the whole or part of the chargeable consideration for the transaction being determined for the purposes of Part 4 of the Finance Act 2003 in accordance with section 51(1).

(2) In this regulation, 'arrangements' includes any scheme, agreement or understanding, whether or not legally enforceable.

19 Right of appeal

(1) An appeal may be brought against a refusal by the Inland Revenue to accept an application.

Amendments: SI 2009/56.

20 Notice of appeal

(1) Notice of an appeal under regulation 19 must be given –

    (a)   in writing;
    (b)   within 30 days after the date on which the notice of the decision to refuse the application was issued; and
    (c)   to the officer of the Board by whom that notice was given.

(2) The notice of appeal must specify the grounds of appeal.

(3) The provisions of paragraphs 36A to 36I of Schedule 10 to the 2003 Act apply to appeals under this regulation.

Amendments: SI 2009/56.

21 Settling of appeals by agreement

(1) If before an appeal under regulation 19 is determined, the appellant and the Inland Revenue agree that the decision appealed against –

    (a)   should be upheld without variation,
    (b)   should be varied in a particular manner, or
    (c)   should be discharged or cancelled,

the same consequences shall follow, for all purposes, as would have followed if, at the time the agreement was come to, the tribunal had determined the appeal and had upheld the decision without variation, varied it in that manner or discharged or cancelled it, as the case may be.

(2) Paragraph (1) does not apply if, within 30 days from the date when the agreement was come to, the appellant gives notice in writing to the Inland Revenue that he wishes to withdraw from the agreement.

(3) Where the agreement is not in writing –

    (a)   paragraphs (1) and (2) do not apply unless the fact that an agreement was come to, and the terms agreed, are confirmed by notice in writing given by the Inland Revenue to the appellant or by the appellant to the Inland Revenue; and
    (b)   the references in those paragraphs to the time when agreement was come to shall be read as references to the time when the notice of confirmation was given.

(4) Where –

    (a)   the appellant notifies the Inland Revenue, orally or in writing, that he does not wish to proceed with the appeal, and

(b)   the Inland Revenue do not, within 30 days after that notification, give the appellant notice in writing indicating that they are unwilling that the appeal should be withdrawn,

paragraphs (1) to (3) have effect as if, at the date of the appellant's notification, the appellant and the Inland Revenue had come to an agreement (orally or in writing, as the case may be) that the decision under appeal should be upheld without variation.

(5) References in this regulation to an agreement being come to with an appellant, and to the giving of notice or notification by or to the appellant, include references to an agreement being come to, or notice or notification being given by or to, a person acting on behalf of the appellant in relation to the appeal.

Amendments: SI 2009/56.

22 Direction by the tribunal postponing payment

(1) If the appellant has grounds for believing that the amendment or assessment overcharges the appellant to tax, or as a result of the conclusion stated in the closure notice the tax charged on the appellant is excessive, the appellant may –

(a)   first apply by notice in writing to HMRC within 30 days of the specified date for a determination by them of the amount of tax the payment of which should be postponed pending the determination of the appeal;

(b)   where such a determination is not agreed, refer the application for postponement to the tribunal within 30 days from the date of the document notifying HMRC's decision on the amount to be postponed;

an application under sub-paragraph (a) must state the amount believed to be overcharged to tax and the grounds for that belief.

(3) If, after any determination on such an application of the amount of tax payment of which should be postponed, there is a change in the circumstances of the case as a result of which either party has grounds for believing that the amount so determined has become excessive or, as the case may be, insufficient, he may, if the parties cannot agree on a revised determination, apply, at any time before the determination of the appeal, to the tribunal for a revised determination of that amount.

(4) Any such application is to be subject to the relevant provisions of Part 5 of the Taxes Management Act 1970 (see, in particular, section 48(2)(b) of that Act).

The fact that any such application has been heard and determined by any Commissioners does not preclude them from hearing and determining the appeal or any further application under this regulation.

(5) The amount of tax of which payment is to be postponed pending the determination of the appeal is the amount (if any) which appears to be appropriate.

(6) Where an application is made under this regulation, the date on which any tax of which payment is not postponed is due and payable shall be determined as if the tax were charged by an assessment of which notice was issued on the date on which the application was determined.

(7) On the determination of the appeal –

(a)   the date on which any tax payable in accordance with that determination is due and payable shall, so far as it is tax the payment of which had been postponed, be determined as if the tax were charged by an assessment of which notice was

issued on the date on which HMRC issues to the appellant a notice of the total
amount payable in accordance with the determination; and

(b)   any tax overpaid shall be repaid.

Amendments: SI 2009/56.

23 Agreement to postpone payment

(1) If the appellant and the officer of the Board by whom the notice of the decision to
refuse the application was given agree that payment of an amount of tax should be
postponed pending the determination of the appeal, the same consequences shall follow,
for all purposes, as would have followed if, at the time the agreement was come to, the
tribunal had made a direction to the same effect.

This is without prejudice to the making of a further agreement or of a further direction.

(2) Where the agreement is not in writing –

(a)   paragraph (1) does not apply unless the fact that an agreement was come to,
        and the terms agreed, are confirmed by notice in writing given by the officer of
        the Board in question to the appellant or by the appellant to that officer; and

(b)   the reference in that paragraph to the time when the agreement was come to
        shall be read as a reference to the time when notice of confirmation was given.

(3) References in this regulation to an agreement being come to with an appellant, and
to the giving of notice to or by the appellant, include references to an agreement being
come to, or notice being given to or by a person acting on behalf of the appellant in
relation to the appeal.

Amendments: SI 2009/56.

24 Payments and returns

(1) This regulation applies where the Inland Revenue accepts an application.

(2) If the application relates to deferring the payment of tax that has already been paid,
the amount already paid shall be repaid together with interest as from the date of
payment.

(3) The purchaser must make a return or further return ('the return') to the Inland
Revenue –

(a)   within 30 days after the occurrence of a relevant event;
(b)   if relevant –
        (i)   within the period of 30 days mentioned in regulation 13(2)(a);
        (ii)   subject to regulation 27, in accordance with the scheme for payment
                mentioned in regulation 13(2)(b); or
        (iii)   after the final payment has been made in accordance with that scheme,
                within 30 days after the purchaser obtains new information the effect of
                which is that additional tax or less tax is payable in respect of the
                transaction than has already been paid.

(4) The return must be accompanied by payment of any tax or additional tax payable.

(5) If the effect of the return is that less tax is payable in respect of a transaction than
has already been paid, the amount overpaid shall on a claim by the purchaser be repaid
together with interest as from the date of payment.

25 Form and contents of returns

(1) A return under regulation 24(3) must be in writing and must contain the following information –

   (a)   a self-assessment of the amount of tax chargeable in respect of the transaction as a whole on the basis of information contained in the return;

   (b)   a statement of the amount of tax payable in respect of so much of the chargeable consideration for the transaction as is not, or is no longer, contingent or uncertain.

(2) The amounts mentioned in paragraph (1) must be calculated by reference to the rates in force at the effective date of the transaction.

26 Adjustment of payments made as mentioned in section 90(5)

Where –

   (a)   a payment is made as mentioned in section 90(5), and

   (b)   an application is accepted in respect of other chargeable consideration taken into account in calculating the amount of payment,

section 80 (adjustment where contingency ceases or consideration is ascertained) does not apply in relation to the payment and, instead, any necessary adjustment shall be made in accordance with these Regulations.

27 Returns and payments where consideration consists of works or services

(1) This regulation applies where a return or further return is required to be made in accordance with regulation 24(3)(b)(ii) and the carrying out of the works or provision of the services in question is expected to be substantially completed within a period of less than 6 months after the date on which the return or further return is required.

(2) Where this regulation applies, the applicant and the Inland Revenue may agree that the scheme of payment mentioned in regulation 13(2)(b) should be varied so that the next return or further return due to be made in respect of the consideration, or element of the consideration, consisting of the carrying out of such works or the provision of such services may be made within 30 days after the substantial completion of the carrying out of the works or the provision of the services.

(3) If the carrying out of the works or provision of the services in question is not substantially completed within a period of less than 6 months after the date on which, apart from the variation of the scheme of payment, the return or further return would have been required –

   (a)   the variation shall cease to have effect; and

   (b)   returns or further returns must continue to be made in accordance with regulation 24(3)(b)(ii).

28 Applications accepted by the Inland Revenue having no effect

For the purposes of Part 4 of the Finance Act 2003 and these Regulations, an application which has been accepted by the Inland Revenue –

   (a)   shall have no effect if –
      (i)   it contains false or misleading information; or
      (ii)   any facts or circumstances relevant to it are not disclosed to the Inland Revenue; and

(b)   shall cease to have any effect if the facts and circumstances relevant to it materially change.

PART 5
DISTRAINT BY COLLECTORS: FEES, COSTS AND CHARGES

29 Interpretation of Part 4

In this Part –

'close possession' means physical possession by a distrainor or a person acting on his behalf of the goods and chattels distrained;

'walking possession' means possession in accordance with an agreement between a distrainor and a distrainee by which, in consideration of the distrainor not remaining in close possession, the distrainee undertakes neither –

(a)   to dispose of any of the goods and chattels distrained; nor

(b)   to permit their removal by any person not authorised by the distrainor to remove them.

30 Ascertainment of fees, costs and charges

(1) The fees chargeable on or in connection with the levying of distress under paragraph 2 of Schedule 12 to the 2003 Act are those specified in the Table in Part 1 of Schedule 3.

(2) The costs and charges recoverable where such distress has been levied are those specified in the Table in Part 2 of that Schedule.

(3) This is subject to the provisions of Part 3 of that Schedule.

31 Deduction of fees, costs and charges by the collector

The fees, costs and charges specified in Schedule 3 shall be deducted by the collector from the sums received on or in connection with the levying of distress or where distress has been levied.

32 Disputes as to fees, costs and charges

(1) In any case of dispute as to the fees chargeable, or costs and charges recoverable, under Schedule 3, the amount of those fees, costs and charges shall be assessed in accordance with this regulation.

(2) The relevant authority shall carry out any such assessment and may give such directions as to the costs of the assessment as he thinks fit.

(3) In paragraph (2), 'the relevant authority' means –

(a)   in England and Wales, the district judge of the county court for the district in which the distress is, or is intended to be, levied;

(b)   in Northern Ireland, the Master (Taxing Office).

PART 6

33 Interpretation of Part 5

In this Part –

'the appropriate judicial authority' has the meaning given by paragraph 32(3) of Schedule 13 to the 2003 Act;

'the court' has the meaning given by paragraph 40(2) of Schedule 13 to the 2003 Act;

'items subject to legal privilege' has the meaning given by paragraph 35(2) of Schedule 13 to the 2003 Act;

'notice of application' means the notice of intention to apply for an order to which a person is entitled under paragraph 33(1) of Schedule 13 to the 2003 Act;

'order' means an order under paragraph 32 of Schedule 13 to the 2003 Act;

'working day' means any day other than a Saturday, Sunday or public holiday.

34 Approval of decision to apply for an order

Before the hearing of an application for an order, an officer of.Revenue and Customs who is a member of the Senior Civil Service in –

    (a)   the Cross-Cutting Policy branch of Her Majesty's Revenue and Customs , or

    (b)   the Special Compliance Office of Her Majesty's Revenue and Customs,

must approve in writing the decision to apply for that order.

Amendments: SI 2005/1132.

35 Notice of application

(1) Notice of application must be given in writing and must contain the following details –

    (a)   the date, time and place of the hearing of the application;

    (b)   the specifications or descriptions of documents which are the subject of the application;

    (c)   a description of the suspected offence to which the application relates; and

    (d)   the name of the person suspected of committing, having committed or being about to commit the suspected offence.

(2) Notice of application must be given to the person entitled to it not less than five working days before the hearing of the application.

Amendments: SI 2005/1132.

36 Notice of an order, or notice of an application, treated as having been given

(1) Where notice of an order, or notice of application, is delivered to a person, or left at his proper address, notice shall be treated as having been given to that person on the day on which it is delivered or left or, where that day is not a working day, on the next working day.

(2) Where notice of application, or notice of an order, is sent to a person's proper address by facsimile transmission or other similar means which produce a document containing a text of the communication, notice shall be treated as given when the text is received in a legible form.

(3) For the purposes of this regulation, a person's proper address is –

    (a)   the usual or last known place of residence, or the place of business or employment, of that person; or

    (b)   in the case of a company, the address of the company's registered office; or

    (c)   in the case of a liquidator of a company, the liquidator's address for the purposes of the liquidation.

37 Complying with an order

(1) A person complies with an order by producing the documents specified or described in the order to the officer of Revenue and Customs specified in the order within –

(a)   the period mentioned in paragraph 32(2) of Schedule 13 to the 2003 Act; or
(b)   such further period, if any, as is agreed with that officer.

(2) For the purposes of paragraph (1), documents are produced to an officer of Revenue and Customs if they are either –

(a)   delivered to the officer; or
(b)   left for the officer at an address specified in the relevant order.

(3) Where documents are sent to an officer of the Board at the address specified in the relevant order by post, they shall be treated, unless the contrary is proved, as having been produced to the officer –

(a)   if first class post is used, on the second working day after posting;
(b)   if second class post is used, on the fourth working day after posting.

38 Resolution of disputes as to legal privilege

(1) This regulation applies where there is a dispute between the Commissioners of Her Majesty's Revenue and Customs and a person against whom an order has been made as to whether a document, or part of a document, is an item subject to legal privilege.

(2) The person against whom an order has been made may apply to the appropriate judicial authority to resolve the dispute.

(3) All the documents to which an application under paragraph (2) relates must be lodged in the court at the same time as the application is made and shall be held by the court until the appropriate judicial authority resolves the dispute.

(4) The court shall give the Commissioners for Her Majesty's Revenue and Customs notice of an application made under paragraph (2) not less than five working days before the hearing of the application, and the Board shall be entitled to appear and be heard at that hearing in addition to the person making the application.

(5) On the hearing of an application made under paragraph (2), the appropriate judicial authority shall –

(a)   resolve the dispute by confirming whether the document, or part of the document, is or is not an item subject to legal privilege; and
(b)   order the costs of the application to be met by the Commissioners for Her Majesty's Revenue and Customs except where it holds that no document, or no part of any document, to which the application relates is an item subject to legal privilege.

(6) Where a person makes an application under paragraph (2) within the period mentioned in regulation 37(1), he shall be treated as having complied with the order in relation to the documents to which the application relates until the appropriate judicial authority resolves the dispute.

(7) A dispute may be resolved at any time by the Commissioners for Her Majesty's Revenue and Customs and the person against whom an order has been made reaching an agreement, whether in writing or otherwise, and, for all purposes, the consequences

of such an agreement shall be the same as those which would have ensued if, at the time when the agreement was reached, the appropriate judicial authority had resolved the dispute.

Amendments: SI 2005/1132.

Schedule 1

Self-Certificate

Stamp duty land tax

Certification that no Land Transaction Return is required for a land transaction

This is a self-certificate under Section 79(3) of Finance Act 2003

Effective date of transaction	Title number/folio number
/ /	
Property or land address	Name and address of purchaser's solicitor/agent
Name(s) and address of purchaser	Name(s) and address of vendor

Please turn over

SDLT 60   HMRC 03/06

Reason no Land Transaction Return is required

√

☐ Transfer or conveyance of a freehold interest in land for no chargeable consideration.

☐ Grant of a lease in England & Wales or Northern Ireland for a term of seven years or more and for no chargeable consideration (that is, no premium and no rent of any monetary value).

☐ Transfer or assignment of a lease for no chargeable consideration.

☐ Grant of a lease where all the following are satisfied:
  • the term of the lease is less than seven years, and
  • the amount of any premium is not such as to attract a charge to SDLT at a rate of 1% or higher (ignoring the availability of any relief), and
  • the amount of any rent is not such as to attract a charge to SDLT at a rate of 1% or higher (ignoring the availability of any relief).

☐ Transfer or assignment of a lease where both the following are satisfied:
  • the term of the lease when granted was less than seven years, and
  • the amount of any consideration for the assignment is not such as to attract a charge to SDLT at a rate of 1% or higher (ignoring the availability of any relief).

☐ Land transaction (other than the transfer of a freehold interest in land, or grant or assignment of a lease) where the amount of the consideration is not such as to attract a charge to SDLT at a rate of 1% or higher (ignoring the availability of any relief).

☐ Land transaction exempt from SDLT under Schedule 3 paragraph 3 Finance Act 2003 (transactions in connection with divorce or dissolution of a civil partnership formed under the Civil Partnership Act 2004).

☐ Land transaction exempt from SDLT under Schedule 3 paragraph 4 Finance Act 2003 (variation of testamentary dispositions).

☐ Transfer or conveyance of a freehold interest in land consisting entirely of residential property where the chargeable consideration, together with that of any linked transaction(s), is less than £1,000.

☐ Acquisition by a beneficiary entitled under a will or on intestacy, where the only consideration given is the assumption of 'secured debt' as defined in paragraph 3A of Schedule 3 Finance Act 2003.

☐ Transfer of interest in a partnership for chargeable consideration not exceeding the zero rate threshold.

Note: in Scotland
  • for 'a freehold interest in land' read 'ownership of land'
  • 'a lease' includes missives of let constituting a lease
  • for 'assignment of a lease' read 'assignation of a tenant's interest under a lease (including missives of let constituting a lease)'

Declaration

This certificate must be signed by the person acquiring the interest. Signature by an agent is not acceptable. Where there is more than one transferee all of them must sign the certificate, except in certain circumstances (please refer to guidance notes).

I certify that for the reason given (as ticked) I do not need to submit a Land Transaction Return to HM Revenue & Customs.

If you give false information in this certificate you may face financial penalties and prosecution.

I declare that the information I have given in this form is true and complete to the best of my knowledge and belief.

Signature of purchaser(s)

Name (printed)

Capacity in which signing

Date

/   /

Stamp Duty Land Tax

Schedule 2

Regulation 9

Land Transaction Return

PART 1

MAIN FORM

HM Revenue & Customs

Land Transaction Return

For official use only

Your transaction return

How to fill in this return

The guidance notes that come with this return will help you answer the questions.

- Write inside the boxes. Use black ink and CAPITAL letters.
- If you make a mistake, please cross it out and write the correct information underneath.
- **Leave blank any boxes that don't apply to you** – please don't strike through anything irrelevant.
- Show amounts in whole pounds only, rounded down to the nearest pound. Ignore the pence.

- Fill out the payslip on page 7.
- Do not fold the return. Send it back to us unfolded in the envelope provided.
- **Photocopies are not acceptable.**

If you need help with any part of this return or with anything in the guidance notes, please phone the Stamp Taxes enquiry line on **0845 603 0135**, open 8:30am to 5:00pm Monday to Friday, except Bank Holidays. You can get further copies of this return and any supplementary returns from the Orderline on **0845 302 1472**.

Starting your return

ABOUT THE TRANSACTION

1 Type of property

Enter code from the guidance notes

2 Description of transaction

Enter code from the guidance notes

3 Interest transferred or created

Enter code from the guidance notes

4 Effective date of transaction

D D M M Y Y Y Y

5 Any restrictions, covenants or conditions affecting the value of the interest transferred or granted? Put 'X' in one box

Yes   No

If 'yes' please provide details

6 Date of contract or conclusion of missives

D D M M Y Y Y Y

7 Is any land exchanged or part-exchanged? Put 'X' in one box

Yes   No

If 'yes' please complete address of location

Postcode

House or building number

Rest of address, including house name, building name or flat number

8 Is the transaction pursuant to a previous option agreement? Put 'X' in one box

Yes   No

ABOUT THE TAX CALCULATION

9 Are you claiming relief? Put 'X' in one box

☐ Yes ☐ No

If 'yes' please show the reason

☐ Enter code from the guidance notes

Enter the charity's registered number, if available, or the company's CIS number

☐☐☐☐☐☐☐☐☐☐☐☐☐☐☐

For relief claimed on part of the property only, please enter the amount remaining chargeable

£ ☐☐☐☐☐☐☐☐ . 0 0

10 What is the total consideration in money or money's worth, including any VAT actually payable for the transaction notified?

£ ☐☐☐☐☐☐☐☐ . 0 0

11 If the total consideration for the transaction includes VAT, please state the amount

£ ☐☐☐☐☐☐☐☐ . 0 0

12 What form does the consideration take?
Enter the relevant codes from the guidance notes

☐☐ ☐☐ ☐☐ ☐☐

13 Is this transaction linked to any other(s)?
Put 'X' in one box

☐ Yes ☐ No

Total consideration or value in money or money's worth, including VAT paid for all of the linked transactions

£ ☐☐☐☐☐☐☐☐ . 0 0

14 Total amount of tax due for this transaction

£ ☐☐☐☐☐☐☐☐ . 0 0

15 Total amount paid or enclosed with this notification

£ ☐☐☐☐☐☐☐☐ . 0 0

Does the amount paid include payment of any penalties and any interest due? Put 'X' in one box

☐ Yes ☐ No

ABOUT LEASES

If this doesn't apply, go straight to box 26 on page 3.

16 Type of lease

☐ Enter code from the guidance notes

17 Start date as specified in lease

D D M M Y Y Y Y

18 End date as specified in lease

D D M M Y Y Y Y

19 Rent-free period
Number of months

☐☐

20 Annual starting rent inclusive of VAT (actually) payable

£ ☐☐☐☐☐☐ . 0 0

End date for starting rent

D D M M Y Y Y Y

Later rent known? Put 'X' in one box

☐ Yes ☐ No

21 What is the amount of VAT, if any?

£ ☐☐☐☐☐☐☐☐ . 0 0

22 Total premium payable

£ ☐☐☐☐☐☐☐☐ . 0 0

23 Net present value upon which tax is calculated

£ ☐☐☐☐☐☐☐☐ . 0 0

24 Total amount of tax due – premium

£ ☐☐☐☐☐☐☐☐ . 0 0

25 Total amount of tax due – NPV

£ ☐☐☐☐☐☐☐☐ . 0 0

Check the guidance notes to see if you will need to complete supplementary return 'Additional details about the transaction, including leases', SDLT4.

ABOUT THE LAND including buildings

Where more than one piece of land is being sold or you cannot complete the address field in the space provided, please complete the supplementary return 'Additional details about the land', SDLT3.

26 Number of properties included

27 Where more than one property is involved, do you want a certificate for each property? Put 'X' in one box

Yes   No

28 Address or situation of land
Postcode

House or building number

Rest of address, including house name, building name or flat number

Is the rest of the address on the supplementary return 'Additional details about the land', SDLT3?
Put 'X' in one box

Yes   No

29 Local authority number

30 Title number, if any

31 NLPG UPRN

32 If agricultural or development land, what is the area (if known)? Put 'X' in one box

Hectares   Square metres
Area

33 Is a plan attached? Please note that the form reference number should be written/displayed on map. Put 'X' in one box

Yes   No

ABOUT THE VENDOR including transferor, lessor

34 Number of vendors included (Note: if more than one vendor, complete boxes 45 to 48)

35 Title Enter MR, MRS, MISS, MS or other title
Note: only complete for an individual

36 Vendor (1) surname or company name

37 Vendor (1) first name(s) Note: only complete for an individual

38 Vendor (1) address
Postcode

House or building number

Rest of address, including house name, building name or flat number

ABOUT THE VENDOR CONTINUED

39 Agent's name

40 Agent's address
Postcode

Building number

Rest of address, including building name

41 Agent's DX number and exchange

42 Agent's e-mail address

43 Agent's reference

44 Agent's telephone number

ADDITIONAL VENDOR

Details of other people involved (including transferor, lessor), other than vendor (1). If more than one additional vendor please complete supplementary return 'Land Transaction Return – Additional vendor/purchaser details', SDLT2.

45 Title Enter MR, MRS, MISS, MS or other title
Note: only complete for an individual

46 Vendor (2) surname or company name

47 Vendor (2) first name(s)
Note: only complete for an individual

48 Vendor (2) address

Put 'X' in this box if the same as box 38.
If not, please give address below
Postcode

House or building number

Rest of address, including house name, building name or flat number

988   *Stamp Duty Land Tax*

ABOUT THE PURCHASER including transferee, lessee

49 Number of purchasers included (Note: if more than one purchaser is involved, complete boxes 65 to 69)

50 National Insurance number (purchaser 1), if you have one. Note: only complete for an individual

51 Title Enter MR, MRS, MISS, MS or other title
Note: only complete for an individual

52 Purchaser (1) surname or company name

53 Purchaser (1) first name(s)
Note: only complete for an individual

54 Purchaser (1) address
Put 'X' in this box if the same address as box 28.
If not, please give address below
Postcode

House or building number

Rest of address, including house name, building name or flat number

55 Is the purchaser acting as a trustee? Put 'X' in one box
Yes   No

56 Please give a daytime telephone number – this will help us if we need to contact you about your return

57 Are the purchaser and vendor connected?
Put 'X' in one box
Yes   No

58 To which address shall we send the certificate?
Put 'X' in one box
Property (box 28)   Purchaser's (box 54)
Agent's (box 61)

59 I authorise my agent to handle correspondence on my behalf. Put 'X' in one box
Yes   No

60 Agent's name

61 Agent's address
Postcode

Building number

Rest of address, including building name

62 Agent's DX number and exchange

63 Agent's reference

64 Agent's telephone number

SDLT 1   PG 5

ADDITIONAL PURCHASER

Details of other people involved (including transferee, lessee), other than purchaser (1). If more than one additional purchaser, please complete supplementary return 'Land Transaction Return – Additional vendor/purchaser details', SDLT2.

65   **Title** Enter MR, MRS, MISS, MS or other title
Note: only complete for an individual

66   **Purchaser (2) surname or company name**

67   **Purchaser (2) first name(s)**
Note: only complete for an individual

68   **Purchaser (2) address**

Put 'X' in this box if the same as purchaser (1) (box 54).
If not, please give address below
Postcode

House or building number

Rest of address, including house name, building name or flat number

69   **Is purchaser (2) acting as a trustee?** Put 'X' in one box

Yes   No

ADDITIONAL SUPPLEMENTARY RETURNS

70   **How many supplementary returns have you enclosed with this return?** Write the number in each box. If none, please put '0'.

Additional vendor/purchaser details, SDLT2

Additional details about the land, SDLT3

Additional details about the transaction, including leases, SDLT4

DECLARATION

71   **The purchaser(s) must sign this return.** Read the guidance notes in booklet SDLT6, in particular the section headed *'Who should complete and sign the Land Transaction Return?'*.

If you give false information, you may face financial penalties and prosecution.
The information I have given on this return is correct and complete to the best of my knowledge and belief.

Signature of purchaser 1   Signature of purchaser 2

Please keep a copy of this return and a note of the unique transaction reference number, which is in the 'Reference' box on the payslip.

Finally, please send your completed return to:
HM Revenue & Customs, Stamp Taxes/SDLT, Comben House, Farriers Way, NETHERTON, Merseyside, Great Britain, L30 4RN, or the DX address is: Rapid Data Capture Centre, DX725593, Bootle 9

Please don't fold it – keep it flat and use the envelope provided. Fill out the payslip on the next page and pay in accordance with the 'How to pay' instructions.

How to pay

ℹ️ Please allow enough time for payment to reach us by the due date. We suggest you allow at least 3 working days for this.

MOST SECURE AND EFFICIENT

We recommend the following payment methods. These are the most secure and efficient.

1. Direct Payment
Use the Internet or telephone to make payment. Provide your bank or building society with the following information
- payment account
- sort code 10-50-41
- account number 23456000
- your reference as shown on the payslip.

2. BillPay
You can pay by Debit Card over the Internet. Visit **www.billpayment.co.uk/hmrc** and follow the guidance.

3. At your bank
Take this form with payment to **your** bank and where possible to **your own** branch. Other banks may refuse to accept payment. If paying by cheque, make your cheque payable to 'HM REVENUE & CUSTOMS ONLY'.

4. At a Post Office
Take this form with your payment to any Post Office. If paying by cheque, make your cheque payable to 'POST OFFICE LTD'. The Post Office also accept payment by Debit Card.

5. Alliance & Leicester Commercial Bank Account
Alliance & Leicester Commercial Bank customers can instruct their bank to arrange payment.

OTHER PAYMENT METHODS

✉️ **By post**
If you use this method
- Make your cheque payable to 'HM REVENUE & CUSTOMS ONLY'.
- Write your payslip reference after 'HM REVENUE & CUSTOMS ONLY'.
- Send the payslip and your cheque, **both unfolded**, in the envelope provided to
  HM Revenue & Customs SDLT
  Netherton
  Merseyside
  L30 4RN

By DX
As above, but send to
Rapid Data Capture Centre
DX725593
Bootle 9

FURTHER PAYMENT INFORMATION

You can find further payment information at **www.hmrc.gov.uk/howtopay**

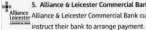

Alliance & Leicester *Trans cash*   **Payslip**   HM Revenue & Customs   bank giro credit
COMMERCIAL BANK
Bootle Merseyside GIR 0AA

	Reference	Credit account number		By transfer from Alliance & Leicester account number
159 209 24		610 5041	£	

Amount due
(no fee payable at PO counter)
CHEQUE ACCEPTABLE

For official use only

Name _____

Cashier's stamp and initials

Signature _____   Date _____

BANK OF ENGLAND
HEAD OFFICE COLLECTION A/C
HM REVENUE & CUSTOMS

CASH
CHEQUE
£

10-50-41

SDLT1/P

Please do not fold this payslip or write or mark below this line

PART 2
ADDITIONAL VENDOR/PURCHASER DETAILS

HM Revenue & Customs

Land Transaction Return
Additional vendor/purchaser details

When to fill in this return
You must fill in this return for each additional vendor and/or purchaser. The guidance notes will help you answer the questions.

If you need help with any part of this return or with anything in the guidance notes, please phone the Stamp Taxes enquiry line on **0845 603 0135**, open Monday to Friday 08:30 – 17:00, except Bank Holidays. You can get further copies of this return from the Orderline on **0845 302 1472**.

Reference
Insert the reference number from the payslip on page 1 of the Land Transaction Return, SDLT1, here.

For official use only

Vendor or Purchaser
1 Please indicate if this return is for an additional vendor or an additional purchaser. Put 'X' in one box

Vendor   Complete section below only

Purchaser Complete section below and the section over the page

Complete in all cases
2 Title Enter Mr, Mrs, Miss, Ms or other title
Note: only complete for an individual

3 Surname or company name

4 First name(s)
Note: only complete for an individual

5 Address
Postcode

House or building number

Rest of address, including house name, building name or flat number

Please turn over for additional purchaser details

Additional purchaser details

Only complete this section if this return is for an additional purchaser.

6 Are the purchaser and vendor connected?
Put 'X' in one box

[ ] Yes   [ ] No

7 Is the purchaser acting as a trustee? Put 'X' in one box

[ ] Yes   [ ] No

8 Declaration

The purchaser(s) must sign this return.
Read the notes in Section 1 of the guidance notes, SDLT6
Who should complete the Land Transaction Return

If you give false information, you may face financial
penalties and prosecution.

The information I have given on this form is correct and
complete to the best of my knowledge and belief.
Signature of purchaser

PART 3
ADDITIONAL DETAILS ABOUT THE LAND

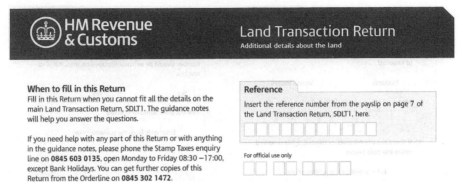

When to fill in this Return

Fill in this Return when you cannot fit all the details on the main Land Transaction Return, SDLT1. The guidance notes will help you answer the questions.

If you need help with any part of this Return or with anything in the guidance notes, please phone the Stamp Taxes enquiry line on **0845 603 0135**, open Monday to Friday 08:30 –17:00, except Bank Holidays. You can get further copies of this Return from the Orderline on **0845 302 1472**.

Reference

Insert the reference number from the payslip on page 7 of the Land Transaction Return, SDLT1, here.

For official use only

About the land

1 Type of property

Enter code from the guidance notes

2 Local authority number

3 Title number, if any

4 NLPG UPRN

5 Address or situation of land

Postcode

House or building number

Rest of address, including house name, building name, flat number or continuation from the SDLT1

Please turn over ➤

SDLT 3   PG 1   HMRC 06/06

About the land continued

6 If agricultural or development land, what is the area (if known)?

Hectares ☐   Square metres ☐

Area

☐☐☐☐☐☐☐☐☐.☐☐☐

7 If there are any minerals or mineral rights reserved enter the code below

☐☐ Enter code from the guidance notes

8 Is a plan attached? Please note that the form reference number should be written/displayed on map. Put 'X' in one box

☐ Yes   ☐ No

9 Interest transferred or created

☐ Enter code from the guidance notes

PART 4
ADDITIONAL DETAILS ABOUT THE TRANSACTION, INCLUDING LEASES

Inland Revenue

Land Transaction Return
Additional details about the transaction, including leases

When to fill in this return
You must fill in this return where additional information about the transaction and/or lease can be provided.
The guidance notes will help you answer the questions.

If you need help with any part of this return or with anything in the guidance notes, please phone the Stamp Taxes enquiry line on **0845 603 0135**, open 8:30am to 5:00pm Monday to Friday, except Bank Holidays. Calls are charged at local rates. You can get further copies of this return from the Orderline on **0845 302 1472**.

REFERENCE
Insert the reference number from the payslip on page 7 of the Land Transaction Return, SDLT1, here.

For official use only

ABOUT THE TRANSACTION

1 If this transaction is part of the sale of business, please say if the sale includes Put 'X' in relevant boxes
- Stock
- Goodwill
- Other
- Chattels and moveables

What is the total amount of the consideration for the sale of the business apportioned to these items?
£ . 0 0

2 If the property is for commercial use, what is it? Put 'X' in the appropriate box(es)
- Office
- Hotel
- Shop
- Warehouse
- Factory
- Other
- Other industrial unit

3 Have you applied for and received a post transaction ruling in accordance with Code of Practice 10, or asked us for advice on the application of the law to this transaction? Put 'X' in one box
- Yes
- No

If 'yes' have you followed it when completing this return? Put 'X' in one box
- Yes
- No
- Ruling not received

4 Is any part of the consideration contingent or dependent on uncertain future events?
- Yes
- No

5 Have you agreed with the Inland Revenue that you will pay on a deferred basis?
- Yes
- No

6 If there are any minerals or mineral rights reserved enter the code below
Enter code from the guidance notes

7 If the purchaser is VAT registered, give their VAT reference number

8 If the purchaser is a company please give the following details
Tax reference number

Company registration number

If registered abroad, give its place of registration

SDLT4 V2   PG 1

Please turn over
BS11/04

ABOUT THE TRANSACTION CONTINUED

9 **Give a description of the purchaser**
Enter code from the guidance notes

ABOUT LEASES

Complete if the transaction notified on SDLT1 is for the grant of more than one lease

10 **Type of property**

Enter code from the guidance notes

11 **Address or situation of land**

Put 'X' in this box if the same as box 28 on SDLT1

If not, please give address below
Postcode

House or building number

Rest of address, including house name, building name,
flat number or continuation from the SDLT1

12 **Local authority number**

13 **Title number, if any**

14 **NLPG UPRN**

15 **If the transaction is for land, what is the unit and area of measurement?** Put 'X' in one box

Hectares ☐ Square metres

Area

16 **Is a plan attached? Please note that the form reference number should be written/displayed on the map.**
Put X in one box

Yes ☐ No

17 **Interest transferred or created**

Enter code from the guidance notes

18 **Type of lease**

Enter code from the guidance notes

continued at the top of the next column

ABOUT LEASES CONTINUED

19 Start date as specified in lease

D D M M Y Y Y Y

20 End date as specified in lease

D D M M Y Y Y Y

21 Rent free period
Number of months

22 Annual starting rent inclusive of VAT (actually) payable

£ ⬚⬚⬚⬚⬚⬚⬚⬚⬚ . 0 0

End date for starting rent

D D M M Y Y Y Y

Later rent known? Put 'X' in one box

Yes   No

23 What is the amount of VAT, if any?

£ ⬚⬚⬚⬚⬚⬚⬚⬚⬚ . 0 0

24 Total premium payable

£ ⬚⬚⬚⬚⬚⬚⬚⬚⬚ . 0 0

25 Net present value upon which tax is calculated

£ ⬚⬚⬚⬚⬚⬚⬚⬚⬚ . 0 0

26 Total amount of tax due - premium

£ ⬚⬚⬚⬚⬚⬚⬚⬚⬚ . 0 0

27 Total amount of tax due - NPV

£ ⬚⬚⬚⬚⬚⬚⬚⬚⬚ . 0 0

28 Any terms surrendered

29 Break clause type Put 'X' in one box

Landlord   Tenant only

Either

30 What is the date of the break clause?

D D M M Y Y Y Y

31 Which of the following relate to this lease?
Put 'X' in relevant boxes. If none, leave blank

Option to renew

Market rent

Turnover rent

Unascertainable rent

Contingent reserved rent

32 Rent review frequency

33 Date of first review

D D M M Y Y Y Y

34 Rent review clause (type) Put 'X' in one box

Open market   RPI

Other

35 If Schedule 17A para 7FA 2003 has been used in calculating the NPV, what is the date of the rent change?

D D M M Y Y Y Y

Please turn over ➤

ABOUT LEASES CONTINUED

36 **Service charge amount if known**

£ ▢▢▢▢▢▢▢ . 0 0

37 **Service charge frequency** Put 'X' in one box

▢ Monthly   ▢ Annually

▢ Quarterly   ▢ Other

38 **Other consideration – tenant to landlord**
(for example, services, building works)
Enter the relevant codes from the guidance notes

▢▢   ▢▢   ▢▢   ▢▢

39 **Other consideration – landlord to tenant**
(for example, services, building works)
Enter the relevant codes from the guidance notes

▢▢   ▢▢   ▢▢   ▢▢

Schedule 3

Regulation 30

Fees, Costs and Charges

PART 1
FEES CHARGEABLE ON OR IN CONNECTION WITH THE LEVYING OF DISTRESS

Action taken in connection with the levying of distress	Fees
For making a visit to premises with a view to levying distress (whether the levy is made or not).	A sum not exceeding £12.50.
Levying distress where the total sum charged is £100 or less.	£12.50.
Levying distress where the total sum charged is more than £100.	12½ per cent on the first £100 of the amount to be recovered;4 per cent on the next £400; 2½ per cent on the next £1,500; 1 per cent on the next £8,000; ¼ per cent on any additional sum.

PART 2
COSTS AND CHARGES RECOVERABLE WHERE DISTRESS HAS BEEN LEVIED

Action taken where distress has been levied	Costs and charges
1 Taking possession.	
Where close possession is taken	£4.50 for the day of levy only.
Where walking possession is taken.	45p per day, payable for the day the distress is levied and up to 14 days thereafter.
2 Removal and storage of goods.	The reasonable costs and charges of removal and storage.
3 Appraisement.	The reasonable fees, charges and expenses of the person appraising.
4 Sale.	
Where the sale is held on the auctioneer's premises, for the reasonable cost of advertising, auctioneer's commission (to include all out-of-pocket expenses other than charges for advertising, removal and storage)	15 per cent on the sum realised plus the reasonable cost of advertising, removal and storage.

Where the sale is held on the debtor's premises, for the auctioneer's commission (not to include out-of-pocket expenses or charges for advertising).	7½′ per cent on the sum realised plus out-of-pocket expenses actually and reasonably incurred and the reasonable costs of advertising.

PART 3
MISCELLANEOUS PROVISIONS RELATING TO FEES, COSTS AND CHARGES

1 In any case where close possession is taken, an individual left in possession must provide his own board.

2 For the purpose of calculating any percentage fees, costs and charges, a fraction of £1 is to be reckoned as £1, but any fraction of a penny in the total amount so calculated is to be disregarded.

3 In addition to any amount authorised by this Schedule in respect of the supply of goods or services on which value added tax is chargeable there may be added a sum equivalent to value added tax at the appropriate rate on that amount.

INDEX

References are to paragraph numbers.